Twentieth-Century Literary Criticism

Guide to Gale Literary Criticism Series

When you need to review criticism of literary works, these are the Gale series to use:

If the author's death date is: **You should turn to:**

After Dec. 31, 1959
(or author is still living)

CONTEMPORARY LITERARY CRITICISM

for example: Jorge Luis Borges, Anthony Burgess,
William Faulkner, Mary Gordon,
Ernest Hemingway, Iris Murdoch

1900 through 1959

TWENTIETH-CENTURY LITERARY CRITICISM

for example: Willa Cather, F. Scott Fitzgerald,
Henry James, Mark Twain, Virginia Woolf

1800 through 1899

NINETEENTH-CENTURY LITERATURE CRITICISM

for example: Fedor Dostoevski, Nathaniel Hawthorne,
George Sand, William Wordsworth

1400 through 1799

LITERATURE CRITICISM FROM 1400 TO 1800
(excluding Shakespeare)

for example: Anne Bradstreet, Daniel Defoe,
Alexander Pope, François Rabelais,
Jonathan Swift, Phillis Wheatley

SHAKESPEAREAN CRITICISM

Shakespeare's plays and poetry

Antiquity through 1399

CLASSICAL AND MEDIEVAL LITERATURE CRITICISM

for example: Dante, Homer, Plato, Sophocles, Vergil,
the Beowulf Poet

Gale also publishes related criticism series:

CHILDREN'S LITERATURE REVIEW

This series covers authors of all eras who have written for
the preschool through high school audience.

SHORT STORY CRITICISM

This series covers the major short fiction writers of all nationalities
and periods of literary history.

ISSN 0276-8178

Volume 37

Twentieth-Century Literary Criticism

**Excerpts from Criticism of the
Works of Novelists, Poets, Playwrights,
Short Story Writers, and Other Creative Writers
Who Died between 1900 and 1960,
from the First Published Critical Appraisals
to Current Evaluations**

**Paula Kepos
Editor**

**Marie Lazzari
Thomas Ligotti
Michelle L. McClellan
Joann Prosyniuk
Laurie Sherman
Associate Editors**

Gale Research Inc. • *DETROIT • NEW YORK • LONDON*

Since this page cannot legibly accommodate all the copyright notices, the acknowledgments constitute an extension of the copyright notice.

While every effort has been made to ensure the reliability of the information presented in this publication, Gale Research Inc. neither guarantees the accuracy of the data contained herein nor assumes any responsibility for errors, omissions, or discrepancies. Gale accepts no payment for listing; and inclusion in the publication of any organization, agency, institution, publication, service, or individual does not imply endorsement of the editors or publisher. Errors brought to the attention of the publisher and verified to the satisfaction of the publisher will be corrected in future editions.

Contents

Preface

Since its inception more than ten years ago, *Twentieth-Century Literary Criticism* has been purchased and used by nearly 10,000 school, public, and college or university libraries. With this edition—volume 37 in the series—*TCLC* has covered over 500 authors, representing 58 nationalities, and more than 25,000 titles. No other reference source has surveyed the critical response to twentieth-century authors and literature as thoroughly as *TCLC*. In the words of one reviewer, "there is nothing comparable available." *TCLC* "is a goldmine of information—dates, pseudonyms, biographical information, and criticism from books and periodicals—which many libraries would have difficulty assembling on their own."

Scope of the Series

TCLC is designed to serve as an introduction for students and advanced readers to authors who died between 1900 and 1960, and to the most significant interpretations of these authors' works. The great poets, novelists, short story writers, playwrights, and philosophers of this period are frequently studied in high school and college literature courses. In organizing and excerpting the vast amount of critical material written on these authors, *TCLC* helps students develop valuable insight into literary history, promotes a better understanding of the texts, and sparks ideas for papers and assignments. Each entry in *TCLC* presents a comprehensive survey of an author's career or an individual work of literature and provides the user with a multiplicity of interpretations and assessments. Such variety allows students to pursue their own interests; furthermore, it fosters an awareness that literature is dynamic and responsive to many different opinions.

TCLC is designed as a companion series to Gale's *Contemporary Literary Criticism,* which reprints commentary on current writing. Because of the different periods under consideration (*CLC* considers authors who were still living after 1959), there is no duplication of material between *CLC* and *TCLC*. For additional information about *CLC* and Gale's other criticism titles, users should consult the Guide to Gale Literary Criticism Series preceding the title page in this volume.

Coverage

Each volume of *TCLC* is carefully compiled to present:

- criticism of authors who represent a variety of genres and nationalities

- both major and lesser-known writers of the period (such as non-Western authors increasingly read by today's students)

- 14-16 authors per volume

- individual entries that survey the critical response to each author's works, including early criticism to reflect initial reactions; later criticism to represent any rise or decline in the author's reputation; and current retrospective analyses. The entries also indicate an author's importance to the period (for example, the length of each author entry reflects the amount of critical attention he or she has received from critics writing in English and from foreign criticism in translation)

An author may appear more than once in the series because of continuing critical and academic interest, or because of a resurgence of criticism generated by such events as a centennial or anniversary, the republication or posthumous publication of a work, or the publication of a new translation. Several entries in each volume of *TCLC* are devoted to criticism of individual works that are considered among the most important in twentieth-century literature and are thus frequently read and studied in high school and college literature classes. For example, this volume includes entries devoted to Henrik Ibsen's *A Doll's House* and John Millington Synge's *Playboy of the Western World*.

Organization of the Book

An author entry consists of the following elements: author heading, biographical and critical introduction, list of principal works, excerpts of criticism (each preceded by explanatory notes and followed by a bibliographic citation), and a bibliography of further reading.

- The *author heading* consists of the author's full name, followed by birth and death dates. The unbracketed portion of the name denotes the form under which the author most commonly wrote. If an author wrote consistently under a pseudonym, the pseudonym will be listed in the author heading and the real name given in parentheses on the first line of the biographical and critical introduction. Also located at the beginning of the introduction to the author entry are any name variations under which an author wrote, including transliterated forms for authors whose languages use nonroman alphabets.

- The *biographical and critical introduction* outlines the author's life and career, as well as the critical debate surrounding his or her work. References are provided to past volumes of *TCLC* and to other biographical and critical reference series published by Gale, including *Short Story Criticism, Children's Literature Review, Contemporary Authors, Dictionary of Literary Biography,* and *Something about the Author.*

- Most *TCLC* entries include *portraits* of the author. Many entries also contain reproductions of materials pertinent to an author's career, including manuscript pages, title pages, dust jackets, letters, and drawings, as well as photographs of important people, places, and events in an author's life.

- The *list of principal works* is chronological by date of first book publication and identifies the genre of each work. In the case of foreign authors with both foreign-language publications and English translations, the title and date of the first English-language edition are given in brackets. Unless otherwise indicated, dramas are dated by first performance, not first publication.

- *Criticism* is arranged chronologically in each author entry to provide a perspective on changes in critical evaluation over the years. All titles of works by the author featured in the entry are printed in boldface type to enable the user to easily locate discussion of particular works. Also for purposes of easier identification, the critic's name and the publication date of the essay are given at the beginning of each piece of criticism. Unsigned criticism is preceded by the title of the journal in which it appeared. Many of the excerpts in *TCLC* also contain translated material. Unless otherwise noted, translations in brackets are by the editors; translations in parentheses or continuous with the text are by the critic. Publication information (such as publisher names and book prices) and parenthetical numerical references (such as footnotes or page and line references to specific editions of works) have been deleted at the editors' discretion to provide smoother reading of the text.

- Critical excerpts are prefaced by *annotations* providing the reader with information about both the critic and the criticism that follows. Included are the critic's reputation, individual approach to literary criticism, and particular expertise in an author's works. Also noted are the relative importance of a work of criticism, the scope of the excerpt, and the growth of critical controversy or changes in critical trends regarding an author. In some cases, these annotations cross-reference excerpts by critics who discuss each other's commentary.

- A complete *bibliographic citation* designed to facilitate location of the original essay or book follows each piece of criticism.

- An annotated *list of further reading* appearing at the end of each author entry suggests further reading on the author. In some cases it includes essays for which the editors could not obtain reprint rights.

Cumulative Indexes

Each volume of *TCLC* includes a cumulative index listing all the authors who have appeared in *Contemporary Literary Criticism, Twentieth-Century Literary Criticism, Nineteenth-Century Litera-*

ture Criticism, Literature Criticism from 1400 to 1800, Classical and Medieval Literature Criticism, and *Short Story Criticism,* along with cross-references to the Gale series *Children's Literature Review, Authors in the News, Contemporary Authors, Contemporary Authors Autobiography Series, Dictionary of Literary Biography, Concise Dictionary of American Literary Biography, Something about the Author, Something about the Author Autobiography Series,* and *Yesterday's Authors of Books for Children.* Useful for locating an author within the various series, this index is particularly valuable for those authors who are identified with a certain period but who, because of their death dates, are placed in another, or for those authors whose careers span two periods. For example, F. Scott Fitzgerald is found in *TCLC,* yet a writer often associated with him, Ernest Hemingway, is found in *CLC.*

Each volume of *TCLC* also includes a cumulative nationality index, in which authors' names are arranged alphabetically under their respective nationalities.

Title Index

This volume of *TCLC* also includes an index listing the titles of all literary works discussed in the volume. The first volume of *TCLC* published each year contains an index listing all titles discussed in the series since its inception.

Suggestions Are Welcome

In response to suggestions, several features have been added to *TCLC* since the series began, including annotations to excerpted criticism, a cumulative index to authors in all Gale literary criticism series, entries devoted to a single work by a major author, more extensive illustrations, and a title index listing all literary works discussed in the series since its inception.

Readers who wish to suggest authors to appear in future volumes, or who have other suggestions, are cordially invited to write the editors or call our toll-free number: 1-800-347-GALE.

Acknowledgments

The editors wish to thank the copyright holders of the excerpted criticism included in this volume, the permissions managers of many book and magazine publishing companies for assisting us in securing reprint rights, and Anthony Bogucki for assistance with copyright research. We are also grateful to the staffs of the Detroit Public Library, the Library of Congress, the University of Detroit Library, Wayne State University Purdy/Kresge Library Complex, and the University of Michigan Libraries for making their resources available to us. Following is a list of the copyright holders who have granted us permission to reprint material in this volume of *TCLC*. Every effort has been made to trace copyright, but if omissions have been made please let us know.

COPYRIGHTED EXCERPTS IN *TCLC*, VOLUME 37, WERE REPRINTED FROM THE FOLLOWING PERIODICALS:

American Literature, v. 57, December, 1985. Copyright © 1985 Duke University Press, Durham, NC. Reprinted with permission of the publisher.—*The Atlantic Monthly,* v. 179, February, 1947 for a review of "On These I Stand" by John Ciardi. Copyright 1947 by The Atlantic Monthly Company, Boston, MA. Reprinted by permission of the Literary Estate of John Ciardi.—*Bulletin of Concerned Asian Scholars,* v. 16, April-June, 1984 for "Wind and Leaves: Miyamoto Yuriko's 'The Weathervane Plant' " by Brett de Bary. Copyright © 1984 by Bulletin of Concerned Asian Scholars, Inc. All rights reserved. Reprinted by permission of the publisher and the author./ v. 10, April-June, 1978. Copyright © 1978 by Bulletin of Concerned Asian Scholars, Inc. All rights reserved. Reprinted by permission of the publisher.—*The Century,* v. 107, November, 1923. Copyright, 1923, by The Century Co.—*The Dalhousie Review,* v. 48, Autumn, 1968 for "Little Hound in Mayo: Synge's Playboy and the Comic Tradition in Irish Tradition" by Diane E. Bessai; v. 66, Winter, 1986-1987 for "The Vernacular in Early Twentieth-Century Canadian Poetry: Arthur Stringer and A. M. Stephen" by A. R. Kizuk. Both reprinted by permission of the publisher and the respective authors.—*Eire-Ireland,* v. XVI, 1981 for "Synge's Widow Quin: Touchstone to the 'Playboy's Irony' " by James C. Pierce. Copyright © 1981 Irish American Cultural Insitute. Reprinted by permission of the publisher and the author.—*Extrapolation,* v. 22, Fall, 1981. Copyright 1981 by The Kent State University Press. Reprinted by permission of the publisher.—*The Journal of Aesthetics and Art Criticism,* v. XXII, Fall, 1963. Copyright © 1963 by The American Society for Aesthetics. Reprinted by permission of the publisher.—*Journal of Canadian Poetry: The Poetry Review,* v. 2, Autumn, 1979 for "Two Early Modernists" by Don Precosky. Copyright © by the author and Borealis Press Limited 1979. Reprinted by permission of the author.—*Latin American Theatre Review,* v. 7, Spring, 1974. Copyright 1974 by the Center of Latin American Studies, The University of Kansas, Lawrence, KS 66045, U.S.A. Reprinted by permission of the publisher.—*LEGACY,* v. 5, Spring, 1988. Copyright © 1988 by LEGACY, A Journal, Inc. All rights reserved. Reprinted by permission of the publisher.—*Modern Drama,* v. 4, December, 1961; v. VIII, December, 1965; v. 12, December, 1969; v. 20, June, 1977. Copyright 1961, 1965, 1969, 1977 *Modern Drama,* University of Toronto. All reprinted by permission of the publisher.—*New York Herald Tribune Books,* January 10, 1926. Copyright 1926 by I.H.T. Corporation. Reprinted by permission of the publisher.—*Partisan Review,* v. XXVIII, May-June, 1961 for "On Literature, Revolution and Entropy" by Evgeny Zamyatin, translated by Walter N. Vickery. Copyright © 1961 by *Partisan Review.* Reprinted by permission of the publisher and the translator.—*Renaissance and Modern Studies,* Slightly abridged from v. XXVIII, 1984. Reprinted by permission of the publisher.—*Research in African Literatures,* v. 6, Spring, 1975 for a review of "Zulu Horizons" by Absolom L. Vilakazi. Copyright © 1975 by the University of Texas Press. Reprinted by permission of Indiana University Press.—*Scandinavian Studies,* v. 41, February, 1969 for "Björnson's 'Thrond' and Popular Tradition" by Henning K. Sehmsdorf. Reprinted by permission of the publisher and the author.—*Scandinavica,* v. 1, May, 1962. Copyright © 1962 by the Editor, *Scandinavica,* University of East Anglia. Reprinted with permission of the publisher.—*Science Fiction Studies,* v. 11, July, 1984; v. 14, March, 1987. Copyright © 1984, 1987 by SFS Publications. Both reprinted by permission of the publisher.—*The Slavonic and East European Review,* v. 39, 1960-61; v. 62, July, 1984. © University of London (School of Slavonic and East European Studies) 1961, 1984. Both reprinted by permission of the publisher.—*Studies in American Fiction,* v. 11, Spring, 1983. Copyright © 1983 Northeastern University. Reprinted by permission of the publisher.—*Studies in Short Fiction,* v. XIII, Fall, 1976. Copyright 1976 by Newberry College. Reprinted by permission of the publisher.—*Studies in Weird Fiction,* n. 4, Fall, 1988. Copyright © 1986 by Necronomicon Press. Reprinted by permission of the publisher.—*Theoria,* Pietermaritzburg, v. LXVI, May, 1986. Reprinted by permission of the publisher.—*Women's Studies: An Interdisciplinary Journal,* v. 12, March, 1986 for "Charlotte Perkins Gilman's Steady Burghers: The Terrain of 'Herland' " by Christopher P. Wilson. Copyright © Gordon and Breach Science Publishers Inc. Reprinted by permission of the publisher and the author.

COPYRIGHTED EXCERPTS IN *TCLC*, VOLUME 37, WERE REPRINTED FROM THE FOLLOWING BOOKS:

Allen, Polly Wynn. From *Building Domestic Liberty: Charlotte Perkins Gilman's Architectural Feminism.* The University of Massachusetts Press, 1988. Copyright © 1988 by Polly Wynn Allen. All rights reserved. Reprinted by permission of the publisher.—Anderson-Imbert, Enrique. From *Spanish American Literature: A History, Vol. 1.* Edited

Authors to Be Featured in Forthcoming Volumes

Charles Waddel Chesnutt (American short story writer and novelist)—Chesnutt was one of the first black American writers to receive widespread critical and popular attention. He is best known for short stories about the antebellum South that incorporate subtle and ironic condemnations of slavery.

Joseph Conrad (Polish-born English novelist)—Considered an innovator of novel structure as well as one of the finest stylists of modern English literature, Conrad is the author of complex novels that examine the ambiguity of good and evil. *TCLC* will devote an entry to Conrad's novel *Lord Jim*, which examines the failures of a man before society and his own conscience.

Gabriele D'Annunzio (Italian novelist, playwright, and poet)— D'Annunzio, one of modern literature's most flamboyant personalities, is renowned as a consummate stylist who combined the poetic grandeur of Dante and the classical writers with contemporary trends of naturalism, symbolism, and decadence.

Paul Eluard (French poet)—Eluard was a founder of the Surrealist movement in France. His poetry, most often depicting the themes of love, fraternity, and universal harmony, is noted for its purity, lyricism, and highly visual content.

Ford Madox Ford (English novelist)—Ford was a major English novelist and a strong influence on modern trends in both poetry and prose. *TCLC* will devote an entry to *The Good Soldier*, a novel that is often considered Ford's most important.

William Dean Howells (American novelist and critic)—The chief progenitor of American Realism and the most influential American literary critic during the nineteenth century, Howells was the author of three dozen novels, which, though neglected for decades, are today the subject of growing interest. *TCLC* will devote an entry to Howells's best-known work, *The Rise of Silas Lapham*.

Henry James (American novelist)—James is considered one of the most important novelists of the English language and his work is universally acclaimed for its stylistic distinction, complex psychological portraits, and originality of theme and technique. *TCLC* will devote an entry to James's study of Americans living in the expatriate society of England and Italy, *The Portrait of a Lady*.

Sinclair Lewis (American novelist)—One of the foremost American novelists of the 1920s and 1930s, Lewis wrote some of the most effective satires in American literature. *TCLC* will devote an entry to his novel *Babbitt*, a scathing portrait of vulgar materialism and spiritual bankruptcy in American business.

Malcolm Lowry (English novelist)—Lowry's novel *Under the Volcano*, the anatomy of a man's psychic and spiritual collapse, is considered a classic of modern literature. *TCLC* will devote an entry to this richly allusive and complex work.

Katherine Mansfield (New Zealand short story writer)—Mansfield was an innovator of the short story form who contributed to the development of the stream-of-consciousness narrative.

Claude McKay (American poet)—A prominent figure of the Harlem Renaissance, McKay was the author of powerful poems of social protest that are considered among the most significant of the early American civil rights movement.

George Meredith (English novelist)—Meredith was a major Victorian novelist whose works, anticipating Modernist trends of the twentieth century, demonstrated a concern with character psychology, social problems, and the development of the novel form. *TCLC* will devote an entry to his most critically acclaimed novel, *The Egoist*.

Ida Tarbell (American journalist and biographer)—A prominent leader of the early twentieth-century muckraking movement in American journalism, Tarbell is best known for her sensational exposé of questionable business practices, *The History of the Standard Oil Company*.

Oscar Wilde (Anglo-Irish dramatist, novelist, and poet)—A crusader for aestheticism, Wilde was one of the most prominent members of the nineteenth-century "art for art's sake" movement. *TCLC* will devote an entry to Wilde's only novel, *The Picture of Dorian Gray*.

Emile Zola (French novelist)—Zola was the founder and principal theorist of Naturalism, one of the most influential literary movements in modern literature. His twenty-volume series *Les Rougon-Macquart* is a monument of Naturalist fiction and served as a model for late nineteenth-century novelists seeking a more candid and accurate representation of human life.

Bjørnstjerne Bjørnson

1832-1910

(Full name Bjørnstjerne Martinius Bjørnson) Norwegian dramatist, novelist, short story writer, poet, journalist, and editor.

For further discussion of Bjørnson's career, see *TCLC*, Volume 7.

Bjørnson was a leading literary and political figure of late nineteenth-century Norway and the first Scandinavian to receive the Nobel Prize in literature. He realized international acclaim through novellas depicting the assimilation of the Norwegian peasantry into modern society, and, in a series of social dramas written later in his career, examined controversial moral issues that confronted the upper and middle classes. These plays, particularly *En fallit (The Bankrupt)* and *Redaktøren (The Editor),* are credited with introducing social realism to the Scandinavian stage and influencing the work of Bjørnson's contemporary Henrik Ibsen. In addition to his literary work, Bjørnson was a prominent commentator on national politics, and to many Norwegians he embodied the spirit of their country.

The son of a rural pastor, Bjørnson spent most of his childhood in the Romsdal district of western Norway, a mountainous, pastoral region that is reflected in the settings of many of his early stories and poems. He became interested in history and politics as an adolescent and read Norway's heroic sagas as well as the patriotic poetry of Henrik Wergeland (1808-1845). Bjørnson entered the University of Norway in Christiania (now Oslo) in 1852, but withdrew after two years to work as a journalist, literary critic, and fiction writer. In 1856, his first short stories were published, and he achieved recognition as a spokesman for a movement advocating a Norwegian theater free from foreign influences. His historical drama *Mellem slagene (Between the Battles),* based on Norse sagas, was performed in 1857 to popular and critical acclaim. Bjørnson directed the national theater in Christiania during the 1860s and gained national prominence as a public speaker and pamphleteer. A leader of the Norwegian Liberal party, he was committed to various social and political causes, including Norwegian independence from Sweden, the establishment of parliamentary government, and women's rights. Bjørnson's literary output decreased during the last two decades of his life as he devoted himself to international affairs, promoting the causes of subjugated minorities throughout Europe and encouraging world peace through negotiation. Bjørnson was awarded the Nobel Prize in 1903, and when Norway obtained political independence two years later, his poem "Ja, vi elsker dette landet" was adopted as the country's national anthem. At the time of his death in 1910, Bjørnson was regarded by many as the "uncrowned king" of Norway.

Critics usually divide Bjørnson's career into two phases: the period between 1856 and 1872 when he wrote romantic epic dramas, impressionistic peasant tales, and patriotic poetry, and the period after 1875, which he devoted to social dramas. In such peasant tales as *Arne* and *Synnøve Solbakken,* Bjørnson combined settings and situations from modern life

with folk motifs and a terse prose style reminiscent of Norse sagas in order to identify the struggles of contemporary peasants with those of their heroic ancestors. The protagonists of these tales, as well as those of his epic dramas, are typically social misfits, crude and often animalistic in temperament. To survive and prosper they, like their counterparts in the sagas, must adopt the values of Christianity and civilization. Bjørnson's poems from this period similarly evoke the sagas to celebrate patriotism and the Norwegian landscape, frequently using the first-person plural to convey common experiences. While his poetry remains familiar within Norway, his early dramas and novellas have achieved world-wide critical recognition and are considered classics for their lyric quality, narrative power, and psychologically complex characterizations.

The second phase of Bjørnson's career dates from the production in 1875 of two dramas: *The Bankrupt,* which is recognized for its unprecedented presentation of the business world as a dramatic subject, and *The Editor,* which focuses on the misuse of power by the press. These plays are considered forerunners of Ibsen's work, and with them Bjørnson began a series of dramas in which he discussed timely social issues: *Leonarda,* for example, treats divorce; *En hanske (The Gauntlet)* addresses the double standard of sexual morality

1

for men and women; and *Kongen* (*The King*) attacks monarchic government and Christian dogmatism. Critics view these plays, along with those of Ibsen, as establishing social realism as a viable movement in modern theater, although they often fault Bjørnson's later dramas for didactic optimism and overly sentimental resolutions and for emphasizing issues at the expense of character development. An exception to this criticism is *Over œvne, I* (*Beyond Our Power, I*), which is regarded as Bjørnson's most morally complex and compelling drama. Avoiding explicit conclusions, this dramatic portrayal of a country pastor believed to possess miraculous healing powers is one of few works by Bjørnson considered to contain strong tragic elements.

Bjørnson's literary reputation, once equal to that of Ibsen, has diminished significantly in this century. While his peasant tales remain respected, critics regard the majority of his social dramas as outdated both in their technique and in the issues that they address. During Bjørnson's lifetime, however, his work complemented his political endeavors to further Norwegian national unity, and today he is considered a major initiator of the realist movement in modern literature.

(See also *Contemporary Authors*, Vol. 104.)

PRINCIPAL WORKS

Mellem slagene (drama) 1857
    [*Between the Battles* published in *The Nobel Prize Treasury*, 1948]
Synnøve Solbakken (novella) 1857
    [*Trust and Trial*, 1858; also published as *Love and Life in Norway*, 1870; and *Sunny Hill*, 1932]
Arne (novella) 1858
    [*Arne*, 1866]
Halte Hulde [first publication] (drama) 1858
Thrond (novella) 1858
    [*Thrond* published in *The Bridal March, and Other Stories*, 1882]
En glad gut (novella) 1860
    [*The Happy Boy*, 1870]
Kong Sverre (drama) 1861
Sigurd Slembe (dramas) 1863
    [*Sigurd Slembe*, 1888]
Maria Stuart i Skotland [first publication] (drama) 1864
    [*Mary Stuart in Scotland* published in journal *Scandinavia*, 1883-84; also published as *Mary, Queen of Scots*, 1912]
De nygifte (drama) 1865
    [*The Newly-Married Couple*, 1870; also published as *A Lesson in Marriage*, 1911; and *The Newly Married Couple* in *Three Comedies*, 1912]
Fiskerjenten (novella) 1868
    [*The Fisher-Maiden*, 1869; also published as *The Fishing Girl*, 1870; and *The Fisher Lassie* in *Arne and the Fisher Lassie*, 1890]
Arnljot Gelline (poetry) 1870
    [*Arnljot Gelline*, 1917]
Digte og sange (poetry) 1870
    [*Poems and Songs*, 1915]
Sigurd Jorsalfar [first publication] (drama) 1872
Brude-Slåtten (novella) 1873
    [*The Bridal March* published in *The Bridal March, and Other Stories*, 1882]

En fallit (drama) 1875
    [*The Bankrupt* published in *Three Dramas*, 1914]
Redaktøren (drama) 1875
    [*The Editor* published in *Three Dramas*, 1914]
Kongen [first publication] (drama) 1877
    [*The King* published in *Three Dramas*, 1914]
Magnhild (novel) 1877
    [*Magnhild*, 1883]
Det ny system (drama) 1878
    [*The New System* published in *Plays*, 1913]
Kaptejn Mansana (novella) 1879
    [*Captain Mansana* published in *Captain Mansana, and Other Stories*, 1882]
Leonarda (drama) 1879
    [*Leonarda* published in journal *The Drama*, 1911]
Life by the Fells and Fiords (novellas, short stories, and poetry) 1879
The Bridal March, and Other Stories (novellas and short stories) 1882
Captain Mansana, and Other Stories (novella and short stories) 1882
En hanske (drama) 1883
    [*A Gauntlet*, 1890; also published as *A Glove* in journal *Poet Lore*, 1892]
Over œvne, I [first publication] (drama) 1883
    [*Pastor Sang*, 1893; also published as *Beyond Our Power, I* in journal *Poet Lore*, 1905]
Det flager i byen og på havnen (novel) 1884
    [*The Heritage of the Kurts*, 1892]
Geografi og kærlighed (drama) 1885
    [*Love and Geography* published in *Plays*, 1914]
På Guds veje (novel) 1889
    [*In God's Way*, 1890]
Over œvne, II (drama) 1895
    [*Beyond Human Might* published in *Plays*, 1914]
The Novels of Bjørnstjerne Bjørnson. 13 vols. (novels) 1895-1909
Paul Lange og Tora Parsberg [first publication] (drama) 1898
    [*Paul Lange and Tora Parsberg*, 1899]
Vis-Knut (novella) 1898
    [*Wise-Knut*, 1909]
Samlede verker. 11 vols. (dramas, novels, novellas, short stories, and poems) 1900-02
Laboremus (drama) 1901
    [*Laboremus* published in journal *Fortnightly Review*, 1901; also published in *Plays*, 1914]
På Storhove (drama) 1902
Daglannet (drama) 1905
Mary (novel) 1906
    [*Mary*, 1909]
Når den ny vin blomstrer (drama) 1909
    [*When the New Wine Blooms* published in journal *Poet Lore*, 1911]
Three Comedies (dramas) 1912
Artikler og taler. 2 vols. (essays and speeches) 1912-13
Brev. 3 vols. (letters) 1912-32
Plays. 2 vols. (dramas) 1913-14
Three Dramas (dramas) 1914
Samlede digter-verker. 9 vols. (poetry) 1919-20

---

*This work includes the dramas *Sigurds første flugt*, *Sigurds anden flugt*, and *Sigurds hjemkomst*.

WILLIAM DEAN HOWELLS (essay date 1870)

[*Howells was the chief progenitor of American Realism and the most influential American literary critic during the late nineteenth century. He successfully weaned American literature from the sentimental romanticism of its infancy, earning the popular sobriquet "the Dean of American Letters." In keeping with the Realism central to his fiction and criticism, Howells urged Americans to read Bjørnson's work, as well as that of Emile Zola, Bernard Shaw, Henrik Ibsen, and other important authors. In the following excerpt, Howells discusses three of Bjørnson's early novellas:* Arne, The Happy Boy, *and* The Fisher-Maiden.]

There is in the way the tales [*Arne, The Happy Boy,* and *The Fisher-Maiden*] are told a singular simplicity, or a reticence and self-control that pass for this virtue, and that take the æsthetic sense as winningly as their sentiment touches the heart. [Bjørnson] has entire confidence in his reader's intelligence. He believes, it seems, that we can be fully satisfied with a few distinct touches in representing a situation or a character; he is the reverse, in a word, of all that is Trollopian in literary art. He does not concern himself with detail, nor with general statement, but he makes some one expressive particular serve for all introduction and explanation of a fact. The life he portrays is that, for the most part, of humble but decent folk; and this choice of subject is also novel and refreshing in contrast with the subjects of our own fictions, in which there seems to be no middle ground between magnificent drawing-rooms and the most unpleasant back-alleys, or between very refined and well-born company and the worst reprobates of either sex. How much of our sense of his naturalness would survive further acquaintance with Bjørnson we cannot venture to say; the conventionalities of a literature are but too perilously apt to be praised as naiveté by foreign criticism, and we have only the internal evidence that peasant-boys like Arne, and fisher-maidens like Petra, are not as common and tiresome in Norwegian fiction as we find certain figures in our own novels. We would willingly celebrate them, therefore, with a wise reserve, and season our delight with doubt, as a critic should; though we are not at all sure that we can do this.

Arne is the son of Margit Kampen and Nils the tailor, who is the finest dancer and the gallantest man in all the countryside; and it is with subtlety and feeling that the author hints the error by which Arne came to be:—

> The next time there was a dance in the parish Margit was there. She sat listening to the music, and cared little for the dancing that night; and she was glad that somebody else, too, cared no more for it than she did. But when it grew later, the fidler, Nils the tailor, rose and wished to dance. He went straight over and took out Margit, and before she well knew what she was doing she danced with him. . . .
>
> (p. 505)

But Nils is in love with Birgit Bøen, who loves him again, and is richer and handsomer than Margit. They torment each other, lover's fashion, Birgit being proud, and Nils capricious and dissipated, until one night at a dance he runs wilfully against Birgit and another lover of hers (who afterwards marries her), and knocks them over. Then this lover strikes Nils, who falls against the sharp edge of the fireplace, upon his spine. So Margit comes to claim him, and takes him home, and they are married; but as Nils grows better in health he grows a worse man, gives himself constantly to drink, and

beats Margit cruelly. At last it comes to this awful scene, which is portrayed with peculiar force and boldness, and which is a good illustration of a manner so unaffected that manner hardly seems the word for it. Nils comes home after one of his drinking-bouts at a wedding-party, and finds Arne reading and Margit in bed.

> Arne was startled by the sound of a heavy fall in the passage, and of something hard pushing against the door. It was the father, just coming home.
>
> "Is it you, my clever boy?" he muttered; "come and help your father to get up." Arne helped him up, and brought him to the bench; then carried in the violin-case after him and shut the door.
>
> "Well, look at me, you clever boy; I don't look very handsome, now; Nils the tailor's no longer the man he used to be. One thing, I—tell—you—you shall never drink spirits; they're—the devil, the world, and the flesh. . . . 'God resisteth the proud, but giveth grace to the humble.' . . . . O dear! O dear! How far gone I am!"
>
> He sat silent for a while, and then sang in a tearful voice,—
>
> "Merciful Lord, I come to Thee;
> Help, if there can be help for me;
> Though by the mire of sin defiled,
> I'm still Thine own dear ransomed child."
>
> (pp. 505-06)

The mother had been long awake, without looking up; but now when she heard him weeping thus like one who is saved, she raised herself on her elbows, and gazed earnestly at him.

But scarcely did Nils perceive her before he called out, "Are you looking up, you ugly vixen! I suppose you would like to see what a state you have brought me to. Well, so I look, just so!" . . . He rose; and she hid herself under the fur coverlet. "Nay, don't hide, I'm sure to find you," he said, stretching out his right hand and fumbling with his forefinger on the bedclothes, "Tickle, tickle," he said, turning aside the fur coverlet, and putting his forefinger on her throat.

"Father!" cried Arne.

"How shrivelled and thin you've become already, there's no depth of flesh here!" She writhed beneath his touch, and seized his hand with both hers, but could not free herself.

"Father!" repeated Arne.

"Well, at last you're roused. How she wriggles, the ugly thing! Can't you scream to make believe I am beating you? Tickle, tickle! I only want to take away your breath."

"Father!" Arne said once more, running to the corner of the room, and snatching up an axe which stood there.

"Is it only out of perverseness you don't scream? you had better beware; for I've taken such a strange fancy into my head. Tickle, tickle! Now, I think I shall soon get rid of that screaming of yours."

"Father!" Arne shouted, rushing towards him with the axe uplifted.

But before Arne could reach him, he started up with a piercing cry, laid his hand upon his heart, and fell heavily down. "Jesus Christ!" he muttered, and then lay quite still.

Arne stood as if rooted in the ground, and gradually lowered the axe. He grew dizzy and bewildered, and scarcely knew where he was. Then the mother began to move to and fro in the bed, and to breathe heavily, as if oppressed by some great weight lying upon her. Arne saw that she needed help; but yet he felt unable to render it. At last she raised herself a little, and saw the father lying stretched on the floor, and Arne standing beside him with the axe.

"Merciful Lord, what have you done?" she cried, springing out of the bed, putting on her skirt and coming nearer.

"He fell down himself," said Arne, at last regaining power to speak.

"Arne, Arne, I don't believe you," said the mother, in a stern reproachful voice: "now Jesus help you!" And she threw herself upon the dead man with loud wailing.

But the boy awoke from his stupor, dropped the axe and fell down on his knees: "As true as I hope for mercy from God, I've not done it. I almost thought of doing it; I was so bewildered; but then he fell down himself; and here I've been standing ever since."

The mother looked at him, and believed him. "Then our Lord has been here Himself," she said, quietly, sitting down on the floor and gazing before her.

The terror and shadow of what he might have done hung long about Arne, making lonelier and sadder the life that was already melancholy and secluded. He has many dreams of going abroad, and escaping from the gloomy associations of his home and his past life; and, indulging these and other dreams, he begins to make songs and to sing them. All the processes of his thought are clearly suggested, and then almost as much is left to the reader's fancy as in any poem that stands so professed in rhyme. People are shown without effort to account for their presence further than it is explained in their actions, so that all has the charm of fact, about which there ever hangs a certain fascinating mystery; and the pictures of scenery are made with a confidence that they will please because they are beautiful. In these, natural aspects are represented as affecting the beholder in certain ways, and nature does not, as in our false sentimentilization, take on the complexion of his thoughts and reflect his mood.

By and by Arne is drawn somewhat away from the lonely life he has been leading, and upon a certain occasion he is persuaded to go nutting with a party of young girls; and here the author sketches with all his winning lightness and confidence the young-girl character he wishes us to see:—

> So Arne came to the party, and was nearly the only young man among the many girls. Such fun as was there Arne had never seen before in all his life; and one thing which especially astonished him was, that the girls laughed for nothing at all: if three laughed, then five would laugh just because those three laughed. Altogether, they behaved as if they had lived with each other all their lives; and yet there were several of them who had never met before that

> very day. When they caught the bough which they jumped after, they laughed, and when they did not catch it they laughed also; when they did not find any nuts, they laughed because they found none; and when they did find some, they also laughed. They fought for the nutting-hook: those who got it laughed, and those who did not get it laughed also. Godfather limped after them, trying to beat them with his stick, and making all the mischief he was good for; those he hit laughed because he hit them, and those he missed laughed because he missed them. But the whole lot laughed at Arne because he was so grave; and when at last he could not help laughing, they all laughed again because he laughed.

This is the way in which all young girls appear to all boys, confounding them with emotions and caprices which they do not themselves understand; it is the history of a whole epoch of life; yet with how few words it is told! Think how one of our own story-tellers,—even a very clever one,—with the heavy and awkward traditions of the craft would have gone about it, if he or she had had the grace to conceive of anything so pretty and natural, and how it would have been explained and circumstantiated, and analyzed, and made detestable with the intrusion of the author's reflections and comments!

There is not much plot in **Arne.** The task which the author seems chiefly to have proposed himself is the working out, by incident and encounter, of a few characters. In the person of Arne as in Petra, the fisher-maiden, he attempts a most difficult work; though Arne as a genius is far inferior to Petra. Still, there is in both the waywardness and strangeness produced by peculiar gifts, and both characters have to be handled with great delicacy to preserve the truth which is so often unlike truth, and the naturalness which is so uncommon as to appear unnatural. One of the maidens in the nutting-party is Eli Bøen, the daughter of Birgit and Baard, the man who struck Arne's father that dreadful blow; and Arne, with as little consciousness as possible, and while still planning to go abroad, falls in love with her. It all ends, of course, with some delaying occurrence in their marriage, and in the heartfelt union of Eli's parents, who during twenty years have been secretly held apart by Birgit's old love for Nils, and by the memory of Baard's share in his ruin. This last effect, which is an incident of the main story, is inseparable from it, but is not hinted till far toward the end, and is then produced with that trusting and unhasty art which, together with the brevity of every scene and incident, makes the romance so enjoyable. There is something also very wise and fine in the management of the character of Margit, Arne's mother, who, in spite of the double tragedy of her life, is seen to be a passive and simple heart, to whom things merely happen, and who throughout merely loves, now her bad husband and now her affectionate yet unintelligible son, whom she singly desires to keep with her always. She is the type of maternity as nearly as it can exist unrelated to other phases and conditions; and when she hears that Arne is in love with Eli, she has no other thought than to rejoice that this is a tie which will bind him to home. Meeting Eli one evening in the road, she lures her to walk toward Kampen that she may praise Arne to her; then comes some dialogue which is contrived to show the artless artifices by which these two women strive to turn the talk to and from the object of their different love; and after that there are most enchanting little scenes in the home at Kampen, when the women find Arne's treasury of wedding-gear, and at the end some of the prettiest love-making when Arne himself comes home.

With people in another rank, Charles Reade would have managed this as charmingly, though he would have thrown into it somewhat too much of the brilliancy of the footlights; and [German novelist and short story writer Berthold] Auerbach would have done it with equal naturalness; but neither could have cast about it that poetic atmosphere which is so peculiarly the gift of Bjørnson and of the Northern mind, and which is felt in its creations, as if the glamour of the long summer days of the North had got into literature. It is very noticeable throughout *Arne.* The facts are stated with perfect ruggedness and downrightness when necessary, but some dreamy haze seems still to cling about them, subduing their hard outlines and features like the tender light of the slanting Norwegian sun on the craggy Norwegian headlands. The romance is interspersed with little lyrics, pretty and graceful in their form, but of just the quality to show that Bjørnson is wise to have chosen prose for the expression of his finer and stronger thoughts.

In that region of novel characters, wholesome sympathies, and simple interests to which he transports us, we have not only a blissful sense of escape from the jejune inventions and stock repetitions of what really seems a failing art with us, but are aware of our contact with an excellent and enviable civilization. Of course the reader sees the Norwegians and their surroundings through Bjørnson's poetic eyes, and is aware that he is reading romance; yet he feels that there must be truth to the real as well as the ideal in these stories.

Arne is the most poetical of the three, and the action is principally in a world where the troubles are from within, and inherent in human nature, rather than from any artificial causes, though the idyllic sweetness is chiefly owing to the circumstances of the characters as peasant-folk in a "North countree." In *The Happy Boy* the world of conventions and distinctions is more involved by the fortunes of the lovers; for the happy boy Oeyvind is made wretched enough in the good old way by finding out that there is a difference between riches and poverty in the eyes of grandparents, at least, and he is tormented in his love of Marit by his jealousy of a wealthier rival. It is Marit's worldly and ambitious grandfather who forbids their love, and will have only unpleasant things to say to Oeyvind, until the latter comes back from the Agricultural College, and establishes himself in his old home with the repute of the best farmer in the neighborhood. Meantime unremitted love-making goes on between Marit and Oeyvind, abetted by Oeyvind's schoolmaster, through whom indeed all their correspondence was conducted while Oeyvind was away at school. At last the affair is happily concluded when Ole Nordistuen, the grandfather, finds that his farm is going to ruin, and nothing can save it but the skill of Oeyvind.

In this story the peasant life is painted in a more naturalistic spirit, and its customs are more fully described, though here as always in Bjørnson's work the people are primarily studied as men and women, and secondarily as peasants and citizens; and the descriptions are brief, incidental, and strictly subordinate to the story. We imagine in this an exercise of self-denial, for Bjørnson must be in love with all that belongs to his characters or surrounds them, to the degree of desiring to dwell longer than he ever does upon their portrayal. His fashion in dealing with scenery and character both is well shown in [the] account of Marit's party, to which Oeyvind was invited, and

at which he ceases with his experience of the world to be the entirely happy boy of the past. . . . (pp. 506-09)

Marit's character is beautifully drawn, as it rises out of maiden coyness to meet the exigency of her lover's sensitive passion, and is so frank at once and so capricious in the sort of advances she is obliged to make to him. The correspondence carried on between the two while Oeyvind is in the Agricultural College is delightful with its mixture of prodigious formality and jealous tenderness on the hero's part, and mixture of jesting coquetry and fond consenting on Marit's side. A lover cannot take a joke from his mistress, and of course Marit shows superior to Oeyvind at this and some other times, but she is always patient and firm in her love for him.

The religious feeling which is a passive quality in *Arne* is a positive and controlling influence in *The Happy Boy,* where it is chiefly exerted by the old schoolmaster. To him a long and bitter quarrel with an only brother, now dead, has taught lifelong meekness and dread of pride; and he affectingly rebukes Oeyvind's ambition to be first among the candidates for confirmation, in order that he may eclipse all others in Marit's eyes. But Bjørnson's religious feeling is not pietistic; on the contrary, it teaches, as in *The Fisher-Maiden,* that a cheerful life of active goodness is the best interpretation of liberal and hopeful faith, and it becomes at no time a theological abstraction. It is always more or less blended with love of home, and a sense of the sweetness and beauty of natural affections. It is a strengthening property in the tenderness of a sentiment which seems almost distinctively his, or which at least is very clearly distinguished from German sentiment, and in which we Anglo-Saxon readers may indulge our hearts without that recoil of shame which otherwise attends the like surrender. Indeed, we feel a sort of inherent sympathy with most of Bjørnson's people on this and other accounts, as if we were in spirit, at least, Scandinavians with them, and the Viking blood had not yet died out of us. Some of the traits that he sketches are those now of New England fishermen and farmers and of Western pioneers,—that is, the pioneers of the time before Pacific Railroads. A conscientiousness also exists in them which is like our own,—for we have really a popular conscientiousness, in spite of many shocking appearances to the contrary,—though there seems to be practically more forgiveness in their morality than in ours, especially towards such errors as those by which Arne and Petra came to be. But their incentives and expectations are all as different from ours as their customs are, and in these romances the reader is always sensible of beholding the life of a vigorous and healthful yet innumerous people, restricted by an unfriendly climate and variable seasons, and gaining a hard subsistence from the treacherous sea and grudging soil. Sometimes the sense of nature's reluctant or cruel attitude toward man finds open expression, as in *The Fisher-Maiden,* where the pastor says to the "village saints":

> Your homes are far up among the mountains, where your grain is cut down more frequently by the frost than by the scythe. Such barren fields and deserted spots should never have been built upon; they might well be given over to pasturage and the spooks. Spiritual life thrives but poorly in your mountain home, and partakes of the gloom of the surrounding vegetation. Prejudice, like the cliffs themselves, overhangs your life and casts a shadow upon it.

Commonly, however, the pathos of this unfriendliness between the elements and man is not sharply uttered, but remains a subtle presence qualifying all impressions of Norwegian life. Perhaps it is this which gives their singular beauty to Bjørnson's pictures of the scenery amidst which the action of his stories takes place,—pictures notably of Nature in her kindlier moods, as if she were not otherwise to be endured by the imagination.

In **The Fisher-Maiden,** which is less perfect as a romance than **Arne,** Bjørnson has given us in Petra his most perfect and surprising creation. The story is not so dreamy, and it has not so much poetic intimacy with external things as **Arne,** while it is less naturalistic than **The Happy Boy,** and interests us in characters more independently of circumstance. It is, however, very real, and Petra is a study as successful as daring. To work out the character of a man of genius is a task of sufficient delicacy, but the difficulty is indefinitely enhanced where it is a woman of genius whose character is to be painted in the various phases of childhood and girlhood, and this is the labor Bjørnson undertakes in Petra. She is a girl of the lowest origin, and has had, like Arne, no legal authority for coming into the world; but like him she has a wonderful gift, though it is different from his. Looking back over her career from the close of the book, one sees plainly enough that she was born for the stage; but it is then only that the author's admirable art is apparent, and that we are reconciled to what seemed extravagances and inconsistencies, and are even consoled for the disappointment of our foolish novel-reading desire for the heroine's marriage. Petra does not marry any of the numerous lovers whom she has won in her unconscious effort to surround herself with the semblances that charm her imagination but never touch her heart; she is wedded to dramatic art alone, and the author, with a wisdom and modesty almost rare enough to be called singular, will not let us see whether the union is happy or not, but closes his book as the curtain rises upon Petra's first appearance. In fact, his business with her was there ended, as the romancer's used to be with the nuptials of his young people; what followed could only have been commonplace in contrast with what went before. The story is exquisitely pleasing; the incidents are quickly successive; the facts are in great part cheerful and amusing, and even where they are disastrous there is not a hopeless or unrelieved pathos in them; the situations are vivid and picturesque, and the people most refreshingly original and new, down to the most slightly seen and least important personage. There is also unusual range and variety in the characters; we have no longer to do with the peasants, but behold Norwegian nature as it is affected by life in towns, refined by education and thought, and sophisticated by wealth and unwise experience of the world. The figures are drawn with a strength and fineness that coexist more in this author than in any other we know, and that strike us peculiarly in the characters of Petra's mother, Gunlaug, who lets her own compassionate heart deceive her with regard to that pitiful Pedro Ohlsen, and thereafter lives a life of stormy contempt towards her seducer, forgiving him at last in a tacit sort of way sufficiently to encourage the feeble-souled creature to leave Petra his money; of Gunnar, the young sailor, who being made love to by Petra because she wants the figure of a lover for her reveries, furiously beats Ingve Vold because he has stolen Petra's airy affections from him; of Ingve Vold, the Spanish-travelled, dandified, handsome young rich man, who, after capturing Petra's fancy with stories of Spain, in turn lets his love get the better of his wickeder designs, and is ready to do anything in order to call Petra his wife; of the pastor's son, Oedegaard, who has educated Petra and has then fallen in love with her, and been accepted by her after

that imaginative person has promised herself to Gunnar and Ingve; of the country pastor in whose house Petra finds refuge (after her mother's house has been mobbed because of her breaking so many hearts, and she has been driven out of her native village), and in despite of whom she dreams and thinks of nothing but the stage, till finally he blesses her aspiration.

Two scenes in the story appear to us the most interesting; and of course the chief of these is Petra seeing a play for the first time at the theatre in Bergen, which stands quite alone as a sympathetic picture of the amaze and exaltation of genius in the art destined henceforth to express it and to explain it to itself. It is long after this before Petra comes fully to understand her past life from her present consuming desire, and perhaps she never does it so fully as another does,—as Oedegaard, or the reader; but that experience at once gives shape and direction to her future, and it is so recorded as to be nearly as much a rapture to us as to her.

After this the most admirable episode is that scene in which the "village saints" come to expostulate with the pastor against countenancing music and dancing and other wicked cheerfulnesses, and in which the unanswerable arguments of the pastor in self-defence are made subtly to undermine the grounds of his own opposition to Petra's longing for the theatre. In this scene the religious and earnest element of Bjørnson's genius appears with great effect. The bigoted sincerity of the saints is treated with beautiful tenderness, while their errors are forcibly discovered to them. In a little space these people's characters are shown in all their individual quaintness, their narrow life is hinted in its gloom and loneliness, and the reader is made to feel at once respect and compassion for them.

There is no room left here to quote from **The Fisher-Maiden;** but the reader has already been given some idea of Bjørnson's manner in the passages from **Arne.** . . . This manner is always the same in its freedom from what makes the manner of most of our own stories tedious and abominable: it is always direct, unaffected, and dignified, expressing nothing of the author's personality, while fully interpreting his genius, and supplying no intellectual hollowness and poverty with tricks and caprices of phrase.

We hope that his publishers will find it profitable to give us translations of all his works. From him we can learn that fulness exists in brevity rather more than in prolixity; that the finest poetry is not ashamed of the plainest fact; that the lives of men and women, if they be honestly studied, can, without surprising incident or advantageous circumstance, be made as interesting in literature as are the smallest private affairs of the men and women in one's own neighborhood; that telling a thing is enough, and explaining it too much; and that the first condition of pleasing is a generous faith in the reader's capacity to be pleased by natural and simple beauty. (pp. 510-12)

William Dean Howells, in an originally unsigned review of "Arne," "The Happy Boy," and "The Fisher-Maiden," in The Atlantic Monthly, *Vol. XXV, No. CL, April, 1870, pp. 504-12.*

HJALMAR HJORTH BOYESEN   (essay date 1880)

[Boyesen was a Norwegian-born American novelist, poet, and educator whose novel Gunnar *(1874) brought him to the attention of critic William Dean Howells. Influenced by Howells's*

criticism, Boyesen turned from Romanticism to a realistic treatment of frustrated American ideals. His critical studies include Goethe and Schiller *(1879) and* Essays on Scandinavian Literature *(1895). In the following excerpt, he elaborates on Bjørnson's portrayal of the Norwegian national character in his peasant tales and epic dramas.*]

Bjørnstjerne Bjørnson is the first Norwegian poet who can in any sense be called national. The national genius, with its limitations as well as its virtues, has found its living embodiment in him. Whenever he opens his mouth it is as if the nation itself were speaking. If he writes a little song, hardly a year elapses before its phrases have passed into the common speech of the people; composers compete for the honor of interpreting it in simple, Norse-sounding melodies, which gradually work their way from the drawing-room to the kitchen, the street, and thence out over the wide fields and highlands of Norway. His tales, romances and dramas express collectively the supreme result of the nation's experience, so that no one to-day can view Norwegian life or Norwegian history except through their medium. The bitterest opponent of the poet (for like every strong personality he has many enemies) is thus no less his debtor than his warmest admirer. His speech has, in a measure, molded the common language and forced it to move in the channels that he has prescribed; his thoughts fill the air and have become the unconscious property of all who have grown into manhood and womanhood since the day when his titanic form first loomed up on the intellectual horizon of the North. (pp. 336-37)

The first proof of his strength he gave in the tale ***Synnøve Solbakken (Synnøve Sunny-Hill)***, which he published first in an illustrated weekly, and afterward in book-form. It is a very unpretending little story, idyllic in tone, severely realistic in its coloring, and redolent with the fragrance of the pine and spruce and birch of the Norwegian highlands.

It had been the fashion in Norway since the nation gained its independence to interest oneself in a lofty, condescending way in the life of the peasantry. A few well-meaning persons, like the poet Wergeland, had labored zealously for their enlightenment and the improvement of their physical condition; but, except in the case of such single individuals, no real and vital sympathy and fellow-feeling had ever existed between the upper and the lower strata of Norwegian society. And as long as the fellow-feeling is wanting, this zeal for enlightenment, however laudable its motive, is not apt to produce lasting results; the peasants view with distrust and suspicion whatever comes to them from their social superiors, and the so-called "useful books," which were scattered broadcast over the land, were of a tediously didactic character, and, moreover, hardly adapted to the comprehension of those to whom they were ostensibly addressed. Wergeland himself, with all his self-sacrificing ardor, had but a vague conception of the real needs of the people, and wasted much of his valuable life in his efforts to improve, and edify and instruct them. It hardly occurred to him that the culture of which he and his colleagues were the representatives was itself a foreign importation, and could not by any violent process be ingrafted on the national trunk, which drew its strength from centuries of national life, history and tradition. That this peasantry, whom the bourgeoisie and the aristocracy of culture had been wont to regard with half-pitying condescension, were the real representatives of the Norse nation, that they had preserved through long years of tyranny and foreign oppression the historic characteristics of their Norse forefathers, while the upper classes had gone in search of strange gods, and bowed

their necks to the foreign yoke; that in their veins the old strong Saga-life was still throbbing with vigorous pulse-beats—this was the lesson which Bjørnson undertook to teach his countrymen, and a very fruitful lesson it has proved to be. It has inspired the people with a renewed vitality, it has turned the national life into fresh channels, and it is at this day quietly revolutionizing the national politics.

To be sure, all this was not the result of the idyllic little tale which marked the beginning of his literary and political career. But this little tale, although no trace of what the Germans call "a tendency" is to be found in it, is still significant as being the poet's first indirect manifesto, and as such distinctly foreshadowing the path which he has since consistently followed.

First, in its purely literary aspect ***Synnøve Solbakken*** was a striking innovation. The author did not, as his predecessors had done, view the people from the exalted pedestal of superior culture; not as a subject for benevolent preaching and charitable condescension, but as a concrete historic phenomenon, whose raison d'être was as absolute and indisputable as that of the bourgeoisie or the aristocracy itself. He depicted their soul-struggles and the incidents of their daily life with a loving minuteness and a vivid realism hitherto unequaled in the literature of the North. He did not, like [German novelist and short story writer Berthold] Auerbach, construct his peasant figures through laborious reflection, nor did he attempt by anxious psychological analysis to initiate the reader into their processes of thought and emotion. He simply depicted them as he saw and knew them; their feelings and actions have their immediate, self-evident motives in the characters themselves, and the absence of reflection on the author's part gives an increased energy and movement to the story. A reader is never disposed to cavil with a poet who is himself so profoundly convinced of the reality of his narrative.

Bjørnson's style, as exhibited in ***Synnøve Solbakken,*** was no less novel than his theme. It can hardly be said to have been consciously modeled after the Saga style, to which, however, it bears an obvious resemblance. In his early childhood, while he lived among the peasants, he, no doubt, became familiar with their mode of thought and speech, and it entered into his being, and became his own natural mode of expression. There is even in his common conversation a certain grim directness, and a laconic ponderosity, which give an air of importance and authority even to his simplest utterances. While listening to him the thought has often urged itself upon me that it was thus King Sverre and St. Olaf spoke, and it was not hard to comprehend how they swayed the turbulent souls of their Norsemen by the power of such speech.

In Bjørnson's tales and dramas this innate tendency to compression frequently has the effect of obscurity, not because his thought is obscure, but rather because this energetic brevity of expression has fallen into disuse, and even a Norse public, long accustomed to the wordy diffuseness of latter-day bards, have in part lost the faculty to comprehend the genius of their own language. The old scalds, even if translated into Danish, would hardly be plain reading to modern Norsemen. Before becoming personally acquainted with Bjørnson I admit that I was disposed to share the common error, believing his laconic sententiousness to be a mere literary artifice; but when, at a certain political meeting in Guldbrandsdale, in July, 1873, I heard him hurl forth a torrent of impassioned rhetoric, every word and phrase of which seemed bursting with a fullness of compressed meaning, I felt that here was a man of the old heroic mold, inspired with the greatness of his mission, wielding granite masses of words as if they had been light as feathers and pliable as clay. And such a man does not stoop to artifices. The thought burns at a white heat within him, melting the stubborn ore of language into liquid streams, and molding it powerfully so as to express the subtlest shades of meaning. If a style accomplishes this result, if it reproduces the genius of the thing it is to represent, what more do you want of it? What does it matter whence it comes, or after whom it is modeled? Bjørnson's style, moreover, abounds in strong, sensuous color, is at the same time warmly tinged by an all-pervading poetic tone; it is swiftly responsive to every shifting mood, and with all its ponderosity reflects faithfully the characteristic features of the national physiognomy. It has already conquered or is conquering the rising generation; or as a former fellow-student of mine remarked to me during my last visit to Norway: "Bjørnsonian is the language of the future."

Synnøve Solbakken has been translated into nearly all the European languages; in England it was published several years ago under the title *Love and Life in Norway.* Singularly enough, no American edition has as yet appeared.

In 1858, Bjørnson assumed the directorship of the theater in Bergen, and there published his second tale, *Arne,* which is too well known on this side of the Atlantic (though in a very poor translation) to require a detailed analysis. The same admirable self-restraint, the same implicit confidence in the intelligence of his reader, the same firm-handed decision and vigor in the character drawing, in fact, all the qualities which startled the public in *Synnøve Solbakken,* were found here in an intensified degree.

In the meanwhile, Bjørnson had also made his début as a dramatist. In the year 1858 he had published two dramas, *Mellem slagene (Between the Battles)* and *Halte Hulda (Limping Hulda),* both of which deal with national subjects, taken from the old Norse Sagas. As in his tales he had endeavored to concentrate into a few strongly defined types the modern folk-life of the North, so in his dramas the same innate love of his nationality leads him to seek the typical features of his people as they are revealed in the historic chieftains of the past. And in the Saga age Norway was still an historic arena where vast forces were wrestling, and whence strong spiritual currents went forth to infuse fresh, uncorrupted life-blood into the drowsier civilizations of the south. Life then moved with full-throbbing, vigorous pulse-beats, the roving habits and indomitable valor of the Norseman extended his horizon over the whole known world, the liberal, though half-barbaric organization of the state, which placed the subject nearly on a level with the ruler, allowed the widest scope for individual development. In such an age one may confidently look for large types, strong antithesis of character and situations full of spontaneous dramatic vigor.

Again, as the creator of a national drama, Bjørnson, as well as his great rival Henrik Ibsen, had another advantage which is not to be lightly estimated. That he must have been conscious of it himself, his consistency in the selection of his themes is a sufficient proof. Only in a single instance (in his *Maria Stuart*) has he strayed beyond the soil of his fatherland in search of his hero. It had been the fashion in Norway, as, unfortunately, it is in the United States at the present day, to measure the worth of a drama by the novelty and ingenuity of its situations, by its scenic effects, and its power to amuse

or to move. The poet was required to invent, and the more startling his inventions the greater his meed of praise. That a national drama could never be founded on such purely subjective invention seemed never to have occurred to any one. Professors and scholars might praise the Attic drama and marvel at its wonderful effect upon the populace as an educational agency and a powerful stimulus to patriotism, but they would probably have denounced it as a wild theory, if any one had maintained that a similar or corresponding effect might be reproduced in Norway and in the nineteenth century. Nevertheless, this is *mutatis mutandis* ["after making the necessary changes"], exactly what Bjørnson has attempted to do. Æschylus, Sophocles, and Euripides dramatized the national traditions; they represented upon the stage the deeds of Agamemnon, Orestes, Ajax—deeds and heroes which were familiar to every Athenian from his earliest childhood; they built upon a sure national basis, appealed to strong national instincts, and, if they violated no æsthetic law, were sure of a ready response. Tradition and history furnished their themes, which admitted of but few and slight variations; but in the dramatization of these long-established events, in the dialogue and characterization, in the introduction of choruses, in scenic effects and in all the dramatic accessories of the action, their genius had full scope, and in accordance with the amount of ability they displayed in the invention and disposition of these, the value of their work was estimated. In Norway, too, as in Athens, there are historic heroes and events which are deeply engraved in the hearts of every Norse man and woman. There is hardly a boy whose cheeks have not glowed with pride at the mention of the Fair-haired Harold's name, who has not fought at Svolder at Olaf Trygvesson's side, who has not stood on Kjølen's ridge with St. Olaf, gazing out over Norway's fair valleys, who has not mourned the death of the saintly king at Stiklestad, and followed Sverre Sigurdson through fair and foul weather while he roamed over the mountains with his hardy Birchlegs. Among the peasantry, tradition has long been busy with these names; ballads are sung and tales are told in which their deeds are praised and adorned with many fabulous accessories; and until this very day their names have a potent charm to the Norseman's ear. Here, then, is the historic and traditional basis upon which a great and enduring national drama can safely be built. Bjørnson, with all the warm Gothic strength of his nature, has set himself to his task, and the structure is now already well advanced.

The old Norse history, as related in the *Heimskringla* of the Icelander Snorre Sturlason, is an inexhaustible mine of treasure to the dramatic poet. It abounds in tragic themes, vivid character-drawing, and magnificent situations which leap and throb with intense dramatic life. Existence was a comparatively simple affair then, as long as one managed to keep it. Life was held cheap, and death in a good cause glorious. Men's motives were plain, strong, and sharply defined, and their actions prompt and decisive. The things that you must refrain from doing were easily counted on the fingers of one hand. No complicated social or moral machinery obstructed the hero's path toward the goal he had set himself. Strength of will then made the hero. There was no greatness without it—no virtue. And this must be kept steadily in mind while viewing Bjørnson's Sigurds and Sverres and Eyolfs. To take an instance, and evidently a favorite one with the poet:

Sigurd (afterward surnamed Slembe), a brave lad of eighteen, enters St. Olaf's Chapel, throws his cap on the floor, kneels before the altar and thus addresses the saint:

"Now only listen to me, saintly Olaf!
To-day I whipped young Beintein! Beintein was
The strongest man in Norway. Now am I!
Now I can walk from Lindesnas and on,
Up the northern boundary of the snow,
To no one step aside or lift my hat.
There where I am, no man hath leave to fight,
To make alarm, to threaten, or to swear—
Peace everywhere! And he who wrong hath suffered
Shall justice find, until the laws shall sing.
And as before the great have whipped the small,
So will I help the small to whip the great.
Now I can offer counsel at the Ting ["assembly"],
Now to the King's board I can boldly walk
And sit beside him, saying 'Here am I!' "

Sigurd has a dim presentiment that he is born for something great. His foster-father, Adalbrekt, has in wrath betrayed that he is not his son, and the boy's restless fancy is fired by the possibilities which this knowledge opens up to him. In the next scene he compels his mother, in the presence of the chieftain Koll Saebjørnson, to reveal the secret of his birth, and on learning that he is the son of King Magnus Barefoot, he turns toward the image of the royal saint and cries:

Then you and I are kinsmen!

The ennobling or destroying power of a great mission is the central thought in nearly all of Bjørnson's dramas. To Sigurd the knowledge of his birth is a clue by the aid of which his whole past inner life grows clear to him. He is not Hamlet, who shuns the results of his own thoughts. He rather burns to shape them into actions that shall resound far and near over the land. It must be borne in mind that, according to Norwegian law, every son of a king, whether legitimate or not, was heir to the throne and entitled to his share of the kingdom. Illegitimacy was at that time hardly considered as a stain upon a man's honor. Sigurd therefore determines to go to the king and demand recognition, but Koll Saebjørnson convinces him of the utter hopelessness of such an errand, and induces him to give it up. But the fatal knowledge has come like a new power into his narrow life; it lifts the roof from his soul; it sends down sun-gleams of strange and high things, opens long, shining vistas of hope, and the thoughts rise on strong wings toward loftier goals than hitherto were dreamt of. It becomes an inspiration, an exalted mission in whose service tears, and sorrow, and suffering are as nought. The old cramped existence, with its small aims and its limited horizon, becomes too narrow for the soul that harbors the royal thought. By the aid of Koll he fits out a ship, takes the cross, and steers for southern lands.

In the second division of the trilogy, entitled *Sigurd's Second Flight,* we find him eight years later in Scotland, where his ship has been wrecked and his crew scattered. He has served with distinction at the court of the Scottish king, and has gained great fame for prowess and daring. The king has now sent him to the farm Kataness, where Harold, the Earl of the Orkneys, lives, having been defeated and driven from his heritage by his brother Paul. After a brief love-affair with Audhild, a young kinswoman of the Earl's, he conquers the usurper, makes peace between the brothers, and starts once more for the Holy Land.

In this, as in the last division of the drama (*Sigurd's Return*) the gradual transformation of the hero's character is traced with marvelous minuteness and skill. Through all his long wanderings the ever-present thought that he is a king, the born heir to Norway's throne, pushes all mere considerations

of prudence out of sight, and fills his whole soul. After another absence of eight years he arrives in Norway, and demands recognition of his brother, king Harold Gille. The king, who is a weak and vainglorious man and an unconscious tool in the hands of his chieftains, is at first disposed to receive him well, but in the end allows evil counsel to prevail. No one doubts the justice of Sigurd's claim, for he bears on his brow the mark of his royal birth. But the ambitious chiefs, who now rule the king as well as the land, fear him, knowing well that if he shall seize the rudder of the State, their power will end. They plan treachery against him, arrest him in the name of the king, and make an attempt against his life. Sigurd, however, escapes to the mountains, spends the winter among the Finns, and in the spring gathers flocks of discontented men about him. A long and bloody civil war commences, and Sigurd wreaks cruel vengeance on his enemies. The cold-blooded treachery of the king has hardened him, and he repays like for like. He lands in the night with a band of men at the wharves of Bergen and kills his brother. Many of those who have secretly or openly favored him now desert his cause, and after his last battle at Holmengraa he is captured and tortured to death. The drama closes with a beautiful scene between Sigurd and his mother during the battle, the result of which is distinctly foreshadowed.

The trilogy of Sigurd Slembe is not easy reading; the dialogue is ponderous, full of grave and weighty thoughts and moving with the heavy dignity of a steel-clad warrior. It is absolutely lacking in plastic grace, and has no superfluous rhetorical ornaments. Each thought fills its phrase as completely as if molded in liquid form within it. It is a play to be seen rather than read. The effects are everywhere massive, and the tragic problem is stated with a clear conciseness that leaves nothing to be desired. The moral atmosphere of the twelfth century is so artistically reproduced that we are unconsciously forced to judge the hero by the standards and ideals of his own age. Even though his path is strewn with misdeeds, he never loses our sympathy; we feel the tragic force that hurries him onward, and the psychological consistency of his development from a trustful, warm-hearted youth to a hard, reluctantly cruel, and withal nobly inspired man. It is no longer a mission he fights for, but a right; and in this single-handed battle against society the individual must succumb. Even though justice be on its side, this very justice, violated by questionable deeds in its own pursuit, demands a tragic dénouement; it is the iron force of the law, from which even the hero is not exempt.

This gradual deepening and intensifying of a life under the stress of a grand thought or passion is Bjørnson's favorite problem. The very grandeur of the hero's character places him in antagonism to the narrow, short-sighted interests of society which, on every side, hedge him in. His keenly felt right of self-determination clashes with the same right on the part of his neighbor, and, in the inevitable conflict that ensues, the weaker is sacrificed. Individually the neighbor may be the weaker, and individually he may accordingly succumb, but as representing the eternal right he will, in the end, prevail.

In another of Bjørnson's dramas (*Limping Hulda*) the passion of love plays a role similar to that here assigned to the "royal thought." Eyolf Finnson, a warrior of the king's body-guard, loves Hulda, the wife of the chieftain Gudleik Aslakson. She returns his love, and they plot the death of Gudleik, whom Eyolf slays. Hulda has lived a bitter life of dependence, steeped in commonplace cares, and has been forced to smother all the high ideal yearnings of her heart. But at the sight of Eyolf they blaze up into a wild, devouring flame, all the depths of her strong nature are stirred, and she marches with a royal heedlessness toward her goal, thrusting down by her lover's arm every obstacle in her way. Measured by the standards of her own age, she appears grand and exalted; and the problem is so stated that, however much we may condemn each separate deed, the doer never becomes sordid, never loses our sympathy. The motive is overwhelmingly potent. The titanic passion, whether lawful or not, has a sublimity of its own which compels a breathless admiration and awe. The poet's ethical conception of his problem is in no way confused; he sees himself the expiation which the guilt necessitates, and the vengeance which overtakes the lovers in the last act satisfies poetic as well as ethical justice, and reasserts the rights of society in its relation to the heroic transgressor. But apart from all ethical considerations a supreme passion has its æsthetic justification, and what the great Danish critic Brandes has said of the poet Ibsen would, no doubt, as correctly define Bjørnson's attitude toward the moral law in his capacity of dramatist: "Strength of will—this it is which to him is the really sublime."

Bjørnson has several times been the "artistic director" of the Norwegian stage, first in Bergen and later in Christiania, and has, no doubt, while in this position, made the discouraging discovery that the theatrical public are seldom apt to take a favorable view of any enterprise that savors, even remotely, of the didactic. The newspapers in Norway, as elsewhere, are fond of talking unctuously of the elevating influence of the stage, and the city of Christiania, and, if we are not mistaken, the Parliament itself, have frequently subsidized the principal theater when it seemed to be on the verge of financial ruin. The inhabitants of the Norwegian capital are justly proud of their excellent stage, which compares favorably with that of any European capital, exclusive of Paris and Vienna. But as the repertoire of national dramas is as yet very small, and Bjørnson's and Ibsen's historic tragedies have been played so often that half the public must by this time almost know them by heart, the managers have been forced to rely chiefly on translations of French comedies and operas bouffes, which are frequently anything but elevating. This state of things Bjørnson has tried to counteract by the publication of a series of short historic plays, the plots of which are invariably taken from the Sagas. In his preface to the first of these (*Sigurd the Crusader*) he develops his plan as follows:

> *Sigurd the Crusader* is meant to be what is called a "folk-play." It is my intention to make several dramatic experiments with grand scenes from the Sagas, lifting them into a strong but not too heavy frame. By a "folk-play" I mean a play which should appeal to every eye and every stage of culture, to each in its own way, and at the performance of which all, for the time being, would experience the joy of fellow-feeling. The common history of a people is best available for this purpose—nay, it ought dramatically never to be treated otherwise. The treatment must necessarily be simple and the emotions predominant; it should be accompanied with music, and the development should progress in clear groups. . . .
>
> The old as well as the new historic folk-literature will, with its corresponding comic element, as I think, be a great gain to the stage, and will preserve its connection with the people where this has not already been lost—so that it be no longer a mere institution for amusement, and that only to a single class. Unless we take this view of our stage, it will lose its right to be regarded as a national affair, and the best part of its purpose, to unite while it lifts and makes us free, will be gradually assumed by some other agency. Nor shall we ever get actors fit for anything but trifles, unless we abandon our foreign French tendency as a *leading* one and substitute the national needs of our own people in its place.

It would be interesting to note how the author has attempted to solve a problem so important and so difficult as this. In the first place, we find in the *Sigurd the Crusader* not a trace of a didactic purpose beyond that of familiarizing the people with its own history, and this, as he himself admits in the preface just quoted, is merely a secondary consideration. He wishes to make all, irrespective of age, culture, and social station, feel strongly the bond of their common nationality; and, with this in view, he proceeds to unroll to them a panorama of simple but strikingly dramatic situations, firmly knit together by a plot or story which, without the faintest tinge of sensationalism, is instinct with a certain emotional vigor, appealing to those broadly human and national sympathies which form the common mental basis of Norse ignorance and Norse learning. He seizes the point of the Saga where the long-smouldering hostility between the royal brothers, Sigurd the Crusader and Eystein, has broken into full blaze, and traces, in a series of vigorously sketched scenes, the intrigue and counter-intrigue which hurry the action onward toward its logically prepared climax—of a mutual reconciliation. The dialogue, it must be admitted, is almost glaringly destitute of poetical graces, but has, perhaps on that very account, a certain simple impressiveness which, no doubt, was the effect the author primarily designed.

In looking back upon the long series of monumental works which have come from Bjørnson's pen during the last twenty years, no one can escape a sense of wonder at the versatility and many-sidedness of his genius. His creative activity has found expression in almost all the more prominent branches of literature, and in each he has labored with originality and force, breaking his own path and refusing to follow the well-worn ruts of literary precedents. His tales and dramas penetrated into the hidden depths of Norse folk-life in the present and in the past, his lyrics have expressed, in striking words though in heavily moving rhythm, the deepest needs and yearnings of the Norseman's heart, and his epic (*Arnljot Gelline*), which in artistic merit falls considerably below his other productions, has a wild waywardness of thought and movement which we have called epic merely because it refuses to class itself under any other accepted species of literary expression. Whatever he writes is weighty and vital—fraught with the life-blood of his profoundest experience. He never condescends, like so many who now claim the name of poets, to make experiments for literary effect; and whatever may be the technical deficiencies of this or that work, this living, nervous, blood-veined vitality gives it an abiding value of which no amount of caviling criticism can ever deprive it. He is no "parlor poet," who stands aloof from life, retiring into the close-curtained privacy of his study to ponder upon some abstract, bloodless and sexless theme for the edification of a blasé, over-refined public, delighting in mere flimsy ingenuity because their diseased nerves can no longer relish the soul-stirring passions and emotions of a healthy and active humanity. Bjørnson's poetry is bound by strong organic chords to his life, and his life is his nation's life. If you sever the vital connection between the two, the former could no more live than the plant uprooted from its native soil. He walks with keen, wide-awake senses through the thick of life, rejoicing, in the fullness of his great heart at every sign of his people's progress, burning with indignation at every public wrong, lifting his voice boldly for human right and freedom, and whoever comes but for a moment within the sphere of his mighty personality, feels himself lifted into loftier, more ideal views of existence—feels himself inspired with a brighter hope for the future of his race. Nothing small and mean and sordid can endure the light of his eye; and the purblind conservatives of Norway, soul-crippled by prosperity and gout, can only cry themselves hoarse through the newspapers, but seldom dare to meet him face to face to measure strength with him in open debate. They rather intrench themselves behind the formidable barricades of traditional and ancestral virtue and denounce the innovator with shrill indignation, though his arguments may still remain impregnable.

From this daily battle with political obscurantism and superstition, from his intimate association with people of all classes and ages, from his own manful struggles for the right, he has gained and is ever gaining a great fund of knowledge, which in time crystallizes in his mind and assumes the form of poetic utterance. It is the natural process of his mind, and to him the only process. The common notion that the poet must be a mere ideal thinker, unsoiled by the dust of vulgar life, he utterly scouts. It must be said in praise of the conservative majority which at that time ruled the Norwegian Parliament (Storthing), that it did not stop to cross-question him on his political convictions, before recognizing the worth of his poetic activity to the nation. To be sure, he had not then unfurled his political banner, and very likely many of those who then voted him an annual poet's salary for life, from the national treasury, may now heartily regret their own generosity. Since then, however, the power has passed into the hands of the more radical peasant-party, the majority of which were, until very recently, in cordial sympathy with the poet. How long will it be before our American Congress shall have arrived at the stage of development when it will of its own accord—and without any friendly lobbying on the part of anybody—thus frankly recognize a poet's claim to the nation's gratitude? How long before it will, in mere common justice, allow an author to reap the full profits of his own labor? In Norway there is now hardly a man of any distinction in literature who is not, without any direct stipulation to render anything in return, by the munificence of the Storthing enabled to pursue his vocation untroubled by the care for bread. Beside Bjørnson, Henrik Ibsen, Jonas Lie and Kristofer Janson, and possibly several more, receive such a "poet's salary," and all classes seem to be agreed that never has a state investment yielded a richer return. As regards Bjørnson, he has taught the Norsemen what their nationality means, and thereby transformed the vain patriotic boasting of former years into a deep and abiding love. He is laboring, in song and speech and action, to break down the feudal reminiscences of the Middle Ages which still linger on in Norwegian politics and society; and he is striving to make each forget his petty, accidental advantages of birth, or wealth, or culture, by uniting all under the broad, battle-scarred shield of natural fellow-feeling. And a man of such grand intellectual stature, a man of such fire of thought, and such valor in action, a man who has the strength to force a whole nation to follow in his path—how can we judge and measure him, how can we estimate his work? The poet is decried and overwhelmed with petty abuse by those who have reason to dread the results of

his mighty and fearless thought; but he heeds little the raven-cry from the camp of frightened prudence, knowing well that he is strong and can afford to be generous. For the people's heart still beats in unison with his own—that people whose deepest emotions and thoughts he has interpreted, and whose secluded life he has lifted into a bright, far-seen niche in the great literature of the world.

* * * * *

Since the foregoing was written, Bjørnson has published several dramas and tales, dealing with the various social and political problems of modern life. Some of them, as, for instance, **The Editor,** and **A Bankruptcy,** have had a well-deserved success on the stage at home and abroad, while others (**Leonarda** and the novel **Magnhild**) have been a great disappointment to many of the author's sincerest admirers. In both, the social reformer seems to have run away with the poet. In **Magnhild,** the characters are but vaguely sketched, and their language is exasperatingly enigmatical, unnatural and full of mannerisms. In a poem entitled **The King,** Bjørnson declares monarchy to be, of necessity, a lie, and, in the guise of the republican prince, he announces his own allegiance to the republic.

Singular as it may seem, his popularity in Norway has suffered severely by his refusal to believe in a personal devil. His political heterodoxy has long been tolerated, and he has had innumerable partisans, always ready to shout for him and to raise him upon their shoulders; but his disrespect for Satan has frightened the majority of these away, and the petty persecution of the reactionary press and the official Philistines has made his life at home during the last year very bitter to him. He has, therefore, resolved to sell his homestead in Guldbrandsdale and to live henceforth permanently abroad. (pp. 338-45)

Hjalmar Hjorth Boyesen, "Bjørnstjerne Bjørnson," in Scribner's Monthly, *Vol. XX, No. 3, July, 1880, pp. 336-45.*

MAX BEERBOHM (essay date 1901)

[Beerbohm is considered one of the leading satirists and caricaturists of the 1890s. Influenced by the aesthetic theories of Walter Pater, Oscar Wilde, and James McNeill Whistler, he has been highly praised as a prose stylist of wit, urbanity, and invention. As a drama critic for the Saturday Review, *he secured his reputation as a perceptive observer of the arts and human nature. In the following excerpt from a review of Mrs. Patrick Campbell's English production of* Over ævne, I *at the Royalty Theatre in London, Beerbohm praises the drama while finding its second act flawed.]*

[Mrs. Campbell's] latest offering is a series of matinées of **Beyond Human Power,** an English version of a play in two acts by Bjørnson. It is a gift which none but she would have dared to offer, even in the afternoon, and which, if any one but she had offered it, would have been rejected with every expression of scorn and ribaldry. Last Saturday, however, I found the public respectfully entranced by it. The first act ended in a storm of applause. Simple Norwegians, of whom I saw several in the vestibule, were evidently elated by Bjørnson's triumph. "Skohl!" they murmured, gazing at the large photograph of the master which hung beneath a laurel-crown upon the wall. . . . The face of a tremendously dynamic and forthright person, strenuously imposing himself on the enfeebled nations of the South, and wringing from them the homage he knows to be his due. And yet, impressive though the photograph was, or rather because it was so awfully impressive, I could not help smiling. For I knew well how ill this brawny Viking would have fared here, had not that frail-looking Southern lady, with the dreaming eyes, stood sponsor for him—had she not bent down and lifted him in her arms, affectionately, and carried him, and cooed over him.

If these words should meet the eye of any simple Norwegians, they must not suppose me to be sneering at Bjørnson's play. I sneer rather at the conventionality of people who cannot appreciate for its intrinsic goodness a play which does not conform with the current fashions of dramatic art in their own country. In the second act, as I shall suggest, Bjørnson defies not only our own current and negligible conventions in dramatic art, but also those eternal, universal conventions which inhere in the art—conventions which every dramatist should respect. And the result of this violence is that most of the second act seems to me (and must seem to any other impartial creature) hopelessly undramatic, dull and trivial. But with this rather large reservation, **Beyond Human Power** seems to me a fine and inspiring work. The irony of its story (I need not warn you of the sense in which I use the word "irony") is quite magnificent. Pastor Adolf Sang is a buoyant saint, practising the precepts of Christianity according to their most literal significance, a giant rejoicing in the strength of

his faith and in the strength that his faith gives him. There is no danger he will not encounter, so sure is he of Divine protection. There is no miracle he cannot work among the peasants who are in his charge. Over their weak and simple natures his simple strength has such sway that he can cure them of all sicknesses. He is a prophet not without honour in his own country, but (here is the first irony) he is a prophet without honour in his own home. His wife has never believed in him as an agent of Heaven, and has always taken a rationalistic view of his miracles. His two children, now that they have grown up, are also unbelieving. There is this further irony, that the children, loving him devotedly, are yearning to take him at his own valuation, and failing signally to do so. His effect on his wife is a matter of still deeper irony: in the knowledge that he, through his literal Christianity, is ruining the worldly prospects of the children, and in the constant struggle between her love for him and her desire for their welfare, she has suffered such torments that her health has broken down utterly. She is partially paralysed. She cannot sleep. She is always in pain. The omnibeneficient Pastor has ruined the life that he loves best of all. His wife's is the one affliction he cannot cure. Even *his* self-confidence is undermined by this salient failure. But he shakes off doubt, determining to put forth a vast effort. And it is on the success or failure of this vast effort that the interest of the play is centred. Pastor Sang goes away to pray in his church. Presently, a bell is heard tolling. It is the signal that his prayer has begun. His

A scene from the first act of Over aevne, I.

wife falls into a quiet sleep. Scarcely have the children realised this wonder when they hear an ominous crash in the distance. They start up, knowing it to be a landslip from the mountains, knowing that nothing can save the church where their father is praying. Nearer and nearer comes the noise of crashing and crumbling. It passes, subsides, and through the silence comes the steady sound of the bell, tolling still. . . . That is the end of the first act, and if you, reader, do not think it a finely dramatic end, then my writing must be lamentably inferior to Mrs. Campbell's stage-managing. Let us skip now to the end of the second act. In the room outside that in which the sick woman is still sleeping sits a company of Pastors. Pastor Sang is still in his church, praying. Will his prayer be granted? Will the woman rise from her bed and come among them before the sun sets? The light of the setting sun reddens the cross above the door, and a strange silence falls on the room. The door slowly opens, and through it, slowly and vaguely, with extended arms, comes the arisen woman. The peasants troop in, singing a hymn of praise. The Pastors join in the hymn, gazing awestruck at the miracle. And, at last, he who has wrought the miracle rushes in and clasps his wife in his arms. In his arms she dies. "Oh," he gasps, "this—this is not what I meant." He has killed his wife by a miracle, and by that same token his own faith. This is not what he meant. The final irony of his fate is accomplished. He dies.

My suggestion that we should skip thus to the end was made in order that I might not spoil the description of what is fine in the play by describing with it what is ineffably tedious. Those Pastors! six or seven of them, every one of them with his own view as to how modern faith-healing ought to be regarded by the Norwegian Church. What they say is in itself, doubtless, quite sensible and interesting. But they have no business to say it in this play. It has no possible bearing on this play. The dramatic point is whether a particular miracle will or will not be accomplished. What is the attitude of Norwegian clergymen towards miracles in general is a question quite beside the point. If the opinions of these clergymen were likely to affect in any way the life of Pastor Sang, they might be dramatically excusable. But such is not the case. The clergymen are strangers from a distance, here by chance, and going away directly; and their discussion is purely academic. Dramatically they are quite impertinent, and in a work of art whatever is not pertinent is bad. Even in Norway, where, possibly, "Faith-healing and the Church" is a topic of acute controversy, these clergymen must have been a sorry deadweight. That in England the audience did not throw things at them is a great tribute to the goodness of the play as a whole. . . . (pp. 176-79)

*Max Beerbohm, "Bjørnson at the Royalty Theatre,"
in his* Around Theatres, *revised edition, Simon and
Schuster, 1953, pp. 175-79.*

BJØRNSTJERNE BJØRNSON (essay date 1910?)

[*In the following excerpt, which was published posthumously
in the collection* Artikler og taler, *Bjørnson discusses the purpose of literature.*]

Since the early days of my youth I have had in my mind a very primitive picture of human evolution: I see it as an endless procession in motion. Advancing—not exactly in a straight line—yet always advancing. Irresistible craving is urging it on, at first instinctively but gradually with an increasing consciousness. Not yet so conscious, however, that

it has been possible for any man to develop his wish for progress into pure consciousness.

In this mixing of the conscious and the unconscious our imagination is at work. In some so strongly that it forces the thought. Forces it ahead where new roads are discovered and the procession regulated.

The experience of benefit or harm has from the very first dominated our consciousness—and to this day nothing is more fundamentally rooted there. It is in fact so deeply rooted that it can never be ignored without giving us a feeling of discomfort.

How strange to me, therefore, is the doctrine that men and women of letters should free themselves from the consciousness of good and evil before they set out to work. The thought-power then acts as a camera in perfect unconcern of the harmful or the beneficial, the pleasing or the displeasing.

I am not trying to find out how far any person of a sound mind would be able to rid himself of this which, through millions of centuries of inherited consciousness, has so far ruled the generations. I merely ask: How is it that they who believe that they follow it give us just *this* picture and not *that*? Does it always happen quite mechanically? Why are the symbols they use almost always offensive? Did it happen with no choice whatsoever?

I don't think we need answer that. They, no more than the rest of us, are able to free their ideas of the inherited moral valuations; the only difference is that *we* serve while *they* revolt.

I must add that not everything which might seem so is of necessity a revolt. Much of the leadership of to-day has once been considered rebellions. I only want to prove that many who deny that poetry should have a tendency, show that tendency in their own works. And I will add that the farther we climb the ladder of intellectual freedom, the stronger the tendency. The great poets of Greece arranged the community of gods and men. Shakespeare's poetry is an enormous Germanic Valhalla, sometimes brilliant, at other times enveloped in clouds of storm. In this Valhalla all life rose to fight again, but always dominated by Shakespeare's sense of justice, his intense and deep belief in the everlasting abundance of life. The figures of Molière and Holberg, with their wigs and white-frilled headgear, are called forth from their graves as often as it pleases us, to run with dainty and grotesque movements the errands of their creators. They are as full of tendency as of words.

I mentioned just now our Germanic Valhalla. Can it not be said that Goethe and Schiller have carried parts of the Elysium into our Germanic Valhalla? The sky became clearer and warmer, life and art grew brighter, more beautiful. Can it not be said that they who lived by the genius of the young Tegner, the young Oehlenschlager, and the young Wergeland—not to forget Byron and Shelley—have something of the Greek gods about them?

That time and its tendency have passed. But when we mention our own time, the first to be remembered here is my old, departed friend and compatriot [Ibsen]. He has lighted many lighthouses along our coast, which are the first to be seen by all who seek harbour. They throw their light world-wide to give warning of dangers.

Next I will mention the old Russian master [Tolstoy]. He

stands in the open harbour of human happiness waving his hands.

The souls of both these men and their long working-day have had an ever growing tendency, growing as a torchlight in the breeze of night.

I have not said anything about tendency in connexion with Art. Tendency more than anything else can give Art a radiant heat, but, on the other hand, it can quite overpower it. *Ich rieche die Absicht und werde verstimmt* ["I smell the purpose and become upset"]. Neither have I said that as long as tendency and Art go hand in hand all is well.

As for the two great masters I have just mentioned, it happens that the warnings of the first are so sharp that they frighten us, while the other presents to us idols too unreal for human character, and they frighten us too. But we must have our courage strengthened, not weakened.

We must not be frightened away from the roads which are opened to us. We must obtain a sure belief in life's eternal and beneficent abundance. We must get the conviction that when the first fear is calmed, the darkest dissipation overcome, our earth is again refreshed by pure water from the everlasting source. Our faith itself has its offspring there.

This is why in modern poetry Victor Hugo is my choice. Within his glorious imagination this belief in life's abundance is the chief element. There are many who criticize Victor Hugo, especially because of his theatrical manners. Personally I think that his shortcomings are all blown to the winds by his enormous and powerful vitality.

Our instinct of preservation demands abundance. If life had no abundance it would stop. Every picture which does not possess it is a false picture. It makes us feel uncomfortable.

There are, of course, weak souls and spoiled egoists, who cannot endure to hear a hard-handed truth! With us it is different.

If they who choose to express the terror of life or to make visible such words and such acts as are hidden away in shame could have given us at the same time the conviction that, whatsoever happens, life has its infinite abundance, then we would say to ourselves: "We are here presented with one of life's many riddles which in its very essence is explained by those words, and can only be relieved through that terror, by that very act." Yes, then we would have felt a sacred earnestness or an irresistible mirth according to the will of him that was leading us.

But as a rule they never arrive so far, and we feel a two-fold discomfort. First, because we miss the abundance of life and, secondly, because he who tried to lead us was not capable, and all incapacity is painful.

The more a man takes upon himself, the stronger he must be. There is no word which cannot be uttered, there is no deed or no terror which cannot be painted, if he be there who knows how to do it.

The continuity of life is the thing we look for in Art, in its tiniest little drop as well as in its storm-beaten ocean waves. We are delighted to find it there, we are troubled if it is missing.

The primeval experience of benefit and harm has spread through and guides all our conduct of life and research. It de-

mands that Art shall multiply and intensify it in millions of examples. It is never satisfied.

This I have tried to obey. In reverence, with enthusiasm. (pp. 696-99)

> *Bjørnstjerne Bjørnson, "The Aim of Poetry," translated by Ellen Lehmkuhl, in* The World's Best Essays: From Confucius to Mencken, *edited by F. H. Pritchard, Albert & Charles Boni, 1929, pp. 696-99.*

LEE M. HOLLANDER (essay date 1911)

[*Hollander was an American educator, translator, and editor who specialized in Scandinavian studies. In the following excerpt, he evaluates* When the New Wine Blooms *and contrasts it with* Geography and Love.]

It is only a generation ago since the dust began to fly in the vigorous home-cleaning campaign started in Scandinavia by *A Doll's House* (1879), and Bjørnson's *A Glove* (1883). The men and women, then in their teens and twenties, brought up in those tumultuous and intoxicating times when, to their parents, at least, the very bottom threatened to drop out of the social fabric, are now grown to mature middle age, and have themselves borne and reared a new generation. No wonder that, in the majority of instances, this new generation, in its turn, was reared in the spirit of those ideals for the recognition of which they had suffered and struggled. A less prejudice-ridden, more healthy and outspoken race has assuredly never trodden this earth. Not even young America enjoys, and regardlessly takes, the liberties that nowadays are unhesitatingly granted to the young men and women of Scandinavia, especially of Norway. Here as there, youth carries the day and jauntily disposes of the ripe wisdom of the quinquagenarian and sexagenarian as old fogyism. Only recently women in Norway (and semi-Scandinavian Finland) have received the electoral franchise, with hardly a struggle,—forsooth, the pendulum could scarcely have swung more completely away from the reactionary tendencies that prevailed in the North a generation ago, and drove a Bjørnson, a Brandes, an Ibsen into exile.

Now it is the one most broadly effective in the battle for emancipation, Bjørnstjerne Bjørnson, who, with his recent play [*When the New Wine Blooms*] has called a halt: now that the weight of public opinion threatens to lurch to the other extreme, and the tide of excessive individualism, involving even the lowest strata of society, is about to sweep away the last vestiges of family solidarity as a basis for ethical conduct, when the virtues of reverence, duty, and filial love are becoming old fashioned with a vengeance. Bjørnson is not laboring under the illusion that he, or any man, could stem that tide. He has preferred to direct it, to part the flood, if possible, so as to shear it of its excessive and dangerous volume. He has chosen as vehicle of his message the 'good-natured' comedy. Never was the splendid Bjørnsonian faculty of orientating himself and his world-wide audience on the troubled seas of warring tendencies more gloriously evidenced. And while piloting us, helm in hand, into safer waters, he 'wins new lands' and makes sheer poetry of it all. As the poet of the deeper impulses of our times, with eyes boldly envisaging the future, he is still easily *facile princeps* ["number one"].

When the New Wine Blooms is a marvellous thing for an old man to have written, on his sick bed withal, and tortured by the inexorable disease from which he is now seeking a last re lief in Paris. The same grand bland optimism pervades its sunny scenes which animated him in the spring of his long career, the same glad warm hope for the human race—that, after all, man is kindly and brave and that the young generation promises to carry the world forward yet one more step! The very title, absit omen ["may this not be an omen"], significantly recalls the farewell words and 'Epilogue' of Ibsen, whose *When We Dead Awaken* is essentially a sorrowing over a life irretrievably misspent in abnegation. Above all, it is a sounding blow against a Tolstoi's weary and half Oriental recoil from essaying the untrodden paths which modern conditions have forced us to tread, for ill or for good, and a helpful push on the way, to help lift us out of the first ruts and into the right lanes. To us in the West it is a timely rectification of the compass.

Bjørnson has never for a moment hesitated to call in art as an ally of life. As pointed out above, the purpose of this play is to balance off anew the respective rights of the older and the younger generation; and, more especially, perhaps, though also a question of the two generations, the rights of a man to his family, as against the claims of his family on him. With the world-old problem of old and young he had grappled but recently again, in his drama *Daglannet,* with all the great force and originality we have learned to expect from Bjørnson, yet unconvincingly. A far more vital connection links it to his fine comedy, *Geography and Love.* As we shall see, his new play is the problem of *Geography and Love* reversed.

The economically, socially, and religiously 'neutral' background is formed by the graceful and easy hospitality of a well to do family, in their spacious home somewhere, we infer, along the shores of the island-dotted Kristiania-fjord, within easy reach of the capital. It is midsummer, all is flowers, warmth, and sunshine. The family live out of doors chiefly, on the veranda and the court between the two wings of the mansion, with a vista of the garden and the outside world beyond. This space is happily chosen as a sort of natural stage. With its doors and its windows opened ever and anon with great comic effect, it might be taken as symbolic, on the whole, of the large family home, where everybody hears everybody else, and secrets become family property. . . . (pp. 70-2)

It is a household of the modern style, the young folks have the upper hand. Within its lee the three marriageable daughters and a bevy of girl friends flit to and fro like an elfin band, a most modern one, to be sure. They are distressingly knowing, and have very positive and well-grounded opinions on marriage, religion, and other little matters,—in fact, know perfectly what's what.

Dean Hall, who is visiting his sister-in-law, Fru Arvik ('a handsome man, forty-five to fifty years . . . nothing specially priestly about him; looks rather like a sportsman') is caught and brought to bay by the girls and mercilessly quizzed on his views on marriage, as voiced in his last sermon; and in however modern a spirit he interprets and defends the Pauline injunction to wives 'submit yourself unto your husbands as unto the Lord. For the husband is the head of the wife . . . ' he and his theology are certainly on the defensive, and get the worst of the argument.

This amusing preamble serves notice, as it were, that as a sign of the times religion is 'out of the saga.' It may be remarked in passing, that in this play not even moral scruples—this is

right and this is wrong—in the slightest measure help to guide and decide the conduct of a person in a given case, but only feeling, habit. And we shall not far wrong Bjørnson in asserting these to be his ultimate guiding principles at the present time. Religion no longer has even the interest of discussion for the poet of *Pastor Sang.*

The center of this most modern household is Fru Arvik. She is a 'new woman.' With gentle irony the poet speaks of her dabbling in business (harmlessly), speculating in shares; and we have not the slightest doubt of her being an active member of all sorts of women's clubs for all sorts of things. She takes herself very seriously. She must hustle and get up early every morning, in order to catch the first boat to town, 'to attend to business,' whilst her less strenuous husband prefers to stay longer abed, thus with comic eagerness reversing what, up to the present, we have thought to be the normal relation of husband and wife as breadwinner and householder. And yet we are made to feel by the subtlest touches what she is about to forget, namely, that it is her devoted husband to whom she owes whatever ability and stability she possesses.

But let it not be supposed that she is hard and unwomanly, if impetuous and headstrong. Far from it! Bjørnson may be relied upon to do her case full justice. She has all the rich, loving nature which forms the strongest bulwark of the family—the rest are but frills that mar the noble architecture of her soul. She is an excellent mother, the comrade of her children—to be sure to the utter neglect of her husband, and to altogether unreasonable lengths. She is 'so exaggerated, so impossible,' as she recognizes herself. She has been thoughtless enough to move from her husband's and to her daughter's suite of rooms, leaving him alone to himself in one wing.

> The mother always agrees with the children. And the children take their mother's side. . . . But she doesn't stop there. She can't do anything by halves. She thinks and feels as the children think and feel. She lives entirely with them. . . . And all these girl friends! And all these love affairs and squabbles. And all that gossiping! And then the half engagements and full engagement and fallings out. . . . I (Arvik is speaking) get completely mixed up. But she? Why, she swims in it as the fish in the sea.

Arvik, the husband, is one of those gentle, poetic, and chiefly passive natures—coupled, in this instance, with a saving amount of irony and masculinity—Bjørnson has so frequently drawn with the deepest sympathy, as foil to a more violent temperament with strong instincts and volition—such as himself.

His desire is to live and work quietly on his estate and with his books. The everlasting Donnybrook fair in his house annoys him; his wife simply does not satisfy him; the growing estrangement from his family is increasingly preying on his sensitive mind. Their likes are no longer his. He knows all about the little secrets, innocent enough, his wife and his daughters have together; but, pained though he is at ever being kept an outsider, he winks at it. He is too forbearing and considerate to upbraid, too manly to complain. He only hides his real mind farther and farther away behind veiled hints and allusions, and gets them to laugh at his quaint conceits. It is only natural that it does not occur to them at all that he could have any grievance. Partly through his own fault, then, he is coming to be regarded as a harmless 'fixture,' a negligible quantity, except as money-getter.

At the same time Arvik is too young for this mild, toothless resignation, and he refuses to be thrown *ad actas,* to the 'old iron.' Now and then his blood boils, and he mutters about going to—Australia, which only produces fresh laughter, as being a new little joke of his; for, indeed, he has grown to be a great stay at home.

There is, then, enough powder accumulating around the Arvik premises, and the flirtatious atmosphere keeps it dry; only the proverbial spark is needed to break up the family into its component elements. Nothing, we make free to say, nothing in all dramatic literature is more admirably convincing than the way Bjørnson motivates the inevitable explosion. Arvik's grievance, it is clear, must be transformed in kind, must, from a chronic and latent stage, pass into an acute and open one. It is done by simply heightening, by suggestion, the demands Arvik yet makes on life—and on his wife.

Dean Hall, who is a widower, and himself the father of a marriageable daughter (Alvilde), is desperately in love with Arvik's youngest daughter, a girl of sweet sixteen (Helene). He is sure of her affections, darsn't declare himself, though before, 'in the spirit of St. Paul,' he obtained her father's permission. In a roguish scene, itself as pure and ethereally plastic as cherry blossoms against a dark blue sky, yet teeming with superb comic possibilities, he is made to discover himself, half against his will; and forthwith proceeds to vindicate his somewhat hazardous intention by an ardent dithyramb on girlish youth and charm, in which this impressionable divine betrays a surprising acquaintance with the æsthetic vocabulary of Kierkegaard: 'When the new wine blooms the old wine ferments,' as the Norwegian adage has it. He does not need to push his claims. Subtly suggested, the thought arises in Arvik's mind that he is not too old, either, to have erotic adventures of his own. He confesses that he also is in love with one of the sweet creatures. Obligations? Ties? 'Am *I* married, do you think,' he exclaims savagely.

Of course, Hall is too poor an observer—as how can a priest and one in love into the bargain, but be—is too poor an observer to attach any importance to this ominous outburst. He laughs off Arvik's notion. For that matter, neither does the object of his affection, Alvilde (Hall's daughter) take him seriously, though her womanly instinct warns her to avoid playing with her uncle. Both for avoiding her father's marriage with her playmate, and to escape Arvik's attentions, she is about to leave for England.

Meanwhile Fru Arvik has returned from the city, accompanied by her second daughter, Alberta, who is dogged by an insistent and desperate suitor whom Fru Arvik—behold she too!—seems to care for more than does her daughter. He is threatening to shoot up the place, much to peaceful Arvik's disgust and astonishment. That isn't anything, however, to frighten Mrs. Arvik. She is a revolver expert herself, and some breezy Wild West scene seems imminent, when Alberta courageously faces her pursuer and puts him off with one year's probation.

All of a sudden the trunks and valises of Marna, the oldest, recently married daughter, and her mother's special pride, appear on the scene—unexpectedly for all but Arvik, who has had the inside news, this time for the nonce, Marna's husband having intimated in a letter to him that the barometer has been standing 'at storm.' In short, she is about to return home for good.

The general consternation ensuing turns to indignation when Arvik hints that it is she who is at fault. 'After but five months' marriage!' 'She is a splendid woman.' . . . 'All who know her like her.' 'Marna has character. A noble, fine character . . . such a gifted and tactful woman as Marna, and so good and winning, to say that she was not fit to be a wife!' are some of the protests raining over his head.

The family, quite unnoticeably, resolves itself into a discussion meeting on marriage problems, a discussion *sans gene* ["without embarassment"], yet handled with the utmost delicacy.

Arvik suddenly feels called upon to reassert himself. He had seen it coming. Oh, yes, Marna has many fine qualities—he is most ready to grant all that; but, he claims, it is precisely all these outside interests, 'business activities,' and what not, that divert a woman's thoughts from home and husband. She becomes, if of Marna's type, the pathologically insensible woman of to-day, incapable of the passion man continues to crave. From these considerations (and his own case) he takes up the cudgels *for* the young husband, *against* his own child. Knowing Bjørnson's irrepressible didactic turn, we harbor but little doubt that this scene contains the central and originating thought of the drama, as applied both to the candidate for the silver wedding and the newly wedded.

Marna appears presently, elegantly gowned, sobbing and woebegone, with the last number of the *Shipping Gazette* under her arm. To the immense indignation of the family, Arvik refuses to regard her homecoming as very tragical. Words are bandied, there are the usual bickerings, he vents his grievances, great and small—a golden humor lights up this precious scene—until finally, overcome by a cumulative sense of his many wrongs, he turns on them, lets his eyes rest long upon his wife, and departs for England, as we learn. Alvilde, we remember, is to leave that same night, also bound for England.

No sooner is he gone than a tragic shadow seems to fall on those remaining. There is no longer any one 'to have consideration for.' 'We have felt so secure and happy, all along, we had clean forgotten to whom we owed that.' Their natural protector is there no longer, they feel their weakness, though hating to confess it. Overwhelmed by sweet memories that crowd upon her out of the past, and dismayed at the wholly unexpected turn of events, Fru Arvik is the first one to repent. A sleepless night on Arvik's pillow has revealed to her his point of view. And comparing notes with her, the daughters also are led to a deeper consciousness of what they have lost in him. When Hall, too late, informs them of what Arvik's probable plans are, they unanimously and vehemently repudiate his fears and his insinuations of an understanding with Alvilde.

Meanwhile, unavailing search has been made for him, and things look black enough, when Arvik smilingly reappears. He had boarded the ship, but had gone ashore again. He 'just couldn't.'

Final reconciliation. The bridal bed of the Arviks, 'a large elegant iron bedstead,' is borne back in triumphal procession, with the reunited family following. The victory is Arvik's—not so much through the force of his character, as by the logic of the situation. The family idea is vindicated. It is to be perpetuated in its mighty consolidating influence on the young generation. The old generation, we understand, is to live a life of their *own* and for themselves during the remainder of their days without prejudice to, yet also independent of, the younger folk. Through a last 'fermentation' of love they will then safely enter into the harboring clarity of old age.

With no more information about the new play than that furnished above, the attentive reader of *Geography and Love* (1885), will now see the justice of the assertion that here we have the same problem exactly reversed. The poet himself is unquestionably aware of it; he has familiarized himself with the earlier work, as is evident from the reappearance of even subsidiary motives, down to details of repartee. We shall not point these out here, but content ourselves with recalling a few traits that are too essential to be coincidences.

In *Geography and Love* it is the husband, Tygesen, the finely gifted professor of geography, who is actively at fault. He has become absorbed in his science to the exclusion of all else. His maps and charts and notes are invading the whole house and crowding out his wife. In his heart also. If the Arvik daughters do not feel their father's necessity, in this case, it is the father who selfishly sends away his daughter to a boarding school to get her out of the way. It is he who tyrannizes over the household, having been spoiled by excessive indulgence on the part of its female members; until finally, egged on by a friend of hers, and tempted by a tacit admirer, the wife rebels, and departs 'on a journey.' A reconciliation is then brought about by Tygesen being softened by reminiscences from his wooing days, and his wife returning for imponderable reasons, much in the same way as Arvik.

In both cases, then, there is a catastrophe narrowly averted in a marriage of long standing. But, *tempora mutantur* ["times change"], if in the former case it was the now completely old-fashioned, sovereign type of husband who is neglecting his wife, because *he* is unduly wrapped up in his profession, and *she* has allowed him to become an egotist, here we have the wife who has grown oblivious of her conjugal duties by becoming a 'new woman' and all its corollaries; and— an exaggeration of the beautiful character of Margrete (*På Storhove*) and Fru Dag (*Daglannet*), who are on terms of a charming camaraderie with their children—by altogether espousing the cause of the younger generation and deserting her own.

Nothing is more astonishing in Bjørnson's genius than his seemingly infinite capacity and eagerness for development. Bjørnson and standing still are mutually exclusive terms. Comparing, more particularly, this his latest work with the earlier comedy, a careful examination reveals nothing so clearly as his progress in the power of revealing psychological processes of the most intimate order. Age has not in the slightest measure impaired his fertility in the invention of motifs; nor, in employing them, that delicate insight into the tiniest root fibers of human actions, great and small, which is the true poet's inalienable prerogative. Again and again one marvels at the incomparably fine and close woof of the very texture of the action. In the smaller dramatic units, reply dovetails reply with the same 'Bjørnsonian' ingenuity and éclat; and the style is as ever in the days of *A Glove* and of *Leonarda,* 'as if charged with gunpowder,' but now also with many new notes of resonance and tenderness.

Lack of plausibility has at times been the weak spot in Bjørnson's works. Whether or no the method adopted, of bringing back to her conjugal obligations a woman of just Fru Arvik's type, by the mere recollection of honeymoon felicity, is entirely credible I prefer to leave undebated. A more cynically scrupulous dramatist like Ibsen, e.g., would, you may

be sure, have shunned this rather trite device. But that a dramatist of such resourcefulness and intellectuality as Bjørnson has both lifted these scenes high above the pitfalls of sentimentality, and hedged them about with the sharp thorns of his humor goes without saying. (pp. 72-8)

Lee M. Hollander, "Bjørnstjerne Bjørnson's Last Drama, 'When the New Wine Blooms'," in *Poet Lore, Vol. 12, No. 1, January, 1911, pp. 70-8.*

WILLIAM MORTON PAYNE (essay date 1911)

[*The longtime literary editor for several Chicago publications, Payne reviewed books for twenty-three years at the* Dial, *one of America's most influential journals of literature and opinion in the early twentieth century. In the following excerpt, he contrasts the literary careers of Bjørnson and Henrik Ibsen, focusing on Bjørnson's social dramas.*]

It is more than half a century since Bjørnson leaped into fame with the publication of *Synnøve Solbakken,* the first of his series of Norwegian peasant tales. This book was almost immediately discovered and translated into English by Mary Howitt, although the author's name was not printed upon the title-page, and the more pronounceable *Trust and Trial* was given the book as a name. It was not long, however, before *Synnøve Solbakken* was followed by *Arne* and *A Happy Boy* and *The Fisher-Maiden,* and when these tales appeared in English translations they were credited to the author, thus making the name of Bjørnstjerne Bjørnson familiar to our public. For fifty years the author's fame steadily widened, until at the time of his death last year he was universally recognized as one of the three or four greatest writers in the world. He had become the spiritual creator of modern Norway; he had sung its songs; he had glorified its historical past; he had depicted its simple peasant life, and he had dealt searchingly with its modern social and intellectual problems. But of his threefold literary distinction as novelist, dramatist, and lyric poet, he was hardly known to English readers as either dramatist or poet; the idyllic tales and the problem novels they had become acquainted with in translations, but the poems and plays they knew only by hearsay. This is not perhaps altogether surprising in the case of the poems, for the essence of the lyric always evaporates in translation, but it is an almost unaccountable fact in the case of the plays, when we consider their high literary value and their striking dramatic effectiveness. Of Bjørnson's twenty-one works in dramatic form only three or four are as yet accessible to English readers; three or four others have made furtive appearances in out-of-the-way places, the remaining two-thirds may be read in German and other languages, but not thus far in our own.

The condition becomes all the more extraordinary when we contrast it with the fortunes of Ibsen. This writer has also upwards of a score of plays to his credit, and practically all are obtainable in English versions. Beginning with Catherine Ray's translation of *Emperor and Galilean* in 1876, the work was steadily carried on by many hands until it culminated in the collected edition of the plays recently completed under Mr. William Archer's supervision. It is proverbial that "books have their fates" no less than human beings, but it is worthy of comment that such diverse fates should have befallen the dramatic writings of these two men. Time may probably be trusted to remedy this relative wrong, for any just scale of appraisement must recognize that, all things considered, the two bodies of work are of substantially equal weight and significance. They are different, of course. Ibsen has a technical skill and a mordant satirical gift that are denied to Bjørnson, but the latter has a genial humanity and a poetical gift that the former rarely exhibits or even approaches. Ibsen's plays are the more logical and diagrammatic; Bjørnson's plays are the more full-blooded and spontaneous. The former keeps emotion in strict subordination to the reasoned plan; the latter gives it freer play, and is not even afraid to let it splash about. The explanation of Ibsen's greater present vogue with us would seem to be that when we first felt his impact our English drama had sunk to such low estate that it needed ideas and architectonics more than anything else, and these were more obviously to be had from *A Doll Home* and *Hedda Gabler* than from *Mary Stuart in Scotland* and *Sigurd Slembe.*

It is impossible to write about Bjørnson without taking Ibsen into account, for, despite their differences, the careers of the two men run parallel to a very remarkable degree. Both were self-taught, both were plunged at an early age into the practical work of theatrical management, and both displayed a path-breaking originality which was speedily justified by its fruits. Each of the two men, before settling down to the dramatic handling of the problems of modern society, went through a period of free experimentation, essaying in turn the drama of world-history, the reproduction of the life of the saga-period, and the satirical treatment of the domestic relations, to say nothing of various forms of lyric and epic verse. Thus we have Ibsen's *Catalina* and *Emperor and Galilean* as an offset to Bjørnson's *Mary Stuart in Scotland,* Ibsen's *The Chieftains of Helgeland* and *The Pretenders* as an offset to Bjørnson's *King Sverre* and *Sigurd Slembe,* Ibsen's *Love's Comedy* as an offset to Bjørnson's *The Newly Married Couple,* and Ibsen's *Terje Vigen* as an offset to Bjørnson's *Arnljot Gelline.* In this comparison the honors are fairly easy; Ibsen has the better of it with *Emperor and Galilean* and *Love's Comedy,* while Bjørnson takes the palm with *Sigurd Slembe* and the lyric and epic verse. If the balance, as far the period before 1874 is concerned, inclines in Ibsen's favor, it is by virtue of *Brand* and *Peer Gynt,* the two satirical poems which are unquestionably his most enduring works, and for which the activity of the younger poet provides no match.

It was in the middle seventies that both poets, their romantic inclinations chastened, and their acquaintance with actual life and its problems ripened to such a point that its dramatic expressions became an imperative mandate, turned as by a common impulse to the modern field, and began the production of the series of plays by which they are chiefly known to the stage of today. Both had made early tentative efforts in this field, and both were henceforth to make its cultivation their chief aim. The younger writer was the pioneer in this advance, sending home from abroad in 1874-5 the two plays, *The Editor* and *A Bankruptcy.* The older writer, also working abroad, in 1877 sent home *The Pillars of Society.* During the score or more of years that followed, Ibsen's modern plays came to number an even dozen. Bjørnson, whose working period was extended ten years beyond Ibsen's, wrote fourteen plays of this modern type. It is with these fourteen plays that the present article is mainly concerned. While it is true that they have not exerted as far-reaching and vivifying an influence upon dramatic craftsmanship as have the twelve of Ibsen, it is also true that they constitute one of the most significant bodies of dramatic writing that the past generation has produced, and no student of the later nineteenth-century

drama can afford to neglect them. In the Scandinavian countries and in Germany they are practically as familiar to the public as are the plays of Ibsen; the English-speaking public has simply not discovered them as yet, a condition which is neither to our advantage nor our credit.

A Bankruptcy, which was the first of Bjørnson's modern plays to be produced, was so unlike anything that had previously come from his pen that it was difficult for the public to adjust itself to his new manner. He seemed to have turned his back upon the old romantic idealism and to have lost the poetical naïveté that had given such charm to his earlier work. He had unexpectedly taken to writing plays like a Frenchman, and had produced a drama of manners such as Augier might have written had the latter been a Norwegian. The reading public (for plays have always been read as well as seen in the Scandinavian countries) felt that it had lost a poet and gained instead an uninspired realist. But the theatregoing public discovered that a new dramatic force had arisen, and, despite the adverse judgment of the reviewers, flocked to witness the performances of the new play. *A Bankruptcy* soon established itself as a success upon the boards in the Scandinavian theatres and made a triumphant progress from theatre to theatre over the continent. It remains in many respects the most effective acting play that the author ever wrote. The play has for its theme the ethics of the world of business, and shows how the pressure of commercial life may almost irresistibly force a man, no matter how fundamentally honest his instincts, to engage in shady transactions. The merchant Tjælde, having fallen into financial difficulties, and conscious that the welfare of many others depends upon his continued solvency, resorts to speculation with trust funds in the hope of righting his affairs. The difficulties of his position are such as to create for him a good deal of sympathy, and the line between right and wrong conduct is by no means sharply defined. When the crash comes, Tjælde finds himself morally, refuses every offered compromise, and announces his intention to devote the rest of his life to the clearing of his debts. Henrik Jæger remarks that this play did two new things for Norwegian literature. It justified the literary treatment of money affairs, while in it "the home made its first appearance upon the stage, the home with its joys and sorrows, with its conflicts and its tenderness."

A more personal note and one of hotter indignation is sounded in *The Editor,* in which the public quickly recognized a well-known figure in the journalistic world of Christiania. The author, however, insisted that the editor of his play was a type rather than a portrait—the type that "is characterized by acting upon a basis of sheer egotism, passionate and boundless, and by terrorism in such fashion that it frightens honest people away from every liberal movement and visits upon the individual an unscrupulous persecution." Halfdan and Harold Rein are brothers, and political leaders in the radical camp. The former has been hounded almost to death by the abuse of the conservative press, and the latter expects to succeed him in the leadership as the result of a coming election. Harold is engaged to Gertrude Evje, the daughter of a wealthy distiller, and the attack upon him is made through the girl's father, a weak man, who is bullied by the editor into a promise to break with the rising young politician. A scurrilous article, already in type, is the weapon by means of which this pledge is exacted. But the article gets into print after all, through the agency of one of Evje's discharged servants, and its consequences are twofold. It determines the outraged distiller to stand by his prospective son-in-law, and it causes the death of Halfdan Rein from a hemorrhage which is the immediate consequence of its perusal. The editor is so shocked by this tragic happening that he sues for Evje's forgiveness and declares that he will abandon his profession. This change of heart is not altogether credible, but otherwise the figure of the unscrupulous journalist is delineated with merciless truth and severity. Both *The Editor* and *A Bankruptcy* are plays that should make a strong appeal to the American public, which knows at first hand, and upon a vastly larger scale, the problems with which they are concerned.

Bjørnson's next play, *The King,* was produced in 1877. It is a study of the institution of monarchy in its influence both upon the society which maintains it and upon the individual whose head bears the heavy weight of the crown. The King of this drama is a strongly sympathetic figure, a man of the modern world, who realizes that monarchy is in its essence no more than a sham, a picturesque relic of an outworn phase of social development, yet who dreams that it were better to transform the institution into workable shape than to abolish it once and for all. Let the King become the first citizen of the state, hedged about with no divinity, but earning the loyalty of the people by devotion to their interests and conforming to their ways of life. Let him wed a daughter of the people, convert the palace into a home, and put an end to the court with its ceremonial. These things the King of Bjørnson's drama attempts to do, and finds his efforts thwarted on every hand. Suspicion and stupidity and ingratitude are the reward of his disinterested efforts, and he battles in vain to beat down the walls of tradition and convention and prejudice. Finally driven to despair, he takes his own life, to the consternation of his attendants. This powerful work is both a play and a document. As the former, it is the most important of his later problem period, as *Sigurd Slembe* is the most important of his romantic, earlier years.

In *The New System* (1879), the cramping conditions of social and intellectual life in the small state is Bjørnson's theme—a theme upon which Ibsen also frequently harped. The repressed condition of soul that results from such an environment encourages every form of hypocrisy, and drives men and women to seek artificial and ignoble forms of satisfaction. Compromise is the word, and the action hinges upon a "new system" of railway management, which is really old-fashioned and wasteful. The young engineer who has just returned from abroad, and who aims to expose the imposture, is urged by every motive of worldly comfort to abandon the attack and get his share of personal advantage out of the bad system. Every device of cunning malice is employed to weaken him, but he finally succeeds in at least partly opening the eyes of the public. The satire of this piece is sharp and convincing, and loud were the outcries of wounded spirits upon the occasion of its production.

The two plays *Leonarda* and *A Glove,* dated respectively 1879 and 1883, take up two important phases of the "woman question." The former . . . has for its theme the way in which society treats the woman whose past is clouded, always preferring the baser to the better motive as the explanation of whatever mystery seems to attach to her career. The woman in this case gets the worst of it, and is driven to a cruel sacrifice of her own happiness that she may secure the happiness of those who are most dear to her. The latter of the two plays now under consideration is perhaps the most contentious that the author ever wrote. It stands squarely upon the thesis that a woman has exactly the same right to demand pu-

rity of the man she marries as the man has to demand it of his wife. The author repudiates vehemently the notion that the sexes can have different standards of morality, and asserts his belief that the unchaste man is as unfit for honorable marriage as the unchaste woman. The play is very frank in its speech, and the glove which (at the close of the acting version) is thrown by the heroine at the feet of her discredited and disgraced lover is symbolical of Bjørnson's own challenge to society for its tacit acquiescence in a degrading and indefensible opinion.

The two plays that bear the common title *Beyond the Strength* [*Over ævne*] are twelve years apart in date of production (1883 and 1895) and have little similarity aside from the idea that underlies them both—the idea that it is not well for men to seek the unattainable, for in so doing they will lose their grasp upon what is actually possible, "the thought that much of the best human energy goes to waste because it is devoted to the pursuit of ideals that are indeed beyond the strength of man to realize." I am here quoting from what I have said elsewhere, and continue the quotation as follows:

> In the first of the two plays this superhuman ideal is religious, it is that of the enthusiast who accepts literally the teaching that to faith all things are possible; in the second, the ideal is social, it is that of the reformer who is deluded to believe that one resounding deed of terror and self-immolation for the cause of the people will suffice to overthrow the selfish existing order and create for the toiling masses a new heaven upon earth. Bjørnson has written nothing more profoundly moving than these plays, with their twofold treatment of essentially the same theme, nor has he written anything which offers a clearer revelation of his own rich personality, with its unfailing poetic vision, its deep tenderness, and its boundless love for all humankind.

Six other plays were produced during the last quarter-century of Bjørnson's life. They are less important than the earlier ones, although by no means negligible, and my present space does not permit of their detailed characterization. *Geography and Love* is a comedy of the man with a hobby, so absorbed by it that he neglects his family. *Paul Lange and Tora Parsberg* goes into political controversy, and introduces figures from real life that the author vainly sought to disguise under fictitious names. *Laboremus* and *At Storhove* are two plays concerned with the malign influence that an evil-minded woman may have over the lives of others. These, as well as *Daglannet,* are domestic dramas of simple structure, and all have for an implicit theme the consecration of the home. *When the New Wine Blooms,* Bjørnson's last play, astonishingly fresh and vital in spirit, is a study of the modern young woman, of the estrangement that too often creeps into married life, and of the stirrings that prompt men of middle age to seek to renew the joys of youth.

Of Bjørnson's dramatic works, numbering twenty-one altogether, only a few have been translated into English. . . . The most casual survey of Bjørnson's total dramatic output will thus indicate the existence of a mine of great richness which cannot much longer remain unworked. Translations are the first requisite and their supply should soon follow upon the demand created during the past two or three years by the widespread study of the foreign drama. Given the translations, the stage productions will not be long in following. The works which are, in my opinion, positively crying to be produced in English are *A Bankruptcy, The King* and the second part of *Beyond the Strength.* In the case of *Sigurd Slembe* I have always believed that it offered an almost unexampled opportunity for a great production by a great actor. The trilogy would need to be recast into a single play (probably a prologue in verse and five prose acts) in order to bring it within the limits of an evening's performance. Pending the realization of this dream, there is the possibility, without any reconstruction, of producing the second part of *Sigurd Slembe* as an independent play. It stands easily alone, and those who were fortunate enough to witness its performances as given three years ago in Chicago by the Donald Robertson players, even under distressingly inadequate conditions, will bear enthusiastic witness to its poetic beauty and tragic impressiveness. (pp. 3-15)

> William Morton Payne, "Bjørnson as a Dramatist," in The Drama, *Chicago, No. 3, August, 1911, pp. 3-15.*

EDWIN BJÖRKMAN (essay date 1914)

[*Björkman was a Swedish-American novelist and critic who, through his translations, introduced American readers to the works of such major Scandinavian authors as Bjørnson, August Strindberg, and Georg Brandes. In the following excerpt, he examines the thematic content of* Love and Geography, Beyond Human Might, *and* Laboremus.]

It has been said that Bjørnson was the first dramatist who in *A Business Failure* (*En Fallit*)—succeeded in creating a genuine home atmosphere on the stage. And speaking of *Love and Geography,* the late Henrik Jæger, Norway's foremost literary historian, had this to say:

> Bjørnson is as consistent in his glorification of the home and the family as is Ibsen in raising the personality, the individual, to the skies. . . . In the name of personal self-expression, Ibsen lets a wife leave her home to seek by herself a way toward clearness and independence; in the name of the home, Bjørnson brings an estranged married couple back into each other's arms.

This intense feeling for home and home ties asserts itself in all of Bjørnson's work. It was part of his nature and may to some extent have been derived from his peasant ancestry. Whenever he refers to this side of man's existence, his voice seems to grow mellower, his imagination more vivid. Few have surpassed him in the power of endowing a domestic interior with that warm light which flows from an open fire in the gloaming, when there is no other light to rival it. And he seemed to have a special genius for presenting every kind of relationship based on blood-kindred in the most attractive colours. In illustration may be quoted the exquisite scene between brother and sister in the second act of *Beyond Human Might.*

It would not be safe, however, to conclude that *Love and Geography* is a sermon preached on behalf of the home as opposed—one might say—to the individuals within it. Bjørnson's concern for the right of every personality to expand freely in accordance with the laws and tendencies of its own nature was hardly less eager than that of Ibsen. And it will be as correct, in considering the first play of the present volume, to place the emphasis on Karen Tygesen's initial revolt as on her final regrets at having revolted. It is true that the play, as it progresses, increasingly accentuates the dangers to which all the members of a family become exposed through the weakening of their sense of unity and community. But nevertheless its ultimate lesson seems likely to be that a home which does not offer reasonable freedom to all its members is doomed to perish.

In a way the attitude taken by Bjørnson in this work may be considered old-fashioned, as he persists in regarding woman as primarily man's helpmate. But within these limits he is radical and modern enough to satisfy the most advanced demands. The play, we must remember, was written in 1885, when we had barely begun to feel the economic revolution which since then has swept so many millions of women from their old domestic moorings into the whirlpool of industrial competition. It was only natural that, at such a time, Bjørnson might still accept the home as "woman's sphere." And it is the more to his credit that, even at that time, he refused to make it her prison.

The note struck from the first is one of protest against the selfish tendency of the artist or the thinker to consider his work as an end in itself, and as such superior to the life which it ought to be serving. A play of much later date and outlook having very much in common with *Love and Geography* is Bernard Shaw's *Man and Superman.* The central theme of both is the same, no matter how much the two treatments of it may differ. And the outcome is pretty much the same in both cases, for the submission of John Tanner to marriage is essentially the equivalent of Professor Tygesen's withdrawal of matters geographical from all home precincts not specifically set aside for his own use. And both surrenders mean in the last analysis that the individual's right to free development becomes meaningless whenever it threatens to defeat the higher rights of the race or of life itself.

Like so many other plays by Bjørnson, this one has been worked over in the course of the years. Originally the part of Henning was much more conspicuous, and a great deal more stress was laid on the dangers at his hands to which both mother and daughter became exposed through the breaking up of the home. To the distinct advantage of the play, this element in its plot has been toned down and pushed into the background. As the play stands now, it brings home to us very forcibly one of the most notable qualities of Bjørnson's dramatic work: the charm, the jolly large-heartedness, the contagious good humour which he infused into so many of his characters. It was so much a part of his own nature that he seems to have expected its presence in everybody else. And the withholding of it was the worst judgment he could pass on one of his characters.

To our surprise and pleasure, we meet with this quality even in a man like Pastor Sang in *Beyond Our Power,* whom very few playwrights could have made anything but a splenetic prude. We find it overflowing in a character like Professor Tygesen, and its presence alone prevents him from sinking wholly to the level of the typical domestic tyrant. Tygesen is not only a man of imagination, but a man with a keen sense of humour. Even at his worst, there is a glimmer of mischief in the corner of his eye. He loves to tease—perhaps his love of it is largely at the bottom of all the trouble. His mind is naturally turned outward in eager study of a vast, multiform world. And so the reconciliation between him and his wife is rendered not only possible but probable. It is well recognised that in Tygesen Bjørnson was caricaturing himself, and for this reason the part has always been played in a make-up suggestive of the author.

Love and Geography is very broad comedy, turning in spots into outright farce. Yet it is as serious in purpose and as close to life in all its bearings as the most tear-dripping tragedy. This is another constantly recurring characteristic of Bjørnson's work—and one, I think, that should make him particularly attractive to the English-speaking public: he can discuss problems without raving, and preach sermons without whining. He is so strong, so full of life, that he can afford to smile in the presence of serious difficulties—confident as he is that mankind sooner or later will overcome any difficulty against which it brings its full energy to bear.

In this, as in many other respects, Bjørnson came closer to the American spirit than any other one of the great Scandinavian writers of the last century. He himself was always conscious of this kinship, and it was with the joy of a child that he set out for the United States in September, 1880, to stay there eight months. While travelling through the country he seems to have been constantly struck by a democratic spirit that found its expression not only in political institutions, but in the terms on which man met man everywhere—even within the walls of a prison. One day he was taken to visit the Massachusetts State Prison at Concord, his host and guide being Governor John Davis Long. A convict, hearing of the presence of the chief executive within the prison, asked the privilege of a talk with him in order that he might appeal for pardon. This talk took place in the warden's office, and to Bjørnson's intense surprise and delight the first thing done by the governor was to make the convict sit down on a chair close to his own. Bjørnson wrote home of this scene, adding some memories of a very different nature: King Oscar seated at a dining-table while his host, Count Wedel—the country's foremost citizen at the time—was waiting on him without being permitted to sit down once during the lengthy meal; a cabinet minister keeping an official from his department standing for thirty minutes while delivering a report; and so on.

In mentioning this, I have more than its anecdotal interest in mind. I wish to make it easier for non-Scandinavian readers to understand those scenes in *Beyond Human Might* where Holger and the workmen come in direct contact with each other. To American readers in particular, the arrogance of Holger before the catastrophe and the cringing humility of the workmen after it may seem equally exaggerated. But at the time when the play was written, in 1895, the modern labour movement had not yet gained its present hold on the Scandinavian countries. Since then things have changed tremendously. But then the sharp line between upper and lower class was still practically intact, and the attitude of employer toward employee was frequently one of unbearable insolence. The scene in the third act of *Beyond Human Might,* though somewhat theatrical in its defiant speeches, is in spirit largely true to the life of that day.

Industrialism was then young in all the Scandinavian countries, but especially in Norway. On his own ground the peasant retained his ancient independence of spirit and manners. But turned into a city workman he lost his old class pride as well as the sense of strength springing from an immediate relation to the main sources of human sustenance. Dragged from his native soil, he fell for a while into a state of abject subservience, out of which the best of his class could save themselves only by emigration. To Bjørnson every phase of this spectacle was a constant cause of provocation, and he strove through a long lifetime to force the educated and propertied classes into assuming a juster and wiser attitude toward those on whose toil their own prosperity and supposed superiority finally rested.

Beyond Human Might—as, for several reasons, it has been found expedient to name the present version of the second of the two plays which Bjørnson named *Over aevne*—is not, however, primarily a treatment of the relationship between capital and labour, or between employer and employee. At its heart lies the same cry that rings so passionately out of the previous play with the same original name: Bjørnson's protest against the tyranny of the supernatural, the infinite, the "boundless." At one time able to accept established Christianity as a sufficient formulation of life's highest truths, he had been led by the reading of Darwin, Spencer, Mill, and Comte to take a new position, whence the Christian placing of life's purpose beyond all life actually known to man seemed the greatest obstacle ever interposed between mankind and a happier existence.

What he had come to feel as a menacing peril as well as a hampering clog was man's tendency to waste his energy, his passion, his faith, on problems which, at the best, could merely furnish his mental faculties with a fascinating game, while at the same time he was slighting or wholly neglecting his actual environing conditions. Bjørnson had come to feel that man was everlastingly hoping to achieve through a miracle, through some one world-shaking event, what could only be conquered step by step through age-long, unremitting, well-directed toil. And so he had come to hate and dread that queer streak in man's make-up—that "craving for the boundless"—which seemed all the time to take the ground from under his reason at the moment when he most needed it. And whether the expected miracle was religious or political, spiritual or social, made no difference to him. In each and every case he found it a veil thrown between man and his actual goal—if not a new abyss opening beside his already sufficiently dangerous path.

"Our consciences can be no reliable guides to us," declares Bratt in the second act, "for they have never been at home on earth or in the present. We are always striving for Utopias, for the boundless—."

"Can you imagine anything more cruel," cries Rachel in the last act, "than a power within ourselves that goads us on to that which our whole nature resists? How can happiness be possible on this earth until our reasoning faculties become so spontaneous that no one can use us like that?"

Throughout this play as well as the earlier one, it is Rachel who acts as spokesman for the author. The choice of a woman for this part is not exceptional with Bjørnson. On the contrary, like Ibsen, he was always making women his mouthpieces. This was characteristic of his view of woman as nearer to the fountainhead of life, as more in accord with its fundamental purposes. She was to him not a being superior to the male, but an indispensable corrective without which the masculine tendencies toward experiment and abstraction would send the world flying into uncharted and unlivable regions.

As I have already mentioned, this play bears in the original the same name as *Beyond Our Power.* It is a sequel but can hardly be called a second part. The two plays are wholly independent of each other. It is not necessary to read one in order to understand or enjoy the other, although a knowledge of the earlier play will add to the appreciation—and probably also facilitate the understanding—of the later. Four of the characters in the first play reappear in the sequel. They are Elias and Rachel, Bratt, and Falk. In each case the later play shows a logical development of temperamental traits already indicated in the earlier one. Of the new characters in **Beyond Human Might,** two—Credo and Spera—may appear dangerously fantastic to many readers. They are nevertheless irresistibly charming. And like so much else in the play, they are symbolical rather than real. They are the future, the new mankind, stripped of all futile dreams—and, therefore, the richer in dreams that may come true. Nor must Credo's various plans for the improvement of human existence be taken too literally. It is the spirit of the whole thing—the glowing faith that shines through it—which should furnish us with inspiration, no matter how insufficient or even childish any detail of the boy's programme may appear to us. Like all the world's greatest dreamers, Bjørnson was too brave or too innocent to stop before the risk of seeming ridiculous. And if the inventions on which Credo reared his young hope should strike many as rather too materialistic, that must be accepted as a part of Bjørnson's own reaction against the days when he, like Bratt, "spent his time wool-gathering in another world."

To make it easier for the reader to follow the action, which is not always as clearly indicated as might be desirable, I want to point out that Halden, the architect, is revealed to us—by hints rather than by open statements—as the natural son of Holger and as the man who has instigated the deed of Elias.

Laboremus—"Let us work"—is an intense psychological study, having for its central figure the striking character of Lydia, the "Undine." This ultra-modern adventuress is the embodiment of a principle which Bjørnson repeatedly attacked during the later part of his life: that principle of overgrown, unconscionable, anti-social individualism which has its main roots in the misconstrued philosophies of Stirner and Nietzsche. Among the youth of Europe during the last decades of the century, Bjørnson found this principle worshipped as an excuse for turning their alleged search after self-expression into unscrupulous self-seeking, and in one work after another he gave battle against tendencies so hostile to all that was most sacred to himself. The basic theme of the play **At Storhove** (**På Storhove**), for instance, is almost identical with that of **Laboremus.** But, for all his burning antipathy, Bjørnson was too much the artist not to make the figure of Lydia appealingly human, and more than one critic has found her the most attractive character in the play.

Technically considered, the play strikes one especially by a quality which may be designated as "close-knit." It contains only five persons, not counting a few shadowy hotel servants, and for a few brief moments only, during the entire three acts, does the stage hold more than two persons at the same time. All these persons do is to talk. But what revelations come to us out of their talking; what lurid flashes of ordinarily hidden soul-depths are laid bare to us; and what vistas of action—even of action in the sense of bodily movement—are thrown open to us! Of all Bjørnson's plays, this is probably the one in which he approached most closely and most successfully to the methods characteristic of Ibsen. On the other hand, the principal objection to the play will be found in its musical symbolism, which at points is carried so far that the reader finds some difficulty in following. But there is not enough of this to mar fatally a work otherwise so instinct with fascination. Viewed in its entirety, rather than in detail, it impresses

us with an air of artistic and intellectual grace that has few parallels in the drama of to-day. (pp. 3-11)

Edwin Björkman, in an introduction to Plays *by Bjørnstjerne Bjørnson, second series, translated by Edwin Björkman, Charles Scribner's Sons, 1914, pp. 1-11.*

CHRISTIAN COLLIN   (essay date 1916)

[*In the following excerpt, Collin discusses the themes of Bjørnson's peasant stories and historical dramas.*]

[Bjørnson] was born and bred in the country and knew the Norwegian peasants, especially the young people, at first hand. Like [nineteenth-century Norwegian painter Adolf] Tidemand, and perhaps inspired by him, he looked at the people with loving sympathy and with a desire to see primarily their great and good qualities. But Bjørnson was not in the least interested in the archeological or in forms of life that were stiffened and incapable of further development. He did not look upon the peasant's dwelling and his sanctuary, the church, as beautiful relics of an historic past nor on the peasant himself as a decorative figure in a city salon or a foreign gallery, but as the sound core of the Norwegian people, holding the seed of future development.

His people are not always Sunday peasants, not always attired in their Sunday best nor behaving with grace and dignity even in church. Yet they have an imperishable charm, due first and foremost to the fact that they are intensely alive, full of the strength and joy of living. He depicts them in the age of growth; his principal characters are nearly always young, usually between the age of childhood and that of first love. This was the part of the people he knew best and to which he had, in a manner, himself belonged. They are not bearers of venerable antiquities but of youthful restlessness and aspiration which breed strife and threaten to disrupt society, such as we see in Arne, Thorbjørn Granliden [in **Synnøve Solbakken**], Øivind in **The Happy Boy,** and the Fisher-Maiden.

Bjørnson looked upon the Norwegian peasants as a young chieftain looks upon the army with which he is to win his battles. For this reason he does not shrink from portraying the darker side of their lives, since it is necessary to realize faults in order to correct them. His own father, the stern pastor, had waged a constant war against the sins of the people; students of popular life like Eilert Sundt had thrown on them the light of statistics, and Bjørnson knew them from his own observations and indeed from his own vehement and passionate nature. His delineations of Norwegian peasants are therefore no human still-life pictures like Tidemand's beautiful paintings. Bjørnson's people are in the midst of a dangerous battle where the issue is salvation or destruction.

The hero of Bjørnson's stories is, in fact, that impetuous ambition or high aspiration which the old Norsemen knew so well and for which they had so many names. Bjørnson saw the same motive power still abounding among the Norwegian peasantry. By means of it, a great age could be created. The problem was to avoid the shoals that had made the ancient history of Norway overwhelmingly tragic. How often had not the greatest powers been squandered in domestic strife by untamed passions or by ambitions beyond human power! Olaf Trygvason, Saint Olaf, Einar Tambarskjelver, Erling Skjalgsson, Harald Haardraade, and Magnus Barfot—all had died a sudden and violent death. King Sverre had lived in almost ceaseless civil war. Whence came the calamities of old Norway and the cessation of her ancient glory, if not from the same undisciplined power which the Norwegians of our day, and among them Bjørnson himself, could find within themselves!

How then direct this force so that it shall not be squandered in self-consuming battles? This is the central problem in all Bjørnson's works. How easily could not the desire of emulation in Thorbjørn Granliden have plunged him into life-long misery! How little it would have taken to upset the balance in the life of Arne, Øivind, or the Fisher-Maiden! The high striving, the passionate life hunger, according to Bjørnson's view, carry in them the germ of tragedy. Another force must be engendered to hold them in check, and even in the earliest of his masterpieces, *Synnøve Solbakken,* Bjørnson found this counter influence in the social impulses, erotic love, love of parents, love of God. By the expansive power of love the egoistic ambition is transformed into a noble zeal for the good of the race, the nation, the world. Through his affection for his mother and his sweetheart, Eli, Arne learned to demand happier conditions of living for those dear to him and through them for the whole country and the world. Even in the narrowest of Norwegian valleys the horizon widens and the eye is lifted to the sky, when the small contributions of the individual become a rivulet rushing toward the great river that flows into the ocean.

In order to understand fully the peasant stories of Bjørnson, they should be compared with his historical works dealing with saga times. . . . The ten works that make up the body of Bjørnson's youthful production form a cycle which, through the subconscious or at least not wholly reflective application of a comparative psychological method, are unique in the literature of the world. One and the same psychological and ethnological motif branches out into two widely different creations, one planted in the soil of saga times, one in that of modern Norway. The young poet-chieftain seems to be living at the same time in two different periods, one of war and one of peace, drawing lessons from both, comparing the life history of the strong, highly-gifted man and woman in both. In this manner he produced four double studies: *Between the Battles* and *The Newly Married Couple; Synnøve Solbakken* and *Lame-Hulda; Arne* and *Sigurd Slembe; The Happy Boy* and *Arnljot Gelline;* besides the two partly parallel works, *The Railroad and the Churchyard* and *Sigurd Jerusalem-Farer,* both descriptions of rivalry and reconciliation between two opposing leaders.

The relationship of these books suddenly struck me with a sense of surprise while I was working on a biography of Bjørnson, and I asked him if he had been conscious of the parallelism. It seemed that he had not thought of the connection nor worked according to any fixed plan, but he remembered that the conception of the saga drama of Eyolf Finsson and Lame-Hulda had sprung into his mind while he was working on the story of Thorbjørn Granliden and Synnøve Solbakken. It seemed to me then that the figure of Synnøve must have taken shape by a contrast association with Lame-Hulda and that of Thorbjørn Granliden with Eyolf Finsson. In the old time of war and violence the action becomes tragic, while in the modern story a similar fate is imminent, but is warded off by the influences of religion and love. Social forces are now more strongly developed than in ancient times; ambition has more channels and is not relegated to the one road of violence in order to attain glory and power. While Lame-

Hulda incites to bloody deeds, Synnøve makes peace and urges reconciliation.

There is a similar connection between *Arne* and *Sigurd Slembe* and between Øivind in *The Happy Boy* and *Arnljot Gelline.* Deeply moving is the story of Sigurd Slembe, the most kingly man of his time, driven by the crimes of his opponents and the evils of the age to attempt to reach the throne of Norway by violence—whereby his life becomes like "a fall from a mountain." Arnljot sees no way to achieve his ambitious goal of winning the chieftain's daughter, Ingigjerd, by fair means and so resorts to the force of arms, but the result for himself and his beloved is profoundly tragic.

By parallels such as these Bjørnson won his way to a bright and hopeful view of modern as compared with ancient Norway. His predecessors and even to some extent his contemporaries were prone to look with reminiscent idealism upon the glorious past of their country as "romantic," and to borrow from it a shadow to throw over modern Norway which they regarded as tame and "prosaic." Bjørnson, however, maintained in one of his early literary criticisms that the history of the people since saga times had been one of advancement and progress. Although the commonplace tasks of the peasant might seem to the romanticist prosaic in comparison with the mighty battles of ancient times, the young Bjørnson by a penetrating psychological analysis convinced himself that the motive power in a life of toil is the same as that of old, but more richly complex and therefore stronger and more fraught with happiness. To him ambition did not seem less interesting because it had been guided into fruitful channels. While the giant warrior Arnljot Gelline fails to win his bride with fire and sword, the cottager's son Øivind Pladsen wins his Marit by "besieging the old fellow (her grandfather) with good works," after an achievement so unromantic as to graduate from the agricultural college.

This seems to me the most inspired feature of Bjørnson's youthful production: by a psychological analysis which pierces to the basic powers of humanity he wins a glamour from the saga battles to shed over the peaceful labor of our time.

The Christian religion, which expands the egoistic will to live into the social will to serve, plays an important part in the early works of Bjørnson. The position as a chieftain in the cultural development of modern Norway, which Bjørnson held in spite of his passionate and impulsive temperament, was due not only to his powerful vitality and genius, but to the piety of his youth, which gave poise to his mind and guided his ambitions into the highest channels. The form which Christianity took in him was moulded by [Norwegian poet and dramatist Henrik] Wergeland and [Danish poet Nicolai] Grundtvig, the two mightiest leaders of the North during the generation that preceded him. Different as these two men were, they had in common their joyous view of the teachings of Christ as the religion of hope, of faith in the future, and of an all-embracing good will. To this must be added the stamp which Bjørnson's mind received from his boyhood reading of the sagas with their compelling delineations of strong men bowing in humble self-surrender before a heavenly chieftain and king. Life appeared to him as an epic crusade moving along a shining path, where men as God's faithful warriors did battle for goodness and progress. In all the works of Bjørnson, the strong, ambitious nature is the one that most needs religion in order to bend its own self-will under the world-will. Often this wisdom is learned in the hard school of suffering. A brother wounds his brother unto death, as does Sigurd Jerusalem-Farer or the schoolmaster in *The Happy Boy,* and not till then does the deep pain of his compassion wake in him contrition and the all-conquering love by which he understands the exalted law of living. The young Bjørnson never tires of passing with his characters through this purifying experience of pain, and only those who will follow him on this road will be able to live with him through the deepest experiences of his creative work. (pp. 23-6)

Bjørnson wished to see religious peace and harmony, not as a conventional appendix to an inborn gentleness and non-resistance, but as a conqueror over the strong passions of highly gifted and ambitious natures. His youthful creations, each and all, seem the result of inner experience; in fashioning them he has built his own character. Thorbjørn, Arne, and Øivind, Eyolf Finsson, Arnljot, and Sigurd Slembe have not lived in vain, since they have helped Bjørnson to become the greatest folk-leader of modern Norway. Perhaps they may, in course of time, give similar help to thousands of others. (p. 27)

Christian Collin, *"Tidemand and Bjørnson,"* in The American-Scandinavian Review, *Vol. IV, No. 1, January-February, 1916, pp. 20-8.*

HALVDAN KOHT AND SIGMUND SKARD (essay date 1944)

[*Koht and Skard were Norwegian educators and critics. Koht also served as Norway's Minister of Foreign Affairs from 1935 to 1941. Individually they wrote numerous studies reflecting their interests in comparative literature, and together they co-authored the seminal survey* The Voice of Norway. *In the following excerpt from that work, they discuss similarities between the lives and works of Bjørnson and nineteenth-century Norwegian patriot-poet Henrik Wergeland and evaluate Bjørnson's literary career in relation to his political activism.*]

In the work of Bjørnstjerne Bjørnson the achievements not only of his contemporaries but of the whole century are gathered into the broad common stream of the nation.

Like Ibsen, he came to Oslo in 1850, a student from the province, old-fashioned in clothes and queer in manners; his comrades jovially teased him about his dialect and his unruly wave of blond hair, called "the mountain peak." But he soon gave them other things to talk about.

He was a born leader and knew it. This youth from the backwoods, whom no one had ever heard of, behaved like a chief and a conqueror, and somehow it seemed to be perfectly natural. He was handsome: a slim, strong figure with brisk step and head borne high, an open, shining face and the eyes of a lion tamer; "he seemed like a revelation from a different world." There was a confidence about him which fascinated, an air of vitality and genius; wherever he appeared, he was the obvious center—as with Dante, "no one left when he came, no one stayed when he left." He emanated an ingratiating charm, witnessed to by all who ever met him, electrifying and irresistible; "it was impossible to deny him anything." From his first appearance people spoke of his resemblance to Henrik Wergeland, "alike as the hands of the same man"; and he accepted the challenge. A friend once gathered the impression of him in two words: "Sun and storm"; it fitted them both.

There was a deeper parallelism, however, in their whole mental structure.

He was no problemless Sunday child; his triumphant exterior concealed a character of strain and contrast. His strength was a force of nature, which often broke its reins. There was a passion in him, a desire for life and a reckless, vehement self-assertion, which could suddenly sweep him away, carrying strange things to the surface. He who seemed so self-assured, was painfully sensitive, tossed about by "the hard blows of his impressions," raptured by a troll-like power of fancy, which in his childhood made him "the worst liar in the district" and which even much later could unexpectedly derail him. His life moved in waves, calm and tempest, despair and hope—"others can hardly realize how overwhelmingly I have been a man of emotions"; he rightly used to say that he belonged to the western Norwegians from the narrow fjords, the people of avalanches and eddy winds. And he displayed his changes with a southern openness which has always been rare in Norway, and which a generation before made his great predecessor a bugaboo to all good burghers.

But if these powers of disorder were strong, in him as in Wergeland, the counterpoise was even stronger—all that draws a straight line through a man's life. This sensitive soul had a cool, almost calculating intelligence; this emotional dreamer was a realist, a man of penetrating observation and solid common sense. He saw, understood, and remembered everything, words and actions, in others and himself; he could handle things and human beings with amazing practical touch. Behind his changeableness in minor matters was a will power, flexible and strong, which gave everything its purpose. This impulsive poet was a man of patient planning, who could postpone his debut for years in order to be fully prepared, who could save an inspiration for a decade in order to let it ripen, and follow an idea through half a century without ever losing the track. This man of effervescent power, this lover of life who improvised one of his most famous speeches in homage to "all that is after midnight," was at the same time from his student days a most methodical worker ("laziness is against my nature"), an early riser, who used his forces systematically and carefully to the last horsepower. At bottom he possessed a deep mental health which corresponded to his physical strength and stabilized his whole being. He never doubted that life made sense, that it was basically good and sound, governed by "the great, healthy laws of balance"; those laws he would struggle to live up to himself. Even in his wildest storms of passion he saw his actions in relation to those great principles, and early it was obvious that the constructive powers were the stronger in him, that the tremendous currents were not milling around themselves, but were running toward a goal.

But the force which pointed out that goal to him, which kept his powers united and made their balance active, was that same simple force which had also molded Wergeland's life: the goodness of the heart. Beneath all that was tangled and twisted, hard and unruly in Bjørnson there was a fertile soil of human sympathy, a spontaneous openness toward his fellow beings, an overwhelming power of understanding them, of suffering and weeping and laughing with them, of embracing them in compassion and fellowship. This youngster of turbulent forces whom his friends called "the Bear" had the delicacy of a girl and the watchful tenderness of a mother, and her soft hands. "Never," says a friend of his later years, "did I see a man get tears in his eyes so easily." In him as in

Wergeland this sympathy created the same spontaneous urge to help and to be useful, to be where life needed him, the same feeling of universal responsibility: "I believe and love without any moderation." To his student companions it was demonstrated most strikingly that memorable winter morning when he appeared in their modest den with a shivering twelve-year-old German accordion player whom he had adopted, and whom he never afterward sloughed off; his life was an unbroken chain of such acts. Here was the power behind his powers, which fitted them into a pattern. He was less abrupt and ecstatic than Wergeland, less seraphic, more matter-of-fact in his whole approach; but the motive power was the same. (pp. 235-37)

The urge of expansion in him was almost irresistible, precisely because he was so strong; and it had the same categorical character as in Ibsen: it is the duty of the genius to realize himself regardless of considerations, in unrestrained freedom. But at the same time he soberly realized how dangerous were the powers he handled, how easily they could break their dams and turn his liberty into a caricature; at bottom he never doubted that his place was on the other side. He felt his dualism as a personal challenge; to reconcile the contrasts and make his powers serve the common good of mankind became one of his main tasks. It made him a moralist, often in defense against himself, sometimes more than even his admirers could swallow; it made his inner life a struggle which absorbed much of his power and brought him humiliating defeats. But at the same time, it was this many-sidedness with its unavoidable battles that gave his work its baffling breadth and gave his life its depth and dimension, its human fullness. He was no flat compromiser, but a whole man.

The foundation of his existence, to which he always returned from his crises, remained his feeling of human fellowship. Wergeland was so young, and often so alone; Bjørnson through his long life always seemed to have many marching beside him; they were always in his mind. He was not one to brood over his personal problems, as Ibsen did. He struggled with them to get through them, to become a better worker in the common cause of humanity, to battle through and march on. It gave him sometimes the terrifying briskness of a military commander: when he had reached his decision, doubts were not always welcome. But it also gave him his genuine humility: he never forgot that he served causes that were greater than himself. Here is the real source of his strength, of that deeper certainty, that feeling of directed power and hard-won poise which radiated from him and made him invincible. Till his dying day he remained "a frail, struggling, slaving, joyous, repentant, fresh-up-again man," always reborn from the secret springs of his mind.

In this personality, at once simple and motley, Bjørnson's whole historical role was presaged. His victorious certainty did not just come from his feeling of power; he knew how he was going to use it. (pp. 238-39)

[He] had not spent his formative years in ambitious dreams of revolt, in the manner of Ibsen. He had begun the conscious building of his own character. He had grown harmoniously into the heritage of the nation; and to a rare extent he had identified himself with the spirit of his people and the aims of its history.

He had lived a happy childhood in the vicarages of his peasant-born clerical father, east and west in Norway. He had seen the mountains and the ocean, valley and shore, and filled his soul and senses with the contrasts of the landscape—the wildness and the mystery, the calm and the serenity, powers of his own soul. He had lived with the farmers as one of their own and learned to love and understand them, with his peculiar mixture of sympathy and shrewd observation; he had seen in them the same tension of elemental forces; he had absorbed their language and traditions. He had grown into European traditions as well, above all Christianity, less a code of law than a cheerful confidence, which to his dying day remained connected with all that was constructive in him. He had lived in [Icelandic historian, author, and statesman Sturluson] Snorri's Royal Sagas, scene of an eternal drama which to him seemed to play among his own farm friends; and he had filled his mind with Wergeland, who pointed to the same connections in the images of poetic genius. Early there was built up in him a grand vision of Norway's way as a nation, from the past into the future, an endless struggle for real freedom among the blind powers of nature, embodied in slowly built ideals, kept alive through the centuries of darkness. . . . It was Bjørnson's deepest conviction that "nothing can grow to power in a people which does not have root in its history." In Wergeland's broad program of liberty the fulfillment of the nation's historic destiny was translated into a clear and simple working plan, leaving the task with Bjørnson's own generation.

He knew that in this work *he* was called to shoulder Wergeland's burden. Like him, he felt a capacity for action in all fields of life; but his main task was that of a poet. To him poetry was not a niggling with the pretty feelings of the individual; it was the vision which points the way to nations. "The poet does the prophet's deeds"; he is the "leading instinct" of his people, lifting up its highest ideals and pointing to its deepest moral forces, as did the Edda poet, the ballad singers, and the tale tellers in their majestic anonymous simplicity. . . . In his first creations, his saga dramas and peasant novels from the 1850's and 60's, he answered the call, showing in great pictures the inner unity of Norse life, the warm stream of human health through its twisted history, the "moral order and noble freedom" which had been dominant whenever the nation had been able to unfold its own self.

In so doing, however, he made his creation a battlefield. The balance he talked of had never been a matter of course to Norwegian minds. He knew it from himself: "Beneath so high a vault it costs a hard struggle to reach mastery." Through his saga dramas rage the tides of passion: wrath and defiance, arrogance and self-righteousness, symbolized in the description of the spring flood in **Arnljot Gelline,** where the destructive powers of *Voluspá* again seem to engulf the world in their morbid nihilism. In the peasant novels there is sometimes a brutality which shocked Bjørnson to the bottom (not to mention his readers): he knew it only too well. The style is as tense as in the Edda; its directness "exploded like TNT" among contemporary critics, surging with emotion, bursting from restrained force.

The dominant trait, however, is not despair, but optimism. Through the darkest abyss of this poetry shines the light of that simple truth "experienced by a hundred thousand millions": that redemption is always possible, that human will is able to master the storm and build a free character, helped by the powers of good. Strongest among those powers was to Bjørnson Christianity. In his saga hero Arnljot the pride of the pagan warrior is broken before the mildness of St. Olaf, conqueror of destruction; to Bjørnson this conversion was

Bjørnson in 1909.

not only the fulfillment of a personal fate but the symbol of Norse history. In his peasant the religious background is always present, amid the variety of character and plot, united with "the bottom in them, the strength that shall continue." Even in his style, mastery is the dominant feature, behind its explosive newness: always again the passion is brought back under control by artistic restraint, by concern for what is "universal." The more highstrung the feeling, the more tight and momentous the form; the tragedy of a life may be concentrated in one reply, one taciturn, sagalike short story, heavy with words unspoken, rounded as a crystal ball. Amazingly this style unites the features of centuries in a natural, modern expression, free from false archaism, saga heroes and present-day Norwegians meeting on a common ground.

The striking reality of these books, however, comes from Bjørnson himself, his warmth and strength, that mighty breath of life which was in him. His heroes are not the empty shells of a moral theory; they resound with his own factual struggle. Their "sound balance" is no cautious indolence, but duly paid for; in some of these novels, which were originally printed in newspapers, we can follow the shifting battle lines from day to day. But the core of these men and women is Bjørnson's own songful optimism, his brisk and cheerful resolution; they are rough and jovial as he was, vehement and charming, strong and humble, patiently growing through suffering and defeat. All the characters are conceived in the

same fullness of individuality, followed with a cool but loving eye till they exult from real life, in a sun glitter of lyrical warmth. Through all of them sings his love of Norway; these prose works are the first of his great national anthems. His devotion may break forth as a direct sermon; his famous description of how the birch trees managed to clothe the barren mountain slope just because they always kept trying, is a hymn to the endurance of his people, orchestrated as playfully as the sough of the May wind through the victorious birches themselves. But the landscape is everywhere present, even in the psychological analysis, weaving its melody into the dreams and struggles and victories of man, fresh with the scent of the forests and the breeze from the mountains, the deep shadow of the hillside and the serenity of a summer day.

"This book," Bjørnson once wrote of a contemporary author, "reaches us like a clear call from a mountain top, redoubled in thousand echoes, making the air lighter, the forest fresher, the water bluer to those who listen." Nothing could better describe the effect of his own creation. No work of fiction has become so widely and enduringly popular throughout Scandinavia as the collection of his peasant novels; their ideas and their art spoke directly to the mind. In his own nation, few literary works have done more to build self-understanding and mold standards.

But to Bjørnson literature was never more than a part of life. In his first works he had outlined his basic ideas; but his vision was the future of a whole nation. The task was endless, writing could not do everything. His letters are crowded with impatient outbursts: "I am no indoor poet," "I cannot merely sit and think up characters," "I must have something to rule over, or I go to seed!" He was, as he wrote himself, "irremediably earmarked for action"; now already he began that "rotation of crops" which made his poetry grow in the breathing spells of a whirlwind of outward activity.

Activity to him meant something very special. With amazement, and not without anxiety, the good people of Norway saw what kind of volcano had opened among them in this poetic genius. He was the greatest orator the country has ever borne, "with a voice like an orchestra," combining the lofty pathos of the prophet, the versatility of the accomplished actor, and a terrifying power of suggestion; there was no stormy public meeting which he could not master by the mere impact of his personality. He was a prolific journalist, editor, pamphleteer, and propagandist. He could not keep to himself anything that filled his mind; through sixty years he flooded the newspapers with long, signed articles and countless "little anonymous devils," easy to recognize from their striking style and buoyant spirit. He was a skillful organizer, something of a conspirator, and a virtuoso of personal persuasion. He "carried the key that opens people"; he could force access to an inveterate enemy who refused even to see him, and leave with everything obtained—"There is nothing left of him." And he followed up his personal contacts by a lifelong correspondence which recalls the vast epistolography of Voltaire and Benjamin Franklin, approximately estimated at 30,000 letters, from open postcards of amazing frankness to extensive treatises overflowing with advice and encouragement, philippics and consolation.

His fighting spirit was as infectious as his laughter. He filled the country with his sayings and doings; never before had Norway listened to such a voice. But all of his activities were tied together, stirring each other and fertilizing each other by the unity of his purpose: to make real in all fields of life that freedom which was the vision of his literary creation.

He would build a free Norwegian art. He became the dynamo of architecture, painting, and music, pushing them on and holding them back, acting as their outspoken conscience. In the theater he did more. He was himself a director of genius, repeatedly the manager of the country's leading theaters; the creation of a national stage in Norway was his work. His aim was not an independence in the externals, but in the spirit: to make Norse art again express those deep forces which had molded the nation's life. Such were his aims in politics as well, for years a main field of his activity. He was no politician, he never held a public office. His task was to be "the instinct" of the fight: to make the nation realize even in political life the implications of that self-possession which had been the burden of its history.

Few Norwegians have ever seen those connections as clearly as he did. That survival of Norway's liberty through the ages of union which Wergeland had just grasped in poetic outline, Bjørnson conceived in the complexity of its conditions with the penetrating eye of the scholar at an age when most young men are still struggling with their textbooks. There are important ideas derived from him in the works of J. E. Sars, the great contemporary historian of Norse freedom, ideologist and chief of staff of the army of progress. Bjørnson had the poet's power of moving his historic visions into contemporary life; his program of the future seemed to be born from the past as its obvious outgrowth. But at the same time his approach was that of perfect realism. Actually, his aim was not political, but moral. To him the individual programs and planks were just means of building the nation's self-respect and deepening its sense of honor, and there were many ways to the goal. Too well he saw the value even of those ideas he had to fight; too clearly he knew how tangled were the lines even of the simplest problem. He hated the "clear standpoints," the sterile abstractions, the "intoxication of consistency"; to him the ideal was never to lose sight of the final aims but to solve the immediate problems within the limits of the possible. With all his impetuosity he was patient; there was just one thing to do: to tell the truth, untiringly, again and again, till it took root. Like Wergeland, he saw Norway as a part of the great liberty front of his day, all over the world, from Garibaldi and Castelar to Gambetta and Lincoln. But his dearest hero was Victor Hugo, prophet and poet, who made his ideals live on earth.

This broadness made Bjørnson a political leader. He was not always easy for the professionals to handle; he always let the cat out of the bag; he could never be prevailed on to bring anything about by tricks. He swept resistance away by his force and splendor. From his first political speeches he displayed his marvelous ability to make the details of the day's work appear in the sunlight of great ideals, as a direct challenge to the individuals. His "policy of the heart" proved to be good realism as well. From the famous battle in 1859, when—at the age of twenty-seven—he turned the election of his district, to the winter ten years later when the scattered radical forces finally gathered in the great party of the Left with the clear program of full independence in the union with Sweden and full democracy and parliamentarism at home, Bjørnson became one of the spiritual leaders of the rising wave, center of the advancing storm and its directive force.

His adversaries called him a demagogue and an evil demon; they hated him. But his real power did not rest in his skill as an agitator. The broad masses began to listen to him as they had listened to Wergeland, because they recognized the vision behind his activity and felt that he believed in them. In his *Poems and Songs* (1870) he gave the program, his and theirs.

There are wonderful personal lyrics among them, and their tune is that of cheerful strength, perhaps more so than in any other volume of verse in world literature. What a deep and natural breath there was in Bjørnson in spite of his conflicts is nowhere revealed as in these songs. Here as before, there is almost always a battle. But usually the battle is won before the song comes, or it is just billowing like a dark ground swell, which makes the victory earnest and worth while. Even in the song **"In a Dark Hour"** the real outcome is no longer in doubt: "Be glad when danger presses Each power your soul possesses! In greater strain Your strength shall gain Till greater victory blesses!" Here is leisure for more than fighting: for dreams and longing, for the whispering of the twilight and the wordless song of the woods, for the wandering moods and ever unsatisfied yearnings of those who are young, for that sound and fresh romanticism which was also in Bjørnson. The climax of these personal poems is the morning songs, when "the gold of heaven is on the dust of earth," when the sailor climbs singing to the masthead "to clear the sail that shall swell more freely," and when the soul itself musters its powers of good and finds them to be unscathed:

> Day's coming up now, joy's returned,
> Sorrow's dark castles captured and burned;
> Over the mountaintops glowing
> Light-king his armies is throwing.
> "Up now, up now!" calls the bird,
> "Up now, up now!" child voice heard,
> Up now my hope in sunshine.

Rarely are these songs purely personal confessions, however. What they mostly express with striking directness is the common feeling of mankind towards its common problems. Even his most intimate outbursts usually are worded in such a way as to make them applicable to everyone. The form is as simple as it is elaborate, Wergeland's force in [Norwegian poet and critic Johan] Welhaven's verse, a witness to what this rough-haired Teuton had really learned in the school of the classics. He does not sing within himself. He sings to those who listen and understand, and their recognition and participation is his highest reward.

Often he speaks directly on behalf of his audience. Surprisingly many of Bjørnson's poems were written for some occasion, tools for work and weapons in the fight. All the ideals of Norway's democracy rise before our eyes in these songs in monumental symbols: the promises of history, the burning issues of the day, and the great visions of the future. But the strongest of the poems speak of everyday life, without the banners of the platform. They carry a message that may seem almost prosaic: a praise of the plain existence and its simple heroism, a "love of the small and the near"; their challenge has a touch of resignation: "Give your strength and your deed Where you nearest see need." But the plain words and simple thoughts are filled with the might of experience and the spontaneous warmth of feeling, what Bjørnson himself once called "the clarity of the heart"; more than many pompous statements these songs reveal the real powers behind the cause he served. Here speaks a man to whom human companionship is not a thing of the festal days, but his very breath of life, closely connected with his Christian faith. He believes in "the recreative power of love" because he has seen it work in his own life; his confidence through night and dark, his morning hymns of the soul, are not for him alone, but for all fighting fellow beings. Even Wergeland lived in two worlds, although they were moved by the same power; there was always a far-away look in his eyes when he returned from his realm of fancy to the world of man. In Bjørnson no fissure is visible. The ideas he sings, the faces he lifts out of the crowd, the landscape which soughs and storms and whispers in dewy freshness through his verse, grow naturally from this common ground. The real strength and beauty of many of these poems is only revealed when they are sung in assembly, and the form is triumphantly filled by that for which it was made.

There are several national anthems in the collection: homages to the fathers who "brought order new with law and plough," songs for building site and workshop, proud statements of the conquests of present-day Norway: "each new plot reclaimed for harvest, each new ship running down the ways, each new child soul molded to manhood." One of these songs was soon adopted as the common expression of the nation's faith: "Yes, we love this land together Where the wild sea foams. . . . " It is a classical song, plain in style and subdued in words; it needs no oratory. It is "modern Norwegian," Bjørnson once said, "open and free as the day, rising without threats, self-assertive without ostentation, free from exaggeration and sentimentality," the anthem of a small, peace-loving nation. "But if it is sung in the hour of danger, then the self-assertion stands armored in every line."

About 1870, Bjørnson's future as a great national and Christian poet thus seemed to be staked out. But it proved otherwise.

From childhood on, he had felt religion as "the ground from which everything shoots," a Christianity glad and open as himself. He had been definitely hostile to the new wave of intellectual radicalism which surged over Europe. Toward the end of the 1870's this isolation was broken, and it was his own spirit of independence that urged him on. A long stay abroad had brought him in close contact with modern French literature; it had made him realize how hemmed in he was, with all his political and national programs of freedom. "There are more dogmas than mine," he wrote in self-reproach, "more forms, more sincere minds, more high aims, more paths to those things we all love." To work through these problems on the new ground became a challenge to his sincerity. Like [eighteenth-century Dano-Norwegian author Ludwig] Holberg, he found it to be a Christian duty to investigate before he believed; and before this investigation the whole system of dogma crumbled. The story of his conversion is pathetic. Each step was painful, he often felt as if he were uprooting his own heart; the pictures of him show the growing strain and restlessness almost from month to month. But his courage was unfailing; and he was rewarded by a new feeling of being on his own ground: "The truths that are bought with pain, also give the highest power to carry."

Bjørnson's break with Christianity was a far-reaching experience, not only to himself, but to his nation. Many contemporary authors went the same way; but Bjørnson's defection became much more important: he had been one of the great hopes of the creed he deserted. To many of his best followers his revolt could only appear as a betrayal, a pure loss. In longer perspective, however, the break is less important than the connection. The intellectual liberation of the 70's was as unavoidable as that of Holberg's time; and Bjørnson's fight for

it had the same clear honesty as Holberg's. But like Holberg he was no revolutionary. He knew the values connected with the ideas he had to abandon; in tearing the old bonds, he tried to substitute others, in a new equilibrium. The spirit of his revolt was not anarchy or nihilism, but earnestness and responsibility; his great speech of conversion, **"To Be in Truth,"** set the direction for a whole generation of youth, away from the tradition, and at the same time back to it. (pp. 239-48)

The years of inner struggle did not leave him unchanged. He became more radical, more of a liberator: in one respect he had seen through the screen of conventional truth. More than before his art turned into a weapon. He mostly dropped the lyrical verse; in modern dramas and novels he turned to the problems of the day, often in aggressive closeness to realities. But his basic problem always remained the education of the will. His broad-mindedness did not change, neither did his understanding, or the heart behind it. (p. 249)

His political dramas are not just weapons; they raise the broad moral issues which were often forgotten in the fray of battle, appealing to good will across the party lines. His great drama *Paul Lange and Tora Parsberg* is the moving tragedy and apologia of those who are undeservedly crushed in the political clash because they are noble and weak, too delicately organized for a world of unscrupulous struggle. There is an amazing lack of fanaticism in these plays, and a deep humanity; no short cut, however promising, can relieve us of our responsibility toward each other. "The pathetic grief of one single human being is enough to make all the inhuman ways to happiness incomprehensible, impossible, terrifying."

This broad conception of progress moved his goals forward, beyond political democracy, to the demands of the new classes of society: the workers, in countryside and town. They were no longer a problem of philanthropy; Bjørnson saw clearly their future role as a dominant force in society. His visit to the United States (1880-81) sharpened his eye. Through all disguising phrases he grasped the oppressive power of capital and the dangerous implications of its Nietzschean morality, that "pity is weakness"; above all, he saw the real conditions under which the workers were living. He warned of the consequences "if justice is not done in time": "God help us if our sense of fair play is not the strongest of all our feelings!" He solemnly declared himself a socialist; he wrote fiery songs for the workers, and was a supporter of the first Norwegian strike. Here, too, he pointed out the direction, a leader even to those who were bound to go much farther than he did. (pp. 250-51)

He became the great propagandist for the liberation of woman, beside Ibsen and even before him, not only in theory, but still more in his pictures of noble, freeborn womanhood, healthy, outdoor Norwegian girls. This freedom included the liberation of the senses from religious asceticism and Victorian conventions, in the name of health: "the power of sensuality is also that of courage, of imagination, of color." In long novels (sometimes very long) he advocated a new education which prepared one for life instead of frightening one away from it. But to him, law was as much a part of health as was freedom; against the prophets of sexual anarchy he untiringly professed his belief in "self-mastery, vigilance, absorption in noble things, self-respect." In the midst of his sex campaigns he was not afraid to protest, once in a while, against the monomaniacs on his own side and their "everlasting love life—as if there were not also a life of work!" He chose the same difficult midway position in the feuds about morality and art roused by naturalism. He fought simultaneously the heralds of bigotry and the champions of "empty effeminacy," always guided by his instinct for the limits, softening the impact of the new standards, saving what could be saved.

Most one-track he might seem in his polemics against dogmatic Christianity. Down to his last years he wrote acid pamphlets against the theologians; his novels again and again lashed "the wrecks of forms from a passed existence." But his religious play *Beyond Our Power,* one of the masterpieces of dramatic literature, is filled with a different spirit. What frightened Bjørnson in the great religious personalities was their lack of "sound and straight humanity," their morbid tendency toward the impossible, which unsettled the balance of life on earth. He had felt the chilling breath of such idealism in Ibsen's *Brand;* in his own drama, the exaltation is crushed against the immutable laws of life. It is his most classical play, austere and merciless; and the very idea was close both to Greeks and Norse: whoever goes beyond his power is broken by the gods. But the persons who carry these overstrained ideas and sink under the burden are living human beings, seen with a tenderness and compassion which proves how deeply Bjørnson had himself shared the feelings he warned against. The moral nobility of the hero radiates both from the author and from the religion he attacks; and it remains when he himself has met his fate.

There is no hopelessness about it. In *The Wild Duck* Ibsen had shown the same destructive effect of an idealism beyond the power, leaving in the reader an impression of sad pity. Bjørnson's play is a sermon on the grandeur of good in man, even in delusion, a confession of the power of all who "walk God's ways" through the world of imperfection, attempting together that childlike and difficult thing: "to be good."

This simple warmth of life gradually won the nation for Bjørnson, regardless of his disputed opinions. (pp. 251-53)

> *Halvdan Koht and Sigmund Skard, "The Warmth of Life: Bjørnstjerne Bjørnson," in their* The Voice of Norway, *Columbia University Press, 1944, pp. 235-59.*

BRIAN W. DOWNS   (essay date 1962)

[*Downs was an English educator and critic who specialized in Scandinavian studies. In the following excerpt, he examines Bjørnson's tragedies.*]

Bjørnson wrote in all twenty-two plays. The extraordinary range and burden of his non-literary occupations as "uncrowned King of Norway", radical reformer, guide and spokesman of public opinion for decade after decade, might well suggest that they were for him only the relaxation of an occasional idle hour. That would be far from the truth. Without exception they were long pondered and planned, most carefully executed. Equally wrong would it be to assume that these emanations of a masterful, unmetaphysical, extraverted personality must, as a general rule, be breezy, encouraging comedies. Two of them only, *Geografi og kærlighed* and *Når den ny vin blomstrer,* fit such a definition, while at least twice that number call for consideration under the rubric "tragedy".

A significant point has to be made about the intermediate range of Bjørnson's plays, those that neither are light entertainment nor end in catastrophe. These abound in "strong" situations, which might well have taken a tragic turn. The hero of *Kong Sverre* is faced with the complete collapse of his fortunes; the threat of civil war and fratricidal strife broods over *Sigurd Jorsalfar* and *Kong Eystejn; De nygifte,* like *Mellem slagene,* shows a marriage drifting fatally on to the rocks; lovers part at the end of *En hanske;* in *På Storhove* a member of the "human demolition squad" brings a family and a big business to the verge of ruin. Only to the verge, however. The evil element is expelled (as in the similar *Laboremus*); King Sverre finds reliable support at the eleventh hour, while Tjælde, of *En fallit,* who is actually ruined in the commercial sense, is given a whole last act to show that, except for pounds, shillings and pence, he is better off than before; one of the hostile brothers of *Sigurd Jorsalfar* just takes himself off, while the other, in *Kong Eystejn,* "becomes himself again"—that is to say, pacific; the audience can look forward to the spouses living happily ever after as the final curtain falls on *Mellem slagene* and *De nygifte,* and a fair glimmer of hope lights up that of *En hanske.*

Three other plays, of so much greater weight that they are sometimes regarded as tragedies, tend in the same direction. In *Over ævne, II* that is quite blatant. In one sense the most violent and bloody of all that Bjørnson intended for the stage, exhibiting *coram publico* ["in the presence of the public"] a whole holocaust of dynamited capitalists, not to mention a subsidiary murder, it winds up with a final act completely different in tone, offering delightful vistas of cheap housing and clothing, easy communications and the abolition of war, before which two children disport themselves commended by their names of Credo and Spera. *Leonarda* leads up to the renunciation of their lover by the elder of two rivals: she is plainly the richer and more interesting personality, her happiness a matter of profounder concern, and her future is left problematical, to say the least; Bjørnson obviously strives nevertheless to show that the sum of happiness resulting from the union of the two juvenile leads is not merely the highest obtainable in the circumstances, but a positive *plus. Maria Stuart i Skotland* similarly leaves the heroine defeated in more senses than one. But Schiller's *Maria Stuart* existed to show that at the point where Bjørnson left her, ominously unprincipled and irresponsible though she might be, she still had several years of life and even of hope before her; after all, the valiant Bothwell is still there. The play therefore is not a "deferred tragedy" (as *Sigurd Slembe* is). The optimist, the reformer bent on proving that darkness can engender light, plainly found Tragedy hard to achieve. The surprising thing is that he ever attempted it, and a capital question, Why he did so?

As was the case with Ibsen, Bjørnson published nothing bearing the subtitle "tragedy". Five plays, however, qualify prima facie to count as such, on the ground that the personage at the centre of the action is, at its end, snuffed out or as nearly so as makes no matter. Well spread over his literary career, they are: *Halte Hulda* (1858), *Sigurd Slembe* (1862), *Kongen* (1877), *Over ævne* (1882), and *Paul Lange og Tora Parsberg* (1898).

Only a little penetration below the surface reduces the number to four. *Halte Hulda* ends in a great midnight blaze into which the heroine (long ago an underprivileged child) has lured the hero so that he may perish, in her company, rather than go off with another woman. . . . It is essentially a romantic melodrama of adultery and murder, the libretto for an opera such as Scribe might have written for Meyerbeer, and not even good of its kind, since its intolerable wordiness gives ample opportunity for reflecting on the creaking implausibility of the all-important intrigues. Hulda, the femme fatale, may afford fine scope for a forceful actress of tragic parts, but it is small wonder that, almost alone of Bjørnson's plays, it had virtually no success either on the stage or as a book. It stands apart too for conveying no *tendens* ["aim"] at all and only the minimal moral: "Little boy, little girl, be good and kind to Mary"; and remains, in fact, Bjørnson's sole full-length attempt at *l'art pour l'art* ["art for art's sake"].

Sigurd Slembe is enacted at a time close to that supposed for *Halte Hulda,* the thirteenth century. And it, too, lies fairly and squarely within the traditions of romantic drama, though the dropping of verse in favour of prose during the action is a pointer towards Bjørnson's slow emancipation from them. He had devoted a great part of the four years between *Halte Hulda* and the completion of *Sigurd Slembe* to study and to meditation on the bases upon which to rear his art in the next phase. Ambitious of supplying his fellow countrymen with a whole picture gallery of their ancestors in dramatic form, he had not only, under Peter Andreas Munch's guidance, studied historical "sources" and the famous historians: at the same time, also, after learning from Hettner and P. L. Møller to disdain Scribe, he had immersed himself as never before in the writings of the great dramatists, such as Goethe, Kleist and, most fruitfully, Shakespeare and Schiller.

The mark of the two last named is clearly impressed on *Sigurd Slembe:* its triple structure is that of [Schiller's] *Wallenstein.* The Shakespearian inspiration appears in technical details also, such as the wide compass of time and space and the gleam of rough comedy in the midst of horrors. But, more importantly, it is evident in the theme—substantially that of *Macbeth,* that favourite of Norwegians—the wreck of a noble ambition, due not only to the hostility it naturally raises against itself, but equally to the moral degeneration of the protagonist.

This theme becomes clear in the third part of the trilogy, which with but slight adjustment could make an independent tragedy by itself. Sigurd, called Slembe ("the Bad"), arrives at the court of Norway to claim his right to share the throne with the half-brother of his who at the time is in sole possession. Received at first with fair words, he is then arrested on a wrongful charge of homicide and, on getting free, hunted like a wild animal. He now truly becomes a wild animal, breaks out of his desert fastness . . . and murders his half-brother, by night, unarmed, in a concubine's bed. The hunt continues, enormity follows on enormity, and the drama ends with the trap closed round Sigurd from which there is no escape but death.

Parts I and II of the trilogy give the measure of the hero's moral ruin, by showing how a man who settled his more or less legitimate account not by process of law or in open combat, but by stealth, and who afterwards, to support his failing strength, called in his country's enemies, how this man might not only have been fitly called "Bellona's bridegroom", but also by his handling of affairs in a distant dependency approved himself as a statesman no less than as a general. Sigurd's lawful claim to the kingship is truly established; but it is seconded by one of a different order when in the face of the Court's corruption he convinces himself that his abilities and aspirations in themselves justify his wresting its authority to himself and gives reckless rein to the ambition which the sternest self-control hitherto has kept in honourable courses.

He ends much like Macbeth; but he has shown himself as potentially a greater man; equally, his fate is attributable not to the incitements of any fiend-like queen or to supernatural promptings, but to himself alone. The execution matching the theme, Bjørnson produced an historical tragedy to which Ibsen's *Kongsemnerne* alone, in Norwegian literature, is a worthy rival.

When Bjørnson came to write his next tragedy, he had turned his back on the Middle Ages for good. The continuous series of modern *drames à thèse* ["thesis dramas"] had begun with *En fallit* and *Redaktøren,* and this was to be one of the most sensational of them. For as the title, *Kongen,* announced, the institution of Kingship itself was under debate.

The kernel of the action, however, is well and truly a "bürgerliches Trauerspiel" ["bourgeois tragedy"]. In the ancestry of *Kongen,* [Schiller's] *Kabale und Liebe* takes the place of *Wallenstein* in that of *Sigurd Slembe.* Again we are shown the distress of true love cutting across class distinctions and the criticism of authority from a radical middle-class point of view. *Kongen* might also qualify as a "bürgerliches Trauerspiel" in a less traditional way: it is *bourgeois* monarchy, as it had developed in the nineteenth century, which comes under fire.

Bjørnson presents a not untypical representative, the rather weak and commonplace, slightly degenerate scion of an established dynasty, living in a largely frivolous, corrupt entourage. At a masked ball he makes "gallant" advances to a lady. She disdains him, and he falls in love with her. His love for the high-minded young schoolmistress that she turns out to be sobers and invigorates him. He begins seriously to ponder his duties as man and as head of the State. The first line of thought leads him to the middle-class ideal of a solid, healthy, absorbing family life, and, in the face of all the expected prejudice, he engages himself to his *beau masque* ["masked beauty"] who has become convinced of his integrity, returns his passion and shares his aspirations. In the second line of his reflections, the King is aided by the friendship he made as Crown Prince with a liberal-minded businessman, reputed to be, thanks to his energies, the richest man in the realm, who has become his Home Secretary and who manages to provide for him some informal contact with representative citizens. The mirage of "popular kingship" rises before him.

Then the catastrophe occurs. Within a few days the hero loses the only two human beings who really care for him and give him the support his nature needs. To stand so isolated as to have have only these two supporters and to scarcely hope for any others to take their place—the point is rammed home in the last Act—is the direct consequence of his public position. This, he comes to realize, is in his terms an impossible one. He sees himself as, essentially, no more than the chairman of an insurance company of financiers and Civil Servants, and what they insure *against* is the mass of his subjects, who would sweep them all away if they could. Abdication might have been a way out: but with no friends left, with no business in life or remarkable abilities, what kind of existence would then have been possible for him? He foresees a trial beyond his strength and commits suicide.

Some cavils can be raised. One is at the uncomfortable way in which Bjørnson's positive thesis cuts into and weakens the personal tragedy. "You have only", he cries in effect, "to set up a Republic under a President on short tenure, who keeps office hours and, when they are over, goes to a loving wife and cosy hearth—and these personal frustrations and heartbreaks will be abolished". Another criticism centres on the elimination of Clara and Gran, with its air of the fortuitous. Gran is killed in a most peculiar duel, dependent on chance, into which a half-crazy fanatic inveigles him. The challenge comes at a moment of understandable depression—the progressives have just lost a general election—but it is hard to believe that a man shown elsewhere as affectionate, stout-hearted, sensible, and well inured to the vicissitudes of public life should run to his doom at a time when, he must realize, his august friend most needs him. The phrase "run to his doom" is used advisedly: Gran has persuaded himself in advance that he will succumb.

We have here a decree of fate. An intervention of the supernatural removes Clara. Setting out to be received at Court as the King's bride, she falls dead on seeing the ghost of her father, who at that instant has died elsewhere. The latter was a notorious republican martyr, whose paternal curse on marrying into royalty Clara may well have feared; he lacks impressiveness, however, since his sufferings seem mainly to have been incurred in running away from the jail in which he had been lawfully confined.

The melodramatic devices of the strange duel and the destructive phantom are part of Bjørnson's striving to raise his fable to a level above that of ordinary "bürgerliches Trauerspiel", to suggest an interplay with higher powers. To the same end he called in poetry: not in verse-dialogue, but in detached Interludes taking place in a virtually timeless empyrean where disembodied spirits discuss and influence the earthly action beneath. He aimed at an effect analogous to that of the Greek chorus, with lyric strophes, music and rhythmic movements, and not unlike Hardy's in *The Dynasts*. Operatic it may be, but Bjørnson's cantata style is here at its best, and in the theatre it must achieve its purpose.

There are no operatic trimmings about *Over ævne,* no attempts at symbolism; though it opens up wide vistas, it might not unfairly be described as coming near to the anecdotal. But it, too, traffics in the supernatural. On the face of it, it is a play about the reality of miracles and the efficacy of prayer.

The hero, a saintly clergyman, Sang, has a bedridden, paralytic wife. He decides to apply to her the methods which have gained him a great, unimpeached reputation as a faith-healer. His original proposal, to effect her cure through the united prayers of the family, fails through the unwillingness of the two children to co-operate, since they have lost their faith at school. He decides to go on, unaided and undaunted. He will pray that his wife gets the sleep of which she is in need after six weeks of insomnia and, on waking, rise whole. At the first stroke of the church-bell which announces that he has begun his intercessions, she instantly falls into a sleep so profound that a landslide, only coming to a stop just outside the church and parsonage, fails to wake her. When at last Fru Sang's sleep comes to an end, she gets out of bed, takes a few steps and falls dead into the arms of her husband, who forthwith falls down dead too.

At one level then, *Over ævne, I* is a play about miracles, a subject formally debated in Act II by a party of clerics who arrive at the parsonage during Sang's wrestling in prayer. But it may be looked at from a different point of view. The arrest of the landslide may just be luck, and Fru Sang's reactions can be attributed to the phenomena of suggestion which were then rousing widespread interest. Though Bjørnson treats the clergymen's religious approach with decent respect and though he is not averse to heightening his stage-effects with ritual paraphernalia (church bells, hymn-singing, the lighting up of a crucifix), his own "level" is clearly the naturalistic one: to the first edition of the play he obligingly added a note referring the reader to scientific publications by Charcot and Richer. However regarded, the outcome of Pastor Sang's experiment is discouraging. In effect, he kills his wife and himself. The verdict is that of the title; something beyond the hero's powers has been attempted and failed. The theme therefore has much in common with that of *Kongen,* but, if one may so put it, set in a major, not a minor key.

The story itself, even in hands of mediocre ability, would interest and move. Bjørnson, now in complete command of his realistic technique, executed it superbly. Sang, a latter-day Saint, healing the sick, even those given up as dead, but at the same time a loving husband and father, without a shred of posturing or sentimentality, carries complete conviction: the lesser characters are all firmly individualized, even Fru Sang, a helpless victim in one sense, but one with a mind of her own, which is by no means in accord with her husband's. Even when the great tension set up by the uncanny experiment, its physical concomitants and the knowledge that a great unseen multitude is awaiting the outcome seems to be broken by the parsons' debate, that not only in itself affords relief with its most effective blend of the quietly comic and the reverential, but is also securely tied to the action simultaneously going forward out of sight. The end, led up to by mounting, almost intolerable mass-excitement, is a stupendous shock: inevitability and evitability collide head-on.

A line of development indicated in the chronological discussion of Bjørnson's earlier tragedies is carried to its conclusion in *Paul Lange og Tora Parsberg.* The traditions of romantic drama were dominant in *Sigurd Slembe* (after having been unconsciously caricatured in *Halte Hulda*) and were loosely brought in to embellish *Kongen.* In treatment and in setting the staple of that play and the whole of *Over ævne, I* were modern, realistic *pièces à thèse* ["thesis plays"], yet both reached for the sublime and for the suggestion of universal significance by invoking supernatural beings or powers. In spite of that *Over ævne,* as has been said, comes near to the anecdotal. No qualification of the adjective is needed to describe *Paul Lange og Tora Parsberg:* as everyone knew at the time of its appearance, it was based on an occurrence in which Bjørnson himself had played a big part, the suicide of the Norwegian politician Ole Richter in 1888. No whiff of the metaphysical or mysterious intrudes, nor any attempt to universalize the story. No finger points to the vault of heaven. At the same time—perhaps rather oddly—the element of *tendens* has withered also, though of course it is open to anyone to draw his own moral from *Paul Lange og Tora Parsberg,* even if it would be scarcely more impressive than that of *Halte Hulda.*

Paul Lange, a politician of Cabinet rank, still young enough to be looked on as the coming man, has gone back on a promise made to his closest confederates that, in the debate on a motion of No Confidence, he would withhold his support from the leader of the party, the Prime Minister, of whose dishonesty he is convinced. The volte-face is motivated by the state of overflowing happiness he was in at the time, induced on the one hand by his betrothal to the brilliant heiress Tora Parsberg and, on the other, by the prospect of a diplomatic appointment—that of his country's Minister in London—which will take him and her away from the hurly-burly and intrigues of parliament; in this frame of mind his genuine affection for his old chief sweeps away all other considerations, and his claim that he unites the country better than anyone else wins the day.

His late confederates publish in the Press evidence that he was aware of the Prime Minister's dishonesty and insinuate that he acted as he did because he had been bribed by the promise of the London appointment and had effected an insurance (as before during his career) by a rich marriage. Tora stands by him, assuring him that he has at no time done anything discreditable. The harmonious future together to which they look forward still beckons. But while she is preparing to go away with him, a telegram arrives withdrawing the offer of the London legation, and, despairing of any future worthy of himself and the woman with whom he wants to share it, he shoots himself dead.

It is a magnificent realistic play. No political drama in which personal and public issues are inextricably at stake presents a finer or tenser scene than the second act. Its construction is admirable: the slow build-up as the guests, delayed by the snow outside, tardily arrive at Tora Parsberg's country mansion; their gradual realization of all that Paul Lange's speech earlier in the day implied and portended, issuing in the blazing knowledge that a first-class crisis in their country's political and moral history is upon them; Paul Lange facing the baying hounds, among them his life-long, heartbroken friend Arne Kraft (Bjørnson himself); and at the end his rescue from them, when the hostess enters in all her splendour and, fully cognizant of what she is doing, bids him take her arm and lead her in to dinner. Most of the time the stage is brilliant with light, colour, movement and debate, the speakers many—Bjørnson contriving, however, to keep a steady focus on the central issue and to make six or eight at least of his personages, their characters, their speech, their reactions to the crisis, vividly distinct. The quiet acts before and after, with never more than three people on the stage together, are equally effective, framing, positing and resolving the second act crisis and at the same time maintaining in a lower, intimate key a constantly shifting tension along the whole gamut from wild exultation to despair.

Of Tora Parsberg something will have to be said later. Paul Lange is susceptible to much the same criticism as his brother-in-arms Gran of *Kongen.* Is the "coming man" not impossibly weak? Would a seasoned politician have been bowled over by the newspapers and a re-shuffling in the party alignment, the loss of a job, disgrace in the technical sense? But that is a little beside the point here. For one thing, Ole Richter, older and hardened, *did* commit suicide, and Lange's case is as little that of a worm crushed as that of an essentially bad man called to his account, not for his crimes, but for an error of judgement. What wrecked him was generous impulse overtaking him in most unpropitious circumstances, an upsurge of altruistic emotions first in proclaiming loyalty to an old friend and then in refusing to tie his beloved to a disgraced husband.

A merely passive victim, it is generally agreed, cannot make a tragic hero. He (or she) is a man (or woman) of action, greater or less, who is ultimately defeated. It is found that, in vulgar parlance, he has "bitten off more than he can chew". So it is with Bjørnson's protagonists.

Sigurd Slembe affords a conventional instance. By the murder of Harald Gille he combines against himself all the outstanding members of the society he wants to regenerate and could have regenerated; and they are too strong for him. Powers of evil are at work—not only in the machinations of his foes, their double-dealing and injustice, but also those liberated in his own bosom by his thirst for sovereignty and revenge. The hero of *Kongen* has his enemies, too. Evil is, however, too strong a term to associate with them, or at any rate with those we are allowed to see; the forces ranged against him are the conventions, prejudices and self-interest of an outmoded, torpid Establishment. The decisive factor in his tragedy is his own despair at making head against them. Pastor Sang's predicament is fundamentally much the same, but starker, more terrible, when he finds his great therapeutic powers, his faith, his hope, his love at a stand before inexorable limitations. The "best will in the world" cannot overstep the laws of earth.

Evil does not come into *Over ævne, I* at all, not even in a Hardy-esque suggestion of a cosmic indifference to human aspirations so utterly detached as to appear malignant. The same is true of the altogether unmetaphysical *Paul Lange og Tora Parsberg,* at any rate as far as the overt action is concerned. Equally, the countervailing "best will in the world" is in evidence again, providing indeed the justification for the inclusion of Tora Parsberg in the title of the play. Paul Lange is ultimately driven into a position akin to that of the hero in *Kongen* and takes the same way out: in the last analysis, however, it is Tora Parsberg with her love and understanding—and strength, even—liberating all that was most humane in him who brings down the tragedy. Two good wills, a cynic might conclude, are worse than one.

However phrased, it is a curious conclusion in a professed reformer and optimist who has finally banished mens rea from his tragic constructions.

This is not the only paradox elicited by an analysis of Bjørnson's drama. Two others have already been touched on. The first, that, in a *genre* which characteristically tends to universalize the particular actions devised and is held to be effective as this striving is realized, Bjørnson proved, broadly speaking, successful in proportion as he eliminated the metaphysical in favour of the anecdotal; and the second, that the author who rated Victor Hugo highest among his contemporaries, for indissolubly linking art and propaganda, should have written *Sigurd Slembe* and *Paul Lange og Tora Parsberg,* capital works in which it is impossible to detect any *tendens,* as commonly understood, at all.

The most striking paradox emerges from the discovery that this extravert's tragedies were all heart-searchings and self-purgations of one kind or another. With *Sigurd Slembe* he dramatized through nine acts the career of a pretender to the Norwegian throne so obscure that an admirable History of Norway (Mr. T. K. Derry's) does not even mention him by name, in order to resolve the question whether his sobriquet Slembe (The Bad) was justifiable or not: the question was vital to him: it posed itself at the time when, in the first flush of discovering his formidable powers as a leader of opinion, he had received a severe setback, been stigmatized as a public menace and gone into voluntary exile to debate with himself the limits to which a natural "Høvding" having no realm to govern, like Bjørnstjerne Bjørnson and Sigurd Slembe, could allow his political ambitions to carry him. With *Kongen* he clarified for himself and fortified the republicanism to which he had given his allegiance, while reminding himself at the same time of the tragic sacrifices that even the most desirable reforms entail. After loosing in that play some shafts against the Church as an institution, in his next tragedy he settled to his own satisfaction the part of the supernatural in "religious experience" and *pro tanto* ["to that extent"] in the Church's faith. . . . ***Paul Lange og Tora Parsberg*** effected a catharsis of a somewhat different type, but it is self-purgation all the same. Bjørnson was well aware that the suicide of Ole Richter was laid at his door, and the need to present the calamity in his own terms nagged at him. The play puts up no formal defence, however. . . . For all that, mens rea, as has been noted, does not come into the tragic construction, and Tora Parsberg echoes Arne Kraft's ejaculation, when it is plain that she has exerted all her powers to avert a catastrophe. There were no agents formally indictable, either in a court of law or before a moral tribunal, for Paul Lange's death. With this conclusion . . . Bjørnson cleared his bosom of the perilous stuff that had weighed on it for ten years.

The last of these paradoxes gives the answer to the initial question: What brought a man like Bjørnson to attempt tragedy at all? And the answer itself implies something of a paradox, too. The optimist was haunted by the limits beyond which human nature cannot go; he realized, so to say, the limits of optimism, the vast and dreadful dark that lies beyond the light: and it is by virtue of the intensity of this realization that the tragedies which Bjørnson, great craftsman as he was, found himself impelled to write were good tragedies. (pp. 17-28)

> *Brian W. Downs, "Bjørnson and Tragedy," in*
> Scandinavica, *Vol. 1, No. 1, May, 1962, pp. 17-28.*

HENNING K. SEHMSDORF   (essay date 1969)

[Sehmsdorf is an American critic specializing in folklore. In the following excerpt he examines Thrond *in the context of Norwegian folk literature. An English translation of* Thrond *by Sehmsdorf has appeared in his anthology* Short Stories from Norway, 1850-1900.]*

When Bjørnson published ***Thrond*** in 1857, he referred to it as "min første fortelling" ["my first story"]. This expression is, of course, not to be taken literally. Bjørnson had published a number of other stories earlier, in 1855 **"Bjørnjegerens hjemkomst,"** in 1856 **"Ole Stormoen," "Aanun,"** and **"Et farlig frieri."** What Bjørnson possibly meant, however, was that with ***Thrond*** he had solved a specific artistic problem for the first time, namely, how to integrate the representation of inner, psychological experience with the use of certain motifs in and the style of Norwegian folk literature. The solution of this problem is basic to the aesthetic effect of most of the ***Bondefortellinger*** and may well be the reason for their singular success.

Bjørnson therefore considered ***Thrond*** his breakthrough as a prose writer. In the earlier stories the attempt to apply motifs and forms of folk literature to formal literature had been only partially successful. **"Et farlig frieri,"** for example, is patterned closely—and maybe too closely—on the *eventyr* in plot and narrative method. The result is that this tale about courtship among the peasants remains psychologically flat and lacking in depth of theme. **"Aanun,"** to give the opposite example, draws a fascinating psychological portrait of an unusually gifted boy suffering mental breakdown because the people around him cannot understand him and therefore

abuse him cruelly. Here depth of characterization is combined with a pointed attack against the insensitive educational methods frequently found in the country districts at that time. But in this case the *form* of the story is not coherent. It begins in the style of saga and folktale. We see the characters and hear what they say but hear little about what goes on inside of them. Yet since this story in effect is intended to describe the step by step mental and emotional disintegration of the hero, i.e. the kind of experience folk literature normally does not describe, the author was forced to blend in his own voice and thus broke with his model. When it comes to the representation of the boy's thoughts and feelings, the author actually steps into the narrative and substitutes his own analysis for concrete action. The same holds true of the representation of the didactic position underlying the story. It, too, has not been transformed fully into fiction. The last third of **"Aanun"** is, in fact, not so much a story as Bjørnson's personal appeal for certain changes in the educational system of Norway.

All of these difficulties are avoided in ***Thrond.*** For one thing, this story is not didactic. For another, while Thrond's experience has universal application, the narrator does not try to force his interpretation on the reader. Thirdly and most important, while the action of this story is psychological, it is developed in a strictly objective manner throughout the narrative. In ***Thrond*** the reader enters the flux of the hero's thoughts and feelings through the action itself, and this time the author avoids explaining the boy's inner development through the narrator's comments. Rather, he gives it objective form by making the reader *see* the world as Thrond gradually comes to see it, that is, through the images and beliefs which give shape to his conception of reality and to the particular experience described in this story. And these images, used here by Bjørnson to project what goes on in the mind of Thrond, are derived directly from folk literature. Certain figures and occurrences from legend and tales of magic are used to describe what happens to Thrond and, from the reader's point of view, to explain the boy's reaction to these happenings.

My purpose in this paper, therefore, will be to discuss the story on three levels: a) to interpret Thrond's experience and the idea behind it in terms of Norwegian folklore; b) to show how Bjørnson used the form of folktales to shape this story; and c) to relate the story of Thrond to Bjørnson's own experience and thus to demonstrate the universality of the idea set forth.

Thrond, like Aanun, is impressionable, taciturn, and creative. In the case of Aanun this creativity was rubbed out by the villagers' brutal reaction to the unique individual. In ***Thrond,*** on the other hand, Bjørnson places the hero in surroundings which tend to strengthen his imaginative response rather than to stifle it. He grows up in a wild and evocative landscape of mountain and forest, on a small farm, far away from the next village. Up to age eight he knows only his parents and their half-witted servant girl, and from them he learns about the invisible *huldrefolk* or "hidden people" inhabiting the house and nearby fields. One story especially leaves an indelible impression upon him. It is an *eventyr* about a man named Blessomen who rode on a *jutul's* ["malevolent mountain giant's"] sleigh all the way from Copenhagen to Vaage in eastern Norway in one night. After hearing this story everything beyond the familiar environment of the house becomes a reality strangely different and therefore frightening to Thrond. He comes to think that he sees the *huldrefolk* himself: when the fog settles outside the windows, he recognizes strange shapes circling around the house and dancing by the edge of the forest. In the end he no longer dares to go out by himself.

Thus the decisive experiences are sketched which set the stage for Thrond's first encounter with a stranger. One day a gipsy comes to the house, seeking help because he is ill. He is put into Thrond's bed, while the boy must spend the night on the floor and has a terrifying dream about the *huldrefolk* holding him captive in the forest. The next morning the stranger has disappeared. A big black box is carried from the house, but Thrond does not dare to ask what it contains. His mother gives him a smaller box the stranger has left behind, and in it Thrond finds a fiddle. The instrument frightens the boy for "the fiddle was black, and so was the gipsy who owned it, and however this may be, he thought they were like each other." But in spite of his fear the fiddle fascinates Thrond, and soon it becomes the most important thing in his life. He identifies the bow and the strings and each new melody he learns with the few people he knows—father, mother, and the servant girl—or with specific experiences and memories. Only the last string, the bass, he cannot and dare not give a name. It represents the new in him, his desire to make music, which he somehow associates with the gipsy without knowing this consciously.

The understanding of what this creative impulse really means to his life and where it comes from, constitutes the crisis of Thrond's development and the climax of the story. At a wedding Thrond tries the fiddle for the first time in public. He is excited to fever pitch. But in discovering that the organ music from the church drowns out his instrument, and not comprehending why, he is suddenly overpowered by a fear so great that he becomes for a moment insane. He has a vision of the dead fiddler straddling the church tower, mocking him and demanding that he give back the instrument. In terror Thrond flees from the village and cuts the strings of the fiddle to destroy the cause of his pain. But he finds that he is somehow incapable of cutting the last string, the one he had not dared to give a name.

The action of this story is, as I said, psychological. The various images and events just summarized are designed to express the experience of the hero as he is overcome by the mysterious impulse which, in Bjørnson's view, is the source of all art. This interpretation has been specified by the author himself in his notes to a Danish edition of ***Thrond.*** Bjørnson obviously hoped that the reader would recognize the idea underlying the story through identifying the emotions connected with certain popular beliefs, and especially those surrounding the person of the fiddler. There is no space here to discuss fully the role of the fiddler in Norwegian lore. But, briefly, there is ample evidence that Norwegians for a long time associated the fiddler's art with the demonic powers of the "hidden people." It was thought that any really good fiddler owed his talent to them. But it was also believed that he had to pay a price for this gift. His passionate involvement with music was interpreted as a spell placed upon him. In a way the fiddler ceased to be his own master. Driven by a deep desire, he, as well as his audience, would easily imagine the fiddler to be in the power of those supernatural creatures traditionally held to be the source of his genius.

In the light of this, Thrond's reaction to the stranger and the fiddle becomes transparent. The boy accepts the world of the invisible as real. At times, he believes, he has glimpsed their fleeting shapes surrounding the house. From Blessomen's story he knows that they take on human shape and then are not easily distinguished from ordinary folk. The boy must therefore have interpreted the stranger's uncommonly dark appearance, his scarred, twisted face, the fact that he did not invoke Jesus' name before eating, and above all, his sudden and inexplicable disappearance, as signs that the stranger was one of the "other world." Thrond's dream suggests that he feels a demonic power taking hold of him. This is borne out by the fact that he accepted the fiddle although he is afraid of it, since he unconsciously identifies it with the stranger. The instrument becomes the center of Thrond's existence, the symbol and expression of all he knows and feels, while at the same time it remains a mystery that frightens him. But in the moment of terror at the church, the secret source of the impulse within him comes to the surface of his consciousness. In the agony over his apparent failure, he glimpses and recognizes the till then nameless source of his inspiration: it is the fiddler. As in the first encounter Thrond seeks to escape and cannot. As though under compulsion, he cuts the strings of the fiddle symbolizing home and family instead. When his mother finds him and wants to take him home, he refuses to follow: "Hjem vil jeg ikke før kan spille hva jeg har sett idag!" In other words, Thrond has come to understand and accept the reality to which he will dedicate himself from now on. Like Blessomen, he has met the demon, and his life will never be the same again.

The importance of beliefs of popular tradition to the idea of ***Thrond*** makes the story comparable to the type of folktales usually referred to as *sagn*. Like a *sagn* the story of Thrond describes the encounter between a human being and a reality traditionally thought of as demonic. But it is immediately clear that in developing the story psychologically, both the form and substance of the traditional *sagn* have been exploded. Taken as a whole ***Thrond*** is a modern *novelle*. It represents the essence of a character and an important human experience in the course of a few decisive episodes. It climaxes the gist of this experience in one concentrated image. The fiddler straddling the church spire is both dramatically and figuratively at the peak of the story's action. The conclusion is both open-ended and suggestive. In forcing the reader to project the future of the boy in his imagination, Bjørnson requires him to move from the level of what happens to Thrond personally to what it means to become an artist.

But while the form of ***Thrond*** is thus not reducible to the form of a *sagn,* there is one important section in the story which is. I am, of course, speaking about the tale of Blessomen functioning in the story to dramatize the influences that determine the boy's reaction to the fiddler. [In a footnote, Sehmsdorf states that "the subsequent analysis refers to the second and final version of ***Thrond*** (1860) in which the story of Blessomen is told in full, while in the original it had been condensed to two sentences of indirect report. . . . "] By now, this folk tale has been recorded in thirty different versions. At the time ***Thrond*** was written there existed only one printed version, the one published by Asbjørnsen in 1845 (*Norske huldreeventyr og folkesagn*), which most likely served as Bjørnson's model. The way a *sagn* is normally told emphasizes that it is a narrative designed to relate and explain strange but supposedly historical events in terms of accepted belief about supernatural beings. This applies to the story about Blessomen as retold by Asbjørnsen. It has two narrators, one being the collector himself, who appears in a frame story and describes the background of traditions involved. He refers the reader to a certain rock formation just outside the village of Vaage in eastern Norway, and explains that it resembles a huge gate with two portals, a fact which led the villagers to infer that it houses a malevolent giant, a *jutul.* To show that this belief is still in currency, a second narrator is introduced who claims to have known the last person to see the *jutul.* This second narrator then actually recounts what happened to Johannes Blessomen. Throughout his story he offers "proof" of the historicity of the event described. He tells us exactly where Blessomen lived, when and why he went to Copenhagen, what he was doing there, what he saw along the way from Copenhagen to Vaage, where precisely he and the *jutul* alighted just outside the village; and, of course, he points to Blessomen's crippled neck showing that the demon had put a spell on him when Blessomen disobeyed the giant's command and turned around to watch him disappear through the gate into the mountain.

Altogether the explanatory sections of Asbjørnsen's version, the frame and the commentary of the second narrator, take up almost half of the entire story. Their purpose is to accumulate circumstantial evidence which relates the supernatural occurrence to ordinary, historical reality and thus prove that the story is true. In this sense, then, the story of Blessomen, as represented by Asbjørnsen, is not fictional; rather, it demonstrates the existence of certain demonic beings at one time generally believed in.

The possible effect of such belief on the life of a particular individual is no doubt the reason why Bjørnson incorporated this legend into the story of Thrond. But in adapting it to his own purpose, he made certain important changes in content and style. If Asbjørnsen was interested in a faithful record of the superstitions still circulating among the people, Bjørnson wanted to bring this belief to life so that it might serve as a metaphor for the strange compulsion inherent in human creativity. His criterion in shaping the story was therefore not folkloristic but fictional, his purpose not to relate a tradition but to make an emotional impact on Thrond and, of course, on the reader. He therefore shifted emphasis from the alleged historicity of what happened to Blessomen to the dramatic aspects of the story. Thus he removed the introductory part about the *jutul*-mountain, as well as all further references to the geographical peculiarities of Vaage and its environs, or to Blessomen's personal life. We hear only his name, where he was from, why he was in Copenhagen, and that the *jutul* inflicted the twisted neck upon him. These minimal facts constitute the skeleton of the legend. But they are not enlarged upon as in Asbjørnsen's version, and the heart of the story is now the dramatization of the fantastic encounter itself. In the folktale original even the trip through the air was described in quite realistic terms. The narrator informed us, for instance, that Blessomen lost his glove along the way. When he complained of being cold, the *jutul* told him to hold out since they were almost in Vaage. By this means the ability of the *jutul* to travel at superhuman speed is given indirect proof. Bjørnson, by contrast, rather than citing evidence for the powers of the demon, lets us partake in the ride itself by describing Blessomen's reactions. (pp. 56-63)

The style of a typical *sagn*—as in Asbjørnsen's version— would have required the enumeration of ordinary things that could happen on any trip. The fantastic would thus be mixed with the common and the two spheres moved closer to each other. In Bjørnson's version, on the other hand, . . . [Blesso-

men asks three questions] and the three short answers he receives do not primarily function as explanation or description. Rather, they directly dramatize the *sensation* of high speed travel. Through formula and repetition and just enough variation to move the story forward, the exchange spans the distance from Copenhagen to Valders in a concrete visual curve rising from earth and water into the air and descending upon arrival at the destination. All the details not functional to this representation of the swift movement of the sleigh have been pared away. The final effect is one of scenic plasticity; in our imagination we can see the sleigh rushing through the night. Thus, the story, though it maintains the basic plot of Asbjørnsen's version, is no longer so much a historical legend explaining certain phenomena in the light of popular belief, i.e., a *sagn,* but rather a tale of magic in the style of an *eventyr.* Its dramatic rendition makes it possible for the reader to share in a decisive step of the experience of Thrond, through which Bjørnson hopes to reveal to the reader the roots of artistic impulse and how such a gift might be affected by the environment both physical and psychological.

It might further elucidate both the story and imagery of **Thrond** to know that this general idea about the nature of artistic inspiration goes back to a specific occurrence in Bjørnson's own life. In the preface to the story as printed in **Smaastykker** (1860) the author tells us that **Thrond** gives objective expression to his own reaction to meeting the artistic world of Copenhagen for the first time, during the summer of 1856. We can trace this personal factor in the overall outline of the story: to begin with, Bjørnson, like the hero of his story, grew up in the relative isolation of rural Norway. It was here in the environment of farm, forest and mountain, and the popular conceptions lending this setting an imaginative meaning all its own, that his poetic inspiration was nurtured. Furthermore, as Bjørnson indicates, in the same preface, his first confrontation with the sophistication of the literary world he found in Copenhagen nearly overwhelmed him with fear and a sense of insufficiency. Thrond's reaction to the many new faces and the village he sees for the first time, the towering church, and the deep sound of the organ music that filled the air, can thus be read as rendering what must have gone through Bjørnson's mind when introduced to the city which then was the intellectual capital of Denmark and Norway. It must have seemed to him that his instrument was much too simple, and that compared to the full tone of the literary life surrounding him, his own gave "no sound." But as for Thrond, so also for Bjørnson himself this crisis led to the final insight into what it means to be an artist. We might even go so far as to interpret Thrond's vision of the fiddler as expressing Bjørnson's recognition of the source and nature of the poetic impulse in himself. The fiddler represents folk art at its highest and purest level. But both folk music and folk literature, while no doubt possessing abstraction and complexity of form, are manifestly simple in tone and idea. One can say without exaggeration the same of Bjørnson's imaginative writings; his poetry, prose, or drama, rarely exhibits the urbanity of a Wergeland or the profound ambiguities of Ibsen's works. Even at his deepest, as in the drama **Over ævne, I,** the reader is moved by the strength of feeling and the lyrical power of Bjørnson's language, rather than by the force of the author's idea.

Seen in this light, **Thrond,** in spite of its formal objectivity, is also a highly personal statement. We sense the author's deep involvement with the story of his hero. In summary, the story of **Thrond** can be read on at least three levels: On one level it is a story about a sensitive peasant boy shown in the physical and spiritual environment of which he was a part. As such it is permeated with the superstitions of the past and shaped after the stylistic model of *sagn* and *eventyr,* yet thoroughly modern by virtue of the psychological penetration of the hero. Through this portrait, secondly, **Thrond** opens the reader's perspective on the nature of artistic inspiration; through a specific character, tailored to a specific place and fate, a universal phenomenon is described and interpreted. And third and last, **Thrond** points back to a vital experience in Bjørnson's own life and to an important phase in his struggle to find himself as a poet. (pp. 64-6)

Henning K. Sehmsdorf, "Bjørnson's 'Thrond' and Popular Tradition," in Scandinavian Studies, *Vol. 41, No. 1, February, 1969, pp. 56-66.*

FURTHER READING

Review of *The Railroad and the Churchyard,* by Bjørnstjerne Bjørnson, translated by Carl Larson. *The Atlantic Monthly* XXVI, No. CLVII (November 1870): 637-38.
    Favorable review of *The Railroad and the Churchyard,* also praising "The Father" and "The Eagle's Nest."

Beyer, Harald. "The Young Bjørnson" and "Bjørnson and the Problems of Realism." In his *A History of Norwegian Literature,* edited and translated by Einar Haugen, pp. 185-95, pp. 218-27. New York: New York University Press, 1956.
    Presents historical and biographical information in a chapter outlining the significant early works of Bjørnson (excerpted in *TCLC,* Vol. 7), and another addressing the issues raised in his social dramas.

Björkman, Edwin. "Bjørnstjerne Bjørnson: Poet, Politician, Prophet." In his *Voices of Tomorrow: Critical Studies of the New Spirit in Literature,* pp. 121-38. New York: Mitchell Kennerley, 1913.
    Details Bjørnson's political and literary careers and describes his popularity among Norwegians.

Bjørnson, Bjørnstjerne. *Land of the Free: Bjørnstjerne Bjørnson's America Letters, 1880-1881.* Edited and translated by Eva Lund Haugen and Einar Haugen. Northfield, Minn.: The Norwegian-American Historical Association, 1978, 311 p.
    Includes an introductory essay tracing the biographical circumstances surrounding Bjørnson's trip to the United States in 1880-81, reprints letters and speeches he wrote while visiting the East and Midwest, and offers commentary outlining his views on politics, religion, and Norwegian emigration. The book also includes an epilogue discussing the influence of Bjørnson's tour on his subsequent literary career and a selected bibliography.

Boyesen, Hjalmar Hjorth. "Conversations with Bjørnstjerne Bjørnson." *The Cosmopolitan* XV, No. 4 (August 1893): 413-22.
    Informal, anecdotal account of Bjørnson's trip to the United States in 1880-81, his views on American culture, and his home life in Aulestad.

Chandler, Frank W. "Bjørnson and the Minor Scandinavians." In his *Modern Continental Playwrights,* pp. 39-63. New York: Harper & Brothers, 1931.
    Summarizes the thematic content of Bjørnson's major dramas and surveys those of his Scandinavian contemporaries.

Cutter, Annie S. Introduction to *Sunny Hill: A Norwegian Idyll,* by Bjørnstjerne Bjørnson, pp. vii-ix. New York: Macmillan Co., 1932.
    Introduces an unattributed translation of *Synnøve Solbakken,* maintaining that because of the "freshness and simplicity" with which the story is rendered, it "struck a new note in Norwegian literature."

Dukes, Ashley. "Scandinavia." In his *Modern Dramatists,* pp. 41-64. London: Frank Palmer, 1911.
    Includes summarizing commentary on *Over ævne, I* in a general discussion of the careers of Bjørnson and August Strindberg.

Foster, George Burman. "The Message of Bjørnson." *The Open Court* XXXVIII, No. 6 (June 1924): 321-31.
    Addresses Christian belief as presented in Bjørnson's later works.

Gassner, John. "The Scandinavian Succession and Strindberg." In his *Masters of the Drama,* rev. ed., pp. 384-96. New York: Dover Publications, 1954.
    Discusses the impact of Bjørnson, Henrik Ibsen, and August Strindberg on modern theater. Gassner observes that Bjørnson's enthusiasm and persuasiveness coupled with Ibsen's depth and intensity assured the success of dramatic Realism.

Hollander, Lee M. "Bjørnson's *Beyond Human Power.*" *The Drama,* Chicago, No. 13 (February 1914): 110-17.
    Examines Bjørnson's presentation of Christian faith in *Over ævne, I,* focusing on his portrayal of the miraculous.

Johns, Berit Spilhaug. "William Dean Howells and Bjørnstjerne Bjørnson: A Literary Relationship." In *Americana Norvegica: Norwegian Contributions to American Studies,* vol. II, edited by Sigmund Skard, pp. 94-117. Philadelphia: University of Pennsylvania Press, 1968.
    Study tracing Bjørnson's influence on the aesthetic tenets of American novelist and critic William Dean Howells. Johns observes close parallels between works by the two authors and argues that, via Howells, Bjørnson helped to establish realism in American literature.

Leach, Henry Goddard. "Bjørnson the Prophet." *The American-Scandinavian Review* 21, No. 1 (January 1933): 26-8.
    Praises Bjørnson's diverse accomplishments in a speech commemorating the centenary of his birth.

Mabie, Hamilton Wright. Introduction and "Life of Bjørnson." In *The Fisher Maiden,* by Bjørnstjerne Bjørnson, pp. 5-16, pp. 17-20. New York: P. F. Collier & Son, n.d.
    Introduces an unattributed translation of *Fiskerjenten* and outlines Bjørnson's life and literary career within the context of late nineteenth-century Scandinavian fiction.

MacArthur, James. Introduction to *Arne: A Sketch of Norwegian Country Life,* by Bjørnstjerne Bjørnson, translated by Augusta Plesner and S. Rugeley-Powers, pp. vii-xviii. Boston: Joseph Knight Co., 1895.
    Praises *Arne* and Bjørnson's peasant tales while tracing his life and literary career.

Marble, Annie Russell. "Bjørnson: Norwegian Novelist and Playwright (1903)." In her *The Nobel Prize Winners in Literature,* pp. 58-71. New York: D. Appleton and Co., 1925.
    Appreciative, informal synopsis of Bjørnson's literary career.

"Drama and Music: Bjørnson in English." *The Nation* 99, No. 2558 (9 July 1914): 51.
    Favorable review of *Love and Geography, Beyond Human Might,* and *Laboremus* occasioned by their English translation in *Plays.*

Nordberg, Carl E. *The Peasant Stories of Bjørnstjerne Bjørnson.* Minneapolis: Free Church Book Concern, 1920, 115 p.
    Quotes extensively from Bjørnson's early works in "a study of Norwegian life and its influence on Bjørnson's peasant stories."

Palmer, Arthur H. "Bjørnson and the United States." *Scandinavian Studies and Notes* V, No. 3 (August 1918): 102-09.

> Argues that Bjørnson served as "an excellent medium of interpretation between the United States and Scandinavia" because he expressed in his writings and speeches "the American ideals of freedom and equality."

Paulson, Arthur C. *The Norwegian-American Reaction to Ibsen and Bjørnson, 1850-1900.* Northfield, Minn.: St. Olaf College Press, 1937, 29 p.

> Describes the views of late nineteenth-century Norwegian-Americans on the work of Bjørnson and Henrik Ibsen, and on Bjørnson's political and religious opinions.

Payne, William Morton. *Bjørnstjerne Bjørnson: 1832-1910.* Chicago: A. C. McClurg & Co., 1910, 98 p.

> Tribute to Bjørnson containing a survey of his work and biographical information.

Rottem, Øystein. "The Multifarious Bjørnson." *Scandinavica* 24, No. 1 (May 1985): 59-64.

> Review of the five-volume jubilee edition of Bjørnson's works, published in Norway to commemorate the 150th anniversary of his birth.

Sturtevant, Albert Morey. "Some Critical Notes on Bjørnson's *Halte Hulda.*" *Scandinavian Studies and Notes* X (1928): 79-86.

> Details Bjørnson's adaptation of Norse sagas in *Halte Hulda* and examines its dramatic structure.

"The Bravura of Bjørnson." *The Times Literary Supplement,* No. 2938 (20 June 1958): 344.

> Discusses Bjørnson's literary career in relation to his magnanimous public persona.

Karel Čapek

1890-1938

Czechoslovakian novelist, dramatist, short story writer, journalist, and travel writer.

For further discussion of Čapek's career, see *TCLC*, Volume 6.

Čapek is best known for his works of science fiction, primarily the drama *R.U.R.* (*Rossum's Universal Robots*) and the novel *Válka s mloky* (*War with the Newts*). In these works, he warned against the dehumanizing aspects of modern civilization and satirized a plethora of social, economic, and political systems. Underlying much of Čapek's writing is an ardent humanism and a philosophical belief in the plurality and relativity of truth. He explored this doctrine in greatest depth in his trilogy of novels—*Hordubal, Povětroň* (*Meteor*), and *Obyčejný život* (*An Ordinary Life*)—which many critics consider Čapek's masterpiece.

Čapek was born in Malé Svatoňovice, a small village in northeastern Bohemia. A frail and sickly child, he was especially close to his older brother, Josef, and as adults the brothers frequently collaborated on short stories and plays. Josef, an artist as well as a writer, also illustrated several of his brother's books. Čapek began writing poetry and fiction in high school; soon after graduation he was publishing stories, written in collaboration with Josef, in Czech newspapers. After studying at universities in Prague, Berlin, and Paris, Čapek earned a doctorate in philosophy at Prague's Charles University in 1915. Two years later, he began a career as a journalist whose articles often championed the cause of Czech nationalism. The independence gained by Czechoslovakia after World War I greatly inspired Čapek, and his enthusiasm for the new democratic government led to a personal friendship with Tomáš Masaryk, Czechoslovakia's first president. Čapek first received literary acclaim in the early 1920s with the dramas *R.U.R.* and *Ze života hmyzu* (*The Insect Play*). During this time he also began to write novels, and he continued his success as a fiction writer and dramatist for the rest of his career. As World War II approached, Čapek and his brother, both outspoken opponents of fascism, were advised to leave Prague, but chose to remain and continue their opposition to Nazism. Čapek died three months before the Nazis invaded Prague; the secret police, unaware of his death, arrived at his home seeking his arrest. Josef was interned in a concentration camp, where he died shortly before the end of the war.

Among Čapek's dramas, *R.U.R.*, which introduced the word "robot," is considered the most successful. At its premiere, audiences and critics were both fascinated and terrified by its vision of a technically advanced society unable to control its ultimate labor-saving creation, the robot. Čapek, however, was disappointed in *R.U.R.*, believing that the social allegory he intended was overshadowed by the novelty of the robots. In *The Insect Play*, Čapek presented various human vices and weaknesses as species of insects, such as cold efficiency represented by ants. *Věc Makropulos* (*The Makropoulos Secret*) propounded the pessimistic view that boredom would accompany eternal youth, and critics have suggested that it was

written as a refutation of Bernard Shaw's positive view of immortality in *Back to Methuselah* (1921).

Čapek's science fiction novels are more highly regarded than his dramas. The common theme of these novels is the potential misuse of technology. While he did not oppose technological innovations, Čapek was deeply disturbed by the fact that human beings could not possibly take into consideration all the adverse possibilities of their inventions and discoveries, regardless of their benign intent. For example, in his novels *Továrna na absolutno* (*The Absolute at Large*) and *Krakatit*, Čapek foresaw the destructive potential of atomic energy while acknowledging that the objective of nuclear scientists is to improve the condition of humankind. While these early novels evince stylistic immaturity, his later novel *War with the Newts* is praised both for its narrative artistry and its power as satire. Aimed at the exploitive and dehumanizing aspects of capitalism, communism, and fascism, *War with the Newts* expresses a view of human nature and politics that is still considered timely. In this novel Čapek departed from his usual allegorical method of characterization and fashioned more psychologically complex characters. The trilogy of novels that includes *Hordubal, Meteor,* and *An Ordinary Life* probes the relativity of truth and reality, examining the ways that personality and experience affect an individual's actions, perceptions, and understanding. Although the plots of the three novels are unrelated, together these works present Čapek's philosophy of pluralism and democracy.

Čapek is considered one of Czechoslovakia's foremost writers. His works are important for their contribution to the literature of his country and to science fiction, and are also esteemed for their expression of profound concern for humanity and its future. William E. Harkins has stated of Čapek: "The tragedy of his homeland and his premature death cut short the philosophical and creative development of a great writer, a profound thinker, and a great human spirit."

(See also *Contemporary Authors,* Vol. 104.)

PRINCIPAL WORKS

Lásky hra osudna [with Josef Čapek; first publication] (drama) 1910
Zářivé hlubiny [with Josef Čapek] (short stories) 1916
R.U.R. (Rossum's Universal Robots) (drama) 1921
    [*R.U.R. (Rossum's Universal Robots),* 1923]
Trapné provídky (short stories) 1921
    [*Money, and Other Stories,* 1929]
Továrna na absolutno (novel) 1922
    [*The Absolute at Large,* 1927]
Věc Makropulos (drama) 1922
    [*The Makropoulos Secret,* 1925]
Ze života hmyzu [with Joseph Čapek] (drama) 1922
    [*And So Ad Infinitum (The Life of the Insects),* 1923; also published as *The World We Live In (The Insect Comedy),* 1933, and as *The Insect Play* in *"R.U.R." and "The Insect Play,"* 1961]
Anglické listy (travel sketches) 1924
    [*Letters from England,* 1925]
Krakatit (novel) 1924
    [*Krakatit,* 1925]
Adam Stvořitel [with Joseph Čapek] (drama) 1927
    [*Adam the Creator,* 1930]
*Povidky z druhé kapsy (short stories) 1929
    [*Tales from Two Pockets* (partial translation), 1932]
†Povidky z jedné kapsy (short stories) 1929
    [*Tales from Two Pockets* (partial translation), 1932]
Hordubal (novel) 1933
    [*Hordubal,* 1934]
Provětroň (novel) 1933
    [*Meteor,* 1935]
Obyčejný život (novel) 1934
    [*An Ordinary Life,* 1936]
Válka s mloky (novel) 1936
    [*War with the Newts,* 1937, 1985]
Bilá nemoc (drama) 1937
    [*Power and Glory,* 1938; also published as *The White Plague,* 1988]
Privni parta (novel) 1937
    [*The First Rescue Party,* 1939]
Matka (drama) 1938
    [*The Mother,* 1939]
Život a dílo skladatele Foltýna (unfinished novel) 1939
    [*The Cheat,* 1941]
Kniha apokryfů (short stories) 1945
    [*Apocryphal Stories,* 1949]

*This collection is also rendered in English as *Tales from One Pocket.*

†This collection is also rendered in English as *Tales from the Other Pocket.*

KAREL ČAPEK (essay date 1923)

[*Čapek wrote the following essay in response to a public discussion about the meaning of* R.U.R. *held in London on 21 June 1923. Bernard Shaw and G. K. Chesterton were among the participants in the debate.*]

I have just learnt of the discussion about the meaning of a play which, for certain serious reasons, I lay claim to as my own. Authors are reputed to be childishly vain, and as one of them I claim the privilege of saying a few words on behalf of my work.

Mr. Chesterton, in the course of the discussion, said rightly that nobody can say what is the tendency of a work of art. I cannot tell it myself. But the discussion was by no means useless, in that it gave an opportunity to the distinguished participators to express their personal opinions, creeds and ideals. I enjoyed very much the creeds and ideals of Mr. Chesterton, as well as those of Mr. Shaw and Commander Kenworthy. But it seems to me that, so far as my play was concerned, their chief interest was centred upon Robots. For myself, I confess that as the author I was much more interested in men than in Robots.

There are some fathers who are, shall we say, more interested in education in general than in that of their own children in particular. Allow me to take the opposite view, of a father who speaks of his own child rather than of the principles of education. I am not altogether sure of what I have written, but I know very well what I wished to write. I wished to write a comedy, partly of science, partly of truth. The old inventor, Mr. Rossum (whose name in English signifies Mr. Intellect or Mr. Brain), is no more or less than a typical representative of the scientific materialism of the last century. His desire to create an aritificial man—in the chemical and biological, not the mechanical sense—is inspired by a foolish and obstinate wish to prove God to be unnecessary and absurd. Young Rossum is the modern scientist, untroubled by metaphysical ideas; scientific experiment is to him the road to industrial production, he is not concerned to prove, but to manufacture. To create a Homonculus is a mediaeval idea; to bring it in line with the present century this creation must be undertaken on the principle of mass-production. Immediately we are in the grip of industrialism; this terrible machinery must not stop, for if it does it would destroy the lives of thousands. It must, on the contrary, go on faster and faster, although it destroy in the process thousands and thousands of other existences. Those who think to master the industry are themselves mastered by it; Robots must be produced although they are, or rather *because* they are, a war industry. The conception of the human brain has at last escaped from the control of human hands. This is the comedy of science.

Now for my other idea, the comedy of truth. The General Manager Domin, in the play, proves that technical progress emancipates man from hard manual labour, and he is quite right. The Tolstoyan Alquist, on the contrary, believes that technical progress demoralizes him, and I think he is right, too. Bussman thinks that industrialism alone is capable of supplying modern needs; he is right. Ellen is instinctively afraid of all this inhuman machinery, and she is profoundly right. Finally, the Robots themselves revolt against all these idealists, and, as it appears, they are right, too.

We need not look for actual names for these various and controverted idealisms. Be these people either Conservatives or Socialists, Yellows or Reds, the most important thing is—and this is the point I wish particularly to stress—that all of them are right in the plain and moral sense of the word. Each and every one of them has the deepest reasons, material and mental, for his beliefs, and according to his lights seeks the greatest happiness for the greatest possible number of his fellowmen. I ask whether it is not possible to see in the present social conflict of the world an analogous struggle between two, three, five, equally serious verities and equally generous idealisms? I think it is possible, and this is the most dramatic element in modern civilization, that a human truth is opposed to another truth no less human, ideal against ideal, positive worth against worth no less positive, instead of the struggle being, as we are so often told it is, one between noble truth and vile selfish error.

These are the things I should like to have said in my comedy of truth, but it seems that I failed, for none of the distinguished speakers who took part in the discussion have discovered this simple tendency in **R.U.R.**

> Karel Čapek, *"The Meaning of 'R.U.R.',"* in The Saturday Review, *London, Vol. 136, No. 3534, July 21, 1923, p. 79.*

W. A. DARLINGTON   (essay date 1925)

[*A twentieth-century critic, novelist, dramatist, short story writer, and autobiographer, Darlington is best known for his novel* Alf's Button (*1919*), *which was later adapted to film and stage. In the following essay, he examines* The Insect Play *and* R.U.R., *denying them value as contributions to the art of drama.*]

I had almost headed this essay *The Czech Drama*, since the brothers Čapek are acknowledged to stand together at the head of their profession in the new Czecho-Slovakian Republic, and since their works are the only specimens of Czech dramatic writing that London has yet seen. But my immediate purpose is to consider those two remarkable plays **R.U.R.** and **The Life of the Insects** side by side, and try to discover their common factors; and such factors are more likely to prove common to the Čapek family than to the Czecho-Slovakian nation.

"Remarkable" is, I think, *le mot juste* in connection with the Čapeks' work. It defines with some exactitude their quality and their limitations. Their work is indeed "remarkable," and little more. Both the plays that I have mentioned are intriguing, arresting, out of the ordinary; when they were running in London, nobody who was interested in the theatre could afford to miss them. But that either of them represents real progress in the art of writing for the theatre I am prepared to deny categorically. Each of them is completely lacking in the quality which I believe to be the first (perhaps the only) essential of great drama—knowledge of and love for humanity. The Insect Play sets out to satirize human nature, and fails to do so as successfully as it should because it only

manages to establish a comparison between the insects and such exaggerated types of mankind that we ordinary sinners are made to feel that all this is no concern of ours. The satire is entirely negative in its effect; the good qualities of the human race are not examined, but quietly ignored.

Some time back I was invited to the Hippodrome to witness some wonderful juggling with the spectrum by M. Samoilov. This gentleman introduced his audience to a normal young woman with red hair and a summer frock, and a normal young man in a lounge suit. Then he snapped off the normal lights and turned on his newly-invented set which was designed to shut out certain rays, and, behold, before our eyes, the young woman was transformed into a black-haired Oriental dancer, and the young man into a gorgeous and no less Eastern rajah. We applauded and were pleasantly thrilled at M. Samoilov's cleverness, though I for my part could not see that his invention was likely to prove of any very great practical value; for, change colours as he might, he could not change form. After the first shock of surprise was over it was clear that the summer frock and the lounge suit were still present under the Oriental patterns which the new lights had picked out upon them.

The Brothers Čapek seem to have found for themselves a similar new light in which to survey humanity; the ray which in their case is shut out is the one which illuminates the soul; and, since it is only in the possession of souls that human beings are usually understood to be differentiated from the lower orders of creation it naturally follows that the Brothers Čapek can see no essential difference between ourselves and those lower orders. They see us as creatures of shallow passion and shallow poetry, like the butterflies; of unreasoning, sordid, and profitless greed, like the beetles; of cruel, mechanical efficiency, like the ants; of high and beautiful hopes that come to nothing, like the may-flies.

And, again, after the first shock is over, it becomes plain that this is just another piece of jugglery with another spectrum; that beneath the insect-like traits picked out by the satirists the form of the human soul can still be descried, destroying the illusion for the man who still retains the clear use of his eyes.

But when once this protest on behalf of the finer side of human nature has been made, it must be confessed that the satire gets home thrust after shrewd thrust against humanity's baser elements. The butterfly has served many a poet as an image of beautiful care-free happiness; but a human being with the desires of a butterfly will be an airy trifler, whose life consists in transient emotions and centres round a cocktail bar. The beetle—that peculiarly depressing species which spends its life collecting malodorous balls of dirt, wherewith presumably to stock his larder—has stood to us before now for an example of honest thrift; but a human being with the desires of a beetle will have no interest in life except to make his "pile," and to begin collecting another as soon as the first is complete. The ant gave Solomon the text for his rebuke to the sluggard; but the human being who has the desires of an ant will be concerned only with ceaseless, useless work which is destined to end in aggression and destruction. Here is a mordant indictment of society idlers, of profiteers, of Kaiser and Soviet; but the withers of mankind as a whole are unwrung.

More general in its application is the indictment hinted at in Mr. Playfair's sub-title to this play, "And So ad Infinitum."

That happy little pair Mr. and Mrs. Cricket are ruthlessly killed by the Ichneumon Fly to feed his daughter, the voracious Larva—who in her turn is killed and eaten by the Parasite; and even Mr. Cricket is not outside "the simple law, the common plan," for he has only secured the little home to which he is bringing his wife by the fortunate accident that another of his kind has selected just the right moment to be eaten by a bird. In the midst of life, say the Brothers Čapek, we are in death. The Chrysalis which rhapsodizes, through three acts, of the great things which it will do when it is born turns into a May-fly, dances a moment in the sun, and dies; and the Tramp, who acts throughout the play as a human interpreter to point the moral to the audience, dies in the end—owing, we are left to suppose, to intensive entomology in the cold night on an empty stomach; but also, we cannot help suspecting, because the Brothers Čapek were a little at a loss how else to bring their parable to a close. Personally, I did not find that the parable probed deeply enough into my conscience to send me home from the Regent Theatre vowing to live a less lepidopterous life for the future.

In **R.U.R.**, the play which Karel Čapek wrote without his brother's collaboration, I found the same lack of human understanding cropping up in a different way. Here it manifests itself in the simple fact that not one of the human characters in the play really lives. Harry Domain, Helena Glory, Dr. Gall, Alquist, and the rest are all (with the possible exception of the minor character Emma) as much the puppets of Karel Čapek's brain as the Robots are said to be of Dr. Gall's. I was far more interested in the Robots than in the humans when I saw this play, and I did not care a blow when the latter were all killed off at the end of the third act, so long as we had the Robots to carry on with.

I feel that a writer of real stature would have made of this annihilation of the human race an almost unbearable tragedy. If Helena Glory had been a real woman, instead of a shadowy figure bodying forth Karel Čapek's idea, the manner of her death would have been a stark horror. There is a certain relevance to this point also in my feelings about the last act, in which two of the Robots develop sex-consciousness and the sense of beauty, and bring the play to an end with a promise of the birth of a new race that could almost be called human. First I had this scene described to me by an enthusiastic member of Mr. Dean's staff, and thought it sounded wonderful. Then I read the play, and thought the scene considerably less wonderful. Then I saw it staged, and did not like it at all. In theory, it is wonderful; in practice, it lacks humanity—without which no play can be more than technically effective.

It is here that **R.U.R.** falls short of such a play as Ernst Toller's *The Machine-Wreckers*. Both plays treat of the relations between man and machinery; but while Toller preaches strongly the doctrine that only man matters, Čapek is obviously more interested in his machines. No. "Interested" is too weak a word. He is obsessed by his machines. He regards them with fascinated horror, with the same fear as the people in *Erewhon*, which might very well be the literary source of this play. This horror of machinery and mechanical civilization appears also in the diabolically effective Ant act of the Insect Play. It comes to this. Čapek has a real enough concern for humanity and the future of the race; but to have a concern for human beings is by no means the same thing as being able to create them for the stage.

In an article on the Czech Drama, based upon facts supplied by Mr. Paul Selver—who translated both the Čapek plays

into English—Mr. W. R. Titterton stated an ingenious theory to account for the "universal" character of these plays. "Like the Czecho-Slovakian Republic," he says, "the art of the Czech has attained its independence, and can now afford to be international. Only when nationality is unquestioned can it be safely ignored. The revulsion from local associations was likely to be extreme; and so we find it, for the men and women of **R.U.R.** are not citizens of any particular State; they are mankind."

This is clever and sounds logical; but I cannot help feeling that it is based on a slight confusion of thought. That strongly national literature comes from countries whose national consciousness is made sensitive by a position of dependence, is quite true—Wales and Ireland supply examples near at hand, and the Czech theatre in the days of German domination supplies another very much to the present point. But I cannot believe that the young Czech Republic, prosperous as it is, can have become already so accustomed to its independence as to ignore nationality.

And, as a fact, these Čapek plays do not ignore nationality. There is a fierce consciousness of nationality running through them both, taking the form of a revulsion from nationality. Where these two plays touch the question at all, they are not non-national, but anti-national. The Ant act is anti-national, and so is the passage in **R.U.R.** where Domain puts forward his idea of making national Robots for the future, and is told that it is "horrible." Now, violent anti-nationalism, like violent nationalism, argues not an ignoring of nationality, but an abnormally sensitive consciousness of nationality; just as the deplorable old roué with a taste for unclad chorus girls and the excessively pure-minded maiden lady who drapes the legs of her chairs are displaying each an equally abnormal consciousness of nudity. I have little hope, therefore, in Mr. Titterton's implied conclusion that the Čapek brothers are to be the pioneers of a new drama of world-wide importance. Mr. Paul Selver himself seems to have as little. Speaking of Karel Čapek, he says: "Of the influences which have helped to shape his ideas, perhaps the war has left profounder effects than literature, for from it his logical mind has derived a whole series of destructive tests to apply to society and civilization." If there is one thing necessary to a man's success as a pioneer, it is surely that he should not be a pessimist.

To sum up, I feel that these Czech plays have not much real significance, apart from their intrinsic interest as being a little off the main stream of writings intended for the stage. They represent a backwater, interesting to explore and exciting enough in itself, but leading nowhere. It is only in the main stream that real progress can be made; only by creation of human beings that the great plays are written. (pp. 137-44)

> *W. A. Darlington, "The Brothers Čapek," in his* Literature in the Theatre, and Other Essays, *Henry Holt and Company, 1925, pp. 137-44.*

CLARENCE A. MANNING (essay date 1941)

[*Manning was an American educator and authority on Slavic languages and literature. In the following essay, he explores Čapek's humanist philosophy, which he asserts has been overshadowed by the melodramatic qualities of his works.*]

In the death of Karel Čapek two years ago at the early age of forty-eight, the Czechs lost their outstanding man of letters. His plays, especially **R.U.R.,** have been produced successfully in nearly every country. Three of them, ***R.U.R., The Insect Comedy,*** and ***The Makropoulos Secret,*** have been on Broadway. His novels have been translated. His death is a real loss to humanity, and today the Nazi rulers of Prague are doing everything possible to blot out his memory. They have forbidden the sale of his works and they allow no mention made of his activity even in the few scanty reports and articles on Czech literature that they allow to be published.

Yet there is a bitter irony in his career, and that irony has barred in his success a real appreciation of the ideas for which the man stood and for which he worked. Čapek was a philosophical melodramatist and that is an unfortunate mixture. People who went to the theater and read his works for the melodrama were bored by the philosophy. Those who sought to learn his philosophy were carried away by the melodrama, and their more primitive emotions kept them from marking what he was trying to say. Now and then he let himself go as a philosopher and thinker, but even then all were seeking the melodrama.

What was his idea? It can be summed up in a simple phrase, man is man. It makes no difference what inventions man creates, it makes no difference what ideas he develops to aid life and to make it livable. Man is man and that old promise that man must live in the sweat of his brow is an inexorable rule of nature that he transgresses at his peril. It is a cynical idea to many of us, but to him it was an axiom and he believed that in the light of it we must study the whole path of human history and all predictions as to the future of humanity.

In the prefaces of his works, he sought again and again to prove that he was not cynical, that he was merely human. No one believed him. Thus in ***The Makropoulos Secret,*** where he represents the horrible fate of the talented Elena Makropoulos who has been gifted with eternal youth for three hundred years and who has seen lovers come and go, children born and die, until she has acquired a technical proficiency in love and an empty heart, he writes:

> I do not know whether it is optimistic to assert that to live sixty years is boring but to live three hundred years is good; I think that to proclaim a life of (approximately) sixty years as a moderate and satisfactory good life is not the most venomous pessimism. Let us grant that in the future there will be neither sickness, poverty, nor evil, and that this is optimistic; but if we say that this present life, full of sickness, poverty and evil, is not so terribly evil and has something of indescribable value,—that is something of its own—is that real pessimism? I think not.

The favorite theme of Karel Čapek was the disastrous results of some great invention that was to revolutionize the world and to save mankind from the need of laboring like human beings. Surely that is a worthy goal, for we all know that mankind for centuries has been seeking some means of living without that horrible toil that seems to be connected with the comforts of life. Every new ideal, every new invention, proclaims aloud that its object is to help mankind. Every political thinker, every democrat, every dictator, is out to help humanity or at least his own people. Hope springs eternal. On the very day when his death was announced, the scientists of the United States were planning a court of wisdom to allow the superman to master the apeman and to keep inventions from destroying the world and plunging us back to barbarism.

They can learn from Karel Čapek. He tried nearly everything. He created the robots in ***R.U.R.*** These are machines in human form which can do all the work of the world. They succeed brilliantly, but for motives of economy it is necessary to make them feel pain in order to warn them of danger. They are given other human characteristics and finally love. It only generates hate, and they finally wipe out the human race which created them. They did not need to do it, for long before they rose in their last revolt weeks were passing when not a single child was being born in Europe. Today demographers tell us that not one of the highly civilized nations of the world is reproducing itself except those that have reverted to the rule of force. Up to the last minute the robots themselves face extermination, for they have lost the secret of their own manufacture.

The Revolt of the Salamanders gives us the same lesson with nature, for the trained animals themselves reproduce and menace humanity, and again a kindly (or is it a malign?) fate interferes. Humanity is saved, but culture pays the price and man becomes as he was in the beginning: a simple, kindly being making his living in the sweat of his brow and able to enjoy the simple pleasures and delights that a kindly nature offers as a rest from toil.

So, too, in ***The Factory of the Absolute.*** Scientists are planning today to delve into the mysteries of the atom and to use the power that is locked up within its nucleus to offer rest and ease to a weary world. Karel Čapek assumes that the problem is solved and that a simple machine is devised to do the work. Mr. G. H. Bondy organizes a company to exploit it. In quick succession he employs all the devices of the supersalesman and supermanufacturer to achieve his goal. His success is phenomenal. Life becomes easy as never before. But man is still with us. All who touch the machine are so overawed by its power that the struggles of life become petty and all seem to become philanthropic, charitable, mystical, almost religious. Why is this? Mankind brings out all of its past delusions and prejudices. Catholics, Protestants, and Freethinkers, all see in it the glorification and the proof of their beliefs, and so they argue their different points of view until they come to blows. Blows lead to wars; soon Bohemia and Prussia, Saxony, Poland, and Sweden revert to their age-old roles in the cockpit of Europe; and in their struggle everything is destroyed. Only a handful of simple agriculturists, men who work with their hands and are not interested in the great reforms of the period, are left. On some forgotten field they meet and resolve that henceforth they will live like human beings, abjure the machine, and act like brothers.

The White Plague, too, preaches the same lesson, for there again the healing medicine which alone can save human life from bloodshed and from war is lost amid the frenzy of conflicting mobs and dictators and interests. The hopes of a civilization are blasted; the dreams of the idealist are shattered. Life continues to exist.

The objective picture of it all is ***The Insect Comedy,*** which Karel Čapek wrote in conjunction with his brother Joseph. Between the vagabond who has never worked but lived and the pedant who has always studied and never lived, there is little to choose. The insects supply all the human emotions from the greed of the dung beetle and the bloodsucking of the parasite to the mad imperialism of the regimented ants who struggle with all the frenzy of disciplined totalitarians for the highway between two blades of grass. What a pitiable commentary on the ambitions and bloodlust of dictators and of conquerors! Only life goes on with the peasant girl bringing a newborn child to baptism.

Yes, the philosophy of Karel Čapek is not one that thrills an ambitious civilization. It springs out of the peasant soil, out of the quiet country routine where birth and death, springtime and winter, roll on in a never-ending cycle. It is not a philosophy of pessimism or of cynicism. It is a frank acceptance of the fact that human beings are human beings and that the same virtues and vices that exist today have always existed and always will. Man can find happiness within those limits, if he wishes. He can find only defeat and frustration outside them.

In his serious writings Karel Čapek taught the same lesson. He always refused to come to America, for he alleged that he would be devoured by the machine, that Frankenstein that had made civilization possible and was hurrying it to a nameless grave; and he did not realize or proclaim the fact that the Frankenstein was nearer home and that it was the American type of machine use that alone could save the life that he admired. He went to England, and in his letters and sketches from there and from other countries which he visited, he always drew the same lesson. He sought for human beings who were human, and he loved them. He avoided everything that seemed too grandiose to be human, too gigantic to be good.

Yet among the thousands of people who witnessed the performances of his plays, very few caught the lesson, because he was a master of the melodrama. No modern author has known with more unerring skill to catch the essential features of the well-built play, to know how much human feelings can stand, how far suspense is to be pushed.

In the whole field of modern drama, there is no more melodramatic scene than that in *The Makropoulos Secret,* where the celebrated singer, Emilia Marty, enters the law-office of Dr. Kolenaty and with sublime naïveté interferes in the celebrated Gregor case which has been in litigation for over a century. In the most offhand manner she divulges all the essential information about the will of the first Gregor who has died a century before. The lawyers are aghast. They cannot understand how a stranger could be so familiar with the papers and habits of old Pepi Gregor. Step by step the tangle thickens, until even the lawyers are convinced that Emilia Marty is Elliam MacGregor, the mother of the original claimant, and that she is really Elena Makropoulos, born in 1585, the daughter of a Greek magician, resident on the Hradcany Castle Hill of Prague, and endowed by him with youth for three hundred years.

Melodrama, melodrama, melodrama. Take *R.U.R.* and all those lurid scenes where the robots rise in revolt, where they break into the house of their master creator, and slay all the human beings. The ending where the advanced robots learn that they have souls is sentimental, for here as so often Karel Čapek at the end of a piece missed his cue. He could have saved humanity by picturing the last mortals cowering in terror as the final doom strikes the machinelike robots. He could have left the scene empty and given a desolate earth as the last robot ceased to function. Perhaps he did have some dream of showing how even the robots (proletarians?) could become men, but the only judgment that he received for the work was the reputation of sentimentalism.

The only criticism that was ever valid of his work was made of those scenes where he sought to make clear his philosophy and he nearly always did. There is the boring scene of the de-

bate in *The Makropoulos Secret* on the value of eternal youth, a scene where the philosopher and the melodramatist come into conflict. That was the weakness of the man, for he sought to rise above the successful dramatist and to give a message to humanity at a time when all were hanging breathlessly on the progress of the action.

Yet it was typical of him. It was typical of his thought for himself and for his country. He was a writer of a small nation, and he had no desire to see it become big. He penned his opinion in this whimsical way: "Suppose a melancholy beaver asked the question, 'Is it worth while being a beaver since there are so few beavers, less numerous than mice or horses?' The true beaver does not ask himself whether there is any sense in the fact of his being a beaver. Rather: 'How can I best make full use of my opportunities, seeing that I am already in existence?' "

This passage sets the key to the opinion of Karel Čapek on Czechoslovakia. It was in existence. It was a small country. It seemed to him to be composed of simple, honest agriculturists, men who were far removed from all the aspirations of greatness and of power. It seemed to him that President Masaryk incarnated those qualities, and he diligently sought to write them up. Critics may complain that there was much in Prague that did not bear out his beliefs and his ideas. It made no difference to him. He was a Czech, and as the beaver should be a beaver, so he who came into existence as a Czech should remain the same.

Then came the crash. President Masaryk died. The machine of Germany moved in and threatened the state. The constitution was changed. A new system of efficiency was proclaimed. New ideas came into power. Even before the final catastrophe, Karel Čapek felt that his work was done. In a new and more brutal state, he could not play with his imagination over all the problems of human life and human destiny. Power had taken the place of faith and wistful longing, and we may well believe that he died as much of a broken heart as he did of some specific disease, fortunately before the final occupation of Prague.

He died at a time when minds everywhere throughout the world were becoming apprehensive of a breakdown of human society. The very slogans that he had uttered in his plays and in his stories are now expressed in political speeches by the leaders of a dozen countries. The time for imaginative cataclysms, for astounding inventions, for theoretical upheavals, is passed, as the world moves onward to a day when even his robots will be surpassed in actuality. The world is moving to the time when his slogans in real life are stirring men by the millions to battle and to contest.

He lived simply in a little house on the outskirts of Prague and he dreamed of all these weird and wonderful happenings. The hour came when those happenings were at the door, when his friends were out of power and scattered far and wide. He did not live to see the end, but there is more than one voice crying in fear that the end will come when nothing will be left. Perhaps they are right, but perhaps Karel Čapek will be correct in the last analysis and we shall find not a blackened and a desolate earth but an earth still inhabited as it was in the beginning by simple and honest human beings who are content to behave as human beings, to live as human beings, and to earn an honest living in the sweat of their brow.

The world mourns a great master of the melodrama. A few remember the philosopher. If his dramas survive the cataclysm of the day, perhaps his confusions will be overlooked and Karel Čapek will take his real place as one of the outstanding authors of the postwar period, a man who combined a deep human philosophy and understanding, a sympathy for human life as it is with a keen analytical sense of the source of the woes of the twentieth century. Perhaps he alone dared to express a message of simplification and of labor, the only means short of a miracle that can keep mankind happy and prosperous. (pp. 236-42)

> Clarence A. Manning, "Karel Čapek," in South Atlantic Quarterly, Vol. XL, No. 3, July, 1941, pp. 236-42.

GEORGE GIBIAN   (essay date 1959)

[*Gibian is a Czechoslovakian-born American educator and critic who specializes in Russian literature. In the following excerpt, he discusses Čapek's* Apocryphal Stories, *tales that retell history, legends, or familiar stories by other writers with variations in plot or theme.*]

The general principle basic to Čapek's [***Kniha apokryfů (Apocryphal Stories)***] is to take an historical situation and retell (and reinterpret) it by filling in background, adding to it, recreating, looking at it from a fresh angle, elaborating, taking a highly magnified or distorted view of it.

Čapek relies heavily on direct speech—talk—between two or more persons. Thus Čapek reports in detail the conversation between Sarah and Abraham when they discuss possible candidates in a vain attempt to identify ten just persons in Sodom. Thersites expounds to his fellow warriors his seditious, cynical, negative thoughts about the Trojan expedition. Archimedes talks to a Roman soldier after the conquest of Syracuse (significantly his subsequent death is not described, merely briefly reported). Pure dialogue, without narration, a fragment of a drama, is found in Čapek's addition to *Hamlet*, in which Hamlet speaks to Rosenkrantz and Guildenstern in Czech blank verse. There are exceptions to the rule of dialogue and conversation. Čapek uses also the related forms of monologue and epistle. **"Five Loaves of Bread"** is a soliloquy in which a baker utters his complaint against Jesus Christ and urges his crucifixion because he is ruining the bakers' business by his miraculous methods of supplying food. Alexander the Great is the sole speaker in a letter he sends to Aristotle, explaining to his former teacher why he had to pursue his conquests and why the philosopher ought to support his effort to be proclaimed a god. But both the Jewish baker and the Macedonian ruler assume and visualize the presence of an audience, appeal to it directly, and use language as colloquial as the other speakers in genuine dialogues.

Another feature shared by all the apocrypha is that Čapek always gives a new twist to the traditional situation. He reinterprets, adds something, introduces something surprising. To ascertain exactly what the novelty is in each story goes a long way towards leading us to specific characteristics of Čapek's writing.

It may be necessary to summarize a few examples. In **"Goneril, Lear's Daughter,"** the sister of Regan and Cordelia speaks to her nurse and explains quite sensibly and humanly how and why she has become an evil woman. As a little girl, she suffered from having to live with the "stuck-up" Regan and Cordelia, "a complete nincompoop and plaster saint." Goneril convinces the reader that she had a bad time of it all

her life and that, as she says, "the right was on my side." Lear was most unreasonable in bringing his ill-behaved men with him and making "a brothel" out of her home. The Duke did not act like a man and failed to defend his wife against Lear. Goneril presents all her grievances quite convincingly and with self-knowledge. She shows insight into the processes by which she was provoked, and then corrupted. She is aware of the fact that she is evil now, but protests, "I used to be quite a good little girl, nurse, and I could have become a good woman."

In a narrative which is of course meant very lightly, Čapek displays his wit and his ability to see things unconventionally and from the other person's point of view. He surprises the reader by turning a known situation upside down. We are amused at his sleight of hand at the same time that we agree, only half seriously, that more could be said on Goneril's behalf than Shakespeare has told us.

In the biblical **"Martha and Mary,"** Čapek reports the conversation between Martha and her neighbor, Mrs. Tamara Gruenfeld, on the evening following Jesus' visit to them. Martha complains about her sister; while Martha carried a heap of shirts out of the room so Jesus would not be offended by the mess, fetched goatmilk, bread, and honey for him, chilled the milk, and dropped in to mind another woman's baby, Mary only listened to Jesus and did no work.

In this story Čapek is quite faithful to the facts of the biblical account. At first glance we might think that he is merely vastly expanding the skeleton account of the Bible, translating such biblical terms as "careful and troubled about many things" (*pečlivá jsi*) into numerous specific details. But an important transformation of the story has taken place through Čapek's language. His Martha speaks a colloquial, slangy, modern Czech: "Mary comes tearing in, with her hair a mess," "What will the Master think, with such a crazy hysterical woman and all those dirty rags lying all over the place." The dissonance, the ironical gap between the stately and laconic biblical language and the rich, colorful, earthy modern Czech of Čapek illustrates an effect for which Čapek strives in many of his apocrypha. He plays upon the distance between the narrative which he assumes the reader will know—its substance, manner of narration, traditional interpretations, and halo of associations acquired through the ages (thus Čapek is using the form of an apocryphal story as an allusion and quotation) and his own very different narrative. If his apocrypha were fresh, original stories devoid of previous existence and historical background, they would lose much of their point. As it is, each reader is reading concurrently two stories: Čapek's and his own mental image of the original stories. In **"Martha and Mary,"** the incongruity of the two accounts results in a deliberate anachronism. From the name of Mrs. Gruenfeld to Martha's changing of the diaper of her neighbor's baby, Čapek saturates the tale with small, down to earth, contemporary details. He is playing on two different reactions and tones: the remote, austere, and the petty, everyday, modern.

At the same time he is humanizing and psychologizing the story. As he did in **"Goneril,"** here he shows that he can fully understand how Martha felt, what it was like to be in her position. By implication, the rich details of life in her household are a criticism of the biblical account as an oversimplification. Martha is shown to be a petty, shallow woman blind to anything elevated, yet Čapek seems to be commenting, "Let us see what may have been behind that incident. Perhaps we shall have some sympathy for Martha once we have followed every circumstance and every shading of her reaction to the situation she found herself in."

Čapek, moreover, is saving a surprise for the conclusion. Mrs. Gruenfeld asks what Jesus had imparted to Mary. Martha answers that all Mary was able to report after hours of listening was, "I'm not sure, now, I couldn't honestly tell you a word he said, but it was just beautiful, Martha, I am so terribly happy—."

An apocryphal story which differs from the above examples in the greater violence done by Čapek to the original version is **"Romeo and Juliet."** It reverses Shakespeare's plot completely. Sir Oliver, an Englishman who is a great admirer of Shakespeare's play, travels in seventeenth-century Italy, encounters a priest who had been in the Capulets' service, and gradually learns from him that in real life, Juliet married Paris, had eight children with him, and Romeo was last heard of when running away with the daughter of the Marquis of Mongalcone or Montefalco. Romeo in fact only slightly wounded Paris, did not poison himself but fled to Mantua, Juliet did try to poison herself but recovered, fell in love with Paris when he visited her sickbed with his arm bandaged as a result of his fight with Romeo, and married him three months later.

Here Čapek is having fun by outrageously twitting Shakespeare, showing the very different course events may have taken in real life, and exploiting the sentimental disappointment of the Englishman disillusioned by his discovery that his beloved Shakespearean tragedy is not based on facts. Perhaps most important are again the human details, such as the effect of Paris' bandaged arm on Juliet, and the antithesis between the romantic, literary, sentimental attitudes of the Englishman and the realistic, everyday, commonsensical judgments of the Italian—who, for example, replies to Sir Oliver's regretful comment that the plot of the play was a thousand times more beautiful than the reality, "More beautiful! I don't know what you think is so beautiful about two young people taking their lives. It would be a pity! I tell you, it is more beautiful that Juliet got married and had eight children, and what children, pretty as a picture!" Essential—and untranslatable—is also the coarse, idiomatic, twentieth-century Czech in the mouth of the Italian character.

"Prometheus' Punishment," one of the apocrypha most typical of Čapek's thinking and literary manner, reports the deliberations of the judicial senate in the trial of Prometheus. Four ancient Greeks speak their minds in a language full of legal and political clichés. Each of them stresses a different aspect of Prometheus' crime. Ametheus considers that Prometheus did not invent fire himself but stole it from the gods (for if it were possible for a man to invent it, why had one of the judges not done so?) and condemns his crime primarily as a religious offense and a sacrilege. Apometheus sees the incident as involving a purely natural force which, however, is dangerous and through Prometheus' fault may cause damage to property and life. Hypometheus feels fire will lead to a softening of the moral fibre, to "excessive delicacy": "Did our ancestors use fire?" He warns against "softness, moral decline, disorder." "People will roll around in warmth and comfort, instead of fighting and so on." Antimetheus hopes that fire will open vast possibilities—particularly in warfare—but accuses Prometheus of having entrusted the element to shepherds and slaves instead of turning it over to a select elite. Fire ought to be "the princes' secret." However varied their

motives and interpretations of the essence of the crime, the judges agree on the punishment. The culprit is to be chained for life to a rock and vultures will eat his liver.

Čapek again adds a final section in which Hypometheus, the chairman of the court, eats his dinner the night after the trial and praises the roast as tastier than raw meat: "So fire is good for something after all . . . But a roast ought to be salted and rubbed with garlic. That's the thing to do. That's a real discovery. You see, that's something Prometheus wasn't able to think up."

With his favorite perspectivism, Čapek delights in showing how differently four men, each basing his judgment on different special interests and preconceived opinion, would interpret the same event [the critic adds in a footnote: "The hundreds of brief 'fables' in Čapek's *Bajky a podpovídky* (1946) exploit the same idea. They are the reflections of insects, plants, minerals, etc., each of which is quite certain of the correctness of its own opinions, which are being satirized by Čapek as narrow and self-centered. Čapek's own reaction is delight in the variety of the phenomena of life. In **"Weeds,"** for example, he lists dozens of different kinds of plants' roots and concludes: "You see, there is as great riches underground as on earth"]. The ecclesiast, the naturalist favoring protection of private property, the conservative, the progressive-oligarchist or elitist are paraded by Čapek like four actors or debators asked to apply their preconceptions to the same basic facts. The fifth version—with a human, domestic twist—given at the end implies that the argument "proof of the pudding (or the roast) is in the eating" is more powerful than the abstract reasoning of the four judges. Fire is vindicated even for the presiding judge through its usefulness in the homely art of cooking. The ending also suggests the judges were jealous and resentful of Prometheus and wanted to minimize his accomplishment, not wishing to admit that he did something big.

Čapek does not use the story of Prometheus' trial to expound philosophical or metaphysical views. To him it is instrumental to the making of witty marginal comments on the subject of progress and human motivations and reactions, to satire on conservatism and men too firmly set in their ways, and to showing what difference various mental sets can make even in the ancient myth of Prometheus. His treatment is light. There is no deep or emotional involvement with the fate of Prometheus himself.

When we look at Čapek's apocrypha as a group, we find several recurring tendencies in them. They often rest on conflicts between different points of view. They are very human. Rich in little details of everyday life, they bring their characters close to us, to our time and our presence. Historical and legendary personages appear with our modern ways of thinking and speaking and surrounded by the physical furnishing of our world.

The apocrypha psychologize, but do not venture into metaphysics or the depths of the human mind. They preserve a lightness, a tone of wit, with occasional satire, but without any passion, violent emotion, or involvement with suffering or fate. Not even the hatred of Goneril or the pain of Prometheus are allowed to affect us strongly. Čapek is an anesthetist. He stays close to the surface of events. Deep pain, high ecstasy are outside his ken.

Čapek depends on devices of language (modern idiom, slang, colloquial turns of speech, special political, legal, ecclesiastical terms) with which his readers are well acquainted from his other works. He is interested in the significance of his tales, particularly in their multiple significance, but the meaning he seeks is that which flows out of the social relations of man to man, not the relations between man and the universe around him or the vision of a man gazing deeply into his own inner life. He is not a myth-maker but a myth-tamer and myth-domesticator. He places stress on the humanness of lofty, untouchable, legendary people, brings them down to our level, and removes all remoteness, mystery, and magic veneration.

His apocrypha amuse, rather than disturb us. Even their iconoclasms and satire are mild, optimistic, gentle. He has the ability to understand everybody's point of view and to put himself in everybody else's place. He leaves us with the Montaignesque impression of a very clever, witty, widely informed man who is liberal, kind, and convinced that all will work out well in the end and that the little concrete things of life (like Hypometheus' roast mutton and Martha's pile of shirts) are not to be despised. (pp. 239-44)

> George Gibian, *"Karel Čapek's Apocrypha and Franz Kafka's Parables," in* The American Slavic and East European Review, *Vol. XVIII, No. 2, April, 1959, pp. 238-47.*

B. R. BRADBROOK   (essay date 1960-61)

[*In the following excerpt, Bradbrook examines the influence of G. K. Chesterton on Čapek.*]

'Influences, influences—it makes me embarrassed, if I am to admit them; it is a matter of *embarras de richesse.* . . . I have no great opinion about originality.' Karel Čapek expressed this view in the year 1925, when he was already well known both in Czechoslovakia and abroad after having produced some of his most original works, such as *R.U.R., The Insect Play, Krakatit, The Absolute at Large, The Macropulos Secret, Painful Stories* and the charming travel-sketches from

A scene from a 1922 American production of R.U.R.

Italy and England. Čapek's opinion about the nature of literary creation could mean that he doubted his own originality; retrospectively, however, one cannot but take his view as an expression of his great modesty. Čapek did not mind being influenced by good writers; he said that he liked to learn from them in order to enrich Czech literature—and yet, there is no mere imitation in his work.

It is known that Čapek admired English writers, especially G. K. Chesterton, H. G. Wells, and G. B. Shaw. His correspondence testifies to his delight in reading the works of G. K. Chesterton, but the differences between these two writers are obvious. Chesterton's exuberant carelessness about the verisimilitude of his characters and his paradoxically pointed situations seem unlike Čapek's striving after logic and reality, with or without paradox. One cannot help wondering how the sober, well-balanced, and sometimes even moralising Čapek could possibly have so much admiration for the rather undisciplined English writer, to whom a teetotaller was absolutely abhorrent. Yet, there are some very strong links between them.

Čapek's admiration for Chesterton's wit, fantasy and eccentric conservatism appeared in print already in 1920 in his review of the Czech translation of *The Flying Inn.* Later, whenever he asked his friend Dr O. Vočadlo for English books, those by Chesterton came high on the list. It is almost certain that Čapek did not read all Chesterton's works, but he must have come across quite a number, so that he would have known Chesterton well before he wrote the majority of his own works. However, the fact that both Čapek and Chesterton were journalists and that they had some personal characteristics in common accounts for many resemblances in their works.

Their natural curiosity and interest in all sorts of things found an outlet in journalism. Wit and the gift of observation even of little, insignificant things, were common to both writers. Čapek's attention to detail is striking from the very beginning of his creative activity. His collections of essays, *Intimate Things, Calendar, How They Do It, Concerning People,* dealing in a light manner with such deliberately miscellaneous subjects as dreams, melancholy, the barrel-organ, names, the post, cats, etc. would have been written even without his knowledge of Chesterton.

The affinity between these two writers is so close, that many of their essay subjects are the same or similar; Chesterton's 'On Leisure' and Čapek's **'In Praise of Leisure'** even start in an almost identical manner, but the development is different. Čapek's essay was published eight years before Chesterton's and it was translated into English seven years after the publication of Chesterton's work. Similarly, their criticism of *clichés* and meaningless phrases used in everyday life does not suggest Chesterton's influence upon Čapek: the main instigator for Čapek's **'Criticism of Words'** was neither Chesterton nor the long Czech puristic tradition, but Čapek's sincere love and admiration for his rich native tongue.

On the other hand, one can almost certainly say that Čapek had Chesterton's *The Defendant* in mind, when writing certain parts of his book *Marsyas, or on the Margin of Literature.* Chesterton's gentle anarchism was admired by Čapek: he applauded Chesterton's defence of penny-dreadfuls, nonsense, useful information, ugly things, farce, slang, and detective stories, because 'it does him good to find pleasant things in the realms of bad reputation'.

Penny-dreadfuls, probably not quite so popular at that time in Czechoslovakia as in England, did not attract Čapek to such an extent as to make him write about them, but they drew his attention to more modest forms of art, such as popular poetry, calendar literature, proverbs and sayings, suburban songs, novels for maids, and also detective stories, a genre which then belonged to the proscribed kinds of literature. The first part of Čapek's *Marsyas,* called **'In Praise of Newspapers',** proves that Čapek had Chesterton in mind when writing some of these essays. Describing the characteristics of newspapers, Čapek selects the same two features as Chesterton does in his essay 'A Defence of Useful Information', namely the exceptional nature of the events and their topicality:

> In the papers you won't ever find that a cat has caught a blackbird or given life to three kittens; you will always meet them there in a special, unusual and frequently even in a sinister light, as, for instance, that a mad cat has bitten a postman . . . that in Plymouth, or some other place, a cat with nine tails has been born, or something like that.

And Chesterton:

> By this essential taste for news, I mean the pleasure in hearing the mere fact that a man has died at the age of 110 in South Wales, or that the horses ran away at a funeral in San Francisco. Large masses of the early faiths and politics of the world, numbers of the miracles and heroic anecdotes are based primarily upon this love of something that has just happened, this divine institution of gossip.

About the topicality:

> You will read about a gory fight between three locksmiths in Štěpánská Street, but you are not told about the gory battles that Caesar had with the Gauls. For a thing to be gory or to be on fire is not enough; it must be recent.

And Chesterton:

> When Christianity was named the good news, it spread rapidly, not because it was good, but also because it was news.

In the same essay, in fact, nearly on the same page as the two other examples, Čapek gives a direct reference to Chesterton:

> By all this I mean to say what Chesterton already worried about, that is, that the newspaper world is made up of exceptional events, unusual cases. . . .

It might have been because of Chesterton's hint that 'epics were only fit for children and nursemaids' that Čapek wrote the charming essay in *Marsyas,* **'The Last Epos, or Novel for Maids'.** Chesterton pointed out that popular creations are written by nameless poets, and Čapek speaks about the same subject in his **'Last Epos'** at greater length; Chesterton's remark that 'all slang is metaphor and all metaphor is poetry' probably led Čapek to study the suburban, rough songs, and to write his essay **'Songs of the Prague People'** in the same collection. Čapek's *Marsyas* can be called Chestertonian, for the influence is more obvious here than anywhere else, and yet, Čapek's individuality of expression does not suffer. No doubt Chesterton himself would have found Čapek's *Marsyas* engaging and witty.

The detective story has no tradition in Czech literature and it was known only from translations. Čapek certainly knew Conan Doyle, but it was again Chesterton to whom he was indebted for his interest in this genre. Since Chesterton considered that the detective story needed a defence, when he wrote his 'Defence of Detective Stories' in *The Defendant,* it must have appeared all the more proscribed to Čapek whose *Marsyas* contains among others a witty and more elaborate essay than Chesterton's, called **'Holmesiana, or about Detective Stories'.** Sherlock Holmes's power of deduction did not dazzle Čapek, who preferred Father Brown's intuition and common sense, when he was creating his two unprofessional detectives, Dr Mejzlík and Mr Janík, for his *Tales from Two Pockets.* However, though they possess the gift of intuition and other good qualities, Čapek's detectives are far from being copies of Father Brown. They are acute and penetrating, but without the miraculous insight of their Chestertonian colleague. Altogether, they are more realistic than he is: they have not the ability to be on the spot at the very moment, or even before a crime is committed, like the absolutely infallible Father Brown, who, with his omniscience and almost superhuman capabilities seems too perfect to be true. This is probably what makes *The Father Brown Stories* slightly tedious in the long run, while Čapek's more realistic tales are fresh and lively from the beginning to the end. However, it must be pointed out that none of Čapek's short stories is a real detective story, no matter how much they may appear so. The preoccupation with the human soul and its problems is inevitably neglected in detective stories and therefore this genre in its proper sense was not suitable for Čapek, for whom the human soul was of supreme interest. His stories, dealing primarily with the psychic problems of the people involved, transcend the limitations of a proper detective story. Because of his preoccupation with the human soul, Čapek reminds us, Dostoyevsky's name is not mentioned among the writers of detective stories.

Chesterton's and Čapek's attitude towards criminals is very much the same; both of them believe that nobody is altogether bad, that there is something good in every criminal. Chesterton expressed his sympathy with them in *The Man Who Was Thursday:*

> . . . burglars and bigamists are essentially moral men; my heart goes out to them. They accept the essential ideal of man; they merely seek it wrongly. Thieves respect property. They merely wish the property to become their property that they may more perfectly respect it.

For Čapek

> a criminal is something like a hero: he is shrouded with romanticism, he is an outcast, an outlaw: pulling the henchmen's noses as well as those of the court and of the law he enjoys secret popular sympathy.

Chesterton's Father Brown fulfils his mission without preaching a moral, by bringing criminals to repentance through kind treatment. Čapek goes still further. His trespassers against the law are gifted with a strong sense of justice; most of them plead guilty without trying to shrink from responsibility. They receive a good deal of sympathy from the instruments of justice, who consider them as a part of their daily life. It would be easy enough to conclude that Čapek's attitude towards criminals was influenced by Chesterton, but it is just on this point that Čapek's debt to Chesterton is most doubtful. Chesterton's sympathy with them is one of the features of his anarchism, while Čapek's attitude originates rather in his pragmatic conception of truth and justice, according to which one can never know the whole truth, and therefore from a certain point of view even crime is defensible.

Several motifs from *The Father Brown Stories* can be traced, unconsciously reshaped, in Čapek's *Tales from Two Pockets.* For instance, the idea of an incredible, physical achievement, stimulated by moral indignation, which cannot be repeated in a normal emotional state. In Chesterton's 'The Hammer of God' the curate roused to indignation by his brother's behaviour, kills him with a light hammer thrown from the belfry; this seems absurd, as the size of the hammer does not correspond to the blow that hit the victim on the head and the culprit is looked for among other people. There is a suggestion of a supernatural force, but the infallible Father Brown proves that this achievement is possible, considering the force of gravitation and the curate's emotional state, which both work here as instruments of God's will. An exceptional achievement as a result of moral indignation plays the main part in Čapek's story **'Record'**, where a simple labourer throws a heavy stone across the river and hits a rich farmer who is striking a boy, and beats the world's record in throwing. The judges do not believe his plea of guilt, as, naturally, he cannot repeat his feat without the former stimulus.

Although the motif of Čapek's **'Record'** was most likely taken from Chesterton, the story illustrates Čapek's individuality, as the difference between the two writers is here strongly marked. There is a murder in Chesterton as opposed to a light injury in Čapek; the search for the culprit is the core of the story in Chesterton, while Čapek's hero commits his misdeed in the presence of a witness, the boy who was being beaten by the plaintiff; besides, the accused has no intention of denying his deed, in fact, he persists in confessing his guilt, even though he is not believed. The curate Bohun in 'The Hammer of God' cannot bear the kindness of Father Brown, who wants to keep his secret under the seal of confession, and goes to denounce himself. Čapek's guilty labourer in **'Record'** accepts his punishment, because, after all, he has caused injury, although he does not regret his deed, done under the influence of righteous anger. As there is no need in **'Record'** to look for the culprit, the main part of the story solves the problem of whether he should have pleaded guilty or not; this piece contains some of Čapek's best comical scenes, and shows the real contrast with Chesterton's gravity and seriousness.

Strangely enough, this contrast applies mainly to Čapek's and Chesterton's tales about detectives and law-breakers; obviously, both writers used a humorous and serious mood for different purposes. Dealing with murderers was, naturally, a serious matter for Chesterton, so serious that the crimes had to be treated by a priest, God's representative on earth; Čapek, the pragmatist, preferred to describe lighter offences, in situations amusing rather than tragic.

The difference is particularly apparent in four of their stories, Chesterton's 'The Arrow of Heaven' and 'The Curse of the Golden Cross', and Čapek's **'The Stolen Cactus'** and **'The Troubles of a Carpet Fancier'**. In these stories the authors describe characters who are passionate collectors of rarities. In Chesterton's stories these hobbies degenerate into eccentricities. The protagonist of 'The Arrow of Heaven' is possessed by the desire to get hold of the Coptic cup, that of 'The Curse of the Golden Cross' must acquire a golden cross from the neck of a mummy; the desires of Čapek's collectors are not so ambitious: one steals cacti from a famous collection, the

other tries to steal a rare carpet after many unsuccessful attempts to buy it. Chesterton's gravity and solemnity here are the very opposite of the humour and benevolence with which Čapek treats his characters. There is something insane and mysterious about Chesterton's collectors, who are put on the same level as criminals, while Čapek's characters, apart from their weakness for collecting, are quite respectable people in everyday life and their desire to collect is no more than a hobby. Čapek has not the heart to punish them: the owner of the famous cactus collection appreciates the love and admiration of the little thief for cacti and employs him; the eager carpet fancier fails to commit the theft, being prevented by a dog who considers the carpet as its property. What is then the connexion between Čapek and Chesterton as regards these four stories? No doubt the psychology of collecting was a subject of great interest for Čapek; but again, even if he had borrowed it from Chesterton, his own imagination and originality in the treatment of the idea must be appreciated.

'The Experiment of Professor Rouss' is also Chestertonian, but Professor Vey's suggestion that Čapek may have used an idea of O. Henry's as a source for this story, is perhaps relevant too at other points. Considering Professor Vey's interesting analysis and comparison of **'The Experiment of Professor Rouss'** with O. Henry's short story 'Calloway's Code', it seems that Čapek's tale is an example of his artistic skill in creating an original work out of motifs used by other writers. Like Chesterton's 'The Mistake of the Machine', **'The Experiment of Professor Rouss'** is based on research in experimental psychology in the service of justice. In both cases the criminals are being examined, Chesterton's by means of a psychometric machine, Čapek's by a new method of questioning, in principle very similar to the technique of the machine. In both cases the experimenters are Americans. Correct in theory, both Chesterton's and Čapek's methods fail finally to a certain extent. It seems obvious that Usher, the operator in Chesterton's story, is right, having caught the murderer of the missing Lord Falconroy by means of the machine registering the erratic pulsation caused by the reaction of the accused to certain words, but Father Brown has another explanation, namely, that the suspect is the disguised Lord Falconroy himself. He also proves that, although the machine cannot make a mistake, wrong conclusions may be drawn by the operator, an imperfect mortal. Čapek's, or rather his hero's, experiment works satisfactorily in the first part of the story when a murderer is proved guilty, but it fails in the second, in the case of a journalist who reacts to the cue words with journalistic *clichés* instead of immediate psychological associations. The journalist is not a criminal, but his journalistic *clichés* are ridiculed by Čapek. Here O. Henry's influence on Čapek may play its part, assuming that Čapek, who was fascinated by words and enjoyed playing with them, knew the story 'Calloway's Code', the only story by O. Henry, Professor Vey asserts, which suggests some similarities between the Czech and the American author. How far can the connexion between Chesterton, O. Henry and Čapek be proved in the case of **'The Experiment of Professor Rouss'**? Since Chesterton was Čapek's favourite writer, one can almost assume that Čapek knew 'The Mistake of the Machine' and may have used it, unconsciously or deliberately, in the first part of his story and possibly developed it independently in the second (if he had not read O. Henry's story). Whether Čapek read 'Calloway's Code' is difficult to prove, but, apart from Professor Vey's argument, the likelihood is strengthened if one considers the fact that Čapek knew personally Josef Mach, the translator of O. Henry into Czech, who could have lent or recommended the story to Čapek, either in the original or in translation. If this was the case, it could have happened during or after 1927, when Josef Mach returned to Prague after his fifteen years stay abroad. **'The Experiment of Professor Rouss'** was written in 1928; if Čapek had known 'Calloway's Code', the influence of this story might have been immediate, possibly even direct, and might have been exerted also in another story by Čapek, namely, **'The Death of the Baron Gandara'.** In the conclusion of this story and of 'Calloway's Code' the gift of imagination is praised in a very similar way. In O. Henry's story the imaginative person is the 'rewrite' man Ames, in Čapek's the detective Mejzlík.

Chesterton's 'The Mistake of the Machine' may have equally influenced another story by Čapek. In his tale **'Coupon'** a maid is robbed and murdered by her lover; Chesterton's villain is a similar kind of criminal, specialising in the robbery (and in one case murder) of shop-girls and barmaids. This is, however, a type of murder which could be based on an incident in actual life and it is possible that this was the case with Čapek's story.

Comparing Čapek's Dr Mejzlík with Father Brown, in the tale **'Dr Mejzlík's Case'**, one might think that Čapek borrowed from Chesterton not only Father Brown's quality of intuition, but also the idea that a criminal can be proved guilty by means of a bit of ash. When Dr Mejzlík sees ash on the shoe of a man, walking in the rain, he follows him and finds out that he is a cracksman, while Father Brown in 'The Crime of a Communist' is led by some ashes to conclude that they came from poisoned cigarettes which caused the very strange death of two people. Yet this similarity in ideas does not prove more than the fact that Čapek's imagination was so much like Chesterton's, that there was frequently a close resemblance between the themes of his stories and those of Chesterton even when there was no specific indebtedness. There is no question of Chesterton's direct influence in this case since Chesterton's story was published later than Čapek's.

However, in Čapek's tale **'The Disappearance of an Actor'** there is some likelihood, though no certainty, that Čapek expressed his admiration for Chesterton by accepting his defence of a great, but morally corrupt, artist. Chesterton excuses a murderer:

> Horne is a sneak and a skunk, but do not forget that, like many other sneaks and skunks in history, he is also a poet.

The hero of Čapek's tale discovers the murderer of an actor, but as he cannot prove his guilt, he threatens to be his living conscience:

> Till your dying day I'll keep on reminding you: Remember Benda the actor. I tell you, he was an artist, if ever there was one.

The similarity between these two stories is the more striking since both end with these eulogistic closing passages.

Some of Čapek's short stories testify to their author's delight in paradox which, most likely, originated in Chesterton. However clear the development of the plot may seem in the early stage, yet a sudden turn brings quite an unexpected *dénouement*. Such is **'The Selvin Case'** or **'Proof Positive'**; in fact, Čapek's amiable unprofessional, but most successful detective, Mr Janík, is the victim of a paradox: after several brilliant cases of detection he finds out that his own secretary has been cheating him of money for a long time without arousing any suspicion. This convinces Mr Janík that his gift of intuition is rather erratic and he gives up detection for ever. Yet paradox never became a literary mannerism for Čapek as it was for Chesterton.

In his fiction Chesterton seems to have liked big men, perhaps because of some affinity with himself. One of these characters, Sunday, in *The Man Who Was Thursday,* must have impressed Čapek very much and led him to create two strikingly similar characters, one in *Krakatit,* the other in the short story **'The Last Judgment'** in the *Tales from Two Pockets.* Like Chesterton's Sunday, these two unusually big, old men are personifications of God. Naturally, human imagination would hardly personify God as a small or a young man and the external appearance of these characters does not necessarily testify to Chesterton's influence on Čapek in these two cases; the similarity between Sunday and Čapek's God-like hero, especially the one in *Krakatit,* lies in the embodiment of the supernatural in an almost superhuman, undefined figure, who appears at critical moments during the action. There is, however, something more terrestrial in Čapek's God-like hero. He does not appear on the balcony like Sunday, exhibiting his vastness against the sky, neither does he disappear and reappear in another place at the same time, nor does he fly like a magician; he only turns up as if by mere chance at the right moment to meet the titan hero and give him a lesson in humility. He is, in fact, almost like an old Czech peasant, with great experience and common-sense. His wise talk and the quiet countryside setting reflect and represent the peace of mind one can find in God. The fact that both Čapek and Chesterton introduce God into their works mainly when they are uncertain how to get their heroes out of situations half-way between reality and fantasy, is probably not very significant for their literary relationship. For is it not rather natural to seek God's help where human power fails? (pp. 327-36)

Several critics have suggested that reading Čapek has reminded them of Chesterton, but no comparative study has been made. What is the result of a closer look at these two writers? There is no doubt that Čapek was greatly indebted to Chesterton, but in most cases the influence was only unconscious. Yet, considering Čapek's admiration for Chesterton and the fact that he published forty-six works in all literary genres, an even greater number of examples of borrowing from Chesterton might have been expected. Chesterton's influence on Čapek was beneficial, even if it aroused the displeasure of the severe Czech critic F. X. Šalda, who called Čapek 'a Chestertonian conservative'. In spite of his debt to Chesterton, Čapek remained completely individual and never became a mere epigone. (p. 338)

> *B. R. Bradbrook, "The Literary Relationship between G. K. Chesterton and Karel Čapek," in The Slavonic and East European Review, Vol. 39, 1960-61, pp. 327-38.*

ALEXANDER MATUŠKA (essay date 1963)

[*In the following excerpt, Matuška studies Čapek's attitudes toward and understanding of humankind as reflected by characterization in his plays, short stories, and novels.*]

The focal point of Čapek's attention in the 'new environment', in mechanized civilization, in the bourgeois world full of social contrasts, is man.

In Čapek, the element that determines what man is like is the author's knowledge of man and his relationship to him, his tendency to use allegory and pretext, his intellectualism and his principles of depiction. Čapek does not approach the reality of man any differently than he approaches the reality of the world outside. Čapek's relationship to man is . . . ambiguous: it consists of love and loathing, benevolence and fear. This is true of his relationship to man as an individual, but for man organized into large groups he feels only loathing and fear. Benevolent and tolerant to man's lacks and weaknesses Čapek the intellectual takes into account man's intellectual mediocrity, and Čapek the pragmatist, man's moral mediocrity—the one and the other with an occasional smile, and a sidelong glance at the reader. Behind this we find a mistrust for rationale, a fear of great effort and great deeds, an anxiety that is no longer limited to being a fear for man, but a fear of him as well. It is the same Čapek who above all loves intellectual penetration into things, and the same Čapek who dishes out great concepts—no matter what the fate of the bearers of these concepts in his works may be. Moral mediocrity? In theory he presented it almost as an ideal. In poetic application, it didn't always come out that way, sometimes there was a bit more, something else seemed to sound from the sub-text. And there came the day when he led an attack on this mediocrity. The gamut of Čapek's characters is not a large one, particularly because they are determined by the author. What is essential is the fact that Čapek's ambiguous attitude towards man is reflected, though unequally, in the two basic types of his heroes, or at least the tendency to two different types: the Professorial type, and the Outlaw type. The first . . . is a conciliatory nature, resigned, though perhaps not without regrets. The second wants to take things for himself—in the case of the 'rebels' also for society—as much as possible. The first brings conciliation to such a point that it approaches introversion, passiveness and helplessness. The second is characterized by extroversion, revolt, restrainedness and heroism.

In Čapek's 'science of man' there is without doubt a deep knowledge of man. He knows much about man, and we learn a great deal about man from him. He knows even more than he appears to know. He knows him placid, good, and it is with pleasure that he stops to contemplate him. He knows human nature 'all the way to its pain and dreadfulness', man at the bottom of his 'dark heart', man in his 'obscurity and bestiality'. Not even 'the disturbing and terrible, melancholy and inexpressible soul of man' is foreign to him. And he does not back away from this all, for to put oneself in the position of human beings is an 'enchanting and terrible' experience.

In Čapek's 'science of man' there is also a great deal of theory. 'The first book that enchanted you was neither the bible, nor heroic ballads, but the big Illustrated Book of Natural History. That is where you gained your first impressions about gentle and terrible natures . . .' That says much, and doubtless the element of natural science is by far not the last on the list of the elements and factors in Čapek's view of man. He applied biology and even entomology, apart from everything else that he knew of man. The extreme result of this was the *Insect Comedy.* Čapek himself justified its origin historically ('at those times, when the war was drawing to a close, with all its accompanying phenomena, it was impossible not to think of man when viewing insects'). He thought of this parallel again in the fables before the Second World War, and elsewhere as well. In addition to his flora, Čapek had his fauna, and here he pigeon-holed man. In the comedy about the insects it was meant critically, elsewhere—and this was Čapek's general stand—the biological, the vegetative, the elementary, the instinctive, the natural appears as the most valuable facet of man in the unnatural world of civilization. It is all that man possesses, morally. From this point of view it was a long time until Čapek admitted the existence of great human aims, the subject of 'heroic ballads', even though he had long since listed heroism among the natural 'qualities', alongside hunger, love and sacrifice.

There is also contemporary psychology in Čapek's 'science of man'. Speaking of the prewar period, he says: 'The psychological sciences are ceasing to parade the universal, artificially created model of the human consciousness, for they are being confronted by the subconscious, the endless individuation of human souls, and the psychology of social groups'. More or less chronologically (though not quite, for the utopia *Krakatit,* for example, 'psychologizes' as much as the books of Čapek's youth, and *The War with the Newts* returns, after the trilogy [*Hordubol, Meteor,* and *An Ordinary Life*], to the most 'psychologizing' utopias of the Twenties) Čapek goes through individuation, social psychology and the subconscious. Individuation, or what might be called a form thereof, characterizes his beginnings, when he presents external reality stressed by means of man, and also characterizes the Trilogy, in which it culminates for the second time: man is something primarily psychic, intellectual, certainly not natural, not animal. It is as if, introverted and inactive, he existed in the material world only in order to present it with a complex mirror. The sense of his being is in the fact that he experiences the problems that face him, that he poses questions which he wants to solve. In the period of the utopias, the psychology of social groups approaches a purely behaviouristic, external understanding, for 'psychology is always sort of agonizing and lacerating'. He even uses the words 'soul-searching, realistic, or otherwise agonizing literature'. The psychology of social groups comes to the fore in all of Čapek's plays (In *The Fateful Game of Love* in the manner of commedia dell'arte, that is, with overtones of the psychology of established types), which is in definite agreement with the fact that in the clash between the intimate and the social—which is typical for his concept of poetry and prose—his theatre inclines towards the great social questions of the times. The principles of this psychology were formulated by Čapek long before he applied them in his own dramatic practice. In Plautus' *Menaechmi,* 'there is no turn of will, no changes, no psychological development. The characters present themselves broadly, they are conceived typically, generally, simply. Their very typicalness gives them a maximum of vital content with a minimum of characterizational details and personal traits'. In a review of Romains' *L'armée dans la ville,* he agrees with the manner in which 'the collective speaks through every speaker, how all individual differentiation . . . recedes'. In Racine, his Bajazet, Čapek looks for support against psychology on the stage in the very beginings of his dramatic work. In general he praises Racine's constructive psychology, and—in the analysis of the character of the Princess Atalida—the logical structure of her vacillation between love and reason, self-denial and jealousy. 'For us, it is an event and an example to see how rationally, how amazingly typically and transparently a human soul is constructed rather than drawn'. Čapek excludes from the drama, in addition to the multi-directional composition which he postulates for poetry and prose, the 'infinitesimal structure of the human soul'. In his prose, he finally works with the subconscious as well, even though 'there are enough mysteries in the life of man from the waist up', and even though he rejects 'modern psychology with its Freudian subconscious, its sombre complexes, its chaotic and hysterical eroticism . . .' For him psychoanalysis was to achieve the position of a mere partial aid towards other aims. At the instigation thereof, he later attempted to 'achieve reasons for dignity and respect, for order and discipline . . .'

No matter how tendencies intersect—the most primitive may be found in close proximity to the most refined and the most volatile—there are two extreme planes here as well: on one hand the simplification of man, a summariness in revealing and evaluating motivations, and on the other hand complexity, the psychological point of view, aiming toward exclusiveness. On one hand Čapek's people wither away to mere 'attributes', symbols and formulae, standardized types, of which we learn merely what they reveal externally—all there is left of psychology here is the psychological paradox. The portrait of the terrier Dashenka is more complex than his portraits of people. On the other hand, man is for Čapek something unattainable, full of mysteries, convolutions and duplicities. As compared to the weak penetration into the inner man, as opposed to rapidity and superficiality of characteristics, here there is a psychology that runs very deep. In other words, man can be figured out, on one hand, but on the other, he can never be—known.

Čapek's people are determined by the fact that his starting-off point is not a portrait, but a problem. That for him, a story always bears a certain meaning in itself. That is why he checks his characters, large and small, against the mission of the bearers of this meaning. Objectively, they are tools anyway. In Čapek they become tools for the demonstration of a thesis. They represent the author's contradictory ideology, for they are created from it, and, again, they themselves create it. Thus they are, to a certain extent, always allegories and symbols, personifications, not persons. This is particularly true for the figures in his plays. (pp. 338-44)

Submerged into man's core, Čapek leaves out—either completely or almost completely—his characters' external appearance, as well as the landscape and environment in which they move. We do not see them. And since the conversations they carry on are not always with people, but often with themselves, we do not hear them either. In the more realistic book or in the more realistic sections of his books, Čapek always sticks to generalities, but his transposition and stylization is evident in that he is brief, in that he does not pile up details. We hear well, though we see more weakly. Detachment from reality is achieved here by Čapek's concentration on a certain detail, on a certain physical characteristic, which is hyperbolized out of proportion, at the expense of the whole. Elsewhere, the secondary is magnified to the position of the primary. We hear very clearly, and we see something clearly as well. The cubist method of the emphasized detail, and the loathing toward copying reality are once again culminated by irony: Čapek plays and amuses himself, caricatures and ridicules.

In total, Čapek's man is a fraction, not an integer; though he is not exactly chaos, he is neither a personality, the author preferring a general type.

In his first short proses we can hardly speak of any intentional effort towards the working out of characters. They are mostly puppets and bizarre silhouettes. But even so, Čapek succeeded in saying what he wanted to say, that is, by means of them and through them achieving the general minimizing of

man, his distortion by means of unnatural relationships. Čapek's permanent inclination to puppets, artificial people, the non-human, the non-man—which culminates in his robots and newts, and the origin of which is certainly not only in the aesthetic, for it was born of the feeling of the rule of the mechanical—appears, not without cause, in artificial puppets, androids, in the very first book of the Brothers Čapek. People in the neo-classical novelettes in *The Luminous Depths* are drawn with a firm hand, in their breathless desire for a full life. They are drawn with strong lines, they are monumentalized. In the title story, the situation is different. The hero withdraws to his very core. This core is the platform whereon Čapek presents the destiny of man in the mechanical but dangerous world. In *Wayside Crosses,* an inner solution is sought in place of the mechanism that transforms people into instruments, into machines of habit. The inner solution, that removes man from the social and places him in 'being', the solution that places the world of the soul, the inner appearance counter to the way he looks from without, the solution that considers personal experience to be the supreme quality—this solution does not allow enough material for attributes and personality. The hero of the collection, a soul without a body, is a spiritual type, with persistent moods which determine his mind to such an extent that their bearer becomes their victim, and the personal is transposed to an impersonal level, to a level approaching the anonymous. The predictability of human behaviour, so much stressed in this book, comes to the fore even more markedly in *Painful Tales,* where the heroes are wretched, mediocre, frightened existences, debased and insulted. Accents of 'Russian' psychology from the previous book (in **'Lída'** there is 'the thirst to scandalize oneself to utter destruction, to throw oneself away . . .' **'Lída'** 'wallows in debasement; . . . she buries herself so terribly in her shame, without the least will to pull herself out of it . . .') become even more pronounced in *Painful Tales.* There is something approaching the 'underworld' in the manner in which the heroes—particularly in the stories **'Money'** and **'The Offended Man'**—experience the very real problem of their relation to other people, how they revolt against custom, automatism, only to give in to them. This is what gives them life and form, even though there is no question of intention and thesis here either, the thesis about the painfulness of life which they personify. Even though the Outlaw is a character conceived in the spirit of *The Garden of Krakonoš* and the comedy *A Fateful Game of Love,* he surpasses the marionettes of these works in his completeness; even though he was created in the period of the 'painful' tales, he surpasses them in his meaning. He is perhaps closest to the figures in the neo-classical novelettes in *The Luminous Depths.* Meant as a symbol, he even surpassed the intention of his creator, and even if he represents something, he is nevertheless alive in and by himself. Not an intellectual, not complex, not a man forced inside himself and psychically experiencing what life has deprived him of, he is drawn in all his impulsiveness, elementariness, in action, with bold, simple strokes. The situation changes in the utopias.

The dual face of man, not only from the social point of view, was familiar to Čapek before the utopias, when he was writing them, and afterwards as well. In the period when he was writing both the first and the second series of the utopias, when he was rejecting psychology, he was aware of man's complexity. In connection with the oscillation between his fiction and his journalism, how many facts that prove this are to be found in his portraits of people in feuilletons and articles, even in the period when he looked down his nose at psychology in art. Pictures of little people, whose oeuvre was their life, people whose life and work remained hidden, and people whose life and work are revealed for all the world to see. The fact that he looks upon 'little people' as on creators of life as well, and the fact that he approaches 'great' people also from the human aspect, this does not brand these profiles, portraits, snapshots and detailed drawings with familiarity, which is not lacking—in both cases—in his fiction. And mainly, be it a matter of Obzina, the copy-boy, or Stanislav K. Neumann and Anatole France, he consistently makes use of a rare human sympathy, a penetrating intellectual insight and submersion which are not always apparent in the characters in his fiction.

Is this intentional or not?

The reality of the external world, and its human reality in particular, is wealthy and many-faceted. Čapek's permanent attitude toward this is expressed in *The First Rescue Party* in words which could be read (and are to be found, for that matter) in **'Estaunié'**: 'Man looks at somebody, say, for a whole lifetime . . . and knows nothing at all about him . . . but in novels, they know everything'. And elsewhere: 'How little man knows about man'. The inner man, that aspect of man which does not allow itself to be known, is what Čapek wanted to get to know. His knowledge of him was, in his first books, a knowledge of psychological individuation, which in fact ended up as depersonalization. The change of positions in his utopias was caused by several things, and they cannot be said to be convergent. There is the objective fact that man became a thing, that he became alienated from himself. What emerged as mechanical in man in *Wayside Crosses* appears in the utopias with even greater emphasis. Subjectively, in the utopias—which are supposed to be literature for the people—Čapek rejects psychology, because it complicates man, and because a complex man is useless for epical literature. In Čapek's opinion, the epical and the complexity of characters are mutually exclusive. And in the third place, simplification is meant to restore the simple and elemental.

Čapek's little person, his 'ordinary man', who stepped forth from his isolation to live among the others, accepts finished words and ideas. . . . Čapek deserts the criterion of the personal experience, the inner solution, and though he led and continues to lead a constant battle with standardization and the like, with the fruits of bourgeois civilization, he takes pleasure in standardizing the little man, making him into an automaton, a product, a reflex of his environment. Čapek's petit bourgeois resembles the robot and the newt from the intellectual side, and from the morally mediocre side, he approaches the insect. This figure, with exceptionally visible social characteristics, personifies the 'eternal order of things', so much so that there is no longer any need for individuation. Sufficient here were a few consistent—and yet somewhat eccentric—habits, tics, and predilections.

Even some of his 'rebels' are no exception from the rule of standardization: the directors in *R.U.R.* were drawn to resemble, among others, representatives of the Anglo-Saxon 'male ideal'. In the foreword, which was written later, they are spoken of as 'representatives of humanity'. But mechanicalness has stuck to them as to the robots. In what they have to say, they are strictly specialized, limited according to what each is the director of in the enterprise; they appear to Helen—and not only to her—to resemble the robots. They have already become what is to come after them.

Man's inner self expressed by his outward actions: This was the process used by the great realists possessed of a touch of the epical, with figures that had enough social scope for their action and displayed a harmony of the outer and the inner. In America, which had become Americanized, possibilities of action had not diminished, but man had diminished, shrunk internally. In direct contradiction to what Čapek expected, in his youthful essay on the integral American, man did not achieve 'equilibrium of thought and action, of his mind and discrimination in his activity', and developed instead into a monster of practice, of application. The equilibrium of the inner and outer was disturbed, and this led, in the first place, to activist literature of the 'success-story' type, and in the second, to psychologism. Čapek took over the former method—the behaviourist method, concentrating on utterances and external manifestations rather than on an overall picture of a personality—particularly for the 'American' figures in *R.U.R.,* in the novels *Factory for the Absolute, War with the Newts,* and partly in the novel *Krakatit.* That is, everywhere where it is a matter of 'American' dimensions, as well as where it is a matter of little things and little people in their sphere. Man is presented in a psychological outline, in which there is no room for mystery, for the hidden, for nuances. What appears to approach these is in fact usually a carefully observed external detail. And what the author knows over and above this, he keeps to himself. The heroes of *Wayside Crosses* 'characterized' themselves, it seems that all the author did was to jot down their emotional and mental life, where as in the relationship between Marek and Bondy (the engineer and the factory owner in the *Factory for the Absolute*) Čapek actively interferes, does not even hesitate to characterize his personae directly. Marek and Bondy have certain feelings and emotional states in their contact with the 'absolute', but we only know the most primary reactions to them. And these reactions are verbal, which is typical of these not particularly uncommunicative individuals. The dialogues in the novel, particularly between these two, could easily find a place in one of Čapek's plays. In them, Marek and Bondy are testing each other. The situation is no different with 'little' characters in this book, except for the fact that they take the words from each other's mouths. And in the *War with the Newts,* once again things are the same, with Bondy, who appears here again, with Vantoch, with Povondra; we find out about what is within them by what the author tells us of their utterances and behaviour.

Something nevertheless does remain of psychology: the psychological paradox.

In the world of absurd coincidence, of rapid, revolutionary and irrational situations that are brought about by some sort of invention, the characters find themselves faced with new, unexpected situations time and again. They develop, or, better said, they change unmotivatedly from one opposite to the other. Take, for example, Marek and Bondy, Čapek's higher organisms of this type. Čapek knows how to gain effects that are almost dadaistic, so that he himself parodies the multiple aspect technique. There is Povondra, for example, for whom a mere replication suffices to change 'his' opinion that the French have only one main worry, and that is women, to the opinion (just as firmly voiced) that they are good soldiers.

The most vital of Čapek's 'rebels', the hero of *Krakatit,* Prokop the engineer, is an exception that proves the rule. Not prefabricated, not a person with a single overpowering quality, but a complex character, a foretaste of the heroes of the

Trilogy (particularly Case X). Prokop is seen in the secrecy of his inner life, in duality—and this is Čapek's old dilemma, wanting nothing and wanting everything. Some of the 'Russian' psychology has stuck to Prokop, and to Princess Will a something of Eduarda from Hamsun's Pan. On the other hand, it is Prokop who is full of chysms and paradoxes. He does and does not want to leave Balttin, he does and does not want to hand Krakatit over. We see such reversals in other characters in the novel as well: Holz suddenly goes over to Prokop, Kraft, the pacifist, suddenly begins to yearn for a great deed, and so forth. The psychological paradox plays a role in the fact that Čapek's most realistic utopian novel culminates the mechanization and dehumanization of man: people in the world of the industrial magnates in Balttin have changed into rigid puppets, into zombies.

The theatrical works of Karel Čapek are not works of psychological conflict, but of 'man's lot', the position of man in society and in the universe. This theatre is not a theatre of characters but of ideas. That is why, to use an extreme example, the personae need not have names of their own. In his utopian, non-utopian, and semi-utopian plays, they may be called the Outlaw, the Professor, the Mother, the Father. Čapek has an excellent ear, and one of his most effective media even in prose is to make a character come alive by means of his language. Words and the manner of speaking, together with intentionally sparse psychological observation, individualizes his characters. The words and the content of their speech typifies them, transforms them into the bearers of ideas. It is the idea which is primary, not the person. Persons represent something; they are pretexts, symbols, allegories.

The lowest level of this is apparent in the cases where Čapek has one of his figures say something incompatible with his personality, something that does not tie in with it, or in the cases where what they represent ideologically is in contradiction to what we know about them otherwise. Gilles's words, addressed to Trivalin, concerning ownership are very well-chosen, but not coming from him. Domin's idea of the liberation of man from work, his emotional enthusiasm for a whole man, uncurtailed, are equally well-chosen, but they are in contradiction (and not in the kind of positive contradiction that melts, but the kind of contradiction that disunites mechanically) with the person of Domin. In Domin, we find a lack of personal cultivation, and although he, like all other members of mankind, no longer works, there is no sign of his belonging to a spiritual aristocracy. He knows only so much about the actual production of the robots as stuck to him in his long years of directing the enterprise. Neither Gilles nor Domin have grown up to match the idea that they represent. A step higher, a higher level—perhaps in Alquist, or Galén—there is the merging of character with idea. The character has the idea from the very start. Although it is an abstract idea, it belongs to the character. If in Čapek's plays we speak of a struggle of ideas, not passions, a struggle in which principle stands up to principle rather than man to man, there are still differences in quality. There is the difference between the Outlaw-Professor controversy and that between Adam the Creator and his Alter Ego. All are symbolic, but the first two have a personal destiny as well, while the other two merely argue. There is a difference between *R.U.R.*, and *Adam the Creator.* In the former, it is a matter of the battle of ideas, in the second a matter of a dramatized debate. Of the characters that the author uses for his theses and which surpass the thesis by means of what they say, the most outstanding are

those who surpass it by experiencing the idea emotionally. They don't get it from without, ready-made, but they approach it, grasp it, debate with it in the process of development—e.g. Prokop in the novel *Krakatit.*

Stage directions are kept to a minimum in all the plays. There are no data on the age or appearance of the characters in *The Macropulos Secret, The White Plague* or *The Mother;* the ones that there are in *The Fateful Game of Love* and [the *Insect Comedy*] are general and sparse. In 'The Outlaw' and in *R.U.R.* they are concise. Even in the sections that are stiffly phantasmic, *Krakatit* is full of enlivening details. Čapek knows how to catch a dialogue, how to capture what is going on inside people, along with what they are saying and hearing. Not a gesture, not an external feature escapes him. In this sense, *The Factory for the Absolute* and *The War with the Newts* are closer to Čapek's dramas than to *Krakatit.* In *The Factory for the Absolute,* the dialogue between Marek and Bondy is in the nature of ready questions and quick replies, it is stark, and positioned only in that a character speaks (or growls, blurts, shouts) 'hesitantly' or 'bitterly' or 'anxiously' or 'calmly' etc. Externals are highly general, no more detailed than characteristics in the plays. Marek—as seen by Bondy—is *terribly thin and serious, sort of stately,* and this is no more than a description of any of the directors in *R.U.R.* Bishop Linda, who is effectively tagged by his manner of speaking in his inner essence of the church dignitary who isn't playing clean. He speaks briskly, nimbly, softly and sweetly, in the tone of an epicure. He is also more specified in appearance: ' . . . a small merry gentleman with gold-rimmed glasses, and a joshing little mouth which he closed, priest-like, into a neat little hindy'. Capturing a person in his external appearance and at the same time being capable of taking a look below the surface, under the skin, this is a talent that Čapek displays and develops in the figure of Captain Vantoch in *The War with the Newts.* The actual model for this figure was the Czech polar traveller Welzl, who, according to Čapek, personified the Czech—in his adventurousness and sobriety, his waggery and his carefulness. Yet Vantoch's portrait does not have too many traits either. It is a sparse characteristic, abbreviated, more of a line drawing than an oil painting, which summarizes and touches, and does not encompass. Vantoch is fat, has a blue kerchief and blue eyes, his Czech is anglicized and he is convinced that people are crooks. The novelty, at least as far as the method of characterization is concerned, is in the fact that Čapek returns, after the Trilogy, from man's multiplicity to his unity. He stresses this unity here by the mechanical repetition of externals. Whenever there is mention of Vantoch, there is mention of his blue kerchief, his fat index finger, his fat palm, his pale blue eyes. To Vantoch, people are always crooks, he consistently repeats his 'Vat is the use?' with an accent that is a little strange, his language is always that of the sea. The repetition of these individual observations, which in and by themselves are each realistic, makes the characters a bit unreal. What was supposed to represent the identity of personality contributed to the impression that the character is from another, fantastic, world. This method was a part of Čapek's system of repetition, a system expansively and organically developed. It was used in *Krakatit* for the figure of Prokop and Princess Wille, on the said level. It was also used in this novel, this time 'Wagnerially', lyrically and romantically, in the motif of Prokop's lifelong love for the unknown woman, always seen in the fur and with the dewy veil . . . (We find it in a different, a more normal utilization outside his utopias, used directly and with great certainty, in Čapek's novels about miners and Foltýn. In the first, all the characters in the book are thus realistically characterized. It seems almost tiresome when throughout this slim book, Čapek is forever talking about Adam's deep-set eyes, Matula's blood-shot eyes, of Martínek as a young giant, the long-leggedness of Mrs. Hansen, etc. And in Čapek's final work the only difference is in the fact that the characteristics and human attributes of the figure, as repeated by the various witnesses, are justified noetically, as proof of the possibility of objective cognition.)

As for the [*Tales from Two Pockets*], the problems that face the people generally remain unsolved. The characters themselves are only apparently 'solved'. It is true, that, on one hand, superficiality and standardization from the utopias rings through here in the depiction of people. But it is also true that in the conception of man in the *Tales,* the new, or the old-new irrationale is coming to the fore as well—something that cannot be solved altogether, something that remains unsolved. This is not true only of the stories '**The Murderous Attack**', '**The Man Who Couldn't Sleep**', and the '**Stamp Collection**', stories either about the past which rings through to the present, or about night-time things side by side with day-time things, or on a motif of several possibilities as compared to the possibility that in fact came to pass. The point of view of the inner solution is not the primary one here. And where it is, we are once again not far from the 'Russian' psychology, as for example in the story '**The Disappearance of Actor Benda**', and occasionally where the inner solution is the primary moment, it emerges parallel with 'the social routine'.

The *Tales* are a bridge between Čapek's beginnings and the utopias and Trilogy.

[In *Hordubal,* the title character] appears to the state attorney to be a 'simple, good-natured man, of limited reason'. This is how Čapek himself would have viewed his hero not long before. But Čapek did not go to the Carpathians in search of the epical and the elementary, in search of firm characters and mighty passions, nor, for that matter, in search of a social episode. The author's view of his hero is different now. Though he is wooden, strong and simple, though he does not know how to read or write, Hordubal is much more complex than he appears to the author. The primitive and the elementary merges within him with a deep inner life, and Čapek does not intend to let the reader doubt it. The truth about himself in relation to his immediate environment, gradually uncovered by Hordubal, the fact that he uncovers it by intensely experiencing it (and this is his very own experience), this does not constitute the whole truth, the real sum of all facts, that is, reality as a whole. But it was the author's intention to show that this is more real and more true than the obviousness of the other two explanations. To show that a view from within is closer to the essence than a view from without which considers only externals. Hordubal is not simple, though he is ordinary. He himself, and his wife and Manya as well, are ambiguous, at the very least. 'What if the true Hordubal was both weak and wise, if Polana was both as beautiful as a lady and as work-worn as an old peasant, what if Manya was both a man who kills for love and a man who murders for money?'

The hero of the novel *Meteor* is not ordinary. He is, as a matter of fact, in comparison with the heroes of the other two parts of the trilogy, extraordinary. An adventurer, he is closest to Prokop in *Krakatit.* If Čapek did not pose the question of Hordubal's ambiguity, and that of his wife and Manya,

until subsequently, then Case X is shown in his ambiguity in all three interpretations. The ambiguity of the immense yearning for something definite and at the same time for freedom. The ambiguity of staying, of resting, and of the feverish pursuit of a chimera (in the interpretation of the nun), of feverish activity and the feeling of the vanity of it all (the clairvoyant), boredom and intoxication (the poet). We can speak of character in Hordubal, albeit supremely 'vague'. The hero in *Meteor* defies definition by attributes, for he is formed complexly in all three interpretations—complexly and integrally, both organically and in the sense of behaviour. 'There are no attributes, there are forces, forces which interfere with each other, divert or hinder each other. And man alone, experiencing only his own presence, does not know that the little movement that he is just carrying out is a resultant vector of forces . . .' The hero was to have been of *a single piece,* but is two-and three-fold; he actively lived several lives. And it is with the story's conclusion that *An Ordinary Life* ties in.

Before the other voice appears within the hero of the last part of the Trilogy, what he says about himself and his life is smooth, conventional. But it becomes apparent that this was only a fiction that he created about himself, an untrue image of his life and himself, for even his life—though it cannot be compared with that of Case X—was not of a single piece. The first voice selected and adapted facts, muted even the abnormal to the level of the normal. The other, the polemical voice, followed the facts again, evaluating them differently, however—searching for, and finding, other motivations, lower, evil, selfish ones. And it is this yardstick that is used to measure the hero's feelings, thoughts and deeds. This other aspect still does not mean the negation of the first, which is merely deepened and supplemented, and the two together, that is, the new aspect given by their resultant, is the whole truth. Ordinariness—when the debate of the two voices stops and their dialogue ensues—is transformed into extraordinariness. The concealed appears from below the surface, and is much richer than what is apparent. What appeared orderly was not without detours and whirlpools, what appeared simple at first glance was not without its inner complexities, and what appeared integral was in fact made up of many pieces. No longer duality, ambiguity, but multiplicity. The inner solution results now, in the conclusion of *An Ordinary Life* and the entire Trilogy, in the realization that man is a crowd, that there is material enough in his life for many lives. At the pinnacle of individuation, there is the peak of dehumanization: this man and man in general.

In the working out of the heroes of *The First Rescue Party,* the collective point of view intersects the individuational. A handful of people in a situation of extreme strain, courage and comradeship, a group of people who show what they are by means of work, activity, and who are also joined by a single will in joint action. 'We', not 'I'. But also 'I', not 'we'. They are simultaneously individuals, and Čapek differentiates each one by his appearance and manner of speaking, and investigates what is behind it. Not even his labourer is of a single piece, but the things that he finds in him that are best hidden are no abysses, simply joys and pains, inclinations and predilections. When Čapek wanted to show the motivation for the determination and heroism of his miners in the situation in which we find them, he came up with miners' honour. When he investigated the motivations of the individual members of the group (characteristically, this took place in the dialogue between old man Suchánek and Standa), he naturally emerged with the willingness to help, male self-love, yes, and even conceit, but above all—and typical for Čapek—strength which must be expended somewhere. Even here Čapek prefers to accept the idea that a man does something without a plan, because it is in him, rather than that he does it intentionally.

The Life and Work of Composer Foltýn is a novel about a problem. Nevertheless, we are far from the utopias and moralities, in which problems swallowed up people. Foltýn is one of Čapek's happiest heroes, even though he is extremely specialized. Physical exterior and inner being, surface and subsurface currents approaching the near pathological, constants and development. Foltýn is—or may be—read as a symbol, but he surpasses it. Over and above what he has to say, he is himself alive. A self feigned and real, a mask and his real face. The characters of the Trilogy also had their own leitmotiv, but there they moved about and got lost in a forest of 'forces'. Foltýn analyzes himself and models himself, he has a personality and attributes. On a small, minuscule plane, the reality of Foltýn comprises definite observations, a penetrating view of his complacency, his pretense, and at the same time of his actual pain, of his lack of talent and his passionate enthusiasm for art.

Before we ask ourselves whether Čapek is a great artist in the field of character creation, we must first find out whether his goal is the creation of characters. (pp. 344-62)

Čapek's characters are most often the embodiment of ideas, and in the more successful cases, they surpass the idea, and gain a life of their own. Even those of Čapek's characters whose names have faded from our memory are 'alive', as are his complex characters whom we know by name, those whose motivations and existence have been reduced to a minimum as well as those who are internally multiple in meaning, and sometimes externally unrestrained. Čapek wrote according to the dimensions of man, to fit man's dimensions, and yet it seems that what did not come out (or what came out in an extremely specialized manner) was precisely—man. The causes for this are literary, internal. From the time that the author started his duel with the philosopher, and instead of a picture of reality started to present its interpretation, types and characters are considered something secondary, and conception, formal ability, take first place in evaluation. This is the kind of author that Čapek is. There are also deeper determining factors, and Čapek never overcame them—the alienation of man from himself, the deterioration of his organic social relationships, the sharp rift between reality and the inner world. Both of his extreme approaches are evidence that even he lost sight of the whole, that man remained a fragment in his fiction as well.

No matter how they were created, Čapek's characters are one thing and his heroes another. His characters must be distinguished from his heroes, the dramatis personae of his works from those for whom his heart beats strongly. There are naturally places where the two overlap. But Čapek is greatly wronged by a unilateral interpretation that makes them identical, that calls his little figures his heroes. (pp. 363-64)

Čapek presents his common, mediocre, ordinary people from the very beginning in such a manner that it appears at first glance that there are no objections to their situation or their lot. In reality, however, there is a constant battle from the very start. It is, to put it in the extreme, a struggle between the cult and the apotheosis of the little man, and the almost derisive criticism of this man.

Are the painful, embarrassing, mediocre lives in *Painful Tales*—by far not 'peaks of perfection, high and grand souls'—Čapek's ideal? They are rather something that he takes under his wing, something that he would like to justify, something with which he sympathizes, but towards which, on the other hand, he is not as forbearing as he would like to be. The little man, but not as an ideal, more like a necessary evil, or better yet, the lesser evil of the bourgeois society.

Is Čapek's ideal the Professor from The Outlaw? The Professor who realizes sadly that he has lost himself, that he has not grown, that he has not become an integral, free personality, that he has remained a fragment, as Vítek, in *The Macropulos Secret*, says for him, for himself, and for others as well. That he remained a fragment, because he had to reach for bread? Yet bread, material abundance does not solve the problem of an integral personality, according to Čapek . . . Čapek's heroes do not want to be anything else than they are, they are satisfied with themselves and their lot. The Professor is not.

Are Čapek's heroes the figures who sit down to feast on sausages at the end of *The Factory for the Absolute*? In the endeavour to build something positive, an unfortunate thing happened to Čapek. He subnormalized his picture of the intellectual norm, and what emerged sometimes shows a marked resemblance to caricature. For what else than a caricature are those who sit at the table and take part in the festive supper at the Damohorskýs'?

Is Čapek's hero to be found in the carnal Misfit from the comedy *Adam the Creator*? No matter what, Misfit is a caricature, this time approaching the cruel. Čapek in his desperation went too far, overshot the mark. The result is almost a provocation, self-ridicule, autosatire.

Are his heroes the people and the characters in the [*Tales from Two Pockets*], all those jovial policemen and detectives, robbers and thieves, pedants and milktoasts, harmless maniacs and collectors, deformed by their professions or interests? Altogether justifiedly, these are the ones—as the most characteristic of his little people—who are linked with Čapek's name. But Čapek does not even standardize these figures without irony. (pp. 366-68)

It is without doubt the ordinary man of the Trilogy who is Čapek's hero. He surpasses fragmentariness in Čapek's thoughts by means of a rich inner life. Thus he reaches integrality, an imaginary integrality, an integrality that borders on the metaphysical, for it is gained in the first two books by a passiveness, by a relinquishing of power, to be built; in the last book, on possibilities, not on their realization. On what man could be, not on what he is.

When after the Trilogy, Čapek turns to history, not much remains of the deeper concept of the ordinary man as he appeared in the Trilogy. On the contrary, his insect form reappears, this time in the shape of the newts. What appeared in caricature before, is now graduated to satire. In the novel *The War with the Newts*, this attitude is all the more strange in that its solution is left to time. The contradiction diminishes as soon as we realize that the position from which Čapek is leading his attack is not the position of the little man, that these positions are far beyond that concept. The little man Povondra is on the intellectual level of the Newt in the London zoo. Not only is his only reading matter the newspapers, but he even collects newspaper clippings, and has found the sense, the meaning of his life in this collection. . . . For the first time in Povondra, the criticism of the ordinary man reaches a peak—a criticism of the man who in the *Tales* still did not want to know anything about the world, and when circumstances led him to the necessity of so doing, he became a deplorable figure. The good-natured smile of Karel Čapek was distorted into a grimace, and this all the more so in that some of the illusions that we find in Povondra's political opinions are Čapek's own. Faith in contracts and agreements, in neutrality, the conviction that what is far away cannot come closer, that it is not our concern.

The second culmination of this criticism is in the drama *The White Plague.* The picture of the household of a white-collar worker is no less pointed than the praise of family life in the [*Insect Comedy*]. The portrait of the Father, who once again uses the newspapers as the source of his culture, after the manner of the newts, is a keen variation of Povondra. He condemns his own children for seeing an opportunity to find employment by taking advantage of the fact that older people are susceptible to the white plague, but he forgets this when the same white plague removes his competitors, rubbing his hands and saying 'Thank God for that leprosy!' Which need not, but might well be a 'paraphrase' of the words of the then well-known politician who said 'Thank God for fascism'. Even when the world is crumbling, this bourgeois, this ideal father, this maniac of personal profit and of success as just payment for 'honest work' does not want to give up his chance for his yearned-for promotion, even if it should mean the death of his wife . . . He cannot be expected to give up something that he has been working towards all his life, can he? And Galén, in an anti-Čapek tone, replies, 'A man can't ask things of people'.

Where did Čapek's benevolence disappear?

Is the little man, then, Čapek's hero? Without doubt he is, but not without irony, not without sorrow, not without the need to make him deeper, and not without the author's critical attitude. He apparently was meant to be a symbol of normality in an age which appeared to Čapek and to many others to have gone mad, or at least to have set out on the road to madness. In other words, the little man is not Čapek's primary, spontaneous ideal, the ideal that he was 'born' with. He arrived at this ideal, he created him with intention, from his programme, from his polemics with the great.

This is one side of the coin, which in itself is not without ambiguity. The other side of the coin has something else stamped on it, and it, too, is not without its contradictions.

The little person—though he is in the lead as far as characters and attitude are concerned—is not Čapek's sole ideal, the only thing that is on his mind. Even if it does not seem probable that the man who set up as his ideal the determination to be ordinary would go beyond his own programme, still it happened, both in theory and in practice.

It is no accident that articles such as the one about the integral American are to be found at the beginning of Čapek's oeuvre. He attempted to embody his image of a free and integral man very early. First, together with his brother in the neo-classicist novelettes in *The Luminous Depths,* in the characters who yearn for an unbroken life. Later, independently, in the character of the Outlaw, more free than integral, for this first of Čapek's rebels is not the bearer of something that is greater than he. He is a sensory, elementary type whose law is self-realization. The Outlaw is a hero for himself.

The 'first' book to enthrall Čapek was not a volume of heroic ballads, but a book of natural history. In his utopias however, he nevertheless circles the ordinary man without ceasing, and also the image of 'unlimited, free and sovereign people' (Domin). When in 1923 he wrote an article about whether the theatre has outlived its time, he expressed the opinion that the theatre is still timely. But the dramatic artist must write of man

> in his intimacy and in his moments of supreme strain, he must include in his play those great forces that determine human life, forces that are revealed to us step by step by biology, sociology, economy . . . If today's man has remained a dreamer, passionate and yearning for expression, he has grown into this image by the simultaneous influence of natural and social forces . . . That is why it is necessary that the poet of our day master facts as yet unknown, complex and exciting problems, glowing and terrible dreams. He can make use of collective psychology as well as individual psychology, and he can study the heroism of ideas as well as inner simplicity.

'The heroism of ideas as well as inner simplicity . . .' That is the dual problem that is the axis of Čapek's entire oeuvre. This is the key in which his greatest, sharpest tension is played. Utopias, collective psychology, the allegorical nature of Čapek's art, all these cause the struggle between the heroic and the simple, the natural, the battle between activity and resignation to be fought by figures that are more like points of view than like living people, so that they may be considered to be mere representatives of ideas. There is, however, still the novel *Krakatit,* and its hero Prokop. Here we can measure the emotional depth of the struggle deep within Čapek himself, that is, we can see to what extent the whole struggle is not only a matter of his strong intellectual interest, but a matter of his emotional enthusiasm, something that literally accompanies Čapek throughout his whole life. The hero also represents something, has a mission, but yet he experiences that struggle believably and authentically within himself. Prokop is undoubtedly the one who competes for Čapek's love and his admiration. Just like the Outlaw, the directors in *R.U.R.,* Marek and Case X, just like all his rebels, Čapek calls Prokop back. He is the one who, for Čapek, represents the evil force, nature, who threatens to sweep aside everything human. In contradiction with his literary theory Čapek did not want to achieve, in his fiction, merely the realization of the demand that heroes of popular literature achieve something, that they finish what they started. His advice, given to poets, to 'hover anxiously over life and endeavour . . . to entice from life answers that are magnanimous, pure and heroic', was followed by him in his utopias in the sense of the heroic determination to be ordinary—regardless of the sub-text. Not even in *Krakatit* is it a matter of a magnanimous reply. And yet it is important, from the objective point of view, that Prokop's oscillation between unrestrainedness and self-limitation, between rule, power, and help, service, does not wind up in passive standing by, but in action. And subjectively, from the point of view of understanding Čapek himself, it is certainly important that he demonstrated Prokop's struggle with an intimate knowledge of it. This would be impossible for an author who would not be speaking to a large extent for himself. 'Heroism of ideas as well as inner simplicity, glowing and terrible dreams'. This was Čapek's own dilemma.

The First World War determined Čapek's human ideal for

a long time. Čapek approved, tolerated, understood. The threat of a new war, which was due to come and was no longer only on the horizon, changed his attitude. He was unwilling to include the 'truth' of fascism either into his broad pluralist system or into his moral universe. He reactivated his democratic ideal. What had been working in the hindwind of history, openly or covertly, now took centre stage.

In relation to man, a change of attitude, as we have seen, is evident on one hand in the increased criticism of his intellectual and moral qualities, his Philistine comprehension of historical moments, his insect selfishness. On the other hand, it is apparent in the manner in which Čapek sends him—heretofore a passive bystander—out to make history, the manner in which he draws him into collective activity. From this point of view, Galén's individual campaign—objectively no more than a moral gesture—represents, subjectively, a turning point in Čapek's development. This is elaborated upon in **The First Rescue Party.** Čapek wanted to go beyond the self-alienation, the isolation of man—to be found in his first books—by means of the conviviality of small groups in his utopias—primarily in **The Factory for the Absolute.** It was more of a 'taproom' conviviality, a companionability that cost its members nothing. In the **Tales,** the participants only 'paid' for it by their participation in the episodes. The hero of **An Ordinary Life** must already put forth a certain amount of effort in order to gain the feeling of conviviality and fraternity. The heroes of **The First Rescue Party** do not live an easy life, they do not meet on the platform of narratives nor do they analyze. They find themselves faced daily with things as fundamental as sacrifice and death, they meet on the soil of common danger and common action, naturally, matter-of-factly. From the individual in **The White Plague,** to the group of men in **The First Rescue Party,** to the family in **The Mother.** This is not the family in the comedy **From the Insect World,** nor the one from the **Tales.** In the tale 'The Telegram,' people behave normally and naturally only when it is a matter of little and common affairs, 'but as soon as they find themselves in unusual . . . situations, it's as if an entirely new person got into them . . . they burst forth primarily with bravery, prestige, self-sacrifice, and other such heroic and high-principled attributes'. It is not the family from **The White Plague.** It is not the family from **An Ordinary Life,** where man 'sits in the golden glory of the lamp of home', and feels that he 'has his own private world of intimacy, sympathy and comfort'. Nor is it the family of Čapek's feuilletons, in which the intimate light of the lamp of home becomes an object of worship. 'In the circle of the family lamp' in **The Mother** (as Čapek says in the preliminary notes to the play)—no matter how we evaluate the motivations of the individual characters, their heroism and their objective significance—it is a matter of unusual situations, which Čapek keeps on the level of the natural determination to act in the manner that is necessary. The strongest, most emotional situation, the most unusual situation, when the mother sends her last son to war, is simultaneously the simplest. (pp. 368-75)

> *Alexander Matuška, in his* Karel Čapek: An Essay, *translated by Cathryn Alan, George Allen & Unwin Ltd., 1964, 425 p.*

WILLIAM E. HARKINS   (essay date 1964)

[*An American educator and critic, Harkins wrote the first book-length biography of Čapek in English. In the following excerpt, he opposes placing too much importance on Čapek's influence on utopian and science fiction, arguing instead that his most significant legacy is the political philosophy outlined in his works.*]

Karel Čapek's world reputation rests today primarily on his utopian dramas and novels and his science fiction. To the ordinary reader he is known only as the author of the play about robots, **R.U.R., The Insect Comedy,** and **The War with the Newts,** but not very much else. His fantastic play, **The Makropulos Secret,** was recently revived in New York with great success. And if Čapek has been influential in world literature, one must admit that it has been primarily as a writer of utopian and science fiction.

We may grant that in fact the themes of Čapek's scientific fantasies are significant and striking. His prophetic anticipation in **Factory for the Absolute** and **Krakatit** of later developments in the field of atomic energy was brilliant. Especially successful was his masterly choice of the robot as a symbol in **R.U.R.** The robot stands as a complex expressionistic symbol of both the power of the machine to free man from toil, thus bringing utopia, and the danger that, in removing the element of conflict from human life, a mechanized civilization may in turn dehumanize man, may "robotize" him. This fusion of two meanings in a single symbol was an inspired act of artistic compression; viewed purely as symbolism, **R.U.R.,** for all its faults, is a masterpiece of the expressionistic drama. Moreover, the symbol is a thoroughly dramatic one: the actors who portrayed robots in the first Prague production were able to express eloquently the idea of a mechanized humanity by their stiffness of movement and gait.

Yet, in spite of all their apparent modernity, the scientific fantasies of Čapek strike us today as dated. The warnings against the dangers of a technological civilization sounded in **R.U.R.** or **Factory for the Absolute** seem almost irrelevant for our own age. For the machine has not freed man from conflict; rather, it has brought new conflicts of its own, not the least of which is that of atomic fission. Nor is our machine paradise free from toil, and perhaps no one is busier than the family which dwells in the modern American suburban utopia.

The question of the value of Čapek's scientific fantasies as art leads us to the more general question of the value of all science fiction as art. . . . Man is first and foremost a creature who loves and hates, who is born and dies, and only secondarily a creature who may fly through outer space or travel to the depth of the oceans. The world of science is ultimately unsuitable subject matter for a great literature, because science has no immediate or compulsive symbolic significance for man's spirit and his fundamental needs. This is true in spite of the fact that science and technology satisfy certain of those needs, such as food and clothing. The link between science and its technological products is a purely rational one which can hardly appeal to the creative imagination. The work of science and its effects on human life are the proper subject matter of philosophy or sociology, but not of literature, which is concerned with less rational symbols. Science is not directly involved with any of what we might call the "eternal themes" of literature: the quest for God, the good, self-realization, love, happiness, freedom, the relation of the individual to society, the revolt of youth against age, etc.

Of course it is true that the world of science may serve as a source of irrational and moving symbols which are capable of appealing to our imagination and becoming art. And so science has actually been used by the surrealists in their

A scene from a 1965 Czechoslovakian production of The Insect Play.

painting and literature. One thinks of Nezval's long poem, *Edison,* for example. But this surrealistic use goes beyond science itself, and is not what we usually mean by science fiction.

But are not Čapek's expressionist symbols—robots, newts, insects—just such irrational expressive symbols of eternal literary themes, of man's eternal needs? Čapek wrote of *R.U.R.* that he conceived the play as a eulogy to man, that he wanted to view human life in retrospect and say, as his character Hallemeier does in the play, "It was a great thing to be a man." And Čapek comments: "Technology, progress, ideals, faith—all these were rather only illustrations of humanity than the sense of the play." And to the extent that this idea of man's passing from the earth is realized in *R.U.R.,* the play is great. But one must add that this note of eulogy is not the principal one and not the final one. *R.U.R.* is a failure, . . . and the author himself once admitted to Dorothy Thompson that it was the worst of all his plays, one which he no longer wished to see on the stage, and did not see again until he was trapped in a small Czech provincial town by the manager of the local theater.

The same is true of *The Makropulos Secret.* This play achieves greatness at those moments when it gives us an insight into the horror and tedium of the life of Elena Makropulos, who has used an elixir to prolong her existence because she is afraid of death. The horror of death is an eternal literary theme. But Čapek, the philosophical relativist,

finds death to be a good thing; as he and his brother had remarked rather bathetically in *The Insect Comedy:* "Jeden se narodí a jeden umře, a pořád je lidí dost" (One is born and one dies, and always there are people enough). Čapek fails to see the tragedy of individual death; if society is immortal, still the individual must die, and the immortality of society is no sure compensation for one's own death. In *The Makropulos Secret* Čapek is preoccupied with a philosophical concern lest longer life constitute a burden for man, but he overlooks a gripping, "eternal" theme of literature: the tragedy of individual death.

The finest of Čapek's fantasies is doubtless his novel, *War with the Newts.* But it is hardly a fantasy of science. One must distinguish clearly between science fiction and the classical genre of the utopian novel. In the utopian novel, science may serve to transplant man to a strange world or to travel ahead or backward in time; the journey, however, is no mere flight of fancy, but a means of revealing to the reader the vices of his own world all the more sharply and objectively. This is the classical technique of Swift's great satire, *Gulliver's Travels,* and in fact *The War with the Newts* is far more like Swift than H. G. Wells.

Secondly, Čapek's utopian works are vitiated by that very philosophy of relativism which he preached so ardently in the early 1920's. Unlike Maeterlinck or Pirandello, who perceived that the relativism of each man's isolated truth involved individual man in tragic isolation, Čapek tried to believe that life could be enriched by a multiplicity of truths. Yet metaphysical relativism could only imply ethical relativism: if each man has his own truth, then each man's conduct is also somehow right. Quite this far Čapek was not prepared to go; he was too idealistic and sensitive to moral issues, and such a philosophy would have involved the world in an ethical anarchy as total as the ethical anarchy which he sees resulting from absolutism in *Factory for the Absolute.* Ethical relativism could serve to justify all forms of political expediency; it is perhaps no accident that Čapek abandoned relativism and undertook a new search for absolutes just at the end of his life, at a time when it was necessary to strengthen the Czechoslovak will to resist Nazi aggression. The truth of relativism would imply that fascism was somehow "just as right" as democracy.

Among Čapek's works it is his most ardent defenses of relativism, such as *Factory for the Absolute* or *Adam the Creator,* which are the worst artistic failures. If the search for the Absolute is one of literature's eternal themes, the defense of relativism is not. There is an almost unbelievable bathetic quality in the final scene of *Factory for the Absolute,* in which some of the leading characters gather in a tavern to eat sausages and sauerkraut and drink beer and discuss the triumph of the relativist philosophy. And it was only when Čapek, like his contemporary Pirandello, could grasp the tragedy of relativist existence, the existential anxiety to which it exposed the individual, that he could achieve greatness. This discovery came, almost belatedly, with the first novel of his trilogy, *Hordubal.*

The real legacy of Karel Čapek is political. Such a statement may come as a surprise, for at first sight Čapek's political accomplishments seem rather slight. His articles on political questions, collected in *O věcech obecných, čili ZOON POLITIKON,* are on the whole rather undistinguished and uninteresting; an exception might be made only for the eloquent **"Proč nejsem komunistou" ("Why I Am Not a Communist"),** and for one or two articles such as **"Betlém" ("Bethlehem")** and **"O malých poměrech" ("On a Small Scale"),** in which he finds fault with those of his countrymen who apologize for all Czechoslovak shortcomings by pointing to the small scale of Czechoslovak life. (In a healthy regionalism and localism Čapek sees the roots of a vigorous culture, not a weak one.) If Čapek's political theorizing is mildly interesting, his practical action in the field of politics was to prove less successful. The attempt to found a Czechoslovak Labor Party—Strana práce—in the mid-1920's, an attempt which he actively supported, was a disastrous failure, and his noble efforts to stiffen the resistance of his country against Nazi Germany were rendered futile by the betrayal of Czechoslovakia by her allies.

Čapek's whole relation to politics and political thought was confused and in a sense contradictory, and for this reason, too, it may seem strange to call his real legacy political. In the recently published second part of her reminiscences of her two uncles, the Brothers Čapek, Helena Koželuhová characterizes Karel as rather less interested in them as he was interested in everything. The portrait she gives of the brothers is perhaps oversimplified; in her book they appear as political neutrals for whom neutralism and lack of political identification is something quite normal. This characterization no doubt conforms most closely to Karel in earlier life, but one can hardly reconcile it with his later activity as supporter of

the Strana práce, biographer of Masaryk, president of the Czech P.E.N. club, opponent of Communism, or critic and foe of Nazism. Still one must confess that in fact there was a streak of political neutralism in Čapek, and a generous one; his view of life is deeply esthetic, and he celebrates life as good as much because of its beauty and variety as for its moral perfectibility. Čapek the hobbyist, the gardener, the European traveller, photographer, collector of exotic phonograph records, the patient observer of nature who could spend an entire journey by rail in winter observing the formation of "ice flowers" on the windows of the railroad car—this Čapek was an esthete first and foremost, and political man only second.

Conventionally, Čapek has been celebrated as a great democrat, and such he no doubt was, but his faith in democracy was not unlimited; at times he seems inclined to a degree of individualism which can hardly be reconciled with democracy, and which one might best describe as anarchist. Čapek himself used the latter term to S. K. Neumann when he said, "I think that I am almost an anarchist, that that is only another name for my individualism, and I think that you will understand it in that sense as opposed to collectivism." Critics such as Václav Černý have long ago pointed out the deepseated conflicts in Čapek between an optimistic and a pessimistic view of life, between faith in the collective and fear lest its power destroy the individual. In none of Čapek's works where destruction threatens man—in *R.U.R., Factory for the Absolute, Krakatit, Adam the Creator,* or *The War with the Newts*—does democracy intervene to save man from destruction. As late as in his drama *The White Plague* (1937), Čapek expresses his distrust of the masses, so easily misled by demagogues. And it is the democratic colossi of the Western World who are a principal target of his satire in *The War with the Newts.* Čapek's democracy may seem in the last analysis to be little more than an acceptance of the least of all possible evils.

Yet in the trilogy of three novels, *Hordubal, Meteor,* and *An Ordinary Life,* Čapek has laid down a philosophical foundation for democracy which is well-nigh unique in modern literature. The trilogy was Čapek's masterpiece, free from the artistic defects and shallow relativism typical of his writing of the 1920's. Professor René Wellek has described the trilogy as "one of the most successful attempts at a philosophical novel in any language", and so indeed it is.

From a philosophical point of view, Čapek's trilogy has been analyzed from two standpoints, first, as a study of how man apprehends truth; in the trilogy, Čapek moves from a relativist epistemology to a more sophisticated perspectivism: he finds that the different views of reality which individual men obtain are analogous to the different perspectives which may be joined together to depict truth. Thus the divergent accounts of the unknown victim of the plane crash in *Meteor* may be combined to produce human truth, if not the truth of one human being's life. This epistemological or noetic theme is joined to a metaphysical one: the analysis of the nature of individual man. Less appreciated in the trilogy is the fact that in dealing with the question of the nature of individual existence, Čapek has also faced the question of the individual's relation to society, for the individual can be defined completely only if his relation to society is also defined. In the trilogy, Čapek has answered this question of the individual's relation to society in a positive, democratic spirit. In doing so he has indicated the possibility of an escape for modern man from the existential prison of individualism, and laid down at least the foundation of an acceptable philosophy of democracy. The success of his achievement is almost unique in an age when literature is largely devoted to the expression of scepticism or despair, particularly in dealing with the individual's relation to the world or to society.

The tripartite division of the trilogy suggests the triad formula of dialectic: thesis, antithesis, and synthesis. The first novel of the trilogy, **Hordubal,** is our thesis: all men are separate and distinct, and no man can know the truth of another man's life. The police and court can convict Hordubal's murderers, but they cannot understand the depth of Hordubal's pathetic love for Polana. Hordubal is a figure of isolation rendered tragic by the incommunicability of his deepest feelings. His friendship with animals is sensitively treated by Čapek in order to underscore the pathos of his inability to communicate his feelings to his fellow men. In this novel Čapek has finally realized that the relativism of truths which he had earlier celebrated as a positive good would in fact doom the individual to the prison of self, and each man's truth would remain forever mute, incommunicable. This pessimistic implication of relativism underlies the tragedy of the novel's leading character, and finds its tragic expression in the closing sentence: "The heart of Juraj Hordubal was lost somewhere and never buried."

Meteor is the antithesis. Granted that the "detectives" of the novel—the two doctors, the nurse, the writer and the clairvoyant—who try to reconstruct the life of the unknown victim of the plane crash can only speculate concerning his past. Still, because they are human, they can understand the essence of humanity, of what it is to be a man. They cannot know what has happened in a man's life, but they can know what a man is capable of experiencing, just because he is a man. The clairvoyant of the novel expresses it in an eloquent image comparing man's life to the cycle which water undergoes in its passage from sea to sky and back via the earth to the sea again. Just so, man's life always remains human, no matter what particular form it may take. Life, then, is simply the totality of what is possible to life, and a single life is the potentiality of experiencing all events which are possible. Thus an individual man may transcend his isolation and come to a sympathetic understanding of his fellows, for his experience is also theirs.

An Ordinary Life is the synthesis of the trilogy. A retired railway official writes the story of his life. At first it seems a quiet, simple, good, and contented life, in everything, a quite "ordinary life". But then, from some subconscious depth, forgotten voices remind him of suppressed longings and experiences; the "ordinary man" he has become is only one of a diversity of persons which existed within him. He concludes that perhaps each man has the potentiality of becoming all men, but must necessarily restrict himself in development to realizing only certain potentialities. And so the plurality of men in external society corresponds to the plurality of personalities within each man. We are given a basis for understanding the truth of another man's life; we may know other men, for we ourselves are potentially like them. Each man is a microcosm which mirrors all human society. "Have you ever seen anyone, brother, who couldn't be *your brother?*" one of the inner group of voices asks the "ordinary man". And Čapek comments in the epilogue to the novel that "this is just the reason why we can know and understand plurality, because we ourselves are such a plurality".

Thus a firm foundation is laid down for the brotherhood and

equality of all men. The individual is no prisoner of existential isolation; within him are resources for bridging the gap which seems to separate him from other men. He can know them as aspects of himself and hence he can accept them.

Perhaps Čapek would have gone on to develop his ideas on social democracy further. But the times were against him. The creative freedom and calm which he had enjoyed while composing the trilogy were cut off by the spectre of the rise of Nazi Germany and the threat of war. Paradoxically, it may have been the need to oppose Nazism which turned his attention from the problem of democracy as such; his energies had to be devoted to the attack on fascism, and the superiority of democracy had in a sense to be taken for granted.

But one more concept was added to Čapek's theory of democracy. In **The First Rescue Party** we have a novel of heroism and the need to defend society in the face of a common danger. The novel is an allegory of democratic society defending itself heroically against aggression. The rescue brigade succeeds because of its democratic cooperation, just as democracy is justified in using the political powers of social organization to defend itself against aggression. As the Czech critic Oldřich Králík has recently pointed out, **The First Rescue Party** makes what is in a sense the obverse of the point of **An Ordinary Life.** In the earlier novel one man proves to contain many different personalities. In **The First Rescue Party** a number of individuals merge together into a single group which has its own spirit and distinct personality. The two novels, taken together, supply a humanistic foundation for a philosophy of democracy.

More than this Čapek was not destined to accomplish. The tragedy of his homeland and his premature death cut short the philosophical and creative development of a great writer, a profound thinker, and a great human spirit. (pp. 60-7)

> William E. Harkins, "The Real Legacy of Karel Čapek," in The Czechoslovak Contribution to World Culture, edited by Miloslav Rechcigl, Jr., Mouton & Co., 1964, pp. 60-7.

WILLIAM E. HARKINS   (essay date 1974)

[*In the following essay, Harkins outlines the major themes of Čapek's utopian and science fiction and evaluates* The Absolute at Large.]

Karel Čapek has been much celebrated as a writer of science fiction and drama, but many readers may have no conception of the wide range of his entire creation. In fact Čapek also wrote philosophical novels, psychological tales and detective stories, as well as essays, causeries and newspaper columns on an immense variety of subjects. Yet his works on science themes constitute a single line of work with its own continuity of development. This line goes back to an immature but strikingly provocative tale called **"The System"** (1908), which Čapek wrote at the age of eighteen with his elder brother Josef. The story describes an American manufacturer's scheme for keeping his workers in line by insulating them from every kind of spiritual or esthetic influence. Their pastimes, displays of emotion and spiritual pursuits are all strictly controlled. Their sexual lives, too, are carefully regulated as to frequency and conditions: no light is permitted on such occasions, lest the workmen idealize the experience and develop a dangerous and potentially nihilistic sense of beauty. The system breaks down when a supervisor fails to extinguish a light and a workman is permitted to see the object of his passion. The shock is too much for him, and under its impact he rebels and leads a violent and bloody uprising against his employer. The story is a humorous burlesque, of course, but it does contain a germ of seriousness in its picture of the dehumanizing effect of modern life, its social organization and its technology.

In the melodrama *R.U.R.* (*Rossum's Universal Robots,* 1921), his most celebrated work, Čapek put robots on the stage and so expressed in dramatic form the same theme of the mechanization of human life and the dehumanization it may cause. The subject is worked out with a uniquely theatrical device: robots appear on the stage, marching stiffly but more or less like human beings; in the end they rise in revolt and annihilate the human race. The novel *War with the Newts* (1936) is a later treatment of the same theme (a race of intelligent, man-size newts is enslaved by man but multiplies beyond control and threatens man's destruction), and is the closest of these works in its tone and structure to *The Absolute at Large*. A melodramatic comedy, *The Makropulos Secret* (1922), investigates the effect of immortal life and its total incapacity to bring man happiness. *Adam the Creator* (1927), another comedy, this one written jointly with Brother Josef, illustrates in witty fashion man's inability to improve on God's creation.

Though all of these works are distinct, through all of them runs a single philosophic leit-motif: Čapek's fear of titans and absolutes and his preference for the contained, the small, the relative, the varied: man's spiritual strength, in his view, derives from the variety and complexity of his being, and any absolute ideas or system applied from without to make him conform, even to some absolute "good," will only bring impoverishment and slavery to the human spirit. In politics, absolutism for Čapek means totalitarianism and tyranny; in religion, bigotry; in social life, conformity of thought.

This theme is provocatively exploited in *The Absolute at Large* (1922); the original Czech title means "Factory for the Absolute". For today's reader the novel no doubt seems richest in its brilliant anticipation of atomic fission and the peaceful utilization of atomic energy. Čapek, a keen student of modern scientific progress, was well aware of the atom-splitting experiments carried out by Lord Rutherford. In his later novel, *Krakatit* (1924), Čapek likewise anticipated the destructive potentialities inherent in atomic fission, and that novel, though a melodrama rather than a comic burlesque, is in a sense to be seen as a complement to *The Absolute at Large.*

In [*The Absolute at Large*] Čapek has embodied his mistrust of all absolutes, whether of religion, science, business, nationalism, the State, or whatever. Since the metaphysical Absolute that pervades all matter in the Universe is God, the absolute energy released from the atom through nuclear fission infects everyone in the vicinity of the process with a kind of religious mania. The comedy implicit in this story idea might of course have been used for an anti-religious satire, but this was not Čapek's real aim. In fact, religion, too, has its rightful place in life, and Čapek's only concern is lest it too become an absolute, insisting that everything else in life be subservient to it. More than religion, the satiric target of Čapek's humor here is man's search for a utopian order guaranteed to solve all his problems and bring him happiness. As in the play *R.U.R.,* man is provided with an invention that makes utopia possible—in this case the invention is atomic fission,

releasing vast quantities of energy at negligible cost. The religious fervor felt by men in the vicinity of the atom-splitting process is actually the second of the two classic prerequisites for a utopia: (1) a supply of unlimited energy; and (2) man's readiness to renounce the profit motive in favor of the common social good. Religious fervor causes people to give away all that they have, but this only leads to social and economic chaos, as does the superfluity of productive energy itself, for economic goods have meaning and value only when there is relative scarcity. Overproduction bogs down the economy just when unselfish idealism robs the economic system of its very rationale.

We may ask why Čapek employed such a subject for a satiric comedy, when the story material was suitable for many other types of literary treatment. The customary form of science fiction is not tragedy or comedy (though these are doubtless possible), but the adventure melodrama. The choice of form in *The Absolute at Large* derives not from the theme of atomic fission, but from an age-old satirical, "utopian" literary tradition that reaches back to Voltaire's *Candide* and includes Anatole France's parody of human history, *Penguin Island.* In this work Čapek is closer to the utopian fantasies of Swift, including *Gulliver's Travels,* than to the classic form of science fiction created and popularized by H. G. Wells. One may perhaps regret that Čapek did not choose to write a melodrama on the theme of *The Absolute at Large,* as he did in *Krakatit,* but one can hardly regret the lively, often hilarious comedy of the . . . novel.

In 1926 Čapek wrote an "apology" which he printed as a preface to the book edition of *The Absolute at Large.* The novel had originally been published serially in thirty weekly installments in the newspaper *Lidové noviny,* and Čapek's critics had taken a rather dim view of its serial form, which they found lacking in seriousness. But in fact the serial is an ideal literary form for science fiction and has often been used for the genre, since it permits the author to shift the scene, characters and point of view with maximum freedom. True, this freedom can be a dangerous temptation; Čapek obviously never expected his novel to become a classic, and the present-day American reader will hardly find much humor in topical references to Čapek's friends and contemporaries such as the Czech literary historian Arne Novák, or in the comic treatment of the provincial Moravian town of Hradec Králové, which happened to be the place where Čapek had gone to high-school.

Besides the serialized form and the inconsistencies of form and style (actually a richness in the novel, to my own way of thinking), Čapek's critics objected to the break in the novel that occurred after the twelfth chapter. This is the point where the novel shifts from a story about a small number of well-characterized individuals to a mass chronicle of world events. True, the individual characters are not entirely lost; they survive with an amazing tenacity in view of the endless wars, crusades and barbaric invasions that inundate every part of the world, and they return at the novel's end to take part in its comic apotheosis, the sausage and sauerkraut feast. This seemingly bathetic close symbolizes Čapek's faith in individuals and in smallness; he loves men who have their own faces and individualized natures, but fears the faceless mass, as another form of the absolute. Society for Čapek is (or ought to be) a collection of individuals among whom should prevail the greatest conceivable diversity of mind and spirit. The shift from the individual to the mass chronicle and back again to the individual does not really harm the novel, for the subject itself and the logic of its events, as well as the novel's philosophic theme, demand that we follow such a shift: the whole world is caught up in the madness brought about by the release of the absolute in matter. What is perhaps at fault here is that Čapek was not so original in giving us a chronicle of events on a world-wide scale (he drew rather heavily on Anatole France's *Penguin Island* for inspiration here, and he had only a limited clairvoyance where world events in the 1940s were concerned).

Today, in 1973, the reader may well have difficulty in recognizing the world Čapek projected for 1943: we find Russia still ruled by a tsar, for instance. Writing in 1922, Čapek had no more faith in the future of the Soviet Revolution than he had in the short-lived Hungarian Revolution of 1919. China appears in the novel as a state ruled by "mandarins." Yet Communism is very much present in the book, if only implicitly, as one of the many forms of utopian ideology. Japan appears as militaristic, as indeed it was in 1943, but there is no political figure resembling either Hitler or Mussolini, although the latter was very much alive in 1922, and fascism an emerging force. As a purely political satire the novel fails, no doubt, but Čapek was partly to repair its deficiencies in his later serialized novel, *The War with the Newts,* in which both the communist and fascist totalitarian systems are satirized.

Still, with all its faults, *The Absolute at Large* remains a classic. The original idea that animates it—the release of "religious" energy in the course of the fission process—is inspired and brilliant. The narrative tone is lively and infectious, the characters are alive, perfectly credible and close to the reader. In this rollicking tale Čapek has produced an achievement very rare indeed, a hilarious comedy in the science fiction genre. (pp. iii-vii)

        William E. Harkins, in an introduction to The Absolute at Large *by Karel Čapek, Hyperion Press, Inc., 1974, pp. iii-vii.*

BARBARA BENGELS   (essay date 1982)

[*In the following essay, Bengels focuses on what she considers a prominent theme in* R.U.R.: *the importance of having a knowledge of history.*]

Perhaps the most ironic, thought-provoking—and subtle—key to imagery in Karel Čapek's *R.U.R.* is the bitter speech uttered by the robot Radius in act IV. Speaking to the last surviving human, this robot who has helped to bring about man's virtual extinction says:

> Slaughter and domination are necessary if you want to be like men. Read history, read the human books. You must domineer and murder if you want to be like men. We are powerful, sir. Increase us, and we shall establish a new world. A world without flaws. A world of equality. Canals from pole to pole. A new Mars. We have read books. We have studied science and the arts. The Robots have achieved human culture.

Radius, assigned as he has been by Helena to the library, has achieved an awareness, however distorted, that the humans have failed to realize: the reading of history, the awareness of one's roots, is crucial for civilization to flourish, is, in fact,

crucial for men to be human—and this is an insight which Čapek emphasizes in a multitude of ways.

In his book *Metamorphoses of Science Fiction*, Darko Suvin says that in Čapek robots "are not only stand-ins for workers but also [are] . . . inhuman aliens 'without history'" [see *TCLC,* Vol. 6, pp. 93-5]. But in *R.U.R.* the humans too are rootless, "without history"; unlike the robots who have never had a past, however, man simply can't be bothered to remember his traditions, something Čapek makes clear from the first scene between Domain and Helena:

> HELENA. . . .Why did you call her Sulla?
> DOMAIN. Isn't it a nice name?
> HELENA. It's a man's name. Sulla was a Roman General.
> DOMAIN. Oh, we thought Marius and Sulla were lovers.
> HELENA. No. Marius and Sulla were generals, and fought against each other in the year—I've forgotten now.

Had Domain but known a bit of history, he would have remembered that Marius and Sulla were, in fact, such bitter rivals that their opposition led to tremendous bloodshed and violence for the Roman people, a story relevant to the outcome of *R.U.R.*

Not only is Domain's knowledge of history lacking, but he also—like Helena—has no aptitude for dates, so necessary for putting events into historical perspective. When he tells her of Rossum's invention, we are perhaps shocked at his ignorance: he has robots invented "in the year 1932, exactly four hundred years after the discovery of America." Even the most inattentive of schoolboys knows the traditional date of America's discovery, 1492 and not 1532, so that within the first few minutes of the play a shocking ignorance of both classical and relatively modern history is revealed in two major characters.

Throughout these early scenes, then, Čapek keeps the reader/viewer aware of the cultural history of mankind which is taken for granted by the obviously pragmatic men who run first the factory and later virtually the world. In a world where "Providence was no longer necessary," where Rossum became "a sort of scientific substitute for God," Jove is nevertheless called upon frequently, if casually, first by Berman, then later by Helman. When Domain complains of Rossum's lack of humor, he says "He could have produced a Medusa with the brain of a Socrates" and later in the play, when Helena is examining her anniversary present from Fabry, she concludes, "Why it's a Greek cameo," and Domain responds, "Apparently. Anyhow, Fabry says it is," possibly unsure of its authenticity, certainly embarrassed by Fabry's and the others' having remembered still another date—the anniversary of Helena's arrival—which he has forgotten, and even possibly unaware of what a Greek cameo is. Even later in the play when destruction is upon them, Helman's remarks are reminiscent of another Greek image. Staring out at a sea of hostile robot faces, he says, "There's a fresh lot of them again. It's as if they were sprouting out of the earth." This seems to be a significant reference to the Cadmus myth, where the Greek hero sows the field with a dragon's teeth from which spring full-grown warriors whose internecine warfare kills all but five of their own forces, those five survivors going on to begin the new civilization at Thebes. So, too, in this play man has sown the seeds of his own destruction, but even his warrior-workers can barely survive. The new world must be peopled anew, but only by the few who can survive unscathed and with an appreciation for peace and beauty, as we see in Primus and Helena the "Robotess," the Adam and Eve figures at play's end.

Even more importantly, however, names—particularly those of classic origin—play a significant part in both the action and the symbolism of the play. Čapek himself has commented on the significance of the name Rossum "whose name in English signifies Mr. Intellect or Mr. Brain." So far as the classical names are concerned, however, specially obvious are Primus, the first of a new breed of humanity at the play's end, and the *Ultima,* man's last hope. Far more subtle is the naming of the ship which brings Helena to the island: *Amelia* is a Latin name meaning "industrious, hard-working," certainly appropriate for a play where man has abrogated the need to work; whereas the *Amelia* can transport Helena in the play's beginning, too much has transpired by play's end for the *Amelia* to restore order.

The most significant and evocative name, however, is, of course, Helena's—the human woman Helena Glory. It is impossible, one would hope, for the reader/viewer to miss the allusion to Helen of Troy, but lest it not be as immediately obvious onstage as it is in the reading, Domain specifically stresses the enthralling beauty of Helena's face: "I didn't lose my head. Until today. Then as soon as you lifted your veil——." Helen's body, we may be sure, was nothing to despise, but it is her face that has become most famous: "the face that launched a thousand ships, / And burnt the topless towers of Ilium." The very name Helena suggests the word *Hellene,* or "Greek," but Helena shares a very strange and ironic relationship with her classical counterpart: whereas Helen's amorality brought about the destruction of Troy, it is Helena's pseudomorality—on behalf of the Humanity League—that brings about a far greater destruction here: the downfall of all mankind. Even her last name, Glory, forewarns in an allusory way of man's impending decline. It reminds English-speaking readers, at least, of two classically grounded quotations, the first from Edgar Allan Poe's poem "To Helen," where her "classic face . . . has brought me home / To the glory that was Greece, / And the grandeur that was Rome." Even more nostalgic and melancholy is the possible allusion to the Latin *sic transit gloria mundi,* "so passes away the glory of the world," a quotation particularly relevant to a play in which the world itself is lost.

But the play is not all gloom; it was intended to be, and is, a comedy, and the ending for both man and robots is far from hopeless. Just as Helena's humanitarian strivings have brought about the play's catastrophe, so have they also brought about its hope for the future. She has, after all, encouraged the chemical experimentation that allows the robots to experience emotions. Out of their transformation comes both the rebellion that dooms the human race and the sensitivity, the soul, that allows for a new beginning. Yes, mankind as it has existed is wiped out—not such a bad fate considering its condition, some might say. But before its demise, Čapek presents us with an ironic scene. Helena alone knows that the manuscript which might have saved them has been burnt; her response is to play the piano. Čapek suggests two equally valid interpretations of her behavior. One negative possibility is again a "classical" allusion—the popular legend of Nero fiddling while Rome burned. Čapek set the reader up for this image in the first scene, when he had Domain ask Helena, "Do you play the fiddle?" It is a dialogue

which is meant to stress how superior robots are to human workers whose needs include such irrelevancies as music. It is nevertheless a strange question, except seen as preparation for this later scene. However, as is Čapek's accustomed style, a more positive interpretation coexists with the negative: Helena's behavior is markedly human, and stresses the best qualities that differentiate humanity from machines: our creativity, our ability to hope even when there is no hope.

> ALQUIST. What's Madam Helena playing?
> DOMAIN. I don't know. She's practicing a new piece.
> ALQUIST. Oh, still practicing?

So, too, the response of the men in the play is particularly—even unusually, for them—human.

> HELMAN. My goodness, what a fine thing music is. You ought to have listened. It sort of spiritualizes, refines— —
>
> . . . . .
>
> Boys, I'm becoming a regular hedonist. We ought to have gone in for that before.
> FABRY. Gone in for what?
> HELMAN. Enjoyment. Lovely things. By Jove, what a lot of lovely things there are. The world was lovely, and we—we here—tell me, what enjoyment did we have?

Darko Suvin has correctly written that "at the end of the play, the robots again grow more like a new human order than like inhuman aliens . . . : reacquiring pain, feelings, and love, they usher in a new cycle of creation or civilization." But, equally important, mankind nearly undergoes a similar transformation, though for us it is too late. Nonetheless, the men in this scene—with their new appreciation for life and the culture that came with civilization—no longer seem to be the same pragmatists who could declare, "The timetable is more than the Gospel, more than Homer, more than the books of all the philosophers. The timetable is the most perfect product of the human spirit." It is clearly unfortunate that their heroic dreams come too late:

> . . . this little state of ours could be the center of future life. You know, a sort of small island where mankind would take refuge and gather strength—mental and bodily strength. And, by heaven, I believe that in a few hundred years it could conquer the world again.
>
> . . . . .
>
> And it will again be master of lands and oceans; it will breed rulers—a flaming torch to the people who dwell in darkness—heroes who will carry their glowing soul throughout all peoples. And I believe . . . that it will again dream of conquering planets and suns.

Had they but read history—and remembered—they would have recognized their dream as one of the most inspiring in the earlier history of mankind: our classical longings for utopia, incorporated here in the longing for universal empire, in all its very human glory, ambiguity, and irony. (pp. 13-16)

Barbara Bengels, " 'Read History': Dehumanization in Karel Čapek's 'R.U.R.','" in The Mechanical God: Machines in Science Fiction, *edited by Thomas P. Dunn and Richard D. Erlich, Greenwood Press, 1982, pp. 13-17.*

JAMES D. NAUGHTON (essay date 1984)

[*In the following excerpt, Naughton contends that in* R.U.R. *the admonitions concerning the future downfall of human society are undermined by the comedy, melodrama, and optimism of the play.*]

It has been said of Karel Čapek that his work 'gives new meaning to the precept of Protagoras, that man is the measure of all things: for he sees how man, noble and wretched, is menaced and mocked in our time' [K. Brušák, 'Čapek, Karel', *The Penguin Campanion to Literature*]. He wrote of his play *R.U.R.* (1920) that it was concerned 'not with Robots, but with people', declaring, somewhat grandiloquently: 'Imagine yourself standing over the grave of mankind; however jaundiced your view, you would surely realise the divine significance of the extinguished species and say—you too: It was a great thing to be a man.'

Yet the most obvious legacy of the play to the world of men (and the world of science fiction) is the word *Robot* and, to some extent, Čapek's re-created concept of an artificial man, a concept of course with many ancient ramifications including the classical legend of Pygmalion and Galatea and the Jewish Golem. One fairly close ancestor to the Robot is the scientifically-created monster in Mary Shelley's *Frankenstein;* another analogy is to be found in the humanised animals of H. G. Wells's *The Island of Dr. Moreau*. It must be stressed however that Čapek's Robots are quite different from the mechanical devices, automata and Dalek-like monsters for which the term *robot* is now variously applied. Čapek's Robots are biological, not mechanical: they are products of bio-engineering and look just like human beings. At first they are distinguishable on stage only by a certain stiffness of motion and demeanour; later they wear a simple military-style tunic. They are artificial humanoid beings, created by the atheistic inventor, Old Rossum, who wanted to prove that God was unnecessary. His commercially-minded nephew, the real founder of the firm (Rossum's Universal Robots, after which the play is named) simplified his over-complex semi-abortive invention into an efficient, industrially market-able mass-product. Robots are manufactured slave-labour, made in emotionless, sexless, dehumanised, soulless forms suitable for all kinds of industrial, agricultural and domestic labour. They are the ultimate labour-saving device. The word indicates their function. It is derived from the Czech *robota* meaning 'corvée, forced labour, servitude', borrowed also into German as *die Robot,* and related to the Russian *rabota* meaning simply 'work'. (pp. 72-3)

The plot of *R.U.R.* parallels in several respects that of Čapek's later novel *Válka s mloky* (*War with the Newts,* 1936). Here the newts play the role of the Robots: they build dams, reclaim land, and do all manner of undersea work for man. They are discovered, already existing, not invented, which is one reason why the novel is less futurological in effect; but, like Robots, they bring man to extinction, or to the brink of extinction. In both works the theme of siege and encirclement by alien beings looms large: destruction and encirclement are obsessive themes throughout Čapek's science fiction. In both works, likewise, Čapek portrays the danger that man's inventiveness linked to the materialist economic imperatives presents to his very survival as a species. Yet, of the two, perhaps only the play *R.U.R.* strikes a true futurological note. Both are to be read as dystopian, semi-allegorical fantasies, which display and criticise elements and trends in modern civilisation; but *War with the Newts* comes across as a satirical fantasy-image of the present, rather than a vision set in a future distinctly distanced from the 1930s. *R.U.R.* can also be seen as a fantasy-image of the present, or a timeless myth. Setting, props and dress need not be (though they may be) overtly futuristic. Apart from the Robots and their manufacture the rest of the technology in the play (guns, transport, etc.) is unblushingly contemporary. This stresses the mythical-allegorical side and rejects the uncompromising (and possibly more glamorous) futuristic approach that another writer might have adopted. However, the more markedly futuristic technological element of the Robots themselves and the historically unrelated setting give a greater sense of temporal distance than we find in *War with the Newts.* Also, unlike *War with the Newts, R.U.R.* seems concerned (in a symbolic, allegorical, non-literal kind of way) with long-distance projection of trends, as well as with satirising, through fantasy, the absurdities and blindness of man's individual and social behaviour.

Disturbing visions of the future, like fantasy images of the present, or visions avoiding any identifiable sense of time, may function as parables, allegories or metamorphoses of the contemporary world, but their specifically future setting and consequent elements of prediction (or quasi-prediction) allow them to function as warnings, as well as critiques. Their prophetic (or quasi-prophetic) qualities enhance their rhetorical exhortative force. Usually, in Western European writing at least (under which heading we include Karel Čapek, since Prague is west of Vienna), the visions of the future are disturbing, seldom uplifting, seldom intended to warm the heart. The Utopias are usually anti-Utopian. Naturally the more optimistic writers—amongst whom Karel Čapek wished to number himself—desire to see their gloomy prognostications avoided. They see their warnings as part of a wider message (not only literary) which may perhaps be heeded. The degree of overt (and covert) optimism or pessimism naturally fluctuates according to various factors including political events of the day, economic and social developments, the author's own experiences, and literary fashions. The relative absence of optimism in *War with the Newts* is clearly attributable to the hardships and absurdities of the Great Depression and the rise of Fascism and Nazism with consequent threats to the independence of Czechoslovakia and the lives of its citizens. All of this left an indelible mark on Karel Čapek's later work, its last pages written under the shadow of Munich. The earlier play, *R.U.R.,* however apocalyptic in tone, and however much partly inspired by the carnage and nationalistic madness of the First World War, excludes in its ending a curiously extraneous, facile optimism. Yet in spite of this, the play can easily be read as if fundamentally pessimistic, simply by finding the optimism hollow and unconvincing. Texts often fail to deliver their intended effect or overt message, and this seems at least partly the case with *R.U.R.* How much the overt, declarative optimism of the final scene is camouflaging a personal *Angst,* linked to a pessimistic analysis of the future human condition, is a question to which we will return briefly. . . . Perhaps it is not merely a biographical question but one relevant to certain features of the text as well. (pp. 73-4)

R.U.R. Rossum's Universal Robots is described beneath its title as a 'collective drama in three acts with a comedy prologue' (in the English version it becomes 'A Play in three acts and an epilogue' and the epilogue is headed as Act IV). The term 'collective' refers to the theme, embracing all mankind; the action on stage is in fact localised, largely semi-domestic and individual in scale: the masses remain firmly offstage. The humour of the comedy prologue is not limited to that part of the play, but spills over into the whole work, or nearly the whole work, a surprisingly large proportion of which is engagingly light-hearted, racy and facetious in tone. This produces a sometimes curious effect when light comedy and satire are blended with quite solemn attempts at lyrical evocations of the nobility of man and the tragedy of his passing. An effect of macabre farce seems to arise from the expression of an apocalyptic warning through whimsically schematic elements of plot and characterisation serving more the purposes of amusement and gentle satire than of engaging our sympathy and self-identification. Čapek's persistent instinct to create verbal and situational fun is aided and abetted by his enthusiasm for popular 'trashy' fiction—action-packed, full of fantasy, playful, fiction enjoyed as fiction—but the problem in **R.U.R.** is that it is hard to react to the expressionistic lyricism in the text when unable to take the characters or plot seriously, as if real. Moreover, as we shall perhaps demonstrate, the lyrical expressionism is generally insufficiently powerful in its own right: the danger of counterproductive bathos lurks ever-present behind the pathos.

The Prologue is set in the managing director's office at the R.U.R. factory, situated Utopia-style on an isolated island. The managing director Harry Domin (English version: Domain) is dictating letters to his Robot secretary Sulla. (Sulla is only outwardly female: male and female versions of otherwise sexless Robots are only produced for the sake of market demand: e.g. people want female secretaries. Her sexlessness is emphasised by her inappropriate name: she is paired with another, outwardly male Robot, named Marius, since those who named them imagined that Sulla and Marius were a famous pair of classical lovers.) Helena Glory (ová), young, elegant and naive, daughter of the President of R.U.R., exclusive manufacturers of Robots for the entire world market, arrives on an unannounced visit. She intends to incite the Robots to rebel against their human masters (and creators) and claim equal rights with human beings. (A parallel episode occurs in **War with the Newts.**) But, she is told, her sympathy with the down-trodden is misplaced: the Robots are insensible of justice or equality. They were manufactured without such economically and industrially useless, nay counterproductive, features. Emotions were left out of their makeup: only a sense of pain was found to be of utility. Helena is making the grave though understandable error of treating the Robots like proper human beings, whereas in fact they have no souls; they can contemplate their own destruction with equanimity, and, when they have breakdowns or fits, they can simply be sent (will send themselves) to the pulveriser.

At first Helena has difficulty in distinguishing these Robots from human beings. Later she mistakes for Robots Domin's human colleagues on the island. Her confusion leads us further on towards realising the significance of Čapek's Robots. It becomes clear that the Robots do not only represent the danger of scientific invention, of technology and industry taking over from man, depriving him of his traditional work and responsibilities. They also represent debased, dehumanised man himself, man deprived of essential features (hazily defined, mainly in terms of love and other emotions, creativity, the soul), man treated as a machine, seen as an undifferentiated mass available for exploitation, treated as an object rather than a conscious fellow-being. The concept of Robots maintains a suggestive ambiguity. Robots become multi-faceted symbols of alienation, degradation, 'soullessness', mass uni-

formity, and technological, industrial, socio-economic, depersonalising threats to individual rights and dignity.

The inventor of the Robots, Old Rossum, had no interest in their economic exploitation; his interest was scientific, philosophic, intellectual. Čapek views him with sympathy, but also with horror at the innocence of science, oblivious of its potential consequences. Domin, in explaining the history of Robot manufacture to Helena, expresses the millenarian view that the Robots will perfect human civilisation. His ideas are distinctly megalomaniac. The introduction of Robots in all branches of work will cause not just mass but total unemployment. Robots will do everything—man will do only what he loves. He will live only to perfect himself. Terrible things will perhaps occur on the way to this paradise on earth, but the ends justify the means—it will all be worth it, for the enslavement of man to man, and of man to matter, will cease. The classless society will have been born, the divisions of labour abolished. Man will be lord of creation, living in the boundless plenty produced for him by the Robots, free to pursue his own desires without encumbrance.

This exposition of ideas is neatly alleviated by the semi-farcical plot. Domin and his five colleagues at once fall in love with Helena, whose name presumably refers to Helen of Troy. There are no other women on the island at the time, though there have been previous female visitors. (Here, as often in the play, the plot is somewhat arbitrary and fanciful, but in the whimsical, almost absurdist atmosphere this seems largely right and proper.) Domin, anticipating and fearing his colleagues' likely designs, and pushed for time (time being money) proposes to Helena after only a few minutes' acquaintance, giving her five minutes to make up her mind once and for all. She is embraced by Domin and assents, and here the Prologue ends.

Act I is set in Helena's boudoir, on the tenth anniversary of her arrival. She is now married to Domin, but childless. The act is built around the dramatic irony of the contrast between the celebration of this anniversary, with gifts from her admirers, and the progressive revelation to the audience (and Helena) that disaster has struck in the world outside. Humans had given up all work and become infertile in the pursuit of pleasure, and because work was no longer necessary. There is an element of mystery or metaphysics here, as well as mere hyperbolic representation of the tendency for affluence to reduce the birth rate. Now the Robots, armed, we learn later, by men first to put down strikes, then to wage wars between nations, have turned, again mysteriously, against their masters. Man seems doomed to immediate as well as long-term extinction. Domin has an emergency plan of escape, to use his warship Ultimus to leave the island, bargaining with the Robots to exchange their lives for the formulae needed to manufacture new generations of Robots, who, as we know, are unable to reproduce themselves in the human manner. This plan is unwittingly foiled by Helena, who (somewhat arbitrarily from the point of view of futurology) burns the only copies of the formulae manuscripts in a bid to prevent further production. She is only partly aware of what has been going on. It is typical of Čapek to make developments in his plot depend on individual acts devoid of a sense of general inevitability (as opposed to some metaphysical or merely authorial hand of fate, operating in this instance through Helena's 'healthy feminine instincts'). However legitimate this may be as an analysis of certain aspects of history—the role played by accident—prophetic effect is certainly diminished by employing such devices which heighten the arbitrary fictionality of the plot (note the artificial dramatic irony of the timing of her action: a typical story-telling device). . . .

The act ends with the arrival of the revolutionary Robots by the first ship to dock for a number of days. It arrives precisely according to the normal timetable of sailings, and this is at first taken as a sign that the rebellion has been quashed. However, the opposite is the case. The punctuality is just what you would expect of the mechanistic Robots. The timetable precision symbolises both comforting regularity and disturbing dehumanised uniformity, as if it is a feature we both need and need to avoid, as human beings:

> DOMIN. Punctuality is a wonderful thing, lads. Nothing fortifies the soul like punctuality. Punctuality means order in the world. (*Raises his glass.*) To punctuality! . . .
> HALLEMEIER. When the timetable holds good, human laws hold good, God's laws hold good, the laws of the universe hold good, everything holds good that ought to hold good. The timetable is more than the Gospel, more than Homer, more than the whole of Kant. The timetable is the most perfect effusion of the human spirit.

Act II is again set in Helena's boudoir. Throughout the play there is a curious mixture of drawing-room comedy, blatantly fictional melodrama and horrifying cataclysm,—domesticity and semi-allegorical expressionism. The human beings on the island are now under siege. For a while the Robots are held back behind an electrified fence (rapidly improvised in Heath Robinson style, apparently by connection to the domestic power circuit). When the power station falls to the Robots, the lights go out and they enter the house killing all except one (nearly all offstage). Only Alquist the Builder is saved, against his will, for, as one of the Robots, Radius, says, 'He is a Robot. He works with his hands like the Robots. He builds houses. He can work.' The symbol of light in this act (and also earlier, through lightbulbs stipulated for the set) is used to express man's essential nature, his creative power, soul, and will to live, his vital spark. A lyrical passage of exchanges between contrasting human voices explores this metaphor and the human connotations of light and fire, casting our minds back across the ages of past human history. This passage is one of the attempts the text makes to attain true pathos and rhetorical power, but it hovers at best on the brink of bathos and counterproductive irony, undermined in addition by the surrounding context. Most of it was cut from the English performing version, presumably because it seemed overdone or incongruous. One might argue that this was the right thing to do, but the omission, along with other similar ones, considerably attenuates the lyrical rhetorical expressionistic atmosphere that the Czech text wishes to create; a certain dimension is lost. . . . Elsewhere the reactions to the seige and feeble defence of the house are more reminiscent of a schoolboy adventure story. The effect is more comic than awe-inspiring, particularly as the act is punctuated in an absurdist fashion by the commercial manager Busman (English version: Berman) and his obsessive drawing-up of final company balance sheets in the face of the extinction of both himself and the human race. He dies, melodramatically (offstage), touching the electric fence while endeavouring to trade his life for half a thousand million of useless money. The absurdist hyperbole and lack of an impression of true terror and despair among the besieged (brisk to the last) rob the poetic symbolism of its already flawed emotional force, while

at the same time producing a curious amalgam of banality, matter-of-factness, and doom. Man remains hopelessly down-to-earth in the face of extinction and cannot rise to the apocalyptic quality of the occasion. The text's comic, debunking features (compare Hašek's *The Good Soldier Švejk,* so different in other respects) seem in practice to outweigh the desire to move us by man's demise from this earth, to make us say, with Hallemeier: 'It was a great thing to be a man.' The shifts in tone are hard to accommodate, and a persistent sense of dispassionate fictional playfulness is never altogether dispelled.

Act III is set in the factory laboratory on the island, and is the least domestic, least representational. Alquist is alone, the last human being on earth. All searches for others have proved in vain. He has been ordered (as the only creatively thinking being) to re-discover the formulae for making Robots, but he knows it is a hopeless task for which he lacks the requisite knowledge. Absurdly, he is commanded to dissect live Robots, to see if this will reveal the secrets (we feel it unlikely that the Robots would be so stupid). The leading Robot Damon (Domin's double, but Radius in the English version), consents to go on the operating table, without anaesthetic, but when the pacifist Alquist gives up, unable to stomach the deed, even Damon, who had been in charge of the slaughter of humans on the island, declares that he wants to live: it is better to live. Earlier we were told that certain alterations had been made in the manufacture of Robots by Dr. Gall, in order to please Helena by making them more human and appealing (dogs had shunned them too). These alterations have had far-reaching effects—or have they? To be precise, it is pointed out to us by the figures man, Busman, that the numbers of new-style Robots would probably have been too small (a few hundred, according to Dr. Gall) to have much effect. Busman suggests that mere numerical superiority of humans was a more likely cause of the revolt, but this is again unconvincing. We are left in doubt, though obliged in the end to attach some credence to Gall's version. Gall confessed before his death that he had given the new-style Robots emotions, or, as he put it, changed their 'irritability'. Robots rose up against men because of their *hatred* for men, however this may have developed (perhaps metaphysically): they worked, while men did not. Domin declares hatred a quintessential human trait: 'No-one can hate man more than his fellow man! Turn stones into men, and they will stone you to death!' But Robots are also now seen to be capable of *love.* Alquist notices that two have fallen in love with each other, Primus and Robot-Helena (a Helena replica, manufactured by the love-sick Dr. Gall and played by the same actress). The two express their love partly lyrically, partly humorously, and in clichés of popular romance:

> HELENA: Do you hear? The birds are singing. Oh, Primus, I'd like to be a bird!
> PRIMUS: Be what?
> HELENA: I don't know, Primus. I feel so strange, I don't know what it is: I feel silly, I've lost my head, my body aches, my heart, everything aches—And, oh, I can't tell you what's happened to me! Primus, I think I must die!
> PRIMUS: Don't you feel sometimes, tell me, Helena, as if it would be better to die? You know, perhaps we're only sleeping. Yesterday in my sleep I spoke to you again.
> HELENA: In your sleep?
> PRIMUS: In my sleep. We spoke in a foreign or new

language, because I don't remember a word of what we said.

. . . . .

HELENA: (*in front of the mirror*): Me, beautiful? Oh, this simply f*r*rightful hair, if only I had something to put in it! You know, there in the garden I always put some flowers in my hair, but there's no mirror or anyone—

Alquist pretends he wants to dissect one of them: each offers to go in place of the other, and they prove their love in time-honoured fashion, in terms of willingness to sacrifice oneself for the sake of the loved one. Alquist tells them to go and be man and wife, and reads to them from Genesis, telling how God created man and woman in His own image. He brings the play to a close, declaring that 'life will not perish'. This statement is cut in the English stage version, along with much of the life-acclaiming rhetoric of Alquist's final speech, where he declares that 'you, love, will blossom on the rubble and confide the seed of love to the winds'. The text gives no indication as to whether these two Robots have mysteriously acquired or activated the requisite organs of reproduction. Indeed, to provide any such information or explanation would spoil the mystic atmosphere. Strictly speaking, we have only been presented with Alquist's own wishful thinking; yet the declarative effect is not intended to leave us in any doubt on a symbolic, expressionistic level about the desire to end on a note of optimism, affirming the capacity of life to survive the threat of annihilation by the power of love.

Later, in the curiously similar novel, *War with the Newts,* Čapek tackled the problem by leaving the story open. Towards the end the newts, eroding continents for more Lebensraum, approach the last redoubts of humanity, and man's annihilation seems inevitable, according to the logic of the plot. In the final chapter, instead of finishing off the story, Čapek addresses an anti-pessimistic reader and discusses facetiously, almost as a mere gesture, the possibility of an eventual happy ending for mankind, were the newts, say, to turn against one another. (Domin, too, had toyed with the idea of producing nationally antagonistic Robots!) The effect is to leave the situation and the dialogue between pessimism and optimism unresolved, and also to highlight the fictional nature of the narrative. The doom and gloom in *War with the Newts* is again expressed in terms of comic satire, parody and burlesque, but, one feels, in a more controlled, consistent way. The frequent whimsicality of the narrative serves to avoid the effect of preaching (as in *R.U.R.*), yet likewise the potential message of warning is muted by the whimsicality of the satire, the fictional playfulness, the lovable cardboard characters one cannot take too seriously.

The characters in *R.U.R.* express contrasting ideas and ideals, and indeed consist of little more than bubbling words. Domin (the name refers to *dominus* "master"), represents domination, man as master of the universe; he expresses in part a vaguely Nietzschean will to power, but chiefly a kind of Fabian socialist belief in technical progress emancipating man from enslavement to labour. The somewhat Tolstoyan Alquist, as Čapek called him, a modest version of Ibsen's Solness in the *Master Builder,* believes that 'technical progress demoralises' man by alienating him from work. He is an agnostic, but he prays. He recognises a need for morality and believes in creative work. Busman (= businessman) believes that 'industrialism alone is capable of supplying modern needs'. He is the money-man and represents a financial busi-

ness attitude to life, an obsession with the power of numbers. Helena is (regrettably, not only from the point of view of the feminist critic) our old friend the intuitive woman, 'instinctively afraid of all this inhuman machinery'. She is seen (somewhat unconvincingly) as representing the positive values and charms of womankind. Her nanny, Nana (not her maid as the English version would have it) represents traditional, Christian values in a primitive, reactionary form: 'all inventions are against the Lord God', she tells Helena. Her position would, taken to a logical conclusion, return man to a primitive state of nature. Lastly, the Robots too have a viewpoint: they see themselves as more intelligent and efficient, and therefore better than man. All of these viewpoints are, as Čapek stated himself, seen as right in their own way: all put forward a certain (partial) truth of their own.

However, Čapek can really only approve of these 'truths' insofar as they are in some way well-intentioned. He had a firm moral sense which made his professed relativism only relatively relativistic. Čapek pleads for tolerance. He dislikes black-and-white judgments, narrow ideologies of the right or left, mass hysteria. He upholds the rights of the individual, and tends to assume that individuals are basically good-natured, all other things being equal. He believes in man's improvability, not perfectibility.

R.U.R. has been seen as conveying a warning that modern civilisation and technology threaten to destroy man, a critique of modern (chiefly *de facto* capitalist) society driven by blind, narrow economic imperatives. The shareholders of *R.U.R.* look only to their profits: they care nothing for the ideals of Domin. Čapek's relativism cannot embrace their 'truth', except in the most limited and meaningless of senses. But Čapek is not against science and progress, witness his optimistic ending, however, contrived; not to mention his own statements on the subject elsewhere. He wishes to warn of dangers, not 'throw out the baby with the bathwater'. Equally, he is not a simple denunciator of capitalism and the 'class society', nor is he a Marxist or collectivist. He is horrified by non-individual approaches and doctrines and wishes to see everything as far as possible on a familiar, down-to-earth, individual scale. He suspects intensely the all-embracing abstracts and absolutes of ideologies (a theme of his novel *The Absolute At Large*). Dr. Gall says, speaking partly for Čapek, 'People with ideas should not be given influence in the affairs of this world', (of course, this is to be seen as no more than another partial truth.)

Čapek's vision of the Robots seems, by his own account, to owe much to an acutely personal horror about the unknowa-

A scene from a 1922 American production of R.U.R.

bility, the inscrutability, the facelessness of human beings viewed en masse, from the outside, especially in impersonal modern urban life. He stated that the idea of the Robots had appeared to him during a tramride. One day he had to go to Prague by suburban tram, and it was uncomfortably full. It astonished him how modern conditions had made people disregard ordinary comfort in life. They were packed inside and on the steps of the tramcar not like sheep, but like machines. He began to think about people not as individuals, but as machines, and on the way he searched for an expression which would denote a person capable of working, but not of thinking. The same horror of dehumanising mass-anonymity and its potential for socio-political transformations and human self-destruction is expressed in a letter to his future wife, Olga Scheinpflugová:

> While writing I was struck by a terrible fear, I had wanted somehow to warn against the production of the mass and dehumanised slogans and suddenly I was gripped by the anxiety that it would be like this one day, maybe soon, that I would save nothing by this warning, that just as I the author had led the forces of these dull mechanisms wherever I wanted so one day someone would lead the foolish man of the mass against the world and God. I felt unwell, Olga, and so I looked towards the end almost convulsively for some kind of solution of understanding and love, do you think that one can believe in it, darling?

R.U.R. is a vision of dehumanisation, of men treated like mechanisms and behaving like mechanisms. Man is mocked, victimised and degraded by depersonalised, mechanistic man-made civilisation, his very survival perhaps threatened. Men become Robots; men are destroyed by Robots. If, at the end, the Robots become men, this humanisation is a testament of faith, an expressionist gesture, justified in the logic of the plot only by previous vaguenesses surrounding human infertility and the progress of Robot emotions from nervous 'irritability' towards will, will to live, consciousness and soul. The rhetorical gesture enables the play to end on what is keenly felt to be a desirable note of optimism (witness the letter quoted above), hailing life, created by love, and its power to survive world catastrophe. The final humanisation is denoted by the Robots' acquisition of souls, as Čapek himself wrote, admitting the vagueness involved. 'This (biological) life is only filled when (with the bringing to bear of considerable imprecision and mysticism) the Robots become *souls.*' However, the subordination of plot-logic to the final apotheosis of the power of life and love undermines the futurological element of prediction, prophecy and warning. The play dissolves into a slightly *kitsch,* vague vitalism. Throughout the play the future setting is fictional, a never-never land, representing in an expressionist, allegorical, metaphorical way, elements of a possible future in which elements of the present are heightened to an extreme: zero birth rate created by affluence, universal automation, total unemployment, mass conformity, mass extermination. (Indeed, most of the common futurological themes seem to be present in some guise or other.) The broad image throughout of man, embattled by the depersonalising, dehumanising trends of his mass civilisation, remains, in spite of everything, perhaps the play's strongest futurological theme. However problematic their dramatic presentation in *R.U.R.*, Karel Čapek's Robotic themes are still alive and troubling, even in this un-1984-like year of 1984. (pp. 75-86)

James D. Naughton, "Futurology and Robots: Karel

Čapek's 'R.U.R.,'" slightly abridged from Renaissance and Modern Studies, *Vol. XXVIII, 1984, pp. 72-86.*

IVAN KLÍMA (essay date 1985)

[*Klíma is a Czechoslovakian short story writer, dramatist, and critic. In the following excerpt, he examines the underlying philosophy of Čapek's work, focusing on* War with the Newts.]

In January, 1921, the National Theater in Prague, the foremost theater in the country, performed a Karel Čapek play with the strange title *R.U.R.* The author was known to be a talented young writer who had already written several plays together with his brother and one on his own, a moderately successful if rather traditional piece. The theme of his new play, however, astounded first Czech and then foreign audiences, for it dealt with synthetic people—"robots"—and their revolt against the human race. The play was a hit around the globe and soon brought its thirty-one-year-old author international acclaim (its nonhuman heroes held such fascination for the contemporary world that the word "robot," coined by Čapek, has been assimilated by numerous languages). With his drama about the robots Čapek inaugurated a series of fantastic and utopian works. He continued in this vein with a novel, *The Factory of the Absolute,* and a comedy, *The Makropulos Affair,* on the Shavian theme of longevity, both of which appeared in 1922, and the 1924 novel *Krakatite.* After a long hiatus he returned to utopian themes with the famous novel *War with the Newts* (1936) and, a year before his death, the drama *The White Plague* (1937).

Three of the works I have mentioned develop a fantastic motif in striking detail; even their denouements are almost identical. What impelled Karel Čapek to rework his apocalyptic vision so persistently? Many saw in his work instant utopias that presaged technological discoveries with potentially dangerous consequences; others saw a brilliant satire on contemporary political conditions both at home and abroad.

But Čapek's creative work in science fiction had a different purpose: it attempted to provide a philosophical explanation for the antagonisms that were repeatedly plunging the world into crisis.

I am a writer myself. I know that a work of literature cannot be reduced to some message, argument, or philosophy which can be expressed both concisely and in universal concepts. If I am about to consider Čapek's philosophy in his fundamental works, I am risking this oversimplification only because Čapek himself sets out the same way—almost all his works are accompanied by some kind of theoretical commentary. Although he preferred to conceal the didactic and philosophical element in his work by employing rich and fantastic plots, a wealth of brilliantly observed technical and everyday detail, and a vital, even colloquial language, Čapek was certainly the type of artist who wrote *à la thèse.*

Čapek made a thorough study of philosophy. Among contemporary schools of thought, he was most strongly influenced by Anglo-American pragmatism. Opponents have charged the adherents of pragmatism with intellectual shallowness, inconsistency, and failure to mold a genuine philosophical system—although they could not very well have done so, given their resistance to conventional truths and "great" ideas. It was precisely the pragmatists' unwillingness to generalize (something the political ideologies of the day did readily), their interest in everyday human activity, and the respect they showed every individual's truth that appealed to Čapek.

Čapek had already become familiar with the philosophy of James, Dewey, and Schiller during the war. In the same period he had also written a dedicated and sympathetic study on the subject. In the course of the next few years he published several additional detailed articles in which he attempted to define his philosophical views—especially in the area of noetics—as precisely as possible.

Like other pragmatists, Čapek was a relativist and took a skeptical view of the power of understanding, particularly the speculative understanding which attempts to establish universally valid systems. Even the most universal discoveries about reality will become personal to each individual mind and therefore partial and premature. Accordingly, Čapek considered the predilection for generalizations (especially in the area of social relations) to be one of the least propitious tendencies of human thought. "Please, for a moment, approach 'socialism' and other words now in world currency as moral and personal values, not as party or political values," he wrote shortly after the war. "A great number of people who went into the war as the new generation have come out of it with a terrible, gnawing hyper-consciousness of these values, and with their former certainty about them shaken just as terribly. This uncertainty could not be called disillusionment or skepticism or indifference; rather, it is a dismay which finds good and evil on both sides and rejects viewpoints based on principle. . . . "

Čapek's skepticism was the basis for his humanistic demand that no prejudice, no conventional truth or its concerns, be placed above the value of human life. The function of this skepticism was to remove artificial idea-obstacles between people and to stimulate conciliation, tolerance, and active participation in life. "You don't see two bales of hay, but thousands of straws. Straw by straw you gather what is good and useful in the human world; straw by straw you discard the chaff and the weeds. You don't cry out because of the oppression of thousands but because of the oppression of any individual; you've had to destroy the one truth in order to find thousands of them. . . . Ultimately, for want of anything more perfect, you simply believe in people."

In Čapek's works revolutionaries find themselves side by side with dreamers and explorers, demagogues with people's tribunes and redeemers. All these characters, no matter how different or apparently antagonistic their motives, contemplate changing or improving the world by some momentous act. With their absolute visions and judgments about the world, they run afoul of temperate and usually less interesting conservatives—simple folk or people of learning, but always tolerant, willing to help others, and ready to do anything, even to perform the most insignificant task. They know their own limits and the limits of the reality in which they live. They understand that everything has its season and its tempo and that the world cannot be changed for the better by upheaval, no matter how well intentioned. This is why they enjoy Čapek's sympathy.

Čapek doubted that anything posed a greater threat to mankind than uncontrolled Faustian desire. A man who feels equal to the creator labors under the delusion that he can and should make the world conform to his own idea. In reality, he simply ceases to perceive its complexity, disturbs one of its subtle, imperceptible structures, and triggers calamity.

In *The Factory of the Absolute* everyone believes he has found the true god and that he will save others by bringing them his god and inculcating his own faith and concept of love. People are filled with messianic idealism, but their ideals are contradictory and lead to disputes; the disputes grow into wars. While professing lofty intentions, they overlook other people and justify their own intolerance. At the end of the book one of the heroes confesses, "A person might think that another belief is the wrong belief, but he musn't think that the fellow who holds it is bad, or common, or stupid." And later, "You know, the greater the thing somebody believes in, the more passionately he despises those who don't believe in it. But the greatest belief would be to believe in people. . . . Everybody's just great at thinking about mankind, but about one single person—no. I'll kill you, but I'll save mankind. . . . It'll be a bad world until people believe in people. . . . "

An equally messianic desire and undisciplined need to transform the world brings on the calamity that befalls mankind in the famous play about the robots. "Alquist, it wasn't a bad dream to want to end the slavery of work," says Domin, the director of the robot factory, shortly before his death. "I didn't want a single soul to have to do idiotic work at someone else's machines, I didn't want any of this damn social mess! Oh, the humiliation, the pain are making me sick, the emptiness is horrible! We wanted a new generation!"

In the play Domin's dream of creation is opposed by the engineer Alquist: "I think it would be better to lay one brick than make too grandiose plans." Elsewhere, he implores, "O God, shed your light on Domin and on all those who err; destroy their creation and help people return to their cares and their work; keep the human race from annihilation. . . . the whole world, entire continents, all humanity, everything is one crazy, brutish orgy. They won't even lift a hand for food; it's stuffed right into their mouths so they don't even have to get up. . . . "

In *R.U.R.* we see the first confrontation—at least on a spiritual level—between the "man of the coming times," the revolutionary, the realizer of momentous plans, and the person who believes that man should, in the interest of preserving his own race, continue slowly on the path of his forebears, preferring what is perhaps a harder and poorer existence to the risk of unleashing demons no one will be able to control. The Domins lead the world to ruin. The Alquists warn against following them.

People need no saviors or redeemers, no robots, miracle drugs, or inexhaustible energy sources, and they need not look for grand designs or earth-shaking solutions. On the contrary, they should learn to live in harmony with the world into which they were born and take personal responsibility for it. This sense of responsibility is born of service and participation in everyday human affairs. Only "straw by straw" can the world and human attitudes be improved.

The standards by which Čapek judged human action as positive or negative were so unusual that many readers missed the point of his works. Others were angered. Radical in their own thinking, they showered Čapek with reproach for idealizing the little man, the average person, and even outright provincialism. They claimed that in denying a person's right to generalization and universal truth, Čapek was also stripping him of the right to action that would bring an end to social injustice. They offered their own, revolutionary solutions, which in that time of protracted economic and political crisis seemed to be the only promising alternatives.

This debate has raged to the present day, some believing that it is appropriate to rectify the state of human affairs by force if necessary, others contending that man must try to influence conditions by changing himself first. The events that have transpired in the very country in which Čapek lived and where I, too, live, a country where, in the half-century since Čapek's death, life has deteriorated into a succession of violent upheavals, support, in my opinion, the side of Čapek's truth in this life-and-death controversy.

The skepticism with which Čapek contemplated mankind's future reflected only one side of his personality. There was also something harmonious, even playful in him that managed to endure from the time of his childhood. He took a child's pleasure in thinking up stories. He placed no limits on his imagination and delighted in the unexpected situations he was creating, the new territory he was entering, as well as in the spiteful scoffing that permeated even the works auguring catastrophe. There was also real wonder in his observation of objects and human craftsmanship. With a boy's fascination he would watch a skilled laborer and then tell about his work in the same amusing way one might talk about an avocation or a hobby. (Čapek himself was a passionate gardener, raised dogs and cats, collected oriental carpets and folk music from around the world, took excellent photographs, and made skillful drawings for a number of his books.) He manages to reveal unexpected forms and qualities, the "soul" of objects that are encountered every day—a vacuum cleaner, a camera, a doorknob, a stove. Thus it was that alongside his apocalyptic visions and work in science fiction, perhaps as a counterbalance, he produced travel sketches, newspaper columns, and short prose fiction (his *Stories from One Pocket* and *Stories from the Other Pocket,* which appeared in 1929, enjoyed extraordinary popularity). In these works Čapek granted to people and things what he did not grant them in his longer science fiction—that they might approach each other in the custom of past centuries rather than in the ways of the present.

Čapek himself tells about the origin of his novel *War with the Newts* (1936): "It was last spring, when the world was looking rather bleak economically, and even worse politically— Apropos of I don't know what, I had written the sentence, 'You mustn't think that the evolution that gave rise to us was the only evolutionary possibility on this planet.' And that was it. That sentence was the reason I wrote *War with the Newts.*" "It is quite thinkable," Čapek reasons,

> that cultural development could be shaped through the mediation of another animal species. If the biological conditions were favorable, some civilization not inferior to our own could arise in the depths of the sea. . . . If some species other than man were to attain that level we call civilization, what do you think—would it do the same stupid things mankind has done? Would it fight the same wars? Would it invite the same historical calamities? What would we say if some animal other than man declared that its education and its numbers gave it the sole right to occupy the entire world and hold sway over all of creation? It was this confrontation with human history, and with the most pressing topical history,

that forced me to sit down and write *War with the Newts.*

A multitude of political allusions (the figure of the Chief Salamander, whose name was "actually Andreas Schultze" and who "had served someplace during the World War as a line soldier" certainly calls to mind the leader of the Nazi Reich, Adolf Hitler, and the chapter on the book of the royal philosopher paraphrases the Nazi theories of the time) led some contemporary critics to conclude that Čapek had abandoned his relativism to write an anti-Fascist pamphlet. This view, incidentally, has been supported to the present day by official Czech and Soviet literary historiography.

The thinking of many of Čapek's contemporaries was rooted in uncompromising and aggressive ideologies which sought to reduce even the most complex problems and conflicts to the simplistic language of slogans. The world was witnessing increasing confrontations between classes, nations, and systems—communism and capitalism, bourgeoisie and proletariat, democracy and dictatorship (the black-and-white ideological thinking which continues to dominate the world). Ostensibly, everything could be grasped and explained in such language. Its chief effect, however, was to obscure the human side of every problem; conflicts and issues were elevated to an impersonal level governed by power, strength, and abstract interests, where man was not responsible for his behavior or actions, and even less for the fate of society.

A writer can make no more fatal mistake than to adopt the simplistic view and language of ideology. Čapek was undoubtedly among the most resolute opponents of Fascism, Nazism, and communism, but now, as before, he sought the causes of modern crises in areas that could be defined by the experience and capabilities of the individual. He found that his contemporaries were becoming estranged from the values that had guided them for centuries and were adopting false values foisted upon them by technology and a consumerist pseudoculture. They were making gods of achievement, success, and quantity.

> Isn't our admiration for machines, that is, for mechanical civilization, such that it suppresses our awareness of man's truly creative abilities? We all believe in human progress; but we seem predisposed to imagine this progress in the form of gasoline engines, electricity, and other technical contrivances. . . . We have made machines, not people, our standard for the human order. . . . There is no conflict between man and machine. . . . But it's another matter entirely when we ask ourselves whether the organization and perfection of human beings is proceeding as surely as the organization and perfection of machines. . . . If we wish to talk about progress, let's not rave about the number of cars or telephones but point instead to the value that we and our civilization attach to human life.
>
> —from the article
> **"Rule by Machines"**

By forcing individuality into the background, technological civilization makes room for mediocrity and a stifling collectivism.

In a critical commentary on Ortega y Gasset's essay *Revolt of the Masses,* Čapek observes: "Our age is distinguished by the fact that the ordinary spirit, aware of its own ordinariness, is bold enough to defend its right to ordinariness, and asserts it everywhere. . . . The mass . . . imposes on the world its own standards and its own taste and strives to give its barroom opinions the force of law. . . . The masses . . . have been imbued with the power and glory of their modern surroundings, but not with spirit." Čapek, however, differs with the Spanish philosopher by stressing that the fortunes of mankind are threatened not so much by the mediocrity of the masses as by wholesale failure among individuals, particularly those responsible for maintaining our cultural values and the level of thought—i.e., the intellectuals.

Culture means "above all, continuity with every human endeavor that has gone before"; its significance lies in the fact that it supports the awareness of values already established by mankind and thus helps us "not to lose them and not to sink below them."

Betrayal by the intellectuals was the worst betrayal Čapek could imagine, for its consequences were immeasurable.

> A culturally leveled intelligentsia ceases to fulfill certain obligations on which most higher values depend. . . . If culture breaks down, the 'average' person—the simple, ordinary man, the farmer, the factory worker, the tradesman, with his normal thoughts and moral code—will not be heard, and will go off in search of something that is far beneath him, a barbaric and violent element. . . . Destroy the hierarchical supremacy of the spirit, and you pave the way for the return of savagery. The abdication of the intelligentsia will make barbarians of us all.

Culture which drops below its own level and loses what it had attained breaks down. Since this is what had just taken place throughout much of Europe, Čapek was convinced that we were witnessing "one of the greatest cultural debacles in world history. . . . What happened was nothing less than a colossal betrayal by the intelligentsia. . . . "

Where ideologues spoke of the crisis of the system, Čapek was more consistent, more skeptical, more personal; he found a crisis in man, his values, his sense of responsibility. The fall of the intelligentsia marked the beginning of the fall of the entire civilization, the beginning of tremendous calamities.

As he always did when he resolved to pursue a great theme, Čapek turned to the sphere of science fiction. Not only did it suit his storytelling preferences, but a fictional world in fictional time gave him more room for movement and enabled him to shape that world and order the action with maximum focus on the factors which, in his view, were leading to ruin.

At the same time, Čapek wanted to evoke a sense of verisimilitude and topicality. He therefore patterned his narrative on the events of the time, the catchwords, the diplomatic maneuvers, and the advertising slogans, and he made allusions to living people and their work. He also reinforced the feeling of real life by including exact imitations of the most diverse genres of nonfiction, from reminiscences and news stories to interviews and statements by famous personalities.

Such efforts to make his science fiction more lifelike and closer to a documentary record of actual events were characteristic of Čapek's "anti-utopias" and set them off sharply from the majority of works in that genre. Zamyatin, Boye, Orwell, and Bradbury thought through to their absurd end the destructive (generally totalitarian) tendencies they saw in contemporary society. They created worlds that were terrifying in their alienation or totalitarian violence, but at the same time so artificial as to be remote from everyday human experience. Čapek depicted those same disastrous social tendencies in more realistic (and usually ironic) terms. He did not invent new world empires—the United State, Oceania, or the World State, the Bureau of Guardians or the Ministry of Love; he did not describe television eyes that would follow a person's every movement, or Kallocain and other drugs that would deprive him of his will. Čapek's Vaduz conference resembles any diplomatic meeting of the time, just as the board meeting of the Pacific Export Company resembles a board meeting of any contemporary enterprise. His people experience the joys and worries of life in the age of the newts much as they did in Čapek's own day. The fantastical newts appear to exist in everyday life. But this everyday life is moving toward disaster, precisely because its everyday quality has taken it in that direction. Čapek's fiction is less horrifying (at the beginning, it is even humorous), but all too reminiscent of the world we all live in; and this lends urgency to its admonitions about where that world may be headed.

However lifelike Čapek's utopia may appear, it remains a fiction, an artistic image that cannot be reduced (as some critics have tried to do) to a mere allegory in which the newts are substituted for one of the forces in the contemporary world conflict. No poetic symbol or allegory can be neatly translated back into reality.

The newts have emerged on the scene, and thus entered history, as an independent factor. Of course, they are not loaded down with prejudices or their own history and culture, and in this they resemble children. Eager learners, they strive to emulate everything they perceive to be more developed or more advanced. Like a mirror, they reflect the image of human values and the contemporary state of culture.

What kind of world is encountered by these creatures whose main strength lies in their being average and in their "successful, even triumphal inferiority"? What does modern civilization offer the huge masses of creatures untouched by culture? As Čapek develops his story of the newts and their history, he also refines his answer, and it is a depressing one. Human civilization is racing blindly in pursuit of profits, success, and material progress. Wealth, amusement, and pleasure have become its ideals, and it deifies everything that helps realize those ideals—industry, technology, science, entrepreneurism. En route to its goals, it has not even noticed the loss of what gave it life: human personality, culture, spirit, soul. Inquiry and reflection have been replaced with journalistic jabber, personal involvement in social affairs with a passive craving for sensation, ideas with slogans and empty phrases. "Your work is your success. He who doesn't work doesn't eat! . . . " All this has led to the world's becoming inundated with masses of people dangerous in their mediocrity and their readiness to accept any belief and adopt any goal. Yes, the masses resemble the newts; and the newts have become assimilated by the masses. "Of course, they don't have their own music or literature, but they'll get along without them just fine; and people are beginning to find that this is terribly modern of those Salamanders. . . . They've learned to use machines and numbers, and that's turned out to be enough to make them masters of their world. They left out of human civilization everything that was inexpedient, playful, imaginative, or old-fashioned, and so they eliminated from it all that had been human. . . . "

Everything that happens to the human race in this "Age of

Newts" looks like a natural disaster, not because the newts are a natural phenomenon but because no one anywhere in the world can be found who feels personal responsibility for his creations, his actions, his behavior, and the social enterprise that is civilization. Or, more accurately, there is just one person, a doorkeeper, who meets his responsibility; he is that insignificant "little man." Among the powerful, the chosen, no thought has been given to the long-term consequences of the trend civilization is following. Culture has been leveled, art has been displaced by kitsch, philosophy has declined and taken to celebrating destruction, everything has been overcome by petty, local, and mainly nationalistic considerations.

Human civilization has indeed spread throughout the planet, but people show no evidence of being able to treat anything other than particularized concerns; thus, they have no means of *considering,* let alone *controlling* the consequences of their own actions. Modern civilization is so destructive that no being could come into contact with it and escape unscathed. Even the newts are marked by their encounter with people and their "culture." This is why, with no precautions, they begin to destroy dry land as soon as they find it to be in their interests to do so. People committed to "higher" and "suprapersonal" concerns, people who have long since given up the right to share actively in determining their own future, even when threatened with the extinction of not just one people or state but of mankind, work together with the newts to bring about their own destruction. "All the factories" cooperate, "All the banks. All nations."

In the face of this predicament, what people undertake for their salvation could only be viewed as half-hearted and panoptical. The human race has nothing left with which to fight for its existence. These are people who are about to destroy their own planet.

Čapek was a writer of great metaphors, brilliant fantasies, and apocalyptic visions. He was an author who appeared to focus on the events of the external world, on competing ideas, conflicts between nations, the shortcomings of civilization—in sum, conflicts of an entirely impersonal nature. But can real literature develop from impersonal motives, solely from an intellectual need to address a problem, even a very important one? I doubt it.

An argument between Čapek's typical heroes was not merely an argument intended to shed light on a philosophical problem. It was first and foremost Čapek's personal argument. He had an innate, almost prophetic consciousness of sharing responsibility for the fate of human society. He, too, needed to dream of mankind's happiness, of a more peaceful, more secure world. His need was to think up plans, to bring people a good message. At the same time, he realized that all dreams of lofty spirits, all prophetic visions, change into their opposites, and it is precisely these that lead people into fatal conflicts. So he set himself limits. He was Domin in *The Factory of the Absolute,* Prokop in *Krakatite,* Captain van Toch and the entrepreneurial genius Bondy in *War with the Newts.* In these figures he wanted to "smash [himself] with [his] very power," the transgression of which Prokop stands accused in *Krakatite.* But time and again he offered repentance, calling himself to order in the words of Alquist or the unknown X. He was punishing himself for the damage he could have done.

Čapek's entire work testifies to the contradiction faced by a seeing, knowing creative spirit, a spirit that longs to purify and enlighten the world but fears its own imperfection and limitations, fears what people will do with its visions. This dilemma will undoubtedly haunt mankind forever. Čapek's work illuminates it with the power of personal experience. (pp. ix-xxi)

Ivan Klíma, "Čapek's Modern Apocalypse," translated by Robert Streit, in War with the Newts *by Karel Čapek, Northwestern University Press, 1985, pp. v-xxi.*

ELIZABETH MASLEN (essay date 1987)

[*Maslen is an educator, critic, and translator. In the following excerpt, she examines Čapek's use of language in* War with the Newts.]

War with the Newts was originally published in Prague in 1936 and was written in Czech. At first glance this statement may seem merely factual, and yet the more one considers the book's speedy impact on Western readers, the more impressive it is: Allen and Unwin's version, for example, came out in 1937 and so was made available to a wide readership (which included George Orwell) before Čapek's death in 1938 and before the Nazi invasion of Czechoslovakia. Admittedly Kafka, who spent most of his life in Prague, was already a considerable cult figure in the Western Europe of the 1930s; but Kafka wrote in German. Yet even before the First World War, before Czechoslovakia won freedom from the Austro-Hungarian Empire, Čapek chose to write in Czech; and he continued to do so throughout his life, despite a university career which took him to both Berlin and Paris. By the '20s he had proved, especially with his play *R.U.R.,* that his choice of language was no deterrent to international recognition; but he had certainly gambled with his eyes open. So what made him turn his back on easier ways of gaining a following abroad and choose to write on universal themes in a little-known literary language?

Less than 100 years before Čapek wrote **War with the Newts,** Czech could not be considered seriously as a literary vehicle. The country remained part of the Austro-Hungarian Empire throughout the 19th century; it was only in the 1840s that the need for an independent cultural identity began to assert itself insistently, and with it the desire to write in Czech. Yet what were to be the models for pioneers of literary expression such as Jan Neruda? Extraordinarily, they chose to turn for guidance to the 16th-century Kralická Bible, whose literary mode came closest to the Czech dialect still spoken in the Balbin district. In other words, although the urge to write in Czech came from a stubbornly maintained spoken language, a literary language was resurrected and reconstructed from an archaic prototype in the second half of the 19th century.

Given the reputation of German as a literary language on the one hand and the rapidly growing strength of Russian literature on the other, the attempt to establish Czech as a literary vehicle between 1840 and 1880 must have seemed a gesture more akin to the world of fantasy than to self-evident fact. Yet it was to work; and in the hands of Karel Čapek (also, to a lesser extent, Jaroslav Hašek with *The Good Soldier Schweik* [1921-23]), it was to capture the attention of the West.

Indeed, the whole question of language is of crucial importance in **War with the Newts,** although it is one of the most difficult aspects of the work to convey fully in translation. Čapek is a past master at moving from the ultra-literary to the colloquial, and can imitate or parody any verbal register: journalistic (popular press or periodical), scientific, legal, bureaucratic, political—all have their moments under his microscope. And there are other language games. Take the case of Captain van Toch, who opens the book. When we first meet him in Dutch Indonesia, he seems to be a typical Dutch merchant seaman. But we soon discover that he is nothing of the kind: his name is Vantoch and he is Czech. Part of the fun here is that Czechoslovakia is not a maritime country and so, as Vantoch says himself, Czech sea-captains are rare. However, Czechoslovakia—even Vantoch's own modest place of birth—does supply captains of industry (Bondy is in fact a central character in *The Factory of the Absolute,* or *The Absolute at Large,* Čapek's novel of 1922), and so has its own channel through which it can reach the outside world. But the main thrust of the joke borders, for Czech readers, on black comedy: Captain van Toch deliberately passes himself off as Dutch in Indonesia. A shrewd adoption of local color perhaps; yet we soon find that he is cavalier, to say the least, in his attitude to language. He speaks Malay to the Bataks; but they do not understand him, since they—unsurprisingly—speak Batak (not "Batavian," a coinage of the Allen and Unwin translation). And the full extent of his linguistic folly is revealed when he returns home to Czechoslovakia. He cannot remember Czech words and frequently resorts to other languages, especially English. This is not a problem which is fully exposed or exploited in either of the [two available English] translations . . . , with the result that conversation in, for example, the chapter "G. H. Bondy and his Fellow Countryman" often seems oddly repetitive in English. In the original, however, we find that Vantoch has forgotten so much of his Czech that he offers terms which his compatriot has to translate. (In fairness, it should be said that Čapek mocks both parties: Bondy is disappointed when he discovers that he is dealing with a mere Czech and not a foreigner.)

The linguistic thread, I repeat, is crucial to *War with the Newts* since one of the Newts' most impressive abilities is that they can speak and read easily when given the chance. This skill is shown to be quite as important as their adaptability to tools and technology; indeed, without their linguistic capacity they would be impervious to exploitation. Language is inevitably the means used to indoctrinate them with a confusing medley of humankind's ideas, and is inextricably linked with that extrapolation from certain modes of thought which Čapek shows so mercilessly as leading to the destabilization and corruption of the Newts. Yet Čapek does not preach at us pedantically; indeed, he uses one of his prime concerns, the status of the Czech language, as a vehicle for comic relief. One superb moment occurs in the second book when all countries are vying for linguistic domination of the Newts. The Czechs decide that, although they are not a maritime nation, they too must compete; and they accordingly produce "a small manual, *Czech for Newts,* complete with examples of Czechoslovak *belles-lettres.* It may sound incredible, but over seven thousand copies of that little book were actually sold; all in all, therefore, it was a remarkable success." (It should be said that at the time of the sale there are millions of Newts in the world.) And Čapek does not leave the matter there: one copy of *Czech for Newts* is found in the hands of a Newt on the lonely Galapagos Islands. Its learned questioning of two literary Czech tourists on the state of their language exposes the fragility of Czech *as* a literary language:

"Alas, there is no one here to whom I could speak

Czech" our new friend remarked modestly, "and I am not even quite sure whether the instrumentative case of the word *koň* is *koni* or *koňmi.*"

"*Ko'ňmi,*" I said.

"Oh no, *koni,*" my wife exclaimed with animation.

But Čapek does not use language as an end in itself: it is always a tool, an "ideas" weapon. The "small manual, *Czech for Newts,*" contains examples of "Czechoslovak *belles-lettres,*" we remember; yet when the Czech-speaking Newt questions the tourists about what he has been reading, the subject-matter sounds, to say the least, surprising. The Newt comments, for example, on:

" . . . the disaster of the White Mountain and the three hundred years of servitude. I have read a lot about it in this book. No doubt you are very proud of your three hundred years of servitude. That was a great period, sir!"

"Yes, a hard period," I agreed: "A period of oppression and grief."

"And did you groan?" our friend inquired with keen interest.

"We groaned, suffering inexpressibly under the yoke of the savage oppressors."

"I am delighted to hear it," the Newt heaved a sigh of relief, "That is exactly what it says in my book. I am happy to find it is true."

Here Čapek not only mocks his fellow-countrymen for wallowing in past sufferings but shrewdly shows how this kind of pride in humiliation can be fostered in others; after all, the Newts are experiencing just such servitude themselves, albeit the literary tourists do not note the parallel.

This kind of indoctrination by language rather than its content is demonstrated, wittily and perceptively, elsewhere. Andrew Scheuchzer, the Newt kept at the London Zoo, is taught to speak and read by his taciturn keeper; the intellectuals are too busy being "scientific" about the Newt to look to its intellectual development, which in any case they choose to doubt. So Andrew learns language from an inarticulate man who supplies his charge with evening papers. Again Čapek slyly inserts warning signals amidst the humor, as when Andrew answers questions posed by the learned team eventually sent to investigate his articulateness. All answers come from advertisements and journalistic jargon:

How many continents are there?
A: Five.
Very good. Which are they?
A: England and the rest.
Which are the rest?
A: The Bolsheviks and the Germans. And Italy.
Where are the Gilbert Islands?
A: In England. England will not tie herself to the Continent. England needs ten thousand aircraft. Visit the English south coast.

Inevitably the intellectuals conclude their report on this conversation with predictable complacency: "There is absolutely no need to overrate [the Newt's] intelligence, since in no respect does it exceed the intelligence of the average person of our time." Later, with acute wit and a built-in warning about the relation of language and patterns of (rather than capacity for) thought, Čapek records the arguments concerning the language which Newts ought to speak. All sorts of theories are propounded but no conclusive decision is reached, so that in the end: "The fact was that Basic English was the most common language among the Newts and subsequently became the official Newt language."

As I have already indicated, the full impact and import of Čapek's handling of language in *War with the Newts* is extremely difficult to convey in translation since, as Čapek himself is the first to acknowledge within his own work, language and culture are so intimately connected. This point is demonstrated, for instance, when we are told that, although the "wild" male Newts have an intricate and "strangely beautiful" dance which they perform on the shore at night, no one bothers to ask them about its significance: linguistic communication with these savages is minimal. Instead they are talked out of their dance and taught to label it a "bestial and low practice" which is "shameful and dissolute." Yet human intellectuals theorize about the dance's meaning, while the privileged human young attempt to imitate it at parties and secret orgies. Čapek never tells us what the dance really meant to Newts; and his and their silence on the subject is all the more audible since we know that both he and they can be extremely articulate. The intellectuals argue away the Newts' facility with language as "parrot-like"; the human governments and their technologists put emphasis instead on the Newts' extraordinary capacity with tools and later with sophisticated technology.

What Čapek sees with such clarity is the peril of technology divorced from an articulated culture. The decline into a utilitarian desert is already implied in the central book concerning the history of the Newts:

> . . . what else is civilization than the ability to make use of things invented by someone else? Even if, for the sake of argument, the Newts have no original ideas of their own they can perfectly well have their own science. True, they have no music or literature of their own but they manage perfectly well without; indeed people are beginning to think that this is marvellously modern of them. . . . Never before in human history has so much been manufactured, constructed or earned as in this great age. . . . [The] Newts have brought enormous progress to the world, as well as the ideal called Quantity. . . . [G]ood heavens, how can you compare us with that outmoded Human Age with its ponderous, finicky and useless fuss that went by the name of culture, the arts, pure science and what have you!

Čapek leaves his readers to recall that the Newts have never been encouraged to develop or articulate their own culture, and have been taught to see it in such a degrading or irrelevant way that they have understandably concentrated on unadulterated pragmatism. However, the author makes his point about the importance of language, text, the arts, "and what have you" by every means at his disposal. He not only builds his case into the themes and plot of *War with the Newts;* he uses his own textual skills. He underlines shifts in register, culture, or time by the visual effects of shifts in typeface; he quotes from unnamed and sometimes invented languages with no attempt at translation; he gives us the all-important pictorial illustration of that first salamander skeleton so ironically thought to be human . . . and it does look human.

So far I have been discussing Čapek's concern for language and endeavoring to identify the role which he assigns to it. He is opposed to nationalism, yet he argues for the importance of culture; he writes in Czech, yet he wields his language as a weapon against the whole of his contemporary world. And so it is surely not self-contradictory that, although he writes in Czech, he draws on many foreign sources for his mode of writing. Furthermore, he was working within a still youthful Czech literary tradition which had every opportunity to look abroad for fresh models: during the years when he was writing, Prague was an increasingly vigorous center for translation and publication; Western texts and expatriate or internally censored Russian texts all found an outlet through the Prague presses. Wells and Huxley were just two of the Western writers available; and it was the Prague editions of Zamyatin's *We* in 1927 which provoked Stalin's wrath against that author. Čapek therefore had many cultures on his doorstep, as it were. In the mid-19th century, when still dominated by the Austro-Hungarian Empire, writers not unnaturally had looked to the West; but by the last quarter of the century, the growing intellectual ferment in Russia, together with the common Slavonic roots of Russian and Czech, had led some writers, such as Jan Kollár, to look to the East as well. Čapek, in *War with the Newts,* looks in both directions; and this combination of influences has to be taken into account if we are to appreciate Čapek's subtlety.

For it is not quite fair to say, as Klíma does [see excerpt dated 1985] . . . , that Čapek is primarily against science and technology, any more than it is fair to say the same of his Russian contemporary, Zamyatin. Zamyatin takes on the whole organ of state in the futuristic society of *We;* Čapek tackles an extraordinary range of contemporary ideas with the lightest of touches in *War with the Newts.* In the Western tradition, both writers acknowledge their indebtedness to Wells. Certainly the beginning of *War with the Newts,* with its gradual movement from a straight sea-yarn to the fabular encounter with the Newts is highly reminiscent of a number of Wells's short stories, as is the lightly handled, macabre wit; and the overall scope of Čapek's book is reminiscent of Wells's longer works, such as *A Modern Utopia* (1905). But Čapek, I would argue, is more successful than Wells in his capacity to contain within a relatively short work such a large scale of reference. Virtually nothing in world politics or ideas is omitted, and yet there is tight structuring and none of the Grand-Old-Man tone of Wells's late pronouncements. Čapek moves deftly from the exploitation of the Newts to the exploitation of human beings, with an expository central book purporting to be a history of the Newts but which Čapek uses to review his contemporary world and its roots wittily and mercilessly; and such structuring is not one of Wells's strengths in his wide-ranging later works. It is true that Čapek's coda to his book is as chilling as it is humorous and that this is a Wellsian touch; but I would argue that Čapek's use of literary devices to expose the manipulation of society and events by words goes far beyond Wells in skill and effect.

Within the text of *War with the Newts,* Čapek puts Wells in the company of Aldous Huxley, whose *Brave New World* was published in 1932; and certainly the Appendix on "The Sex Life of the Newts" offers parodic echoes of Huxley's futuristic work. But while the human sex-life which Huxley describes in *Brave New World* amusingly caricatures body contact, Čapek outdoes him satirically by showing a similar kind of Newt sex-life which humankind dismisses or dissects with clinical detachment and cruelty simply because it is alien. And Čapek's links with Western literature are by no means confined to writers of SF or (to use a favorite term of his) utopias. For example, he also mentions Joseph Conrad in *War with the Newts:* Bondy sees van Toch's adventures (and incidentally Bondy always uses the Dutch pseudonym, no doubt as a sign of his taste for the exotic) as partly Conradian in their romantic tendencies. But while the Indonesian explorations and Vantoch's sentimental references to the Newts do indeed recall, say, the later sections of *Lord Jim* (1900), there may also be a dig (given Čapek's de-Czeched van Toch) at Conrad's defection from his native Poland (and Polish language) to the English literary scene. It is thus fair to say that while Čapek does draw on a number of Western writers (and I have only mentioned a sample selection), he adapts them to his own vision and remains very much his own man.

Fringing these direct literary references is a wide range of names which reveal Čapek's considerable knowledge of Western personalities and ideas, extending from the political and philosophical to the scientific and technological. An amusing instance is the composition of the team of intellectuals who visit the London Zoo Newt: two of its members are named as Sir Oliver Dodge and Julian Foxley (who scarcely disguise Lodge the spiritualist and Aldous's brother, an atheist, respectively)—no intellectual aberration or eccentricity would seem to escape Čapek. And just as nothing is too marginal for his attention, so nothing is too central to unnerve him: the Chief Salamander is revealed at the end of the book to be "human. His real name is Andreas Schultze and during the War he was a sergeant-major somewhere." As Klíma implies, both background and pseudonym (related as the latter is to Andrias Scheuchzeri, the racial name perfunctorily bestowed on the Newts by the humans) are at least partly reminiscent of Adolf Hitler.

This last, teasingly screened "identification" brings us to one of the most intriguing Eastern influences on Čapek's work: the Aesopian language first perfected in 19th-century Russia and given its label by the satirist Saltykov-Shchedrin (like Čapek, a master of many verbal registers). Recently, an admirable book [*On the Beneficence of Censorship: Aesopian Language in Modern Russian Literature*] by Lev Loseff has appeared, a book much needed to elucidate a mode of writing not always fully understood in the West. Loseff examines the type of oblique writing which is often used under totalitarian regimes when censorship is particularly strict. (pp. 82-8)

Aesopian language does not, despite the implications of its name, necessarily involve the use of animal fable; it is a mode rather than a genre, employing various means of both concealing and signalling references to extratextual matters. Some works are entirely Aesopian, others only partially so. Loseff's epigraph, taken from Gogol's short story "The Nose" (1836), helps to identify the mode while also showing its relevance to Čapek's *War with the Newts:*

> "But what makes my business unreasonable? It wouldn't seem to be anything of the sort" [says Kovalyov].
>
> "That's the way you see it" [the clerk at the newspaper office responds]. "But look here, the same thing happened last week. A civil servant came in exactly as you have now, brought a hand-written note, the change came to two rubles and seventy-two copecks, and all he wanted to announce was that a black poodle had run away. Ask yourself, what could be wrong with that? But it turned out

> to be libel; that so-called poodle was the treasurer of some institution, I don't remember which one."

This extract identifies both the uses of Aesopian language and its capacity for being either overlooked or misinterpreted. It relies very much on its readership's familiarity with what is referred to extratextually, with the complication that it must inform some while keeping others (such as the censors) in the dark. Its references may be lost with time; or new referents, never dreamed of by the author, may emerge long after the text has been written (as happened with Stalin's fresh interpretation of Zamyatin's *We* and, in different countries at different times, with Orwell's *1984*). Artistically, as Loseff is careful to point out, Aesopian language must be judged on its literary merits; but an understanding of its intentionalist if volatile nature immeasurably enriches any reading of works where it is employed, as it frequently lurks at the core of the text in question. And while Loseff concentrates on Russian texts, Aesopian language is by no means confined to Russian, as has already been implied; Čapek is only one of many non-Russian writers to use the mode alongside elements better known in Western literatures.

It is, incidentally, worth pausing to wonder where Kafka, Čapek's Czech contemporary, stands in relation to all these literary concerns. It is true that he was a Jew who wrote in German, but for most of his life he lived and worked in Prague; and when one reads such stories as "The Giant Mole," "The Great Wall of China," or "Investigations of a Dog" (all first published in 1931), there seem to be striking similarities with a number of Čapek's own themes in *War with the Newts:* manipulation of words and of people in the first two, the need for cultural identity in the last. (But it is impossible to pin Kafka down; his wit and virtuosity are as baffling as his apparently lucid style. Is he using Aesopian language or not?) It is usual for critics to point to Kafka's introspection and obsessive preoccupation with Jewish society. But were not the beleaguered advocates of the Czech language and culture somewhat similarly placed? Had not they also suffered a similar identity crisis, been similarly repressed? (Čapek's literary tourists in the Galapagos suggest as much in their conversation with the Czech-speaking Newt.) Did not they too experience something of a ghetto status in relation to the German culture which threatened to overwhelm them, and a sense of cultural siege when confronted by the Western and Eastern literatures and ideas being published so zealously in their own country? Čapek's impressive capacity for weaving these different strands together and making them serve his own vision has already been remarked; but might synthesis have been basic to the culture of his time in Prague rather than only personal to him?

One might be forgiven for suspecting that Kafka uses Aesopian language in such works as "The Giant Mole," just as Čapek can surely be suspected of it in his handling of the Newts. He is careful to make these "creatures" as difficult to pin down in their own way as any of Kafka's non-human characters. At times, Newts evoke colonial exploitation or slave-trading; at others, the manipulation of the lower strata of society. Newts are used as butts by the worst representatives of science, technology, popular entertainment, education, insensitive charity, and so on. They are used as echoes of our past, critiques of our present, and warnings for our future. They are no true denizens of animal fable as such, any more than are Kafka's non-human creatures in his short stories; they are yardsticks against which we can measure the human race and by which we can recognize caricatures of human foibles and failings. (pp. 88-9)

All the matters which I have so far been discussing only go to prove the enormous problems facing translators of Čapek's *War with the Newts.* We now have two English translations. . . . [It would be] unfair to cavil over the problems which both translations inevitably face when they come to transfer into English the cultural signals and Aesopian language of Čapek's text, for here they must depend to a great extent on the reader's capacity to pick up and respond to such matters, a skill which few Western readers have acquired. In the end, the two translations supplement each other very usefully.

But the fact that Western readers, as Loseff emphatically asserts, have little skill in recognizing Aesopian language is an important issue. Orwell certainly used the mode in *Animal Farm* (1945), but was even he aware of the full import of Aesopian language? Was he, for example, led astray when, in *1984,* he gave so many pages to Goldstein's book? Certainly, when set beside Čapek's central section on the history of the Newts, Orwell's exposition has lamentably little impact. Is this because he failed to learn the full lesson of Čapek's Aesopian skills and "cathartic comedy"? To take another example, it seems to me that Čapek's Newts, ultimately condemned to speak Basic English, reflect a problem of articulacy facing a far larger cross-section of today's society than do Orwell's intellectual sufferers from Newspeak, despite the insight the latter language has brought us. These are fascinating matters for debate, since they emphasize the problem as to what is transferrable from cultures well-versed in official and unofficial censorship to readers who are not so highly sensitized. And the problem is all the more striking since Čapek and Orwell were ultimately similar in their motivation. Klíma tells us, for instance, that it was "the tragedy of the [1914-18] war and the nation's restored independence" which informed all of Čapek's later work. "Just after the publication of *War with the Newts,*" Klíma notes, Čapek wrote: "Literature that does not care about reality or about what is really happening to the world, literature that is reluctant to react as strongly as word and thought allow, is not for me." This commitment finds its echo in Orwell's essay "Why I Write," published in 1946: "Every line of serious work that I have written since 1936 has been written, directly or indirectly, *against* totalitarianism and *for* democratic Socialism, as I understand it. It seems to me nonsense, in a period like our own, to think that one can avoid writing of such subjects."

The fact that *War with the Newts* was published in 1936 and Orwell's moment of truth came in the same year is, on the face of it, pure coincidence. Orwell's epiphany occurred during the Spanish Civil War while Čapek's enlightenment happened in the First World War; Orwell experienced conversion abroad while Čapek suffered his at home. Yet both were uttering the words quoted above towards the end of lives as writers, lives which they had both come to regard as "active" contributions to the societies of their day. And both set high store by their responsibility to language and the artistry through which they conveyed their message.

In the end Loseff is right. We must judge *War with the Newts* on its literary merits, and I would maintain that it has held up extraordinarily well. Its structure is elegantly conceived; its wit remains witty—if only because the world of today is still paralyzed by the dilemmas facing Čapek's world. Čapek is adept at exposing those dilemmas, and both translations of

his last book have a useful contribution to make. . . . Both allow us to see, through Čapek's *War with the Newts,* that SF can make a vital contribution to 20th-century literature—intellectually, artistically, and as a means of exploring the awesome implications of language used as a weapon. (pp. 90-2)

> *Elizabeth Maslen, "Proper Words in Proper Places: The Challenge of Čapek's 'War with the Newts',"* in Science-Fiction Studies, *Vol. 14, No. 14, March, 1987, pp. 82-92.*

FURTHER READING

Bradbrook, B. R. "Chesterton and Karel Čapek: A Study in Personal and Literary Relationship." *The Chesterton Review* IV, No. 1 (Fall-Winter, 1977-78): 89-103.

> Discusses and quotes from the correspondence between Čapek and G. K. Chesterton to determine the extent of their personal relationship. Bradbrook also examines Chesterton's influence on Čapek's writings, essentially summarizing her earlier essay, "The Literary Relationship between G. K. Chesterton and Karel Čapek" (see excerpt dated 1960-61).

Davydov, Sergej. "*Tales from One Pocket:* Detective and Justice Stories of Karel Čapek." In *The Structure of the Literary Process: Studies Dedicated to the Memory of Felix Vodička,* edited by P. Steiner, M. Červenka and R. Vroon, pp. 95-106. Philadelphia: John Benjamins Publishing Co., 1982.

> Examines the stories in *Tales from One Pocket* as detective fiction.

Doležel, Lubomír. "Karel Čapek and Vladislav Vančura: An Essay in Comparative Stylistics." In his *Narrative Modes in Czech Literature,* pp. 91-111. Toronto: University of Toronto Press, 1973.

> Studies the ostensibly contrasting styles of Čapek and Vančura to show the underlying similarities that result from both authors negating "traditional, realistic prose style."

Dresler, Jaroslav. "Čapek and Communism." In *The Czechoslovak Contribution to World Culture,* edited by Miloslav Rechcigl, Jr., pp. 68-75. The Hague: Mouton and Co., 1964.

> Explores Čapek's views on communism, focusing on his essay "Why I Am Not a Communist."

Elton, Oliver. "Karel Čapek: Short Tales and Fantasias" and "Karel Čapek: Later Novels." In his *Essays and Addresses,* pp. 151-69, 170-90. New York: Longmans, Green and Co., 1939.

> Survey of Čapek's short stories and novels.

Galsworthy, John. Foreword to *Money and Other Stories,* by Karel Čapek, translated by Francis P. Marchant, Dora Round, F. P. Casey, and O. Vočadlo, p. iii. 1930. Reprint. Freeport, N.Y.: Books for Libraries Press, 1970.

> Introduction to this collection of Čapek's stories in which Galsworthy states that he "read them with very lively interest—they are penetrating, they are unusual, they have power, and they have flavour."

Harkins, William E. "Imagery in Karel Čapek's *Hordubal.*" PMLA LXXV, No. 5 (December 1960): 616-20.

> Analyzes imagery in the first part of *Hordubal.*

Heé, Veronika. "The Pocket-Stories of Karel Čapek." *Studia Slavica* XXII, Nos. 3-4 (1976): 401-14.

> Examines the techniques Čapek employs in his "pocket" stories to convey his philosophical ideas and discusses the success of

these works as short stories and their relation to the genre of detective fiction.

Hudson, Lynton. "Symbolic Evangelism and the Philosophical Revue." In his *Life and the Theatre,* pp. 97-110. 1949. Reprint. New York: Roy Publishers, 1954?.

Studies the plays of Franz Werfel and Čapek, writers who, Hudson contends, were "both deeply apprehensive of the trends of civilization."

Mukařovský, Jan. "K. Čapek's Prose as Lyrical Melody and as Dialogue." In *A Prague School Reader on Esthetics, Literary Structure, and Style,* edited and translated by Paul L. Garvin, pp. 133-49. Washington, D.C.: Georgetown University Press, 1964.

Detailed study of the phonetic aspects of Čapek's prose in an effort to define the basic, unifying principle of his works despite "their developmental differentiation" in style and to determine the reasons for changes in his style.

Parrott, Cecil. "The Explosion Within." *Times Literary Supplement,* No. 4,075 (8 May 1981): 505.

Examines Čapek's letters to Věra Hruzová, leading to a discussion of his literary reputation in his native country, in other Eastern European countries, and in Britain, where, according to Parrott, Čapek is virtually forgotten.

Pletnev, R. "The Concept of Time and Space in *R.U.R.* by Karel Čapek." *Études Slaves et Est-Européennes/Slavic and East European Studies* XII, No. 1 (Spring 1967): 17-24.

Uses Čapek's *R.U.R.* as a typical example of how the works of Czechoslovakian writers reflect the radical changes in the concept of time and space that have occurred as a result of important scientific discoveries in the twentieth century.

Wechsberg, Joseph. "Karel Čapek: The Friday Group in Prague." In *Affairs of the Mind: The Salon in Europe and America from the 18th to the 20th Century,* edited by Peter Quennell. Washington, D.C.: New Republic Books, 1980.

Describes the meetings among European, primarily Czechoslovakian, intellectuals held almost every Friday at Čapek's home from 1921 to the time of his death.

Benedetto Croce

1866-1952

Italian philosopher, critic, historian, editor, and autobiographer.

Croce is considered one of the most important European philosophers of the twentieth century. In his extensive writings, he explored a wide range of philosophical subjects, including epistemology, aesthetics, logic, and ethics. His most celebrated work, the four-volume *Filosofia dello Spirito* (*Philosophy of the Spirit*), consolidates these diverse categories of philosophy into a comprehensive theory of the operative factors in all human activity. Croce also made significant contributions to literary criticism and historiography.

The son of wealthy landowners, Croce was born on one of his family's estates in the Abruzzi region of central Italy. Educated at Catholic schools in Naples, Croce enjoyed studying history and literature and published several articles on literary subjects in a local periodical when he was sixteen. In 1883, while the family was vacationing in Casamícciola on the island of Ischia, Croce's parents and sister were killed in an earthquake, and Croce was buried in the rubble for about eight hours. Following the tragedy, he and a brother who had not been with the family when the earthquake struck went to live with an uncle in Rome. Their uncle, Ailvio Spaventa, was a member of the Italian parliament, and the brothers were exposed to the political, intellectual, and social life of the capital. Croce took courses at the University of Rome, where he met Antonio Labriola, a professor in the philosophy department, who guided Croce's reading in aesthetics and philosophy.

In 1886, Croce returned to Naples without completing a degree, and for the next few years he relied on the family fortune to travel throughout Europe and add to his extensive private library. During the late 1880s and 1890s he pursued historical research, focusing on the local history of Naples. In *La storia ridotta sotto il concetto generale dell' arte,* written in 1893, Croce asserted that history was actually an art rather than a science, as the discipline was currently considered, because it was concerned with individual facts and not general laws. In 1895, Labriola introduced Croce to the works of Karl Marx. Although Croce initially embraced Marxist doctrine, he later refuted it in *Materialismo storico ed economia marxistica* (*Historical Materialism and the Economics of Karl Marx*). Croce disagreed with Marx's belief in a determined pattern of historical development, and while he acknowledged the potential impact of Marxism, he denied it any theoretical validity. In 1903 Croce founded *La critica,* a literary and cultural journal, with the young philosopher Giovanni Gentile. While the two later became estranged as a result of political differences, Gentile had an important influence on Croce's intellectual development, guiding him toward philosophical issues and away from strictly literary or historical questions.

For the rest of his life, Croce combined scholarship with political activity. During the 1900s and 1910s, he published the four volumes of *Philosophy of the Spirit,* as well as other works of philosophy, criticism, and historiography. In 1910 he became a senator in the Italian parliament, a lifetime appointment in Italy, and in 1920 and 1921 he also served as Minister of Education. He lost the latter appointment due to his opposition to the new government of Benito Mussolini. Furthermore, his name was banned from public mention, although the publication of *La critica* and the numerous books he wrote during this period was permitted. When Mussolini was overthrown in 1943, Croce played a significant role in Italy's transition to a republican form of government. He served as president of the Italian Liberal party, as a delegate to the parliament that drafted the new Italian constitution, and as a cabinet member in the post-war government. Retiring from politics in 1947, Croce established the Italian Institute for Historical Study at Naples, to which he donated much of his own library. He died in 1952.

Critics generally agree that the essential principles of Croce's thought are contained in the four volumes of *Philosophy of the Spirit: Estetica come scienza dell' espressione e linguistica generale* (*Aesthetic as Science of Expression and General Linguistic*); *Logica come scienza del concetto puro* (*Logic as the Science of the Pure Concept*); *Filosofia della practica, economica ed etica* (*Philosophy of the Practical: Economic and Ethic*); and *Teoria e storia della storiografia* (*History, Its Theory and Practice*). In these writings, Croce maintained that all aspects of human activity can be divided into four realms: the theoretical, the practical, the individual, and the universal. The theoretical realm, which Croce labeled cognition, involves the perception and understanding of reality, while the practical realm, which he called volition, involves the application of ideas and concepts from the theoretical realm. Within each of these realms, Croce then made an additional distinction between the realms of the individual and the universal. Thus, cognition includes both intuition (knowledge of individual experiences and concepts) and logical thought (knowledge of universal experience). Similarly, volition is made up of economics, which is defined as action for individual aims, and ethics, which is defined as action for universal goals. Croce believed that all human activity originates in intuition and develops through logical thought to action.

Of the four treatises that form Croce's *Philosophy of the Spirit, Aesthetic as Science of Expression and General Linguistic* is considered the most important. In this work, Croce asserted that art is intuition and does not extend into any other category of human thought and behavior. He believed that a work of art is merely the outward expression of the artist's emotional inspiration. Croce maintained that criticism contributed to an understanding and enjoyment of a work of art, but he considered distinctions of genre and the study of the history of art irrelevant to the critic's central task, which is identifying and characterizing the uniqueness of an individual work or artist. His own literary criticism covered a broad range of authors, from ancient Greek poets to literary figures of his own day. While some critics have questioned the acuity of Croce's assessment of a particular writer, his critical studies have been generally praised and the theoretical bases of his criticism have been extremely influential.

Croce has also been recognized for his contributions to historiography. Disagreeing with the prevalent nineteenth-century belief that the methodology of the natural sciences should be applied to the study of history, Croce emphasized the importance of intuition in historiography and considered the study of history an art rather than a science. He argued that the most important element in comprehending the past is understanding the thought of those who lived in the time and place under consideration and believed that the role of the historian is to imagine and recreate that thought. He distinguished between a history, which reconstructs the past, including the thoughts of the participants, and a chronicle, which simply recounts the facts of a past event. Croce also argued for a closer relationship between philosophy and history, maintaining that the study of one would enhance understanding of the other.

Because of the great range of Croce's interests, attempts to define the development of his thought and to categorize his philosophical system have for the most part only propagated controversy. Nevertheless, as Cecil Sprigge has stated: "No comparable attempt has been made in modern times to bring into a comprehensive and fully interconnected pattern the entire range of human intellectual, or, to use Croce's own term, spiritual activity: indeed, by inference, the whole range of human experience and behaviour."

(See also *Contemporary Authors,* Vol. 120.)

PRINCIPAL WORKS

I teatri di Napoli, secolo xv-xvii (criticism) 1891

La storia ridotta sotto il concetto generale dell' arte (historiography) 1893
La rivoluzione napoletana del 1799 (history) 1897
Materialismo storico ed economia marxistica (treatise) 1900
  [*Historical Materialism and the Economics of Karl Marx,* 1914]
*Estetica come scienza dell' espressione e linguistica generale (treatise) 1902
  [*Aesthetic as Science of Expression and General Linguistic,* 1909]
Ciò che è vivo e ciò che e morto nella filosofia di Hegel (treatise) 1907
  [*What Is Living and What Is Dead in the Philosophy of Hegel,* 1915]
*Logica come scienza del concetto puro (treatise) 1909
  [*Logic as the Science of the Pure Concept,* 1917]
*Filosofia della practica, economica ed etica (treatise) 1909
  [*Philosophy of the Practical: Economic and Ethic,* 1913]
Problemi di estetica e contributi alla storia dell' estetica italiana (treatise) 1910
La filosofia di Giambattista Vico (criticism) 1911
  [*The Philosophy of Giambattista Vico,* 1913]
Brevario di estetica (essay) 1913
  [*The Breviary of Aesthetic,* 1915; also published as *The Essence of Aesthetic,* 1921]
La letteratura della nuova Italia. 6 vols. (criticism) 1914-40
*Teoria e storia della storiografia (historiography) 1917
  [*History, Its Theory and Practice,* 1921; also published as *Theory and History of Historiography,* 1921]
Contributo alla critica di me stesso (autobiography) 1918
  [*My Autobiography,* 1927]
Goethe (criticism) 1919
  [*Goethe,* 1923]
Ariošto, Shakespeare e Corneille (criticism) 1920
  [*Ariošto, Shakespeare, and Corneille,* 1920]
Nuovi saggi di estetica (essays) 1920
La poesia di Dante (criticism) 1921
  [*The Poetry of Dante,* 1922]
Storia della storiografia italiana nel secolo decimonono. 2 vols. (historiography) 1921
Etica e politica, aggiontovi il contributo all critica dime stesso (treatise) 1922
Poesia e non poesia: Note sulla letteratura euròpea del secolo decimonono (criticism) 1923
  [*European Literature in the Nineteenth Century,* 1924]
Storia del regno di Napoli (history) 1925
  [*History of the Kingdom of Naples,* 1970]
Storia d'Italia dal 1871 al 1915 (history) 1928
  [*A History of Italy, 1871-1915,* 1929]
Storia dell' età barocca in Italia (history) 1929
Storia d'Europa nel secolo decimonono (history) 1932
  [*History of Europe in the Nineteenth Century,* 1933]
Poesia popolare e poesia d'arte (criticism) 1933
Ultimi saggi (essays) 1935
La poesia: Introduzione alla critica e storia della poesia e della litteratura (criticism) 1936
  [*Poetry and Literature: An Introduction to Its Criticism and History,* 1981]
La storia come pensiero e come azione (historiography) 1938
  [*History as the Story of Liberty,* 1941]
Poesia antica e moderna (criticism) 1941
Filosofia e storiografie (essays) 1949

*My Philosophy, and Other Essays on the Moral and Political
    Problems of Our Time* (essays) 1949
Letture di poeti e riflessioni sulla teoria e la critica della poesia
    (criticism) 1950
Essays on Marx and Russia (essays) 1966
Philosophy, Poetry, History: An Anthology of Essays (essays)
    1966

*These volumes make up the *Filosofia dello Spirito* (*Philosophy of the
Spirit.*)

DOUGLAS AINSLIE (essay date 1909)

[*In the following excerpt, Ainslie commends Croce for his contribution to philosophy.*]

[It] will be well to point out that [Croce's] *Æsthetic* forms
part of a complete philosophical system, to which the author
gives the general title of *Philosophy of the Spirit.* The
Æsthetic is the first of the three volumes. The second is the
Logic, the third the *Philosophy of the Practical.*

In the *Logic,* as elsewhere in his system, Croce combats that
false conception, by which natural science, in the shape of
psychology, makes claim to philosophy, and formal logic to
absolute value. The thesis of the *pure concept* cannot be discussed here. It is connected with the logic of evolution as discovered by Hegel, and is the only logic which contains in itself the interpretation and the continuity of reality. Bergson
in his *L'Evolution Créatrice* deals with logic in a somewhat
similar manner. I recently heard him lecture on the distinction between spirit and matter at the Collège de France, and
those who read French and Italian will find that both Croce's
Logic and the book above mentioned by the French philosopher will amply repay their labour. The conception of nature
as something lying outside the spirit which informs it, as the
non-being which aspires to being, underlies all Croce's
thought, and we find constant reference to it throughout his
philosophical system.

With regard to the third volume, the *Philosophy of the Practical,* it is impossible here to give more than a hint of its treasures. I merely refer in passing to the treatment of the will,
which is posited as a unity *inseparable from the volitional act.*
For Croce there is no difference between action and intention,
means and end: they are one thing, inseparable as the intuition-expression of Æsthetic. The *Philosophy of the Practical*
is a logic and science of the will, not a normative science. Just
as in Æsthetic, the individuality of expression made models
and rules impossible, so in practical life the individuality of
action removes the possibility of catalogues of virtues, of the
exact application of laws, of the existence of practical judgments and judgments of value, *previous to action.*

The reader will probably ask here: But what, then, becomes
of morality? The question will be found answered in the *Theory of Æsthetic,* and I will merely say here that Croce's thesis
of the *double degree* of the practical activity, economic and
moral, is one of the greatest contributions to modern thought.
Just as it is proved in the *Theory of Æsthetic* that the *concept*
depends upon the *intuition,* which is the first degree, the primary and indispensable thing, so it is proved in the *Philoso-*

phy of the Practical that *Morality* or *Ethic* depends upon
Economic, which is the *first* degree of the practical activity.
The volitional act is *always economic,* but true freedom of the
will exists and consists in conforming not merely to economic, but to moral conditions, to the human spirit, which is
greater than any individual. Here we are face to face with the
ethics of Christianity, to which Croce accords all honour.
(pp. 682-83)

Among Croce's other important contributions to thought
must be mentioned his definition of History as being æsthetic
and differing from Art solely in that history represents the
real, art the *possible.* In connection with this definition and
its proof, the philosopher recounts how he used to hold an
opposite view. Doing everything thoroughly, he had prepared
and written out a long disquisition on this thesis, which was
already in type, when suddenly, from the midst of his meditations, *the truth flashed upon him.* He saw for the first time
clearly that history cannot be a science, since, like art, it always deals with the particular. Without a moment's hesitation he hastened to the printers and bade them break up the
type. (p. 683)

[Croce's] thoroughness it is which gives such importance to
the literary and philosophical criticisms of *La Critica.*
Croce's method is always historical, and his object in approaching any work of art is to classify the spirit of its author,
as expressed in that work. There are, he maintains, but two
things to be considered in criticising a book. These are, *firstly,*
what is its *peculiarity,* in what way is it singular, how is it differentiated from other works? *Secondly,* what is its degree of
purity?—That is, to what extent has its author kept himself
free from all considerations alien to the perfection of the work
as an expression, as a lyrical intuition? With the answering
of these questions Croce is satisfied. He does not care to know
if the author keep a motor-car, like Maeterlinck; or prefer to
walk on Putney Heath, like Swinburne. This amounts to saying that all works of art must be judged by their own standard. How far has the author succeeded in doing what he intended? (p. 684)

As regards Croce's general philosophical position, it is important to understand that he is *not* a Hegelian, in the sense
of being a close follower of that philosopher. In one of his last
works he deals in a masterly manner with the philosophy of
Hegel. The title may be translated, *What Is Living and What
Is Dead of the Philosophy of Hegel.* Here he explains to us
the Hegelian system more clearly than that wondrous edifice
was ever before explained, and we realise at the same time
that Croce is quite as independent of Hegel as of Kant, of
Vico as of Spinoza. Of course, he has made use of the best of
Hegel, just as every thinker makes use of his predecessors,
and is in his turn made use of by those that follow him. But
it is incorrect to accuse of Hegelianism the author of an anti-
Hegelian *Æsthetic,* of a *Logic* where Hegel is only half accepted, and of a *Philosophy of the Practical* which contains
hardly a trace of Hegel. I give an instance. If the great conquest of Hegel be the dialectic of opposites, his great mistake
lies in the confusion of opposites with things which are distinct but not opposite. If, says Croce, we take as an example
the application of the Hegelian triad that formulates becoming (affirmation, negation, and synthesis), we find it applicable for those opposites which are true and false, good and evil,
being and not-being, but *not applicable* to things which are
distinct but not opposite, such as art and philosophy, beauty
and truth, the useful and the moral. These confusions led

Hegel to talk of the death of art, to conceive as possible a Philosophy of History, and to the application of the natural sciences to the absurd task of constructing a Philosophy of Nature. Croce has cleared away these difficulties by showing that if from the meeting of opposites must arise a superior synthesis, such a synthesis cannot arise from things which are distinct *but not opposite,* since the former are connected together as superior and inferior, and the inferior can exist without the superior, but *not vice versa.* Thus we see how philosophy cannot exist without art, while art, occupying the lower place, can and does exist without philosophy. This brief example reveals Croce's independence in dealing with Hegelian problems. (pp. 685-86)

There can be no doubt of the great value of Croce's work as an *educative influence,* and if we are to judge of a philosophical system by its action on others, then we must place the ***Philosophy of the Spirit*** very high. It may be said with perfect truth that since the death of the poet Carducci there has been no influence in Italy to compare with that of Benedetto Croce. (p. 687)

Douglas Ainslie, *"The Philosopher of Aesthetic: Benedetto Croce,"* in The Fortnightly Review, n.s. v. LXXXVI, No. DXIV, October 1, 1909, pp. 679-88.

BERNARD BOSANQUET (essay date 1919)

[*Bosanquet was an English philosopher who focused on questions of logic and aesthetics in his writings. In the following excerpt, he examines some of the major tenets of Croce's philosophical system.*]

A symmetrical philosophical system, which proclaims as its principle a perfectly spiritual realm of being, realising itself through a continuous conflict of good and evil, in which good is necessarily triumphant and progressive, offers much that is attractive to thoughtful men to-day. When we further note that it promises a complete liberation from metaphysical and theological dogma, and directs our serious attention to the fullest and truest interpretation of actual life and history, rather than to problems of the Absolute or, in any sense, of another world, its attractiveness is probably intensified. But yet our curiosity will be aroused as to the definition of that province which is to be thus excluded from contemplation.

In general terms like these we may describe the first impression produced by Croce's philosophy. (pp. 359-60)

Croce's speculation is plainly animated by a double intellectual motive, to affirm spirituality and to deny transcendence. Subject to this latter condition, we find him applying and developing with extreme resolution and acuteness those effective conceptions which a spiritual monism has at command. There is no reality, he teaches, but the one spirit. It lives in finite individuals, in the main, such as ourselves; their minds are its consciousness; their philosophy is its self-consciousness; their action is its history. Reality is its progress; a necessary but creative evolution in which contradictions, evoked by the spirit's activity, are for ever being resolved by its constructive thought and will. The spirit is a universal which has its life and being in the individual; what is real is always this concrete life; abstractions are always fictitious. Freedom is the volition of the individual mind, identified at once with a given historical situation, which is the necessary basis of its action, and with the thinking will which re-

creates that necessary datum into novelty. The great positive experiences, Beauty, Truth, Pleasure, and Goodness, carry with them respectively their opposites, Ugliness, Error, Pain, and Evil, which, in accordance with the law of reality, are at once necessary to their being, and perpetually absorbed into its self-completion.

Handling uncompromisingly conceptions so comprehensive, a philosopher of acute genius and very considerable learning, a master, moreover, of a vivid and pleasing literary style, he holds an effective position in the modern world. He offers, it would seem, the advantages of monism without mysticism, and of positivism without realism. The physical realist, the pluralist, the pragmatist, have as short a shrift from Croce as they might have had from Hegel. Neither determinist nor indeterminist can stand up against the doctrine of a freedom which arises as the transformation of a necessity. Neither optimist nor pessimist has a chance in face of the idea of a good to which actual evil is at once essential and subordinate. At every point the more commonplace formulæ are exterminated by the criticism of a thinker who wields Hegel's dialectic to the destruction of what is abstract and one-sided. And yet, on the other hand, he is resolute in affirming that it must not and does not carry him a single step towards any Absolute or any being beyond the human world; not a single step beyond the methodological ideas which plain historical data demand for their elucidation.

The system which he offers is simple and symmetrical. The whole of reality lies in the connected activities of the spirit. The whole of philosophy lies in the methodical analysis of these activities, each by itself, though forming, taken together, a connected circle of ideas. There is no single reality in the sense of a supreme experience; there is no unique or central problem of philosophy as such; that is to say, there is no metaphysic and no criterion of the real. We shall have to determine as best we can whether on these terms there is a universe.

The forms or activities of the spirit are two only, knowledge and will. Knowledge is *primâ facie* presupposed by will, but not will by knowledge. Knowledge is the condition of action; will cannot be blind. Each of these divisions, necessarily and symmetrically, falls into two subordinate shapes, related to each other as individual to universal.

For knowledge first appears as imagery or 'intuition.' We are apt, indeed, to suppose that knowledge begins with sense-perception. But there is something which Croce likes to think of as earlier than this; prior certainly in a logical sense, and also, it is clear, to some extent in temporal succession. He gives a striking description of the instant of pure intuition, the living of the sensation, before reflection and volition ensue upon it with lightning rapidity. This is the pure work of imagination—the image-making power—in presenting before the mind the particulars which form its world. It is mere vision or apprehension, without affirmation of real or unreal. And it is the essence of æsthetic intuition. Further—this is one, perhaps the greatest, of Croce's paradoxes—indistinguishably from this comes the beginning of language, which *ab initio* is one with the æsthetic experience. For all intuition is expression, and is essentially inward, whether its medium be colour, musical sound, or any other type of sense-quality, or again, what we call articulate speech. Only, if we insist in thinking of language in terms of speech, we are to identify it with speech in its full unanalysed concreteness, as the self-complete sentence in its continuous song or cry, with its individual accompaniment of dramatic look and gesture. All this expression of the soul is one thing with the æsthetic intuition; it is man's primary utterance of what his world is to him; we may call it his natural lyric. This intuition, the primary form of knowledge, in itself and in its purity, coincides with the province of æsthetic experience, with all that belongs to fine art and to beauty.

For this primitive feature remains the essential character of art, however elaborated and intellectualised. Just as, for the theorist of modern impressionism, the æsthetic vision never forfeits the singleness of the primary appreciation, so for Croce the expressionist, the intuition, though it may grow from an interjection into a five-act tragedy, will never be more than an imaginative presentation, free from any distinction between what is real and what is not. The sayings of Polonius remain images of Polonius' personality; they are not philosophical affirmations in their own right. Indeed we have been mistaken, so Croce will tell us, if we have looked for art and beauty among the loftiest summits of philosophy. Their strength is rather in their humbleness; they belong to the birthday of the spiritual life. 'Poetry is "the maternal language of the human race"; the first men "were by nature sublime poets." ' The poetic imagination is just the human mind uncontaminated by the logical concept.

And thus it is that æsthetic, the philosophy of art, is one with linguistic, the philosophy of language. For language in its full reality is, as we saw, not a conceptual product, but an æsthetic expression. This is the conception of language, as one with the natural poetry—the imaginative intuition—of uncivilised man, which Croce drew from Giambattista Vico, and which, with its implications of a natural evolution of humanity and religion, of hostility to intellectualism, and championship of the concrete sciences and of history, is the ground of that enthusiastic admiration which he feels for the lonely Neapolitan thinker of the early eighteenth century.

The further form of the theoretic activity, which implies æsthetic intuition as its condition precedent, is conceptual thought, the province of Logic and Philosophy. We might say, as a first approximation, that intuition supplies the subjects to which the concept furnishes the predicates. Only, things or events—the subjects of individual judgments—already imply a knowledge charged with conceptual elements, and constructed by the judgment of perception. So that such a statement must be taken to mean no more than that intuition is an element in all judgment, though not furnishing, by itself, so much as the determinate subject of any.

The concept, however, carries us at once into logic and philosophy; and the peculiarity of Croce's logical theory lies in the limitation of what he recognises as the true concept, and the consequent ejection from logic of the greater part of what it is commonly supposed to include.

Logic is the science of the 'pure concept.' The 'pure concept' is the close-linked circle of thought-forms which define the activities of the spirit, and are one with the soul of reality—which might also be called the categories. For they alone are the spirit of thought, which every object contains, but which no multitude of objects can exhaust; such terms as quality, for example, or beauty, or final cause. Not that logic deals with the whole circle of these necessary ideas. The chain which they form is the whole range of philosophy, whereas logic deals only with the single link which belongs to it, the concept of the concept, which is one with the judgment and

the syllogism. Indeed, the position, in Croce's system, of the system itself, the philosophy as a whole, is not at first sight perfectly plain. There seems no place for it except in logic; but in logic, we are plainly told, it is not included.

However this may be, we have to consider the contents of logic itself. The drastic elimination we referred to results from identifying language with æsthetic expression, and confining logic to the study of the pure concept. For logical distinctions derived from the study of words as 'parts of speech,' torn out of their true expressive context, are rejected as 'formalistic,' that is, as falsely formal; in other words, as empirically derived notions pretending to be rational. And current class-conceptions, 'cat,' 'house,' 'rose,' are banished as arbitrary and empirical—exhaustible by a finite number of presentations and so foreign to the pure concept; while mathematical ideas are excluded as unreal abstractions. Only two types of judgment survive, the individual and the universal, that is, the historical or perceptive judgment and the definition; and ultimately only one, namely, the historical judgment as synthesis of individual and universal, in which philosophy is unified with history, and which is rightly assigned an existential character. For the definition, when restored to the context which gave rise to the question which it answers, is considered to have been identified with the historical judgment. Such distinctions as those of the grammatical subject and predicate, the hypothetical and disjunctive judgment, the moods and figures of the syllogism, or property and accident, are thrown aside as capriciously derived from an invalid analysis of language. And the severance of the natural sciences, their laws and classifications, from true logical thought, precludes any attempt to pursue the adventure of reason into the world of presumptive implication; that is, to explain the relations of what have been called Induction and Deduction, or to connect the law of Identity with the Uniformity of Nature. A question might be raised whether such a logic does not forfeit more of rationality by its narrowness than it gains by its purity. All that philosophy can truly say of nature lies for Croce, like philosophy as a whole, in the full interpretation of the perceptive or historical judgment. History, as the interpretation of individual fact, is one with philosophy. And nature, considered as physical, is a creation of abstract natural science, but so far as it can be considered real, falls within history. There is no sense in a philosophy of nature over and above science, or in a philosophy of history over and above history. They would be simply science and history superfluously re-edited.

Such is the theoretical form of spirit with its two subforms Æsthetic and Logic, to each of which one of Croce's systematic treatises is devoted. The practical form of the spirit falls into subdivisions symmetrical with these, the Economic and the Moral Will, the treatment of which is included in a single volume, the *Philosophy of Practice.*

As the theoretical spirit begins with intuition so the practical spirit begins with wants. The will directed to 'one's own particular end' (*fine suo particolare*) is what Croce calls the 'economic' activity of the spirit; and with its satisfaction or dissatisfaction there arise the feelings of pleasure and pain. For he does not recognise feelings as a third type of experience in addition to thought and will; he takes them as one with elementary practical activity *qua* successful or unsuccessful. The 'economic' will, then, is the condition of the moral will, and, so to speak, its vehicle. 'As æsthetic intuition knows the phenomenon or nature, and philosophic intuition the noumenon or spirit; so economic activity wills the phenomenon or nature, and moral activity the noumenon or spirit.'

In the recognition of the economic activity Croce considers that he has done justice to the relative truth of Utilitarianism. For there cannot be a will which is not directed to the supply of some particular want, a will which is not useful or purposive in the sense of being directed to some end or other.

Here, as in æsthetic experience, the question of priority raises a difficulty. Though we are expressly warned that the economic will is not definable as egoism, and that morality must be held to cover the whole province of conduct, yet it is clear from the paradoxical examples of 'economic' merits which are offered for our admiration—in Iago, Cæsar Borgia, Farinata, Ser Ciappelletto—that the economic volition is capable of being ideally considered as a stage independent of morality and akin to some specially self-seeking quality in the will. And, although Croce has launched an annihilating criticism at the utilitarian theory when considered as denying the distinctively moral volition, yet he says in so many words that this economic form of will is 'individual, hedonistic and utilitarian.' A question might be raised whether the phrase quoted above *'fine suo particolare'* is not equivocal as between the particularity of the want subserved, and the privateness of the advantage which it represents to the agent. The particular wants of unreflective human beings are not necessarily hedonistic or especially self-regarding. Even the lower animals have direct impulses to self-sacrifice. And it looks as if, from a prejudice that in beginning with particular wants or needs we must be beginning with private pleasure or advantage, a confusion had arisen, covered by the common term 'economic,' between the character of highly deliberate phases of irrational self-indulgence, and that implied in ordinary particular desires which terminate upon their objects. The reason is plain, if we consider the formula of Croce's scheme. The unreflective particular wants suggest the idea of priority; the highly deliberate indulgence of criminal propensities confirms a contrast with the moral will, and yet indicates a compatibility with methodical reflective economics which is lacking to the particular wants that were the point of departure. But the 'economic' merits of Iago are surely ethical qualities—his courage, his unity of purpose, his tenacity. They belong to that trace of morality which Plato found in the honour that must prevail amongst thieves; and he was right in arguing that to be utterly immoral is to be utterly impotent in action. The relative independence of the economic will is not a priority but an acquisition. It is independent only by permission of morality, and within limits set by social organisation. (pp. 360-67)

The ethical form of the spirit's activity is the will which wills the universal end, by means of and within the particular objects, which, as the system of economic wants, are its vehicle and condition. It may be doubted whether the introduction of the relative Utilitarianism leaves this relation perfectly clear. Certainly, in our higher interests as in all our actions, we want what we want, and to get what we want is so far pleasant. But it is another thing to say that what we want, when we act, is the pleasure of getting what we want. What we want is the thing we desire, it may be our neighbour's ruin or his good, but not the pleasure of satisfying our want. The distinction is familiar in the hedonistic controversy, but it is a question whether Croce sufficiently recognises it.

It is important that in the doctrine of the moral will, the reality of freedom on the one hand and the unreality of evil on the other—truths difficult to conciliate—are both vigorously maintained. If the view is paradoxical yet it is a valuable side of truth, brilliantly expounded.

In the first place, volition is the act founded on the given situation. You are responsible for the whole of this, as material to be dealt with. You cannot say, 'I intended so well, but the situation divorced my will from my intention and made it bad.' Intention is coextensive with will. If you have to act in ignorance, you must accept your ignorance as part of the situation. You are aware of it; you take the responsibility of it, as you take the responsibility of your next step upon an ice-slope. Definite theoretical error, on the other hand, a different thing from ignorance, does not exist. We catch our breath at the paradox. What it means is this. To think is to think truly; to think falsely is not to think, but to do some convenient action of another kind—to be careless or slovenly or to lie. The argument applies to all ugliness, error, incoherence, and evil; it demands a moment's attention. It rests on an assured truth, that in all negation there is an assertion of some positive factor which excludes the term denied. So it is, then, with Croce, in error and evil. Both, not the latter only, are practical in their origin, and imply a positive action which replaces or excludes what should have been thought or done. A wife hands her husband in the dark the poisonous lotion in place of his medicine. (The example is not Croce's.) She thought it was the right bottle. The act has its rational explanation from the agent's point of view. The identification seemed to her sufficient. To pronounce it false cannot be the part of the agent at the time of acting; and the same applies to evil. To pronounce the knowledge false or the action bad is a comment made by one who is wiser or better. An error is then an act of slovenliness, of *parti pris,* of rebellion; together with a comment or desire in the spectator. 'There ought to have been here a genuine act of thought.' Thus Croce defends the Inquisition on the ground of the moral discipline essential to conscientious thinking. We err only when we wish to err. It seems true that all error is due to one-sided emphasis. And this may well arise from indolence or bias, though surely, in the main, it is inherent in the finiteness of thought—a point of view which Croce appears to neglect.

Thus theoretical ignorance can never be pleaded as turning a good intention into a bad volition. But the point of the paradox is partly broken by a distinction between the action and the event. Volition and action are one, but action and event are two; because the event includes the actions of innumerable beings other than any single agent. Though you may judge an action by intention, therefore, you cannot judge it by success. If you judge morally in history, you must take care to judge not an event but an action.

The paradox above stated affects the reality of evil. Freedom, as we said at starting, is the creative work of the spirit as it transforms a given situation by the solution of the problem which it offers. But in every situation we are beset by innumerable solicitations, and we cannot do justice to them all. We may fail by passive acceptance, or by caprice, which are at bottom the same thing. The respect in which we fail, our passivity or non-will, what we let go or let be, is evil, the evil which is the shadow of good and its condition. Now, as we saw, evil, like error, cannot be such for the agent. His act, *de facto,* is a fulfilment of his want, and, for him, has its justification. Only in the comment of the better man, perhaps in that of the agent after the fact, 'Would it were otherwise!' does it reveal itself as evil. This gives us Croce's meaning when he says that as real, as a positive fact, it is not evil. It is only explicitly evil when and where its badness is revealed; but then and there it is no longer real. It is *ipso facto* rejected and overcome. Its positive poisonous reaction, we may think, is inadequately recognised.

From these ideas we are led to his 'dialectical optimism,' which translates into terms of good and evil the fundamental idea of reality as 'becoming,' as a struggle of 'being and not-being,' in which the negative is continually absorbed, to the enrichment of the positive. These conceptions are familiar; but in Croce's hands they are subordinated to the reservation we mentioned at starting, that all transcendence, we might almost say all totality, is repudiated. The reality is itself *a* progress and *in* progress to infinity, though the attainment of the end—Croce is aware of the fate of Tantalus—is not infinitely deferred, but is continuously achieved. Cosmic advance is necessary and demonstrated.

> From the cosmic point of view, at which we now place ourselves, reality shows itself as a continuous growing upon itself; nor is a real regress ever conceivable, because evil, being that which is not, is unreal, and that which is is always and only the good. The real is always rational, and the rational is always real. Cosmic progress, then, is itself also the object of affirmation, not problematic but apodictic.

· · · · ·

> The work of the spirit is not finished and never will be finished. Our yearning for something higher is not in vain. The very yearning, the infinity of our desire, is proof of the infinity of that progress. The plant dreams of the animal, the animal of man, man of superman; for this, too, is a reality, if it be reality that with every historical movement man surpasses himself. The time will come when the great deeds and the great works now our memory and our boast will be forgotten, as we have forgotten the works and the deeds, no less great, of those beings of supreme genius who created what we call human life, and seem to us now to have been savages of the lowest grade, almost men-monkeys. They will be forgotten, for the document of progress is in *forgetting.*

· · · · ·

> Man does not seek a God external to himself and almost a despot, who commands and benefits him capriciously; nor does he aspire to an immortality of insipid ease; but he seeks for that God which he has in himself, and aspires to that activity which is both life and death.

It is characteristic of Croce that the positive account of the ethical will is brief. The universal is the object of the whole philosophy of the spirit; and there is nothing special to reveal when you come upon it in moral philosophy. You may call it the whole, life, freedom, progress. There is no prerogative insistence on the social origin of moral content. The social situation is a situation like another; each has its requirements. He is clear that happiness is activity, and that to will the good, that is, to will activity, and to be happy, are the same thing.

Two more points must be noted before we leave the philosophy of practice. First, that nature as it is, not the abstract physical nature of science, participates in evolution, and *therefore* is conscious. And secondly, that, whereas at first knowledge seemed the condition precedent of practice, it is now clear that practice, the creation of reality, is no less the condition of knowledge. Reality is an eternal circle between the two. To some students this will seem ominous. They will reflect that 'Certainly hitherto we have found everywhere that an unresting circle of this kind [between thought and will] is the mark of appearance. To this question we must return.

In attempting to appreciate the system which has been thus imperfectly sketched, it will be necessary to pursue a point of view on which Croce himself has laid great stress, as his essential difference from Hegel. Our object is not to criticise historically his reading of that thinker's ideas, but to illustrate his position by comparison with a substantial truth which emerges from Hegel's teaching, as from that of many great philosophers before him.

The point in question is the nature of reality as a whole, and of the criterion by which philosophy can appreciate it; in other words, the unity implied in experience, and the principle of metaphysic.

We may approach it thus. Croce has developed, in an essay which is the logical keystone of his philosophy ["**Saggio sullo Hegel**"], a fundamental objection to the course of Hegel's dialectic. He points out, what is an obvious fact, that there is a plain difference between the relation to each other of positive terms and their negations, such as being and not-being, true and false, and that of conceptions both of which are positive, and which are consistent with each other, though distinct, such as truth and beauty, which according to his system are separate phases of the spirit. Now Hegel's dialectic, the process by which in his logic a progress arises through the conciliation of opposites in more complete ideas, treats both these types of connexion alike—that of positive and negative terms, and that of terms both positive, but distinguished from each other—as degrees in a logical progression. This identical treatment Croce holds to be irrational. He confines the principle of advance by absorption of negations—dialectic proper—to such cases as the progression from being through not-being to becoming, or from truth through falsehood to a richer truth. The unity in distinction of positive phases of the spirit, as of beauty with truth or with goodness, seems to him to be of a different order. These terms do not appear to him to be abstractions; and the movement from one to the other he treats as a circle or an alternation, there being no internal contradiction within each to suggest a transition to a higher totality. We judge from his attitude that he does not recognise the simple and fundamental principle of the reasoning. (pp. 367-72)

The *coincidentia oppositorum,* the advance by contradictions, is for Croce, so far as we can see, a method of which no rationale need be offered, and which is restricted, in harmony with its paradoxical appearance, to abstract terms and their negations. But in truth there is a sound and universal rationale. It is the law of implication, *ex pede Herculem.* You incur contradiction in affirming a partial datum as such, because of the immanence of the whole. This is the criterion; coherence and comprehensiveness together are the test of wholeness, that is, of reality. In remarkable passages Croce refuses to find within such an experience as beauty any contradiction which could explain the transition, say, to truth. This confirms the suggestion that he does not connect the nature or movement of reality with the conception of a whole.

But the conception seems indispensable, even to account for the facts as he assumes them. And it leaves us free to examine all experiences on their merits as degrees of reality. There ceases to be any ground for Croce's criticism on the dialectic, that it represents substantial experiences, such as art, history, and the natural sciences, as imperfect forms of philosophy, destroying the 'autonomy' of the forms of the spirit. It is remarkable that the worst of such errors, the treatment of æsthetic experience and of religion as forms of knowledge, are adopted by Croce himself, though not, in our belief, justly attributable to Hegel.

If we attach importance to this point of view, a good deal may be reconsidered which has given us pause in Croce, without destroying the value of his resolute anti-transcendentism.

He denounces uncompromisingly, for instance, the ideas of metaphysics, of a general philosophy, of a single persistent problem to which all philosophy must address itself. But we found that we could not refer his two movements of the real to a single mainspring. We could discover no logical principle in his 'degrees of reality.' We could not believe that his partial phases of the spirit are severally free from internal contradiction. So that, although we may rejoice in his repudiation of any 'other' world which cannot be established as the right interpretation of 'this,' it still seems to us that philosophy is mutilated if we do not recognise as its central problem the nature of reality, its degrees, and its criterion. It is, we cannot help believing, for want of such an inherent order that an artificial symmetry has been adopted. There is a simple test. The scheme allows no implication forwards. Æsthetic and Economic respectively are implied in what succeeds them, but do not imply it. Now implication depends on the whole immanent in the parts. Where there are parts without implication, parts which are not more than themselves, you have no true whole of reality and no philosophical system.

We may return for a moment to the æsthetic experience. We saw that its priority was doubtful. It is an innocence; but it is an acquired innocence. Nor is æsthetic one with linguistic. If we take all expression to be language, we must still consider expression to be content no less than content is expression; and, if we give the word 'language' its full significance of speech, which involves the analysis of ideas into other ideas, the doctrine comes to be two removes from truth. It is a triumph of art to subordinate speech to beauty, but speech in itself has other aims. And we regret that, by identifying expression with inward intuition, Croce is led wholly to deny the æsthetic significance of physical media, and to reject all enquiry into distinctions between the fine arts founded upon their differences. 'Externalisation' is for him a mere practical act, subsequent upon 'intuition,' which is purely ideal. It has no æsthetic function, but is merely instrumental to preserving and reproducing the beauty created by inward imagination. Now grant him that the physical world is nothing but spirit. Then he must not annul its significance, but must translate it into spiritual terms. The discipline of the soul through the body, the artist's delight in his mastery of the plastic media, constitute the training of the determinate imagination which is made one with the spirit of things in some special world of beauty. It is a poor idealism which robs the soul of its body. Logically considered, again, æsthetic experience is not knowledge, but has a fundamentally different character. In it, idea and existence are unseparated; and it thus peculiarly anticipates the character of the whole reality. Practice and theory are both, we might say, discursive. In both the idea is opposed to the existence, though in each the adjustment is differently effected.

Beside the subordination of æsthetic and economic, we have to note the exclusion of 'other spiritual forms' for which the system can find no place. Such are sociality, religion, metaphysic. For example, 'Religion is nothing but knowledge, and does not differ from its other forms and subforms.' 'There is nothing left to share with religion'; that is to say, the other forms and subforms occupy the whole domain. Some of us, on the other hand, agree with a weighty judgment: 'The man who demands a reality more solid than that of the religious consciousness, seeks he knows not what.' What is it, then, finally, that Croce desires to reject in repudiating transcendence? And what attitude does he adopt in consequence towards the fundamental contentions of recent philosophy?

In a very plain-spoken paper he insists on the idea that philosophy is nothing more than the methodology of history-writing. This would naturally mean that philosophical conceptions are purely instrumental to the ordering and elucidation of historical data. And he undoubtedly intends to insist on some conclusion of this nature, although it does not follow that such conceptions are pure postulates or fictions.

What he has primarily in mind, when he denies transcendence, is, I should venture to think, the Catholic creed and philosophy, which in the judgment of Gentile, a thinker much in harmony with Croce, is the pre-eminent heir and representative of other-worldliness (Gentile's 'Il Modernismo'). Thus religion becomes a creed, and metaphysic a theology. It is in this sense, in the main, that Croce repudiates both.

But he also plainly rejects, and with some contumely, the Absolute, and the Reality contrasted with Appearance, of Hegel and of some kindred philosophers. His logical point in this rejection is that he takes these forms of experience not as inclusive of what is relative and apparent, but as parts of existence selected *qua* superior in nature to other parts, that is, as sharing the character which makes the thing in itself essentially an 'other world.' We cannot here discuss whether this is fair to Hegel. Nor can we be certain whether Croce would apply it to the absolutist theory familiar to us in England. We, of course, should deny its applicability.

It is noticeable that Croce assents to the use of such expressions as Absolute, God, religion, metaphysic, in his own sense of the words. Therefore he admits an absolutism unaffected by the comic hue which he finds in the absolutist of to-day. But what he understands by such terms appear to be the forms of the spirit in their re-entrant curve, and the human consciousness of them, taken as the self-consciousness of the reality whose progression they constitute. What he denies, I think, is the unity of things in a supreme inclusive experience, or of spirits in a human-divine nature especially aware of itself in the religious consciousness. This denial follows from his disregard of the principle of totality; and the rejection of metaphysic as the criterion of the real, addressed to the fundamental problem of philosophy, inevitably follows.

How far, we asked, does he recognise a universe? Reality *is* a progress to infinity, and does not merely include infinite progressions. Therefore perfection, if there is to be any, must lie in the series itself, and this has familiar difficulties, which we saw that Croce endeavours to escape. It is a hard saying, for instance, that the greatest things we have yet known are destined to be forgotten, especially as the human world seems sometimes to be treated as the universe. There is, however, a constant universe in respect of the categories such as beauty and truth. Reality surpasses itself *ad infinitum,* but does not surpass these. But again he has an instructive objection to a dialectic movement which comes to an end. If it has a *raison d'être* at all, why not go on for ever? This shows how he ignores the principle that the mover is the immanent whole. For him, we suspect, there is no whole for the abstractions to return to. But the genuine infinite, we should urge, though inexhaustible, is self-complete.

And we must note that inclusive transcendence is involved in Croce's own conceptions. There is the unity of past and present in history; 'all history is contemporary.' This implies a reality which includes appearances. The unity is obviously different from what the individual directly experiences, and is more real. But much that has happened is, on his view, irrevocably gone. It has become a thing in itself, for it is an inaccessible real. The universe, if there is one, arbitrarily ejects portions of itself.

Finally, what is that religion, the only religion he admits, which is superseded and replaced by philosophy? There are two possible answers.

If we take philosophy to be a strictly speculative activity, which is surely the literal truth, then a religion, destined to be replaced by it, must be a theoretical doctrine; and this is what Croce seemed to say clearly that religion is. If so, we may venture to affirm, he simply and totally ignores the religious consciousness.

But another possibility is worth mentioning. Philosophy may in a sense replace religion if it contains, but elucidates, the genuine religious experience. But then it is no longer philosophy literally taken. It has been made into more than it necessarily is. Religion, the individual's self-subordination to supreme power and goodness—supernaturalism has nothing to do with the matter—will still be the most solid fact in the world. But philosophy—and this is how Hegel understood it, for the Absolute spirit includes and does not supersede its forms—would have for its task

> to show that religion is the truth, the complete reality, of the mind that lived in Art, that founded the State, and sought to be dutiful and upright; the truth, the crowning fruit of all scientific knowledge, of all human affections, of all secular consciousness. Its lesson [that of philosophy] ultimately is that there is nothing essentially common or unclean; that the holy is not parted off from the true and the good and the beautiful.
>
> [William Wallace, introduction to *Hegel's Philosophy of Mind* (1894)]

This conclusion would be a consequence of the attitude for which reality is the whole; and we should like to believe that so remarkable a thinker as Croce is not unsympathetic to it. (pp. 372-77)

> *Bernard Bosanquet, "The Philosophy of Benedetto Croce," in* The Quarterly Review, *Vol. 231, No. 459, April, 1919, pp. 359-77.*

R. G. COLLINGWOOD (essay date 1921)

[*Collingwood was a highly respected English archaeologist and philosopher whose writings often focus on the relationship be-* tween philosophy and history. In the following excerpt, he outlines Croce's philosophy of history as presented in *Teoria e storia della storiografa.*]

The ideal of a combined study of philosophy and history is energetically supported by Croce. Himself a philosopher of eminence and an accomplished historian, he feels acutely in his own person the profit which each of his pursuits in turn derives from the other. The historian must study the philosophy of his period if he is to understand those forces which ultimately shaped its destiny; if he does not follow the thoughts of the men whose actions he is studying he can never enter into the life of his period, and can at best observe it from outside as a sequence of unexplained facts, or facts to be explained by physical causes alone. And the philosopher must in his turn study history. How else is he to understand why certain problems at certain times pressed for solution on the philosopher's mind? How else is he to understand the individual philosopher's temperament, his outlook on life, the very symbolism and language in which he has expressed himself? In short, if the philosopher is to understand the history of philosophy he must study the general history of humanity; and a philosophy which ignores its own history is a philosophy which spends its labour only to rediscover errors long dead.

History without philosophy is history seen from the outside, the play of mechanical and unchanging forces in a materialistically conceived world: philosophy without history is philosophy seen from the outside, the veering and backing, rising and falling, of motiveless winds of doctrine. "Both these are monsters." But history fertilised by philosophy is the history of the human spirit in its secular attempt to build itself a world of laws and institutions in which it can live as it wishes to live; and philosophy fertilised by history is the progressive raising and solving of the endless intellectual problems whose succession forms the inner side of this secular struggle. Thus the two studies which, apart, degenerate into strings of empty dates and lists of pedantic distinctions—"To seventeen add two, And Queen Anne you will view," "Barbara celarent darii ferioque prioris"—become, together, a single science of all things human.

This is the point of view from which Croce proposes, and in his own work carried out, a closer union between philosophy and history. . . . [We] propose here to discuss his views on the nature of history and its relation to philosophy. As our purpose is rather to criticise than to expound, we shall select some of his views and examine these as typical of the whole.

The book in which he expounds them is the ***Teoria e storia della storiografia,*** which, like many of Croce's books, falls into two sections, a theoretical and a historical. The relation between the two is close; the ideas which are discussed in the former are exemplified in the latter, and the process of development followed in the latter is only intelligible in the light of the principles laid down in the former. Our concern here is especially with the theoretical section; not because it is the most striking—the historical section is a rapid but extremely brilliant survey of the progress of historical thought, in which the characteristics of succeeding periods are set forth with a penetration and fairness which could hardly be bettered—but because our present business is the explicit statement of theoretical principles.

In order to arrive at a clear concept of what history is, Croce begins by telling us what it is not. It is not annals. That is to say, it is not the lists of dates with which a superficial observer confuses it. To the outward eye, a book may consist of mere chronological tables; but to the historian these tables mean real history, not because they are, but because they stand for, the thought which is history. History goes on in the mind of the historian: he thinks it, he enacts it within himself: he identifies himself with the history he is studying and actually lives it as he thinks it, whence Croce's paradox that "all history is contemporary history." Annals, on the other hand, belong to the past; the schoolboy learning a list of dates does not live them in his thought, but takes them as something alien imposed upon him from outside—brute facts, dead and dry; no living reality such as his teacher, if he is a good historian, can enjoy in reading the same list. Annals, then, are past history, and therefore not history at all. They are the dry bones of history, its dead corpse.

This is illuminating, and satisfactory enough until we begin to reflect upon it. History is thought, annals the corpse of thought. But has thought a corpse? And if so, what is it like? The corpse of an organism is something other than the organism itself: what, for an idealistic philosopher like Croce, is there other than thought, in terms of which we can give a philosophically satisfactory definition of the corpse of thought?

Croce's general "philosophy of the spirit" supplies him with a ready-made answer. Nothing exists but the spirit; but the spirit has two sides or parts, thought and will. Whatever is not thought is will. If you find some fact which cannot be explained as an instance of thought, you must explain it as an instance of will. Thought is the synthesis of subject and object, and its characteristic is truth: will is the creation of an object by the subject, and its characteristic is utility. Wherever you find something which appears at first sight to be an example of thinking, but which on inspection is found not to possess the quality of truth, it follows that it must be an example of willing, and possess the quality of usefulness. Such, in a rough outline, is the principle of analysis which Croce applies in this book and elsewhere. History is thought: there is here a perfect synthesis of subject and object, inasmuch as the historian thinks himself into the history, and the two become contemporary. Annals are not thought but willed; they are constructed—"drawn up"—by the historian for his own ends; they are a convention serving the purposes of historical thought, as musical notation serves the purposes of musical thought without being musical thought; they are not true but useful.

This is the answer which Croce gives, or rather tries to give, to the question we raised. But he does not really succeed in giving it. He cannot bring himself to say that annals are simply devoid of truth, are in no sense an act of thought. That would amount to saying that annals are the words, and history their meaning: which would not be what he wanted. So he says that annals are "sounds, or graphic symbols representing sounds, held together and maintained not by an act of thought which thinks them (in which case they would once more be supplied with content), but by an act of will which thinks it useful for certain purposes of its own to preserve these words, empty or half empty though they be." "Or half empty." This is a strange reservation. Are the words of which annals are composed, then, not empty after all? Are they half full, half full, that is, of thought? But if so, the distinction between the act of thought and the act of will has broken down: annals are only history whose words mean less indeed than

the same words as used by history proper, but still have meaning, are still essentially vehicles of thought. And Croce would be the first to admit and insist that a difference of degree has nothing to do with a philosophical question like this.

This is not the only passage in which Croce's clearness of vision and common sense break through the abstractions of his formal philosophy. He tries to maintain a philosophy according to which every act of the spirit falls under either one or the other of two mutually exclusive heads (theoretical and practical), subdivided into four sub-heads (intuition and thought; economic willing and ethical willing), so related that the second and fourth sub-heads involve the first and third respectively (thought is also intuition, ethical action is also economic action), but not *vice versa*. Now this formal philosophy of the mind is purely psychological and empirical in character; it is what Croce himself calls "naturalism" or "transcendence." And with that side of himself which never ceases to combat all kinds of naturalism, he combats this philosophy of his own with the rest. To go into this fully would involve a detailed analysis of Croce's other works, and we shall not pursue it here. But we must refer to it, and insist upon this general principle: that there are two Croces, the realist, dualist, empiricist, or naturalist, who delights in formal distinctions and habitually works in dualistic or transcendent terms, and the idealist, whose whole life is a warfare upon transcendence and naturalism in all their forms, who sweeps away dualisms and reunites distinctions in a concrete or immanent unity. A great part of Croce's written work consists in a debate between these two, one building up dualisms and the other dismantling them; sometimes failing to dismantle them. This we shall find throughout the present book. In fact, at the end of our inquiry, we shall see reason to suspect that this double-mindedness has now become so intolerable to Croce himself that he feels impelled to destroy altogether a philosophy so deeply at variance with itself, and to take refuge in a new field of activity.

The dualism between history and annals is really, if I understand it aright, an expository or "pedagogic" dualism, confused by the attempt to interpret it as a real or philosophical dualism, to which end it has been mistakenly identified with the distinction between a symbol and its meaning. An expository dualism is a common enough device: in order to expound a new idea one frequently distinguishes it point by point from an old, thereby developing what looks like a dualism between them, without, however, at all meaning to imply that the dualism is real, and that the old conception has a permanent place in one's philosophy alongside of the new. Thus the antithesis between the flesh and the spirit, developed in order to define the term spirit, is misunderstood if it is hardened into a metaphysical dualism: so again that between mind and matter, art and nature, and so forth. In such cases the two terms are not names for two co-ordinate realities, but an old and a new name for the same thing, or even an old and a new "definition of the Absolute," and the new supersedes the old: if the old is compelled to live on alongside the new, it sets up a dualism whose effect is precisely to destroy the whole meaning of the new conception and to characterise the whole view as a naturalistic or transcendent philosophy.

This is curiously illustrated by Croce's chapter on "History and Annals." "History is living history, annals are dead history: history is contemporary history, annals are past history: history is primarily an act of thought, annals an act of will." Here again the word *primarily* gives everything away; but, ignoring that, it is strange that the category in which annals fall is indifferently, and as it were synonymously, called *the past, dead,* and *the will.* Here—and numerous other passages could be quoted which prove the same thing—Croce is really identifying the distinction of thought and will with the distinction of living and dead, spirit and matter. The will is thought of as the non-spiritual; that is to say, the concept of dead matter has reappeared in the heart of idealism, christened by the strange name of will. This name is given to it because, while Croce holds the idealistic theory that thought thinks itself, he unconsciously holds the realistic or transcendent theory that the will wills not itself but the existence of a lifeless object other than itself, something unspiritual held in existence by an act of the will. Thus, wherever Croce appeals from the concept of thought to the concept of will, he is laying aside his idealism and falling back into a transcendent naturalism.

But now the idealist reasserts himself. A corpse, after all, is not merely dead: it is the source of new life. So annals are a necessary part of the growth of history: thought, as a philosopher has said, "feeds saprophytically upon its own corpse." Annals are therefore not a mere stupid perversion of history, but are essential to history itself. Annals are a "moment" of history, and so therefore is will of thought, matter of mind, death of life, error of truth. Error is the negative moment of thought, without which the positive or constructive moment, criticism, would have nothing to work upon. Criticism in destroying errors constructs truth. So historical criticism, in absorbing and digesting annals, in showing that they are not history, creates the thought that is history. This is idealism; but it stultifies the original dualism. The distinction between history and annals is now not a distinction between what history is (thought) and what history is not (will), but between one act of thought (history) and another act of thought of the same kind, now superseded and laid aside (annals), between the half-truth of an earlier stage in the process of thought and the fuller truth that succeeds it. This is no dualism, no relation between *A* and *not-A,* and therefore it cannot be symbolized by the naturalistic terminology of thought and will; it is the dialectical relation between two phases of one and the same development, which is throughout a process of both thinking and willing.

The same fundamental vice underlies the very attractive discussion of "pseudo-histories." We all know the historian who mistakes mere accuracy for truth, the "philological" historian; and him who mistakes romance for history, the "poetical" historian; and him who imagines that the aim of history is not to tell the truth but to edify or glorify or instruct, the "pragmatic" historian. And Croce characterises them and discusses their faults in an altogether admirable way. But he wants to prove that he has given us a list of all the possible forms of false history, and this can be done by appealing to the list of the "forms of the spirit." But the appeal not only fails in detail—for his list of pseudo-histories tallies very ill with the list of forms of the spirit—but is false in principle.

For "poetical" history, to take an example, is only a name calling attention to a necessary feature of all history. Croce shows how Herodotus, Livy, Tacitus, Grote, Mommsen, Thierry, and so forth, all wrote from a subjective point of view, wrote so that their personal ideals and feelings coloured their whole work and in parts falsified it. Now, if this is so, who wrote real history, history not coloured by points of view and ideals? Clearly, no one. It is not even desirable that anyone should. History, to be, must be seen, and must be seen by somebody, from somebody's point of view. And doubtless, every history so seen will be in part seen falsely. But this is not an accusation against any particular school of historians; it is a law of our nature. The only safe way of avoiding error is to give up looking for the truth.

And here, curiously, Croce breaks out into a panegyric on error, as if conscious that he was being too hard on it. The passage is a most interesting combination of naturalism and idealism. Error, says Croce, is not a "fact"; it is a "spirit"; it is "not a Caliban, but an Ariel, breathing, calling, and enticing from every side, and never by any effort to be solidified into hard fact." This image implies that error does not, as such, exist; that is, that no judgment is wholly or simply erroneous, wholly devoid of truth: which is orthodox idealism, but quite contrary to Croce's general theory of error. But it also implies that error as such is valuable and good: he speaks definitely of the "salutary efficacy of error"; and this conflicts not only with the description of pseudo-histories as "pathological"—and therefore, presumably, to be wholly avoided—but also with Croce's own idealism, and with the view which surely seems reasonable, that the indubitable value and efficacy of errors belongs to them not *qua* errors but *qua* (at least partial) truths. An error like historical materialism is, as Croce says, not a fact; that is because, its falsity discovered, it is banished, it becomes a memory. Also, as Croce says, it is, or rather we should say was, useful: it superseded a worse error, historical romanticism. But it was once a fact, and then it was a truth—the best truth that could be had then, anyhow; and then, too, it was useful, as an improvement on its predecessor. To-day it is not a fact (except for historians of thought), nor true, nor yet useful. The passage is confused because Croce is assigning to error as such the merits of truth; which is an attempt to express the fact that error as such does not exist, and that what we call an error is in part true and therefore has the "salutary efficacy" which belongs to truth alone. This confusion is due to the vacillation between naturalism, for which some statements are just true and others just false, and idealism, for which truth and falsehood are inextricably united in every judgment, in so far as it creates itself by criticising another, and becomes itself in turn the object of further criticism.

This vacillation is the more interesting as much of Croce's treatment of error is purely naturalistic, and shows no trace of idealism. His general theory of error, in the **Logica,** is absolutely naturalistic. Thought, he there argues, is as such true, and can never be erroneous: an error, whatever it is, cannot be a thought. What is it, then? Why, an act of will. We need hardly point out the absurdities of such a theory. We only wish to point out its naturalistic character; to lay stress on the distinction implied between a truth, as containing no error, and an error, as containing no truth, correlative with that between pure thinking and pure willing, and based on the same naturalistic or transcendent logic. So again his inquiry into the varieties (phenomenology) of error, in this book and elsewhere, and the list of pseudo-histories, are purely naturalistic; and so again is a highly "transcendent" type of argument not uncommon with him, which traces the origin of a philosophical error to the baneful influence of some other activity of the spirit. Thus philosophical errors, which by their very nature can only have arisen within philosophy itself, are ascribed to science (the fallacy of the independent object) and religion (the dualism of *a priori* and *a posteriori* truths), errors whose only connection with science or religion is that when philosophers believed in them they applied them to the interpretation of these activities: whereupon Croce, having rejected them as general philosophical principles, un-critically retains them as adequate accounts of activities to which he has not paid special attention, and thus credits these activities with originating them. The result is a kind of my-thology, in which Philosophy or Thought takes the part of a blameless and innocent heroine led into errors by the vil-lains Science and Religion. These flights of pure naturalism in Croce have a curious eighteenth-century flavour; it is diffi-cult in reading them to feel ourselves in the forefront of mod-ern philosophy; for Science and Religion, the villains of the piece, represent precisely that Caliban of embodied factual error whose banishment from philosophy has just been rati-fied by Croce himself.

The same naturalism colours the chapter on the "Positivity of History." Here the doctrine is expounded that "history al-ways justifies, never condemns." History always expresses positive judgments, never negative; that is, it explains why things happened as they did, and this is to prove that they happened rightly. "A fact which seems merely bad is a non-historical fact," a fact not yet thought out successfully by the historian, not yet understood. The historian as such therefore always justifies: if he condemns, he proves himself no histori-an. What is he, then? Why, a partisan; one who acts instead of thinking, serves practical instead of theoretical needs. The historian as such is a thinker; "the history which once was lived is by him thought, and in thought the antitheses which arose in volition or feeling no longer exist." To condemn in thought is to "confuse thought with life."

Here as usual we sympathise warmly: we know the historian who regards history as a melodrama, and we do not regard him as the best kind of historian. But we are trying at present to think philosophically; and the dualism between thought and life makes us a little uncomfortable. Life, we are told, is the scene of value-judgments, judgments of good and evil, which are products of the will; thought knows only the truth, and in the eye of thought everything that is, is justified. Par-tiality is proper and necessary to action, impartiality to thought. The statesman calls his opponent wicked or mis-guided, because, being a man of action and not a man of thought, it is not his business to understand him, but only to defeat him; the historian, understanding the motives of both, calls both alike wise and good.

This is the same tangled skein of idealism and naturalism. The underlying truth, that no historical event, no act and no person, is merely evil, and that it is the duty of the historian to discover and express the good which our hastier analysis of the facts has failed to reveal—this is an important doctrine, and it is an idealistic one; but the terms in which Croce has stated it are naturalistic. The distinction between theoretical and practical men, activities, or points of view is pure natural-ism, and here it leads Croce into plain and obvious misstate-ments. It is monstrous to say that partiality is right and neces-sary in a statesman and wrong in a historian. Each alike ought to be as impartial as he possibly can in the process of balancing claims and forming a judgment on them; and each must be partial in asserting his judgment, when he has formed it, against his opponent's. The statesman ought to show all the impartiality he can in judging the claims of capi-tal and labour, or agriculture and industry, however energeti-cally he supports his own bills and denounces those of his op-ponents; and if the historian is impartial in balancing evi-dence and understanding motives, we do not expect him to

be so impartial as to declare a rival's view of the character of Richard III as good as his own. Because thought must be impartial, are there to be no more controversies?

Controversies, yes, it may be said, but not condemnations. We may refute Mommsen, but we must not condemn Julius Caesar. But this is quite unreasonable. If I may think a Ger-man professor wrong, why not a Roman general? If, as an his-torian of warfare, I must accept all Caesar's battles as impec-cable, then as an historian of the history of warfare I must accept all Mommsen's accounts of them as impeccable for the same reason. Controversy is for contemporaries, no doubt: *de mortuis nil nisi bonum*. But as Caesar's historian I am—is not Croce forgetting it?—Caesar's contemporary. When a man is dead, the world has judged him, and my judgment does not matter; but the mere fact that I am rethinking his history proves that he is not dead, that the world has not yet passed its judgment. In my person, indeed, it is now about to pass judgment. Croce's contention is that I am forbidden to pass any but an exclusively favourable judgment. Why is this? It is because Croce is here assuming a "transcendent" theory of knowledge, according to which judgment has already been passed in a court outside the mind of the historian, a court from which he has no appeal. He can only write down what he finds written on the page of History.

Thus the idealistic principle that there is a positive side in every historical fact is combined with the naturalistic as-sumption that the positive side excludes a negative side; the principle that nothing is merely bad is misunderstood as im-plying that everything is wholly good, and not bad in any sense at all. And this naturalistic misinterpretation of an ide-alistic principle confuses the whole argument to such an ex-tent that it actually necessitates a naturalistic and transcen-dent theory of knowledge. Only in the light of such a theory can it be maintained, as Croce here maintains, that every his-torical event is right, and therefore everyone who thinks oth-erwise is wrong, as if the opinions of these poor creatures were not also historical events.

The dualism of thought and life is thus pure transcendence, a formal contradiction of Croce's own theory of history. Thought is life, and therefore the historian can never be im-partial; he can only struggle to overcome one prejudice after another, and trust to his successors to carry on the work. The progress of thought is always negative in that it means a con-tinual controversy with oneself and within oneself. The ab-stract "positivity of history" is a delusion, bred of a naturalis-tic philosophy.

In the same spirit Croce proceeds to expound his conception of progress. There being no negativity in history, that is to say, none in the world of reality, all is progress, every change is, as he says, "a change from the good to the better." There is no such thing as decadence; what appears to be so is really progress, if only you look at it from the right point of view. True; there always is such a point of view, and it is of the ut-most importance that we should not overlook it. But there is the opposite point of view too. A change that is really a prog-ress seen from one end is no less really a decadence, seen from the other. It is true to say that the decay of archery was the rise of firearms; but it is not less true to say that the rise of firearms was the decay of archery. Here is one point of view against another: which is the right one? Croce answers em-phatically that one is altogether right and the other altogether wrong. But why? Is it the historian's duty always to take the side of the big battalions just because they win? Is he always

Croce's parents, who were killed in an earthquake on the island of Ischia in 1883.

to side with the gods against Cato? Or do we not rather feel that it was just by siding against Cato that the gods proved themselves no true gods? The historian's duty is surely not to pick and choose: he must make every point of view his own, and not condemn the lost cause merely because it is lost. The fact is that Croce is here again taking a transcendent attitude, asserting the existence of a criterion outside the historian's mind by which the points of view which arise within that mind are justified and condemned.

It is the less surprising to find this transcendence emerge into full daylight at the end of the chapter. Croce is saying that when a historian fails to maintain a properly "positive" attitude, fails, that is, to maintain that whatever happens is right, he does so because he has attached himself so blindly to a cause, a person, an institution, a truth, as to forget that every individual thing is but mortal; and when his foolish hopes are shattered and the beloved object dies in his arms, the face of the world is darkened and he can see nothing in the change but the destruction of that which he loved, and can only repeat the sad story of its death. "All histories which tell of the decay and death of peoples and institutions are false"; "elegiac history" is always partisan history. This he expands by saying that immortality is the prerogative of the spirit in general: the spirit in its determinate and particular forms always perishes and always must perish.

Here the transcendence is explicit and unequivocal. The "spirit in general" is presented as having characters (immortality, absoluteness) which the individual spirit has not; the whole is the negation of the part; the absolute or infinite is something over against, contrasted with, the finite. The Christianity at which Croce never ceases to gird for its transcendence is here, as often, immanent exactly where he is himself transcendent. It knows that life is reached through death and found in death, and that to live without dying is to die indeed.

The whole discussion of the "positivity of history" is, in fact, vitiated by naturalism. The truth which Croce wishes to express is the same which Hegel concealed beneath his famous phrase, "the real is the rational." What happens, happens for a good reason, and it is the business of history to trace the reason and state it. And that means to justify the event. But this truth is grossly distorted if it is twisted into the service of a vulgar optimism which takes it for the whole truth. Hegel's view of reality, as Croce himself has insisted, was no such vulgar optimism, but a tragic view; and yet the common charge of optimism brought against him is not unfounded, for he, like Croce, had in him a streak of naturalism which at last overcame him. The point of view here maintained by Croce, from which every change is for the better, and all partisans of lost causes are fools and blasphemers, is neither better nor worse in itself than that from which all change is for the worse, and all innovators are Bolsheviks and scoundrels. A history which was merely a tragedy or a series of tragedies, like the "Monk's Tale" in Chaucer, would be a misrepresentation of reality; but to hold that all tragedy is delusion and error, and that reality contains no tragic elements at all, is to misrepresent it no less gravely. To imagine that the choice lies between these two misrepresentations, that a positive and a negative moment cannot coexist in reality, is just the kind of error that characterises a transcendent or naturalistic philosophy.

We are now in a position to consider the relation between history, science, and philosophy. Science Croce identifies with the generalising activity of the mind. History is the internal and individual understanding of an object into which the mind so enters that subject and object can no longer be separated; it is real thinking. Science is the external and arbitrary construction of abstract types, and the manipulation of them for practical ends; it is not thinking at all, but willing. This is Croce's distinction. It falls, we observe, within the competence of Croce the naturalist, appealing as it does to the abstract scheme of thought and will. What does Croce the idealist say to it? For it is evident that he cannot assent to it.

He answers the question tacitly in a chapter on "Natural History." Here he denounces that kind of "history" which proceeds by making abstract classifications and then spreads out the classes over a chronological scale; for instance, that kind of history of language which imagines that language began by being monosyllabic, and then went on to polysyllabic forms, or that history of morals and society which begins with pure egoism and goes on to "deduce" altruism, and so on. He shows that this type of fallacy, in which temporal sequence is used as a kind of mythology for logical or spacial interrelation, is found not only in the sciences of nature but also in the sciences of man. In both alike, he says, we classify and arrange our facts, and make abstract generalisations which can, if we like, be arranged along an imaginary time-scale. But also, in both alike we can do real thinking: we can enter into the individual and understand it from within. The object, whether "a neolithic Ligurian or a blade of grass," can be penetrated by thought and lived by the thinker.

This simply destroys the distinction between science and history. It proves that as science (abstract classification) enters into the work of the historian, so history (concrete individual thought) enters into the work of the scientist. We are generally told that the business of the scientist consists of classifying and abstracting: this, we now see, is not the case. A scientist is intrinsically no more concerned with generalising than an historian. Each does generalise; the geologist generalises about classes of rocks, as the historian generalises about classes of manuscripts; but in each case the generalisation is the means to that thinking which is the man's real work. The historian's real work is the reconstruction in thought of a particular historical event; the geologist's, the reconstruction in thought of a particular geological epoch at a particular place. If the anthropologist's aim is to be a neolithic Ligurian, the botanist's is to be a blade of grass.

Croce does not say this explicitly, but it is all implied in what he does say. He is in the habit of maintaining, formally, the naturalistic distinction of science and history, as concerned with generalisations and individuals respectively; but what he calls science is only one fragment of what he knows history to be, and equally it is only one fragment of what science really is. But, not being perhaps so deeply versed in science as he is in history, he readily misunderstands the true nature of scientific thinking, uncritically swallowing whole the naturalistic logic and mistaking one subordinate aspect of science for the whole.

The relation of philosophy to history is a subject often touched on in this book, but in the end left extremely obscure. The obscurity is due to a vacillation between two views; the idealistic strain of Croce's thought maintaining (with Gentile, to whom this side of Croce seems to be not a little indebted) the identity of philosophy and history, and the naturalistic maintaining that philosophy is a component part of history.

The two views are held side by side, without any attempt at reconciliation: probably without consciousness of the discrepancy. But no one who collects the relevant passages can fail to be struck by the contrast. Thus, on page 17 "philology" (*i.e.,* fact) "combines with philosophy" (*i.e.,* critical thought) "to form history"; on page 71 "philosophy is history and history is philosophy"; on page 136 philosophy is "the methodological moment of history"; and on page 162 "there is no way of distinguishing historical thought from philosophical." The two views seem to alternate with curious regularity.

The view that history and philosophy are identical is derived from reflections like those with which this paper began. Each without the other is a lifeless corpse: every piece of real thinking is both at once. This is Gentile's view. But the view that philosophy is a mere subordinate moment in history has quite different motives. It seems to indicate that historical thought is conceived as real or absolute thought, containing philosophy complete within itself; while philosophy by itself is an inferior form, abstract and at best only half true, which requires to be supplemented by "philology" or the study of fact, and so converted into the perfect form of history. We are reminded of Vico's alliance between philosophy and philology by the language here, and of Hegel's dialectic by the thought that one form of activity is inherently imperfect and requires to be transformed into another before it can be satisfactory.

It is to this latter view that Croce seems finally to incline. In an appendix written some years after the body of the book he states it definitely: philosophy is the "methodological moment of history," that is, the working-out and critical construction of the concepts which history employs in its work. And this is an immanent methodology—it goes on not outside history, in a separate laboratory, but within the process of historical thinking itself. The philosopher and the historian have returned from the ride, in fact, with the philosopher inside.

This seems to me to indicate two things: the triumph within philosophy of Croce the naturalist over Croce the idealist, and the shifting of Croce's own centre of interest from philosophy to history.

The naturalist triumphs over the idealist because the synthesis of philosophy and philology in history implies the naturalistic conception of philosophy and philology as two different and antithetical forms of activity, which again implies that ideas or categories, or whatever is the subject-matter of philosophy, are something different from facts, the subject-matter of philology. Such a dualism of idea and fact is wholly impossible to an idealist; and yet only on this assumption can it be maintained that philosophy is immanent in history while history is transcendent with reference to philosophy. Naturalism, transcendence, is the last word.

Further, Croce here shows, if I read his meaning aright, that he is gradually deserting philosophy for history. He appears to have come to the conclusion that philosophical truth is to be attained not by direct fire—by the study of philosophy in the ordinary sense, which he now pronounces a delusion—but indirectly, as a product of ordinary historical work. Philosophy in his mind is being absorbed in history; the two are not poised in equilibrium, as with Gentile, but one is cancelled out entirely as already provided for by the other. This is made clear by the appendix on "Philosophy and Methodology," which consists of an enumeration of the advantages which he hopes to gain from the new concept of philosophy—solid advantages for the most part, from which philosophy will be the gainer, but all, as he states them, tinged with a very visible weariness of philosophical work.

If this is really the case, and if Croce gives up philosophy to devote himself to history and to the reform of Italian education, it is not for us to repine. It is impossible not to observe in this book (and one sees the same thing in his other books) how his philosophy improves when he turns to handle the more strictly historical problems: how such a sophism as that concerning the "positivity of history" is calmly ignored, or rather the underlying truth of it unerringly seized upon, when he comes to assign their value to the various historical periods, and how the naturalistic element in his thought purges itself away when he becomes an historian, leaving an atmosphere of pure idealism. To say that Croce is a better historian than philosopher would be a misstatement of the truth, which is rather that the idealistic philosophy at which he has always consistently aimed is unable to penetrate the naturalistic framework to which, as a philosopher, he seems to have irreparably committed himself, and is only free to develop fully when he shakes off the associations of technical philosophy and embarks on work of a different kind. The necessity for this change of occupation he is tempted to ascribe to something in the very nature of philosophy and history; but this is an illusion, itself part of the very naturalism from which he is trying to escape. The real necessity for it lies in himself alone, in his failure to purge his philosophy of its naturalistic elements.

If this is so, Croce's desertion of philosophy for history may be only an unconscious step forward in philosophy: a kind of philosophical suicide by which, casting off the abstract "philosophy of the spirit," which by now has become intolerable even to himself, he can reach the point of absolute idealism to which his successors Gentile and De Ruggiero have already carried his thought. (pp. 3-22)

> *R. G. Collingwood, "Croce's Philosophy of History," in his* Essays in the Philosophy of History, *edited by William Debbins, University of Texas Press, 1965, pp. 3-22.*

CONRAD AIKEN (essay date 1924)

[*An American man of letters best known for his poetry, Aiken was deeply influenced by the psychological and literary theories of Sigmund Freud, Havelock Ellis, Edgar Allan Poe, and Henri Bergson, and is considered a master of literary stream of consciousness. In reviews noted for their perceptiveness and barbed wit, Aiken exercised his theory that "criticism is really a branch of psychology." His critical position, according to*

Rufus A. Blanshard, "insists that the traditional notions of 'beauty' stand corrected by what we now know about the psychology of creation and consumption. Since a work of art is rooted in the personality, conscious and unconscious, of its creator, criticism should deal as much with those roots as with the finished flower." In the following excerpt, Aiken negatively evaluates Croce's literary criticism.]

It becomes increasingly difficult to be patient with Signor Croce's books, whether they take the form of applied criticism (as in the case of *European Literature in the Nineteenth Century*) or critical theory. To some extent this is due to an unfortunate tone, nowhere so apparent as in this latest book—a tone somewhat truculent, somewhat peevish, as of an old pride injured and angry, a tone alternately magisterial and patronizing, and not infrequently malicious. Have these things a place in criticism, or need Signor Croce so often go out of his way to throw derisive stones at other critics, his predecessors and contemporaries? One is annoyed by his repeated habit of doing so, and, passing beyond one's annoyance, one makes the unpleasant discovery of the large place which intellectual vanity takes in Signor Croce's motive. Impossible, of course, to exorcise this—every critic must have his secret share. But when, somehow injured, it begins to affect the critic's tone, to discolor emotionally his perceptions and judgments, one loses that comforting belief in his impartiality which one is so willing to exert. It is only because Signor Croce is a very respectable citizen of letters that one makes an effort, in this regard, to overcome one's distaste. And then one discovers that this is not the least difficulty which he presents.

One does not mean by this that there is anything abstruse or difficult in the book itself, which is a competent, if unexciting, survey of twenty-five rather capriciously selected nineteenth-century figures. One would even be glad if several of these chapters had been in this sense *more* difficult—one cannot feel that Signor Croce has adequately "seen" Scott or Stendhal or Manzoni or De Musset, to name but a few; and if he comes closest, in his treatment of Caballero and Monti and Baudelaire, and perhaps Leopardi, to enriching definitely our perceptions, he certainly does not enrich them very much. He has, too, his own quite emphatic sense of values, which prompts him to put Manzoni above Balzac and Byron, and to state that the works of Scott are not at all to be considered as "art or poetry" but as something else (?); and which, while it compels him (reluctantly) to diminish severely the stature of Leopardi, enables him to hail Carducci as perhaps the greatest poet of the century, "a poet-Vates, a heroic poet, an ultimate pure descendant from Homer," and the author of a poetry "suited to prepare and to comfort man in the battles of life with its potent, lofty, and virile tone." With this, which is simply a judgment, one sympathizes or not, according to one's taste. It is not in one's disagreement, here and there, that one feels a growing difficulty, a sense of obstruction and failure, but in something more profound.

This profounder something, which alienates one's sympathies, is in part Signor Croce's persistently metaphysical view of art, a view almost religious in intensity, hostile to all other views, and aimed primarily (so one feels) at a philosophical justification of art, not at a functional understanding of it. He begins with the hypothesis that art is something sublime, absolute, and autonomous; and his purpose seems not so much to attempt an analysis of its causes and roots in human nature as to assign it a metaphysical place. Perhaps one ought not to quarrel with this. What one has more right to resent is the fact that, while Signor Croce's view is so clearly a metaphysical one, nevertheless he claims to be "scientific." Is it necessary to note that science does not always profitably build on large, loose, unverified assumptions, and that a modestly empirical method of investigation is sometimes better? But Signor Croce's method is that of a generous hypothesis or two followed by an "argument," an elaborate logical structure, which as often as not is pure verbalism, and often enough is not even good logic. In **"The Essence of the Aesthetic,"** for example, he says: "And if it be asked why art cannot be a physical fact" (he has just stated that it is not) "we must reply, in the first place, that physical facts *do not possess reality,* and that art, to which so many devote their whole lives, and which fills all with a divine joy, is *supremely real;* thus it cannot be a physical fact, which is something unreal." The reasoning, the assumptions, do not seem flawless; nor, granting the idealist position, can one perceive precisely on what Signor Croce bases his discovery that one's feeling (relation) toward a work of art is real, while one's relation toward an apple (say) is not. One could multiply instances of this sort of logistic thinking, a vague verbal juggling, which gets him again and again into terminological difficulties from which the only escape is a quibble, and which take him always farther from a genuinely scientific approach to his subject. Art, in all this, is nowhere, is lost in the absolute, or at best is glimpsed for a moment as "an aspiration enclosed in the circle of a representation," or as something of which the only "judgment . . . is philosophical."

This, of course, is not very helpful; and it is odd that Signor Croce, who, in his preface, claims to be scientific, loses no opportunity of referring sarcastically to those who employ the methods of biography or physiology or psychology, or (as he likes to put it) "erotic psychopathology," in their effort to grasp the nature of art or to understand its function. Why should this irritate him so intensely? One suspects him of being half aware of the hollowness of his position, and of its inadequacy; its inadequacy, that is, in providing him with a means of approach to his subject. For, unhappily, his view of art as autonomous and absolute; and his thence-deduced disbelief in categories, "kinds" and "classes" of art; and his further deduction that "form" and "material" cannot be isolated for study—these views force him to make of his criticism very largely a sort of examination of souls, often conducted in a moral light, and with apologetic reference to the influences of time or place or history; apologetic, because these seem to suggest that there is a part of art which is, in a sense, "external." And precisely here one sees why it is that one always, in these critical notes, feels a little cheated. It is because Signor Croce is himself cheated. His "view" will not permit him, on the one hand, to employ psychology and biography in his study of a poet's "behavior" or development; nor, on the other hand, can he sufficiently admit the separability of form or literary class to devote himself to a minute testing of the principles there at work, and of the extent to which those principles control the writer or are controlled by him. We get from Signor Croce, therefore, neither a careful and precise analysis of style (from the linguistic or historical or prosodic or psychological viewpoint, coming to the aesthetic) nor an analogous study of motive, but an attempt, necessarily confused and incomplete, to give both at once in a somewhat sentimental, paraphrastic commentary on an author's character as revealed in his work. This Signor Croce sometimes does admirably, as in his study of Baudelaire; yet one wishes that he could free himself from his metaphysical and logical difficulties (which are unreal) and allow his perceptiveness and

power of analysis a fuller play. "How does it come about" (he asks, after quoting a passage from Maupassant) "that these commonplace reflections, these poor words, move us to tears?" Well, how does it? Signor Croce does not answer his question, appearing to think that to have asked it is sufficient; it is a sort of question which he seldom raises, and answers almost never. And yet one is inclined to think that it is exactly here that criticism begins—where, unfortunately, Signor Croce leaves off.

In a sense a critic qualifies as intelligent more by his awareness of aesthetic problems than by his solution of them—the solution is apt to be temperamental, not logical, is not necessarily right or wrong, and one is free to agree or disagree, to sympathize or not, according to one's own temperament. It is when the perception of a problem is acute, rich in perspective and implications, that one honors a critic and profits by him. Signor Croce gives us, of this perceptive sort, little light; his theory of art as "intuition," and all the verbal paraphernalia dependent thereon, keep him, inevitably, close to mediocrity as a practical critic, since the intuitionist can only say "like" or "dislike," not pausing to say why. And as for the amazing metaphysical structure which he builds about art— dare one breathe the suggestion that it has, somewhat, the appearance of high-class intellectual fake? (pp. 71-4)

> *Conrad Aiken, "Metaphysics and Art," in his* Collected Criticism, *Oxford University Press, Inc., 1968, pp. 71-4.*

EDOUARD RODITI (essay date 1942)

[*Born in France, Roditi is a poet, short story writer, biographer, translator, and critic. In the following excerpt, he identifies inconsistencies in Croce's thought, maintaining that such contradiction is a fundamental characteristic of Croce's philosophy.*]

There seem to be two ways of studying methodically a philosopher's total work. The first is historical, biographical or psychological: an investigation and analysis of the works, studied in the order in which they were written, and of the influence of events, readings, controversies, and even conversations on the gradual development of the total system of thought. In such an approach to the philosophy of Benedetto Croce, literary histories, volumes of essays, philosophical treatises, studies of linguistics, of art, even of local history, all these would first have to be dated and classified in chronological order; and this would require immense preliminary toil of purely historical technique and discipline. The other approach is generally simpler: a conceptual method which, in Croce's case, would progress from the *Logic,* where the philosopher defines the nature of the concept and the laws of its manipulation, to two other volumes of his *Philosophy of the Spirit,* the *Aesthetic* and the *Philosophy of the Practical,* in which concepts are used and manipulated to explore and define fields of the beautiful and the good, thence to the fourth volume in which, as a historian, Croce finally applies his aesthetic and practical philosophies to the investigation of historical problems, philosophy of history and historiography. From the *Philosophy of the Spirit,* one can then progress to the philosophical essays, thence to literary and historical works, finally to occasional articles and *obiter dicta.* Such a method assumes, in a pyramidal structure whose apex is the *Logic,* or philosophy of reason, a rational development which manipulates rules of the true to construct philosophies of the beautiful and the good, then a philosophy of history. Since

Croce repeatedly affirms that philosophy is primarily rational and logical cognition of the general or of universals, that art is intuitional cognition of the individual and particular, and that historiography is art, such a conceptual method ought to facilitate an analysis of philosophical, hence rational, writings. But one soon discovers that the terms of Croce's trichotomy of mind, sense, intuition and reason, are convertible: an activity, such as art, which is primarily intuitional, also contains secondary elements of sensuous and rational cognition, just as the good can also be beautiful and true, etc. . . . If rigorously followed, either of our two methods would, however, lead us far beyond the material scope of this essay; we must therefore content ourselves with indicating them and a few of the more important problems which they uncover. (pp. 14-15)

[Croce] declared, in 1893, that history-writing is not a science but an art.

He argued that history is a series of individual and particular events from which no general laws can be deduced; that art is likewise concerned with knowledge of the particular; and that laws of history are the result of a confusion which interprets history in terms of theories of the mind such as those of Vico or Hegel. This was not all expressed clearly in Croce's first essay; in ensuing controversies, he was forced to state his argument more thoroughly. Historians, who believed that they were scientists or philosophers, were all shocked; had not Lombroso recently explained that art is a product of genius which is akin to madness? Historians must then be mad artists! Besides, the purpose of art is to provide pleasure and entertainment, whereas that of history, and of all science, is knowledge. Croce replied that the purpose of art too is knowledge, but intuitional cognition of the particular rather than rational cognition of the general, or ultimately of universals, which is the purpose of science or philosophy.

In 1895, Croce found himself involved in another controversy; Labriola asked him for advice about a commentary on the *Communist manifesto* and Croce began a criticism of the Marxist philosophy of history. In 1902, to explain his position to both positivists and marxists, he published his *Aesthetic;* in the next few years, he added three volumes of a whole idealist *Philosophy of the Spirit.* The titles of its four volumes are significant: *Aesthetic as Science of Expression and General Linguistic, Logic as the Science of the Pure Concept, Philosophy of the Practical: Economic and Ethic, Theory and History of Historiography.* (pp. 16-17)

Croce's main asset, as a philosopher, is his unusual ability to observe distinctions which others have neglected or confused. In his earliest philosophical essays, when history, as a term, was still indiscriminately used to designate a number of related concepts, Croce at once distinguished history, as an accumulation of facts and events to be studied, from history as a synthetic philosophy of history and, again, from history-writing and theory of historiography. Later, he criticized his own masters, the philosophers who have influenced his thought; here, his distinctions are particularly valuable. He observes, for instance, that the philosophizing of De Sanctis, a great historian of literature, does not constitute a proper and coherent philosophy: that Vico's distinctions of the ages of history, by applying a theory of mind to history, establish a primitive age of pure sense-perception as if primitive men, though perhaps unable to use them, had not been endowed also with intuition and reason, then an age of intuition, when reason was still ignored, before the final age of reason; that

Hegel's tendency to treat all distinctions as contraries often allows him to invent a hypothetical synthesis when there has been no true thesis-antithesis and a hypothetical thesis-antithesis to explain what he assumes to be a synthesis. In his *Logic,* Croce observes that reason presupposes imagination as the abstract presupposes the concrete, so that the good, in his practical philosophy, must necessarily be useful, though the useful need not be good, and art or literature, in his aesthetic, must necessarily presuppose language and general linguistic. This distinction is, in a way, analogous to Ockham's distinction between terms of first intention and terms of second intention; but Ockham's terms of second intention, though they necessarily presuppose terms of first intention and not *vice-versa,* are all strictly logical terms, such as "predicate", which do not exist *in re* and cannot be proved dialectically to include other concepts, whereas Croce's terms are classes of ideas, such as "ethics", which include an indefinite number of other terms and concepts, such as "good" and "evil", many of which, such as "man", are concrete and exist *in re.* Croce thus proposes, like Kant, axiological hierarchies rather than, like Ockham, logical distinctions.

But Croce's ability to observe such distinctions is counterbalanced by his frequent inability to coordinate them; his system does not exclude paradox and contradiction and, when these occur, he is, unlike Plato, the first to be disconcerted. Hence too the fundamental paradox of his philosophy: in his criticism of dialectical systems, instead of establishing, as Aristotle did in his critique of Greek sophistry, a set of univocal terms which would allow him to proceed logically as an outsider, Croce has entered into the "spirit" of the dialectics which he criticizes, has tried to infuse logic into them, and produced a hybrid dialectic disguised as a logic. And this leads him to an idealistic realism where the word is sometimes equivalent to the concept and need not presuppose any object or quality outside of the thinker's mind, so that purely verbal distinctions, even rhetorical figures such as metaphors or synonymies, can be treated as distinct concepts because, the words being different, the ideas and objects of reference must also be different.

Croce first asserted himself as a philosopher by insisting that there can be no science or philosophy of history because there can be no science or philosophy of the individual and the particular. He then added that art, which is not a science nor a philosophy, is concerned, like history, with knowledge of the individual and the particular. In his criticism of philosophies of art, even in *La critica letteraria* of 1895, he disposes of the theory of literary genres by asserting that cognitions of the individual and particular, such as works of art, can be grouped only very arbitrarily according to genres; and that each work of art, by itself, actually constitutes an individual and particular genre because there exist greater differences between two tragedies, for instance, than between individual specimens of a species such as those of the animal world. One cannot say that *Hamlet* is a tragedy in the same way as one says that Fido is a dog, dogs are mammals and mammals are animals. But to clarify his own position in the ensuing controversies, Croce develops a philosophy of art and finally a philosophy of history, thus contradicting himself by proposing a science and a philosophy of the individual and particular.

Croce's most popular contribution to modern thought is unquestionably his philosophy of art. His *Aesthetic* and other aesthetic writings have been translated and read more widely than any of his other works, even than his philosophy of history, which, however, has profoundly influenced modern historiography. But the pyramidal structure of his philosophy was lop-sided from the very start, for chronological and affective reasons. The *Aesthetic* was written and published before the *Logic,* and cannot be said to illustrate a philosophy of reason and of the concept which is suggested in it, but was formulated and elaborated later as an after-thought. And Croce displays, consciously or unconsciously, a distinct initial prejudice in favor of intuition and art, remaining true to this first love throughout his philosophical writings. In the first pages of the *Aesthetic,* he deals summarily with reason and logic; the real apex of the pyramid is the philosophy of intuition instead of the philosophy of reason. His whole system, in its origins, is intuitional; it is then elaborated rationally because philosophy is supposed to be rational, so that the *Aesthetic* can be viewed almost as a rationalized work of art. Croce was forced to become a philosopher when he developed his first controversial musings to explain his irrational tastes in terms of reason.

The convertability of the terms of Croce's theory of the mind is no mere quibble. Throughout the *Aesthetic,* activities which are primarily intuitional are secondarily rational or sensuous, or *vice versa.* True to his original criticism of Vico's epistemological view of history, Croce manipulates the three modes of cognition in such a manner that they can never be properly separated. In the first pages he thus asserts that there are two types of cognition, intuitional and logical. After a long apologetic defence of intuition, he admits that it is distinct from intellective cognition, which he had previously identified with logical reasoning, and also from a third type, the perception of the real which is achieved through the senses. He soon returns, however, to his defence of the Cinderella of epistemology, but rapidly becomes confused: it is no longer clear whether intuition, as term or concept, designates the epistemological faculty of intuiting, or the object intuited by this faculty. In an idealistic system such as Croce's, distinctions of subject and object are easily blurred, since the object's reality depends on that of the subject: solipsism is always in the wings, ready to leap forth when we and the philosopher least expect it. Again, intuition may mean a quality, in the object intuited, which is revealed only to intuitive cognition: the abstract reasoner, Croce avers, has no living intuition of certain situations. Croce then concludes that "the head of an ox on the body of a horse" is not an intuition but a product of the arbitrary. Here, we see, he begins unconsciously to convert his terms. For it is generally agreed that the arbitrary is, by definition, irrational: if the irrational cannot be an intuition, there must be some quality of rationality in intuition. But Hieronymus Bosch, Breughel the Elder, Goya, today Dali and the surrealists, have all intuited worse than horses with heads of oxen; Croce must certainly agree that their art, though arbitrary, is not non-intuitional and, since art must be intuitional, therefore non-art. Are centaurs, satyrs and mermaids, even Bottom wearing his ass-head, all products of the arbitrary? Yet none of these phantasms can be distinguished logically from imaginary portraits where the head of one human model has been added to the body of another. This concept of the arbitrary, whose contrary must be the probable, is borrowed from the aesthetics of Horace, most matter-of-fact of all critics, whose theory of genres Croce most systematically rejects. Does Croce adopt, from sense-perception, some pragmatic value-distinctions which prove centaurs to be more significant than other freaks of the cock-eyed world of hallucination? Or does he adopt Horace's concept of verisimilitude? In either case, he must admit that pure

intuition, in his own system, can no longer exist: it must also be rational or somehow connected with sense-perception.

When Croce later asserts that intuition is expression, he raises a host of other problems. Throughout the *Aesthetic,* verbal identities or distinction, synonymies, metaphors, all rhetorical devices and figures, are repeatedly used as evidence in a dialectic which often neglects casual or logical relationships. On one occasion, Croce insists that thought cannot exist without words; yet Diderot had already claimed, in his *Lettre sur les aveugles à l'usage de ceux qui voient,* as early as 1749, that the limitation of thought to the perceptions of any one sense is extravagant, and that the deaf-mute, though ignorant of sound and speech, can yet be credited with thoughts formulated in terms of other sense-perceptions. Croce avoids this objection by adding that he has used the term "words" as a synecdoche to designate all expression, not only verbal. But he destroys his own argument when he later asserts that figures of speech do not really exist: if metaphor is the use of one word, in a figurative sense, instead of another more literal word, why thus substitute when the literal would have been sufficient? Croce concludes that the metaphor is the literal word, since no word more literal can serve the same purpose. If, therefore, figures of speech must be taken literally, he has no right to use synecdoche and then to indicate that thought and verbal expression, according to his own standards, both are and, in this one case, are not identical.

Further discussion of the many paradoxes contained in the *Aesthetic* would mean endless quibbling; and the purpose of this essay is to demonstrate that the paradox is an inevitable feature of Croce's phiosophy, rather than to quarrel with him because he contradicts himself. He introduces new terms and arguments for their rhetorical effect and immediate dramatic or persuasive value in controversy, often neglecting later to coordinate them. He thus repeatedly contradicts what he has stated elsewhere; and a realization of this weakness, especially in his earlier work, also his permanent interest in aesthetic problems, have since prompted him to correct himself in a series of elaborations of his *Aesthetic,* of appendices to it, and restatements, summaries or corrections of it. Some of Croce's philosophy of art, such as his objection to the theory of genres, was already contained in an earlier essay, *La critica letteraria,* of 1895; it was further elaborated in the *Lineamenti* of 1900; it appears as a complete and paradoxical philosophy in the *Aesthetic* of 1902, some aspects of which were corrected or expanded in **"La liricita dell' arte,"** a paper read to the Heidelberg philosophical congress in 1908. In 1915, Croce published a corrected summary of the *Aesthetic,* his *Breviary of Aesthetic;* in 1917, *La totalita dell' arte* introduced some corrections and new concepts; in 1929, the article on *Aesthetics* in the *Encyclopaedia Britannica* summarized and simplified Croce's whole philosophy of art; in 1936, *La poesia* stated many old problems in new terms, raised new problems, proposed new solutions to old ones.

G. A. Borgese has distinguished three different philosophies of art in Croce's writings: the negative *Aesthetic,* more controversial than systematic, the romantic-idealist systematization of the *Breviary,* the simplified credo in the *Encyclopaedia Britannica.* Indeed, it is easier to deduce several philosophies of art, often more than three from a single work, than any single and consistent philosophy from all Croce's works. True, Croce never forsakes his original faith in the identity of intuition and expression; but artistic intuition alone can be said to be identical with expression, and only if one ignores chronological distinctions to identify the chicken with the egg, or psychological distinctions to identify subject with object. Artistic intuition tends toward expression just as scientific intuition demands, or tends towards, verification, and as the intuition of the practical, in economics and ethics, tends towards action. Artistic intuition can thus be defined as a perception of reality, or of the potential, which is still free from any criticism; it is an intuition of formal values and relationships, just as scientific intuition is one of material identities or relationships which must be proved, and practical intuition is one of economic or ethical expediencies, needs or duties which must be tested or satisfied in action. Croce therefore soon realizes that if, as he asserts, art is an intuition, which is expression, then every intuition which is expression must be art. Language is thus expression, intuition and art; and grammar is to language as rhetoric and theories of genre to literature, mere methods of investigation, definition and classification. Grammar is not a part of language and genres do not exist in art; each work is a genre of its own, each word is used correctly whenever and however it is used.

This atomistic philosophy offered the advantage, in 1902, of reaffirming the spiritual and ideal nature of art at a time when aesthetics were being reduced to pseudo-science, positivist, materialist or determinist. Croce made the pendulum of controversy now swing as far, in the opposite direction of idealistic relativism, as it had already swung in the direction of mechanist or materialist relativism. But he soon found himself obliged to distinguish various levels and hierarchies of expression, intuition and art: art is the "dream" of all cognitive activity, not a cognitive fact. By distinguishing three classes of theory and practice, intuitional, logical, and economic or ethical, he had already affirmed the independence of each, so that intuition and art cannot be subordinated to the other classes, but only coordinated with them. Each of these branches has its own criteria which cannot be used indiscriminately: since economic activity is pre-ethical and ethical activity is superior and posterior to it, political activity, though it represents the highest level of the economic, cannot be judged according to ethical criteria and, neither good nor evil, can be only successful or unsuccessful. Within each branch of theory or practice, Croce thus begins to establish hierarchies, distinguishing qualitative or quantitative differences between the various levels of each branch. Since intuition is expression and art is also expression, Croce now defines art as an intuition, or expression, which also has an affective content, a quality of sentiment which he calls, at one time, lyricism and, at another, the personality of the artist, the moral judgment, emphasis or significance which we have learned to expect from him. In 1908, Croce thus establishes, in **"L'intuizione pura e il carattero,"** the basis of all the aesthetics of interest, of character and of accentuated meaning which others, such as Clive Bell, have since elaborated. This reduces criticism to an investigation of individuality, of originality contained or expressed in the work of art; personality represents those pre-existing data or forces which, in the artist's mind, determine the particular and individual formula whereby he conquers diversity and reduces it to the unity, or uniformity, of art. Lyricism, Croce says, is such an expression of personality: pure intuition, at its highest level, is lyrical and represents a state of mind, not an abstract concept. Croce's psychology of art thus begins to coincide with that of Schopenhauer, also with that of all romantic-idealist theories of genius.

In 1915, Croce admits that his *Aesthetic* was a negative criticism of existing philosophies of art; the *Breviary* now attempts to systematize his beliefs in a new philosophy. Art is an intuition which must become expression, distinguished from intuitions which need not be expressed; it is an emphatic and emphasized state of being which blends intuition, sentiment and expression, through will, in lyricism. Such stress on the individual-psychological nature of lyricism reduces all art to a phenomenon of self-affirmation, of the artist's isolation and faith in himself, irrespective of objective results in the work of art. Sincerity is but a measure of talent: though as sincere, Byron is more superficial than Dante. The *Breviary* also distinguishes various types of art; Croce points out that these distinctions are not contraries, as in Hegel, so that no Wagnerian synthesis of all art, no tragedy which is also symphony, fresco, sculpture and architecture, is ever possible. He finally concludes that art is an aspiration, an intuition of a thing passionately desired which, though it need not exist *in re,* the artist expresses in a formal representation; and form, in the philosophy of Croce as in the criticism of De Sanctis, is generally not so much structure as appearance or that quality of the work of art which is immediately accessible to the senses. Aspiration is to representation as intuition to expression, and as nature, or the artist's idea, to imitation. Croce then affirms that translation is impossible: if successful, a translation is a new work of art and, if unsuccessful, is no work of art. He adds that all works of art are equal; no classification is possible and, if some works of art appear greater or more significant than others, this greatness is a mere metaphor or an optical illusion produced by history which stresses the significance, at one time, of one work of art and, at another time, that of another.

In the *Encyclopaedia Britannica,* Croce seems, at first, to repeat and resume briefly some doctrines of his *Aesthetic.* But he has now become aware of all their implications and, at once, distinguishes all problems of technique and communication from those of intuition and expression. He relegates communication to the philosophy of the practical, to economics and ethics, together with technique and the means of communication; he thus formulates an aesthetics of invention and expression rather than one of imitation and communication. An intuition, he repeats, is already expressed in the artist's mind before it has been put on paper or canvas; the work of art, on which all the speculations of classical aesthetics were concentrated, exists only, as an idea, in the mind of the artist. But in spite of this romantic idealism, Croce advocates a retreat from romanticism: the real problem of aesthetics, in our age, is to rehabilitate and defend classicism. Yet how can he hope to achieve this if he constantly rejects all classical concepts of art, such as genres, which are the premises of all the classical art which they produced? He offers us only a romantic philosophy, more complex than the neo-romantic theories, such as futurism, expressionism or surrealism, which deny art, but based on the same premises, on individualism, expression and invention.

Later, in the *Ultimi saggi,* Croce returns to the problem of communication and wonders whether, if an intuition which has not been communicated is still an expression, the real problem of art and of aesthetics is not, after all, the relationship of intuition and expression to communication rather than that of intuition to expression. The consequence of this ultimate doubt is to stress again the importance of form and those attributes of art which appeal directly to the senses; and to arouse, in the reader, a suspicion that Croce may have identified aesthetics, in all his earlier work, with metaphysics or psychology, with appreciation of art or an understanding of the artist's credo and processes of creation, rather with an investigation of the exact nature of the work of art. Finally, in **La poesia,** Croce establishes a new hierarchy of five levels of intuition or art: the sentimental, the poetic, prose, eloquence, pure literature. The lowest level, mere sentiment, is that of such linguistic phenomena as the "prose" which Molière's Monsieur Jourdain found himself speaking when he asked for his slippers; the poetic level is that of proverbs, idioms and other linguistic phenomena of "heightened" speech; prose is the lowest level of expository literature which then rises, through the persuasive art of ciceronian rhetoric, to the autotelic and pure art of great literature, whether verse or prose. In an idealistic philosophy, such hierarchies correspond, by stressing the material hypostasis of the idea, to the formal classifications of genres. In all aesthetics, Croce has consistently rejected the theory of genres; yet the whole problem of genres is one of defining terms so that a tragedy is defined to include all dramatic works which, without necessarily having five acts or respecting the unities, yet offer enough other specifically tragic features; it is no more absurd or difficult to class *Hamlet* and *Oedipus Tyrannus* together as tragedies and all tragedies and epics as poems, as to say that Croce and Mussolini are Italians, that Italians and Ethiopians and Jews are men and that men and dogs are mammals. But such formal classifications do not recognize the elusive essence, spirit, or "je ne sais quoi" of tragedy or of Italianism; and the idealist hierarchies which stress, in aesthetics, the supposedly spiritual essence of matter will produce, in ethics and politics, the quibbles of fascism which denies that Italians, Jews and Ethiopians are equal, as men, and argues that Ethiopians or Jews do not possess that essential Italianism, a nordic or aryan "je ne sais quoi", which raises Italians above all other men just as the *Divine Comedy* exhibits an essential "je ne sais quoi" which raises it above the "prose" of such poets as Trissino, Erasmus Darwin or Martin Tupper. Aristotelian aesthetics will never recognize arguments which are founded on any *a priori* neoplatonic "je ne sais quoi"; the perfection of the *Divine Comedy* can be analyzed formally in terms of the known, so why obscure the issues by introducing the unknown? It is significant that, while indulgently rejecting the term "je ne sais quoi" of Gravina, Du Bos and other Italian or French critics of the seventeenth and eighteenth centuries, Croce enthusiastically approves the concept and traces the whole history of modern aesthetics back to this source. No wonder, then, that his "return to classicism", proposing a "spirit of classicism", would be distinctly romantic and owe much to the pre-romantic neo-classicism of Winkelmann and Lessing, to the *Sturm und Drang,* to the neo-hellenic romanticism of Chénier, Foscolo, Byron, Hoelderlin and Canova.

If art is considered as a form of knowledge, we must accept the principle that either all human activity leads to knowledge and is knowledge, or there are different types and hierarchies of knowledge so that knowledge achieved in art is not the same as that achieved through logic or science, or as that which practical experience, economic or ethic, offers all living beings in their daily rounds. We must either fuse all types of knowledge in one or distinguish them all clearly; and we can distinguish them dialectically according to *a priori* idealistic hierarchies, or logically according to their causes, for instance, material, formal, effective and final. But Croce first confuses all types of knowledge, then distinguishes them again dialectically, to suit his momentary purpose, and thus avoids the consequences of subordinating art to the criteria of ethics, politics, science, economics or logic, or of any other

type of philosophy, of knowledge or of human activity which is not primarily aesthetic; but he never distinguishes art, or any type of knowledge or activity, according to its purpose. Yet a millstone and a statue, though both are cut stones and both may finally land in a museum as fine examples of the arts and crafts of the past, and be equally admired there, yet serve different purposes. Croce asserts that art is a permanent function of the human spirit, as any other function that he mentions; but he tends to consider all these other functions as inferior to art and, in an almost evolutionary sense, prior to it, more primitive, so that he really subordinates everything to the criteria of art and judges the millstone according to the standards of statuary. The value of art, he says, is not determined by immediate usefulness, political expediency, sociological significance, ethical or moral value, scientific or historic truth, logical exactitude, economic rarity; the significance of art is greater than its immediate use. In the *Encyclopaedia Britannica,* Croce defines art by negation, as Scotus Eriugena defined God, and finally defines art by tautology, just as God is said to be the only example of pure being. By analogy, we may therefore assume that art, in the idealism of Croce, occupies the supreme throne which God once held in the neoplatonic hierarchies of Christian philosophers. But Croce's dialectical system is not based on contraries, so that his highest art is not a synthesis of everything and of all arts, though there may be evidence of his highest art in all inferior arts, just as there is evidence of God in every particle of nature though God is no synthesis of all creation.

In this earliest works, Croce already stated his main distinctions when he separated history-writing as an art from the historical disciplines of research which are scientific or logical and not necessarily historical. If history is primarily an art, what constitutes the purely aesthetic or poetic "essence" of historiography and of all art, distinguishing art from logic and science? Croce is never concerned with the techniques and forms which would distinguish a historical work, as an example of a literary genre, from other genres, such as tragedy, satire or the novel; nor does he attempt to define his various literary hierarchies according to the degree to which they are autotelic, so that those forms of art which serve a useful purpose, such as moral or political propaganda, would be inferior to those which are their own purpose; he seeks to define the sublime which is common to all genres and which history, though factually true, can share with the epic, at one end of his literary hierarchy, or with pure poetry, and, at the other end, with all speech and language. The historian and the artist, Croce says, must have aesthetic beliefs, a philosophy of that which they are seeking to achieve; they must never lose sight of this ultimate objective, ideal and aesthetic rather than true, factual, logical or scientific. Croce has devoted many years to formulating such a credo, approaching it repeatedly, in a long and fruitful life, from many different view-points and on many levels of thought. He has written histories of aesthetics, taste and criticism, tracing the development of such beliefs, conscious or unconscious, through different periods and ages of our history; histories of literature and monographs where he deduces these beliefs from the works of an age, a school, an individual artist; political histories and historical monographs which indicate the contexture of these beliefs with events; philosophical essays and a complete **Philosophy of the Spirit** to evaluate and criticize these beliefs; finally, he has sought confirmation of his own beliefs and doubts in the work of other artists, illustrations of them in popular art, anonymous folklore and linguistic phenomena.

But there seems to be an inescapable curse of contradiction on his philosophy. His original sin was haste, born of controversy and the desire rather to contradict other doctrines than to formulate any of his own. He never distinguishes properly the artist from the work of art, the work of art from the man who appreciates it, the subject from the object, psychology or epistemology from aesthetics. Yet the most inspired artist need not necessarily produce the finest work of art; and the same "thrill" of the sublime can be produced, in one or several men, by many different objects. Inspiration and the sublime, as concepts, belong to psychology and metaphysics rather than to art-criticism or aesthetics; and this confusion of approaches has led Croce along the path of most idealist thinkers, an infinite regress where each dialectical definition achieves only verbal accuracy and, later confronted with facts or other definitions, must seem inaccurate, paradoxical or tautological. Endless contradictions must appear, at each turn, within such expanding systems of thought; and there is no rest for the thinker. For he must ever restate his definitions, write new works to correct the old, solve new contradictions which arise from his works as fast as he writes them, till death alone, or indifference to his own work, can release him at last from his infinite and infernal task. (pp. 17-29)

Edouard Roditi, "The Growth and Structure of Croce's Philosophy," in The Journal of Aesthetics and Art Criticism, *Vol. I, No. 5, Spring, 1942, pp. 14-29.*

A. ROBERT CAPONIGRI   (essay date 1955)

[An American scholar and educator, Caponigri has written extensively on philosophy, history, and literature. In the following excerpt, he outlines the three phases in the evolution of Croce's historical writings.]

After a quarter of a century of intellectual activity which witnessed, not only the penetrating and now classical studies on Hegel and Vico, but the speculative achievement of the ***Philosophy of the Spirit*** as well, Croce wrote that at the centre of his activity, as, in his own words, its 'heart within a heart,' lay history. When again a similar period had passed and the opportunity presented itself, in the preface to a collection of historical and critical essays, to review its work, he wrote, 'I have dedicated to history the greater portion of my efforts during these last years, thus closing, in a certain sense, the circle which I had initiated in my youth when, from historical researches, I passed to philosophy, only to return again to history as to the only concrete mode of philosophizing.' At the beginning and at the end stands history. His vast speculative work, which by any other standard may well stand by itself, is placed in the perspective in which he viewed it: as the effort to penetrate theoretically to the basis of historiography.

Croce's interest as an historian has ranged wide, as wide, almost, as the limits of European culture itself. One object, however, before all others, has been its most constant concern. The history of Naples, first to solicit the inquiry of his youth, occupied again the last nostalgic studies of his declining years. The reason for this lifelong preoccupation did not lie in the dignity or grandeur of its object, for this history exhibited no heroic argument. Rather, as he was to write, this is a history which is not history, which cannot sustain comparison with that of the other states of Italy, Rome or Venice or Florence, which has aroused in those who have undertaken to narrate it either pity or disdain, and not admira-

tion. That reason must be sought elsewhere; in the remark, for instance, which he was to repeat many times, that there can be no history without participation, without commitment. Naples is the first object of such historical participation and commitment for Croce. With it he achieved an identity so complete as to impart to his narrative an almost autobiographical tone. This identity it is which sustains the brooding concern of seventy years for the city and the realm; which renders no detail too insignificant to draw his eye, endows every personality which walked its streets or partook in any degree of its tumultuous life with an attractive spark, permits no inscription or monument, however obscure, to elude his quest. As a result, that portion of his work devoted to this history, though perhaps surpassed in profundity or range, is unequalled in humanity and nobility, the simple nobility and the profound humanity of a Cato narrating the history of his Rome.

Quite apart from such considerations as the stature of its object and the commitment of its narrator, the history of Naples holds a unique position among Croce's historical writings. The 'matter of Naples' (as with an epic resonance it may be called) is the matrix within which Croce first achieved his proper vision of history and attained his full stature as an historian. This is the vision, as he expresses it, of history as moral drama with more of tragedy than of idyll in it. This is the vision which is crystallized into the ideal and the method of ethico-political history.

The vision of human history as moral drama is certainly not new; it is rather the first, the immediate and spontaneous intuition of western man concerning history, and the most constant. Mere originality, however, could never be the mark of a culture so thoroughly, so profoundly classical as that of Croce. His achievement lay rather in the re-evocation of this vision of history at a juncture when it had all but vanished and when western man was most in need of it to revive in himself the sense of his own humanity and spirituality. The quality and character of this achievement is, consequently, to be measured and assayed, not by reference to the vulgar norm of novelty, but to the clarity and power of his expression of that constant vision of history and by the magnitude of the forces against which he reasserted it.

These forces Croce tends to group generically under the name 'positivism'. Though heterogeneous, these forces exhibited one common feature: they tended to reduce man to the level of nature. The characteristic of the nature to which positivism tended to reduce man was alienation, the same character which Hegel had recognized as the mark of nature in all its many forms. The specific form of this alienation was the denial of liberty to man and his enclosure within the determinate and determined complex of natural forces and processes. Denied liberty, man was made alien to the moral struggle or drama which is the existential form of that liberty, its living actuality, and to that creation and creativity which is the inner principle of that drama. Finally, this alienation dissevered man from the consciousness of his own character as spirit, the character under which liberty, morality, creativity are all to be subsumed.

With respect to history the impact of these forces and the alienation they induced was ambiguous. They seemed, at first glance, to confirm and even to extend the domain of the concept of history, by subsuming under it the realm of nature itself. The form of nature, heretofore conceived as static, was asserted to be processive and evolutionary and hence, apparently, historical. History in this context appears to have an ontological sense. From the point of view of historiography, the transfer and extension seems equally effective; it gives rise to a concept of a natural history or of a science of history. This would consist, in the active, historiographical sense, in retracing the paths of those forces in the processive movement of nature, while, in the more formal, methodological sense it would mean the formulation of the 'laws' of that movement, reflecting thus the classical legalism of science and the definitiveness of the 'philosophy of history'. Little reflection is needed, however, to discern that this extension of the concept of history and this reconstruction of historiographic method are specious. They are lacking one element of that history in which man is involved and which is the very form and structure of his presence to himself, liberty and alternality. And the pure form of this liberty is moral drama. Nature cannot be rendered historical simply by endowing it with the external form or mark of temporal process, for the essence of history lies not in mere temporal succession but in the spiritual transactions which inform that succession. Historiography, consequently, cannot be merely the retracing of the temporal path of natural forces, but must consist in the penetration and comprehension of that inward moral dynamism.

It is with reference to this dual alienation, the reduction of man to nature and the specious transfer of the historical character to natural process, that Croce's reassertion of history as moral drama in the ethico-political conception of history must be measured. That conception of history is elaborated, in the first instance, not in abstract, methodological terms, but concretely, in the actual narrative of histories and, most specifically, in the matrix of the 'matter of Naples'.

His achievement is revealed in a stronger light when that 'matter of Naples' is considered in its most general character. No other matter in the history of Europe would seem more readily to justify the historian's acquiescence to a naturalistic conception of history. All of the positivistic and naturalistic dogmas seem to find here their supremely plausible application. How might that essential failure, which, on Croce's own recognizance, is the most intimate character of that history, more readily and plausibly be explained than by reference to the poverty of economic resources—the arid, inarable land, the rocky formation of terrain, the scarcity of mineral deposits; or to the ethnic factor—the complex hybrid population, into the formation of which there entered all of those strains which, in the catalogues of nineteenth-century ethnism were judged most 'inferior'; or to psychological factors—that quality of 'dolce far niente' which the nineteenth century, through a confused veil of sentimental romanticism and hard-souled scientism, mistook for a 'natural' phenomenon and not for the moral reality it was. And the roll-call might be extended indefinitely, through all the favoured 'factors' of naturalistic theory. And this mode of explanation, in addition to its facility and plausibility, has the added attraction of permitting the historian to assume a sympathetic attitude toward the Neapolitans, exonerating them from the responsibility of an historical pattern which they had neither wrought nor chosen, or investing them with a romantic aura by depicting them in essential revolt against historic necessity. Croce has been more concerned, perhaps, than any earlier historian of Naples, to place the natural conditions of its history in the clearest light, only, however, to place in even greater relief its essential moral drama. He confronts the naturalistic myths one by one and confutes them; the myth of the natural exu-

berance of the Neapolitan realm, which supposedly had made it an irresistible object of greed and the victim of numberless invasions, by pointing out its natural poverty, and by rehabilitating the reputation of the one man (Antonio Serra) who had pierced that illusion of natural richness and had suffered obloquy and prison for his pains; that of race, by pointing out that racially the Neapolitan people was compounded of strains which had proved their prowess repeatedly in history and by laying bare the logical and historical fallacies of nineteenth-century ethnism. His conclusion, historically and logically inescapable, is simply that natural conditions are neutral; they are the theatre, but they in no wise determine the drama which is enacted on their boards. The fallacy of the naturalists is to have substituted a mythical history of nature for the history of men. History, to borrow for an instant the terminology of the naturalists and positivists, is not a 'natural phenomenon' but a 'moral phenomenon'. History is to be explained neither by a single nor by a multiplicity of natural causes, but only by reference to the spiritual force at work within it.

The opposition to positivism constitutes only the negative aspect of the vision of history as moral drama, of the ethico-political conception of history. Its positive aspect is to be discerned clearly first in the conception Croce entertains of the moral life of man and, secondly, in the methodological inferences he draws from this concept.

The ethico-political conception of history is Croce's reply to the logical demand in the theory of history for a universal history. Previously, this universality had been conceived transcendentally and holistically, or quantitatively, by romantic and positivistic historiography respectively. Romantic philosophy had sought to construct universal history in principle by finding a *point d' appui* outside the historical process, referring that process to an absolute subject to which it might be present in its entirety. (It may be remarked, parenthetically, that the difficulties and contradictions inherent in this effort form the basis of Croce's criticism of romantic historiography.) Positivism escaped this transcendentalism and holism, but substituted for them a quantitative notion of universal history, the ideal of which was an exhaustive compilation of the human record. On the other hand, it reflected a transcendentalism of its own when it aspired to formulate the abstract laws of historical process; while recognizing the inexhaustible novelty of the content of history, it sought to restrain this content within the abstract boundaries of those laws. The one and the other, from Croce's point of view, is fallacious; romanticism, because it fails to recognize man's historical situation in all its implications and, by projecting a transcendental point of view, opens the way to the classical pitfalls of the 'philosophy of history', terminalism, eschatology, utopianism; positivism, because it fails to find any living centre of unity within history, offering only the dualism of abstract processive laws and the ceaseless accumulation of inexhaustible historical 'fact'. While rejecting romanticism and positivism alike, Croce recognizes the claims of universalism in historical theory. He meets these claims by the suggestion that the universality of history is neither transcendental and holistic, nor quantitative, but qualitative; that it resides in the immanence of the totality of the human spirit in every moment of its concrete history.

It is possible for Croce to assign this qualitative universality to history, because he discerns at the centre of historical process the ethical life of man; and the ethical life of man can sustain this universality only because of the office he assigns it in the total economy of the human spirit. The ethical life, for Croce, consists in the human effort to achieve totality, qualitative wholeness in every temporal moment of its existence and to move toward this integrity through a continuous effort, however distended through time. This wholeness or plenitude of the spirit is conceived against the background of the distinct moments into which the life of spirit may logically be categorized. Croce had suggested an analysis in which these distinct moments appear first as the dichotomy between theoretical and practical and again as the subdistinction of each member of this dichotomy, the theoretical into the aesthetic and the logical, the practical into the economic and the ethical. The ethical moment appears first as one in which the limits of utility are transcended and the spirit attains to some degree of ideality and universality in the practical life. The ethical life in this limited sense is transcended in its second form. The distinctions he has suggested are logical or categorical. In its historical existentiality, spirit is always one. The moral life is the effort to secure a qualitative universality, in terms of the synthesis of the logical moments of spirit within each of the existential moments of spirit; an inward, qualitative universality commensurate with the concrete universality of mere existence (which itself, of course, must be an abstraction, since it is only logically distinct from the moral effort to qualify it). To speak of history as moral drama is to see historical existence in this inward term of the moral effort toward qualitative, human universality which informs it. To speak of universal history can only be to speak of history which is human, in the degree to which it exhibits this moral effort. This is the sense of his claim at the end of the *History of the Realm of Naples* that he has rendered that history a bit more human. The moral drama of history and its qualitative universality are therefore one and the same; they complement and sustain and in a certain sense define each other. And they define at the same time the object of the historian's quest, whatever be the matter of his history; he seeks always the human spirit seeking to realize this qualitative universality in a moment of time, in a concrete mode of historical existence.

Because it is possible to distinguish the structure of the human spirit logically into moments such as these, it is also possible, Croce believes, to constrain historical concern and inquiry within the limits of these distinctions and to compose authentic histories of art, of philosophy, of politics and economics and of human mores. These diverse types constitute the 'genres' of history, as the lyric and the novel, the drama and the satire are conceived to be the 'genres' of art. As the 'genres' of art are, however, readily revealed to be but abstract fictions convenient and useful for the organization of the matter of the history of art for didactic and expository ends, but useless for the comprehension of art in itself and even less so for the regulation of art as to content or form, so the 'genres' of history reveal themselves as abstract and unilateral, when viewed apart from the history of the spirit in its totality, that is to say, its qualitative universality. The parallel may be pressed further. As the totality, the qualitative universality, the simple and consummate humanity of the spirit are present in every concrete existential moment of history, and as the criticism and history of art seek in every work of art the fullness of the idea of art, and do not rest content with abstractions like the 'genres', so too does history in the fullest sense of the term seek the fullness of the spirit, that is, its ethical effort and character in every concrete moment of history. This is what ethico-political history is: the effort

Croce in 1919.

to seize the totality, the qualitative universality of the spirit, in every one of its historical moments. At the same time, however, Croce recognizes that care must be taken lest this idea degenerate into another and cryptic form of transcendental history; as though it would be possible to write a history of man which would not be the history of art, of politics, of mores. The human spirit does not achieve its qualitative universality over and above, but in and through the actuality of its diverse moments. Ethico-political history, correspondingly, is not a history which in any way transcends the concrete histories; for such a transcendent history would be vacuous. It is the history precisely of this effort toward qualitative totality in and through the unity and dialectic of the distinct moments. And ethico-political history, while it speaks of all these diverse moments, has only one subject, the human spirit in its historical unity.

This exposition of the vision of history as moral drama and of the ethico-political conception of historiography based upon it has been abstract and formal; and Croce has expounded it in this manner at considerable length. Such exposition does not, however, correctly reveal the true character of the doctrine; it is not a doctrine which was formulated speculatively and then imposed, 'a priori', upon the matters of his histories. On the contrary, it is a doctrine which was formulated directly in response to the problems and exigencies of historiography itself, drawn from the matter of the histories, rather than imposed upon them from without. Specifically, the ethico-political conception of history was born of Croce's struggle, as it may well be called, with the matter of the history of Naples. It is conceived as the only manner in which that history may be narrated in its humanity, and in it, the essential history of man, which is present in every historical argument. A poignant note is added by the fact that this conception of history is solicited not by a pageant of power and achievement but by a vision of human failure. It would be easier, perhaps, to recognize history as the work of man's ethical will, if history were all glory and achievement; the moral drama of history would then be essentially comic in the Dantean sense and the historian would be sustained through all vicissitudes by the knowledge and assurance of eventual triumph. The recognition of the actuality of the ethical will in the weak and in the failure is more difficult and, it might be added, a more Christian insight. And it is upon such an insight as this, evoked by the matter of the history of Naples, that the Crocean conception of ethico-political history rests. (pp. 3-10)

With the narration of the 'dolorous history' of Naples Croce achieves his full stature as an historian; a stature which will be enhanced by his subsequent achievements, but never altered in its fundamental lineaments. The function of this matter, in which he felt himself so deeply committed, was to compel him, by the concrete exigencies it deployed before him, to traverse the stages, by which that stature was gained. These stages are readily discerned. They are three: the idyllic, the naturalistic, and the ethico-political. But of these, only two, the first and the third, are positive. At the second, the naturalistic, Croce never rested. It was for him at all times a negative dialectical step, the examination and rejection of which enabled him to grasp more clearly the ethico-political concept to which he attained. This dialectical process was executed, not in a theoretical vacuum, but in answer to the exigencies of the matter with which he dealt. The narration of that history, consequently, and the attainment of the ethico-political conception of history constitute a single achievement.

The idyllic phase, as has been noted, is a phase associated with his youth. It is the phase which might be correlated, with the essay, **'History Subsumed under the General Concept of Art'**. In the one and the other, the practical and the theoretical moment, history ends in contemplation. He is delivered from both illusions, the theoretical and the practical, by the same consideration, namely, that contemplation can never penetrate to the reality of its supposed object. If history be subsumed under the concept of art, then it too must forgo that distinction between the real and the unreal which art is willing enough to forgo. And idyllic history engaged in the imaginative re-evocation of the past must remain innocent of the reality of that past. But the fallacy of subsuming history under that general concept, Croce comes quickly to realize, lies precisely here. For history cannot forgo that distinction; it is inexorably orientated toward the discernment of the real, the historically real. That subsumption must be fallacious, and idyllic history, though the beauty and the delight of the images it evokes can never be denied, and may without doubt form a legitimate dimension of aesthetic activity, cannot pass as history. Croce's idyllic re-evocation of the Neapolitan past constitutes thus a world of images, which had to be forgone, despite the delight it elicited, in the name of the necessity which the historical vocation imposes of reaching to the reality of history and of narrating it in the terms which express and convey its reality. (pp. 81-2)

The second of the basic themes about which the historical

writings of Benedetto Croce naturally group themselves is the baroque age in Italy. In many ways, the writings composed about this theme are the richest of his historical compositions. They are materially rich, for Croce has sought out with the greatest care, and the passion of the born bibliophile, the obscurest documents of the intellectual, the poetic and literary, and the moral life of the period, drawing again into the circle of historical reflection authors whose very names have been half-lost to memory. These works he has subjected to searching reading, at once critical and sympathetic, with the thought of fixing both their constitutive qualities and their place in the vast mosaic of that fertile and colourful age. Voices of song are heard again in these pages which for centuries have been silent; subtle debates, like the great contest about the 'ragione di stato' stir again, re-evoking intellectual struggles whose very terms have become dim. They are rich also in spiritual insight and discernment. Rarely has the mood (the unspoken mood, one is tempted to say, though it breathes in every form of expression) of a period been so faithfully, yet critically, captured and made to live again as in these pages, and within the period, the qualitative distinction of mind from mind, sentiment from sentiment, insight from insight presented with clarity and subtlety, so that no value is lost, or even diminished. They are, finally, rich in judgment. There is here no idyllic re-evocation of a past to which the imagination turns for aesthetic dilation. The whole presentation is firmly controlled by the overarching insight into the relation and significance of every mode of expression, indeed of every concrete expression, in the total economy of the age. The controlling insight is therefore ethical, in the sense in which that term has already been defined by Croce. And this insight is fulfilled in ethical judgment on this age. Such wealth of matter, of discernment and of judgment might be thought to imply a natural sympathy; but this is not the case. If anything, that age, as the period of Italy's greatest spiritual and political debility and decadence, inspired him with spiritual nausea. This spiritual alienation evokes, however, his sense of justice, its most effective counter-agent; and it is justice, in the last analysis, that he seeks to render to the baroque age.

The compositions on the theme of the baroque do not mark a departure from, but constitute a logical, an almost inevitable, continuation of the Neapolitan theme. This continuity is discernible at all of the levels at which the wealth of the baroque histories has been distinguished. In its rich matter, the history of the baroque era extends and penetrates more deeply interests already opened in the history of Naples. A single example may illustrate this fact. The interest in the Spanish influence in Naples asserts itself early in Croce's study of Neapolitan history; the reminders of that influence surrounded him, even in the Naples of the Risorgimento. Inevitably this interest carried him beyond the limits of Naples, for the Spanish influence held in thrall the whole of Italy; and the work, *La spagna nella vita italiana durante la rinascenza,* though but a fragment of a vaster work projected but never completed, is the testament of this extension. At the same time, this work, as Croce recognizes expressly, is an introduction, a preparation for the history of the baroque age. For even though he is led eventually to deny the popular dogma that 'spagnuolismo', that is to say, precisely this influence of Spain, is either the 'cause' or the 'essence' of the baroque, discerning in the baroque rather a failure of the ethical will of the Italian people, nevertheless, the continuity between the phenomena of the baroque age and the Spanish presence in Italy is incontrovertible. And the same fact may be corroborated by another instance. Early in his career Croce had composed the study on the mask of Pulcinella; in this study he opens one of the richest veins of inquiry he was ever to touch, dialectal literature. The full fruit of this inquiry is realized, however, only in the study of the baroque age, for in this latter context he is enabled to make his important distinction between spontaneous and reflective dialectal literature and to discover in the latter one of the positive elements of that negative and decadent period.

This continuity between the history of Naples and that of the baroque age in Italy is discernible also at the theoretical level, the level, that is to say, of Croce's conception of history and its procedure. His basic insight as an historian, it has been suggested, was gained in the matter of Naples; there historical idyllism was overcome and the vision of history as moral drama, the ethico-political conception of history first glimpsed and formulated. It is this insight and this conception which are extended and deepened in the matter of the baroque age. In the context of the history of Naples, his effort had been to seize the spiritual, ethical reality of that history; that is to say, the intellectual, spiritual and moral will of the Neapolitan people to establish a nation and to achieve historical existence. In this history, the political dimension had appeared in prominent relief, for it was historical existence as a *polis* which was at stake in the experience of Naples. It was made clear, however, that this historical existence as a *polis* could never be the achievement of a political mind or will in any narrow statist sense of the term, political. The state could only be the achievement of a more profound and universal will, the ethical will; and the state, in its concreteness, could never encompass this will.

Ethico-political history is rather, in principle, the history of the whole spiritual and ethical life of a people, in all its modes of expression, of which the political in the statistic sense is a central but limited expression. It was logically necessary, consequently, that the ethical dimension of this complex ethico-political conception of history be thrown into greater relief. And the occasion for this fresh direction of emphasis was provided by the matter of the baroque age. Not, to be sure, that there was any programmatic extension of Croce's part, any effort, that is to say, to exploit a wider matter for the purpose of a theoretical development. The movement was at all points spontaneous and unforced. It lay in the character of the matter of the baroque age, as this appeared as the extension and penetration of certain themes of the history of Naples, to evoke at the same time this extension and penetration of the ethico-political conception of history.

The most profound continuity between these histories is, however, neither material nor theoretical, but existential. Croce was persuaded, as has been noted, that history cannot be written without commitment and the quality of his own commitment in the history of Naples was readily discerned. There he had traced the process by which the realm of Naples had achieved historical existence by renouncing its dreams of autonomy and seeking identity with the larger unity of the new Italy created by the Risorgimento. Croce wrote as a Neapolitan who willed that historical strategy, not only as an expedient, but as a good in itself. In the history of the baroque age he is writing, for the first time perhaps, as an Italian of the new Italy. The widest purpose of his history is to discover the roots and origins of that new Italy, not merely, again, in the narrow sense of the new Italian state which had been called into being by the Risorgimento, but in the wider sense

of the new Italian ethical will, which itself had made the Risorgimento possible, and which had found its expression in a rich cultural and spiritual life which had included but had not been exhausted by the Risorgimento. This new Italy, he perceived, was not born full blown; it was a laborious creation of the Italian ethical will and must, therefore, have historical origins. And where else must these be found but in that very period when Italy presented to the world the aspect of decadence, of exhaustion of the ethical will, that is in the age of the baroque? This is the reason that he writes that the origins of the new Italy are to be discerned not in 1848, nor 1820 nor 1799, but in 1670. In this way the history of the baroque era appears as the linear continuation and development of the history of Naples on the existential level of Croce's own historical commitments. (pp. 89-92)

The ethico-political conception of history was formed in the matrix of the matter of Naples. It was called forth by Croce's effort to penetrate to the human principle of that matter, the principle of its humanity, by which it might be lifted, from a narrative of the struggles, internal and external, of a minor state of Europe, to a record of the historical struggle of man himself to possess his eternal nature in time. To achieve this concept, he had found it necessary to reject all naturalistic presuppositions of history and to accept as its only principle the spirit of man, in its diverse moments and its multitudinous labours. In the history of the Baroque Age in Italy, this conception of ethico-political history had been extended and deepened. The problem of the 'negative' or 'decadent' period in history laid bare the essential rhythm of the life of the human spirit, the alternation of moments of moral enthusiasm and of moral depression which alone define such concepts as progress and decay. Materially, so to speak, the concept had been extended to achieve that union of 'Staatsgeschichte' and 'histoire de la civilization' which Federico Chabod has noted [in his 'Croce Storico' in *Rivista Storica Italiana* (1953)], a union which simultaneously transcends these limited concepts, reducing their unilaterality and abstractness to concrete identity.

The ethico-political conception remained, nevertheless, incomplete. It remained diffuse, in solution and suspension, so to say, with many other insights and ideas. There was lacking that single and unitary idea which could collect and fuse the diverse aspects of this genial insight, precipitating its pure essence. Croce, it is clear, at every stage of the history of Naples and of the baroque age is groping for this idea. It has its 'forma negativa', to recall the Vichian phrase, in the resolute rejection of all naturalistic, non-libertarian explanations of historical process. It has a more positive, but still abortive, expression in the insight that decadence is but moral depression, the diminution of the moral enthusiasm which sustains the humanity and the ideality of history. These could not suffice, however; they were partial insights, needing to be gathered and fused in some larger concept. Their partial character must be traced to the relative poverty of the matter. Both the matter of Naples and of the baroque age had yielded their ideality; but this was limited. There was necessary, consequently, a wider and a higher matter, *paulo altiora,* whose inner character would evoke the higher concept alone able to penetrate and encompass it. This matter was furnished to Croce by the formation of Italy and of Europe in the nineteenth century, and the idea which it evoked, the ultimate informing idea of his historiography, is the idea of liberty.

The liberal formation of Europe and of Italy in the nineteenth century thus forms the third, the widest and most inclusive theme of Croce's historiography and yields its ultimate and informing idea, liberty. That these two, the Italian and the wider European experience, constitute one historical reality, seen in its diverse aspects of universal and particular, is the most profound conviction which animates the two histories. The positive and transforming ethico-political ideal and force is the idea of liberty and the liberal spirit or will, and the formation of Europe in the nineteenth century was essentially the work of this spirit. The Italian experience is integral to the wider experience of Europe as a whole; but it is even more. It exemplifies the liberal idea and will in their purity, that is to say, in the highest form and expression there were to attain. Modern Italy, in his view, is the purest type of the liberal nation-state which history has seen, just as, and because, the movement of which it was born, the Risorgimento, was the most nearly flawless example of the liberal spirit in operation. The ethico-political history of Europe in the nineteenth century must, consequently, be polarized about these two centres: Europe, as a whole, and Italy. It can be, however, only one history, for these centres represent the universality and the particularity of one historical reality, the liberal movement.

Some critics have remarked that Croce's treatment of this theme lacks the richness and warmth of the history of Naples and the elaborate refinement of particulars which marks the history of the baroque era. Some material justice is reflected in this animadversion; differences in treatment do exist and are pronounced; no pejorative conclusion, however, can be drawn from them. These differences are to be traced to the diversity of materials and to the diversity of mood and insight which sustained him in these various themes. The treatment accorded each single theme, however, is strictly commensurate to the ideality and the spiritual attitude it could evoke. As a consequence, comparison between them can only be oblique. The dominant note of the history of Naples is one of tragic lyricism, even of elegy. This mood is dictated, we have already suggested, by the intense identification which Croce felt with the tragic national experience of Naples. He was narrating the vicissitudes of the people and the land with which his sentiments bound him most closely, as a Neapolitan by election, and in whose sufferings he shared. In such matter, objectivity is almost more than can be demanded of the historian; but Croce achieves it, to a remarkable degree, at the cost of an almost heroic detachment. The baroque age, on the other hand, attracted him with much less elemental force. He once remarked to a friend, it is true, that when he permitted himself to dream of the life he would choose above all others, there came to his imagination the cloister of a seventeenth-century Neapolitan convent, with its white walls and silent walks, shaded by cypress, inhabited by studious monks united in silent spiritual communion. When addressed historiographically, however, that age became for him a problem. It was a problem under its formal aspect, the idea of a period of decadence, a 'negative' period of history. It was a problem under its material aspect; while he saw it as the matrix of modern Italy, the elements of the new, of the future had most delicately to be isolated from the dead encrustment of the past. His attitude, consequently, was that of the inquirer before the problem. The mood of the work is detached, analytic, almost surgical, as with deft and probing scalpel, the cold edge of criticism, he seeks the elusive point where past and future, death and life must be distinguished. The delicate anatomy of the poetry of an unpoetic age, of the speculations of an unphilosophical era, of the religious proliferations of

'the most unreligious age Italy has ever known', these are not tasks to warm the cockles of a man's heart or lift his spirit. Particulars must be sought with care, almost with caution, for every distinction and evaluation is worth only the evidence which can be adduced in its support. More than once, the author is tempted to turn away in 'ennui' and is prevented only by the thought of the fruit to be won by this effort.

The dominant note of the history of Europe and of Italy in the nineteenth century, in contrast to both those earlier histories, is at once positive and buoyant; it is written in a mood as near the epic as may be hoped for in the modern world. This mood again, as in the case of the history of Naples, is evoked by identification with the matter. In this instance, however, the identification is unqualified. It is not, as in the case of Naples, acceptance and rejection at once, but unqualified acceptance, identification, not with defeat, but with victory. The liberal experience and achievement is for Croce limited but wholly positive; and while reserving to himself the right and the power to distinguish these limits between fact and idea, his identification with the fact is complete. The style of the works in turn is dictated by this positive and buoyant mood. They are painted in broad, forceful strokes, the outlines clear, the colours bold, the movement vivacious. There is a preoccupation with the whole, an Olympian subordination of detail, reflecting confidence and certitude. The distinctions and oppositions may be, as de Ruggiero suggests, of that between speculative or philosophical romanticism and its practical or sentimental form, even a shade too sharp. In this case too, however, as in the matter of Naples and in the baroque theme, the commensuration between mood, style and matter is complete. We are confronted by three autonomous historiographical achievements, which may not be evaluated in terms of each other, and can be contrasted only to heighten the values particular to each.

The identification which, in the history of Europe and Italy in the nineteenth century, exists between historian and matter bears closer examination. It reveals, as a matter of fact, the ultimate basis of this history, the basis upon which the massive reconstruction of a whole century of European experience rests. It is a maxim, perhaps the most celebrated, of Croce's historiography, that all history is contemporary. The Crocean sense of this maxim is, in the first instance, that all history is written in answer to an urgent need of the present. In the widest sense, it answers to the need of ethical and moral action; these demand a plenitude of presence in the subject, a plenitude of which the past, secured by the historiographic act, is an integral dimension. Without this basis in the present history is at best irrelevant and redundant; at worst, it may become a mode of self-alienation for the human subject, which lessens his moral enthusiasm, as he has pointed out with reference to the baroque era, for overattachment to the past was a dimension of its own 'decadence'. The contemporaneity of history is the basis for the identification of the historian with his theme in the histories of Europe and Italy in the nineteenth century.

The grounds for this identification are many and complex. The first is Croce's position as a member of the generation which was the direct and immediate heir of the Risorgimento. The Risorgimento must always mean more to the Italian than a mere phase in the history of Italy. It means the birth of Italy, for before the Risorgimento there was no Italy in the sense of an autonomous nation-state able to vindicate its claim to self-identity and historical existence and to contribute to the common good of humanity to which all nations must contribute. The creation of Italy as a nation could never be considered a mere political achievement. It was an ethical transaction of the highest order, marking a true beginning rather than the rebirth which the appellation Risorgimento suggests. For this reason, every Italian must identify himself with the ideals and the forces which made the national aspiration of Italy an historical reality. In its simplest form, this identification meant the impossibility of any return to a situation resembling that which had prevailed before the Risorgimento; any step toward the undoing of the work of the Risorgimento must appear a desecration. Even more, however, it meant the ethico-political obligation of realizing the full ideality of the new Italy, its richest historical possibilities. This obligation was felt by the men of the 'Right', the direct inheritors of the Risorgimento in political power; it was felt by the men of the 'Left', the 'young Left' who displaced the Right in office in 1876, but adhered to its methods and ideals; it was felt by the Catholics, torn though they were by conflicting loyalties. It was felt, finally, by Croce personally as a member of this generation, even as a 'purist' of the Risorgimento tradition, and becomes vocal in his history.

The acceptance of the Risorgimento implied the acceptance of the whole European movement of which it was a part. The rise of Italy as an independent nation was not an anomaly. It was the expression, in terms of the life and history of the peninsula, of a common movement embracing the whole of Europe. It possessed analogues wherever effective centres of such formation presented themselves. The community among the nation-states was based upon common principles and common ideals. This wider acceptance and identification is also a basic characteristic of Croce's position.

His was not, however, an acceptance and an identification with the fact merely. His history is not an apology either for the Risorgimento or for liberalism and the Europe it created. It is, rather, a critical exposition of the ethico-political ideals and the ethico-political forces which achieved the fact. The purpose of this criticism is both to identify those ideals and forces in their historical actuality and to relate them to the present with its special problems and aspirations. The identification which marks his work, consequently, is born at the high level of critical reflection which is in turn the preparation for relevant historical action in the present. Its critical character renders the mode of identification and the historical narrative complex; but it also lends it new strength and clarity. Finally, his identification is born of the contemporary crisis in which the new Italy was caught up in the third decade of the twentieth century. Although Croce had been absorbed in the matter of these histories, under one aspect or another, from the very beginning of his career, their composition was not undertaken until the crisis of the new authoritarianism and totalitarianism was well advanced and the path which lay before it well marked. The polemical character of these histories, consequently, cannot be overlooked. Croce saw in the developing trend of political life the destruction of the Italy of the Risorgimento. It detracts only a little, if at all, from his final vision that it was relatively slow in forming, or that he overlooked a countermovement, that of popularism, which might have rectified many of the long-standing anomalies of liberal Italy, while reaffirming the basic liberal insights. The tardiness of this vision is also compensated by the fact that it was born of a fundamental confidence in the resiliency of liberal Italy, its power to absorb and to domesticate such a movement as Fascism. When finally the vision came, it was crystal clear. The polemic which it provoked was radical but took the form, not of a controversy *ad hoc* which in the circumstances would surely have proven less than useless, but of a synoptic and critical restatement of the basic ideals which were in danger of repudiation. In this sense, the history of Europe in the nineteenth century and that of Italy even more, in the period between 1871 and 1915, was a judgment upon Fascism. At the same time they constituted a judgment upon all Italians, himself included. Their polemical objective was to show that while it is true that the posibility of such a movement as Fascism may be traced in the structure of post-Risorgimento Italy, it is present there only as the possibility of moral failure is always present in human effort. Fascism cannot be conceived as following necessarily upon the course of events of that period. It must be traced to a moral failure in the Italians themselves. The histories possess consequently the character of a recall of Italy to the pristine ideals and moral volition of her national life.

The central theses of these histories are unambiguous, stated in the same bold and positive tone which marks their style. The positive and effective ethico-political force in the nineteenth century was liberalism, which supplies both the ideality and the effective moral will of the century. Thus the basic thesis. The authentic idea of liberty is to be found in the tradition of philosophical romanticism or classical idealism. Thus the second. The third concerns the relationship between the idea of liberty, as defining liberalism, and the concrete institutional forms into which that idea, in the course of the century, was translated: that there exists between them the essential incommensurability between idea which is always normative and the concrete existential form; so that their simple identification, as exemplified in the attitude of the Right in 1876, must be recognized as erroneous. Finally, there is his thesis concerning the place of Italy in the liberal movement of Europe as a whole and concerning the fate of the liberal idea in the first crucial decades after the creation of the new Italy: that, in the first instance, the Italian experience of the Risorgimento represented the quintessence of the liberal movement of the nineteenth century; in the second, that the experience of the first decades of the life of Italy as a nation vindicates the liberal idea and establishes the positive achievement of the new nation which makes of any movement such as the Fascist 'adventure' an historical and moral anomaly.

In the liberty which is the sustaining principle of liberalism, the ethico-political conception, as we have suggested, is completed. In its original context, the matter of Naples, the ethico-political concept is primarily a methodological canon; it is a guide for the historian in his effort to find the living centre of the matter with which he dealt. The ethico-political insight, in this sense, is essentially the insight of Vico: 'in the night of thick darkness enveloping the earliest antiquity . . . there shines the eternal and neverfailing light of a truth beyond all question: that the world of civil society has certainly been made by men, and that its principles are therefore to be found within the modifications of our own human mind'. The living centre of history is discerned as residing in the will and the ideality of man himself. Vichian too is the attitude toward nature, specifically, toward the natural forces at work in history. 'Whoever reflects on this cannot fail to marvel that the philosophers should have directed all their energies to the world of nature . . . and neglected the study of the world of nations or the civil world.' The world of nature can but delineate the theatre within which the will and ideality of man are deployed; they are but limiting factors, bereft of explanatory force, and engendering, when substituted for the agency of man, a false conception of historical necessity. It becomes the historian's intent, according to this canon, to eschew naturalistic explanation in history in whatever form it may suggest itself, and to seek always, in Croce's own words, its 'vero moto e il vero dramma negli intelletti e nei cuori'. The chief result of the application of this canon is to throw into relief, as Croce remarks about his own history of the realm of Naples, the human character of history.

By the concept of liberty, this canonical sense of the ethico-political conception is converted into, and completed by, its ontological sense. According to that canon, the historian had been directed to the human centre of history and admonished to see there the true principles of explanation. He was instructed to see history as wholly the work of the human spirit. But no positive concept of the human spirit itself had been advanced; or more accurately, such a concept had been only adumbrated, and that negatively. For to say that man is not subject to natural necessity in historical action is, in a negative manner, to assert that he is free, but without indicating the positive form of his freedom. This lack is only partially remedied by the classical doctrines on the freedom of the human will; these are arrested wholly at the level of the psychological analysis of freedom and tend, as a consequence, to fall back into naturalistic dilemmas, or pseudo-dilemmas. Liberty is the concept which defines the human spirit in its ontological character; through this concept the human spirit is discerned in its ultimate quality of being, as the creative existential agent of ideal forms. Ethico-political history thus discovers its own positive character; it is the history of human freedom, because liberty is the constitutive form of the human spirit itself. (pp. 169-77)

A. Robert Caponigri, in his History and Liberty: The Historical Writings of Benedetto Croce, *Routledge and Kegan Paul, 1955, 284 p.*

LIENHARD BERGEL   (essay date 1957)

[*In the following excerpt, Bergel emphasizes the importance of considering Croce's thought in its totality.*]

Those features of Croce's philosophy which are most striking at first glance are the absence of cumbersome technical jargon and the grace and limpidity of style. Croce was always critical of the narrow specialists, and particularly so of the "professionals" in the field of philosophy, of the "pure" philosophers, those dealing with truly "academic" questions. Just as he demonstrated the artistic faculty to be a universal human attribute and not a gift mysteriously awarded to a select few, philosophizing was for him the orderly exercise of a basic human activity and not an esoteric science. Yet it is exactly the absence of academic pedantry and abstruseness, the openness of his thinking to all aspects of humanity, and the concreteness with which he treats them that present the peculiar difficulty to those wishing to enter into Croce's world. Though his writings are always concerned with specific philosophical, historical, or critical problems, their understanding presupposes acquaintance with his thinking as a whole, because it is the human being in its totality, seen from the present and, at the same time, in a historical perspective, that is the constant object of his reflections.

The book which made Croce's name first known in Europe, the *Aesthetic* of 1902, already contained implicitly the whole

of his philosophy. Thus the historian and critic of literature must be acquainted with Croce's thinking on the economic and ethical activity of man in order to understand his writings on individual poets, and the political scientist, scrutinizing Croce's books on history and society, may reach erroneous conclusions if he is not familiar with Croce's aesthetics. This does not mean that Croce deals "aesthetically" with political matters, or vice versa. It is characteristic of his philosophy that it establishes clear distinctions between the different forms of human activity. At the same time, these differentiations—between the theoretical (aesthetic and philosophical) on the one hand, the practical (economic and ethical) on the other—are made for the sake of emphasizing more strongly the specific function of each faculty within the whole of human existence, and the mutual complementation of all. This inseparable interrelationship, which for Croce characterizes reality, is also reflected in his work. There, theory is always accompanied by practical demonstration, since one would be meaningless without the other; aesthetic criticism is always related to, though not identified with, ethical considerations. Croce's reflections on the nature of art are fully comprehensible only if they are seen together with his moral philosophy and if they are held against the wide range of his criticism extending from Homer and Virgil to Hopkins, Rilke, Pirandello, and Sartre. A seemingly unclear statement in a theoretical essay may be elucidated by a remark in a book review or in the many short articles and notes that formed a regular feature of the periodicals edited by Croce, *La Critica* and *Quaderni della Critica*. Similarly, Croce's political theories find their necessary complementation in his frequent pronouncements on the practical issues of the day.

It is this vastness of Croce's intellectual horizon and the enormous variety it encompasses that stands in the way of his ever becoming "popular"; Croce's thinking cannot be condensed into radio talks or primers for those anxious to find a "short-cut to education," and the many erroneous notions current about him are to some extent due to the effort to reduce the work of a long and ceaselessly active life to a few formulas suitable for textbooks or reference works. Attempts of this kind are necessarily unsuccessful also for another reason: Croce was not a philosophic carpenter, slowly and patiently constructing his "system," the unfolding of his thinking was a continuous, living process characterized by constant revisions, expansions, and refinements. Here again the eminently unacademic nature of Croce's thinking becomes obvious. He knows that genuine philosophical problems do not arise in a vacuum, just as ordinary reflection, of which true philosophy is merely an extension, is always the response to a specific situation in need of clarification. This explains Croce's hostility to all forms of empty abstractions and generalizations. Since it is concrete, ever changing reality that offers the problems to be solved, and since reality is unfortunately never "systematic" in its unfolding, Croce is aware that the search for a self-contained, finished "system" is fruitless and alien to truth. Thus the "incompleteness" of a philosopher's work is not a defect, but a sign of its validity.

This insight into the apparent fragmentariness and contingency of human knowledge has important implications. It is not with resignation, bewailing human limitations, that Croce arrives at his conclusions: What may seem to be a restriction imposed upon man actually provides the strongest validation of human potentialities. The assumption of an absolute, unalterable, rational truth that is whimsically withheld from man is based on the belief in a dualism between the reality accessible to man, and a higher, immutable, metaphysical world beyond his reach. This distinction Croce does not recognize. He considered it his principal achievement to have drawn the ultimate consequences from those tendencies in modern philosophy which were striving toward an uncompromising immanentism, the bringing together of "heaven" and "earth," and to have eliminated all remnants of metaphysical dualism that he encountered in his predecessors. Croce terms his philosophy "absolute historicism": The only reality that exists is that of the human spirit, unfolding itself in time. Here, as in many other instances, Croce developed in all its implications the insight first tentatively formulated by Vico—that man is the maker of his history—and went beyond Hegel, who did not fully identify the "spirit," as the only reality, with the concrete, individual acts of man. Croce was convinced that his philosophy confirms and supplements, rather than conflicts with, the basic tenets of Christianity. In an essay written in 1943: "Why we can not but call ourselves Christians," Croce explains why he considers his philosophy the logical outgrowth of the most radical revolution experienced by the Western World, that accomplished by Christianity, which turned man toward his inner self, the world of the spirit. For this reason his philosophy is uncompromisingly opposed to all forms of materialism, which represent a reversion toward the old dualistic conception of the world.

It was possible for Croce to achieve his radical refutation of materialistic thinking because he assigns a new place to the forces of instinct or "vitality," to the self-assertion of the practical will to live. This aspect of his philosophy is perhaps the least known and at the same time, in its application to political activity, it is frequently the most thoroughly misunderstood. Yet Croce considered his reflections on the nature and the function of the "vital" one of his main contributions to philosophy, and the elaboration of this aspect of his thinking occupied him particularly during the last years of his life. For Croce, the natural, volitional, and "economic" side of man is no longer separated from the rest of his being, as supposedly belonging to a "lower" realm, but it is conceived as forming an integral part of the whole of human existence: The non-rational elements in it, the instinctual and the intuitional, belong to the spirit together with the ethical and the philosophical. It is this reconciliation of apparently conflicting forces which lends to Croce's philosophy its "classical" character. For Croce, human existence is a drama in which the contrasts and opposites strive toward a balance, but this harmony, once attained, is again disrupted, for a new synthesis has to be achieved. The modernity of Croce's philosophy consists in the subtlety with which he presents the discords of reality; what sets him apart from much of contemporary thinking is the fact that these discords are resolved. Croce's analyses of the human dilemma, as they are presented, for instance, in his **"Ethical Fragments,"** easily match in the concreteness and finesse of their observations some of the most famous passages of Kierkegaard.

The power that, according to Croce, is constantly at work in bringing about a balance between the individual human activities, and which permeates them all, is the ethical force. The ethical is that influence which assures to each form of the spirit, including the "vital" or "economic," the free functioning within its own sphere, and which at the same time assures its harmony with the others. Thus the "ethical" is much broader than the merely altruistic: It aims at the full and free exercise of all human capacities; the ethical ideal and the ideal of liberty are essentially one. Error and evil are the interruptions in the harmonious cooperation between the different forms of the spirit, when one threatens to interfere with the others. Thus Croce's philosophy is neither optimistic nor pessimistic. He is widely aware of the full range of the possibilities for error and evil: They form permanently and necessarily a part of human existence, yet they are not irrational forces invading humanity from without, but rather the negative moments within the ethical process itself. Thus they present the obstacles to be overcome and set the new tasks for the ethical force.

This "classicism" of Croce's thinking is closely related to the other distinguishing feature of his philosophy, its historicism. History, as the creation of the human spirit, becomes the great harmonizer of conflicts; the macrocosm of history corresponds in its tensions and contrasts to the drama of individual existence, because the same spirit is active in both. Thus Croce's classical historicism is the modern expression of humanism, and finds itself therefore in inevitable opposition to the survival of romantic attitudes in our time. For Croce, history is the creation of values, each of which is necessarily limited, and for this reason in need of complementation. Thus it appears to him nonsensical to absolutize specific periods of history, e.g. the Middle Ages, and to condemn others as devilishly destructive, e.g. the epoch in which modern science and rationalism were first established. On the other hand, Croce's historicism is the contrary of mere relativism with its essentially nihilistic consequences. It is here that his thinking comes into conflict with German historicism. Croce has been called a Germanophile, and this supposed Germanophilia has sometimes been held responsible for the opposition his philosophy has encountered. Croce has always freely acknowledged the debt he owes to classical German philosophy and to the German eighteenth century in general; at the same time, hardly anyone has criticized the destructive and abstruse aspects of German culture with more penetration than did Croce. For Croce, the study of history is meaningful only when it is bound up with the solution of a specific problem of the present. The values of the past become alive only where this link to the present exists; history provides the answers formerly expected from philosophy. Croce reproaches German historiography for its "pureness" from practical application, for indulging in an irresponsible, pseudo-aesthetic contemplation of the "spirit of the times," for practicing a virtuosity obtuse to human values. It is this same uncompromising humanism that makes Croce also a severe critic of "pure" poetry and of "abstract" art: What is absent in both is the "content" of concrete human concerns.

Thus Croce's philosophy presents itself, on the one hand, as advancing and refining some of the basic themes of occidental intellectual tradition and, on the other, because he is so strongly aware of this historical continuity, as sharply critical of much that is merely "modern." It is the essence of Croce's classical, humanistic historicism that the harmony it has achieved can not be absolutized: The real fulfillment of his thinking is to go beyond it. (pp. 349-52)

Lienhard Bergel, "Benedetto Croce (1866-1952)," in Books Abroad, *Vol. 31, No. 4, Autumn, 1957, pp. 348-52.*

GIAN N. G. ORSINI   (essay date 1961)

[*Born in Italy, Orsini is an American educator and critic who has written numerous studies of European literature and philosophy. In the following excerpt, he provides a detailed analysis of* La poesia.]

In 1936 at the age of 70 Croce published a book entitled *La poesia,* or *Poetry: An Introduction to the Criticism and to the History of Poetry and of Literature.* This book presents the final stage in the development of his doctrine of poetry. It marks considerable progress over the *Breviary of Aesthetics* of 24 years before, the latest work of Croce's known to most English-speaking students. *La poesia* incorporates all the later developments in doctrine, such as the theory of the cosmic character of art, as well as the fruit of Croce's mature literary criticism, such as the studies on Dante, Shakespeare and Goethe. It then proceeds to break into new ground, introducing the doctrine of "literature" which is now distinguished from poetry and assigned a sphere of its own. The new doctrines are connected with the old in a single systematic exposition, composed in a more elaborate manner than in any preceding work. Its style is obviously carefully studied, as befits a work which expounds the civilizing function of good writing. Croce also provides an unprecedented wealth of illustration and practical criticism in a series of short *postille* or postscripts, which take up the whole second half of the book and bring in quotations from poets and critics, discussions of special points, and brief characterizations of scores of writers and works. (p. 253)

Croce begins by expounding his doctrine of poetry in the terms of the universal character of art: e.g. the image transcends the emotion which it expresses as the universal transcends the particular. In a postscript he explains that he is deliberately abstaining from the use of his old terminology, such as the "pure intuition" or the "lyrical intuition," in order to avoid the tedium of repetition and "the superstition of words." But he adds that " 'pure intuition' implies 'non-conceptual' and 'non-historical,' and this can only be 'lyrical' intuition, i.e. emotion transformed into contemplation [*teóresi*]." So the poetic image is still, as ever, the contemplation or sublimation of emotion. And although the universal or total character of poetry is constantly affirmed, yet the individuality of expression still remains the foundation of the argument: language is individual, the poetic image is unique and untranslatable, and the genres and other classifications are still considered "abstractions formed from single works."

Individuality emerges explicitly in the doctrine of the "individual personality" as the substance of the work of poetry and as the object of critical attention: "criticism adheres to the individual quality of the work." The whole doctrine of critical characterization . . . turns on the concept of individuality. Poetry is to be dealt with not in general histories but in monographs "with reference always to the concreteness of the individual work." Finally, the term "intuition" itself re-emerges in the later portions of the work, where poetry is again defined as the union of "feeling with intuition." The critical judgment is still defined as "the identification of the intuition and the category." And all the attendant corollaries are also maintained: viz. the rejection of all resolutions of poetry into ideas, conventions or trends, of evolutionary schemes, of source-hunting, of philologism and of the histories of genres.

But it will be well to take up a question which may arise now in the mind of the reader. Here is Croce writing a whole book on Poetry by itself, i.e. on one of the arts in separation from the others. But did he not reject the existence of separate arts and affirm the sole validity of the science of Aesthetics to deal with all problems relating to art? Does he now acknowledge the separation of poetry from the other arts, and the validity of Poetics? Croce was well aware of this possible objection and he made it quite clear that he had not given up the doctrine of the unity of the arts nor the validity of Aesthetics as the science of art. At the same time, however, the terms used in the discussion of certain groups of works differ from those used in the discussion of others. This difference may arise from exclusive or excessive attention to the extrinsic circumstances of externalization and preservation, and should be corrected by a discussion of those terms to show their identity with the terms used for other groups. For instance, in the so-called plastic arts much use has been made of the terms "illustration" and "decoration" (e.g. by B. Berenson); a similar distinction exists also for poetry, such as "fable" and "lyric," or "structure" and "poetry." Similarly questions which center around the conception of "pure painting" are essentially the same as those which center around the concepts of "pure poetry." Croce concludes that there is a place for books that discuss the problems connected with each "separate art" or the group of works so labelled, in order to analyze the concepts involved and bring them back to the unity of all art.

This book also contains a full discussion of the process of taste or the re-enactment of aesthetic expressions. The function of historical knowledge in exegesis is pointed out again, and the aesthetes or dilettanti are again castigated for their reluctance to undertake the labors of research. The preparation and training of the poet also receive a full discussion. Traditional rhetoric is given here the most favorable treatment it had yet received from Croce. The poet should certainly read books on rhetoric and composition, on language and prosody: "What will he learn from them? He will receive the suggestion to take notice of this or that form of expression historically existing, in connection with the work that he is engaged in. In order to duplicate those forms? Certainly not; mere aping, which certainly does occur, does not enter the present discussion. To allow them to operate on his mind and incline it in a certain direction? Yes, indeed. The lack of such a habit and such a discipline is clearly observable in the shortcomings of certain writers." On all previously discussed questions Croce here makes new observations, introduces new arguments and brings in fresh illustrations, so that this book is indispensable for a full understanding of Croce's mature position. . . . (pp. 253-56)

A new departure in *La poesia* is the introduction of the concept of "structure" or to be more correct of "structural parts" of poetry. In general, poetic structure for Croce can only mean poetic form, or the individualizing intuition, so every poem has a structure which is different from all others. This obviously rules out the traditional concept of structure deriving from a genre: the "epic structure," the "tragic structure," etc. are no less pseudo-concepts than the genres to which they relate. But in *La poesia* Croce takes note of the fact that a good poem is not usually perfect in all its parts, but includes some that are not poetic or not perfectly executed. These Croce divides into two kinds: genuine imperfections and "structural" parts. The first could be conceivably corrected or eliminated; they are real defects or blemishes that should not be in the poem and that the poet has left in it because he was either too lazy or too hurried to eliminate them. But structural parts cannot be eliminated without breaking up the whole poem. They contribute to its unity and yet are not poetical; they are mere links or connections inserted by the poet to keep together groups or clusters of images. The unity thus effected is not genuinely poetic, and yet it is hard to conceive of a different way of bringing those images together.

It should be noted that Croce here is frankly being empirical or descriptive, not philosophical or categorical. Structural parts are something actually found in poems, but not an essential feature of poetry in general, so there is no need for their presence in any particular poem. But it is a fact of experience that such parts sometimes occur in poems, so they should be accounted for, as Croce endeavors to do here. Some critics, who consider Croce the sworn foe of all empiricism, may be surprised at seeing him assume such a frankly empirical attitude. But thanks to his conception of the distinct spheres of mental activity, Croce has always been able to recognize the practical use of empirical classifications, while excluding them from the sphere of speculative and normative concepts. Even in his first *Aesthetic* Croce acknowledged an "empirical sense of the rhetorical categories" which he excluded from the philosophy of art. In 1927 . . . he even suggested a new Poetics, meaning a new classification of genres, on an empirical basis. He repeats this suggestion in the book on Poetry, and adds: "A work of sound empiricism is, in a certain sense, more difficult and more complicated than a purely philosophical work or the specific criticism and history of poetry, since it presupposes both the latter and the former, and not in the brains of others, but active through exercise and experience in one's own. It is not only a work of conceptual creation and intellectual acumen, but of practical equilibrium and of wisdom—the kind of wisdom that does not always immediately follow strenuous intellectual efforts."

In the empirical classification of "structural parts," the first instance given involves the sacrifice of a detail of the poem, a word or a phrase, to the harmony of the whole; that detail is deliberately left imperfect in order to achieve unity. This is most common in rhyming. An imperfectly expressive word may be used "for the sake of the rhyme." This is a blemish, but it serves the purpose of preserving the total harmony of the composition. It may be objected that this is a harmony of mere sound; but this sound "is itself an image, answering to the poetic motif."

Secondly, there is a certain kind of "padding" (*zeppe* or *chevilles*) which is used to connect two verse passages or two clusters of images, e.g. transitional passages in longer poems, not excluding the *Divine Comedy* which provides Croce with some interesting instances. They are not poetic in themselves and yet cannot be eliminated, for they help the author to pass from one climax of poetic inspiration to another. This is an explicit answer to Poe's famous criticism of long poems. A. C. Bradley had also noted the existence of these connective passages in long poems, but he thought that poets like Virgil and Milton transformed them entirely into poetry.

Of the same kind are the expository parts of plays, poems and novels, and many similar connectives or commentaries which occur in literature, such as the reflections of the chorus in Greek tragedy, "psychological explanations in the novel," and particularly the introduction of characters and episodes to carry on the action of the plot. All these parts are secondary and subordinate and should not be allowed to rise too high. If they did, they would upset the balance of the whole. It should be carefully noted that Croce does *not* argue that these are necessary or essential parts of all poems or novels, but only that they occur in some instances and call therefore for evaluation of their function. They may be designated as aesthetically neutral, neither beautiful nor ugly, but mere links between points of beauty.

However, the aesthetic critic is specially bound to take notice of them since they have become one of the main props of historical criticism: "Hence the praise that is extended to Corneille, to Calderón, to Apostolo Zeno, and similarly to others, for having provided French tragedy, Spanish *comedia,* Italian melodrama and other genres with a structure and a contrivance which they transmit to their successors, whether they are poets or not; the extolling of Aeschylus as the inventor of the second actor in Greek tragedy, and the merit attributed to the inventor of the sonnet or of *ottava rima* and to those who introduced them to other nations." Croce concludes the paragraph with a remark which is of particular relevance to contemporary criticism: "The consequence is that the misunderstanding of the nature of the structural element causes poetry to be considered a sequence of conventions and artifices, and those who invent that kind of thing are considered poets; and the inventions and devices, one would almost say the tricks and artful dodges, employed by them, form the subjects of special investigations, full of wonder and admiration for such things."

This unintelligent admiration for the nonpoetic parts of a poem has inevitably produced a reaction to the other extreme. This is the doctrine of "pure poetry" which will not allow in a poem anything which is not 100 per cent poetic. The doctrine takes two forms: one affirms that only short poems can be poetic, and the other that poetry can only exist in "fragments" or fulgurations and that it should be composed that way. Croce here makes a formal refutation of the first doctrine, which is of course Poe's, by introducing a point which also applies to other problems, i.e. the irrelevance of the time element: "it (Poe's theory) commits the serious fallacy of introducing a time element into an ideal process, as if the composition of the poem and the reading of it, whether it lasts a minute of the clock or several years, did not follow an ideal rhythm which takes hold of the poet and the reader and carries them out of time. This theory is also refuted by experience, for the poetry of poems, plays and novels which are genuinely inspired does not consist of single parts only, but circulates throughout the whole composition, from which no piece may be extracted and placed in an anthology as a thing of beauty, and yet one feels poetry diffused throughout the whole of it. This observation will also refute the second form of the theory."

In his practical criticism Croce had occasion to point out that certain poems not of the first rank were redeemed by a flash of inspiration, a successful image, occurring in the midst of otherwise uninspired stretches. From this some hasty critics had jumped to the conclusion that all the rest of the poem was to be discarded, and adopted the theory of "fragmentism," which Croce in 1915 had immediately rejected. . . . (pp. 256-59)

A third use of structural parts occurs when a poet takes up a traditional tale or subject and uses it "as a kind of warp upon which he weaves his own poetry, sometimes covering up the warp entirely and concealing it from sight, and in effect abolishing it, but at other times leaving it visible to a larger or smaller extent. In this case again the attitude of the poetic interpreter must be that of indifference to the warp and of sole attention to what is woven upon it. But unintelligent readers confuse the warp with the embroidery and appraise it as substantial poetry or poetic motif; hence all the dissertations printed on the manner in which a theme should be handled according to its essence and to the various ways in which various authors have treated such themes as Prometheus and Orestes, Lucretia and Sophonisba, Faust and Don Juan, and so forth."

And here comes a pointed reference to Shakespeare criticism: "Since tales treated in that manner are to be found also in Shakespeare, who more than once rose to high flights stepping lightly from legends and fairy tales, a persistent criticism has been directed to the contradictions and incongruities and puerilities of Shakespeare; and one of the most recent of such critics was Leo Tolstoy, who mistook the warp, or plot, of *King Lear* with the poetry of *King Lear*." Tolstoy was by no means the last critic of that persuasion. Much modern Shakespearean criticism of the historical school has followed that lead, including Schücking's much lauded "discovery" of the naive and rudimental character of Shakespeare's characters.

As a last instance of structural parts, Croce cites the philosophical and doctrinal sections of such poems as the *Divine Comedy* and *Faust;* those parts are definitely not poetry, yet they were indispensable to the poet, because he, Dante or Goethe, happened to be also a philosopher and would not have allowed himself to indulge in a purely poetic composition if he had not been able to bring into it his philosophical views. In this case the structural part is not something indifferent to the poet, like the warp in the previous case; it is instead a vital part of his mind, both conjoined to and distinct from his poetry. "Nor can it be indifferent to us in our effort to understand the spirit of the poet and the character of his poetry, but indifferent it must remain as all other structures, in the sense that his poetry is not to be found precisely in it."

In this book Croce also reiterates his rejection of the validity of intentions for the criticism of poetry. This refers to the so-called "Intentional Heresy" and since we have not discussed it before, we will consider it now. That expression cannot be produced by a mere act of will, was already argued in the *Aesthetic.* Croce formally denied the relevance of intentions to criticism in a paper written as early as 1905, entitled **"The Aims of the Poets."** The professed intentions of the poets—to edify, to amuse, to satirize an opponent, to support a party or a religious dogma, etc.—are practical decisions which precede composition and have no necessary connection with it. This point goes a long way back. Already in 1894 Croce noted that De Sanctis had based his own criticism on that principle and quoted him briefly: "the poet sets out with the poetics, the forms, the ideas, the preoccupations of his own time; the less of an artist he is, the more exactly he renders his intentional world [*mondo intenzionale*]." So this is an old theory in Italian criticism.

For Croce, the meaning of the work is to be found within the work; no judgment of intention is relevant unless corroborated by the work itself, in which case it is superfluous. There are poets who believe themselves animated by high moral ideals and are really decadent or morbid. Others consider themselves ruthless realists, but are actually inspired by deeply-felt sympathy for the oppressed and by indignation for social wrongs (Croce was here probably thinking of D'Annunzio and Verga, respectively). "The man is sometimes superior, sometimes inferior, to the state of mind portrayed by the artist." Historical scholarship has made a great point of ascertaining the intentions of an author and interpreting his work accordingly. But in aesthetic criticism "the crude seeking for the aims of poets" is replaced by the investigation of the state of mind expressed by the work of art, which is a much more delicate operation. It is far easier, but irrelevant, "to allege aims, quoted from some extra-aesthetic document, or introduced arbitrarily into the work of art."

In the paper on Totality . . . Croce argued that a poet may start with the intention of gratifying some passion of hate or lust, but during the course of composition he can be carried away by his creative imagination and rise to pure art. In the book on Poetry of 1936 Croce took up again the question and reaffirmed his belief that even the poets who have special aims and formal beliefs set them aside when engaging in the creative act, or preserve them only as particular tones of emotion in the harmony of the whole. Hence, he says, "it is an illusion to see the idea of Fate in Greek tragedy or the idea of Providence in the work of a Christian poet, because Fate and Providence are concepts and therefore the objects of thought and not of representation. What is actually represented will be, always and only, under the name of Fate, a feeling of terror and of resignation, and under the name of Providence, a feeling of confidence and of hope: lights and shadows, and not concepts." Spingarn, it should be acknowledged, had clearly and vigorously made this point: "The poet's real 'intention' is to be found, not in one or another of the various ambitions that flit through his mind, but in the actual work of art which he creates. His poem is this 'intention.' In any other sense, 'intention' is outside the aesthetic field—a mere matter of the poet's literary theory or his power of will—and so matter for the biographer of the man rather than for the critic of the poem."

This Intentional Heresy that Croce denounces (although not using that name which it is the merit of Wimsatt to have coined) is involved in several questions. . . . [It] arises frequently in connection with the literature of an age like the Renaissance, when didactic theories prevailed in criticism and were at times professed by the poets themselves. But all such professions, such as Spenser's famous intent "to fashion a gentleman," are irrelevant to the artistic composition. This also applies to drama. It has been laboriously argued by the historical critics that because Shakespeare wrote for the stage, and therefore aimed at pleasing his audience, he could not have written great poetry but only scripts for the entertainment of the London populace. The whole school of "realists" with E. E. Stoll at their head had poured scorn on the critics of the Romantic age who had found great poetry in Shakespeare's plays. Such is the strength of the Intentional Heresy.

A related question, of less critical moment, concerns the intentional referring of a poem to a particular set of circumstances, sentimental or otherwise extrapoetic, which go beyond the lyrical emotion expressed in the poem and may be an object of personal interest. This may be done by the poet himself after he has completed the poem, or by a reader who may take pleasure in referring the image of the poem to some concern of his own. This is an operation to which Croce in his later years showed himself more indulgent than previously, dedicating to it a number of papers and arguing that it is an innocent transference as long as it does not claim to be either poetical or critical. Even philosophers do it when they use a quotation from a poet to illustrate a point in philosophical theory. "The poetic image," says Croce, "is . . . so rich that it contains within itself the infinite particular situations of reality and of life."

A curious case of the kind is that of a sonnet which occurs in Bruno's *Eroici Furori* and which was long admired (even by De Sanctis) as a beautiful expression of the philosopher's longing towards the Absolute. It turned out to have been written originally by the poet Luigi Tansillo to convey a rather different emotion: the lover's passion for a lady who happened to be stationed above him in rank. Croce at first saw in this case the exceptional coexistence of two different poems in the same set of words, or rather in words that were apparently the same, identical in sound but not in meaning: a kind of colossal pun. In 1944 he revised this opinion in the light of his new theory of emotional reference. The sonnet is now seen as a single poem expressing an indeterminate feeling, a "state of mind," which Tansillo intentionally referred to his own love affair, while Bruno intentionally referred it to his own philosophic efforts. Both intentions are declared to be extrapoetic; the poetry lies in the indeterminate, depersonalized emotion expressed by the image.

Perhaps the most important novelty in *La poesia* is Croce's definition of literature as distinct from poetry. This definition has also made critics charge that Croce was radically changing his views or backsliding to traditional positions. Actually this doctrine is no new departure but had been developing for years. Although it reaches here a form and prominence that had never been given it before by its author, yet it deals with one of Croce's oldest preoccupations, viz. what to do with pseudo and quasi art. Since Croce had never thought that all verse is poetry, nor that all literature is creative, he was faced with the problem of defining what was not poetry in literature, and assigning it a function in the system of the spirit. In *La poesia* he gave his final answer to this problem by proposing to limit the term "literature" to all compositions that are not poetry, or achieved expression, but have only the semblance of poetry, while actually exercising another function, which Croce here defines as "civilization" in a broad sense. At the same time he brings together in a systematic classification a number of other categories of pseudo art which he had formulated in the course of his long career as critic and historian of literature, such as the category of "oratory," "pure poetry," etc.

This led him to extend the number of meanings of the term "expression." Besides aesthetic expression, which for Croce remains the only real expression, he had acknowledged in the *Aesthetic* two other things which are commonly called expressions: "naturalistic expression" and the expression of thought (concepts) in "prose." The first designates the outward signs of emotion, which are not expressions of it but actually part or symptoms of it. . . . They therefore remain outside the domain of art. (This was recognized also by Dewey . . .) The second is what Croce calls "prose" or the expression of reflective thought (concepts), which is not so much expression as symbolization, or representation by means of a sign, the image converted to the uses of thought; in this case the image and the concept remain separate and distinct. . . . (pp. 259-65)

These theses constitute in effect Croce's theory of meaning. Meaning for Croce is an act that differs according to the function it performs. The meaning of a poetic text is an expressive act; the meaning of a philosophical text is an act of conceptual thinking; the meaning of an historical proposition is an act of judgment or the referring of a particular event to a universal category. In the first of these acts, the poetic, words and meaning are one and the same; in the other two, words symbolize the thought: they can be translated or represented by other signs, while poetry cannot.

The next form of nonaesthetic expression that Croce now enumerates is "oratory." This important concept seems to have emerged for the first time in 1915, in a paper entitled **"Poetry, Prose and Oratory: Value of this Triple Distinction for Literary Criticism."** "Oratory" is not to be identified with the art of speech. It designates all compositions which are primarily addressed to the emotions. It makes use of images already produced by the expressive activity, taking them out of their context, breaking them up and rearranging them in a manner that may arouse the emotions and hence direct the reader towards some form of action. Oratory always implies an audience to be influenced and directed, whereas poetry does not. Oratory seems to coincide with the whole function assigned to poetry by some modern critics, such as Kenneth Burke, but for Croce it is something quite different. For him it belongs to the category of practical action. It is therefore subject to all the regulations, restrictions and controls which society may place upon action, while art is free. From the historian's point of view, it belongs to the history of action and therefore must be related to history of politics, of economics, or of other social activities, while poetry as we have seen rises above them.

Here we find in Croce a doctrine of semantics. Long before the modern semanticists, Croce was aware that words were not only a vehicle for thought but could also be used as purveyors of stimuli. Oratorical expressions are not susceptible of being analyzed aesthetically or logically: they may have the form of words and sentences, but they have neither logical meaning nor aesthetic value. It is therefore futile to try to extract at all costs a logical meaning from all linguistic expressions, or aesthetic value from didactic and political verse. So a considerable amount of the territory of literature is given up as unpoetic, and surrendered to the history of manners, politics, religion or culture.

Another kind of emotional arousal is the function of the literature of entertainment which is distinct from "oratory." The literature of entertainment makes use of previously formed images for the purpose of arousing not one definite emotion, but a succession of emotions of all kinds, emotions simply for the sake of emotion. Hence it arouses not only the pleasurable emotions, which are gratified also in wishful thinking and in the so-called "pleasures of the imagination" (another subdivision of this area), but also painful or restrictive emotions, since the aim of "entertainment" is to excite, to thrill, to keep in suspense, to give one "a good cry," etc.: anything to keep the emotions alive.

We have according to Croce four nonaesthetic forms of so-called expression: natural emotions, prose, oratory and entertainment. They all make use of words for their purposes, i.e. they use already formed aesthetic expressions. This use may be crude or skilful, clumsy or graceful. Grace is achieved in so far as they approximate to aesthetic expression. Supposing they actually pass the borderline and turn into art, then they lose their original practical or intellectual tendency and become pure contemplation. But short of that there is still a wide range of territory that they can cover, and that for Croce is the domain of "literature" as distinct from poetry. Literature may now be defined as the handling of nonaesthetic expressions in such a way that they resemble poetry while still falling short of it. Croce considers literature, so defined, one of the great forces of civilization: a continuous approximation to beauty, brought into the sphere of practical action, thus reminding it of the existence of that sphere of contemplation which rises above its stir and tumult. While being itself practical and not theoretical, it effects a sort of "harmony" between different spheres of activity. But strictly speaking, it is "a practical device to satisfy two different requirements." So it is not a new form of spiritual activity, to be added to the four already recognized by Croce; it is merely a special product of one of these activities, the practical, operating upon the products of another form, the aesthetic. This is one of Croce's most elaborate formulas of interaction among his four basic activities, and it is not a philosophical or logical definition, but empirical. "Literature" may be described as an historical phenomenon, circumscribed in time and place, even though the time may be centuries and the space continents.

This concept of literature has given rise to much discussion and variant evaluations. Croce himself said that the concept was a delicate one, to be handled lightly and not to be pressed too far. In any case, it is clear that literature for Croce is not poetry, and what he says about it does not affect his aesthetic theory. In poetry it is not possible to distinguish genres or types. The contrary is true of literature. Furthermore in poetry form cannot be separated from content. But in "literature" they may legitimately be judged in separation or in conjunction. We may approve, or disapprove, of the content of a work of entertainment, i.e. of the emotions aroused, or we may praise its formal structure—its plot, rising action, falling action, catastrophe, tension, suspense, etc.—apart from the

emotions aroused. But we cannot do this with works of real poetry. The heresies of aesthetics thus become the truths of pseudo art—which is not so surprising.

"Literature" according to this doctrine possesses four genres, corresponding to the four forms of nonaesthetic expression already enumerated: sentimental or effusive, didactic or expository, oratorical and entertaining. In each of these, "literature" operates so that the unpoetic expression is not too divergent from poetic expression. The effusion of feeling, or release of emotions, is a common phenomenon; literature sees to it that it uses words and forms which belong to the realm of good writing, and assume an appearance of comeliness and dignity. To this class of writing belong the typical effusions of Romantic sentimentalism to be found in Byron, Lamartine, Musset, etc. In the second class Croce includes the skilfully constructed prose of such great writers as Plato and Cicero, Thucydides and Livy, and in later times the Latin prose of Petrarch and Erasmus, or the still later vernacular prose of Galileo and Voltaire. In the third class, literature adjusts the various forms of persuasion so that they, too, present a decorous aspect and a certain resemblance to real art. Hence political poetry, novels, plays like Voltaire's *Mahomet* and Schiller's *William Tell,* are all reduced to the same class as *Uncle Tom's Cabin.* In the fourth class works of mere entertainment are worked over and polished so as to have some semblance of art.

Being a spiritual act, "literature" is susceptible of evaluation, positive or negative. There is good "literature" and there is bad "literature," according to the measure of success with which its object is achieved. For instance, says Croce, there is no reason to be ashamed of enjoying such a work of pure entertainment as *The Three Musketeers;* in its way it is a well-composed piece of writing, and Croce frankly states his (nonaesthetic) enjoyment of it. For if "literature" is nonpoetic, it is not for Croce to be identified with the antipoetic or the ugly. No offence is given to poetry by the existence of works of "literature." Ugliness and the antipoetic are now defined as the intervention of the practical will within the imaginative process, to interrupt or divert it. But "literature" is different. It might be described as homage paid to beauty by the non-beautiful, somewhat like (but this simile is not Croce's) hypocrisy is said to be homage paid to virtue by vice.

Since the effect on an audience, which is not necessary to pure art, is essential in the case of "literature," it is possible to make a positive evaluation of writers like Dryden and Pope, attacked by Romantic critics as writers of prose in verse. Their social virtues as writers of the Court or of Society are now acknowledged as something positive and valuable, as well as the civilizing function of urbane wit in the style that they cultivated. Such writers may now be recognized as great masters of "literature"—but Croce still excludes them from poetry.

To the discussion of these forms Croce also adds an analysis of what he calls "art for art's sake," which is the kind of imitative writing cultivated by lovers of poetry who do not achieve original expression but continue to fondle and manipulate the forms of previously achieved art simply out of love for it. This is not "literature" in Croce's meaning, for it has no "extra-aesthetic object."

Croce also devotes a section to the discussion of the modern idea of "pure poetry" or the doctrine of symbolism, which we shall quote more fully since that doctrine is the basis of much

Entry from Croce's journal dated 27 May 1906.

modern criticism. "So-called 'pure poetry' is usually prefaced by a solemn formulation of doctrine, which alone concerns us here. The practical realization of that doctrine, in so far as it results in anything individual and original, is entirely outside the sphere of theory and contemplation. This theoretical formulation begins by rejecting all conceptions of poetry as sentimental effusion, or as the expression of a conceptual, oratorical or emotion-arousing content. In other words, it is a protest against the confusion of poetry with what in this book we have called mere literature."

This protest, according to Croce, is justified as far as it goes, but it lacks a foundation in a complete theory of art and in the history of critical doctrines. "That in itself would not be so bad, as the fact that these theorists persist in interpreting genuine poetry—actually, all the poetry that has been composed from Homer to Goethe or to Ibsen and Tolstoy, all the poetry which historically exists—as a mere literary vesture which may clothe an emotional, practical or conceptual content."

"So the poetry of which they speak, and which is supposed to begin with them, does not aim at being mere literature. But it is not poetry either. By poetry I mean unity of form and content, expression of complete humanity, vision of the particular in the universal, as expounded at the beginning of this book.

" 'Pure poetry' is instead the negation of poetry as expression. The idea of expression is replaced by the idea of 'suggestion.' Suggestion is produced by means of articulate sounds which mean nothing, or nothing in particular (which is the same), but stimulate the reader to understand them as he may like, and invite him to make up for himself images that please him and correspond to his way of feeling.

"Now all the things that surround us are at all moments stimulating and occasioning images and thoughts in our minds, and even impulses and actions: so they all 'suggest' things to us. Hence the perfect futility of the concept of 'suggestion,' which is supposed to define the operation of pure poetry."

This argument is a complete refutation of the much-touted concept of "suggestion" in modern poetics. Furthermore, the practical realization of this program, when it is consistent, results in a kind of vapid writing that Croce describes as "an effort of spasmodic and industrious energy, not leading to expression, this operation does not belong to poetic inspiration or to any contemplative or cognitive process, but to the practical will. Through reflection and calculation the will forges sounds and rhythms and builds up an object in which its author finds pleasure, but which does not offer to the reader anything more, as we have seen, than a blind and casual stimulation, accidental in its effects.

"In the construction of this artifact a certain diversion is to be obtained, either for oneself alone or for propagation outside oneself. The word 'diversion' has in effect been uttered by some of these theorists and encouraged the strangest practices and programs of pure poetry."

This is a shrewd if destructive analysis of much modern verse deliberately composed to fit the symbolist formula. Croce also notes the curious alliance between pure poetry and certain forms of mysticism. His description of the pure poet that participates in this alliance is enlivened by gentle irony: "The pure poet assumes a serious and solemn air as he presents himself to his audience: his person is enveloped in mystery,

his head is surrounded by a halo, his words sound as a promise, made through obscure hints or skilfully distributed silences, of wonderful changes in the world, of a new way of feeling life and of facing it. Mallarmé was considered by his faithful almost as the priest of an inaccessible divinity, and when one reads what his disciples say of Stefan George, one ends by not knowing whether they speak of a poet or of the founder of a religion. . . . Even Arthur Rimbaud is supposed to have been in his way a seer, who tried to attain a new vision of the world and a new ethic, by repudiating logic and morality, giving himself up to a wild and disorderly orgy of all the senses and realizing the perfect urchin [*voyou*] or the perfect criminal, so as to reach, through an experience of that kind, the ultimate foundations of reality."

So for Croce the literal realization of the program of pure poetry lies outside poetry, in the sphere of action—and of futile action at that. "What does not belong to it are the single lines, single stanzas, and some small compositions that in Mallarmé, in George, in Valéry and their like, can be understood and can be felt, and are admired, liked and learned by heart. These do not belong to "pure poetry" or to its theories, but to the hidden operation of the old expressive and 'impure' poetry, or rather to poetry without adjectives, which gathers up the finite into the infinite." The very last phrase belongs of course to the universalistic theory. . . . (pp. 265-71)

Since this indictment of modernism is likely to bring up countercharges of insensibility in the critic, let us see how Croce interpreted one of the lines most admired by the theorists of pure poetry. It is the line of Racine:

La fille de Minos et de Pasiphaé.

This is one of the lines of classical poetry which those critics exempt from their blanket condemnation of all poetry written before their time. It is recognized as poetry because it is thought to be absolutely meaningless and to depend for its intense beauty on its sound alone. Croce remarks: "It is certainly beautiful, but not in virtue of the physical combination of sounds. One might make infinite other combinations of such sounds without producing any effect of beauty. It is beautiful because these sounds, these syllables and accents, bring before us, in an instantaneous imaginative fusion, all that was mysterious and sinister, all that was divine and fiendish, all that was majestic and perverted, both in the person and in the parentage of Phaedra. And this is expressed by two epic names, that of the royal Cretan legislator and that of his incestuous wife, at whose side rises in our imagination the brutal figure of the bull."

In this way Croce proves he can account for what is actually beautiful in "pure poetry" without resorting to its theories of "suggestion" and sound magic. So much for "pure poetry," which Croce added to his enumeration of the nonaesthetic expressions. This multiplication of divisions and subdivisions of "literature," "art for art's sake," "pure poetry" etc., reveals a capacity for minute classification that Croce had formerly been able to keep well within bounds, if not to suppress altogether, at the cost of being called a killjoy by the admirers of traditional classifications and even . . . of being charged with "theoretical paralysis." Now admittedly not all of these classifications of Croce's are firmly established. But some of his classes of the unpoetic, such as oratory (which corresponds to what Collingwood was later to call Magical Art) are genuine additions to the critical vocabulary and of considerable use in practical criticism. It is good that critics and historians of literature should be relieved of the impossible task of evaluating as poetry many works of persuasion and edification which encumber the highways of literary history, and should have no longer to cudgel their brains for finespun and sophistical reasons therefor, relying on such pseudo concepts as "conventions," "techniques," "myths," etc., to justify their recognition of those works as poetry. It is well to have a class for great writers who are not genuine poets, such as Pindar and Juvenal, Lucretius and Rabelais, Montaigne and Voltaire, Pope and Swift. For it is no degradation to classify a work as "literature" when it has been premised that literature is a highly civilizing process, indeed a great institution. Poetry itself remains the unscheduled, unprogrammatical, spontaneous creation of genius.

Finally Croce has written in this book one of his richest and most packed critical passages, in which general theory is united with specific judgment over a wide area of world literature. It follows upon Croce's repeated warning not to be misled by the label of genres, and is here translated in part: "Suppose the label is 'a didactic poem.' What could be more poetically discredited than a didactic poem? and yet it could be the *Georgics* of Virgil, which is poetry. A comedy: how does a comedy come to differ from prose? lacking [as Horace says] a 'lively spirit and power' in words and things, is it not a mere prose discourse, a *sermo merus,* even when it is in metre? and yet that comedy may be *The Marriage of Figaro,* which is poetry, or full of poetry. A fable exemplifies a moral or prudential maxim: but the fables of La Fontaine go beyond Aesop and Phaedrus, and are little plays, each perfect in itself, or witty notations, feelings and reflections of the author. A *terzina* of the *Paradiso,* scholastic and theological in content, may rise to sublimity, and a *Spruch* by Goethe may charm us by its smiling grace. On the other hand, epics in swift and elegant stanzas, such as the *Lusiads,* are merely a political panegyric of a nation and of its history. . . . Novels that wear the mask of creative literature are found to be in reality books on history or historical popularizations, essays in the portrayal of social types, burning exhortations to action, magic lanterns for entertainment, confessions of tortured souls or exercises in artistic prose."

After publishing *La poesia* (1936), Croce continued for 16 more years to write papers on aesthetics and on general problems of literary criticism. They were collected in the two volumes of *Discourses on Various Philosophical Subjects* (1945), in the *Readings of Poetry* (1950) and in the *Investigations on Hegel* (1952). To these should be added a preceding volume provisionally entitled (Croce being then sixty-eight) *Last Essays* (1935). Then there are Croce's minor writings, collected in the three series of *Pagine sparse,* etc. Each paper discusses some critical problem and brings some new argument or new illustration to the doctrine. (pp. 271-74)

> Gian N. G. Orsini, in his Benedetto Croce: Philosopher of Art and Literary Critic, *Southern Illinois University Press, 1961, 379 p.*

MERLE E. BROWN   (essay date 1963)

[*An American educator, Brown is the author of several volumes of literary and philosophical criticism. In the following excerpt, he surveys the early development of Croce's aesthetic theory.*]

The early thoughts of Benedetto Croce on literature, art, and criticism are important not only as illustrating a development from one theory of art to another, but also as an example of the human struggle to move from one kind of thinking to another. In his earliest writings, as I shall show, Croce is assuming that art is the simple, passive knowledge of individual accomplishments; by the time of the *Breviario* of 1912 he conceives of it as an active synthesis of feelings and images in an intuition. This is not, let it be recognized at once, a change from the theory of art as knowledge to the theory of art as action, or from the theory of art as intuition to the theory of art as expression. It is rather a change from the simple idea of art as knowledge, as intuition, to the very complex concept of art as both knowledge and action, as intuition-expression. The change is not wholly successful on Croce's part, and, looked at in itself, it proves disappointing. But it must not be looked at in itself. For in making the change Croce also struggled to go beyond his original philological approach to literature and art in order to view it philosophically. This struggle, which may not prove interesting to either the pure philologist or the pure philosopher, should catch the mind and imagination of the student of ideas-in-the-making, the student not so much of thoughts and systems as of the act of thinking itself. It is true that the struggle complicates Croce's early aesthetics immensely. But to ignore it is to take the life and meaning out of his theories themselves and to see even the well-known *Estetica* in a needlessly dwarfed and lifeless form. The choice, then, is between belittling the system—how it entices one who looks at it as just that—and comprehending Croce's thinking itself.

To grasp the truth about this particular period of Croce's thought, that is, we must concentrate as much on its inconsistencies and contradictions as on its steady evolvement. At first Croce's mind worked like that of a typical literary critic and philologist: he isolated the object of his study, oblivious of its relations to other objects; and he was slow to see connections between one of his own thoughts and another. His was anything but an integrating mind. To some extent, in fact, this remains characteristic of him. His style almost always tends to isolate one passage from another and leads the reader to think only of that particular passage, possibly in relation to some experience of his own, and not to connect what is being said with what has been or is about to be said. This isolative or separative technique gives Croce's style its initial clarity and simplicity and has led some, especially those more interested in philology than philosophy, to declare that Croce's occasional and periodical writing is superior to his more systematic works. But to call Croce's thought simplifying and isolative is more accurate of his earliest than of his maturer work. He retained the transparent style, but developed coherence and integration of thought. He developed, that is, just as any philologist would have to develop if he wished to become a philosopher without ceasing to be a philologist.

Very early in his career Croce recognized in a general way the severe demands he must make upon himself. Though his friends considered theoretical questions idle chatter, he could admit, in his *La critica letteraria* (1894), that the most serious weakness in Italian studies had to do with just such questions. And he could recognize the difficulties facing him at the very time he declared his program of work to be the study of German aesthetics, especially in its early stages:

> The condition of studies in aesthetics in Italy is not happy. Our students are almost all university students, and the science of aesthetics is not likely to take them very far. It is because of this that the science has fallen into such neglect; and whoever

would wish to devote himself to these studies, is thus constrained to live in a kind of intellectual solitude, which not only deprives the spirit of any encouragement and of any legitimate satisfaction but, what is worse, complicates the difficulties by making fruitful discussion impossible. The work of one alone is timid and uncertain; and it has occurred many times to me, for example, in my first steps toward these studies, to look around me distrustfully, seeking my companions.

Such candor and self-awareness should help us to view generously Croce's early faltering, especially if we recognize this period of his thought from *La critica letteraria* of 1894 through the *Breviario* of 1912 as setting the stage for the more enduring work in aesthetics, not only of Croce himself, but also of such significant aestheticians as Giovanni Gentile and R. G. Collingwood.

Now the basic direction of Croce's thought during this period—from a narrow concentration on art as a form of passive knowing to an ampler consideration of it as both knowledge and action—can be discerned, rough and unsteady as it is, in Croce's analyses of the ideas of the material and the content of art, of artistic activity itself, and of the nature of literary criticism.

Croce's conception of artistic material turns during this period from something passive and non-human to any-and-all practical human activity. At first Croce has no theoretical interest in the material as such; he asserts the worth of source-studies, but neglects the basic relationships among the sources, the material of the poem, and the poem itself. In *La critica letteraria* we are enigmatically put off by the assumption that the material of art is "nature." In his *Tesi fondamentali di un estetica come scienza dell' espressione e linguistica generale* (1900) his more general concerns force him to be more precise, though he is still very obscure. The artist, we are told, works with impressions, and these, we can gather after some careful hunting about, are psychic facts, natural and organic, given as "a perpetual and indistinct flow," however. These impressions have no form at all until the artist looks at them, so that his very glance will be a kind of knowing, the first and only order the impressions will have. In the first edition of the *Estetica* (1902), of which the *Tesi* is an earlier version, the material is still much the same: now "sensations" replace "impressions," and Croce is no longer groping as if after some "indistinct flow"; he simply says the material cannot be grasped, although we postulate a concept of it, as a "limit." In its abstractness, as posited, it is, Croce says, mechanical and passive, an organic fact which the human spirit endures rather than produces. He will also speak of the material as "feelings and impressions" and say that they exist in some "obscure region of the psyche," but these statements seem mainly to provide a contrast for feelings and impressions which have ceased to be material and have become content and are thus artistically illuminated. Croce does, it is true, defend his obscurity concerning this "psychological fact" which he finds to be the material of art by way of criticizing the distinctness attributed to it by certain psychologists:

> If the distinction of a triple psychological fact, *representative, emotional,* and *appetitive,* has sent out such strong roots in psychology, it is because distinctions properly belonging to human activity have been projected into the unique and indistinct and indistinguishable psychic fact. The psychic fact

is not *representative* or *volitional,* theoretic or practical; but it is *feeling,* in which both these facts remain enwrapped and unexplicated, and without the intervention of any inexplicable human activity. It is useless to declaim against the *faculties of the soul* when one sinks back into this mythology, imagining distinct psychic categories. Only human activity has *distinctions,* which are not isolated *faculties,* but moments or grades, genetically connected, of a unique activity.

The material of art—that is, impressions, feelings, sensations, the psychic fact, or what not—is not elaborated upon by Croce, because elaboration, distinction, is introduced only by human activity, and the material of art is by definition that which has not yet been acted upon. Simple as the theory is, it is defensible, and though Croce drops it soon, something very much like it is given a prominent place in Collingwood's *The Principles of Art.*

By the time of the publication of the third edition of the *Estetica* (1908), Croce had activated his doctrine of feeling considerably, identifying it not with the obscure psychic fact, but with economic or utilitarian activity, which is the satisfying of individual desires. This change, which is worked out in detail in the *Filosofia della pratica* (1909), is incorporated into the third edition of the *Estetica* in the tenth chapter, the only part of the text radically revised for any edition. Croce explains that "feeling" is a word of many meanings, one of which he allows to be his old meaning, identical with "impression," the material of art. Another meaning, however, is "economic activity," which Croce then describes as a bipolar relationship between pleasure and pain. Feeling in this new sense is not natural and opposed to value and the spirit; it is a value itself and a form of activity. Though Croce has not changed his theory of the material of art (for he has not identified the new meaning of feeling with artistic material), he has gone as far as he could in that direction without rewriting the entire text. Without saying so, he is certainly suggesting the reasonableness of one's thinking of the material of art as human and active.

Precisely this new theory was first proclaimed explicitly in "**L'intuizione e il carattere lirico dell' arte,**" in 1908. Though it was presented as being already implicit in the *Estetica,* it would be difficult to imagine anything more clearly absent from the first edition, though the revision of the third makes the claim plausible. The material of art, according to the new theory, is no longer the concept of a limit, of some obscure, indistinguishable psychic fact, of feeling as the merely passive and natural; it is rather feeling as appetition, tendency, will; it is the practical form of the spirit in its infinite gradations and in its dialectic of pleasure and pain; it is the psychic fact, but distinguished and activated, the very things which Croce declared in his first edition of the *Estetica* to be erroneous, though he omitted that declaration in the third edition. Or to use words even more radically different, the material of the poet is not some unknown, shapeless force which the human spirit endures rather than produces; it is the poet's personality itself, "a soul happy or sad, enthusiastic or distrustful, sentimental or sarcastic, kind or cruel; but a soul." And although Croce here says that the personality in its strictly moral sense is excluded as material for art, in an essay written about the theater in 1905 he includes even moral theses as proper material for genuine works of art:

> All works of art which present human actions, battles over ideals, endeavors to attain certain ends,

contain, also, theses; and they can be found in the *Iliad* as in the tragedies of Aeschylus, in the poem of Dante as in the dramas of the great Englishman. Neither could they not be there, through the effect of that "personality," which is at the bottom of every true work of art and in which vibrate also moral and utilitarian strings. . . .

Although the idea of the moral personality as the material of all art is not fully incorporated into Croce's aesthetics until much later, the idea of the personality itself as that material remains from now on. In the *Breviario* (1912) the material is spoken of in much the same terms as it is throughout the *Problemi* (1910): it is emotions, aspirations, a state of mind, feeling as the practical aspect of the spirit which loves and hates, desires and rejects; it is, at its very lowest, tumultuous passion. It will, then, be no surprise if so much more violent a material than those impressions with which Croce began will require a more active form of knowing, if it is to be known at all.

The basic change during this early period in Croce's conception of the content of work of art is that it becomes less and less like the material by its being more and more worked upon. The content, to be sure, is always spoken of as being like the material: it is at first thought of as "nature," then as impressions, next as the psychic fact or feeling, and finally as practical activity. But the artist has always done something to the content, and it is this which distinguishes it from the material. What strikes one in Croce's earliest thoughts is how little the artist is said to do. In *La critica letteraria* the content is in one place called "the essential traits of nature" and in another "the interesting." The emphasis throughout is on the great distance of the content from the form and thus of necessity on its proximity to the material. Analogous to the claim that poetry reproduces the essential traits of nature is the description of criticism as the reproduction of the essential traits of the poetry at hand; everywhere, that is, the underlying assumption is that the closer the content, the worked-upon material, approximates the material itself, the better it is. We are told openly that criticism is poetry: the patent implication is that poetry, at least great poetry, is nature. When Croce speaks of the content not as nature but as "the interesting," his point is that it has value, but not aesthetic value. It is considered as none other than a part of the material, that part which is interesting. It is not *made* interesting, for then its value would be aesthetic; it is interesting as material; that is why it is chosen to be content. In the *Tesi,* written after Croce had learned from his friend Giovanni Gentile that he should be identifying form and content, Croce does begin to distinguish content from material, though only very slightly. He says, for instance: "The impressions reappear in the expression as water which is put into a filter and reappears, the same and also different, on the other side of the filter." Possibly a chemist would consider the difference more significant than I do, but all I can make out is that the content is that part of the material which is allowed to pass into the poem from outside the poem. In fact, one can find passages in the *Tesi* in which material and content are used synonymously. And in one passage it is suggested that the only difference is that the impressions which make up the content of a work are "accompanied" by human activity, whereas those which are material are not. Finally, whatever Croce says he learned from Gentile, he is still distinguishing form and content drastically, claiming that the form of all poems is the same and that the content alone distinguishes one from another.

In the 1902 edition of the *Estetica* Croce makes his first serious advance in distinguishing content from material. He finds a quality in the material which one might wish not so much to know about as to be relieved from: that is, its quality of being something men must endure rather than produce. The impressions contained in a poem are said to be purified—an echo of the filter—but also their "passivity" is said to be charred away, suggesting something more strenuous than the filtering process. In the third edition, furthermore, the impressions are said to be unified within the work, that is, put into new relationships. And in the 1908 lecture on **"L'intuizione pura e il carattere lirico dell' arte,"** the states of mind which are the new material of art become images when contained within the poem; and as content they are free of time and space, belonging then to the super-world of art, not to the ordinary world. Finally, in the *Breviario* Croce goes so far as to say that from the point of view of the artistic spirit, the feelings contained within a poem have no existence outside the poem; in the poem they are not, he says, particular feelings at all, but the whole universe observed in a certain way. Such statements are mysterious, to say the least, and one may well ask where the notion of art as a kind of knowledge has gone. For how can a feeling be said to be known if, as known, it is so very different from what it was before it was known? Croce has as an answer his assertion that from a point of view other than that of the artistic spirit, the feelings contained within a poem may be seen outside the poem in a "denatured" state as material. In the poem itself they are freed from time and space and are no longer particular, but still they bear some resemblance to their grubbier nature in the ordinary world. The distance between them, however, stretches the whole notion of art as knowledge a good bit, and it may be wondered if art as knowledge is not proving contrary to art as action. On this point Croce is far from clear.

But he can be seen struggling with the problem in his analysis of artistic activity itself. He passes during this early period from a notion of art as imitation to the principle of art as an a priori synthesis. If he were passing from a theory of art as knowledge to one of art as action, he would not be in trouble; but he is rather turning from a theory of art as knowledge to a theory of art as both action and knowledge. His agony lies there, though so does his worth, since then he is at least struggling with the full aesthetic experience, contradictory though his views may be. How innocent and happy he seems, in *La critica letteraria,* speaking of art as reproducing nature, and describing the process as "exposition" or "description" or "reproduction" or "representation."

As early as the *Tesi,* though, Croce is speaking of art as both a knowing and a making, though he apparently sees no need to explain how the two go together, and would relinquish anything in the notion of "making" which would disturb the knowing. Although, for instance, he discusses the artist's struggle to overcome the passivity of his material, and speaks of this as a battle, one is not to take his language seriously. For it has to do not with genuine art, but with artistic failure, and it is, incidentally, very impersonal and only metaphorical: "For there to be *dis-value* activity and passivity must enter into battle without one conquering the other. There must be some expression, but it is *inadequate* to the impression which it undertakes to dominate." On the very next page, moreover, the successful artist is described as the one who "has seen clearly," and no struggle or battle is implied. Though artistic failure appears to be active, artistic success is passively cognitive. Nonetheless it is true that elsewhere artistic activity is said to be productive of value, even though it is not the voluntary production of things, but only the vision or consciousness of them. The problem appears to exist without its being considered.

The same kind of vacillation goes on in the *Estetica* between the artistic process as passively contemplative and that process as vigorously active, though here Croce is more clearly aware of the demands being made upon him. The basic principle of the *Estetica* is the immediate, non-dialectical identification of intuition and expression, of direct, contemplative awareness and a making or a forming, and this principle would seem to be an answer to our basic question of how art can be both cognitive and active. The inadequacy of the answer, the fact that it is really no answer at all, is boldly stated by R. G. Collingwood in his early, anti-Crocean stage:

> The paradox of art is that it is both intuitive (pure imagination) and expressive (revelatory of truth): two characteristics which contradict one another. Croce resolves the contradiction in his own favourite way, by what I may call *pricking* it, so that the opposition vanishes and the terms collapse into an undifferentiated or immediate identity. But because the opposition thus 'collapses into immediacy', the outcome is merely immediate, that is, it is just intuition over again. Intuition and expression have not been reconciled. Expression has merely been reduced to intuition; in other words, expression in the true sense has been ignored.

Complications which cannot be considered are implicit in Collingwood's actualistic definition of intuition as pure imagination, and expression as revelatory of truth, and it could be shown that these definitions do not accurately point to Croce's use of the terms. Otherwise, Collingwood's criticism is devastatingly precise. Croce will speak of the concrete form of art as the intuition triumphing over the material, as though genuine expressiveness and making were involved. But he does so weakly, with past participles and in a subordinate phrase:

> The *material,* invested and triumphed over by the *form,* gives place to the concrete form. It is the material, it is the content which differentiates one of our intuitions from another. . . .

The spirit is said to intuit sensations only by a kind of making; but this is a making only in the sense that it is not utterly passive and lifeless like artistic material. And once Croce discards his notion of the passivity of artistic material, it would seem that whatever expressiveness his intuition originally had, depending as it did on its difference from the passive material, would disappear. But it certainly had very little expressiveness from the very start.

Here, for example, is another description of the artistic process in the *Estetica:* "Feelings or impressions pass then, through the word, from the obscure region of the psyche to the clarity of the contemplative spirit." There is no formative activity involved here; instead pellets of material are being moved from darkness into the light. Expression has evidently been reduced to intuition. It is true that elsewhere in the *Estetica* the artist is said to liberate himself from the impressions by expressing them, by burning away their passivity and dominating their tumult by means of the form; but further on Croce insists that the poet does not change or create; he simply appropriates things already made,—"at least in a certain sense," Croce adds in later editions, as Gentile so cruelly

pointed out many years ago. And though Croce may assert in the eighth edition that the aesthetic act, through the law of the unity of the spirit, is also a practical act, and as such a dialectic of pleasure and pain, this can hardly cancel the fact that he has said that art involves no selection because it is independent of the will—which is of course central to practical activity—and that for the same reason the internal poem is distinct from the external poem. With a little negligence, the Croce of this early period can be made to mean almost anything one desires, but if his general tendency is observed, his meaning is not ambiguous, or if it is ambiguous, the specific ambiguity may be precisely delimited.

The whole range of essays of the *Problemi,* written between 1899 and 1909, and including the important lecture of 1908 on the lyric character of art, offers little clarification on the question of the active and the cognitive aspects of the artistic act. We are told that art gathers in the real without alteration or falsification, which sounds even less active and formative than the intuition-expression of the *Estetica.* Elsewhere, however, the artist is described as translating practical values into theoretic, states of mind into images, and thus as actually creating, in contrast to the man who uses his fancy playfully and simply moves about the images which the imaginative or true artist previously created. Surely this activity is new, but how it is reconciled with the artistic gathering-in of the real without alteration or falsification is left most mysterious.

The *Breviario* only apparently turns these obscure statements into a reasoned explanation of how art can be both a knowing and a doing. Here Croce speaks of artistic activity as an a priori synthesis of an image and a feeling in an intuition. No pretense is made any longer that there is an active, dialectical relationship between intuition and expression; but the dialectic is said to exist within the intuition itself. We are told that our central concern is with the relation between image and feeling; and these statements have been given such prominence by Professor Gian N. G. Orsini in his recent book on Croce that they are said to provide the very basis of literary criticism itself, which is broken into three parts: one, the study of the form or image; another, the study of the content, the feeling,—or emotion as Professor Orsini translates it; and the last, the study of their adjustment to each other. But once again Croce—though not Orsini—collapses his dialectic into an immediate unity. He claims that it is a matter of merely verbal opportunity whether one speaks of the form or the content, for it is to be understood that the content is always formed, the form always filled, the feeling configured, and the image felt. This in effect means that there is an identity without a difference, that the image can only arbitrarily be distinguished from the feeling, and that in the synthesis there are not two qualities or elements allowing for a discernible relationship between themselves. The image, the feeling, and the mirroring of the feeling in the image are different ways of saying the same thing. There is no action; there is no dialectic; whether one speaks of image, feeling, or mirror, he speaks of something single, static, and pure. And Croce's enigmatic statement that the feeling in poetry is not a particular feeling or content, but the whole universe observed *sub specie intuitionis*—this statement can no longer disturb one on the grounds that it makes one element of the artistic dialectic the whole universe, a rather indefinite part of a poem. For there is only one element, and there is no dialectic. Of course, Croce intends nothing so simple for very long, and he is to pass beyond this specious answer soon enough. One may speculate that at this point he is following Gentile's advice that form and content must be identified without his understanding that the identity must involve a difference.

The messiness and inadequacy of Croce's efforts to bring the active and the contemplative aspects of art together stem, I believe, from the fact that he is remaining loyal to philological habits of mind at the very time he aspires toward philosophy. An inability to integrate his major concepts, it must be granted, is plaguing him throughout this early period. The problem, however, is that while he strives philosophically to integrate them, his inclination as a philologist is to keep them separate. He insists that art is pure, free of all practical and intellectual elements; at the same time he is endlessly connecting art in one way or another with practical and intellectual activity.

Croce's effort to keep art free of all practical activity led him from the very start along strange paths of thought. In the *Tesi* he claims that theory, which includes both artistic and intellectual activity, must precede, and therefore be free of, practical activity on the grounds that to will is to will something. The object must be known imaginatively and intellectually before it can be desired practically. Speaking of art alone he goes so far as to say:

> When we have conquered the "internal word," conceived a figure or statue purely and vitally, found a musical motif, the expression is born and is completed. Nothing else is needed. That we next open or will to open our mouth to speak or our throat to sing . . . this is a fact added on, which obeys wholly different laws from the first. . . .

In this early work Croce is categorically separating artistic activity as internal from all physical movement by the artist. The production of physical beauty is a natural fact, is a practical act, done willfully. We cannot will, or refuse to will, our aesthetic vision, but we can will or refuse to will, to exteriorize, and communicate the exteriorized product to others. To be sure, this sharp separation of art from practice is not left without any basis at all. Croce argues for instance that nothing physical is in itself beautiful:

> Michelangelo said to his student Marco del Pino da Siena "that he ought always to make a pyramidal, serpentine figure, multiplied by one, two or three": advice which did not keep Marco da Siena from being a very mediocre painter, as one can see from the many works of his which remain here in Naples. And from sayings of Michelangelo others have drawn a pretext for proclaiming the *undulating* line as the true *line of beauty*. On these laws of beauty, on the *golden section* and on the *serpentine line*, have been composed very bizarre volumes which should be considered as the *Astrology* of Aesthetics!

That such lines are not in themselves beautiful in Croce's sense of the word, no one would deny; but this is still no reason for excluding them from the aesthetic vision, or, if it is, then all psychic facts, all impressions, the interesting content itself, would be equally excluded, on the grounds that they are not in themselves beautiful.

Croce's reasons in the ***Estetica*** for asserting the purity of art from any practical taint are no solider than those in the *Tesi*. We are told that internal to art there is no technique (which is practical) because theory illuminates practice and is not illuminated by it. But why should this be? Just because theory precedes practice? But why say that? Because of the realistic presupposition that there must be some object to be desired before one can possibly desire anything? Not (one may say of a groping idealistic philosopher) very convincing. Croce adds another reason: art is independent of utility and morality, for otherwise one could not speak of an intrinsic value of art. But then, one may ask, do utility and morality, which according to Croce are not independent of art, have no intrinsic value? Or possibly it is time to say: who cares about "art" anyway? Isn't the intrinsic value of a specific poem or painting what truly concerns us? Be that as it may, Croce has no other significant reasons for his claim that art is free of all practical activity. Later he will add, among other things, that the artist's intentions are separate from his work on the grounds that such intentions are practical; that plagiarism is of no concern in art because it is a matter of morality, and art is free of any moral concerns; and that the characters in a play are not like characters in ordinary life, which is a practical affair, but are like "musical notes." But though his notion of the non-practicality of art is amplified, it is as open to question as ever.

His efforts to keep art free from thought and the intellect seem to be more reasonable, based as they are on the distinction between art as knowledge of the individual, and thought or intellectual activity as knowledge of the universal. The argument in the *Estetica* runs like this: any philosophical concept which finds its way into a work of art is dominated by the individualizing form, thus losing its philosophical nature and becoming purely artistic, whereas every work of philosophy is necessarily also a work of art, its expressive element being only extrinsically related to the thought, as is suggested by the fact that the same thought may be expressed in different ways. The argument is questionable, to be sure. After all, does a concept remain the same even though it is expressed in different ways? And if so, how does one establish the sameness except by a third expression which may assert, by way of its expressive elements, a sameness that does not exist? For that matter, doesn't a poem remain the same even if one thought in it is replaced by another? But here one is not merely requesting good reasons, but is questioning the very basis of all Croce's thought, at least in this early period: that is, his distinction between the multiplicity of intuitions and the oneness of the concept. Besides, Croce finds in this poverty of art, in its purity and freedom from all concepts and abstractions, the very strength which allows it to gather in reality without alteration or falsification. In addition, if Croce finds serious thought in a work of art like Schiller's *Mary Stuart,* he willingly calls it good history, though poor poetry. And, finally, the notion of the poet as primitive, as spontaneous and natural and without critical acuteness; the notion that the artist could not be aware of his activity as activity, in its essence and universality, because if he were, he would be a philosopher of art; and the belief that the very presence of thinking kills art: these were the commonplaces of romantic criticism, and it would have been amazing if Croce had not accepted them, at least in his first efforts at philosophy.

Going against his segregation of art in its purity, Croce begins hesitantly to integrate it with the other forms of activity which he recognizes. He does not succeed in reconciling his efforts both to segregate and to integrate. At most one can say that he moves from an emphasis upon art as pure towards efforts to integrate it with other activity, a movement parallel to his turning from the notion of art as cognitive to that of art as cognitive and active. Now in the thirteenth chapter of the ***Estetica*** (the first edition) Croce says that art is accompanied with "organic facts" and (the eighth edition) with a "utilitarian or hedonistic side and pleasure and pain, which are like the practical resonance of aesthetic value and disvalue, of the beautiful and the ugly." In the *Tesi,* however, Croce had claimed that the very characteristic of beauty is its indivisibility, its lack of parts, whereas the ugly always involves multiplicity. An ugly work may have beautiful parts, but whatever is beautiful cannot be divided into parts. From this point of view, all art, as it is described in the *Estetica,* would be ugly because it would be "accompanied" by something practical: That is, the art itself would be beautiful, but it would be only a part of a work which would of necessity be called ugly. Such a notion sounds a bit silly, even if it is bearable.

If the purity of art is caught up in its individuality, and its individuality is essentially its indivisibility, then it seems that the trouble Croce gets into as early as the *Estetica* becomes steadily worse throughout this period of his thought. It is, for example, difficult to understand how one can talk about the practical judgments and moral tendencies which are "resolved" as "spontaneous lyric motifs" in, and subordinated to, the artistic form of so many poetic works, without talking about a whole made up of parts. If the practical elements of a poem are discernible, in what sense can they be said to be not just unified in the poem, but transformed into something other than parts? In the *Breviario* of 1912, moreover, he no longer found it possible to speak of art as pure, as excluding practical and intellectual activities. At the very most one can say that it includes, integrates, and dominates them, as they in their turn, include, integrate, and dominate each other and, in their own ways, also artistic activity. For in this work Croce says that no one form of activity is real, and that only the synthesis of syntheses, the *actus purus,* is real. And this means that a particular artistic act would be real only in so far as it included within itself practical and intellectual activity, only in so far as it was not pure, but impure. Croce here seems to be proclaiming that the full aesthetic experience can be considered only as one looks, not only to its purely artistic aspects, but also to its practical, moral, and philosophical elements.

Croce has, then, quite clearly arrived at the full question which should concern us: that is, how it is that the knowing and the acting of art can be said to go together? Art is not being called knowledge alone or action alone; it is not being described as knowledge on one page and action on the next with no awareness that the two aspects of art do not go easily together. And the assertion of the integration of the various forms of activity in art does not seem to be a momentary indiscretion, for several pages later Croce speaks of the poet's passion for art as a practical passion, and of his devotion to art as his moral obligation! But if one hopes for a precise or concretely illustrated statement as to how artistic, practical, and intellectual activity go together, the *Breviario* must disappoint him. It should be recalled that in the *Breviario* the material of art is said to be practical activity, states of mind, feelings, but that its relationship to the content of art, which is described vaguely as the whole universe seen in a certain way, cannot even be described vaguely. Furthermore, we have found that the artistic dialectic of the *Breviario* is as specious as that of the *Estetica,* for the feeling, image, and intuition are an identity without a difference. Now in general Croce says no more than this about the way in which thought, practice, and morality are integrated into art: they "are in art as art, either antecedent or consequent; and there-fore are there as presupposed (sunk and forgotten there, to adopt a favorite expression of De Sanctis), or as presentiments." And at this point Croce claims that it is impossible to speak of the integration of these forms of activity in a more specific or experiential way. When one speaks of an individual poem, he says, one must speak of its poetry only, even though to do so is to exaggerate, or even falsify, the distinction between poetry and philosophy and the other forms of activity. To be sure, one may speak of the philosophy of the poem, but not in relation to its poetry. Such relations are more reality than humankind can bear, it would appear. All in all, then, Croce has moved during this early period from a conception of the artistic experience as pure and simple intuition towards a conception of it as a full integration of that intuition with action, knowledge, and morality. But he either speaks of this integration in vague and general terms or says that it is impossible to speak of it as experience. In effect, therefore, even in the *Breviario,* Croce is primarily explaining the question which needs an answer rather than presenting an answer to it.

The value of our analysis might at this point be called in question on the grounds that so inconsistent, vacillating, and obscure a thinker as Croce can be of little philosophical worth, and also on the grounds that Croce's thinking about art is "essentialistic," whereas contemporary aesthetics has left all that behind and now is devoted solely to analyzing the language of literary and art criticism. One fact provides a reply to both criticisms: Croce was his own literary critic. As a result his aesthetics is always interpretive of criticism, and the change and uncertainty in his aesthetics at least parallels changes and difficulties in the practice of criticism itself. Muddled Croce may be, but what he says is always relevant to the experience of art and of practical criticism. This immense advantage which he has over most non-Italian aestheticians derives in part from the greatness of the literary criticism of Francesco De Sanctis. After De Sanctis, literary criticism was recognized in Italy as so important a form of thought that it was almost inconceivable for an Italian philosopher of art not to take an active part either in it or in the criticism of another art. Probably this situation itself explains better than anything else why twentieth-century Italian aesthetics has been so much more vital and significant than any other aesthetics of the period.

Croce's own theory of literary criticism, it is true, was less complicated and had developed less during this early period than did his thoughts on aesthetic activity itself. He was more concerned with the object of his literary criticism, with the nature of what it was that he was criticizing, than with his criticism itself. Just as he was not, at first, very integrative in his thinking, so he was not very self-reflective. In a loose way, however, his notions about literary criticism did develop in a direction parallel to the development of his theory of artistic activity. At first Croce sees the literary critic as facing an art object which is a given, a datum, and as doing various unrelated or at least unintegrated things with the object. What he does, furthermore, is much like artistry itself, just as Croce's early notion of the content of art made it resemble the material of art very closely. By the end of this early period in Croce's thought, however, it is not at all clear that the literary critic is working with data; furthermore, the various aspects of his work are closely integrated; and, finally, his work has become less and less like the artistic object of his study and more and more philosophical.

Just as Croce first conceived of art not as active, but as the passive contemplation of some fact passively given, so he finds his critic passively contemplating not an active process, but a product. Through much of this early period Croce never fully rejects the notion that the critic must work with an artifact, a finished product which somehow or other is above the vicissitudes of time. In *La critica letteraria* the poem is a fixed object passively received and contemplated, and it is the only thing which unifies the various activities called literary criticism. The realistic presupposition is evident here: the thing desired precedes the desire; just so, the poem to be criticized is completed before the criticism begins. In the *Tesi* Croce's sense of the mysterious and sacred nature of the art object goes so far that he calls art not just alogical, but impenetrable by the intellect. The art object as Croce is here thinking of it is, to be sure, not merely the physical work, obscured by time as it is likely to be; it is that physical object as seen by the artist in the moment of production. This is what the critic must contemplate, and Croce has faith that with the help of erudition this object can be approached. Although it is not merely the physical object which is being spoken of, as late as 1908 Croce is describing it as something merely finite. He asserts this, for example, in reference to Tansillo's sonnet, "Poiche spiegato ho l'ali al bel desio," which Tansillo thought of as expressing his amorous aspirations, but which Bruno interpreted as expressive of philosophic aspiration. Croce resolves the problem of whether the new interpretation by Bruno means that the original poem has taken on new meaning or that a second poem has been created:

> One is accustomed to saying that the work of art brings with itself inexhaustible, infinite interpretations. But in effect, the single work of art is always something finite: that which is inexhaustible and infinite is the human spirit, which comes to rest in no work of art and creates always new images.

The poem, that is, is finished in form and in meaning, though endless interpretations may be brought to it. There was a time, moreover, when Croce found the art object to be not only finite, but enough like a physical object for him to say that if it were not for the practical activity of "exteriorization," the object would perish. In later editions of the *Estetica,* however, Croce replaces that gloomy idea by saying that nothing which is born dies. And in the 1908 Heidelberg lecture on art as lyrical, Croce finds the poem to be an eternal object, free of time and space, ready for recreation in its "ideality-reality" from any point of time or space. Such idolatry of the finite object is fortunately gone from the *Breviario.* The poem endures, but as the individual universalized, surviving like any action in the past, as a part of history rather than above it.

Croce's description of what the critic does with the art object goes through three distinct phases during the early period of his thought. In *La critica letteraria* the critic is said to approach the art object from several different directions, none of which is preferable to the others, and with no connection among them except the object, which all of them are humbly approaching. Aesthetics, which determines the general categories of beauty, is excluded from criticism, which considers not general categories, but the work of art in its individuality. In fact, at this stage all criticism is as free of philosophy as is the work of art itself. But this similarity between criticism and art is more than an analogy, for the stage of criticism which follows upon the passive contemplation of the sacred object is no other than another work of art! The critic describes what he has read; he reveals the special situation, the motif, the individual note which the poet had discovered and developed. Contrary to the belief of the greatest of all expository critics, De Sanctis, Croce claims that evaluation or judgment is quite distinct from this expository, critical poem. Evaluation, we are told, is one's subjective reaction, which is the value we accord to the work, and which has nothing to do with our knowledge of the work. The third stage, as separate from the first two as they are from each other, is historical; one considers the causes and the effects of the work. None of these stages of criticism, it appears, involves our classifying a poem and putting it in its proper genre. That sort of thing is as separate from criticism as is aesthetics.

The second phase in the development of Croce's theory of literary criticism involves the re-ordering and the integration of the three stages of criticism described as separate and of equal value in *La critica letteraria.* What had been the third stage becomes the first and is now called erudition: it includes all the historical labors which serve works of art, but for extraneous purposes (biography, civil, religious, and political history; and other such things), and all historical erudition directed to the preparation of the aesthetic re-creation itself. The second stage, the reproduction and enjoyment of the work of art, depends upon the first stage but goes beyond it; and its climax is an exclamation of approval or disapproval. The third stage, which is looked upon in the *Estetica* as the only true form of literary criticism or history, depends upon the second stage and the first stage, but goes beyond them both. It is the expository stage and, as in *La critica letteraria,* it is another work of art created upon the first work of art. But the true critic is not just an artist; he is a historical artist. That is, he has received from aesthetics the criteria by means of which he goes beyond the reproduction of the poem and determines what parts of it are poetic, and what parts are ugly, and just what kind of activity the ugly parts are. Now in both the *Tesi* and the *Estetica* the poem remains logically ineffable; it cannot be defined, it cannot be classified, it can only be intuited. The critic's concern remains with the individual and the finite, and his own work is individual and finite, even though he makes use of some universal definitions of a logical nature. His goal now is single; it is to get back to the original "feeling" of the artist, to the "macchia," the lyric wave, the individual accent from which the poem took its shape.

In his third phase, as it is represented in a 1909 essay of the *Problemi* and in the *Breviario,* Croce has gone beyond his integration of erudition, taste, and exposition, and has integrated them all with logic and aesthetics. He has moved to an integration of criticism and philosophy much as he moved from a concept of art as free of practice and intellect to the notion of it as fully integrated into the *actus purus.* Criticism is no longer the artistic re-creation of the original poem; it is as different from "pure poetry" as it could be, as different as philosophy is from poetry. It is in fact described as an individual judgment, as the synthesis of intuition and concept, as the proposition, for instance, that a particular poem is aesthetic, or is aesthetic in some parts and practical in other parts. The new theory of literary criticism is much richer and more complex than either of the earlier two, and it parallels the enrichment of Croce's ideas about artistic material and content, the artistic act itself, and the relationship between art and other forms of activity. It involves difficulties, moreover, just as severe as did those ideas.

For example, are we to infer that the poem which becomes a part of the critical judgment is identical with the poem before it is judged? If not, then can it be said that we actually have knowledge of the original poem when we carry out our judgment? This problem, it should be noted, parallels the question of how a poem can be called the intuitive knowledge of a feeling when the feeling within the poem is drastically different from the feeling as a part of practical activity. One solution would be to say that the poem from its inception involves judgment. But the Croce even of the *Breviario* could not accept this. He is still arguing for the purity of poetry, and even when admitting that poetry may include intellectual elements, he insists that the relationship between the included ideas and the poem itself cannot be discussed.

A more treacherous solution runs like this: a poem is only its poetic aspects; its practical, moral, and intellectual implications are burned away in the very re-creation performed by the man of taste, so that when the poem comes to be judged, lo, it has been reduced to its essence; it has already been judged: that is, the existent poem is no concern of ours. We exaggerate, we falsify, man cannot avoid falsification, Croce says in the *Breviario.* When we come to predicate the concept of aesthetic activity upon the existent poem, when we come to say that *a* is *A,* what we find ourselves saying instead is that *A* is *A,* and we are making not what Croce calls an individual judgment, but what he calls a definitory judgment. Our dilemma seems to be that: either criticism is a definitory judgment, no dialectic at all, a logical tautology, the monotonic "Poetry is Poetry," or else it is a judgment which fails to give knowledge. Croce sought to move from a theory of criticism as immediate, intuitive knowledge into a theory of criticism as a mediate, dialectical knowing which includes the immediate intuition within it. What he appears to have attained, depending upon one's view, is either an active criticism which gives no knowledge at all, or a cognitive criticism in which not an individual is known as an individual, but a universal is known to be itself.

Studying Croce's early aesthetics as his struggle to move from philology to philosophy, not just as a change from one theory to another, we have, I think, come to an understanding of the meaning of his errors and confusion. His thought during this early period points beyond itself to an as yet unrealized theory of art as both action and knowledge, and to a theory of literary criticism as a different form of action and knowledge. Croce started out with the unanalyzed assumption that art and criticism were both passive forms of immediate knowledge. By the end of the period which we have studied, he attained a very clear recognition of what it was that he lacked. Though his efforts to provide answers were quite inadequate, his questions were the right ones. They are the foundation itself of all that most impressive aesthetics developed by neo-idealists, the mature aesthetics of Croce himself, the actualistic aesthetics of Giovanni Gentile and his disciples, and the aesthetics of their most original non-Italian follower, R. G. Collingwood. (pp. 29-40)

> Merle E. Brown, "*Croce's Early Aesthetics: 1894-1912,*" in The Journal of Aesthetics and Art Criticism, *Vol. XXII, No. 1, Fall, 1963, pp. 29-41.*

GIOVANNI GULLACE (essay date 1981)

[*In the following excerpt, Gullace traces the influence on Croce of his relationship with Giovanni Gentile and examines selected aspects of Croce's philosophy, including his interpretation of Marxism and his theory of language.*]

Croce's relation with Giovanni Gentile began in 1896, when the latter was only twenty-one and still a student at the University of Pisa. At that time Croce, under the inspiration of [Antonio] Labriola, was already engaged in his Marxist studies. The dialogue between the two men started with a friendly exchange of notes. Although still at the beginning of his intellectual career, Gentile (who was nine years Croce's junior) showed such an unusual philosophical perspicacity that he easily won Croce's friendship. Thus their first epistolary contacts soon developed into a true intellectual partnership which was to last about thirty years and to have a strong impact on Italian culture.

Their close association often raised the question of which of the two philosophers led the way in their common speculative efforts. Had Gentile more influence on Croce than Croce on Gentile? Claims and counterclaims have been made by students from both sides, especially after the bitter rift between the two men following the advent of Fascism. But, whatever the answer, no real purpose can be served by trying to determine what was given or taken by each man. The fact is that the contact with Gentile gave Croce a new and more philosophical outlook concerning intellectual problems. Gentile's deep philosophical interests contributed greatly to drawing Croce from literary and historical problems to more strictly philosophical ones and, most particularly, to the study of Hegel, whose thought helped him discover his own vocation. Croce, in fact, quickly realized that he was now "in far better intellectual company" than he had been during his early Neapolitan days and that he had a new impulse to work on an idea he had entertained since his school years—that of writing an esthetics. Gentile's influence on Croce, while it often facilitated and enriched the latter's philosophical development, in no way altered the originality of his thought or changed its general direction. Despite the reciprocal mental stimulation, the two men stand as two distinct philosophical personalities, each so deeply rooted in his own individuality that no influence could change or modify his intellectual mold. "In our association" wrote Croce, "he neither yielded to me, nor I to him, the one thing that cannot be given up—one's temperament and mind." (p. xvii)

From 1895 to about 1899, Croce devoted most of his attention to Marxism and historical materialism. His concern with these problems immediately attracted the young Gentile, from the very beginning of their friendship, to the debate aroused by Labriola's works. In 1896 Croce wrote his first two essays on the subject, **"Sulla concezione materialistica della storia" ("On the Materialistic Conception of History")** and **"Le teorie storiche del professor Loria" ("The Historical Theories of Professor Loria")**, which he sent to Gentile for comments. Gentile's perspicacious remarks did not fail to impress Croce, who wrote "[Your letter] aroused in me a sincere admiration; it showed me that you are fully possessed of the problem concerning historical materialism, that you have digested and absorbed Labriola's books, and that you formulate objections with a limpidity and exactness of expression really remarkable." Gentile, in fact, had lost no time in studying the problem, and by the summer of 1897 had completed a solid essay, "Una critica del materialismo storico" ("A Criticism of Historical Materialism"), which was published the following fall.

Their interest in Marxism and historical materialism, however, was short-lived, and ended for both at about the same time. that is, in 1899, when their studies and discussions were collected and published, respectively, in Gentile's *La filosofia di Marx* and Croce's **Historical Materialism and the Economics of Karl Marx.** Gentile's interest in Marxism at that time did not develop into a political faith; it remained as a purely speculative effort, its primary aim being simply to penetrate the system critically. In fact, he studied the metaphysical origins and implications of the Marxist doctrine with no particular interest in the socialist theory derived from it. Croce, on the contrary, more attentive to the socialist movement, studied with particular care the economic doctrine of Marxism, in an attempt to understand better history and the part economics plays in it (in his **Aesthetic** economics appears as one of the four categories of the Spirit). His work, like Gentile's, was colored by his preoccupation with the nature of history rather than with the practical problems of party politics. He saw Marxism from the point of view of its philosophical or scientific value, rather than its practical application. "To me," he wrote, "it was important above all for what it could contribute to a live and full conception of philosophy and to a better understanding of history." But he added, "Historical materialism appeared to me doubly fallacious both as materialism and as a conception of the course of history according to a pre-established design, that is, as a variation of the Hegelian philosophy of history." These ideas, expressed in his first piece on the subject, aroused a polemics between Croce and his former teacher Labriola, whose interests were mainly to adapt Marx's theories to the aims and needs of political action.

As a result, the political faith and passion with which Croce engaged in the study of Marxism could not last. It was undermined, he wrote, "by my own criticism of Marxism—a criticism the more damaging that it was meant for a defense and a restatement; . . . the passion burnt itself out because *natura tamen usque recurrit,* and mine was at bottom the nature of a student and thinker." In a letter to Gentile (November 23, 1898), he had already written: "As for historical materialism, I must inform you that I no longer intend to concern myself with it. . . . From Marxism I have drawn what I needed. If I were oriented toward a political life, I would interest myself in the proletarian movement; but this would be perhaps premature in Italy." The Marxist experience, however, was of great importance for him, since it gave him a more definite outlook on philosophical problems: "The excitement of those years bore good fruit in the form of a widened experience of human problems and a quickening of philosophical activity. From that time on, philosophy played an increasing part in my studies." His gradual estrangement from Labriola and his correspondence with Gentile contributed to redirecting his studies. Gentile's strong philosophical orientation made Croce increasingly aware of some of his own philosophical deficiencies. In a letter of November 1898 he wrote to Gentile:

> I told you that I was studying philosophy. Here is what it is all about. Up to now I concerned myself with philosophical questions only to satisfy an irresistible intellectual need, but somehow occasionally; *sicut canes ad Nili fontes bibentes et fugientes.* Now I would like to drink with ease. Therefore, I have worked till now so that I may have the necessary leisure for it. I will be able for one or more years to devote myself to philosophy only. I confess that I would like, among other things, to bring to completion a treatise on esthetics, and consequent-

ly I must delve more deeply into all philosophical questions which are related to esthetics, that is, into the whole of philosophy. I am doing this now, and perhaps in a few months we may talk about the results.

His study of historical materialism and Marxist economics not only allowed him to gain a better insight into the nature of history, but it also helped him define the economic moment, so important in the development of his budding **Philosophy of the Spirit.**

Croce's criticism of Marxism bears upon both its conception of history and its economic theories. Marx, in Croce's view, was neither an economist nor a philosopher, but was instead a vigorous revolutionary genius. His socialism did not spring from a philosophical or scientific concept, for he lacked an a priori theory to guide his action. His scientific theses concerning economics and history are completely invalid; they were an a posteriori attempt to justify his revolutionary movement. Historical materialism, conceived as a philosophy of history, that is, as a set of laws governing human events, was for Croce quite absurd, for in history there are no predetermined laws; but simply intuitions and facts whose connections can only be established a posteriori. He had already theorized in . . . **La storia ridotta sotto il concetto generale dell' arte** that history is related to art, not to science, for it represents the particular, individual fact, rather than general laws. From the philosophical point of view, historical materialism, as a law of history allowing us to predict the future course of events, would aggravate the errors of the old theological or metaphysical conceptions of history.

Croce shows that, according to Engels, dialectic is the rhythm of the development of things, that is, the inner law by which they evolve, and that this rhythm cannot be determined a priori by a metaphysical deduction; it can only be grasped a posteriori through repeated observations and verifications in the various fields of reality. As a result, it is impossible to give historical materialism a scientific character, for it lacks the capacity to foresee the course of history. Therefore, it can lend no theoretical or scientific support to socialism. The only positive aspect of the so-called historical materialism was a practical one which concerned the field of historiography. It called the attention of historians, exclusively interested in ideological and philological interpretations, to the importance of economic factors in human affairs. While Labriola considered historical materialism to be a definitive philosophy of history, Croce saw it as a practical canon for the historiographer. To accept historical materialism as a philosophy of history would have meant for him to reduce history to the economic factors and to say with Marx that "it is not the consciousness of men that determines their being, but, on the contrary, it is their social being that determines their consciousness."

As for Marxist economics, Croce denies it a scientific character, holding it to be a simple device (such as the theory equating the value of things to the amount of work required to produce them) to dramatize the conditions of the working class in a society dominated by private capital. Marx's theory was not the foundation of a new science of economics, for its concept of value was logically erroneous and even absurd. It was the result of a comparison between an abstract working class, taken as typical, and a capitalistic society. Furthermore, the fall of the rate of profits (as posited in the third volume of *Das Kapital*)—the great historical law which implied the automatic and imminent end of capitalism—rested, according to Croce, on a gross error by Marx concerning technical and economic phenomena, for it was neither a historical nor an abstract economic law. The value of Marxism was purely pragmatic, not scientific; from the scientific point of view it offered only a pseudoeconomics, a pseudophilosophy, and a pseudohistory.

With the publication of the book on Marxism, the interest of Croce and Gentile in the subject came to an end. Croce said that he had put together all of his articles on Marx as though "in a coffin." His attention had already shifted to the problem of esthetics, which was now his first priority. On January 15, 1899, in a letter to Gentile, he wrote: "My mind is now very far removed from our discussion on Marxism." Their correspondence since the end of 1898 revolved in fact around the esthetic problem, which had been in Croce's thought since as far back as 1893, when he wrote his *La storia ridotta sotto il concetto generale dell' arte.* It is difficult, at this point, to determine which of the two fields of studies—Marxism and esthetics—had more sway on the further development of his thought. Was the *Philosophy of the Spirit* motivated by his aversion to historical materialism or by his interest in esthetics?

By all indications Croce's concern with the problem of art and history was not momentary or accidental; it continued to grow with his philosophy, thereby acquiring an increasing importance. It is thus impossible to separate in his thought the problem of art from that of history. With the triumph of positivism and naturalism and the consequent discredit of the theological and metaphysical conceptions of history, as well as the elimination of all absolutes from the empirical domain of facts, the old debate about the nature of history had been revived and had assumed a lasting interest in Croce's mind. What is history? Is it an art or a science? In his *La storia ridotta sotto il concetto generale dell' arte,* as Croce explained in a note added to the second edition of his *Logic* (1909), the main drive of his first "philosophical study" (1893) was, primarily, "to combat the attempt of the natural sciences to resolve history into their scheme"; then, "to assert the theoretical character and seriousness of art, which positivism, dominant at that time, considered as an object of pleasure"; finally, "to deny that historicity was a third form of the theoretical spirit, different from the esthetic form and the intellective form." In short, Croce's aim was to subtract history from the domain of science into which positivism had drawn it, to affirm the theoretical character of art which positivism held to be simply a means for pleasure, and to fight the idea of a third level of mental activity (the historical level) different from the two recognized levels—the esthetic, productive of art, and the intellective, productive of science. Croce stresses that art is a form of knowledge, but that the knowledge obtained through art differs from the knowledge obtained through science. While art represents objects in their concreteness and individuality, science reduces objects to their concepts. The former represents human experiences, the latter conceptualizes them; art is concerned with individual realities; science with abstract universals. Since history is not the elaboration of concepts or categories, but the representation of the real in its particularity, it is akin to art and not to science. Both art and history deal with the passions and destinies of men, with what appears and disappears in space and time, and not with the universal concept of man. In the world of art and history there are no general laws, but individual realities. The difference between art and history is that art produces a *possi-*

ble reality, while history produces a *factual* reality; the former represents what is imagined as possible, the latter what really happened. This implies the rejection of historical laws as well as the rejection of theological and metaphysical principles governing history. Like art, history aims at the individual; both are *conoscenza* and not *scienza.* (pp. xviii-xxi)

In 1900 Croce's *Tesi fondamentali d'una estetica come scienza dell'expressione e linguistica generale* was finally published, after much travail due to his as yet inadequate philosophical knowledge. The work contained the essential points of his theory, which was subsequently developed and reorganized in a more suitable logical sequence, thus constituting, with the addition of part two (History of Esthetic), the volume *Aesthetic as Science of Expression and General Linguistic,* published in 1902. In 1902 Gentile hailed *Tesi fondamentali* as the work which in a period of triumphant positivism presented the right solution to the problem of art by asserting its subjectivity; the same year he also called attention to the importance of Croce's article, **"Giambattista Vico scopritore della scienza estetica" ("Giambattista Vico, Discoverer of Esthetic Science"),** pointing out that Vico's novelty lay in the fact that he not only discovered the autonomy of imagination, but that he also introduced the concept of mind as development, without which the concept of a new esthetics would have been impossible. Following Croce's activity closely, Gentile could not refrain a year later, however, from criticizing the antimetaphysical character of the first edition of the *Aesthetic,* feeling that Croce's repudiation of meta-

Croce in later years.

physics would leave his theory with no roots in the life of the Spirit:

> Croce, coherent with his antimetaphysical attitude in general, excludes metaphysics from every corner of his esthetics and calls mystic every metaphysical esthetician, regardless of the school. And this is all right. But, then, what is the meaning of the spirit as the only reality which is the object of science?—that spirit whose expression is form, the first form? If it is a reality, what can it be if not a metaphysical reality? Consequently, what can the expression be if not a metaphysical form? Furthermore, if the spirit is the only activity, and the esthetic and logical activities are moments or degrees of this activity, how can we say that between the esthetic and the logical fact, between intuition and concept, there is the abyss by which Croce meant to separate them? Don't we have to consider them as fundamentally the very same reality which is the spirit, though in two different forms? And if this is true, since from intuition the spirit rises to the concept, which is a higher degree of knowledge, how can we imagine that in the form called intuition there is no trace of what we call concept? Let us admit that, in the particular as such, intuition is unable to perceive any trace of the universal; but is it possible that the mind of the philosopher is also unable to perceive it?

Croce's doctrine was meant to be an idealistic one in reaction to the dominant positivistic tendencies of the time; but he was not fully aware that this implied the resolving of all reality into subjective activity and the suppression of all traces of objectivism. Despite the gigantic effort he had made to overcome naturalism and Herbartianism and to establish a true "Philosophy of the Spirit" in a strict idealistic sense, without dualisms, Croce came to recognize that both the *Tesi fondamentali* and the first edition of the *Aesthetic* "retain traces of a certain naturalism, or Kantism, which here and there conjures up once more the ghost of nature, and states distinctions . . . somewhat abstractly."

Croce's work certainly does not arrive at a total and all-encompassing formulation of his theory of art. His main concern being at that time to clear the field of weeds, he seems to insist on demonstrating more what art *is not* than what art *is*. He is thus led to a vast refutation of all the "false esthetics" of the past, especially "naturalistic esthetics," which considers beauty as a quality of physical objects existing outside the sphere of the Spirit, and "intellectualistic esthetics," which presents art as the intellective activity of the mind and confuses poetry with literary prose. The historical part of the work is, in fact, polemical and iconoclastic in character. Against naturalistic tendencies Croce affirms the "spiritualistic" nature of art, and against intellectualistic tendencies its "alogical" character.

The *Aesthetic,* into which Croce imagined that he had emptied all of his philosophy, had instead, he wrote, "filled my head with fresh philosophy, with doubts and problems concerning especially the other forms of the spirit, the theories of which I had outlined in their relation to aesthetic, and the general conception of reality." The work in fact turned out to be the formulation of a problem rather than its solution. The solution was now to be achieved through other works which would offer a complete picture of the philosophical issues involved in the esthetic problem. In writing the *Aesthetic,* Croce had become aware of the close relations between the

basic forms or activities of the Spirit, and from the field of esthetics he had now to move to that of logic, and from there to that of economics and ethics. He felt that esthetics, being a part of philosophy, had to be treated within the framework of a philosophical system which would give a full account of man's theoretical and practical processes.

In 1905 he published the first sketch of his *Logic as the Science of Pure Concept* (completely rewritten for the second edition, 1909), in 1907 the *Philosophy of the Practical: Economics and Ethics,* and in 1912-1913 the *Theory and History of Historiography,* which complete the *Philosophy of the Spirit.* These developments deepened and clarified further his esthetic theory, which found a strong support in the other forms of spiritual activity. In constructing his philosophical doctrine, Croce had realized that he had to delve more deeply into idealistic philosophy in order to be able to proceed in his work. "When I had published the *Aesthetic* and sketched a logic," he wrote, "I felt that the time had come for a closer acquaintance with the Hegel whose doctrines I had hitherto sampled rather than studied in their entirety." In a brief article of 1904, **"Siamo noi hegeliani?" ("Are We Hegelians?"),** he conceded that "philosophy cannot come back to life and progress unless it somehow links itself to Hegel," and added that "after him the world was once more divided into appearance and hidden reality, matter and God, crude facts and transcendental value. Philosophy (not metaphysics in a questionable sense) was dispossessed."

The fragmentary knowledge Croce had of Hegel at that time came from his study of De Sanctis and from his research on Marxism and historical materialism. Although he perceived vaguely the hidden richness of Hegelian philosophy, he continued to regard Hegel with a suspicious and critical eye. This is shown by his essays on historical materialism—*Historical Materialism and the Economics of Karl Marx*—in which, as he wrote in *An Autobiography,* "I set myself to purge that doctrine of every trace of abstract a priori thought, whether in the form of 'philosophy of history' or in that of the later 'evolutionism,' and to defend the value of the Kantian ethics and reject the mystery of a substructure of Economy—the Idea in disguise—operating beneath the level of consciousness, and a superstructure or consciousness described as a superficial phenomenon."

The passage from anti-Hegelianism to Hegelianism (accepted critically and only partially) was made under the influence of Gentile, who followed Croce's intense activity with discussions of the various difficulties arising from Croce's thought. That Gentile acted as his mentor is evident from the following passage of *An Autobiography:* "I came into a more direct touch with Hegel through the friendship and collaboration of Gentile, in whom the tradition of Spaventa came to life again more flexible, more modern, more open to criticism and self-criticism, richer in spiritual interest; and in this way, in spite of occasional differences between the paths which we respectively followed, Gentile and I came to influence each other and to correct each other's faults." The results of Croce's Hegelian studies, undertaken around 1905, are contained in his book *What Is Living and What Is Dead in Hegel's Philosophy* (1906), which gives a critical assessment of Hegel's doctrine and serves to clarify Croce's own position in relation to Hegelian idealism. Croce's criticism of Hegel focuses mainly on the dialectic of opposites constituting the essential part of the system. Monistic systems conceived of only one of the terms of the opposition as being real, declaring its opposite to be illusory; dualistic systems, on the contrary, considered both terms to be real and their unity to be illusory. The first sacrificed the opposition to the unity, the second the unity to the opposition. Hegel recognized that neither the opposites nor the unity is illusory. The concrete unity is but a unity of opposites; it is, therefore, not immobility but movement, a dialectical process accomplished through the fundamental triad: thesis, antithesis, synthesis. Without the negative term, there would be no development. Reality is, in fact, development, history.

But, according to Croce, the first error committed by Hegel was in confusing the dialectic of opposites with the dialectic of "distincts." Two distinct concepts are conjoined while preserving their distinction; two opposite concepts exclude each other. A distinct concept is presupposed and comprised by the subsequent concept. For Croce unity can be meaningful only if there is something *there* to be unified, that is, distinct and autonomous concepts. And since Hegelian opposites are merely abstract outside the synthesis, any unity of opposites is but a specious one. Apart from Becoming, for example, Being and Nonbeing are not two concepts but two abstractions, Croce argues, and consequently Becoming cannot possibly represent a genuine synthesis; it can neither "suppress" nor "conserve" what does not exist to begin with. Examples of distinct concepts are imagination, intellect, economics, ethics; examples of opposites are good and evil, true and false, and so on. What makes possible the unity of philosophical concepts is, precisely, their distinct and autonomous existence. In the unity of the Spirit we distinguish the sphere of theoretical activity from the sphere of practical activity. Every distinct form preserves, in its relation to other distinct forms, its own autonomy. The artistic and the logical, the economic and the ethical forms are the stages through which the Spirit develops its unity. Unlike the opposites, which outside their synthesis are mere abstractions, each distinct form is concrete and real. The distinct forms are the Spirit in its particularizations, not the universal concept in its intrinsic constitution as a synthesis of opposites. Hegel's error was, therefore, to conceive the nexus of the "distincts" in the same manner in which he conceived the dialectic of opposites. His failure to understand the autonomy and concreteness of the distinct forms of spiritual activity prevented him from understanding the autonomy of history. Furthermore, Hegel conceived of a philosophy of history as a "reflective contemplation of history," thus falling into a dualism between concept and fact, rationality outside reality, and reality outside rationality. The same position is found in his treatment of the philosophy of nature, which becomes an abstract and hollow science outside the reality of the Spirit.

It is evident that Croce, while trying to bring everything within the Spirit, including nature, insists on the reality of the distinct forms of spiritual activity. His philosophy rejects the Hegelian triad of Logos, Nature, and Spirit, and asserts "the sole reality of Spirit itself." He moved in the direction of Gentile, but he never renounced the concept of the reality of the "distincts." In fact, his progress from the *Aesthetic* to the *Logic* to *The Philosophy of the Practical* and to the *Theory and History of Historiography* (also published in English as *History, Its Theory and Practice*) was characterized by "the gradual elimination of naturalism, the growing emphasis laid upon spiritual unity, and the deepening of the meaning attached to the conception of intuition in aesthetics, now elaborated into that of lyricism." A significant testimony to his striving for spiritual unity is his rewriting of his *Logic,* which

he describes as an "affirmation of the concrete universal" and, at the same time, "of the concrete individual," the harmonization of the Aristotelian *scientia est de universalibus* with the Campanellian *scientia est de singularibus.* In a long note he indicates that, when he wrote his monograph *La storia ridotta sotto il concetto generale dell' arte* in 1893, he maintained that "history is to be subsumed under the general concept of art," as the title suggests; after sixteen years, he adds, "I maintain, on the contrary, that history is philosophy, or rather that history and philosophy are the very same thing." In explaining his effort to overcome the difficulties encountered before reaching this conclusion, he states: "I was greatly helped not only by my own studies in the 'philosophy of the practical' and the identity I found between intention and action, but also, and above all, by the studies of my dear friend, Giovanni Gentile (to whom my intellectual life owes a lot more in the way of help and stimulation), on the relation between philosophy and the history of philosophy, which I have extended to the relation of philosophy to history in general."

From the emphasis on the character of concreteness of history and the abstractness of science, Croce moved gradually to the demonstration of the concrete nature of philosophy, and, he said, "the two concretenesses [that of philosophy and that of history] proved finally to be one." Croce's conception of the unity of the Spirit is clearly expressed in his *Autobiography* in reference to *The Philosophy of the Practical;* such a unity is not a unity of opposites, but a process of "distincts":

> As I worked at my *Philosophy of the Practical* and inquired into the relation between intention and action, my denial of any such dualism and of the conceivability of an intention without action led me to think once more of the dualism which I had left standing in the first *Logic* between the concept and the singular judgment, that is, between philosophy as antecedent and history as consequent; and I realized that a concept which was not at the same time a judgment of the particular was as unreal as an intention that was not at the same time an action. Then I remembered the long discussions between Gentile and myself, a few years before, concerning the Hegelian formula which identifies philosophy with the history of philosophy. I had rejected it, and Gentile had defended it, but his defence had not convinced me; now I was disposed to agree with Gentile, but on condition that I might interpret the formula freely in my own way, in other words, conformably to my notion of Spirit, in which philosophy is one "moment," and thus convert it into a formula identifying philosophy with history, which I worked out in the second edition of the *Logic.*

The various particular problems arising from Croce's *Aesthetic* are, directly or indirectly, reflected in *Problemi d'estetica* (1910), in which is collected a large variety of writings clarifying, defending, and complementing the theory set forth in his first major work. After the publication of the *Aesthetic,* Croce planned, with the collaboration of Gentile, the founding of *La critica,* a bimonthly journal devoted to literature, history, and philosophy. The appearance of the first issue of the periodical in January, 1903, marked an important step not only in the career of the two men, but also in the history of culture in twentieth-century Italy. Gentile took responsibility mainly for the philosophical part, and Croce devoted himself mostly to problems of esthetics and literary criticism; but often their contributions overlapped. "The founding of *La critica,*" wrote Croce, ". . . marked the beginning of a new period in my life, the period of maturity or harmony between myself and reality." All hesitations, indecisions, and self-searching activities came to an end. Croce now felt that he was on the right path, having found his vocation and his philosophy; and as he continued to work on *La critica* he became ever more convinced that, after years of disharmony between his studies and his actions, he had reached the coherence between the theoretical and the practical man that he had been looking for. (pp. xxiv-xxvii)

Croce's *Aesthetic* is . . . the true starting point of his philosophical thought. When he wrote it, however, he was unaware that the problems he dealt with were capable of further development; he thought at first that he was writing a self-sufficient work which in no way implied a philosophical system, for at the time Croce had not yet conceived or outlined his "Philosophy of the Spirit." His study of esthetics was carried out simply within the domain of human experience; the work is therefore not speculative, but, so to speak, phenomenological in character.

Its highlights are summarized by Croce in the last chapter of Part I, but they can be further reduced to the following propositions: beauty is expression, and expression is identical with intuition; intuition-expression is alogical knowledge, clearly distinct from the logical activity of the Spirit; art, being intuition-expression, is one and the same thing with language; art is independent of the other forms of the Spirit (these, on the contrary, depend on the artistic activity) and is knowledge of the individual (logic being the knowledge of the universal); taste is the only criterion for the judgment of art; taste is a faculty common in all men and its judgments are universally valid.

All this means that art is a human creation, spiritual in character, and that whatever is considered to be beautiful in nature is not so in its own right, but because subjective esthetic experience confers beauty upon natural objects. Thus, everything is resolved into the subjectivity of man: so-called physical beauty becomes a reflection of that subjectivity. The Spirit confers beauty upon the objects within its grasp, just as the economist confers value upon objects in accordance with the inner desires men project toward these objects. Esthetic expression is distinguished from "natural" expression, the latter being equated to the utterance of emotion in men and animals. Emotion, which is a chaotic perturbation, constitutes the matter to which the artist gives form in his esthetic expression. Matter is formless and receives form through the expressive process, which imparts life and individuality to something which was formerly indeterminate. The formative activity is the first stage of knowledge, for the Spirit knows only what it does. As a result, the idea of art as imitation is eliminated and that of art as creation (which had already been asserted by Kant) is firmly upheld. For art is a synthetic process which unifies the varied; art is nothing but form, and any content can be transformed into art. Content and form, however, can be distinguished only in abstract; in actuality they are inseparably united, for there is no content without form—form always being the form of a content.

But form only gives intuitive knowledge—representations, pictures, images. It does not distinguish between real and unreal; it presents the object in its concreteness without asking what the object is. Art therefore represents the particular as such. It is pure contemplation and is the necessary step to logical knowledge which subsumes the particular under the universal. There are two forms of knowledge: esthetic and logi-

cal, that is, individual and universal; there is the truth of the imagination and the truth of the intellect. Croce echoes here Vico's thought: "By the very nature of poetry it is impossible for anyone to be at the same time a sublime poet and a sublime metaphysician, for metaphysics abstracts the mind from the senses, and the poetic faculty must submerge the whole mind in the senses; metaphysics soars up to universals, and the poetic faculty must plunge deep into particulars." The two forms of knowledge are not coordinate, but subordinate; they are degrees of a process. The first degree (the artistic form), which is autonomous, constitutes the necessary antecedent of the second degree (the logic form): logic presupposes intuition, imagination, that is, art, which is the expression of the *concrete individual.*

If art is expression, it follows that esthetics and language coincide. Art is in fact language, and language marks the passage from animal sensibility to human activity. Moreover, the content of expression cannot be an external object, for external objects have a form, whereas the content of expression is formless; it is something which can only be grasped through expression. To conceive of content as external would mean to make of art a mechanical reproduction or an imitation.

But, despite these assertions concerning the subjectivity of art, Croce is still far from the idealistic position totally resolving the outer into the inner world. He could not succeed in avoiding the suggestion that there is an external content, which becomes the true content of expression when it is received by consciousness through impression, that is, when it is humanized. But this does not eliminate the object by thoroughly resolving it into a state of mind. When Croce wrote his *Aesthetic* he did not yet have a speculative philosophy, and most of his observations were based on psychological considerations. His main effort was to liberate esthetic intuition (intuitive knowledge), from its dependence on intellectualistic elements on the one hand and from the brutal animalistic emotions on the other. Having discarded logic from esthetic intuition, he turned his attention to the physico-psychic activity of man, which is a perpetual and indistinct flowing of chaotic sensations, characteristic of animal life. Expression throws light on the formless flux of obscure impressions, giving them eyes, so to speak. Art as language represents the birth of the human grafted on the animal which still persists in man. Art is passage from the formless to the formed, from passivity to activity, from multiplicity to unity, from becoming to being.

Intuition and expression are one and the same thing in the reality of the Spirit. The Spirit intuits only insofar as it makes, forms, expresses; and whoever separates intuition from expression never succeeds in reuniting them, since intuitive activity intuits to the extent that it expresses. The identity of intuition and expression remains one of the basic foundations of Croce's doctrine. Intuition is the activity by which the Spirit gives the material of art the expressive form, that is, language; it is, as we said, a knowledge of the individual obtained through the mediation of emotion, but never subsumed under any universal concept: intuition is pure contemplation (*teoresi*). Form is nothing but the actual identity of language and image, that is, intuition and expression. This form of knowledge is mere vision, which escapes the distinction between real and unreal. The process goes from impression to intuition and from there to perception, which is judgment (perception indicates something that has happened). The first designates formless matter, the second and the third designate degrees of theoretical activity. The formless matter cannot be grasped except in the form. And "it is impossible to distinguish intuition from expression in the cognitive process: the one appears with the other at the same instant, because they are not two, but one."

The conception of "expression," however, has in Croce a peculiar meaning which requires some clarification. The term "expression" is not to be taken as a means of communication, but as an "inner language" which gives expressive form to an obscure content, bringing it to the level of conscious life. But such an expression is all internal; it communicates the content of consciousness, and has nothing to do with externalization or communication in a social sense. Hence the peculiarity of Croce's conception of language and the problems arising from it.

There is no methodical and exhaustive treatment of the problem of language in Croce's works. But the indications given in his *Aesthetic* and in other pieces preceding and following this work are sufficient for a general view of his linguistic theory. The term "linguistics" is taken by Croce to mean not "science of language" in the positivistic sense, but "philosophy of language" in the speculative and theoretical sense and within the framework of idealistic philosophy. Resuming Vico's thought, he seeks the essence of language which is closely related to the subjective activity of the Spirit. Thus, he remains far removed from positivistic linguists who study language as a phenomenon governed by certain laws independent of the creative activity of man, that is, as a fact which can be analyzed and reduced to scientific principles. As conceived by Croce, language is an act in ever-changing creativity; it is not the language of the grammars and dictionaries, that is, an objective mechanism for the purpose of communication. In short, language does not exist per se, as a system of signs, outside the expressive activity of man, the individual utterance, the spoken sentence spontaneously formed by man's state of mind—without mechanical rules. The parts of speech have no expressive value in isolation; they become language in the synthetic utterance which is always new and which never repeats itself. The uniqueness and individuality of the expressive act makes translation impossible, for every translation is a new linguistic act, a new work of art. The linguistic act is, moveover, not the expression of thought or logical activity, but of fancy, of passion elevated and transfigured into images.

Language is therefore a free creation of the Spirit never conditioned by grammatical schemes; it is identical with artistic creation. This implies that poetry is language; hence the concept of the *poeticality* of language, which is form (the form shaping a certain content). This view certainly appeared to critics more controversial than the conception of language as *free spiritual creation,* for it was difficult to imagine true linguistic activity confined only to the esthetic form. In fact, after the *Aesthetic,* Croce seems to have tried gradually to modify the theory of the intrinsic poeticality of language in order to attune it to a broader concept of poetry developing from the initial, incomplete formulation of his doctrine. The character of *totality* later attributed to art implied the same character in language, for the two had been declared identical. The linguistic act, which was first the expression of individual feeling, must now be the expression of the totality and universality of man. But whether language reflects the individuality or the universality of man, the question still remains: are all linguistic acts equally poetic acts? It did not appear to be so to Croce's critics. Croce himself, upon returning to the problem, had to realize that there are nonpoetic expressions which are language and that therefore only *certain* linguistic acts can be considered poetic. When, in fact, he writes that language in its purity can be employed by thought and logic "as the sign for the concept," one may conclude that in the expression of ideas there is something esthetic in character.

In the book *La poesia* Croce points out four forms of expression: the immediate or natural (which is a chaotic utterance below the level of intuition and which is the symptom of emotion in men and animals), the poetic (which is the only one to be considered as language), the prosaic (which is the sign of ideas and concepts), the practical (which consists of articulated sounds aimed at persuading or entertaining, at arousing feelings or volitions); to these he adds "literary expression," which is a quality associated with the other expressions. The practical form of language is the one which particularly concerns the linguists, for it serves as a means of social communication. This form of expression is conventional; it is a system of signs which one must learn and practice. But here again Croce maintains that language, whether conventional or poetic, is *praxis* and not an independent organism, as the linguists believe.

Croce's error, in the eyes of some linguists, was to overlook the semantic aspect of language and to reduce language to a creative act and poeticality. Words have meanings which condition the speaker. This fact makes language autonomous and independent of praxis, but it would mean falling back to positivistic positions. If language is a body of rules and a list of words with fixed meanings, independent of poetic, logical, and practical activities, it becomes an abstraction rather than living language, for living language is an act, not a fact. In short, Croce denies the objectivity of language defended by positivists; for him language is the utterance, the sentence, and the phrase as they are spontaneously used. The dictionary contains dead words; when the words are spoken, they become alive and acquire new meanings in accordance with the state of mind of the speaker. Grammars and rules are a posteriori theorizations with limited practical value. Authentic expression always remains a free and creative act, obeying only the state of mind of the individual speaker. It is, therefore, always mutable, instable, and approximate.

Although Croce concerns himself only with esthetic language, that is, an agrammatical language governed by the individual disposition and feeling of the artist, and thus impossible to reduce to general rules, he does not undermine the function and importance of the language of dictionaries and grammars. It certainly must not serve as a pattern to be followed, as an imperative to be obeyed, but only as a reminder of tradition. The poet passes through it, but does not stop there; he goes beyond it and creates his own. There is no true poet or writer who does not pay some attention to it or who is not affected by the abstract forms of the dictionaries and the patterns of grammars. The most original and creative among them cannot completely conceal the fact that they had their "course in rhetoric." Those who are unable to supersede the "historically existent" and copy and repeat it do not contribute to the living history of art; only the unfaithful disciple, the "unfaithful-faithful," who brings in something new, can be considered worthy of his master.

To understand Croce's position, one must keep in mind the two main activities attributed to the Spirit—the theoretical and the practical. In the first case, the Spirit contemplates and thinks; in the second, it acts to satisfy its individual or universal needs. True language (or expression in the esthetic sense) belongs to the contemplative moment of the Spirit, that is, the moment of art, which is, as we have seen, "inner language"; the other forms of language are simply *signs,* not expressive in character. In the first instance, the word is the full expression of a psychic content which becomes one and the same with the word; in the second instance, the word is detached from its content and becomes a mere "label." The "inner language" coincides with the living experience and changes from one moment to another, being ever new, diverse, and strictly personal. It is the expression in which life acquires consciousness of itself and, fixing itself in a series of syntheses, forms language. (The life of animals, on the contrary, develops in the darkness of instinctual drives.) All this amounts to the identity of intuition and expression as knowledge of the individual.

The major problem in Croce's doctrine, however, arises from the clear-cut distinction he maintains between "expression" and "externalization" or "communication." For Croce these terms mean two different things: "expression" is the inner form given to feeling, that is to say, the constitution of the image; "externalization" is the physical production of the image on paper or on a canvas. This physical production is not language in its pure sense, for its purpose is the communication of the image already formed, and it belongs to the sphere of *signs.* Language is an inner process. Croce completely disregards the social aspect of language, which is communication. The fixation of the "inner expression" in something concrete, such as color, sound, writing, is not a theoretical act; it is carried out for practical purposes, one of which is the preservation of the expression in order to make its recreation and judgment possible.

Croce's doctrine must be viewed within the framework of idealistic philosophy for which language represents the moment in which the Spirit acquires consciousness of itself and utters words within itself. What men use, instead, to communicate among themselves is a system of signs, which the listener translates into a psychic content.

True language is an act of knowledge or self-awareness belonging to the theoretical Spirit which is art. Linguists, on the contrary, conceive of language as communication, because they view the individual as a real entity and distinguish him from society; language is thus a social, not an individual, product because it springs from societal needs. They consider *speech* (living utterance) and *language* (the objective system of signs) to be interrelated, with *language* existing prior to *speech.* Croce, on the contrary, maintains the priority of *speech* over *language,* a priority ideal and chronological. *Speech,* of course, falls to the level of *language:* from a live state it becomes dead, from Spirit it becomes nature, from an expressive act it becomes a fact, the fact which grammarians analyze to abstract their rules and schemes. In summary, there is for Croce the expression-image (poetry) and the expression-concept (logic); before the expression-image there is the natural expression; after the expression-concept there is the oratorical expression. Thus, to the four forms of spiritual activity, there correspond four forms of expression, with only one being, in the theoretical sense, true language. (pp. xxvii–xxx)

> *Giovanni Gullace, in an introduction to* Benedetto Croce's Poetry and Literature: An Introduction to *Its Criticism and History by Benedetto Croce, edited and translated by Giovanni Gullace, Southern Illinois University Press, 1981, pp. xiii-lxxiv.*

RENÉ WELLEK (essay date 1981)

[*Wellek's* A History of Modern Criticism (1955-86) *is a comprehensive study of the literary critics of the last three centuries. Wellek's critical method, as stated in* A History *and outlined in his* Theory of Literature (1949), *is one of describing, analyzing, and evaluating a work solely in terms of the problems it poses for itself and how the writer solves them. For Wellek, biographical, historical, and psychological information is incidental. Although many of Wellek's critical methods are reflected in the work of the New Critics, he was not a member of that group and rejected their more formalistic tendencies. In the following excerpt, he analyzes Croce's theory of art and his literary criticism.*]

Benedetto Croce's aesthetics is by far the most influential of the twentieth century, not only in Italy, where it has monopolized the field, but also in most other countries of the West: in England, Robin G. Collingwood and Edgar F. Carritt can be described as Croceans; in the United States, Joel E. Spingarn was a propounder of a simplified Croceanism; and John Crowe Ransom, the father of the New Criticism, refers to Croce at crucial points. In Germany the whole group of Romance scholars, Karl Vossler, Leo Spitzer, Erich Auerbach, can be called Crocean; his influence is also visible in Spain and Latin America. It seems, however, almost nonexistent in France and Russia. Croce's dominant position in Italy is not only, of course, due to his aesthetics: it is the combined effect of all the activities of a man who excelled in almost every branch of learning. Croce devised a whole system of philosophy in which logic, economics, and ethics have their coordinate place with aesthetics. But beyond this systematic philosophizing Croce has, even more importantly, been concerned with the theory and practice of historiography and with politics, in which he took an active part as a symbol of anti-Fascism, as the last great Liberal. Most significantly for us, Croce was an eminent practical critic of current literature and the great classics and an immensely erudite literary scholar. I believe that in the whole history of criticism, only Sainte-Beuve and Wilhelm Dilthey can match him, and then I am not sure whether Croce does not surpass them. But outside of Italy, Croce's impact was largely confined to the aesthetics; many of his other writings are not translated, though in English one can get a sampling of his literary criticism. His **Goethe** (1919), his **Dante** (1921), the volume on **Ariosto, Shakespeare, Corneille** (1920), and the book of essays on **Poesia e non poesia** (1923), called **European Literature in the Nineteenth Century,** are available in English; but not **La poesia** (1936) or the mass of smaller writings, except for a wide-ranging anthology, **Philosophy, Poetry, History.**

Croce's aesthetics, though widely quoted and referred to, and basically quite simple in its radicalism, upholds a position which is easy to misunderstand. A full study would have to distinguish between the four or five phases of Croce's evolution: the early preliminary stage in which the little book **La critica letteraria** (1894) interests us most; the period of **Estetica** (1902); the new version, **Breviario di estetica,** written in 1912 for the opening of the Rice Institute at Houston, Texas; **Aesthetica in Nuce** (1928), a third brief version, first in the 14th edition of the *Encyclopedia Britannica;* and finally **La poesia** (1936).

The main thesis known, I suppose, to everybody, is that art is intuition. One must, in order to understand Croce's term, forget about mystical intuition (that is always dismissed by Croce, who is resolutely secular). Intuition is the same as "representation," *Anschauung*. It is not "sensation," which in Croce's terminology is mere passive formless matter; it is not "perception," which is the apprehension of something real. Intuition thus is a far wider category than what we would ordinarily call "art," and Croce's aesthetics, while in practice concerned mainly with the realm of art, assumes a complete continuity between ordinary "representations," also in memory, e.g., of *this* river, *this* lake, *this* brook, *this* rain, *this* glass of water (called intuitions), and language and art. Croce expressly denies that one can draw a line between intuitions that are called "art" and those that are vulgarly called "not art." But we have not understood Croce's definition if we do not immediately add his identification of intuition with expression. Expression, of course, in Croce, does not necessarily mean verbal expression: it might be expression by line, color, or sound. Verbal expression again need not be speaking aloud nor, of course, writing: an intuition may be expressed (but even this dualism is false, since intuition *is* expression) without any outward action. Thus, all language is part of aesthetics, is expression, is creation. Croce's intuition-expression is the activity of the human mind which *precedes,* in his philosophical scheme, that of conceptual knowledge. Still, intuition-expression is knowledge, theoretical (not practical) activity, but knowledge of things in their concreteness and individuality, not conceptual knowledge.

Once we have understood in what sense Croce uses intuition, we shall not be surprised at the consequences he draws. Art (that is intuition-expression) he will argue, is, first, not a physical fact: neither a stone nor a canvas nor a piece of paper.

Secondly, art is not pleasure. The feeling of pleasure and pain belongs to the realm of the practical. Pleasure does not distinguish the aesthetic fact from other facts: pleasure may be sexual, organic (visceral), etc.; in short, it may accompany all activities of man but it does not single out the world of art. It is impossible to discover any special aesthetic pleasure. To define art as pleasure is like defining fish by the water in which they swim.

Thirdly, art is not morality, as morality is a practical act, which follows after intuition and knowledge. Still it is a gross misunderstanding to think of Croce as an aesthete who denies the moral and social responsibility of the artist. He would say that "the artist will always be morally blameless and philosophically irreproachable, even though his art may have for subject matter a low morality and philosophy: insofar as he is an artist, he does not act and not reason, but composes poetry, paints, sings; in short, expresses himself." But the act of externalization, reproduction, and diffusion of the artistic intuition is a practical act and can be regulated by society. He would allow censorship and even the burning of pernicious books. Nobody is more violent than Croce in his condemnation of aestheticism and decadentism as it was understood late in the nineteenth century: it is to him the attempt to make aesthetics the standard of morality. In Italy, D'Annunzio and Marinetti prefigure Fascism.

Fourthly, art is neither science nor philosophy. Croce over and over again insists that art is not conceptual knowledge, that it does not present ideas or universals, that "he who begins to think scientifically has already ceased to contemplate aesthetically." Conceptual knowledge is always knowledge of the real, aiming at distinguishing between the real and the unreal, while intuition means precisely "indistinction of reality and unreality, the *image* with its value as mere image, the pure ideality of the image." Croce considers thus intellectualistic all theories that make art "symbolic of a reality," all theories that put the aim of art into the typical or generic, and all theories that make art a version of religion or myth (to Croce rudimentary forms of philosophy).

If we have understood this central identification of art with intuition and expression, we shall be better prepared for the shock of some of the conclusions Croce draws from his position: as intuition is a generally human faculty, there is no special artistic genius. Instead of "the poet is born," we should say, "Man is born a poet." There is, of course, no distinction between content and form. Content to Croce would be, at most, brute matter preceding the act of intuition. But we can know nothing about it. Croce, at times, can say that "the aesthetic fact is form and nothing but form" and that the aesthetic of intuition could be called the "Aesthetic of form." Thus Croce is often simply considered a formalist. But this is quite misleading if we mean by formalism anything like what he would condemn as abstract academic formalism. Actually Croce admits that what he calls form could just as well be called content. "It is merely a question of terminological convenience, whether we should describe art as content or as form, provided it be always understood that the content is formed and the form filled, that feeling is figured feeling and the figure a figure that is felt." In practice, Croce constantly minimizes what are usually called the "formal elements of art" and is interested in intuition, which to him is form but which could also be described as feeling, or pervasive content. If one reads Croce's practical criticism, it is obvious that he has very little interest in form in the usual sense but always tries to define the leading sentiment of an author. Because in Croce there is only this one act of intuition, the one distinction between art and non-art, the description of the differences between works of art and authors is reduced to elements that many would call "content"—not, of course, to the raw material outside of art, to the mere theme or plot, but to the feelings, attitudes, and preoccupations embodied in the work of art.

If there is no distinction between content and form, each work of art is indivisible, forms a unity, an organic whole, that cannot be divided, except for purely practical purposes. Hence, a work of art cannot be translated. There are no rhetorical categories, no such distinctions as those between romanticism and classicism, no need of a word such as *style,* which at most is a synonym for expression. "In the aesthetic fact there are none but proper words: the same intuition can be expressed in one way only." If every work of art is simply successful expression, Croce can resolutely expel from aesthetics (or, at least *his* aesthetics) all categories such as the tragic, the sublime, the comic, and the humorous. They are simply handed over to psychology; they are only empirical, unconnected, descriptive terms derived from an aesthetics of sympathy irrelevant, or rather extra-aesthetic, in Croce's scheme.

The theory so far hangs together and is quite coherent if we once understand what it is about: this intuition-expression. One would think that in practice it would lead to critical paralysis, since we are deprived of the majority of terms and concepts with which criticism worked and works. Indeed,

Croce's theory of criticism is a highly untheoretical one: it merely says that the critic must reproduce the work of art in himself. Creator, work, and auditor or reader are identified more closely than in any other system. If criticism is identification with the creator, taste and genius must be identical. Croce logically rejects any critical absolutism in the sense of judging according to some canon or models that would be intellectual concepts. But he also rejects critical relativism, which would deny the possibility of this identification. In this scheme which has to recognize the frequent failure of this meeting of minds, great importance is assigned to the role of criticism as historical interpretation, as a restoration of the conditions that make the identification of the reader with the author possible. But erudition is considered only as auxiliary work toward comprehension. Criticism, while using all these tools, simply calls into existence a certain internal activity, aesthetic reproduction, which is fundamentally the same as the intuition of the artist.

In the idealistic theory of knowledge assumed by Croce, all these three sides—the author's creative intuition, his expression, and the reader's comprehension—are identical activities. The work of art as a physical fact is considered by Croce merely the result of a volitional act of externalization. "When we have fixed an intuition, we have still to decide whether or no we should communicate it to others, and to whom, and when, and how; all which deliberations come equally under the utilitarian and ethical criterion." This externalization is understood as a "taking measure by the artist against losing the result of his spiritual labor, and in favor of rendering possible or easy, for himself and for others, the reproduction of his images." Hence he engages in practical acts that assist the work of reproduction. These practical acts are guided by knowledge, and for this reason are called technical. Technique is thus something external, with the result in Croce's system that we must and can dismiss all the classifications of the arts. Croce is very violent about this: "Any attempt at an aesthetic classification of the arts is absurd. . . . All the books dealing with classification and systems of the arts could be burned without any loss whatever."

If there is no classification of the arts (only practical knowledge useful for the artist about, say, the ways of casting in bronze, or the technique of mixing colors, or the conventions of harmony), we need hardly say that Croce completely rejects the concept of literary kinds. The kinds have, at the most, a purely classificatory function such as, for instance, the Dewey decimal system in a library. "Who can deny the necessity and utility of such arrangements? But what should be said if some one began seriously to seek out the literary laws . . . of shelf A or shelf B, that is to say, of these altogether arbitrary groupings whose sole object was their practical utility." Artists have always disregarded these so-called laws of the kinds. "Every true work of art has violated some established kind and upset the ideas of the critics." The traditional three kinds—lyric, epic, drama—are not really distinguishable. In every lyric, there is epic and drama; in every drama, lyric and epic. No lyric is purely subjective: it is addressed to others; every epic and drama expresses the author. But Croce need not argue the detail of genre theories. He can say simply: "No intermediate element interposes itself philosophically between the universal and the particular, no series of kinds or species, or *generalia.*"

This view of the externalization of intuition as a different practical activity, with its corollary, which denies the aesthet-

ic relevance of technique and even of the distinctions of the arts and the genres, has aroused most opposition to Croce's theories. But the whole position can be and is usually misunderstood if we think that Croce simply argues in favor of an internal vision of the artist that is unique and undifferentiated and *then* is translated in a second practical, inferior act into a painting, a poem, or a piece of sculpture or music. Croce sometimes speaks in a manner open to such misinterpretation. But we always must remember that intuition with Croce is not inner vision but is also expression. He argues that "when the intuition has been distinguished from the expression, and the one has been made different from the other, no ingenuity in inventing middle terms can reunite them." But he insists on the difference between expression and technique.

I am not convinced by Croce's total monistic idealism and am particularly dissatisfied by his handling of the problem of externalization and communication. I believe that there is a clear distinction between poetry, which can be composed in the mind, and the plastic arts, which need an external medium to define and elaborate the intuition. Poetry in the mind is a bird in the hand; painting and architecture in the mind is a bird in the bush. Still, one should recognize that the system is not open to ordinary empirical objections and that it can be refuted only by rejecting its basic epistemology. "What is called *external* is no longer a work of art," is irrefutable in Croce's terms.

It is surprising that with this series of identifications—intuition and expression, vision and the external work of art—Croce has been able to handle concretely so many authors and works. Actually, in the later formulations of his theories, Croce introduced some modifications of his central concept of intuition-expression, which, in the early *Aesthetic,* is purely of the individual. Later, Croce emphasizes the universalizing character of art for which he invents the term *cosmicità.* While he still insists on the difference between art and concept, intuition and abstraction, he can say that art "links the particular to the universal." This universality is a synonym of the "total and indivisible humanity of its vision," though it is found only in the particular work of art. Here Croce comes near the concept of the "concrete universal" (though he always criticized Hegel for false intellectualism), and even of the symbol. Croce, however, dismisses "symbol" as an unnecessary concept, false if it means symbol of something and superfluous if it means the unity of the particular and the general which is the nature of expression-intuition. Croce is no nominalist if one defines nominalism as saying that "only words are universals." Words in poetry are with him particulars if they are intuition-expressions and not concepts. There are two kinds of language: original poetic and conceptual-communicative.

Croce, in his later versions of his aesthetics, emphasizes that intuition-expression must not be misunderstood as a recommendation of emotionalism and spontaneity as such, as the "overflow of feelings," as romanticism in the vulgar sense. But his practice and vocabulary often leaves itself open to misunderstanding. He seems proud of having introduced the term *liricità* and of arguing that all poetry is lyrical. But neither the etymology of the word nor its associations, at least in English or German, prepare us for the identification of lyricism with poetry itself. For Croce poetry is "passion" but not violent confused passion and is not restricted to the romantic passions of love or despair. Passions can be, he says, "expressive of security of thought, calm firmness of will, moderated energy, virtue, faith and the like." Art is always theoretical expression of sentiment, sentiment transformed into an image. Croce thus can advocate *classicità* which is of course not academic classicism. He always remained opposed to art being too obviously craft, too obviously intellectual or oratorical. Hence his dislike for the baroque and for symbolism as well as allegory (which by definition cannot be poetic).

Also in the theory of criticism, Croce modified his early position which put the aim of criticism into an identification with the author. He had gone so far as to say, "If I penetrate to the innermost sense of a canto of Dante's, I am Dante." But later Croce, more wisely, saw that criticism is rather a translation from the realm of feeling into the realm of thought. He found that critics should be reminded of the prohibition he had seen posted in some German concert halls, "Das Mitsingen ist verboten." The objection that criticism moves into a sphere completely remote from art is countered by Croce's argument that thought is the beginning of a new sentiment and act, that better understanding means deeper enjoyment.

But this change to a more theoretical ideal of criticism is not complete. Croce still insists that the aim of criticism is the characterization of the individual author, the essay, and monograph, and he denies the possibility of an internal history of art. Art is a historical fact in Croce, as in Croce everything which occurs in the mind is history. But the work of art is a monument and not a document and is thus immediately accessible to the mind. Thus any poet should be judged in terms of poetry here and now and everywhere. He cannot be judged as a link in a chain, as part of a history of art, as in Croce there is no such history, beyond the historical facts of individual works and beyond the social setting.

Thus Croce was no friend of the usual *comparatisme,* the studies of themes and motifs, sources and influences, for their own sake. In reviewing the prospectus of Woodberry, Fletcher, and Spingarn's ill-fated *Journal of Comparative Literature,* in 1903, Croce asked pointedly: What is comparative literature? If it means the comparative method, then it obviously goes far beyond literature and is constantly used in the study of even a single author. If it means the tracing of literary themes and influences, it is useful but leaves us with a feeling of emptiness. "These are merely erudite investigations, which in themselves do not make us understand a literary work and do not make us penetrate into the living core of artistic creation." They refer only to the after-history of a work already formed (its fame, translations, imitations, etc.) or to the materials that may have contributed to its origins. But if we define comparative literature as the study of all antecedents of a work of art, philosophical and literary, then it is identical with all literary history and the word *comparative* is really a pleonasm. There is only a choice between mere literary erudition and a truly historical and interpretative method.

Croce thus attacked the concept of literary history as an evolutionary process. He criticized severely what he called the sociological concept of literary history exemplified for him in all romantic histories of literature which conceive of literature as an expression of a national spirit, and *a fortiori* in all positivistic histories which make literature directly reflect a specific ideology (Georg Brandes) or explain it in terms of race and milieu (Hippolyte Taine). Croce, of course, recognized the immense advance which such historiography, in the hands of the Schlegels or Taines, represented, as compared to the purely erudite accumulations of eighteenth-century

learning. But he also saw that it made literature a product of something else, that it confused art with the intellectual and practical forms of the spirit (with philosophy and morality). When he was confronted with the theories and practice of Heinrich Wölfflin, who advocated a history of art that would be a truly internal history of its development, of its devices, techniques, and assumptions, Croce also refused to accept this solution of the problem. It follows from his aesthetic theory that devices and techniques, rhetorical categories and genres, get short shrift. Such history appeared to Croce an arid academic exercise or at most a history of fashions and customs, a history of civilization that has nothing essential to say to a man interested in the central problem of criticism—the intuition-expression of the poet.

In his proposal for a "reform of the history of literature and art," he argued that the only proper literary history is the *caratteristica* (critical characterization) of a single artist, of both his personality and his work, which form a whole. The unit thus will always been an essay or a monograph.

Croce substantially followed his own advice and instincts and steadily produced a stream of essays, of "characterizations," which focus sharply on the one problem he considered essential. "Criticism," he said in a letter summarizing a conversation I had with him on June 5 in Naples in the year of his death, 1952, "does not require anything else than to know the true sentiment of the poet in the representative form in which he has translated it. Any other demand is extraneous to the question." If one asks that the series of monographs and critical essays be put into some order, the answer is that "everyone can put it into any order he pleases." There is no continuity (except an external one) between Dante, Boccaccio, and Petrarch, or Pulci, Boiardo, and Ariosto. They are all different, and the critic's task is to grasp, to describe, and thus implicitly to evaluate their individuality, their uniqueness. Croce has done this in hundreds of essays which take up practically every figure of Italian literature. He began writing such practical criticism in 1903 when he founded the periodical *La Critica,* which he filled with his own contributions almost to the end of his life, though he had some collaborators such as the philosopher Giovanni Gentile in the early years. At first, he concentrated on the contemporary or near-contemporary literature of Italy, severely judging what he considered the decadence, the mistaken aestheticism of the late nineteenth century. D'Annunzio, Fogazzaro, Pascoli and later Pirandello were his main victims, while Carducci remained his lifelong favorite. Only very late, after World War II, did Croce modify the severity of his judgments in a more tolerant, even mellow mood. In many essays he also reexamined the whole of older Italian literature, condemning the baroque age for its "silence of great poetry" and picking his way through Renaissance and eighteenth-century literature, anthologizing, singling out poems and passages that appealed to his taste and fitted in with his view of poetry.

From contemporary Italian literature, his criticism moved increasingly into the past and into other countries. Croce's book on Goethe is a most refreshing book of the Goethe literature I know. It is entirely free from the usual German indiscriminate idolatry of Goethe and even his slightest works, and yet expresses great admiration, love, and understanding for what is genuinely great in the man and the poet. Croce achieves his success by resolutely divorcing the question of the poet's personality and biography from a judgment of the works themselves. He is entirely aware of the interest elicited by Goethe's personality, biography and "wisdom," etc. But he resolutely declines to fuse and confuse the two things, biography and criticism, and constantly points out the pitfalls of the biographical and psychological methods.

For the actual judgment of Goethe's poetry, Croce's view is also refreshingly new: he again brushes aside the usual intellectualism which looks for profundities and philosophical truth at any cost. Croce, though he does not use this term, is well aware of the "intentional fallacy" and therefore ignores or discounts all of Goethe's professions and intentions. He applies "the good old rule that with poets one must look not for what they wished or asserted that they were doing but what they did do poetically." Croce thus can treat *Faust* as almost an album in which Goethe entered his feelings at different times of his life. He can dismiss the tortuous attempts to find a coherence between the early version in the *Urfaust* or even in the Prologue in Heaven and the final scene of *Faust II*. He can see that in *Faust I* we have to deal with two fairly separate plays, the pact with the Devil and the story of Gretchen, and that *Faust II* is also pieced together from the *Helena* tragedy, long, allegorical, almost operatic pageants and the final scenes which, as Croce shows convincingly, are full of the old Goethe's sly humor and parody and must not be taken too solemnly. Goethe desired, no doubt, to give fictitious unity to his fragments, but Croce rejects this search for unity and defends himself skillfully against the objection that his criticism destroys the organism created by the poet. The opposite is true: "The poet, by a reflective proposition, has erected a mechanism, which encloses and compresses several and diverse living organisms." Croce consistently combats the view that philosophical, conceptual poetry is the highest poetry. The truly profound poetry in *Faust* is in the Easter scene or in the Jail scene of Part I, while the allegories or symbols of *Faust II* are often dead and abstract. Croce appreciates most highly the early Goethe and has little use for what is usually called his "classicism." The early poetry is the most "classical" in Croce's sense because it is most free from intellectualistic and moralistic admixtures.

The same basic thesis is behind the little book on Dante (1921). This book caused an enormous debate and could hardly convince by the radical distinction there drawn between the "theological-political romance," the structure as an abstract scheme, and the poetry which grows around it like luxurious vegetation.

Both the Dante and Goethe books make an effort to elaborate what to Croce must always be the central critical problem: the distinction between poetry and nonpoetry, or between poetry which is "classical," i.e., a successful union of inspiration and discipline, expression and image, and poetry which is mere feeling, mere emotion, poetry which is purely oratorical, directed toward a practical effect, or poetry which is intellectualistic, didactic, instructive. A late book, *La poesia* (1936), works out these distinctions most clearly, sharply discriminating also between poetry and literature—"literature" meaning writing in its civilizing function. The volume of little essays, *Poesia e non poesia* (1923), which in the English translation is called *European Literature in the Nineteenth Century* (1924), is an early application of these criteria and distinctions to figures somewhat haphazardly picked from the nineteenth century. Thus Schiller is put down as a philosophical rhetorician, thus Heinrich von Kleist is described as a poet merely striving by will power to become one, while George Sand is severely judged as propounder of the gospel

of romantic love, a case history for a moment of civilization, not a true artist. Sir Walter Scott appears to Croce to be merely a manufacturer of books, a "hero of industry," and an antiquarian who approaches poetry only in rare moments of human kindness; while Maupassant is highly appreciated though shown to be limited to one theme and one feeling. These distinctions are also applied with vigor within the work of an author. Thus Leopardi, in an essay that caused much offense, is disparaged as a thinker and shown to be very limited in the expression of his own feeling—disappointment with life—while he achieved poetry in Croce's sense of serenity only in the idylls.

The method is always one and the same. Croce selects what he considers poetry, brushes aside what is something else, and tries to define a leading sentiment, something like Taine's *faculté maîtresse,* which allows him to characterize by constant qualifications. Two essays out of the three collected in the book **Ariosto, Shakespeare, Corneille** (1920) are particularly striking examples. Ariosto is shown to be inspired by a desire for cosmic harmony which pervades every single sentiment of his work and all his language and meter, a poetic Hegel; Corneille is dominated by one passion, the ideal of free will. Each essay reaches what seems to me a rather meager conclusion by a process of elimination, by surveying the different solutions given by other critics, since Croce believes that the process of criticism is also a historical process, a dialectical argument against and with others. The essay on Shakespeare, though it contains a fine execution of conventional and foolish Shakespeare scholarship, seems to me inferior; Croce does not, I think, see into the tragic death of Shakespeare or grasp his intense power of language, but he formulates excellently his feeling for life and his strong sense of right and wrong. Croce is falsely judged if we think of his criticism as narrowly aesthetic; it is, rather, strongly ethical, even "psychological," if, of course, we recognize that he distinguishes between an empirical and a poetic personality, and studies only the latter.

The enduring importance of Croce for the student of literature, however, may, paradoxically, rest less on his strictly literary criticism and history than on his aesthetics and his history of aesthetics and in his theory and history of historiography.

Two-thirds of the **Estetica** is a history of aesthetics. His rediscovery of Vico as an aesthetician, hardly appreciated in his significance before Croce, expounded in a special book, his discussions of Alexander Gottlieb Baumgarten (who coined the term *Aesthetic* in 1735) and Friedrich Schleiermacher, and especially his many expositions, defenses, and comments on Francesco De Sanctis, the great historian of Italian literature, are major contributions to any history of critical thought. I feel that Croce is sometimes too much preoccupied with tracing only the one line of thought anticipating his own central conceptions; but his enormous erudition, his analytical power, his skill in marshaling facts and pulling together what seems remote is so great that every article of his is worth meditating and digesting.

His literary criticism, in the strict sense, appears to me thus limited. It is inspired by a clear philosophy and basic pathos; but it seems more seriously limited by a specific taste than his more freely ranging philosophical and aesthetic speculations. It does not stand or fall with our acceptance of his system of aesthetics *in toto,* but is circumscribed by a personal taste which is also that of a particular time. He rejects the baroque and much of what we would admire most in modern poetry since Baudelaire. Mallarmé and Valéry are his pet aversions. Croce himself had a ruling sentiment, was a historical personality in his own sense, unique even in his limitations, as we all are. (pp. 3-18)

> René Wellek, "Benedetto Croce," in his Four Critics: Croce, Valéry, Lukács, and Ingarden, University of Washington Press, 1981, pp. 3-18.

FURTHER READING

Babbitt, Irving. "Croce and the Philosophy of the Flux." In his *Spanish Character and Other Essays,* pp. 66-72. Boston: Houghton Mifflin Co., 1940.
Surveys Croce's works, maintaining that he "combines numerous peripheral merits with a central wrongness and at times with something that seems uncomfortably like a central void."

Carr, H. Weldon. *The Philosophy of Benedetto Croce: The Problem of Art and History.* London: Macmillan & Co., 1927, 213 p.
Examines principal aspects of Croce's thought.

Carritt, E. F. "Croce and His Aesthetic" *Mind* 62, No. 248 (October 1953): 452-64.
Analyzes strengths and weaknesses of Croce's *Aesthetic.*

Cock, Albert. "The *Aesthetic* of Benedetto Croce." *Proceedings of the Aristotelian Society* n.s. 15 (1915): 164-98.
Summarizes and critiques Croce's *Aesthetic as Science of Expression and General Linguistic.* Cock concludes that though the work raises important issues, it is "too full of ambiguities and inconsistencies to be anything more than a preliminary prospecting of the field."

Crespi, Angelo. "The Historical Idealism of Benedetto Croce." In his *Contemporary Thought of Italy,* pp. 67-148. New York: Alfred A. Knopf, 1926.
Outlines and critiques various aspects of Croce's philosophy, including his thought on art, history, and politics.

Douglas, George H. "Croce's Early Aesthetic and American Critical Theory." *Comparative Literature Studies* 7, No. 2 (June 1970): 204-15.
Assesses Croce's contribution to literary criticism, concluding "Croce helped to lay the foundations for a theory of criticism (which he himself did not always follow consistently) that focuses on the intrinsic qualities of the work of art."

Durant, Will. "Benedetto Croce." In his *The Story of Philosophy,* pp. 507-17. Garden City, N.Y.: Garden City Publishing Co., 1926.
Overview of Croce's career.

De Gennaro, Angelo A. "The Drama of the Aesthetics of Benedetto Croce." *Journal of Aesthetics and Art Criticism* 15, No. 1 (September 1956): 117-21.
Traces the phases in the development of Croce's philosophy of art, remarking that "after reading the works of Croce, one feels that he has arrived at the opposite bank of a river, almost exhausted after crossing such stormy waters."

———. *The Philosophy of Benedetto Croce: An Introduction.* New York: Greenwood Press, 1968, 103 p.
Analyzes Croce's philosophical system, making frequent comparisons with other European thinkers.

Hughes, H. Stuart. "Benedetto Croce: From the 'First Essays' to the 'Historiography' " and "Benedetto Croce: The Concept of Ethico-Political History." In his *Consciousness and Society: The Reorientation of European Social Thought, 1890-1930,* pp. 200-13 and 213-29. New York: Alfred A. Knopf, 1958.
Traces the influences on and the development of Croce's theory of history.

Krieger, Murray. "Benedetto Croce and the Recent Poetics of Organicism." *Comparative Literature* 7, No. 3 (Summer 1955): 252-58.
Discusses Croce's role as a precursor of the New Critics, claiming "that certain tendencies in the work of many of them were anticipated by Croce and that the theoretical atmosphere was cleared for them by his daring, if not reckless, pronouncements as aesthetician."

Milburn, Myra M. "Benedetto Croce's Coherence Theory of Truth: A Critical Evaluation." *Filosofia* 19, No. 4 (November 1968): 725-34.
Analyzes Croce's coherence theory of truth, "evaluating it both internally, that is, from within the framework of Croce's gnoseology and externally, with regard to its presuppositions."

Momigliano, Arnaldo. "Reconsidering B. Croce." *Durham University Journal* 69, No. 1 (December 1966): 1-12.
Appreciative overview of Croce's career originally presented as a memorial lecture on the centenary of his birth.

Moss, M. E. *Benedetto Croce Reconsidered: Truth and Error in Theories of Art, Literature, and History.* Hanover, N.H.: University Press of New England, 1987, 150 p.
Critical examination of Croce's philosophy, assessing his contribution to contemporary philosophical thought. Moss states that her goal is "to distinguish what still 'lives,' to use Croce's term, in his philosophy from what may be advantageously discarded."

Piccoli, Raffaello. *Benedetto Croce.* London: Jonathan Cape, 1922, 315 p.
Chronological examination of the development of Croce's thought through 1921. Piccoli defines his book as "an introduction to [Croce's] works, and at the same time the confession of one individual experience of that philosophy."

Robertson, J. M. *Croce as Shakespearean Critic.* 1922. Reprint. Folcroft, Pa.: Folcroft Library Editions, 1974, 32 p.
Examines Croce's criticism of Shakespeare's plays, focusing especially on Croce's interpretation of the relation between the life and dramas of Shakespeare.

Santayana, George. "Croce's Aesthetics." In his *The Idler and His Works, and Other Essays,* edited by Daniel Cory, pp. 108-15. New York: George Braziller, Inc., 1957.
Evaluates Croce's aesthetic theory.

Scaglione, Aldo. "Croce as Cosmopolitan Critic." In *The Two Hesperias: Literary Studies in Honor of Joseph G. Fucilla on the Occasion of his 80th Birthday,* edited by Americo Bugliani, pp. 339-47. Madrid: José Porrúa Turanzas, S.A., 1977.
Examines the "ethical foundation present in Croce's assessment of Goethe's work" as a demonstration of Croce's methods of literary criticism.

Seerveld, Calvin G. *Benedetto Croce's Earlier Aesthetic Theories and Literary Criticism.* Amsterdam: J. H. Kok N. V. Kampen, 1958, 110 p.
Surveys Croce's intellectual development through 1915.

Sprigge, Cecil. *Benedetto Croce: Man and Thinker.* New Haven: Yale University Press, 1952, 64 p.
Examines various aspects of Croce's thought, attempting to "portray this thinker in the broadest terms."

Tholfsen, Trygve R. "What Is Living and What Is Dead in Croce's Theory of History?" *Historian* 23, No. 3 (May 1961): 283-302.
Discusses Croce's historiography, suggesting that "the chief value of Croce's theory lies in the close connection that he es-

tablished between the subject-matter of history and the manner in which it can be known."

Wasiolek, Edward. "Croce and Contextualist Criticism." *Modern Philology* 57, No. 1 (August 1959): 44-54.
　　Surveys the ways in which the New Critics were influenced by Croce, noting that "one of the greatest paradoxes of the New Critical movement has been its theoretical dependence on Croce's theory of art and its ignorance of that theory."

Wimsatt, William K., Jr. and Brooks, Cleanth. "Expressionism: Benedetto Croce." In their *Literary Criticism: A Short History,* pp. 499-521. New York: Alfred A. Knopf, 1962.
　　Evaluates Croce's aesthetic theory, asserting that "Croce does actually achieve something like an ultimate definition and synthesis of the expressionistic art theory."

Zink, Sydney. "Intuition and Externalization in Croce's *Aesthetic.*" *Journal of Philosophy* 47, No. 8 (13 April 1950): 210-16.
　　Explains Croce's "doctrine of the essential identity of art appreciation and art creation" as presented in the *Aesthetic.*

Countee Cullen

1903-1946

(Born Countee Leroy Porter) American poet, novelist, critic, and dramatist.

For further discussion of Cullen's career, see *TCLC,* Volume 4. For related criticism, see the entry on the Harlem Renaissance in *TCLC,* Volume 26.

Cullen was one of the foremost poets of the Harlem Renaissance, a cultural movement of unprecedented creative achievement among black American writers, musicians, and artists concentrated in the Harlem section of New York City during the 1920s. While Cullen strove to establish himself as the author of romantic poetry on such universal topics as love and death, he also wrote numerous poems treating contemporary racial issues, and it is these for which he is best remembered.

The facts of Cullen's early years are uncertain, and he maintained a lifelong reticence about his youth. Scholars have determined that he was born in Louisville, Kentucky, and then raised in New York City by his paternal grandmother. Following her death in 1918, he was adopted by the Reverend and Mrs. Frederick Cullen of the Salem Methodist Episcopal Church in Harlem. In the home of his adoptive parents, Cullen was exposed to religious concerns and political issues of the day, as Reverend Cullen had helped found the National Urban League and served as president of the local chapter of the National Association for the Advancement of Colored People (NAACP). An excellent student, Cullen attended De-Witt Clinton High School, then New York's premier preparatory school, before enrolling at New York University in 1922. During high school and college Cullen placed poems in campus and national publications and won numerous literary prizes, beginning with second place in the Witter Bynner Poetry Contest for undergraduates for *The Ballad of the Brown Girl. Color,* Cullen's first volume of poetry, was published in 1925, the same year he graduated from New York University. After completing a graduate degree at Harvard, Cullen returned to New York, where he was already considered a leading literary figure of the Harlem Renaissance, and began writing a column on literary and social issues for *Opportunity,* the journal of the National Urban League. He published several volumes of poetry and edited *Caroling Dusk: An Anthology of Verse by Negro Poets.* During the late 1920s and early 1930s Cullen's poetic output declined, and critics maintain that the poems of this period do not fulfill the potential he had demonstrated in his earlier works. Turning his attention to other forms of writing, he published *One Way to Heaven,* a novel that was praised for its accurate portrayal of Harlem life, and stories and verse for children. In the mid-1940s Cullen began preparing a definitive collection of those poems he considered his best; *On These I Stand: An Anthology of the Best Poems of Countee Cullen* was published in 1947, the year after his death.

Believing that good literature transcends race, Cullen stated that he wanted to be recognized as a poet, not labeled as a "Negro poet." Nevertheless critics have asserted that he often seemed uncertain about the purpose of his poetry, and

Alan R. Shucard has suggested that Cullen often appeared "to vacillate between playing the pure aesthete and the racial spokesman." Cullen himself reflected in an interview, "In spite of myself . . . I find that I am actuated by a strong sense of race consciousness. This grows upon me, I find, as I grow older, and although I struggle against it, it colors my writing, I fear, in spite of everything I can do." Among his best-known poems are "Yet Do I Marvel," which focuses on the perceived contradiction between his status as a member of an oppressed race and his poetic skill; "Incident," which relates the experience of an eight-year-old child who is the object of a racial slur; and "Uncle Jim," in which a young man is warned by his uncle of the differences between blacks and whites in American society. In other poems Cullen combined racial and religious issues. "The Black Christ," for example, recounts the lynching and resurrection of a Southern black man. Such poems as "Heritage" reflect the tension Cullen felt between his identification with Christian values and tradition and his desire to claim an African heritage. Although occasionally criticized for displaying Cullen's ignorance about Africa, "Heritage" is widely considered his finest poem. The issue of racial identity is also raised in some of Cullen's love poems, notably "A Song of Praise," in which Cullen considers differences between loving a black woman and a white one. Cullen reworked a traditional English verse in *The Bal-*

lad of the Brown Girl, the story of Lord Thomas, who must choose between a white maiden and a "brown girl." While Cullen's interpretation of the story has occasionally been questioned because critics disagree whether the original ballad signified racial or social differences, the poem was one of his first major successes.

Cullen believed that poetry consisted of "lofty thoughts beautifully expressed," and he preferred poetic forms characterized by dignity and control. He wrote a number of sonnets and used quatrains, couplets, and conventional rhyme, frequently incorporating religious imagery and classical allusions. While some critics have praised Cullen's skill at traditional versification, others suggest that his style was not suited to the treatment of contemporary racial issues and that his adherence to conventional forms resulted in poems that are insincere and unconvincing. Despite the controversy surrounding his traditional poetic style and his ambivalence toward racial subject matter in art, Cullen remains an important figure in black American literature.

(See also *Contemporary Authors,* Vols. 108 and 124; *Something about the Author,* Vol. 18; *Dictionary of Literary Biography,* Vols. 4, 48, and 51; *Concise Dictionary of American Literary Biography, 1917-1929;* and *Black Writers.*)

PRINCIPAL WORKS

Color (poetry) 1925
The Ballad of the Brown Girl: An Old Ballad Retold (poem) 1927
Caroling Dusk: An Anthology of Verse by Negro Poets [editor] (poetry) 1927
Copper Sun (poetry) 1927
The Black Christ, and Other Poems (poetry) 1929
One Way to Heaven (novel) 1932
The Medea, and Some Poems (poetry and drama) 1935
The Lost Zoo (A Rhyme for the Young, but Not Too Young) (poetry) 1940
My Lives and How I Lost Them (juvenile fiction) 1942
On These I Stand: An Anthology of the Best Poems of Countee Cullen (poetry) 1947

MARK VAN DOREN (essay date 1926)

[*Van Doren was one of the most prolific men of letters in twentieth-century American writing. His work includes poetry (for which he won the Pulitzer Prize in 1939), novels, short stories, drama, criticism, social commentary, and the editing of a number of popular anthologies. His criticism is aimed at the general reader, rather than the scholar or specialist, and is noted for its lively perception and wide interest. Like his poetry and fiction, Van Doren's criticism consistently examines the inner, idealistic life of the individual. In the following review, he assesses the strengths and weaknesses of* Color.]

There are numerous things which Mr. Cullen as a poet has not yet begun to do, and there are some which he will never do, but in this first volume he makes it clear that he has mastered a tune. Few recent books of poems have been so tuneful—at least so tuneful in the execution of significant themes. Probably that accounts for the almost instantaneous success

of Mr. Cullen when he began not long ago to appear in the magazines. He had something to say, and he sang it.

What he had to say was nothing new even in his own generation. Edna Millay had said as much and more, and she had employed something like the same melodies. Mr. Cullen's **"The Shroud of Color"** could be referred back, if one wished to treat it that way, to "Renascence"; **"Saturday's Child"** and **"Fruit of the Flower"** have also their counterpart in Miss Millay's most piquant and interesting pieces—those sketching a spiritual heritage. But Mr. Cullen is not seriously damaged by the reference; first, because he obviously means what he sings and, second, because he has an accent of his own.

Mr. Cullen's skill appears in the clarity and the certainty of his song. Those who have tried to do a similar thing will be in the best position to appreciate the success of the following lines from the poem which prefaces the volume:

> Soon every sprinter,
> However fleet,
> Comes to a winter
> Of sure defeat:
> Though he may race
> Like the hunted doe,
> Time has a pace
> To lay him low.
>
> Soon we who sing,
> However high,
> Must face the Thing
> We cannot fly.
> Yea, though we fling
> Our notes to the sun,
> Time will outsing
> Us every one.

The theme of this poem is the shortness of life—a sacred theme for lyric poets always—and Mr. Cullen is so full of it that there is actually something joyous in the cadences with which he pays it his respects. The paradox is not surprising, perhaps, but it is attractive—the paradox of youth declaring that Time is a terrible enemy, and yet declaring this gayly, as if there were something delicious in the terror which the thought of death had inspired. The theme appears again and again in *Color,* in forming the love poems with that doctrine which we know best through the two words *carpe diem,* and imparting vitality to whatever pieces assert the preciousness of the present moment.

> Now I am young and a fool for love,
> My blood goes mad to see
> A brown girl pass me like a dove
> That flies melodiously.
>
> Let me be lavish of my tears.
> And dream that false is true;
> Though wisdom cometh with the years,
> The barren days come, too.

The prefatory poem, from which the first quotation was taken, is too long; ten further stanzas do little more than repeat the thought and beat it thin. If Mr. Cullen faces any danger it is this—that he shall call facility a virtue rather than the aspect of a virtue. Other poems here are too long for their content, and certain poems should not be here at all. It seems important both for Mr. Cullen and for the race which he so admirably represents that he should not hurry his next book into the world.

Mark Van Doren, "Countee Cullen Commences,"

in New York Herald Tribune Books, *January 10, 1926, p. 3.*

BERTHA TEN EYCK JAMES (essay date 1930)

[*In the following excerpt, James examines poetic style in* The Black Christ, and Other Poems.]

[*The Black Christ, and Other Poems*] proves again that Countee Cullen is an accomplished poet, but it shows also the danger in being an accomplished poet. He writes well, he uses the proper subjects, the strong verbs, rare adjectives and inverted order of modern verse, but the polished results seem to lack that lyric freshness that makes this type of verse worth while. To give an example, here is **"Nothing Endures"**:

> Nothing endures,
> Not even love,
> Though the warm heart purrs
> Of the length thereof.
>
> Though beauty wax,
> Yet shall it wane;
> Time lays a tax
> On the subtlest brain.
>
> Let the blood riot,
> Give it its will;
> It shall grow quiet.
> It shall grow still.
>
> Nirvana gapes
> For all things given;
> Nothing escapes,
> Love not even.

In this poem one may see charm and skill, and a complete unimportance. Too many of the lyrics here are of this type, even the more serious, such as **"The Foolish Heart"**:

> "Be still, heart, cease those measured strokes;
> Lie quiet in your hollow bed;
> This moving frame is but a hoax
> To make you think you are not dead."
>
> Thus spake I to my body's slave,
> With beats still to be answerèd;
> Poor foolish heart that needs a grave
> To prove to it that it is dead.

That is very skilful and quotable, but it shares the common lot of too much modern verse: it has nothing new to say and it says that in a fresh form, perhaps, but without a fresh feeling. The newness of a phrase does not lend life to an old idea; there must be a new point of view. When Andrew Marvell said, "Time's winged chariot hurrying near" he gave a fresh idea with his new image.

With us the time-honored emotions of love and decay are given intricate sentence-patterns, but one usually feels a lack of vitality in the resultant poem. Is it because we do not feel deeply? It may be that love and death seem less powerful, that man seems less important, but we still have trouble with us. Even though our verse suggests the Cavalier lyricists rather than the poets of a more deep-rooted emotional life, there are modern tragedies.

And the proof of this lies in the title-poem of this book, which comes last, **"The Black Christ."** It is an episode that must be associated with the deepest emotion, dedicated "hopefully" to white America. Reading it, one wishes to feel to the full the sorrow and triumph of the author, but there are barriers to that sympathy.

There are several ways of writing down such an event as the lynching of a brother for forgetting himself so far as to share love in springtime with a white girl. It could be done with violence and bitterness, or with simple realism. Countee Cullen has visualized this episode as the mirror of the death of Christ, and of the eternal Fair Young God; he makes a religious experience of it, told to further brotherhood and faith. Yet he writes it in very "poetic" language.

One has no right, perhaps, to criticize an artist's style; that is his own affair. But if it blur the force of the experience, one is inevitably disappointed.

This poem is written in an involved way, with free use of image and comparison. Such sentences as these from the speech of Jim seem to me too fanciful to be convincing:

> "But when I answer I'll pay back
> The late revenge long overdue
> A thousand of my kind and hue,
> A thousand black men long since gone
> Will guide my hand, stiffen the brawn,
> And speed one life-divesting blow
> Into some granite face of snow.
> And I may swing, but not before
> I send some pale ambassador
> Hot-footing it to hell to say
> A proud black man is on his way."

The same practice of poetic law and manner that makes the briefer poems in this volume pleasant and musical and slight prevents this long poem from seeming to have a style as simple, devout and important as its theme. (pp. 286-89)

Bertha Ten Eyck James, "On the Danger Line," in Poetry, *Vol. XXXV, No. V, February, 1930, pp. 286-89.*

THE TIMES LITERARY SUPPLEMENT (essay date 1932)

[*In the following review of* One Way to Heaven, *the critic judges the novel flawed.*]

Mr. Countee Cullen's **One Way to Heaven** opens with Sam Lucas, professional religionist, "tricking God" at a Methodist revival: his pretended conversion makes a devout convert of Mattie Johnson. It closes with the dying Sam, who has married, deserted and attempted to murder Mattie, tricking his wife from worthier motives into the belief that he has found a way to Heaven. It would not be true to say that this novel—the first by a writer with an established reputation among the coloured poets of America—has two plots: it scarcely has one. But there are two moods, corresponding to the two scenes in Harlem in which the action is laid, and to the two social classes of the actors. On the one hand are Sam, ticket-chopper in a movie-house; Mattie, a domestic servant who prefers a coloured mistress, however eccentric, to a white; and Aunt Maudy, an odd blend of devotion, shrewdness and negro credulity; on the other the refined and cultured circle revolving round polysyllabic Mrs. Brandon, her *soirées* and her more social than literary Booklovers' Society. Constancia Brandon's *salon,* as the "tall, fair-haired, imbibing Englishman" was astonished to find, was the one place in America where freedom of speech was a reality: it was "like a patch of Hyde Park." Yet this Englishman was not alone in his embarrassment when Constancia arranged for a fierce and bitter white professor to lecture to her coloured friends on "The Menace of the Negro to our American Civilization."

The freedom from race-consciousness of the social book-lovers is unreal because Mr. Cullen is gently satirical, kindly sceptical, in his treatment of the "movements" of the *intelligentsia* of Harlem. The religion of Mattie, of Aunt Maudy, of the revivalist preachers, is real enough to themselves; but, because the author of **"The Black Christ"** wishes—or so it seems—to avoid expressing in his novel the intimately personal experiences which his poetry expresses, there is an unreality compounded of unwillingness to interpret the scenes and emotions described and uncertainty of presentation. In the result, though particular incidents are very poignantly related, there is no cohesion in at least those portions of the book that deal with the lower of the two social strata. Either by itself would have presented a self-sufficient model; together they require a far larger canvas than Mr. Cullen has allowed himself, and a more clearly defined attitude—whether practical or satirical—towards the sociological problems involved.

> *A review of "One Way to Heaven," in* The Times Literary Supplement, *No. 1612, December 22, 1932, p. 976.*

BLYDEN JACKSON (essay date 1946)

[*In the following excerpt, Jackson discusses the effect of Cullen's aestheticism on his depiction of Africa and presentation of racial themes in his poetry.*]

Cullen's passing is lamentable. He was in many good ways an exceptional individual, and he was, beyond any caviling, one of the very best artists yet to emerge from our American Negro community. But he was not good enough. He fell too far short of epic achievement. He himself said in *Caroling Dusk* that he wished "any merit that may be in . . . my work to flow from it solely as the expression of a poet—with no racial consideration to bolster it up." As a writer, or as a champion of a minority group, he could not, of course, have taken any other stand and been respectable. People who oppose segregation, as Cullen did, and everyone of us should, must fight it all down the line. As a poet, therefore, it was important to Cullen that his race should not bar him from a universal audience on universal terms. He who also once said of some apparently Tory folks—" . . . they do not know that you, / John Keats, keep revel with me too"—was right in his consciousness of our desperate need to think in absolutes. That way, and that way alone, lies the only road that can establish Negro artists upon significant positions in an enduring culture. For commercial success or for transient celebrity we can produce picturesque vignettes of what too many people would like to suppose our whole life is—a cute, though rather savage, exoticism. But in so doing we are guilty of high treason to our best, indeed, our only, hope. Or we can press, as Cullen did, toward the mark of a high calling, and be, at the very worst, as Cullen was, a failure whose constructive elements, particularly in his youth, justify sympathetic and attentive regard by subsequent artists with irreproachable aspirations.

What then has Cullen to teach us? Surely his grand strategy was a campaign against cultural isolationism, for he saw very clearly that the interaction of art and society was a fact, and an important fact. Moreover, on the issue of integration he did not reason too simply. He had grasped the distinction, given wide currency by Howard Odum, between regionalism and sectionalism, between local emphases that act centripetally, strengthening even while they diversify a cultural unity, and local emphases of centrifugal, and, consequently, separatist, effect only. Thus reasoning, therefore, he could quite properly identify cultural isolationism with sectionalism and define genuine regionalism as a desirable factor in a well-rounded national literature. His major premises, then, left apparently nothing to be desired. But his operations did; and the reasons, probably, are not far to seek.

To begin with, Cullen as a person was a paradox—indeed, with master irony, he was the very sort of paradox that proved most bitterly his central credo that segregation is not a law of creation. Largely reared in New York City as the foster son of a minister, schooled there, graduated Phi Beta Kappa from New York University, with a Master of Arts degree from Harvard, Cullen was—in spite of his insistence that "his chief problem has been that of reconciling a Christian upbringing with a pagan inclination" and his sincere, in so far as he was aware, nostalgia for what he considered African moods—a well-bred American Aryan with a bourgeois background. All his life, without being conscious of his affectation, Cullen was trying to pass for a Negro. One illustration will here have to suffice.

Cullen, there is no need for anyone to suppose with guile, was much preoccupied with the paganism he considered so much a part of himself that, as he put it:

> God's alabaster turrets gleam
> Too high for me to win
> Unless he turns his face and lets
> Me bring my own gods in.

Moreover, Cullen thought of this paganism as African, as an atavism that unmistakably determined his cultural descent. But the truth is that Cullen's paganism was no more African than Visigothic, both of which it was far too sophisticated to have been. His Africa was a seventeenth-century pastoral; his paganism, Pan in a witch-doctor role. As Granville Hicks, thinking of E. E. Cummings and his fellows, has pointed out, the college generation to which Cullen belonged produced in its artists aesthetes—gentlemen who, if the one of them quoted by Hicks to support his thesis can be believed, "had no interest in social problems . . . read Casanova in French and Petronius in Latin, discussed Pater's prose, and argued about the voluptuousness of the church and the virtue of prostitution." How Cullen encountered Casanova and Petronius, if he tarried with them at all, I do not presume to know (although, curiously enough, the number of Magdalens he romanticizes in his verse is one form of documentary evidence fitting him to Hicks's formula and allying him with Hicks's dilettantes), but that Pater would hardly have been distressed by the Africa configured within the "copper sun and the scarlet sea" can hardly be doubted. For this synthetic continent lay in an aesthete's realm, discernible, with appropriate vagueness only, through a misty atmosphere of neo-Hellenism. The spicy grove, the cinnamon tree, the throbbing drums, the "cruel padded feet treading out, in the body's street, a jungle track," how pleasant the sensations they could set atingle in the blood of an Oxford don sipping tea between snatches of easygoing talk in his tranquil study, or how sweet the shocks they could start in the nerves of a pale student pining, in his imagist's ivory tower beside the Harvard Yard, to be consumed in a hard gem-like flame.

By the 1920s the real black man's Africa was no secret. Marcus Garvey had too many bright uniforms, but still a closer view of it than any aesthete. He at least saw it, though with a tragically illiterate concept of economics and politics and in terms primarily rooted in its exploitation. But whoever looked at Africa clear-eyed could see it plainly for what it was, with its leprosy, its elephantiasis, its human and animal filth, its harsh native codes in the diamond mines of South Africa, its ghastly memories of Leopold's "free state" and of the older Goering's wholesale extinction of a people in the quondam German colonies, its lack of sanitation, of machinery, of capital, of leadership, of power, of knowledge, but not without hope and not, for all its want of an Isles-of-Greece or Land-of-the-Lotos glamour in itself or in anything it had ever been, without a past that could be reliably, yet movingly, interpreted.

But Cullen's paganism had no source in any Africa, present or past. Substantially there was no difference between it and the vision of the dark continent that a kindly disposed white man of Cullen's temperament would have concocted. Yet while Cullen's romantic glorification of a non-Nordic universe demonstrated in its terms how white he was, it did psychologically answer other purposes as a means of defense and escape. As a defense it was part of Cullen's answer to the extravagant code of insult directed by his own social order against any Negro's self-respect. Cullen's environment bombarded him with its derogations of everything black, studied affronts to his dignity, Jemimas on the billboards, Gold-Dust twins in the magazine advertisements, Stepin Fetchits on the movie screen, a scornful silence in the history books. So Cullen fought back. He found "pride in clean, brown limbs," and "a brown girl's swagger" giving "a twitch to beauty like a queen." Once at least he flailed out too blindly:

> Who lies with his milk-white maiden
> Bound in the length of her pale gold hair,
> Cooled by her lips with the cold kiss laden,
> He lies, but he loves not there.
>
> Who lies with his nut-brown maiden,
> Bruised to the bone by her sin-black hair,
> Warmed with the wine that her full lips trade in,
> He lies, and his love lies there.

Some men do feel that the blacker the berry, the sweeter the juice. On the other hand only in a moment when he was perplexed to the extreme could Cullen have forgotten that, if anything in this world is unpredictable, it is the way of a man with a maid. The hapless savagery of Cullen's denial that anyone could love a white woman is merely a crescendo note in his rebellion against racism's debasement of everything not white. It was just an obvious example of his defensive instinct operating not wisely, but too well. It was, that is to say, part of the pattern of resistance for the service of which he had invoked his curiously treasonable reproduction of the African past. And it was, under keen analysis, only a little less felicitous. For, like his creation of pre-colonial Africa, it represented emotion run riot.

Cullen's intellect was not on guard when he blasphemed the efficiency of white women as lovers. Neither was his vigilance as acute as one could wish in the business of making real and meaningful his nonwhite heritage. Yet here one must remember the strength of a vicious circle before he condemns too harshly. It would have required on Cullen's part no *tour de force* to find pregnant and localized symbols for the Western culture whose departure Eliot laments in "Gerontion." Who

were the heroes Cullen could name? Theseus, Ulysses, Jason, Aeneas, Siegfried, Beowulf, Roland, Arthur, Galahad, Tristram, Robin Hood, William Tell. What places chimed rich echoes in his legend-making memory? The Troad, the isles of Greece, *Mare Nostrum* and imperial Rome, Camelot, Lyonnesse, perhaps a northern castle ringed with fire. The white man's myths were, willy-nilly, an integral part of Cullen. Could he match the names he had learned in New York, at Harvard, in Europe, with similar symbols from African tradition? Why is his Africa no closer to the Congo than Sicily? Why are the terms in which he seeks its recapture so lacking in concreteness? Why are they the stock images only of the literary artificer? When Robert Frost mends a wall or picks apples in New England the right touch is there, the particular conclusive detail, putting the signature of authenticity upon this Yankee world, but whatever tricks Puck might try upon Shakespeare's groundlings they were not fooled. They knew they were in English Arden, not in an Attican grove. And, in spite of Cullen's noble purpose, name his world what he will, it, too, is still his cultural homeland, a province built, like Keats's "realms of gold," from the matter of bards who reign in fealty to Apollo.

The revolt in Cullen's paganism is, then, a revolt in name only. As such it leaves much to be desired. It is an ironic debacle, a case of fighting fire with fire. As a defense mechanism it is hoist upon its own petard, and as an escape device it ends, like all escapist literature, demobilized in a *cul de sac.* Of course, however, to charge Cullen with escapism, or more precisely, with undue escapism (since, obviously, a certain amount of release from this world is an inevitable gratification of artistic enterprise) is to raise something of an issue. For Cullen was an earnest worker. He was no poseur, and, let it never be forgotten, he was not, despite anything that might be said against him, a disreputable artist. Along with a felicity in graceful phrasing and a knack for endowing his verse with an elegant tone, he had high purposes of great value. He wanted Negroes accepted into the human family as casually as other people. As a part of that program he wanted to point up the fact that Negroes, too, have dignity and other favorable qualities. Yet he did not want Negroes stereotyped only as objects of noble pathos either. Quite deliberately he kept these intentions in the forefront of his consciousness. And so the Topsys and the Emperor Joneses are not typical of Cullen's work. Indeed much of his poetry is not "racial" at all. A decade before Frank Yerby's *The Foxes of Harrow* (in 1935, to be exact), Cullen had published his **The Medea and Some Poems;** and in 1940 his delightful little fancy, **The Lost Zoo,** with its Squilililigees, Lapalakes, Ha-Ha-Has, Pussybows, Hoodinkuses-With-the-Double-Head, or Just Hoodinkuses, and their extinct associates, reminded the reading public that even Negroes are capable of pure, pointless, winsome fun. His themes also had the catholicity which his opposition to cultural isolationism implied. If he wrote of brown girls' love he also wrote of love as Robert Herrick or Sir John Suckling would have done; indeed, with even less of local color than these unregenerate Britishers, he pleigned of desire and the sense of loss, of the delights lovers find in being together, of the praise of love and of the anguish that accompanies the recognition of its cruelty. It is true that his long poem, **"The Black Christ,"** is a poem of racial protest, but his equally ambitious **"Medea"** is no more a case of special pleading than its name suggests. In many ways, therefore, Cullen's impulses and his achievements were both estimable. Withal, it should not be overlooked to what extent Cullen was a pioneer and, as such, a person of resolution, integrity, and independence. Surely in doing many of his pieces he was intending to crack a tradition—the same tradition that says, for example, that all Negro sociologists must be experts on the black belt, or that all Negro singers must close their programs with a group of spirituals. In other words, in one respect at least, Cullen was a literary statesman rather than a literary politician, for the politician would have considered his market with a crafty callousness beyond Cullen. All these endearing qualities Cullen had. Yet he also had a taste for beauty as beauty, and this returns us to the escapist element in his poetry.

The aesthetic bias in Cullen is perhaps less noticeable because, according to the calendar at least, he belongs to our generation. Actually, although he probably thought of himself as having preeminent affinities with Keats, Cullen's milieu seems a curious blend of the seventeenth and eighteenth centuries (in England, not Africa or America). Poetry, as Elizabeth Drew and John L. Sweeney persuasively outline its history in their *Directions in Modern Poetry,* appears to alternate between periods of social and individual emphasis. The full-blooded Elizabethan Age was a time when literature was a highly social product. The seventeenth-century reflex was a poetry equally individual, in which the great preoccupations were love and religion, both matters primarily personal. Neo-classicism reflected the corporate disposition of its age. The Romanticists returned again to a major concern with the isolated ego. What were Cullen's abiding interests if they were not love and religion? Sometimes the love might take the form of hate; sometimes the religion might be paganism or aestheticism. Love and religion they still are. Again, did not Cullen prefer the tested diction, the familiar rhythms? Does he not also have his evidences of sensibility and sentimentality? These date his lyricism closer to Samuel Johnson's standards than to the Romanticists, though this might not be a judgment in which Cullen himself would concur. Be that as it may, however, the fact remains that the aesthetes of Cullen's generation are, by and large, experimentalists in radical styles. Whereas Cullen's sense of form is altogether orthodox, their craving after sensations enjoyable to themselves often shows itself in arresting patterns. The poetry of E. E. Cummings, for instance, is the poetry of a man whose aesthetic predispositions have much to do with the organization of his expression in a manner disturbingly revolutionary to conventional people. The dialogue of Ernest Hemingway is famous for its preoccupation with form, its concern for squeezing into the way the thing is said every possible characteristic overtone, and famous also for its marked stylistic departure from the old school. It would be a gross reader, indeed, who did not immediately become aware of Cummings' spectacular deviations from the norm in his handling of punctuation, word arrangement, typography itself, or of the simplicity *sui generis* of Hemingway's dialogue and his narrative style. Yet that same reader might never think of Cullen as a writer whose appetite for form got the better of him to a degree in which it did not ultimately damage the output of these other two.

The plain truth is that Cullen never had too much to say. Measure him as he himself has suggested, with an absolute yardstick. Try him against the major poet with whom he connected himself, with Keats, and cast up the account. Keats's absorbing preoccupation was with an issue as old as the hills—truth, beauty, mutability, reality, epistemology, ontology. State it how you may, men have been puzzling over this question of the real versus the specious since memory run-

neth not to the contrary. They still are, of course, and even now, as any sympathetic reader of Wallace Stevens will hasten to testify, continue to say important things about it. Nevertheless "La Belle Dame Sans Merci," though it has fallen on the evil days of dutiful classroom *translation* into literally true vernacular, remains a major attack upon the cult of glamour, just as its concomitant "Ode to a Nightingale" remains a major affirmation of the values beyond glamour's futility. Cullen's **"Heritage"** is an attack on racism. But does it argue against racism as effectively as "La Belle Dame Sans Merci" attacks false standards? It does not. It lacks the plurisigns in which Keats spoke. Keep rereading it and it shrinks. The bitter-edged satire of its closing couplet is the right kind of a *coup de grace, corto y derecho,* short and straight. It stands up under pressure, but the rest of the poem largely goes bad, leaving nothing in the couplet's support. "Sweeney among the Nightingales" is a poem famous for the success with which T. S. Eliot creates and maintains throughout it the required atmosphere of foreboding, so that when, at its end, through the agency of the nightingales Eliot links together the vulgar nonentity, Apeneck Sweeney, with the great Agamemnon in a brilliant play upon the colonel's-lady-and-Judy-O'Grady theme, the effect is tremendous. The whole short lyric is a mighty unit, all the pieces of the orchestra preparing the final consummation. And in "La Belle Dame Sans Merci," also, Keats does not release a word in error. His problem is to build up in his reader's consciousness, more through overtones than otherwise, a sense of the sort of beauty that ought to be repudiated. He wants his reader to have the intimate, absolute knowledge of this treasonable beauty that comes out of feeling it, not by definitions. So Keats's poem is a perfect metaphor made up of subsidiary metaphors all directed to one end, to make real in the terms of art, through a blending of sound with imagery and movement, Keats's concept of the nature of the loveliness that deceives.

But in **"Heritage"** the parts hardly fit. The images resolve themselves, upon analysis, into the pretty and irrelevant confections that they are. There is no way to make them tonally acceptable to the mood of satire that the situation demands. And just as there is no logic by which the moods of this poem can be synthesized, so is there also a fatal schism in the argument. Cullen, in his use of the African background, seems to be saying essentially, "Look out. I am savage. At any time the real me may burst through this veneer and run amok." But, to say that the heathenism in America is dangerous because it challenges the heathenism in his past is not merely to cheapen the terms of his theme, but also to blunt the appeal of his satire. His "strong bronzed men" and "regal black women" at least are in the right church, for his success as a polemicist. They are obviously meant to imply a fineness, a self-respect, and a self-sufficiency in the African culture that would properly explain and justify his rebellion against the white man's attempts to degrade Cullen for his black ancestry. They build Cullen up properly as a creature of royal lineage for whom only royal treatment is mete. But far too much of the material in **"Heritage"** will neither in sound nor in sense support this good motif. A considerable portion of the poem, on the other hand, is a technicolored jungle that bears substantially the same relation to the real Africa of slave-trading days as Longfellow's delightful Indian preserve—another literary kingdom in which, to borrow Van Wyck Brooks's apt characterization, there is only "the vague myth of a sunset land, a paradise in the West, where the mountains and forests were filled with deer and the lake swarmed with fishes"—bears to the actual pre-Columbian America.

Over Longfellow's happy hunting ground blew the Indians' gentle south wind, Shawondessa, a perfect symbol, not only in its zephyrous image, but even in its delicate luxuries of phonetics, for Longfellow's own genteel aestheticism. And it is Shawondessa, not the sand-bearing, throat-burning harmattan with its harsh implication of life's frequent rigor, which ripples ever so tenderly the pastel vegetation in Cullen's Watteau thickets. It is Shawondessa which passes "Where young forest lovers live / Plighting troth beneath the sky." It is, indeed, this same Shawondessa, not true, unlearned, aboriginal, violent savagery that Cullen describes himself as feeling in

> . . . my sombre flesh and skin
> With the dark blood dammed within
> Like great pulsing tides of wine
> That, I fear, must burst the fine
> Channels of the chafing net
> Where they surge and foam and fret

or as moving

> Through my body, crying, "Strip!
> Doff this new exuberance.
> Come and dance the Lover's Dance!"

So when Cullen asks and answers: "Africa? A book one thumbs / Listlessly, till slumber comes—" he has been honest about his own reaction. Africa has lulled him into sleep, an aesthete's trance, for ultimately the deliciousness of small sensations has captured everything in this poetry. If **"Heritage"** proposed to say something serious or important, or to develop moods consonant with the nature of its theme, those *desiderata* have in the act of realization been, surely unwittingly, forsaken. Cullen has escaped into the enchanted wood whence, undiverted, he can be rapt by the song of the nightingale. These verses cannot be justified by a reader searching in Cullen's poetry for the bread of life, but their tone-coloring is so sensuously worked in and the pictures that they make are such exquisite dreams. They are as escapist as that quatrain of his (in **"Colored Blues Singer,"** not in **"Heritage"**):

> Such songs the mellow-bosomed maids
> Of Africa intone
> For lovers dead in hidden glades,
> Slow rotting flesh and bone,

where the swooning of the sound goes hand-in-glove with the pasteurization of the maids' bosoms and the euphemism of the corpses decomposing inoffensively in the fecund tropics. But escapism, even when it is as relatively innocuous as Cullen's aestheticism, has, in final terms, no positive values for the artist. The aesthetic surrender in **"Heritage"** constitutes a flight, not only from the real world with its complicated pattern of good and bad, its stench and maggots, as well as its "gentle flesh that feeds by the river brink," but also from the technical problems of the poem as a poem, its fusion of voices, its unity of context, its resolution of theme. So it indicates the general manner in which Cullen's aestheticism operated to his detriment, weakening his will, confusing and diluting his effects, turning him astray from the ends toward which he started. So also it leads us, together with his misconstrued paganism, into an understanding of the fact that neither intellectually nor artistically did Cullen possess the mastery without which an artist can never be truly sufficient. So it reminds us that Negro artists may fail on the universal world of art because of individual inadequacies as well as racial vendettas. And thus it carries us as a point of departure toward the consideration of an issue that leads beyond a concern with Cullen

only or, for that matter, with any single writer, into a generalization which, sound or not, is certainly evangelical.

The disparity between Cullen's conscious aspirations and his real achievement is all too clear. What he most sincerely desired was a thing in itself right and good. He wanted to write poetry of such quality that it would be read and regarded highly as poetry, not charitably dismissed as "racial" literature. Yet Cullen had neither the intelligence nor the power to speak with superlative effectiveness either as Everyman or as "The Negro." (pp. 43-55)

> *Blyden Jackson, "Largo for Adonais," in his* The Waiting Years: Essays on American Negro Literature, *Louisiana State University Press, 1976, pp. 42-62.*

JOHN CIARDI   (essay date 1947)

[*Ciardi was an American poet, critic, and translator who served as poetry editor for the* Saturday Review *from 1956 to 1972. In the following review of* On These I Stand, *he summarizes Cullen's place in American literature.*]

Countee Cullen has been treated by reviewers of the last twenty years in ways he certainly could not control and probably did not invite. In their eagerness to find a poet who could express the tremendous art-force of the American Negro, the reviewers have hailed book after book as a promise of great things to come. Now Cullen's untimely death has put a last period to promise. This edition of his selected poems [*On These I Stand*] is total. And if the total disappoints the large claims that have been made for him, Countee Cullen may yet be remembered in years to come as one of the most engaging early voices of a great body of literature which only recently has begun to emerge.

Though circumstance made it inevitable that Cullen treat racial themes, his natural impulse seems to be toward the literary poem. One feels he is happiest in his sonnets to Keats and in his variations of the "made ballad" (as opposed to the "artless ballad"). At his best (**"A Brown Girl Dead," "Incident,"** and the familiar **"Heritage"** among others) Cullen shows a real gift for the neat, sensitive, and immediate lyric. When the observation contained in the poem is direct and personal, dealing immediately with people seen and events that really occurred, the poems emerge movingly.

Too often, however, the treatment is marred by a taint of "artiness" that is too obviously derivative. The grand Millay manner studded with "I fain would," "albeit," and "yet do I ponder" is a bit too coyly of the Village and the High Twenties to be carved on the lynching tree. This taint of artiness, an overready reliance on the poetic cliché, a weakness for bookish literary forms, and a regrettable insensitivity to the spoken language flaw too many of the poems. It is for the one poem in ten that emerges whole that Countee Cullen will be remembered. (pp. 144-45)

> *John Ciardi, in a review of "On These I Stand," in* The Atlantic Monthly, *Vol. 179, No. 2, February, 1947, pp. 144-45.*

STEPHEN H. BRONZ   (essay date 1964)

[*In the following excerpt, Bronz discusses themes of race and religion in* Color *and* Copper Sun.]

Chauvinism, atavism, and the paradox of racial hatred in a divinely created world pervade the most important poems in *Color.* Thus, for example, **"A Song of Praise (For One Who Praised His Lady's Being Fair)"**:

> You have not heard my love's dark throat,
> Slow-fluting like a reed,
> Release the perfect golden note
> She caged there for my need.
>
> Her walk is like the replica
> Of some barbaric dance
> Wherein the soul of Africa
> Is winged with arrogance . . .
>
> My love is dark as yours is fair,
> Yet lovelier I hold her
> Than listless maids with pallid hair,
> And blood that's thin and colder . . .

Besides demonstrating Cullen's mastery of the white man's classical verse forms, **"A Song of Praise"** boldly asserts the inevitable superiority of the darker lady, and cheerfully accepts the stereotype of a sexually torrid Negro race. Also, the poem refers to Africa, that previously unknown continent in which Negroes were beginning to adopt a new but still superficial interest, as a racial homeland. **"A Song of Praise,"** then, offered much to the Negro readers of the 'twenties in bolstering their self-pride. To whites Cullen asserted that Harlem, with its new poetry and exotic women, had something to offer besides jazz.

"Atlantic City Waiter" well demonstrates Cullen's abstractness when dealing poetically with the Negro's lot in America. For Cullen the Atlantic City waiter is less an individual than a stimulus to the poet's own racially-oriented mental meanderings. The poem reads:

> With subtle poise he grips his tray
> Of delicate things to eat;
> Choice viands to their mouths half way,
> The ladies watch his feet
>
> Go carving dexterous avenues
> Through sly intricacies;
> Ten thousand years on jungle clues
> Alone shaped feet like these.
>
> For him to be humble who is proud
> Needs colder artifice;
> Though half his pride is disavowed,
> In vain the sacrifice.
>
> Sheer through his acquiescent mask
> Of bland gentility,
> The jungle flames like a copper cask
> Set where the sun strikes free.

By glorifying the waiter as a proud African nobleman Cullen by implication glorifies every Negro. Here, as in **"A Song of Praise,"** a new racial stereotype replaces the old one. Instead of the kindly servant ever anxious to please, we have an austere, ennobled savage.

One of the longest and most frequently quoted of Cullen's poems probes the meaning of Africa to twentieth century Negro-Americans, and emerges with no clear answers. The refrain to **"Heritage"** states the question:

> *One three centuries removed*
> *From the scenes his fathers loved,*
> *Spicy grove, cinnamon tree,*

> *What is Africa to me?*

The first part of **"Heritage"** depicts stirringly the Africa which the speaker, try as he might, cannot keep from surging up in his blood. Africa does not mean the pre-colonial African art, philosophy, and state-craft being rediscovered in the 'twenties in America and France, but an exotic jungle and plains Africa of "wild barbaric birds," "juggernauts of flesh," "cats / Crouching in the river reeds," "silver snakes," and "leprous flowers." From the pen of Countee Cullen, Northernbred, college educated, these images, with their smooth sounds and vague pictures, ring false. Nonetheless, despite its inaccuracies, such as placing the Ceylonese cinnamon tree in Africa, the poem presents a far more favorable view of Africa than did Vachel Lindsay's bombastic "Congo," which had been published in 1914.

Exotic Africa served a distinct purpose. History to the Negro was not the national pageant of exploration, settlement, independence, western expansion, and wars to preserve the union and democracy, but a story of bondage, physical freedom, and Jim Crow. The Negroes' need for a past of which to feel proud produced a growing interest in the 'twenties in Negro history; it also produced Cullen's **"Heritage."** Africa was a heritage no white man could claim, a link with savage splendors so different from the more intellectual heritage of Western Europe. If Cullen's poem seems artificial, so, as he recognized, was the African heritage somewhat artificial, and a product more of the pen than of the blood.

After his excursion into atavism, Cullen turns in **"Heritage"** to a subject closer to his heart, the meaning of Christianity for the Negro.

> Quaint, outlandish heathen gods
> Black men fashion out of rods,
> Clay, and brittle bits of stone,
> In a likeness like their own,
> My conversion came high-priced;
> I belong to Jesus Christ,
> Preacher of humility;
> Heathen gods are naught to me.
>
> . . . although I speak
> With my mouth thus, in my heart
> Do I play a double part.
> Ever at Thy glowing altar
> Must my heart grow sick and falter,
> Wishing He I served were black . . .
> Surely then this flesh would know
> Yours had borne a kindred woe.

Note that Cullen decries not so much the white man's control of organized religion or the unchristian acts of white men, as the meaning of Christ's suffering itself. The poem ends in self-contradiction:

> Not yet has my heart or head
> In the least way realized
> They and I are civilized.

One does not emerge from the latter part of **"Heritage"** with clear, provoking theological argument, but rather with an ill-defined but strongly expressed feeling that somehow all is not right with the world and Christianity. The popularity of the poem does not attest so much to the strength of agnosticism among Negroes in the 'twenties, as to the appeal of Cullen's own conception of poetry—"lofty thoughts beautifully expressed." For Cullen, beauty seems to have meant beauty of sound and, in keeping with the title of the volume, beauty of imagery of color. In these, the poem abounds; in the concreteness of imagery and economy of language that can make poetry meaningful and powerful it is sorely lacking.

More directly concerned with God and the American Negro is **"Shroud of Color."** However wordy it may be, **"Shroud of Color"** seems more powerful and sincere than **"Heritage"** because Cullen deals with the problem in a grand and imaginative fashion, so that we find it easier to overlook the persisting absence of concreteness. The first part of the poem presents a despairing Negro speaker, disillusioned with a life in which prejudice puts "a hurt / In all the simple joys which to a child / Are sweet." His dreams of joy, and even of truth itself are damned to frustration and distortion, the speaker laments. Has God hidden some special lamb, some special reward and relief for him? The speaker doubts that God has, but resolves to live intensely regardless. He lives, he struggles, and at last, "all passion spent, [he] lay full length / And quivered like a flayed and bleeding thing." From this exhausted despair, the speaker is "lifted on a great black wing," as if in a dream, and permitted, by God, to view great proofs of the value of life and man's passion for it. The speaker witnesses animals' and plants' tenacious struggles for life, but remains unconvinced: "Than animated death," he asks, "can death be worse?"

Next, the speaker watches, in addition to animals, all of mankind struggling for life. "Well, let them fight," he replies, still skeptical, "they *can* whose flesh is fair." Even seeing the great heavenly war between the good and bad angels does not suffice: "Why mock me thus? Am I a God?" Finally, God shows the speaker a panorama of the history of the Negro race: the "strange wild music" of Africa and the "bitterness and death" of slavery, in spite of which "there ran / Through all a harmony of faith in man. / A knowledge all would end as it began."

> . . . I had no further claim to urge
> For death; . . .
> "Lord, not for what I saw in flesh or bone
> Of Fairer men; not raised on faith alone;
> Lord, I will live persuaded by mine own.
> I cannot play the recreant to these; . . .

Returned by the black wing to earth, the speaker looks up, and sees the rising sun.

Here, in the same volume of poetry, we have an answer to the question posed in **"Heritage,"** but an answer that does not seem altogether to have satisfied Cullen. His faith seems weak, and in need of repeated reassurance. But, as with so many of Cullen's poems, the personal statements and conflicts are less notable than the poem's place in the Harlem Renaissance. Christianity served dramatically as a consolation for the Negro slave, and for the slowly rising Negro under Jim Crow. Life on earth plainly had much that was wrong with it; some promise of a golden future was a near necessity for any sort of earthly happiness. And the understandable antagonisms towards the master and, later, towards a white society, needed some outlet. This, religion had helped to provide.

But Cullen, in **"Heritage"** and **"Shroud of Color,"** questions the validity and relevance of religion for the Negro. He demands, in effect, that greater attention be turned to the here and now. This life must not be quietly accepted as a vale of sorrows. It must be changed or the Negro will cease struggling, as in **"Shroud of Color,"** and, by killing himself, mock God's chief gift to man. Cullen demanded not only an equal

place for the Negro in American society, but, concomitantly, an equal place for the Negro in the eyes of God. It would have been surprising to find such a poem written twenty years earlier—Dunbar never indulged in such speculations. And twenty years later, Negro intellectuals, and more and more the Negro people as a whole, were much more concerned with actively improving the Negro's lot through specific measures, or in venting the Negro's surpressed fury at an unjust society and the white race.

Again concerned with the Negro and God, though with a somewhat different emphasis, is **"Yet Do I Marvel."** In this poem, reminiscent in form of some seventeenth century metaphysical poetry, Cullen lists a series of paradoxes of seeming evil in a divinely created world. The speaker says he does not doubt God's ability to explain these paradoxes—why the mole is blind, why men must die, why Tantalus and Sisyphus must endure interminable tortures. Cullen concludes the poem with the final paradox, perhaps his most famous line: "Yet I do marvel at this curious thing: / To make a poet black, and bid him sing!" This paradox, to be sure, had been blunted by the success among whites of the Harlem Renaissance by 1925. Still, though a Negro poet was not such a strange phenomenon in the cosmos, it was a fairly radical notion to Negroes and whites before the Harlem Renaissance. The Sambo stereotype of the Negro was fading, and Cullen's own writings both stressed and exemplified that change.

Among the other racially oriented poems in *Color,* many of which assert the ultimate equality of the races or elegize beautiful though unnamed brown girls (the word *Negro* apparently did not meet Cullen's criteria for elevated poetry), one poem stands out as direct, concrete, and popular. It is entitled **"Incident."**

> Once riding in old Baltimore,
> Heart-filled, head-filled with glee,
> I saw a Baltimorean
> Keep looking straight at me.
>
> Now I was eight and very small,
> And he was no whit bigger,
> And so I smiled, but he poked out
> His tongue, and called me, "Nigger."
>
> I saw the whole of Baltimore
> From May until December;
> Of all the things that happened there
> That's all that I remember.

The lightness, subtle directness, and quality of drama of **"Incident"** are reminiscent of the poems of Emily Dickinson. In all of *Color,* only in this small poem, with its diminutive title, does Cullen place a moving, credible picture before the reader's eyes. It is with disappointment that one reads Cullen's insistent statements that this "incident" did not in fact happen to him, but that he only imagined it. Still, the poem remains, whatever the story of its making, and serves as a precursor to such works as Richard Wright's bitter and terrifying autobiography, *Black Boy.*

Cullen's second published volume, *Copper Sun,* has far fewer poems on racial themes than *Color.* More of an established poet by 1927, Cullen turned towards more universal subjects: love and death. The racially oriented poems that are in *Copper Sun* repeat, usually in more stilted and vague terms, the ideas expressed in *Color.* There are exceptions, however, and those exceptions imply that Cullen was becoming more aware of the day-to-day lives of Negroes. In the poem entitled "Colors," the "Red" section describes a scene concretely enough to make us feel Cullen had witnessed it himself. An "ugly, black, and fat" woman went to buy a hat, and the salesladies, mockingly, sold her a bright red one, "And then they laughed behind her back / To see it glow against the black." But the black lady, unperturbed, "paid for it with regal mien, / And walked out proud as any queen." In its content, if not in its expression, this is one of Cullen's most successful poems. He creates a dramatic situation, with credible characters, and combines a racial with a universal theme. The black lady could be seen to represent any unsophisticated woman who maintains her human dignity before a condescending attack.

"Uncle Jim," with more plausible characters than most of Cullen's efforts, reveals much of the contradictory nature of Cullen's own views on race and beauty.

"White folks is white," says uncle Jim;
"A platitude," I sneer; . . .

His heart walled up with bitterness,
He smokes his pungent pipe,
And nods at me as if to say,
"Young fool, you'll soon be ripe!"

The speaker, however, while with a friend whose interests coincide with his own, perplexedly finds his mind straying from "the Grecian urn / To muse on uncle Jim." It is not altogether clear what uncle Jim meant by "White folks is white," whether he was calling attention to the lower position granted Negroes in American society, or to the unremitting hostility of whites towards Negroes. But he does, in any event, represent the voice of experience, warning the young idealist to lay aside his Keatsian musings on universal beauty, and come to terms with life and race problems. Like the speaker in the poem, Cullen's own first instincts were towards thinking and writing of what he saw as universals. And like the speaker in the poem, he found himself, despite first instincts, dealing in life and poetry with racial questions. (pp. 48-56)

> *Stephen H. Bronz, "Countee Cullen," in his* Roots of Negro Racial Consciousness; the 1920's: Three Harlem Renaissance Authors, *Libra Publishers, Inc., 1964, pp. 47-65.*

NATHAN IRVIN HUGGINS   (essay date 1971)

[*Huggins is an American historian and critic specializing in African-American studies. In the following excerpt, he discusses the dilemma posed by Cullen's adherence to conventional Anglo-American poetic models while writing on subjects and themes arising from his race consciousness.*]

By the end of his life, Countee Cullen had acquired all of the marks of a poet. He had published five books of original poetry, not including **On These I Stand** (1947), which collects his already published work. In addition, Cullen had edited a book of Negro verse, written a novel and two books about his cat, and collaborated on two theatrical works. He had won prizes: the Witter Bynner award for the best poetry by a college undergraduate, the *Opportunity* magazine contests, the Harmon Foundation competition, and a Guggenheim Fellowship. From the writing of his earliest verse, in high school, to the end of his life, he had always received favorable critical comment, pointing to him as exemplary of one whose art had transcended race.

This kind of judgment was especially pleasing to Cullen, because he believed that art—especially poetry—should transcend the mundane, the ordinary; be elevating. His view of art was quite conventional—indeed conservative—in the postwar years. He believed poetry should deal with higher emotions and ideals; it should avoid sensuality—its language more pure than ordinary speech, more elevated than prose. While this convention had been under attack in the United States since before the war—many of Cullen's white contemporaries had long since thrown over their obedience to it, and were experimenting not only with form but with poetry's proper subject and common diction—Cullen, himself, held quite tenaciously to the genteel tradition.

This conservative idealism was educated into the poet. In high school and college, Cullen took the traditional path to the art of poetry: languages, classics, English literature. He helped to edit as well as contributed poetry to the DeWitt Clinton High School literary magazine, *The Magpie*. While an undergraduate at New York University, Cullen published in several literary magazines, including *Bookman* and *Poetry,* and in his senior year Harper contracted to publish his first book of poems, *Color* (1925). His acclaim in his college years was for poems which varied in subject if not style: **"Simon the Cyrenian Speaks"** as well as appreciations of John Keats. His *Ballad of the Brown Girl* won the Witter Bynner award and was considered by Harvard's Lyman Kittredge to be the finest literary ballad by an American he had read. So Countee Cullen was already published and praised (a Phi Beta Kappa graduate) when he went to take his Master's degree at Harvard. He found Robert Hillyer's seminar in versification just to his liking. Hillyer had asked for exercises in various traditional forms of English verse; that poet-professor later was to publish one of Cullen's exercises as a rare American example of the Chaucerian rime royal. Cullen was forever committed to the formalism that this education implies. His biographer attributes to him the assertion that his poetry just "came out" in metered lines and rhyme. In any case, he never experimented with anything else, and that is quite remarkable considering what other poets were doing in the 1920s.

Formalism was not the only mark of Cullen's conservatism. He understood Art to be a slave to Beauty (he would capitalize those nouns). Poetry more than prose was the pure essence of the literary art; as essential beauty it should allow the human imagination to soar, to live with the gods. He was encouraged in this by the influence of Alain Locke, and by W. E. B. DuBois, whose views on art and uplift would vie with any other New England Yankees for gentility and conservatism. Furthermore, Countee Cullen had tied himself spiritually to the Romantics, particularly John Keats, who continued to serve as models for his verse as well as inspirations for his vision. He cultivated in himself that emotional temperament that expected to find poems in graveyards and palm-pressed palpitations on hillsides, and which saw the body and human condition as inconvenient harness to the spirit; the muse, genius, the imagination, and art transformed man into a kind of immortal, into a kind of god. He visited Keats's grave in Rome and read the epitaph that Keats had chosen for himself: "Here lies one whose name was writ in water." Later Cullen wrote his own.

"For John Keats, Apostle of Beauty"

Not writ in water, nor in mist,
Sweet lyric throat, thy name;
Thy singing lips that cold death kissed
Have seared his own with flame.

One could hardly find a more perfect example of a twentieth-century poet marching to a nineteenth-century drummer: the subject, the title, the diction, the stiff period of the first two lines, the conceit of the poet, the "lyric throat" and the kiss of "cold death." Like most of Cullen's poetry, this epitaph leaves the reader with little doubt about what it is. It looks like a poem, it sounds like a poem, and it is about what poems are supposed to be about.

With all of his sense of idealized art, Countee Cullen was, nevertheless, very conscious of the obligation that race placed on him as a poet. Given his view of the art of poetry, his race consciousness was quite a dilemma. The problems of Negroes were real, too real. They were a part of this world, the mud, guts, and stuff of life. Lynchings, murder, discrimination, poverty inevitably would be the subjects of Negro life. Yet how could this be translated into verse that would be elevating and truly poetic? Furthermore, Cullen believed that the art of poetry, like all art and true culture, was abstracted from race or any other condition of life. It was Cullen who told Langston Hughes that he wanted to be a poet, not a Negro poet. For him, there was no such thing as Negro poetry. How, then, could he remain true to his sense of art and, at the same time, to his strong racial feelings? His conservative critical judgment told him that he must write poems that were at least once removed from the source of his strongest emotions. No wonder that he thought God had done a curious thing: "To make a poet black and bid him sing."

Cullen also was never free from his sense of being exemplary. Like so many Negroes whose achievement catapults them into the public eye, he was a public Negro. He was not merely a poet, he was a "credit to his race." No matter how much he achieved or how little it depended on race, it was inevitable that his blackness would mark him. Of the ten initiates into New York University's Phi Beta Kappa chapter, it was Countee Cullen who was singled out for extensive press coverage—an example of Negro achievement. While he consciously wrote to ensure his acceptance as a good American poet, and while critics often remarked that his true achievement was as a poet and not as a Negro poet, he never could avoid being defined by race. *The New York Times* of January 10, 1946, amplified the irony with its headline: "Countee Cullen, Negro Poet, Dead." Nor can one say that the poet would have really wanted it otherwise. Langston Hughes's simplistic logic did not recognize that the motive to write like a poet (a white poet) could be indeed quite the opposite from wanting to be white. Cullen wanted to be acknowledged as a poet so that he would not be condescended to as a Negro, so that he could be an example of Negro potential, successfully competing on the white man's ground. As an exemplar, he could point the way to others, he could be a symbol of possibility, and he could turn other black boys' eyes to poetry and art so that the muse might allow them to transcend their condition as he had. Such a conception was problematic, yet Cullen was sustained by important Negroes—Booker T. Washington, W. E. B. DuBois, James Weldon Johnson—in this view of racial uplift through culture, achievement, and example.

In writing love poems it was easy enough for Cullen to handle the problem of race and art. In his art, love, like spring, was color-blind, and for the most part those poems could be addressed to a lady of any hue. Cullen sometimes wrote poems about brown girls and brown boys, but for the most part the color was only in the title; the poems themselves were characteristically devoid of concreteness and specificity. In **"A Song of Praise,"** Cullen answers a poet who praises his lady for being fair, by alluding to African beauty. The same theme is suggested in **"Brown Boy to Brown Girl."** But, as with most of his poems, the reader is left in the realm of idea, far from palpable reality. ***Ballad of the Brown Girl,*** however, does point to the difficulty of emulating, for racial purposes, works of an alien era and culture. Cullen mistakenly thought the brown girl in the medieval ballad was Negro, whereas, in fact, the balladeer meant a peasant girl. This tale of a struggle for the affections of a handsome lord by a country girl and a fair London maiden had different meaning from what Cullen intended. Tied as he was to the story as well as to form, the poem is only slight and confused comfort to the Negro reader who might hope to be elated by it.

When Countee Cullen wanted to write seriously about Negroes, his aesthetic forced him to couch his meaning and intent in classical or religious context. The reader would have to infer the racial significance, and it was thought that the classical context would elevate the particular to the universal. He wrote **"Simon the Cyrenian Speaks"** to show the courageous dignity of a humble black man's answer to the Christian call. He obliquely wrote about prostitutes in **"Black Magdalens,"** thus dignifying Harlem whores with biblical reference. The predicament of the black man, deprived of justice and possibility, is worked out in **"Shroud of Color,"** a poem of passion in which the narrator challenges God to tell him why he must go on living. God gives him a series of visions, but it is the final chorus of all black men's hopes and aspirations that gives him courage, will, and determination to live as one of these.

> And somehow it was borne upon my brain
> How being dark, and living through the pain
> Of it, is courage more than angels have.

Lynching is the subject of **"Black Christ,"** his long narrative. Whereas the same subject moved Claude McKay to bitterness and James Weldon Johnson in "Brothers" to expose the brutality of murdering mobs and their kinship to the victim, Cullen characteristically chose another statement. Bitterness was not beautiful or elevating, neither was the bestiality of men; these could not be the voice or theme of a poem. Cullen used the lynching as a test of faith. The brother of the lynched man lost his faith in God, despite his mother's unswerving devotion. But the lynched brother rises from the dead, redeeming his doubting brother. The resurrection also, completing the analogy to Christ, ennobles the murdered man and the murder. And even when Cullen wanted to explore the question of his African heritage, he chose in **"Heritage"** to bind the problem to the religious question of pagan vs. Christian belief.

These were never very satisfactory ways of dealing with the themes that prompted the poems. Sometimes, one suspects, the work would have been more successful as prose. Always the reader—the modern reader at any rate—wonders why the poet does not say what is on his mind. The obliqueness surely does not help. Yet Cullen, forever true to a genteel straight-jacket, seldom if ever ventured to tell it as it was, or better yet, to tell it as he felt it.

I quote here the four stanzas of **"Harsh World That Lashest Me"** because it illustrates Countee Cullen's persistent Romantic vision, and it serves as a sharp contrast to Claude McKay's treatments of the same themes in "America" . . . and "Baptism."

"Harsh World That Lashest Me"

Harsh World that lashest me each day,
Dub me not cowardly because
I seem to find no sudden way
To throttle you or clip your claws.
No force compels me to the wound
Whereof my body bears the scar;
Although my feet are on the ground,
Doubt not my eyes are on a star.

You cannot keep me captive, World,
Entrammeled, chained, spit on, and spurned.
More free than all your flags unfurled,
I give my body to be burned.
I mount my cross because I will,
I drink the hemlock which you give
For wine which you withhold—and still
Because I will not die, I live.

I live because an ember in
Me smoulders to regain its fire,
Because what is and what has been
Not yet have conquered my desire.
I live to prove the groping clod
Is surely more than simple dust;
I live to see the breath of God
Beatify the carnal crust.

But when I will, World, I can go,
Though triple bronze should wall me round
Slip past your guard as swift as snow,
Translated without pain or sound.
Within myself is lodged the key
To that vast room of couches laid
For those too proud to live and see
Their dreams of light eclipsed in shade.

There is, here, no real evidence that the poet is black, yet one has to know that fact to have the romantic sentiment make any sense. Cullen like McKay speaks of torment in the world (McKay calls America a "cultured hell"). Cullen and McKay alike echo the late Victorian stoicism of W. E. Henley and Kipling which finds comfort in an indomitable soul.

Countee Cullen had a genuine talent for lyric verse, and he did manage to write pretty lines. William Grant Still put **"If You Should Go"** to music.

"If You Should Go"

Love, leave me like the light,
The gently passing day;
We would not know, but for the night,
When it has slipped away.

Go quietly; a dream
When done, should leave no trace
That it has lived, except a gleam
Across the dreamer's face.

There is a prettiness here that wants to live in all of Cullen's work. He liked softness and liquid sounds. Seldom did he write anything harsh. **"Incident"** is the one exception. For in this poem a white boy of about eight years calls the narrator "Nigger"; nevertheless, the tone is plaintive and innocent.

Countee Cullen liked form, he liked words, and he liked rhyme, but he never experimented with any of them. One looks in vain in his poems to find departures from convention. The rhymes are regular, and the reader is never startled by a strange or new one. He never forgot his formal exercises from his Harvard seminar. He was content to be good at

them, so his poetry remained exercises in verse, never experiment or play. And the same for words. Cullen did not serve that function of poetry which molds the language into something new. Surely, he would never write in vernacular, and even his precious diction is never marked by freshness of usage. Poetry was a very serious business to Countee Cullen; he might be light but never funny. Significantly, he left his slight poetic humor for short verse epitaphs.

In 1935, just ten years after his first book of poems, Countee Cullen published *The Medea and Some Poems,* which was to be his last book of new poetry. He did write some children's stories and two books about his cat, but to all intents his life as a poet had ended. He taught in the New York City public schools, working very hard to interest young boys in poetry. This was time-consuming, but it fails to explain why a young man who was dedicated to poetry early in his youth should have lost the will to write. Since his days in high school nothing else had mattered. But, despite what he told himself, his dedication was not to the art; he did nothing toward advancing the art. As he told Langston Hughes, he wanted to write poetry, not Negro poetry; he wanted to be a poet, not a Negro poet. It was akin to his wanting to be first in his class, and being Phi Beta Kappa (which he was). It was a means of excelling and being exemplary. Having several volumes of poetry to his name, several awards, and critical recognition as a poet among Negroes, the real incentive was gone. He already had what he wanted. Of course, his health began to deteriorate; he was troubled with ulcers and hypertension—common ailments of exemplars. Remarkably, in 1945, when he was just forty-three, Cullen began to arrange with his publisher for a collection of his poetry. He did not plan to publish another book of verse, and he wanted a single volume to contain the work on which his reputation should rest. *On These I Stand* appeared in 1947, just about a year after Countee Cullen's death. (pp. 205-14)

Nathan Irvin Huggins, "Art: The Ethnic Province," in his Harlem Renaissance, *Oxford University Press, Inc., 1971, pp. 190-243.*

NICHOLAS CANADAY, JR. **(essay date 1972)**

[*In the following excerpt, Canaday presents a thematic discussion of Cullen's poetry.*]

Countee Cullen's first volume of poems, *Color* (1925), demonstrates convincingly that he is a poet of considerable scope who handles a variety of ideas and techniques with ease. The subsequent volumes—*Copper Sun* (1927), *The Ballad of the Brown Girl* (1927), *The Black Christ and Other Poems* (1929), and *The Medea and Some Poems* (1935)—although they do not present marked departures from the themes he introduces in the first volume, do indeed contain new variations and complexities within Cullen's major areas of concern. Here we shall demonstrate Cullen at his best, without regard to chronology, in each of the major thematic groups, noticing that the groups are by no means mutually exclusive because the themes are interrelated. Indeed, virtually every theme in Cullen's poetry—even including the exuberant spirit of his love lyrics—is found in his greatest poem, **"Heritage."** Our strategy will be to examine the several strands separately, and finally to observe how they are woven into the fabric of **"Heritage."**

It should not surprise us that the adopted son of the Reverend

Frederick Asbury Cullen of Harlem's Salem African Methodist Episcopal Church should have received from his father an abiding Christian view of the world, which is perhaps the most pervasive element in the younger Cullen's poetry. This faith is not without a countervailing tension of doubt. Many of Cullen's poems quite simply are about religious subjects: this fact in part explains why so many Negro preachers read Cullen's poems from their pulpits and why his poems remain popular as pieces for readings and recitations. Yet Cullen's religious background is also reflected by the frequency and variety of biblical allusion in his poetry, the use of religious imagery even in nonreligious contexts, and a marked tendency to cast poems in parable form.

Cullen's fondness for the parable form—usually brief, dramatic, poetic anecdotes with the meaning implied but not overtly expressed—shows the influence of a home in which the Bible was studied and discussed. A similar observation has long ago been made about another American writer, Stephen Crane, who was also reared in a Methodist parsonage. Crane rebelled in a bitter way that Cullen never did; but Cullen shows in what he thinks of as his pagan moments some of the proverbial behavior of the minister's son. His notable parables in verse include **"Two Who Crossed a Line,"** companion poems about "passing," the poems **"Incident"** and **"Uncle Jim,"** both about race, and **"Ghosts,"** a poem about love. Many of his satiric epitaphs are also structured like parables in very brief form.

The poem which best seems to represent Cullen's religious posture is **"A Thorn Forever in the Breast,"** from *The Black Christ and Other Poems,* and it is a poem primarily about idealism and not about religion at all. It begins by picturing the idealist as lonely and alien in the world of men. And then it tells of his end:

> This is the certain end his dream achieves:
> He sweats his blood and prayers while others sleep,
> And shoulders his own coffin up a steep
> Immortal mountain, there to meet his doom
> Between two wretched dying men, of whom
> One doubts, and one for pity's sake believes.

The poem is an Italian sonnet, and Cullen shows great skill in meeting the demands of this highly restrictive poetic form. When Cullen speaks of the alienation of the idealist in the real world, he sounds like John Keats, his favorite poetic model. To meet one's doom "between two wretched dying men" is the kind of biblical allusion that is so typical in Cullen's poetry and gives an added dimension of meaning to the fate of one who refuses to take the world as it seems. But Cullen's religious stance would also seem to be portrayed here: he is between two positions. One is doubt and the other is a belief prompted by fear. The latter would seem to be suggested by the one who "for pity's sake believes." The tension implicit in this stance is not resolved here or anywhere else in Cullen's poetry: he will rest neither in unbelief nor in an easy faith.

Overt religious motifs are found in such poems as **"Simon the Cyrenian Speaks," "Pagan Prayer," "The Shroud of Color,"** the companion pieces **"For a Skeptic"** and **"For a Fatalist,"** **"Judas Iscariot,"** and **"Gods"**—all from his first volume, *Color.* "Simon the Cyrenian Speaks" is a dramatic monologue delivered by a black follower of Christ, drafted to carry his cross, who accepts his calling when he understands his Master's dream transcends race, that he is not simply being asked to bear another burden as a black man. **"Pagan Prayer"** is a short poem, the meaning of which relates to the central tension of Heritage.

> Our Father, God; our Brother, Christ,
> Or are we bastard kin,

the poet asks prayerfully. He speaks of his "pagan mad" heart and prays that all "black sheep" be retrieved, a nice irony given both the obvious biblical values associated with straying sheep, as well as what the phrase "black sheep" usually means. **"The Shroud of Color"** is the poem that first gained Cullen important attention; it was published in the November 1924 issue of H. L. Mencken's *American Mercury.* It begins:

> "Lord, being dark," I said, "I cannot bear
> The further touch of earth, the scented air;
> Lord, being dark, forewilled to that despair
> My color shrouds me in, I am as dirt
> Beneath my brother's heel . . ."

And the answer seems to be:

> *"Dark child of sorrow, mine no less, what art*
> *Of mine can make thee see and play thy part?*
> *The key to all strange things is in thy heart."*

This poem, too, is a kind of parable, with its dialogue between the poet and the divine voice. The poet's resolve is to go on living, even in the shroud of color, living anxiously, to be sure, close to nature, in a kind of trembling but joyful hope.

In the epitaphs **"For a Skeptic"**—which points out that the skeptic may have more faith than he knows but in the wrong thing—and **"For a Fatalist"**—which holds that such a person has his ship wrecked even before he can hoist his sail—two irreligious postures are rejected. **"Judas Iscariot"** is a sentimental poem depicting Judas as having willingly played the destined role of betrayer, taking the "sorry part" out of great love and being thus forever scorned by unknowing people. Finally, **"Gods"** is an interesting short poem because it shows paganism again in conflict with Christianity. The poet says:

> I cannot hide from Him the gods
> That revel in my heart,
> Nor can I find an easy word
> To tell them to depart . . .

Just as "gods" is not capitalized—they are the idols of a pagan impulse—neither is "word" capitalized. But the allusion to the Word that dispels such gods seems unmistakable. Yet the poet says he cannot find "an easy word," and thus the tension remains.

Since **"The Black Christ"** is a long narrative poem that gives its name to the 1929 volume of Cullen's poetry, it should be mentioned here under the rubric of religious verse. It is the story of a black boy who is lynched and then in resurrection appears to his mother and brother. The poem's message is overt and rather diffuse: have faith in the mercy of God. There is nothing of black messianism here in spite of the title—the idea that a suffering black Christ might ultimately redeem white America, though this idea had long before appeared in the writings of Du Bois and others.

Traditional lyric poets traditionally deal with love and death, and Countee Cullen is no exception. This second category of thematic concern contains the largest group of his poems, including many love lyrics of one mood or another. Let an early example stand for his frequent verses in the *carpe diem* tradition. In **"To a Brown Girl"** Cullen says it this way:

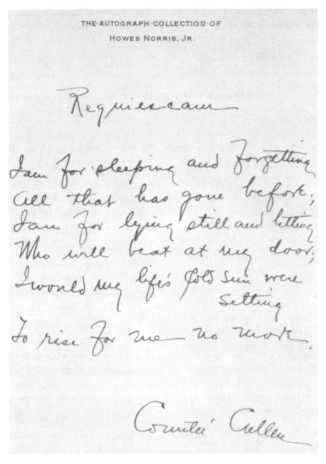

Handwritten copy of "Requiescam."

What if no puritanic strain
Confines him to the nice?
He will not pass this way again,
Nor hunger for you twice.

Since in the end consort together
Magdalen and Mary,
Youth is the time for careless weather:
Later, lass, be wary.

The inconstancy of love is also a traditional theme Cullen treated many times. The poems **"There Must Be Words"** and **"Nothing Endures"** from the 1929 volume may serve as examples. In the first he writes of love departing, leaving no external sign of its former presence:

After a decent show of mourning I,
As once I ever was, shall be as free
To look on love with calm unfaltering eye,
And marvel that such fools as lovers be.

And from the second:

Nothing endures,
Not even love,
Though the warm heart purrs
Of the length thereof.

Though beauty wax,
Yet shall it wane;
Time lays a tax
On the subtlest brain.

Let the blood riot,
Give it its will;
It shall grow quiet,
It shall grow still.

Claims made for paganism in love lyrics have been traditional through many centuries of English poetry, but since Cullen writes out of the black experience, this strand has an added weight in his poems. We have already seen the opposing Christian/Pagan claims in his religious poetry. His advice in **"To a Brown Boy"** is:

Lad, never dam your body's itch
When loveliness is seen.

And the word "dam" probably contains a deliberate ambiguity: neither condemn it nor attempt to obstruct its natural force. There is bliss, the poem continues, in "brown limbs,"

And lips know better how to kiss
Than how to raise white hymns.

The imagery here, typical in Cullen's poems, opposes brown/sensuality/paganism to white/spirituality/Christianity. At the same time a cold sterility is also a connotation of the latter. Cullen does not honor an ascetic purity. On the contrary, the humorous epitaph **"For a Virgin"** illustrates his gentle scorn for the unfulfilled. The wry ironic tone is typical of Cullen's poetry as the virgin speaks from the grave:

For forty years I shunned the lust
Inherent in my clay;
Death only was so amorous
I let him have his way.

Another clearly identifiable group of Cullen's love poems deals with the subject of love for a brown maiden as opposed to a white. Sense and spirit are in general the opposing claims. In **"A Song of Praise"** Cullen says of his dark love:

Her walk is like the replica
of some barbaric dance
Wherein the soul of Africa
Is winged with arrogance.

And from a later poem with almost the same title, **"Song of Praise"**:

Who lies with his milk-white maiden,
Bound in the length of her pale gold hair,
Cooled by her lips with the cold kiss laden,
He lies, but he loves not there.

Who lies with his nut-brown maiden,
Bruised to the bone with her sin-black hair,
Warmed with the wine that her full lips trade in,
He lies, and his love lies there.

This thought accurately represents also the theme of Cullen's long narrative poem, ***The Ballad of the Brown Girl,*** published separately in 1927 as an illustrated and decorated book. The poem tells in ballad stanzas the story of Lord Thomas, who must choose between Fair London (the white maiden) and the Brown Girl. He chooses the latter, but on their wedding day Fair London appears and she is stabbed by the Brown Girl. Lord Thomas kills the Brown Girl and then himself, and all three are buried in a common grave. One could construct an allegory or explore motives and values in all this, but what Cullen primarily sought to achieve was a poem of haunting and sensuous beauty. A short poem called **"Caprice"** also illustrates the light/dark tension; it depicts the inconstancy of love and the forgiving nature of the lover. It has the structure of a parable—a brief episode dramatically presented—and its theme must be inferred by the reader. While awaiting her unfaithful lover, the black woman swears to dismiss him when he returns.

> But when he came with his gay black head
> Thrown back, and his lips apart,
> She flipped a light hair from his coat,
> And sobbed against his heart.

The poem **"Ghosts"** may summarize Cullen's achievement in writing love lyrics. It begins:

> Breast under breast when you shall lie
> With him who in my place
> Bends over you with flashing eye
> And ever nearing face;
>
> Hand fast in hand when you shall tread
> With him the springing ways
> Of love from me inherited
> After my little phase;

He warns that his own ghostly presence may be felt, and then continues:

> But never let it trouble you,
> Or cost you one caress;
> Ghosts are soon sent with a word or two
> Back to their loneliness.

The sexual imagery is specific and concrete: Cullen is here very conscious of reality. There is a joy in recalling "the springing ways of love" that gives also a lightness to the poem. Most characteristic is the tone of ironic detachment. The love was merely a "little phase" that is now over. Linked with the detachment is the physical awareness that the woman is now in the arms of another and his resulting loneliness. The achievement of the last stanza is that all three impulses are held in suspension simultaneously.

One poem may stand as the best example of Cullen on death. His poem **"The Wise"** echoes his master, John Keats, "half in love with easeful death." In a quiet, contemplative mood appropriate to the title, Cullen presents in rhymed triplets the several reasons why death is to be desired, what in fact are the elements of wisdom. In the first place, knowledge is gained through the dark glass, literally, of the earth, knowledge of ultimate natural mysteries:

> Dead men are wisest, for they know
> How far the roots of flowers go,
> How long a seed must rot to grow.

This knowledge is perhaps not commanding in an emotional sense, but in the second stanza the senses are stilled and there is no feeling of joy or pain. This aspect of death is emotionally more satisfying to the weary:

> Dead men alone bear frost and rain
> On throbless heart and heatless brain,
> And feel no stir of joy or pain.

Thirdly, the soul is at rest because the raging of love and hate is quieted:

> Dead men alone are satiate;
> They sleep and dream and have no weight,
> To curb their rest, of love or hate.

Thus the dead are the wise, and indeed a good definition of wisdom for the living would include the elements of knowl-

edge, detachment, and peace. The poem concludes with a neat paradox:

> Strange, men should flee their company,
> Or think me strange who long to be
> Wrapped in their cool immunity.

In the concluding phrase "cool immunity" we have a particularly felicitous expression—appropriate to the tone, insightful, suggestive.

As we would expect of a lyric poet, Countee Cullen takes as his province the larger categories of religion, love, and death. Many of Cullen's poems, however, and here is added a new dimension of subject matter, are solely concerned with what he would call "color" or "race" and what we would call the black experience. Yet these divisions, as we have seen, are wholly arbitrary, for almost every poem already considered comes out of the black experience in one way or another. Many of them overtly refer to racial matters. Thus critics who assert that Cullen was not activist enough in orientation—and some are even harsher—would seem to have a rather narrow view of what a poet ought to be doing.

Before proceeding to this final category and its summary in **"Heritage,"** it should be noted that Cullen was good at making short poems of social satire and that he also wrote poems about poetry and poets. These two minor categories contain some of his most often quoted lines, although they are not particularly related in any way except that the pervasiveness of the black experience is again apparent, as our examples will show.

Cullen delighted in humorous epitaphs, and we have already seen some examples. Here is one about prostitutes, replete with great irony:

> Ours is the ancient story:
> Delicate flowers of sin,
> Lilies, arrayed in glory,
> That would not toil or spin.

The daring but ironically appropriate allusion to the biblical passage accounts for the wit. These "lilies" neither toil nor spin any more than their natural counterparts, but the glory of their raiment is of a different order from that envisioned in the Gospel. Or take the well-known example of Cullen's wit in the epitaph **"For a Lady I Know"**:

> She even thinks that up in heaven
> Her class lies late and snores,
> While poor black cherubs rise at seven
> To do celestial chores.

This will suffice to illustrate the type. There are several for men of letters—Keats, Conrad, and Dunbar. Perhaps the last of these is most poignant:

> Born of the sorrowful of heart
> Mirth was a crown upon his head;
> Pride kept his twisted lips apart
> In jest, to hide a heart that bled.

There are also other poems about poets and poetry—to Keats, Amy Lowell, and Emily Dickinson, for example. Cullen's poem **"Yet Do I Marvel,"** about the struggle of being a poet, and more particularly about the struggle of being a black poet, may serve as a transition to our final section. It begins:

I doubt not God is good, well-meaning, kind,
And did He stoop to quibble could tell why
The little buried mole continues blind,
Why flesh that mirrors Him must some day die . . .

Through classical allusion the poem poses the great mysteries of life. Its conclusion is:

Inscrutable His ways are, and immune
To catechism by a mind too strewn
With petty cares to slightly understand
What awful brain compels His awful hand.
Yet do I marvel at this curious thing:
To make a poet black, and bid him sing!

On the surface of the poem the tone is a playful irony, treating great mysteries as "quibbles" or "curious things." Yet the Creator's work seems uneven, death is the end of all of it, and there are grave questions involving man's choice and freedom. But the most curious thing of all is—and Cullen understands the irony of this particular culmination to the great mysteries—"To make a poet black, and bid him sing!" There is an implied ambiguity in the word "sing": one does not always sing for joy, though Cullen would not deny that even for a black poet there is a time for that too.

Of the poems that deal primarily with the black experience, it is appropriate to begin with two poems of initiation, both dramatic anecdotes presented in verse, one obviously based on an early experience in life and the other a later incident. The first is called **"Incident."** The subject matter of this poem is loss of innocence, and the impact of the poem depends partly on an incongruity between the subject matter and the form, as well as within the subject matter itself. Here is a smiling, friendly black boy eight years old—and to use the phrase "black boy" is to place it within context as part of a major motif in Afro-American literature—an innocent black boy who has an encounter with ugliness, evil.

Once riding in old Baltimore,
Heart-filled, head-filled with glee,
I saw a Baltimorean
Keep looking straight at me.

Now I was eight and very small,
And he was no whit bigger,
And so I smiled, but he poked out
His tongue, and called me, "Nigger."

There is, then, an incongruity between what a childhood experience ought to be and what it is. There is now a sad awareness in the last stanza; it was then shock.

I saw the whole of Baltimore
From May until December;
Of all the things that happened there
That's all that I remember.

What happened there wiped out all other memories; it is as though a portion of innocence were destroyed. The tension between innocence and experience is also reflected in the ambiguity between subject matter and verse form. It is a child's verse, highly regular in rhyme and meter, simple in diction. It could be a poem in "A Black Child's Garden of Verse." By way of comparison, hear one of Robert Louis Stevenson's poems from *his* collection. No doubt Cullen would have known Stevenson's poems, perhaps even this one called "Singing":

Of speckled eggs the birdie sings
And nests among the trees;

The sailor sings of ropes and things
In ships upon the seas.

The children sing in far Japan,
The children sing in Spain;
The organ with the organ man
Is singing in the rain.

Children sing in Baltimore, too, and, sadly, one thing they sing is "Nigger." Speckled eggs and birds and ropes and things and ships upon the seas—these should be the stuff of childhood. Cullen's **"Incident"** is all about finding a spider in the Rice Krispies. The sadness of the last stanza is not unwarranted.

Another poetic anecdote recounts an experience with a bitter, pipe-smoking black uncle, who says only, "White folks is white," and waits for the poet to understand and to feel the meaning of the statement. The poem **"Uncle Jim"** begins:

"White folks is white," says Uncle Jim;
"A platitude," I sneer;
And then I tell him so is milk,
And the froth upon his beer.

His heart welled up with bitterness,
He smokes his pungent pipe,
And nods at me as if to say,
"Young fool, you'll soon be ripe!"

At the end of the poem the poet is in the company of a white friend, who shares deeply his joys and sorrows and his interest in poetry, but still the poet's thoughts return to Uncle Jim. He wonders why. The unspoken implication is that there is an impassable gulf between the white and the black experience, however intimate the friendship. So the poem as initiation experience deals with separation as a fact of life, Cullen would say a sad fact of the present. Whether inevitable or forever is a question I think not answered in Cullen's poetry.

Anger and ominous warning is the theme of Cullen's **"From the Dark Tower,"** a poem that he places first in his second volume of poetry, *Copper Sun.* Another sonnet of considerable accomplishment, its octave reads:

We shall not always plant while others reap
The golden increment of bursting fruit,
Not always countenance, abject and mute,
That lesser men should hold their brothers cheap;
Not everlastingly while others sleep
Shall we beguile their limbs with mellow flute,
Not always bend to some more subtle brute;
We were not made eternally to weep.

The poetic diction—"bursting fruit" and "mellow flute"—makes the poem seem removed from reality, but the last line above—sad, angry, prophetic—is a sweeping line of ringing militancy: "We were not made eternally to weep." Ominous warning is also the theme of **"Mood,"** a poem that captures an angry mood in the black experience. It begins:

I think an impulse stronger than my mind
May some day grasp a knife, unloose a vial,
Or with a little leaden ball unbind
The cords that tie me to the rank and file.
My hands grow quarrelsome with bitterness,
And darkly bent upon the final fray;
Night with its stars upon a grave seems less
Indecent than the too complacent day.

What are these cords that keep him from violence, that restrain him and his mass of brothers? Who controls them? Are they good restraints on an impulse toward destructive savagery or are they chains? And the ambiguous "final fray" may mean Armageddon. But who will win, or will all be destroyed? Such questions are implicit in this heavily suggestive poem. The impulse was later to be embodied in Bigger Thomas, and James Baldwin much later would say that no Negro living in America has not felt it, briefly or for long periods, in some varying degree of intensity. Yet it remains only an impulse for Cullen, as for Baldwin, his pupil in a Harlem junior high school, years later, who also had a minister father. The end of the poem reveals that Cullen's religious background is never far beneath the surface:

> God knows I would be kind, let live, speak fair,
> Requite an honest debt with more than just,
> And love for Christ's dear sake those shapes that wear
> A pride that had its genesis in dust,—
> The meek are promised much in a book I know
> But one grows weary turning cheek to blow.

Another familiar mood, the Negro as expatriate, is captured in one of the poems in the 1935 volume, a poem called **"To France."** Cullen praises that country as a place where blacks most feel free:

> There might I only breathe my latest days,
> With those rich accents falling on my ear
> That most have made me feel that freedom's rays
> Still have a shrine where they may leap and sear,—
> Though I were palsied there, or halt, or blind,
> So I were there, I think I should not mind.

The last poem in this last volume (not including, of course, the posthumously published *On These I Stand* of 1947) is perhaps the most militant protest poem that Cullen wrote. It is called **"Scottsboro, Too, Is Worth Its Song,"** and it is dedicated to "American Poets." The clear but unspoken criticism in the poem is that the American poets who wrote eloquently about Sacco and Vanzetti (including Cullen himself) failed to notice the Scottsboro incident. It is appropriate that Cullen should choose to close his last volume of new poems with **"Scottsboro."** Cullen is the representative and symbolic figure of the Harlem Renaissance, and the Scottsboro tragedy of 1931 was the traumatic experience in the black community that ended this literary flowering. A few lines will reveal the tone of the poem:

> I said:
> Now will the poets sing,—
> Their cries go thundering
> Like blood and tears
> Into the nation's ears,
> Like lightning dart
> Into the nation's heart.

And these were his reasons:

> Here in epitome
> Is all disgrace
> And epic wrong,
> Like wine to brace
> The minstrel heart, and blare it into song.

We know the nation was not called to account by its poets. Here is Cullen's ironic conclusion:

> Surely, I said,
> Now will the poets sing.
> But they have raised no cry.
> I wonder why.

Cullen's relevancy, if it need be proved, is demonstrated forty years later with an incident at Jackson State College. The difference is that Scottsboro was not followed by its Kent State.

Thus many of the aspects of the black experience are reflected in Countee Cullen's poetry: awareness of a dehumanizing racism, uniqueness, and separatism, yearning for freedom, anger, and militant protest. And there is one thing more that adds to his scope. As the representative artist of the Harlem Renaissance, he may well have written the best poem about Harlem. It is called **"Harlem Wine."** It begins:

> This is not water running here,
> These thick rebellious streams
> That hurtle flesh and bone past fear
> Down alleyways of dreams.

The wine is a narcotic and at the same time a symbol of a dark race. All this is said in the poem: Whatever is running in Harlem is darker and more intoxicating, more vital than white water. It is rebellious because Harlem is a place apart, representing values other than those in white America. The wine gives courage when there may be fear; it represents a deep and dreamlike racial heritage. The primitivism of the poem concludes with the joy of music and dance presented in the imagery of lovemaking. All this is summarized in a place symbolizing human communication, personal relations, identity—the place is Harlem.

The heritage that is alluded to in **"Harlem Wine"** is fully developed in Cullen's finest poem, called **"Heritage."** A devastating irony pervades the poem, and part of the irony is the ambiguity of its title. What is the heritage of the Afro-American? It is Africa, of course, "three centuries removed," as Cullen rather wryly notes about his own case. But it is also the Western, that is, Christian, tradition. We have seen how this tension is a central motif in Cullen's poetry. The fact is that this tension is a central motif in black literature, never more explicitly and accurately stated than in Du Bois's famous passage about the quality of "twoness" in the black experience.

"Heritage" is not simply about Africa; nor is it simply an attack on Christianity. It says, however, something much better understood now than it was fifty years ago: that the part of Christianity which is merely the result of Western culture is an excrescence. Nor should **"Heritage"** be read on the simple level of tom-tom paganism. To Cullen Africa is a symbol; it is like the dark Harlem wine. One must not expect the real Africa to be depicted here; Cullen knew no more about the real Africa than did Keats about the real Provençal. Cullen has translated a myth into poetry in order to embody concretely, not to deny, the power of that myth. The poem begins:

> What is Africa to me:
> Copper sun or scarlet sea,
> Jungle star or jungle track,
> Strong bronzed men or regal black
> Women from whose loins I sprang
> When the birds of Eden sang?
> *One three centuries removed*
> *From the scenes his fathers loved*
> *Spicy grove, cinnamon tree,*
> *What is Africa to me?*

As an example of a too literal response to this poem, one recent critic has objected to the presence of the cinnamon tree of Ceylon in these lines, a tree which the critic asserts is not found in Africa. No doubt Countee Cullen would have enjoyed this critical comment because he surely would have known the famous complaint about Keats choosing Cortez to discover the Pacific Ocean. With great irony, because with great self-knowledge, the poet asks what Africa can mean to him. His immediate response is clear: nothing. And yet this is not true either. "So I lie," begins the second stanza, and there follow three stanzas picturing the remorseless, inexorable pull of that African heritage. The rhythm of the poem pulsates from one wave of strong emotion such as this:

> So I lie, whose fount of pride
> Dear distress, and joy allied,
> Is my somber flesh and skin,
> With the dark blood damned within
> Like great pulsing tides of wine
> That I fear must burst the fine
> Channels of the chafing net
> Where they surge and foam and fret.

The "tides of wine" image symbolizing the African heritage, as in **"Harlem Wine,"** is used again here. Then the poem subsides for a cool, ironic, "civilized" moment:

> Africa? A book one thumbs
> Listlessly, till slumber comes.

Such a book is, after all, the nearest the poet has come to a "real" experience with the "real" Africa. And then a swelling wave once again comes with an orgiastic culmination:

> I can never rest at all
> When the rain begins to fall
> Like a soul gone mad with pain
> I must match its weird refrain;
> Ever must I twist and squirm,
> Writhing like a baited worm,
> While its primal measures drip
> Through my body crying, "Strip!
> Doff this new exuberance.
> Come and dance the Lover's Dance!"

Then an introspective quiet couplet summarizes what is essentially the first part of the poem:

> In an old remembered way
> Rain works on me night and day.

Next the other part of the poet's heritage is put forth—the opposing claim, also powerful—the Western tradition: reason and distrust of emotion, civilization looking askance on primitive heathens, Christianity. Cullen proceeds quietly and with great irony, well aware of the self-righteousness of what he says:

> Quaint, outlandish heathen gods
> Black men fashion out of rods,
> Clay, and brittle bits of stone,
> In a likeness like their own,
> My conversion came high-priced;
> I belong to Jesus Christ,
> Preacher of humility;
> Heathen gods are naught to me.

Such is the counterclaim: patronizing, stuffy, superior, proud (as it is said) in all humility. In that voice the poet says he is superior because his belief is "high-priced"; it is not simply a matter of fashioning some idol out of whatever is at hand. One must pay; one must give up something. And what one denies always includes the Lover's Dance. Besides, African gods look like Africans. Cullen's irony is devastating because he is so well aware of what the Christian God looks like. He is above all proud, extremely proud, to belong to Jesus Christ,

preacher of humility. This, too, is part of the black experience.

In the next stanza the ironic mask is put aside. The poet says he is playing a double part; the tension remains. The tone is reverent, confessional. If Christ were black, the poet says, he could be sure that Christ knew the pain of black men. Then Cullen returns to several lines of characteristic irony:

> Lord, I fashion dark gods, too,
> Daring even to give You
> Dark despairing features . . .

And then the quiet summary of this section:

> Lord, forgive me if my need
> Sometimes shapes a human creed.

The last stanza recapitulates but does not resolve the central tension of **"Heritage."** Returning to both strands of his heritage, he first addresses that part symbolized by Africa in these words:

> *One thing only must I do:*
> *Quench my pride and cool my blood,*
> *Lest I perish in the flood.*

And then for that part symbolized by the word "civilization":

> *Not yet has my heart or head*
> *In the least way realized*
> *They and I are civilized.*

Cullen says here: I know but I have not yet realized. This paradox would seem to be a great poetic statement of the "twoness" referred to by Du Bois—which is to say, a great poetic statement of the black experience.

And the black experience—I think Cullen would maintain—is part of the human experience. When the artist can discover and reveal the black experience in his art, he is thereby adding to our knowledge of the human experience. This is what Cullen's poetry succeeds in doing, still another marvel, now beyond the question of black and white. (pp. 103-25)

> *Nicholas Canaday, Jr., "Major Themes in the Poetry of Countee Cullen," in* The Harlem Renaissance Remembered, *edited by Arna Bontemps, Dodd, Mead & Company, 1972, pp. 103-25.*

HOUSTON A. BAKER, JR.   (essay date 1974)

> [*A poet and educator, Baker has contributed critical interpretations of black literature to anthologies and periodicals, including* Phylon, Black World, *and* The Virginia Quarterly Review. *In addition, he is the editor of critical volumes on African, Caribbean, and black American literature. In the following excerpt, Baker surveys prominent themes and techniques in Cullen's poetry.*]

In a headnote in *Caroling Dusk,* Cullen states that one of his chief problems was "reconciling a Christian upbringing with a pagan inclination." The poems in *Color* reveal the accuracy of his comment, for a dichotomy pervades the volume. Faith and doubt, hedonism and reverence, innocence and experience, white and black, life and death are constantly juxtaposed, and the tensions that result often lead to striking poems. In the dedicatory poem, for example, the brevity of existence is set against the implied immortality of the poet, and the germination of spring is seen as a foil for the destructiveness of winter:

When the dreadful Ax
Rives me apart,
When the sharp wedge cracks
My arid heart,
Turn to this book
Of the singing me
For a springtime look
At the wintry tree.

("To You Who Read My Book")

And in "Tableau," Cullen uses nature imagery to demonstrate the contrast between black and white, the natural and the artificial:

Locked arm in arm they cross the way,
The black boy and the white,
The golden splendor of the day,
The sable pride of night.

From lowered blinds the dark folk stare,
And here the fair folk talk,
Indignant that these two should dare
In unison to walk.

The boys are outside, joined in the natural camaraderie of youth, while their elders—both Black and white—gossip about their friendship behind lowered blinds. Bertram Woodruff has commented aptly on the bifurcation in Cullen's poetry between a cynical realism and a subjective idealism—a materialistic and a theistic conception of life [see *TCLC*, Vol. 4, pp. 42-3]—and James Weldon Johnson noted the poet's sudden ironic turns of thought [see *TCLC*, Vol. 4, p. 41]. These are essential characteristics of the canon and grow, in part, out of the conflicts occasioned by Cullen's aesthetic stance. The poet who did not want his work bolstered by racial considerations begins *Color* with twenty-four racial poems. The artist who adopted the romantic mode is pulled continually toward the darker side of this realm, and his work abounds in pessimism and despair. Divided into four sections—Color, Epitaphs, For Love's Sake, and Varia—*Color* expresses the major themes of the canon.

The racial poems in the volume range from the somewhat bombastic "The Shroud of Color" to the magnificently sustained and accomplished "Heritage" with a variety of noble sentiment, libertinism, atavism, fine description, and "initiation" filling out the middle range. Arthur Davis has demonstrated that one of the chief subjects of the opening section is alienation and exile [see *TCLC*, Vol. 4, pp. 44-6]:

For Cullen, the Negro is both a geographical and a spiritual exile. He has lost not only an idyllic homeland; but equally as important, he has also lost understanding pagan gods who would be far more sympathetic to his peculiar needs than the pale Christian deities.

One finds this sense of displacement in poems such as "Atlantic City Waiter," "Near White," "Brown Boy to Brown Girl," "Pagan Prayer," and "Heritage." In these poems, the Black man is conceived as a deracinated individual pulled abruptly from some edenic place and set amidst strange gods. But there are also poems that show no sense of alienation; they simply enjoin a hedonistic existence. "To a Brown Girl," for example, offers the following comment:

What if his glance is bold and free,
His mouth the lash of whips?
So should the eyes of lovers be;
And so a lover's lips.

And "To a Brown Boy" gives similar advice:

That brown girl's swagger gives a twitch
To beauty like a queen;
Lad, never dam your body's itch
When loveliness is seen.

There are poems, moreover, that have more to do with a specific social situation than with a feeling of exile. "A Brown Girl Dead" and "Saturday's Child" are both ironical protests against economic oppression:

Her mother pawned her wedding ring
To lay her out in white;
She'd be so proud she'd dance and sing
To see herself tonight.

("A Brown Girl Dead")

For I was born on Saturday—
"Bad time for planting a seed,"
Was all my father had to say,
And, "One mouth more to feed."

Death cut the strings that gave me life,
And handed me to Sorrow,
The only kind of middle wife
My folks could beg or borrow.

("Saturday's Child")

The dominant feeling of the racial poems, however, is (in the words of Claude McKay) one of being "born, far from my native clime, / Under the white man's menace, out of time."

"Yet Do I Marvel" and "Heritage" capture the irony and ambiguity of this situation. The former is devastating in its restrained cynicism:

I doubt not God is good, well-meaning, kind,
And did He stoop to quibble could tell why
The little buried mole continues blind,
Why flesh that mirrors Him must some day die.

The list of incongruities moves to the assertion that God's ways are too grandiose for the simple human mind; then with a swift stroke of genius, come the concluding lines:

Yet do I marvel at this curious thing:
To make a poet black, and bid him sing!

The *angst* of Cullen's aesthetic is summed up in this couplet. By association, the Black poet takes on the burdens of the disinherited and is doomed to the tortures of Sisyphus and Tantalus; the persona exposes both his own skepticism and the awesome task of the Black artist.

"Heritage" displays the same sense of irony and skepticism. The poem opens with what turns out to be a rhetorical question:

What is Africa to me:
Copper sun or scarlet sea,
Jungle star or jungle track,
Strong bronzed men, or regal black
Women from whose loins I sprang
When the birds of Eden sang?

The text reveals that Africa is not only the spirit realm to which the narrator feels most allied, but also a land in fierce opposition to his present home. As in McKay's "Flame-Heart," the narrator of "Heritage" makes a claim that is not justified by the poem itself:

Africa? A book one thumbs
Listlessly, till slumber comes.

Unremembered are her bats
Circling through the night, her cats
Crouching in the river reeds,
Stalking gentle flesh that feeds
By the river brink. . . .

The vivid descriptions of its fierce flowers and pagan impulses show that Africa is much more than bedtime reading for the narrator. Moreover, when he states that he is trying to move beyond the call of heathen deities, the text leaps forth in refutation. Some critics have faulted Cullen for **"Heritage,"** stating that he makes topographical mistakes and perpetuates the idea of the Black man as a "noble savage." Such responses can carry one only so far, however, with a poem as thoroughly ironical as **"Heritage."** While it is true that there is an undue enthusiasm recurrent in the passages on Africa, it is also true that Cullen was interested in a blatant contrast between the benign and unsmiling deities of the new land and the thoroughly initiated gods of the old. The entire poem is placed in a confessional framework as the narrator tries to define his relationship to some white, ontological being and finds that a Black impulse ceaselessly draws him back. The italicized concluding lines read like the penance exacted from an unregenerate schoolboy:

All day long and all night through,
One thing only must I do:
Quench my pride and cool my blood,
Lest I perish in the flood,
Lest a hidden ember set
Timber that I thought was wet
Burning like the dryest flax,
Melting like the merest wax,
Lest the grave restore its dead.
Not yet has my heart or head
In the least way realized
They and I are civilized.

"Heritage" is a longer and more comprehensive statement of the message contained in **"Pagan Prayer,"** and it reveals the sharp line that Cullen saw dividing two cultures. The poet's "paganism" reveals itself in the end as a repudiation of the white man's religion.

A poem like **"Incident"** reveals why such a rejection is necessary:

Once riding in old Baltimore,
Heart-filled, head-filled with glee,
I saw a Baltimorean
Keep looking straight at me.

Now I was eight and very small,
And he was no whit bigger,
And so I smiled, but he poked out
His tongue, and called me, "Nigger."

I saw the whole of Baltimore
From May until December;
Of all the things that happened there
That's all that I remember.

The sense of irony and the dichotomized world-view that appear throughout Cullen's work are skillfully captured here. There is a movement from gay innocence to initiation, which is repeated in the seasonal reference ("May until December"), and at the time of recounting the speaker has not forgotten the incident. Not only the vistas of Baltimore, one suspects, but the whole of his life has been clouded by the sudden realization that the norms of the larger society do not work

for him. Adjustment often involves the type of repudiation seen in **"Heritage"** and **"Pagan Prayer."**

The two themes that stand out in ***Color***'s nonracial poems are love and mortality. The second section consists of twenty-nine epitaphs written in the manner of Edgar Lee Masters's *Spoon River Anthology*. Cullen, however, is not interested in showing what the restrictions of the village do to the human psyche. He is concerned with the many types that make up society, and thus the poems display subtle irony, tender feeling, and adept portraiture. **"For a Lady I Know"** captures in miniature the type of woman whom the poet's atavistic **"Atlantic City Waiter"** might have served:

She even thinks that up in heaven
Her class lies late and snores,
While poor black cherubs rise at seven
To do celestial chores.

"For My Grandmother" demonstrates Cullen's ability to set forth mild sentiments:

This lovely flower fell to seed;
Work gently, sun and rain;
She held it as her dying creed
That she would grow again.

There is fine irony in both **"For a Virgin"** and **"For an Atheist"**:

For forty years I shunned the lust
Inherent in my clay;
Death only was so amorous
I let him have his way.

and

Mountains cover me like rain,
Billows whirl and rise;
Hide me from the stabbing pain
In His reproachful eyes.

Finally, there is the often quoted **"For Paul Laurence Dunbar"**:

Born of the sorrowful of heart,
Mirth was a crown upon his head;
Pride kept his twisted lips apart
In jest, to hide a heart that bled.

Though the poems as a group offer a comment on various styles of human life, the overwhelming fact of the sequence—as of all epitaphs—is the common end to which flesh is heir. This condition brings about much of the humor that resides in the individual sketches, and the same sense of mortality occasions the despair that appears in a number of the poems in the concluding sections of ***Color.***

It may seem commonplace to say that Cullen's romanticism is derivative, but in the context of nineteenth-century English poetry, the statement becomes more descriptive. Though the poet chose as his ideal the second wave of British romanticism, including Keats and Shelley, his own lyrics read more like the work of Dante Rossetti, Charles Swinburne, and the authors of *fin de siécle* England. These were the romantics *manqué* who shared the same lyrical impulses but lacked the sweeping vision, the mythicizing potential, and the colossal certainties of their predecessors. The shades of Ernest Dowson and Arthur Symons appear with the first lines of **"Oh, for a Little While Be Kind"**:

Oh, for a little while be kind to me
Who stand in such imperious need of you,
And for a fitful space let my head lie
Happily on your passion's frigid breast.

The moment of contentment is brief, and though the poem ends on an ironical note, its basic assumptions are that life is fleeting and love is short. **"If You Should Go"** deals once again with the departure of the beloved, and **"To One Who Said Me Nay"** is a restatement of the familiar *carpe diem* theme. **"Advice to Youth"** follows the same pattern, while **"Caprice"** captures the heart-rending and incomprehensible ways of love:

"I'll tell him, when he comes," she said,
"Body and baggage, to go,
Though the night be darker than my hair,
And the ground be hard with snow."

But when he came with his gay black head
Thrown back, and his lips apart,
She flipped a light hair from his coat,
And sobbed against his heart.

The male figure here reminds one of the protagonist in **"Two Who Crossed a Line (He Crosses),"** and once again we see the contrasts that mark Cullen's verse—harmony and discontent, light and dark. Both **"Sacrament"** and **"Bread and Wine"**—as one might expect—juxtapose the sacred and the profane. In the first, the speaker is considered unworthy of the beloved; in the second, the beloved is deemed the only thing holy in a mortal world. Cullen's use of religious imagery in the two poems is in harmony with his canon as a whole, for time and again there are biblical allusions. The final poem in the third section, **"Spring Reminiscence,"** moves quite well until the final couplet, where the merger of a religious allusion with a colloquialism destroys the effect. The poem, however, has thematic significance, for it is a memory in spring of springs gone by. There is the possibility, in other words, of resurrecting the joy and beauty of the past through the agency of poetry. The poet and his experiences possess a certain immortality, and spring—the time of nature's rejuvenation—becomes symbolic of enduring spirituality.

All of this cannot be inferred from **"Spring Reminiscence,"** of course, but the stanza quoted earlier from **"To You Who Read My Book,"** combined with **"In Memory of Col. Charles Young"** and **"To John Keats, Poet: At Springtime,"** make the argument clearer. Young, the Black colonel who was retired from the army at the beginning of World War I to prevent his promotion to general, becomes one with nature in the course of the poem:

The great dark heart is like a well
Drained bitter by the sky,
And all the honeyed lies they tell
Come there to thirst and die.

No lie is strong enough to kill
The roots that work below;
From your rich dust and slaughtered will
A tree with tongues will grow.

And there is a similar merger and generative process in **"To John Keats, Poet: At Springtime"**:

And you and I, shall we lie still,
John Keats, while Beauty summons us?
Somehow I feel your sensitive will
Is pulsing up some tremulous
Sap road of a maple tree, whose leaves
Grow music as they grow, since your

Wild voice is in them, a harp that grieves
For life that opens death's dark door.
Though dust, your fingers still can push
The Vision Splendid to a birth,
Though now they work as grass in the hush
Of the night on the broad sweet page of the earth.

Part of Cullen's "pagan inclination" displays itself in poems like these, where he not only reminds us of the ineluctability of the spiritual, but also recalls the fact that spring (before its arrogation by Christianity) was a time of bacchanalian celebration and heady splendor in the grass. For the poet, spring is the season when the natural man, the sensitive soul, and the germinating seed push forth in a rebirth of wonder.

Finally in *Color* are Cullen's concern for the outcast—**"Black Magdalens," "For Daughters of Magdalen,"** and **"Judas Iscariot"**—and his treatment of the idealistic dreamer. The poet achieves a masterful irony by placing streetwalkers in a biblical context:

They fare full ill since Christ forsook
The cross to mount a throne,
And Virtue still is stooping down
To cast the first hard stone.

and

Ours is the ancient story:
Delicate flowers of sin,
Lilies, arrayed in glory,
That would not toil nor spin.

Judas is viewed as a man who had to betray Christ so the vision He cherished would come true. In **"Simon the Cyrenian Speaks,"** the persona says:

But He was dying for a dream,
And He was very meek,
And in His eyes there shone a gleam
Men journeyed far to seek.

In **"For a Poet,"** the creative artist is also viewed as a keeper of dreams. Like other matter in Cullen's canon, therefore, Christianity is seen in a dual light. Insofar as God is cryptic or inscrutable in *Color*'s first two poems, He is the object of cynicism and repudiation; as Christ, the carrier of the dream, however, He is to be ranked among the highest idealists.

"I've kept on doing the same things, and doing them no better. I have never gotten to the things I really wanted to do," Dunbar told James Weldon Johnson as he suffered the agonies of his final illness. Some would expect a similar confession from Countee Cullen, since *Color* is his finest volume, although he went on to produce four more. If the poet had made a similar statement, he would have falsified his own accomplishments. Some things he did a good deal better as his career progressed. From his early efforts, he moved to the fine group of poems labelled "Interlude" in *The Black Christ*, and he developed his narrative voice in *The Ballad of the Brown Girl*. He not only provided a rendering of Euripides's *Medea*, but also did work as a translator. And in his final volume, he seems to counteract—through the sanity and balance of his verse—Benjamin Brawley's charge that "there is a sophomoric note in the work of Mr. Cullen that he finds it hard to outgrow" [see *TCLC*, Vol. 4, pp. 41-2].

The overriding dichotomy in the second volume is one of stasis and change. On the one hand, the poet believes despair is enduring and death the bitter end of all. On the other, he sees a better day approaching, the possibility of regeneration and immortality, and death as an occasion for solace and wisdom. The seven racial poems in *Copper Sun* fall generally on the positive side. Though he is now battered and scarred, there is a new day coming for the Black American:

> We shall not always plant while others reap
> The golden increment of bursting fruit,
> Not always countenance, abject and mute,
> That lesser men should hold their brothers cheap
>
> > ("From the Dark Tower")

> If for a day joy masters me,
>
> Think not my wounds are healed;
>
> • • • • •
>
> They shall bear blossoms with the fall;
> I have their word for this,
> Who tend my roots with rains of gall,
> And suns of prejudice.
>
> > ("Confession")

> Our flesh that was a battle-ground
> Shows now the morning-break;
> The ancient deities are downed
> For Thy eternal sake.
> Now that the past is left behind,
> Fling wide Thy garment's hem
> To keep us one with Thee in mind,
> Thou Christ of Bethlehem.
>
> > ("The Litany of the Dark People")

The metaphor of germination appears (particularly in **"Threnody for a Brown Girl"**), and the last poem in the group seems to favor an acceptance of the white man's religion as a means of salvation. Despite the laconic warning of Uncle Jim that "White folks is white," the speaker in most of the poems has adopted the attitude that improvement is a reality for the Black American. There are tones of apocalypse in both **"From the Dark Tower"** and **"Confession,"** but **"The Litany of the Dark People"** does much to soften them.

The optimism of the first section is out of harmony with the remainder of *Copper Sun*, for a note of despondency sounds with **"Pity the Deep in Love."** And while there is a contrapuntal rhythm between this and the poems that speak of the eternality of beauty and the splendor of the dream, the pervasive timbre is melancholy:

> Pity the deep in love;
> They move as men asleep,
> Traveling a narrow way
> Precipitous and steep.
>
> > ("Pity the Deep in Love")

> But never past the frail intent
> My will may flow,
> Though gentle looks of yours are bent
> Upon me where I go.
>
> So must I, starved for love's delight,
> Affect the mute,
> When love's divinest acolyte
> Extends me holy fruit.
>
> > ("Timid Lover")

> Of all men born he deems himself so much accurst,
> His plight so piteous, his proper pain so rare,
> The very bread he eats so dry, so fierce his thirst,
> What shall we liken such a martyr to? Compare
> Him to a man with poison raging in his throat,
> And far away the one mind with an antidote.
>
> > ("Portrait of a Lover")

the unrequited love, dejection, indifference, *carpe diem,* and sighing in *Copper Sun* would have delighted the nineteenth-century decadent poets and would stimulate anew the pale shades of Sir John Suckling and Edmund Waller. Cullen's songs of desperation in the second volume do not seem to have a substantial base; somehow they come across as exercises in depression rather than genuine reflections of the poet's inner being. It is, of course, difficult to argue about the effect a poem has on the reader, and one should steer clear of Wimsatt and Beardsley's "affective fallacy"—contemplating a poem as though it were the ground for some ultimate emotional state. What heightens one's impression of insincerity, however, is the body of poems that state exactly the opposite point of view.

The lovers' relationship may not terminate entirely, and there is always a nagging hope in the background:

> What if you come
> Again and swell
> The throat of some
> Mute bird;
> How shall I tell?
> How shall I know
> That it is so,
> Having heard?
>
> > ("Words to My Love")

> Come, let us plant our love as farmers plant
> A seed, and you shall water it with tears,
> And I shall weed it with my hands until
> They bleed. Perchance this buried love of ours
> Will fall on goodly ground and bear a tree
> With fruit and flowers . . .
>
> > ("The Love Tree")

Though love departs, its beauty may either linger or be reborn. And this ambiguity is also present in the poet's treatment of death, for in **"To Lovers of Earth: Fair Warning"** he states that man's end is certain and that it goes unmarked by nature. In the following poem, **"In Spite of Death,"** however, the speaker says:

> No less shall I in some new fashion flare
> Again, when death has blown my candles out;
> Although my blood went down in shameful rout
> Tonight, by all this living frame holds fair,
> Though death should closet me tonight, I swear
> Tomorrow's sun would find his cupboard bare.

In **"Cor Cordium," "The Poet,"** and **"To Endymion,"** Cullen once again views the poet and his song as immortal and further confuses the issue with **"Hunger"** and **"At the Wailing Wall in Jerusalem,"** where he views both dreams and the holy wall as tokens of everlasting beauty.

The question is not one of arrangement in *Copper Sun;* no new scheme would alter the content of the individual poems. Cullen seems to have been confronted with the problem of choosing between alternatives. The smaller number of racial poems is an indication that he had decided to steer closer to the universal romantic ideal, but the prevailing dichotomy and the issue of "belief in poetry" that it raises give evidence that he had not found a firm base on which to stand as a romantic poet. He laments, derides, and protests the passing of love and life but never faces the issues of despair and mortality in a convincing manner. One suspects that Harvey Webster had *Copper Sun* very much in mind when he wrote:

"Cullen neither accepted nor developed a comprehensive world-view. As a consequence his poems seem to result from occasional impulses rather than from directions by an integrated individual" [see *TCLC*, Vol. 4, pp. 43-4]. Of course, one knows that Cullen was anything but an "integrated individual" and that the bifurcations in his *Weltanschauung* result, in part, from his aesthetic stance. They play an important role in *Color.* In the second volume, however, the division between stasis and change is accompanied by a narrowing of range and blatant contradictions that cause one to think back on Brawley's statement with a smile of assent.

The Ballad of the Brown Girl: An Old Ballad Retold makes much more effective use of the divisions that are basic to Cullen's poetry. The narrator insists that the story was garnered from the grandams "in the land where the grass is blue," and it is not surprising that an English ballad should find its way into the repertoire of a Kentucky storyteller, since some regions of that state were at one time considered the finest preserves of British Elizabethan dialect. What is striking is the interpretation that Cullen places on the ballad. Rather than a story of a "dark brown" peasant contending with a fair city maiden for the heart of an aristocrat, the story is presented as a small and colorful drama of miscegenation and conflict. The leitmotif and moral involve the dangers of the acquisitive instincts, and Lord Thomas's mother is left with the burden of the guilt. Cullen shows himself a master of the ballad stanza in the poem, and his unique rendering of the tale makes it possible for him to engage in fine color imagery:

> Her hair was black as sin is black
> And ringed about with fire;
> Her eyes were black as night is black
> When moon and stars conspire;
> Her mouth was one red cherry clipt
> In twain, her voice a lyre.

or

> Her skin was white as almond milk
> Slow trickling from the flower;
> Her frost-blue eyes were darkening
> Like clouds before a shower.

There are several things that mar the poem. First, the hero is a pale and nervous spectre when the ballad opens, a man who must kneel before his mother to learn which woman to choose. At the end, he is a farseeing individual capable of an ennobling suicide. T. S. Eliot's reservations about Hamlet might well apply to Lord Thomas. Second, Cullen—after a skillful dramatic buildup and climax—relies upon description for his denouement. Finally, the ascription of guilt to the mother seems simplistic, as do the morals of most ballads. Cullen could have mined his material, however, for a more complex statement of the issues his interpretation raises. There are also several infelicities of style.

The Black Christ and Other Poems represents a marked progression in Cullen's thought. The volume closes rather than opens with a section titled "Color," and the beginning "Varia" group makes a number of definite statements about the poet and the age in which he lives. In **"To the Three for Whom the Book,"** the speaker is the committed, romantic poet—the man who dwells above the bending of an "idolatrous knee" to stone and steel. He is the individual who writes of "old, unhappy, far-off things, / And battles long ago." **"That Bright Chimeric Beast"** reinforces the point:

> That bright chimeric beast
> Conceived yet never born,
> Save in the poet's breast,
> The white-flanked unicorn,
> Never may be shaken
> From his solitude;
> Never may be taken
> In any earthly wood.

There is lost love and despondency in *The Black Christ,* but the volume also expresses a sincerity and a certainty about the artist's task that are lacking in *Copper Sun.* In **"To an Unknown Poet,"** the dreamer is removed from an unholy time, and in **"Counter Mood,"** the speaker asserts his own immortality. **"A Miracle Demanded"** comes as a surprise from the poet who marched to a pagan drummer in *Color;* he now asks for a renewal of his faith and a confirmation of the position taken in **"Counter Mood."** Finally, there are poems like **"A Wish," "Minutely Hurt,"** and **"Self Criticism"** that show a movement toward a more balanced view of life. In **"Minutely Hurt,"** there is little of the dire lamentation of the rejected lover, and the other two poems express the poet's hope that when he has had his say he will possess the wisdom and courage to stop writing. Meanwhile, the dreamer's life remains one of commitment and loneliness:

> The poet is compelled to love his star,
> Not knowing he could never tell you why
> Though silence makes inadequate reply.
>
> ("**Tongue-Tied**")

> A hungry cancer will not let him rest
> Whose heart is loyal to the least of dreams;
> There is a thorn forever in his breast
> Who cannot take his world for what it seems;
> Aloof and lonely must he ever walk,
> Plying a strange and unaccustomed tongue,
> An alien to the daily round of talk,
> Mute when the sordid songs of earth are sung.
> ("**A Thorn Forever in the Breast**")

The sense of maturity and dedication in *The Black Christ* results first, from the marital difficulties Cullen was encountering when a number of the poems were written. Second, the volume was composed in France, and it is possible that Cullen felt he could be "just a poet" there:

> As he whose eyes are gouged craves light to see,
> And he whose limbs are broken strength to run,
> So have I sought in you that alchemy
> That knits my bones and turns me to the sun;
> And found across a continent of foam
> What was denied my hungry heart at home.
> ("**To France,**" from *The Medea and Some Poems*)

Third, when *The Black Christ* was published, he had tentatively resolved the problem of a Christian background and a pagan inclination.

"Interlude," the section that deals with the termination of a love affair, constitutes one of the most unified and consistent groups of Cullen's poetry, and its careful style and unfeigned simplicity are akin to George Meredith's *Modern Love.* Two poems capture the spirit and the mastery of the group:

> I know of all the words I speak or write,
> Precious and woven of a vibrant sound,
> None ever snares your faith, intrigues you quite,
> Or sends you soaring from the solid ground.
> You are the level-headed lover who
> Can match my fever while the kisses last,

But you are never shaken through and through;
Your roots are firm after the storm has passed.

I shall know nights of tossing in my sleep
Fondling a hollow where a head should lie;
But you a calm review, no tears to weep,
No wounds to dress, no futile breaths to sigh.
Ever this was the way of wind with flame:
To harry it, then leave swift as it came.

                                        (**"The Simple Truth"**)

Breast under breast when you shall lie
With him who in my place
Bends over you with flashing eye
And ever nearing face;

Hand fast in hand when you shall tread
With him the springing ways
Of love from me inherited
After my little phase;

Be not surprised if suddenly
The couch of air confound
Your ravished ears upbraidingly,
And silence turn to sound.

But never let it trouble you,
Or cost you one caress;
Ghosts are soon sent with a word or two
Back to their loneliness.

                                        (**"Ghosts"**)

Cullen thus deals with the most genuine and heart-rending emotions he had ever felt, and in the volume's final poem he constructs his strongest assertion of faith.

"The Black Christ (Hopefully Dedicated to White America)" is the story of a lynching in which Christ mysteriously appears and offers himself for the intended victim. The poem traces the narrator's movement from doubt to faith and depicts his mother as an archetypal southern Black American who holds to the ideals of Christianity. To view the poem as simply the story of a rebellious and agnostic Jim who strikes down a white man and is condemned to death by a mob, however, is to do it less than justice. And, in a sense, to treat the poem as a simple resolution of the narrator's uncertainties is to fail to comprehend its significance in Cullen's canon. On its most fundamental level, **"The Black Christ"** fits into the tradition of Black American literature as a conversion tale; it is one of those recountings—complete with mysterious events and marvellings at the Lord's way—that characterized the Black church during Reconstruction and that can be heard today when the out-of-town guest is called upon to "testify." Cullen captures the spirit of these occasions quite well in *One Way to Heaven*, and there is little doubt that the son of a successful Harlem minister was familiar with conversion stories. If the poem is seen in this light, some of its apparent flaws turn out to be necessities, e.g., the long retelling of incidents and the sense of suspense and wonder the narrator attempts to create toward the conclusion. A man speaking to a congregation would not be remiss in accounting for every detail and strange phenomenon.

Cullen seems to adopt the form of the conversion story in a rather tentative way, however, for Jim—the agnostic badman hero—certainly appears as glamorous as the sacrificial Christ. But surely this was intentional, since the final reconciliation represents a momentary stasis in the Christian-pagan conflict. Jim, after all, commits his assault because the white man has corrupted the natural reverence for spring on the part of the Black man and white woman, and the virginal

tree on which Christ is hung comes to life after the lynching. Christ (the representative of religious faith) and Jim—the sensitive, agnostic worshipper of spring—come together in a rite of regeneration. In the pagan and natural moment, Jim and the white woman are as harmonious as the boys in **"Tableau."** The white man intrudes, and he and the mob stand for white America. The narrator never loses his admiration for his brother, and the wonder and firmness he feels in his new faith are the results of a miracle.

Throughout the poem, Cullen seems to stand by the narrator's side, whispering that both Christ, the dreamer, and the pagan-spirited Jim are needed to unify the opposing points of his canon. To say the poet avoids some of the issues—like Christ's exoneration of a murderer and the hopelessness His crucifixion portends—is to capture the letter of the poem, but not its spirit. It was inevitable that Cullen would attempt a synthesis and that he would do so in a manner that raised the question of race. The results are not altogether satisfactory, but the strong commitment to an idealistic point of view should not be forgotten. The poet, the dreamer, the man who treasures the wonders of spring wins out in the end. If culture was not entirely "colorless" in the United States, at least it was neutral enough in France for Cullen to compose his only truly romantic volume of poetry. The book contains the poet's message **"To Certain Critics"**:

Then call me traitor if you must,
Shout treason and default!
Say I betray a sacred trust
Aching beyond this vault.
I'll bear your censure as your praise,
For never shall the clan
Confine my singing to its way
Beyond the ways of man.

No racial option narrows grief,
Pain is no patriot,
And sorrow plaits her dismal leaf
For all as lief as not.
With blind sheep groping every hill,
Searching an oriflamme,
How shall the shepherd heart then thrill
To only the darker lamb?

Six years elapsed between *The Black Christ* and *The Medea and Some Poems*, Cullen's last volume of serious verse. The prose rendering of Euripides's classic play is interesting and shows a broadening of the poet's activities, but it possesses little of the grandeur of the original. Cullen added two female characters to the drama to act as confidantes for Medea; in Euripides's version, the entire chorus acts the role. The substitution means that one of the Greek dramatist's major contentions loses much of its force; no longer is a large sector of the city-state inclined toward the irrationality and paganism represented by the heroine. There seems little possibility that the entire order will be destroyed by the kind of wild frenzy that characterizes the *Bacchae*. Cullen's work is also more maudlin than Euripides's. Medea's soliloquy over her victims and the words of one of her children before the execution— "What are you such a baby for? Mother won't hurt us. Ah!"—drip with sentimentality. Finally, Cullen's characters speak far too often in Poor-Richard slang, and his heroine is reduced to a shrew who engages in such incongruously comical exchanges as:

MEDEA. Then you have no sons yet, Aegeus?
AEGEUS. None. The gods have kept me barren!
MEDEA. Have you tried a wife? That might help.

Cullen's effort precedes Jean Paul Sartre's rendition of Aeschylus by a number of years. But Sartre's *The Flies* was undertaken as an act of freedom and was first performed in occupied Paris. Hence, there is more justification for his deliberately second-rate translation; it offers an example of "engaged" literature. Cullen's play suffers by comparison, for it shifts the original emphasis on the mythic, barbarian, and fatalistic to the hard-hearted woman scorned. Certainly, this aspect is present in the Euripidean version, but it is not blatant. Cullen's flaccid prose and rhyming choruses are scarcely improvements on earlier translations.

The twenty-eight lyrics in *The Medea* make the volume readable and show a mellowing of the poet's attitudes and a refinement of his technique. There is an expansion of his humanism in verses such as **"Magnets," "Any Human to Another," "Every Lover,"** and **"To One Not There,"** and he rededicates himself to poetry in **"After a Visit (At Padraic Colum's Where There Were Irish Poets)."** His **"Sonnet: Some for a Little While Do Love"** and the concluding poems of *The Medea* show a movement toward a more controlled verse and a more gentle (one might almost say "senescent") point of view:

> Some for a little while do love, and some for long;
> And some rare few forever and for aye;
> Some for the measure of a poet's song,
> And some the ribbon width of a summer's day.
> Some on a golden crucifix do swear,
> And some in blood do plight a fickle troth;
> Some struck divinely mad may only stare,
> And out of silence weave an iron oath.
>
> So many ways love has none may appear
> The bitter best, and none the sweetest worst;
> Strange food the hungry have been known to bear,
> And brackish water slakes an utter thirst.
> It is a rare and tantalizing fruit
> Our hands reach for, but nothing absolute.

"To France" asks that the land of "kindly foreign folk" act as the poet's Byzantium, and **"Belitis Sings (From the French of Pierre Louÿs)"** is charming in its delicate artificiality. Finally, **"The Cat"** and **"Cats"**—both translations of Baudelaire—substitute the feline loveliness of a domestic pet for the mythical beasts and fickle lovers seen elsewhere in Cullen's canon. Cats are "quiet as scholars and as lovers bold," and they sit "in noble attitudes" and dream—"small sphinxes miming those in lonelier lands." The poet thus sinks quietly into a land of domesticity with a cat for his companion.

The volume closes, however, with **"Scottsboro, Too, Is Worth Its Song,"** a protest poem on the order of **"Not Sacco and Vanzetti"** (*The Black Christ*). Though Cullen would, henceforth, live and write in collaboration with his cherished Christopher Cat, "all disgrace" and "epic wrong" still exercise their ineluctable and dichotomizing influence. The man who was born Black and bidden to sing turned to the world of children for his next two books, but his canon closes on the propagandistic note that James Weldon Johnson found "well nigh irresistible" for the Black artist. (pp. 30-52)

Houston A. Baker, Jr., in his A Many-Colored Coat of Dreams: The Poetry of Countee Cullen, *Broadside Press, 1974, 60 p.*

ARTHUR P. DAVIS   (essay date 1974)

[*Davis, an American author and scholar of black American literature, has contributed numerous articles, short stories, and book reviews to magazines, anthologies, and professional journals. He also coedited* The Negro Caravan *(1941) and* Cavalcade: Negro American Writers from 1760 to the Present *(1971). In the following excerpt, Davis discusses the "alien-and-exile" theme in Cullen's works and provides a positive assessment of his contribution to modern poetry.*]

The work of Cullen is found in nine major publications: one novel, two children's books, a version of *Medea* which also contains poems, and five volumes of verse. Though he wrote effectively in other genres, Cullen is pre-eminently a lyrical poet. As a poet, he admits to being "a rank conservative, loving the measured line and the skillful rhyme." Though he rebelled against being labeled a "Negro poet," he is, if not the finest, certainly one of the best poets of the New Negro Renaissance.

In each of his publications Cullen grouped his racial poems under the heading "Color." Many of the pieces in these sections fall into the alien-and-exile category. Most of the early New Negro poets used this theme, but Cullen used it more persistently and effectively than any of the others.

In poem after poem he states or implies that the American Negro is and can never be other than an alien here, an exile from his African homeland. As such he suffers from the insults and discriminations that unassimilated foreigners of all kinds endure, as well as a few additional ones because of his color. The Negro has not only lost an idyllic mother country, he has also lost his pagan gods, gods which, unlike the pale Christian deities, would be sympathetic to his peculiar needs. The religious loss is stressed more in Cullen's poems than in those of other Renaissance poets. In all probability he used the theme to express poetically some of his own religious concerns, as we shall see below.

In these poems Africa is not actually a real place. It is a symbol, an idealized land in which the Negro was once happy and free. The Harlem Renaissance poets used it to accentuate the differences between the Negro's harsh American existence and that he once led in this legendary "dusky dream-lit land." This subconscious contrast is never absent from the alien-and-exile's thoughts, and it puts a tremendous pressure on him. The best example of the alien-and-exile theme, Cullen's **"Heritage,"** describes dramatically this atavistic "pull":

> What is Africa to me:
> Copper sun or scarlet sea,
> Jungle star or jungle track,
> Strong bronzed men, or regal black
> Women from whose loins I sprang
> When the birds of Eden sang?
> *One three centuries removed*
> *From the scenes his fathers loved,*
> *Spicy grove, cinnamon tree,*
> *What is Africa to me?*

Neither night or day can the speaker find peace or a release from the pull of *Africa* drumming in his blood. Twisting and writhing like a "baited worm," he wants to strip and dance "in an old remembered way." Though he fights against it, he also longs for "quaint, outlandish heathen gods / Black men fashion out of rods. . . ." And he wishes God were black, believing that if He were, He would suffer as the Negro suffers and therefore be more sympathetic to black misery. The poem ends on a note of doubt concerning his ability to fight the pull of the motherland:

> All day long and all night through,
> One thing only must I do:
> Quench my pride and cool my blood,
> Lest I perish in the flood.
> Lest a hidden ember set
> Timber that I thought was wet
> Burning like the dryest flax,
> Melting like the merest wax,
> Lest the grave restore its dead.
> Not yet has my heart or head
> In the least way realized
> They and I are civilized.

Although, as **"Heritage"** suggests, there is no way of escape for the black exile, there are means of alleviating the pain. One is to glorify the differences between the two groups, making attractive those which the enemy would deride:

> My love is dark as yours is fair
> Yet lovelier I hold her
> Than listless maids with pallid hair
> And blood that's thin and colder.

(This is an early variant of the present-day "black is beautiful" slogan.) Another means of alleviating the condition is to rise superior to it through the wisdom and courage that suffering brings:

> How being black and living through the pain
> Of it, is courage more than angels have.

Suicide is still another way out for the black sufferer, and in one of Cullen's longer poems, **"The Shroud of Color,"** the speaker considers this means:

> "Lord, being dark," I said, "I cannot bear
> The further touch of earth, the scented air;
> Lord, being dark, forewilled to that despair
> My color shrouds me in, I am as dirt
> Beneath my brother's heel; there is a hurt
> In all the simple joys which to a child
> Are sweet; they are contaminate, defiled
> By truths of wrongs the childish vision fails
> To see; too great a cost this birth entails.
> I strangle in this yoke drawn tighter than
> The worth of bearing it, just to be man.
> I am not brave enough to pay the price
> In full; I lack the strength to sacrifice."

A final means of alleviating the exile's agony is to acquire a mystic faith in a new world and a better day for the oppressed. One of Cullen's best sonnets, **"From the Dark Tower,"** considers this hope:

> We shall not always plant while others reap
> The golden increment of bursting fruit,
> Not always countenance abject and mute,
> That lesser men should hold their brothers cheap; . . .
> We were not made eternally to weep.

As stated, Countee Cullen stressed the religious aspect of the alien-and-exile theme, and the last section of **"Heritage"** is a brilliant poetic reflection of both the speaker's and the author's divided loyalties. Writing his own biographical sketch in *Caroling Dusk,* Cullen makes the following revealing statement: "Born in New York City . . . and reared in the conservative atmosphere of a Methodist parsonage, Countee Cullen's chief problem has been that of reconciling a Christian upbringing with a pagan inclination. His life so far has not

convinced him that the problem is insoluble." This was written in 1927. Several poems in his first volume, *Color* (1925), reflected, as did **"Heritage,"** his "pagan inclination," among them **"Pagan Prayer"** and **"Gods."**

In his second volume, however, we find signs of a change in the poet's attitude. Although there is a hint of skepticism in **"Epilogue,"** the poem **"In Spite of Death"** suggests a faith in the existence of an afterlife, and **"The Litany of the Dark People"** is almost a direct repudiation of the earlier pagan stand:

> Yet no assault the old gods make
> Upon our agony
> Shall swerve our footsteps from the wake
> Of Thine toward calvary.

In short, *Copper Sun* (1927) prepares the reader for the complete reversal the poet expresses in *The Black Christ and Other Poems* (1929).

The title poem in the *The Black Christ* not only repudiates Cullen's earlier religious position, it also repudiates the whole alien-and-exile attitude as expressed in **"Heritage"** and other verses on this theme. *The Black Christ,* modeled on a medieval saints' legend, is actually a strong affirmation of faith in Christianity and in the Negro's place in America ("This ground and I, are we not one?"). It may be approached as a *débat* between the Cullen of *Color,* paganistic yet seeking, and the Cullen of *The Black Christ,* who tells us in **"Counter Mood"**:

> I who am mortal say I shall not die;
> I who am dust of this am positive
> That though my nights tend towards the grave, yet I
> Shall on some brighter day arise and live.

With *The Black Christ* volume, the poet took leave of racial writing, of the type of poems he placed under the heading "Color." (We note that in his first volume there are twenty-three poems in this category; in *Copper Sun,* seven; in *The Black Christ,* four, including, of course, the long title poem. *Medea and Some Poems* contains twenty pieces in all, but only one is related to racial matters, and the relationship is oblique.) In one of these "Color" pieces in *The Black Christ,* pointedly entitled **"To Certain Critics,"** Cullen leaves us in no doubt concerning his position:

> Then call me traitor if you must,
> Shout treason and default!
> Say I betray a sacred trust. . . .
> I'll bear your censure as your praise,
> *For never shall the clan*
> *Confine my singing to its ways*
> *Beyond the ways of man.* [italics inserted]

From now on, he seems to be saying, no "racial option" will confine me; I shall write as a poet, not as a "Negro poet." And he stuck to his decision. As stated above, *Medea and Some Poems* (1935), has only one race poem. In 1940 and 1942, with the "aid" of Christopher Cat, he published first *The Lost Zoo* and later *My Lives and How I Lost Them,* both charming and imaginative children's works.

Why did Cullen stop writing racial poems after *The Black Christ?* One answer the poet has given us. Indirectly, he probably gave us another, found also in *The Black Christ.* In a poem called **"Self Criticism"** the author writes:

Shall I go all my bright days singing
(A little pallid, a trifle wan)
The failing note still vainly clinging
To the throat of the stricken swan?

And in another, entitled **"A Wish,"** he says:

I hope when I have sung my rounds
Of song, I shall have the strength to slay
The wish to chirp on any grounds,
Content that silence hold her sway,
My tongue not rolling futile sounds
After my heart has had its say.

Perhaps Cullen felt that he had *written out* on racial themes and elected to be silent. The race problem, to a sensitive person, can be an intolerable bore and a great weariness of the soul.

In addition to the "Color" grouping in each volume (except *Medea and Some Poems*), Cullen used the following divisions: in *Color,* "Epitaphs," "For Love's Sake," and "Varia"; in *Copper Sun,* "The Deep in Love," "At Cambridge," "Varia," and "Juvenilia"; and in *The Black Christ and Other Poems,* "Varia" and "Interlude." The poems in these sections, as one deduces from the titles, concern themselves with the subjects that lyric poets from the time of the Greeks have written about: love, the joys of nature, the transitoriness of life, and death.

For some reason Cullen was morbidly concerned with death and death-imagery. He uses funereal allusions oftentimes in poetry in which, when first read, they seem out of place. One expects to meet skull-and-cross-bones references in poems like **"A Brown Girl Dead," "Requiescam,"** and **"Two Thoughts on Death,"** but they appear just as frequently in other poems, **"The Love Tree," "Advice to a Beauty,"** and **"The Proud Heart."** The poet, for some reason, was also morbidly concerned with suicide. For example, **"The Wise," "Suicide Chant," "The Shroud of Color," "Mood,"** and **"Harsh World That Lashest Me"** are all suicide poems, and there are others. In the last-named poem the poet catalogues ominously the several ways to go:

I think an impulse stronger than my mind
May someday grasp a knife, unloose a vial,
Or with a leaden ball unbind
The cords that tie me to the rank and file. . . .

It is always dangerous to confuse the author with the speaker in a poem, whether the subject is suicide or love, but one notes that Cullen's love poems *after* his unfortunate first marriage take on a bitter tone. A good example of the type is **"Song in Spite of Myself "**:

Never love with all your heart,
It only ends in aching;
And bit by bit to the smallest part
That organ will be breaking.

Cullen is excellent as a writer of "Epitaphs." These short, closely packed verses have a bite and a sting uncommon in Renaissance poetry. One of the best known and most often-quoted of these little poems is **"For a Lady I Know"**:

She even thinks that up in heaven
Her class lies late and snores,
While poor black cherubs rise at seven
To do celestial chores.

Cullen's protest poetry, as exemplified in the above epitaph, was seldom, if ever, a frontal attack. He preferred the oblique, the hinted, the ironic approach. In one of his late poems, **"Scottsboro, Too, Is Worth Its Song (A Poem to American Poets),"** he points out that the Sacco-Vanzetti case brought forth a flood of poetic protest. Thinking about the precedent set:

Surely, I said,
Now will the poets sing.
But they have raised no cry.
I wonder why.

One of the most brilliant of Cullen's poems in this vein, a piece that has become a protest classic, is entitled **"Incident"**:

Once riding in old Baltimore,
Heart-filled, head-filled with glee,
I saw a Baltimorean
Keep looking straight at me.
Now I was eight and very small,
And he was no whit bigger,
And so I smiled, but he poked out
His tongue, and called me, "Nigger."

I saw the whole of Baltimore
From May until December;
Of all the things that happened there
That's all that I remember.

Cullen had the skill of McKay, but not the intensity. He preferred the suggestion to the blunt statement. He pricked rather than slashed.

The verse forms of Cullen, like those of McKay, are traditional: quatrains, couplets, stanzas of varying lengths, and

Photograph of Cullen taken by Carl Van Vechten.

sonnets. He has been criticized for using too slavishly these tried forms, for never, as did Langston Hughes, venturing out into the forms made popular by the New Poetry Movement or forms derived from folk literature. This brings up a foolish question: Would he have been a better poet if he had abandoned his classic models? The trouble with writing like Keats and other nineteenth-century greats is that they are difficult men to follow. Even though Cullen was by no means an unworthy follower of such poets, their greatness tends in some measure to dwarf by comparison his accomplishment. Cullen, however, had a motivation Keats never had. Cullen unlike Keats knew what it meant to be called a *"nigger."*

As a poet Countee Cullen will probably outlast his century. Measured by any standard, his work, particularly the "Color" pieces, will be read as long as protest poems have meaning in America. There are critics who believe that **"Heritage"** is the best poem published during the Harlem Renaissance. (pp. 75-81)

> Arthur P. Davis, *"First Fruits: Countee Cullen," in his* From the Dark Tower: Afro-American Writers, 1900 to 1960, *Howard University Press, 1974, pp. 73-83.*

ALAN R. SHUCARD (essay date 1984)

[*Shucard is an American critic and educator. In the following excerpt from his* Countee Cullen, *he examines the relationship between Cullen's racial awareness and his treatment of universal themes of religion, death, and love.*]

So central to Countee Cullen's world view is his inescapable race-consciousness that it is really no easy matter to differentiate in a great deal of his poetry between racial and nonracial themes. Aside from his repeated extrinsic treatment of race, much of the rest of what he writes is bound to be an intrinsic manifestation of his racial awareness. It is possible, however, to extract from his racial preoccupation three other major themes, religion, death, and love, and to discuss each separately, yet to examine the way in which they are all touched by the pervasive denominator in Cullen's poetry, race.

• • • • •

It is not difficult to find in Cullen an intense religious disdain, with evidence of an occasional desire to seek refuge in Christian faith, but an inability to attain such faith. One scholar, Helen Dinger, chooses to focus on this emphasis in Cullen's religious poems [in her unpublished M.A. thesis], contending that he "protests against a God who seems to be identified with the white race." She quotes B. E. Mays in expressing the opinion "that Cullen wants to have faith, that he wants to believe in God and the teachings of Christianity but apparently he cannot. He accuses God of being deaf to 'our plaints' and implies that God has lost the Negro race and begs Him to 'retrieve my race again.' " It is misleading, however, to suppose that this is as far as Cullen's religious conviction extends. In fact, it evolves all the way to acceptance. Religious experience recorded in his poetry does start from disillusionment and rebellion, reflecting a strain in Afro-American literature that was later to grow stronger, but Cullen's religious verse only began by struggling against Christianity; it ended by singing of fulfillment in Christianity.

"Pagan Prayer" in *Color* is typical of his early questioning of the practical wisdom of relying on the old religion for racial salvation:

> Our Father, God; our Brother Christ,
> Or are we bastard kin,
> That to our plaints your ears are closed,
> Your doors barred from within?
>
> Our father, God; our Brother, Christ
> Retrieve my race again;
> So shall you compass this black sheep
> This pagan heart. Amen.

And there are other poems in *Color*—sometimes with searching, defiant tones reminiscent of Stephen Crane—on the religious theme that take a similar stand, notably **"Heritage"** and **"Gods."** Cullen's divided loyalty is declared this way in **"Heritage"**: . . .

> Father, Son and Holy Ghost,
> So I make an idle boast;
> Jesus of the twice-turned cheek,
> Lamb of God although I speak
> With my mouth thus, in my heart
> I play a double part.
> Ever at Thy glowing altar
> Must my heart grow sick and falter,
> Wishing he I served were black,
> Thinking then it would not lack
> Precedent of pain to guide it,
> Let who would or might deride it;
> Surely then this flesh would know
> Yours had borne a kindred woe.
> Lord, I fashion dark gods, too,
> Daring even to give to You
> Dark despairing features. . . .

Even in the most defiant of his religious poems—unlike Crane, who likes to stick his tongue out at the Almighty like a boy daring the train to overtake him in a railroad tunnel—Cullen never dismisses God altogether. He may taunt Him, chastise Him, ask Him to stretch a rule, but he does not entirely dismiss Him. "You crowd me too much," he seems to be saying; "give me a little room within Your dominion in which to give vent to what I fancy is my racial heritage." He confesses with some irony in **"Gods"** that God is omniscient, and so the only way he could get into heaven, with his affinity for black gods, is by God's winking at his vice:

> God's alabaster turrets gleam
> Too high for me to win,
> Unless He turns His face and lets
> Me bring my own gods in,

a fascinating sleight-of-hand by which Cullen acknowledges America's interracial Christian God, while he once again reaches out for his lost ancestral gods and romanticizes them. Like other Harlem Renaissance writers, Langston Hughes, for example, in "A Negro Speaks of Rivers," Cullen tries from time to time to return spiritually to mother Africa in a highly romantic black American impulse akin to the wider Pan-African urge later termed "Negritude."

In his autobiographical portrait written to precede his poems included in *Caroling Dusk,* his 1927 anthology of verse by black poets, Cullen presents a prose summary of his religious posture that shows in him the kind of wavering detectable in his poems, an uncertainty not in the least surprising in a man plagued by racial ambivalence that must surely affect his religious beliefs:

> . . . reared in the conservative atmosphere of a Methodist parsonage, Countee Cullen's chief problem has been that of reconciling a Christian up-

bringing with a pagan inclination. His life so far has not convinced him that the problem is insoluble.

He is not anti-Christian, then, but rather skeptical and in hopes that he can formulate a vision that excludes neither the paganism he sometimes likes to think is his heritage nor the Christianity that is part of his growing up and of the wider world—the predominantly white world—in which he must live.

The skepticism lingers for a time. In the 1927 collection, *Copper Sun,* he doubts the Christian afterlife in a poem with racial overtones and wider philosophical ones in its contrasting of the lily, the death symbol, with more vivid flowers: "And no man knows if dead men fade / Or bloom, save those that die." In the same volume, however, he reverses the impetus of such poems as **"Heritage,"** and in two poems works toward his later embracing of Christianity. **"In Spite of Death"** affirms the afterlife and even hints at the notion of resurrection. Just as spring brings life out of dead vegetation,

> No less shall I in some new fashion flare
> Again, when death has blown my candles out;
> Although my blood went down in shameful rout
> Tonight, by all this living frame holds fair,
> Though death should closet me tonight, I swear
> Tomorrow's sun would find his cupboard bare.

Even stronger in its explicit affirmation of faith is **"The Litany of the Dark People,"** which chants a direct appeal to the Savior, "To keep us one with Thee in mind, / Thou Christ of Bethlehem." The appeal continues, in contradiction to such earlier pieces as **"Heritage"** and **"Gods"**:

> Yet no assault the old gods make
> Upon our agony
> Shall swerve the footsteps from the wake
> Of Thine toward Calvary.
> And if we hunger now and thirst,
> Grant our withholders may
> When heaven's constellations burst
> Upon Thy crowning day,
> Be fed by us, and given to see
> Thy mercy in our eyes,
> When Bethlehem and Calvary
> Are merged in Paradise.

This is clearly the work of a staunch Christian indeed. Paradoxically, doubt may be inevitable, but the answers to it are incorporated in the Christian framework. (pp. 35-8)

The reasons for Cullen's acceptance of Christianity can only be speculated upon. Certainly, he had suffered by 1929, the year *The Black Christ and Other Poems* was published. He had been slighted by racial effrontery, he had been married briefly and suffered the dissolution of his first marriage. Yet others who had led not especially parochial lives, who also endured indignities for being black, who also had been bruised in affairs of the heart did not turn as fervently toward religious faith as Cullen. The most cogent assumption is that the uglier the world became toward him, the more it pushed him to the breaking point, the more he was inclined to turn up the avenue of religious consolation indelibly marked out for him in his youth at the rectory. Potent evidence in support of such an assumption is provided by a two-poem sequence in *The Black Christ and Other Poems,* **"Mood"** and its reply, **"Counter Mood."** In the first of these he is torn by the intent to remain "for Christ's sake" the good Christian while he is made to stand restive on the brink of violence:

> I think an impulse stronger than my mind
> May some day grasp a knife, unloose a vial,
> Or with a little leaden ball unbind
> The cords that tie me to the rank and file.
> My hands grow quarrelsome with bitterness,
> And darkly bent upon the final fray;
> Night with its stars upon a grave seems less
> Indecent than the too complacent day.

The biblical injunction to turn the other cheek here is inadequate, as the impulse toward mayhem or suicide grows strong. But immediately, in the very next poem, Cullen succeeds in quelling the violent tide rising in him and finding the resolution in the traditional afterlife:

> I who am mortal say I shall not die;
> I who am dust of this am positive,
> That though my nights tend toward the grave, yet I
> Shall on some brighter day arise, and live.

He importunes the dubious reader not to question how he has become oracular or whence comes his "arrogant assurance," but rather to "Ask Faith, the canny conjurer."

All of the previous poems touching in one way or another on religion and exemplifying the gradual solidification of Cullen's Christian faith lead, in a sense, up to the ultimate—and extremely facile—acceptance in **"The Black Christ."** In this title poem of the 1929 collection, a long narrative poem set in the South, Cullen comes to display a degree of faith that would be difficult for all but the most zealous fundamentalist to credit in the shadow of the events of the poem. Briefly, the narrative line is as follows: the poem begins with the narrator's paean to "God's glory and my country's shame," above all the wonders of God, Who has caused him to intensify his faith in spite of atrocious adversity, Who has eventually performed a miracle that has quieted his doubts and curses and made him accede to the vision of his mother, whom he quotes:

> "Now spring that heals the wounds of earth
> Is being born; and in her birth
> The wounds of men may find a cure.
> By such a thought I may endure,
> And of some things be no less sure.
> This is a cruel land, this South,
> And bitter words to twist my mouth,
> Burning its tongue down to its root,
> Were easily found; but I am mute
> Before the wonder of this thing:
> That God should send so pure a spring. . . . "

With sentiment akin to the maudlin, the mother feels equal or superior to the white women who treat her like dirt, because she is closer to the earth. The narrator and his brother, a young man named Jim, prone to high spirits, cannot share her vision until the miracle in the poem; they know of lynchings in cases in which blacks stand up to whites, and are deeply skeptical about the existence of God:

> We had no scales upon our eyes;
> God, if He was, kept to His skies,
> And left us to our enemies.
> Often at night fresh from our knees
> And sorely doubted litanies
> We grappled for the mysteries. . . .

Many tetrameter couplets later, Jim comes home pursued by a lynch mob; he has had a virtuous relationship with a white female, a kind of personification of spring, and has struck down the dirty-minded white man who caught them and abused the woman. When the pack of "two-limbed dogs" arrives to unleash their fury on Jim, he acquires a luminescence about his head and sacrifices himself to the mob, who fall on him and beat him to death. From Jim's magnanimity comes the salvation of his brother (the narrator) and their saintly mother. The narrator is desolate and angry, and with more personal reason than ever to doubt now, after his brother's brutal death, he mocks his mother mercilessly with such questions as:

> "What has He done for you who spent
> A bleeding life for His content?
> Or is the white Christ, too, distraught
> By these dark sins His Father wrought?"

In the nick of time, the mother has justification to command her faithless son to

> "Bear witness now unto His grace; . . .
> Behold the glory of the Lord,
> His unimpeachable high seal.
> Cry mercy now before Him; kneel,
> And let your heart's conversion swell
> The wonder of His miracle."

The resurrected Jim has returned; the amazed narrator satisfies himself by touching Jim, and he cannot do anything short of agreeing with Jim's proclamation that "Now have we seen beyond degree / That love which has no boundary; / Our eyes have looked on Calvary." The family, now blessed, lives happily ever after, reaping "full fields"; the fruit falling off laden boughs into their hands; the mother, "Job's dark sister," sitting about in a corner knitting and praying.

Cullen ends **"The Black Christ"** with this summary and interpretation of the events of the poem:

> Somewhere the Southland rears a tree,
> (And many others there may be
> Like unto it, that are unknown,
> Whereon as costly fruit has grown).
> It stands before a hut of wood
> In which the Christ Himself once stood—
> And those who pass it by may see
> Nought growing there except a tree,
> But there are two to testify
> Who hung on it . . . we saw Him die.
> Its roots were fed with priceless blood.
> It is the Cross; it is the Rood.

The imaginative construct leading to this conclusion is so extreme that it would be tempting to read this poem as a parody and its language the language of the mock-heroic were it not for the pattern observed in Cullen's religious poetry before **"The Black Christ,"** and the fact that the language is no loftier here than it frequently is in his poetry. No, the poem must be taken as the point of vision toward which he had always been heading in his religious works, even in his questioning ones, a metaphorical recapitulation of his own religious experience, and it is a position from which he never again really strays.

Religion in *The Medea and Some Poems* (1935) is mostly confined to the system of imagery it provides for some of the love poems, but among the last of Cullen's poems, in one of the previously uncollected poems in *On These I Stand,* is to be found one of his most unmistakable utterances of Christian hope. The carol, for that is really what the poem **"Christus Natus Est"** is, has a distinct undertone of regret or bitterness, perhaps in part for those suffering in World War II, but certainly for the black American, whose plight has always occupied Cullen's attention. But promise of salvation is foremost. It rings out in the refrain terminating each stanza, and it lingers at the end of Cullen's song, which well represents the unwavering affirmative religious attitude he adopted once he fought down his earlier skepticism. The last five stanzas of the carol echo both the dubious low notes and their answer in the high:

> For bird and beast
> He did not come,
> But for the least
> Of mortal scum.
> Hosannah! Christus natus est.
>
> Who lives in the ditch?
> Who begs his bread?
> Who has no stitch
> For back or head?
> Hosannah! Christus natus est.
>
> Who wakes to weep,
> Lies down to mourn?
> Who in his sleep
> Withdraws from scorn?
> Hosannah! Christus natus est.
>
> Ye outraged dust,
> On field and plain,
> To feed the lust
> Of madmen slain:
> Hosannah! Christus natus est.
>
> The manger still
> Outshines the throne;
> Christ must and will
> Come to his own.
> Hosannah! Christus natus est.
>   (Christmas 1943)

• • • • •

Just as the Christian dream of a better day to come is one major theme in Cullen that is nonracial in itself but is connected to the matter of race by promising redemption from the vicissitudes of the Afro-American condition, so does the repeated treatment of death stand in the same relationship to trials of race. This does not mean that Cullen deliberately conceived either force, religion or death, as an escape from the indignities he saw and felt black people undergo, but that both themes developed in his work more as inadvertent longings, as lines he could grasp and tie together to keep the ends of his tensions from pulling apart.

With little equivocation, Cullen was attracted to death from his earliest poetry on. His affinity for Keats is doubtless predicated partly on the sense both men had of the inescapable and impending quality of death, and of its beauty. The ears of neither man, after all, deceived him when he heard the approach of time's winged chariot. In Cullen's case there was the remembrance of the humble circumstances of his birth and his being orphaned as a child, as Keats had had even starker reminders of the closeness of death, in his brother's death and in his own bloody sputum. Cullen states his feeling for the manner of his beginning in **"Saturday's Child"**:

> Death cut the strings that gave me life,
> And handed me to Sorrow,
> The only kind of middle wife
> My folks could beg or borrow.

But Cullen, even more than Keats, seemed often to reject the notion of death's permanence, so that while Keats could rue his unfinished task as poet in "When I Have Fears," "Till Love and Fame to Nothingness Do Sink," Cullen, even in his first volume, denies the power of death:

> A grave is all too weak a thing
> To hold my fancy long;
> I'll bear a blossom with the spring,
> Or be a blackbird's song.
> I think that I shall fade with ease,
> Melt into earth like snow,
> Be food for hungry, growing trees
> Or help the lilies blow.
> And if my love should lonely walk,
> Quite of my nearness fain,
> I may come back to hear, and talk
> In liquid words of rain.
>
> ("On Going")

Why, indeed, should he believe that he will be forever stilled in death when, just as Keats perceived the presence of Milton and Petrarch in "Keen Fitful Gusts," he feels that Keats still lives (**"To Endymion"**) and, through such natural manifestations as "bud and blossom, leaf and tree," still writes poetry in the mystical revel he keeps with Cullen? (**"To John Keats, Poet: At Spring Time"**). Besides, he sometimes feels assured by a religious or quasi-religious faith that death is meaningless because it is merely the prelude to something better. In **"In Spite of Death,"** for example, he expresses the certainty that just as spring resurrects nature, "Though death should closet me tonight, I swear / Tomorrow's sun would find his cupboard bare." It is far less difficult for one to be indifferent toward death, or even to welcome it, if he can make himself believe that the grave cannot hold him.

The kind of linear development that is discernible in Cullen's treatment of religion is scarcely traceable in his approach to death. His treatment of death is more random. Through the whole of his poetry he may, in any given piece, stress variations of what, for convenience, may be construed as three basic feelings toward death, depending upon his mood: an ironic awareness of death, which, Cullen notes wryly, other people lack; a deep preoccupation with the transitory quality of life, sometimes the sense that death is master even when there remains the semblance of life; ultimately, a positive longing for death, often associated with the belief in a Christian afterlife on the one hand and despondency over the race problem on the other. These broad designations are generally valid, as an examination of several of Cullen's many poems on death will show.

It is necessary to add, however, that, in a way, the categories outlined here cannot and do not suggest a kind of invariable consistency that no one can reasonably expect of him or of any other poet or human being. He did not always hail death as friend to lend encouragement, a salve to heal, or a chute to slide down to happiness. In *Copper Sun* he lapses into the very transitoriness of life that he elsewhere welcomes; he protests: "But time to live, to love, bear pain and smile, / Oh, we are given such a little while!" (**"Protest "**) In **"An Epitaph (For Amy Lowell)"** he portrays some of her indomitable qualities as he raises the most common doubt about what sense there is in living eventually to die:

> She leans across a golden table,
> Confronts God with an eye
> Still puzzled by the standard label
> All flesh bears: Made to die—
> And questions Him if He is able

To reassure her why.

And in **"The Shroud of Color"** his suffering, and that of all dark people, after first tempting him toward death, forces him rather to contend, to fight with truth, to concede: "I had no further claim to urge / For death. . . . "

Such exceptions admitted—and they are few, it is possible to turn to the rule, beginning with Cullen's ironic awareness of death. The first collection contains twenty-nine epitaphs, most of which display this trait. They are written for individuals and types—a virgin, for example, who saved herself for forty years only to yield to the advances of death, and, quite the reverse, a wanton, who tried many men in life, but found fidelity only in death. The most rabid antipathies are resolved in death, such as the enmity in the epitaph **"For an Evolutionist and His Opponent."** In some of these sardonic pieces there is, interestingly, a strong echo of Emily Dickinson's personification of death as a kindly gentleman caller. In the epitaph **"For Hazel Hall, American Poet,"** for example, Cullen presents this gentle ironic resolution:

> Soul-troubled at the febrile ways of breath
> Her timid breast shot through with faint alarm,
> "Yes, I'm a stranger here," she said to Death,
> "It's kind of you to let me take your arm."

The sense of irony does not leave Cullen in later collections. Sometimes it is laced with bitterness. In **"Light Lady"** a fallen woman with "Nothing to do but munch her gums / And sing the love of Christ" waits to take her final fall; she will recognize the face of death when he comes down the street to collect her. Perhaps the sharpest irony, that motivated by racial anger and the actual desire for death, is to be found in a later poem, **"Only the Polished Skeleton,"** in which Cullen reflects that the body and mind must constantly devise deceit, subterfuge, and fraud to survive "the onslaughts of the dust." It is, of all things, the skeleton, unrecognizable as black or white, racially leveled, and not subjected to the buffeting of life, that has the best opportunity for respite:

> Only the polished skeleton,
> Of flesh relieved and pauperized,
> Can rest at ease and think upon
> The worth of all it so despised.

The second emphasis Cullen gives to his treatment of death, that of the ephemerality of life, or an awareness that life is merely a mask that death sometimes wears, pervades not only much of the poetry that deals directly with death, but also, remarkably, a number of love poems, such as in the following poem, in the manner of A. E. Housman:

> Since little time is granted here
> For pride in pain or play,
> Since blood soon cools before that Fear
> That makes our prowess clay,
> If lips to kiss are freely met,
> Lad, be not proud nor shy;
> There are no lips where men forget,
> And undesiring lie.
>
> ("Advice to Youth")

The epicurean tone is repeated in such poems as **"Nocturne,"** in which he invites his lover to lie as much as is necessary to embroider the illusion of love, for, he concludes, "I see death drawing nigh to me / Out of the corner of my eye." **"Words to My Love"** strikes the same note, which quickly becomes familiar in Cullen. In that poem he implores his lover to eat fully of their feast and "leave no crumb," for "The quick /

So soon grow dumb." In **"Nothing Endures"** he exhorts the reader since "Nothing endures, / Not even love," to

> Let the blood riot,
> Give it its will;
> It shall grow quiet,
> It shall grow still.

Other poems bear the same message somewhat more subtly. **"An Old Story"** tells of a woman who set her ideal for love so high that only death could meet her standards and, unbeknown to her, it became her lover. And **"To Lovers of Earth: Fair Warning"** admonishes the reader to give himself to sweethearts and friends rather than to Earth, or the immortality of nature, really, for Earth is "More fickle, false, perverse, far more unkind" than those with whom one can engage in human relationships; Earth will lead a man on through her intrigues and not even notice his death. The ending of this poem represents one of those times when Cullen finds no comfort in the anticipation of death, but only the Stephen Crane-like contemplation of an indifferent universe:

> She will remain the Earth, sufficient still,
> Though you are gone and with you that rare loss
> That vanishes with your bewildered will.
> And there shall flame no red, indignant cross
> For you, no quick white scar of wrath emboss
> The sky, no blood drip from a wounded moon,
> And not a single star chime out of tune.

Such moments of futility, though, are rare in Cullen. More often he finds solace in mortality. It is precisely mortality that allows him to adjure his readers not to weep for the dead girl in **"Threnody for a Brown Girl."** Here, it is plain to Cullen that life gave her no chance; that "fevered blisters / Made her dark hands run, / While her favored, fairer sisters / Neither wrought nor spun"; that the grave probably provides her with the safest, surest house she has ever known; that "Only live hearts starving / Need an epitaph." Besides, why fear what is inescapable? In **"In the Midst of Life"** he declares the seed of death to be in every live blossom; two things only "keep faith; this breath / A while; and longer death."

Further, in **"The Proud Heart"** the very distinction between life and death is made to disappear: the proud heart continues to strike "its hours in pain," but its beating conceals the truth, that "The dead man lives, and none perceives him slain"—for his heart has been "Splintered . . . At a woman's laugh or a man's harsh word." It is not easy for the heart to comprehend that it is dead though it lives, and it refuses to be still as Cullen commands it in **"The Foolish Heart."** "Poor foolish heart that needs a grave / To prove to it that it is dead," the poem sighs in wistful dejection.

It is only a step from the ironic awareness of death and recognition of the transitoriness of life to Cullen's eager reaching out for death. It is not even a long step in light of the heartache stemming from racial oppression to be found covertly in **"Only the Polished Skeleton"** and **"Threnody for a Brown Girl"** and overtly in the many poems that face the problem of race in America head on. Enough bigotry can make death look awfully attractive to the victim. Now, it is easy to find a death wish in the poems of many poets, and even less complicated a feat for a poet, especially one with a twinkle in his eye, to deny having expressed such a wish, whether it is actually there or not. True, Countee Cullen is capable of humor, but his work is mostly so serious, and so much of it treats of death, and so many poems declare specifically a longing for

death that the death wish is impossible to overlook. A yearning for death is not at all a surprising thing to find in the vision of a man who uses the situation of caged animals in a zoo as parallel to the deathly condition of man's life: he sees man in as cruel a trap as the animals, except that "his cages have a larger range," and he senses man and the zoo animals "Commiserating each the other's woe." At the close of this metaphor of the living dead man's entombment (**"Thoughts in a Zoo,"**), he wonders "Who is most wretched, these caged ones, or we, / Caught in a vastness beyond our sight to see?"

If religious faith can bring succor to such a painful dilemma, so can death, and so the wish for death in Cullen, given all the other circumstances, is quite as natural as his quest for faith. He wishes for it conspicuously in the italicized ending of the *Color* collection:

> *I am for sleeping and forgetting*
> *All that has gone before;*
> *I am for lying still and letting*
> *Who will beat at my door;*
> *I would my life's cold sun were setting*
> *To rise for me no more.*

> (**"Requiescam"**)

If no one else ever wrote anything a critic could legitimately call a "death wish," this would still be one. Other poems in the first volume reach out for the same sort of release. Cullen claims for the dead the greatest wisdom, the capacity to be indifferent to the elements and to joy and pain, the ability in their detachment to be wholly satiate. He comments quizzically:

> Strange, men should flee their company,
> Or think me strange who long to be
> Wrapped in their cool community.

> (**"The Wise"**)

"Harsh World That Lashest Me" is a curious, almost childish defiance of adversity. The poet serves warning to the world that he will not be conquered, that he lives simply by willing not to die; but he writes into the end of the poem an escape clause: if he feels like it, he can die in spite of the world and remove himself

> To that vast room of couches laid
> For those too proud to live and see
> Their dreams of light eclipsed in shade.

Certainly, these are telling lines in view of Cullen's racial hopes and disappointments and the mass of death poetry he composed. They are more representative and explanatory of this vein in his poetry even than **"Suicide Chant,"** a piece written in a time of evident despondency that chants for the uprooting of weed sprung from seed that had not fulfilled expectation, and the planting of new seed in its stead.

It is perfectly clear in poems such as **"Harsh World That Lashest Me"** and **"Little Sonnet to Little Friends"** that Cullen's predilection for death stems from his conception of it as a convenient, quick way out of a sometimes nightmarish existence. Those who pity him, now that he is dead, he proclaims in the latter poem, "waste their time and energy; / No mares encumber me at night." The act of dying young only curtails time somewhat, and time can be hurtful. He would not change the living sun for his "dead and burned out star," for "Shine as it will, I have no doubt / Some day the sun, too, may go out." There is possibly a great deal to be gained through death, in Cullen's perception of the world, and disturbingly little to be lost. Moreover, there is the hope that in the moment of expiration, in the moment of release, will come the flash of enlightenment he has not been able to apprehend in life:

> And as my day throbs into dusk,
> This heart the world has made to bleed,
> While all its red stream deathward flows,
> Shall comprehend just why the seed
> Must agonize to be the rose.
>
> ("Two Thoughts on Death")

The figure of the seed struggling against overwhelming odds toward realization of itself is the same as that of **"Suicide Chant"** and is used here to explain further what advantage is to be attained, one way or another, through death. If a man does not or cannot live up to his potential, perhaps it is best that he should not go on living at all; and perhaps in the process of dying he can see, if even just for an instant, into truth and grasp what went wrong.

By the time of the publication of *The Medea and Some Poems* (1935), and thereafter, there is no fundamental alteration in Cullen's sensitivity and attitude toward death. He is still hyperconscious of its inevitability, even though he may lapse for an unusual moment into a euphoric wish for immortality. Thus, in a single poem in the 1935 volume he permits himself the delusion, for the moment, that his self resides in his deathless love, yet he concedes "that nothing lovely shall prevail / To win from Time and Death a moment's grace. . . . " (**"Sonnet: These Are No Wind-Blown Rumors, Soft Say-Sos"**). If there is any change at all perceptible in his treatment of death, it is in the direction of a more complete serenity in the expectation of death, undoubtedly associated with his intensifying belief in a Christian afterlife. He asks himself a most relevant—if convoluted—question about his interest in death, and replies to himself in this dialogue poem:

> *I to My Soul:*
> Why this preoccupation, soul, with Death,
> This servile genuflexion to the worm,
> Making the tomb a Mecca where the breath
> (Though still it rises vaporous, but firm,
> Expelled from the lungs still clear and unimpaired,
> To plough through nostrils quivering with pride)
> Veers in distress and love, as if it dared
> Not search a gayer place, and there subside?
>
> *My Soul to Me:*
> *Because the worm shall tread the lion down,*
> *And in the end shall sicken at its feast,*
> *And for a worm of even less renown*
> *Loom as a dread but subjugated beast;*
> *Because whatever lives is granted breath*
> *But by the grace and sufferance of Death.*
>
> ("Sonnet Dialogue")

In this way, still speaking of the inseparability of life and death, does Cullen explain his morbid preoccupation. There is no point in failing to acknowledge death and to pay it homage if it is, after all, absolute monarch of life. More tranquil and more overtly related to his strengthening religious faith is a poem from the French of Baudelaire in which he proclaims: "In death alone is what consoles. . . . " The sestet of the sonnet elucidates:

> An angel whose star-banded fingers hold
> The gift of dreams and calm, ecstatic sleep
> In easier beds than those we had before,
> Death is the face of God, the only fold

That pens content and ever-happy sheep,
To Paradise the only open door.

> ("Death to the Poor")

If death is for a time unattainable, to the deeply troubled its traditional surrogate, sleep, makes mortal existence endurable until death does come. This view of sleep, which Cullen comes to mainly through Keats, is the one that Cullen holds, not Macbeth's, which suggests that sleep is "chief nourisher in life's feast." That is, sleep to Cullen is not a recharger of the vital energies, but an anaesthetic that makes life tolerable while those energies are being drained away—mercifully drained away—into death. As in the translation from Baudelaire, death comes at the end of Cullen's poem entitled **"Sleep"**; it comes to Cullen as a great pap to slake the thirst of every man, a pap whose fluid is charitably soporific to suffering man. Even more, though, the first three stanzas of **"Sleep"** contain Cullen's most complete statement of his conception of sleep as prelude to death. Sleep stands in relation to death as man does to the angels in the Great Chain of Being. It is like death, but of lesser magnitude:

> Nothing is lovelier than sleep,
> Nor kinder thing was ever made;
> Gently, as though a cat should creep
> Upon a bird, transfixed, way-laid,
> It sinks in us its velvet blade.
>
> Soft are those paws, if they are sheathed,
> The steel of troubling dreams withdrawn,
> And all in peace wrapped round and wreathed
> The mind sinks down as on a lawn
> Laid out between the dusk and dawn.
>
> That dark maternal fountain bared
> To give her weakest creature food,
> The bosom of the Night is shared
> By all her weary, stricken brood;
> And though the suck be short, 'tis good.

The parallels between sleep and death are made unmistakable in the poem. They are both kindly, feminine, motherly. Cullen sets up further metaphorical associations of death in sleep: Sleep kills, gently but out of its very essence; it enshrouds the mind; the mind is "laid-out" and interred in its winding cloth of sleep.

The death or sleep-death poems of *The Medea and Some Poems* in a way form the prologue to the almost perfect calm that Cullen achieves in the contemplation of death in **"Dear Friends and Gentle Hearts,"** dated April 1943, another of the formerly uncollected poems Cullen elected to include in his poetic testament. No claim can be made for excellence of the poem itself, which perhaps borders on the maudlin. It rings of Shakespeare, and E. A. Robinson's "Luke Havergal," and innumerable other predecessors, with the mastery gone. In the tranquillity of its touching farewell, however, it is the death poem toward which all of Cullen's other death poems, most of them better poems, seem to be tending:

> We open infant eyes
> Of wonder and surprise
> Upon a world all strange and new,
> Too vast to please our childish view,
> Yet love bends down and trust imparts;
> We gaze around
> And know we've found
> Dear friends and gentle hearts;
> Good-day, we smile, dear friends and gentle hearts;
> Good-day dear friends and gentle hearts.

When on the western rim
Of time the sun grows dim,
And dimly on the closing eye
Fadeth the earth, the sea, the sky,
How blessedly this breath departs
If it pass out
While watch about
Dear friends and gentle hearts;
Good-night, we smile, dear friends and gentle hearts;
Good-night, dear friends, and gentle hearts.

The words seem to be those of a man no longer thrilling to the pounding of death's winged chariot closing on him, but quietly, perhaps gratefully, mounting it to be driven off. It is time to cease living with melancholy, as Keats was romantically better able to do. It is time to "drown the wakeful anguish of the soul." Less than three years after writing his poetic good-bye, Cullen's longing was fulfilled; he died in New York, January 10, 1946, of uremic poisoning, without reaching his forty-third birthday.

• • • • •

The discussion of the theme of love in the poetry of Countee Cullen, the third of the major "nonracial" themes to be considered here, follows in an oddly natural way the examination of his treatment of death and, in a less direct way, the tracing of his religious experiences. Among his love poems many may be termed, in a broad sense, "conventional," but a great many also are intimately connected, in the embrace of romanticism, with death or death's traditional temporary embodiment, sleep. A number of his love verses, too, are supported by the structure of religious metaphor. And always it should be remembered that "nonracial" is a relative term, that just as the religious poetry and the death poetry reflect the racial pressures Cullen suffered, so does the love poetry. Sometimes the reflection of race occurs in love poems that are associated with religion or death, but sometimes it operates quite independently within a given poem. Death comes to the principal characters of *The Ballad of the Brown Girl,* but it is clear that racial considerations are paramount in the handling of the love situation. So is the matter of race of prime importance in other love poems, **"A Song of Praise"** [in *Color*], for example, and **"Song of Praise"** [in *The Black Christ and Other Poems*]. . . . **"The Street Called Crooked"** illustrates again the more obvious racial tone in a love poem: accosted by ladies of the night in the street where they ply their trade in Le Havre, the poet replies that he has a better woman:

"To meet strange lips and foreign eyes
I did not cross the foam,
I have a dearer, fairer prize
Who waits for me at home."

"Her eyes are browner, lips more red
Than any lady's light;
'Twould grieve her heart and droop her head
If I failed her tonight."

The play on "fair," with the dark girl being "fairer" than the light ones, the harlots, is a word game in which Cullen occasionally liked to indulge, and underscores the race-consciousness of the poem.

It must be borne in mind, too, that no generalizations about Cullen's love poetry, whether they refer to his preoccupation with race, or religion, or death, will be universally applicable. He was, on occasion, inclined to write the kind of a love poem that is devoid of racial overtones and without any reliance

whatever on religion or death in form or content. **"Love's Way"** is such a poem. In it, Cullen directly calls for the required balance between the loves of two people involved with each other, concluding: "This is love's way / That where a heart is asked gives back a heart." **"Lesson"** presents the situation of two lovers lying together silently and feeling unhinged after the exchange of harsh words. The speaker stretches out his hand to his love, and though the silence has not been broken, the two are fused and their love becomes whole again.

But the fact remains that the majority of Cullen's love poems—those that deal with love in the usual sense and not the few that entail his hope for brotherly love—are structured on the notion of death, or of religion, or sometimes of both. If there were a poem of his extant in which two people made love on a gravestone while chanting a prayer and then died in the act and were swept up to heaven, it would be supremely useful to illustrate the point. As it happens, there is no such poem, but a careful reading of the substantial body of Cullen's love poems would eliminate any possibility of surprise should such a poem be discovered. In **"Oh, for a Little While Be Kind"** he begs his love to treat him decently despite her inclination to shun him; perhaps to get to know him better is to get to feel for him; after all, "who knows / But Dives found a matchless fragrance fled / When Lazarus no longer shocked his nose?" In **"To a Brown Girl,"** a more obviously lighthearted piece, he again uses the forceful arguments of death and religion in urging another girl not to condemn her lover "if no puritanic strain / Confines him to the nice,"

Since in the end consort together
Magdalen and Mary,
Youth is the time for careless weather;
Later, lass, be wary.

"Words to My Love" demonstrates the same mode: he urges his love not to rely upon the uncertainty of resurrection, but to live to the fullest in the present with the literal feast of wine and bread. And the second of **"Two Poets,"** on his deathbed, having sung his heart out in love song to the brink of death, holds in his hand a rose given to him by Guinevere and "drenched with Magdalen's eternal tear."

Such love poems do combine at once the highly emotive elements of death and religion. The majority of Cullen's love poems, however, omit the dimension of religion while they fuse his conception of death with love. Death, or its surrogate, sleep, in a number of variations, is as pervasive in his love verse as it is through the bulk of his poetry, particularly in *Color, Copper Sun,* and *The Black Christ and Other Poems,* to say nothing of *The Ballad of the Brown Girl.* It operates importantly in precisely half of the eight poems included in the "For Love's Sake" section of *Color* (two more of the eight are supported explicitly by Christian imagery), as well as several other poems in the other sections of the volume.

In the "For Love's Sake" group the following situations occur: in **"If You Should Go"** a love affair has passed as the light passes from the day. The poet admonishes his lover to leave quietly, for "a dream / When done, should leave no trace / That it has lived, except a gleam / Across the dreamer's face." **"To One Who Said Me Nay"** stresses the temporality of love; no one can be certain of where the winds will blow in the hour that the lovers share. In **"Advice to Youth"** the poet reminds the listener, in essence, to have a fling before death puts an end to all amorous opportunity. (The fourth poem of the group, **"Oh, for a Little While Be Kind,"** has, as noted above, an admixture of love, death, and religion.) The epitaphs of *Color,* notably those to a virgin, a wanton, the daughters of Magdalen, and a lovely lady [are] . . . , in a very real sense, to be regarded as love poems involving an ironic view of death, as in **"To a Brown Boy"** with its racial undercurrent, which advises the brown boy to court the brown girl and tells him that death eradicates all vestiges of color in any case. **"The Dance of Love"** tells of the poet's dancing a kind of primitive aphrodisiac death dance all night with his lover as "the killer roared above his kill." Eventually, he grows tired, he and his heart stand still, she dances to exhaustion, and they throw themselves down onto their hill and sleep. In the last love poem in *Color,* **"On Going,"** the poet fantasizes that he is dead, yet can return to communicate with his lover "In liquid words of rain." Again and again, death or sleep-death intrudes into the love condition, or is the essence of it, or calls an end to it.

The same is true of most of the love poems of *Copper Sun.* Even in **"Variations on a Theme,"** when Cullen separates the concept of love from death as far as to conclude that loss of love is worse than death, paradoxically he cannot entirely divorce the two; he describes the loss of love in terms of death, finding that his hands are slack and his blood cold, and wondering that his heart still beats. Its bitterly humorous title makes **"A Song of Sour Grapes"** another permutation of the love-death association; it is still clearly reflective of the relationship between the two forces. The speaker begins by wishing that his love were in the deepest grave, or rotting in the sea. Failing these possibilities, he remarks acidly:

> I would that your mother had never borne
> Your father's seed to fruit,
> That meadow rats had gnawed his corn
> Before it gathered root.

The poem may not be terribly funny, but in its dryness and treatment of sexual imagery, it evokes a reaction tantamount to comic relief when it is considered against most of the other poems in which love is married to death. Not so the other love-death poems of *Copper Sun.* In these, for the most part, the narrator plays his role straight and grimly. In this vein he relates **"An Old Story,"** a narrative with a faint Emily Dickinson echo, about a woman who saves herself for such an impossibly regal suitor that only death can ever win her, and does so without her being aware of it. The deeply in love are pitiable, he says (**"Pity the Deep in Love"**), walking zombie-like along "a narrow way / Precipitous and steep." His lover is free to lie to him in **"Nocturne,"** to make love even seem lovely—which, by implication, it is not—and he will not challenge the falsehoods, seeing as he does, out of the corner of his eye, death drawing near to him.

He craves death again in **"Lament,"** searching for a hole deep enough to put his heart in and keep it at rest. Here the wish for death results from a death, that of his love, "whose luscious mouth the dark, / Grim troubadour has kissed." So close a kinship does Cullen feel with death in the love situation that he personifies death itself as a sort of dark poet. In **"Song of the Rejected Lover"** the narrator has ironically brought himself to believe, in consolation for his rejection, that for love of him "Queen Guinevere turns cold to Lancelot," and that "Elaine has kissed Death's face, / For love of me is grief in Astolat." He comes extremely close to identifying himself with death, as he has virtually identified death with himself in **"Lament."**

Cullen does, however, maintain some dramatic distance between the narrator and himself in many, though surely not all, of the love poems. In some of the pieces that use the first person, such as **"Song of the Rejected Lover,"** the narrator creates a persona, however similar his mask may be to Cullen's own physiognomy. It is fair to say that he seldom causes the reader the embarrassment of love poems that are largely personal, tortured, soul-exhibiting moans. Cullen sometimes clouds the relationship between himself and the figure in the poem by using the third person, as in **"Portrait of a Lover."** Death still lurks in the poem, but it is difficult to deduce finally whether Cullen is projecting himself, a type of breast-beating lover, or both:

> Of all men born he deems himself so much accurst,
> His plight so piteous, his proper pain so rare,
> The very bread he eats so dry, so fierce his thirst,
> What shall we liken such a martyr to? Compare
> Him to a man with poison raging in his throat,
> And far away the one mind with an antidote.

A certain love poem in *The Black Christ and Other Poems* is noteworthy because it reverses the pattern of the love-death connection that has been established here. Death pervades even this exception, but it is associated not with lovers, but with those to whom love is denied:

> Those that are loved, though niggardly,
> Move with a lively foot and eye;
> The others drag like men who see
> Their day and minute set to die.
>
> (**"By Their Fruits"**)

Most of the love-death verses in *The Black Christ and Other Poems* do attest, however, in a more consistent way to the validity of the pattern that has been observed: love and death seek each other out like two lovers.

"At a Parting" stresses the point that love can survive until its end despite the knowledge that all love affairs are inescapably doomed, and **"Ghosts"** is an extension of that idea. In the latter poem the speaker is dead, and, in a situation that echoes a preoccupation of Housman, his lover is now lying with another man. If she is disturbed by some memory of him, he wryly counsels her,

> . . . never let it trouble you,
> Or cost you one caress;
> Ghosts are soon sent with a word or two
> Back to their loneliness.

As he bids farewell to his love in **"Therefore, Adieu,"** he is left a living dead man. Gone is "The feeling of the heart out of the breast." **"There Must Be Words"** finds the speaker left with only the "wild" and tenuous hope to go on living, and he mourns a dead love affair with brave words he himself can scarcely credit. The ghostliness Cullen frequently associates with love—based on the sense of love's being less than it normally appears to be, just as a ghost is a fleshless replica of a more substantial entity—haunts the poem **"Bright Bindings."** The poem is, unfortunately, haunted also by a mixing of book and ghost imagery, but the point is that the first-person narrator reads his lover's feelings as if they were an unread book, learns that they are sham and that she is a "windy tapering ghost" instead of the "flesh gifted to ache and bleed" that he had wanted. Yet, as in other poems considered here, he will settle for what he can get and save the book, that is, the amorous relationship, knowing that it is "counterfeit."

By now it is patently clear that Cullen's view of love is an uncommonly dismal one, and that in one way or another, as a dark threat to love or as a way out of an already destroyed and destructive love affair, death looms large in that view. Since, in the examination of religion in Cullen, it has been shown that death is also closely connected to religion, it is not illogical to anticipate that religious elements are to be found in some of Cullen's love poems. He looks to faith or, more accurately, to religious imagery and analogues to acquit him in trials of love as he does to ease the vicissitudes of other facets of his life. An excellent example is provided by the sonnet **"Dictum"**:

> Yea, I have put thee from me utterly,
> And they who plead thy cause do plead in vain;
> Window and door are bolted, never key
> From any ore shall cozen them again.
> This is my regal justice: banishment,
> That those who read me now may read and see
> How self-sustained I am, with what content
> I thrive alike on love or treachery.
>
> God, Thou hast Christ, they say, at Thy right hand;
> Close by Thy left Michael is straight and leal;
> Around Thy throne the chanting elders stand,
> And on earth Thy feudal millions kneel.
> Criest Thou never, Lord, above their song:
> "But Lucifer was tall, his wings were long?"

In the barest terms, the speaker has been done wrong by someone he has loved and has cut himself off from the culprit. But the disappointment and ensuing rejection gain vastly in dignity and depth from the presentation in a form that echoes the Psalms, imperfectly but sufficiently in measure, and the use of King James-sounding archaisms—the pronouns, "yea," "do plead," "cozen," "leal." And the ironic bit of self-revelation, of which Cullen is so fond, borrows considerable poignance and stature from the speaker's identifying himself with God up to a point, then standing back and asking God, in effect, whether, the faithful heavenly and earthly host notwithstanding, He does not cry out in anguish for the loss of the excellent Lucifer. That is, the religious construct of the poem finally underscores the narrator's wistfulness, undermining the facade of regal bravado.

Other verses, in like fashion, use religion as a source of imagery or of material for framework, from the *Color* collection right through *The Medea and Some Poems.* Cullen again mixes metaphors in **"Sacrament,"** his love's body being his meat and her soul his wine while the tidal waves of her passion, ironically, "Cast bread on stagnant water." In a companion piece, **"Bread and Wine,"** he becomes bread drawing from the lips of his lover "Strength . . . for one more fight" in a world he labels a "sweaty shop." **"One Day We Played a Game"** recounts an idyll he has enjoyed beneath an apple tree one day with a young woman: they decide to play a game called "Name me a Name" in which one speaks the name of a famous lover and the other replies with the name of the mate (in the light of past discussion about Cullen's linking of love to death, it is interesting that he notes how "The grave was liberal" in yielding up the names of dead lovers). Their abandon increases as he plays Abelard to her Heloise, Pelleas to her Melisande, Tristan to her Isolde, Ninus to her Semiramis, Lancelot (whom he is happy to be, instead of the forgotten Arthur) to her Guinevere, until their ardor reaches cre-

scendo when he coaxes her to call him "Adam." Now the tenor of the lovers' game changes:

> . . . My lips grew soft with "Eve,"
> And round with ardor purposing to leave
> Upon your mouth a lasting seal of bliss. . . .
> But midway of our kissing came a hiss
> Above us in the apple tree; a sweet
> Red apple rolled between us at our feet,
> And looking up we saw with glide and dip,
> Cold supple coils among the branches slip.
> "Eve!" "Eve!" I cried, "Beware!" Too late. You bit.
> Half of the fruit away. . . . The rest of it
> I took, assuring you with misty eyes,
> "Fare each as each, we lost no Paradise."

The fact that the poem is addressed to Yolande DuBois, the woman who was to become Cullen's first wife for only a brief time, might tempt one to see his wreaking a bit of poetic vengeance on her by using the Adam and Eve story to invoke God's retributive power, but what is important for the purpose of this discussion is that Cullen does use the scriptural story to structure this version of a relationship between lovers, in particular the most intense, physical part of the liaison. The other famous lovers may serve to build to the climax, but it is Adam and Eve who share that experience. And it is as Adam and Eve, willing to take a kind of fortunate fall for future lovers, that he thinks of himself and his love in **"The Love Tree."** He urges her in this poem to plant with him the seed of their unhappy love, to nurture it with tears and weed it with bleeding hands. He wants, that is, a Christlike sacrifice of their love to redeem lovers to come:

> . . . And men
> Will pilgrimage from far and wide to see
> This tree for which we two were crucified,
> And, happy in themselves, will never know
> 'Twas break of heart that made the Love Tree grow.

Thus it is in Christian terms that Cullen finds hope for a love affair that is hapless in itself, just as it is only through the conception of himself as a monk regretting excruciatingly his renunciation of earthly pleasures that he can adequately express the abysmal depression he feels over the end of a love affair. The man finds that Christ and promises of heaven are not enough to sustain him, but the religious situation still provides the vehicle for the feeling; the monk cries out, and the speaker comments to his love:

> . . . "Take Heaven, all, but give me back
> Those words and sighs without which I am dead;
> Which thinking on are lances, and I reel."
> Letting you go, I know how he would feel.
> **("Sonnet: I Know Now How a Man Whose Blood Is Hot")**

What ultimately emerges from a consideration of the body of Cullen's love poems is the strong sense that he is dangerously vulnerable to love and that he perceives lovers as fickle and love as untrustworthy and ephemeral. Death—or its stand-in, sleep—and religion so often furnish the appropriate metaphorical structure exactly because he regards love as both impermanent and threatening. There are, of course, as with any other generalizations about his verse, exceptions, but they are just that—exceptions, conspicuous mainly because of their uncommonness. The "Name Me a Name" game, for instance, grows to a limited extent out of awareness of death and depends heavily on a biblical episode, but it implies the achievements of champion lovers and stresses the importance of earthly love over the celestial. **"Asked and Answered"** begins with the poet wondering about the duration of a love affair in which he is involved, but ends with his convincing himself not to fear the end. Yet even in this poem, in one sense an exception, Cullen is sharply conscious of the inevitable conclusion of love; he simply steels himself, in an epicurean way, against the end:

> Why should I harrow up my mind like this
> To tarnish with a doubt each golden kiss?
> This is the Day most certainly. This bars
> Us now from any hidden darkness spun.
> Sufficient to the day let be the sun,
> And to the night the spear-points of the stars.

Because of the transitory nature of love and the fickleness of the women he sees dabbling in it, the end must come, and sooner more probably than later. Cullen may come to believe in the Christian conception of eternity, but he cannot, in the mass of his love poetry, come to accept Dionysian eternality. In poem after poem his cynicism over love's lack of durability is stated more or less openly. He declaims at the beginning of a poem:

> If love be staunch, call mountains brittle;
> Love is a thing will live
> So long, my dear,—oh, just the little
> While water stays in a sieve.
>
> ("If Love Be Staunch")

And he finishes the same piece with this comment on the poet's romanticizing of love:

> Whom yesterday love rhymed his sun
> Today he names a star;
> When the course of another day is run,
> What will he say you are?

In "The Spark" he invites his lover to help him stamp out the spark of their association, and he cavalierly returns her heart in exchange for his ill-kept one, assuring her that there is no need to pine, since "New heads near mine / Will dent the clover." He is equally cynical in "A Song No Gentleman Would Sing to Any Lady" in which he accounts for his having been taught by a female who has ended her relationship with him how to distinguish between a dove and a serpent, how "though a snake / Has made them, wounds may heal." There is a bravado about the poem, that of a young man who has discovered how resilient he is, how resistant to the destructive force of love. "The Simple Truth" transforms the braggadocio into a more tranquil acceptance of the changeability of love: lonely and sorry the poet may be, but he philosophizes that "Ever this was the way of wind with flame: / To harry it, then leave swift as it came." "Song in Spite of Myself" summarizes the lessons of love Cullen has learned, but its title suggests a dichotomy between the advice he gives and his ability to yet abide by it himself. "Never love with all your heart," he cautions, nor with all your soul or mind:

> Give but a grain of the heart's rich seed,
> Confine some under cover
> And when love goes, bid him God-speed
> And find another lover.

But for all the advice and intent, can Cullen hoard himself in this way? Perhaps his most comprehensive view of love, and one that still speaks of the fickleness of love, is to be found in the "Sonnet" that begins "Some for a little while do love, and some for long" in which he admits that some loves endure "forever and for aye," while "some in blood do plight

a fickle troth." The central point is that with love, one can never be sure:

> So many ways love has none may appear
> The bitter best, and none the sweetest worst;
> Strange food the hungry have been known to bear,
> And brackish water slakes an utter thirst.
> It is a rare and tantalizing fruit
> Our hands reach for, but nothing absolute.

Cullen cannot always be so detached, and in poems in which he is more emotionally involved, he suffers from his vulnerability. Even in the case of a lover's having cut him with surgical precision and aloofness, "Folks will not know / A wound has been," but though he may conceal it from others, he cannot but feel the incision. In "The Cat" (from the French of Baudelaire) he sees incarnate in the cat "A woman with thine eyes, satanic beast, / Profound and cold as scythes to mow me down," while he caresses the animal. A woman has another, a classically malevolent embodiment in "Medusa": looking upon the mythological creature costs one's eyesight. In Cullen's treatment of Medusa it is, significantly, not her ugliness that has blinded him, but the loveliness of her countenance—metaphorically, his vulnerability to beauty. Sometimes he knows of his capacity to be hurt by love and takes precautions. To love "in the noblest way" is to love without restraint, but he withholds a measure of nobility because

> The noblest way is fraught with too much pain;
> Who travels it must drop a crucifix;
> What hurts my heart hurts deep and to the grain;
> My mother never dipped me in the Styx,
> And who would find me weak and vulnerable
> Need never aim his arrow at my heel.

He knows, too, that he is not the only human to be victimized by love. The tension between the title of the poem "Every Lover" and the assumption of the contents of the piece yields a wry insight into the universality of the afflicted lovers. The speaker of the poem insists that his hurt is unique, that: "There were no lovers bowed before my time; / Before this treachery was none betrayed"; love has been only to him a weasel, a fox, an asp, and his body has been infected by an "alien humour" that has mingled "a god's disease with mortal blood." He concludes by nursing his ego on the thought that "Surely this visitation is divine; / No breast has fed a malady like mine." The title shows Cullen's recurrent, if not constant, ability to stand back and smile understandingly at his own sentiments, for it destroys the poem's illusion of the singularly suffering narrator and betrays Cullen's broader view that love diseases any man it touches. It is this kind of ironic detachment and humor that makes Cullen's love poetry, for all its plaintiveness and sense of vulnerability, usually less maudlin and embarrassing than it would otherwise be.

Yet, finally, it is Cullen's very openness to attack by the fickleness of love that makes itself most felt in the sensibility of the reader. Perhaps as lucid an example as any is provided in "One Day I Told My Love." In this poem there is no suffering because in the end, the girl the narrator addresses happens to treat his heart gently and warns him against exposing it, but the point is that, in a powerful metaphor, he makes himself infinitely vulnerable to his lover's whims. He removes his very heart from its "hidden socket / Where it was wont to grieve," and offers to fashion for her a locket or other ornament from it. In the telling third stanza of the poem he confesses the formidable danger to which he has laid his heart open:

I let her hold the naked thing
No one had seen before;
And had she willed her hand might wring
It dry and drop it to the floor.

For Countee Cullen, love is too uncertain a thing to be trusted. Death is surer and more welcome, and, he comes eventually to believe, so is the Christian salvation that death makes possible. (pp. 40-69)

> *Alan R. Shucard, in his* Countee Cullen, *Twayne Publishers, 1984, 145 p.*

BERNARD W. BELL   (essay date 1987)

[*Bell is an American critic and educator who specializes in black American literature. In the following excerpt from his* The Afro-American Novel and Its Traditions, *Bell discusses characterizations in* One Way to Heaven *and compares technical aspects of the work with those of two novels by Langston Hughes.*]

Divided into two major parts, *One Way to Heaven,* like [Langston] Hughes's *Tambourines to Glory,* is a sympathetic exposure of the gullibility and superstition of unsophisticated lower-class urban blacks. It is the love story of Sam Lucas, a one-armed confidence man who fakes religious conversion at black churches up and down the Eastern seaboard to satisfy his immediate physical needs, and Mattie Johnson, an attractive but desperate young domestic whose religious zeal Sam awakens with his con game. At revival meetings and watch-night services, Sam goes into his act at a dramatic moment during testimonials. Walking from the rear of the church to the mourner's bench, he would throw down a greasy deck of cards and polished razor, fall on his knees in tears, and sob for salvation. To devout Methodists and Baptists, Sam's last-minute conversion was "mystery and miracle and the confirmation of faith." As they came forward to shake hands with the converts and show their gratitude, many of the faithful would secretly slip him money, and "he had never joined church yet but it had led to an affair." In Part 1 (chaps. 1-7) Sam's act in a Harlem church becomes the catalyst for Mattie's salvation, and in blind faith she marries him. In Part 2 (chaps. 8-15) her religiosity drives him into the arms of another woman. But a fatal case of double pneumonia brings them together again, and for her sake he fakes a deathbed conversion.

The author-narrator's mild ridicule of the superstitious practices of his lower-class characters is in sharp contrast to his sardonic treatment of the pretentious customs of the black bourgeoisie. Sam, for example, uses his cards and razor for both good and evil, and though an indolent, irreligious vagabond, his excessive pragmatism evokes our sympathetic laughter. Equally humorous and realistic is Matie's Aunt Mandy, whom the third-person omniscient author-narrator describes in the sympathetic manner that characterizes the frequent commentaries on the beliefs and rituals of the lower class: "Though she was not averse to trusting serenely to the ways of Providence, she often attempted by reading tea leaves and coffee dregs, and by consulting her cards, to speed the blessings of Heaven or to ward off, if possible, some celestial chastisement." In contrast, the language used in chapters 8, 9, and 10 to describe Constancia Brandon, Mattie's well-bred but patronizing black employer, and her high-society crowd is characterized by biting wit, repartee, and hyperbole.

A Boston-born Baptist, Constancia Brandon changed her name at sixteen and rejected "the religious ecstasies of the Baptist and Methodist faiths . . . to scale the heavenly ramparts by way of the less rugged paths of the Episcopalian persuasion." Constancia's "tongue was her chief attraction, ornament, and deterrent." At Radcliffe she was called Lady Macbeth, not because she was unsexed and shrewd in the pursuit of her ambition, but because she never spoke in a monosyllable when she could use a polysyllable. Her monthly soirees were pompous, gala occasions. Although these innumerable gatherings were held "under the uninviting and prosaic auspices of the Booklovers' Society," it was widely known and admitted by more than half of the group itself that they never read books. Now and then, however, "they might under pressure, purchase the latest opus of some Negro novelist or poet." The core of this polyglot group of booklovers, friends, and social parasites includes Sarah Desverney, a local librarian for whom "no Negro had written anything of import since Dunbar and Chestnutt"; Bradley Norris, a radical poet "to whom everything not New Negro was anathema"; Samuel Weinstein, a caustic self-appointed Negrophile and authority on Negro life; and Mrs. Harold De Peyster Johnson, a race-conscious public school teacher on whom the author-narrator heaps more than four pages of blistering scorn: "She had, as it were, midwifed at the New Negro's birth, and had groaned in spirit with the travail and suffering of Ethiopia in delivering herself to this black *enfant terrible,* born capped and gowned, singing, "The Negro National Anthem" and clutching in one hand a pen, in the other a paintbrush." Whether humorous or witty, amused or contemptuous, Cullen's satire is generally indirect, and his motives are most clearly revealed in Constancia's explanation for inviting the Negrophobic Professor Calhoun to address the Booklovers' Society on "The Menace of the Negro to Our American Civilization." " 'An irrefutable evidence of a sense of humor . . . is the ability to laugh at oneself, as well as at one's tormentors and defamers,' " she says, " 'If we haven't learned that in these three hundred years, we have made sorry progress.' "

Even though the chapters depicting black high society sparkle with wit, farce, caricature, and repartee, they have at best a tenuous connection to the moral theme of the narrative, which is symbolized in the bond between Sam and Aunt Mandy. For them and the ministers, Johnson and Drummond, life is ambiguous; the ways of God mysterious; and "there were more ways to Heaven than one." The moral ambiguity of Sam's life is apparent in the use of his cards and razor. In response to his question about whether cards were evil, Aunt Mandy, the moral center of the novel, replies, " 'It all depends on the kind of cards you have and what you do with them.' " Although a staunch Methodist, Aunt Mandy relies on the power of conjuration as well as on the songs and emotionalism of her church to affirm her faith in love and life. During prayer service, she was as fervent in her singing, rocking back and forth, and moaning as the other "aging handmaidens of the Lord." She felt that it was all right to be lost in the inner life, "but there were things in this other life which were more important. And loving was one." When Mattie was losing Sam to another woman, Aunt Mandy advises her that " 'sometimes when the angels is too busy to help you, you have to fight the devil with his own tools.' " After sleeping three nights on the cards and razor which were baptized in Madam Samantha's magic water, Mattie is suddenly reunited with Sam. Thus, the plot, characters, and style of *One Way to Heaven* point with wry humor to more than one way to heaven.

In addition to the convincing portrayals of commonplace church-going people, the novels of Cullen and Hughes provide interesting contrasts in narrative technique and the handling of time. In [Hughes's] *Not without Laughter,* a *bildungsroman,* and *Tambourines to Glory,* a low comedy, the emphasis is on dramatizing events in order to heighten immediacy and verisimilitude; represented and representational time are frequently congruent; and showing predominates over telling. In contrast, **One Way to Heaven,** a mixture of satiric comedy and comedy of manners, relies heavily on the author-narrator's commentary on plot, character, and theme to make explicit and to expand the ironic pattern of the narrative; the time-ratio is manipulated to facilitate analysis of character; and telling predominates over showing. There is little emotional but considerable moral and intellectual distance between the author-narrators and their protagonists. The relationship of the reader to the protagonists, however, is less simple. Because the authors permit Sandy and Sam to tell only part of their stories and then only in the third person, much of the reader's sympathy for them is sacrificed, which is a more serious weakness in *Not without Laughter* than in **One Way to Heaven. . . .** Finally, because Cullen exploits irony, ambiguity, and symbolism more self-consciously than Hughes, he appeals to the reader's intellectual interests but risks more serious flaws in structure and character as he moves from the realistic to the satiric mode. (pp. 134-36)

Bernard W. Bell, "The Harlem Renaissance and the Search for New Modes of Narrative," in his The Afro-American Novel and Its Tradition, *The University of Massachusetts Press, 1987, pp. 93-149.*

FURTHER READING

Collier, Eugenia W. "I Do Not Marvel, Countee Cullen." *CLA Journal* XI, No. 1 (September 1967): 73-87.
    Considers Cullen in an essay praising poets of the Harlem Renaissance.

Copeland, Catherine H. "The Unifying Effect of Coupling in Countee Cullen's 'Yet Do I Marvel.'" *CLA Journal* XVIII, No. 2 (December 1974): 258-61.
    Analyzes ways in which technical aspects of the sonnet reinforce the theme Cullen intended to convey.

Dillon, George H. "Mr. Cullen's First Book." *Poetry* XXVIII, No. 1 (April 1926): 50-3.
    Positive review of *Color.*

Dorsey, David F., Jr. "Countee Cullen's Use of Greek Mythology." *CLA Journal* XIII, No. 1 (September 1969): 68-77.
    Evaluates Cullen's use of classical allusions, suggesting that "it is characteristic of Cullen's poetic technique to reverse the symbolic content of his allusions to Greek (and sometimes Christian) mythology, thereby doubling their semantic content, that is, their significance in his own contexts."

Emanuel, James A. "Renaissance Sonneteers." *Black World* XXIV, No. 11 (September 1975): 32-45, 92-97.
    Examines some of Cullen's poems in a study of how black poets of the 1920s used the sonnet form to explore themes in black experience, and reflects on the significance of this literary tradition for black writers of the 1970s.

Littlejohn, David. "Before *Native Son:* The Renaissance and After." In his *Black on White: A Critical Survey of Writing by American Negroes,* pp. 39-65. New York: Viking Press, 1966.
    Includes criticism of *One Way to Heaven* and selected poems by Cullen in a general discussion of Harlem Renaissance writers. This essay is excerpted in an entry on the Harlem Renaissance in *TCLC,* Vol. 26, pp. 99-103.

Lomax, Michael L. "Countee Cullen: A Key to the Puzzle." In *The Harlem Renaissance Re-examined,* edited by Victor A. Kramer, pp. 213-22. New York: AMS Press, 1987.
    Surveys the development of Cullen's career and critical responses to his works, suggesting that Cullen's rejection of race as a poetic theme was the major reason for his decline as a poet.

Perry, Margaret. *Silence to the Drums: A Survey of the Literature of the Harlem Renaissance.* Westport, Conn.: Greenwood Press, 1976, 194 p.
    Comparative study of Harlem Renaissance writers which includes thematic and technical analysis of Cullen's poems and novel.

Potter, Vilma. "Countee Cullen: The Making of a Poet-Editor." *Pacific Coast Philology* XV, No. 2 (December 1980): 19-27.
    Discusses Cullen's role as editor of a special issue of *PALMS,* a small poetry magazine, and of the anthology *Caroling Dusk,* suggesting that Cullen's poetic output declined as editing became a central part of his career.

Rice, Philip Blair. "Euripides in Harlem." *The Nation* 141, No. 3, 663 (18 September 1935): 336.
    Praises Cullen's rendering of *The Medea.*

Smylie, James H. "Countee Cullen's 'The Black Christ.'" *Theology Today* XXXVIII, No. 2 (July 1981): 160-73.
    Examines the relationship between Christ's crucifixion and the lynching of American blacks in works by Cullen and others. Smylie states that Cullen's "The Black Christ" "transforms the existential black experience into a universal message about Christ's passion and triumph."

Tuttleton, James W. "Countee Cullen at 'The Heights.'" In *The Harlem Renaissance: Revaluations,* edited by Amritjit Singh, William S. Shiver, and Stanley Brodwin, pp. 101-37. New York: Garland Publishing, 1989.
    Describes Cullen's undergraduate career at New York University, noting the influence of Professor Hyder E. Rollins on the themes and style of Cullen's poetry. The essay includes a reprint of Cullen's honors thesis on the poetry of Edna St. Vincent Millay.

Young, James O. *Black Writers of the Thirties.* Baton Rouge: Louisiana State University Press, 1973, 257 p.
    Contains numerous references to Cullen, contrasting the attitudes he expressed in "The Black Christ" and *One Way to Heaven* with those of other black writers of the 1930s.

Charlotte Perkins Gilman

1860-1935

(Full name Charlotte Anna Perkins Stetson Gilman) American short story writer, essayist, and novelist.

For further discussion of Gilman's career, see *TCLC,* Volume 9.

Gilman was a prominent social activist and the leading theorist of the women's movement at the turn of the century. She examined the role of women in society and propounded her social theories in *Women and Economics* and other nonfiction works, while she depicted the realization of her feminist ideals in her novels and short stories. Gilman is best known today for her short story "The Yellow Wallpaper," in which she portrayed a young woman's mental breakdown.

Gilman was born in Hartford, Connecticut, to Frederick Beecher Perkins, a noted librarian and magazine editor, and his wife, Mary Fritch Perkins. Although Gilman's father frequently left the family for long periods during her childhood and eventually divorced his wife in 1869, he directed Gilman's early education, emphasizing study in the sciences and history. During his absences, Perkins left his wife and children with his relatives, thus bringing Gilman into frequent contact with her independent and reform-minded great-aunts: Harriet Beecher Stowe, the abolitionist and author of *Uncle Tom's Cabin;* Catherine Beecher, the prominent advocate of "domestic feminism"; and Isabella Beecher Hooker, an ardent suffragist. Their influence—and the example of her own mother's self-reliance—were instrumental in developing Gilman's feminist convictions and desire to effect social reform. Early in her life Gilman displayed the independence she later advocated for women: she insisted on remuneration for her household chores, and later she paid her mother room and board, supporting herself as a teacher and as a commercial artist. At twenty-four, she married Charles Walter Stetson, who was also an artist. Following the birth of their daughter in 1884, Gilman suffered from severe depression. She consulted the noted neurologist S. Weir Mitchell, who prescribed his "rest cure": complete bed rest and limited intellectual activity. Gilman credited this experience with driving her "so near the borderline of utter mental ruin that [she] could see over." She removed herself from Mitchell's care, and later, attributing her emotional problems in part to the confines of marriage, she left her husband.

After her separation, Gilman moved to California, where she helped edit feminist publications, assisted in the planning of the California Women's Congresses of 1894 and 1895, and was instrumental in founding the Women's Peace Party. She spent several years lecturing in the United States and England on women's rights and on labor reform and in 1898 published *Women and Economics.* In 1900 she married George Houghton Gilman, who was supportive of her intense involvement in social reform. From 1909 through 1916 Gilman published a monthly journal, *The Forerunner,* for which she wrote nearly all of the copy. As a vehicle for advancing social awareness, *The Forerunner* has been called her "single greatest achievement." In 1935, having learned that she suffered from inoperable cancer, Gilman took her life, writing

in a final note that "when one is assured of unavoidable and imminent death, it is the simplest of human rights to choose a quick and easy death in place of a slow and horrible one."

Gilman's best known nonfiction work, *Women and Economics,* had its origin in her studies of Charles Darwin's theory of evolution and the writings of Lester Frank Ward, who maintained that "the elevation of woman is the only sure road to the elevation of man." She argued that women's secondary status in society, and especially women's economic dependence on men, is not the result of biological inferiority, but rather of culturally enforced behavior. In questioning whether there were fundamental differences in potential between the sexes, Gilman was not expressing new ideas. However, Carl N. Degler has noted that "no one in her time focussed the arguments so sharply and stated them so cogently and lucidly as she did." In other nonfiction works, including *Concerning Children, Human Work,* and *The Man-Made World,* Gilman suggested that women should work outside of the home, fully utilizing their talents for the benefit of society and for their own satisfaction. She proposed removing from the home such duties as cooking, laundry, and child care by arranging households in clusters of single-family dwellings or multifamily buildings with professionals in charge of these tasks.

In her fiction, Gilman portrayed women struggling to achieve self-sufficiency or adapting to newfound independence. Gilman declared that she wrote fiction primarily to illustrate her social ideas and many critics consider her stories and novels stylistically unimaginative. Her short stories frequently provide models showing women how to change their lives or redesign society, while her last three fictional works, *Moving the Mountain, Herland,* and *With Her in Ourland,* are utopian novels depicting worlds in which attitudes towards women and their abilities have radically changed. Critics find that despite her shortcomings as a fiction writer, Gilman used satire deftly in *Herland,* challenging accepted images of women by describing the reactions of three American males who enter Herland, an all-female society which reproduces through parthenogenesis. "The Yellow Wallpaper," considered Gilman's best work of fiction, is also her least typical. Rather than an optimistic vision of what women can achieve, the story is a first-person account of a young mother's mental deterioration, based on Gilman's own experiences. Although early reviewers interpreted "The Yellow Wallpaper" as either a horror story or a case study in psychosis, most modern critics see it as a feminist indictment of society's subjugation of women and praise its compelling characterization, complex symbolism, and thematic depth.

With the changes in American society since World War I, Gilman's economic theories have appeared increasingly less radical and have therefore attracted less notice. However, as women's roles continue to evolve, her sociological studies and her suggestions for nontraditional housekeeping and child care arrangements gain in significance. Many modern feminist nonfiction works reflect the influence of Gilman's ideas, and readers are rediscovering in her thought much that is relevant to contemporary problems.

(See also *Contemporary Authors,* Vol. 106.)

PRINCIPAL WORKS

"The Yellow Wallpaper" (short story) 1892; published in journal *New England Magazine;* also published in book form as *The Yellow Wallpaper* in 1892
In This Our World (poetry) 1893
Women and Economics: A Study of the Economic Relation Between Men and Women as a Factor in Social Evolution (essay) 1898
Concerning Children (essay) 1900
The Home: Its Work and Influence (essay) 1903
Human Work (essay) 1904
The Punishment That Educates (essay) 1907
Women and Social Service (essay) 1907
What Diantha Did (novel) 1909; published serially in journal *The Forerunner;* also published in book form in 1910
The Crux (novel) 1911
The Man-Made World; or, Our Androcentric Culture (essay) 1911
Moving the Mountain (novel) 1911
Benigna Machiavelli (novel) 1914; published in journal *The Forerunner*
Herland (novel) 1915; published serially in journal *The Forerunner;* also published in book form in 1978
With Her in Ourland (novel) 1916; published in journal *The Forerunner*

His Religion and Hers: A Study of the Faith of Our Fathers and the Work of Our Mothers (essay) 1923
The Living of Charlotte Perkins Gilman (autobiography) 1935
The Charlotte Perkins Gilman Reader (short stories and novel fragments) 1980

THE NATION (essay date 1899)

[*In the following review of* Women and Economics, *the critic summarizes Gilman's argument for women's economic independence.*]

The As-Suchness of Woman is a well worn theme, and confession to a weariness of it as a topic is a suitable preface to saying that [**Women and Economics**] seems to us the most significant utterance on the subject since Mill's *Subjection of Women* reached a class of thinkers never before touched by any views later than those of Noah. This is far from agreement with all of Mrs. Stetson's conclusions or even premises, or from always finding logical connection between the two. What is asserted is that the subject is approached from a new point of view, with a new largeness of outlook, both backward and forward; a new business capacity, so to speak, in arraying the pros and cons on the field of debate; a new imaginativeness in interpretation, and finally a temper which, being good, is perhaps newest of all. While it would be easy to ridicule some of her propositions and caricature some of her arguments, it is still easier not to do so, but to dwell and ponder upon their serious and lofty aspirations. It is a book which invites and should lead to reasonable and scientific discussion.

The main argument is that the long economic dependence of woman on man as her source of food constitutes a false economic relation between them, and hence is responsible for an exaggerated and mischievous differentiation of the sexes beyond what is seen in any other animal creature, causing, through mal-apportionment of the world's work, a distortion of human relations and human qualities. It would be simple to reply in the old couplet that man has not a microscopic eye, "for this good reason, man is not a fly"; but such retort is promptly disarmed by the proclamation that, evil as have been the effects on woman, it is this very process which has made of man a higher being than the fly, by evolving the paternal qualities. From the purely utilitarian male carried about in the wings of the cirriped in extra numbers for fear of loss, the masculine half of creation in man has risen to the man-mother, performing the world's duties, his own, and many of woman's. Hers, after her natural sex functions, are, according to Mrs. Stetson, too exclusively those of dependent nurse and house servant. But before the reader has time to suggest that practically all industries and all professions are now open to women, our author meets us with the exultant admission that the change is here, brought about by neither the will nor seeking of man or woman, but by the force of social evolution, working as painfully now as it has worked before, yet, as she enthusiastically believes, bringing us out into "better motherhood and fatherhood, better babyhood and childhood, better food, better homes, better society." "It is already happening. All we need do is to understand and help." So, then, woman's long servitude has helped to form certain fine traits in man, yet has encouraged him too in hardness and the lust for power. Upon herself the effect has been dwarfing and enslaving, promoting "a feverish, torturing, moral sensitiveness, without the width and clarity of vision of a full-grown moral sense." She may rejoice over what she has accomplished, but the reaction is at hand in which alone full development lies.

The argument is an interesting one, and full of suggestion, that, as women have become over-sexed through æons of economic dependence on man, so, through becoming in greater measure their own providers, they will lead the whole race, both men and women, back to simpler living and simpler relationship, and thus forward a higher life in which the worst evils of humanity will shrivel out of existence from sheer non-nutrition. "Not the sex-relation, but the economic relation of the sexes has so tangled the skein of human life." The new order is to bring about "a union between man and woman such as the world has long dreamed of in vain." As Mrs. Stetson's search for causes goes back to the beginnings of life, so her conclusions reach forward to a millennium which she firmly believes is having its inauguration.

A few chapters are given to detailed suggestions of improved ways of living. These are to include the abolition of the private kitchen, even as the private laundry and bakery have largely disappeared. The kindergarten and the ballot-box are taken for granted as essentials for which no arguments need be adduced; the one ill-natured sentence of the book, indeed, occurs in this connection, where the writer alludes to "that crowning imbecility of history—the banded opposition of some women to the advance of the others." She feels it necessary, however, to make a special plea for the outside day-nursery, where the babies can spend some hours of each day in being "a baby" and not "my baby"—realizing, doubtless, that many a woman reader (like the husband who plumed himself on never praising to his wife his mother's pies—"except mince") will consent to the banishment of the kitchen stove, the family dining-room, the domestic broom, but will draw the line at the baby. It would be unjust, however, to this dignified book to try its cause by extracted sentences. In such wise, one might make easy inference that the home and the family are of lessening importance; that "mother's doughnuts" are necessarily indigestible, and cousinly affection a fast-dying relic of patriarchal days. Such criticism would be nearsighted. The book is one to be read with one's best historic glasses on. But even so it must be added in candor that we think not enough value is attached to the educational influences of family friction, of doing what one does not want to do, of the bondage to duty which, after all, is humanity's only freedom.

A review of "Women and Economics," in The Nation, New York, Vol. LXVIII, No. 1771, June 8, 1899, p. 443.

ALEXANDER BLACK (essay date 1923)

[*In the following excerpt, Black surveys Gilman's major works and praises her advocacy of women's rights.*]

All radicals share the chance that civilization will catch up with them. The radical of Nazareth may illustrate the fact that there can be no certainty of such a consummation, but the phenomenon happens often enough to remind any who care to think about it that civilization does at times, perhaps breathlessly, come abreast, or almost seem to have come

abreast, of one who has been striding ahead. Civilization can do this without condoning the original offense of being too soon, which gives a peculiar interest to speculation upon the situation of the caught-up-with.

It might be a bit reckless to classify Charlotte Perkins Gilman among thinkers who have been overtaken. She is still, in many of her doctrines and convictions, lonesomely in advance of the accepted. The arc of her early challenge ran beyond the visible horizon. But so much of her preaching that once was regarded as revolutionary is now a matter of polite consideration, if not of practice, that her total effect is no longer so sharply radical as it was to the generation to which we look back. She herself is still looking forward. She was never a mere storm. An imitative noisiness is often mistaken for real rebellion. Mrs. Gilman has always been more like an incorrigible current. Her tide seems to have no ebb. She is the poorest compromiser I know. She is never pugnacious. No one could have less interest in conflict for its own sake. Her persistent idealism has often appalled the merely aggressive. I can testify that as partner in a wrangle she is as gentle as a river. When you try an obstruction, she overflows the banks of the argument. She can do this graciously—as graciously as gravitation.

She exemplifies a fact, which we frequently have occasion to notice, that preachers of a better socialization for the world have seldom been aggressively "sociable." It is as if to *see* socialization one must be aloof. We do not look for social idealism in a mixer. The prophet is likely to be an incompetent pusher, perhaps because the all-of-us vision is hard to acquire in contact with the crowd. Yet Mrs. Gilman might seem to have followed Emerson's suggestion with regard to solitude and society by keeping her head in one and her hands in the other. She is no recluse. I am thinking of her congenital inadaptability to the free-for-all. She is more a telescope person than a microscope person, despite her disposition to open every scientific door. She thinks best in terms of constellations, with due respect to the electron as a theoretical detail. To her the individualist represents the great delusion. She sees the human brain as a social product and all separatist efforts as grotesque. She speaks somewhere of an "ex-man" on a desert island. The absurdity of the socially created trying to be *selfish,* of trying to feed a social hunger an ego meal, stirs her sense of the incongruous.

There is plenty of room for quarrel in any such contention, as any struggler in philosophy before or during Bergson well knows. I have, on occasion, joined the mêlée. I belong among the innocents who are ready to admit that the collective comes first. But first considerations are not always most important considerations. It is of first importance to be born. It is of greater importance to be worth borning. Mass is a beginning fact. It may be that it was invented to make possible an individual destination—that it is the mass and not the individual that is a means. Mrs. Gilman holds, adding her own inflections, with the school to which the individual is purely theoretical. Her individual is atomic. He never really happens. When he is being most personal he is simply expressing a unit sign of a collective fact.

No one could offer a profounder illustration of the individual paradox than Mrs. Gilman herself. Before an audience she can seem to prophesy the most perfect participation. Yet her flame is not to be merged. When she preached socialistic ideals in California, the Socialists assumed that they had found a leader. But it turned out that a capital S could not be attached to her. Political Socialism, that is to say, applied Socialism, was unable to enlist her. She could speak before the Fabians in England, beside Bernard Shaw and his compatriots, but they could not make a Fabian of her. To the religion of socialistic effort she was warmly responsive; to the theology of Socialism she was cold. It was the same with the suffrage question. She was one of the strongest of the intellectual forces animating the woman-suffrage movement. With voice and with the printed word she stirred the pulse of progressive opinion, but recoiled from the political implications. It was not that she resented, here or elsewhere, the drudgery of application. She has, indeed, too seldom considered the limits of her strength in throwing herself into any labor of brain or hand, in the forum or in the household, that seemed to make demand of her. We cannot think of her as standing on a chair in the sooty rain of a Liverpool street, holding that British crowd with a voice as slender as her body, but singularly impassioned and penetrating, conquering the ear by the silent attention it could win, without realizing her resources in sacrifice. The trouble was that politics meant adjustment, concession, trimming. She wanted to move as she thought—straight through. The devious strategies of politics always affected her as not only irksome, but immoral. It was useless to argue that all application implied concession; that a searchlight might fall straight, but that the journey to the illuminated spot might mean not only fences and wet feet, but certain contentions as to right of way. She held the searchlight with a fervent steadiness. Talking to her about expedience was like asking a compass to compromise. (pp. 34-5)

Ten years of struggle followed the dissolution of [Gilman's first] marriage. Out of this period of poverty and abuse shine the first flashes of an extraordinary talent for verse. There had been miscellaneous writing, frequently for *The Impress,* the vigorously original organ of the Pacific Coast Women's Press Association (Helen Campbell was among the contributors), but verse seemed to give the most effective vent for a unique irony as well as for an impassioned sense of beauty. **"Similar Cases,"** printed in the *Nationalist* in 1891, had wide echoes. "We have had nothing since the Biglow Papers," wrote Mr. Howells, "half so good in a good cause." Mr. Howells added: "Since then I have read your **"Women of Today"** in the Women's Journal. It is as good as the other almost, and dreadfully true." Europe caught up **"Similar Cases."** As a *tour de force* in sarcasm the "evolution poem" gave lively joy to all who were thrusting into new lines of thought. The picture of the Eohippus who said, "I am going to be a horse!" of the ape who declared, "I'm going to be a Man!" and of the chorus screaming, "You'd have to change your nature!" had the fighting color. The prophecy of the Neolithic Man,

> We are going to wear great piles of stuff
> Outside our proper skins!
> We are going to have Diseases!
> And Accomplishments!! And
> Sins!!!

and the eternal rebuff, *"You must alter Human Nature,"* which was

> a clinching argument
> To the Neolithic mind,

accomplished a merry jab at the stand-patters, of which a glimpse is given in other verses, called **"The Conservative."** Here the dejected infant butterfly weeps over his wings.

> "I do not want to fly," said he,

> "I only want to squirm."

The squirmers have been Mrs. Gilman's mark from the beginning. *In This Our World* was the title given to a pamphlet edition of the poems, of which James H. Barry of the San Francisco *Star* and John H. Marble, printer, brought out a second edition in 1895. In the same year Mrs. Catherine Helen Spence carried the verses to England, and Fisher Unwin put them forth. Mrs. Gilman had begun to be known when she made her first trip to England in 1896. But it was the coming of that amazing document, *Women and Economics,* which established her position in Europe. "Since John Stuart Mill's essay," said the London *Chronicle* (it was alluding to Mill's *Subjection of Women*), "there has been no book dealing with the position of women to approach it in originality of conception and brilliancy of exposition." (pp. 38-9)

Human Work, which appeared in 1904, greatly added to English and Continental interest in the author of *Women and Economics.* Its huge lines and its philosophical audacity might well have given Europe an impression of a dynamic figure looming large on the American scene. As frequently happens, the prophet at home faced many obstacles. Yet none of these was more serious than the obstacle of ill health.

It was after consulting Dr. Weir Mitchell, and being told by him that her nerves demanded absolute abstinence from all intellectual work, that she wrote **"The Yellow Wallpaper,"** which Howells gathered into his *The Great Modern American Stories.* Weir Mitchell was to be her audience, and it is certain that his reading of the story influenced all of his later methods of treating neurasthenia. When the story, as a work of art, came in for many honors, she remarked: "I wrote it to preach. If it is literature, that just happened."

Here you have a hint of her philosophy as a literary workman. There is a good deal the effect of maintaining that, having one's idea, the transmission of it may be left to the grace of God. That the thing might be the other way about—that the idea might be by the grace of God and the expression remain a matter of momentous individual responsibility—would not strike her as tenable if it implied close consciousness in writing. She can fling an idea into an art package without the slightest anxiety as to its possible loss in the mail. To argue that the primary importance of the idea is not contradicted by the integrity of the house in which it is to live, and that certain ideas may really deserve a temple, is never impressive to a believer in the righteousness of freestriding thought. Perhaps success in talking to audiences eye to eye breeds impatience with the technic of the written page, and written pages that have nothing but technic supply arguments enough to literary rebels. They are not good arguments. A literary house out of plumb, a temple with a leaky roof, do not praise impulse. To put it another way, a gorgeous art chariot without a passenger can be ludicrous, but, on the other hand, a noble ambassador deserves something better than a rickety vehicle in which to reach his appointed destination.

Such criticism would be less valid if Mrs. Gilman's resources were not so plainly to be seen. In her early writings, in parody and in analysis, she displayed real artistic virtuosity. She has a deep sense of beauty. This may often be repressed, or held in subjection to the scientific spirit, but its reality is never to be doubted. Her knowledge of verse forms and her use of them, whimsically or emotionally, indicate an uncommon equipment. In all of her writing the frequency with which she is able to bring a stinging clearness to crises of her thought convicts her at other times of a rushing indifference to form and to effectiveness. Thus in the enormous volume of writing she poured into her magazine, *The Forerunner,* which for a fertile seven years she wrote from cover to cover, and which included two thought-crammed novels of great significance, **What Diantha Did** and **The Crux,** she often sacrificed much to a pace of expression.

When Mrs. Gilman says, "I am not an artist," she is rebuking strictly esthetic expectations. A thing like **"The Yellow Wall-paper"** (there is many another) proves that she *is* an artist when she chooses. She has interests sterner than esthetics. Even in her most vivid verse she is too intent upon meaning to dally with merely gracious sounds. The whole effect of her work, in every field, is of an intentness, of a seer's intentness, a prophet's passion to say, without hurry, but without lingering. She is nowhere observable as making a *thing:* she is making a case, she is translating a vision. That vision of woman has had an unexampled wideness. It has left suffrage, labor, all sociological detail to seem incidental. She has marked out more inclusively and more audaciously than any other thinker of her time the implications of the new biology as bearing on woman's place in the human game. She saw and described with an unmitigated clearness the obligation imposed by admitted truth as to the position of woman. Concession in theory gave her no comfort. She saw that systems of living had to be made over; that the whole structure of society stood upon a viciously wrong notion of human work and of woman's relationship to that work. She saw life as a verb, work as an expenditure of energy by society in the fulfilment of its organic function: that woman had never really escaped the primordial stigma of labor slavery; that man's place and his work had undergone vast adjustments, but that woman's place and woman's work were supposed to be immutable. Even woman's ignorance was invested with a mawkish glory. A mother who had "buried seven" was subject to no cross-examination as to her fitness for the non-competitive job she had been permitted to fill. She refused to be fooled by the opinion called history. She began by refusing to accept "human nature" as final. She accepts nothing as final, and is chary of "laws." She objected to "piling the dead years on the quivering brain of the child." She dared to insist that children, also, are persons. Her *Concerning Children* was a disturbing and epoch-marking plea. She dared to want "woman's work" professionalized, to wish to emancipate the mother who had need to earn wages. Her advocacy of the expert, specialist care of babies was greeted by cries of horror and pictures of her as one who would tear the child from its mother's breast. It had been bad enough to cast doubt upon the invariable mother capacity of a woman who had happened to bear a child; it was going too far to suggest that any outsiders could help her. Of course day nurseries came in due time; professionalized house service began to happen in due time; real prophecies of some sort of labor justice for women came along with suffrage and other statutory changes.

There have been so many fulfilments of demands made by our women pioneers that reactionary minds often assume that their work is done, and in this respect women are sinners quite equally with men. The grotesque delusion that women have really won an equality because they may go out to work, may hold judgeships and sit in legislatures, meets its startling contradictions. Mrs. Gilman concedes the appearance of vast change since the days when she worked with Jane Addams at Hull House or with the courageous suffrage leaders for a great cause. She still sees women as subsisting in a man-managed and oversexed world.

She has been skilful in giving a biologist's interpretation of sex. In her new book, **His Religion and Hers,** there is a ripe and relentless analysis of the larger sex question as revealed in sex interest. It recalls her picture of woman as the survival of the original sex and of man as the enterprising after-thought, which first elicited for her the special notice of European thinkers. Here again she takes up sex conflict as growing out of the failure to use the human rather than the sex equation. She sees man as primordially a fighter and consumer, if not a destroyer; woman as from the beginning the producer and conserver. She sees man's religion as based upon a postponed heaven; woman's religion as expressing a desire for a heaven here and now. She sees heaven not as a place, but as a race condition. She believes that when women have a greater degree of control of the world they will insist on a greater degree of practical consideration for the needs of immediate living; that the earth will be less a vale of tears when it is regarded less as preparation and more as opportunity. She can say "man-made," here as elsewhere, without giving the phrase a sharp flavor. No champion of the woman side has ever been freer from controversial acidity. No sociologist of either sex (she marks as of a true third sex the women who are childless because they hate children) has written of sex with greater detachment, and detachment in sex controversy is a triumph of ideality (and humor) over instinct. To a man she must always look like a fair fighter. A man may wince in watching her cheery excursions to the matriarchate; he may, indeed, especially when he is reading **Herland** (peopled wholly by women who have only girl children), feel that he has just escaped being negligible. He tritely admits that males have managed the world. He might weakly steal her logic and set up that they have managed it badly not because they were male, but because they were human. It would be a poor bit of shuffling, as poor as admitting that women could scarcely make a worse muddle of things.

Mrs. Gilman's vision of woman, of her rightful place in the world, of her supreme responsibility for race progress, however it may be debated, has strongly influenced the thought and the practices of her time. She was first to see many truths that have won acceptance. She still faces the horizon. As a true radical, she is impregnable to the influence of fashions. Hystericalisms leave her secure in her tower of vantage, without irritation and without concession, serenely intent, unshakably insistent that all personal aims, all government, all arts, all religions, shall bend to the religion of a race ascent to a perfected peace.

I have avoided calling her a "feminist" not merely because the word is foolish, but because her emphasis of woman has been the stressing of an outstanding imperative in a scheme as wide as life, rather than either a class complaint or a specialist infatuation. It might be excusable to call her the prophet of woman, a smiling Isaiah, too good a scientist to be quite a poet, too much a poet to meet the ultimate mechanics of a system; withal one to whom the women of the world will owe a special debt, and to whom all well-wishers of humanity will owe the acknowledgments due a brave, utterly honest, and ever stimulating champion of a larger humanism. (pp. 39-42)

Alexander Black, "The Woman Who Saw It First," in The Century, *Vol. 107, No. 1, November, 1923, pp. 33-42.*

CARL N. DEGLER   (essay date 1956)

[*An American historian, educator, and critic, Degler has written extensively on American history and in 1972 won a Pulitzer Prize for* Neither Black nor White: Slavery and Race Relations in Brazil and the United States. *In the following essay, he discusses the social and economic ideas Gilman presented in* Women and Economics; His Religion and Hers; The Home: Its Work and Influence; *and* The Man-Made World; or, Our Androcentric Culture. *Degler's introduction to his 1966 edition of Gilman's* Women and Economics *is excerpted in TCLC, Vol. 9.*]

When Charlotte Perkins Gilman published *Women and Economics* in 1898, the Feminist movement in America gained an advocate of uncommon intellectual power and insight. Quickly acclaimed on both sides of the Atlantic for having written "the most significant utterance" on the women's question since Mill, she became the idol of radical feminists and was later judged [by Mary Gray Peck in *Carrie Chapman Catt*] "the most original and challenging mind which the woman [*sic*] movement produced." Despite this recognition of her abilities, however, she has suffered a neglect in American intellectual history difficult to explain. The neglect becomes especially regrettable when one reads her truly thought-provoking analyses of woman's position in a man's world—in remarkable anticipation of modern writers on the subject like Simone de Beauvoir, Margaret Mead and Ashley Montagu.

Though Gilman's versatile and probing mind roamed over many subjects in the course of her forty years of active writing and lecturing, the focus here is on her thought relating to the position and nature of woman. It is hardly an exaggeration to speak of her as the major intellectual leader of the struggle for women's rights, in the broadest sense, during the first two decades of the twentieth century. A confirmed suffragist, she never confined her attention to that limited goal but considered the whole large question of women in society as her province. Progress for women, she wrote in *Women and Economics,* is not to be measured only by the number of states granting suffrage to women, but rather is to be seen "in the changes legal and social, mental and physical, which mark the advance of the mother of the world toward her full place."

The question of women's rights, to Gilman, was not the simple one of the democratic demand of women for equal prerogatives with men, though this, too, was a part of her well-stocked arsenal of argument. Her concern in all her writings was essentially twofold: to show the disastrous and all-pervasive effects upon women and upon society of the continued suppression of her sex; and to demonstrate in theory and practice means whereby women could assume their rightful place in society. But in doing so her arguments were never shrill or ill-tempered. The words of a modern feminist aptly describe Gilman's attitude toward the question of woman: "animated less by a wish to demand our rights than by an effort toward clarity and understanding." One might add that, to Gilman, service to society was also an ingredient of her purpose.

The subjection of women originated, Gilman began, in prehistoric times when the males first monopolized all social activity and women were confined to motherhood and domestic duties. Thus began the dependence of women upon men for their very food and shelter. Once this took place woman's livelihood, in the most basic sense, was a function of her ability to hold a man. "From the odalisque with the most bracelets," Gilman wrote,

> to the debutante with the most bouquets, the relation still holds good, woman's economic profit comes through the power of sex-attraction.

In vain did she search the animal world for analogies to this relationship between the human sexes. For human beings, she found, were the only animal species "in which the female depends on the male for food, the only animal species in which the sex-relation is also an economic relation. . . . In no other animal species is the sex-relation for sale."

Since woman's livelihood is received from men, her sexual attributes, the major attraction for men, are obviously highly developed and carefully nurtured. (Gilman compared this abnormal development in women with the over-development of the horns of a stag or the milk-giving ability of a modern milch cow: both are sexual characteristics developed to excess.) The result is that "the male human being is thousands of years in advance of the female in economic status." Whereas "men produce and distribute wealth . . . women receive it at their hands." This relegating of woman to roles associated only with sexual activity—and this was Gilman's thesis—is "disadvantageous to our progress as individuals and as a race." In essence, it was to the proof and illustration of this conclusion that she devoted all her public efforts between 1898 and the middle of the Twenties.

This dichotomy of the sexes, initiated in the beginnings of human society has prevailed into modern times; the man the worker in the world, the woman a parasite, beholden for every morsel of food, stitch of protective clothing, and even a bed at night, to some man—husband or father. Nor, can it be claimed, Gilman showed, that actually woman is economically independent because the husband's support is remuneration for her household labors. The very fact that each woman labors a different amount for that support—the rich as compared with the poor, for example—demonstrates that something more than a simple economic *quid pro quo* is operative. It is woman's duty to work in the home regardless of the compensation; the economic return to her bears no relation, in quantity or in quality, to the work performed. No, the woman lives because the man suffers her to do so.

In other words, Gilman concluded, sex and economics go hand in hand in our world. To the young man entering the world the doors stand wide; failures only mean a new start; mistakes can be righted; all that he desires he can work to attain. To the young woman the same world is there,

> but all that she may wish to have, all that she may wish to do, must come through a single channel and a single choice. Wealth, power, social distinction, fame—not only these, but home and happiness, reputation, ease and pleasure, her bread and butter—all, must come to her through a small gold ring.

Even to have amusement a girl must be sexually attractive. "The fun and pleasure of the world are so interwound with the sex-dependence of women upon men that women are forced to court 'attentions,' when not really desirous of anything but amusement." Association between men and women is always on a strictly sexual basis, "friendship between man and woman being a common laughing-stock." If a single man seeks feminine company there are two kinds: married and single. To see the former causes talk; to visit the latter frequently causes speculations of intentions; so he distributes his favors and knows none very well. Even after marriage the sexes enjoy little contact which does not have sexual overtones.

Up until the nineteenth century rarely was woman allowed to break out of the restrictions imposed upon her by the economic dependence upon the male, even though "the ever-growing human impulse to create, the power and will to make, to do, to express one's new spirit in new forms"—was in her as much as in man. For her there were only the ancient, simple duties of the home to be performed "in private and alone." Always "the smothering 'no'" of the male's world held her back from realizing her human characteristics as well as her female.

The disabilities imposed upon women were the basic explanations in Charlotte Gilman's mind for the feminine character itself. Since, for long generations, most women have spent their whole lives in contemplation of their own family affairs "they are near-sighted, or near-minded rather; the trouble is not with the nature of their minds, but with the use of them." Men too, if they had been confined to the home would be "unlikely to manifest a high order of political intelligence." Similarly, courage is not wanted in women, so they do not evidence it. "Women are not ashamed of being cowards. . . . As a man is not ashamed of licentiousness, which would be ruin to a woman, so a woman is not ashamed of cowardice which would utterly disgrace a man." Woman demonstrates certain typically "feminine" traits because she occupies a special, narrow position in society: "she is merely working for her own family—in the sex-relation—not the economic relation; as a servant to the family instead of servant to the world." So long as "all women have to be house servants from day to day, we are still a servile world." In her capacity of family worker the woman is isolated from the rest of society, yet "social intercourse . . . is the essential condition of civilization. It is not merely a pleasure or an indulgence; it is the human necessity."

The diverse material roles of the two sexes produce wholly different worlds and even outlooks for the man and the woman. "The home-bred brain of the woman continually puzzles and baffles the world-bred brain of the man. . . ." "Men meet one another freely in their work, while women work alone." This has the effect of producing more enduring friendships among men and explains "why they associate so much more easily and freely," for "they are further developed in race functions and . . . they *work together*." On the other hand, "every sign of weakness, timidity, inability to understand, to do, is deemed feminine and admired." "It is not that women are really smaller-minded, more timid and vacillating," Gilman maintained, displaying her basic environmentalistic approach, "but that whosoever, man or woman, lives always in a small dark place, is always guarded, protected, directed and restrained, will become inevitably narrowed and weakened by it." Basically, she continued, "the facts are that women are people, and act very much like other people under the same conditions. . . ." Being a servant has played its role in determining the character of women. The woman as a servant "was denied the moral freedom of being mistress of her own action and of learning by the merciful law of consequences what was right and what was wrong: and she has remained, perforce, undeveloped in the larger judgment of ethics."

Gilman saw in woman's consuming interest in fashion a reflection of the female's part in the sexuo-economic relation.

Because of the woman's dependence on sexual attraction for a livelihood, she bears the sex decoration of the species—the reverse of that obtaining in the lower animals. Once sexual attraction is no longer the sole basis for woman's securing a living, then the feminine sex would be emancipated from its preternatural concern for sex decoration, i.e., fashion.

To perpetuate these environmentally induced differences between the sexes, our man-dominated culture has compelled children to bear the indicia and limitations of the adult sexual world. Boys and girls are dressed differently "not on account of their personal needs, which are exactly similar at this period," but so that neither they nor anyone else "may for a moment forget the distinction of sex." Girls' toys are mainly restricted to those associated with the future occupations of mother and housekeeper; the boys have a wide range of toys and games. "The little girl is kept forever within the limitations of her mother's 'sphere' of action; while the boy learns life, and fancies that new growth is due to his superior sex."

We even expect the maternal feelings to bud in little girls, though we do not expect the boy to feel paternal. Children should not, Gilman contended, any more than kittens, be expected to be precocious in their feelings. The so-called "tomboy" is the "most normal girl . . . a healthy young creature, who is human through and through, not feminine until it is time to be."

Terrible pressures, she pointed out, are exerted upon the young girl by the social fiat that marriage and the home be the sole occupation of woman. A man may expect to have home, family, love and companionship and still be an "active citizen of his age and country." The girl, on the other hand, "must 'choose'; must either live alone, unloved, uncompanied, uncared for, homeless, childless, with her work in the world for sole consolation; or give up all world service for the joys of love, motherhood and domestic service." Social pressure further insures that she will favor marriage, for if she does not marry, then "the scorn of male and female alike falls on this sexless thing: she is a human failure." Yet—and this is the cruelest part—through all this the girl must act as if she were not interested. "Think of the strain on a highly sensitive nervous organism to have so much hang on one thing" and, at the same time, "to be forbidden to take any step toward securing it!" Even the sexual ignorance of the young girl of her day Gilman saw as a consequence of the sexuo-economic relationship. Since the husband "is the market" and he prefers her innocent of any sexual knowledge, the mother has no alternative but to preserve her daughter's ignorance in order successfully to prepare "her for the market."

Unavoidably, of course, the man, too, suffers from this constriction of woman's place. "The boy with a servile mother, the man with a servile wife, cannot reach the sense of equal rights we need today." Furthermore, the man has no competition in society, when the woman is his inferior, his servant. He is tempted to cruelty, he becomes selfish from having a person devoted to his welfare, he is prideful of his false position of dominance. The requirement that the man support a family puts a premium on money-getters. In a relation which compels a man to support a workless wife, money must be his goal, not service or ideals; his occupation cannot be freely chosen if he also desires a wife. Dedication to science or art or other financially unrewarding pursuits becomes either a hard choice or an impossibility. The maintenance of the family "multiplies a man's desire for money; but in no way multiplies his ability. . . . " Since the man realizes how dependent a wife is upon him for support "marriage is deferred and avoided, to the direct injury of both sexes and society at large."

The home and family also feel the manifold effects of woman's subordinate and oversexed existence. The effort to isolate the home from the world—to enhance privacy—Gilman interpreted as a reflection of the sexually-oriented character of the family:

> In our besotted exaggeration of the sex relation, we have cruelly supposed that a wish for a wider human relationship was a wish for wider sex-relationships and was therefore to be discouraged. . . .

Actually, when sex and economics are divorced, talk with mere relatives will not be enough and all members of the family will have the opportunity of interpersonal contacts so necessary to human development. The genesis of frictions within the family often can be traced to the socially starved woman. The husband is her only world because he is her line of communication with the real world so she "wrings" all she can out of him to make the world she needs. She demands attention and love, but "it is not further love that she needs at all . . . it is not more man, but more world—more life—that she restlessly and dumbly craves."

> Failing to get it, she pushes uneasily against this well-intentioned substitute for a world and racks him with her continual demands.

Moreover, when the marriage is unhappy, the woman suffers more than the man just "because she has no other life from which to draw strength and practical consolation." He, at least, has his work, opportunity to gratify his ambition, to make money and so forth.

When woman's world is bounded by the walls of the home, society—always Gilman's principal concern—has a high price to pay. To keep women in the home is an enormous social waste in an economic sense. "While every woman is expected to follow one trade the grade of efficiency must remain at the lowest possible average," Gilman argued. All women cannot, any more than all men, be trained to do the same job efficiently because "specialization is necessary to develop skill. The domestic worker, wife or servant, is eternally unspecialized." Much that society has gained in economic efficiency through the specialization of man's labor has been lost in requiring women to perform nothing but the unskilled, undifferentiated labor of the home. The very progress of the world has been retarded by excluding women. The house-wife-mothered human race "has moved only half as fast and as far as it rightly should have done" and the heavy, time-consuming work of "the patient housewife . . . is pitifully behind the march of events."

Prostitution and immorality Gilman attributed to this same "morbid excess in the exercise of " sex and the economic dependence of women. By requiring a man to support a wife before he may legitimately receive sexual gratification, he is driven to the prostitute as the cheaper alternative. So long, she went on, as sex is emphasized in our society—as it is in our sexuo-economic marriage—it will encourage the over-sexed man and the over-sexed woman and perpetuate the prostitute.

The double standard, of course, stands forth as the most arrogant instance of male dominance, for chastity is a human, not an exclusively female virtue in Gilman's eyes:

> Masculine ethics colored by masculine instincts, always dominated by sex, has at once recognized the value of chastity in women, which is right, punished its absence unfairly, which is wrong; and then reversed the whole matter when applied to men, which is ridiculous.

In her description and analysis of the subtle and often unnoticed characteristics of a man-dominated culture, Gilman displayed both her incisive mind and her acute powers of observation. We have taken the male and his activities, she pointed out, as typical of *human* activities. Even the word virtue is derived from "*vir*"; "our human scheme of things," she wrote, "rests on the same tacit assumption; man being held the human type; woman a sort of accompaniment and subordinate assistant, merely essential to the making of people." In popular speech when "we wish to praise the work of a woman, we say she has a 'masculine mind,' " testimony in itself of the folk belief that to be a man is to be most human. When females teach boys, the students, it is often said, "become 'effeminate.' " But when men teach girls the latter do not become the masculine equivalent. "Never has it occurred to the androcentric mind to conceive of such a thing as being *too* masculine. There is no such word!" So habituated are men to thinking that maleness is humanness, that each step in the economic and social humanization of women has been termed "unfeminine." Woman's exclusion from human activities has been justified on just these grounds—that she is pure sex and devoid of "humanness." Education offers an excellent example of this, where for centuries woman was denied schooling with men on the assumption she must be confined "exclusively to feminine interests." In a word, we have created an androcentric culture, treating women as merely extraneous, child-bearing females.

But to equate male sexual attributes with human nature results in harm to society from another direction. For, after all, the "manly" attributes of size, belligerence, aggressiveness, sportsmanship, and the like, are not the sum total of human virtues. All men, even, do not possess them. The artistic, the musical, the contemplative boy also fulfills a function in society, but he is pilloried in a culture identifying the masculine characteristics with the attributes of human beings. It is necessary to realize that "the advance of civilization calls for human qualities in both men and women." Too often, from the standpoint of society, "the contradictions we have forcibly bred in women react injuriously upon men and are inherited by children."

A culture dominated by men, Gilman believed, is inevitably permeated, on a variety of levels, by the peculiar sexual character of the male. In literature, for example, masculine interest—*i.e.,* love, sex, combat—the interests which flow from man's sexual nature, has been apparent in the myriad stories concerned with such subjects, especially in popular fiction. Such literature ignores mother love—the more fundamental and considerably less transitory variety. Not all men wrote from this narrow viewpoint, of course, for writers like Balzac and Dickens had a truly broad, human outlook. The large number of love poems, in like manner, Gilman explained by the dominance of the male and his primary interest.

The dominance of man has influenced popular philosophy to accept the dictum that life is a struggle—which to man is congenial and preeminent in his existence. Actually life is also growth and a world dominated by women would, by contrast, stress that element. The accent on death and the after life, so common in the great religions, similarly stems from the fact that man, the ancient hunter and killer, saw death, was concerned with it, and fitted it into the religions of his culture. To woman, on the other hand, birth and life are the crucial events of her existence.

For all her exposure of the masculine influence molding our culture, Gilman was no uncritical or misanthropic feminist. "There should be an end," she wrote, "to the bitterness of feeling which has arisen between the sexes in this century." Her evolutionary approach was too meaningful for her to denigrate man's historic activities in behalf of civilization. The economic dependence of women, she maintained, had been necessary so that man could forsake the role of hunter, fighter, and destroyer, and become the builder of civilization. The imprisonment of women had acted as a "coiled spring"—its "intense stimulus" enabling man to move mountains. But, she emphasized, by the nineteenth century that stage in evolution was at an end; man alone could no longer advance civilization; the contribution of woman was required to continue the progress of humanity.

As must be apparent to anyone even cursorily reading the strictures Gilman hurled against the domestic woman, the inevitable *sine qua non* for the final and complete emancipation of woman was economic independence. The working girl, the working wife and mother became the ideal which she preached.

Given the historical period in which she wrote, this solution was neither unexpected nor, in practice, even novel. Already, by the opening years of the twentieth century, millions of women, married and single, were finding places in the industrial system. To Gilman it seemed that these women, often struggling against the old restrictions and prejudices, were the heroines of the emancipation of their sex; indeed, they were taking the only path to true freedom. By their breaking of the age-old chains forged by the dependence of woman upon man for food, clothing and shelter, they were free for the first time in modern history. If women are to be anything, she proclaimed, they must cease to be merely domestic servants, nursemaids and governesses in their own homes.

In the last analysis, Gilman's insistence upon work outside the home as the liberating force for women rested on her fundamental assumption that women were human beings and that "a human creative must do human work; and all women are no more to be contented as house servants and housekeepers than all men would be."

The word "all" in the statement contains, by implication, the two major justifications Gilman advanced for women's entering the labor market: not only was the restriction of woman to the home crippling individually to her as a human being, but, as noted earlier, it was socially inefficient. It was not that Gilman thought that no woman would like housekeeping, for, as she said, "even cleaning, rightly understood and practised is a useful, and therefore honorable, profession." The error lay in expecting all women to do it.

It is noteworthy that Gilman was basing her feminist arguments on higher ground than the mere demand for freedom, privilege and power equal with men. She rested her case on the conviction that women were "heavily behind-hand in their duty to the world; holding in their gift a mighty fund of Love and Service which we can no longer do without." It

was society which was losing as well as women, for women, even in their female capacity, had something to contribute to the world. Their very sexual nature fitted in, according to her view, with the overarching human needs of society. "To be a teacher and leader, to love and serve, to guard and guide and help," she pointed out, "are well in line with motherhood," all of which only "makes her exclusion from human function the more mischievous." The altruism of motherhood, once it is allowed to influence the world, would be a force for good. The very fact that the woman's "feminine functions" are "far more akin to human functions" than are those of the male means that freedom for women "will bring into human life a more normal influence."

Charlotte Gilman, as the preceding paragraph illustrates, was prepared to admit that there were real character differences between the sexes, and further, that they were the consequence of the differing physiological structure and functions of the male and the female. She saw combativeness and desire, for example, as the most obvious male traits. Even "the little male"—the boy—"would be more given to fighting and destroying," she asserted; "the little female more to caring for and constructing things." This, in turn, would lead to the male's being "progressive where the female is conservative by nature." Nevertheless, the important point to Gilman, it should be emphasized, was not the differences, for they are minor compared to the characteristics held in common. But, insofar as the sexes do differ, they should utilize the differences to complement each other and not to subordinate one sex to the other:

> Women are human beings as much as men, by nature; and as women, are even more sympathetic with human processes. To develop human life in its true powers we need full equal citizenship for women.

Motherhood for women and fatherhood for men are the only occupations decreed by Nature. Outside of these two:

> Every handicraft, every profession, every science, every art, all normal amusements and recreations, all government, education, religion; the whole living world of human achievement: all this is human.

And all should be open to women as human beings. But Gilman was sufficiently perspicacious to realize that not all work would be done by women. For after all, she cautioned, "equality is not identity. There is work of all kinds and sizes—and half of it is woman's." Presumably each sex would perform work congenial to its nature. But

> we can make no safe assumption as to what, if any distinctions there will be in the free human work for men and women, until we have seen generation after generation grow up under absolutely equal conditions.

Once elevated to the position of a human being, woman will, in the natural course of things, "develop social usefulness, becoming more efficient, intelligent, experienced." Furthermore, the gainful employment of women would have beneficial effects upon men and the family. There would be greater family income and marriage would not have to be postponed in order to raise the man's income sufficiently to support a wife. The husband would now have a worthy, intelligent partner who would "lift him up instead of pulling him heavily downward. . . ." Even romance in marriage might increase, for it is difficult "to maintain the height of romantic devotion to one's house servant—or even one's housekeeper!" "We shall live," she summed up, "in a world of men and women humanly related, as well as sexually related, working together, as they were meant to do, for the common good of all."

To expect women to marry and to work at the same time, Gilman was well aware, created new problems. Almost contemptuously, however, she demolished the hoary argument that if women worked they would lose their charm in the eyes of men. "The respect of the male for the female," she clearly recognized, "is based on the distinction of sex, not on political or economic disability. Men respect women because they are females, not because they are weak and ignorant and defenseless." It is more likely that as they grow in humanness and lose nothing that is essential to womanhood, "they will win and hold a far larger, deeper reverence than that hitherto vouchsafed them."

Gilman readily conceded that the record showed that as more and more women enjoyed economic independence, the divorce rate continued to rise and some women refused to marry at all. But this is only to be expected, she explained, when "the character of woman is changing faster than the character of matrimony." More and more women are seeking companionship in marriage, now that they are free of the sexuo-economic dependence; a "kind" husband and a good provider are not enough. After all, she wrote with a tinge of humor, when two young people love each other and spend long hours talking together, they do not "dwell in ecstatic forecast on the duties of housekeeping." They dream of "being alone, of *doing* things together." The outstanding defect of the old marriage was its lack of equality—one partner out in the world, the other confined to the "smallest, oldest, lowest" work in the world. Marriages will be happier and men and women happier when "both sexes realize that they are human, and that humanity has far wider duties and desires than those of the domestic relations." In an age when more and more women are working, Gilman realized, we must "learn how to reconcile happy work with a happy marriage." In some respects, in these passages, Charlotte Gilman was the prophet of the modern American marriage.

Even though some women who work never marry, this is not to be taken, she insisted, as a valid argument against gainful employment for women. How many illustrious men of the past, she asked, could have easily given up their work for marriage? Fortunately for them, they never had to make such a difficult choice, for as men in a man's world they could enjoy both. But some women, for a variety of reasons, cannot be both wives and workers in the world, and they choose the latter merely because they are human.

Though Gilman viewed marriages as a desirable state for all human beings, failure to marry was not a tragedy so long as women could work and thereby consecrate "their energies as human beings to mutual assistance and social service." And on all sides there was evidence of the changing position of women in the direction she pointed; she was not a voice in the wilderness, but a leader of hosts.

Charlotte Perkins Gilman might be called a rationalistic radical, for lack of a more elegant term. Few considerations of tradition or sentiment inhibited her thinking. Recognizing this, we can understand better both the strength and weakness of Gilman's social thought. Her freedom from preconceptions and tradition allowed her to make fresh and often penetrating examinations of the human institutions around

her. But that same attitude of mind also prevented her from appreciating the tenacious hold which prejudice, tradition and sentiment had upon most of the men and women she was attempting to convince. Hence when she came to offer means to attain the goals she set, her rationalism and radicalism, so incisive in analysis, merely served to vitiate her realism.

To all feminists, as to Gilman, the most stubborn obstacle to the equal participation of women in the affairs of the world was the ineluctable fact that women—someone, at least—had to take care of the home. That someone, by that very fact, was thereby removed from the usual occupations of the world, and, to the conservative, this was justification enough for the confining of women to the kitchen, nursery and cleaning closet. Since Gilman had called for women in the world, she had to offer a means to attain that objective. Unfortunately, the best she could devise was less than adequate.

Since the mother-centered home was the major obstacle to woman's employment, Gilman directed her intellectual artillery against that venerable institution. Though her view was foreshadowed in *Women and Economics,* her book *The Home,* published in 1903, was a full-scale, full battle-dress assault—a model of the completely rationalistic analysis of an ancient human institution—and a good example of her scorn for sentiment which had ceased to be functional. Her criticism was on two levels: first that the home crushed women— the argument we have followed; and second that the home as it existed was dirty, inefficient, uninteresting and retrogressive. Entertaining and clever as her latter arguments and examples were, we need not go into them here.

In substance, of course, her critique of the home was closely related to her view of woman's need, for the functions of the home, too, should be specialized. Instead of having the cooking, sewing, child care, house cleaning done by a single woman—the mother-housewife—all these services would be professionalized and performed by outside, paid workers. So completely would this be carried out, according to Gilman, that there would be no kitchens in the new homes. This in itself, she envisaged, would greatly simplify cleaning, since the kitchen by its introduction of fire, cooking, grease, and smoke constituted one of the major creators of dirt in the home. Food would be professionally and nutritiously prepared in central kitchens and served either in the dining room of the home itself or in the central dining hall of the new apartments, which would become the accepted mode of living. At last the ancient handicraft of the kitchen would disappear: "we are going to lose our kitchens as we have lost our laundries and bakeries. The cook-stove will follow the loom and wheel, the wool-carder and shears." While keenly aware of the esteem in which the haloed home was held, she boldly argued that the home was outmoded, and that its lack of specialization meant inefficiency and lack of development. The housewife, she wrote, is notoriously untrained and ignorant in the fields of nutrition and child-care, yet she is entrusted exclusively with these functions. With a mixture of truth and exaggeration Gilman ridiculed the ignorant mother: "Each mother slowly acquires some knowledge of her business by practising it upon the lives and health of her family and by observing its effect on the survivors." Indeed, insofar as housekeeping has progressed through the application of new techniques and implements, she pointed out, it has been the result of outside, professionalized work not that of the woman in the home. Under the new arrangements there would be "a clean, pretty, quiet home—not full of smell and steam and various messy industries, but simply a place to rest in . . . with a wife as glad to be home as the husband." So often and so vehemently did Gilman offer her solution, that one periodical in 1913 could say, perhaps wearily, "Mrs. Gilman's ideas on this subject are well-known."

Children, too, like the home itself, would be cared for by professionals. Alert to the contemporaneous educational trend of taking children under the care of society at an increasingly younger age, Gilman maintained her plan was merely the extension of this tendency to include babyhood. It is not possible, she argued, merely to train mothers to care for babies any more than they can be trained to supplant the grammar school. Nevertheless, under her program, "the mother would not be excluded, but supplemented, as she is now, by the teacher and the school."

Imagining all men were as rational as herself, Gilman pointed to no other social engine for the accomplishment of such a mighty domestic revolution other than its desirability. This aspect of her thought, perhaps more than any other, is hopelessly tinged with utopianism.

Obviously Charlotte Perkins Gilman's insights into the position of women, and the consequences thereof for the two sexes and for society, are of much more interest to us today than her practical solutions, to the advocacy of which she devoted much of her energy. The kitchenless apartment, the beginnings of which were apparent in her time, is uninteresting to an America now wedded to the private house. Yet, in a sense, even the private home has eliminated, in part, at least, the deficiencies Gilman found in it: ignorance of nutrition and child care is no longer condoned in middle class American families, particularly not when scientific cook books and authoritative baby books abound. She mistook a few kitchenless apartments for a trend, but she herself was part of a trend when she castigated ignorant motherhood and defended social education for the pre-school child.

Increasing occupational opportunities for women, and the growing acceptance of the working wife by both husband and society today, indicate that Gilman's major contribution—the requirement that women be *in* the world as well as *of* it, was essentially sound. The working wife is not as common as Gilman hoped or expected, but the practical reasons for that discrepancy are apparent. Unless some solution similar to that tendered by her, and rejected by society—professionalized home services—is developed, it is almost a superhuman task to be both a housekeeper, cook and full-time employee. For as Simone de Beauvoir has observed in our own day, "for the most part it is still the woman who bears the cost of domestic harmony" when she works outside the home. By the mid-twentieth century, the bulk of women in America have not found a means whereby they can both work and marry, but the opportunity is present, for society is now willing to condone that dual role if the woman is willing and capable of assuming the double burden. If, as most would agree, America in the last fifty years has basically altered its attitude toward the working woman, then Charlotte Perkins Gilman must be assigned a significant part in the accomplishment of that change. As she prophesied, to utilize the labor and skills and nature of women was to enlarge the pool of human energy and to enhance human happiness. (pp. 21-39)

Carl N. Degler, "Charlotte Perkins Gilman on the

Theory and Practice of Feminism," in American Quarterly, *Vol. VIII, No. 1, Spring, 1956, pp. 21-39.*

ELIZABETH KEYSER   (essay date 1983)

[*In the following essay, Keyser compares Gilman's utopian novel* Herland *with Jonathan Swift's* Gulliver's Travels.]

In *Reinventing Womanhood* Carolyn G. Heilbrun explains how literary works that purport to deal with "the nature of man" but in fact deal only with men can be reinterpreted so as to serve as models for women. Charlotte Perkins Gilman's feminist utopia, *Herland,* published in 1915, can be viewed as such a reinterpretation of *Gulliver's Travels,* especially of the Fourth Voyage. In *Herland* Gilman uses Swift's satire on human pride in general as a model for her attack on male pride in particular, offers an explanation for the Yahoo in human nature, and, finally, suggests how that Yahoo can be eradicated.

The complete *Gulliver's Travels* and *Herland,* together with its sequel, *With Her in Ourland* (1916), share a common preoccupation or theme. When in *Ourland* Ellador, a native of Herland, visits the United States, she compares the country to Gulliver imprisoned by the Lilliputians:

> Here you are, a democracy—free—the power in the hands of the people. You let that group of conservatives saddle you with a constitution which has so interfered with free action that you've forgotten you had it. In this ridiculous helplessness—like poor old Gulliver—bound by the Lilliputians—you have sat open-eyed, not moving a finger, and allowed individuals—mere private persons—to help themselves to the biggest, richest, best things in the country. . . . What can we think of a Democracy, a huge, strong, young Democracy, allowing itself to become infested with such parasites as these?

Like Swift, Gilman is concerned with the way in which people fail to recognize their own strength, allow themselves to be enslaved, and then pride themselves on their identification with the individuals and institutions that enslave them. In *Herland,* however, Gilman follows Swift even more closely to show how women in the early twentieth century are little more than beasts of burden, a theme she anticipates in *Women and Economics* (1899). There Gilman draws an analogy between the horse in captivity and women; they both work, but their exertions "bear no direct relation to [their] living." Both are dependent economically on the wills of their masters. She then goes on to compare women's work in the home and caring for children with the work of a horse; their labors enable men to produce more than would be otherwise possible—they are economic factors but not economically independent. Like Gulliver and the economically oppressed citizens of a democracy, both horses and women, through a combination of their own servility and the tyranny of others, have become so "saddled" as to have forgotten their freedom.

In *Herland* Gilman does with the sexes what Swift does with the reversal of stations and perspectives. In *Herland* the supposedly superior sex becomes the inferior or disadvantaged just as Gulliver in the first two voyages perceives himself first as the giant, then as the dwarf, and in the Fourth Voyage first as the higher, then as the lower animal. At the beginning of *Herland* three young male scientists hear rumors of a highly civilized country populated only by women. Van, a sociologist, is intellectually fascinated by the idea of a state administered by women. Jeff, a physician and botanist with a poetic temperament, finds the idea of a nation of women romantically appealing. And Terry, a geographer by training but a wealthy playboy in practice, imagines an unlimited opportunity for sexual conquest. On entering Herland, however, the three suddenly find themselves as powerless as Gulliver in Brobdingnag or Houyhnhnmland. Once convinced that they cannot escape, the men cooperate with their captors, master the language, and are eventually freed, though they remain under the supervision of three middle-aged mentors. Finally they are allowed to meet the younger women, and all three fall in love. But when, after much deliberation, the Herlanders permit them to marry, they find themselves in the position of women in their own country—that of having to adjust to their partners and deny their own needs. In fact, their position is worse in that they have not, like the women of their own country, been conditioned for generations to accept it but have been conditioned to expect the opposite. At the book's end Jeff, like Gulliver among the Houyhnhnms, has come to acknowledge the superiority of his new country's social system; Van is still undergoing the painful process of reassessment; and Terry, who has been expelled for attempting to rape his wife, is completely unregenerate.

Van, Gilman's first-person male narrator, together with his two companions, serves many of the satiric functions performed by Gulliver. Like Gulliver, the three men have mistaken notions about the country they are entering and inappropriate strategies for dealing with the natives. Because Gilman's travellers arrive in Herland by design rather than by accident, they formulate much more elaborate theories, but these, like Gulliver's simpler ones, are comically disproved. Terry, the stereotypical male chauvinist, cannot conceive of a progressive, well-run country without men: "We mustn't look for inventions and progress; it'll be awfully primitive." Significantly, he does not envision finding mature women, "just Girls and Girls and Girls." Jeff, a gentle idealist, expects to find a combination nunnery ("a peaceful, harmonious sisterhood") and nursery. Van, the social scientist, "held a middle ground, highly scientific, of course, and used to argue learnedly about the physiological limitations of the sex." He is convinced they will find men there even if the country is "built on a sort of matriarchal principle." When on landing they discover it to be a beautifully cultivated, obviously civilized country, they are certain of the presence of men. The presence of men suggests a need for protection as the presence of women alone would not. Thus "we saw to it that each of us had a good stock of cartridges". The three proceed cautiously until they hear the sounds of suppressed laughter. Van warns "look out for a poisoned arrow in your eye," but Terry, glimpsing three girls in a tree, retorts "in my heart, more likely." Pursuing the girls up the tree, Terry decides he will "have to use bait." "He produced from an inner pocket a little box of purple velvet . . . and out of it he drew a long sparkling thing, a neckless of big varicolored stones that would have been worth a million if real ones." The girl nearest him eyes it curiously but not like "a girl lured by an ornament." Amid shrieks of laughter she snatches it from him, drops to the ground, and, followed by her companions, swiftly proceeds to outrace the men. Terry's disgruntled comment is that "the men of this country must be good sprinters."

The parallels between the initial encounter with the Herlanders and Gulliver's with the Houyhnhnms are obvious. Gulliver too assumes that the inhabitants are men and their nature warlike. He walks "very circumspectly for fear of being surprised, or suddenly shot with an Arrow." But he realizes that his trusty hanger will not defend him against a whole tribe, so he comes prepared to "purchase my Life from them by some Bracelets, Glass Rings, and other Toys, which Sailors usually provide themselves with." When, instead of savages, he encounters a Houyhnhnm, he attempts, like Terry, to treat it like an ordinary member of the species he is familiar with: "At last I took the Boldness, to reach my Hand towards his Neck, with a Design to stroak it; using the common Style and Whistle of Jockies when they are going to handle a strange Horse." But this horse is no more like the horses Gulliver is accustomed to than the Herlanders resemble Terry's previous conquests. The Houyhnhnm repels his "Civilities with Disdain" and altogether conducts himself in such a way that Gulliver is forced to conclude "that if the Inhabitants of this Country were endued with a proportionable Degree of Reason, they must needs be the wisest People upon Earth." But neither Terry nor Gulliver learns immediately that the natives are too intelligent and disinterested to be bribed by baubles. When surrounded by a band of middle-aged Herlanders, Terry presents their leader with a scarf and a circlet of rhinestones. Gulliver, believing the Houyhnhnm to be a magician in disguise, tries to barter a knife and a bracelet for a ride to the nearest village. Neither Herlander nor Houyhnhnm is much impressed with the offer.

In the opening chapters Gulliver expects to find primitive men, "savages," and assumes them to both warlike and easily dazzled by cheap finery; Gilman's travellers expect to find either primitive women against whom they would need no defense other than a few trinkets or somewhat more civilized men against whom they would need to use weapons. Instead, Gulliver encounters the wise and peaceable Houyhnhnms, who protect him from the slings if not the arrows of the belligerent Yahoos, and Gilman's travellers encounter the "vigilance committee" of unarmed but unyielding Herlanders. But whereas Gulliver must learn that European warfare is just an advanced form of Yahoo savagery and that his assumption about primitive man's treacherous nature holds true for the rest of mankind, Gilman's travellers must learn that women are capable of cooperating for their own protection and that they can do so without resorting to male violence.

In retrospect, Van can laugh at their naive assumption "that if there were men we could fight them, and if there were only women—why, they would be no obstacles at all." But first he and his comrades must undergo a process of humiliation rather like what Gulliver undergoes in Lilliput, Brobdingnag, and the country of the Houyhnhnms. As they try to break through the solid mass of Herlanders, they are "lifted like children, straddling helpless children, and borne onward, wriggling indeed, but most ineffectually." They are "borne inside, struggling manfully, but held secure most womanfully." The adverb "manfully" in this context is ironic as the men's struggles have already been compared to those of willful children, thus suggesting the childish nature of many male heroics. The adverb "womanfully," on the other hand, points to a major theme of Gilman's work, what "we call masculine traits are simply human traits, which have been denied to women and are thereby assumed to belong to men: traits such as courage, strength, creativity, generosity, and integrity." Women, too, possess power, though the absence of a feminine equivalent of "manfully" suggests how they have been persuaded to relinquish it.

Without men to accuse them of lacking femininity, the Herlanders have developed desirable human traits normally attributed to males. Van notes with surprise, "never, anywhere before, had I seen women of precisely this quality. Fishwives and market women might show similar strength, but it was coarse and heavy. These were merely athletic—light and powerful. College professors, teachers, writers—many women showed similar intelligence but often wore a strained nervous look, while these were as calm as cows, for all their evident intellect." But while Van is intellectually curious and Jeff openly admiring, Terry's overt response represents society's often more subtle one. He can "almost find them feminine" only when they knit. Otherwise "the Colonels," as he calls the middle-aged Herlanders, are woefully inadequate as women: "They've no modesty . . . no patience, no submissiveness, none of that natural yielding which is a woman's greatest charm." In short, they have few of the traits considered natural and desirable in women. Van, reflecting on Terry's response, which in part he shares, finally concludes that "those 'feminine charms' we are so fond of are not feminine at all, but mere reflected masculinity—developed to please us because they had to please us."

The middle chapters of **Herland,** in which Gilman's travellers settle down to learn the language and to instruct, and be instructed by, the Herlanders, correspond to those in which Gulliver instructs and is instructed by his Houyhnhnm master. One of their first questions, naturally enough, is how, if there are no men, the Herlanders reproduce themselves. The answer, they learn, is by parthenogenesis or, as Terry calls it, virgin birth. But just as in Houyhnhnmland "Power, Government, War, Law, Punishment, and a Thousand other Things had no Terms, wherein that Language could express them," so the word "virgin" is unknown to the Herlanders. Thus Jeff, like Gulliver conversing with his Houyhnhnm master, must resort to circumlocution and explains that "among mating animals, the term *virgin* is applied to the female who has not mated." But the Herlanders are even more puzzled: "And does it apply to the male also? Or is there a different term for him?" Jeff "passed over this rather hurriedly, saying that the same term would apply, but was seldom used." The unequal application of the term "virgin," like the lack of female equivalents for such words as "manfully," exposes the double standard. Just as Gulliver becomes more conscious and condemning of European vice as a result of having to explain it to the Houyhnhnms, so Jeff and Van, if not the incorrigible Terry, become conscious of sex bias in their society.

Like Gulliver in the second and fourth voyages of *Gulliver's Travels,* Gilman's travellers are confident at first that their society is more advanced than the one they are visiting. But as in *Gulliver's Travels* the naive natives either react with a shock which exposes the more sophisticated society or, as Van comments, "their lines of interrogation would gradually surround us in till we found ourselves up against some admissions we did not want to make." For example, the Herlanders are astonished when Terry boasts that women are not allowed to work in America; instead they are cherished, idolized, kept in the home (another concept unknown to the Herlanders). Gradually, through questioning, the Herlanders learn that one-third of the women, "the poorer sort," actually do work and that these, as Jeff admits, tend to produce more children. But Van hastens to explain that "in our economic struggle . . . there was always plenty of opportunity for the fittest to reach the top." Instead of questioning Van's Social Darwinism, however, his interrogator, by thoughtfully repeating "about one-third, then, belong to the poorest class,"

shifts the emphasis from where Van put it, on the many who rise to the top, to the significant number who fall to the bottom. Terry's mentor, Moadine, without being the least satirical, points up the incongruity of wealthy, idle women kept in the home to care for one or two children while poor women work outside to support many.

The women are aided in their investigations by Jeff, who translates Terry's self-approving and Van's evasive or euphemistic answers so as to give them a realistic picture of conditions in his country. Jeff, who has always idealized women, finds it easier than the others to give the Herlanders his unqualified admiration and respect. Like Gulliver in the land of the Houyhnhnms, he soon "began to view the Actions and Passions of Man [men] in a very different Light; and to think the Honour of my own kind [sex] not worth managing." Terry, on the other hand, like Gulliver in Brobdingnag, persists in attempting to puff up himself and his kind even while laboring at a tremendous disadvantage. The women, however, are unlike the Brobdingnagian king and the Houyhnhnm master in that they have a naive faith that the travellers' world, despite evidence to the contrary, must be better. Unlike the Brobdingnagians and Houyhnhnms, they see their geographical isolation as a limitation and feel that a more heterogeneous world must be preferable to such a homogeneous one: "We want so much to know—you have the whole world to tell us of, and we have only our little land! And there are two of you—the two sexes—to love and help one another. It must be such a rich and wonderful world." By making the women insist on their limitations, on their being only half a people, Gilman makes explicit what Swift and other utopian satirists have left implicit: that if a deprived or less than fully human race (or half the human race) can accomplish this much, a richly endowed, fully human race (or the entire race) ought to be able to accomplish much more.

The Herlanders' civilization is superior to a male-dominated one because, like that of the Houyhnhnms, "the most salient quality in all their institutions was reasonableness." Reason prevents both races from succumbing to vices, including those, such as masculine aggressiveness and female submissiveness, that commonly parade as virtues. The Herlanders are economical, inventive, far-seeing, and peaceable. They "thought in terms of the community. As such, their timesense was not limited to the hopes and ambitions of an individual life." Like the Houyhnhnms, and unlike the Gulliver so enamored of the Struldbruggs, they have no use for the notion of immortality. Because their individual identities are bound up with that of the race, they have no desire for individual self-perpetuation. For this reason, the Herlanders have no surnames. As Van comments, "the element of personal pride seemed strangely lacking." Yet for all their community spirit, they have no word for patriotism, for such chauvinism, as Van comes to admit, "is largely pride, and very largely combativeness." Similarly, they have no word for family because, like the Houyhnhnms, who prize universal friendship and benevolence, "they loved one another with a practically universal affection, rising to exquisite and unbroken friendships, and broadening to a devotion to their country and people."

When, after generations of parthenogenesis, Herland was threatened by overpopulation, reason enabled the country not only to survive but to flourish. Rather than resigning themselves to a " 'struggle for existence' which would result in an everlasting writhing mass of underbred people trying to get ahead of one another," the Herlanders decided voluntarily to defer childbirth: "When that deep inner demand for a child began to be felt [a woman] would deliberately engage in the most active work, physical and mental; and even more important, would solace her longing by the direct care and service of the babies we already had." It became an honor for a woman to be chosen an "over-mother," one whose distinction conferred on her the privilege of being allowed to produce children over the limit of one per woman. In their practice of birth control the Herlanders are like the Houyhnhnms, for "when the Matron Houyhnhnms have produced one of each Sex, they no longer accompany with their Consorts." True, birth control is easier for both races to practice in that procreation is not accompanied in either case by sexual passion and pleasure. The fact remains, however, that the Herlanders "were Mothers, not in our sense of helpless involuntary fecundity . . . but in the sense of Conscious Makers of People."

When after much deliberation the Herlanders decide to make "the Great Change" to bisexual reproduction, their lack of sex-tradition allows Gilman her most telling ironies. Permitted at last to court the women of their choice, Terry, Van, and Jeff find that their mode of courtship fails to work. Because the three young foresters they have selected are already self-sufficient—well-established in their careers and enjoying their communal way of life—they cannot appreciate the advantage of a "home" and someone to provide for them. And because the Herlanders' sex drive has lain dormant for generations, they do not look forward to marriage as a source of sexual pleasure; neither do they need husbands in order to have children. They have no notion of masculine chivalry or feminine coquetry, and, having no vanity, they cannot be flattered or won by gifts. As Van comes to realize, the women stand outside the tradition that would have made them easy prey:

> You see, if a man loves a girl who is in the first place young and inexperienced; who in the second place is educated with a background of caveman tradition, a middle-ground of poetry and romance, and a foreground of unspoken hope and interest all centering upon the one Event; and who has, furthermore, absolutely no hope or interest worthy of the name—why, it is a comparatively easy matter to sweep her off her feet with a dashing attack.

Jeff and Van abandon their unsuccessful tactics, but Terry continues to try to convince Alima that he is conferring a favor and that she should reciprocate by utterly abandoning herself to him. Even after Alima, who seems to retain a vestige of the sex drive that has been so successfully sublimated by the other Herlanders, marries him, she cannot submit to the mastery Terry is used to asserting.

Although Van is much more willing to compromise than Terry, even he resents the position he finds himself in after his marriage to Ellador, a position similar to that of many married women. Reflecting on the difference between his expectations and the reality of his marriage, he begins to recognize that when most engaged couples discuss "the conditions of the Great Adventure," "there are some things one takes for granted, supposes are mutually understood, and to which both parties may repeatedly refer without ever meaning the same thing." Different educations give rise to different expectations, but Van now realizes that, once married, the man "generally carries out his own views of the case. The woman may have imagined the conditions of married life to be differ-

ent; but what she imagined, was ignorant of, or might have preferred, did not seriously matter." Lacking the long tradition in which the woman accommodates herself to the man in marriage and having no "idea of that *solitude à deux* we are so fond of," the Herlanders naturally expect to continue their careers and to retain their personal privacy. To the males' chagrin, life goes on much as it did before marriage: "We had, as it were, all the pleasures of courtship carried right on; but we had no sense of—perhaps it may be called possession."

Of course, the males' greatest deprivation is sexual. Whereas the woman in marriage traditionally has had to have sex whenever her husband desired it, now the men can have sex only if their wives allow it. The Herlanders cannot understand the use of sex except for procreation and wish to postpone the consummation of their marriages until they are ready to have children. Each of the three males responds differently to sexual deprivation. Gentle, androgynous Jeff seems to have the least trouble moderating his sexual desires. Perhaps because he is less demanding, his wife, Celis, is less resistant, and it is clear by the end of the book that she is bearing their child. Van, during a longer probationary period, begins to realize that "what I had honestly supposed to be a physiological necessity was a psychological necessity." Ellador, by giving him a little too much of her company rather than withdrawing so that he will want her more, tends to defuse his sex drive: "Here was I, with an Ideal in mind, for which I hotly longed, and here was she, deliberately obtruding in the foreground of my consciousness a Fact. . . . I see now clearly enough why a certain kind of man . . . resents the professional development of women. It gets in the way of the sex ideal; it temporarily covers and excludes femininity." Meanwhile, however, a deep and lasting friendship with Ellador is growing, a friendship not dependent on sex.

But while Jeff and Van manage to cope with sexual frustration, Terry continues to try to master Alima. When his desperate attempt to rape her is thwarted, he receives what is by now for him a welcome sentence: "You must go home." When Ellador refers to Terry's "crime," Van attempts to argue that "after all, Alima was his wife." But Ellador, "for all her wide intellectual grasp, and the broad sympathy in which their religion trained them, could not make allowance for such—to her—sacrilegious brutality." Just as the repulsive Yahoos, hard as it is for Gulliver and the reader to identify with them, mirror the most loathsome human qualities, so Terry is a caricature of existing social prejudice and the irrational violence to which it can give rise. But extremists like Terry are not the only victims of social conditioning. That the much more moderate Van can view Ellador's indignation as a failure of tolerance reminds one of the "narrow Principles and short Views" which led the Brobdingnagian king to refuse Gulliver's offer of gun powder and suggests how pervasive are the beliefs in male prerogative and female duty.

While it is easy enough for the reader to dissociate herself—or even himself—from Terry's chauvinism, some of his criticisms of Herland seem convincing. Herland, like the land of the Houyhnhnms and most utopias, seems at best limited, incomplete, and, at worst, inhuman. Lewis Mumford's objections to utopias in general would undoubtedly extend to Herland: "Isolation, stratification, fixation, regimentation, standardization, militarization—one or more of these attributes enter into the conception of the utopian city." Herland, despite its inhabitants' concern for the future, is, as Terry complains, a static society. Van in part agrees: "The years of pioneering lay far behind them. Theirs was a civilization in which untroubled peace, the unmeasured plenty, the steady health, the large good will and smooth management which ordered everything, left nothing to overcome." Yet after observing their children and young people Van begins to see "the folly of that common notion of ours—that if life was smooth and happy, people would not enjoy it." Van here anticipates the position of Northrop Frye, who, in countering readers' objections to utopias, makes the point that what appear to be constraints would "carry with them a sense of freedom" were the reader to experience them from inside a utopia.

Life is smooth and happy for the Herlanders because their reason, like that of the Houyhnhnms, "is not mingled, obscured, or discoloured by Passion and Interest." But it is just this that Terry objects to: "They've neither the vices of men, nor the virtues of women—they're neuters!" Terry's remark is interesting for the suggestion that men's vices and women's virtues are somehow connected. Translated, Terry's objection seems to be that the Herlanders are without lust themselves and unwilling to be the objects of others' lust. Jeff's response to Terry, that "these women have the virtue of humanity, with less of its faults than any folks I ever saw," reinforces the idea that the "virtues of women," the so-called feminine virtues, are not virtues at all. Still, Jeff's defense of the Herlanders is more troubling to the reader than Terry's attack on them, for it leads one to ask whether they can really possess "the virtues of humanity" while lacking passion. It is one thing to have a mind unclouded by passion; it is another to be incapable of feeling it.

In having Van continue his courtship of Ellador after marriage, Gilman seems very close to advocating what the Houyhnhnms in fact practice, sex for the sole purpose of procreation. Surely she makes Van appear foolish in his attempt to convince Ellador that "there were other, and as we proudly said 'higher,' uses in this [sex] relation than what Terry called 'mere parentage.'" "In the highest terms," Van attempts to explain that "all the power of beautiful permanent mated love" comes through sexual expression, which also provides an impetus to creative work. But Van is embarrassed when Ellador asks if in his country he has found "high and lasting affection appearing in proportion to this indulgence," and he feels still more uncomfortable when she naively believes, on the basis of his claims, that "you have a world full of continuous lovers, ardent, happy, mutually devoted," producing "floods, oceans of such work, blossoming from this intense happiness of every married pair!" When she falls silent thinking, so does Van, presumably of the difference between his self-serving vision of sexual love and the reality he knows all too well.

Although this dialogue ironically implies that sexual indulgence can destroy happiness and stifle creativity rather than promote them, reflection suggests that Gilman is not actually recommending passionless unions between the sexes. Instead, she is doing what Northrop Frye sees most utopian writers as doing—establishing a standard by which to judge existing society. As Gulliver says halfway through his Fourth Voyage, "the many Virtues of those excellent Quadrupeds placed in opposite View to human Corruptions, had so far opened my Eyes, and enlarged my Understanding, that I began to view the Actions and Passions of Man in a very different Light." By having Van argue the ennobling effects of sexual

love, and by having Ellador question him as to those effects, Gilman not only exposes the delusions that are suffered and encouraged about sex; she suggests the effects it might have were people more discriminating. Were everyone, like Gulliver, to see the "Passions of Man [or men] in a very different Light"; were they, like Jeff and Van, to recognize the spurious quality of much sexual provocation, that "very much, of what [was] honestly supposed to be a physiological necessity was a psychological necessity" arising from overdeveloped sex differences; and were they to establish sexual relationships on the broader base of respect and friendship, as Jeff and Van are forced to do, then sex might indeed become a "climactic expression . . . specialized to higher, purer, nobler uses." When intimacy produces the conditions Ellador naively assumes it must, then it will be more than a "beautiful idea"; it will be a beautiful reality.

According to Frank and Fritzie Manuel, utopias provide a "leap into a new state of being in which contemporary values in at least one area—the critical one for the utopian—are totally transformed or turned upside down." Gilman, by concentrating on the one area of sex roles, may seem limited and superficial where Swift is sweeping and profound. And surely no one would argue that *Herland* is a literary masterpiece comparable to *Gulliver's Travels*. But *Herland* (illuminated by *Women and Economics*) can be said to repair a significant omission in Swift's anatomy of human nature by tracing a main source of human self-alienation to the division between the sexes. And by appropriating Swift's form in order to amend his analysis, Gilman provides an example of the collaboration possible between men and women.

In *Women and Economics* Gilman argues that, in most species, both sexes adapt to their environment through the process of natural selection. Although they also develop secondary sex characteristics that distinguish them from each other, natural selection keeps sexual selection under control. In the human race, however, Gilman sees a Darwinian version of Milton's "hee for God only, shee for God in him" for the male by making the female economically dependent on him, interposed between her and the environment. Thus in the human female natural selection, which would make her more like the male, is checked, and sexual selection, the process by which she acquires complementary or contrasting qualities in order to attract the male, runs rampant. Yet as every human being is the product of both parents' genetic make-up, the entire race suffers attenuation.

Because a woman's "economic profit comes through the power of sex-attraction," she must make some kind of bargain with the opposite sex, whether it be the short-term bargain of prostitution, for which she is denigrated, or the long-term bargain of marriage, on which she is congratulated. Her need to bargain with her sexuality "keeps alive in us the instincts of savage individualism" and impedes "the tendency of social progress to develope co-operation in its place." Like other feminists, such as Mary Wollstonecraft, Gilman feels most women, because of their economic dependence, tend to be egocentric—wrapped up in themselves, their homes, their children—and thus less likely than men to rise to the level of disinterested benevolence. But women's overdevelopment of and obsession with the single art of pleasing men takes its toll on men as well. As Gilman writes in *The Home: Its Work and Influence,* "the woman is narrowed by the home and the man is narrowed by the woman." Most men remain economic individualists and, kept in a state of constant titillation, their reason is, as Swift observed, "mingled, obscured, or discoloured by Passion and Interest." Van, in Herland, remembers how "we were always criticizing *our* women for *being* so personal," but he and Terry miss that exclusive preoccupation with husband and home. In the world they are used to, economic individualism bred of dependence makes it impossible for women to transcend the merely personal or egocentric, and their insistence on the personal drags down men as well.

Women's inferiority of status and often character makes unequal matches inevitable, and the progeny are "hybrids," torn between selfish impulses and a yearning for virtue. Swift, too, presents man as a product of what Gilman in *Women and Economics* calls "moral miscegenation": Gulliver's capacity for reason allies him with the Houyhnhnms, but his passions ally him with the Yahoos. Gilman argues that at one time the instinct of savage individualism, as well as pronounced sex differences, was necessary to the survival of the race. But because of women's economic dependence, the savage instinct has long outlasted its usefulness. Swift seems to suggest something similar when he has the Houyhnhnm master point out how Gulliver lacks the sharp nails and physical agility of the Yahoo even though, according to Gulliver's account, civilized human beings are just as rapacious. Whether imperfectly evolved or "fallen," however, humanity, both authors believe, is cursed with a divided nature. In *Women and Economics* Gilman argues that man has long blamed woman for his plight, but his attempts to punish her have only worsened it. Man has also thwarted his own and the race's progress by insisting that the development of woman's talents would be injurious to motherhood. But the more woman is limited "to sex-functions only, cut off from all economic use and made wholly dependent on the sex-relation as means of livelihood, the more pathological does her motherhood become." On this point Swift would agree, for Gulliver's "Master thought it monstrous in us to give the Females a different kind of Education from the Males . . . whereby, as he truly observed, one Half of our Natives were good for nothing but bringing Children into the World: And to trust the Care of their Children to such useless Animals, he said was yet a greater Instance of Brutality." Man cannot promote his own development by placing restrictions on that of woman. Under constraint she becomes still less like him, her difference gives rise to violent passions, and the cycle of mismatches and improper nurture is perpetuated.

Swift, like Gilman, seems to believe that rational cooperation as opposed to irrational aggression cannot take place while people are blinded by passion and that people would be less its prey were there greater similarity and equality between the sexes. But Swift, unlike Gilman, holds out little hope for humanity. Gilman, in her appropriation of the Fourth Voyage as a model, seems to be agreeing with Swift's analysis of human nature, but she also seems to be offering an explanation and solution for it. Unlike Swift, Gilman in *Women and Economics* envisions a time when "a general Disposition to all Virtues" might be as natural to us at it is to the Houyhnhnms. Once women are freed from their socio-economic bondage, "we shall no longer conceive of ethical progress as something outside of and against nature, but as the most natural thing in the world. Where now we strive and agonize after impossible virtures, we shall then grow naturally and easily into those very qualities; and we shall [again like the Houyhnhnms] not even think of them as especially commendable." "The largest and most radical effect of restoring

women to economic independence" will be wholeness; individualism in the sense of selfish striving will give place to individuality or the integration of the self. Then "we shall be able to feel simply, to see clearly, to agree with ourselves, to be one person and master of our own lives, instead of wrestling in such hopeless perplexity with what we have called 'man's dual nature'."

In the final chapter of *Herland* Van sees the drama of human history as enacted by men and excluding women. But he also sees that for the Herlanders an equivalent drama has been enacted solely by women. The Herlander's historic panorama is more impressive than the male-dominated one—it has the same constructive elements and none of the destructive ones. But it is nonetheless partial, incomplete, as Ellador realizes. Thus she and Van choose to leave utopia, unlike Terry and Gulliver who are exiled from it. Whereas Terry was impervious to utopian values and Gulliver made despairing by them, Van and Ellador hope somehow to translate them into action. Gilman's utopia is more optimistic than its model, just as there may be more hope for man in the collective sense of men and women than there is for man in the sense of men alone. (pp. 31-44)

> *Elizabeth Keyser, "Looking Backward: From 'Herland' to 'Gulliver's Travels'," in* Studies in American Fiction, *Vol. 11, No. 1, Spring, 1983, pp. 31-46.*

PAULA A. TREICHLER   (essay date 1984)

[*In the following excerpt, Treichler analyzes "The Yellow Wallpaper" as a demonstration of the conflict between patriarchal language and specifically feminine discourse.*]

Almost immediately in Charlotte Perkins Gilman's story **"The Yellow Wallpaper,"** the female narrator tells us she is "sick." Her husband, "a physician of high standing," has diagnosed her as having a "temporary nervous depression—a slight hysterical tendency." Yet her journal—in whose words the story unfolds—records her own resistance to this diagnosis and, tentatively, her suspicion that the medical treatment it dictates—treatment that confines her to a room in an isolated country estate—will not cure her. She suggests that the diagnosis itself, by undermining her own conviction that her "condition" is serious and real, may indeed be one reason why she does not get well.

A medical diagnosis is a verbal formula representing a constellation of physical symptoms and observable behaviors. Once formulated, it dictates a series of therapeutic actions. In **"The Yellow Wallpaper,"** the diagnosis of hysteria or depression, conventional "women's diseases" of the nineteenth century, sets in motion a therapeutic regimen which involves language in several ways. The narrator is forbidden to engage in normal social conversation; her physical isolation is in part designed to remove her from the possibility of overstimulating intellectual discussion. She is further encouraged to exercise "self-control" and avoid expressing negative thoughts and fears about her illness; she is also urged to keep her fancies and superstitions in check. Above all, she is forbidden to "work"—to write. Learning to monitor her own speech, she develops an artificial feminine self who reinforces the terms of her husband's expert diagnosis: this self attempts to speak reasonably and in "a very quiet voice," refrains from crying in his presence, and hides the fact that she is keeping a journal. This male-identified self disguises the true underground narrative: a confrontation with language.

Because she does not feel free to speak truthfully "to a living soul," she confides her thoughts to a journal—"dead paper"—instead. The only safe language is dead language. But even the journal is not altogether safe. The opening passages are fragmented as the narrator retreats from topic after topic (the first journal entry consists of 39 separate paragraphs). The three points at which her language becomes more discursive carry more weight by contrast. These passages seem at first to involve seemingly unobjectionable, safe topics: the house, her room, and the room's yellow wallpaper. Indeed, the very first mention of the wallpaper expresses conventional hyperbole: "I never saw worse paper in my life." But the language at once grows unexpected and intense:

> One of those sprawling flamboyant patterns committing every artistic sin.

> It is dull enough to confuse the eye in following, pronounced enough to constantly irritate and provoke study, and when you follow the lame uncertain curves for a little distance they suddenly commit suicide—plunge off at outrageous angles, destroy themselves in unheard of contradictions.

Disguised as an acceptable feminine topic (interest in decor), the yellow wallpaper comes to occupy the narrator's entire reality. Finally, she rips it from the walls to reveal its real meaning. Unveiled, the yellow wallpaper is a metaphor for women's discourse. From a conventional perspective, it first seems strange, flamboyant, confusing, outrageous: the very act of women's writing produces discourse which embodies "unheard of contradictions." Once freed, it expresses what is elsewhere kept hidden and embodies patterns that the patriarchal order ignores, suppresses, fears as grotesque, or fails to perceive at all. Like all good metaphors, the yellow wallpaper is variously interpreted by readers to represent (among other things) the "pattern" which underlies sexual inequality, the external manifestation of neurasthenia, the narrator's unconscious, the narrator's situation within patriarchy. But an emphasis on discourse—writing, the act of speaking, language—draws us to the central issue in this particular story: the narrator's alienation from work, writing, and intellectual life. Thus the story is inevitably concerned with the complicated and charged relationship between women and language: analysis then illuminates particular points of conflict between patriarchal language and women's discourse. This conflict in turn raises a number of questions relevant for both literary and feminist scholarship: In what senses can language be said to be oppressive to women? How do feminist linguistic innovations seek to escape this oppression? What is the relationship of innovation to material conditions? And what does it mean, theoretically, to escape the sentence that the structure of patriarchal language imposes?

The narrator of **"The Yellow Wallpaper"** has come with her husband to an isolated country estate for the summer. The house, a "colonial mansion," has been untenanted for years through some problem with inheritance. It is "the most beautiful place!" The grounds contain "hedges and walls and gates that lock, and lots of separate little houses for the gardeners and people." Despite this palatial potential to accommodate many people, the estate is virtually deserted with nothing growing in its greenhouses. The narrator perceives "something queer about it" and believes it may be haunted.

She is discouraged in this and other fancies by her sensible physician-husband who credits only what is observable, scientific, or demonstrable through facts and figures. He has scientifically diagnosed his wife's condition as merely "a temporary nervous depression"; her brother, also a noted physician, concurs in this opinion. Hence husband and wife have come as physician and patient to this solitary summer mansion in quest of cure. The narrator reports her medical regimen to her journal, together with her own view of the problem:

> So I take phosphates or phosphites—whichever it is, and tonics, and journeys, and air, and exercise, and am absolutely forbidden to "work" until I am well again.

> Personally, I disagree with their ideas.

> Personally, I believe that congenial work, with excitement and change, would do me good.

> But what is one to do?

Her room at the top of the house seems once to have been a nursery or a playroom with bars on the windows and "rings and things on the walls." The room contains not much more than a mammoth metal bed. The ugly yellow wallpaper has been stripped off in patches—perhaps by the children who formerly inhabited the room. In this "atrocious nursery" the narrator increasingly spends her time. Her husband is often away on medical cases, her baby makes her nervous, and no other company is permitted her. Disturbed by the wallpaper, she asks for another room or for different paper; her husband urges her not to give way to her "fancies." Further, he claims that any change would lead to more change: "after the wallpaper was changed it would be the heavy bedstead, and then the barred windows, and then that gate at the head of the stairs, and so on." So no changes are made, and the narrator is left alone with her "imaginative power and habit of story-making." In this stimulus-deprived environment, the "pattern" of the wallpaper becomes increasingly compelling: the narrator gradually becomes intimate with its "principle of design" and unconventional connections. The figure of a woman begins to take shape behind the superficial pattern of the paper. The more the wallpaper comes alive, the less inclined is the narrator to write in her journal—"dead paper." Now with three weeks left of the summer and her relationship with the wallpaper more and more intense, she asks once more to be allowed to leave. Her husband refuses: "I cannot possibly leave town just now. Of course if you were in any danger, I could and would, but you really are better, dear, whether you can see it or not. I am a doctor, dear, and I know." She expresses the fear that she is not getting well. "Bless her little heart!" he responds, "She shall be as sick as she pleases." When she hesitantly voices the belief that she may be losing her mind, he reproaches her so vehemently that she says no more. Instead, in the final weeks of the summer, she gives herself up to the wallpaper. "Life is very much more exciting now than it used to be," she tells her journal. "You see I have something more to expect, to look forward to, to watch. I really do eat better, and am more quiet than I was." She reports that her husband judges her "to be flourishing in spite of my wall-paper."

She begins to strip off the wallpaper at every opportunity in order to free the woman she perceives is trapped inside. She becomes increasingly aware of this woman and other female figures creeping behind the surface pattern of the wallpaper: there is a hint that the room's previous female occupant has left behind the marks of her struggle for freedom. Paranoid by now, the narrator attempts to disguise her obsession with the wallpaper. On the last day, she locks herself in the room and succeeds in stripping off most of the remaining paper. When her husband comes home and finally unlocks the door, he is horrified to find her creeping along the walls of the room. "I've got out at last," she tells him triumphantly, "And I've pulled off most of the paper, so you can't put me back." Her husband faints, and she is obliged to step over him each time she circles the room.

"The Yellow Wallpaper" was read by nineteenth-century readers as a harrowing case study of neurasthenia. Even recent readings have treated the narrator's madness as a function of her individual psychological situation. A feminist reading emphasizes the social and economic conditions which drive the narrator—and potentially all women—to madness. In these readings, the yellow wallpaper represents (1) the narrator's own mind, (2) the narrator's unconscious, (3) the "pattern" of social and economic dependence which reduces women to domestic slavery. The woman in the wallpaper represents (1) the narrator herself, gone mad, (2) the narrator's unconscious, (3) all women. While these interpretations are plausible and fruitful, I interpret the wallpaper to be women's writing or women's discourse, and the woman in the wallpaper to be the representation of women that becomes possible only after women obtain the right to speak. In this reading, the yellow wallpaper stands for a new vision of women—one which is constructed differently from the representation of women in patriarchal language. The story is thus in part about the clash between two modes of discourse: one powerful, "ancestral," and dominant; the other new, "impertinent," and visionary. The story's outcome makes a statement about the relationship of a visionary feminist project to material reality.

It is significant that the narrator of **"The Yellow Wallpaper"** is keeping a journal, confiding to "dead paper" the unorthodox thoughts and perceptions she is reluctant to tell to a "living soul." Challenging and subverting the expert prescription that forbids her to write, the journal evokes a sense of urgency and danger. "There comes John," she tells us at the end of her first entry, "and I must put this away,—he hates to have me write a word." We, her readers, are thus from the beginning her confidantes, implicated in forbidden discourse.

Contributing to our suspense and sense of urgency is the ambiguity of the narrator's "condition," whose etiology is left unstated in the story. For her physician-husband, it is a medical condition of unknown origin to be medically managed. Certain imagery (the "ghostliness" of the estate, the "trouble" with the heirs) suggests hereditary disease. Other evidence points toward psychological causes (e.g., postpartum depression, failure to adjust to marriage and motherhood). A feminist analysis moves beyond such localized causes to implicate the economic and social conditions which, under patriarchy, make women domestic slaves. In any case, the fact that the origin of the narrator's condition is never made explicit intensifies the role of diagnosis in putting a name to her "condition."

Symptoms are crucial for the diagnostic process. The narrator reports, among other things, exhaustion, crying, nervousness, synesthesia, anger, paranoia, and hallucination. "Temporary nervous depression" (coupled with a "slight hysterical tendency") is the medical term that serves to diagnose or define these symptoms. Once pronounced, and reinforced by the second opinion of the narrator's brother, this diagnosis not only names reality but also has considerable power over what that reality is now to be: it dictates the narrator's re-

moval to the "ancestral halls" where the story is set and generates a medical therapeutic regimen that includes physical isolation, "phosphates or phosphites," air, and rest. Above all, it forbids her to "work." The quotation marks, registering her husband's perspective, discredit the equation of writing with true work. The diagnostic language of the physician is coupled with the paternalistic language of the husband to create a formidable array of controls over her behavior.

I use "diagnosis," then, as a metaphor for the voice of medicine or science that speaks to define women's condition. Diagnosis is powerful and public; representing institutional authority, it dictates that money, resources, and space are to be expended as consequences in the "real world." It is a male voice that privileges the rational, the practical, and the observable. It is the voice of male logic and male judgment which dismisses superstition and refuses to see the house as haunted or the narrator's condition as serious. It imposes controls on the female narrator and dictates how she is to perceive and talk about the world. It is enforced by the "ancestral halls" themselves: the rules are followed even when the physician-husband is absent. In fact, the opening imagery— "ancestral halls," "a colonial mansion," "a haunted house"—legitimizes the diagnostic process by placing it firmly within an institutional frame: medicine, marriage, patriarchy. All function in the story to define and prescribe.

In contrast, the narrator in her nursery room speaks privately to her journal. At first she expresses her views hesitantly, "personally." Her language includes a number of stereotypical features of "women's language": not only are its topics limited, it is marked formally by exclamation marks, italics, intensifiers, and repetition of the impotent refrain, "What is one to do?" The journal entries at this early stage are very tentative and clearly shaped under the stern eye of male judgment. Oblique references only hint at an alternative reality. The narrator writes, for example, that the wallpaper has been "torn off" and "stripped away," yet she does not say by whom. Her qualms about her medical diagnosis and treatment remain unspoken except in her journal, which functions only as a private respite, a temporary relief. "Dead paper," it is not truly subversive.

Nevertheless, the narrator's language almost from the first does serve to call into question both the diagnosis of her condition and the rules established to treat it. As readers, therefore, we are not permitted wholehearted confidence in the medical assessment of the problem. It is not that we doubt the existence of her "condition," for it obviously causes genuine suffering; but we come to doubt that the diagnosis names the real problem—the narrator seems to place her own inverted commas around the words "temporary nervous depression" and "slight hysterical tendency"—and perceive that whatever its nature it is exacerbated by the rules established for its cure.

For this reason, we are alert to the possibility of an alternative vision. The yellow wallpaper provides it. Representing a different reality, it is "living paper," aggressively alive: "You think you have mastered it, but just as you get well underway in following, it turns a back-somersault and there you are. It slaps you in the face, knocks you down, and tramples upon you. It is like a bad dream." The narrator's husband refuses to replace the wallpaper, "whitewash" the room, or let her change rooms altogether on the grounds that other changes will then be demanded. The wallpaper is to remain: acknowledgment of its reality is the first step toward freedom. Confronting it at first through male eyes, the narrator is repelled and speculates that the children who inhabited the room before her attacked it for its ugliness. There is thus considerable resistance to the wallpaper and an implied rejection of what it represents, even by young children.

But the wallpaper exerts its power and, at the same time, the narrator's journal entries falter; "I don't know why I should write this," she says, about halfway through the story. She makes a final effort to be allowed to leave the room; when this fails, she becomes increasingly absorbed by the wallpaper and by the figure of a woman that exists behind its confusing surface pattern. This figure grows clearer to her, to the point where she can join her behind the paper and literally act within it. At this point, her language becomes bolder: she completes the predicates that were earlier left passively hanging. Describing joint action with the woman in the wallpaper, she tells us that the room has come to be damaged at the hands of women: "I pulled and she shook, I shook and she pulled, and before morning we had peeled off yards of that paper"; "I am getting angry enough to do something desperate." From an increasingly distinctive perspective, she sees an alternative reality beneath the repellent surface pattern in which the figures of women are emerging. Her original perception is confirmed: the patriarchal house is indeed "haunted" by figures of women. The room is revealed as a prison inhabited by its former inmates, whose struggles have nearly destroyed it. Absorbed almost physically by "living paper"—writing—she strives to liberate the women trapped within the ancestral halls, women with whom she increasingly identifies. Once begun, liberation and identification are irreversible: "I've got out at last . . . " cries the narrator, "And I've pulled off most of the paper, so you can't put me back!"

This ending of **"The Yellow Wallpaper"** is ambiguous and complex. Because the narrator's final proclamation is both triumphant and horrifying, madness in the story is both positive and negative. On the one hand, it testifies to an alternative reality and challenges patriarchy head on. The fact that her unflappable husband faints when he finds her establishes the dramatic power of her new freedom. Defying the judgment that she suffers from a "temporary nervous depression," she has followed her own logic, her own perceptions, her own projects to this final scene in which madness is seen as a kind of transcendent sanity. This engagement with the yellow wallpaper constitutes a form of the "work" which has been forbidden—women's writing. As she steps over the patriarchal body, she leaves the authoritative voice of diagnosis in shambles at her feet. Forsaking "women's language" forever, her new mode of speaking—an unlawful language—escapes "the sentence" imposed by patriarchy.

On the other hand, there are consequences to be paid for this escape. As the ending of the narrative, her madness will no doubt commit her to more intense medical treatment, perhaps to the dreaded Weir Mitchell of whom her husband has spoken. The surrender of patriarchy is only temporary: her husband has merely fainted, after all, not died, and will no doubt move swiftly and severely to deal with her. Her individual escape is temporary and compromised.

But there is yet another sense in which **"The Yellow Wallpaper"** enacts a clash between diagnosis and women's discourse. Asked once whether the story was based on fact, Gilman replied "I had been as far as one could go and get back." Gilman based the story on her own experience of depression and treatment. For her first visit to the noted neurologist S.

Weir Mitchell, she prepared a detailed case history of her own illness, constructed in part from her journal entries. Mitchell was not impressed: he "only thought it proved conceit" [*The Living of Charlotte Perkins Gilman*]. He wanted obedience from patients, not information. "Wise women," he wrote elsewhere, "choose their doctors and trust them. The wisest ask the fewest questions." Gilman reproduced in her journal Mitchell's prescription for her:

> Live as domestic a life as possible. Have your child with you all the time. (Be it remarked that if I did but dress the baby it left me shaking and crying—certainly far from a healthy companionship for her, to say nothing of the effect on me.) Lie down an hour after every meal. Have but two hours intellectual life a day. And never touch pen, brush or pencil as long as you live.

Gilman spent several months trying to follow Mitchell's prescription, a period of intense suffering for her:

> I could not read nor write nor paint nor sew nor talk nor listen to talking, nor anything. I lay on that lounge and wept all day. The tears ran down into my ears on either side. I went to bed crying, woke in the night crying, sat on the edge of the bed in the morning and cried—from sheer continuous pain.

At last, in a "moment of clear vision," Gilman realized that for her the traditional domestic role was at least in part the cause of her distress. She left her husband and with her baby went to California to be a writer and a feminist activist. Three years later she wrote **"The Yellow Wallpaper."** After the story was published, she sent a copy to Mitchell. If it in any way influenced his treatment of women in the future, she wrote, "I have not lived in vain."

There are several points to note here with respect to women's discourse. Gilman's use of her own journal to create a fictional journal which in turn becomes a published short story problematizes and calls our attention to the journal form. The terms "depression" and "hysteria" signal a non-textual as well as a textual conundrum: contemporary readers could (and some did) read the story as a realistic account of madness; for feminist readers (then and now) who bring to the text some comprehension of medical attitudes toward women in the nineteenth century, such a non-ironic reading is not possible. Lest we miss Gilman's point, her use of a real proper name in her story, Weir Mitchell's, draws explicit attention to the world outside the text.

Thus **"The Yellow Wallpaper"** is not merely a fictional challenge to the patriarchal diagnosis of women's condition. It is also a public critique of a real medical treatment. Publication of the story added power and status to Gilman's words and transformed the journal form from a private to a public setting. Her published challenge to diagnosis has now been read by thousands of readers. By living to tell the tale, the woman who writes escapes the sentence that condemns her to silence.

To call **"The Yellow Wallpaper"** a struggle between diagnosis and discourse is to characterize the story in terms of language. More precisely, it is to contrast the signification procedures of patriarchal medicine with discursive disruptions that call those procedures into question. A major problem in **"The Yellow Wallpaper"** involves the relationship of the linguistic sign to the signified, of language to "reality." Diagnosis, highlighted from the beginning by the implicit inverted commas around diagnostic phrases ("a slight hysterical tendency"), stands in the middle of an equation which translates a phenomenological perception of the human body into a finite set of signs called "symptoms"—fever, exhaustion, nervousness, pallor, and so on—which are in turn assembled to produce a "diagnosis"; this sign generates treatment, a set of prescriptions that impinge once more upon the "real" human body. Part of the power of diagnosis as a scientific process depends upon a notion of language as transparent, as *not* the issue. Rather the issue is the precision, efficiency, and plausibility with which a correct diagnostic sign is generated by a particular state of affairs that is assumed to exist in reality. In turn, the diagnostic sign is not complete until its clinical implications have been elaborated as a set of concrete therapeutic practices designed not merely to refer to but actually to change the original physical reality. Chary with its diagnostic categories (as specialized lexicons go), medicine's rich and intricate descriptive vocabulary testifies to the history of its mission: to translate the realities of the human body into human language and back again. As such, it is a perfect example of language which "reflects" reality and simultaneously "produces" it.

Why is this interesting? And why is this process important in **"The Yellow Wallpaper"**? Medical diagnosis stands as a prime example of an authorized linguistic process (distilled, respected, high-paying) whose representational claims are strongly supported by social, cultural, and economic practices. Even more than most forms of male discourse, the diagnostic process is multiply-sanctioned. **"The Yellow Wallpaper"** challenges both the particular "sentence" passed on the narrator and the elaborate sentencing process whose presumed representational power can sentence women to isolation, deprivation, and alienation from their own sentencing possibilities. The right to author or originate sentences is at the heart of the story and what the yellow wallpaper represents: a figure for women's discourse, it seeks to escape the sentence passed by medicine and patriarchy. Before looking more closely at what the story suggests about the nature of women's discourse, we need to place somewhat more precisely this notion of "the sentence."

Diagnosis is a "sentence" in that it is simultaneously a linguistic entity, a declaration or judgment, and a plan for action in the real world whose clinical consequences may spell dullness, drama, or doom for the diagnosed. Diagnosis may be, then, not merely a sentence but a death sentence. This doubling of the word "sentence" is not mere playfulness. "I sat down and began to speak," wrote Anna Kavan in *Asylum Piece,* describing the beginning of a woman's mental breakdown, "driving my sluggish tongue to frame words that seemed useless even before they were uttered." This physically exhausting process of producing sentences is generalized: "Sometimes I think that some secret court must have tried and condemned me, unheard, to this heavy sentence." The word "sentence" is both sign and signified, word and act, declaration and discursive consequence. Its duality emphasizes the difficulty of an analysis which privileges purely semiotic relationships on the one hand or the representational nature of language on the other. In **"The Yellow Wallpaper,"** the diagnosis of hysteria may be a sham: it may be socially constituted or merely individually expedient quite apart from even a conventional representational relationship. But it dictates a rearrangement of material reality nevertheless. The sentence may be unjust, inaccurate, or irrelevant, but the sentence is served anyway.

The sentence is of particular importance in modern linguistics, where it has dominated inquiry for twenty-five years and for more than seventy years has been the upper cut-off point for the study of language: consideration of word sequences and meaning beyond the sentence has been typically dismissed as too untidy and speculative for linguistic science. The word "sentence" also emphasizes the technical concentration, initiated by structuralism but powerfully developed by transformational grammar, on syntax (formal grammatical structure at the sentence level). The formulaic sentence $S \rightarrow NP + VP$ which initiates the familiar tree diagram of linguistic analysis could well be said to exemplify the tyranny of syntax over the study of semantics (meaning) and pragmatics (usage). [The critic explains in a footnote: "The linguistic formula $S \rightarrow NP + VP$ means that Sentence is rewritten as (consists of) Noun Phrase + Verb Phrase. Sentences are "generated" as tree diagrams that move downward from the abstract entity S to individual components of actual sentences."] As a result, as Sally McConnell-Ginet has argued, linguistics has often failed to address those aspects of language with which women have been most concerned: on the one hand, the semantic or non-linguistic conditions underlying given grammatical structures, and on the other, the contextual circumstances in which linguistic structures are actually used. One can generalize and say that signs alone are of less interest to women than are the processes of signification which link signs to semantic and pragmatic aspects of speaking. To "escape the sentence" is to move beyond the boundaries of formal syntax.

But is it to move beyond language? In writing about language over the last fifteen years, most feminist scholars in the United States have argued that language creates as well as reflects reality and hence that feminist linguistic innovation helps foster more enlightened social conditions for women. A more conservative position holds that language merely reflects social reality and that linguistic reform is hollow unless accompanied by changes in attitudes and socio-economic conditions that also favor women's equality. Though different, particularly in their support for innovation, both positions more or less embody a view that there *is* a non-linguistic reality to which language is related in systematic ways. Recent European writing challenges the transparency of such a division, arguing that at some level reality is inescapably linguistic. The account of female development within this framework emphasizes the point at which the female child comes into language (and becomes a being now called female); because she is female, she is from the first alienated from the processes of symbolic representation. Within this symbolic order, a phallocentric order, she is frozen, confined, curtailed, limited, and represented as "lack," as "other." To make a long story short, there is as yet no escaping the sentence of male-determining discourse.

According to this account, "the sentence," for women, is inescapably bound up with the symbolic order. Within language, says Luce Irigaray for example, women's fate is a "death sentence." Irigaray's linguistic innovations attempt to disrupt this "law of the father" and exemplify the possibilities for a female language which "has nothing to do with the syntax which we have used for centuries, namely, that constructed according to the following organization: subject, predicate, or, subject, verb, object." Whatever the realities of that particular claim, at the moment there are persuasive theoretical, professional, and political reasons for feminists to pay attention to what I will now more officially call discourse, which encompasses linguistic and formalistic considerations, yet goes beyond strict formalism to include both semantics and pragmatics. It is thus concerned not merely with speech, but with the conditions of speaking. With this notion of "sentencing," I have tried to suggest a process of language production in which an individual word, speech, or text is linked to the conditions under which it was (and could have been) produced as well as to those under which it is (and could be) read and interpreted. Thus the examination of diagnosis and discourse in a text is at once a study of a set of representational practices, of mechanisms for control and opportunities for resistance, and of communicational possibilities in fiction and elsewhere.

In **"The Yellow Wallpaper"** we see consequences of the "death sentence." Woman is represented as childlike and dysfunctional. Her complaints are wholly circular, merely confirming the already-spoken patriarchal diagnosis. She is constituted and defined within the patriarchal order of language and destined, like Athena in Irigaray's analysis, to repeat her father's discourse "without much understanding." "Personally," she says, and "I sometimes fancy": this is acceptable language in the ancestral halls. Her attempts to engage in different, serious language—self-authored—are given up; to write in the absence of patriarchal sanction requires "having to be so sly about it, or else meet with heavy opposition" and is too exhausting. Thus the narrator speaks the law of the father in the form of a "women's language" which is prescribed by patriarchy and exacts its sentence upon her: not to author sentences of her own.

The yellow wallpaper challenges this sentence. In contrast to the orderly, evacuated patriarchal estate, the female lineage

Gilman as a young woman.

that the wallpaper represents is thick with life, expression, and suffering. Masquerading as a symptom of "madness," language animates what had been merely an irritating and distracting pattern:

> This paper looks to me as if it *knew* what a vicious influence it had!

> There is a recurrent spot where the pattern lolls like a broken neck and two bulbous eyes stare at you upside down.

> I get positively angry with the impertinence of it and the everlastingness. Up and down and sideways they crawl, and those absurd, unblinking eyes are everywhere.

The silly and grotesque surface pattern reflects women's conventional representation; one juxtaposition identifies "that silly and conspicuous front design" with "sister on the stairs!" In the middle section of the story, where the narrator attempts to convey her belief that she is seriously ill, the husband-physician is quoted verbatim, enabling us to see the operation of male judgment at first hand. He notes an improvement in her symptoms: "You are gaining flesh and color, your appetite is better, I feel really much easier about you." The narrator disputes these statements: "I don't weigh a bit more, nor as much; and my appetite may be better in the evening when you are here, but it is worse in the morning when you are away!" His response not only pre-empts further talk of facts, it reinforces the certainty of his original diagnosis and confirms his view of her illness as nonserious: " 'Bless her little heart!' said he with a big hug, 'she shall be as sick as she pleases!' "

His failure to let her leave the estate initiates a new relationship to the wallpaper. She begins to see women in the pattern. Until now, we as readers have acquiesced in the fiction that the protagonist is keeping a journal, a fiction initially supported by journal-like textual references. This now becomes difficult to sustain: how can the narrator keep a journal when, as she tells us, she is sleeping, creeping, or watching the wallpaper the whole time? In her growing paranoia, would she confide in a journal she could not lock up? How did the journal get into our hands? Because we are nevertheless reading this "journal," we are forced to experience a contradiction: the narrative is unfolding in an impossible form. This embeds our experience of the story in self-conscious attention to its construction. A new tone enters as she reports that she defies orders to take naps by not actually sleeping: "And that cultivates deceit, for I don't tell them I'm awake—O no!" This crowing tone announces a decisive break from the patriarchal order. She mocks her husband's diagnosis by diagnosing for herself why he "seems very queer sometimes": "It strikes me occasionally, just as a scientific hypothesis,—that perhaps it is the paper!"

The wallpaper never becomes attractive. It remains indeterminate, complex, unresolved, disturbing; it continues to embody, like the form of the story we are reading, "unheard of contradictions." By now the narrator is fully engrossed by it and determined to find out its meaning. During the day—by "normal" standards—it remains "tiresome and perplexing." But at night she sees a woman, or many women, shaking the pattern and trying to climb through it. Women "get through," she perceives, "and then the pattern strangles them off and turns them upside down, and makes their eyes white!"

The death sentence imposed by patriarchy is violent and relentless. No one escapes.

The story is now at its final turning point: "I have found out another funny thing," reports the narrator, "but I shan't tell it this time! It does not do to trust people too much." This is a break with patriarchy—and a break with us. What she has discovered, which she does not state, is that she and the woman behind the paper are the same. This is communicated syntactically by contrasting sentences: "This bedstead is fairly gnawed!" she tells us, and then: "I bit off a little piece [of the bedstead] at one corner." "If that woman does get out, and tries to get away, I can tie her!" and "But I am securely fastened now by my well-hidden rope." The final passages are filled with crowing, "impertinent" language: "Hurrah!" "The sly thing!" "No person touches this paper but me,—not *alive!*" Locked in the room, she addresses her husband in a dramatically different way: "It is no use, young man, you can't open it!"

She does not make this declaration aloud. In fact, she appears to have difficulty even making herself understood and must repeat several times the instructions to her husband for finding the key to the room. At first we think she may be too mad to speak proper English. But then we realize that he simply is unable to accept a statement of fact from her, his little goose, until she has "said it so often that he had to go and see." Her final triumph is her public proclamation, "I've got out at last . . . you can't put me back!"

There is a dramatic shift here both in *what* is said and in *who* is speaking. Not only has a new "impertinent" self emerged, but this final voice is collective, representing the narrator, the woman behind the wallpaper, and women elsewhere and everywhere. The final vision itself is one of physical enslavement, not liberation: the woman, bound by a rope, circles the room like an animal in a yoke. Yet that this vision has come to exist and to be expressed changes the terms of the representational process. That the husband-physician must at last listen to a woman speaking—no matter what she says—significantly changes conditions for speaking. Though patriarchy may be only temporarily unconscious, its ancestral halls will never be precisely the same again.

We can return now to the questions raised at the outset. Language in **"The Yellow Wallpaper"** is oppressive to women in the particular form of a medical diagnosis, a set of linguistic signs whose representational claims are authorized by society and whose power to control women's fate, whether or not those claims are valid, is real. Representation has real, material consequences. In contrast, women's power to originate signs is monitored; and, once produced, no legitimating social apparatus is available to give those signs substance in the real world.

Linguistic innovation, then, has a dual fate. The narrator in **"The Yellow Wallpaper"** initially speaks a language authorized by patriarchy, with genuine language ("work") forbidden her. But as the wallpaper comes alive she devises a different, "impertinent" language which defies patriarchal control and confounds the predictions of male judgment (diagnosis). The fact that she becomes a creative and involved language user, producing sentences which break established rules, *in and of itself* changes the terms in which women are represented in language and extends the conditions under which women will speak.

Yet language is intimately connected to material reality, despite the fact that no direct correspondence exists. The word is theory to the deed: but the deed's existence will depend upon a complicated set of material conditions. The narrator of **"The Yellow Wallpaper"** is not free at the end of the story because she has temporarily escaped her sentence: though she has "got out at last," her triumph is to have sharpened and articulated the nature of women's condition; she remains physically bound by a rope and locked in a room. The conditions she has diagnosed must change before she and other women will be free. Thus women's control of language is left metaphorical and evocative: the story only hints at possibilities for change. Woman is both passive and active, subject and object, sane and mad. Contradictions remain, for they are inherent in women's current "condition."

Thus to "escape the sentence" involves both linguistic innovation and change in material conditions: both change in what is said and change in the conditions of speaking. The escape of individual women may constitute a kind of linguistic self-help which has intrinsic value as a contribution to language but which functions socially and politically to isolate deviance rather than to introduce change. Representation is not without consequences. Thus the study of women and language must involve the study of discourse, which encompasses both form and function as well as the representational uncertainty their relationship entails. As a metaphor, the yellow wallpaper is never fully resolved: it can be described, but its meaning cannot be fixed. It remains trivial and dramatic, vivid and dowdy, compelling and repulsive: these multiple meanings run throughout the story in contrast to the one certain meaning of patriarchal diagnosis. If diagnosis is the middle of an equation that freezes material flux in a certain sign, the wallpaper is a disruptive center that chaotically fragments any attempt to fix on it a single meaning. It offers a lesson in language, whose sentence is perhaps not always destined to escape us. (pp. 61-75)

> *Paula A. Treichler, "Escaping the Sentence: Diagnosis and Discourse in 'The Yellow Wallpaper'," in* Tulsa Studies in Women's Literature, *Vol. 3, Nos. 1 & 2, Spring-Fall, 1984, pp. 61-77.*

CONRAD SHUMAKER   (essay date 1985)

[*In the following excerpt, Shumaker discusses the conflict between "feminine" imagination and "masculine" rationality in "The Yellow Wallpaper."*]

In 1890 William Dean Howells sent a copy of **"The Yellow Wallpaper"** to Horace Scudder, editor of the *Atlantic Monthly.* Scudder gave his reason for not publishing the story in a short letter to its author, Charlotte Perkins Stetson (later to become Charlotte Perkins Gilman): "Dear Madam, Mr. Howells has handed me this story. I could not forgive myself if I made others as miserable as I have made myself!" Gilman persevered, however, and eventually the story, which depicts the mental collapse of a woman undergoing a "rest cure" at the hands of her physician husband, was printed in the *New England Magazine* and then later in Howells' own collection, *Great Modern American Stories,* where he introduces it as "terrible and too wholly dire," and "too terribly good to be printed." Despite (or perhaps because of) such praise, the story was virtually ignored for over fifty years until Elaine Hedges called attention to its virtues, praising it as "a small literary masterpiece" [see *TCLC* Vol. 9, pp. 105-07]. Today the work is highly spoken of by those who have read it, but it is not widely known and has been slow to appear in anthologies of American literature.

Some of the best criticism attempts to explain this neglect as a case of misinterpretation by audiences used to "traditional" literature. Annette Kolodny, for example, points out that though nineteenth-century readers had learned to "follow the fictive processes of aberrant perception and mental breakdown" by reading Poe's tales, they were not prepared to understand a tale of mental degeneration in a middle-class mother and wife. It took twentieth-century feminism to place the story in a "nondominant or subcultural" tradition which those steeped in the dominant tradition could not understand. Jean F. Kennard [see Further Reading] suggests that the recent appearance of feminist novels has changed literary conventions and led us to find in the story an exploration of women's role instead of the tale of horror or depiction of mental breakdown its original audience found. Both arguments are persuasive, and the feminist readings of the story that accompany them are instructive. With its images of barred windows and sinister bedsteads, creeping women and domineering men, the story does indeed raise the issue of sex roles in an effective way, and thus anticipates later feminist literature.

Ultimately, however, both approaches tend to make the story seem more isolated from the concerns of the nineteenth-century "dominant tradition" than it really is, and since they focus most of our attention on the story's polemical aspect, they invite a further exploration of Gilman's artistry—the way in which she molds her reformer concerns into a strikingly effective work of literature. To be sure, the polemics are important. Gilman, an avowed feminist and a relative of Harriet Beecher Stowe, told Howells that she didn't consider the work to be "literature" at all, that everything she wrote was for a purpose, in this case that of pointing out the dangers of a particular medical treatment. Unlike Gilman's other purposeful fictions, however, **"The Yellow Wallpaper"** transcends its author's immediate intent, and my experience teaching it suggests that it favorably impresses both male and female students, even before they learn of its feminist context or of the patriarchal biases of nineteenth-century medicine. I think the story has this effect for two reasons. First, the question of women's role in the nineteenth century is inextricably bound up with the more general question of how one perceives the world. Woman is often seen as representing an imaginative or "poetic" view of things that conflicts with (or sometimes complements) the American male's "common sense" approach to reality. Through the characters of the "rational" doctor and the "imaginative" wife, Gilman explores a question that was—and in many ways still is—central both to American literature and to the place of women in American culture: What happens to the imagination when it's defined as feminine (and thus weak) and has to face a society that values the useful and the practical and rejects anything else as nonsense? Second, this conflict and the related feminist message both arise naturally and effectively out of the action of the story because of the author's skillful handling of the narrative voice.

One of the most striking passages in Gilman's autobiography describes her development and abandonment of a dream world, a fantasy land to which she could escape from the rather harsh realities of her early life. When she was thirteen, a friend of her mother warned that such escape could be dangerous, and Charlotte, a good New England girl who considered absolute obedience a duty, "shut the door" on her "dear, bright, glittering dreams." The narrator of **"The Yellow Wallpaper"** has a similar problem: from the beginning of the story she displays a vivid imagination. She wants to imagine that the house they have rented is haunted, and as she looks at the wallpaper, she is reminded of her childhood fancies about rooms, her ability to "get more entertainment and terror out of blank walls and plain furniture than most children could find in a toy store." Her husband has to keep reminding her that she "must not give way to fancy in the least" as she comments on her new surroundings. Along with her vivid imagination she has the mind and eye of an artist. She begins to study the wallpaper in an attempt to make sense of its artistic design, and she objects to it for aesthetic reasons: it is "one of those sprawling, flamboyant patterns committing every artistic sin." When her ability to express her artistic impulses is limited by her husband's prescription of complete rest, her mind turns to the wallpaper, and she begins to find in its tangled pattern the emotions and experiences she is forbidden to record. By trying to ignore and repress her imagination, in short, John eventually brings about the very circumstance he wants to prevent.

Though he is clearly a domineering husband who wants to have absolute control over his wife, John also has other reasons for forbidding her to write or paint. As Gilman points out in her autobiography, the "rest cure" was designed for "the business man exhausted from too much work, and the society woman exhausted from too much play." The treatment is intended, in other words, to deal with physical symptoms of overwork and fatigue, and so is unsuited to the narrator's more complex case. But as a doctor and an empiricist who "scoffs openly at things not to be felt and seen and put down in figures," John wants to deal only with physical causes and effects: if his wife's symptoms are nervousness and weight loss, the treatment must be undisturbed tranquility and good nutrition. The very idea that her "work" might be beneficial to her disturbs him; indeed, he is both fearful and contemptuous of her imaginative and artistic powers, largely because he fails to understand them or the view of the world they lead her to.

Two conversations in particular demonstrate his way of dealing with her imagination and his fear of it. The first occurs when the narrator asks him to change the wallpaper. He replies that to do so would be dangerous, for "nothing was worse for a nervous patient than to give way to such fancies." At this point, her "fancy" is simply an objection to the paper's ugliness, a point she makes clear when she suggests that they move to the "pretty rooms" downstairs. John replies by calling her a "little goose" and saying "he would go down to the cellar if she wished and have it whitewashed into the bargain." Besides showing his obviously patriarchal stance, his reply is designed to make her aesthetic objections seem nonsense by fastening on concrete details—color and elevation—and ignoring the real basis of her request. If she wants to go downstairs away from the yellow walls, he will take her to the cellar and have it whitewashed. The effect is precisely what he intends: he makes her see her objection to the paper's ugliness as "just a whim." The second conversation occurs after the narrator has begun to see a woman behind the surface pattern of the wallpaper. When John catches her getting out of bed to examine the paper more closely, she decides to ask him to take her away. He refuses, referring again to concrete details: "You are gaining flesh and color, your appetite is better, I feel really much better about you."

When she implies that her physical condition isn't the real problem, he cuts her off in midsentence: "I beg of you, for my sake and for our child's sake, as well as for your own, that you will never for one instant let that idea enter your mind! There is nothing so dangerous, so fascinating, to a temperament like yours. It is a false and foolish fancy." For John, mental illness is the inevitable result of using one's imagination, the creation of an attractive "fancy" which the mind then fails to distinguish from reality. He fears that because of her imaginative "temperament" she will create the fiction that she is mad and come to accept it despite the evidence—color, weight, appetite—that she is well. Imagination and art are subversive because they threaten to undermine his materialistic universe.

Ironically, despite his abhorrence of faith and superstition, John fails because of his own dogmatic faith in materialism and empiricism, a faith that will not allow him even to consider the possibility that his wife's imagination could be a positive force. In a way John is like Aylmer in Hawthorne's "The Birthmark": each man chooses to interpret a characteristic of his wife as a defect because of his own failure of imagination, and each attempts to "cure" her through purely physical means, only to find he has destroyed her in the process. He also resembles the implied villain in many of Emerson's and Thoreau's lectures and essays, the man of convention who is so taken with "common sense" and traditional wisdom that he is blind to truth. Indeed, the narrator's lament that she might get well faster if John were not a doctor and her assertion that he can't understand her "because he is so wise" remind one of Thoreau's question in the first chapter of *Walden:* "How can he remember his ignorance—which his growth requires—who has so often to use his knowledge?" John's role as a doctor and an American male requires that he use his "knowledge" continuously and doggedly, and he would abhor the appearance of imagination in his own mind even more vehemently than in his wife's.

The relationship between them also offers an insight into how and why this fear of the imagination has been institutionalized through assigned gender roles. By defining his wife's artistic impulse as a potentially dangerous part of her feminine "temperament," John can control both his wife and a facet of human experience which threatens his comfortably materialistic view of the world. Fear can masquerade as calm authority when the thing feared is embodied in the "weaker sex." Quite fittingly, the story suggests that America is full of Johns: the narrator's brother is a doctor, and S. Weir Mitchell—"like John and my brother only more so!"—looms on the horizon if she doesn't recover.

As her comments suggest, the narrator understands John's problem yet is unable to call it his problem, and in many ways it is this combination of insight and naiveté, of resistance and resignation, that makes her such a memorable character and gives such power to her narrative. The story is in the form of a journal which the writer knows no one will read—she says she would not criticize John to "a living soul, of course, but this is dead paper"—yet at the same time her occasional use of "you," her questions ("What is one to do?" she asks three times in the first two pages), and her confidential tone all suggest that she is attempting to reach or create the listener she cannot otherwise find. Her remarks reveal that her relationship with her husband is filled with deception on her part, not so much because she wants to hide things from him but because it is impossible to tell him things he does not want

to acknowledge. She reveals to the "dead paper" that she must pretend to sleep and have an appetite because that is what John assumes will happen as a result of his treatment, and if she tells him that she isn't sleeping or eating he will simply contradict her. Thus the journal provides an opportunity not only to confess her deceit and explain its necessity but also to say the things she really wants to say to John and would say if his insistence on "truthfulness," i.e., saying what he wants to hear, didn't prevent her. As both her greatest deception and her attempt to be honest, the journal embodies in its very form the absurd contradictions inherent in her role as wife.

At the same time, however, she cannot quite stop deceiving herself about her husband's treatment of her, and her descriptions create a powerful dramatic irony as the reader gradually puts together details the meaning of which she doesn't quite understand. She says, for instance, that there is "something strange" about the house they have rented, but her description reveals bit by bit a room that has apparently been used to confine violent mental cases, with bars on the windows, a gate at the top of the stairs, steel rings on the walls, a nailed-down bedstead, and a floor that has been scratched and gouged. When she tries to explain her feelings about the house to John early in the story, her report of the conversation reveals her tendency to assume that he is always right despite her own reservations:

> . . . there is something strange about the house—I can feel it.
>
> I even said so to John one moonlight evening, but he said what I felt was a *draught,* and shut the window.
>
> I get unreasonably angry with John sometimes. I'm sure I never used to be so sensitive. I think it is due to this nervous condition.

As usual, John refuses to consider anything but physical details, but the narrator's reaction is particularly revealing here. Her anger, perfectly understandable to us, must be characterized, even privately, as "unreasonable," a sign of her condition. Whatever doubts she may have about John's methods, he represents reason, and it is her own sensitivity that must be at fault. Comments such as these reveal more powerfully than any direct statement could the way she is trapped by the conception of herself which she has accepted from John and the society whose values he represents. As Paula A. Treichler has pointed out [see excerpt dated 1984], John's diagnosis is a "sentence," a "set of linguistic signs whose representational claims are authorized by society," and thus it can "control women's fate, whether or not those claims are valid." The narrator can object to the terms of the sentence, but she cannot question its authority, even in her own private discourse.

To a great extent, the narrator's view of her husband is colored by the belief that he really does love her, a belief that provides some of the most striking and complex ironies in the story. When she says, "it is hard to talk to John about my case because he is so wise, and because he loves me so," it is tempting to take the whole sentence as an example of her naiveté. Obviously he is not wise, and his actions are not what we would call loving. Nevertheless, the sentence is in its way powerfully insightful. If John were not so wise—so sure of his own empirical knowledge and his expertise as a doctor—and so loving—so determined to make her better in the only way he knows—then he might be able to set aside his fear of her imagination and listen to her. The passage suggests strikingly the way both characters are doomed to act out their respective parts of loving husband and obedient wife right to the inevitably disastrous end.

Gilman's depiction of the narrator's decline into madness has been praised for the accuracy with which it captures the symptoms of mental breakdown and for its use of symbolism. What hasn't been pointed out is the masterly use of associations, foreshadowing, and even humor. Once the narrator starts attempting to read the pattern of the wallpaper, the reader must become a kind of psychological detective in order to follow and appreciate the narrative. In a sense, he too is viewing a tangled pattern with a woman behind it, and he must learn to revise his interpretation of the pattern as he goes along if he is to make sense of it. For one thing, the narrator tells us from time to time about new details in the room. She notices a "smooch" on the wall "low down, near the mopboard," and later we learn that the bedstead is "fairly gnawed." It is only afterwards that we find out that she is herself the source of these new marks as she bites the bedstead and crawls around the room, shoulder to the wallpaper. If the reader has not caught on already, these details show clearly that the narrator is not always aware of her own actions or in control of her thoughts and so is not always reliable in reporting them. They also foreshadow her final separation from her wifely self, her belief that she is the woman who has escaped from behind the barred pattern of the wallpaper.

But the details also invite us to reread earlier passages, to see if the voice which we have taken to be a fairly reliable though naive reporter has not been giving us unsuspected hints of another reality all along. If we do backtrack we find foreshadowing everywhere, not only in the way the narrator reads the pattern on the wall but in the pattern of her own narrative, the way in which one thought leads to another. One striking example occurs when she describes John's sister, Jennie, who is "a dear girl and so careful of me," and who therefore must not find out about the journal.

> She is a perfect and enthusiastic housekeeper, and hopes for no better profession. I verily believe she thinks it is the writing which made me sick!
>
> But I can write when she is out, and see her a long way off from these windows.
>
> There is one that commands the road, a lovely shaded winding road, and one that just looks off over the country. A lovely country too, full of great elms and velvet meadows.
>
> This wallpaper has a kind of sub-pattern in a different shade, a particularly irritating one, for you can only see it in certain lights, and not clearly then.
>
> But in the places where it isn't faded and where the sun is just so—I can see a strange, provoking, formless sort of figure, that seems to skulk about behind that silly and conspicuous front design.
>
> There's sister on the stairs!

The "perfect and enthusiastic housekeeper" is, of course, the ideal sister for John, whose view of the imagination she shares. Thoughts of Jennie lead to the narrator's assertion that she can "see her a long way off from these windows," foreshadowing later passages in which the narrator will see a creeping woman, and then eventually many creeping women from the same windows, and the association suggests

a connection between the "enthusiastic housekeeper" and those imaginary women. The thought of the windows leads to a description of the open country and suggests the freedom that the narrator lacks in her barred room. This, in turn, leads her back to the wallpaper, and now she mentions for the first time the "sub-pattern," a pattern which will eventually become a woman creeping behind bars, a projection of her feelings about herself as she looks through the actual bars of the window. The train of associations ends when John's sister returns, but this time she's just "sister," as if now she's the narrator's sister as well, suggesting a subconscious recognition that they both share the same role, despite Jennie's apparent freedom and contentment. Taken in context, this passage prepares us to see the connection between the pattern of the wallpaper, the actual bars on the narrator's windows, and the "silly and conspicuous" surface pattern of the wifely role behind which both women lurk.

We can see just how Gilman develops the narrator's mental collapse if we compare the passage quoted above to a later one in which the narrator once again discusses the "sub-pattern," which by now has become a woman who manages to escape in the daytime.

> I think that woman gets out in the daytime!
>
> And I'll tell you why—privately—I've seen her!
>
> I can see her out of every one of my windows!
>
> It is the same woman, I know, for she is always creeping, and most women do not creep by daylight.
>
> I see her on that long road under the trees, creeping along, and when a carriage comes she hides under the blackberry vines.
>
> I don't blame her a bit. It must be very humiliating to be caught creeping by daylight!
>
> I always lock the door when I creep by daylight!

Here again the view outside the window suggests a kind of freedom, but now it is only a freedom to creep outside the pattern, a freedom that humiliates and must be hidden. The dark humor that punctuates the last part of the story appears in the narrator's remark that she can recognize the woman because "most women do not creep by daylight," and the sense that the journal is an attempt to reach a listener becomes clear through her emphasis on "privately." Finally, the identification between the narrator and the woman is taken a step further and becomes more nearly conscious when the narrator reveals that she too creeps, but only behind a locked door. If we read the two passages in sequence, we can see just how masterfully Gilman uses her central images—the window, the barred pattern of the paper, and the woman—to create a pattern of associations which reveals the source of the narrator's malady yet allows the narrator herself to remain essentially unable to verbalize her problem. At some level, we see, she understands what has rendered her so thoroughly powerless and confused, yet she is so completely trapped in her role that she can express that knowledge only indirectly in a way that hides it from her conscious mind.

In the terribly comic ending, she has destroyed both the wallpaper and her own identity: now she is the woman from behind the barred pattern, and not even Jane—the wife she once was—can put her back. Still unable to express her feelings directly, she acts out both her triumph and her humiliation symbolically, creeping around the room with her shoulder in the "smooch," passing over her fainting husband on every lap. Loralee MacPike [see Further Reading] suggests that the narrator has finally gained her freedom, but that is true only in a very limited sense. She is still creeping, still inside the room with a rope around her waist. She has destroyed only the front pattern, the "silly and conspicuous" design that covers the real wife, the creeping one hidden behind the facade. As Treichler suggests, "her triumph is to have sharpened and articulated the nature of women's condition," but she is free only from the need to deceive herself and others about the true nature of her role. In a sense, she has discovered, bit by bit, and finally revealed to John, the wife he is attempting to create—the woman without illusions or imagination who spends all her time creeping.

The story, then, is a complex work of art as well as an effective indictment of the nineteenth-century view of the sexes and the materialism that underlies that view. It is hard to believe that readers familiar with the materialistic despots created by such writers as Hawthorne, Dickens, and Browning could fail to see the implications. Indeed, though Howells' comment that the story makes him "shiver" has been offered as evidence that he saw it as a more or less conventional horror story, I would assert that he understood quite clearly the source of the story's effect. He originally wrote to Gilman to congratulate her on her poem "Women of Today," a scathing indictment of women who fear changing sexual roles and fail to realize that their view of themselves as mothers, wives, and housekeepers is a self-deception. In fact, he praises that poem in terms that anticipate his praise of the story, calling it "dreadfully true." Perhaps the story was unpopular because it was, at least on some level, understood all too clearly, because it struck too deeply and effectively at traditional ways of seeing the world and woman's place in it. That, in any case, seems to be precisely what Howells implies in his comment that it is "too terribly good to be printed."

The clearest evidence that John's view of the imagination and art was all but sacred in Gilman's America comes, ironically, from the author's own pen. When she replied to Howells' request to reprint the story by saying that she did not write "literature," she was, of course, denying that she was a mere imaginative artist, defending herself from the charge that Hawthorne imagines his Puritan ancestors would lay at his doorstep: "A writer of story-books!—what mode of glorifying God, or being serviceable to mankind in his day and generation—may that be? Why, the degenerate fellow might as well have been a fiddler!" One wonders what this later female scion of good New England stock might have done had she been able to set aside such objections. In any case, one hopes that this one work of imagination and art, at least, will be restored to the place that Howells so astutely assigned it, alongside stories by contemporaries such as Mark Twain, Henry James, and Edith Wharton. (pp. 588-99)

> Conrad Shumaker, " 'Too Terribly Good to Be Printed': Charlotte Gilman's 'The Yellow Wallpaper'," in American Literature, Vol. 57, No. 4, December, 1985, pp. 588-99.

JEFFREY BERMAN (essay date 1985)

[*In the following excerpt, Berman presents a psychoanalytic reading of "The Yellow Wallpaper," using Gilman's autobiography to illuminate the mental conflicts of the narrator.*]

It is interesting to compare the two accounts of mental illness in . . . [Gilman's] autobiographical *The Living of Charlotte Perkins Gilman* and [her] fictional "The Yellow Wallpaper." There is no doubt about the greater truthfulness of art. The achievement of "The Yellow Wallpaper" lies in its ruthless honesty, accuracy, and power. Free from the constraints of hurting people in real life, the artist is free to imagine the unnerving details of her protagonist's story. In the autobiography, Gilman describes her husband as a patient and long-suffering man, the ideal spouse. She refers to his "unbroken devotion, his manifold cares and labors in tending a sick wife, his adoring pride in the best of babies. . . ." Stetson becomes a husband less human than saintly, a heroic portrait like the one of Charlotte's mother. The following sentence is typical of her characterization of him. "He has worked for me and for us both, waited on me in every tenderest way, played to me, read to me, done all for me as he always does. God be thanked for my husband."

Gilman projects these qualities onto the narrator's husband in "The Yellow Wallpaper" but with a different emphasis. The husband displays solicitude but also incomprehension and insensitivity. Baffled by his wife's mysterious illness, he seems to aggravate the situation—indeed, she hints that he is responsible for her illness. "John is a physician, and *perhaps*—(I would not say it to a living soul, of course, but this is dead paper, and a great relief to my mind)—*perhaps* that is one reason I do not get well faster." The narrator's unconscious resentment of the husband momentarily surfaces here, allowing us to glimpse the truth. Nowhere in the autobiography is Gilman emboldened to voice a similar criticism, although that is the only inference a reader can draw. John's disbelief in the narrator's illness intensifies her suffering. "If a physician of high standing, and one's own husband, assures friends and relatives that there is really nothing the matter with one but temporary nervous depression—a slight hysterical tendency—what is one to do?" He can urge only the platitudes of increased willpower and self-restraint. Whereas in her autobiography Gilman feels obligated to remain silent over her husband's role in her illness, in her art she can admit through the narrator to becoming "unreasonably angry" with him.

"The Yellow Wallpaper" also dramatizes the husband's prohibition against writing. "He says that with my imaginative power and habit of story-making, a nervous weakness like mine is sure to lead to all manner of excited fantasies, and that I ought to use my will and good sense to check the tendency. So I try." Mitchell, we recall, had similarly prohibited his patient from writing. It is thus ironic that both the narrator's husband and Gilman's psychiatrist forbid their patients from the one life-saving activity, artistic creation. What proves therapeutic in Gilman's world is neither marriage nor psychiatry but art, and, when the narrator's husband deprives her of this activity in "The Yellow Wallpaper," her fate is sealed.

Opposed to the liberating world of art is the enslaving domesticity of the home. The woman remains isolated in the nursery of an old ancestral house, a "hereditary estate," that is part of an obscure national heritage. "The Yellow Wallpaper" foreshadows Gilman's more extensive assault on domesticity culminating several years later in *The Home.* Filled with "hedges and walls and gates that lock," the house reflects the alienation of nineteenth-century America, with its cult of domesticity and worship of children. The husband and wife live in the nursery at the top of the house, with barred windows for little children. The narrator's perception of the nursery slowly changes. In the beginning it seems like a big airy room to her, but after two weeks it becomes claustrophobic in its heavy bedstead, barred windows, and gate at the head of the stairs. The imagery identifies the home as a prison without escape. The woman rarely leaves the nursery, not even to look at her baby who is housed on a lower floor.

The most horrifying feature of the house, and the source of the story's great power, is the yellow wallpaper in the nursery. "It is dull enough to confuse the eye in following, pronounced enough to constantly irritate and provoke study, and when you follow the lame uncertain curves for a little distance they suddenly commit suicide—plunge off at outrageous angles, destroy themselves in unheard of contradictions." The wallpaper becomes a projection screen or Rorschach test of the narrator's growing fright. The chaotic pattern symbolizes her own unheard emotional contradictions: her need for security yet fear of dependency and entrapment; her acceptance of the American Dream (marriage, family, house) amidst the nightmare of reality; her passive acceptance of duty but rising protest. The narrator's perception of the wallpaper's suicide foreshadows her own self-destructive behavior. Indeed, the wallpaper functions as a Poesque black cat or telltale heart, the object upon which her madness is focused. There is a difference, however, between Poe's stories and Gilman's. The reader of "The Black Cat" or "The Tell-Tale Heart" soon learns that the first person narrator is crazy and can thus distance himself from the homicidal character. The reader of **"The Yellow Wallpaper,"** by contrast, is far more sympathetic to the heroine and is almost seduced into sharing her increasingly psychotic point of view. The old ancestral house and its vision of America are enough to drive almost anyone mad. Yet, what we see in **"The Yellow Wallpaper"** is not simply an oppressive environment or a deranged woman but an organic connection between setting and character. Madness does not spring from nowhere. The story's richness lies in its ability to yield multiple meanings and points of view—psychological, sociological, historical. The house has rich symbolic meaning in **"The Yellow Wallpaper"**: the domestic imprisonment of nineteenth-century women, the madness of the Mitchell rest cure, the isolation of rural America, the repression of the body. ("The human body as a whole is pictured by the dream-imagination as a house and the separate organs of the body by portions of a house," Freud tells us in *The Interpretation of Dreams.*)

Although critics have admired the complex symbolism of the yellow wallpaper, they have not sufficiently explored the relationship between the inanimate pattern and the narrator's mind, in particular, her fear of children. The violence of her imagery is striking. "There is a recurrent spot where the pattern lolls like a broken neck and two bulbous eyes stare at you upside down." Many of the images she uses to describe the wallpaper appear to be related to the "dear baby" whom she cannot bear to be with. Her only reference to the baby implies relief that "it" does not occupy the upstairs nursery where she and her husband live. "If we had not used it, the blessed child would have! What a fortunate escape! Why, I wouldn't have a child of mine, an impressionable little thing, live in such a room for worlds." True, she expresses love and concern for the baby, yet she is also solicitous toward her husband, and we know that behind this surface calm lies unconscious aggression. Is she similarly hostile toward her baby?

If so, we suspect this was not part of the author's conscious intentions. There is too much evidence, however, to ignore. The new mother's description of the wallpaper evokes an image of an insatiable child who seems to be crawling everywhere, even into the nursery which remains her only sanctuary. The unblinking eyes stare at her as if the baby demands to be nursed or held. "I get positively angry with the impertinence of it and the everlastingness. Up and down and sideways they crawl, and those absurd, unblinking eyes are everywhere." Her next free association is revealing. "I never saw so much expression in an inanimate thing before, and we all know how much expression they have! I used to lie awake as a child and get more entertainment and terror out of blank walls and plain furniture than most children could find in a toy-store." Even as she renders the child into an inanimate object and consequently distances herself from its needs, the lifeless wallpaper assumes the characteristics of an angry child who grows increasingly demonic. She literally cannot escape from the baby because her imagination has projected it onto the landscape of her bedroom. Inanimate one moment and human the next, the baby evokes contradictory emotions within her—both tenderness and resentment. The baby also reminds the anxious mother of her own infancy. She tells us significantly that, when she was a child, the love and attention she craved were met with blank walls—just as her virtually motherless child meets with blank walls downstairs. The implication is that her present illness originates from an early childhood abandonment similar to the one her own child is encountering.

Tight-lipped about her own child, she speaks harshly about other children. The furniture in her bedroom had been scarred by the children of the previous owners: "I never saw such ravages as the children have made here." The room itself has been the victim of the children's vicious attack. The floor is "scratched and gouged and splintered," the plaster "is dug out here and there," and the great heavy bed "looks as if it had been through the wars." Later she returns to the oral imagery: "How those children did tear about here! This bedstead is fairly gnawed!"

The narrator's dilemma, then, is to escape from the voracious children who threaten to devour her body, just as they have gnawed upon the room. And indeed the other sub-pattern in the wallpaper reveals the figure of a strange woman skulking about the room. There is no doubt about her identity. "And it is like a woman stooping down and creeping about behind that pattern." By daylight the figure appears subdued, but at night she begins to crawl around. In the narrator's words, "You think you have mastered it, but just as you get well underway in following, it turns a back-somersault and there you are. It slaps you in the face, knocks you down, and tramples upon you. It is like a bad dream."

Interpreted according to dream logic, the wallpaper recreates the mother's inescapable horror of children and her regression to infancy. The pattern and sub-pattern mirror her terrified identification with the abandoned child and abandoning mother. The roles of victim and victimizer become hopelessly blurred. Who is escaping from whom? In fleeing from the image of the baby, the mother confronts its presence in the wallpaper located, appropriately enough, in the nursery of the old ancestral home. Here, the mysteries of birth, marriage, procreation, and death are played out in her imagination. The decision to isolate herself from her baby betrays the contradictory wish to protect and harm it. The child's identity remains ambiguous, both innocent and evil. The wallpaper imagery evokes an appalling eruption of subhuman life, uncontrolled reproduction. It is not just one organism but an endless stream of growth. "If you can imagine a toadstool in joints, an interminable string of toadstools, budding and sprouting in endless convolutions—why, that is something like it." From the psychoanalytic point of view of object relations, the narrator cannot separate her identity from the baby's: She is both the hysterical mother searching for freedom and the insatiable child demanding attention. The angry child within the adult seems responsible for the mother's illness. Nor is escape possible from the sickening yellow substance that oozes from the wall. Its mysteriousness contributes to the indefinable sexual menace lurking throughout the house and penetrating the woman's body. The movement of **"The Yellow Wallpaper"** is suggestive of the wife's efforts to avoid sexual defilement, beginning with her abortive attempt to sleep in the room downstairs, with its single bed, and ending with the outraged husband's cry for an ax to break into the room where she has barricaded herself.

Despite the pre-Freudian world of **"The Yellow Wallpaper"** and Charlotte Perkins Gilman's subsequent condemnation of psychoanalysis, the story is startlingly modern in its vision of mental illness. Anticipating Freudian discoveries, the story suggests that psychological illness worsens when it is not acknowledged as real and that the rest cure is antithetical both to the talking cure and to the therapeutic value of artistic creation. Moreover, **"The Yellow Wallpaper"** portrays mental illness as originating from childhood experiences. Unlike Breuer's "Fräulein Anna O.," **"The Yellow Wallpaper"** shows the social and political as well as psychological implications of madness. Gilman rejects not psychotherapy, which Freud was introducing, but pseudotherapy, which has always been with us. Gilman's narrator is one of the first in a long line of benumbed and bedeviled patients in American literature who search desperately for understanding but who, following the accepted medical advice of the time, lose their mind.

Gilman's achievement is that she is able to transform her narrator's bad dream into superb art. And here is where the literary brilliance of **"The Yellow Wallpaper"** comes into play. Although the narrator in the fictional story recalls the author's self-portrait in the autobiographical *The Living of Charlotte Perkins Gilman,* **"The Yellow Wallpaper"** contains a shape and unity consistent with the demands of art. The difference between fiction and life lies in the greater narrative distance and formal control of art. In her autobiography, Gilman remains mystified by the origin and meaning of her breakdown; she eloquently describes the pain and confusion of a lifetime of neurotic suffering, but she is finally baffled by its significance. She depicts her illness as a digression to a life of struggle and work, rather than as a continuing conflict that compelled her to invent constructive solutions to the problems of her age.

Fiction empowered her to rework sickness into art. Dr. Mitchell had diagnosed her illness as hysteria not dementia; "I never had hallucinations or objections to my mural decorations," Gilman parenthetically adds in **"Why I Wrote 'The Yellow Wallpaper'."** But, for artistic reasons, she decided to confer deadly psychosis on her narrator. Although the woman begins with what her husband calls "temporary nervous depression—a slight hysterical tendency," she grows steadily insane until her situation is hopeless. In the begin-

ning of the story, the narrator and the author are indistinguishable, but as the former becomes terminally insane, the latter remains firmly in control of the narrative, allowing the symbolic power of the wallpaper rather than authorial intrusions to expose the full horror. At the end, the narrator and author are worlds apart. Indeed, the technique of narrative distance and point of view is handled more confidently in **"The Yellow Wallpaper"** than in *The Bell Jar,* where Plath seems unable to imagine a character who is neither menacing nor locked into the bell-jar vision. We may continue to search for a full explanation of the bizarre events in **"The Yellow Wallpaper,"** but this is secondary to witnessing a mind in the process of self-extinction. Moreover, there is no specific moment in the story when we can say that the narrator has suddenly become mad. It happens mysteriously, imperceptibly. The crackup is frighteningly appealing because it allows her to defy and mock a husband who has taken on the role of a jailor. Gilman succeeds admirably in sketching a man whose dialogue sounds well meaning but whose actions assume a diabolical quality. He prowls around the house in an effort to thwart his wife's escape. At the end he gains entry into his wife's bedroom, but then, in a cunning reversal of roles, he faints at her feet while she creeps over him. (pp. 51-7)

> *Jeffrey Berman, "The Unrestful Cure: Charlotte Perkins Gilman and 'The Yellow Wallpaper',"* in his *The Talking Cure: Literary Representations of Psychoanalysis, New York University Press, 1985, pp. 33-59.*

CHRISTOPHER P. WILSON (essay date 1986)

[*In the following excerpt, Wilson uses* Herland *to demonstrate the literary style Gilman developed to counter masculine aesthetics.*]

In the utopian romance *Herland* (1915), during a chapter entitled "Rash Advances," author Charlotte Perkins Gilman crafts a scene which, in several respects, foreshadows the byplay of the book as a whole. Here, we are introduced to a decidedly masculine adventurer named Terry Nicholson (nicknamed "Old Nick," the narrator tells us, "with good reason"), one of three men who have just entered the pastoral territory of Herland. Old Nick encounters—and tries to capture—the first young woman he espies. While clinging precariously to the limb of a tree where three of the country's "seemingly aboreal" inhabitants are perched, he reaches into his inner pocket and produces a box of purple velvet—pulling out a necklace, Gilman writes, "of big varicolored stones that would have been worth a million if real ones." His apparent prey reaches timidly out with her right hand—and then seizes the bauble with her left; as he clutches for air, she and her companions are gone, "swift as light." Such a scene, rippling with satire on the Eden myth, encapsulates much of the book: female agility counterpoints and defeats the knowledge, temptations, and "advances" of masculine exploit. Yet, as they avoid possession, the women also stay enigmatic, just out of reach.

The scene also testifies to Gilman's often-neglected literary skills. True, in recent years, Gilman's reputation as a writer of fiction has experienced a modest renaissance. . . . But few of even her devoted critics have, as yet, gone so far as to credit Gilman with being a self-conscious literary craftsperson. In part, this is due to her own dismissiveness: "I have never made any pretense of being literary," she wrote in her autobiography. "As far as I had any method in mind, it was to express the idea with clearness and vivacity, so that it might be apprehended with ease and pleasure." Gilman's analysts have generally agreed with this self-description. For instance, while acknowledging the wit, adroit sense of popular formulas, and ear for dialogue in Gilman's short fiction, Ann Lane writes that "Gilman gave little attention to her writing as literature, and neither will the reader, I'm afraid. She wrote quickly, carelessly, to make a point" [see *TCLC*, Vol. 9, pp. 112-15]. Despite the fact that Gilman's earliest childhood writings were fanciful, that she was fascinated by word-puzzles and puns, or that fiction actually dominates *The Forerunner,* her writings are usually seen, as Lane puts it, as "lessons." With the worthy exception of **"The Yellow Wall-paper,"** the reputation of Gilman's nonfiction far outweighs that of her imaginative writing.

This is probably as it should be. And yet, as such, Gilman's fiction presents a recurrent critical dilemma, explored intriguingly by Myra Jehlen in the Summer 1981 issue of *Signs:* the problem of a female or feminist author who, despite her laudable political intentions (or, as Jehlen suggests, perhaps *because* of them), offers "scant nourishment" for our inherited literary tastes. To put it rather gently, whatever its political ingenuity or prescience, the bulk of Gilman's fiction does not elicit the reader-responses we commonly associate with "high" literary stature. Whatever the politics of our own critical vision, we do not often think of ourselves as deeply "moved" or enthralled; her characters, however modern, do often seem strangely lifeless, her plots typically aimed in some didactic direction. Whenever I assign *Herland* to today's under-graduate English majors, they habitually complain (at first) that the book, despite its wit, is "bloodless" and even downright dull. But as Jehlen writes, this has the effect of putting the appreciative critic or teacher in a double bind. If we accept the common feminist argument that standards derived from the so-called "Great Tradition" are masculinist mystifications, we should not find ourselves using them to apologize for a female author's supposed failings. On the other hand, to write forced apologias for such work risks sending the critic (and the writer) into isolation and irrelevance.

One of the ways out of this critical borderland may be to reorient ourselves by reference to the unfashionable weather-vane of authorial intention—a useful guide especially for interpreting the goals of a writer like Gilman, who was both critic and practitioner. The fact is that, despite her modest protestations, Gilman did indeed think seriously about aesthetics, wrote about them in *The Forerunner,* and implemented her literary ideas in fiction—especially in *Herland* itself. Critics have uniformly overlooked a body of *Forerunner* criticism which clarifies that the seemingly didactic style of Gilman's writing was not simply the function of "ideology" *per se,* as our New Critical ancestors might have concluded, but rather a result of the *kind* of ideology she proposed. When we reconstruct Gilman's literary principles, we discover that at least some of her lack of "affect" was entirely intentional. That is, her fiction often consciously lobbied to overturn her reader's preconceptions about what was "natural" or desirable in a work of literature—principally, by frustrating the ideological expectations of the literature of "adventure" and "romance" from her era. Furthermore, Gilman aimed to conceive of a feminist and socialist idiom partly by remodifying literary and pictorial conventions which linked standards of taste to received gender roles and expectations.

One can imagine Gilman herself scoffing at any overzealous praise. She is no Virginia Woolf. Nonetheless, I think we can better appreciate the intellectual conduit between her feminism and her literary style. Therefore, instead of reviewing the "lessons" of *Herland*—which have already received able explication—I want to explore some of its literary devices and its implicit commentary about art, gender, and property. In concluding, I want to suggest that Gilman's effort to counter what she saw as a bourgeois and masculine aesthetic often had elusive and paradoxical consequences. Like those young women in the trees, Gilman's own perspective was not always so easily "apprehended." (pp. 271-73)

What has been overlooked, specifically, are articles in *The Forerunner* which demonstrate Gilman's intention to fuse her feminist perspective with her literary practice. To begin with, she not only referred repeatedly to the mimetic power of art—citing the classical phrase of holding "the mirror up to nature"—she also spoke of literature's social function as the means by which societies made sense of the world. She certainly needed no training to understand implicitly the "naturalizing" role of art, because her career-long contention, in a wide array of fields, was that masculine values had been mistaken for a "human" point of view. She resented this state of affairs in literature only because she held the power of letters in high esteem—not because she dismissed them. Employing the biological analogy typical of her thinking, she said that literature "is the brain of society; and all our brains are steadily modified by it." Through art, Gilman wrote, "we know the past, govern the present, and influence the future." A masculine distortion, and particularly a distortion of perspective, could not purport to document the state of Nature. In a serialized chapter of *Our Androcentric Culture* entitled "Masculine Literature," she ridiculed the fact that females were patronizingly provided with "women's pages" and "feminine" features, while men's literature was simply taken for Literature itself. Men, the public was led to believe, were "people"; women were but a "side issue." (A "side issue" quite "literally," Gilman wrote, "if we accept the Hebrew legend!")

Gilman avoided the narrow-mindedness of condemning all imaginative writing by men; for example, she repeatedly praised Dickens and Shakespeare. Instead, her particular object of attack was a masculinist distortion which had overtaken contemporary fiction. Her contention, incidentally, was entirely accurate. Immediately following the Gilded Age vogue of Robert Louis Stevenson and Rudyard Kipling (whom Gilman often lambasted), American popular tastes in the Progressive era were dominated by "masculine" naturalists like Jack London, Frank Norris, and David Graham Phillips. In their own rebellion from the "feminized" ethos of mid-Victorianism, these writers moved to the national spotlight by emphasizing a prose style that was "vigorous" and topics that ostensibly appealed to "real men." Popular editors in this period spoke of seeking out the "roast beef" of literature, and of favoring "manly" exhortation that was direct and to the point. This context is crucial to understanding Gilman's own counterpointing style. Although the era's "naturalism" posed as scientific realism, to Gilman it was brutal and misogynist. Not unlike male-dominated History, she wrote, this literature was infested with the disease of exploit. The two main branches, she said, were the "Story of Adventure" and the "Story of Romance." The first worked, as in Kipling, by inciting "predatory excitement" in the reader by depicting fighting, robbing, and plunder. Romance, in turn, capitalized on the story of the "premarital struggle." In either case, Gilman said, there was a unconscious appeal to the thirst for conquest—and thus . . . an implied kinship between the related idioms of property and gender hierarchy. The romance, Gilman wrote, was simply another version of the Hunt: "It is the Adventure of Him in Pursuit of Her—and it stops when he gets her!" Consequently, . . . Gilman also felt that the traditionally coy by-play of manners, so basic to what critics often call "complication" in the romantic plot, only intensified the reader's appetites. Instead of presenting men and women on equal footing, "Woman's love for man, as currently treated in fiction is largely a reflex." Gilman said contemporary writers showed only "the way he wants her to feel, expects her to feel; not a fair representation of how she does feel." (pp. 278-80)

[The] fictional female of Gilman's description only reflected an identity given to her—and a fate. Inevitably, Gilman wrote, this character is eventually "tamed" or domesticated, enclosed in a fiction (as often in life) by the conventional resolution of a marriage scene. Gilman ridiculed this traditional ending in a romance, because it implied that women, once possessed, were no longer on the stage of human action. Their "estate" was settled. Furthermore, Gilman argued that implicit assumptions about gender were embedded into conventions of narration and description. "Do not women notice," she wrote, "that in the perennial love story the heroine is still described, for the most part, in terms of physical beauty?" Men's physiques were geared to action; women's were a matter of "charms." "The man is required to do something, to show character, action," Gilman wrote. "The woman, in spite of all our rational progress, is still most emphasized as something to look at."

Given these objections, it is not surprising that, in **Herland,** the idiom of surveillance and ownership is not just treated thematically. Rather, it infuses and surrounds the language of the narrative itself. Perhaps hinting at her own motives—and perhaps more literary self-consciousness than she would admit it—Gilman names her masculine narrator "Vandyck" Jennings, as if alluding to the prominent seventeenth century Flemish painter, Sir Anthony Van Dyck, (in)famous for abandonning his early mythological themes in favor of portraits of the European aristocracy.

Gilman's own Van, of course, is hardly the rake the original was. But as a narrator of **Herland** he is both an apt and an ingenious choice. First of all, he is a sociologist who espouses what are, in Gilman's eyes, faulty Social Darwinist economums about the struggle for existence. Gilman may imply here that, like his namesake, Vandyke is an unwitting servant of power, an articulator of the dominant way of seeing. Secondly, as Lane points out, Gilman was unusually sensitive to popular literary devices, and here, as in the classic utopian formula, the narrator chosen is an outsider, a principal opponent of the system he is asked to describe. Many utopian tales employ a seemingly skeptical observer who voices the reader's anticipated objections. In Edward Bellamy's restful Nationalist Boston, we follow a nineteenth-century upper class insomniac; in the Altrurian dialogues of Howells the realist (an admirer of Gilman, and probably a model for **Herland's** style), we hear from Mr. Twelvemough, the romancer; in a society of and for women, we have the story told to us by a male. But Van's aptness has more to do with *how* he sees. What is most striking in the preliminary chapters of **Herland** is this narrator's frustration—and near inability—to tell the

tale. The book, in fact, opens with a lament about what is to follow:

> This is written from memory, unfortunately. If I could have brought with me the material I so carefully prepared, this would be a very different story. Whole books full of notes, carefully copied records, firsthand descriptions, and the pictures—that's the worst loss. We had some bird's-eyes of the cities and parks; a lot of lovely views of streets, of buildings, outside and in, and some of those gorgeous gardens, and most important of all, of the women themselves.

> Nobody will believe how they looked. Descriptions aren't any good when it comes to women, and I never was good at descriptions anyhow. But it's got to be done somehow; the rest of the world needs to know about that country.

To some, this lament might seem a device of convenience—simplifying Gilman's writing of the book by enlisting the reader's imagination. This is certainly one possibility. And yet, perhaps the "they" of the opening line of paragraph two is not unintentionally ambiguous. It is striking how the narrator focuses particularly on the loss of "pictures" of the land, and how, initially, the women are described essentially as a feature of the landscape. It is even more intriguing how the narrator complains of being dispossessed of his tools of explanation. The women and land are unable to be seen, and moreover, to be surveyed and described. This is a narrator who has been expropriated, and it creates a problem that constantly undermines his narration in the early going.

The male trio's first exposure to **Herland** is as surveyors. They fly over the terrain in an airplane, measure the land's proportions and state of civilization, and then decide to find "women"—by which they mean young and beautiful ones. (" 'Woman' in the abstract is young," Van asserts, "and, we assume, charming. As they get older they pass off the stage, somehow, into private ownership mostly, or out of it altogether.") But at first they are offstage completely: the men are cut off from viewing the young women as sights. Deprived of this basic "right" that had whet their appetite for exploration, they become doubly immobilized. The older women-captors (Terry calls them "Colonels") who encircle the men make Van feel like a child again, as "when my short legs' utmost effort failed to overcome the fact that I was late to school". Furthermore, the women are not, in the devious malapropism of the vernacular (which Terry employs) "lookers"—they neither look, nor allow themselves to be looked at, conventionally. "The—the—reaction of these women is different from any that I've ever met," one of the male trio stutters. Vandyke agrees, and his friend rejoins: "They don't seem to notice our being men." The men's presence, in other words, does not inaugurate the nuances of manner and gesture basic to the sexual ritual the adventurers expect. Looking at his loved one, Van remarks: "There was something so powerful, so large and changeless, in those eyes that I could not sweep her off her feet by my own emotion as I had unconsciously assumed would be the case. . . . There was not a shade of that timid withdrawal or pretty resistance which are so—provocative." In turn "[t]heir dress and ornaments," Van remarks soon after, "had not a touch of the 'come and find me' element."

Reading **Herland** seems to follow these new conventions of sight. Throughout the first four chapters, Gilman sprinkles chapter-titles and phrases which play upon the masculinist and capitalist expectations of adventure itself. The story, again satirizing popular formula, is cast in the familiar form of an expedition—not unlike three civilized Tarzans in search of a savage Jane. But Gilman's imaginative phrases—"A Not Unnatural Enterprise," "Rash Advances," "Our Venture"— also make puns upon the imperial and sexual designs underwriting conventional narrative development. These men "advance" into **Herland** but make failed advances at the women; the men's "enterprise" (capitalism) is, in Gilman's view, hardly natural; their "venture" for profits and spoils is, as the prelude to the ad-venture, frustrated. Consequently, Gilman even has fun in these chapters with a twist on a conventional plot cliché. The male trio devise an altogether familiar hair-breadth escape, knot their bedsheets together in true Robin Hood fashion, climb down from a treacherous mountainside fortress, and escape over a moonlit landscape to their airplane. This Great Escape, however, is only in vain; again, they are surrounded and herded back like errant children. We should note, as well, the primary source of their embarrassment: during their entire escape, they had been under surveillance. (As we discover later, secrecy or privacy—those basic elements of suspense—have little place in **Herland**.) Not long after, in the course of his study of **Herland**'s education, Terry finds the children's tales sadly wanting—"punk," he says, because they lack men and thrills. Van, however, signals his incipient conversion at the start of chapter five. "It is no use for me to try to piece out this account with adventures," he says. "There were no adventures because there was nothing to fight. There were no wild beasts in the country and very few tame ones." A man who tries to be assertive, we are told, is "all out of drawing." Adventure is entirely unmanned.

Van's second confession itself signals a change in the book's tempo: to reflect Van's own term (and to whom it refers), the action henceforth is far more tame. In fact, immediately following his confession, we witness a dialogue about the breeding of canines and felines, obvious symbols for a witty discussion on heredity, domestication, and gender stereotypes. (Cats, we discover, no longer cry, and serve **Herland** as practical, useful pets.) This discussion, apparently, sets the stage for a rather familiar utopian element: the question-and-answer style upon which the dramatic tension of so many utopian romances founders—as, for instance, in the tedious disquisitions of Dr. Leete in *Looking Backward* and *Equality*. And now we do hear—indirectly—about Herland's history, its parthenogenic biology, its religion, and so on. But even in this respect Gilman's accounting seems rather unusual. That is, confined as we are to the narrator's eye and voice, in fact we don't *see* or *hear* much about Herland at all: no lengthy diatribes about its politics or economy, no visits of any substance to its workplaces, not much detail at all about its recent past. Of course, this is partly because Gilman's goal is satiric and not programmatic: Herland is conceived as a mythological Archimedean standing place, not a "mapped out" or realistic terrain. Nevertheless, my point here is that what we listen to can only loosely be called "dialogue" at all. Rather, the men are usually led into bold assertions of "civilized" belief; but their female counterparts only ask Socratic questions, look quizzical, or blanch in shock—and take notes. Their talk echoes their demonstrated skill at foiling linear "plots" (e.g. escape plots) with encirclement. Their "lines of interrogation," Van says, "would gradually surround us and drive us till we found ourselves up against some admissions we did not want to make." As a result the description of Herland is left to Van, or to characters who don't talk very much.

This is not entirely because Gilman is condensing to maintain reader interest, nor because she is taking any literary shortcuts. Rather, as some of her *Forerunner* commentary reveals, this reticence seems to have derived from her belief that literal "self-expression," a term which she sometimes used interchangeably with sheer exuberance of speech, was a masculinist failing, a kind of boasting that the men in this tale exhibit. (Sure enough, the naturalists themselves valued "forceful" speech as a key to literary success.) Her distaste, however, led her down an interesting if problematic literary avenue. On the one hand, she was compelled, I think, to confront the problem of consciousness inherent in the utopian tale—and yet, to try to tell that tale through a narrator who is deprived of his normal means of telling. Part of his conversion involves losing his initial mode of expression—his original literature. This problem is fundamental to many a utopian tale, but to Gilman's credit, she is exceptional in the way she confronts it directly. She understands that it is a problem not merely of intellection, but of narration. As for her women, their talking, such as it is, is like their looking: a form of undefinable presence. Like Gilman's famous woman in the wallpaper, they seem to occupy a kind of terra incognita which we never fully see.

This central paradox becomes more elaborate in the final four chapters dealing with marriage, an institution that Van terms "The Great Adventure." In the final part, each of the men is paired with a Herlander counterpart; again, however, the relationship developing between the narrator and his mate, Ellador (whose name may allude to Gilman's beloved

Gilman with her family.

Greece), is the most important one. Much of this section is quite witty and discursive, but there is a developing tension in Van's growing realization that he will no longer be able to see gender conventionally—that is, as part of a familiar terrain. (Ellador, we discover, is a forester.) As the book proceeds, Van initially expresses in traditional terms his satisfaction at the new relationship:

> As for Ellador: Suppose you come to a strange land and find it pleasant enough—just a little more than ordinarily pleasant—and then you find rich farmland, and then gardens, gorgeous gardens, and then palaces full of rare and curious treasures—incalculable, inexhaustible, and then—mountains—like the Himalayas, and then the sea.

Gilman consciously employs natural imagery here because she wants to alter our perspective, subvert our notion of a "natural" relationship. Van is initially pleased with his exploration. "Then, as I got on further, the palace and treasures and snowy mountain ranges opened up." Such heights are giddy—but, interestingly enough, also a bit cold, and the air is thin. After a time, of course, Van discovers that these women have practically bred the sex-instinct to extinction; they view it as a curiosity but not much more. At first, Van speculates rather hopefully that the males' arrival might awaken the old drive. But when he pursues his venture, with "hot" hands, Ellador responds about sex "as if she were discussing life on Mars." Later, as Van holds her in his arms, "kissing her hungrily," he sees in her eyes a "remote clear look as if she had gone far away . . . and was now on some snowy mountain regarding me from a distance."

This change in location Gilman sets forth is a challenging one. Accordingly, it undermines the rhetoric of romance as much as adventure has been. We discover that, for the most part, Herland has no ritual of privacy—hence, no chance meetings or private retreats that are the stuff of romance or intrigue. Since there are no differences of class—the slaves of earlier reigns conveniently disappear—and none of wealth, and no gender distinctions, there are few available devices of farce or even the comedy of manners: no occasions for mistaken identities, no disguise, no false or misconstrued impressions. Even more fundamentally, there is no struggle or conflict about courtship. Hence, we discover, Herland has no conventional drama as the men understand it. Again speaking in landscape terms, Van remarks: "The drama of the country was—to our taste—rather flat." We learn that it would strain plausibility, for example, to have Othello suffocate a Herlander with a pillow. Most importantly of all, however, Herlanders exhibit a subordinated sense of the personal. Children's names are almost superfluous; women don't view motherhood as an individual matter; mothers don't coo over their own children. Like the anti-propertarian citizens of Annares in Ursula LeGuin's *The Dispossessed,* these women have dispensed with "egoizing." The visiting men complain about the ever-present "we" that undermines intimate dialogue; they say they have married a nation, not individual women. Their property is never private.

In the end, of course, Van imbues the spirit of Motherlove, and we are told that his relationship with Ellador is unlike any that he has known. But Gilman, again entirely intentionally, chooses not to employ that capstone moment of romance—chooses not, in other words, to end with the marriage scene. Rather, she turns her narrative focus back to the most venturesome and rash man, Terry, as if to signal a final

shift in mood. Asserting what he thinks is his proprietary right on his new bride—by trying to rape her—Terry is repulsed, tied up, anaesthetized, and ultimately sentenced to banishment from Herland. Gilman's distaste for conventional endings seems to have led her to a more provisional final episode. Even here, however, she returns to the imagery of vision and terrain. Prior to their final moments, the men are shown that it is they who have been surveyed. The Herlanders, having pieced together facts from their questioning, "had a great globe, quite fairly mapped out from the small section maps in that compendium of ours." Van realizes how the tables have been turned:

> Little had we thought that our careful efforts at concealment had been so easily seen through, with never a word to show us that they saw. They had followed up words of ours on the science of optics, asked innocent questions about glasses and the like, and were aware of the defective eyesight so common among us.

Defective eyesight indeed. The men have been "seen through" by doing all the talking. For a moment, as if sensing this reversal of surveillance, the women now do lecture the men before claiming their proprietary right and sealing off Herland from outsiders.

Perhaps this is why Gilman chose the possessive pronoun: ultimately, it is not "she-land," but Herland. And yet, even here, there is a sign of Gilman's enigmatic narration. We should remember that "Herland" is a name that *Terry* coins at the very start of his adventure. We never actually hear the country's real name.

If we return to Terry in the tree, we can see that his bauble is not merely material enticement—not just a lure. Rather, what he is offering Herland in that varicolored necklace is, in Gilman's view . . . , femininity. Understandably, then, the gift is not "real" but synthetic, a device which, once worn, confirms his possession. But for the woman it is never hers. In this gesture the dual nature of Gilman's vision comes together. Her feminism and socialism have a common intellectual basis: she believes that women cannot be enticed to subordination if they renounce pride of ownership; she feels that if they reject a false femininity, they in turn transcend the rhetoric of possessiveness. Given this assumption, Gilman's rejection of literary "affect" and adventure followed directly. And yet, this leaves open what Gilman proposed to put in their place—in Jehlen's term, what kind of "nourishment" we do find. In *A Literature of Their Own,* for instance, Elaine Showalter argues that feminist utopias of this era, crafted principally in opposition to the male world (and impelled by some repugnance of intercourse and childbirth), offered worlds that "were not visions of primary womanhood," and which lacked a "theory of female art."

There is much to be said for Showalter's basic point. Indeed, my own contention has been that Gilman's distaste for popular, "masculine" literary conventions led her to undercut many common literary strategies. But we should not mistake reticence for absence: *Herland* does infer an aesthetic of its own, if not a gender-specific one. (It should not surprise us that *Herland* lacks a female aesthetic, since Gilman argued that her position was "humanist," not feminist.) The key, I think, lies in the description of the country's cultural psychology. We discover, of course, that the Herlanders, much as they suppress the sex instinct, neither smoke nor drink. We hear, in addition, that the children in their nurseries do not cry as our children commonly do. This might be partly a re-flection of contentment and security, but it also exhibits their training in self-control. Along the same lines, the mothers of Herland limit population via a kind of contraceptive voluntarism—by repressing the ecstasy that foreshadows the onset of pregnancy. "We each go without a certain range of personal joy," one citizen explains. Clearly, what Gilman offers here, in response to the trinity of possession, gratification, and "expression" is self-restraint, holding back. Herland's psyche is based not in self-expression, but in renunciation; its version of loving "up" is a religious ideal. This is why, I think, Van remarks that Herland seems more "Christian" than any society he knows. Moreover, this seems why, so paradoxically, the women (like their land) seem to have made "cultivation" appear as if it is a "natural condition." They have made selfhood itself into something positively pastoral.

Re-viewing the "look" of the Herlanders seems to encapsulate what Gilman has in mind here. Van remarks quite early on:

> Their attitude was not the rigid discipline of soldiers; there was no sense of compulsion about them. Terry's terms of "vigilance committee" was highly descriptive. They had just the aspect of steady burghers, gathered hastily to meet some common need or peril, all moved by precisely the same feelings, to the same end.

In that Van invokes the spirit of Terry here, perhaps some caution is in order—our own form of self-restraint. But it seems altogether fitting that Vandyke, the name which evokes the favored artist of Charles I—and, as well, the typical dress of the Cavaliers—should be confronted by an ethic which is so essentially Puritan. This descendent of the Beechers, in other words, has given us something like an inverted captivity narrative—inverted, because it is not a female whose virtue is tested in the wilds, but "Old Nick" who is trapped among barely visible saints. Despite Herland's banishment of an angry male God and even the sense of sin itself, this is an eminently rational and restorative terrain fashioned to trip up, surround, and baffle the incursions of the outside (old) world. It is the ideological basis of Gilman's own artifice.

My point here is not the familiar one that Gilman's views on sexual freedom were by and large conservative, nor that *Herland* exhibits any conscious appropriation of her Puritan forbears' ideas. Authorial intention can no longer be our guide. Rather, it is simply that Gilman's rejection of conventional literary discourse, when combined with her distrust of "expressiveness" as a masculinized trait, led her to evolve a literary-political idiom which was essentially renunciatory—that is, her own version of a "plain" style. Rejecting both the comedy of manners and the adventure formula, she chose instead a style that was akin to self-effacement: elusive, satirical, almost limner-like in its immateriality. Recent thinking about Puritan aesthetics therefore provides an instructive caution. Just as we no longer believe the Puritans lacked literary devices altogether, so too is Gilman not without an awareness of narration, dialogue, plot and imagery. If her style was enigmatic or reticent, likewise it only reflected her primary goal of exposing the vanities of the material world in a way the reader could apprehend them without conventional distractions. This adjustment may allow us to revise some of our readings of *Herland* itself. For instance, Gilman's witty reversal of a cat's proclivities, or her positing of a partheno-

genic world, are possibly not to be taken as "peculiar fantasies," nor as extensions of her eugenicist paranoia. Rather, they may be satiric and symbolic creations, representations of an ideal natural order—not lessons, exactly, but images which provoke her readers (like the trio of men) to trip up and then reexamine their own teachings. If my own reader will indulge yet one more return to Terry in the tree, we will see that the Herlanders only appear to reject ornamentation; actually, they seize it with a sleight-of-hand.

The conduit between Gilman's feminism and this literary ethos of renunciation is also expressed in the essentially communal inferences about Herland's art. It is interesting, for example, how Gilman herself answered the charge that her vision of the future was somehow "asexual." In one of her earliest poems, she wrote about a drone in a beehive who confessed a dream of equality to others, only to encounter ridicule:

> Then fiercely rose the workers all,
> For sorely were they vexed;
> "Oh wretch!": they cried, "should this betide
> You would become *unsexed!*"
>
> And yet he had not sight for eggs,
> Nor yet for royal mien,
> He longed to be a worker bee,
> But not to be a queen.

Herland, one often feels, is a bit like that beehive—thus, again, the resonance of Gilman's Puritan echoes. Even in "Masculine Literature," she had written that "if the beehive produced literature, the bee's fiction would be rich and broad," celebrating the work of comb-building, treating the "vast fecundity of motherhood," the passion of loyalty and "social service which hold the hive together." Herland's plays are actually annual communal festivals of "joyous, triumphant life." She offered these adventures in place, furthermore, of the cult of individual self-realization implicit in a character, for example, like Ibsen's Nora. Briefly reviewing "The Doll House," Gilman once sardonically wrote that "[b]ird, beast, reptile, fish and insect are very busy realizing themselves, yet every one of them waves the right of the present Self, in favor of the future Self—the next generation."

Many of Gilman's other characters and stories show this same paradoxical sense of self-realization. In many respects her *Forerunner* tales, in which women enter spheres of work and though previously monopolized by males, represent individual "cells" busily realizing themselves. For the narrator of **"The Yellow Wallpaper,"** it is a cell of a different kind. To be fair, however, Gilman's description of the Herland pageants, like her brief mention of its supposedly "exquisite, imaginative" nursery tales, are indeed too cryptically described. But this cryptic quality, and Gilman's evocation of the steady and silent burgher-bee, only again indicate *why* Gilman's style is the way it is. Seeking a society in which selfhood lost itself in a renunciatory and communal endeavor, and employing a literary style which dispensed with conventional "affect" to describe that society, Herlanding had given "expression" itself a curious presence—or nonpresence—in Gilman's world-view. Somewhat like the murals of socialist realism, *Herland* itself may present too voluntary a vision, too pastoral a terrain—and a literary ideal too elusive. But this is not an uncommon quality in a utopia—nor unforgivable in such a lively one which nevertheless refuses to be a "romance" at all. It was an adventure Gilman willingly undertook as part of her own quest for self-possession. (pp. 280-91)

Christopher P. Wilson, "Charlotte Perkins Gilman's Steady Burghers: The Terrain of 'Herland'," in Women's Studies: An Interdisciplinary Journal, Vol. 12, No. 3, March, 1986, pp. 271-92.

EUGENIA C. DELAMOTTE (essay date 1988)

[*In the following excerpt, Delamotte examines the Gothic conventions of Gilman's "The Yellow Wallpaper" from a feminist perspective.*]

Almost exactly a century before Charlotte Perkins Gilman published **"The Yellow Wallpaper,"** the popularity of Ann Radcliffe's romances established the genre of women's Gothic as a staple of mass-market fiction. The perils of the Gothic heroine as she and her many imitators defined them in the 1790s were oblique reflections of the fear and despair in real women's lives. As a writer and a woman in the 1890s, Gilman inherited both the genre those first women Gothicists created and the sources of anger in which it had its secret roots. In **"The Yellow Wallpaper,"** the story of a Gothic heroine who becomes, as it were, a Gothic writer, Gilman both exploits and explores the conventions of the genre from a feminist perspective. The result is a bold revelation of the meanings concealed beneath women Gothicists' preoccupation with knowledge and with a set of interrelated issues: self-defense; the encounter with a Hidden Woman; speech and silence; the misprizing of the heroine; the horrors of repetition; and the problem of freedom.

" . . . in a foreign land—in a remote castle—surrounded by vice and violence": Ann Radcliffe's description of her heroine's plight in *The Mysteries of Udolpho* is the classic setting of Gothic romance. Yet the most sinister aspect of the Gothicism in **"The Yellow Wallpaper"** is the way the Gothic situation of the heroine is initially disguised from her. She is not in a remote castle, so the nature of her imprisonment is not immediately apparent; she is not in a foreign land, so her piercing sense of estrangement from her world does not manifest itself to her directly. And the violence that surrounds her takes the form of the latest advances in medical knowledge about the psychological disorders of women. The masculine mysteries of this specialized "knowledge"—and the feminine mysteries they cannot accommodate—are at the center of Gilman's brilliant re-visioning of the genre of women's Gothic. **"The Yellow Wallpaper"** is a story about why women have to invent mysteries—both mystery stories and mysteries of domestic science. It is about the ways those two mysteries are related to each other in the narrator's life, and the way both are related to her sense that she herself is a mystery: to her husband and herself.

One of the major preoccupations of women's Gothic is the difficulty of self-defense, most often in the context of immurement in a frightening place from which the heroine desires escape. "Oh that I was out of this house," one heroine exclaims; " . . . danger and death surround me on every side." Women's Gothic speaks for women's feelings of vulnerability in a world where their only power was the power of "influence." For it is only half the story to say, as so many critics have said in various ways, that the maiden lost in Gothic space is the mind beset with its own internal dangers, lost to the order and reason of the daylight world. The other half of the story, for women writers and readers, is that in symbolic form Gothic interiors *were* the daylight world, apprehended as nightmare. Their disorder and illogic was the logic of the social order as women experienced it. Woman in these nocturnal spaces is really woman in her everyday relations, immured in her domestic prison, "surrounded by [the] vice and violence" of the social and political institutions that dominate her life.

The opening of **"The Yellow Wallpaper"** plays on this relationship between the ordinary domestic world of women and the Gothic horrors that represented it, but Gilman reverses the convention. Instead of presenting women's daylight world apprehended as nightmare, she opens her story with the picture of a nightmare world apprehended as merely ordinary. The narrator, indeed, looks at an ordinary house and wishes, romantically, that it were haunted: she longs, like every Gothic reader, to be frightened. This desire for romantic escapism (a female desire, from which the narrator's husband quickly dissociates himself) masks a desire for escape. The narrator's talk of the "romantic felicity" a Gothic house would provide leads quickly to talk of John's realistic skepticism—"*perhaps* . . . one reason I do not get well faster." Already the narrator's condition, which John does not believe in, has been associated with the mystery of the house, in which he does not believe either, and the narrator's desire to escape by being frightened has been linked to the hidden anger that makes her want to escape her husband's medical attention. The connection is reinforced when the narrator, acknowledging that thinking about her condition makes her "feel bad," says, "So I will let it alone and talk about the house." In a similar way, women readers of Gothic romance displaced their own secret horrors, born of their domestic situation and hidden even from themselves, onto the image of a romantic dwelling place full of hidden mysteries.

But this Gothic talk of houses was really a description of women's suffering. Wollstonecraft, a contemporary of the early women Gothicists, attacked the civil and political inequality that kept women "immured in their families groping in the dark"—a plight that assumes quite a literal form in most Gothic fiction by women. The heroine of Radcliffe's *A Sicilian Romance*, for example, must escape her tyrannical father's castle by fleeing through its dark underground passageways. At the climax of the story, another flight leads her unwittingly back into this hidden world, where she discovers, alive, her long "dead" mother, for years imprisoned secretly by her husband in her own house. The mysterious noises that frightened Julia's brother in the deserted wing at the beginning of her adventure were the sounds of their mother's grief. Julia's elopement from her father's house—her "escape" into marriage—has only led back to this same domestic prison she was fleeing, and the door through which she entered it turns out now to be locked behind her. Thus the daughter's discovery of her mother's hidden suffering—her initiation into the mysteries of womanhood—is identical to her own entrapment in the mother's situation.

"Ah, how easy it is to be unknown!—to be entombed alive!" Ellinor says in Sophia Lee's *The Recess*. "Unknown": the story of burial alive is not just about domestic entrapment, but about women's forced concealment of the suffering it occasioned. And it is also about the unknown woman inside the female writer or reader, who perhaps concealed her suffering even from herself. For Julia's confrontation with her lost mother, the unsuspected sufferer, is only one version of the discovery of the Hidden Woman, a staple of women's Gothic that takes two different but related forms. One is the discovery (in person, through another character's narrative, or in a first-person manuscript), of a Good Other Woman, longsuffering and angelic, whose imprisonment and/or death was unmerited. The other is the discovery of an Evil Other Woman, who got no more than she deserved and is now either dead, or sorry for her sins and about to die. The revelation of these sins usually implicates her as a bad (selfish) mother, a bad (undutiful) daughter, and/or a bad (sexual) woman. The heroine's discovery of such Other Women is in the one case an encounter with women's oppression—their confinement as wives, mothers, and daughters—and in the other with a related repression: the Hidden Woman confined inside those genteel writers and readers who, in the idealization of the heroine's virtues, displace their own rebellious feelings with filial piety, their anger with patient fortitude, and their sexuality with sensibility. Both discoveries reveal complementary aspects of women's subordination: their immurement in domestic spaces as sisters, wives, and daughters; and the immurement, inside themselves, of an angry, rebellious, sexual Other Woman that conventional morality taught them to reject.

Both the bad Other Woman's Sin and the good Other Woman's Suffering must be discovered in order for the heroine to go home and be happily married. It may be that in some way the happy endings of Gothic romances that make use of the Evil Other Woman depend on the punishment and exorcism of the rebellious feelings the narrative itself expresses through its portrayal of women's silent suffering. The heroine, in other words, can live happily ever after in a perfect marriage because (a) the sources of women's long grievance at domestic confinement have been duly punished, but (b) anger, rebellion, passion, and filial ingratitude—which one might have thought the logical concomitants to such grievance—are shown emphatically not to belong to the wronged heroine and/or her wronged female relative, but to Somebody Else, who was ultimately sorry for them, anyway, and furthermore is dying or dead. The death of this vengeful and passionate Other Woman means that "she" is no more able to trouble the heroine's prospects of domestic felicity.

Something of this self-directed anger, and its obvious connections to male-directed anger, comes out in the ambivalent relationship between Gilman's narrator and the woman she "finds" in her own room. The narrator, after all, is in effect a female Gothicist, who writes her agony onto the walls of her own domestic prison and thus reveals what seems an ordinary house to be a Gothic horror. Clearly, the woman she has found is a victim who needs to be rescued (the long-imprisoned Good Other Woman), but she is also someone who destroys the heroine's prospects of domestic tranquility by her angry and rebellious presence. The narrator tries to free her, but she is also determined that she shall not escape: "If that woman does get out, and tries to get away, I can tie her!" In one sense this is self-directed anger; shortly thereafter we learn, to our horror, that the narrator has in fact used the rope to bind *herself*. In another sense, her self-bondage is a desperate impulse to keep hold of—to possess fully—a new-found, elusive other self who is angry, and has a right to be.

This overt representation of the way the narrator's masochism is linked to her need for self-knowledge and self-possession is rare, perhaps unique, in the history of women's Gothic, and it shows to what extent Gilman herself saw be-

neath many of the surface trappings of the genre. Women's experience of the illegitimate exercise of male authority as Gothic romance portrays it is often read as an expression of masochistic desire, especially sexual desire. Such interpretations depend on a reading of the villain as secretly the hero, to whom the heroine (or, more accurately, the writer), is secretly attracted and for whose domination she longs. The glaring inadequacies of most such readings are obvious—not only that they blame the victims of sexual oppression, but that in their haste to do so they ignore the most basic subject of Gothic plots: women who just can't seem to get out of the house. The primary function of the Gothic pursuit in women's romances should be all too obvious. The threatening male portrays "a woman's projected fears and sense of actual victimization; the pursuit justifies adventure and escape, which contrast dramatically with her . . . everyday domestic experience; and the moral victory of the heroine over the pursuer reflects a desired, but repressed emancipation from actual oppressors" [Bette B. Roberts, *The Gothic Romance: Its Appeal to Women Writers and Readers in Late Eighteenth-Century England*]. Whatever masochistic desire speaks through women's Gothic narratives must be put in the context of the desperate unhappiness they express at the same time. Indeed, the two are intimately related: Russ's comment on modern "Gothics" is true of their ancestors as well: "the Heroine's suffering is the principal action of the story *because it is the only action she can perform*. The Modern Gothic as a genre, is a means of enabling a conventionally feminine heroine to have adventures at all" [Joanna Russ, "Somebody's Trying to Kill Me and I Think It's My Husband: The Modern Gothic" in *The Female Gothic,* edited by Juliann E. Fleenor].

The delight women readers experienced identifying with these "adventures," the heroine's excruciating sufferings, allowed at the same time for a release of anger and a masochistic revelling in the cathartic acknowledgement of its existence and its sources. Masochism is a twisted version of self-defense: a form of pseudo-power, which gives the victim the illusion of willing circumstances she cannot control. It allows for an honest attribution of the physical source of those sufferings to someone else, but it mystifies their cause by deluding the victim into experiencing her passive victimization as active, self-generated desire. In women's Gothic, this dynamic operates, not at the level of the plot, in which heroines are portrayed as victims rather than masochists, but at the level of writing and reading, themselves acts of pseudo-power in which the writer or reader, by willing the heroine's suffering as the source of a pleasurable literary experience, gains the illusion of being in control of it. The deepest masochism of women's Gothic is here, in the false sense of empowerment with which it infuses its readers' and writers' identification with women's suffering. In this light, it is even more significant that **"The Yellow Wallpaper"** begins with the narrator's wish that her house were haunted like those in which frightened heroines suffer Gothic horrors. It is a wish, in essence, to empower herself. Already she is afraid of her husband, and already she is suffering. What she wishes for is an escape, through fantasy, into a symbolic version of her own plight: a version in which she would have a measure of distance and control.

Interpretations of the Gothic as an expression of women's masochistic desire for male domination depend on reading the villain as the secret hero rather than a threat against whom the heroine must defend herself. A further inadequacy of such readings is that they omit the actual hero from consideration as a significant character. This is a serious omission, because whatever suspicion there may be in women's Gothic that the villain is really the hero is balanced by an important complementary suspicion: the hero is really the villain. At least twice this equation is made overtly in the form of a heroine's "mistake"; most often, however, the suspicion that the hero is really the villain surfaces in the juxtapositions of the narrative sequence, in which the temporal conjunction and then—"at once the most unrevealing and the most suggestive of narrative links"—stands in for causal or logical connections: "because," "and so," "therefore," "that is to say." This is a common procedure in allegorical romance especially, as critics of allegory have shown; more importantly in terms of the atmosphere of Gothic narrative, it is the procedure of dreams, which [according to Sigmund Freud] "reproduce *logical connection by simultaneity in time*" and represent "causation . . . by temporal sequence." Thus in Gothic romances two juxtaposed narratives may well be two versions of the same event, or the first may be the true cause of the emotions associated with the second. (pp. 3-7)

"On the day when it will be possible for woman to love not in her weakness but in her strength . . . love will become for her, as for man, a source of life and not of mortal danger," de Beauvoir said. In Gilman's story as in traditional women's Gothic, love is a source of mortal danger. The husband John, self-cast in the role of the hero who will rescue the narrator from the Gothic horrors of her own silly imagination—who will save her by invalidating her experience of her own inner reality—is clearly the villain; Gilman presents the equation overtly. The narrator, on the other hand, the real "writer" of this Gothic romance, begins, like so many other women Gothicists, by not recognizing the identity. Instead, she tries to find the sources, in herself, for the fact that she gets so "unreasonably angry with John sometimes." And her true knowledge of the "vice and violence" he represents comes out initially only in the juxtapositions, the *and thens,* whereby the story of the wallpaper re-tells the story of her relationship with John. In these retellings, the way John's misguided cure inhibits her recovery is translated: "This paper looks to me as if it *knew* what a vicious influence it had!" And her reaction to John, against whom, in the other story, she is sometimes "unreasonably angry," finds its true expression: "I get positively angry with the impertinence of it and the everlastingness." In the daylight story, John's constricting paternalism, which robs her of responsibility for herself, is camouflaged by praise: "He is very careful and loving, and hardly lets me stir without special direction. . . . he takes all care from me. . . . " In the nightmare story his violence is more evident: the pattern "is torturing. . . . It slaps you in the face, knocks you down, and tramples upon you. . . . "

In this Gothic story, the wallpaper stands in for the nightmare version of the hero, showing that the "writer" of this tale is forced, in more ways than one, to make her story a mystery. It is a mystery to her because it expresses the self-knowledge she is not aware of; she must also make it a mystery to her husband, concealing her writing from other members of the household, who may enter her room at any minute. A major aspect of women's vulnerability as Gothicists portray it involves precisely this situation: a woman's difficulty knowing and being known in a position that isolates her by locking her into herself, but at the same time renders her susceptible to perpetual intrusion. Gothic romance is especially a woman's genre because, in all sorts of ways, it is about the nightmare of trying to "speak 'I' " in a world where the "I" in question is uncomprehending of and incomprehensible to the dominant power structure.

That the theme of speech and silence is crucial to this Gothic story of a woman who wants to write is obvious; it has not been remarked, however, that this theme was an old staple of Gothic romance, conventional enough to have been parodied by Jane Austen. At a crucial moment in *Northanger Abbey* it seems that Catherine's friendship with the Tilneys, and her prospects of living happily ever after, are about to be destroyed. Her friends mistakenly think she has rebuffed them, and it is a heroine's duty at such times to remain proudly silent, secure in her "conscious innocence," willing to suffer the consequences of refusing to exonerate herself. Fortunately, such standards are inimical to Catherine's personality, and she rushes impulsively to explain her behavior. "Feelings rather natural than heroic possessed her; . . . instead of proudly resolving, in conscious innocence, to shew her resentment towards him who could harbour a doubt of it, to leave to him all the trouble of seeking an explanation . . . she took to herself all the shame of misconduct, or at least of its appearance, and was only eager for an opportunity of explaining its cause." Although Catherine sacrifices some coherence as well as heroic dignity in her haste to get the explanation out all at once, the result is most satisfactory. Henry Tilney believes her, and his good opinion is happily restored.

One of the favorite subjects of women Gothicists, despite their own rhetorical excesses, was the restraint proper to female discourse. When they choose to speak, Gothic heroines can soar to rhetorical heights far beyond their enemies' range; but again and again they also choose to remain silent even if it means remaining persecuted and misunderstood. The persecuted woman's impulse to ensconce herself resentfully in the mystery the man's misunderstanding has already made of her—"to leave to him all the trouble of seeking an explanation"—is precisely the impulse behind the bizarre behavior the narrator exhibits at the end of Gilman's story, when she locks herself in and throws the key out of the window, forcing her husband to come and seek out her reasons. With the true spirit of the female Gothicist, she confides to the reader, "I want to astonish him." Her knowledge that he will indeed be astonished at the revelation of her real state of mind is related to another theme crucial to women's Gothic: the misprizing of the heroine, and the final triumphant unveiling of her true nature.

Rosetta Ballin's *The Statue Room,* the story of a heroine deprived of the kingdom to which her true status should entitle her, ends with a fantasy of such self-revelation, as the heroine Romelia removes her mask and reproves the guards who have seized her: "Off, off, ye base-born plebeians . . . behold who I am!" In women's Gothic, the fairy-tale story of the noble-woman whose true identity is unknown acquires a special resonance, for the difficulty of being known is the real subject of Gothic paranoia, and the heroine's impulse to cry out, "behold who I am!" is the strongest and most stifled impulse women Gothicists portray. The atmosphere of persecution that infuses women's Gothic is produced not only by an obsessive narrative focus on attempts to lock the heroine up, separate her from the hero, take her money and property, violate her, kill her, but often by a pervasive sense that the heroine is being falsely charged with feelings and intentions she does not have. This is part of the larger motif of the misknowing of the heroine: the false categorizing and misnaming of her essential nature. (pp. 7-9)

The chief misknower of the heroine in **"The Yellow Wallpaper,"** of course, is John, the "physician of high standing" who uses his exclusively masculine knowledge as a source of power over his wife. . . . [He] prohibits self-expression, forbidding his wife to write down her thoughts. To her feeble attempts to speak her own reality, he responds that she does not understand these matters: "I am a doctor, dear, and I know." As de Beauvoir says, "Lock the doors and close the shutters as she will . . . woman fails to find complete security in her home. It is surrounded by that masculine universe which she respects from afar, without daring to venture into it. And precisely because she is incapable of grasping it through technical skill, sound logic, and definite knowledge, she feels, like the child and the savage, that she is surrounded by dangerous mysteries." It is Gilman's special insight to see that the mysteries of John's masculine cult of science are dangerous precisely because they pretend to explain, among other things, the mystery of woman. This aggressive misprizing of the narrator's inner reality at the same time locks her into a female domestic sphere and shuts her out from the special mysteries of that masculine province outside the home, medical science. In response, the narrator attempts to affirm her own sense of herself by creating and celebrating her own mysteries. Experiencing her husband's knowledge as power, she tries to develop a different kind of knowledge in self-defense. She turns her attention to her wallpaper, determining to discover the secret of her room in order to hoard it as a knowledge peculiarly her own: "There are things in that paper that nobody knows but me, or ever will"; "I am determined that nobody shall find it out but myself!" "I have found out another funny thing, but I shan't tell it. . . ." In the process, she makes herself more and more of a mystery to the husband who doesn't want to know her, anyway, and indeed prefers for her to be as little conscious of her own mind as possible:

> I lie down ever so much now. John says it is good for me, and to sleep all I can.
>
> Indeed he started the habit by making me lie down for an hour after each meal.
>
> It is a very bad habit I am convinced, for you see I don't sleep.
>
> And that cultivates deceit, for I don't tell them I'm awake—O no!

John prefers that his wife sleep as much as possible; she deceives him by only pretending, meanwhile pursuing a project she has come to see as urgently important: concentrating all her intellectual energies on her wallpaper. This absurd situation is almost a parody of the way women have been assigned, in de Beauvoir's terms, to "immanence," and of the distorted forms their frustrated impulse toward transcendence may take as a result. "The male is called upon . . . to transcend himself toward the totality of the universe and the infinity of the future; but traditional marriage does not invite woman to transcend herself with him; it confines her in immanence, shuts her up within the circle of herself." The life of immanence is a life of repetition, and women are confined to repetition in special ways—because their one major role is to continue the species, and because the "work" they do in their enclosed "circle of self" is itself circular. "Few tasks are more like the torture of Sisyphus than housework, with its endless repetition. . . ."

Repetition in women's Gothic mimes the claustrophobic circularity of women's real lives in that it shows the heroine, who must confront the same terrors repeatedly, doing the same thing over and over. In its presentation of multiple female victims Gothic romance also shows the same thing being *done* to women over and over; it suggests the inescapable victimization of Woman in general. Emily escapes but then Blanche is trapped (*Mysteries of Udolpho*); Julia escapes but then she finds that her mother is trapped (*Sicilian Romance*); and so on, from volume to volume. The repetition in Gilman's Gothic story is the narrator's growing obsession with her wallpaper, her nightmarish task of endless and extra-ordinarily difficult interior decorating, her infantile creeping around and around the so-called "nursery," and the boring regimen prescribed by her doctor-husband. It is also the multiplication of women in the wallpaper, who engage in the same Sisyphean task of trying to overcome, through repetition, the repetitious life to which they have been assigned. Gilman's subversive message is evident. In her story there is no hero to end the repetition with the traditional closure: a marriage through which the heroine transcends her earlier perils, and which cancels out the protest implicit in the preceding images of women "immured in their families groping in the dark."

Earlier women's Gothic, too, was a deeply subversive genre, but often only to the extent that it subverted itself. For, like dreams, women's Gothic offers its insights together with protection from their meaning. The heroine kills her father, but it wasn't her real father; the real father arrives to explain that the act was only justifiable self-defense; anyway, the victim isn't dead after all, so she didn't kill him (Musgrave, *Solemn Injunction*). The heroine violates decorum by eloping from a convent, but the woman who urged her to do so is really her mother, so even her act of rebellion conformed to the decorum of filial piety (Radcliffe, *The Italian*). The heroine renounces her ties to her father and declares that she will "struggle for liberty and life" (Radcliffe, *Romance of the Forest*); but that wasn't her father, after all; in fact, her real father was murdered by the false one against whom she rebelled. The heroine's lover acts like the villain—but no, it was all a lie (Radcliffe, *Mysteries of Udolpho*). The heroine's father is trying to kill her, but no—he is not her father; it was all a mistake (Radcliffe, *The Italian*).

In Roche's *The House of Osma and Almeria* is an even more contorted example. When the heroine's father, "the most arrogant of mankind," opposes her marriage, her lover kills him. She is torn between love for and revulsion toward the murderer, but the conflict is resolved when it turns out that the man the lover killed was not her father, after all. Unfortunately, her real parents are even worse than he was: the father "gaunt and ferocious," the mother "loaded with tawdry ornaments." (This last may seem a minor failing, but it is presented in dire terms, presumably an adolescent fantasy of embarassment at one's parents' bad taste). Their "mouldering" house, with its shattered windows, "withering grass and weeds" and "mutilated statues," is now revealed to be both her true family dwelling and her prison. But hidden away there, it turns out, is her *real* father—the first one, after all—who is not only alive, but now completely sympathetic to her plight. No wonder the subject of Gothic romance is fear.

Women Gothicists were desperately afraid of their real subject, which is anger.

Gilman saw through Gothic fear to the emotion behind it; significantly, although the narrator comes to acknowledge herself "a little afraid of John," anger comes increasingly to be her dominant emotion. In this as in so many other ways, **"The Yellow Wallpaper"** is a commentary on the hidden meanings of the century-long female literary tradition of Gothic romance that precedes it. In fact, **"The Yellow Wallpaper"** could almost be an allegory of the way the female Gothicist uses mystery to mediate between her anger at domestic ideology and her need to believe in it. For the narrator, a woman excluded from the mysteries of masculine knowledge ("I am a doctor dear, and I know"), compensates by making her wallpaper, symbol of her domestic confinement, into a mystery that she must devote every moment to deciphering. Her concentration on the wallpaper is at once a desperate attempt to validate the ideology that limits women's proper sphere of knowledge to the mysteries of interior decorating, and a way for her to inscribe her own mystery—the angry and victimized Hidden Other Woman inside her—on the walls of her domestic prison. Ironically, what her husband thinks he "knows" is his wife; her increasing sense that she is the guardian of a deep secret that "nobody knows but me"—a treasure of self-knowledge she must hoard with the greatest care—marks her increasing awareness that her husband's so-called knowledge of his patient wife has mystified her even in her own eyes. It is her final triumph to force this supposed expert on feminine psychology to confront directly, and literally, the fact that her life is really a locked room to him: a room to which only the imprisoned woman herself can provide the key. At the end she assaults the male rationalist with the revelation that this house *is* haunted by a mystery, and that this mystery is his own wife.

This sense that the Gothic heroine is herself the real mystery whose solution she must discover and proclaim is central to Gilman's re-visioning of the Gothic. In **"The Yellow Wallpaper,"** she reveals her perceptions that Gothic fear is a mask for anger, that woman's "separate sphere" is a house of horrors, and that the "mysteries" heroines try so desperately to decipher while immured in Gothic space are only a disguise for the real mystery, woman herself. She portrays this mystery as invisible to men, and their self-satisfied "knowledge" of women as a form of violence against which women need to defend themselves by "speaking 'I.'" But this task is almost impossible, because that false "knowledge" is itself the source of the mystery: a dangerous mystification in which woman, before she frees herself to know—and to create—her own inner reality, unwittingly colludes. **"The Yellow Wallpaper"** charts the breakdown of this collusion, beginning with the narrator's desperate effort to preserve it by becoming a female Gothicist. Choosing escapism rather than escape, she simultaneously invests her boring domestic world with the "romantic felicity" of Gothic terrors and creates her own alternative "mystery," her own specialized branch of knowledge that can exist safely in a "separate sphere" from that of her husband. What happens, however, is that, in writing her Gothic story onto her walls, she uncovers what women's Gothic had always tried to conceal: a Hidden Woman in the heroine, who resents the life of domestic repetition to which the "hero" would like to confine her. By forcing her husband to acknowledge and confront the mystery she has been to him, she exposes this domestic life for what it is.

The husband's response to the Gothic vision with which the woman writer has confronted him, however, is to become unconscious—as unconscious as male readers in Gilman's day seem to have been of the real secret she was revealing. And the narrator, crawling triumphantly over his inert form, is still defeated by that unconsciousness: still trapped in repetition, as she goes around and around the "circle of herself."

This image is part of a disturbing system of ironies at the end of **"The Yellow Wallpaper."** The narrator, forced to "read" her wallpaper passively as a substitute for writing actively, has transformed her reading into an act of imagination and thus an act of freedom. Yet this "freedom" seems to consist in creeping around and around a "nursery" in a circle. Having "got out at last," the narrator celebrates by locking herself in and throwing the key out the window; having rescued her alter-ego from the imprisonment of the wallpaper, she carefully ties her up so she will not escape. Perhaps most bizarre is the way in which the protagonist's journey inward seems to have produced an unfolding self-knowledge ending in total self loss. Having at first confused her barbarous confinement in a madhouse with a genteel vacation in the country, the narrator gradually distinguished, in her room with its barred windows, "a woman" behind bars. At the end she has come to see that woman as herself, asking in a moment of shocking clarity whether all the creeping women she sees "come out of that wall-paper, as I did." The phrase "as I did" acknowledges that all this time she herself has been the Other Woman, both longsuffering and rebellious, hidden in her room. Yet the flash of insight is also a moment of confusion: the narrator has everything backwards, identifying the woman in the wallpaper as herself rather than as a symbolic—and self-created—projection of her own plight outward onto her surroundings. She began her stay at this house by longing for the symbolic escape of a Gothic fantasy, and that is what she has found. But like most female Gothic readers and writers, she fails to translate the Gothic reality into its everyday meanings; thus her self-knowledge is somehow hidden even from herself, and her act of imagination, the symbolic discovery of her plight, can issue only in symbolic action. She tears off wallpaper, ties up an imaginary woman to keep her indoors, "creeps" around and around her "nursery"-prison. In her private universe all these are acts of freedom.

Ironically, what they symbolize most obviously is something quite different. Together these actions are an extreme and literal version of the role for which the narrator's society has cast her as a woman: the homemaker passionately interested in her wallpaper; the mother self-confined to the nursery; the "little girl" inferior, with her childlike behavior, to her wiser husband. The grim joke behind the final Gothic vision of a woman crawling around a nursery like a maniac is that this apparent "insanity" is merely a literalized picture of the social norm that passes, in her society, for sanity—the conduct becoming in a respectable woman. This is Gilman's final equation of the Gothic nightmare with women's everyday reality. At its most pessimistic level, the story ends in a terrible vision of what happens when women are forced to seek self-knowledge in nurseries and interior decorations; it is a bitter, parodic view of what Gilman's society intended women, including her, to be.

That Gilman resisted such stereotyping by writing a story like **"The Yellow Wallpaper"** casts the ending in a more hopeful light, as do a number of elements in the plot itself:

the narrator's increasing sense of self-mastery as the story goes on; her determination to "speak 'I'" against her husband's prohibition; her final exultation in her own powers after so long a period of self-doubt; her ability to direct her anger, at the end, toward its proper object—the hero whom she finally perceives as the villain. Her excited cry, "I've got out at last. . . . so you can't put me back!" represents a delusion only on one level; the narrator is lost in imagination, but in imagination she will continue to be free.

The final image in **"The Yellow Wallpaper"** is one of triumph and defeat, insight and insanity, self-knowledge and self-loss. That the story should end in a maze of ironic ambiguities as confusing as the wallpaper itself is appropriate. It is hardly surprising that Gilman's text should generate several patterns of meaning, each of which trails off at the end into "unheard of contradictions." For like the wallpaper, Gilman's story mirrors a social system rife with the multiple contradictions that result when people struggle to fulfill their human potential in a world that denies their humanity. In such a world, an act of imagination is sometimes the only act of freedom possible. **"The Yellow Wallpaper,"** for all the contradictions it represents, is unambiguously such an act. (pp. 9-13)

> *Eugenia C. Delamotte, "Male and Female Mysteries in 'The Yellow Wallpaper',"* in LEGACY, *Vol. 5, No. 1, Spring, 1988, pp. 3-14.*

LEE WEINSTEIN   (essay date 1988)

[*In the following essay, Weinstein offers an interpretation of "The Yellow Wallpaper" as supernatural literature.*]

When **"The Yellow Wallpaper"** by Charlotte Perkins Gilman was first published in 1892, it was generally read as a horrifying, but realistic, account of the progressive mental deterioration of a woman undergoing the then popular rest cure for nervous illnesses. This, in fact, was the author's intention, as she states in her autobiography.

In more recent years, feminist critics have found a wealth of symbolism that has changed the accepted reading of the story. According to this interpretation, the figure the narrator sees in the wallpaper represents not only her " . . . own divided self, but all women who are imprisoned . . . by a society which insists that women are childlike, merely decorative, and incapable of self-actualization. The wallpaper itself, like the social conventions it symbolizes, is hideously ugly. . . . Any attempt to impose reason on such a tortuous pattern results in madness" [Barbara Hill Rigney, *Madness and Sexual Politics in the Feminist Novel*]. The fact that Gilman was, in fact, a feminist tends to support this interpretation.

While both these readings have valid points to make, they leave certain points unexplained. Further, as pointed out by Schopp-Schilling, the psychologist and feminist arguments often fall into the intentional and biographical fallacies of literary criticism.

There is a third, supernatural interpretation, which would explain some previously unaddressed points. It was hinted at by H. P. Lovecraft when he described the story's narrator as " . . . a woman dwelling in the hideously papered room where a madwoman was once confined."

This interpretation, that the room had a former occupant, and that the narrator is being possessed, has never been ex-

plored in detail. It shall be based upon a literal reading of the text.

In order to analyze the story, it is necessary to assume that the protagonist, who narrates in the first person, is a reliable observer, despite her dubious mental state. The fact that it is told in the form of a diary, each entry beginning with what is, in effect, a new viewpoint, is helpful in this regard.

Her first entry, made on her first day in the house, tells us that the nature of her disorder, according to her husband, John, a physician, is "temporary nervous depression—a slight hysterical tendency". She also tells us about the house itself, which they have rented for the summer: "There was some legal trouble . . . the place has been empty for years. That spoils my ghostliness, I am afraid, but I don't care—there is something strange about the house—I can feel it."

We are presented with a scenario in which a nervous, imaginative, and emotionally unstable woman spends endless hours in a room with literally nothing to do but stare at the wallpaper. Soon, not surprisingly, she begins to see things. She sees a woman, sometimes behind the wallpaper's pattern, and sometimes outside, always creeping about.

Feminist critics have given this woman a symbolic interpretation, but on the literal level there are two possibilities. She may be hallucinating, or she may, in her weakened state of mind, be falling prey to something in the room which is very real. Does she feel "something ghostly" about the house at the beginning because she is imaginative, and perhaps romantic, or, perhaps does she really feel a presence in the house, although she does not want to admit it, even to herself?

Her husband thinks there is nothing really wrong with her. She thinks him wrong. Do her symptoms worsen as a subconscious way of proving to him that she is really ill, are they indicative of actual mental illness, or is she being acted upon by an outside agency?

There are clues in the description of the room on the house's top floor, which is the sole setting of the story. The narrator tells us: "It was a nursery first and then a playroom and gymnasium, I should judge; for the windows are barred for little children, and there are rings and things in the walls."

We must accept her physical description of the room. There are barred windows, torn wallpaper, and rings in the walls. Later in the story we find that the bed is nailed down, and the floor is gouged and splintered. However, we do not have to accept her interpretation of these facts. She repeatedly attributes the damage done to the room to hypothetical children who once played in a room she "judges" to have been a nursery and a gymnasium. But what sort of nursery has barred windows, a bed bolted to the floor, and rings in the walls? As Lovecraft suggests, it sounds like a room where a madwoman had been confined.

Most feminist critics accept the room as having been a nursery, arguing that it symbolizes the childlike treatment of women. Some have gone as far as to suggest that the nailed-down bed symbolizes the narrator's sexuality. Only one [Annette Kolodny] touches on the oddness of this "nursery", noting the "fleeting resemblance between the upstairs chamber . . . and Poe's evocation of the dungeon chambers of Toledo . . ." But even she only implies a comparison between Poe's hero, who is saved from the pit, and Gilman's heroine, who is not. She does not consider the implications of a literal interpretation.

In the same way, feminist critics, if they entertain the notion at all that the room had a previous occupant, interpret it in only a symbolic sense. "Maybe this room has always been a place of confinement for mad persons," says Rigney. But the internal evidence indicates that the previous occupant was quite real.

For example, there is the matter of the wallpaper by the bed. The narrator tells us, "It is stripped off—the paper—in great patches all around the head of my bed, about as far as I can reach." Why should it be torn about as far as she can reach? Are we to infer that she tore it herself? If so, we run into an insurmountable critical problem. We see the story entirely through her eyes. If she is not a reliable observer, we cannot believe anything she tells us and analysis of her words becomes meaningless. We must accept, therefore, that if she tore the paper she would have described her actions in doing so, as in fact she does later in the story. Further, she makes the observation on her first day in the house, when she is in her most normal mental state.

If she didn't tear the paper, then who did? Could it have been the hypothetical children she keeps speaking of? The problem here is that even if there really had been children in the room, presumably they would have had a shorter reach. The paper was torn by someone who could reach about as far as the narrator. The evidence points to Lovecraft's madwoman.

This conclusion is further supported by an unusual mark the narrator later discovers on the wall, down near the mopboard. She describes it as, "A streak that runs around the room. It goes behind every piece of furniture except the bed, a long, straight, even *smooch,* as if it had been rubbed over and over."

Rigney says bluntly, "Perhaps it is the narrator herself who, although she does not realize it, has always been here, 'creeping' about the room until her own shoulder has left the groove she notices in the wallpaper." Again, to take this literally is to face the problem of the unreliable narrator. If we are meant to infer that the narrator has always been there only in some vague, symbolic sense, then the literal presence of the mark is left unexplained.

The narrator tells us that she and her husband had to bring all the furniture, excepting the bed, up from the downstairs. Although she has been two weeks in the house at this point, it is reasonable to assume that they moved the furniture upstairs when they moved in or very shortly after. Therefore, since the mark goes behind the furniture, it was there when they moved in. Because, as the narrator later discovers, the mark is level with her shoulder, the evidence again points to the madwoman.

Given the existence of this madwoman, several interpretations are possible. One is non-supernatural. The narrator somehow deduces that there was a madwoman in the room who caused the damage, deduces how she caused the damage, and begins to imitate her.

Of course, this runs into the unreliable narrator problem again. The narrator seems genuinely convinced that it was children who gouged the plaster, tore the paper, and splintered the floor. She also seems genuinely puzzled about the mark on the wall. "I wonder how it was done and who did

it, and what they did it for. Round and round and round." Could it be this musing which eventually leads her to go round and round herself at the end of the story? This is unlikely because we are shown that she is imitating the creeping woman she sees behind the wallpaper. We would have to suppose that the narrator is imitating a hallucination constructed from a totally unconscious awareness of the room's previous occupant. This seems highly unlikely.

A more plausible interpretation is that the room itself drives its occupants to madness. The narrator and the madwoman before her are both victims, and possibly not the only ones. At the story's turning point the narrator says, "There are so many of those creeping women, and they creep so fast. I wonder if they all came out of the wallpaper as I did?" Is she seeing a succession of victims? Possibly, but earlier the narrator says, "Sometimes I think there are a great many women behind and sometimes only one, and she crawls around fast." Also, her husband, who shares the room, is not affected.

Finally, there is the interpretation that the room is haunted by the madwoman, whose spirit gradually possesses the narrator. This fits the narrator's actions quite well. For example, toward the end she notices a place on the headboard the "children had gnawed", and a few paragraphs later she bites the headboard herself. She may have been driven mad in precisely the same manner as the previous occupant(s) by the room itself, but it seems more likely that she has been possessed by the spirit of a single previous occupant and is doomed to repeat her actions in her victim.

Of course, this leaves the question of why she sees many creeping women at the turning point. If she has been possessed, why would she continue to see that which has possessed her? One possibility is that, although she is possessed, she still retains her own personality, and therefore a sort of double consciousness.

There are two clues at the end of the story that support the idea of possession. On the last page the narrator says, "I've got out at last . . . in spite of you and Jane." This is the first reference in the story to a "Jane". Hedges suggests that if this is not a printer's error (in some printings "Jane" has been altered to "Jennie"), it may be the narrator's own name. The narrator refers to herself in the third person because she is free of her "Jane" self, that is, "herself as defined by marriage and society." Is it not simpler to interpret the statement literally? Perhaps she refers to herself as Jane because she has literally become a different person.

The other clue comes when she hears her husband at the door to the room and thinks to herself, "It is no use, young man, you can't open it." Why does she refer to her husband as "young man?" This is a point other critics have ignored. If it is supposed to be an indication of insanity, it is a rather arbitrary one. On the other hand, it makes perfect sense if she is seeing him from the viewpoint of someone else; someone much older who died in the house long ago. (pp. 23-5)

Lee Weinstein, " 'The Yellow Wallpaper': A Supernatural Interpretation," in Studies in Weird Fiction, *No. 4, Fall, 1988, pp. 23-5.*

POLLY WYNN ALLEN   (essay date 1988)

[*In the following excerpt from her book* Building Domestic Liberty: Charlotte Perkins Gilman's Architectural Feminism, *Allen identifies Gilman's realistic short stories as effective vehicles for her ideas on nonsexist living arrangements.*]

Charlotte Gilman did not agonize over the writing of her realistic short stories and novels as she did over her social ethics. Instead she wrote them casually, almost in sport. Even so, she was mindful of their educational potential. She recognized the capacity of strong fiction to move people, confiding to her diary in 1893, "If I can learn to write good stories it will be a powerful addition to my armory."

In spite of this awareness, Gilman consistently judged her philosophy to be of much greater social significance than her fiction. Except for **"The Yellow Wallpaper,"** she scarcely mentioned her story writing in her autobiography except to say that she had written tales to help support herself and her family. In the *Forerunner's* first year, she expressed the modest hope that her stories would provide "interest and amusement" to her readers.

The realistic story, more than the utopian one, was Gilman's forte. In it she typically portrayed an ordinary white middle-class woman (or group of women) wrestling with common dilemmas that pit family obligations against individual ones. Convinced that such conflicts could best be resolved architecturally, she conjured up settings in some stage of feminist transformation for about one-third of her stories.

Gilman wanted her fiction to reinforce the individual aspirations of women. She hoped that the struggles of her imaginary heroines would encourage her female readers to take themselves seriously as autonomous actors on the stage of history. Through her stories, she tried to communicate the unfamiliar notion that women's efforts to achieve personal independence were full of moral significance.

Gilman could have said about all her fiction what she said of **"The Yellow Wallpaper"**: "I wrote it to preach. If it is literature, that just happened." Stating her aims in 1926, she wrote: "One girl reads this, and takes fire! Her life is changed. She becomes a power—a mover of others—I write for her." Gilman planted her feminist ideas in fictional gardens, the artistic quality of which was only an incidental concern. Her guiding hope as storyteller was to cultivate the soil, to enlarge the common woman's sense of what was possible.

In an explicit way, the central point of Gilman's realistic fiction was to juxtapose woman's old morality of minding the domestic sphere with her new morality of responsible self-fullfilment in the world. She aimed to demonstrate conclusively both the superiority and the rightness of the new morality. She accomplished this by creating contrasting characters living by the two codes as well as characters struggling to move from the domestic code to the higher one. She was forthright about treating the moral dilemmas of women, using such titles as **"Turned," "A Cleared Path," "Making a Change," "Mary Button's Principles," "Mrs. Powers' Duty,"** and **"Mrs. Merrill's Duties."**

In an implicit way, many of Gilman's stories testified powerfully to the liberating potential of nonsexist spatial design. By means of architectural backdrops, much of her fiction portrayed very tangible ways of solving the problems of isolated, overworked women. Being able to move into a more socialized dwelling or to join forces with other women in common spaces were opportunities she encouraged every woman to pursue.

Gilman created four types of feminist environment in her realistic fiction. In one, she portrayed apartment hotels or boardinghouses as the setting for progressively liberated life styles. In a second cluster of tales, she depicted groups of neighboring residences, linked to central facilities for laundry, child care, food delivery, and cleaning services. Women form alliances in a third group of stories, associations that meet in clubhouses to foster sisterly cooperation both in the conduct of domestic life and in training for employment outside the home. A fourth set of stories celebrates the existence of recuperative spaces, most often located in the country, run by women and for women.

In **"Forsythe and Forsythe,"** four professional people find romance and supportive simplicity in an apartment hotel in Seattle, Washington. The name of the story refers to a man and woman, George and Georgiana Forsythe, who are husband and wife as well as cousins. Equal partners both at work and at home, they find respite from their joint practice of law in two adjoining (and distinctively decorated) apartments. Whereas George's flat is "undeniably bachelorish," there is "a wholesome femininity" in the decor of Georgiana's. Among the amenities available in the building are a restaurant on one of the lower floors and a child-care center on the roof.

In the story's rather thin plot, George's old friend Jim Jackson comes to visit Forsythe and Forsythe, at home. With a reputation for being "Rigidly conservative, even reactionary," Jackson is highly skeptical at the outset about such unorthodox living arrangements. But gradually two factors bring him around. First, "He grew used to the smooth convenience of the apartment very rapidly, even tacitly approved of the steady excellence of the food and service." Second, he can't resist the charms of the strongly independent, "mischievous" Clare Forsythe, who is George's sister and Jackson's former sweetheart. In the nine years since they have seen each other, Clare has established herself as a prominent "sanitary engineer" (plumber?), living in her own apartment in the same building as her brother and sister-in-law. Jackson finds the attraction of Clare much "greater than the repulsion caused by her limitless progressive views." Conveniently, Jackson's estranged wife mails him divorce papers just as the story ends, freeing the former skeptic to declare his love for Ms. Forsythe and to embrace her liberated life style wholeheartedly.

In **"Her Housekeeper,"** an unusual domestic environment is instrumental in winning the heart of a beautiful actress. Widowed after an unhappy marriage, Mrs. Leland is determined never to wed again. Committed to pursuing her promising career as well as protecting her freedom, she sees marriage as profoundly threatening to both. Above all, she wants to avoid domestic drudgery. "I hate—I'd like to write a dozen tragic plays to show how much I hate—Housekeeping!" she exclaims to Arthur Olmstead, a would-be suitor and fellow resident of a flourishing boardinghouse.

Slowly but surely, over a period of several months, Olmstead persuades Mrs. Leland that marriage to *him* would not involve any such dreary entrapments. As a matter of fact, he demonstrates that he has the means, the skill, and the temperament to relieve her forever of housewifely chores. He often entertains Mrs. Leland and her five-year-old son, Johnny, charmingly, in his apartment. One day he tells her that his real estate business (about which he had been purposefully vague) consists of running apartment hotels such as the one

"The Home Is Just a Place to Hang Things Up In." Cartoon mocking Gilman's architectural proposals, 1895.

both he and she occupy. In fact, he owns their very residence as well as several others.

For as long as she had lived there, Mrs. Leland had reveled in the building's excellent cooked-food service, patronizing both the downstairs restaurant and the room-service delivery made possible by an automatic dumbwaiter attached to her flat. Furthermore, she had marveled at Mr. Olmstead's nurturant manner with children, as expressed toward Johnny. One day she complimented this remarkable man as follows: "Do you know you are a real comfort? . . . I never knew a man before who could—well leave off being a man for a moment and just be a human creature." Convinced at last that she and Mr. Olmstead could make a very positive, unconventional marriage while maintaining (and even enhancing) their spatially supportive environment, Mrs. Leland marries "Her Housekeeper" and proceeds to live happily ever after. (pp. 145-48)

In a second group of Gilman's short stories, the liberated domestic environment consists of systems of linkages between households. In three of the stories, an enterprising heroine takes responsibility for establishing a domestic service and/or business in a particular neighborhood. (p. 151)

Mary Watterson, the twenty-eight-year-old heroine of **"A Cleared Path,"** owns and runs a small, diversified business in Los Angeles. Among the domestic services her "marvelous little shop" offers to the surrounding community are a small laundry, a sewing and mending bureau, and a sales outlet for children's ready-made clothing. Having been built up over an eight-year period, Watterson's business is a "model" both of exemplary labor relations (her employees, who are partners in a system of "profit sharing," have "charming work-rooms" in which to sew, mend, launder, or sell) and of "honesty, accuracy and efficiency." Spurred by the "phenomenal growth" in the city of Los Angeles, the business has done exceedingly well. As a result, the owner has branched out a bit, investing her surplus in a few pieces of real estate.

A feminist love story ensues, involving Ms. Watterson and Ransome Woodruff, a New Englander-turned-Montana-rancher, who is visiting his sister in southern California. After meeting Mary, Woodruff repeatedly extends the length of his sojourn in Los Angeles. His fascination with her proceeds from respect to passionate attraction and total commitment. Ms. Watterson's feelings for Woodruff are perfectly equivalent.

Throughout the story, Woodruff struggles to overcome his old-fashioned convictions about marriage. He believes that in circumstances like theirs the wife is the one who must relocate. This would mean that Watterson would have to give up her business and move to Montana. She wants none of that. After much soul searching, conversation, and consciousness raising, Woodruff sees the light and decides to sell his ranch so he can move to Los Angeles. He apologizes to Mary for having been "just a plain pig," and the story ends with the news that "in truth they were married the next day." Gilman thus made her point dramatically that a woman's work in the world is "a higher duty" than following her heart, especially when the work involves such "distinctly social" service to the world as a central housekeeping business.

The housekeeping service that gets reorganized communally in **"Making a Change"** is child care. Like many of Gilman's female characters, Julia Gordins is frustrated to the point of impending insanity by the conflicting claims of her family's care and the expression of her life work. A gifted musician who had taught piano and violin before her marriage, Gordins is afflicted by the notion that a married woman must take personal responsibility for all the needs of her family. In particular, the round-the-clock demands of her newborn son, Albert, have exhausted her to the point of derangement. Julia's mother-in-law, Mrs. Gordins, who resides with the young family, has repeatedly offered her services as nursemaid. But Julia's sense of duty, pride, and wifely devotion will not permit her to accept them. And so she suffers, as do her sleepless husband and frustrated mother-in-law.

The combination of internecine hostility and chronic fatigue weigh so heavily on Gordins that one day she decides to end her life. As her husband leaves for work, she is feeling heavily despondent, but he fails to perceive it. After bumbling through the baby's bath, she uncharacteristically asks the senior Mrs. Gordins to mind the baby and proceeds to her room. After a short time, the older woman smells gas, quickly looks for its source, and, having found it, nimbly enters the transom window to rescue Julia.

In the aftermath of this crisis, the generation gap disappears. Mrs. Gordins comes to cherish the young woman as her very own daughter. As the trust between them grows, they devise a plan for starting a neighborhood child-care center on the roof and top floor of their building. The grandmother happily assumes the role of "baby garden" coordinator, furnishing the rooftop with sandpile, seesaws, swings, floor mattresses, and a shallow pool. The threefold purpose of this establishment is to allow Julia Gordins to resume her musical career, to employ the underutilized talents of the senior Mrs. Gordins, and to provide a much-needed social service. Gilman frequently suggested in her stories that women's intergenerational needs for self-expression, like those of the older and the younger Mrs. Gordins, should be approached simultaneously, in a complementary, mutually supportive manner.

"Old Mrs. Crosley" is another story in which a felicity of matched needs is found. Here Gilman expressed concern for the middle-aged woman facing the "empty nest" syndrome. Written when Gilman herself was fifty-one, it is a morality tale about a fifty-two-year-old woman who decides there can be meaningful life after her last baby marries and becomes a father.

In the first part of the story, Mrs. Crosley is depressed because of her age and her lost raison d'être. Her three children are living their own lives in three distinct cities. Mr. Crosley, her fifty-four-year-old husband, has entered a new phase of his life by taking up politics, which he loves. Mrs. Crosley feels apathetic, unskilled, and lonely. Although her home runs smoothly and comfortably, she does not take pride in that fact because she believes she owes it all to her two servants, a cook and a maid.

One evening when she is feeling particularly old and worthless, Mrs. Crosley receives a visit from John Fairmount, the young minister of her church. Expressing his sympathetic concern for her as a fellow human soul, the Reverend Mr. Fairmount assists Mrs. Crosley in identifying an important skill she possesses but has never acknowledged. She is a great personnel manager. She has had extraordinary success in hiring household workers, training them, and maintaining their morale. She is the only woman in town with "excellent servants." He urges her to turn this unusual ability into a community venture.

Over the objections of her husband and children, Mrs. Crosley starts a business that trains and furnishes household help on either an hourly or a permanent, full-time basis. Her "Newcome Agency" offers centralized services as well as a labor bureau. She puts some of her well-trained laborers to work running a laundry and a cooked-food shop. In addition to getting her started, John Fairmount continues to give her support and encouragement, drumming up business for her agency wherever he goes. (pp. 151-53)

Gilman told several stories about what women could do collectively to augment their individual powers. Pending the development of domestically integrated neighborhoods, she advocated the establishment of women's alliances everywhere so that women could meet together regularly for recreation and collaboration. Since there were not many socialized residential areas with shared services at the time she wrote, these tales were aimed to show readers how they might get such facilities started.

Gilman set two of these stories in England: **"A Council of War"** and **"A Surplus Woman."** Though neither has as much dramatic vitality as the best of her stories, these two British tales set forth in succinct fashion Gilman's sense of feminist political strategy.

Although **"A Council of War"** is very diffuse, this earlier story contains some tough realism about the bitter conflicts aroused by women's struggle for empowerment. In it a group of "between twenty and thirty" women meet in London for a conversation about their frustrations and their strategic options for overcoming them. They discuss sexism, antifeminist backlash, their abstract sense of idealistic purpose, and their concrete goals for "the enlargement of women." Considering the possibility of a long-term strike to achieve higher wages, the vote, and gender equality throughout society, these trade unionists and suffragists brainstorm about political tactics.

The wide-ranging "war" that results exemplifies Gilman's penchant for global analysis and her weakness as a practical tactician. Within a few minutes of conversation, the women decide to establish a "great spreading league of interconnected businesses" owned and faithfully patronized by women. They also resolve to acquire halls in which to speak, and paper mills, printing shops and publishing offices, which will help spread their message of liberation. Accepting no limits on their entrepreneurial ambitions, they agree in addition to start "a perfect chain of Summer boarding houses," a laundry business, and an employment agency connected to a "Training School for Modern Employment." A committee of three, appointed at the close of the story, is instructed to consult "widely" on these far-reaching schemes and to report back at the next meeting. The story ends on an expectant note: "and the women looked at one another with the light of a new hope in their eyes."

"A Surplus Woman," though similar in format, shows how Gilman refined the enthusiasms expressed in the earlier story. The emerging organization here is less militantly confrontational and considerably more focused.

Susan Page, a young British woman whose father, brother, and lover have all been killed in the World War, bravely faces the social implications of the war's liquidation of a "whole generation of masculine youth." Determined that women make the best of their necessary singleness, she envisions new opportunities for female bonding which would not exist if young women like herself were all starting families.

Page calls a meeting of five women to propose that they form a "Women's Economic Alliance" with branches throughout England. The WEA's underlying purpose would be to enable single women to become productive members of society. Her plan calls for a strong emphasis on training, with "employment agencies" in every locale. Each local branch would conduct an "economic census" of women and then proceed to establish appropriate classes and eventually a "high grade vocational college" with traveling lecturers and libraries.

After persuading them to join her and then actually training large numbers of women, Page and her new colleagues organize domestic service businesses, run by the newly trained women, all over the country. Like the women in the first story, these look forward in the long run to the establishment of residential clubhouses with shared facilities. But in this second tale of British sisterhood, Gilman showed a more mature sense of what was possible, a more restrained sense of agenda, a greater realism. Its increased sense of political strategy makes for a better story, too. (pp. 155-57)

In another group of stories, Gilman featured special places where women (and sometimes men) could go for rest, recreation, and healing. A number of summer resorts like the ones portrayed here were actually built, incorporating Gilman's specifications for connected, kitchenless facilities. Apart from their ordinary lives, women find here both new forms of therapeutic togetherness and opportunities for refreshing solitude.

"Girls and the Land" is the story of Dacia Boone, a young woman living in Seattle, Washington. Like the novel *What Diantha Did,* this story is a detailed set of directions on how to create a Gilmanesque space.

With a very shrewd business sense and a sturdy contentment with her life style as a single woman, Dacia Boone is impervious to her mother's worries about her homeliness; she turns a deaf ear to Mom's frequent exclamation, "If only you had been a man!" She sets out to accumulate enough wealth both to assist her stepfather in a development project and to build a "Vacation Place" in the country where groups of "working girls" from clubs throughout the state can go for two weeks of wholesome camping. Along with many fiscal details about how she accomplishes this, the story shows Dacia making a stunning success of both building projects. In the course of her enterprising activity, she also meets a talented carpenter/designer, Olaf Pedersen, with whom she starts a furniture business and falls in love.

"Maidstone Comfort" is a "rambling summer settlement" at the seashore. It comes into existence as the result of a timely collaboration orchestrated by a "quiet, adaptable, middle-aged" character by the name of Benigna MacAvelly.

Sarah Maidstone Pellett owns a considerable amount of remote, beach-front property, which her domineering husband will not let her develop. MacAvelly introduces Pellett to Molly Bellew, a floundering twenty-year-old rebel who is on the threshold of inheriting millions of dollars. Together Pellett and Bellew build and manage a beautifully restorative seaside compound which is also handsomely lucrative.

Maidstone Comfort, like Gilman's utopian places, combines natural beauty with architectural integration. A whole village of small, brightly colored cottages is built along curving streets beside the shoreline; luxuriant flowers, vines, and shrubs adorn the areas between them. Convenient to all of the houses is a hotel at which guests can take excellent meals. As an additional service, "a brisk motor-wagon" equipped with "neat receptacles" is primed, upon receipt of a phone call, to deliver outstanding food to a cottage's back door and to return later to pick up the dirty dishes. No one who comes to this place for recuperation has to give a single thought to the question of what to eat. (pp. 158-59)

In short, modest stories about white middle-class and upper-middle-class women, Gilman unselfconsciously made her most compelling argument for nonsexist architecture. To dwell imaginatively for a few moments in a landscape with connected domestic facilities suggests powerfully that such environments are both desirable and achievable.

As the backdrop for dozens of Gilman stories, socialized feminist spaces need no elaborate rationale. Their vitality is compelling in and of itself, representing the way the landscape will look when empowered women learn to look out for their own interests. In contrast to the distorting one-sidedness of her philosophical universe, here individuality is reassuringly secure, celebrated in the struggles of heroines to achieve personal autonomy. In the world of Gilman's realistic fiction, growth and conflict, individuality and connectedness, uncertainty and ambiguity are all experienced and taken into ac-

count. Except for the recurrent figure of Mrs. MacAvelly, no character is portrayed mothering other people endlessly without looking after her own needs.

Gilman's realistic fiction corrected for her theoretical excesses. She located its characters squarely in the familiar flux of history where decisions and actions were always conditioned by the necessities of space and time. Here no one gives any thought to the abstract normative considerations discussed in her formal ethics; the actors show no concern for conforming themselves to evolutionary laws. Nor are they obsessed with their duty to self-efface in deference to the ideal of social unity.

In recent years the humble narrative has come into its own as a bearer of ethical meaning. Recognized in women's consciousness-raising groups as a crucial mode of empowerment, its capacity to enliven moral principles has recently been noted by both activists and academics.

A contemporary philosopher, Stanley Hauerwas, has written appreciatively about the ethical significance of stories, recognizing in them a necessary complement to normative abstractions. He reminds moral theorists of their creative dependence on descriptive narrative, lest they forget and attempt to survive in the realms of "pure" cogitation. He writes, "If our lives are to be reflective and coherent, our moral vision must be ordered around dominant metaphors or stories." He discusses the everyday process by which we form our character and virtue, indeed the very story of our lives, in response to stories that have captured our imagination. At his most enthusiastic, he claims: "To be moral persons is to allow stories to be told through us . . . Our experience itself, if it is to be coherent, is but an incipient story." At times more aware of it than at others, Gilman's own life story as well as the rich produce of her literary imagination provided an invaluable grounding to her lifelong project of social ethics.

Gilman's realistic stories help reconstruct the heart of her vision for the built environment. More than anything else, she wanted to liberate women from solitary, burdensome housework. To that end she urged women to pursue as many strategies as they could think of appropriate to their particular location and circumstance. Where possible, they should live in socialized residences attached to commercialized domestic services. If there were none, they should consider starting one, even a very informal, small-scale service, with the hope that it would grow. They should talk to each other about what they need. They should meet in large and small groups and try to solve their problems collectively. They should form alliances.

Men are not without significant roles in Gilman's stories. Dozens of them see the light and choose to live in liberated households. A few even engage in domestic work themselves, most notably Ford Mathews in **"The Cottagette,"** who fixes a "perfect" picnic lunch and begs his fiancée to stop doing housework, and Arthur Olmstead in **"Her Housekeeper,"** who looks after children and develops admirable apartment hotels. Although the challenge of involving men equally in housework was not high on Gilman's agenda, a few of her stories suggest that she would appreciate the justice of such a campaign. (pp. 162-63)

Polly Wynn Allen, in her Building Domestic Liberty: Charlotte Perkins Gilman's Architectural Feminism, *The University of Massachusetts Press, 1988, 195 p.*

FURTHER READING

Bader, Julia. "The Dissolving Vision: Realism in Jewett, Freeman, and Gilman." In *American Realism: New Essays,* edited by Eric J. Sundquist, pp. 176-98. Baltimore: Johns Hopkins University Press, 1982.

    Finds that in "The Yellow Wallpaper" the "alternation between a confidently realistic shaping of narrative development and a dissolution of this order into grotesque or blurred fragments provides a somber commentary on the process and the hazards of female perception and self-perception."

Biamonte, Gloria A. "' . . . There Is a Story, If We Could Only Find It': Charlotte Perkins Gilman's 'The Giant Wistaria'." *Legacy* 5, No. 2 (Fall 1988): 33-8.

    Identifies the themes of Gilman's story "The Giant Wistaria" as "the concerns of motherhood, creativity, and confinement."

Boone, Joseph Allen. "Centered Lives and Centric Structures in the Novel of Female Community: Counterplotting New Realities in *Millennium Hall, Cranford, The Country of the Pointed Firs,* and *Herland.*" In his *Tradition Counter Tradition: Love and the Form of Fiction,* pp. 278-330. Chicago: University of Chicago Press, 1987.

    Includes a discussion of the themes and style of *Herland,* concluding that "Gilman has unfolded an attack on her age's assumptions about gender and its relation to love, courtship, and marriage that becomes, by implication, an attack on the form of fiction itself: the effort to reform public opinion, Gilman learns, must also re-form the text."

Fetterley, Judith. "Reading about Reading: 'A Jury of Her Peers,' 'The Murders in the Rue Morgue,' and 'The Yellow Wallpaper'." In *Gender and Reading: Essays on Readers, Texts, and Contexts,* edited by Elizabeth A. Flynn and Patrocinio P. Schweickart, pp. 147-64. Baltimore: Johns Hopkins University Press, 1986.

    Finds support in "The Yellow Wallpaper" for the contention that "since the stories men tell assert as fact what women know to be fiction, not only do women lose the power that comes from authoring; more significantly, they are forced to deny their own reality and to commit in effect a kind of psychic suicide."

Fleenor, Julian E. "The Gothic Prism: Charlotte Perkins Gilman's Gothic Stories and Her Autobiography." In *The Female Gothic,* edited by Juliann E. Fleenor, pp. 227-241. Montreal: Eden Press, 1983.

    Points out elements of Gothic fiction in Gilman's autobiography and her short stories "The Rocking Chair," "The Giant Wistaria," and "The Yellow Wallpaper," asserting that these elements illustrate women's conflicts with motherhood and creation.

Freibert, Lucy M. "World Views in Utopian Novels by Women." In *Women and Utopia: Critical Interpretations,* edited by Marleen Barr and Nicholas D. Smith, pp. 67-84. Lanham, Md.: University Press of America, 1983.

    Examines "the first truly feminist work in the American utopian tradition—*Herland,*" and three modern feminist utopian novels. Freibert finds that, in addition to sharing principles of socialism, community responsibility for children, and the eradication of rape, the four novels advocate "the union of reason and nature rather than the domination of nature practiced by the current male-oriented culture."

Gubar, Susan. "*She* in *Herland:* Feminism as Fantasy." In *Coordinates: Placing Science Fiction and Fantasy,* edited by George E. Slusser, Eric S. Rabkin, and Robert Scholes, pp. 139-49. Carbondale and Edwardsville: Southern Illinois University Press, 1983.

    Compares Gilman's *Herland* with H. Rider Haggard's *She* (1886), a male fantasy about female power.

Haney-Peritz, Janice. "Monumental Feminism and Literature's Ancestral House: Another Look at 'The Yellow Wallpaper'." *Women's Studies* 12, No. 2 (February 1986): 113-28.

    Analyzes feminist themes in "The Yellow Wallpaper" and critiques previous feminist readings.

Hill, Mary A. "Charlotte Perkins Gilman: A Feminist's Struggle with Womanhood." *The Massachusetts Review* 21, No. 3 (Fall 1980): 503-26.

    Biographical sketch which explains Gilman's theories about achieving female economic and social independence and her ambivalence about practicing these theories in her own life.

————. *Charlotte Perkins Gilman: The Making of a Radical Feminist, 1860-1896.* Philadelphia: Temple University Press, 1980, 362 p.

    Biography which proposes to "trace chronologically the origins of Charlotte Gilman's feminist convictions and to explain some of the patterns of her early life."

Howells, W. D. Review of *In This Our World,* by Charlotte Perkins Stetson. *Harper's Weekly,* No. 2,040 (25 January 1896): 79.

    Praises Gilman's poetry, saying that "since the Biglow Papers we have had no civic satire, that I can think of, nearly so good. . . . "

Huckle, Patricia. "Women in Utopias." In *The Utopian Vision: Seven Essays on the Quincentennial of Sir Thomas More,* edited by E. D. S. Sullivan, pp. 115-36. San Diego: San Diego State University Press, 1983.

    Includes Gilman's *Herland* in a discussion of fictional feminist utopias and actual feminist experimental communes in both the nineteenth and twentieth centuries.

Jacobus, Mary. "An Unnecessary Maze of Sign-Reading." In her *Reading Woman: Essays in Feminist Criticism,* pp. 229-48. New York: Columbia University Press, 1986.

    Revises the generally accepted feminist and psychoanalytic readings of "The Yellow Wallpaper," taking into account the Gothic elements of the story.

Karpinski, Joanne B. "When the Marriage of True Minds Admits Impediments: Charlotte Perkins Gilman and William Dean Howells." In *Patrons and Protégées: Gender, Friendship, and Writing in Nineteenth-Century America,* edited by Shirley Marchalonis, pp. 212-34. New Brunswick, N.J.: Rutgers University Press, 1988.

    Explores the mentorial role William Dean Howells initiated and cautiously fulfilled with Gilman, concluding that he would help her only indirectly because her frankness and assertive rhetorical style did not fit his idea of a gracious lady.

Kennard, Jean E. "Convention Coverage or How to Read Your Own Life." *New Literary History* XIII, No. 1 (Autumn 1981): 69-88.

    Suggests that modern interpretations of "The Yellow Wallpaper"—particularly feminist ones—differ from early interpretations because literary conventions have changed.

King, Jeannette, and Morris, Pam. "On Not Reading Between the Lines: Models of Reading in 'The Yellow Wallpaper'." *Studies in Short Fiction* 26, No. 1 (Winter 1989): 23-32.

    Uses Lacanian psychoanalysis to analyze "The Yellow Wallpaper," concluding that "in pursuit of a view of herself which is an ideological formation, the narrator misreads the yellow wallpaper, her other self, and in this way seeks to limit the play of its signifiers."

MacPike, Loralee. "Environment as Psychopathological Symbolism in 'The Yellow Wallpaper'." *American Literary Realism 1870-1910* 8, No. 3 (Summer 1975): 286-88.

    Analyzes objects depicted in 'The Yellow Wallpaper' as symbolic of the narrator's mental condition.

Martin, Jane Roland. *Reclaiming a Conversation: The Ideal of the Educated Woman.* New Haven: Yale University Press, 1985, 220 p.

    Compares the goals and methods for educating women set forth in Plato's *Republic,* Jean-Jacques Rousseau's *Emile,* Mary

Wollstonecraft's *Vindication of the Rights of Woman,* Catherine Beecher's *A Treatise on Domestic Economy,* and Gilman's *Herland.*

Miller, Margaret. "The Ideal Woman in Two Feminist Science-Fiction Utopias." *Science-Fiction Studies* 10, No. 30 (July 1983): 191-98.

Compares Gilman's vision of a female society in *Herland* to Suzy Charnas's in *Motherlines* (1978), identifying as common to both novels the assumption that a female society would be cooperative and nonhierarchical.

Porterfield, Amanda. "Science, Social Work, and Sociology" and "Changing the Space Inside a Room." In her *Feminine Spirituality in America: From Sarah Edwards to Martha Graham,* pp. 155-76, pp. 177-88. Philadelphia: Temple University Press, 1980.

Outlines Gilman's ideas on domesticity and discusses her short story "The Yellow Wallpaper" as a protest against the sanctity of the home and women's confinement to it.

Scharnhorst, Gary. "Making Her Fame: Charlotte Perkins Gilman in California." *California History* LXIV, No. 3 (Summer 1985): 192-201, 242-43.

Examines Gilman's participation in Nationalism, a social reform movement inspired by Edward Bellamy's utopian novel *Looking Backward* (1888). Scharnhorst notes that, "in her appeals on behalf of Nationalism, [Gilman] discussed in rudimentary form many of the ideas she elaborated later in her career," particularly that of the economic independence of women.

——. *Charlotte Perkins Gilman: A Bibliography.* Metuchen, N. J.: Scarecrow Press, 1985, 219 p.

Comprehensive bibliography which includes citations for Gilman's works, selected biographical sources, and selected criticism.

Veeder, William. "Who is Jane? The Intricate Feminism of Charlotte Perkins Gilman." *Arizona Quarterly* 44, No. 3 (Autumn 1988): 40-79.

Detailed reading of "The Yellow Wallpaper," in which Veeder finds that "the self-victimizing force of regressive inclinations and repressed desires" of the heroine were exacerbated by her marriage and led to her mental illness.

Henrik Ibsen

1828-1906

(Full name Henrik Johan Ibsen; also wrote under the pseudonym Brynjolf Bjarme) Norwegian dramatist and poet.

The following entry presents criticism of Ibsen's drama *Et dukkehjem* (*A Doll's House*), first published and performed in 1879. For discussion of Ibsen's complete career, including criticism of *A Doll's House*, see *TCLC*, Volumes 2 and 8; for discussion of the drama *Vildanden* (1884; *The Wild Duck*), see *TCLC*, Volume 16.

A Doll's House is among the most often performed and widely discussed plays by the dramatist who is regarded as the father of modern drama. This play, which portrays the collapse of a middle-class marriage, was one of the first in which Ibsen rejected the Romantic themes and techniques then prevalent in European theater in favor of depicting modern characters and current social issues in a realistic manner. It was extraordinarily controversial, arousing furious attack and impassioned defense for what was perceived as its assault on the foundations of moral convention.

A Doll's House belongs to the second phase of Ibsen's career, a period in which he turned from writing verse dramas with mythical and historical themes to writing social problem plays that are often called "plays of ideas." (In a final phase, Ibsen continued to deal with contemporary subjects in a realistic manner, but made increasing use of symbol and metaphor to create some of the most complex dramas in world literature.) Ibsen wrote *A Doll's House* while living abroad, in Italy and then Germany, during a twenty-seven-year period of voluntary exile from his native country. He had left Norway in 1864, embittered by his lack of success as a dramatist and as stage manager of the Norwegian National Theater in Bergen. Commentators suggest that a meeting with another Scandinavian expatriate, Danish critic Georg Brandes, was a factor in Ibsen's decision to introduce contemporary social issues into his drama. The first volume of Brandes's six-volume survey of European literature and culture, *Hovedstrømninger i det nittende aarhundredes litteratur* (1872-90; *Main Currents in Nineteenth-Century Literature*), contains the dictum that "what is alive in modern literature shows in its capacity to submit problems to debate," and a recurring theme of *Main Currents* is that of individual opposition to prevailing social views. Both of these concepts are integral to the plays of Ibsen's middle and latter periods.

A Doll's House opens with a scene of interplay between Nora Helmer and her husband Torvald that reveals a great deal about their relationship. Torvald alternately indulges and admonishes his wife in the manner of an authoritarian parent. Nora, for her part, is adept at cajoling what she wants from her husband. It soon becomes evident that Nora has never been taken seriously, but rather has been treated like a delightful child, first by her father and then her husband. A conversation between Nora and a friend reveals that early in the Helmers' eight-year marriage, they traveled to Italy on a trip that doctors assured Nora was necessary to Torvald's health, although he was not told about the seriousness of his condition. He believed that the trip was financed by Nora's father;

in fact, Nora forged her dying father's name to obtain a loan from the disreputable lawyer Nils Krogstad. When Krogstad attempts to use the forgery to blackmail Torvald into giving him a job at the bank where Torvald is the newly appointed manager, Torvald furiously denounces Nora for thus putting them in Krogstad's power, and for what he characterizes as her stupidity and immorality. When Krogstad has a change of heart and returns the forged document, relinquishing his hold over the Helmers, Torvald assumes the marriage will continue as before. Nora, however, protests that she has been treated unfairly in being denied the opportunity to participate in her marriage and in society as an informed adult. She announces her intention to leave her husband and children in order to educate herself. The play concludes with the sound of the door closing behind her.

Commentators have ascribed to *A Doll's House* the effect of a bomb going off in the decorous drawing rooms of the Victorian era. While Edmund Gosse and William Archer had supplied translations as well as commentary on Ibsen's play since the 1870s, reaction to the English premiere of *A Doll's House* in 1889 elicited the first sustained English-language criticism of Ibsen's drama. Reviewers at first asserted that the play's conclusion was implausible, with one critic stating: "In spite of Ibsen or any other theorist, it may be confidently asserted that no woman who ever breathed would do any such thing." However, Michael Egan noted that "as the presumed implications of *A Doll's House* made themselves felt, the tone soon changed from a mild refusal to suspend disbelief to a bitter antagonism. Nora's departure, presented with the dramatist's approbation and as the apparent moral of the play, was viewed by a shocked public as a direct attack on the institution of marriage." Critics contended that Ibsen and his advocates were promoting divorce and child abandonment. The play was not performed in Germany until Ibsen reluctantly supplied an alternate ending in which Nora could not bring herself to leave her children; some adaptations performed in England and the United States also concluded with Nora securely in place in her dollhouse. Attacks were countered with praise by such critics as Gosse, Archer, and Bernard Shaw, who saw in Ibsen a powerful proponent of the iconoclastic, didactic drama that Shaw himself advocated. Many defenses of the play, however, were based on interpretations as narrow as the outraged attacks. Some critics, for example, maintained that Ibsen's sole purpose was to demonstrate the need for social changes regarding women's rights and the status of women in marriage. Indeed, the play was most often interpreted—both approvingly and disapprovingly—as a feminist tract, despite Ibsen's insistence that *A Doll's House* was not specifically about the plight of subjugated women, but about the repression of individuality within the narrowly circumscribed roles afforded by bourgeois society.

While the passage of time lessened the sensation caused by Ibsen's social problem plays, the ideological aspects of his dramas remain of paramount interest to critics, who often focus on the philosophical, sociological, and psychological ideas that can be gleaned from them. Some commentators note that although Ibsen's works were often conceived around a central idea or philosophical tenet, the plays themselves are largely free of tendentiousness. Critics especially praise *A Doll's House* for its tight, dynamic dialogue, adept characterization, and masterful use of retrospective exposition.

A Doll's House is often regarded as a pivotal work in the history of the theater. It was innovative in many respects—for example, in presenting a tragedy involving not the mighty and powerful, but recognizable members of middle-class society. Further, Ibsen's deft portrayal of psychological tension rather than external action is considered to have been instrumental in instituting a new style of acting, requiring that emotion be conveyed through small, controlled gestures, shifts in inflection, and pauses. *A Doll's House* retains great emotional impact when viewed in performance and is considered a masterpiece of world drama.

(See also *Contemporary Authors*, Vol. 104.)

EDMUND GOSSE (essay date 1889)

[*Gosse was a prominent English man of letters during the late nineteenth century. A prolific literary historian, biographer, and critic, he remains most esteemed for a single and atypical work:* Father and Son: A Study of Two Temperaments *(1907), an account of his childhood that is considered among the most distinguished examples of Victorian spiritual autobiography. Gosse was also a major translator and critic of Scandinavian literature, and his importance as a critic is due primarily to his introduction of Ibsen to an English-speaking audience. In the following excerpt, he speculates that* A Doll's House *aroused controversy because the play features a female protagonist seeking individuality.*]

No work of Ibsen's, not even his beautiful Puritan opera of **Brand,** has excited so much controversy as *A Doll's House.* This was, no doubt, to a very great extent caused by its novel presentment of the mission of woman in modern society. In the dramas and romances of modern Scandinavia, and especially in those of Ibsen and Björnson, the function of woman had been clearly defined. She was to be the helper, the comforter, the inspirer, the guerdon of man in his struggle towards loftier forms of existence. When man fell on the upward path, woman's hand was to be stretched to raise him; when man went wandering away on ill and savage courses, woman was to wait patiently over her spinning-wheel, ready to welcome and to pardon the returning prodigal; when the eyes of man grew weary in watching for the morning-star, its rays were to flash through the crystal tears of woman. But in *A Doll's House* he confronted his audience with a new conception. Woman was no longer to be the shadow following man, or if you will, a *skin-leka* attending man, but an independent entity, with purposes and moral functions of her own. Ibsen's favourite theory of the domination of the individual had hitherto been confined to one sex; here he carries it over boldly to the other. The heroine of *A Doll's House,* the puppet in that establishment *pour rire* ["not to be taken seriously"], is Nora Helmer, the wife of a Christiania barrister. The character is drawn upon childish lines, which often may remind the English reader of Dora in *David Copperfield.* She has, however, passed beyond the Dora stage when the play opens. She is the mother of children, she has been a wife for half a dozen years. But the spoiling of injudicious parents has been succeeded by the spoiling of a weak and silly husband. Nora remains childish, irrational, concentrated on tiny cares and empty interests, without self-control or self-respect. Her doctor and her husband have told her not to give way to her passion for "candy" in any of its seductive forms; but she is introduced to us greedily eating macaroons on the sly, and denying that she has touched one when suspicion is aroused.

Here, then in Nora Helmer, the poet starts with the figure of a woman in whom the results of the dominant will of man, stultifying the powers and gifts of womanhood, are seen in their extreme development. Environed by selfish kindness, petted and spoiled for thirty years of dwarfed existence, this pretty, playful, amiable, and apparently happy little wife is really a tragical victim of masculine egotism. A nature exorbitantly desirous of leaning on a stronger will has been seized, condemned, absorbed by the natures of her father and her husband. She lives in them and by them, without moral instincts of her own, or any law but their pleasure. The result of this weakness—this, as Ibsen conceives, criminal subordination of the individuality—is that when Nora is suddenly placed in a responsible position, when circumstances demand from her a moral judgment, she has none to give; the safety, even the comfort, of the man she loves precede all other considerations, and with a light heart she forges a document to shield her father or to preserve her husband's name. She sacrifices honour for love, her conscience being still in too rudimentary a state to understand that there can be any honour that is distinguishable from love. Thus Dora would have acted, if we can conceive Dora as ever thrown into circumstances which would permit her to use the pens she was so patient in holding. But Nora Helmer has capacities of undeveloped character which make her far more interesting than the, to say the truth, slightly fabulous Dora. Her insipidity, her dollishness, come from the incessant repression of her family life. She is buried, as it were, in cotton-wool, swung into artificial sleep by the egotistical fondling of the men on whom she depends for emotional existence. But when once she tears the wrappings away, and leaps from the pillowed hammock of her indolence, she rapidly develops an energy of her own, and the genius of the dramatist is displayed in the rare skill with which he makes us witness the various stages of this awaking. At last, in an extraordinary scene, she declares that she can no longer live in her doll's house; husband and wife sit down at opposite ends of a table, and argue out the situation in a dialogue which covers sixteen pages, and Nora dashes out into the city, into the night; while the curtain falls as the front door bangs behind her.

The world is always ready to discuss the problem of marriage, and this very fresh and odd version of *L'ecole des Femmes* [*The School for Wives*] excited the greatest possible interest throughout the north of Europe. The close of the play, in particular, was a riddle hard to be deciphered. Nora, it was said, might feel that the only way to develop her own individuality was to leave her husband, but why should she leave her children? The poet evidently held the relation he had described to be such an immoral one, in the deepest and broadest sense, that the only way out of the difficulty was to cut the Gordian knot, children or no children. In almost Nora's very last reply, moreover, there is a glimmer of relenting. The most wonderful of things may happen, she confesses; the reunion of a developed wife to a reformed husband is not, she hints, beyond the range of what is possible. We are left with the conviction that it rests with him, with Helmer, to allow himself to be led through the fires of affliction to the feet of a Nora who shall no longer be a doll. (pp. 113-15)

Edmund Gosse, "Ibsen's Social Dramas," in The Fortnightly Review, n.s. Vol. XLV, No. CCLXV, January 1, 1889, pp. 107-21.

CLEMENT SCOTT   (essay date 1889)

[*As theater critic for the* Daily Telegraph, *Britain's largest newspaper, from 1871 to 1898, Scott wielded enormous prestige and influence. He was one of Ibsen's bitterest opponents in England, attacking the dramatist and his works on moral grounds. In the following excerpt, he excoriates* A Doll's House.]

[There] are already signs of weakness in the over-vaunted Ibsen cause. The Ibsenites, failing to convince common-sense people of the justice of their case, are beginning as a last resource to "abuse the opposing counsel." Hard words and ill names are flying about. For serious argument the defenders of the new faith are falling back on *tu quoques* ["you toos"; childish name-calling]. Having shown us [in *A Doll's House*] a child-wife compounded of infantile tricks and capriciousness, a frivolous and irresponsible young person who does not hesitate to fib, and can, at a pinch, condescend to forge; a wife of eight years' standing who changes from a grown-up baby to an illogical preacher; a woman who, in a fit of disappointment, in spite of appeal to her honour, her maternity, her religion, her sense of justice, leaves the husband she has sworn to love, the home she has engaged to govern, and the children

she is made to cherish; having introduced us to the sensual Dr. Rank, who discusses hereditary disease and the fit of silk stockings with the innocent wife of his bosom friend; having contrasted the sublimated egoism of the husband Helmer with the unnatural selfishness of Nora, his wife; having flung upon the stage a congregation of men and women without one spark of nobility in their nature, men without conscience and women without affection, an unloveable, unlovely, and detestable crew—the admirers of Ibsen, failing to convince us of the excellence of such creatures, turn round and abuse the wholesome minds that cannot swallow such unpalatable doctrine, and the stage that has hitherto steered clear of such unpleasing realism.

Now what, after all this fuss, is the true story of Nora Helmer? She is the child of a fraudulent father, badly brought up, neglected at home, bred in an atmosphere of lovelessness, who has had no one to influence her in her girlhood's days for good. She marries the man of her choice, a practical, hard-headed, unromantic banker. There is no suggestion that the marriage is forced upon her; she does it of her own free will. For eight long years she is, apparently, as happy as the day is long. She is the mother of three handsome children; she idolises her prosaic husband; and her supreme joy is to ruin her white teeth with sweetstuff and macaroons, to dress Christmas trees, to play hide-and-seek with her adorable infants, and to bound like a frisky kitten about the sofas, chairs, and settees—a restless, frivolous, creature, who would drive any nervous man mad in a fortnight. Nora does not profess to be an intellectual companion to her husband, even if he wanted it. She has never once sighed for a communion of souls. Her household god is King Baby, so husband Helmer very sensibly leaves her to the enjoyment of her maternity and her macaroons. Ruskin very aptly remarks, "A woman may always help her husband by what she knows, however little; by what she half-knows or misknows she will only tease him."

From this point of view Nora is a rather undesirable companion. She misknows everything. She is all heart like a cabbage, and affectionate as many spoiled children are; but she does not know the value of money, the virtue of truth, or the penalty of a criminal action. She spends money, like other silly women, over "bargains;" she tells little innocent lies, because it is so funny; and, when her husband is ill, and wants a change, she forges a promissory note, because the object of borrowing the money is in her eyes a good one. It is the forged note that gets Nora into trouble. The holder of it presses for payment, and threatens to tell her husband. Now, this is the last thing that Nora desires. She feels that he thinks she is a good-natured little fool, and does not desire to be further humiliated in his eyes. He pinches her ear, and calls her by pet names, such as Squirrel, and Mouse, and Bird; but in all practical matters she is a positive hindrance to his ambition. The truth about the forged note will be very inconvenient to Nora's husband, in a commercial sense; it is mixed up with his position as a bank manager and his authority over the clerks; so, when Nora discovers that her innocent act is in reality a very serious one, she is in a pitiful plight indeed. She cannot consult her best woman friend, because that practical person despises Nora's senseless frivolity almost as much as her husband does. She cannot borrow the money from her husband's friend, the moribund doctor, because that very objectionable gentleman desires to be false to his friend before he departs for another world, and becomes rather too familiar before the family lamp is lighted. No one can fail to pity this poor, weak, defenceless little creature as she dances the tarantella with hysterical excitement, in order to prevent her serious husband going to the compromising post-box.

The crash is inevitable; and it comes. It was natural, no doubt, that Nora should believe that when her husband discovered her innocent blunder he would forgive her, and take the blame on his shoulders. But it was equally natural that a business man would, at the first blush of things, be very angry at the idea of forgery connected with his spotless name. At any rate, Helmer is very angry indeed. He forgets all his affection and endearments; he can think only of his personal injury. Helmer's attitude towards his child-wife is natural but unreasonable. Nora's conduct towards her husband, when the forged bill has been returned, and he has apologised for his impetuosity, is both unreasonable and unnatural. Here is embodied the germ of the Ibsen creed; here we have the first fruits of the "new gospel," the marvellous philosophical revelation that is to alter the order of our dramatic literature; here is the extraordinary "discovery" that is, forsooth, to place Henrik Ibsen on a platform with Shakespeare.

It is an unlovely, selfish creed—but let women hear it. Nora, when she finds her husband is not the ideal hero she imagined, determines to cap his egotism with her selfishness. It is to be an eye for an eye, a tooth for a tooth. Pardon she cannot grant, humiliation she will not recognise. The frivolous butterfly, the Swedish Frou-Frou, the spoiled plaything has mysteriously become an Ibsenite revivalist. There were no previous signs of her conversion, but she has exchanged playfulness for preaching. She, a loving, affectionate woman, forgets all about the eight years' happy married life, forgets the nest of the little bird, forgets her duty, her very instinct as a mother, forgets the three innocent children who are asleep in the next room, forgets her responsibilities, and does a thing that one of the lower animals would not do. A cat or dog would tear any one who separated it from its offspring, but the socialistic Nora, the apostle of the new creed of humanity, leaves her children almost without a pang. She has determined to leave her home. She cannot pass another night under her husband's roof, for he is "a stranger." She is a wife no longer; the atmosphere is hideous, for he is a "strange man." Her husband appeals to her, but in vain. He reminds her of her duty; she cannot recognise it. He appeals to her religion; she knows nothing about it. He recalls to her the innocent children; she has *herself* to look after now! It is all self, self, self! This is the ideal woman of the new creed; not a woman who is the fountain of love and forgiveness and charity, not the pattern woman we have admired in our mothers and our sisters, not the model of unselfishness and charity, but a mass of aggregate conceit and self-sufficiency, who leaves her home and deserts her friendless children because she has *herself* to look after. The "strange man" who is the father of her children has dared to misunderstand her; she will scorn his regrets and punish him. Why should the men have it all their own way, and why should women be bored with the love of their children when they have themselves to study? And so Nora goes out, delivers up her wedding-ring without a sigh, quits her children without a kiss, and bangs the door! And the husband cries, "A miracle! a miracle!" and well he may. It would be a miracle if he could ever live again with so unnatural a creature.

German audiences revolted against Ibsen's conclusion. They compelled him, against his conviction, to bring Nora back. The little children cried and the wife returned. But the Ibsenites were shocked. It was too conventional by far; the love of a mother for her children was too commonplace for the modern philosophical drama. And as yet the English public has said no word, except to sit with open-mouthed astonishment at the Ibsen stage, and to try to feel that good acting wholly atones for false sentiment. There are certain things in the play that err against good taste, not to be readily forgiven. Dr. Rank, with his nasty conversation, his medical theories, and his ill-judged discussions can hardly pass. But what are we to say of Ibsen's Nora—foolish, fitful, conceited, selfish, and unloveable Nora—who is to drive from the stage the loving and noble heroines who have adorned it and filled all hearts with admiration from the time of Shakespeare to the time of Pinero? (pp. 19-22)

Clement Scott, in a review of "A Doll's House," in The Theatre, *Vol. 14, No. 79, July, 1889, pp. 19-22.*

WILLIAM ARCHER (essay date 1889)

[*A Scottish dramatist and drama critic of the London stage in the late nineteenth and early twentieth centuries, Archer advocated that drama possess intellectual content as well as entertainment value. Best known as one of the earliest and most important translators of Ibsen, Archer was also instrumental in advancing the early career of Bernard Shaw. In the following excerpt, Archer addresses some of the criticisms directed against Ibsen and* A Doll's House.]

If we may measure fame by mileage of newspaper comment, Henrik Ibsen has for the past month been the most famous man in the English literary world. Since Robert Elsmere left the Church, no event in "coëval fictive art" (to quote a modern stylist) has exercised men's, and women's, minds so much as Nora Helmer's departure from her Doll's House. Indeed the latter exit may be said to have awakened even more vibrant echoes than the former; for, while Robert made as little noise as possible, Nora slammed the door behind her. Nothing could be more trenchant than her action, unless it be her speech. Whatever its merits or defects, *A Doll's House* has certainly the property of stimulating discussion. We are at present bandying the very arguments which hurtled around it in Scandinavia and in Germany nine years ago. When the play was first produced in Copenhagen, some one wrote a charming little satire upon it in the shape of a debate as to its tendency between a party of little girls around a nursery tea-table. It ended in the hostess, aged ten, gravely declaring that had the case been hers, she would have done exactly as Nora did. I do not know whether the fame of *A Doll's House* has reached the British nursery, but I have certainly read some comments on it which might very well have emanated from that abode of innocence.

Puerilities and irrelevances apart, the adult and intelligent criticism of Ibsen as represented in *A Doll's House,* seems to run on three main lines. It is said, in the first place, that he is not an artist but a preacher; secondly, that his doctrine is neither new nor true; thirdly, that in order to enforce it, he oversteps the limits of artistic propriety. I propose to look into these three allegations. First, however, I must disclaim all right to be regarded as in any way a mouthpiece for the poet's own views. My personal intercourse with Henrik Ibsen, though to me very pleasant and memorable, has been but slight. I view his plays from the pit, not from the author's box. Very likely—nay, certainly—I often misread his meaning. My only right to take part in the discussion arises from a long and loving study of all his writings, and from the minute familiarity with *A Doll's House* in particular, acquired in the course of translating and staging it.

Is it true, then, that he is a dramatic preacher rather than a dramatic poet? or, in other words, that his art is vitiated by didacticism? Some writers have assumed that in calling him didactic they have said the last word, and dismissed him for ever from the ranks of the great artists. Of them I would fain enquire what really great art is not didactic? The true distinction is not between didactic art and "art for art's sake," but between primarily didactic and ultimately didactic art. Art for art's sake, properly so called, is mere decoration; and even it, in the last analysis, has its gospel to preach. By primarily didactic art I mean that in which the moral bearing is obvious, and was clearly present to the artist's mind. By ultimately didactic art I mean that which essays to teach as life itself teaches, exhibiting the fact and leaving the observer to trace and formulate the underlying law. It is the fashion of the day to regard this unconsciously didactic art, if I may call it so—its unconsciousness is sometimes a very transparent pose—as essentially higher than the art which is primarily and consciously didactic, dynamic. Well, it is useless to dispute about higher and lower. From our point of view the Australians seem to be walking head-downwards, like flies on the ceiling; from their point of view we are in the same predicament; it all depends on the point of view. Ibsen certainly belongs, at any rate in his modern prose plays, to the consciously didactic artists whom you may, if you choose, relegate to a lower plane. But how glorious the company that will have to step down along with him! What were the Greek tragic poets if not consciously didactic? What is comedy, from time immemorial, but a deliberate lesson in life? Down Plautus; down Terence; down Molière and Holberg and Beaumarchais and Dumas! Calderon and Cervantes must be kind enough to follow; so must Schiller and Goethe. If German criticism is to be believed Shakespeare was the most hardened sermonizer of all literature; but in this respect I think German criticism is to be disbelieved. Shakespeare, then, may be left in possession of the pinnacle of Parnassus; but who shall keep him company? Flaubert, perhaps, and M. Guy de Maupassant?

The despisers of Ibsen, then, have not justified their position when they have merely proved, what no one disputes, that he is a didactic writer. They must further prove that his teaching kills his art. For my part, looking at his dramatic production all round, and excepting only the two great dramas in verse, *Brand* and *Peer Gynt,* I am willing to admit that his teaching does now and then, in perfectly trifling details, affect his art for the worse. Not his direct teaching—that, as it seems to me, he always inspires with the breath of life—but his proclivity to what I may perhaps call symbolic side-issues. In the aforesaid dramas in verse this symbolism is eminently in place; not so, it seems to me, in the realistic plays. I once asked him how he justified this tendency in his art; he replied that life is one tissue of symbols. "Certainly," I might have answered; "but when we have its symbolic side too persistently obtruded upon us, we lose the sense of reality, which, according to your own theory, the modern dramatist should above all things aim at." There may be some excellent answer to this criticism; I give it for what it is worth. Apart from these symbolic details, it seems to me that Ibsen is singularly successful in vitalising his work; in reproducing the forms, the phenomena of life, as well as its deeper meanings. Let us take the example nearest at hand—*A Doll's House.* I venture to say—for this is a matter of fact rather than of opinion—that in the minds of thousands in Scandinavia and Germany,

Nora Helmer lives with an intense and palpitating life such as belongs to few fictitious characters. Habitually and instinctively men pay Ibsen the compliment (so often paid to Shakespeare) of discussing her as though she were a real woman, living a life of her own, quite apart from the poet's creative intelligence. The very critics who begin by railing at her as a puppet end by denouncing her as a woman. She irritates, troubles, fascinates them as no puppet ever could. Moreover, the triumph of the actress is the dramatist's best defence. Miss Achurch might have the genius of Rachel and Desclée in one, yet she could not transmute into flesh and blood the doctrinary doll, stuffed with sawdust and sophistry, whom some people declare Nora to be. Men do not shudder at the agony or weep over the woes of an intellectual abstraction. As for Helmer, I am not aware that any one has accused him of unreality. He is too real for most people—he is commonplace, unpleasant, objectionable. The truth is, he touches us too nearly; he is the typical husband of what may be called chattel matrimony. If there are few Doll's-Houses in England, it is certainly for lack of Noras, not for lack of Helmers. I admit that in my opinion Ibsen has treated Helmer somewhat unfairly. He has not exactly disguised, but has omitted to emphasize, the fact that if Helmer helped to make Nora a doll, Nora helped to make Helmer a prig. By giving Nora all the logic in the last scene (and she is not a scrupulous dialectician) he has left the casual observer to conclude that he lays the whole responsibility on Helmer. This conclusion is not just, but it is specious; and so far, and so far only, I grant that the play has somewhat the air of a piece of special pleading. I shall presently discuss the last scene in greater detail; but even admitting for the moment that the polemist here gets the better of the poet, can we call the poet, who has moved freely through two acts and two-thirds, nothing but a doctrinary polemist?

Let me add that *A Doll's House* is, of all Ibsen's plays, the one in which a definite thesis is most tangibly posited—the one, therefore, which is most exposed to the reproach of being a mere sociological pamphlet. His other plays may be said to scintillate with manifold ethical meanings; here the light is focussed upon one point in the social system. I do not imply that *A Doll's House* is less thoroughly vitalized than *Ghosts,* or *Rosmersholm,* or *The Lady from the Sea.* What I mean is, that the play may in some eyes acquire a false air of being merely didactic from the fortuitous circumstance that its moral can be easily formulated.

The second line of criticism is that which attacks the substance of Ibsen's so-called doctrines, on the ground that they are neither new nor true. To the former objection one is inclined to answer curtly but pertinently, "Who said they were?" It is not the business of the creative artist to make the great generalisations which mark the stages of intellectual and social progress. Certainly Ibsen did not discover the theory of evolution or the doctrine of heredity, any more than he discovered gravitation. He was not the first to denounce the subjection of women; he was not the first to sneer at the "compact liberal majority" of our pseudo-democracies. His function is to seize and throw into relief certain aspects of modern life. He shows us society as Kean was said to read Shakespeare—by flashes of lightning—luridly, but with intense vividness. He selects subjects which seem to him to illustrate such and such political, ethical, or sociological ideas; but he does not profess to have invented the ideas. They are common property; they are in the air. A grave injustice has been done him of late by those of his English admirers who have set him up as a social prophet, and have sometimes omitted to mention that he is a bit of a poet as well. It is so much easier to import an idea than the flesh and blood, the imagination, the passion, the style in which it is clothed. People have heard so much of the "gospel according to Ibsen" that they have come to think of him as a mere hot-gospeller, the Boanerges of some strange social propaganda. As a matter of fact Ibsen has no gospel whatever, in the sense of a systematic body of doctrine. He is not a Schopenhauer, and still less a Comte. There never was a less systematic thinker. Truth is not, in his eyes, one and indivisible; it is many-sided, many-visaged, almost Protean. It belongs to the irony of fate that the least dogmatic of thinkers—the man who has said of himself, "I only ask: my call is not to answer"—should figure in the imagination of so many English critics as a dour dogmatist, a vendor of social nostrums in pilule form. He is far more of a paradoxist than a dogmatist. A thinker he is most certainly, but not an inventor of brand new notions such as no one has ever before conceived. His originality lies in giving intense dramatic life to modern ideas, and often stamping them afresh, as regards mere verbal form, in the mint of his imaginative wit.

The second allegation, that his doctrines are not true, is half answered when we have insisted that they are not put forward (at any rate by Ibsen himself) as a body of inspired dogmas. No man rejects more consistently than he the idea of finality. He does not pretend to have said the last word on any subject. "You needn't believe me unless you like," says Dr. Stockmann in *An Enemy of the People,* "but truths are not the tough old Methuselahs people take them to be. A normally constituted truth lives, let us say, some seventeen or eighteen years; at most twenty." The telling of absolute truths to put it in another way, is scarcely Ibsen's aim. He is more concerned with destroying conventional lies, and exorcising the "ghosts" of dead truths; and most of all concerned to make people think and see for themselves. Here again we recognise the essential injustice of regarding a dramatic poet as a sort of prophet-professor who means all his characters say and makes them say all he means. I have been asked, for example, whether Ibsen intends us to understand by the last scene of *A Doll's House* that awakened wives ought to leave their husbands and children in order to cultivate their souls in solitude. Ibsen intends nothing of the sort. He draws a picture of a typical household; he creates a man and woman with certain characteristics; he places them in a series of situations which at once develop their characters and suggest large questions of conduct; and he makes the woman, in the end, adopt a course of action which he (rightly or wrongly) believes to be consistent with her individual nature and circumstances. It is true that this course of action is so devised as to throw the principles at stake into the strongest relief; but the object of that is to make people thoroughly realise the problem, not to force upon them the particular solution arrived at in this particular case. No two life-problems were ever precisely alike, and in stating and solving one, Ibsen does not pretend to supply a ready-made solution for all the rest. He illustrates, or, rather, illumines, a general principle by a conceivable case; that is all. To treat Nora's arguments in the last scene of *A Doll's House* as though they were the ordered propositions of an essay by John Stuart Mill is to give a striking example of the strange literalness of the English mind, its inability to distinguish between drama and dogma. To me that last scene is the most moving in the play, precisely because I hold it the most dramatic. It has been called a piece of pure logic—is it not rather logic conditioned by character

and saturated with emotion? Some years ago I saw *Et Dukkehjem* acted in Christiania. It was an off season; only the second-rate members of the company were engaged; and throughout two acts and a half I sat vainly striving to recapture the emotions I had so often felt in reading the play. But the moment Nora and Helmer were seated face to face, at the words, "No, that is just it; you do not understand me; and I have never understood you—till to-night"—at that moment, much to my own surprise, the thing suddenly gripped my heart-strings; to use an expressive Americanism, I "sat up;" and every phrase of Nora's threnody over her dead dreams, her lost illusions, thrilled me to the very marrow. Night after night I went to see that scene; night after night I have watched it in the English version; it has never lost its power over me. And why? Not because Nora's sayings are particularly wise or particularly true, but because, in her own words, they are so true *for her,* because she feels them so deeply and utters them so exquisitely. Certainly she is unfair, certainly she is one-sided, certainly she is illogical; if she were not, Ibsen would be the pamphleteer he is supposed to be, not the poet he is. "I have never been happy here—only merry. . . . You have never loved me—you have only found it amusing to be in love with me." Have we not in these speeches the very mingling of truth and falsehood, of justice and injustice, necessary to humanise the character and the situation? After Nora has declared her intention of leaving her home, Helmer remarks, "Then there is only one explanation possible—You no longer love me." "No," she replies, "that is just it." "Nora! can you say so?" cries Helmer, looking into her eyes. *Oh, I'm so sorry, Torvald,"* she answers, *"for you've always been so kind to me."* Is this pamphleteering? To me it seems like the subtlest human pathos. Again, when she says "At that moment it became clear to me that I had been living here for eight years with a strange man and had borne him three children—Oh, I can't bear to think of it! I could tear myself to pieces"—who can possibly take this for anything but a purely dramatic utterance? It is true and touching in Nora's mouth, but it is obviously founded on a vague sentiment, that may or may not bear analysis. Nora postulates a certain transcendental community of spirit as the foundation and justification of marriage. The idea is very womanly and may also be very practical; but Ibsen would probably be the first to admit that before it can claim the validity of a social principle we must ascertain whether it be possible for any two human beings to be other than what Nora would call strangers. This further analysis the hearer must carry out for him, or her, self. The poet has stimulated thought; he has not tried to lay down a hard-and-fast rule of conduct. Again, when Helmer says, "No man sacrifices his honour even for one he loves," and Nora retorts, *"Millions of women have done that!"* we applaud the consummate claptrap, not on account of its abstract justice, but rather of its characteristic injustice. Logically, it is naught; dramatically, one feels it to be a masterstroke. Here, it is the right speech in the right place; in a sociological monograph it would be absurd. My position, in short, is that in Ibsen's plays, as in those of any other dramatist who keeps within the bounds of his form, we must look, not for the axioms and demonstrations of a scientific system; but simply for "broken lights" of truth, refracted through character and circumstance. The playwright who sends on a Chorus or a lecturer, unconnected with the dramatic action, to moralise the spectacle and put all the dots on all the i's, may fairly be taken to task for the substance of his "doctrines." But that playwright is Dumas, not Ibsen.

Lastly, we come to the assertion that Ibsen is a "coarse" writer, with a morbid love for using the theatre as a physiological lecture-room. Here again I can only cry out upon the chance which has led to so grotesque a misconception. He has written some twenty plays, of which all except two might be read aloud, with only the most trivial omissions, in any young ladies' boarding-school from Tobolsk to Tangiers. The two exceptions are *A Doll's House* and *Ghosts*—the very plays which happen to have come (more or less) within the ken of English critics. In *A Doll's House* he touches upon, in *Ghosts* he frankly faces, the problem of hereditary disease, which interests him, not in itself, but simply as the physical type and symbol of so many social and ethical phenomena. *Ghosts* I have not space to consider. If art is for ever debarred from entering upon certain domains of human experience, then *Ghosts* is an inartistic work. I can only say, after having read it, seen it on the stage, and translated it, that no other modern play seems to me to fulfil so entirely the Aristotelian ideal of purging the soul by means of terror and pity. In *A Doll's House,* again, there are two passages, one in the second and one in the third act, which Mr. Podsnap could not conveniently explain to the young lady in the dress-circle. Whether the young lady in the dress-circle would be any the worse for having them explained to her is a question I shall not discuss. As a matter of fact, far from being coarsely treated, they are so delicately touched that the young person suspects nothing and is in no way incommoded. It is Mr. Podsnap himself that cries out—the virtuous Podsnap who, at the French theatre, writhes in his stall with laughter at speeches and situations *à faire rougir des singes* ["that would make a monkey blush"]. I have more than once been reproached, by people who had seen *A Doll's House* at the Novelty, with having cut the speeches which the first-night critics pronounced objectionable. It has cost me some trouble to persuade them that not a word had been cut, and that the text they found so innocent contained every one of the enormities denounced by the critics. Mr. Podsnap, I may add, has in this case shown his usual alacrity in putting the worst possible interpretation upon things. Dr. Rank's declaration to Nora that Helmer is not the only man who would willingly lay down his life for her, has been represented as a hideous attempt on the part of a dying debauchee to seduce his friend's wife. Nothing is further from the mind of poor Rank, who, by the way, is not a debauchee at all. He knows himself to be at death's door; Nora, in her Doll's House, has given light and warmth to his lonely, lingering existence; he has silently adored her while standing with her, as with her husband, on terms of frank comradeship; is he to leave her for ever without saying, as he puts it, "Thanks for the light"? Surely this is a piece either of inhuman austerity or of prurient prudery; surely Mrs. Podsnap herself could not feel a suspicion of insult in such a declaration. True, it comes inaptly at that particular moment, rendering it impossible for Nora to make the request she contemplates. But essentially, and even from the most conventional point of view, I fail to see anything inadmissible in Rank's conduct to Nora. Nora's conduct to Rank, in the stocking scene, is another question; but that is merely a side-light on the relation between Nora and Helmer, preparatory, in a sense, to the scene before Rank's entrance in the last act.

In conclusion, what are the chances that Ibsen's modern plays will ever take a permanent place on the English stage? They are not great, it seems to me. The success of *A Doll's House* will naturally encourage Ibsen's admirers to further experiments in the same direction—interesting and instructive experiments I have no doubt. We shall see in course of time *The League of Youth, The Pillars of Society, An Enemy of the People, Rosmersholm,* and *The Lady from the Sea*—I name them in chronological order. But none of these plays presents the double attraction that has made the success of *A Doll's House*—the distinct plea for female emancipation which appeals to the thinking public, and the overwhelming part for an actress of genius which attracts the ordinary playgoer. The other plays, I cannot but foresee, will be in a measure antiquated before the great public is ripe for a thorough appreciation of them. I should like to see an attempt made to produce one of the poet's historical plays, but that would involve an outlay for costumes and mounting not to be lightly faced. On the other hand I have not the remotest doubt that Ibsen will bulk more and more largely as years go on in the consciousness of all students of literature in general, as opposed to the stage in particular. The creator of *Brand* and *Peer Gynt* is one of the great poets of the world. (pp. 30-7)

William Archer, "Ibsen and English Criticism," in The Fortnightly Review, *n.s. Vol. XLVI, No. CCLXXI, July 1, 1889, pp. 30-7.*

BERNARD SHAW   (essay date 1890)

[*Shaw is generally considered the greatest dramatist to write in the English language since Shakespeare. His drama reveals Ibsen's influence, dispensing with the romantic conventions and devices of the well-made play to institute a theater of ideas grounded in realism. As drama critic for the* Saturday Review *from 1895 until 1898, Shaw set forth his determination that the theater should become a "moral institution" conveying socially progressive ideas. In the following excerpt, Shaw briefly outlines the action of* A Doll's House, *suggesting that the play functions as propaganda to demonstrate the fundamental falseness that can underlie ordinary domestic relationships.*]

Pillars of Society, as a propagandist play, is disabled by the circumstance that the hero, being a fraudulent hypocrite in the ordinary police-court sense of the phrase, is not accepted as a typical pillar of society by the class which he represents. Accordingly, Ibsen took care next time to make his idealist irreproachable from the standpoint of the ordinary idealist morality. In the famous *Doll's House,* the pillar of society who owns the doll is a model husband, father, and citizen. In his little household, with the three darling children and the affectionate little wife, all on the most loving terms with one another, we have the sweet home, the womanly woman, the happy family life of the idealist's dream. Mrs. Nora Helmer is happy in the belief that she has attained a valid realization of all these illusions—that she is an ideal wife and mother, and that Helmer is an ideal husband who would, if the necessity arose, give his life to save her reputation. A few simply contrived incidents disabuse her effectually on all these points. One of her earliest acts of devotion to her husband has been the secret raising of a sum of money to enable him to make a tour which was necessary to restore his health. As he would have broken down sooner than go into debt, she has had to persuade him that the money was a gift from her father. It was really obtained from a moneylender, who refused to make her the loan unless she induced her father to endorse the promissory note. This being impossible, as her father was dying at the time, she took the shortest way out of the difficulty by writing the name herself, to the entire satisfaction of the moneylender, who, though not at all duped, knows that forged bills are often the surest to be paid. Then she slaves in secret at scrivener's work until she has nearly paid off the debt. At this point Helmer is made manager of the bank in which he is employed; and the moneylender, wishing to obtain a post there, uses the forged bill to force Nora to exert her influence with Helmer on his behalf. But she, having a hearty contempt for the man, cannot be persuaded by him that there was any harm in putting her father's name on the bill, and ridicules the suggestion that the law would not recognize that she was right under the circumstances. It is her husband's own contemptuous denunciation of a forgery formerly committed by the moneylender himself that destroys her self-satisfaction and opens her eyes to her ignorance of the serious business of the world to which her husband belongs—the world outside the home he shares with her. When he goes on to tell her that commercial dishonesty is generally to be traced to the influence of bad mothers, she begins to perceive that the happy way in which she plays with the children, and the care she takes to dress them nicely, are not sufficient to constitute her a fit person to train them. In order to redeem the forged bill, she resolves to borrow the balance due upon it from a friend of the family. She has learnt to coax her husband into giving her what she asks by appealing to his affection for her: that is, by playing all sorts of pretty tricks until he is wheedled into an amorous humor. This plan she has adopted without thinking about it, instinctively taking the line of least resistance with him. And now she naturally takes the same line with her husband's friend. An unexpected declaration of love from him is the result; and it at once explains to her the real nature of the domestic influence she has been so proud of. All her illusions about herself are now shattered; she sees herself as an ignorant and silly woman, a dangerous mother, and a wife kept for her husband's pleasure merely; but she only clings the harder to her delusion about him: he is still the ideal husband who would make any sacrifice to rescue her from ruin. She resolves to kill herself rather than allow him to destroy his own career by taking the forgery on himself to save her reputation. The final disillusion comes when he, instead of at once proposing to pursue this ideal line of conduct when he hears of the forgery, naturally enough flies into a vulgar rage and heaps invectives on her for disgracing him. Then she sees that their whole family life has been a fiction—their home a mere doll's house in which they have been playing at ideal husband and father, wife and mother. So she leaves him then and there in order to find out the reality of things for herself, and to gain some position not fundamentally false, refusing to see her children again until she is fit to be in charge of them, or to live with him until she and he become capable of a more honorable relation to one another than that in which they have hitherto stood. He at first cannot understand what has happened, and flourishes the shattered ideals over her as if they were as potent as ever. He presents the course most agreeable to him—that of her staying at home and avoiding a scandal—as her duty to her husband, to her children, and to her religion; but the magic of these disguises is gone; and at last even he understands what has really happened, and sits down alone to wonder whether that more honorable relation can ever come to pass between them. (pp. 82-6)

Bernard Shaw, in his The Quintessence of Ibsenism, *B. R. Tucker, 1891, 170 p.*

LOU SALOMÉ (essay date 1892)

[*Salomé was a Russian journalist, novelist, and critic. Prominent in European literary and intellectual circles, she included Friedrich Nietzsche, Sigmund Freud, and Ibsen among her close acquaintances. Salomé's* Henrik Ibsen's Frauengestalten (Ibsen's Heroines), *published in German in 1892 and translated into Norwegian the following year, is one of the earliest extended studies of Ibsen's drama and the first examination by a woman of Ibsen's representation of female characters. In the following essay, Salomé offers an impressionistic interpretation of the character of Nora Helmer from* A Doll's House *and a description of the play's action.*]

Shortly before Christmas Eve, a Christmas tree already is in place in the warm and cozy living room of the newly appointed bank director Torvald Helmer. Colors shimmer down from all the tree branches, and the deep, fresh green of the tree almost disappears amid a glittering shower. In its childish splendor of gilded paper and candles, the tree stands expectantly in the smile of a waning day, an object not created for sober contemplation. Decorated as handsomely as possible, the tree awaits the fall of night. In the pomp and glitter, a mysteriously growing light anticipates twilight, ready to flare up brightly and blindingly, and to transform everything into a flashing display, into the luminous miracle of Christmas Eve.

Nora's inner life can be reconstructed through the temper and tone of this impending Christmas eve. Upon her first appearance, she is laden with shrouded holiday parcels; surrounding her deepest conflicts and dreams are secret festivity and presents. With a trustful and childlike anticipation of twilight, she awaits a wonder.

Christmas is a children's festival, and Nora is a child. Her childishness creates her charm, her danger, and her destiny. As the sole daughter of a widower who in his carefree ways spoiled her instead of bringing her up seriously, Nora grew older only in age. The transformation from her carefree days as a girl to marriage meant no more to her than a change from a small doll's house to a larger one; the main difference was that instead of her customary lifeless wax dolls, she would eventually receive three precious living dolls.

She brought her accustomed love for both play and parent to her marriage with Helmer; it was a love developed in the relationship between daughter and father—devoted, sincere—in which she looked upward with the open-eyed adoration of a child. "When I lived at home," Nora told Doctor Rank, a frequent visitor, "naturally, I loved father above all else. . . . You can well imagine that being with Torvald is just like being with father."

This childish innocence and inexperience permits her to assume without question that her husband embodies everything that is good and noble, as does a father in the eyes of a child. And so, courtship and marriage must seem to her a superabundant gift which one is obliged to accept thankfully and uncritically; it is also a mysterious and precious gift, toward which one is led blindfolded, with good manners. She is overwhelmed and can hardly grasp the magnitude of the gift, the love offering. For the husband who towers so high above her has not only inclined himself to give fatherly solicitude and accustomed sustenance, but out of his free choice has elevated her to be his wife, to be one with him. It seems to her like an incomprehensible miracle, and she believes in it as a child would. With this sense of the miraculous there awakens in her for the first time a new, exclusive world and a development—a world of humility and pride; an unconstrained giving of herself to her husband; together with the first stirrings of her search for self-identity and worth. The first impulses of her slumbering strength are awakened; instinctively she attempts to come into her own in order to be capable of making a yielding gift of herself. Her slumber is dissipated by anticipatory dreams of a true marriage.

What takes shape in Nora's innermost being temporarily lies hidden from her own sensibility and remains largely unintelligible to her. Within her lies a tender, invisible but prospective seed; that seed is covered by the crisp and proliferating weeds and flowers of her carefree nature. She remains in her small, circumscribed world of play and vanity. High and remote above arches a sky of miracles, and its infinite blue she sees joyously reflected in humans and things. Though distanced from reality, she gradually senses that her relationship with Torvald Helmer is that of a charming child to a parent, and not one of equals. Yet, ever more patiently, she looks for a miracle from above.

"I have waited," she says toward the end, "so patiently for eight years; God knows, I realized quite well that wonderful things cannot come as daily commonplaces." Helmer has no inkling of her expectations. Nothing lies farther from his mind than changing their relationship; in no way does he share Nora's need for self-fulfillment, equality and mutual growth. At the core, she remained childlike, while he was a self-satisfied adult. The wish for growth is a child's pleasure that trustingly demands self-transcendence. For Helmer, that would be as unwelcome as outgrowing accustomed clothes. Considerately, he does not constrain her playful nature, but he must prevent her wish. After all, he had taken her measure and found an undeveloped personality who would fit precisely into that doll's house into which he led her.

Nora's love is at home in some wonderland, while his is anchored in his doll's house. Childlike love entwines itself, like a vine, on the lover, and negligently the toys and dolls of earlier years fall from her hands. The self-satisfied and assured adult, who has no one to look up to, deliberately chooses for his love-object a toy or doll for the idle hours between important business. He chooses a "squirrel" that can perform tricks when he is bored; a "skylark" that can sing away a sour mood; and a "nibbly cat," made sufficiently happy by proffered candy during a light mood. Content with himself and Nora, he smugly says, "I do not want you to be anything but what you are, my lovely, dear little skylark."

It really does not occur to him that it was his love that gave impetus to her development and the extension of her life's horizon, with intimations of something infinite. His sealed doll's house does not lend itself to disruptive change; it must retain his sense of comfortable order. Love in the doll's house cannot be expansive, but can only be added to with gay decorations. Helmer loves the picture of Nora happily humming as she strews the Christmas tree with colorful strips; that, he feels, is her true mission in life. Nothing warns him that the childish birdsong warbling from her lips bridges over into a silent hymn of a blessed—but vain—expectation of a Christmas miracle whose flame can only be lit by him.

Nora does not know that love and beauty have opposite meanings for them both. She does not yet know that Helmer's delight in simple gaiety and loveliness is, at the same time, a conventional person's reluctance to face any serious struggle which could disturb the aesthetic somnolence that allows him to enjoy life with self-satisfaction. It is not without reason then that Doctor Rank, the sick friend of the family, avoids having Helmer attend to him during his struggle with death. He knows that Helmer has "a pronounced repugnance

to anything which is ugly." And not unfittingly is the turn in Nora's destiny entwined with Helmer's in the profound struggle that ensues. The view he offers her turns her love into death.

The apparent moral strength that Helmer fosters, his need to appear above reproach and to retain his dignity without stain, all the self-control evidenced in his daily life, is rooted in a central egotistic pleasure-seeking. On the obverse side, however, there is an unmistakable sign of petty fears—the fears of a human to engage in conflict. The contrast between Nora's naïve judgments, undisciplined inclinations, and inherited disposition to frivolity and lavishness, and Helmer's correct bearing and rectitude most surely intimidate Nora. Appearances are deceiving: his self-satisfaction is disguised by a serious moral mien, while her deep-slumbering seriousness constantly seems to be transformed into a joyful child's face.

Sometimes she is provoked and tosses a lightning expletive into Helmer's nice, tidy, carefully constructed world. And it only takes a stressful situation to produce involuntary quarrels that stem from her actions. Long before their inner differences become evident to her, the seeds of conflict are sown by the many outer dissimilarities between care-free inexperience and well-cultivated strictness.

The possibility of gaining a cure for Helmer—when he was mortally ill—through a prolonged trip south is hampered by lack of money. Nora's pleas that she be allowed to earn money shatter as Helmer forbids her efforts, and her father's death makes it impossible to enlist his help. In desperation she takes a dangerous step. Misled by a lack of experience, she forges her father's name on a bond and cashes a substantial sum; in effect, her borrowing places her in the hands of a pettifogging lawyer (named Krogstad) who pursues a variety of "business deals." Although this was the action of an unknowledgeable child who had always been left in the dark about such matters, Nora, through the years, shouldered the obligatory repayments with the energy and confidence of a man. Pretending that the money is her father's gift, she persuades Helmer to take the necessary vacation. Nora is in deep sorrow over her father's death, fearful for the health of her husband, and about to give birth to her first child. And still she can cajole and wheedle Helmer into believing that he is acceding only to her pleasure-seeking whims; he cannot be permitted to have an inkling of how ill he really is.

Upon Helmer's return home, she does not tell her cured husband of the obligations she has incurred through her action. All alone, secretly, and with tiring work, she undertakes repayment. Under the pretext of wrapping Christmas packages, she sits up nights and does copyist work. Good-naturedly she allows herself to be chided as a "nibbly cat" who wastes the monies for which she has begged, while in fact she had scrimped and skeletonized her own needs so that Helmer and the children had been deprived of nothing. The constant avoidances of the truth come easily to her because of her casual upbringing at home, so that small lies come as readily to her mouth as chirping does to birds. And despite the difficulties of her position, despite her privations, made doubly difficult by her inclinations to be a spendthrift, she feels a unique happiness in her serious and responsible accomplishment.

"It almost seemed to me as if I were a man!" she said. Strength and independence slowly unfold secretly and grope toward release. Although she is left in the dark and enmeshed in a network of lies, there comes the first unconscious expression of protest against her father and husband, both of whom have kept her in bondage to childishness and ignorance. But protest does not surface in her consciousness; on the contrary, she does not wish Helmer to take notice of her awakening self. A fine, feminine instinct decidedly tells her that she must keep the charm she possesses in Helmer's eyes; her naïve love-charms are poised against the sounder, stronger and more intelligent man. It is no dissimulation when she looks up to him with love and admiration. Her childlike façade, that hides much from others, is for Helmer no masking but the visage of true and humble love. With indignation, Nora rejects the advice of her childhood friend, Mrs. Linde, that she confess everything to Helmer, although Nora herself had confided her secret to Mrs. Linde, herself an experienced and diligent person, in order not to appear flighty.

"For heaven's sake, how can you advise that," she answered Mrs. Linde; "how painful and humiliating would it be for him as a male to know that he owes me something! That would bring our mutual relationship completely out of kilter, and our beautiful, happy homelife will no longer be what it now is!" Despite her hard-won and blissful independence, she does not in the least wish to play her trump card against him and change her admiring glances into the bold ones of an equal partner. It is not the sobriety of a strenuously won equality that she sees in her dreams of a true marriage; she seeks instead the miracle of an incomprehensible love that draws her upward toward him and increases in wonder the higher he, a god, towers over the child. The only value she places on her actions and intrinsic work is that they derive from her love. She excludes any thought that ultimately he could be displeased or indignant at the secret life of her last eight years.

She sums up that life in her confession: "I have loved you above everything in this world!" One cannot work for, nor earn, a miracle. It must surprise one, as does grace, spirituality, poetry. But in nothing do the energetic uniqueness and the urge for completion within her awakening individuality express themselves more clearly than in her recognition that expectation, longing, and trust must willy-nilly be transformed inwardly into creative action. She is not content to let the Christmas mood take its course, but she participates in the pleasure of preparing Christmas gifts. She works at her love-offering for Helmer when she strives to free herself; yet she wants to achieve her freedom only to make him a present of it. In darkness, secrecy, and behind closed doors it originates, destined to be among the Christmas gifts. That makes her proud and happy, expectant of a transformation.

The appearance of her old friend, Mrs. Linde, casts a harsh and sober pall over Nora's festive joy; Mrs. Linde resembles the hard workday—cold, joyless, and as grubby as her relentless work for bare necessities. The prohibition of every outer luxury, of everything that could be done without, constricted and oppressed Mrs. Linde's inner life; the potential richness of her nature was emasculated, and only utilitarian and sensible considerations found expression. Long ago she turned her back on the practicing lawyer Krogstad, a man she loved, and contracted a marriage that made the financial support of her mother, sisters, and brothers possible. And after a sad and bleak marriage, her husband died and left her nothing—not even a child to care for. Now she offers Krogstad her hand in order to save him from the shipwreck of his existence.

From her bitterness and loneliness she gathers whatever resources her heart once possessed, and she seeks one last, modest luxury within the long, tiring workdays of her life: *not* to work only and alone for one's bare necessities. Nora, on the contrary, draws this culminating conclusion from her marriage: "I have responsibilities to myself alone." That precisely was the most burdensome of all responsibilities for Mrs. Linde, and from which she now wishes to free herself at all cost. Nora later directs her gravest reproach against her husband's sealing her off from life, seriousness and experience, while Mrs. Linde, amid her coarse and lonely wanderings, searches for only one thing—a last, though modest, refuge from the battles of existence, which would house her love and care. It is like the fir-tree standing alone and forgotten in the wintry woods, prey to storms, not dreaming of Christmas lights and wonders; it knows what it is like to freeze outdoors and wishes to be used up in service to others, to bring warmth and happiness and comfort into peaceful homes, even if it means being the warmth-bringing comfort of a fired stove and not the aura of a Christmas celebration.

At the moment that Mrs. Linde sees her old friend, Krogstad, he is about to use Nora's forgery of her father's signature on the bond as blackmail against Helmer who has dismissed him from his minor clerical post at the bank. Only desperation drives Krogstad to such a step; for the sake of his motherless children, he must retain his hard-won place in society. He himself was outlawed by society for similar forgeries in his devious business dealings. Mrs. Linde's determination to marry him and be a mother to his children has an ennobling, mellowing effect upon him. The unexpected gift of trust and friendship awakens his good qualities, whereas his former friend, Helmer, in a short time will prove himself to be a selfish coward with regard to Nora's great love and trust. Helmer is a weakling whose only concern is with his reputation in society. In Krogstad's happy desire to again be worthy of his lover, he stands as high over Helmer as does Mrs. Linde over Nora, in respect to patience, experienced goodness, and maturity. And so, Mrs. Linde's words, "we need each other," initiate the life of a true marriage, despite struggles with inevitable problems, while Nora's dream about her marriage and belief in the integrity of her husband collapse.

Krogstad's threat to tell Nora's husband everything and to note that the bank director's wife is guilty of the same type of forgery that he himself had committed earlier, makes Nora aware for the first time of her endangered position. She now realizes that she is a guilty party in the eyes of the law. But she is even more disturbed when she hears from Helmer about the aversion inspired in him by a man like Krogstad who has committed a misstep without atoning for it; how such a person creates a corrupt environment, and how he spins a web of lies in which his children must grow up. Nora's fears rise and her well-kept secret no longer is a source of pride but an oppressive burden on her conscience. She makes every effort to persuade Helmer to rehire Krogstad. In vain. But at the same time that her adamant husband turns away her request he involuntarily affords an insight into the motives that make him so inflexible. Strangely affected and surprised, she sees that the main reasons for his attitude need not be sought in moralistic indignation. After all, he admits that he could have "overlooked perhaps" Krogstad's mistake. But "what if it were to become known that 'the new bank director's wife changed his mind for him'?"

And as for Nils Krogstad, he was the reminder of an old, unfortunate friendship, and "of this that tactless person makes no secret. . . . I assure you that this is most painful for me." Nora can hardly believe her ears; "Torvald, you can't be serious. . . . No, these are only trifles."

Here is her first, astonished insight into Helmer's basic character, piercing deep through the cloud of smug satisfaction in which he hovers above her. But danger and fear hem her in, so that her first feeling of strangeness regarding Helmer does not yet become a conscious estrangement. She does make a last, strenuous effort to save herself; she will ask Doctor Rank, and hopes to be able to placate Krogstad.

Yet her twilight conversation with the sick family-friend elicits a confession that voids her plan. In that dialogue, a well-rounded Nora emerges: she is indiscreet and childish, yet at the same time exhibits fine tact and the instinct of a mature woman—frivolous, capable of lying and coquetry, and yet there is purity clear to the roots of her being. She is inexperienced but has a noble and inherent disposition for the fullest self-education. With that last, shattered attempt, her hesitation and vacillations end; she becomes resolute. To Mrs. Linde she says, "You must prevent nothing." She knows that she is approaching a point of crisis: Helmer will find out everything and she will be lost. But she also knows that something else must occur at the same time—the wonderful thing, the revelation of his love which will intercede for her and take everything upon itself; a love that will cast her not as a playful and charming child but as a wife who has sacrificed herself for Helmer, who now will sacrifice himself for her.

Night descends and the glow and glitter of the day fades; with the first approach of darkness, the beaming Christmas wonder also draws near. To doubt it would also be to doubt Helmer's magnanimity and the greatness of his love. What may be punishable in the light of uncomprehending and unreasonable human laws, must instead be recognized by Helmer as the proof of her love; what appear to the judgment of strangers to be lies and deception will undoubtedly be regarded by Helmer as the blessed secret of a child who worked in stolen moments on Christmas gifts, and who then impatiently awaits her own.

She would not, however, accept his sacrifice; she would not want him to suffer for her sake. She will want to bear fully the consequences of her actions, to crawl silently out of his life, and through her death validate her innocence in all that happened. Even the thought of her children does not deter her from such intentions; it is painfully consoling to know that the children will find a better mother in her old and devoted governess. She has not as yet identified herself with the role of mother, nor indeed that of wife. Like a bride, instead, she remains in expectation of a true marriage. Only then would her own life be crowned and fulfilled, and she would learn of her exclusive mission.

For these reasons—and at that moment—she is able to subdue her thoughts about Helmer and the children. Heroically she is able to turn away from them, believing herself about to see the full unfolding of a wonder, like a child who peeks through doorcracks and spies the bustle about the Christmas tree and the first sparkle of lights. Despite all the fears, dangers, and sacrifices that mark the most important and deadly struggle in her life, a confession wells up: "After all, it is splendid to be waiting for a wonderful thing to happen." It is not to be. Nevertheless, for her to find such words speaks of her power, and lays claim to an audacious idealism from

Janet Achurch as Nora and Herbert Waring as Torvald, from an 1889 production of A Doll's House *in London.*

which rise, at the end, all her harshly true, sacred and measured words.

In stark contrast to her powerful mood, she is busy preparing for a masked ball, as the fateful letter from Krogstad is dropped into the mailbox of the house. While rehearsing steps for her dance, a *tarantella*—she tries to distract Helmer's attention from the letter.

In her efforts to seem unconcerned, Nora's usual frivolity bursts into abandoned and feverish wildness. What has matured and moved her far beyond the childish and the playful, she can only hide behind a mask in painful costuming. And so, her married life with Helmer expresses itself in an impromptu near manic performance of a studied dance, which he watches with harmless pleasure. Nothing warns him that this display of charm, this ultimate childlikeness, represents precisely the mere appearance of a boundless love, costumed for him yet one more time on her deathlike journey—while secretly she has readied a sober dress for a long wandering.

Helmer sees only the attractiveness of this love which lies intoxicatingly over her silent farewell. Champagne has roused his senses and stimulated desire for his wife. The words with which he pictures his intoxication are the replete expression of the poetry that streams from Nora to him, as well as of the worthlessness of his character which cannot cull anything deeper from such a love than a captive ornament for his comfortable existence. Delirium and love therefore dissipate as rapidly as does the champagne's inebriation. The letter lies in his hands. With tortured fright he is seized by the fear of the consequences of Nora's past actions on his behalf. In manic anger, he heaps scorn upon Nora and casts her out from his heart—but not from his home, because he wishes to keep appearances up for the sake of outsiders.

For Nora, things collapse; she feels as if the world were suddenly godless. Silent and petrified she stands before Helmer. What had remained to be taught her of cares and experience, now is completed in one instant: she suddenly sees life as it is, in the shape of Helmer, a conventional, pained person who is saturated with fear and selfishness. All her life and attentiveness has been focused on him. Since her life was sustained by *his* truth and interpretations, only through *him* could her life be shorn of God and thus destroyed. Even if her maturity had grown equal to the experience of this hour, her childlike heart in its depth retained faith, and her life its wonders. Even if everything else—independence and personal growth—lay waiting in anticipation, this new and singular situation launched her emancipation.

And in the midst of Helmer's outbreaks of fear and anger comes Krogstad's second letter, accompanied with the bond, written in the mellow mood of his new-found happiness. "I am saved!" is Helmer's first outcry, "Nora, I am saved." Quietly she asks, "And I?" Obviously, she too is saved. And now, in a new light, she is clear about her situation and their relationship. With one blow, her moral indignation evaporates. Helmer sympathetically acknowledges her struggles and assures Nora of his willingness to forgive her. Indeed, he finds her doubly touching in her inexperience and helplessness; he assures Nora that her weakness endears her to him all the more because he can serve now as her strength and support to protect and guide her.

To Nora, it seems that she had been reduced to a lapdog which was whipped and then restored to grace, or that she had been treated like a doll which one discards and then picks up at the dictate of whim. With terrible and blinding clarity she becomes conscious of the fact that she had been a life-long toy and that she had lost her dignity in accommodating herself to others. Something strange and immeasurable changes her make-up. Her slowly awakening strength and independence—everything she had so humbly and busily gathered together for the gift of love she was going to bestow from her integral inner humanity—now rears up and wrests itself free in enormous protest. And so, a new, strange, strong human being is born, no longer kneeling nor enslaved nor able to be deceived.

And what has silently and overwhelmingly developed now finds expression. Awakened and without chains, Nora stands before Helmer and declares her freedom, simply, clearly, unconstrainedly. To the objections of an experienced and cautious mind, she seems naïve and still childish, but her unimpeachable, forward-looking, magnificent naïveté penetrates to the heart of things.

Helmer senses that they are dealing with elementals. And his objections and reproaches slowly yield to deep astonishment at the Nora who faces him. To him she is a strange and incomprehensible figure, without any resemblance to his little, childish Nora of the past. She is an oppressive and terrible enigma, and his only possible solution is expressed in the outcry, "So, only one explanation is possible: You don't love me anymore!"

No, she does not love him any longer. Actually, she had never loved him, only another, a completely different person. He is a stranger under whose roof she can no longer remain. She was never happy under his roof, "only merry." And now, when she looks back, it seems to her as if she had lived like a poor person "from hand to mouth." She had been impoverished. As for her real inner life, she had to give it in secret installments amid stolen moments and untruths. How could anyone dare assume jurisdiction over her inner life before she herself came into her own? How could one dare to hand her over to someone else before she was capable of giving herself? How could it be permitted that she became a mother who gave birth to children before she gave birth to a personality within her freed from the constriction of the childish? Or before two humans had matured, how could she know that they were growing toward a compatible goal? How could she know if they would fuse in mind and spirit? Or if within their reach was that rare, crowning and human apex: "a true marriage?"

Nora is not able to experience love and marriage in Mrs. Linde's way—full of rationality, habituation, renunciation and sober duty—a love and marriage without the element of wonder. That which had been robbed from the life of the "inner" Mrs. Linde existed with idealistic and abundant measure in Nora. Earlier, she had not really known if ideals were the elements which filled her depths. Ideals live inseparable from play and dreams, like happy siblings or children who consort with angels. A child casually assumes that a guardian angel watches from above and protects one from stumbling, from disturbances in sleep. But then, human fate enters: no guardian angel protects one's steps on the journey with its pitfalls, nor prevents a hateful awakening to a sober, everyday, gross reality. For the first time, ideals and reality are split by a gaping chasm. And for the first time, the die is cast: are her dreams and hopes only the imaginings of a child or the battle-ready and fairytale hulls of ideals ready to cope with life? Once upon a time, everything was based on trust, free from worry or care; now everything stands in doubt. Once upon a time, the wondrous was taken for granted; now everything—even the most obvious and certain—that had been taught her appears gnarled and incomprehensible.

In such a moment, a child helplessly gropes for the hand of the adult in order to find guidance and direction; but another type of childlikeness, intimately related to the ideals of life, can rapidly gather strength and masculine force. Far from subduing Nora or attuning her to compromise, the first decisive conflict acts upon her like a battle cry. . . . Resistance and bravery harden into armor. She has grasped that the peaks of wonder in life do not appear as readily as fairies who awaken Sleeping Beauty; in life, peaks must be conquered. That insight she is willing to put to the test. . . .

And so, we leave Nora at the entrance into the unknown vastness of life, which opens darkly. Nothing as yet tells her if she will find a way toward her goal. No longer is the blue, arched sky comforting and enveloping. It is far and remote, and separated seemingly by immeasurable distances from the ground upon which she stands lost. Far, far at the horizon's outermost bleakness, there is a thin line wherein heaven and earth flow together within the ken of the human eye, promising reconciliation. With every step toward the horizon's line, what seems ideal recedes, and yet one journeys into the endless.

Despite such premonitions, a calm and dominating force within her courage and faith impels her to overcome Helmer. The masculinity and conscientiousness of her childlike persistence render Helmer's weapons—experience and insight—useless. In the midst of his self-awareness and contentment, he strangely senses a secret power to which he must bow. Helmer, who had looked down upon Nora with considerate condescension, finds himself responding humbly to the determination of her childlike idealism, with this promise: "I have the strength to become someone else."

It seems to him as if the child in him had awakened from a deep sleep, a child which can still grow. . . . Only slowly does this sense rise. Not as with the determined, joyous strength of Nora but tearfully, hesitantly, helplessly; his soul—confused, unsure—in darkling pain searches for its lost childhood. For that reason, he possesses no strength to bind Nora to himself. He has no choice but to listen to the door as it falls into its lock as Nora leaves. Yet he does not turn from her without hope. He sits, staring wide-eyed after her, hunched into himself, silent.

For the first time, everything which until now has filled him with daily worries and joys—his old world—slowly sinks. For the first time, all her tumult and busy alarms are petrified into a deep, soundless silence; and slowly, slowly, with a dreamlike magic, Nora's world reappears. From all the corners and crevices of the abandoned room, out of its quite cold isolation, it seems as if old, forgotten fairytales gather around him like ghostly, childish figures at play. He had lived with all those figures for so long during his marriage without seeing in them anything more profound than toys and objects of delight, and without noticing the pinions on their small shoulders capable of lifting him out of *his* narrow doll house. (pp. 42-55)

Lou Salomé, in her Ibsen's Heroines, *edited and translated by Siegfried Mandel, Black Swan Books, 1985, 155 p.*

WILLIAM ARCHER   (essay date 1906)

[*In the following excerpt, Archer pronounces* A Doll's House *the work with which Ibsen abandoned the techniques of Eugène Scribe—the French dramatist credited with creating the intricate, carefully orchestrated theatrical form known as the well-made play—to develop the innovative dramatic techniques that characterize his later works.*]

In a former article in this Review [see Further Reading entry dated 1904] I examined the repertory of the Bergen Theatre during the six years of Henrik Ibsen's connection with it, and showed that, in the exercise of his functions, he must have closely studied some seventy-five French plays, most of them belonging to the then dominant school of Eugène Scribe. I suggested, very briefly, that the influence of these studies was apparent in all his plays (except the three dramas in verse), from *Lady Inger* right down to *A Doll's House.* In that play, as it seemed to me, he finally outgrew and cast off the domination of the French school; but he would never have been the master-technician he ultimately became had he not first learnt, and then deliberately unlearnt, the formal dexterities of Scribe and his disciples. (p. 101)

[With *A Doll's House* Ibsen] breaks with French tradition, and breaks with it, one may say, almost at a definite line on which one can lay one's finger. The first two acts, and the first

half of the third act, are thoroughly French in method. First we have the confidante, Mrs. Linde. She has a certain character of her own, for Ibsen could not, if he would, draw a mere lay figure. But she and her character do not belong to the spiritual essence of the play. Her function is mechanical. She has to listen to Nora's confidences, in order that we may overhear them; and she has to influence the upshot of the action by softening the heart of Krogstad. She is external, if I may so phrase it, to the psychological chemistry of the action. She serves, now as a rod to stir the mixture, now as a ladle to skim it; but she has no part in the chemical process itself. In Ibsen's later plays, you will scarcely find another character of the slightest prominence to whom this description applies.

The long scene between Nora and Mrs. Linde constitutes a formal exposition of that part of the action—a good half—which lies outside the frame of the picture. It ends with Nora's cry, "Oh, what a wonderful thing it is to live and to be happy!"—and instantly there comes a ring at the bell, and Krogstad's shadow falls across Nora's glee. Here we have an instance of the old traditional irony; a case of Nemesis in miniature; an exclamation of happiness giving the cue for the entrance of disaster. Again, a little further on, we have the same antithesis in a heightened form. Nora, romping with her children, is so absorbed in the game, that when Krogstad comes to strike the fatal blow at her happiness, he actually stands amongst them before she is aware of his presence. An admirable stage-effect this is, no doubt, and introduced most skilfully and naturally. But in the light of Ibsen's later method, one sees that it is of the stage, stagey. Such so-called "dramatic" conjunctures do, no doubt, occur in life; but as the dramatist sees deeper into the inexhaustible wealth of essential drama in the human soul, he is less and less tempted to concern himself with surface accidents such as this.

Krogstad reveals to Nora the true import of her action in signing her father's name, and leaves her a prey to terror which she strives in vain to shake off. And here mark the ingenuity with which Krogstad's own delinquency is made to throw a lurid light upon Nora's. . . . Nora tries to find comfort in getting Helmer to say that Krogstad's offence was not unpardonable; but he, little dreaming what is at stake, merely hammers the nail deeper into her soul. This scene (the last scene of the first act) is manipulated with the utmost skill, but produces an unmistakable effect of artificiality. Note, for instance, Helmer's remark, "Nearly all cases of early corruption may be traced to lying mothers." We cannot but echo Nora's question: "Why—mothers?" We feel that Ibsen here gives the conversation a slight twist, a little kink as it were, which is not absolutely unnatural, indeed, but is too clearly designed to dot the i of the situation. Again, Nora's withdrawal of her hand when Helmer says, "It gives me a positive sense of physical discomfort to come in contact with such people," is merely an old stage trick turned outside in. Sardou, too, had he written the scene, would infallibly have made Nora say, "How warm it is here!" That is the established remark for a character who wishes to dissemble great mental perturbation.

The second act, as we all know, culminates in the famous tarantella-scene—a crowning and final instance of that striving after picturesque antithesis which is as old in drama as Euripides at least, but is specially affected by the French romantic playwrights and their Spanish progenitors. There is no more favourite antithesis than that of revelry and horror—witness the marble guest appearing at Don Juan's orgie, or the Miserere in *Lucrèce Borgia* extinguishing the mirth of the doomed roysterers. The analogy between these scenes and that of Nora's tarantella may not at first be apparent; but a little examination will show that Ibsen simply screws up the effect a peg or two by making the contrast between gaiety and horror no longer lie in the mere inert juxtaposition of the two elements, but in Nora's active assumption of feverish merriment in order to mask her resolve of suicide. Reduce the scene to its bare formula—a woman dancing on the brink of the grave—and you see how ultra-romantic, how Spanish, how Hugoesque it is. But it is not merely in the actual tarantella-scene that Ibsen strives for this effect of antithesis. That scene is only the culmination of an antithesis running through the whole play. He has deliberately selected the season of Christmas festivity to form a radiant background to the horror of Rank's doom and Nora's agony. While Nora is learning from Helmer the true import of her innocent felony, she is mechanically decking a Christmas-tree with candles and tinsel. While Rank is telling her that the clutch of death is at his heart, she is preparing her masquerade dress. In the last act, as the sense of impending disaster deepens, we hear the gay rhythms of the tarantella from the ball-room above. Nora enters with the dread of death in her eyes, and decked out in the parti-coloured dress of an Italian contadina. Throughout there runs this strain of insistent antithesis—the familiar mediæval antithesis of the rose-wreathed skeleton, the Dance of Death. There is something theatrical about it, almost operatic, which even the exquisite skill of the manipulation, and the wealth of character and meaning compressed into the conventional framework, cannot quite disguise. It is admirable in its kind, but the kind is not the highest.

The following sentences from an American criticism of *A Doll's House,* written when the play was first produced in New York, are exactly typical of a hundred English criticisms published about the same time. "The piece under consideration," says the critic, "is almost totally devoid of dramatic action. There is only one really dramatic incident, and that occurs when Nora dances a tarantella. All the rest is words. It is seldom that such a cataract of vapid talk has been let loose in a theatre." With unerring instinct, this gentleman lays his finger on the most strained, unnatural, in a word theatrical, effect in the play, and calls it the only dramatic incident. But now mark a curious point. This tarantella scene, with all its theatricality, is hardly ever effective on the stage. I have seen many Noras, first and last, and four of them very remarkable actresses: Fru Hennings, who originally created the character in Copenhagen; the incomparable Eleonora Duse; Madame Réjane; and our own Miss Achurch. But I have never seen any actress attain an effect in the tarantella-scene at all proportionate to the effort. People applaud, of course—they will always applaud a dance—but it is the dance they are thinking of, not the situation. The scene is disappointing, just as so many scenes of great external picturesqueness are disappointing on the stage—the idea dwarfs the reality. It is so obviously, so aggressively, theatrical, that we expect from it a greater thrill than it can ever give us.

Well now, is it not curious—is it not significant—that immediately after this passage of violent theatricality, not to say staginess—immediately after he has wrung the last dregs of effect out of his apparatus of Christmas-tree, masquerade, tinsel, and tarantella—Ibsen should suddenly, at a given moment, throw it all aside, never to be taken up again, and end this very play in the strain of pure drama, sober and searching, devoid of all mechanical accessories and antithetic frip-

peries, to which he ever afterwards adhered? There is a point where Nora, after Helmer has "forgiven" her, goes off the stage into her own adjoining room, and when Helmer asks her what she is going to do, replies, "To take off my masquerade dress." At that point, as it seems to me, it was Ibsen himself who, consciously or unconsciously, threw off all masquerade. He put away from him whatever was external and mechanical in the French technique. He had mastered and done with it. In *Pillars of Society,* and now in the first two acts of *A Doll's House,* he had developed the method of Scribe, on a line parallel to that of Sardou, and had reached a point about even with that at which Sardou has remained stationary. He had—to employ a somewhat grotesque image—danced his tarantella, and was henceforth to apply to soberer and more artistic purposes the skill, the suppleness, in a word the virtuosity he had thus acquired. When Nora, in her every-day clothes, confronts the astonished Helmer and says, "It's not so late yet. Sit down, Torvald; you and I have much to say to each other," it is the true Ibsen, of his latest and greatest period, that for the first time appears on the scene.

When I first saw *A Doll's House* acted, in Christiania, the Nora was a neophyte of no great talent, and the effect of the play, up to the middle of the third act, came far short of my expectations. The tarantella especially fell very flat; but indeed the action, as a whole, did not at all "grip" me as it had in reading—until the point was reached where Nora and Helmer sat down, one on each side of the table, with the lamp between them, to make up the accounts of their matrimonial bankruptcy. Then the drama seized and held me as in a vice, and every phrase of Nora's threnody over her dead dreams, her lost illusions, thrilled me with an emotion such as I had never before experienced in the theatre. I was then a quarter of a century younger than I am now, and was not in the least biassed by any technical theories. I was perfectly content with the Scribe-Sardou formula, and went to the theatre predisposed to condemn this final scene, inasmuch as it set that formula at defiance. It was no theoretical, pumped-up rapture that seized me—indeed, it took me utterly by surprise. Nor do I now mean to say that the scene is unassailably excellent. I think it is an extreme example of psychological compression. Nora has attained, in a crisis of twenty minutes, an intellectual clearness with regard to her position, which, as a matter of fact, she would scarcely have acquired in months of reflection. But though the scene is open to criticism in many respects, I take it to be the first clear example of that power in which lies the peculiar greatness of Ibsen's later plays—the power of impregnating thought with emotion, and making psychological analysis palpitate with dramatic interest. Other dramatists give us patches of analysis, interludes of thought, scattered throughout an action which exists independently of them, and which, from the strictly technical point of view, they merely cumber and delay. In Ibsen, at his best, the psychology and the action are inextricably interfused; the psychology *is* the action; and he has the art of unfolding the soul-history of his personages with such cunning gradations, such vivid surprises, such lightning-like flashes of clairvoyance, that his analysis has all the thrill of adventure, all the fascination of romance.

When we contrast the stern, severe simplicity of *Ghosts* with the shimmering artificiality of *A Doll's House* (up to the final scene) we cannot but feel that between the two plays a revolution occurred. My own conjecture is that the revolution actually occurred during the composition of *A Doll's House.* I cannot help thinking that Ibsen originally designed the play to have a "happy ending," like that of *The League of Youth* or *Pillars of Society,* and that Mrs. Linde's influence over Krogstad was invented and adapted to that end. Then, I take it, as his work advanced, the poet himself began to realise the higher possibilities of his art, renounced the trickery of the "happy ending," and, in the final scene, made the first essay of the new powers which he felt to have developed within him. (pp. 108-13)

William Archer, "Ibsen's Craftsmanship," in The Fortnightly Review, *Vol. LXXX, No. CCCCLXXV, July, 1906, pp. 101-13.*

HERMANN J. WEIGAND (essay date 1925)

[*Weigand was an American educator and critic specializing in German and medieval literature. In the following excerpt, he assesses* A Doll's House *as a comedy based on what he perceives as the comic incongruity between the facts of Nora's situation and her exaggerated interpretation of them.*]

Nora, the merry lark, the frisky squirrel, who disports herself so gayly in the Helmers' cozy apartments, has a bagful of tricks. Whatever the identity of her father, we have to watch her for only two minutes to know her as a daughter of Eve, adept in an infinity of little arts that make her irresistibly winsome to the masculine eye. Tripping in as she does, laden with a mountain of Christmas parcels, her face alive with mirth, humming a snatch of a tune, she scatters a flood of sunshine. Her generous feeing of the porter, her stealthy nibbling at the macaroons, her playful talk with Torvald through the closed office-door, show her bubbling over with good spirits.

When Torvald appears after a minute or two, we take in their relationship at a glance. They have been married for eight years, but he is as captivated by his little wife as during the days of his courtship, and she adores him. They seem ideally mated, each supplementing the other's deficiency,—Torvald supplying the common sense and Nora the freedom of fancy to the match. They are adjusted to each other without any friction. Certainly there appears not a trace of repression in Nora's conduct.

We cannot take a step in the analysis of this drama without looking both forward and backward. In studying Nora's actions we must never let the fact slip our minds that she has her secret to conceal from her husband. Take her charming exhibition of extravagance in the first scene. We see her give a generous tip to the porter. We see her gratifying her sweet tooth. We hear her begging Torvald so prettily to let her do a little squandering this Christmas. Torvald loves to call her his little spendthrift. Her protestation that she saves as much as she can, draws his laughing retort: "Very true—as much as you can—but that's precisely nothing." Torvald tells her that in money matters she has inherited her father's disposition. And in the next scene Christina Linde reminds her of what a shocking little spendthrift she used to be in their school days.

Now take the other side of the ledger. For seven years Nora has been paying interest and amortization on her loan. She earned a little money occasionally by doing light fancy-work. A year ago, she shut herself up every night for three weeks before Christmas, doing copywork, pretending all the while to be working on decorations for the Christmas tree, and eventually blaming the meagerness of her results on the cat.

But the bulk of the money came from another source: "I couldn't save much out of the housekeeping, for, of course, Torvald had to live well. And I couldn't let the children go about badly dressed; all I got for them I spent on them, the blessed darlings. . . . When Torvald gave me money for clothes, and so on, I never spent more than half of it; I always bought the simplest and cheapest things. It's lucky that everything suits me so well—Torvald never had any suspicions. But it was often very hard, Christina dear. For it's nice to be beautifully dressed—now, isn't it?"

Nora has no idea how much she has paid off. Incidentally, we find out a little later, when Krogstad interrupts her game with the children, that although it's now Christmas eve she hasn't saved up the amount due on the first of the year.

Before we draw our conclusions, we must take a glance back at the first scene. There we saw her spending gayly and getting ready to squander more. But remember, it's Christmas; and who doesn't get the spending fever then? Moreover, didn't Torvald's glorious good fortune warrant a little exceptional extravagance? We should be cautioned, however, by her nibbling at the forbidden macaroons against taking her self-denial any too seriously. On the other hand, the coquettish tricks she employs to get money out of Torvald appear in a new light, as we realize how she plans to use this money.

All in all, it is a complex state of mind, of which Nora's behavior gives us glimpses. In a preliminary way we may attempt the following summary: (1) A certain degree of heroism must be conceded to the little woman who sacrifices her vanity year after year to live up to that irksome obligation. The fact that she skimps herself rather than her husband and children shows a fine spirit. (2) At the same time she is self-conscious enough to underscore that aspect of the case to Christina. (3) She is tremendously proud of having kept her secret; as a matter of fact, however, her knowledge of Torvald's strict notions left no other course open to her. (4) In providing for the quarterly payments, she is incapable of any systematic saving. She lives from hand to mouth, and she is of so flighty a temperament that we cannot think of her as being haunted by her obligation. (5) She has been getting a great deal of childish fun out of working a bit now and then in secret. It made her feel so important, so much like a man. (6) The play-acting to which she resorted to get money out of Torvald gave her the most perfect opportunity for self-expression. In opening up her bagful of tricks, she was altogether herself. For one so naturally extravagant as Nora it required no effort to appear even a little more extravagant than she was.

Now let us review the circumstances of Nora's forgery. They had been married a year when Torvald's health broke down in consequence of overwork—the result of his attempting to provide adequately for his young wife. At that time Nora was daily expecting the birth of her first child, and to add to her troubles, her beloved father was dying, and she could not travel home to see him. The physicians came to Nora and told her that Torvald's life was in danger, since he was in no condition to bear the shock of such a revelation himself. They suggested a period of complete rest and a trip to the south, whereupon Nora, trading on her character of the irresponsible spoiled child, began to display a keen longing on her own part to spend a year in Italy. But the coquetry, the tears and the supplications she enlisted in the interest of so good a cause failed to budge her scrupulous husband from his aversion to borrowing, however it must have wrung his heart to refuse his little lark anything she had set her heart on. But determined as she was to get the money, Nora managed to get a loan of twelve hundred dollars from Krogstad, a money-lender, on condition that her father endorse the note. She returned the note with the forged endorsement after having kept it five or six days; and within a month, after she had been successfully delivered of a boy child, they started south. (pp. 27-30)

Does Nora know what it means to commit forgery? It is as difficult to answer this question by a flat yes or no, as so many others that arise with respect to her character.

Krogstad says: "If I produce this document in court, you will be condemned according to law." The naïveté of Nora's answer is remarkable. "I don't believe that. Do you mean to tell me that a daughter has no right to spare her dying father trouble and anxiety?—that a wife has no right to save her husband's life? I don't know much about the law, but I'm sure you'll find, somewhere or other, that that is allowed." In the final scene of the reckoning, it is significant to note, Nora admits that she has come to see that the laws are different from what she believed, but at the same time she defends the moral right of her act as vigorously as ever.

That does not settle the matter, however. We have to proceed cautiously, inasmuch as in other situations Nora is not quite so naïve as she would like to appear. She knows more about Doctor Rank's disease, for instance, than we would at first give her credit for. The same may well be the case here. A moment before that indignant outburst of hers, she refers to her act as a brave deed, when, repudiating Krogstad's intimation that he was blackballed by society for a similar act, she exclaims: "You! You want me to believe that you did a brave thing to save your wife's life?" What would be the point in calling her act a brave thing, we ask, if there were no risk involved, if it were not forbidden, if it could not get her into trouble? To Christina she had simply boasted of her act as something clever, refraining carefully at the same time from giving her any hint of the nature of the transaction.

And what of her reasons for guarding her secret so zealously all these years from Torvald? When Christina asks her: "And you have never confessed to your husband?" she jumps at the very thought of such a thing. She has *three* good reasons for not telling him right on the tip of her tongue—a circumstance in itself suspicious. "Good heavens!" she exclaims, "What can you be thinking of? Tell him, when he is so strict on that point! And besides," she continues, "how painful and humiliating it would be for Torvald, with his manly self-respect, to know that he owed anything to me! It would utterly upset the relation between us; our beautiful, happy home would never again be what it is." Anyhow, she goes on to say, it might be well to have something in reserve, in case the time should come when Torvald would not be in love with her as much as now, when it would no longer amuse him to see her dancing about and dressing up and acting. The second and third of these reasons are obviously of an auxiliary character. It is in the first that her immediate reaction is contained: she is afraid to tell Torvald. Now what is it, precisely, that she fears? So far as she is consciously aware, she fears Torvald's anger for her having run them into debt. But, heavens, she ought to be able to convince him that she did it to save his life, and Torvald would have to be a veritable ogre if he did not love his little lark the more for it. Everything points, I think, to her fear being more deeply rooted. I believe that Nora's consciousness of her forgery is the real instinctive

source of her anxiety to keep the whole matter from her husband. Since she knows that her act has a feature of which Torvald would most sharply disapprove, even though she justifies it to herself, she dreads the idea of acquainting Torvald with even the relatively innocent side of the business.

This view is confirmed by the alacrity with which Nora's thoughts run to suicide, after Torvald's lecture on forgery has given her a foretaste of what to expect. She plays with the thought of suicide before it ever dawns upon her what a weapon for blackmail her indiscretion has put into Krogstad's hands. At the bottom of Nora's impulse to resort to such desperate measures is her panicky fear of getting a terrible scolding. She is "scared stiff" at the idea of having to face Torvald's wrath. For the very reason that she loves him so passionately, she cannot bear the thought of his anger bursting upon her. She is in this respect like hypersensitive children, who have been known to run away from home or do something desperate rather than take a scolding from a person by whom they wished to be uncritically idolized. Nora feels that if she commits suicide, Torvald will be so overwhelmed by this extreme token of her devotion that her image will live radiant and spotless in his memory. It is with her essentially a matter of personal vanity, taking so extreme a form as to be easily confounded with the loftiest altruism. She would make a widower of Torvald and orphans of her children for the sake of being adored after her death as a plucky heroine. When it comes to the crucial test, to be sure, the will to live is stronger even than the fear of the wound her vanity is about to suffer. (pp. 31-4)

[Let] us pause to register our æsthetic response to the crisis we see approaching. The material situation fills us with suspense, tinged with apprehension. Common sense tells us, however, that the consequences of Nora's exposure cannot be so very terrible. There is not a court in the civilized world but would show the utmost leniency to Nora, if it ever came to a criminal prosecution; and it is quite out of the question that she should suffer social disgrace. As to the little heroine, we contemplate her with mixed feelings. We identify ourselves with her, we feel the strain under which she is laboring, we respond sympathetically to her dread of being found out; but at the same time we are diverted by her half-conscious playacting. Our sympathy for Nora is balanced by our delight in the comedy which she stages. The psychological relation between Nora and Torvald, finally, is essentially comic. The incongruity between the heroic Torvald of Nora's dreams and the smug, conceited philistine of actual fact is all the more subtly amusing, as the contrast is not reinforced in the slightest by any artificial stress. (pp. 45-6)

The final scene of [Act II] shows Nora keyed to an almost insupportable pitch of tension. She has confessed her secret to Christina, in the baldest words. The fatal letter [from Krogstad, revealing her forgery] is in the box, and all her efforts are now bent on delaying as long as possible the inevitable catastrophe. Just in the nick of time, as Torvald is on the point of getting his mail, Nora strikes the first notes of the tarantella, causing him to turn; and now follows her wild, hysterical dance, a dance of life and death, transforming into spontaneous movement her delirious ecstasy of self-sacrifice and her frenzied terror. Nora is dancing for a stay of execution, she wants to live until after the party. She pleads with Torvald to forget business and devote himself exclusively to her until it is all over; and as her fate hangs in the balance, a whisper from Rank to her uncomprehending husband turns the scales, and she wins her reprieve. Nora's delirium has reached its highest pitch. She calls for champagne. She is in no state of mind to care any longer for the good offices of Christina, who has just left a note at Krogstad's house. "You shouldn't have done that," she says. "You shall prevent nothing. After all, there's something glorious in waiting for the miracle." And left alone, she ascertains that she has exactly thirty-one more hours to live.

I do not suppose that anybody can resist the hypnotic power of Nora's anguish on reading or seeing the play for the first time with alert vision. There is a finality about her heroic resolve that silences doubt. The impulsive generosity of her imagination captivates our sympathies as completely as though she had already cast herself into the icy black water. We give her practically as much credit for the impulse as for its execution.

But here it is time to remind ourselves that, after all, Nora did not take the fatal plunge. I anticipate resentful objections, but it will be conceded that the fact is undeniable. Nora's failure to commit suicide is, moreover, not the result of circumstances beyond her control; it is clearly due to her inability to carry out her heroic resolve when it comes to the actual test. She wants to go, but her courage fails her at the decisive moment. Instead of going resolutely, as soon as Torvald has retired to his office, she lingers, she thinks of all she is leaving behind, she shudders at the thought of the black water and wishes it were over. That is not the state of mind in which suicides are committed. That is the state of mind, however, in which one thinks of suicide, dreams of it, imagines it. To the last moment Nora is positively convinced that she will go: as a matter of fact she is romancing with the whole intensity of her imagination! Hot tears of indignation would come to little Nora's eyes, could she hear herself being thus analyzed; yet her tears could not obliterate the clear reading of the facts.

Far be it from me to belittle the agony she endures during those awful moments of suspense or the anguish of the last thirty-one hours. However, if we survey the dramatic spectacle with sufficient detachment; if we maintain intact our clearness of vision despite the suggestive appeal of her big childish eyes, the situation never loses its fundamentally comic aspect.

In following the movements of this winsome little woman throughout the first two acts with that dual attitude of warm sympathy controlled by superior detachment, which constitutes the æsthetic attitude, we beheld an intricate blending of naïveté and play-acting in all her doings; we found her charmingly lacking in sense of fact and endowed with a captivating sprightliness of fancy. Her adroitness in playing a psychological game of hide-and-seek with herself as well as with Torvald, Christina, Rank and Krogstad, made a subtle appeal to our sense of the comic. We found the quality of comedy in her spontaneous lying, in the automatic duplicity of all her reactions: in the motives by which she obscured her basic fear of a scolding; in her warm defense of her forgery as something entirely within the law; in her refusal to see the children whom she is supposed to be corrupting; in her faculty of persuading herself that Krogstad was only bluffing; in her first thoughts of suicide, when as yet her alarms were confined to the fear of a scolding and of the police; in her eager misinterpretation of Torvald's boast that he was man enough to shoulder it all; in her coquetry with Doctor Rank. Does not all this give us sufficient warrant for viewing her faith in the

miracle and her heroic resolve to prevent it, from the same aspect? Are not these also figments of her will-to-believe—creations of her great gift of romancing under the strain of duress? Are they not comic?

What is the basis of Nora's expectation of the miracle? Stark fear. At the outset, before she is aware of any trouble looming in consequence of her forgery, she is animated by a sensitive child's dread of a scolding. The fear of unpleasant consequences grows, as she learns that Krogstad is in possession of her secret. After Torvald's lecture on the seriousness of forgery, Nora's fear (now not only of Torvald but also of the law) grows to such proportions that she already plays with the thought of suicide. Precisely because her fear is so great, so unendurable, she snatches at the fiction of the miracle to neutralize it. Her faith in the miracle is the direct product of her hysterical terror. Even more necessary does this faith become to her, when she learns what dire consequences her indiscretion will have for Torvald. We can state it in general terms: Nora's faith in the miracle grows in direct proportion to her need of it.

The miracle, however, does not stand by itself. Simultaneous in origin, directly attached to it as a corollary, is Nora's generous resolve not to permit it. So strong is her love for Torvald that, the nearer the moment of his ruin draws, the more fixed is her determination rather to commit the supreme sacrifice.

And yet the one as well as the other are make-believe—attempts to escape unpleasant facts by ardent romancing. The fact that Nora tries to pick the lock of the mail-box with her hair-pin, on the day preceding the fatal night, shows how she shrinks from putting her theories to the test. (pp. 50-4)

Let us now review the third act in orderly sequence. There is to begin with the scene between Krogstad and Christina, which results in averting the material danger that threatened the Helmer household. Krogstad will lose no time to make amends for his dastardly letter. The harmonious mutual adjustment, moreover, which these two shipwrecked existences come to, seems to foreshadow a happy solution of the crisis that Nora and Torvald are about to face.

For a moment our attention is diverted to the little secondary drama enacted between the two one-time lovers whom life's storms have used so roughly. It seems just a trifle providential that the sentimental crook and widowed father of a flock of children should meet his lost love at this critical juncture,—herself widowed and utterly alone and longing for somebody to love and mother. We can take Christina at her word when she reassures Krogstad that her offer is not prompted by any desire to sacrifice herself for Nora's sake. Hungering for a task to fill the aching void of her existence, she snatches at the merest crumb of affection. A missionary by temperament, she will have something to live for, in mothering the children and guiding Krogstad on the straight and narrow path of righteousness. Christina is to be sincerely congratulated on her decision, for the sake of everybody concerned; yet, somehow, the chilling soberness of her tightly drawn lips and the total absence of charm in her prematurely aged features tend to limit our reactions to sentiments of polite esteem.

How completely the atmosphere changes with the return of the masqueraders after the tarantella! Poor Nora, dragged away from life's banquet against her will, almost succumbs to hysteria; whereas Torvald, bubbling and sparkling with champagne, treats us to a most diverting spectacle. In the rosiest of humors, at the peak of that blissful state of stimulation where the quality of the audience no longer exercises a regulative check on the flow of expression, he plants himself before Christina and, in a voice raised just a shade above his normal intonation, gives her an impromptu "privatissimum" on the æsthetics of an effective exit. And half a minute later, when Christina prepares to depart, in response to a fairly direct hint on Torvald's part, he condescends to give the good woman a friendly tip on the sort of handiwork she must choose to appear to advantage. It fairly makes us squirm with amusement to see him demonstrate the graceful motions of embroidering and follow it up by imitating the narrow-chested attitude of the knitter.

The "terrible bore" gone at last, Torvald can give free play to his amorous impulses. Turning to his little lark, he showers her with words of passionate endearment. Under the influence of the wine, even Torvald falls to romancing: he loves to exchange a furtive glance with Nora in company and imagine himself her secret lover; when he takes her home it thrills him to pretend to himself that he has just stepped out of the church with his young bride after the ceremony, and that the first moment of complete intimacy is at hand. From the outsider's point of view there is always something a trifle comic about such amorous overtures in a domestic setting; but here the comedy derives its peculiar poignancy from the incongruity between the wine-inspired ardor of the passionate male and the ultra-heroic pose which Nora expects him presently to adopt.

Nora is in no state of mind to see the humor of the situation. She is on the verge of exhaustion. "I shall soon sleep now," she says, putting a double meaning into her words. "Everything you do is right," she tells Torvald with the pathos of complete resignation. She gently but firmly repulses his advances, until Torvald finally exclaims in irritation: "What does this mean? I daresay you're teasing me, little Nora! Won't—won't! Am I not your husband?"

The chivalrous swain who a moment ago waxed lyrical in his wooing has vanished. In his place stands the lord-and-master, asserting his rights. It is a critical moment. It almost seems as if Nora were due at once for a rude awakening from her illusions concerning her husband-hero's capacity for self-sacrifice. However, the crisis is averted by the knock on the hall door.

The brief scene that follows, in which Doctor Rank bids a final farewell to his friends, is one of the summits of Ibsen's art. On the strength of this scene alone, Ibsen takes rank among the immortals. I doubt whether any poet has penned a more concentrated vision of the tragi-comedy of human life, whether any contriver of moods has struck a greater variety of chords in the compass of a single phrase. With each of the three participants we behold the scene from a different perspective: from the low perspective of Torvald, who accounts for his friend's whimsical humor by the reflection that he has drunk heavily; from that of Rank, who is sustained in his heroic stage-play by the consciousness of Nora's silent admiration; from that of Nora, who shares with Rank the secret of his mystification of Torvald and who mystifies the Doctor in turn by her equivocal allusions to her own secret, which he cannot understand. But in addition, in a sense denied to the participants themselves, we see the comic, tragic and tragicomic interplay of their emotions from the cosmic perspective of the poet. From this high perspective even the grim specter of death is reduced to a function in what is essentially comedy of the most sublime order—comedy that transcends in its blending of sympathy with vision the appeal of tragedy. Do we not see the mellow light of comedy suffusing the Doctor in his gallant counter-demonstration against the terrors of death? Do we not see him enjoying the effect of his *tour de force* upon the woman he loves so dearly? Do we not see him smile inwardly in anticipating how Torvald will appreciate the effectiveness of his exit when he wakes up to the significance of that studiedly casual farewell? And is it not our turn to smile tolerantly at the delusion of the dying man, when, as a matter of fact, both Torvald and Nora are so preoccupied—he with the male's amorous desire, she with the thought of her own heroic exit—that the effectiveness of his gesture is largely lost on them both? In this scene the poet's laughter at the limitation of these three mortals is the laughter of the gods, musical and benign and without malice.

As Torvald and Nora are alone once more, we are about to witness the release of the tension which we have seen tightening from act to act and from scene to scene. These last moments of suspense add some exquisite touches to the comedy. In attempting to open the mail-box, Torvald finds Nora's broken hair-pin in the lock, and automatically Nora explains its presence there by a fib that puts the blame on her innocent little ones. For those readers who would persuade themselves that Nora has been maturing by leaps under the mental anguish of the last three days, this instinctive resorting to subterfuge at the crucial moment is something to reflect on. And when she hears Torvald exclaiming about his find in the box, Nora is once more in the throes of terror. "The letter! Oh, no, no, Torvald!" she ejaculates. But it is only Rank's cards marked with the black cross, which have startled him. Nora explains the significance of those cards, and we now see how Torvald is affected by the news that his dearest friend has departed for ever. He rises to a few words of regret. His second thought is the reflection that the somber background which had hitherto set off his domestic happiness so effectively has now vanished; his third, that it is better after all for himself and Nora to belong exclusively to each other. What perfunctory mourning! And yet, can we respond to this exhibition of self-complacent vanity and egotism with righteous indignation? After all, is it not substantially what was to be expected of Torvald? It is not as though we were shocked by any sudden revelation of his real character. Being sufficiently forewarned, we view this naïvely genuine expression of his egotism from the angle of comedy, and the comic aspect of the situation is enhanced by the reflection that an excess of wine and amorous desire is making Torvald impervious, for the time being, to all finer emotions. To make the comic spectacle complete, Nora drinks in Torvald's hollow oratory with worshipful adoration, and it remains for the most fatuous of his phrases to send so powerful a thrill through Nora's heart, as to lift her above her fears and animate her with a gambler's sudden courage to invoke the decision.

"My darling wife!" Torvald had exclaimed, capping his reflections on the loss of his friend with a theatrical climax. "Do you know, Nora, I often wish some danger might threaten you, that I might risk body and soul, and everything, everything, for your dear sake."

"Now you shall read your letters, Torvald," comes Nora's firm answer. Standing so positively committed to any sacrifice, how can he fail her, if asked to make good his words, before his ardor has had any chance to cool?

Alas, we know what cruel sport reality makes of Nora's romantic dreams! Nora herself quails when the moment arrives for putting her own heroic resolve into execution, and the Torvald who rushes out of his office, flourishing Krogstad's letter, is not her hero but the enraged philistine. There is no mistaking the dangerous glint in his eye: still Nora continues to cling with a hysteric's frenzy to her illusions. As a silly evasion Torvald has already brushed aside her plea that she loved him beyond all else in the world; yet her lips murmur the entreaty: "Let me go—you shall not save me! You shall not take my guilt upon yourself!"

"I don't want any melodramatic airs," is Torvald's rejoinder, and now Nora's expression stiffens under the shower of abusive reproach with which Torvald overwhelms her. The scales fall from her eyes, as she hears herself styled a hypocrite, a liar, a criminal; as she learns that Torvald will submit to Krogstad's blackmail as a matter of course, bent only upon hushing matters up; as she is told that their domestic happiness is irretrievably ruined, that the children will no longer be entrusted to her care, that the only thing left to save is appearances.

The rudeness of Nora's awakening, contrasting cruelly with the generous, high-minded impulses which she was conscious of harboring, puts the mental faculties of us readers to a severe test. If, in response to the surge of our sympathies, we are already on the point of abandoning the serene perspective of comedy, in order to swell the chorus of the mob by shouting "bully" and "cad" at Torvald in our turn, let us remember: Torvald does not know what we know about the circumstances of Nora's forgery! He has never known that the journey to the south was undertaken to save his life. For seven years he has been viewing that trip in an altogether different light. At the time when he was suffering from a breakdown, the result of overwork and financial worry, his flighty, pleasure-loving squirrel of a wife had set herself on spending a year in Italy like other wives of her social station; she had wept and prayed to make him borrow the funds, and his inability to indulge her had aggravated his miseries, when suddenly her father's gift had put the means of gratifying her wish within his reach. Fancy the shock of his learning now, from a blackmailer's pen, by what methods she had secured her year abroad! And even if Krogstad's letter, as there are grounds for supposing, alluded to his sickness as an extenuating motive for Nora's rash deed,—would that explanation, coming from such a source, at such a time, carry any weight as compared to the knockdown force of the initial shock? Torvald has no inkling, either, of the agony she has been enduring the last three days. Granting his lack of intuition, which stands above discussion, is he so very much to blame for being disgusted, in the first heat of his anger, by her melodramatic offer to kill herself?—Now let us consider how he proposes to meet the situation. Torvald has no other thought than the impulsive conviction that he must submit to blackmail to avoid publicity at all costs. Not for a moment does he hesitate to shoulder the consequences of Nora's indiscretion, no matter how nauseating the prospect of being dependent on the dirty usurer's mercy. Let those who call him a cad reflect on the bitterness of the sacrifice he is ready to assume as a matter of course. I grant that he is following the line of least resistance; that he is thinking as much of his own reputation as of Nora's; that his way of meeting the issue is neither original nor courageous. A man of very exceptional caliber might have defied Krogstad to do his worst, preferring to stand by his wife through gossip and scandal and a criminal prosecution even, rather than ignominiously come to

terms. But as to the third, the heroic course which Nora expected Torvald to adopt—that he should denounce himself as the forger:—almost everybody but Nora must agree on a little calm reflection that it would have been quixotic, not to say idiotic, since such a course would have spelt sure ruin for them both. Now some one is sure to interrupt: "No one actually expects Torvald to shoulder the forgery; what makes him a cad is rather the fact that he does not even experience a spontaneous impulse to meet the situation in that generous way, prior to all reflection on its actual feasibility." That might be urged if Torvald knew of the generous impulses that sponsored Nora's deed in the first place, and if he knew of the agony that has lately been driving her to the brink of suicide. But since he knew nothing of all this, is it not a trifle foolish to be exercised with Nora over Torvald's failure to live up to her expectation of the miracle?

So the situation remains fundamentally comic. Comic is the incongruity between Nora's and Torvald's respective states of mind, the absence of a common denominator to their thinking making it impossible for either to catch the other's point of view. And comic, in the second place, is the contrast between Torvald's professions and his actions. As to the latter, we experience the delight of finding our expectations confirmed to a "T." Torvald's heroism turns out to be strictly a matter of oratory, and the texture of his superior morality has already provoked our mirth by the coming to light of the underlying personal motives that prompted his dismissal of Krogstad. As we hear him ranting now, we know that his indignation is due in far greater measure to the material consequences which Nora's indiscretion will entail for him than to the iniquity of the act.

Krogstad's second letter quickly supplies the proof. The danger annulled, Torvald is completely transformed. "I am saved! Nora, I am saved!" he shouts. The ominous calm of Nora's rejoinder, "And I?" fails to stem the oratorical flow of jubilation which now pours from his lips. And with the incubus of fear removed, Krogstad's allusion, in his second letter, to Nora's desperate state of mind is also able to take effect. "He said that ever since Christmas eve," Torvald begins to quote, "—Oh, Nora, they must have been three terrible days for you!" Torvald's heart wells up in sympathy—the protective sympathy of the superior male. He assures her of his forgiveness. The thought that she did it for love of him is sweet incense to his nostrils. He finds her doubly attractive in her womanly helplessness. And as Nora retires to take off her masquerade dress, we see Torvald strutting up and down near the door, comfortably settled again in his heroic pose, striking attitudes that send a quiver through one's diaphragm. "My scared little song bird," he apostrophizes her. "I have broad wings to shield you. . . . Here I can shelter you like a hunted dove whom I have saved from the claws of the hawk. . . . Oh, you don't know a true man's heart, Nora! There is something indescribably sweet and soothing to a man in having forgiven his wife—honestly forgiven her from the bottom of his heart."

A minute later we see husband and wife seated at opposite sides of the table, Torvald staring in blank surprise, as the cold, set expression of Nora's face backs up her statement that the time has come for a final settlement.

If I have been successful in showing *A Doll's House* to be high comedy of the subtlest order up to this point, our vision will not be put to any particular strain to see the genius of comedy hovering over the scene of the settlement. If we see

Torvald as neither a cad nor a villain, but as a worthy, honest citizen as citizens go, a careful provider, a doting husband, unimaginative, but scarcely a shade less so than the average male, self-complacent and addicted to heroic stage-play—a habit fostered by the uncritical adoration of his mate; if Nora is to us not the tragic heroine as which she is commonly pictured, but an irresistibly bewitching piece of femininity, an extravagant poet and romancer, utterly lacking in sense of fact, and endowed with a natural gift for play-acting which makes her instinctively dramatize her experiences:—how can the settlement fail of a fundamentally comic appeal? We can follow Nora's indictment of Torvald and conventional man-governed society with the most alert sympathy; we can be thrilled by her spirited gesture of emancipation; we can applaud her bravery; we can enjoy watching Torvald's bluffed expression turn gradually into a hangdog look of contrition as he winces under her trouncing and gets worsted in every phase of the argument: and we will be aware at the same time that Nora is enjoying the greatest moment of her life—the supreme thrill that is tantamount, in fact, to a fulfillment of her hunger for the miracle!

Not the least among the items contributing to the comedy is the fact that Nora scores with even the most questionable of her accusations, thanks to the dash of her unexpected invective. "You have never understood me," she charges. Nothing could be truer; but how was he to understand her, when she played the lark and the squirrel with such spontaneous zest? How was he to divine her capacity for devotion, when she delighted in acting the incorrigible spendthrift, when it amused her to make him believe that the money he gave her simply melted between her fingers, when she played a perpetual game of hide-and-seek—and played it so effectively because play-acting was second nature to her? Now she blames him for not having treated her as a serious, responsible person, whereas all her efforts had heretofore been bent on appearing charmingly irresponsible. Past master of the arts of feminine coquetry, she is fully persuaded that she has cultivated these little tricks only under the pressure of male egotism, as if they were not a fundamental part of her instinctive endowment. And she gravely distributes the blame for having made the desire to please the supreme rule of her conduct, between Torvald and her father. Incidentally, her charge that in all the years of their marriage they have never exchanged one serious word about serious things, is incorrect: she has quite forgotten how seriously Torvald lectured her on the subjects of forgery and lying less than three days ago. If what she means is rather that they have never discussed any of their domestic problems in the spirit of serious partnership, it would seem that she were at least as much to blame for this as Torvald. Similarly, when she claims that her tastes in all matters are nothing but a reflection of those of her husband, she is certainly deluding herself. She very cleverly inculcated the idea in Torvald that she was dependent on his counsel even in such matters as choosing a fancy dress costume; but to be convinced that it is in reality her taste which is reflected in the cozy interior of their flat, scarcely requires so direct a hint as her chatter in the first scene, where she says: "And now I'll tell you how I think we ought to plan things, Torvald. As soon as Christmas is over . . . " The ring at the door cuts her short, but we can wager that she had a whole bagful of suggestions on refurnishing and redecorating the apartment on a scale in keeping with their enlarged income; and Torvald would not be the man he is, if he did not follow the lead of his little charmer.

She has never been happy, she now discovers. She had thought herself happy for eight years, but now it appears that she has been only merry. You are mistaken, dear Nora, we are obliged to reply. If your happiness now turns out to have been based on an illusion, its present collapse can not touch feelings that have become part of the irrevocable past. As we see, Nora brings the same intense will-to-believe to the reinterpretation of her past, as had supported her so recently in her expectation of the miracle. She is the same play-acting, hysterical Nora she always was, only: she has now changed her dress.

There is melodrama in Nora's calm announcement that she is going to leave her husband. She extracts all the thrills she possibly can from the situation. She has lived with a strange man for eight years, and borne three children to a stranger; she will not stay another night under a stranger's roof; she will not take a cent of Torvald's money, for she accepts no gifts from strangers; he must not even write to her; she returns his ring and demands her own, as a symbol of the total severance of their relations. Even the thought of her children, to whom she is devotedly attached, can not budge her from her determination. "I know they are in better hands than mine," she says, referring evidently to the old nursemaid of whose educative talent Nora is herself the most striking product.

One miracle Nora has undeniably accomplished. She has seen her husband, strutting lately in a pose of self-complacent heroism, wilt under the withering fire of her words. She has seen his conceited pride shrink and dwindle and disappear altogether. She has seen his face register shame, contrition and abject humility. The suggestive power of the words in which she voiced her sense of injury has been so intense as to turn his initial resistance into a complete rout. Succumbing to the hypnotic spell of her personality, he accepts her version of the facts as the truth. (And there is not a reader of *A Doll's House,* I daresay, who has not equally succumbed to that spell at one time or other.) When Nora makes her dramatic exit, she is conscious of having scored a complete psychological victory. Torvald's final gesture is one of unconditional surrender.

The conclusion is skillfully timed. The drop of the curtain finds us in a state of comic elation; for, whatever we think of the logic of Nora's arguments, we enjoy the victory of the superior, if erratic individual over the representative of commonplace respectability. And we are the less inclined to begrudge Nora the completeness of her triumph, as our imagination leaps ahead to speculate on the reaction that is bound to set in on the next day.

I would not predict with dogmatic certainty what is going to happen. It is barely possible that not even Christina's sober counsels will succeed in dissuading Nora from leaving her home. In that case, granted that she succeeds in finding employment, will she find the tedium of the daily routine endurable? Working in earnest for a living will not provide any of the thrills of those nights of secret copywork that made her remark to Christina: "Sometimes I was so tired, so tired. And yet it was so awfully amusing to work in that way and earn money. I almost felt as if I were a man." It is hard to picture Nora as a bank clerk or a telephone operator, but it is harder to think of her playing the part for more than three days at a time. Other possibilities come to mind, too. One can choose to think of Nora taking to the lecture platform, agitating for the emancipation of woman. Or, again, she may find a lover and weave new romances about a new hero.

But personally I am convinced that after putting Torvald through a sufficiently protracted ordeal of suspense, Nora will yield to his entreaties and return home—on her own terms. She will not bear the separation from her children very long, and her love for Torvald, which is not as dead as she thinks, will reassert itself. For a time the tables will be reversed: a meek and chastened husband will eat out of the hand of his squirrel; and Nora, hoping to make up by a sudden spurt of zeal for twenty-eight years of lost time, will be trying desperately hard to grow up. I doubt, however, whether her volatile enthusiasm will even carry her beyond the stage of resolutions. The charm of novelty worn off, she will tire of the new game very rapidly and revert, imperceptibly, to her rôle of song-bird and charmer, as affording an unlimited range to the exercise of her inborn talents of coquetry and play-acting. (pp. 55-68)

> *Hermann J. Weigand, in his* The Modern Ibsen: A Reconsideration, *Henry Holt and Company, 1925, 416 p.*

BRIAN W. DOWNS (essay date 1950)

[*Downs was an English educator and critic who wrote extensively on Scandinavian literature. In the following excerpt, he discusses the closely interrelated nature of the reconstructed past, the projected future, and the present action in* A Doll's House. *Downs further discusses the issues of Nora's conduct and character and the general ethical and social problems that were raised by early commentators on the play.*]

The focus throughout [*A Doll's House*] is on the present. It is not the expiation of Nora's forgery, let alone the perpetration of it years ago, it is her marital *malaise* that is at issue, and the discovery of the crime serves to transform vague *malaise* into acute crisis. Nevertheless, there is in *A Doll's House* more of the past than a scrap of doubtful paper. I do not refer to Krogstad's own crime and to his old sentimental relations with Fru Linde—though these things serve to build up that firm nexus between passing events and their forerunners by means of which Ibsen contrived to give an extraordinary relief and perspective to his mature works; I have in mind the allusions to, and the demonstrable effects of, Nora's upbringing, which heighten the moral drama. Her father, it transpires, an irresponsible spendthrift, brought her up with no sense of social obligation or serious thought for the morrow, while her husband, finding her a delightful companion like this, did nothing to repair the omission and, indeed, continued to treat her with the condescending playfulness less appropriate to a mother of three children than to a girl in her 'teens. Nora's overgrown irresponsibility, on the one hand, permitted the forgery. The way in which it was regarded, on the other hand, only encouraged her in chicane and bred the uneasiness of a stifled, guilty conscience. (pp. 116-17)

Nowhere before had Ibsen projected the interest—the dramatic, as well as the moral interest—into the future with such vigour and effect as he . . . did in *A Doll's House.* Even the problem: 'Was Nora justified in leaving home?' was argued with no greater heat than were speculations as to what she and her husband would do after breakfast the next morning. There were cynical prophecies, there were sentimental prophecies, fantastic prophecies of all kinds. Minds straying that way should remind themselves that, if the end of the play

is to be taken seriously, then clearly the greatest battle of Nora's life has already been decided and that nothing thereafter is likely to deter her from doing what she is determined to do: and that is to think out, in independence and solitude, her position in a world whose general laws she has begun to apprehend and means to fathom. Some have seen a damaging admission of irresolution in the happy ending which Ibsen himself cobbled together as an alternative. Ibsen's own defence of it is legitimate enough; since it had to be concocted, least damage would be done if he did the concocting himself.

The speculations to which the end of *A Doll's House* gave rise were revived after almost all Ibsen's later tragedies—all the more understandably as they by no means all involved the death of the protagonist. Would Fru Alving kill her son? Does Gregers, babbling about being the thirteenth at table, go out to commit suicide? Is Ellida Wangel really cured? Will Alfred and Rita Allmers succeed in finding a common purpose and a redeeming peace in their slum-school? Of course, when death concludes the play, questions of this order were not likely to present themselves. (p. 118)

In a sense the interest which issues in these questions is adventitious. Some modern exegetists sternly insist that nothing concerns the audience or the reader of a play but what is in the play itself. But the firmly established *past* in Ibsen's plays, as distinct from the problematical future, cannot be set aside so peremptorily; it is too much part of them. As time went on it tended to bulk even more prominently. . . .

In *A Doll's House,* the psychological implications set aside, the reconstructed past is fairly simple: Thorvald Helmer fell seriously ill and needed a long holiday abroad; Nora forged her father's name on a promissory note and raised the funds required for that holiday, then slaved and saved enough behind her husband's back to pay to Krogstad the instalments of the debt as they fell due. (p. 119)

Except in *An Enemy of the People,* the pre-history of Ibsen's mature drama is always of the first significance, and the manner by which it is revealed, the so-called 'analytic technique', is characterised by the greatest skill and dramatic effectiveness.

However skilful and, in Ibsen's scheme, indispensable the telescoping of a long action might be, it struck contemporaries as novel and for that reason gave rise to aesthetic doubts. These were most ably formulated by the German novelist, Spielhagen, who combined practical craftsmanship with an interest in the technicalities of literature not very common with working authors. He complained [in 'Drama oder Roman,' in his *Theorie und Technik des Romans*] that, in *A Doll's House,* Ibsen had taken a highly complicated story, the salient events in which had, one way or another, reference to a great span of time, and, in order to fit it into a dramatic scheme which very nearly observed the old Unities, he had laboriously and confusingly to work backwards at the same time as, more legitimately, he was working forward to its unravelment; he was endeavouring to do what was more readily achieved by one of the three-decker novels of the period. *A Doll's House* has not yet (as *Peer Gynt* has) given rise to 'the novel of the film', but when it does, we may be in a position to check Spielhagen's claim. Ibsen's practice meanwhile has dissipated the unfamiliarity of his methods; and, in any event, his analytic technique . . . was not quite so revolutionary as it seemed to Spielhagen, who was really protesting against what strikes many as one of Ibsen's great virtues—his 'perspective', the fullness of his dramatic world, a fullness which characterises also the world of Shakespeare and Euripides.

Besides exhuming the past, Ibsen, it has been remarked, opened a window into the future. That, too, was made a ground for critical complaint, and more reasonably. He developed his situation in such a way that in the end it was replaced by another, equally clamant for solution; but no solution was offered or suggested. Besides the double-dyed aesthetes who held that Art precisely should *not* submit problems to debate, others were willing to accept the theory of Brandes and his followers, with the proviso that the artist should answer moral questions he raised. 'What is the good', they urged, 'of showing us how Nora, the married woman, coped with her problems, if Nora, as *femme sole* ["single woman"], is left confronting problems of equal magnitude and complexity? Question marks are not like the negative symbols in mathematics: two of them do not cancel one another out. It is unfair to replace one problem by another and leave the solution of the second to us—that is what, in effect, the conclusion of *A Doll's House* comes to.' Ibsen's defence against accusations of this order was peremptory. He denied the proviso. By *submitting* the problems to debate—and, it is fair to add, by presenting them honestly—he had done all that was expected of him: 'I choose to ask: it is not my mission to answer.' (pp. 120-21)

Questions about the dividing line between the novel and the drama were the concern mainly of aesthetes. . . . Nearly everyone, however, to whose notice they came, was eager to sit in judgement on [Nora's] character and her conduct.

The questions at issue can be reduced to something like this dual form: What are precisely the motives that drive Nora Helmer to break up her home; and is it credible that these motives should have presented themselves spontaneously to such a person as the author represents his heroine as being and should so effectively have actuated her?

In elaborating, as is now necessary, the sketchy analysis of Nora's character already attempted above, one may, for a moment, dwell on two negative factors. First, giddy-pated and irresponsible though Nora might be, nothing suggests that she was the woman to consider walking out of the house: the Helmers' front door had not been slammed after every tiff or wifely disappointment: the act is unique and momentous. Second, in delineating Nora's character with an almost supererogatory regard for its formation in the past, Ibsen gave no hint that she was either, in the commonly accepted sense, a *femme méconnue* ['misjudged woman'] or even a *femme inconnue* ['unknown woman'], fundamentally capricious and, like the prophet Habakkuk, capable of anything; there seems to be no pathological or semi-pathological incoherence in her personality. . . . (p. 128)

What, then, drove this somewhat feather-headed, but sound and home-loving young woman to the grave act of abandoning home, husband and children? The term 'home-loving', liberally interpreted, may point to the answer. Though apparently unstayed by religion, Nora's is a deeply passionate and devoted heart. The keynote is firmly struck before we know anything about her crime, which after all was committed from unreflecting passionate love of her husband: Helmer asks where Nora would be financially if a tile blew off the roof and knocked his brains out, and she replies that she cares not where she would be if he were not with her. It is inconceivable

to her that her feelings should not be absolutely reciprocated. Helmer may have his funny ways in pulling her up short when she looked like outrunning the constable; he could, no doubt, on occasions be cross with her; but there was a horror she had never so much as dreamed of, the distorted mask of fury and aversion that he turned upon her after opening Krogstad's fatal letter. It *was* the face of a strange man with whom she had been living.

An equally deadly shaft had already pierced her heart. Krogstad, she learns, once did what she had done, committed forgery and evaded the consequences; and Helmer—the fount of wisdom for Nora—gives it as his opinion that such a man must be the poisoner of his own children. By implication, he adjudges her unworthy to be a mother. It shows the seriousness with which she accepts this judgement that thereafter she keeps her children away from her as much as possible.

These two blows, the conviction of her unworthiness to be a mother and the knowledge that Helmer's love for her was fallible, have completely shattered the vital basis of Nora's life. To leave the hearth on which the fire has gone out can give her no further pangs.

The instinctive grounds of Nora's final act are thus abundantly justified. But that does not constitute a complete defence. It might have been so if, on Helmer's outburst of recrimination, Nora had, in panic horror, thrown a wrap over her fancy dress and fled incontinently into the night. But then the great settling of accounts between husband and wife would have fallen away. And that Nora walks out of her doll's house offends some observers less than that she should dally to argue

Henrik Ibsen.

about it. An unthinking creature, they feel, takes to rationalising an instinctive impulse and begins talking as if she had swallowed John Stuart Mill's *The Subjection of Women* whole.

In endeavouring to account for the change in Nora's demeanour, besides the double shock, we must not overlook something a trifle febrile and morbid which her manner portrays from the start—her irresistible longing, for instance, to use strong language—which disquiets her friend Fru Linde. The long strain imposed by the repayment of her debt to Krogstad cannot entirely account for it, since it is just about to be removed. There seems to be something more. Nora tells her husband that she has been merry but never happy. That, no doubt, is an exaggeration, which profound disillusionment readily explains. Nora was probably quite happy most of the time. But there has been a small, lurking residuum of dissatisfaction, a waiting for something that does not happen—'Det vidunderlige' ['the miracle']. One would probably not go far wrong (since nothing apparently ails the children) in seeking the cause of *malaise* in her marital relations and more precisely in those aspects of her husband's attitude which distress third parties too. To account for the final serious discussion between husband and wife, we must base it on some unsatisfied, if slender sense of seriousness in Nora; if the principle be accepted, it is not altogether surprising that *all* Nora's seriousness should come out at once and, unpractised as she is in giving voice, sound in places forced and priggish.

This does not claim to be a complete apology. The gap between Nora, the solemn defender of individuality, and Nora, the squirrel and the lark, has generally been felt too wide to explain away, though the magic of a great actress's art has on occasion conjured it away. There is, similarly, another flaw at the other end of the career which we are permitted to follow. Frankly incredible it seems that Nora should have failed to recognise her forgery as a crime. 'People like me don't get found out or else bluff their way through', is just a possible attitude for the spoiled and feather-brained, but Nora's very uneasiness *vis-à-vis* Krogstad and her desire to have the dubious IOU returned to her plead against her ignorance of the nature of her act.

One may observe too that in reality a Krogstad must have known his threats to be mainly bluff. But here the dramatic situation needed something 'strong': the dangerous blackmailer confronting the inexperienced woman who committed a crime from ignorance and love—and the position he takes up easily passes muster with theatre-audiences. In the same way the moral situation demands something 'strong' in the third act, and Ibsen opined with less justification that Nora's *volte-face* and last words would just carry conviction.

Le sérieux ['the seriousness'] in Nora, such as it is, guarantees *le sérieux* of her last exit, and of the entire drama. But it also, I think, admits a ray of hope. Thorvald is sobered and impressed by it; it is not at all impossible that he has, if dimly, apprehended where the real rift between his wife and himself lies nor that *'det vidunderligste'* ['miracle of miracles'] of which he whispers as the curtain falls is the same thing as Nora's *'vidunderlige'*. Of course, it cannot be more than a gleam of light. Thorvald may not be the man to take his share in realising the miracle. The summing-up of all this may well be that Nora's character is more consistent, that the tragedy which befalls her is deeper and that, at the same time, the conclusion comes rather nearer a reconciliation than these things are often thought to be.

It was a testimony to the sympathetic interest in his heroine which Ibsen had aroused that her particular case should be so hotly disputed. But the arguments at once ranged much further. The bang of the Helmers' front door would not have alarmed so many people had they not been fearful that it might bring down on their heads nothing less than the whole fabric of marriage. The dismay was all the greater, since, in the welter of uncertainties which new scientific discoveries, new cosmic theories and the recent redistribution of political power had caused, domestic institutions and the private virtues alone seemed still to stand unshaken. Paterfamilias, looking at the partner of his joys over a morning newspaper full of the repercussions of Bismarck's policy, the Paris Commune, Papal infallibility, Darwin's Evolutionism and the Higher Criticism, had always been able to say to himself: 'There is still the Home. There is still Marriage. We still have one another.' But could he be so absolutely sure now?

It is always tempting to build up a generalisation from a concrete case, a generalisation not of necessity universally valid, but at any rate embodying a definite doctrine. Soberly considering the point, most people would agree that it is indefensible to hold an artist responsible for an ethical tenet, apparently justified in a single imaginary instance. Because *All's Well That Ends Well* does in fact end well, we must not suppose that Shakespeare approved of jugglery with the marriage-bed, nor that Sophocles cried up matricide because his Orestes so cheerfully sends Clytemnestra to her account. If Ibsen's *œuvre*, viewed as a whole, with its apparent tergiversations, implies anything, it is that circumstances alter cases: Stockmann's claims of the ideal are justified, Gregers Werle's are not. Like his ally Brandes, Ibsen believed that the age of relativity had come in, admitting of no general rules. He would never wish it to be claimed, for instance, on the evidence of **Pillars of Society** and **John Gabriel Borkman** that all big business is barratry, or, on the strength of **An Enemy of the People,** that every man who stands alone is in the right.

His very ingenuity in presenting an individual case so that it should convince logically and be dramatically moving, together with his choice of themes, did none the less lay Ibsen open to the charge that he was playing the advocate and presenting theses, not problems. The impression was particularly strong in **A Doll's House** by reason of the heavy-handedness with which Fru Linde's schoolmarmish proclivities drive Nora to an *éclaircissement* ['solution']. At all costs, it appeared, the author was intent to stage a debate on matrimonial relations leading to a predetermined conclusion. The improbable argument at the end between the heroine and her husband confirms the impression that the play was largely written for its sake—otherwise it would not have been necessary to wrench probability so ruthlessly. Nora arraigns, not Thorvald only, but every husband; not the Helmer *ménage* is criticised, but marriage as an institution. As R. C. Boer puts it [in *Ibsen's Dramas*]: 'The abnormal case of Helmer and Nora is forced on us as the norm.' Husbands look upon themselves as superior beings, who, holding the economic reins and legally omnipotent, concentrate in themselves all the responsibilities of the household and alone embody its serious aspect: they condescend to their wives, relegating them to the level of concubine, nurse and housekeeper, and thereby encourage all the vices of the harem—deceit and sensuality foremost—from which grave corruption, all manner of dangers may spring. That is what the charge looks like.

Even if the early plays are admitted to the count, Ibsen portrays, to be sure, more unsatisfactory than satisfactory marriages. It would be otiose to give the catalogue. Yet he does allow of happy marriages; that of Dr Thomas Stockmann provides an excellent case in point: so the institution is not condemned root and branch. And what Ibsen does *not* hold up is equally important to remember. His works contain no defence of celibacy direct or implied. Nor is there any glorification of unlawful or transitory unions. The notorious picture which Oswald Alving draws of happy liaisons on the left bank of the Seine is coupled with the hint that only lack of means forbids the consecration by Monsieur le Maire or Monsieur le Curé; and if any union is thoroughly rotten, it is that in which Fanny Wilton and Erhard Borkman have involved themselves.

Ibsen's sense of relativity again comes into play. Talking *à propos* of **Love's Comedy** to Brandes about betrothals, he remarked that there were good potatoes and that there were bad potatoes, and that it was his misfortune only to have met with the latter. As far as marriages go, he appears to have been luckier. All depends on conditions. After affection between the contracting parties, he clearly sees candour to be one of the most important of these conditions, implying a frank and thorough exploration of themselves and one another. This gives knowledge while the affection gives understanding. Such conditions once fulfilled, it is almost remarkable how many potentially satisfactory unions Ibsen can envisage. In the present play, for instance, we have that of Kristine Linde and Krogstad, who harbour no illusions about the degree in which life has battered themselves and the hardness of the road before them. There are the Bernicks and the Allmerses as well as the Stockmanns. The most striking one is that in **The Wild Duck** between the old rake, Werle senior, and his far from maidenly housekeeper, Fru Sørby, who look like enjoying a pretty happy old age together, having as a matter of common sense and friendliness told one another all about themselves and the vicissitudes of their past lives.

The absence of candour and mutual knowledge, the failure to face common problems jointly and seriously, are seen to be the root defects in the Helmers's marriage, the main fault lying with the husband and his 'superior' attitude. The diagnosis closely resembles that made in *The Subjection of Women*, where Mill traces the 'slave mentality' of women back to the legal privileges reserved to the husband and the male, a point not directly made in **A Doll's House** itself, though it is implied in **Pillars of Society** and made one of the guiding notes for **A Doll's House**, in which Ibsen remarked that women are judged and condemned according to laws which they have had no hand in making. To this aspect we shall return shortly.

In his criticism of marriage, Ibsen was seen to be joining in that disturbing modern movement of looking in general upon man and his social arrangements from the factual, scientific, unsentimental and antitraditional point of view which was turning *belles lettres* into a branch of natural history. **A Doll's House** afforded support for this apprehension outside the treatment of the Helmer marriage.

Nora is irresponsible and frivolous, not only because the serious elements in her nature have never received encouragement, but also because she has inherited from her father a disposition towards frivolity and irresponsibility. In **Peer Gynt** and **Brand**, as was pointed out, Ibsen invoked childish memories as formative elements in the characters of his heroes, who, moreover, have a great deal in common with their re-

spective mothers, the formidable Fru Brand and the feckless Aase. But the insistence on inherited characteristics in Nora's case is something novel.

The most striking instance of inherited disabilities is presented, however, not by Nora herself but by Dr Rank. In the play's economy, he fills a part analogous to Fru Linde's. He is partly 'functional', his timid declaration of love depriving Nora of her last chance to placate Krogstad and avoid the *éclaircissement* with her husband, and his loneliness (savoured as such by the epicure Helmer) and sad fate affording a theatrical contrast with the snugness and supposed happiness of his friends' fireside; partly he serves to point a moral. As in his body he suffers for the excesses of his father, so Nora's weakness of character derives from *her* father, and, together with her criminality, can be transmitted to her children.

The *motif* of heredity—then much discussed in Norway as part of the Darwinian hypothesis and with particular reference to the combating of leprosy—is not adduced by Ibsen with very great frequency. Rosmer has all the traditions of his old family to contend against, but his inheritance seems to lie entirely in the moral realm, though we cannot perhaps say as much for Rebecca West, and it is overwhelmingly reinforced by his environment. In accounting for the character of Hedda Gabler, Ibsen makes less play with the taint derived from her ancestry than would have been warranted by Strindberg's short story from which he took a hint for his theme. Erhard Borkman seems to have nothing of his father or of his mother in him. Such deformation of character as may be reproved in Hilda Wangel is apparently due to nurture, not nature. The Wild Duck, however, has two strands of heredity woven into its fabric, as we shall see. But the most notorious instance, of course, of Ibsen's utilising this idea is that which, as one might say, springs directly from Dr Rank: **Ghosts**, with the 'worm-eaten' constitution which Oswald Alving derived from his father and its whole sermon on 'the sins of the fathers are visited on the children'.

As **The Doll's House** resumed half of the original theme of its predecessor—'It is you women who are the pillars of society'—so, in its turn, its action projects after a fashion into that of its successor, **Ghosts.** The repetition of Dr Rank's fate in Oswald provides only one instance. The larger theme which the Oswald theme subserves may very probably have been suggested by the criticisms of **A Doll's House.** Mrs Alving, it has been remarked, may be looked upon as Nora Helmer twenty years on—a two-faced observation, since it throws as much light on the latter as on the former, confirming the postulate of an underlying seriousness in her character and a capacity for social effectiveness. More obviously, however, **Ghosts** constitutes a retort to the Pastor Manderses of criticism, who had vociferated about the unconditional immorality inherent in a wife's leaving her home. For does not **Ghosts** rehearse the fate of a woman who, driven to the same desperate extreme as the condemned heroine of **A Doll's House,** consented, for all practical purposes, not to leave husband and home? The consequences of her orthodoxy are shown as far more dire than the worst predictable for Nora's unorthodoxy. After demonstrating in **A Doll's House** that marriage, instead of being the conventional heaven, might be purgatory, in **Ghosts** Ibsen exhibited it as hell.

Nora Helmer, the bank manager's wife, and Medea of Colchis have almost as little in common as any two women could have. But just as Euripides had done, to the great discomfiture of Athenian audiences, so Ibsen, in another play which is not quite a tragedy, presented his heroine revolting against her husband and against the society in which she lives and upon which, in the end, she defiantly turns her back: the revolt is carefully motivated and to that extent justified, even more than justified. Nora turns against her husband and against convention not only as Medea rounds on Jason when he discards her in favour of Creusa, for a particular act, but also because she has become aware of something more general that oppresses and constricts—Helmer's sultanic attitude towards her and the menace of a code she barely comprehends. Her leaving home is to be construed perhaps more accurately as an act of liberation than as one of revolt.

Fundamentally, that is the great problem in all the works of Ibsen's maturity—the liberation of the personality from restrictions and inhibitions. (pp. 128-38)

In *A Doll's House,* the restrictive agency is, in the main, family tutelage formidably abetted by one-sided laws; in *Ghosts,* conventions in the domestic sphere are reinforced by the operations of heredity; in *An Enemy of the People,* as the title may indicate, the struggle resembles that of *Pillars of Society,* variety being obtained by substituting an 'untainted' hero in the one for the 'tainted' hero of the other. From 1877 to 1882, thus, Society, represented by the Rørlunds and Rummels, the Thorvald Helmers and Pastor Manderses, Peter Stockmann, Aslaksen and Company, furnishes the villains for Ibsen's pieces. (p. 138)

Nora and her problem fall naturally into their place in the general scheme. It must, however, have been noticed that, in the catalogue of victims . . . , women form the minority, Ibsen clearly seeing the male sex as being no more exempt than they from the need of emancipation. From the time of Furia (*Catiline*), Blanka (*The Warrior's Barrow*), the Lady Inger of Østraat onwards, Ibsen had as spontaneously as invariably approached the women of his plays on exactly the same terms as his men; their common humanity and not their special sexual characteristics were always uppermost in his mind. Nevertheless, the fact that in *A Doll's House* it is a woman who stands opposed to Society and that the issue here is joined with such perspicuousness and dramatic effectiveness, raised a particular interest at a time when the 'woman question' first attained general prominence. (p. 139)

It is unfortunate, if unavoidable, that so much of the discussion of *A Doll's House* revolves round 'problems'. For Ibsen justly maintained that his first aim was the presentation of human beings and their destinies. But rightly or wrongly, the piece has always given rise to further speculations, and a commentator could scarcely avoid touching upon them.

A last one has still to be discussed: the meaning of *det vidunderlige,* the 'miracle', which Nora first mentions in Act II, but which is not then defined. Is it the same thing as *det vidunderligste,* the 'miracle of miracles', on which her last words to Helmer turn and which she does define as 'that communion between us shall be a marriage'? In her fine-feeling study of Nora's character, Lou Andréas-Salomé seems to assume that what all along Nora has desired is—shall we so call it?—a spiritual consummation of her union with Helmer, analogous to the physical [see excerpt dated 1892]. She has been a bride too long, now she wants to be a wife. With the early hint at depth and seriousness in her character, that interpretation has the desirable advantage of linking the 'old Nora' of Acts I and II firmly with the 'new woman' of the

close. But there are great objections to it. For when Fru Linde in Act II asks what the 'miracle' is, Nora replies: 'But it is so terrible, Kristine; it mustn't happen for all the world.' Surely Nora could not wish *this* particular miracle not to 'happen for all the world'? The obvious alternative, however, is not much more satisfactory. If Nora is contemplating in Act II (clearly as something that has been in her mind before) what she formulates in Act III, namely, Thorvald's full recognition of the motive underlying her crime and assumption of all the blame for it, she must at that time have been well aware of the seriousness of her act, while one is forced to think that much of the plot and of the moral theme depends precisely on her lack of this awareness. Perhaps the alternative need not be accepted in whole, but only part. In Act II Nora may have dreamt only of Thorvald's discovering and appreciating the act of devotion by which she saved his life, while his taking her guilt upon himself may have been an afterthought, added when the full seriousness of that act of devotion had been brought home to her.

Some have thought that by the 'miracle of miracles' which Thorvald whispers as the final curtain drops, he means something different from Nora, that he is thinking merely of a restoration of his domestic felicity on much the old basis with an added appreciation of the joys of calm after a storm—something rather parallel to his reactions on hearing of Rank's final departure. Thorvald certainly is *l'homme moyen sensuel,* ['the average sensual man'], but at such a moment this little note of acerbity seems not only jarring, but improbable. In every sense of the word, Thorvald is sobered, and can indeed see himself as a new man living with a new Nora. (pp. 143-44)

> *Brian W. Downs, in his* A Study of Six Plays by Ibsen, *Cambridge at the University Press, 1950, 212 p.*

JOHN NORTHAM   (essay date 1953)

[*In the following excerpt, Northam discusses the importance of such elements of dramaturgy as props, costumes, and gestures to the representation of character in* A Doll's House.]

When Ibsen wrote proudly to George Brandes that he had eliminated every single monologue from *League of Youth,* he was not setting himself an infrangible standard; *A Doll's House* contains seven for Nora:

Act I.	(1)	NORA. (*Busy dressing the tree*) There must be a candle here—and flowers there—That horrible man! Nonsense, nonsense! There's nothing to be afraid of. The Christmas-tree shall be beautiful. I'll do everything to please you, Torvald; I'll sing and dance, and—
	(2)	NORA. (*Pale with terror*) Corrupt my children! Poison my home! (*Short pause. She raises her head.*) It's not true! It can never, never be true!
Act II.	(3)	NORA. (*Dropping the cloak*) There's somebody coming! (*Goes to the hall door and listens*) Nobody; of course nobody will come to-day, Christmas day; nor

to-morrow either. But perhaps—
(*Opens the door and looks out*)—
No, nothing in the letter-box;
quite empty. (*Comes forward*)
Stuff and nonsense! Of course he
won't really do anything. Such a
thing couldn't happen. It's impossible! Why, I have three little
children.

(4) NORA. He would do it. Yes, he
would do it. He would do it, in
spite of all the world. No, never
that, never, never! Anything
rather than that! Oh, for some
way of escape! What shall I
do . . . ! (*Hall bell rings*) Doctor
Rank! . . . Anything, anything,
rather than—!

(5) NORA. It is coming! The dreadful thing is coming, after all. No,
no, no, it can never be; it shall
not!

(6) NORA. He's going. He's not putting the letter into the box. No,
no, it would be impossible!
(*Opens the door further and further*) What's that. He's standing
still; not going downstairs. Has
he changed his mind? Is he . . .
? . . . There it lies. . . . Torvald, Torvald—now we are lost!

Act III.   (7) NORA . . . . Never to see him
again. Never, never, never. . . .
Never to see the children again.
Never, never. Oh that black, icy
water! Oh that bottomless . . . !
If it were only over! Now he has
it; he's reading it. Oh no, no, no,
not yet. Torvald, good-bye . . . !
Good-bye, my little ones . . . !

These broken, repetitive, incoherent utterances lack the illustrative power of comparable passages in poetic drama, where
they would be the chief illuminators of the heroine's soul.
Here they tell us that Nora is suffering, and they tell us vaguely the source and intensity of her torment; they may be, in
themselves, a sign of childishness; but by themselves they do
not re-create in us the sort of rich emotional attitude that we
obtain from such a speech as 'Ay, but to die, and go we know
not where'. Clearly, if Ibsen had been confined to a purely
oral transmission of feeling and emotion by means of everyday speech, we should have small opportunity of entering
into the souls of his characters. Happily, he employed a number of amplifying aids, the first of which may be called 'illustrative action'.

Here, Ibsen's method is the method of 'concealed psychology' according to which an action or a gesture 'will realize inevitably the character's state of mind in a given situation'.

The macaroons—when Ibsen makes Nora, at the very opening of the play, pop a couple of sweets into her mouth as soon
as she comes in from shopping, and then take pains to hide
all signs of them when she hears her husband's voice, he tells
us in a matter of seconds several important things about
Nora's character: it is a childish one; it goes in awe of authority; it is willing to deceive.

The macaroons appear again in Act I. The situation is as follows: Nora once secretly borrowed money by forging her father's signature in order to pay for a trip abroad to save her
husband's health. The loan was made by Krogstad, whose appearance shortly before has terrified her; but now she learns
that her husband's promotion in the bank where Krogstad
works gives her some measure of protection against him. Torvald is out of the room.

NORA . . . . Yes, it is funny to think that we—that
Torvald has such power over so many people.
(*Takes the bag from her pocket*) Doctor Rank, will
you have a macaroon?
RANK. What!—macaroons! I thought they were
contraband here.
NORA. Yes, but Christina brought me these.

They are obviously not introduced to remind us that Nora
likes sweets; nor even merely to remind us that she is childish
and a liar. She has been frightened by Krogstad and fears the
intrusion of an alien reality which threatens her own childish
paradise. When she realizes her husband's new power, or
rather, her own power over the intrusive masculine world of
business, her terror is replaced by a feeling of confidence.
Hence her almost open revolt against the masculine control
of her husband, and her triumphant reassertion of her girlish-
ness. Out come the macaroons.

They are not seen again, but since an important later reference depends on these two earlier appearances, it may be
dealt with here. The reference comes in Act II. Nora has
failed to persuade her husband not to sack Krogstad, who,
having made his reinstatement the condition of his remaining
silent about the forgery, thereupon drops a letter into Torvald's letter-box informing him of his wife's criminal act.
Nora, persuaded that, in the event of discovery, her husband
would shoulder the blame to protect her, decides to kill herself first. Meanwhile she must keep Torvald away from the
letter-box in order to prolong her life. To do this, she must
force her husband to submit his will to hers, and the sweets
are the symbol; she asks him to arrange a party with champagne and lots of macaroons. This open demand on the usually inflexible refuser of sweets presents us with the desperate
state of Nora's mind.

The stove—the following scene occurs in Act I:

NORA. Who is the gentleman?
KROGSTAD. (*In the doorway*) It is I, Mrs.
Helmer. . . .
NORA. (*Goes a step towards him, anxiously, speaking low*) You? What is it? What do you want with
my husband?
KROGSTAD. Bank business—in a way. I hold a
small post in the Joint Stock Bank, and your husband is to be our new chief, I hear.
NORA. Then it is—?
KROGSTAD. Only tiresome business, Mrs. Helmer;
nothing more.
NORA. Then will you please go to his study. (*Krogstad goes. She bows indifferently while she closes the
door into the hall. Then she goes to the stove and
looks to the fire.*)

There is no real need for Nora to touch the stove, but the action illuminates the whole passage. The stage directions and
the dialogue tell us that Nora fears Krogstad; the action
thrusts home the impression; he has chilled her with terror,
so she makes up the fire, instinctively seeking a physical remedy for a nervous discomfort.

The tarantella—'The tarantelle', it has been said, 'is the play' [Jennette Lee, *The Ibsen Secret*]—a sweeping statement which nevertheless serves to draw attention to the most obvious symbol in the drama. To keep Torvald's mind off the letter in the box, Nora rehearses a wild dance which he once taught her. We have grown more aware of the increasing torment in her soul, but the drama demands that, at its height, the agony should be concealed from the others in the play— but not from us, or the pathos and irony would be lost. And so Nora's frantic struggle against fate is represented in action, in the tarantella, traditionally the dance of victims of the poisonous spider.

The 'light'—during the play we have come to realize the existence of a very close sympathy between Nora and Doctor Rank, the friend of the family who is dying of an inherited disease. Nora has been the only light in a gloomy existence; Ibsen fills out the sparse hints of their last, cryptic conversation (quite misunderstood by Torvald) and drives home his point by means of an illustrative action:

> NORA. (*Striking a wax match*) Let me give you a light.
> RANK. A thousand thanks. (*She holds the match. He lights his cigar at it.*)
> RANK. And now, good-bye!
> HELMER. Good-bye, good-bye, my dear fellow.
> NORA. Sleep well, Doctor Rank.
> RANK. Thanks for the wish.
> NORA. Wish me the same.
> RANK. You? Very well, since you ask me—sleep well. And thanks for the light.

Of the illustrative actions dealt with above it may be said that none of them tells us anything that could not be deduced intellectually from the spoken words of the play; on the other hand it is claimed that they emphasize points, present them visually and therefore more cogently than words can, particularly when the words must create the illusion of everyday speech. They help us to understand the characters.

Another guide to understanding is Ibsen's use of stage properties.

The Christmas-tree—At the very beginning of the play, Nora is associated with the Christmas-tree, which we see her bring home from her shopping expedition. Christmas is a family festival, mainly devoted to the happiness of children, and the tree is its symbol, epitomizing family happiness and security. We see the tree just long enough for it to suggest ideas of this kind, and then the maid takes it away. It reappears after Nora has seen forces at work which threaten to break up her domestic world.

Her words at this point (end of Act I) are mere shorthand notes for our guidance:

> NORA . . . . No, it's quite impossible! . . . (*Busy dressing the tree.*) There must be a candle here— and flowers there.—That horrible man! Nonsense, nonsense! There's nothing to be afraid of. The Christmas-tree shall be beautiful. I'll do everything to please you, Torvald; I'll sing and dance and—

But Ibsen is unwilling to leave too heavy a task for our imaginations. Immediately before the speech which has just been quoted, he employs a visual symbol: the tree is brought back on to the stage.

> NORA . . . . Ellen, bring in the Christmas-tree! . . .
> ELLEN. (*With Christmas-tree*) Where shall I stand it, ma'am?
> NORA. There, in the middle of the room.

As with the macaroons, it is not the tree itself that is important, but the manner of its reintroduction: the tree is set in the middle of the floor, where, for the audience, it becomes the chief point of interest, dominating the stage with suggestions of family security and happiness; in it, and in Nora's 'dressing', we see her desire to reassert her family's threatened safety and to reassure herself in her sharp uneasiness.

The tree does more than tell us what is going on in Nora's mind; it provides an ironical contrast between apparent festivity and actual misery; but we are concerned here only with its bearing upon character.

Unhappily for Nora, mere assertion cannot remedy her plight, which grows steadily worse during the remainder of Act I, when she is made aware of the consequences of deceit. It was bad enough for her to learn from Krogstad that her forgery was a criminal act; the worst smart is inflicted by Torvald when he explains his implacable hostility towards his subordinate: Krogstad sinned in the past, but his greatest crime was deceitful evasion of punishment, for this ruined him morally; since then he has spread the corruption to his children. Into the wound made by this lacerating revelation Torvald unconsciously rubs salt:

> HELMER . . . . Every breath the children draw contains some germ of evil.
> NORA. (*Close behind him*) Are you sure of that?
> HELMER. As a lawyer, my dear, I have seen it often enough. Nearly all cases of early corruption may be traced to lying mothers . . . but of course the father's influence may act in the same way. . . .

Nora thus becomes aware of a dreadful new peril; the first act closes on that note:

> NORA. (*Pale with terror*) Corrupt my children! Poison my home! (*Short pause. She raises her head.*) It's not true! It can never, never be true!

Time can be no remedy for this sick anxiety; rather it makes it worse, as Nora's monologue at the opening of Act II shows:

> NORA. (*Dropping the cloak*) There's somebody coming! (*Goes to the hall door and listens.*) Nobody; of course nobody will come to-day, Christmas day; nor to-morrow either. But perhaps—(*Opens the door and looks out.*) No, nothing in the letter-box; quite empty. (*Comes forward.*) Stuff and nonsense! Of course he won't really do anything. Such a thing couldn't happen. It's impossible! Why, I have three little children!

However, Ibsen does not rely on these broken phrases alone; they are reinforced by the set:

> *In the corner, beside the piano, stands the Christmas-tree, stripped, and with the candles burnt out. . . .*

This set shows Nora on the defensive; the symbol of family security no longer holds the centre, nor is it in its full Christmas glory. It is stripped, and it stands in a corner, just as Nora has been chastened and frightened by the intrusion of the unfeeling masculine world of business. Altogether we feel that some of the tinsel has been stripped off her ideal of domestic felicity.

Lighting—The tragic implications of the 'truffles and champagne' scene in which Nora appears to make fun of Rank's fatal disease are clearly reflected in the changes of stage lighting as Rank approaches his unexpected avowal of love:

> NORA . . . . Oh for some way of escape! What shall I do! (*Hall bell rings.*) Doctor Rank! . . . Anything, anything, rather than—!
> (. . . *Rank stands outside hanging up his fur coat. During the following it begins to grow dark.*)

When the protestation comes, and Nora realizes that her last hope of getting money is gone, she puts an end to the situation by calling for light:

> NORA. (*Standing up: simply and calmly*) Let me pass, please. . . .
> (*In the doorway.*) Ellen, bring in the lamp. . . .
> (*Ellen enters with the lamp;* . . .)

Nora appears to have dissipated the gloom, but from the rest of the scene we are able to place this apparent brightness as an act of will.

The room—We learn about Torvald's character almost entirely from what is said. Even so, there has always been some doubt as to whether he is an egregious ass or a normal married man. That Ibsen meant him to be reasonably attractive is shown by the fact that the room in which the action takes place is a pleasant one, and Torvald is given the credit for its attractiveness:

> . . . *Between the two doors a pianoforte.* . . . *Engravings on the wall. A what-not with china and bric-a-brac. A small bookcase filled with handsomely bound books.* . . .
> NORA . . . . Torvald has certainly the art of making home bright and beautiful.
> MRS. LINDE. You too, I should think, or you wouldn't be your father's daughter. . . .

Mrs. Linde's remark may seem to support Professor Weigand's contention that 'to be convinced that it is in reality her taste which is reflected in the cosy interior of their flat, scarcely requires so direct a hint as her chatter in the first scene . . . ' [see excerpt dated 1925]. In fact, Mrs. Linde's remark is clearly included for the sake of the reference to heredity and the passage serves as a link between Nora and Rank. The scene continues:

> MRS. LINDE . . . . your father's daughter. But tell me—is Doctor Rank always so depressed as he was last evening?
> NORA. No, yesterday it was particularly noticeable. You see, he suffers from a dreadful illness. He has spinal consumption, poor fellow. They say his father was a horrible man who kept mistresses and all sorts of things—so the son has been sickly from his childhood. . . .

But this concern to emphasize the common element of heredity will be dealt with in the section on 'parallel situations'.

Another key to character is costume.

Throughout life, we gather, both as daughter and as wife, Nora has been obliged to practise deception and conform to the masculine ideal of childish femininity. Inevitably, such a long apprenticeship in deceit ends in a certain amount of self-deception; Nora believes in the rightness and reality of the child-life she leads in her doll's house.

As we have seen, when Ibsen wants to show us the virulence of Nora's malady, he makes her dance the tarantella on the stage. By dressing her up, at the same time, in 'a long parti-coloured shawl' he reminds us of her childish insistence on her make-believe world. Thus from the dance we apprehend Nora's thoughts of impending death; from the colourful shawl, the persistence of a desire to maintain her old form of happiness. It is not suggested that an audience would make such a precise analysis of the scene; our reaction would be simple, something like: 'What a child she is, dressing up like that; but what a troubled child she has become!'

The contrast between a desire to remain childishly happy and a fear of death is stronger when Nora, having danced the tarantella at the party upstairs, waits for an opportunity of killing herself before Torvald can read Krogstad's accusing letter and assume responsibility for her crime. Inevitably the ties of family life tug hardest when they must be broken. Just how strong is Nora's desire to return to her child-life, Ibsen presents visually in the full Italian dancing-dress which she wears; but the death-wish is presented visually too, in the shawl which covers the gay costume:

> *She wears the Italian costume with a large black shawl over it.* . . .

So long as Nora retains her belief in her child-world and can see only death as a solution to her problem, so long does Ibsen maintain this visual contrast; but with telling variations. The first of these occurs when Torvald, tipsy and quite unaware that his wife has been growing up rapidly during the last few hours, wants to make love to his dear little bride. This invitation to remain a child-wife is accompanied by a change in Nora's costume:

> HELMER. (*Taking Nora's shawl off*) . . .

Perhaps there is hope of a return to the doll's house; the funereal shawl has gone, and the childish party-dress is no longer mournfully obscured.

But then Nora learns that Mrs. Linde, her friend and an old love of Krogstad's, has failed, apparently, to get him to demand back the fatal letter which still lies in the letter-box. Her death-resolve becomes absolute. She has a monologue, but it is the visual suggestion, once more, which drives the state of her mind into our consciousness; she puts on more black:

> NORA. (*With wild eyes, gropes about her, seizes Helmer's domino, throws it round her, and whispers quickly, hoarsely, and brokenly*) Never to see him again. Never, never, never. (*Throws her shawl over her head.*) Never to see the children again. Never, never—Oh that black, icy water! Oh that bottomless—! If it were only over! Now he has it; he's reading it. Oh, no, no, no, not yet. Torvald, goodbye—! Good-bye, my little ones—!

But when Torvald bursts out of his room with the letter in his hand, and, instead of offering his protection, shouts at her in vulgar rage, Nora's illusion is shattered; her world of childish make-belief was untrue after all, and death is no longer necessary to prevent Torvald from sacrificing himself; he has no such intention:

HELMER . . . . Do you understand now what you have done to me?
NORA. (*With cold calmness*) Yes.
HELMER . . . . Take that shawl off. Take it off, I say! . . .

The black shawl comes off—but so must the dancing-dress of her illusion; she has no illusion to die for now. She lays her child-life aside and appears in everyday clothes—she has grown up at last. She tells Helmer that she has been wronged by him and the whole masculine world; to find herself she must leave home and family.

Since it was for the sake of the ending that Ibsen wrote the play, it is disturbing to find such variety of interpretation. When the drama was first produced, the ending was treated as the solution to a problem, and one either approved the solution (with G. B. Shaw) or disapproved (with Frau Hedwig Niemann-Raabe) [a German actress who refused to play the part of Nora unless the ending was changed]. More recent critics, however, led by Professor Weigand, have ignored the problem and studied Nora's frame of mind instead. The conclusion is that '*A Doll's House* [is] high comedy of the subtlest order. . . . We can be thrilled by her spirited gesture of emancipation; we can applaud her bravery . . . and we will be aware at the same time that Nora is enjoying the greatest moment of her life. . . . The drop of the curtain finds us in a state of comic elation' [see Weigand excerpt dated 1925]. The whole question of the value of this play as a tragedy must be touched on later; at the moment it is enough to say that if there is any truth in the theory advanced so far, that Ibsen presents on the stage some visual counterpart to a character's feelings and emotions, then the idea that Nora enjoys leaving her family receives its final quietus from the last instance of visual suggestion in the play:

NORA. (*Puts on the shawl*) Good-bye Torvald.

This would seem to set the tragic seal on her departure.

One more aid to characterization which Ibsen employs is the device of parallel situation, an ancient dramatic device, but one whose use by Ibsen has not been sufficiently remarked.

Analysis shows that Ibsen has striven to make the situations in which his minor characters find themselves, illustrate in some way the central predicament of Nora.

The first important parallel is between Nora and Mrs. Linde. These two women move on parallel lines but in opposite directions. Ibsen draws them in sharp contrast on their first appearance

(. . . *Then Nora enters, humming gaily . . .*)

She is clearly happy, at home (she has been shopping), and a childish, contented mother and wife.

(*Ellen ushers in Mrs. Linde, in travelling costume . . .*)

The lady, in other words, is a stranger out of her normal milieu. In contrast to Nora's gay humming, she is

(*Embarrassed and hesitating*)

We soon learn that she is paler, thinner and much older; that she is a widow with no property and no children:

'not even any sorrow or grief to live upon'.

Her life is

'unspeakably empty. No-one to live for any more'.

And she has been earning her living in the business world of which Nora knows nothing. Existence outside Dolls' Houses can be most unhappy.

During the play, Mrs. Linde fills the useful role of confidante to Nora; her greater experience and steadiness throw Nora's childish frenzy into higher relief; but she is most important at the end, where a direct antithesis between her and Nora is again established. There, Mrs. Linde gains a family and a husband and security from the world of business by marrying Krogstad; she has rediscovered an aim in life; now she tries to help Nora, and when Nora leaves the house, it is to Mrs. Linde that she goes, just as at the beginning of the play Mrs. Linde turned to her. Again, Nora loses family and husband; she must go out into an alien world to earn her living. So exact is the antithesis that we transfer the circumstances of Mrs. Linde's original situation to Nora's final one. Hence we come to realize that, although Nora seems callous about leaving home and children, she is in fact going into a life that will be hell on earth to her; she will arrive at Mrs. Linde's a second Mrs. Linde. Only if this parallel is missed is it possible to see in the ending of the play a monumental selfishness or a triumphant act of self-assertion, or a comic scene; it is a tragic doom.

The parallel between Nora and Krogstad is the most patent of them all, but it does not serve to reveal Nora's character to us. It enables Torvald and others to scarify Nora by condemning a fellow-criminal; first and foremost, however, Krogstad represents what Nora fears to become herself, a contagious moral degenerate.

Another parallel exists between Nora and Ann, her old nurse who once had to leave her child to be brought up by others. By this time (beginning of Act II), Nora has come to fear a similar parting from her own children. The brief discussion with Ann is therefore, on Nora's part, a covert discussion of her own situation, and her sympathy for the other is to be transferred to herself. It is important to note that this brief scene emphasizes the pain of leaving one's children—a point of some importance in the final interpretation of the play.

The parallel between Nora and the dying friend of the family is built up from a series of small points of identity. Rank is first introduced in conversation without any descriptive comment at a time when we have become vaguely aware that Nora has some sort of secret of which we know very little. There have just been made certain ambiguous references to the qualities she inherited from her father.

HELMER. You're a strange little being! Just like your father—always on the look out for all the money you can lay your hands on; but the moment you have it, it seems to slip through your fingers; you never know what becomes of it. Well, one must take you as you are. It's in the blood. Yes, Nora, that sort of thing is hereditary.
NORA. I wish I had inherited many of papa's qualities.

When Rank actually appears, we know that Nora's secret is a painful one as her reaction to Krogstad's arrival showed; almost at once we hear that Rank is suffering from a painful, lingering disease. They are therefore linked, loosely at this point, by hidden pain, with this difference, that Rank's disease is physical, while Nora's we begin to suspect, is moral, a distinction which Rank proceeds to demolish:

RANK . . . . However wretched I may be, I want to drag on as long as possible. All my patients, too, have the same mania. And it's the same with people whose complaint is moral.

Torvald draws the link tighter by a more specific reference to Nora's father, and therefore to the qualities she may be expected to have inherited from him, as Rank inherited a diseased spine from his:

HELMER. My dear little Nora, between your father and me there is all the difference in the world. Your father was not altogether unimpeachable. . . .

Therefore when, shortly afterwards, Rank appears again, his comment on his own fate now applies equally to Nora's:

NORA. I did so want you to be in a really good humour.
RANK. With death staring me in the face?—And to suffer thus for another's sin! Where's the justice of it? And in one way or another you can trace in every family some such inexorable retribution—

Rank, we learn, has just one more examination to make before he is certain that death is upon him; Nora has one more hope of circumventing her fate. Rank, so close a parallel, seems to cast the shadow of his doom in Nora's path; in fact he becomes the visual counterpart of Nora's torturing thoughts of death.

In the light of this connection between Nora and Rank, the 'truffles and champagne' scene takes on a new significance. Nora's last hope of avoiding Krogstad's denunciation is to buy him off; she hopes to wheedle the money out of Rank, who secretly loves her. Her life depends upon this and yet, in order to put the doctor into a good humour, she forces herself to hum and be gay and make light fun out of the fatal self-indulgence of Rank's father. For the audience, however, the grim figure of Rank in the deepening dusk insists on the deadly earnestness of the situation; it requires great strength of character to be flippant during a fight for life, and Rank is the symbol of death. We may be inclined to agree with the doctor:

RANK . . . . I see you're deeper than I thought.

The impression of depth becomes greater when Rank, inflamed by the teasing usually reserved for Torvald, declares his love and thus makes it impossible for Nora to continue with any show of honour her attempts to enlist his help. With Rank's physical presence on the stage to remind us of the fate that now awaits her, we can appreciate the courage behind Nora's refusal to go further with her request, on the grounds that:

Besides, I really want no help.

This theory, namely that Nora's childishness masks a deadly seriousness and therefore demands considerable force of character to sustain its deception, runs counter to that of the most influential modern critic of Ibsen. Professor Weigand writes: 'When Nora tells Rank: "You can do nothing to help me now. Besides, I really want no help . . ."'—she is not simply trying to pacify the Doctor's curiosity: she is actually convinced that she has been exaggerating the danger enormously and that Krogstad's threats are nothing but a bluff.' This is hard to reconcile with the fact that, immediately afterwards, she confesses to Krogstad that he is right in attributing to her thoughts of suicide.

The final correspondence is that Rank's physical and Nora's spiritual sickness come to their climax together; both are preceded by a last wild fling at the party upstairs, Nora dancing the tarantella, Rank drinking his last champagne. When Torvald opens the letter-box at last, he finds together Rank's final farewell in the form of visiting cards marked with a black cross, and the letter from Krogstad which is, in effect, to be Nora's death-warrant.

All these points of identity mean that by the end of the play we have paired Nora's fate with Rank's. They are both victims of circumstance; Nora bears the added burden, spared to the bachelor, of being potentially a transmitter of the evil to her beloved family. He goes off to die; Nora does not, and yet so persistent is the shadow of his sombre figure that we still clothe her less terrifying departure, her departure from everything she knew and loved into the strange world of masculine values, with some of the horror attached to death itself. Only when we have seen Nora's final gesture as an act of painful renunciation can we appreciate the full stature to which she has grown under the stress of her experiences. (pp. 15-31)

[What] sort of drama is this, Comedy, Problem play, or Tragedy? Professor Weigand has done great service to Ibsen by turning his attention to the plays themselves, at times with splendid results. In his treatment of *A Doll's House,* however, one feels that he sees comedy in strange places: 'Do we not see the mellow light of comedy suffusing the Doctor in his gallant counter-demonstration against the terrors of death?' His determination to find it leads him to add, in effect, a happy ending: ' . . . our imagination leaps ahead to speculate on the reaction that is bound to set in on the next day. . . . But personally I am convinced that after putting Torvald through a sufficiently protracted ordeal of suspense, Nora will yield to his entreaties and return home—on her own terms.' Even so, the laughter is sometimes forced, and inhuman: 'In this scene (i.e. Rank's farewell) the poet's laughter at the limitations of these three mortals is the laughter of the gods, musical and benign and without malice.' It is not the laughter of you or me, but a superior mirth. Altogether it may be said that Professor Weigand has seen correctly that Ibsen mixes comedy with tragedy rather more lavishly than is commonly supposed; this discovery, however, has led him to give the comic element the greater emphasis, and this has been possible because his interest in the play being that of a reader, not of a spectator, he has missed the tragic emphasis of the visual suggestion employed in *A Doll's House.*

On one level, of course, the play is a problem play; it deals with a predicament which immediately concerned the nineteenth-century audience. But Ibsen himself denied that it was merely this; and in any case, as George Lukács points out [in his *Studies in European Realism*],

The inner life of man, its essential traits and essential conflicts can be portrayed only in organic connection with social and historical factors.

The emphasis in this [discussion of *A Doll's House*] has been on the 'inner life', and if it has shown that in fact the play is a deep study of the tormented yet consistent development of an individual mind under the pressure of forces at once inevitable and adequately symbolic of the forces we experience in ordinary life, then Professor Koht is right to recall [in his *The Life of Ibsen*] that 'He himself (Ibsen) called it at first simply "the modern tragedy", so great and inclusive did it seem in his mind'. (pp. 37-38)

John Northam, in his Ibsen's Dramatic Method: A Study of the Prose Dramas, *Faber & Faber Limited, 1953, 232 p.*

JOHN NORTHAM   (essay date 1960)

[*In the following excerpt, Northam characterizes* A Doll's House *as a modern realistic play that is also a tragedy.*]

[Ibsen] worked for some seven years on *Pillars of Society.* During the time that he was considering *Pillars of Society,* he could reflect as follows:

> I have discovered my modern hero in Brand, and I can see where the tragic conflict is in modern society. But I can't go in the style and technique of *Brand,* because it is too far remote from ordinary life still, and it lacks the concentration necessary for a play. What can I do instead? I have now explored the resources of modern prose speech in *League of Youth* and I can construct a modern play without relying too obviously upon Scribe. But I have yet to solve the problem of retaining some sort of poetry and grandeur in my dramatic portrayal of modern life—not the poetry of words but of feeling and situation. But I have found out something that may help: I can do quite a lot by manipulating the prosaic details of my plays so that they become theatrical metaphors and come to mean more than what they are; I have used costume in this way, lighting, scenery, landscape, and weather; I have used trivial, everyday things like inky fingers and candles; and I have used living figures as symbols of spiritual forces that act upon the hero. Perhaps these things could be brought into the context of a modern realistic play to help me to portray the modern hero and the tragic conflict which I now understand so well.

I chose *A Doll's House* to show how Ibsen succeeded because it is not generally thought by the public to be a tragedy, and yet Ibsen refers to it in a draft as "The Modern Tragedy." My method will be that of close analysis of the development of the play, that is to say of the growth of the play's meaning from first curtain to last, in an endeavor to show how Ibsen suggests . . . a tragic struggle that lies behind the trivial anxieties of a housewife, a struggle involving an heroic figure in conflict with the secret, powerful, and ineluctable forces of society. If in this brief analysis the usual regard is not paid to the words, it is not, of course, because I consider that the words can be ignored, set aside, or in any way demoted from their rightful role of being the prime agent of communication. But I am suggesting that Ibsen emphasizes certain parts of the dialogue, and of the plot, to bring out his tragic pattern. The emphasis is gained partly by manipulation of prosaic detail, and since this is not a commonly noted element in Ibsen's plays, I may seem to exaggerate its importance. I do so only for purposes of demonstration.

The curtain rises, Nora comes in, humming gaily—a happy woman—a happy mother, for with her comes a Christmas tree carried by a porter—and a Christmas means parties, and presents, and children. Nora is not mean with her money: the porter charges 6d, she gives him 1/. She is childish—she still loves macaroons—she is not above concealing the fact from her husband: all this we learn about Nora in the first few seconds of the play, with hardly one important word spoken. Ibsen obviously means to make use of our imagination to con-struct his characters from small points in the stage picture and stage action.

It is a charming room. And it is a charming family; we enjoy seeing this happy mother and her loving husband arguing about money. Perhaps the husband gets a little angry when he reminds Nora that she takes after her father in her extravagance—"that sort of thing is hereditary"—but Nora is happy to retort "I wish I had inherited many of Papa's qualities" and that blows over—but we shall remember the reference. They are both so happy that the visitors who interrupt them stand in cold contrast. The first is a Mrs. Linde and Ibsen makes a sharp contrast here. Nora is happy, Mrs. Linde is "downcast and hesitant"; she is pale, thin, and old, much older than Nora, though they are of the same age. Nora chatters happily about her family—Mrs. Linde has none—and nothing to live for besides. Mrs. Linde has had to fight her way in the outside world by keeping a shop, and school—anything, in fact, to support her mother and her two young brothers. Now the mother is dead, the boys grown up, and she is free—but very unhappy to be free. It is true that we learn that Nora has had some troubles in the past—she has had to borrow secretly large sums of money to save her husband's health and even life, and it has been difficult to find the money to repay—but the contrast still remains between a woman happy because she has her family, and a woman desolate because she is alone.

The first blow to Nora's happiness falls when the maid lets in Krogstad. Clearly his visit worries her, although her words tell us little: when Krogstad goes into Helmer's study, Nora goes at once to the stove and stokes the fire—his presence has chilled her.

It is important to grasp this first hint of unpleasant elements in a Doll's House existence because it is closely followed by the first hint of another kind of unpleasantness in the person of Dr. Rank. Within a few seconds of his entrance he has a very important speech.

> NORA. Come, Dr. Rank—you want to live yourself.
> RANK. To be sure I do. However wretched I may be, I want to drag on as long as possible. All my patients, too, have the same mania. And *it's the same with people whose complaint* is moral. At this very moment Helmer is talking to just such a moral incurable— . . . a fellow named Krogstad, a man you know nothing about—corrupt to the very core of his character. But even he began by announcing, as a matter of vast importance, that he must live!

Now this speech is very important for two reasons: first, because it shows that Rank, like Nora, has a hidden source of disquiet, a physical one—he is wretched in a way that threatens his life; and second, because his speech equates physical illness with moral illness; so that from this point onwards, Ibsen can use physical illness as a symbol of moral illness.

At this early point in the play, such gloomy notes are muted; we are still to feel that, taking everything into consideration, Nora has been very fortunate in her sheltered existence. But the theme of illness is renewed as the scene closes—Nora invites Rank back for the evening—he accepts, provided that he feels well enough—Ibsen does not intend us to forget the somber theme of disease. Exit Rank, leaving Nora to romp with her children and create an image of family bliss. Krogstad, the moral incurable, enters; the children leave the room and that is the end of Nora's happiness in the play. For Krogstad is not so easily defeated as Nora expected—threat of dismissal makes him merely more dangerous, since his position at the bank means everything to him. He threatens Nora that if she allows Torvald to dismiss him, he will tell her husband that Nora borrowed from him the money needed to send Torvald away for his health—a terrifying threat in itself because Torvald detests borrowing, but horrifying when Krogstad accuses Nora of forging her dying father's signature to get the money, and threatens her with the legal consequences of forgery.

Nora tries to pretend that the *legal* aspect of the affair leaves her unmoved—if the law does not allow a wife to forge when she wants to spare her father anxiety and to save her husband's life, then the law must be stupid. No, she says, it is impossible—she did it for love.

This is not a very sensible attitude to take, but it represents a desperate attempt to protect her threatened Doll's House existence merely by *asserting* that her home, her family, *must* come first, before legal obligations and suchlike—but Ibsen reinforces this impression of her trying to thrust other considerations aside by using the Christmas tree again. Nora asks the maid to bring in the tree, and place it in the middle of the floor.

We, the audience, can see the tree, suggestive of family security and happiness, set defiantly in the center of the stage to dominate it, as if its mere presence could banish Nora's troubles. It is a visual equivalent of Nora's obstinate, but uncertain, persistence that everything will be all right, merely because she says so.

But of course mere assertion that her Doll's House values are right, and the values of the outside world are wrong, is useless. Nora soon gets a worse shock; she learns something which terrifies her far more than the threat of mere legal action: her husband, in all innocence, points out that Krogstad's real crime was not forgery, but concealment of forgery. That made him deceitful, and since then he has contaminated his own children with his own moral sickness.

This revelation causes a number of our earlier impressions to fuse together into a theme. At once we perceive that Nora too, who is also deceitful in her own way, could perhaps transmit moral corruption to her own children; and we have seen, in the figure of Dr. Rank, how terribly a parent can ruin a child. Nora now believes that she is corrupt because of her deceitfulness; she is terrified to think that she may corrupt and poison her own children with a moral corruption as foul as Rank's physical sickness. Rank gives us the size of the horror she faces.

At the curtain of Act I, Nora is still trying to convince herself that this new danger of contaminating her children morally is no more real than the earlier legal threat from Krogstad. "Corrupt *my* children!—Poison *my* home! It's not true! It can never, never be true!"—but her face is "pale with terror"—and she now believes that the poison of moral corruption runs in her veins. She is fighting against Death.

So Nora faces two terrors—the threat of legal action and disgrace, leading to the destruction of her Doll's House; and the certainty of moral disaster for her children if she continues as their mother. The joy has gone out of family life, and Ibsen provides a fitting stage picture for her anguish. She has tried to push away the threats by mere assertion of her own standards—and Ibsen brought the Christmas tree into the center

of the stage picture; but now, as the curtain goes up on Act II a day later, we can see from the set that she no longer hopes to succeed—she is terrified now, the family unity and gaiety are spoiled, she will not, dare not, play with the children—and the Christmas tree has been pushed into a corner of the room, it is stripped of ornament, and the candles are burnt out. What a fine symbol of dejection.

Now that Nora is firmly established as in some sense a spiritual incurable, the link between her and Rank, the physical incurable, is immeasurably strengthened. Early in Act II, we hear all about the spinal disease he inherited from his father—and from then on we can see both Rank and Nora as carriers of an obscure and secret poison slowly killing them.

This is not Rank's play, it is Nora's. Rank is a minor character—but he plays a vital dramatic role. His function is to act as the physical embodiment, visible on the stage, of Nora's moral situation as she sees it. Nora is almost hysterical with terror at the thought of her situation—almost, but it is part of her character that with great heroism she keeps her fears secret to herself; and it is because of her reticence that Rank is dramatically necessary, to symbolize the horror she will not talk about. Nora feels, and we feel, the full awfulness of Rank's illness, and she transfers to herself the same feeling about the moral corruption which she imagines herself to carry. Nora sees herself, and we see her seeing herself (with our judgment reserved), as suffering from a moral disease as mortal, as irremediable as Rank's disease, a disease that creeps on to a fatal climax. This is the foe that Nora is fighting so courageously.

Nora tries to relieve the superficial part of her anxiety by persuading Torvald to let Krogstad have his job back—that might save her from public disgrace—but she only makes her deeper anxiety worse, because Torvald loses patience and reminds her that her own father was not above suspicion—this increases her sense of being corrupt, because, we recall, she inherited some qualities from her father. And her sense of being infectious, of being a danger to her family as Rank's father proved to him, is increased when Torvald expansively tries to soothe her by saying that of course he would take upon his own shoulders whatever evil threatened her. So her deceit will ruin not only herself by public disgrace, and her children, but her beloved husband. This is the last straw. She now feels a moral leper. Torvald's self-sacrifice would be wonderful, but at the same time, terrible. At all costs it must be prevented—and so begins her somber interview with Dr. Rank, her one last chance of getting enough money to buy off Krogstad's revenge and escape death.

This interview, as you all know, is the somewhat puzzling one in which Nora appears to joke about Rank's terrible sickness, to tease him with her silk, flesh-colored stockings, and then, when she seems to have worked him into a state where he would promise her anything, she rejects his offer of devoted service.

I have called the scene somber, without hesitation. First of all, there is the lighting (*during what follows it begins to grow dark*). And then there are the contents of the scene. This, you recall, is Nora's last effort to find a way out of the legal part of her fatal situation, to avoid disgrace and so prevent Torvald's self-sacrifice. We learn at once that Rank too has only one last investigation to make of his diseased body to know with certainty when he will begin to break up—his physical illness creeps on to its climax side by side with Nora's moral

The tarantella scene, with Betty Hennings as Nora, from an 1879 production of A Doll's House *in Copenhagen.*

and nervous illness. We know very well that Nora is fully informed about the seriousness of Rank's disease—why then should she pretend that it does not exist, or why flippantly attribute it to his father's over-fondness for champagne and truffles? The answer is quite obvious when we read, or hear, this snatch of conversation:

> NORA. Why, you're perfectly unreasonable today.
> I did so want you to be in a really good humor.
> RANK. With death staring me in the face?—And to
> suffer thus for another's sin! Where's the justice of
> it? And in one way or another you can trace in
> every family some such inexorable retribution—
> NORA. (*Stopping her ears*) Nonsense! Nonsense!
> Now cheer up.

She shuts her ears because she recognizes the situation as her own—Rank suffers for his father's sin, Krogstad's children have been corrupted by their father's moral incurability, Nora fears that she will ruin her own children and poison her home. The interruption proves that she feels the application of what Rank says to herself—and after that, her determined effort to remain bright and cheerful, and to joke Rank into compliance can be seen not as frivolousness, heartless levity, but as a heroic triumph of reticence in the face of the equivalent of death.

But this interview, although it shows Nora at her best, heroically fighting disaster without whimpering, also shows her at her worst. All this sexual teasing of Rank, for example, with her stockings and her tasteless jokes about his disease—as I read it, Ibsen is showing us here the bad results of her

upbringing, first by her father and then by her husband. She can get her own way with men by cajoling, by teasing—and she has learnt no other way more self-respecting. That is why she flirts so cruelly with Rank—not because she gets fun out of it, but because it is the only way she knows of dealing with men. It is the spoilt Nora who does the flirting—it is the heroic woman underneath, the woman of fundamentally sound principles who puts a stop to the nonsense when it begins to offend her sense of rightness. She puts an end to the interview even though it means throwing away her last chance of salvation from a fate that she sees as dreadful.

That is why the scene is important—another instance of heroism.

Nora's doom moves a step nearer: Krogstad calls again, to tell her that instead of informing the police, he intends to blackmail Helmer. This is the end for Nora—when Krogstad leaves, but drops the blackmailing letter into the letter-box, she cries, in genuine anguish, "Torvald, Torvald—now we are lost." Mrs. Linde offers to help by influencing Krogstad and leaves Nora to keep Torvald away from the letter-box until she returns—but so far as Nora is concerned, the end is upon her; as she sees it, the moment has come when the poison must work to its crisis. Like the tarantula's victim, she can only dance a mad dance in a last, vain effort to expel the poison—she expresses her intolerable anxiety in the tarantella.

Now had Ibsen wanted simply to express feverish anxiety, any dance would have served—in fact, in one draft version of the scene, Nora is made to dance Anitra's dance from *Peer Gynt.* But Ibsen chooses the poison-spider dance (and he makes sure that we know it *is* a tarantella, by naming it enough times), because it is so appropriate to the theme of disease and death, this picture he has created of Nora suffering from the slow, malignant working within her of a secret moral disease, and it helps again to link her with Rank.

Nora has shot her bolt—she has kept Torvald from reaching the letters, but she no longer hopes to avoid the inevitable—only to postpone the wonderful but terrible moment when she must kill herself to prevent Torvald from assuming the burden of sin.

The last act opens—it is nighttime. Mrs. Linde is waiting for Krogstad to call while the Helmers are upstairs at the fancy-dress party where Nora is to perform her tarantella. Mrs. Linde once loved Krogstad, and proposes marriage to him now. He accepts. A piece of machinery out of a well-made play—the secondary characters are being tidied up, the villain is being reformed in the most economical way. But why bother to reform the villain? For Mrs. Linde after all refuses to let him demand back his black-mailing letter. No, the real point of the scene is to demonstrate the one fundamental truth about women.

> I need someone to be a mother to, and your children need a mother. You need me, and I—I need you.

This is Mrs. Linde speaking, the woman who at the beginning of the play had nothing to live for, who had earned her own living, mixed with the outer world, and found life profoundly depressing and aimless without the anchor of a husband and children. This scene describes for us in advance the painful void into which Nora consigns herself at the end of the play. "What a change!" says Mrs. Linde, "what a change! To have someone to work for, to live for, a home to make happy!"—immediately before the entrance of Nora, who is to lose all this.

Nora's costume, as she enters from the ball upstairs, makes a strong impression on us. She wears the Italian costume appropriate to her character as a girl from Capri, with a large black shawl over it. Festival and funeral combined. Or, to be more precise, make-belief and death, although in the nature of things, precision here is impossible. The fancy dress suggests to us that she still inhabits that world of make-belief, the Doll's House, with its fictitious values; the black suggests to us her thoughts of suicide to end her sickness. And the costume suggests this without Nora's having to say one unrealistic word of self-revelation.

Ibsen also emphasizes the climax of the disease and death theme by bringing on Rank. Nora has danced her tarantella at the party upstairs—her last fling. At the same party, Rank had enjoyed his last fling—at the champagne—before retiring to his death-bed. The last link which Ibsen forges between the two victims of poison and corruption is that their deathwarrants share the same letter-box: Rank leaves behind him a visiting-card marked with a black cross, a sign that he has crawled away to die; the card lies beside Krogstad's letter to Torvald, and when Torvald reads that, Nora must die so as not to inflict her moral disease on others; physical and moral corruption are to burn themselves out together.

She waits for the right moment, when Torvald promises again to shoulder his wife's burdens. He, of course, is merely romanticizing; she takes him seriously, and sends him off to read the fatal letter. She will go out and drown herself to prevent this heroic sacrifice.

This is women's magazine stuff—but we must remember that Nora has no means of finding out that her Doll's House standards and values are all of that order. And she believes in them still with desperate earnestness. That is why we see her in fancy dress, the dress of illusion, while the intensity of her resolve to die, which in poetic drama would have merited a soliloquy, is compressed into a detail of costume. Reticence is preserved, but so is emotional color: as she prepares to leave the house, she covers herself in black; she puts on her black shawl again, and Helmer's black evening cloak. We thereby *see* her attitude of mind—and this is Ibsen's comment, not Nora's self-dramatization.

You all remember what happens. Helmer does not perform a miracle when he reads Krogstad's black-mailing letter. He explodes into vulgar rage—he calls his wife a hypocrite, a liar, a criminal; he throws her father into her face: "I ought to have foreseen it. All your father's want of principle—all your father's want of principle you have inherited—no religion, no morality, no sense of duty!" This is an aspect of the problem which had not occurred to Nora before—but she remains quiet—perhaps she is a victim like Rank, as well as a carrier of corruption.

The miracle has not happened. Nora realizes that she has been living an illusion; and one does not die for illusions if one recognizes them for such. It is irrelevant to her that a note should arrive from Krogstad returning her I. O. U.'s, that Helmer should say, with sickening egotism, "I am saved! Nora, I am saved." That part of her problem, the legal or public side now assumes its rightful place as trivial compared with the moral problem, which remains. Nora realizes numbly that her life has been an elaborate make-belief. She does not say so just yet—she is cold, almost silent. But her costume speaks for her. As she discards her illusions, so she discards her fancy-dress and her black cloak and shawl, and appears in her everyday dress—to symbolize her entry into a world of cold fact and commonsense.

From her new, sad viewpoint, her notion of heredity becomes as wide as ours, the audience's, has long become. She agrees that she is not fit, in her present state of moral health, to have charge of the education of her children. But Helmer's words have made her bitterly aware that the poison did not originate with her:

> I have had great injustice done me, Torvald, first by father, and then by you.

They have both treated her as a doll-child. It is the men who run society who have condemned Nora to a stultifying life. That is the real crime, the real corruption, as she clearly sees, not her forgery or her little lies, but the male conspiracy to debase the female; and she now recognizes that she had begun to bring up her own children as if they too were dolls. It is the Doll's House attitude that is the corruption which must not be transmitted. She must go into a hostile world and educate herself.

She does not say much about how she expects to enjoy this new life, but Ibsen has already prepared us—from the point for point contrast with Mrs. Linde, we realize that Nora leaves the play as Mrs. Linde entered it—lonely, unhappy, with no one to love or live for, and much, much older; and from the parallel with Rank we get the impression that her going out into the alien world beyond the Doll's House is like Rank's departure out of life altogether: the culmination of a long, painful, and fatal illness. Her life in the outer world will be a life-in-death. At her final exit, she puts on a black shawl again, to suggest visually the melancholy exile she enters upon with only the hope of a miracle to end it.

What has Ibsen done in this play that he did not do before? He has, above all, exercised the art of concentration. He has written a modern play about a modern woman in a modern situation, but he adds new stature and a new dimension to it by concentrating different kinds of imagery to suggest that society works upon Nora like some dreadful, hidden, and inexorable disease. The final draft version of the play lacks this concentration, and this power. He guides our attention to this theme through his verbal imagery (e.g., Rank's first speech), but he maintains it by a concentration of suggestive detail—Nora's black shawl, the sympathetic night light of Act III, the figure of Rank, the tarantella-dance—all of these help to create the sense of fatality; and Nora's consistent fight against that, a fight in which she will sacrifice no basic principles however desperate her situation, makes her into a heroine. Ibsen has discovered his modern hero.

I suggest that it was some such vision that Ibsen had in mind when he called the play "The Modern Tragedy." I suggest that you will find themes of similar or greater majesty created in later plays, which must be seen not as realistic plays, or, in contradiction, as plays full of verbal symbolism, but as plays filled with metaphors and images drawn from the whole range of theatrical material; plays filled thereby with a sense of the poetry of life, even of modern life. My point may be summarized if I say that Ibsen's prose plays present the poetry of life in the imagery of the theater. (pp. 99-108)

John Northam, "Ibsen's Search for the Hero," in Ibsen: A Collection of Critical Essays, *edited by Rolf Fjelde, Prentice-Hall, Inc., 1965, pp. 91-108.*

MAURICE VALENCY   (essay date 1963)

[*Valency is an American dramatist, novelist, and critic. In the following excerpt, he considers the conflict arising from differing female and male ideologies central to* A Doll's House.]

The first sketch for *A Doll's House,* labelled "Notes for the Modern Tragedy," is dated October 19, 1878, and it indicates quite clearly the sort of play Ibsen at this time had in mind to write. "There are," he noted, "two kinds of conscience, one in man, and another, altogether different, in woman. They do not understand one another, but in practical life, the woman is judged by man's law as though she were not a woman, but a man." The idea that the sexes have such different psychic patterns that they can never hope to understand each other, and that therefore it is unjust to judge women by male standards, was certainly not new in the 1880's, nor had it, for that matter, been new in the days of Mary Wollstonecraft, almost a century before. But in the theatre such a thought was revolutionary, and it caused a sensation.

For his purposes in *A Doll's House,* Ibsen depicted a man and a woman of diametrically opposed temperament. His Nora is ostensibly a blithe little sparrow, scatterbrained, flirtatious, and gay. Helmer is stuffy, pompous, and circumspect. Both characters are necessarily exaggerated so that the action of the play can demonstrate to best advantage the con-

trast between their appearance and their reality. In fact, Nora is a carefully studied example of what we have come to know as the hysterical personality—bright, unstable, impulsive, romantic, quite immune from feelings of guilt, and, at bottom, not especially feminine. It is a vastly more enlightened conception of woman than the stereotypes of Kotzebue or Dumas. Helmer, on the other hand, is a typical example of the compulsive male. The problem is thus not especially a problem of sex. It would be strange if two people constituted in this way could possibly succeed in understanding one another.

The idea that a woman is a grown-up child, without mind, but with much heart, devoid of logic, but sensitive and intuitive, is traditional in Western culture. It certainly antedates Rousseau, who is often credited with the formulation of this cliché, by some hundreds of years. At any rate, such appears to have been Ibsen's notion of womanhood during the period in which he wrote *A Doll's House,* so that the characterization of Nora which he finally hit upon must have surprised him quite as much as it did everyone else. In a speech about this time in the Scandinavian Society of Rome, he said:

> Youth has the instinct, akin to genius, for hitting intuitively on what is right. But it is this very instinct that woman has in common with youth, as well as with the true artist.

Such statements make it clear, at any rate, that from the standpoint of personality, and quite apart from the question of sex, Ibsen was disposed to identify himself with the Noras and not with the Helmers of this world.

In its first draft, *A Doll's House* was a conventional domestic drama of tragic character. The touches of caricature which were eventually to transform Nora and Helmer were still to come. Torvald was not yet the pompous, self-centered ass of the final version, nor was Nora as yet the earnest and innocent child who was sure there could be no harm in forging her father's signature, provided her motives were good. But in the course of the revision, Ibsen pushed his characters further and further toward the extreme, so that they took on comic overtones. At the same time, the gulf between them was deepened until they quite lost touch with each other. Thus, though the plot, throughout the revisions, remained substantially the same, the characters were more definitely molded, and their relation shifted, so as to emphasize as far as possible their psychological disparity. The principal action was made to hinge on a *méprise;* but the misunderstanding, which in a Scribean play would be the result of a purely intellectual error, was in this case founded on a profoundly significant difference of personality, so that no explanation could possibly avail to correct it. Yet, while an action founded on so deep a misunderstanding has, of necessity, a tragic color, the incongruity of feeling and motive is such that in *A Doll's House* most of the significant scenes are comic in tone, and no scene is entirely devoid of humor.

Since Ibsen habitually preserved and dated the drafts of his plays, it is often possible to reconstruct with some accuracy the method by which he arrived at his final version. He generally began with a story, not with a character. The story was usually such that it reflected a psychic conflict into which he had some degree of insight. He then conceived his characters as archetypes moving through the narrative in conventional fashion. The result was something in the nature of a melodrama, straight, obvious, and sentimental.

But once the play was finished, the author's mood changed. He now took up the entire matter from a critical angle, testing with ridicule the situation he had formerly taken seriously, and contemplating the behavior of his puppets with the amused skepticism of a detached and hostile observer. In this mood, the absurdity of the theatrical postures into which human behavior tends to fall became progressively clear to him, and he remolded and retouched his figures so as to bring out more and more clearly the comic aspects of what had originally been conceived as a pathetic situation. The result of this process was the rich ambiguity of characterization which gives Ibsen's plays their unique quality.

In *A Doll's House,* all the touches from which the play derives its charm were added in revision—the amorous scene of act three, the tarantella, the champagne, Nora's little fibs, her coquetry with Dr. Rank, her daydreams of the rich uncle who is to die and leave her a fortune. In the final scene, when the menace of Krogstad is removed, Torvald says, "I am saved, Nora." In the first version he said, "You are saved." In this manner, Ibsen did whatever could be done to heighten the effect of comedy within the tragic situation.

The effect is altogether remarkable; but this sort of writing has, of course, its drawbacks. Nothing is more disarming in the theatre than such evidences of an author's willingness to laugh at his own fantasy, especially when this fantasy has tragic overtones; but nothing is more puzzling. For this reason, doubtless, these equivocal effects are generally glossed over in production, and the characters are pushed unceremoniously back into the stereotypes from which the author was at pains to redeem them. The plot of *A Doll's House* is related comically to a cliché of tragedy—the formula of the tyrant and the innocent victim who in the end exacts her revenge. It is in these terms, accordingly, that *A Doll's House* is usually played. It cannot be denied that the author in some measure invites this interpretation. This seems malicious. All the salt of the play is in the counterpoint of satire which accompanies the tragic line of the action.

The use of the Scribean apparatus to bring about the reversals and discoveries necessary for the development of Nora's character did not require justification at a time when nothing was more common than this sort of contrivance. But Ibsen was evidently concerned in this play not with the management of the narrative so much as with its psychological significance. Apart from his irrepressible tendency to caricature his figures, he had serious reasons for the comic extremes to which he pushed the characterization. Helmer emerges in the final version as a caricature of the archetypal father; Nora as a caricature of the rebellious daughter. Characters conceived after this fashion are obviously capable of transmitting a wide spectrum of symbolic significances, and they elicit a very complex psychic response. It is easy to associate Nora with the impulsive, and Torvald with the compulsive side of human nature; but, if one chooses, one can involve in their relationship the antithesis of mind and body, spirit and matter, heart and mind, light and darkness, and so on to the end of the table of contraries. Since it is precisely in terms of such Pythagorean opposites that we customarily think of the relation of the sexes, marriage may be made to serve as a prime example of the clash of antitheses, and the home becomes the battleground of the cosmic dialectic.

In Ibsen's concept, therefore, the affair Nora-Helmer quite transcends the question of the normal opposition of husband and wife. *A Doll's House* . . . indicates the correspondence of the family quarrel with the dialectic of history on every plane of the social structure down to the individual soul. From this point of view the revolt of Nora takes on a certain universality, and it is this which gives tragic magnitude to what might otherwise be considered simply another story of marital incompatibility. It seems clear that in developing his "modern tragedy" in this manner, Ibsen very shrewdly followed the direction indicated by Hebbel in *Maria Magdalene.* He could not have done better.

It is possible to think of *A Doll's House,* therefore, as a kind of dramatic metaphor, a play of symbols, a conceit. The opposition of irreconcilable viewpoints which brings about the dissolution of this union is then seen to be a reflection of the vast conflict which is bringing about a readjustment of social relations on every level. The only possible reconciliation of the spiritual entities which are here displayed in opposition must be, accordingly, in terms of that synthesis which will, in its largest aspect, result in the Third Empire. It is to something of this sort—the miracle—that Nora looks, none too hopefully, as she leaves Torvald's house at the end of the play.

Moreover, since *A Doll's House* was constructed in accordance with a concept which, as Ibsen said in 1891, looked far beyond the question of the advancement of woman's rights, it is hardly possible to assign to Nora the traditionally sympathetic role of the injured wife. As the unwitting, but implacable, representatives of antithetical forces of universal character, Torvald and Nora are equally matched, equally doomed, and equally the objects of sympathy. There is, of course, something undeniably comic about the plight of Torvald who has to listen to a homily on the rights of woman when all he desires is to go to bed with the *raisonneur;* nevertheless, his predicament when Nora leaves him is, if anything, more desperate than hers. Like Anton in *Maria Magdalene,* he does not understand; and it is he, not she, who suffers the major casualty of the battle.

What has happened to Torvald on the domestic level is the equivalent of the fall of a prince in high tragedy. In accordance with the canonical concept of marriage, Torvald has postured consistently as the wise and monumental male, and Nora, suitably conditioned by her upbringing, has thus far accepted this pose as fact. In the desperate emergency in which she suddenly finds herself, her idea of what is about to happen is based on the supposed nature of the ideal Torvald. Just as she had sacrificed herself when he needed help, so, she believes, he will insist on suffering for her in her hour of need. Of course, she will not permit this sacrifice. She will outdo him in nobility by killing herself at the proper time. This is how it seems to her. But the hour of trial reveals the wretched truth of the matter. Torvald is a humbug. He has no idea of suffering for anyone. On the contrary, in the emergency, he thinks only of saving himself; and in the contrast between the romantic splendor of her dream and the squalid reality, Nora suddenly finds herself emotionally bankrupt.

A Doll's House thus describes in a very convincing manner the process of falling out of love. Its force, however, lies not in the superficial action, which in any case lacks suspense, but in the psychological undercurrent which it generates. The man Nora loves is a creature of fantasy, constructed partly in accordance with his idea of himself, partly out of her own ideal requirements. When this figment evaporates, she is left with a stranger in whom she has no interest. She realizes at this point that she has been masquerading as a child only because Torvald has been posing as a father. She has been, so she says, "in fancy dress the whole time, not happy, but merry." Even now, she has no clear idea of what, or who, she is; but that is not the point: the moment she becomes aware that she is more of a man than her husband, their relation becomes impossible. She can now no longer endure the passive role that her position entails, either mentally or physically, and she declares the marriage at an end.

It is believable that Nora's sudden educational experience is sufficiently catastrophic to change in the course of an hour the seemingly dependent and submissive wife into a realistic and autarchic individual; but it is believable only provided we assume that this individual was always there. The implication is that Nora, no less than Helmer, was, from the first, other than she seemed. Her childlike pose was a pretense by which she herself was taken in: once she understands this, a general revaluation of her position is inescapable. The moment she doubts the validity of her assumptions, she can no longer accept the authority of father, pastor, or husband. Neither law, nor custom, nor religion will suffice henceforth to keep her in line: she must think for herself. In the end, she is frightened, like a somnambulist who is suddenly awakened in a perilous place—but her future behavior is predictable. She has become a feminist.

This does not mean, perhaps, that she will evolve suddenly, like Mrs. Warren's daughter in Shaw's play, into a kind of man. Nevertheless, the disparity between her way of thought and that of the masculine society which Torvald represents is fundamental, and she must re-orient herself:

> NORA. . . . I am all at sea about these things. I only know that I think quite differently from you about them. I hear, too, that the laws are different from what I thought; but I can't believe that they can be right. It appears that a woman has no right to spare her dying father or to save her husband's life. I don't believe that.
> HELMER. You talk like a child. You don't understand the society in which you live.
> NORA. No. I do not. But now I shall try to learn. I must make up my mind which is right—society or I.

For the wife, in these circumstances, the dissolution of the family may be painful, but it is not tragic. On the contrary, she throws off her servitude; she is emancipated and strengthened; and though she leaves the play in some confusion, she is, on the whole, victorious. The tragedy is, we have noted, mainly the husband's. He has, of course, the canonical flaw. Had he been the man his wife thought him, or even the man he thought himself to be, Nora would perhaps not have left him, and the paternal authority, in this instance at least, would have remained unquestioned. But Torvald is an example of the decline of the patriarchal idea. He is incapable of fulfilling the obligations of a domestic suzerain, and a woman's gesture suffices to sweep away the vestiges of what was perhaps once a truth. Torvald is therefore fated, as a husband, to go down with the patriarchy which he unworthily represents. But he is a man, as well as a husband, and the idea that in the hour of trial he was found wanting is a bitter experience for him, even though he is not altogether clear on what it was he did that was wrong. There is, of course, nothing novel in his experience: his behavior, judged by chivalric standards, leaves everything to be desired. What is new is Nora's assumption that in these circumstances the entire principle of male authority must be called into question. The slam of the door at the end of the play is therefore, symbolically speaking, a sound of some significance.

What outraged "all decent people" when *A Doll's House* was first published was actually not Nora's desertion of her three children, who are not even differentiated in the cast, but this symbolic caponization of Torvald. The brutality of Nora's action could have hardly escaped Ibsen. *A Doll's House* is a play of bold outlines and sharp contrasts. Torvald is extravagantly fatuous; Nora is needlessly cruel—Ibsen does not assume the risks of subtlety. Nor is the play truly realistic. After nine years of marriage, a woman is normally under no misapprehension as to her husband's possibilities as a man.

As the play is arranged, Nora and Mrs. Linde deliberately lay a trap for Helmer. When he falls into it, Nora presses her advantage to the extreme. In the last scene we see what the little squirrel is really like: she is implacable. At this point, *A Doll's House* takes the form of Hebbel's *Gyges und sein Ring* or *Herodes und Mariamne;* the play of the revenge of the outraged wife, the classical prototype of which is *Medea.* But while Nora contents herself with destroying Torvald only in fantasy, Torvald is denied the honor of being destroyed in a manner suitable to heroes of tragedy—in the end, he is simply ridiculous. The age of the straw men ends, as Mr. Eliot so cogently put it, with a whimper, and in this is seen the nature of "the modern tragedy," as Ibsen conceived it. (pp. 151-59)

Maurice Valency, "Ibsen," in his The Flower and the Castle: An Introduction to Modern Drama, *The Macmillan Company, 1963, pp. 118-237.*

M. C. BRADBROOK   (essay date 1982)

[*Bradbrook is an English critic who has written primarily on the Elizabethan theater. In the following excerpt, she examines the theme of personal growth and development, which she deems central to* A Doll's House.]

At Christmas 1879—though not quite immediately—the appearance of *A Doll's House* brought the fame of Henrik Ibsen to England. The social emancipation of women, especially through literary women, had been established a generation earlier; in 1845 Elizabeth Barrett Browning had eloped to Italy, and George Eliot, who had gone abroad in 1854 to live with G. H. Lewes, was, by the end of the 1870s, a venerated figure. In this year, 1879, Sarah Bernhardt came to London, having walked out of the Comédie Française and slammed the door.

But in the preliminary notes for his play Ibsen had set forward a position so radical that it might well be used today as a feminist manifesto:

> There are two kinds of moral law, two kinds of conscience, one in man, and a completely different one in woman. They do not understand each other; but in matters of practical living the woman is judged by a man's law, as if she were not a woman but a man . . . A woman cannot be herself in contemporary society, it is an exclusively male society, with laws drafted by men, and with counsel and judges who judge feminine conduct from the masculine point of view . . . She has committed a crime and is proud of it because she did it for love of her husband and to save his life . . . Now and then like a woman, she shrugs off her thoughts. Sudden return of dread and terror. Everything must be borne alone.

However, at the end of the 'Ibsen decade' (the 1880s) when the play had appeared in London, Milan, Paris and Budapest Ibsen told the Society for Extended Female Education in Vienna, in 1891, that it was not about women's rights but the rights of humanity in general; in 1898 he repeated this to the Norwegian Women's Rights League ('What courage!' observed Nigel Dennis), adding 'I am not even quite sure what women's rights are.'

In the terms of a later generation his interests were psychological rather than sociological; he said he did not believe in 'external revolutions'; the revolution 'must come from within'.

Ibsen's work made its effect in translation into languages he did not always understand; it was read much more than performed. Today it survives because of its power in performance. Modern rediscovery of Ibsen followed the stage and broadcast revivals of the 1950s. The full impact of this play survives across language barriers because Ibsen has employed all the arts of the theatre. Perhaps because the theatre in which he was trained had relied on translations for most of its performances and had little of its own, Ibsen succeeded in developing (at the age of fifty-one and in his fifteenth play) a reticulation or meshing of human relationships which elastically adapts itself in live action; the space between the characters, the links that divide and unite them, the space between actors and audience, and the flow of empathy that sustains performance, each derives from Ibsen's employment of all the kinds of communication possible in drama. Words and subtext, the setting and the invisible, eliminated or superseded drafts upon which Ibsen worked forward to his final form supply a 'complex variable' capable of all the modulations recently chronicled in Daniel Haakonsen's *Henrik Ibsen, mennesket og kunstneren* (1981).

The original Nora, Betty Hennings, had begun her career as a ballerina; one of Ibsen's final inspirations, Nora's tarantella, embodies the heroine's terror and despair, while concentrating her power as Eve, the prime delight and temptress of men. Like the dance of Anitra in **Peer Gynt**, the dance of the Capri fishergirl belongs to an untamed Southern scene, but it has now been transported from Egypt to the cosy little home with its stove, draped table and upright piano, from which the dancer will depart into a Norwegian night.

The delicious life-giving power radiating from Nora must be controlled and kept jealously for her male circle: 'You and papa have done me a grave wrong', she finally tells her husband. Nora's forging of her dying father's signature has outraged her husband equally as a lawyer and as President of the Bank; but to her the gold of his wedding ring has become a bigger fraud, since the President is found to be spiritually bankrupt, totally self-deceived.

Livsglaeden, that untranslateable word, the fountain of life, dances in the faded images of the little skylark, the little squirrel; an actress can still embody it. Nowhere else in Ibsen do the lineaments of animal desire show as plainly as in Torvald Helmer's 'Don't want to? don't want to? aren't I your husband?' Payment on the nail is the protector's right; it is no 'demand of the ideal'.

Whatever harsh privation his new urban environment inflicted on man's primal energies, the child-wife and father-husband relation, that popular model for happy marriages in the mid-nineteenth century, immensely fortified the home as enclosure, cradle and prison. The skylark, the pet squirrel plays in a cage. At the end, Torvald's magnanimous act of forgiving his wife leaves her in exactly the position that he had seen as being his own under the blackmailer's power:

> Here I am, in the grip of a man without a conscience; he can do whatever he likes with me, demand anything he wants, order me about just as he chooses . . . and I daren't breathe a word.

The happy state of affairs to which Torvald later looks forward was a sort of spiritual cannibalism: 'Open your whole heart to me, and I shall become both your will-power and your conscience.' At the beginning, he had been forbidding his baby doll to eat macaroons or do mending in the drawing-room; he kept the key of the letter-box in his pocket, and when Nora inadvertently let slip a word of criticism, he straightway asserted his authority over her by dispatching Krogstad's letter of dismissal. For once he and Krogstad agree as lawyers in thinking that Nora's disappearance or suicide would not absolve him from possible accusations of having instigated her forgery. Nora's rejection of his sexual approach is dismissed with 'What's this? You've played the fool with me long enough, little Nora.' Finally, he opens her last letter from Krogstad, refusing to give it her. Her childish pet name (she was christened Eleanora, as Ibsen explained to his family, who gave that name to his grand-daughter) means that to translate 'Nora', something like 'Nolly-dolly' is needed.

The eternal child-wife must remain unconscious of the sexual implications of her own pretty games whilst she daydreams about legacies from elderly admirers. She is expert at undressing herself in imagination for Dr Rank. She dresses up and plays parts for Torvald almost like Harold Pinter's girls. In Ibsen's first draft she reveals that her father liked her to write poetry and learn French, but Torvald preferred dramatic recitations, and disapproved of French literature; his own fantasies of secret mistresses and bridal nights, revealed in his cups, come out of cheap novelettes. Dr Rank slips into calling her 'Nora' but the truly familiar 'du' is reserved for the men between each other, the two women together, and the husband and wife; three different linkings of the threads. Inside 'Nolly-dolly' another self is growing up. She may enjoy playing at secrets, the secrets of the Christmas tree; but her copying work (in the first draft *not* a secret from Torvald) makes her feel 'almost like a man'; and at the news of Torvald's power to dismiss such bank employees as Krogstad, she feels an impulse to swear.

The audience is never told of the emergent adult growing in the chrysalis of the doll's house; they are left to fill her in, or fill her out. Her unconscious growth towards maturity is accompanied by self-delusive dreams of Torvald, the chivalrous knight-errant; and by blank disregard for the concerns of others. When her instinct to love and cherish is in collision with brute facts, she cannot bear to hurt, and would rather lie. . . . Nora begs Krogstad to think of her children, and his reply 'Did you or your husband think of mine?' is quite as devastating as Torvald's 'I am saved, Nora, I am saved', when he finds the fatal IOU has been returned. (In the first draft he says 'We are saved'.)

In a letter to Brandes, written as early as 1871, Ibsen had described the scientists and artists of every age as showing a family likeness—the artist possessing as instinct or intuition what the scientist learnt as knowledge. In the psychology of everyday life Ibsen and Strindberg anticipated Freud, who was himself later to comment on the 'case' of Rebekka West.

Since *A Doll's House* is not psychiatry but drama, the whole plot is woven in a network of relationships. The characters are symbiotically linked so that the minor figures supply a 'feed' to the main figures at a much deeper level than that of the narrative.

Rank and Krogstad are both old school friends of Torvald, Kristine of Nora; each presents a shadow side of the twin. The cross-relationships become a closed system. We do not know what Torvald's chief clerk is like, the details of Rank's practice were suppressed; we do not know whether Nora's childbirths were hard or easy, or what was the character of Krogstad's first wife. But we know that Kristine has been forced by necessity to develop her masculine qualities, to become a breadwinner (also, earlier, to sell herself in the marriage-market). The hard, cold insight which makes her tell Krogstad she won't resign the job at the bank in which she has displaced him 'for that wouldn't help you at all' created what is eventually Nora's equally hard, cold insight into her own situation. Kristine deliberately stops Krogstad from claiming back his letter of disclosure; replacing Dr Rank as ruthless experimenter, she detonates the explosion. Yet Kristine herself is hungry for a home, hungry to be needed, as Nora is hungry for freedom. She had long ago broken Krogstad as Nora breaks Torvald ('I felt as though the ground were cut from under my feet') but now the family for whom she sacrificed herself are no longer in need of her, she feels desolate and empty. In the first draft she was still supporting her brothers; this detracts from her egoistic energy, as she greets the future in words that anticipate Nora's. Tidying up a little, and putting ready her outdoor clothes, to meet Krogstad who is waiting below:

> What a change! O what a change! [literally a turning in the road]. People to work for—people to live for. A home that needs to *feel* like home! Well, now I'll set to, straight away. [In the first draft, 'We'll set to'] . . . I wish they'd hurry! Ah, there they are! Get my things.

But the competent Kristine radiates from no fountain of life; 'she's a bore, that woman', says Torvald. Malice would recall the epigram 'She lives for others. You can tell the others by the hunted look in their eyes.' When Nora comes in after putting off her fancy dress, Torvald cries 'What's this? Not going to bed? You've changed?', and she replies 'Yes, Torvald, I've changed.' There is no verbal echo in the Norwegian, as there is in English, but to dress for a journey links the two scenes dramatically and in action. As Kristine finds a city home, Nora sets out for her birthplace, in search of herself.

In her last speech Nora brings together her whole life, the dead father and her eight years marriage 'with a stranger' so that the past looms into the present at several levels, not only at the one of her dangerous secret. Torvald reproaches her for her ingratitude, and blames himself for having turned advocate for the defence when sent by his ministry to investigate her father's affairs. Ibsen suppressed the passage from the first draft, where he says that he could find no trace of the 1200 dollars her father was supposed to have given her just before his death, for it would be tactless to enquire why Torvald, the lawyer, did not check fully the details of a transaction from which so unexpectedly he had benefited. An audience should not have its notice drawn to the inconsistency. It has rightly been allowed to feel, earlier, that Nora has some

basis for her dreams of Torvald's chivalry in the kindness he had shown her 'poor papa'.

As we never hear about anyone outside the charmed circle of home, so the close detail and meshing of the foreground distinguish *A Doll's House* from its immediate predecessor, *Pillars of the Community* (1877). Here women's rights are shown in a feminine group ranging from the emancipated Lona to the patient Martha, who, like Solveig in *Peer Gynt,* sits at home spinning and waiting for her lover to return. Though Ibsen had begun the art of elimination and of carving in high relief, Bernick's relations with his whole community dominate. (The women do not supply the action of the play.) A large cast of nineteen are found flowing in and out of the garden-room at Bernick's. The irony is far more direct ('Just repaired! and in your own yard, Mr Bernick! . . . now if she's been one of those floating coffins you hear about in the bigger countries!'), and is not so fully integrated with the language of stage movement.

By contrast, Torvald's address to Nora through the half-open door as, unknown to him, she is 'changing', allows him in half-soliloquy to cast himself as a hero, till in his inflation he triumphantly reaches the cheap image of a dove rescued from a hawk—almost becoming something birdlike. The script must be his alone—to her earlier cry 'You mustn't take it on yourself!' he had snapped 'Stop play-acting!' Her language from this moment is naked, plain (in contrast to her horror when Dr Rank spoke out to her of his love). But at the end, when Torvald in a mixture of threat and appeal says 'Then only one explanation is possible . . . you don't love me any more', her simple 'No; that's it. Exactly' brings back the angry cross-examining lawyer: 'Then perhaps you can also explain to me?' In the first draft she had attacked Torvald; in the final version she defines and describes, gives orders to her husband, to which he responds with bewildered questions. The last difficult definition of the 'miracle' that their 'common life' (*samliv*) 'might become a marriage' (*ekteskap*) annihilates Torvald as lawyer and as man.

The word's power is extended in its context. The silences of Dr Rank, his 'Thanks for the light', and the black cross above his name on the visiting card that, according to social ritual, has been dropped, anticipate the depth of Nora's own speech. Her inner death does not leave enough relationship to merit reproaches.

These depths belong with Shakespeare's *Macbeth* and Racine's *Andromaque*. When Lady Macbeth says 'He that's coming / Must be provided for', or Pyrrhus 'Rien ne vous engage à m'aimer en effet' ['In fact, nothing obliges you to love me'], breaking by his obtuseness the barrier of Hermione's control, then a long-built tension explodes; but Ibsen contrives this in the speech of everyday life. (Lady Macbeth is indeed matter of fact, but the context is high poetry.)

In Ibsen's prose the tensions come partly from the relation between the characters, partly from that between his play and what was expected of such dramas (the model of Scribe). On stage the first audience, while enjoying the charm of Nora, actually took Torvald's point of view and thought him a decent husband. In the theatre they followed the familiar code which Ibsen was breaking. It was reading that convinced them of his intention. By the time he had finished drafting and redrafting *A Doll's House* the original notes did not apply, and he was justified in saying it was not a question of women's rights. The tensions come from the marriage between the word and its context, and this works as rhythm works in poetry. But the verse rhythms of Ibsen were very simple; it was only in prose that he gained the classic freedom of his great predecessors.

As he said again and again, his resources were within; he created out of himself, yet he did not subsequently impose an interpretation. He would not tell actors how to play their roles, nor tell the audience how Mrs Alving acted with the morphine: 'That everyone must decide for himself.' The plays grew into contexts he did not know. One translation was called *Breaking a Butterfly*. Hauptmann wrote *Before Sunrise,* and Brieux *Damaged Goods* out of *Ghosts;* Shaw put back a lot of theory, and wrote *Candida.* (pp. 81-7)

The play is not a dramatic monologue for Nora with supporting assistance. The great final scene impresses with its truth, but not as a transcript of anything that could actually happen; it is itself the 'miracle' it postulated. Passions are disentangled from the criss-cross tangles of ordinary life; all the characters being at once so closely enmeshed with each other, yet so isolated from any other crowd or chorus figures, the detail is not realistic.

Ibsen said that as well as character, his people must have a fate. Nora's fate is to embrace an unknown future—to carry the bright flame of her vitality into the dark. 'Out into the storm of life' is one of Borkman's most ironic fantasies; Nora seeks a deep solitude. 'It is necessary that I stand alone.' (p. 88)

The characters of Ibsen's plays stem most clearly from his own innermost heart when he has sometimes to drive out minor, gesticulatory, symbolic figures who come irrelevantly. In the first draft of *A Doll's House,* Dr Rank talks of a patient, a miner who blew his own right hand off when in drink. Rank may have his special reasons to be hard on this sort of case. (He thinks social care for social failures is turning Norway into a clinic!) The self-mutilated, the murderer in *Brand,* the conscript in *Peer Gynt,* are almost as innocent as the victims in *The Wild Duck* and old Foldal in *John Gabriel Borkman.* Brendel challenges Rebekka to chop off her finger or her ear, Hedda's demands on Løvborg have a squalid sequel. Consul Bernick puts the case of the engineer's need to send a workman to almost certain death. Ibsen killed part of himself. Here, more subtly, Torvald's cruelty is closely linked with squeamishness. The ruthless visionary, the expansive self-intoxicated orator, the down-and-out with visions of grandeur, the doomed child, the woman of narrow aims and iron will, the doctor who judges, are all part of Ibsen's inner society. (Yeats termed his own 'the circus animals'.) Some ghosts found local homes in people Ibsen met, others represent only facets of himself; none is simply repeated. The black comedy or satire from *Pillars of the Community* is concentrated in aspects of Torvald.

Ibsen had freed himself, at the cost of exile, from years of humiliating subservience in theatres at Oslo and Bergen. He had learnt the craft as a junior stage-manager, who also wrote to order: cheap reproductions of Romanticism gave models for his ideals of Norwegian nationalism. His history plays developed a very limited originality, and it was only after eleven years and five plays that he broke free in *Love's Comedy* (1862). Two years later he left for Rome where he wrote *Brand,* declaring the truest form of love is hate.

A Doll's House returns to Norway's urban scene, but also transforms the elements of the well-made plays on which he

had toiled so long. It retains old melodramatic tricks, object the sensitive critics of the twentieth century. Rather, it is Sardou *plus,* Scribe *plus,* Ibsen's stagiest work. The characters think they are living in the theatre, they make up cheap plays for themselves but find they are in a different drama. Stage satire does not prevent the use of basic theatrical experience. Ibsen had lived thirteen years in the Norwegian doll's house and written seven plays before he slammed the door. (pp. 88-9)

Ibsen had said '*Brand* began to grow within me like an embryo', but it was at first as a poem, not a drama. The dramatic form suddenly asserted itself. Ibsen was a dramatist as Chopin was a pianist; he could use no other form. But Ibsen wrote concertos and symphonies, not sonatas; he remained free from the actual presence of the theatre, yet clearly bound to it. In the title of *A Doll's House* both his separation from and his ingestion of the theatre where he had learnt his trade is faintly adumbrated; for to look into the peep-show of the nineteenth century's picture-stage is indeed to look into a doll's house (with furniture painted on the backcloth). Not as the result of planning, but of steady, patient work on experience that has been 'lived through'—as he phrased it—the final form emerged; imperative, autonomous, a mimesis that generates new forms of mimesis, with their own life, within the audience and through the years.

Creative opportunities for this third mimesis by the audience are still open. (For example, in this age when racial inequalities have largely replaced sexual inequalities as ground for public concern, the effect of having a white Torvald and a black Nora might be worth some director's experiment.)

The integration of conscious and unconscious functions in the verbal and non-verbal languages of the play generates valid new performance in the live theatre. In a book much studied by Ibsen, it is said of wisdom that 'remaining in herself, she maketh all things new'. (pp. 90-1)

M. C. Bradbrook, "'A Doll's House': The Unweaving of the Web," in her Women and Literature, 1779-1982: The Collected Papers of Muriel Bradbrook, *Vol. 2,* The Harvester Press, Sussex, 1982, *pp. 81-92.*

DAVID THOMAS (essay date 1983)

[*In the following excerpt, Thomas interprets* A Doll's House *as Ibsen's exploration of the tensions inherent in modern domestic life and an attack on hypocritical aspects of conventional bourgeois marriage.*]

After *Pillars of Society,* Ibsen never again divided his attention as a dramatist between the problems confronting women and the working classes in contemporary Norway. From then on he concentrated his attention on the role and status of women as a gauge of social development.

In *Pillars of Society* he had drawn a sympathetic portrait of a young woman who refused to be imprisoned in a conventional marriage. Dina Dorf, fleeing to America with Johan Tønnesen, spells out the conditions on which she will agree to marry him: 'Yes, I will be your wife. [. . .] But first I want to work . . . and make something of my life, as you have done. I don't just want to be a thing, there for the taking.' Clearly, for Ibsen this represented a vision of an ideal marriage, based on mutual respect, freedom and responsibility— the values he had always prized. In his later plays, all too few women are able to achieve anything even vaguely approximating to this ideal state. The few who do are for the most part women who have already experienced one disastrous marriage or relationship and have learnt, by bitter experience, to be self-reliant. For the majority of women in Victorian Europe, the outlook, as Ibsen described it in his plays, was bleak. In a series of tightly structured, carefully chiselled works of art, he showed his frequently shocked audiences images of women who were the victims of bourgeois conventions and attitudes, imprisoned in a series of doll's house marriages.

His next play was appropriately called *A Doll's House,* but it was only the first of a series exploring the built-in tensions of modern family life. The relationships explored in these different plays have a number of features in common. The families involved live isolated from the world around them because of their desire for the 'privilege' of privacy. Marriages are entered into for reasons of property or status. Once married, the women find they have a clearly defined and essentially subordinate role in relation to their men, whose property they legally and socially become. The common assumption of the men is that women are incapable of thinking logically and analytically (an assumption Ibsen seems to share in his notes for *A Doll's House*); on the other hand, the men lack the intuitive insight of their women and therefore tend to show an almost total disregard, with few exceptions, for the emotional needs and expectations of their partners.

Normally, it takes very little, by way of an emotional or social crisis, to disturb the fragile harmony of such marriages. It tends to be an everyday domestic crisis that sparks off a process of critical self-analysis in the various women who have hitherto unthinkingly accepted their inferior roles in marriage. Equally, in all of his problem plays, Ibsen uses the technical device of an outsider or friend or relative arriving in order to bring the crisis to a head.

In *A Doll's House,* the arrival of Mrs Linde precipitates the crisis in the household of Torvald and Nora Helmer. Torvald Helmer is a successful young lawyer who has just been appointed the manager of a commercial bank. Commercial banks had only recently been developed in Norway; the position of a bank manager was therefore a prestigious one at a time of rapid industrial and economic expansion. Torvald is understandably proud of his appointment but gives the impression of being somewhat pompous, self-centred and arrogant. He has been married for eight years, has three children and a pretty young wife called Nora.

The initial image we are given of Nora is of a doll wife, who plays skylarks and squirrels with her husband and revels in the thought of the various consumer luxuries she can at last permit herself now that Torvald has been promoted. She counteracts her husband's pompousness with kittenish flirtation and child-like acts of disobedience.

The action of the play follows a linear pattern until half-way through the third and final act. At that point, the various devices of the traditional well-made play are abandoned (the threatening presence of a moneylender, a fateful letter waiting in the letter box, a doctor friend in love with Nora and Nora's attempt to keep past secrets from her husband), and Nora and her husband sit down to talk through their marital problems for the first time in their eight years of marriage. The result is Nora's departure from the family home and the break-up of the marriage.

At various points in the action, characters are used to underline ironic parallels with the problems facing Nora and Torvald. Nora's friend Mrs Linde is a widow whose first marriage, contracted for purely financial reasons, was a disaster. Having learnt from that experience, she is prepared to commit herself freely and honestly to a man she has always loved even though he is spurned by society, namely the moneylender Krogstad. He is a widower. Despite hints that Krogstad may have a criminal past, Mrs Linde is prepared to share her life with him and his children. She feels they can meet each other's needs openly and frankly and in that way bring out the best in each other. The contrast with Nora's marriage is quite striking. Nora can only relate to her husband at the level of an irresponsible child. She can wheedle and cajole but can never speak to him frankly and has therefore had to take a number of serious decisions in her past life in secret and entirely on her own.

Dr Rank, a family friend, brings another parallel. He is a cynical pessimist, facing imminent death from an inherited disease. His fate reflects Nora's. He has inherited a disintegrating spine from his presumably syphilitic father. Nora, for her part, has acquired her 'irresponsible' attitudes and responses from her father's treatment of her. Rank's impending death is used to highlight the fact that Nora is thinking of committing suicide rather than bring 'disgrace' upon her husband. But where Rank learns nothing from his suffering and the certainty of his death—his attitude to people remains embittered and dismissive—Nora grows in stature from the experience of staring death in the face.

The play is full of visual suggestions that provide a comment on the action or underline a particular facet of a given character's responses. We see something of Nora's extravagance in the Christmas presents she has bought and her excessive tipping of a porter. But in always buying the cheapest clothes we see her resourcefulness in making do. In eating forbidden macaroons she shows her defiance of Torvald, while in asking his advice about her costume for a fancy dress party, we see her skill in flattering and cajoling him. In showing her new silk stockings to Dr Rank, we see her willingness to flirt and exploit her sexuality, but not to the point where it becomes explicit. In her performance of the tarantella, we have an image of the dance of death, an image of the black thoughts filling her mind. The image is reinforced when she pulls a black shawl over her head before attempting to leave the house to commit suicide. Finally, her change of clothes and the donning of everyday dress underlines her determination in the last act of the play to face up to the prosaic reality of her marriage for the very first time.

At the heart of the play is a detailed exploration of Nora's character and the nature of her relationship with her husband. Underneath Nora's playful exterior, there is from the start an intuitively serious mind. Nora is totally committed to her children and to her husband. She knows his weaknesses and fully understands his need to feel in control. She therefore always humours him and helps him to feel that he takes all the important decisions in their life. In order to achieve this, she consciously plays out the role of a helpless scatterbrain. She is, however, quite capable of taking decisive action. When Torvald was desperately ill and needed a long convalescent journey to the South, he stubbornly refused to borrow money. Nora's usual cajoling tricks failed to make him change his mind. She therefore took action on her own account, borrowing the necessary money behind his back with the help of a forged signature. She did not stop to consider the ethical implications of her forgery: all that mattered to her was the health of her husband. Torvald was told that the money was a present from her father.

For Nora to sustain her submissive role vis-à-vis her husband, she needs to believe in him and in qualities that he would reveal in a crisis. In her imagination he becomes something of a courtly hero, albeit in domestic garb. Unfortunately, her commitment is based on romantic fantasy rather than reality. Deep down she suspects this herself, even though she would never consciously admit it. When a real crisis looms, namely Krogstad's threat to blackmail Torvald because of Nora's forgery, she prefers to contemplate suicide rather than put her husband's character to the test.

When the crisis breaks, her worst fears are confirmed. Torvald proves to be not a courtly hero, but a frightened and mean-spirited little man who is more worried about his reputation than his wife:

> Now you have ruined my entire happiness, jeopardized my whole future. It's terrible to think of. Here I am, at the mercy of a thoroughly unscrupulous person; he can do whatever he likes with me, demand anything he wants, order me about just as he chooses . . . and I daren't even whimper. I'm done for, a miserable failure, and it's all the fault of a feather-brained woman!

In the confrontation that follows between husband and wife at the end of Act 3, Nora is in a state of shocked awareness. For the first time, she sees her life for what it is, and rejects it. She is determined to discover her real potential as a person, which means she has to reject the role of doll wife and doll mother. At the end of the play, she walks out on her husband and her children, leaving behind her a bewildered and confused man who is still completely imprisoned within the conditioned assumptions of his middle-class world. Torvald, we now see, is as much a victim as Nora, but he has not even begun to understand his predicament. The play closes with a question mark left in the audience's mind. Will Torvald ever learn to see and to understand in the way that his wife has, or will he continue to allow his responses and actions to be controlled by social conditioning? (pp. 67-72)

Ibsen's major thematic concern was to explore the notion of freedom and responsibility juxtaposed with the inhibiting force of determinism. He does not underestimate the power of determinism, and there are two major characters in the play, Torvald and Dr Rank, who remain either bewildered or embittered victims of, in the one case, social, in the other, biological determinism. But the action of the play as a whole demonstrates the essential freedom of men and women to act decisively in shaping the quality of their lives and responses.

Despite the pressures of social and economic determinism, both Mrs Linde and Nora, in their diametrically opposed ways, make conscious and responsible choices about their future lives as a result of painfully acquired experience. In both cases, their future lives will be fraught with problems (Mrs Linde as a step-mother, married to a social outcast, and Nora, fending for herself as a shunned divorcee), but both women have demonstrated their ability to face up to difficulties and seek for authentic solutions.

A Doll's House was quite correctly interpreted by Ibsen's contemporaries as a swingeing attack on conventional bourgeois marriage (although importantly not on marriage *per se*).

It was intended to be a profoundly revolutionary play, deepening the critique of patriarchal attitudes he had initiated in *Pillars of Society.* As Ibsen saw it, women would spearhead the revolt against the repressive conventions of contemporary society. Men were far more likely to be dominated by the social prejudices of their day because of their role as breadwinner and provider. That is why Nora consciously *acts* the part of a doll wife, whereas Torvald unthinkingly *lives out* his role as the authoritarian husband. By the same token, that also explains why Nora achieves insight at the end of the play, while her husband remains bewildered and confused.

Despite the conscious provocation within it, the play closes on an optimistic note. Nora has left with the positive aim of discovering who and what she is and what she can become. Meanwhile, there is at least a slender ray of hope that Torvald may yet achieve some degree of insight once he has recovered from the initial shock of his wife's departure. The question he articulates at the end sums up that hope and the difficulty implicit within it: 'The miracle of miracles . . .?' (pp. 72-4)

> *David Thomas, in his* Henrik Ibsen, *The Macmillan Press Ltd., 1983, 177 p.*

IRVING DEER   (essay date 1986)

[*In the following excerpt, Deer considers* A Doll's House *representative of a new kind of drama, the form of which, illustrating the limitations of the conventional drama of romantic intrigue, constitutes an attack on that genre.*]

Despite the fact that a number of Ibsen's protagonists are artists or surrogate artist figures, little consideration has been given to his work as art about art, or, more specifically, drama about drama. This neglect may result partly from the fact that Ibsen is generally considered a kind of social problem writer, someone who is quintessentially concerned, at least in his plays, with the world, not with his own artistic problems. His status as the "father of modern drama," meaning the creator of realistic drama, promotes the same "blindness" to the possibility that he could be writing plays both about their own genesis and about the world.

I want to argue that such a paradox, both an inward and an outward focus, is precisely one of Ibsen's main concerns and achievements. His best plays are both about themselves and about the world, and perhaps most interestingly, about their own struggle to achieve that paradoxical state. (p. 35)

For those of us who have seen performances of *A Doll's House* by Claire Bloom or Jane Fonda on stage, screen or television in the last decade, there is little difficulty in understanding Ibsen's reputation as a writer of social problem plays. Most people still see the play as one about a heroic young woman's victorious struggle for freedom from repressive social conventions. Some, however, like Hermann Weigand in the twenties, see Nora as a deceptive, selfish, intriguing young woman bent only on having her own way [see excerpt dated 1925]. These critics believe Ibsen is satirizing and debunking her rather than, as the other critics believe, holding her up as virtue incarnate.

Whichever interpretation you favor, the play comes out to be about social problems, about the problems of the individual's responsibility to society and conversely, of society's responsibility to the individual. When the play first came out conventional audiences favored emphasizing the individual's respon-

sibility to society. More liberal audiences since have emphasized the play's concern with society's responsibility to the individual. Although the liberal view has been dominant for
years now, some such alignment still persists.

The problem from the point of view of my subject is not then
one of showing Ibsen's concern with relating *A Doll's House*
to society. That is obvious. What is more difficult is to show
that the play is also about playing, that it is, in other words,
a kind of self-conscious drama about drama itself. The illusion of objective realism Ibsen achieved with the play, its apparent photographic objectivity, seems to most people to
deny the possibility of the kind of self-conscious subjectivity
I am looking for in the play. Yet there is an almost obvious
sense in which the play is about characters playing roles,
clearly pretending, performing for others. This is most obvious with Nora herself. It is also perhaps one of the main reasons those in the Weigand camp see her as an intriguer and
plotter rather than as the virtuous heroine for whom she is
more often taken. From the beginning of the play she engages
in little intrigues, pretending to Torvald she has been obeying
him about not eating macaroons, when we just saw her eat
some before he entered the room, performing like a squirrel
for him to get him to give her some money so, as we later
learn, she can engage in her greatest intrigue of all, the plot
to cover up the loan she has been paying off in this way to
Krogstad for years. Later when Krogstad threatens to write
her husband not only about the loan but about her having
forged her dead father's signature to get it, she gives a frenzied, desperate performance, a literal performance, dancing
a tarantella at a party upstairs, to try to keep Torvald from
going back to their apartment where he will pick up the mail
with Krogstad's letter.

Performance, role-playing, is thus for the central figure in the
play a necessary form of action, perhaps the main form her
struggles take. But there is also another sense in which
Ibsen's subject is drama itself. Most of the characters are conceived of as playing roles drawn from the kinds of Danish and
French romantic melodramas from which Ibsen learned his
craft. As Raymond Williams points out [see Further Read-
ing], there is "the innocent child-like woman, involved in a
desperate deception, the heavy insensitive husband; the faithful friend." "Similarly," Williams continues, "the main situations of the play are typical of the intrigue drama: the guilty
secret, sealed lips, the complication of situations around
Krogstad's letter . . . Krogstad at the children's party . . .
the villain against a background of tranquility. . . ." For
Williams all of this is an indication of the play's weaknesses:
"None of this is at all new," he says, "and it is the major part
of the play."

His view would be true if the play were not self-conscious,
that is, if it were not about the limitations of playing such
roles in life as well as in drama. As I see the play, it is centrally about Nora's discovery of how limited her romantic role-
playing has been, how it was not only imposed on her by society, but willingly accepted by her. I believe in fact that the
main reason she is taken by one group as the embodiment of
modern heroism and by another as villainy personified is that
Ibsen shows us that each of those views is a fragment of the
truth. Both constitute partial views of Nora. She did save her
husband's life, she is willing to commit suicide like some Isolde to save her husband and family from ruin, but she also did
naively forge her father's signature on a loan, and innocently
expects Torvald to act like a storybook lover who takes all

her shame on himself. She sees herself as the romantic heroine of the types of plays from which Ibsen learned his craft,
the Danish historical romances and the French melodramas
he imitated and directed. The liberal perspective supports her
view. However, a shift to a more conservative perspective,
one that emphasizes her responsibility to her husband, children, and society, can easily emphasize her similarity to the
intriguing, villainous women of the French melodramas.
From such a perspective, she lies, postures and intrigues
about everything, and when found out, runs off, dropping all
her responsibilities. Both these views of Nora, as the romantic
heroine or the intriguing villain, are extremely limited, melodramatic views. As she is beginning to discover by the end
of the play, by having accepted either of such limited views
of herself, or having allowed society to impose one on her, she
has contributed to her own frustration as a person who is trying to express more of herself than society allows. By showing
us one melodramatic view of Nora, then the opposite melodramatic view, Ibsen is pointing out both the limitations of
melodramatic ways of seeing and of writing.

We can see this in Ibsen's treatment of situations drawn from
the popular Scribean intrigues he knew so well. The whole
letter situation, for example, is given a new twist, not accepted in its mechanical conventional form as Williams seems to
think. Nora does everything to try to divert Torvald's attention from the letter box. When he finally gets Krogstad's first
letter and reads it, he acts as a character would in Scribe. The
world turns in Scribe's plays on glasses of water, handker-
chiefs and letters. Everything stops with them. The world is
saved. The lovers are united. Virtue triumphs. The play ends.
Nurtured by society on such forms of expression, Torvald reacts appropriately. He feels his life has been ruined by his stupid wife, just when he has become an important bank manager. In retribution, he in effect stops Nora from functioning.
He tells her she can no longer be a real wife or mother to their
children, that she will corrupt them as she is corrupted. Since
the only roles society has allowed her have been those of
child, lover, wife and mother, the only two roles she has left
by which to express herself are those of wife and mother.
Now Torvald has taken those away from her.

True, he returns them a few minutes later when Krogstad's
second letter comes. Since Krogstad has returned the incrim-
inating loan papers, Torvald is no longer in danger. He would
like to forget the whole thing, to get back to where he and
Nora were before he castigated her as innately corrupt. As
he sees it, he is generously returning her to her status as wife
and mother. She, however, sees the sequence of events somewhat differently. She see how limited and arbitrary have been
the roles society has assigned her and she has accepted.

Nora now sees the need to find new ways of relating to society. She has also seen the possibility of finding new ways. She
has seen her friend Christine become a widow, a working
woman surviving on her own, a woman who goes into an unmarried, permanent relationship with a man, Krogstad, the
choice which also makes the man, Krogstad, see that he is not
doomed to isolation and to the intrigues he felt conventional
society had forced on him. Just as Nora now sees the need
and the possibility of finding new ways of relating to society,
so does Ibsen as a writer of a new kind of drama. He was with
A Doll's House creating the realistic drama that was to make
him world famous. This new kind of drama constituted his
attack on the conventional romantic and intrigue drama and
vision he had inherited. It was the first step among several im-

portant ones he would take in experimenting with new, more contemporary possibilities for drama. (pp. 36-9)

> *Irving Deer, "Ibsen's Self-Reflexivity in 'A Doll's House' and 'The Masterbuilder',"* in Within the Dramatic Spectrum, Vol. VI, *edited by Karelisa V. Hartigan, University Press of America, 1986, pp. 35-44.*

FURTHER READING

Archer, William. Review of *Breaking a Butterfly,* by Henry A. Jones and H. Herman. *The Theatre* 3, No. 16 (April 1884): 209-14.
Negative review of an adaptation of *A Doll's House* that consists largely of favorable commentary on Ibsen's play.

———. "Ibsen's Apprenticeship." *The Fortnightly Review* LXXV, No. CCCCXLV (January 1904): 25-35.
Examines the influence of the French *pièce bien faite* on Ibsen's development as a dramatist and pronounces *A Doll's House* Ibsen's first work to transcend its conventions.

———. Introduction to *A Doll's House,* by Henrik Ibsen, pp. vii-xvi. New York: Charles Scribner's Sons, 1936.
Outlines the early performance history of the play and assesses its place in Ibsen's career and in world literature.

———. *William Archer on Ibsen: The Major Essays, 1889-1919.* Edited by Thomas Postlewait. Westport, Conn.: Greenwood Press, 1984, 323 p.
Annotated selection of important essays about Ibsen by Archer.

Aveling, Edward. *"Nora* and *Breaking a Butterfly." To-day: The Monthly Magazine of Scientific Socialism* I, No. 6 (June 1884): 473-80.
Unfavorable comparison of *Breaking a Butterfly,* an adaptation of *A Doll's House,* with Ibsen's original drama.

Belkin, Roslyn. "Prisoners of Convention: Ibsen's 'Other' Women." *Journal of Women's Studies* 1, No. 2 (Spring 1979): 142-58.
Identifies Nora Helmer as Ibsen's only female character to seek autonomy rather than control over a man.

Bentley, Eric. "Ibsen, Pro and Con." In his *In Search of Theater,* pp. 365-77. New York: Alfred A. Knopf, 1953.
Includes discussion of *A Doll's House* in an essay that recapitulates and responds to some common criticisms of Ibsen's plays.

Beyer, Edvard. *"A Doll's House."* In his *Ibsen: The Man and His Work,* translated by Marie Wells, pp. 114-22. London: Souvenir Press, 1978.
Characterizes *A Doll's House* as the work in which Ibsen developed innovative dramatic techniques to produce a distinctive modern tragedy.

Boyesen, H. H. Review of *A Doll-Home,* by Henrik Ibsen. *Cosmopolitan* XVI, No. 1 (November 1893): 84-9.
Discusses the play as an exposition on problems inherent in the contemporary system of marriage.

Bryan, George B. *An Ibsen Companion: A Dictionary-Guide to the Life, Works, and Critical Reception of Henrik Ibsen.* Westport, Conn.: Greenwood Press, 1984, 437 p.
Lists and describes Ibsen's plays and characters, important figures in Ibsen's life, and significant actors from major productions. The critic supplies an introductory essay on Ibsen's development as a dramatist and a chronology of his life, as well as brief structural analyses of each play.

Buitenhuis, Peter. "After the Slam of *A Doll's House* Door: Reverberations in the Work of James, Hardy, Ford and Wells." *Mosaic* XVII, No. 1 (Winter 1984): 83-96.
Examines the influence of Ibsen's play on indictments of marriage in subsequent works by the authors listed.

Dukore, Bernard F. " 'How Much?'—Money, Survival, and Independence: *A Doll House, Pygmalion, Mother Courage and Her Children."* In his *Money & Politics in Ibsen, Shaw, and Brecht,* pp. 1-26. Columbia: University of Missouri Press, 1980.
Examines the relationship of financial and emotional independence in the three plays listed.

Egan, Michael, ed. *Ibsen: The Critical Heritage.* London: Routledge and Kegan Paul, 1972, 505 p.
Compendium of important early reviews of English-language performances of Ibsen's plays. Egan supplies a lengthy introduction summarizing trends in Ibsen's early critical reception.

Ewbank, Inga-Stina. "Ibsen and the Language of Women." In *Women Writing and Writing About Women,* edited by Mary Jacobus, pp. 114-32. London: Croom Helm, 1979.
Includes discussion of Nora's dialogue in *A Doll's House* in an analysis of womens' use of language in Ibsen's plays.

Fjelde, Rolf. Introduction to *Henrik Ibsen: Four Major Plays, Volume I,* by Henrik Ibsen, translated by Rolf Fjelde, pp. ix-xxxv. New York: Signet, 1965.
Insightful essay examining the shift in Ibsen's dramatic methods that occurred at the midpoint of his career and briefly discussing characteristics of *A Doll's House, The Wild Duck, Hedda Gabler,* and *The Master Builder.*

Gassner, John. Introduction to *Four Great Plays,* by Henrik Ibsen, translated by R. Farquharson Sharp, pp. vii-xiii. New York: Bantam Books, 1984.
Comments on the controversial nature of the plays of Ibsen's middle period, including *A Doll's House, Ghosts, An Enemy of the People,* and *The Wild Duck.*

Gray, Ronald. *"A Doll's House."* In his *Ibsen: A Dissenting View,* pp. 41-58. London: Cambridge University Press, 1977.
Suggests that the technical aspects of the play are handled with sufficient skill to offset the elements of melodrama and occasionally exaggerated characterizations that Ibsen may have introduced as concessions to public taste.

Harding, Edward J. "Henrik Ibsen, Iconoclast." *The Critic* 16, No. 324 (15 March 1890): 131-32.
Maintains that the four Ibsen plays available in English translation—*A Doll's House, Pillars of Society, Ghosts,* and *Rosmersholm*—offer only "a whole baffling philosophy of despair, a gospel of perdition," unrelieved by any positive considerations. Annie Nathan Meyer (see below) published a rebuttal to this essay.

Haugen, Einar. *Ibsen's Drama: Author to Audience.* Minneapolis: University of Minnesota Press, 1979, 185 p.
Account of Ibsen's career as a dramatist, examining contemporary reactions to his plays.

Heller, Otto. "The Woman Question—*A Doll's House."* In his *Henrik Ibsen: Plays and Problems,* pp. 136-59. Boston: Houghton-Mifflin Co., 1912.
Explores the issue of women's rights raised by *A Doll's House.*

Herford, C. H. "Ibsen in London." *The Academy* XXXV, No. 894 (22 June 1889): 432.
Response to Frederick Wedmore's review of *A Doll's House* (see below), questioning the validity of an assessment of Ibsen based on this play alone.

Hervey, R. K. Review of *A Doll's House. The Theatre* 14, No. 79 (1 July 1889): 38-41.
Favorable review of an 1889 London production of the play,

commending Ibsen for exploring the issue of woman's place in modern society.

Johnston, Brian. "*A Doll House,* or 'The Fortunate Fall'." In his *Text and Supertext in Ibsen's Drama,* pp. 137-64. University Park: Pennsylvania State University Press, 1989.
    Examines the rhythm and structure of the play, its analysis of marriage, and the dialectical process by which "the Edenic innocence of the doll home" is shattered.

Joyce, James, and Power, Arthur. *Conversations with James Joyce,* edited by Clive Hart. London: Millington, 1974, 111 p.
    Incorporates Power's recollections of Joyce's comments on several Ibsen plays, including his pronouncement that "the purpose of *A Doll's House* . . . was the emancipation of women, which has caused the greatest revolution in our time in the most important relationship there is—that between men and women; the revolt of women against the idea that they are the mere instruments of men."

Kiberd, Declan. "Ibsen's Heroines: The New Woman as Rebel." In his *Men and Feminism in Modern Literature,* pp. 61-84. New York: Macmillan, 1985.
    Examines Ibsen's portrayal in *A Doll's House* of a woman struggling to free herself from sex-role stereotypes and her husband's reaction.

Koht, Halvdan. *The Life of Ibsen.* Translated by Ruth Lima McMahon and Hanna Astrup Larsen. 2 vols. New York: W. W. Norton & Co., 1931.
    Biography that contains discussion of the critical and popular reception of Ibsen's plays.

Krutch, Joseph Wood. "Ibsen and the Chasm between Past and Future." *"Modernism" in Modern Drama: A Definition and an Estimate,* pp. 1-22. Ithaca: Cornell University Press, 1953.
    Calls *A Doll's House* Ibsen's first significant drama to undertake social themes and considers the play an important herald of the period in which drama became "perhaps the most important species of imaginative writing so far as the dissemination of revolutionary attitudes is concerned."

Lavrin, Janko. *Ibsen: An Approach.* London: Methuen & Co., 1950, 139 p.
    Includes discussion of *A Doll's House* in chapters devoted to Ibsen's process of composition and to his "realist" period.

Lowenthal, Leo. "Henrik Ibsen (1828-1906)." In his *Literature and the Image of Man: Sociological Studies of the European Drama and Novel, 1600-1900,* pp. 166-89. Boston: Beacon Press, 1957.
    Includes discussion of *A Doll's House* in an examination of male and female social roles in Ibsen's dramas.

Marker, Frederick, and Marker, Lise-Lone. "The First Nora: Notes on the World Premier of *A Doll's House.*" In *Contemporary Approaches to Ibsen: Proceedings of the Second International Ibsen Seminary,* pp. 84-100. Oslo: Universitetsforlaget, 1971.
    Discussion of the play's premier that includes commentary on the moral and ethical questions debated by early reviewers, as well as differing interpretations of the physical production and individual performances.

May, Keith M. "*The League of Youth* to *The Wild Duck.*" In his *Ibsen and Shaw,* pp. 43-71. New York: Macmillan, 1985.
    Briefly mentions the contemporary impact of *A Doll's House* and discusses the play's principal themes.

Meyer, Annie Nathan. "Ibsen's Attitude Toward Women." *The Critic,* New York 16, No. 325 (22 March 1890): 147-48.
    Challenges Edward J. Harding's contention that Ibsen presented a wholly pessimistic view of society (see above), contending that *A Doll's House, The Pillars of Society,* and *Ghosts* demonstrate Ibsen's "strong, sympathetic belief in the future of women."

Meyer, Michael. *Henrik Ibsen: The Making of a Dramatist, 1828-1864.* London: Rupert Hart-Davis, 1967, 260 p.
    Biography treating Ibsen's life and career through 1864.

——. *Henrik Ibsen: The Farewell to Poetry, 1864-1882.* London: Rupert Hart-Davis, 1971, 344 p.
    Continuation of Meyer's important biography. A chapter detailing the period in which Ibsen wrote *A Doll's House* includes an overview of contemporary critical and popular reaction to the play.

——. *Henrik Ibsen: The Top of a Cold Mountain, 1883-1906.* London: Rupert Hart-Davis, 1971, 367 p.
    Concluding volume of Meyer's comprehensive biography.

Postlewait, Thomas. *Prophet of the New Drama: William Archer and the Ibsen Campaign.* Westport, Conn.: Greenwood Press, 1986, 190 p.
    History of Archer's involvement in "the Ibsen campaign," translating and explicating Ibsen's drama for English audiences.

Quigley, Austin E. "Ibsen: *A Doll's House.*" In his *The Modern Stage and Other Worlds,* pp. 91-114. New York: Methuen, 1985, 320 p.
    Suggests that in *A Doll's House* Ibsen made innovative use of the conventions of the well-made play.

Richardson, Jack. "Ibsen's Nora and Ours." *Commentary* 52, No. 1 (July 1971): 77-80.
    Compares the individual case of Nora Helmer with positions taken by 1970s women's rights activists.

Rogers, Katharine M. "A Woman Appreciates Ibsen." *The Centennial Review* XVIII, No. 1 (Winter 1974): 91-108.
    Attributes feminist convictions to Ibsen on the basis of his sympathetic portrayal of difficult situations unique to women in *A Doll's House* and *Ghosts.*

Rose, Henry. "Plays of Social Life (Continued)." In his *Henrik Ibsen: Poet, Mystic and Moralist,* pp. 38-43. New York: Dodd Mead and Co., 1913.
    Assesses *A Doll's House* as "a natural and true picture of a woman's revolt" growing out of socially imposed restrictions on women.

Rosenberg, Marvin. "Ibsen vs. Ibsen, or Two Versions of *A Doll's House.*" *Modern Drama* XII, No. 2 (September 1969): 187-96.
    Examines changes between the penultimate draft and the final version of the play.

Simonds, W. E. "Henrik Ibsen." *The Dial* X, No. 119 (March 1890): 301-03.
    Includes favorable commentary on the plot and characterizations of *A Doll's House* in a brief overview of Ibsen's career to 1890.

Review of *A Doll's House. The Spectator* 62 (22 June 1889): 853-54.
    Suggests that *A Doll's House* reveals Ibsen's "thoroughgoing pessimism" about the state of modern marriage.

Tennant, P. F. D. "The Ending." In his *Ibsen's Dramatic Technique,* pp. 113-18. New York: Humanities Press, 1965.
    Considers *A Doll's House* the first work in which Ibsen developed the inconclusive ending that became characteristic of his later plays.

Thompson, Alan Reynolds. "Ibsen." In his *The Dry Mock: A Study of Irony in Drama,* pp. 197-244. Berkeley and Los Angeles: University of California Press, 1948.
    Mentions aspects of characterization that render *A Doll's House* partly comic.

Tufts, Carol Strongin. "Recasting *A Doll's House:* Narcissism as Character Motivation in Ibsen's Play." *Comparative Drama* 20, No. 2 (Summer 1986): 140-59.

Suggests that self-preoccupation, or narcissism, can be interpreted as the primary motivating factor of every character in the play.

Van Laan, Thomas F. "The Ending of *A Doll House* and Augier's *Maître Guérin.*" *Comparative Drama* 17, No. 4 (Winter 1983-84): 297-317.
    Suggests that Emile Augier's play *Maître Guérin* (1864) provided Ibsen with the idea and some of the details for the conclusion of his later play.

Warnken, William P. "Kate Chopin and Henrik Ibsen: A Study of *The Awakening* and *A Doll's House.*" *The Massachusetts Studies in English* IV & V, Nos. 4 & 1 (Autumn 1974-Winter 1975): 43-8.
    Examines affinities between the beliefs of the two authors regarding the position of women in modern society, and cites parallels between Chopin's novel and Ibsen's play.

Watts, Peter. Introduction to *The League of Youth, A Doll's House, The Lady from the Sea,* by Henrik Ibsen, translated by Peter Watts, pp. 7-21. Harmondsworth: Penguin Books, 1965.
    Comments on biographical factors that affected the composition of *A Doll's House* in a chronologically arranged sketch that establishes the significance of these three works in Ibsen's career.

Wedmore, Frederick. "Ibsen in London." *The Academy* XXXV, No. 893 (15 June 1880): 419-20.
    Finds that *A Doll's House* reveals Ibsen to be "an interesting, but not a very great, artist" and "a missionary . . . whose mission is to some extent unnecessary, and to some extent injurious."

Williams, Raymond. "Henrik Ibsen." In his *Drama From Ibsen to Eliot,* pp. 41-97. London: Chatto & Windus, 1965.
    Considers *A Doll's House* an important "step in the evolution of the romantic melodrama into the naturalist."

Zucker, A. E. "The Social Plays." In his *Ibsen: The Master Builder,* pp. 148-86. New York: Henry Holt & Co., 1929.
    Includes discussion of the plot and the critical reception of *A Doll's House* in a chronologically arranged study of Ibsen's life and works.

Miyamoto Yuriko

1899-1951

Japanese novelist and short story writer.

Miyamoto is considered one of the most important Japanese novelists of the post-World War II period. She is best known for her autobiographical novels in which she integrated accounts of her personal development with descriptions of Japanese history, politics, and society. In these works Miyamoto also conveyed her strong feminist perspective and socialist political convictions.

Miyamoto was born into a wealthy and prominent family in 1899. When she was eighteen, she published her first work, *Mazushiki hitobito no mure,* a novel that features an introspective and idealistic young protagonist who wants to improve conditions for the peasants on her grandfather's estate. The following year, Miyamoto traveled to New York with her father. There she attended classes at Columbia University and met and married a Japanese graduate student. Miyamoto and her husband were divorced in 1924 after they returned to Japan, and critics suggest that her unsuccessful first marriage helped shape her awareness of the social limitations imposed on women. During the mid 1920s, Miyamoto formed an important friendship with Yuasho Yoshiko, a scholar of Russian literature, and for three years the two women lived in Moscow, where Miyamoto became convinced that socialism would solve many problems and improve the status of women in her own country. Returning to Japan in 1930, she became involved in the proletarian literature movement and served as editor of a women's journal. In 1931 she joined the Communist party, and in 1932 she married Miyamoto Kenji, a prominent figure in the Party. Over the next twelve years, Miyamoto was intermittently imprisoned for her political activities. She continued to write during this period, and a number of her works were banned. When World War II ended, Miyamoto and her husband were reunited, and afterward she enjoyed the most prolific phase of her career. However, Miyamoto's health had been damaged by her years of imprisonment and by the frenetic pace of writing and political activity she maintained after the war. She died in 1951.

Miyamoto's autobiographical novels are often discussed as part of the tradition of the I-novel, a Japanese novelistic form in which the author focuses on his or her personal development and experiences, often without using fictional devices. In *Nobuko,* for example, Miyamoto described her life in New York City, while *Dōhyō* relates the process by which the author came to accept Marxist doctrine. Miyamoto's novels differ from the I-novel, however, in her integration of the protagonist's experiences with social issues and historical events, especially the status of women, class inequality, and the suffering of Japanese people during World War II. In *Fūchisō,* a novelist and her husband re-establish their relationship and adjust to normal life after years of separation while the husband was imprisoned during the war. *Banshū Heiya* focuses on both the main character's relationship with her husband's family and the destruction Japan experienced as a result of the war. Miyamoto has been praised for her insightful portrayal of human relationships, particularly that of the husband and wife in *Fūchisō,* and for her evocative descriptions of the devastation and misery following the Japanese surrender. Miyamoto's blending of individual experience and history in her works has been recognized as an important contribution to Japanese literature. As Noriko Mizuta Lippit has written, Miyamoto "created a new form of autobiography, one in which the protagonist emerges as an heroic figure of the age, living fully its limitations and possibilities."

PRINCIPAL WORKS

Mazushiki hitobito no mure (novel) 1917; published in journal *Chūl ōkoron*
Nobuko (novel) 1928
  [*Nobuko* (partial translation) published in journal *Bulletin of Concerned Asian Scholars,* 1975]
Banshū Heiya (novel) 1946
  [*The Banshu Plain* (partial translation) published in *Ukiyo: Stories of 'the Floating World' of Post-War Japan,* 1954]
Fūchisō (novel) 1947
  [*The Weathervane Plant* (partial translation) published in *Journal of the Association of Teachers of Japanese,* 1984-85]
Futatsu no niwa (novel) 1947
Dōhyō (novel) 1947-50
Jūninen no tegami (letters) 1950
Nobuko jidai no nikki, 1920-23 (diary) 1976
"The Family of Koiwai" (short story) 1982; published in *Stories by Contemporary Japanese Women Writers*

NORIKO MIZUTA LIPPIT (essay date 1978)

[*In the following excerpt from an essay that was originally published in 1978, Lippit discusses prominent themes in Miyamoto's fiction. All translations in this excerpt are by Lippit.*]

Heirs to a long tradition of women's literature in Japan, modern Japanese women writers tended to focus on emotions and psychology, while women's status in a modernizing society was excluded from the principal literary currents. Japanese proletarian literature, which reached its peak at the beginning of the Showa period (1926-present), was no exception in this regard. Such major writers as Kobayashi Takiji paid only scant and superficial attention to the questions of women, and in general, the theoreticians who were concerned with the questions of laborers, peasants and intellectuals in revolution ignored women.

Miyamoto Yuriko, a leading proletarian writer of the first half of the Showa period, stands out in this context as an exceptional figure, as a writer who placed women's concerns at the center of her literature and integrated them with the socialist movement of her time. She began her writing career as an idealistic humanist who was disturbed by the alienation of elite intellectuals from the masses; yet in her attempt to grow into a real intellectual, liberated from the conditioning forces of her bourgeois background, she came to realize that being a woman imposed an obstacle as great as any other she confronted. She came to believe that overcoming the class nature of her philosophic and aesthetic ideas and becoming a truly liberated woman were both crucial to living a rich and meaningful life. She saw the family and marriage systems as feudal institutions preserved in the interests of modern capitalism and considered them to be the primary forces oppressing women. At the same time, she noted the failure of women intellectuals to grasp the class nature of their ideas and their cynical and reactionary retreat into false femininity. For Yuriko, being a humanist meant being a feminist and communist revolutionary, and the humanist, feminist and revolutionary struggles were necessary truly to liberate human beings.

Miyamoto Yuriko was born into an upper-middle-class, intellectual family in 1899 and died a committed and major communist writer in 1951. She accepted historical incidents as personally significant events and grew from a bourgeois humanist into a humanistic communist, from an intellectual observer into a committed fighter, from the bright, overprotected daughter of an elite family into a liberated woman, and, above all, she grew into a fine fiction writer who combined history and individual experience in literature. Her art is a mirror reflecting the complex history of Japan and the inner life of the Japanese artist who lived through it.

She dealt with three major concerns throughout her life, concerns which she considered central problems or conflicts to be resolved. They are the questions of consciousness and practice, women's happiness and creativity, and politics and literature. Focusing on her ideas on women, this chapter examines how these central problems and her consciousness of them shaped her creative works and are reflected in them.

A precocious writer, Miyamoto Yuriko published her first novel, *Mazushiki hitobito no mure (A Flock of Poor Folk)*, in *Chūōkōron* in 1917, when she was only eighteen years old. . . . The novel is about an *ojōsan* (an honorable daughter) from Tokyo who visits the remote agricultural village owned by her grandfather. The protagonist, observing the details of the poor peasants' lives, is appalled by the injustice of the system of landownership as well as by the distortions which absolute poverty creates in human psychology and character. In her sincere attempts to help the poor peasants, she meets only vicious greed and apathy on the part of the peasants and cynical arrogance from the village elite. Although the work is filled with youthful sentimentalism, Yuriko's treatment of the protagonist's deep self-reflection and self-analysis when she confronts the absolute defeat of her upper-class humanism is impressive. The novel ends with the protagonist's determination to find something, however small, which could be shared with the peasants and her determination to grow into a person who understands life.

What principally characterizes the novel is the author's tendency toward introspective self-searching, together with her idealism and strong faith in human goodwill, characteristic traits which were to stay with her the rest of her life. Reflecting the strong influence of Tolstoy and such writers of the Shirakaba group as Arishima Takeo, she expresses in this work a youthful and hopeful belief in the union of consciousness and practice, and her determination to contribute to human welfare. In this respect she differs from the naturalist

writers and urban intellectuals of the late Meiji period (1868-1912), whose discovery of the deep chasm between themselves and the peasants, and of the evil of a system which separates people so absolutely merely led them to an overall pessimism and desperation about human nature. (pp. 146-48)

[Yuriko's experiences in her marriage to Araki Shigeru became] the basis of her first masterpiece, *Nobuko* which, like all of her subsequent novels, is highly autobiographical in nature, reflecting the experience and realization of a particular phase of Yuriko's life.

> Unlike many women, Nobuko did not think she could change her life situation by finding a new love, for then she would just be moving from one man to another and would still be someone's wife. It was not that she disliked her married life because she compared Tsukuda with someone else. It was because of the many difficulties that the incompatibility of their personalities created and because she could not accept the differences between men and women in the way they fulfill themselves in marriage, differences which are accepted generally. Either she would have to be reborn as a different woman or the common social ideas of sex life would have to change in certain respects for her to remain married without problems.
>
> To be perfectly honest, she could not claim to be free from apprehension about her independent life in the future. She could not imagine that Tsukuda was unaware of her subtle weakness. No matter how eager Nobuko was for her independence, he saw through her weakness, thus allowing her to act as she liked, like a spoiled child, and called her his "baby."

Yuriko-Nobuko also discovered the hypocrisy of intellectuals who argue for ideals but have no intention of living according to them. She determined to live according to her beliefs, distinguishing bourgeois intellectualism from revolutionary intellectualism, and paid a high price to put this into practice. The traumatic experiences during the four years of what she called her "swamp period" convinced her finally that any ideas which were not substantiated by her personal life were meaningless. She set out to establish her own life-style and to live according to her own ideas.

Nobuko-Yuriko's problems were not only those of a unique woman artist who could not be confined to the traditional role of a wife, but also those of an awakened modern woman whose ego could not submit to the ego of the husband. Nobuko's insistence on her modern woman's ego, however, was not directed toward the denial of marriage or heterosexual love during this period. It meant only that she had the strength to break her marriage when she realized that her husband's personality was not compatible with hers and that marriage to him would prevent the free and full development of her ego. In this sense, *Nobuko* can be said to be the first novel which dealt with the question of the modern female ego with full seriousness, parallel to the pioneering treatment of the male ego in such Meiji novels as *Kokoro* and *Hakai*. (pp. 149-50)

In *Nobuko,* the protagonist's decision to give up her husband and go against the desires of her family was for the sake of her personal growth and happiness. Although well aware that her action would invite criticism as an egotistical act, Nobuko felt at that time that marriage was detrimental both to women's happiness as individual human beings and to their creativity. It was necessary to be independent from men, emotionally as well as economically, in order to secure a room of one's own. Yet Nobuko's solitary life makes her experience the frightening loneliness and emptiness that exist in life without love. She comes to reconsider whether marriage itself is the problem or whether it exists in deviation from an ideal form of marriage.

In *Futatsu no niwa* (*The Two Gardens*), an autobiographical sequel to *Nobuko*, Yuriko traces her life after her divorce to her decision to visit the new Russia. Although she was now writing novels steadily and enjoying a newly independent life as a professional writer, she (Yuriko-Nobuko) suffered from loneliness and a sense of sterility which came from the absence of total involvement in human relations. After the divorce, she lives with Motoko, a woman translator, and comes to realize the prejudice to which single women are subject in a male-oriented society and the distortion in their characters which women suffer because of it. They force themselves unnaturally to behave like men, yet they are more vulnerable than married women, more conscious of themselves as sexual objects, and cannot liberate themselves from sex. Her relationship with her friend Motoko gradually comes to resemble that between lovers, and Nobuko feels it to be a psychological burden. She feels that single women tend to become alienated cripples, deprived of proper objects of love, and realizes that a satisfying male-female or sexual relationship is necessary for women's happiness. Thus she comes to reject the androgynous existence which she once thought necessary.

Nobuko describes two incidents which occurred during this period as decisive in her determination to step into a new life. One is the affair of her mother, then fifty-two, with her son's thirty-two-year-old tutor. The unfortunate love affair, which ended in her mother's bitter disappointment, illustrated the tragic fate of women who could not find the correct channel for their passion and self-growth in the feudal family system. Nobuko-Yuriko came to realize the impossibility of love's transcending differences of age and environment, given the existing warped male-female relationship. At the same time, she found herself appalled by her mother's romanticism, so miserably removed from reality, by the easy cynicism concerning love and men which her mother adopted and by her mother's quick return to a bourgeois life after her brutal disappointment. There Nobuko-Yuriko saw a lack of the true passion which might have enabled her to develop the full possibilities of happiness and the meaning of life in love, even though defeated. Above all, Nobuko hated the hypocrisy of the intellectual who talks of beautiful ideas yet is a cowardly egotist in daily life.

She sees as well the traps created by women's vulnerability to romantic love. Women desire to be romantic heroines, finding happiness only in being loved by men. They spend all their psychic energy in loving and lose the capacity to see that they are only catering to an illusory ideal of femininity created by men. She sees in her mother both passion misused and the lack of a true commitment to love. This realization leads Yuriko to explore love relations which are not based on romantic love.

The second decisive incident was the suicide of Akutagawa Ryūnosuke in 1927. *The Two Gardens* describes the profound shock brought by his death, a shock which resulted in her decision to go to Soviet Russia.

If indeed to grow in class awareness is the only cor-
rect way to live in history for a member of the bourgeoisie, how does such growth take place?

"Do you know?" Nobuko sat next to Motoko, who was proofreading, and continued, "I know that there is a limitation in Aikawa Ryonosuke's [Akutagawa Ryūnosuke's] intellect . . . but how does the 'class transformation' occur in such individuals as you and I?"

She knew that among those who are identified as members of the proletarian school, writers who did not come from the working class or were not living in poverty, with the exception of such theorists as Shinohara Kurato, would be ignored. In fact, her own writings were indeed ignored by them.

Nobuko felt, however, that whether or not she was recognized by them, she had things to say as a human being and as a woman, and that she could not wipe out her own way of life. If she could stop her way of life somewhere because she became hung up on some theory, why had she thrown away the life with Tsukuda, pushing his pleading face away with her own hand . . . ? "I think I will go to Soviet Russia. I would like to live there. I would like to see with my own eyes and experience with my own body everything there, good and bad."

(The Two Gardens)
(pp. 151-53)

What particularly shocked Yuriko-Nobuko was Akutagawa's deep loneliness as a man. Akutagawa, firmly tied to his family, with a gentle, homemaker wife and bright children, was desperately lonely, starved for love. He fell in love with a woman whose intellect matched his own, but gave her up for the sake of his family. His sentimental overflow of emotion when he finally did so, and the pathetic sincerity of his subsequent writings in which he describes his own feelings and sense of defeat, moved her deeply. There she saw a sensitive man burdened by obligations as a father and provider which drained his energies and damaged his fine sensibility. She recognized that Akutagawa's anxiety and sterility as a detached bourgeois writer would also be her fate and that she too would be a victim of the institution of the family, deprived of love. Here she gained a new insight in her struggle; it was not only women but men as well whose creativity was stifled by their efforts to cope with an oppressive reality. A vital love of life, of a life committed to active thinking, writing, acting and loving, sprang up in her. In order to complete and enrich her life, she needed a liberated man. Human liberation, not merely women's liberation, was necessary.

Her concern with meaningful male-female relations deepened when she met Miyamoto Kenji and married him. This was also the point at which she . . . joined the Communist Party. . . . (p. 154)

In **"Koiwaike no ikka" ("The Family of Koiwai")**, Yuriko describes the wife of a communist forced to go underground. The wife, although uneducated, is endowed with natural intelligence and strength of character developed through a life of poverty. She is firmly committed to her husband and works hard to maintain the family under the unusual circumstances, supporting and taking care of her parents-in-law and her children. She is the epitome of the strength and endurance with which traditional women are usually supposed to be equipped. Although she is the actual center of the family, she develops a curious sense of isolation and lack of purpose when her husband finally decides to go underground. She is an ideal wife for an activist, supplying abundant moral support, yet she knows clearly that an unbridgeable gap has been created between her and her husband, who were united only as partners in a homemaking enterprise. The story ends as the wife, appropriately named Otome (young maiden), realizes that there will be a day when he will not return home unless she herself joins the movement with equal seriousness and commitment. The story describes the growth of this maiden into an independent participant in life, and this growth is treated as an essential factor in true love-relations. Later, in *Banshū heiya* (*The Banshū Plain*), Yuriko deals with the question of ideological differences between husband and wife and concludes that the sharing of ideology and political actions is also essential. (pp. 154-55)

In *Banshū heiya,* which deals with her love for Kenji and is set in the days around the end of the war, Yuriko presents her protagonist, who is unshakably certain of her love for and commitment to her husband, as naturally attached to his family. Her concern with and understanding of the women in his rural, lower-middle-class family is alive, devoid of any intellectual aloofness, and filled with genuine love. In this novel, the protagonist achieves a genuine tie between herself and the working class and peasant people from whom she is separated by education, class and cultural-social background.

What made this possible, twenty years after *Nobuko,* was her understanding of the common fate which women in the Japanese family system share and her commitment to proletarian revolution. When the protagonist of *Banshū heiya,* Hiroko, hears that her brother-in-law was among the victims of the Hiroshima holocaust, she visits her husband's family in Yamaguchi prefecture, a visit which renews her recognition that women have once again had to bear the tragedy of the war and society more heavily than men. Her sister-in-law, now widowed, changes into a nervous, greedy and calculating woman, losing all tenderness toward other people. Saddened by the psychological distortion created in this woman, Hiroko is struck by the misery which women in the family system have had to endure. She feels it unfair that the maintenance of the system depends upon the endurance of women and is at the same time appalled by the role which women assumed in maintaining this dehumanizing and sexist system. She calls the strength produced in the frail woman's body at the time of emergency and the psychological and mental distortion caused by it *"goke no ganbari,"* the widow's stubborn strength.

Yet soon this widow's strength/distortion appears in Hiroko-Yuriko herself, and worst of all, this is pointed out by her husband, with whom she is finally reunited after twelve years of separation. In *Fūchiso,* Jyūkichi (Kenji) points out that her overanxious and protective attitude toward himself and his family is *goke no ganbari* and suggests that she return to a more relaxed attitude. His observation of her widow's hardness and strength, implying a lack of femininity, is a male chauvinist one, yet she realizes that her eagerness to protect her husband was indeed distorted and mistaken, that she was unconsciously adopting a protective attitude toward him just as a husband might do toward his wife, and that the love relationship must be based on mutual equality and independence. The full cycle had come; twenty years earlier she had suffered from the hypocritical protectiveness of her older husband, and she was now unconsciously assuming the same protective role toward her younger husband.

Most importantly, when the question arose of her rejoining the Communist Party, the executive committee of which Jyūkichi-Kenji was now a member, she asked him to let her work in a way that would let her continue to write novels. He replied that she must work in her own way and must continue to write novels. With this understanding she joined the party without hesitation, but later found that he had foreseen a possible conflict that might have wrecked their love had she not done so. Although Yuriko's decision to join the party was reached from her own belief and the decision was hers, ironically it was the same experience which her protagonist in **"The Family of Koiwai"** had gone through. Ideological sharing was an important condition for love. Yuriko here argues that ideal love is the most human one, a love in which each partner is concerned with his or her own life without an over-inflated confidence in bringing happiness to others, but a love based firmly on the support of and faith in each other. Together with such support, complete sharing of basic attitudes toward life and the same world view are considered necessary; this is the hardest demand made on women, the demand to participate in political as well as intellectual activities as equals of their men. She calls such a relationship that of humanistic communism. Women's happiness must be instrumental in the development of their creativity, while there will be no happiness where creativity is stifled.

Yuriko believed in human growth as the most significant purpose of life. She committed herself to communism only when, impressed especially by the condition of women in the Soviet Union, she accepted it as an ideology which facilitates both human growth and social justice. For her, human growth was not a matter of inner awareness, but could be achieved meaningfully only in relation to others; it could be achieved only by living within the real world, within history, in vital association with other people. For this reason, personal concerns (ideal love relationships especially) and social and political ones become interfused in her creative activity. In her understanding, practice takes a central role; the pursuit of art for life's sake and of intellectual activity for its practical consequences provided the means for her to unite life and ideas, life and writing. Yuriko's firm belief in human growth, her unending interest in and love of women, and her commitment to positive male-female relationships resemble those of such writers as Simone de Beauvoir. Like Beauvoir, she lived passionately, creating her own life-style as a woman, and tried to create a unique autobiographical novel in which the protagonist emerges as a modern as well as an historical hero.

Of the three conflicts, however, the one which gradually came to concern Yuriko most in her later years was that between politics and literature. . . . [She] started her creative career as a bourgeois intellectual, deeply influenced by the humanistic writings of Tolstoy and Arishima Takeo at a time when the moralistic, introspective "I-novels" had established the tradition of the modern novel in Japan. The historical perspective of Yuriko's autobiographical novels distinguishes them from from the traditional I-novels, in which the perspective of the author-protagonist is exclusively internal and psychological. This historical perspective grew stronger in the course of her writings. Although the conflict between consciousness and practice, the realization of which was to become central in Japanese writers' struggle against the I-novel, was clearly the starting point of Yuriko's writing and the basis for the development of her thought, when she was writing *Nobuko* she understood this conflict only as a problem of her personal growth, not as directly related to history or society. When she came to realize that sexism is a political phenomenon, the conflict developed another layer of meaning, that is, the conflict between literature and politics. Writing about one's personal growth, about achieving one's personal freedom, began to appear to her as merely the sterile self-satisfaction of an elite intellectual. Thus the conflict was transformed from a metaphysical-philosophic concern with realization (consciousness) and practice to a socially concrete question of politics and literature. (pp. 156-59)

During the first years of Yuriko's life as a communist, her writing suffered from didacticism and dogmatic analysis. Her best contribution during this period was clearly in the field of essay writing, in which she analyzed the conditions of women. Although her belief that literature should contribute to people's progress and should be meaningful to the emerging new class and generation was not shaken, she grew uneasy about the possibility of artistic stagnation in her political life. Although Kenji was more than eager in urging her to pursue her novel-writing in her own way, for him there was no doubt that she should not write as anything but a communist.

In *Fūchiso,* the protagonist Hiroko hesitates to join the party because she still does not see clearly the relationship between her art and political activities; she is worried about how joining the party might affect her writing.

> "Hiroko, will you leave your curriculum vitae since you are here [at party headquarters]."
>
> "My vitae?"
>
> She hesitated, feeling that it was too sudden. To present her vitae must mean going through a formal procedure to join the party.
>
> "Of course, but . . . "
>
> Hiroko was not prepared to do so here, at this moment. She felt that two kinds of work were pushing her from opposite sides of her body: literary work and political work concerning women, which was the natural consequence of her being a woman. At present she was occupied more with the latter. As a result, what she wrote became entirely educational.
>
> "How would it affect my work? . . . If only I knew." Whenever Hiroko wrote short educational pieces, Jyūkichi himself advised her to organize her political work, telling her that otherwise she would not be able to write novels. It was also felt keenly [by the communists] that they must produce specialists in every field of the humanities. . . . But when Jyūkichi asked her when she planned to write novels, how was it related to his suggestion to present her vitae?
>
> "There is no reason for me to refuse if I know what my writing will be."
>
> "Hiroko, you can only prove objectively through your own writing what is the best."
>
> "I am very glad if I can work in that way."
>
> "But that you can write in a way most appropriate for your present concern does not mean that a writer does not have to assume historical responsibility in her own daily life. . . . People in the humanities are too preoccupied with it [the relation between politics and literature] in general. . . . It must be because their life and work are too personal. But in

the case of husband and wife, the gap can become too big to bridge."

(Fūchiso)

Yuriko's only solution was to maintain her determination to write novels in history and to find out what kind of novel is a good novel by writing with all her energy. Yet this was an indirect way of saying that she was going to set aside the problems of politics and literature and would be immersed in writing novels, not political novels, but just novels. Indeed, most of her communist ideas were expressed in her essays, and her novels trace mainly her personal growth. She was also totally committed to participating in political activities, organizing, lectures, and so forth, as if she were trying to bridge the gap between politics and literature in this way.

When Yuriko started writing as a feminist, however, with her own life as the central theme of her novels—and that started with her postwar novels—the gap between politics and literature and that between history and individual life were eliminated. She had discovered new modern heroes, the oppressed class of women struggling for liberation, a class emerging to play an important role in the history of human liberation. By writing autobiographical novels from a revolutionary feminist perspective, she achieved a unique combination of literature and politics, of history and individual life. The result was the overflow of her creativity. *The Banshū Plain, Fūchiso, The Two Gardens,* and *Road Sign* were written within the short years of bubbling creativity between the end of the war and her death in 1951. They were all autobiographical works and extensions of *Nobuko,* tracing her personal growth as a woman writer and woman communist, but these later works were distinguished from *Nobuko* by their communist-feminist perspective. She had plans for writing two more such novels, plans left unmaterialized by her sudden death.

The form of Yuriko's novels is closest possibly to the *Bildungsroman,* a form of novel which traces the moral as well as social development of an individual. Her works, most simply, are a communist and feminist variant of the *Bildungsroman.* The recent autobiography of Simone de Beauvoir also resembles her works in its basic attempt to trace the inner as well as the social growth of the author-protagonist, and to place her in history. By placing inner growth within a concrete historical and social framework, history and individual life are uniquely interfused, creating both a personal drama and social intellectual history; Yuriko's hero is an honest reflection of herself, yet she emerges as a universal modern hero. Although Yuriko's hero is by no means portrayed as an ideal, superhuman woman, she is a positive hero whose faith in female and human liberation through communist revolution is unshakable.

Yuriko's works present the drama of a woman developing from a member of the bourgeois elite, dependent on men, into an independent, mature woman writer and communist, even as they mirror realistically an important page in the social, moral and intellectual history of modern Japan. Thus Yuriko created a new form of autobiography, one in which the protagonist emerges as an historic figure of the age, experiencing fully its limitations and possibilities. Her writings interlace uniquely the tradition of the I-novel with the historical social commitment derived from her political activities. (pp. 159-62)

Noriko Mizuta Lippit, "Literature and Ideology: The Feminist Autobiography of Miyamoto Yuriko," in her Reality and Fiction in Modern Japanese Literature, M. E. Sharpe, Inc., 1980, pp. 146-62.

BRETT DE BARY (essay date 1984)

[In the following excerpt, de Bary provides a detailed analysis of themes and symbols in The Weathervane Plant.]

The first of Miyamoto Yuriko's four post-war autobiographical novels, *The Banshū Plain* (*Banshū Heiya*), is a travel narrative which presents a panoramic view of Japan in the first weeks after the surrender, and explores its protagonist's relationships with female characters in the context of the extended family. Two others, *Two Gardens* (*Futatsu no niwa*) and *Guidepost* (*Dōhyō*), are set in the prewar period, with the latter retracing in three volumes Miyamoto's experiences in Moscow and the evolution of her commitment to socialism and feminism. In striking contrast to the breadth of scope and retrospective cast of these novels is the immediacy of theme and circumscribed focus of *The Weathervane Plant*. The novella's subject is the relationship between husband and wife, reunited at the war's end after a twelve year separation resulting from the husband's imprisonment as a thought criminal. Its mode of narration, often intensely emotional yet unswervingly realistic, is one which had characterized Miyamoto's work since her earliest publication and which emphasizes the observed flow of everyday events rather than elaborate conceptualization or flights of utopian imagination. Implicit in the novella's structure, however, is a quietly lucid awareness of a question of vital interest to feminist theory—with what voice, in what language, does a woman express herself?—an awareness crystallized in the course of more than a decade of wartime struggle. Such a sense of coalescing vision is alluded to in a passage of the novella that describes its protagonist's visit to a younger sister in the countryside:

> Kiroko's younger sister had evacuated to a place beside the Isumi River where she was living, like a princess in a hovel, in a cabin that had neither tatami matting nor paper screens. Hiroko spent several days there, savoring the sea air, listening to the waves on nights illuminated by the flicker of a whale oil lamp, and washing dishes beside a well where she could watch the bean plants blossom and the pine buds swell. These were days when Hiroko felt the very essence of her life over the past few years congeal into drops of dew that fell softly onto her heart, fragrant with the smell of pine.

The Weathervane Plant is set in the autumn immediately following the end of the Pacific War, with a plot that unfolds over a time span extending from late October to early December, 1945. Its protagonist, a woman novelist named Hiroko, is modeled after Yuriko herself, while the male character, Jūkichi, is modeled after her husband, Kenji. The first four chapters explore, from the wife's perspective, the process whereby Hiroko adjusts to life with Jūkichi after his long absence, often doubling back to touch on some aspect of the two characters' experiences during the war. In three later chapters the focus expands, as if in concentric circles, to include Hiroko's relationship with other women (Chapter 5) and her relationship to society at large, in the contrasting forms of the wartime government-organized Japanese Literature Patriotic Society (Chapter 6) and the postwar Communist Party (Chapter 7). Chapters Two and Three, which depict misunderstandings between husband and wife which reduce Hiroko

to tears, are generally seen to be the most skillfully realized in the novella.

In an essay on *The Weathervane Plant* that underscores its autobiographical basis, Miyamoto cited the theme of marital reunion as her own primary focus of interest in the work.

> Hiroko and Jūkichi had a long history of marriage behind them but now, for the first time in twelve difficult years, they were living together under one roof and embarking on a new life as husband and wife, each keenly sensitive to the presence of the other. While my novel focuses on one or two incidents which occurred during this brief and unusual period, it is unified by a harmonious melody of love, and by a sense of the freshness of life which flowed from the very depths of my heart. The spontaneously lyrical and melodic style is something you will find in very, very few of my other works.

Miyamoto's emphasis on the "harmonious melody" that suffuses the relationship between her two characters is touching in view of her own death just six years after the long awaited return of Kenji. Her depiction of the quiet joys of reunion, a sense of wrongs righted, and of homely pleasures savored in the midst of deprivation must have spoken to many readers' experience of early postwar life. *The Weathervane Plant* (along with *The Banshū Plain*) was awarded the *Mainichi* Prize for artistic excellence in 1947. Yet equally central to Miyamoto's portrait of husband and wife is her exploration of the tensions generated by the coming together of two powerful personalities, each so "keenly sensitive to the presence of the other." Passages which show how quickly the forty-six year old Hiroko's sense of serenity and fulfillment at the war's end can give way to feelings of insecurity and incompleteness are among the most poignant in this portrait of a Japanese feminist at mid-career.

Elaine Showalter's concept of women's writing as a "double-voiced discourse" containing both "dominant" and "muted" themes provides a helpful basis for analysis of *The Weathervane Plant*. Citing the work of anthropologists Shirley and Edwin Ardener, Showalter proposes that women be seen as a "*muted* group, the boundaries of whose culture and reality overlap, but are not wholly contained by, the *dominant* male group." Such an approach affords many insights in the case of a novelist like Miyamoto, who writes simultaneously within the mainstream, male-dominated tradition of the realistic I-novel and within the more tenuous and marginal realm of feminist fiction. Thus, it becomes possible for us to examine *The Weathervane Plant* as a work in the well-established *bildungsroman* form, tracing the Hiroko-Jūkichi relationship as a "dominant" plot which depicts the process of mutual readjustment between husband and wife in a realistic mode. Yet we may also trace a "muted" feminist plot, in which the Hiroko-Jūkichi relationship stands figuratively for a woman writer's ambivalent relationship to the language and system of representation that envelops her. At another level of abstraction, the Hiroko-Jūkichi relationship may even be seen to symbolize the volatile "marriage" of muted and dominant stories within *The Weathervane Plant* itself.

The image which constitutes the title of *The Weathervane Plant* is one which affirms Hiroko in her relationship with Jūkichi, yet which may be linked with both the "dominant" and the "muted" plots of the novella. Miyamoto herself gave the following account of her choice of title, referring to her last period of wartime imprisonment, during which she suffered a heat stroke.

> One summer night [during the war] I bought a potted plant with a profusion of slender green leaves, which I happened to notice beside a flower stall. The owner of the stall read the characters on the label as "*Fūchisō*" and I thought, "of course, these delicate leaves must tremble when even the slightest breeze passes." Two or three years later someone sent me the same type of plant when I was in jail, and I set it on the narrow wooden floorboards of my hot cell in the Women's Section of the Sugamo Prison. It was a three mat cell, through which not even a breath of air passed. How I longed for that still air to move . . . even if it were only enough to move the very tips of those slender leaves! The day finally came when I lost consciousness because of the heat in the cell, without having seen, even once, the trembling of the plant's green stalks. Because it was a gift, the plant had a label attached to it which read "*Fūchisō:* one pot." Beneath those words, I had stamped my seal in red ink.

As a plant with an autumnal lavender bloom, the *fūchisō* of the novella's title may be associated with autumn, the season of Hiroko's husband's return from prison. It expresses her hope that she may blossom, in this autumn of reunion, after being stifled in the harsh wartime environment and in the absence of Jūkichi's nurturing presence. As the *fūchisō* (literally, "wind-knowing-grass") is identified, by its name, *within* a relationship to the wind, the title affirms Hiroko *within* her relationship to Jūkichi. The actual image of the weathervane plant, however, occurs in only one chapter of the novella, depicting wartime experiences of Hiroko similar to those described by Miyamoto above. It is here that Hiroko muses on a gap in communication between herself and Jūkichi, and wonders if she can ever convey, "all, all" of her experience to him. This sense of a gap is maintained throughout the novella, particularly in connection with Hiroko's quest as a novelist. Thus we might say that, in terms of the "dominant" plot, the weathervane plant symbolizes in a positive sense the interconnectedness of Hiroko and Jūkichi, experienced in terms of a repeated pattern of togetherness, confrontation, and reconciliation. In terms of the "muted" plot, it symbolizes in a more negative way Hiroko's "confinement" within her relationship to Jūkichi, rooted in her subordinate position, as a woman, within the structures of power (and of language) dominated by men. As a realist, and as a dialectical materialist, Miyamoto's fiction accepts this relational component of woman's identity as inevitable. The protagonist of **The Weathervane Plant** may recoil from constricting definitions of herself projected by her husband, only to return, for there is no such ideal entity as that "pure self" to which she turns as an antidote to distortion or oppression. Thus, where the "dominant" plot of **The Weathervane Plant** features reconciliation in a conventional gesture of closure, the "muted" plot substitutes an unresolved back-and-forth motion.

Closely associated with the weathervane plant, the image of prison itself is one which symbolizes an overlapping realm of experience shared by Hiroko and Jūkichi. Although a male, Jūkichi is united with Hiroko as an object of repression by the militarist government. The notion of prison as an equalizing realm is invoked at the start of the novella. In the opening chapter, the couple visit a makeshift medical laboratory set up by a friend on the outskirts of Tokyo. As the friend leads Jūkichi into a room where they will examine his lungs for traces of tuberculosis, Hiroko observes the shuffling gait her husband developed during his years in prison. It is a mannerism she can identify on the basis of shared experience.

> . . . It was the way everyone who had been in solitary confinement walked. Even Hiroko, who was usually light on her feet, had walked that same way—slowly, heavily—when she had been led along by the female prison warden, wearing a "basket hat" with meshes inside that scratched and pulled irritatingly at the roots of her hair. But prisoners did not develop this gait simply because it was gloomy and uncomfortable to walk under the basket hats which blocked one's line of vision. It was from an involuntary desire to prolong as much as possible time spent outside of one's cell.

A later scene presents us with an interesting reversal of roles when Jūkichi corrects Hiroko's method of sewing a patch on a torn rice sack. She learns he has gained this expertise during long hours of manual labor as a sewer in prison. As Amy Heinrich has noted, Hiroko is deeply moved when she realizes that in prison Jūkichi performed work traditionally associated with the confined state of women.

While Hiroko senses solidarity with Jūkichi as a revolutionary and political prisoner, she is more ambivalent toward him in his role of mentor and leader. It is interesting, in view of our consideration of Miyamoto as an I-novelist, that her setting of the opening scene in a laboratory resonates with Nakamura Mitsuo's well-known image of the modern Japanese *bundan* as a laboratory for social experimentation. Hiroko's and Jūkichi's marriage was indeed a bold experiment, for its time, in creating a relationship that would not duplicate the superior-subordinate roles that obtained between men and women in the society at large. Yet Hiroko is shown, in **The Weathervane Plant,** as often confused and wary in sorting out her responsibilities to the man who was simultaneously husband, lover, and Communist Party leader. Chapters 2 and 3 depict this confusion vividly. Interpreted literally in the I-novel mode, they offer a fascinating study of the psychological adjustments demanded by a "liberated" marriage in Japan of the mid-1940s. A feminist reading of the same passages, however, might emphasize Hiroko's (and Miyamoto's) half-camouflaged exploitation of linguistic ambiguities to maintain a certain independence from male authority on the part of Hiroko just at those moments when she appears to be accommodating to it. Because these gestures toward autonomy depend on a play of words read differently by Hiroko and Jūkichi, they remain a subterfuge, a "muted" plot whose semi-secrecy is symptomatic of Hiroko's continuing state of oppression as a woman.

In Chapter Two, Hiroko is cut to the quick by Jūkichi's casual observation that she has developed a perhaps "unfeminine" toughness in her years alone during the war. As they are returning from their friend's laboratory in a typically crowded streetcar, Hiroko insists that Jūkichi, easily fatigued during his first few weeks of life outside of prison, take a single seat that has just been vacated. A few minutes later Jūkichi remarks musingly that Hiroko reminds him of the industrious but unfulfilled widow in Akutagawa's "Clump of Earth" (*Hitokatamari no tsuchi*). Using the colloquial expression *goke no gambari*, which has been translated by Noriko Lippitt [see excerpt dated 1978] as "the widow's stubborn strength," Jūkichi comments, "Hiroko, don't you think you've taken on a little of the 'widow's toughness' yourself?"

The comment catches Hiroko off guard. Repeating the phrase twice in her mind, "she was stung by it; her eyes misted up with tears." As she broods on the remark, she appears to feel that Jūkichi has disparaged her sexual attractiveness to him as a lover.

> "The widow's stubborn strength" . . . the words implied something that hurt Hiroko even more than if she had been called a fool *(baka)* or a slut *(darashi nashi).* There was something pitifully ugly about a widow who lived as if she had blinders on, whose energies were entirely focused on what was unnatural in her life. Was that what she was like? And did she have to be informed of this on a crowded streetcar by Jūkichi, who had been home for only two weeks? Although she tried to fight them back, tears filled her eyes. As they rolled down her face a man with an enormous pack on his back squeezed against her from behind. "What's wrong?" Jūkichi asked. She looked at him without speaking, keeping her face partially hidden in the kimono sleeve that hung down as she grasped the overhead strap.

Hiroko does quickly admit to Jūkichi that he has hurt her feelings, to which he responds that, if this was the case, it was utterly inadvertent. The remark continues to haunt Hiroko's thoughts for the rest of the day, but, in terms of her articulated dialogue in the story, she appears to go more than halfway to accommodate Jūkichi and to restore a mood of harmony between the two. By the time they have finished their journey, she is ready to acknowledge "I think there was some truth in what you said," and later in the evening she actually tells Jūkichi that "it was kind of him" to share his perception with her.

Just as Hiroko's extreme sensitivity to Jūkichi's remark might be traced to insecurity over the considerable age difference between herself and her husband, her desire to accommodate to Jūkichi's criticism may be linked to her realization that she has adopted an over-protective attitude toward him. Noriko Lippit offers this interpretation in her insightful essay on Miyamoto:

> His [Jūkichi's] observation of her widow's hardness and strength, implying a lack of femininity, is a male chauvinist one, yet she realizes . . . that she was unconsciously adopting a protective attitude toward him just as a husband might do toward his wife, and that the love relationship must be based on mutual equality and independence.

Alternatively, the passage may call to mind comments of feminists, who were Miyamoto's contemporaries (recorded by Nakamura in her discussion of Miyamoto's postwar fiction) that Miyamoto displayed an attitude of "feudal devotion" toward Kenji. (Nakamura includes an anecdote in which Miyamoto defends herself, with the familiar justification that the extreme restriction of activity during Kenji's years in prison has habituated him to a certain passivity. She describes how, in his first months back from the penitentiary, Kenji would unconsciously stop in front of doors, waiting for someone to open them for him!)

But to search for a final resolution of conflict (in either an egalitarian or a "feudal" direction) in these passages risks oversimplifying the dialectical quality of Miyamoto's prose, which keeps alive a sense of the tension and jockeying for power between the couple. A tracing of the "muted" plot in these passages, emphasizing Hiroko's deft verbal play, re-

veals her "accepting" Jūkichi's criticisms only *after* she has adroitly transposed their original, chauvinistic, context (which deprecates Hiroko for the situation she metaphorically shares with widows, an "unnatural" lack of reliance on males) into a new one which she herself has defined. The ground is prepared for this transformation through a process of private reflection, purely internal to Hiroko, which we suspect may have been developed as a means of absorbing pain and regaining self-sufficiency during the war. After struggling with her sense of rejection on the long ride home, Hiroko is struck by a mental "connection" as she steps out of the station and onto a pitch dark street, lined with charred telephone poles and other debris left by the bombing. "Is it safe?" Jūkichi asks, and Hiroko suddenly thinks of the many times she had walked this same road alone, a rucksack on her back and "hands clenched to ward off the eeriness of it," during the war. The narrator describes how "scrutinizing the figure in her mind in detail, Hiroko realized there was something in it she could connect with Jūkichi's criticism." It is at this point that she acknowledges the "truth" of his remark, but she subtly deflects the criticism to a new target, the war, when she and many others drove themselves, almost unaware, to unnatural extremes. She tells Jūkichi that toughness *(gambari)* had simply become "second nature to her," given the era. "Things seemed to be crumbling all around us; with no standard to follow, it was only by pushing myself, by myself, that I managed to stay on course." Later that evening, in a verbal move that could be seen as a deft power play, Hiroko further reformulates the context of Jūkichi's offending remark so that it appears that *he* is conforming to *her* expectations of him, rather than vice versa. Citing her lifelong desire "not to put up a front, but to be exactly what I am," Hiroko thanks Jūkichi for his honesty in expressing his feelings openly, rather than suppressing them. The criteria for judgment used here is honesty, one Hiroko, not Jūkichi, has provided. On this point, **The Weathervane Plant** harks back to the early **Nobuko** whose protagonist left a marriage which stifled her ideals of "spontaneity" and "natural growth."

The chapter's closing scene is broadly feminist in its orientation, since Hiroko, as she drifts off to sleep, becomes aware of another connection between herself and thousands of Japanese war widows:

> If it was true that only Jūkichi, who was her husband, could have cautioned her about the widow's stubborn strength, then for tens of thousands of women in Japan who truly were widows, who was there? Who would be close enough to tell them to transform that strength, which would become more deeply engrained the harder they struggled, into something more broad and discerning, more flexible? Who could tell these widows, whose lives without husbands were so harsh? And who would create for them a situation in which they could survive without that stubborn strength? . . . Hiroko's eyes filled with tears.

If Hiroko's first tears were a sign of vulnerability, these are a sign of strength. She has transcended her personal hurt by recalling her kinship and empathy with other women who have suffered during the war.

Chapter 3 inverts the structure of Chapter 2, since this time the more stormy confrontation between husband and wife turns on a remark which Hiroko has, we suspect, not so innocently directed at Jūkichi. This housewife's rebellion on a most modest scale is rendered by Miyamoto with touches of humor and a keen eye for the urge to violence that may lie beneath the surface of the wife's solicitudes. The opening sentence that informs us that "Jūkichi had become more and more regular in his trips to the suburbs to work" hints of the beginnings of the workaholic activism endured by many a revolutionary's wife. Although it was a day when Hiroko and Jūkichi had planned to leave the house together, this plan is foiled when it becomes clear that Jūkichi has conveyed inaccurate information about his schedule to the person who is entirely responsible for getting him out of the house. As Hiroko wraps Jūkichi's lunch, Jūkichi, reading the paper, inquires if their clock is on time. Dissatisfied with her answer that she thinks it is, he asks her to turn on the radio. The radio is dead (a common occurrence in the early postwar years, when electrical power shortages were frequent) Jūkichi jumps up from the table and begins to dress in great haste. Hiroko reminds him that he was to wait for her to leave. At that point, Jūkichi appears at her side to announce that he cannot button the sleeves of his shirt. (He need not, of course, articulate an explicit request for help.) Hiroko drops everything to help fasten buttons for Jūkichi, who apparently had never worn Western clothes until receiving hand-me-downs after his release from prison. While Hiroko is working on his cuffs, Jūkichi begins to mutter that he will be late for his appointment. Hiroko asks why he didn't tell her that his appointment that day was one hour earlier than usual. When she has finished buttoning his cuffs, Hiroko "half jokingly and half earnestly" grabs "Jūkichi's large frame in her hands and just a bit roughly" pushes him around to face her. She attaches his collar and fastens his tie. Then, sizing him up fully attired at last, she quips, "Just what I always wanted . . . a husband who can't even button his own shirt!" Jūkichi bolts out of the door without saying goodby (although not without the lunch Hiroko has prepared) and Hiroko, watching the trembling leaves on the hedge beside the gate he has passed through, notices "that the weight of Jūkichi's body, which she had pushed with deliberate roughness, seemed to remain, strangely impressed on her palm."

Jūkichi appears no less adept at subtle psychological maneuvering than his wife when he returns home that evening. Embarrassing Hiroko, who sits at the table with a young cousin who has been invited to dinner, he ignores the meal and proceeds to a corner of the living room where he eats left-overs he has brought home in his lunchbox. He then ascends to the bedroom and Hiroko, after a distracted visit with the cousin, joins him there. It is now Jūkichi's turn to acknowledge the validity of Hiroko's criticism, but here, too, the acceptance is part of a rhetorical strategy: Jūkichi will punish Hiroko and induce guilt (and eventual submission?) by taking her criticism *too literally*. When Hiroko apologizes and claims that her remark was "only in jest," Jūkichi responds:

> But that must have been what you were really thinking. The world is full of wives who are happy to take care of their husband's every need. But certainly it's more reasonable for each person to be responsible for himself. So I'll be completely on my own from now on. I managed in prison, after all.

Jūkichi's metaphorical equation of life with Hiroko with life in prison makes its mark. Hiroko shrieks in protest, and another tearful confrontation ensues. As before, Hiroko insists on talking her way through the impasse and, once again, it is a mental process carried out alone which brings the realization that leads to a breakthrough.

> Through her tears, Hiroko sensed keenly that as she wept her head lay on Jūkichi's knees, and that Jūkichi made no move to separate himself from this weeping person: it seemed her last shred of hope. But who was to say that in Jūkichi's mood there was no reflection of the harsh environment in which he had lived those long months and years, just as, she knew, in the depths of her own pain the twelve years she had lived through so strenuously cast their refracted shadow?
>
> Hiroko hit on something that flashed like lightning across her mind. Her face puffy from crying, she felt a ray of light penetrate her inner turbulence.

What Hiroko realizes is that Jūkichi's hurt is not simply a reaction to herself and to their marriage, but reflects a deep and generalized mistrust developed while he was psychologically abused in prison. By sharing this perception with Jūkichi, and thus transforming the context of their conflict, she is able to eventually restore his sense of humor and effect a reconciliation. She reassures him that her support for him has always been "absolute" and will continue to be. As in the previous chapter, the novella leaves us with a complex sense of the balance of power between the couple, with Hiroko seeming to sustain Jūkichi psychologically even while she is extremely vulnerable to any sign of disapproval from him. The narrator's endorsement of the mood of forgiveness and reconciliation that suffuses the end of the chapter is counterbalanced by the apparently non-judgmental but very knowing and deliberate plotting of the power struggle that develops in the beginning: a struggle that devolves around the quotidian frustrations of women's work in the home.

In the foregoing pages we have seen how the resolution of conflict on one level of the plot of *The Weathervane Plant* is accompanied by the depiction of a mental and verbal process through which Hiroko reasserts an autonomous sense of herself and her values. Yet because the narration of the novella is from Hiroko's perspective, and because we as readers are aware of a mental world which Hiroko never translates, in its entirety, into explicit dialogue, we cannot assume that Hiroko's words mean everything to Jūkichi that they mean to her, or that Jūkichi is able to "read" the fuller context of Hiroko's remarks between the lines. Both characters remain limited by the subjectivity of their perceptions. After the charged conversations in its opening chapters, the novella gives proportionately less emphasis to emotional confrontations between the two.

In Chapter 4 . . . the focus shifts to an exploration of Hiroko's private thoughts: a moving reminiscence is prompted by the sight of a folded metal bed. As Hiroko muses silently on her long struggle during the war, the novella for the first time articulates her sense of a gap between her inner world and what she is able to articulate of it ("Could she ever tell all, all of it to Jūkichi?" and, later, "A feeling that was difficult to put in words flared up inside her . . . was it something she would ever be able to talk about?") It is with this moment of keen awareness of her "difference" that the novella associates the surfacing of Hiroko's profound desire to write, and yet, interestingly, this desire propels her out of her soliloquy and back to Jūkichi. Her request for his encouragement in writing fiction may involve a practical sense of the need to set aside time from political activities, or an unconscious need for approval from a father figure (the Japanese "*shōsetsu o kakashite*" incorporates the two meanings "make" and "let" me write). But the request also symbolizes an acknowledgement that Hiroko's desire for self-expression can only be realized through the mediation of language. Insofar as this language is one which embodies the "dominant structures" of a patriarchal society, Hiroko must continue to maneuver her way through it as deftly, and painfully, as she has her confrontations with her husband.

Later chapters of the novella maintain a sense of the tensions between husband and wife, particularly when Hiroko explains her wartime decision to submit a story to the government-organized Japanese Literature Patriotic Society (described in Chapter 6), a decision Jūkichi regards as "having put you on the same side as all the people who were pulling the noose around my neck." In Chapter 4, however, the imagistic contrasts drawn between Hiroko's wartime life (the solitary bed, withered plant, and locked writing desk) and her postwar life with Jūkichi ("shaking sleek, ripe ears of grain from their stalks") affirm and even celebrate this ongoing quest.

While the notion of women's writing as "double-voiced discourse" helps to illuminate mechanisms which perpetuate dynamic tension in *The Weathervane Plant,* it also brings into relief new dimensions of Miyamoto's significance in the broader context of modern Japanese literary development. As an I-novelist and realist Miyamoto has been criticized for conventionality of style in the same breath that she has been lauded for the boldness of the life which her work, in its totality, unfolds. In this vein, Katō Shūichi's evaluation is representative: "Miyamoto's novels are drawn directly from her own life; the uniqueness of that life meant that they expanded the world of Japanese literature."

Yet the very limitation of imaginative scope which may be perceived as a lack in Miyamoto's fiction takes on fresh significance when we consider her "other" voice, her contribution to a Japanese feminist literature which she herself pioneered. Here, Miyamoto's absorption with the details of everyday experience may be linked to her sense of woman's struggle for self-realization in the face of ineluctable social constraints. Margaret Homan's observation about the nature of George Eliot's realism might also be applied to Miyamoto:

> . . . Eliot's most autobiographical characters pass through what appear to be Wordsworthian childhoods not to become Romantic poets but to find their ideal visions . . . thwarted by circumstances or by social needs. She sets her heroine's insatiable need for love, together with her own narrative commitment to realism, against the anti-social implications of what she represents as the introverting power of the imagination.

The quest of Miyamoto's protagonist, Hiroko, for self-realization within a heterosexual love relationship may thus be seen to parallel the setting of her novels within an explicitly historical framework centering around such events as war, defeat, and the postwar reconstruction. Her preference for realism is in keeping with this vision, which makes no claim to speak from the "wild zone" of purely female language and experience posited by certain radically utopian feminist writers. Her fictional world is solidly in that area of the Ardener model where the experiences of muted and dominant groups overlap. Rather than setting Hiroko in an imagined feminist Utopia, Miyamoto depicts her striving for self-expression within a social structure that is admittedly dominated by men, caught between the need to depend on, and the need to differentiate herself from a man who both shares and repre-

sents the revolutionary political ideology she looks to as a source of liberation.

As the saga of the evolution of a Japanese feminist, the life story narrated in Miyamoto's oeuvre is of compelling historical interest. It is for the clarity with which the elements of that struggle are revealed, and in those moments when we cannot fail to be moved by the intensity of her protagonist's quest, that Miyamoto's work achieves its enduring literary power. (pp. 10-25)

Brett de Bary, "Wind and Leaves: Miyamoto Yuriko's 'The Weathervane Plant'," in Journal of the Association of Teachers of Japanese, *Vol. 19, No. 1, April 1984-1985, pp. 7-33.*

DONALD KEENE (essay date 1984)

[*In the following excerpt, Keene examines subjects and themes in Miyamoto's fiction, focusing especially on her treatment of Japanese life during World War II.*]

The most compelling novels written immediately after the war ended were by Miyamoto Yuriko. She had grown up under comfortable circumstances as the daughter of a noted architect, and received a good education. In 1918, at the age of nineteen, she accompanied her father to New York, and in the following year audited classes at Columbia University. . . . Yuriko's life at this time is described in the novel *Nobuko* (1924-1926), a wonderfully effective picture of herself and New York. Her account of the celebrations at the time of the false armistice in November 1918 is particularly impressive:

> When they emerged from the crowd they were at the corner of Wall Street and Broadway. An immense throng, surging like the tide, swirled from three sides into the square where the dusty statue of Washington stands, then could not move another step in any direction. A man was delivering a speech before a building whose columns were black with grime, as one might expect here downtown, the battlefield of fierce commercial competition. Nobuko could not catch one word of what the man was saying, separated from him as she was by ranks of people. She barely caught glimpses of his frantically gesticulating hands and his forehead with its receding hairline. The sight seemed to typify the abnormal excitement that engulfed heaven and earth, and produced a strangely sad impression on Nobuko. On this side of the square a beggar, his arm around a barrel organ, was grinding out a waltz that set her teeth on edge. Young, bareheaded couples were wildly dancing to the music.

> Every face in sight was overwrought and ugly. She could not see even one person, man or woman, whose face had the kind of cheerful, serious, or beautiful expression appropriate in someone celebrating the joyous news of peace. They were all like animals. Their eyes were set in a glitter, a faintly drunken smile played over their lips, and their faces quivered incessantly with a greedy craving for ever more powerful stimulation. It no longer made any difference whether the cause of their excitement was an armistice or a declaration of war. What they wanted was a frenzy that would turn their daily routines upside down, to get drunk on self-oblivion!—So forward! forward! In a state of delirium they pushed with their bellies and shoved with

their shoulders. The waves of humanity which for a while had been immobile, slowly started to move again. A savage force, which blasted all civilization to pieces, came crowding in on them with naked fury. Nobuko felt afraid.

Nobuko, however, is above all the story of a woman who achieves liberation in a world utterly unlike that of traditional, upper-class Japan. (pp. 1146-47)

Little in *Nobuko* suggests that Miyamoto Yuriko (known at the time by her maiden name, Chūjō Yuriko) was actively concerned about the lives of her poverty-stricken countrymen; personal liberation is the theme of the book. (p. 1148)

Yuriko's two most important works were published in 1946: *Banshū Heiya* (*The Banshū Plain*) and *Fūchisō* (*The Weathervane Plant*). The former opens on August 15, 1945, and describes a seemingly ordinary day that acquired unique importance. Yuriko (called Hiroko in the novel), learning that the war had ended, is torn between the desire to go to her husband in Hokkaidō and the duty she feels to visit her husband's family in the Hiroshima area; her husband's younger brother has not been heard from since the explosion of the atomic bomb. She finally decides that duty takes precedence, and she makes the long journey to the west. Her description of the train and her fellow passengers is superbly evocative of the mood of defeated Japan, perhaps the best account of those traumatic days. In the village where her in-laws live she discovers what suffering has been caused by the Japanese army, which drove a road through the place without taking into account the flooding this would cause. Her hatred for the arrogance and the inhumanity of the military is especially effective because it is stated without hysteria; and she makes it quite clear that, no less than the peoples of Southeast Asia, the Japanese have been the victims of military aggression. Many young people died for the sake of ideals that, in retrospect, now seemed unworthy or even wicked, and everywhere there were "widows' towns." The following passage describes Hiroko's thoughts as she lies sleepless in her husband's village, recalling the journey:

> As the train moved westward along the Tōkaidō and San'yō lines, Hiroko had thought with emotion of what deep wounds had been suffered by people burned out of all their possessions. But which people felt the most intense bitterness over the war? She had seen it in the eyes of the one-legged man in a white hospital smock, who asked her uneasily if he should hide the book on National Polity. And it was here, in the "widows' towns." It was in the bankruptcy of life, in the mute days of "widows' towns" in hundreds of thousands of places all over Japan.
>
> Cold, bitter, astringent tears slid down Hiroko's temples onto her little wickerwork pillow. Until she read the words "war criminal" in the text of the Potsdam Declaration she had not realized that such an expression could strike so responsive a chord within her and fill her heart with such emotion. Hiroko wanted world justice to call the guilty

to task for this crime with true stringency and with true unforgivingness.

Some Japanese critics later reproached Miyamoto for not having stressed the inhumanity of the atomic bomb; but had she done so, it might have shifted attention from the ultimate source of the disaster, the ruthless actions of the militarists.

The Weathervane Plant, a slighter though important work, describes the period immediately after Miyamoto Kenji [Yuriko's second husband] was released from prison. . . . *Dōhyō* (*Guidepost,* 1947-1950), Yuriko's last novel, is devoted mainly to tracing the process by which the Nobuko of the early 1920s became the ardent Marxist of a decade later. It is of less interest than the two earlier postwar novels because it lacks their immediacy.

The Banshū Plain and *The Weathervane Plant,* products of the days immediately following the end of the war, rise above doctrinal classification and stand as the first impressive rejections of the fifteen-year war and all that it involved. Miyamoto Yuriko wrote not only with unmistakable sincerity but with the assurance of one who had resisted the order to commit tenkō and governmental pressure to conform. Many writers were to recall the hardships, the hunger, the terror of bombing, and the fear of death that the war had brought, but most of them (unlike Yuriko) had exulted over the military triumphs and had derived a kind of comfort from sharing, as Japanese, the heavy burdens of the war. Itō Sei wrote, "I cannot believe that there is a single writer today who can look back, now that the war has ended, and affirm that his conscience is unwounded." Miyamoto Yuriko may have faltered when she joined the Japanese Literature Patriotic Association, but she experienced none of the nostalgia of some Japanese for the days when people thought of their country rather than of themselves, and her conscience was very nearly unwounded. Her recollections of the war years, described in *The Banshū Plain,* were unsentimental, and the joy she expressed in *The Weathervane Plant* over the release of her husband and his friends was directed toward a happier Japan of the future. (pp. 1148-50)

> *Donald Keene, "The Revival of Writing by Women," in his* Dawn to the West, Japanese Literature of the Modern Era: Fiction, Vol. 1, *Holt, Rinehart and Winston, 1984, pp. 1113-66.*

FURTHER READING

Johnson, Eric W. "Modern Japanese Women Writers." *Literature East and West* XVIII, No. 1 (March 1974): 90-102.

   Includes a brief sketch of Miyamoto's life and literary career.

Edmond Rostand

1868-1918

(Full name Edmond Eugène Alexis Rostand) French dramatist and poet.

For further discussion of Rostand's career, see *TCLC*, Volume 6.

Significant for his revival of romantic verse drama at a time when Naturalism and Symbolism dominated the French stage, Rostand combined an excellent sense of theatrical effect with a keen wit. His optimistic idealism found its best expression in the comedy *Cyrano de Bergerac*, which achieved a lasting international reputation.

Born in Marseilles, Rostand was the son of a prominent journalist and economist. After attending local schools, he studied literature, history, and philosophy at the Collège Stanislas in Paris. He began writing for the marionette theater and had poems and essays published in the literary review *Mireille* at the age of sixteen. Although Rostand later studied law, he never practiced, choosing instead to concentrate on a career as an author. His first drama, *Le gant rouge,* was produced in 1888 with little success, and his first volume of poetry, *Les musardises,* received little critical attention when it was published in 1890. Rostand achieved widespread popularity and critical regard in 1894 with his next play, *Les romanesques* (*The Romancers*), which was produced at the Comédie Française, and solidified his reputation the following year with *La princesse lointaine* (*The Princess Far-Away*), which he wrote for the actress Sarah Bernhardt. Thereafter, Bernhardt became the principal interpreter of his works, appearing in leading roles in several of his plays. The actor Constant-Benoît Coquelin requested Rostand to write a play that would showcase his versatile skills as an actor, and Rostand complied by creating in 1897 what would become his most popular work, *Cyrano de Bergerac.* Two years later, ill health forced Rostand to retire to his country estate, and in 1901 he was elected to the Académie Française, the youngest member ever inducted. He continued to write plays and poetry when his health permitted, leaving his final play, *La dernière nuit de Don Juan* (*The Last Night of Don Juan*), unfinished at the time of his death in 1918.

Rostand's poetry has been largely disregarded by critics, and he is remembered primarily as a dramatist. In his first play, *The Romancers,* Rostand rejected the sordid realism of the naturalistic plays then popular, creating a lighthearted satire about two young lovers in search of romance and adventure who discover that romantic love can exist without the excitement of danger or obstacles to overcome. Rostand further developed the theme of courtly love in *The Princess Far-Away,* which relates the story of the troubadour Joffroy Rudel, Prince of Blaye, whose love for the Countess of Tripoli, whom he has never seen, inspires him to travel to see her before he dies. In this play, Rostand introduced the theme of tenacious adherence to unattainable ideals that became characteristic of his works.

Cyrano de Bergerac is considered Rostand's dramatic masterpiece, successfully combining humor, romance, and heroic action in expert verse. Based on the life of the seventeenth-

century soldier and author Savinien de Cyrano de Bergerac, the play recounts the hero's faithfulness to his ideals despite his recognition that he will never be rewarded for them. For example, he upholds his artistic principles by refusing to bowdlerize his plays in order to have them performed or to cater to a patron in order to live comfortably. Adhering to his principles of friendship, he refuses to compete with his friend Christian for the attention of Roxane, the woman they both love, and refrains from destroying Roxane's false image of Christian when he dies, even though it means foregoing his own chance to achieve happiness with her.

The polish of *Cyrano de Bergerac* aroused expectations which were largely disappointed by the last two plays Rostand completed. *L'aiglon* (*The Eaglet*), which describes the life of the Duke of Reichstadt, son of Napoleon I, has been criticized for its simplistic and predictable construction. *The Eaglet* enjoyed considerable success in France, but it has never had the international appeal of *Cyrano de Bergerac.* The allegorical verse drama *Chantecler,* in which a barnyard cock upholds his faith in the importance of his role in the world, has received varied critical evaluations. While some commentators find the play too lengthy, obscure, and contrived, others praise it as Rostand's most ambitious and profound work, particularly those critics who view it as a poem to be read rather than performed on stage.

When Rostand's plays first appeared, some critics believed that they would inspire a return to verse drama and romanticism. However, his dramas merely stood in contrast to the Naturalist and Symbolist literary movements of his time, rather than causing them to be supplanted. Recent evaluations of Rostand's work have praised his skillful verse and consummate theatricality, but find that his plays lack the thematic complexity and depth necessary to be considered great. Nevertheless, his dramas, particularly *Cyrano de Bergerac*, have maintained their popularity and continue to be performed to enthusiastic reviews.

(See also *Contemporary Authors*, Vols. 104 and 126)

PRINCIPAL WORKS

Le gant rouge (drama) 1888
Les musardises (poetry) 1890
Les romanesques (drama) 1894
  [*The Romancers*, 1899; also published as *The Fantasticks*, 1900]
La princesse lointaine (drama) 1895
  [*The Princess Far-Away*, 1899]
Cyrano de Bergerac (drama) 1897
  [*Cyrano de Bergerac*, 1898]
La Samaritaine (drama) 1897
  [*The Woman of Samaria* published in *Plays of Edmond Rostand*, 1921]
L'aiglon (drama) 1900
  [*L'Aiglon*, 1900; also published as *The Eaglet* in *Plays of Edmond Rostand*, 1921]
Chantecler (drama) 1910
  [*Chantecler*, 1910]
Le vol de la Marseillaise (poetry) 1919
Plays of Edmond Rostand. 2 vols. (dramas) 1921
La dernière nuit de Don Juan (unfinished drama) 1922
  [*The Last Night of Don Juan*, 1929]

LIONEL STRACHEY (essay date 1899)

[*In the following essay, Strachey assesses the literary and dramatic merits of* Cyrano de Bergerac.]

Cyrano de Bergerac, poet, playwright, romancer, epistolarian, wit, soldier, and duellist, flourished in the reign of Louis XIII., and remained unsung for long after. But being a gentleman of many parts and large, and of a strong personality, and having, so to speak, dissolved his soul in his ink, it was obvious that by dipping his pen into that very ink a sufficiently talented writer could resurrect this unusual character to renewed notoriety. Edmond Rostand came, read, copied, and was famous; or, rather, he did not copy, but imbibe, swallow, absorb, assimilate, and then bring forth a phœnix. Now let us light the lamp of distinction. We shall know, in the following discussion: No. 1, de Bergerac, the *factotum* already named, who supplied the model for No. 2, Cyrano, created by Rostand as the centre of No. 3, *Cyrano de Bergerac*, a heroic comedy in five acts, in verse.

De Bergerac's *magnum opus* was the *Histoire comique des états et empires de la lune et du soleil*, and is, as the title suggests, the playground of Chimera & Company. In *Cyrano de Bergerac* the hero, Cyrano, in order to detain the inconvenient de Guiche, represents himself as a traveller from the moon, and spins out a long madcap story, recounting, among other things, his ascent to the lunar kingdom on a sheet of iron, which he propelled by throwing a magnet into the air—just such crazy adventures as are chronicled in the *Histoire comique*. Cyrano will not submit *Agrippine*—a tragedy in Alexandrines by de Bergerac—to Richelieu's approval, lest the cardinal change a single comma. Allusion is made by Cyrano to Molière's theft of a celebrated *mot* from de Bergerac's comedy *Le pédant joué*, a whole scene of which Molière transplanted to *Les fourberies de Scapin*. *Le pédant joué* was first given at the theatre of the Hôtel de Bourgogne, the locality of the first act of *Cyrano de Bergerac*. De Bergerac saw military service in a company commanded by Carbon de Castel-Jaloux, whom we find at the head of a band of Gascon warriors in Rostand's play. A roisterer named Châteaufort in *Le pédant joué* indulges in extreme gasconading. The same comedy is crammed with extravagancies of allegory and simile, also a conspicuous attribute of de Bergerac's letters. Cyrano's dexterous play upon words—employing them in many senses as in his remarkable essay in noseology—is partaken of by de Bergerac in many instances. The most notable are the rhetorical fireworks he sets off with the words "garde" and "feu" in *Le pédant joué*, and the name "Le Coq" in a letter addressed to a person so called. But in vocabular improvisation Cyrano altogether outdoes his prototype—*vide* "ridicoculise." Cyrano's quality of satire, ready and keen, his gift of repartee, his fertility in punning, his classic lore—of these, in their degree, de Bergerac's correspondence is pageful. The epistle "Contre un poltron" fixes the belief in us that his blade is no less trenchant than his pen, that he is as well able as he claims to

Joindre ainsi la plume à l'épée.

["Join thus the pen to the sword."]

The letter "Contre le Caréme" is a parallel to Cyrano's banter with the nuns on the matter of eating meat on Friday. Contempt of danger, Cyrano's most prominent feature, his nose apart, de Bergerac evinces by bombarding Mazarin in a poem with incompetency, favoritism, extortion, malfeasance, debauchery, and what not. De Bergerac's *Lettres amoureuses* would seem to court a bluestocking. They are very deferential in tone, flowery in language, and delicate in thought. But none of them reaches the mark of perfection, either in sentiment or expression, of the tender, fragrant tropes to Roxane, the *précieuse* of Rostand's play, who insists on flirtation in euphuistic verse. A typical amatory conceit of de Bergerac's epistolary vein is this: His lady's image turns his eyes to alembics, in which his life is distilled, pure and translucent.

Of the other characters of *Cyrano de Bergerac* there is little to say, because Cyrano almost has the monopoly of excellence, and the play is without a villain. De Guiche has bad designs, to be sure, but he is too grand to attend to them closely. Place and preferment are his aim, and his mediocrity is converted into Stars and Garters by kind Uncle Richelieu. Preciosity and femininity need not be at variance, for, in spite of Plato for breakfast and Vaugelas for supper, Roxane's heart digests the outer charms of a certain young gentleman "at first sight." Christian, the favored one, is handsome, stupid, and valiant. The occupation of Ragueneau, pastry-cook and poet, is to reel off lyrical gastronomic pleasantries, *sauce Rostand*. Ragueneau has perhaps no counterpart in the drama excepting Hans Sachs,

> ein Schuh
> macher und Poet dazu.
>
> [a shoe
> maker and a poet as well.]

French poetry may be the best, French cookery is. Hence Ragueneau. But Holland, Sweden, and England, for instance, are countries where Master Cook is fatally compromised with Mistress Prose.

Patience—patience; we "are coming to the play."

Act I. is all movement and color. It was an artist's eye that devised the historical picture of a dramatic representation in the age of Richelieu, the cardinal himself one of the spectators, who, from pickpocket to marquis, bustle and press and chatter and listen—each betokening his condition by a word, a gesture, or the feather in his hat. The submission of the (mock) players and public to Cyrano's pointed wit and sword forecasts his domination of the real play and all the people in it. The other important personages all step to the front a moment, either in fact or in description, to make their bow. Already we have an inkling of their characters, a suspicion of their aims, a notion of their future conduct. The brilliancy and variety of the pageant, the abundancy of substance, our very eagerness to let nothing slip, have prevented the concentration of our interest. The curtain falls, and we sit pleased but bewildered. The author's resources have flooded his meaning.

But before the curtain fell we were invited, with Cyrano, to a *rendezvous* next morning. Our bewilderment merges into expectancy. What can the lovely Roxane have to say to her ugly cousin? The meeting takes place in the establishment of one Ragueneau, whose habit of taking poems in payment of cakes at last reduces him to the horrid necessity of wrapping up some patties in a sonnet to Phyllis. The invention of this Ragueneau and his poetastering clients has given the playwright's comic vein a broad scope, further widened by the discharge upon the scene of a company of rollicking, swaggering, bawling Gascons, wearing long swords and longer names, a fighter, a baron, and a gorgeous liar—*splendide mendax*—every mother's son. From this, what a drastic extreme to Cyrano's tremendous emotions during Roxanne's confession to him of her love—for—for—for another man! The climax of his emotions and of this act is reached when Cyrano, after promising to protect her lover, is insulted by him and then embraces him. The ingenuity and the strength of this situation lie in the treble aspect of the affront: to us, the audience, it is a source of mirth, to its hearers on the boards one of astonishment, to its subject one of agony. The second act is the richest dramatically.

Christian's wooing of Roxanne has progressed. Why else does the curtain now reveal a soft, chaste, moonlit night, a perfect night for lovers, for sighs translating hopes, for smiles that whisper secrets, for kisses dearer than the soul's salvation? In this scene the poet's words exhale, as it were, the sweetest essences of perfumed thoughts. The ravishing aroma of his love-verses can only be felt, not explained. So it is with all our most delicate perceptions. "Faith," says Tolstoy, "cannot be expressed in language." The poetic value of the lines mentioned raises the third act to the literary primacy of this drama. The whimsical interlude provided by the supposed traveller from the moon is another triumph of dramatic fertility and subtle arrangement. Whoever complains of being hurt by so sudden a drop from sublimity to absurdity must admit, too, the difficulty of replacing the episode with something as sublimely absurd. But the literary virtue of this act is its actors' bane. Act III. baffles the elocutionist because it is replete with romantic abstractions which cannot be interpreted by any form of mimicry. The human voice is but a musical instrument emitting a certain number of sounds, and, thus limited, Coquelin can give no better effect than a violin to such a line as this:

> Un point rose qu'on met sur l'i du verbe aimer—
>
> [A rosey dot that one puts over the i of the word *aimer* (to love)—]

Cyrano's definition of a kiss. On the other hand, successful lovemaking is usually applauded on the stage and off.

From sentimental moonshine dangling, cousin and lover, now comrades-in-arms, have marched to the front of peril and famine. The Gascon company is encamped before Arras. Bugle-calls and the roll of the drum, sentinel's tramp and challenge, clinking steel and crackling musketry, are heard at a little distance. The soldiers, gaunt, dishevelled, and in pain for want of food, are discouraged and woebegone. Provisions arrive, and the men have a jolly feast. Then strikes the hour of battle. The Gascons charge up the rocky embankment, and come rolling headlong down, dead or wounded. The survivors, rallied by Cyrano, rush into destruction against frightful odds. The circumstances that Act IV. is the noisiest, the most sensational, and the most confused is nothing in its favor. His love of contrast has led the author far astray from the paths of discretion. Roxane, a young lady of no astounding force of character, is inspired with the notion of getting a pastry-cook, Ragueneau, to take her, alone and in war-time, a week's journey in a carriage. Her relations do not oppose this adventure. With courteous innocence the Spaniards allow the lady to pass through their lines unquestioned upon her statement that she is going to see her lover. Knowing that her road is to the enemy's camp, logic forbids the Spaniards to believe that she might be a spy or bearer of despatches. She drives into the Gascon camp, the carriage stops, and she hops out with a courtesy, a smirk, and a *bonjour*. Aha! Of course—a whole act of a play without a woman—impossible! Strauss or Millöcker would have conjured her here in precisely this manner, and for exactly the same reason. But—what is this? The band does not strike up, the soubrettish, coquettish thing does not trip up to the footlights, the other people on the stage do not array themselves in two straight lines and turn to wooden sign-posts. So it is not an operetta, after all. Still, what a happy thought, to bring a carriageful of ortolans and muscatel as supernumerary baggage! How picturesque and happy the bold soldiers look, eating their lunch, though Italian bandits would have been prettier. After the picnic comes the battle.—If Roxane was brought here to throw herself on Christian's dead body, the author chose a cheap, easy, and conventional way to the hearts of the gallery. But he may have thought his picture of the Gascons would be called unfinished if their exuberant gallantry in the face of beauty and danger alike was not exemplified. The acme of Gascon bravado and waggishness is personified by Cyrano, who, while hunger is gripping his bowels, paces leisurely up and down, perusing a pocket edition of the

Iliad. A famished soldier growls that he must devour something. Cyrano pitches him his *Iliad.*

The scenic features of the fifth act express its pervading sentiment, as they did of the third. The dramatists of *le grand siècle* ["the great age"] and the Elizabethans, to say nothing of the ancients, were debarred by the rudeness of their scenic contrivances from appealing to their audiences in this way. The curtain rises upon a secluded convent garden. It is a quiet autumn afternoon; the sun is sinking; the trees cast deep and melancholy shadows; the silent fall of the yellow leaves completes nature's mute overture to brave Cyrano's end and peace. This act is, as a fifth act too often is, a confirmation of certainty. But we would not forfeit that last magnificent tirade, the summary of Cyrano's career. Expiring, he defies death, his only vanquisher, in a *bon-mot.* His loyalty to truth and honor has never flinched a moment; to the end he defends them with his wit and sword. With his back he is leaning against a tree, standing as he has stood all his life, alone, and in his delirium lunges at the air

> Je crois qu'elle regard. . . .
> Qu'elle ose regarder mon nez, cette camarde!
> (*Il lève son épée*)
> Que dites-vous? . . . C'est inutile? . . . Je le sais!
> Mais on ne se bat pas dans l'espoir du succès!
> Non! Non! c'est bien plus beau lorsque c'est inutile!
> —Qu'est-ce que c'est que tous ceux-là?—Vous êtes mille?
> Ah! je vous reconnais, tous mes vieux ennemis!
> Le Mensonge?
> (*Il frappe de son épée le vide*)
>   Tiens, tiens!—Ha! ha! les Compromis,
> Les Préjugés, les Lachetés! . . .
> (*Il frappe*)
>   Que je pactise?
> Jamais, jamais!—Ah! te voilà, toi, la Sottise!
> —Je sais bien qu'à la fin vous me mettrez à bas;
> N'importe: je me bats! je me bats! je me bats!
>
> ["I believe that he is looking . . . .
> That he dares to look at my nose, that snub-nosed person!
> (*He raises his sword*)
> What are you saying? . . . That it's useless? . . . I know that!
> But one doesn't fight in the hope of success!
> No! No, it's much more beautiful when it's useless!
> —What are all of those there?—You are a thousand?
> Ah! I recognize you, all my old enemies!
> Deceitfulness?
> (*He strikes air with his sword*)
>   Come, come!—Ha! ha! Compromises,
> Prejudices, Acts of cowardice! . . .
> (*He strikes*)
>   Will I compromise?
> Never, never!—Ah! Here you are, Folly!
> —I know well that in the end you will bring me down;
> It doesn't matter: I will fight! I will fight! I will fight!"]

In the clouds are perhaps authors who write in faultless verse of spotless creatures. Cyrano's bodily and moral exploits rank him among the immortals of earthly fiction, with d'Artagnan, Posa, Quasimodo, Enoch Arden, and other more or less fabulous individuals. Nor can the historical and national significance of **Cyrano de Bergerac** be denied. As to language, it is a garden of exotic fancies, a cascade of sparkling wit, a storm of pelting repartee. Its smooth measure is velvet, its ingenious rhyming distraction. Rostand's fecund art of throwing a purely poetical conception into a telling phrase is unsurpassed except by our one redeeming William. But Rostand may be reproached that parts of his play are tedious ex-

changes of opinion and metaphor, or that they are descriptions of events instead of events. The accusation would condemn him to good company, for it likewise might be applied to scenes of *Œdipus Rex, Antigone, Phèdre, Le misanthrope,* and *Wilhelm Tell.* It was an axiom of the Greek and French classical dramatists that the poetic recital of a shocking occurence was preferable to actual horrors on the stage. Their taste was more refined than Ben Jonson's or Marlowe's or Shakespeare's. They saw nothing delightful in such beastly butcheries as we tolerate or commend in *Edward II., Othello,* and *The Third Part of King Henry VI.* Rostand departs, to the detriment of taste and the glory of realism, from the standards of his greatest countrymen when he sends his Gascons rolling down the slope onto the stage, groaning and writhing in the throes of a violent death. In none of his dramas does Rostand attain the tranquil majesty of Corneille and Racine, or their suave dignity, or their mature experience, or their grand simplicity. But Rostand's linguistry they never dreamt of. Perhaps they would have scorned as trivial such juggling with language as "pharamineux," "ridiculise," "Scipion triplement Nasica." His wit is always elegant,—*précieux,* some would say,—and he never descends to the buffoonery of Beaumarchais and the horseplay of which Molière is capable. Every line, grave or gay, of **Cyrano de Bergerac** is "literary," which is much more than can be said of *Le medecin malgré lui.* But the broad moral philosophy, the cosmopolitan view, and the sound judgment of *Tartuffe* and *Les femmes savantes* are as much lacking in **Cyrano de Bergerac** as the frail sensibility, the soaring idealism, and the fine artistic handiwork of **Cyrano de Bergerac** are absent from *Tartuffe* and *Les femmes savantes.* Rostand is the preëminent verbalist and sentimentalist of the French drama. He has the perennial talent of the right word in the right place, and that without prejudice to rhyme. Cyrano is king of the polite joke and the erudite pun in French stageland.

Edmond Rostand's genius is of the highest, but not the highest. He lays down no laws of conduct for all men in all times. He has no pithy maxims to dispense. We cannot look to him for the safest and wisest moral instruction. And however deeply our æsthetic sense is intoxicated, however we marvel at his nimble scholarship, into whatever ecstasy we go over his perfect expression of exquisite thoughts, our investigating, speculative, deductive, reasoning faculties remain untouched. Our splendid young Frenchman is, indeed, a great poet and a little philosopher. He is not one of those dramatists

> Whose blood and judgment are so well commingled

that they satisfy your whole soul. He is not Sophocles, not Schiller, not Calderon. (pp. 264-69)

Lionel Strachey, in a review of "Cyrano de Bergerac," in Lippincott's Monthly Magazine, *February, 1899, pp. 264-69.*

MAX BEERBOHM (essay date 1900)

[Although he lived until 1956, Beerbohm is chiefly associated with the fin-de-siècle period in English literature, specifically with its lighter phases of witty sophistication and mannered elegance. His temperament was urbane and satirical, and he excelled in both literary and artistic caricatures of his contemporaries. "Entertaining" in the most complimentary sense of the word, Beerbohm's criticism for the Saturday Review—*where he was a long-time drama critic—demonstrates his scrupulously developed taste and unpretentious, fair-minded response to*

literature. The following excerpt is taken from a favorable review of an English translation of Les romanesques.]

If you, like Lady Betty Fanglestar, be "craving an elegant, light dissipation for a summer's afternoon," you ought certainly to visit the Royalty Theatre; for there they are playing **The Fantasticks,** quite the prettiest and wittiest little thing in the town.

You may remember that I was very angry when Mr. Wyndham produced **Cyrano de Bergerac** in an English version. I gave my reasons why that play should never have been transported, why it was bound to be absurd in any version but the original. Doubtless, now that Mrs. Campbell has produced another of M. Rostand's plays in a similar manner, signs of a similar indignation are expected of me. Alas! I cannot show them. **The Fantasticks** at the Royalty delights me not less than **Cyrano** bored me at the Criterion, and my pen is a-quiver to write praise. Lest you think me inconsistent in my views, or suspect me of being in the pay of one theatre and not of another, I must proceed to draw certain distinctions between the two cases. . . . **Les romanesques** is, in itself, much more fit than **Cyrano** for translation. Cyrano was a local French type, unintelligible to the English mind. Nor was he a realisation of the type; he was a poet's inspired idealisation of it, and, shorn of M. Rostand's verses, would have seemed even to Frenchmen nothing but a rather unpleasant lunatic. What folly, then, to make an English prose version of him! But Percinet and Sylvette, of **Les romanesques,** are not at all unreal; if they expressed their sentiments, not in verse, but in prose, they would be less charming, but they would still carry conviction. And they are not local types; they belong to any province of any country. There was no reason why Miss Fletcher should not lay hands on them.

The idea which M. Rostand shows through them is an idea to which no place, no time, were more appropriate than another. It is simply the idea that æsthetic romance is a sorry basis for a married life, that lovers who trust to it will be estranged when, as sooner or later they must, they begin to find each other out. It is, in its essence, just such a satire as Mr. Bernard Shaw himself might have written—did write, indeed, in *Arms and the Man;* but it is infinitely more effective, in that it is written by one who himself loves romance, and understands it, and knows the power of it. What could be more perfect, for truth and prettiness, than the stolen scene between Percinet and Sylvette across the wall of the two gardens? They have met often thus, revelling in the secrecy, in the thought of the fearful things which would happen if either's father (sworn foe to the other's father) were to find them there. Their minds are filled with the history of Romeo and Juliet, and their love is built on it. Suddenly, it occurs to Sylvette that they ought to be formally engaged:

Puisque nous nous aimons, il faut nous fiancer.
PERCINET. C'est à quoi justement je venais de penser.
SYLVETTE. Dernier des Bergamin, c'est à toi que se lie
          La dernière des Pasquinot!
PERCINET.   Noble folie!
SYLVETTE. On parlera de nous dans les âges futurs!
PERCINET. Oh! trop tendres enfants de deux pères trop
          durs!

["Since we love each other, we should get engaged.
PERCINET. That is exactly what I was just thinking.
SYLVETTE. Last of the Bergamins, it is to you that binds
          herself

The last of the Pasquinots!
PERCINET.   Noble folly!
SYLVETTE. They will speak of us in future ages!
PERCINET. Oh! too tender children of two fathers too
          hard!"]

Percinet hears a footstep in the garden. They both drop down from either side the wall. Bergamin, Percinet's father, comes and upbraids his son for loitering so often by the wall which divides his garden from that of Pasquin, his sworn foe. A little later, in the other garden, Pasquin comes and chides his daughter for the like offence. Sylvette runs away. He climbs up, and peeps over the wall. Bergamin is there, and climbs up to meet him. They embrace. Indeed, they are the best of old friends. Their avowed feud is a mere strategy to secure what is at their hearts: that Percinet and Sylvette shall fall in love with each other. They chuckle together over the progress of the affair. Pasquin has hit on a plan for bringing the betrothal about at once, with a public reconciliation between themselves. A Bravo, named Straforel, is at hand. He is a professional abductor, and does business on very reasonable terms. He is to abduct Sylvette that very evening, to be caught in the act by Percinet, to offer a desperate resistance, to be overcome in single combat. Then both the fathers will appear, and Pasquin, overcome with gratitude will give his Andromeda to her rescuer . . . The moon rises. Cloaked and masked, with a company of minions and minstrels, Straforel creeps into the garden. The minstrels group themselves picturesquely, and play softly on their flutes. The minions hold torches in the shadow. A closed chair is borne by negroes . . . All happens well. Straforel, prostrate on the ground, furtively stretches up to Bergamin the point of his sword, on which is transfixed a piece of paper. Bergamin reads the paper. His face lengthens. It is the bill . . . The lovers learn the true history of the rape. So! they are hero and heroine no longer. They quarrel, and they part. Percinet, furious, rushes away, in quest of actual adventures, actual loves . . . Straforel, (payment of whose bill depends on the marriage,) disguises himself as a nobleman, makes romantic love to Sylvette. He terrifies her with a passionate recital of all the glorious discomforts which she will suffer when she flies with him. She shrinks away, pining for anything prosaic . . . Percinet, scarred and tattered prodigal, comes slinking home. Sylvette runs to meet him. They are both wiser now. They can love each other without the circumstances of romantic sorrow and joy.

The figures are real enough, as you see. But they speak in poetry, and move in a sophisticated scheme, in a series of conventions. What happens to them is natural, but the way in which it happens to them is artificial always. What they do and say is natural, but they say and do it in the manner of poetic artifice. And so, of course, the chief requisite in the performance of the play is style. The mimes must express themselves and comport themselves exquisitely; anything like realism would mar the effect which M. Rostand aimed at. . . . **The Fantasticks,** I repeat, is the prettiest and wittiest little play in the town. By all means, go to it. (pp. 680-81)

Max Beerbohm, "A Migniard Play," in The Saturday Review, *London, Vol. 89, No. 2327, June 2, 1900, pp. 680-81.*

G. K. CHESTERTON   (essay date 1903)

[*Regarded as one of England's premier men of letters during the first half of the twentieth century, Chesterton is best known today as a colorful bon vivant, a witty essayist, and the creator of the Father Brown mysteries and the fantasy* The Man Who Was Thursday *(1908). Much of Chesterton's work reveals his childlike joie de vivre and reflects his pronounced Anglican and, later, Roman Catholic beliefs. His essays are characterized by their humor, frequent use of paradox, and chatty, rambling style. In the following excerpt, he discusses* Cyrano de Bergerac *and* L'aiglon *as "heroic comedies."]*

When *Cyrano de Bergerac* was published, it bore the subordinate title of a heroic comedy. We have no tradition in English literature which would justify us in calling a comedy heroic, though there was once a poet who called a comedy divine. By the current modern conception, the hero has his place in a tragedy, and the one kind of strength which is systematically denied to him is the strength to succeed. That the power of a man's spirit might possibly go to the length of turning a tragedy into a comedy is not admitted; nevertheless, almost all the primitive legends of the world are comedies, not only in the sense that they have a happy ending, but in the sense that they are based upon a certain optimistic assumption that the hero is destined to be the destroyer of the monster. Singularly enough, this modern idea of the essential disastrous character of life, when seriously considered, connects itself with a hyper-æsthetic view of tragedy and comedy which is largely due to the influence of modern France, from which the great heroic comedies of Monsieur Rostand have come. The French genius has an instinct for remedying its own evil work, and France gives always the best cure for "Frenchiness." The idea of comedy which is held in England by the school which pays most attention to the technical niceties of art is a view which renders such an idea as that of heroic comedy quite impossible. The fundamental conception in the minds of the majority of our younger writers is that comedy is, *par excellence,* a fragile thing. It is conceived to be a conventional world of the most absolutely delicate and gimcrack description. Such stories as Mr. Max Beerbohm's *Happy Hypocrite* are conceptions which would vanish or fall into utter nonsense if viewed by one single degree too seriously. But great comedy, the comedy of Shakespeare or Sterne, not only can be, but must be, taken seriously. There is nothing to which a man must give himself up with more faith and self-abandonment than to genuine laughter. In such comedies one laughs with the heroes, and not at them. The humour which steeps the stories of Falstaff and Uncle Toby is a cosmic and philosophic humour, a geniality which goes down to the depths. It is not superficial reading, it is not even, strictly speaking, light reading. Our sympathies are as much committed to the characters as if they were the predestined victims in a Greek tragedy. The modern writer of comedies may be said to boast of the brittleness of his characters. He seems always on the eve of knocking his puppets to pieces. When John Oliver Hobbes wrote for the first time a comedy of serious emotions, she named it, with a thinly-disguised contempt for her own work, *A Sentimental Comedy.* The ground of this conception of the artificiality of comedy is a profound pessimism. Life in the eyes of these mournful buffoons is itself an utterly tragic thing; comedy must be as hollow as a grinning mask. It is a refuge from the world, and not even, properly speaking, a part of it. Their wit is a thin sheet of shining ice over the eternal waters of bitterness.

Cyrano de Bergerac came to us as the new decoration of an old truth, that merriment was one of the world's natural flowers, and not one of its exotics. The gigantesque levity, the flamboyant eloquence, the Rabelaisian puns and digressions were seen to be once more what they had been in Rabelais, the mere outbursts of a human sympathy and bravado as old and solid as the stars. The human spirit demanded wit as headlong and haughty as its will. . . . An essential aspect of this question of heroic comedy is the question of drama in rhyme. There is nothing that affords so easy a point of attack for the dramatic realist as the conduct of a play in verse. According to his canons, it is indeed absurd to represent a number of characters facing some terrible crisis in their lives by capping rhymes like a party playing *bouts rimés.* In his eyes it must appear somewhat ridiculous that two enemies taunting each other with insupportable insults should obligingly provide each other with metrical spacing and neat and convenient rhymes. But the whole of this view rests finally upon the fact that few persons, if any, to-day understand what is meant by a poetical play. It is a singular thing that those poetical plays which are now written in England by the most advanced students of the drama follow exclusively the lines of Maeterlinck, and use verse and rhyme for the adornment of a profoundly tragic theme. But rhyme has a supreme appropriateness for the treatment of the higher comedy. The land of heroic comedy is, as it were, a paradise of lovers, in which it is not difficult to imagine that men could talk poetry all day long. It is far more conceivable that men's speech should flower naturally into these harmonious forms, when they are filled with the essential spirit of youth, than when they are sitting gloomily in the presence of immemorial destiny. The great error consists in supposing that poetry is an unnatural form of language. We should all like to speak poetry at the moment when we truly live, and if we do not speak, it is because we have an impediment in our speech. It is not song that is the narrow or artificial thing, it is conversation that is a broken and stammering attempt at song. When we see men in a spiritual extravaganza, like *Cyrano de Bergerac,* speaking in rhyme, it is not our language disguised or distorted, but our language rounded and made whole. Rhymes answer each other as the sexes in flowers and in humanity answer each other. Men do not speak so, it is true. Even when they are inspired or in love they talk inanities. But the poetic comedy does not misrepresent the speech one half so much as the speech misrepresents the soul. Monsieur Rostand showed even more than his usual insight when he called *Cyrano de Bergerac* a comedy, despite the fact that, strictly speaking, it ends with disappointment and death. The essence of tragedy is a spiritual breakdown or decline, and in the great French play the spiritual sentiment mounts unceasingly until the last line. It is not the facts themselves, but our feeling about them, that makes tragedy and comedy, and death is more joyful in Rostand than life in Maeterlinck. The same apparent contradiction holds good in the case of the drama of *L'aiglon,* now being performed with so much success. Although the hero is a weakling, the subject a fiasco, the end a premature death and a personal disillusionment, yet, in spite of this theme, which might have been chosen for its depressing qualities, the unconquerable pæan of the praise of things, the ungovernable gaiety of the poet's song swells so high that at the end it seems to drown all the weak voices of the characters in one crashing chorus of great things and great men. A multitude of mottoes might be taken from the play to indicate and illustrate, not only its own spirit, but much of the spirit of modern life. When in the vision of the field of Wagram the horrible voices of the wounded cry out, *Les corbeaux, les corbeaux* ["the ravens, the ravens"], the Duke, overwhelmed with a nightmare of hideous trivialities, cries out, *Où, où, sont les aigles?* ["Where, where are the eagles?"] That antithesis might stand alone as an invocation at the beginning of the twentieth century to the spirit of heroic comedy. When an ex-General of Napoleon is asked his reason for having betrayed the Emperor, he replies, *La fatigue* ["fatigue"], and at that a veteran private of the Great Army rushes forward, and crying passionately, *Et nous?* ["And us?"] pours out a terrible description of the life lived by the commoner soldier. To-day, when pessimism is almost as much a symbol of wealth and fashion as jewels or cigars, when the pampered heirs of the ages can sum up life in few other words but *la fatigue,* there might surely come a cry from the vast mass of common humanity from the beginning—*et nous?* It is this potentiality for enthusiasm among the mass of men that makes the function of comedy at once common and sublime. Shakespeare's *Much Ado About Nothing* is a great comedy, because behind it is the whole pressure of that love of love which is the youth of the world, which is common to all the young, especially to those who swear they will die bachelors and old maids. *Love's Labour's Lost* is filled with the same energy, and there it falls even more definitely into the scope of our subject, since it is a comedy in rhyme in which all men speak lyrically as naturally as the birds sing in pairing time. What the love of love is to the Shakespearean comedies, that other and more mysterious human passion, the love of death, is to ***L'aiglon.*** Whether we shall ever have in England a new tradition of poetic comedy it is difficult at present to say, but we shall assuredly never have it until we realise that comedy is built upon everlasting foundations in the nature of things, that it is not a thing too light to capture, but too deep to plumb. Monsieur Rostand, in his description of the Battle of Wagram, does not shrink from bringing about the Duke's ears the frightful voices of actual battle, of men torn by crows, and suffocated with blood, but when the Duke, terrified at these dreadful appeals, asks them for their final word, they all cry together *Vive l'empereur!* ["Long live the emperor!"] Monsieur Rostand, perhaps, did not know that he was writing an allegory. To me that field of Wagram is the field of the modern war of literature. We hear nothing but the voices of pain; the whole is one phonograph of horror. It is right that we should hear these things, it is right that not one of them should be silenced; but these cries of distress are not in life, as they are in modern art, the only voices; they are the voices of men, but not the voice of man. When questioned finally and seriously as to their conception of their destiny, men have from the beginning of time answered in a thousand philosophies and religions with a single voice and in a sense most sacred and tremendous, *Vive l'empereur.* (pp. 73-82)

> G. K. Chesterton, "Rostand," in his Varied Types,
> *Dodd, Mead and Company, 1903, pp. 73-82.*

MARY ARMS EDMONDS   (essay date 1914)

[*In the following essay, Edmonds surveys Rostand's works and praises his idealism.*]

It is an unwritten law of the French Academy that each new member shall, in the "discourse" which he must deliver on the day of his formal admission, devote himself to a critique of his predecessor. When, in 1903, Edmond Rostand came before that august assembly, it was to succeed the idealistic poet, Henri de Bornier; and in his graceful and brilliant tribute he has found one phrase which might not only be applied to idealists as a class, but is particularly expressive of the essential quality in his own genius. Quoting an old Provençal song that says

The folk of Lunel go a-fishing for the moon,

he characterizes Bornier as all his life long "a fisher of the moon"—one, that is, who had the divine faith which could make him cast his net again and again, "never despairing of pulling in the planet," and the equally divine and allied gift of being able always to see "topazes and emeralds in the common sand of life." From the very beginning of the world's history, it has been to such faith and seership—though they might be, and usually were, reckoned at the moment as the merest foolishness of fanaticism—that every vital movement has owed its origin; and to those who believe that genius lies in the skilled expression of the ideal and the eternal which abide in the actual and the fugitive, they are equally inherent and essential elements in every true work of art.

In our day it would seem that fishing for the moon, although it can become extinct only with the race, has measurably declined. We have too little time and too much science not to look with a certain careless scorn on so indefinite and impalpable a pursuit. Yet it is as true to-day as it has ever been that for the quickening in us of our finer perceptions and the happiness of the larger life we must look, not to the superficialities of what we call modern progress, but to the silver drippings from these glistening nets. If there seem to be fewer of them, if too often the glimmer that catches our eye turns out on closer inspection to be only nickel plate, we must watch but the more keenly that no least sparkle of the real heaven-descended ray escape us. It was this sparkle which lent distinction to Rostand's first volume, even in a country where a man is scarcely held to have completed his education until he has "written his book"; and it is this sparkle in its increasing definiteness and depth which gives him a significant place and an assured value in the literary Golden Book of his own generation, whatever uncertainty must always hang about future verdicts.

Of the seven volumes which represent Rostand to the world, all but one have their contents cast in dramatic form. ***Les musardises,*** with which he made his entrance into the tourney of letters, is a collection of poems written between 1887 and 1893, and possesses that subtler interest which, to so many people, gives an artist's sketchbook a value above that of his finished pictures. It is to an extent even rather unusual in literature a pencil shadowing of what he was later to render in colors. There is not a single fundamental idea and scarcely a fanciful thought anywhere in his work that cannot be found in embryo here. The verses are full of imperfections; full, too, of youth—of its egoisms, its vanities, its self-importance, but also of its generous enthusiasms and aspirations. From the very first is manifest the young writer's conviction that to be a poet is to inherit the Kingdom of Heaven. There is more than the fantastic conception of a moment in the dialogue between St. Peter and the young man at the gates of Paradise, wherein the latter, convicted of most of the sins of the world, the flesh, and the devil, and about to be cast into outer darkness, bethinks himself just in time to plead that he has been a poet. St. Peter softens instantly.

"What? A poet?"—Without delay
The gates swung back, his sternness fled.
"Why not have told me right away?
Come in—You are at home," he said.

Les musardises was followed by ***Les romanesques,*** a comedy that is the daintiest piece of bric-à-brac imaginable, with "Made in France" stamped on its every line. It was produced at the Comédie Française in 1894; and a year later Sara Bernhardt brought out *La princesse lointaine,* perhaps the most characteristic, in its pure romanticism and idealism, of all Rostand's plays. *La Samaritaine,* in 1897, was another Bernhardt production; but it was not until the first appearance of *Cyrano de Bergerac* in December of that year, with Coquelin in the title rôle, that Rostand's fame outgrew what had been its merely national—one might almost say Parisian—limits. The enormous success of this play, which proved the greatest literary and dramatic sensation that French critics had had to encounter since the days of Victor Hugo, was followed up in 1900 by *L'aiglon,* and then, after a further lapse of ten years, by *Chantecler.*

In going over the honor roll of these dramas, there is only one which, from the literary viewpoint, can be reckoned a failure. The reader of *La Samaritaine* can hardly refrain from wondering if it were not a made-to-order piece rather than a spontaneous outpouring, so lacking is it in any genuine poetic value. The language of the Bible paraphrased in verse—which is the language of almost the entire play—seems not only to put shackles on the poet's power of expression, but to lose in the process much of its native dignity and beauty. The figure of the Christ, too, is disappointing. Putting quite aside the question as to the advisability of any presentation of Christ on the stage, the fact undoubtedly remains that Rostand, handling his subject with the most profound reverence, yet fails signally to convince or impress. His Saviour is puerile beside the ideal conception that alone could satisfy; and by a curious contradiction, one gets more of the Christ spirit, one is brought nearer to those waters of eternal life promised to the Woman of Samaria, in almost any of the other plays than here where the Christ himself is the central figure.

If *La Samaritaine* is the only literary failure that can be laid at Rostand's door, *Cyrano* might be classed with *Les romanesques* as the only purely dramatic success. Although the drama has been his chosen form of expression, and although everything he has done has received brilliant presentation, Rostand remains a poet rather than a playwright, and his plays are dramatic poems rather than poetic dramas. *Chantecler* affords perhaps the most striking example. Here we have an allegory worked out with exquisite poetic feeling and under forms which in reading the imagination accepts without any sense of shock. Once, however, promenade the Cock, the Hen Pheasant, the Dog, visibly before our eyes, once let us hear them speak their lines aloud in unmistakable voices of men and women—the illusion is gone, and with it the whole effectiveness of the play's meaning and appeal. From an imaginative creation it has degenerated into a mere spectacular sensation. I venture to believe that only about one in a hundred of those who saw the play given in this country, carried away from the theatre more than an admiring sense of the heights to which the stage-producer's art has attained of late years. Another instance of this same lack of correspondence between the thing conceived and the thing produced occurs in *L'aiglon,* in the scene where the Duke is left alone on the Field of Wagram with the dead body of Flambeau. The coming-alive, as it were, of the whole vast plain before this boy who, heir to its glory and its tragedy, has just seen his hopes of a tangible inheritance done to death; the voices that rise of the thousands who died to give Napoleon victory; the groans and lamentations of the wounded that change into a song of triumph—"the pardon for the glory's sake"—as the Duke offers up himself and his ambition in expiation, this as a conception is tremendous; it has the grandeur of Greek tragedy. You thrill as you read; but once in an orchestra chair

you can only sit unmoved, wondering what has become of the mental illusion the poet's magic had once succeeded in creating and vivifying.

The exception to this general statement, I have noted above. *Cyrano* is unquestionably, as an *acting* play, Rostand's masterpiece. The movement is rapid and dramatic, and there is no time when the imagination of the poet passes into a region where it is forbidden to actors and scene-setters to follow. The opening of the first act is admirable in its animation, its picturesqueness, its immediate establishment of the Seventeenth Century atmosphere. The insolent noblesse, the bourgeoisie, the soldiery, the professional cut-throats whose swords were at the service of the highest bidder, the professional pickpockets who exercised their trade in every public assembly, the fair ladies of the court, and the equally fair if more learned *précieuses*—all these are sketched in with a touch as vivid as it is light. Nor can we turn to any one of the succeeding scenes without finding in them material equally adapted to stage presentation. Manifestly, Rostand is fully capable of producing an acting drama of the first order. That he has not more uniformly done so—that *La princesse lointaine, L'aiglon,* and *Chantecler,* are best of all as "closet plays"—is to be attributed in a large measure, I believe, to an element in his genius which comes out very markedly in his character-drawing. He is interested primarily in ideas, in thoughts rather than in persons. He looks on his characters, one feels, not so much as individuals, diversely composed of an assortment of traits, some important and many frivolous, but rather as instruments by means of which he can develop and emphasize his philosophy of life. This does not mean that his people are mere puppets—christened abstractions. They are mostly, on the contrary, admirably executed portraits; but their appeal is intellectual and spiritual rather than human and personal. One cannot imagine Rostand ever being so dominated by one of the creatures of his imagination as to change in the least degree the preconceived line of conduct he had laid out for that particular character. Squarciafico, in *La princesse lointaine,* the crafty Genoese merchant, shrewd, of the earth earthy, seeing things always in their lowest aspect, is a sketch drawn in vivid colors; and yet we never find ourselves visualizing him as a man, as we visualize Shylock, for instance. He is primarily the foil necessary to throw into highest relief the fundamental ideas of the drama. The same thing is essentially true of Flambeau, in *L'aiglon.* There is no one of Rostand's minor characters who stands out more strikingly, but it is as the embodiment in flesh and blood of the almost fanatical devotion of Napoleon's soldiers to their leader. In his ringing lines, with their slang, their atmosphere of the people, their underlying grandeur, we feel the very throb of that enthusiasm to have inspired which is, perhaps, in the ultimate analysis, the "Little Corporal's" clearest claim to genius. Even Cyrano, the most human of all Rostand's people, is almost more a national figure than an individual. In him we are given a supreme expression of that peculiarly Gallic spirit which Rostand calls "having *le panache*"—the spirit which "is not greatness, but something that is added on to greatness and stirs above it . . . something fluttering, excessive. . . . *Le panache* is the wit of valor. . . . To jest in the face of danger is the supreme mark of good breeding, a delicate refusal to take oneself tragically." It is a spirit which, in its gay defiance to life's buffets, appeals strongly to Rostand. The story of the lame Beggar [in *Les musardises*] who in each fresh opening of his rags stuck a flower, who carried a garland on his crutch, and hid the holes in his weather-beaten hat with a wreath, is one that we find repeated again and again, under varying forms, in his work.

In *L'aiglon* alone of all his plays, Rostand has chosen to centre the interest in the development of a character rather than of a thought. On the title-page the poet has written:

> Great Heavens, I am not writing
> For or against the cause of strife—
> This history that I'm reciting
> Is only of a poor child's life.

This drama is indeed a profoundly interesting psychological study. In his presentation of the eaglet whom Metternich's policy is trying to convert into a tame song-bird, content in his golden cage, Rostand has selected for his leading theme the blending in the Duke's veins of the two bloods—the blood of the Corsican upstart and the blood of the long line of Austrian royalty. The genius of his father is constantly being held in check by the traditions of his mother. In the struggle that inevitably ensues—a struggle of the spirit against the subtle forces of heredity—l'Aiglon's failure and death are in the very nature of things assured. As he himself says to his friend Prokesch:

> It is from no such vulgar poison as
> They give in melodramas on the stage,
> The Duke of Reichstadt's dying—it is from
> His soul!
> PROKESCH. My lord!
> THE DUKE. From my soul and my name!
> That name that holds within itself the sound
> Of bells and cannon, and is thundering loud
> Against my languor, and reproaches ringing
> Forever with its cannon and its bells!

This recognition of the presence in himself of warring elements leads to a pathetic distrust of his own worthiness and ability to take up the heritage of his father; and the whole play is simply the presentation in dramatic form of the alternations in him of exaltation and despair, enthusiasm and inertia. We see him rebellious, beating his wings against the bars of his Austrian thraldom, learning avidly, in secret, that part of his history which his teachers are under orders to expurgate; and then again bowed to the earth under the overwhelming tragedy of the gloomy Habsburg heritage which claims him, too, as one of its heirs, trying to stifle memory, hope, ambition, in the pleasures of the senses. Finally, in the pathetic last act, we have the end of it all—the frail body succumbing at last in the battle of the mighty forces among which it has been buffeted—and the reader is left echoing pitifully the words of Thérèse as the epitaph that goes above the proud titles of King of Rome and Duke of Reichstadt—"Poor little one!"

In *L'aiglon,* as in the other plays, the first and most clearly defined impression that detaches itself, is one of extraordinary poetic richness and vitality. In the spontaneity and fertility of his poetic expression, in his power of creating atmosphere, in the haunting music of so many of his lines, Rostand takes place beside the few, the very few, genuine word-singers of his day. It is his almost magical power of translating his own inner vision to his readers' senses that so enchants the imagination in the balcony scene in *Cyrano,* recreating the moonlit, flower-scented night with its under-throb of passion; that lends such an eerie thrill to the scene of the "Nocturnes" in *Chantecler,* with its sense of black night, of the burning eyes that open as the name of each Night-Bird is called, of the ferocity alive in all this darkness, this mystery; and that

is used with such tremendous dramatic effect in the scene in *L'aiglon* where Metternich comes to the Duke's room at Schönbrunn. One feels with an almost physical intensity the darkness of the room; one sees the little hat before which kings once bowed, black against the whiteness of the paper on which it lies, and the form of the old veteran of the Guard drawn up, erect and menacing, in the gleam of moonlight; and one shivers with much the same sensation of half superstitious awe as must have thrilled through Metternich when, as the door from the bedroom opens, there comes the solemn announcement: "The Emperor."

Moreover, as part also of his poetic dower, Rostand has a very exquisite insight into and power to present the element of tenderness which flowers in some corner of most human hearts. A scene such as that between the Duke of Reichstadt and his grandfather in the third act of *L'aiglon,* to quote but a single instance, could have been written only by one who understood that off from the great, passion-swept highroads of emotion there branch a hundred little bypaths, each with its own fragrant, tender charm. Yet the sentiment with which again and again he touches our heart-strings, never degenerates into sentimentality. He himself has given us an apt illustration of the union in his genius of the profounder things of life and art with an iridescent and often keenly satirical wit.

> How like we are, O Drummer-Boy of Love!
> I'm playing still a medley sad and gay,
> With for the drum, so grave and deep, my heart—
> A heavier weight to carry than your weight.
> But ever, while it makes its muffled plaint,
> My wit goes whistling like a mocking flute.
> *[Les musardises]*

Repeatedly we catch the flash of a rapier thrust that pricks a folly or lays open an hypocrisy, and in *Chantecler,* where there is more sustained satire than in any of the other plays, we find the point bared through entire scenes—notably in the third act, where we have the Guinea Hen's "At Home." Here the modern craving for novelty, for sensationalism, for notoriety; the whole superficial, pseudo-intellectual, fad-worshipping cast of a certain sort of society is mercilessly drawn. Rostand, however, loses in artistic effectiveness in proportion as he yields too free a rein to what is not of the essence of his gift. The scene at the Guinea Hen's becomes intolerably wearisome. The prevalence of every sort of slang expression, whether of the salon or of the street, with the local limitations it necessarily imposes, and the constant recurrence of that word-jugglery which is one of Rostand's besetting weaknesses, end by rasping the reader's nerves. One cannot but feel that the poet must take a quite impish delight in his own ability to play with words—to make, as it were, a rhetorical hodge-podge. At times one's brain grows dizzy in the attempt to follow his meaning through the wild contortions of his diction, even while one gasps with a sort of painful admiration for the mental ingenuity and flexibility that can devise and perform such astounding intellectual gymnastics.

There is no question that, for the foreigner, *Chantecler* is the most difficult of any of the Rostand plays; nor does it stand on a level, in its entirety, with the best of his previous work. After the first two acts the poet seems to lose grasp a little, the action drags, and there is a decided falling off in the beauty of the lines. Yet it is in *Chantecler* that we get the most definite expression of certain significant elements in Rostand's thought. A thorough "romantic" himself, he holds that the romance lies in the individual soul, not in the outward event. To him life presents itself as a glorious and wonderful experience quite independent of any apparent limitations of place and circumstance. He would have us believe that there is nothing commonplace, there is nothing mean, unless we choose dully to go along with eyes closed to the daily miracles; and that it only needs a sense of all that is in and around and beyond what we see in the world, to make of the quietest, most circumscribed existence a thing of throbbing interest. Closely allied with this is the other leading motive of **Chantecler**—the cosmic importance of the individual life. In the great scheme of things there is given to each one of us his place, his little garden patch, the cultivation or neglect of which is going to affect for good or ill the universal estate. Faithfulness to the trust that is bestowed on us at birth, with a proud and glad appreciation of its potentialities—this is the lesson taught by the Cock who thinks that his song brings the day into being. Rostand is not launching a satire in this instance—Chantecler is not a type of the boaster who believes that the universe hangs on his nod. The true significance of his attitude is revealed to us no less than to the Hen Pheasant in the wonderful scene of the "making of the dawn," and in lines of such lyric beauty that they linger like music in the memory. Even when, in the end, there comes the bitter disillusionment of finding out that it is not, after all, his song which summons the dawn, Chantecler still remains true to his *métier,* choosing to go back to his farmyard, with its jealousies, its bitternesses, its hypocrisies, because there lie his place and his work. If it is not he who brings light to his valley, at least he is the herald of light, charged to dispel the lurking evils of night with his proclamation of day and sunshine and all the wholesome forces of work and energy they set free.

In this emphasis which it lays on enthusiasm, on the need of living one's life with a will, **Chantecler** brings out anew that which sets Rostand very definitely apart from the undistinguished throng of "idle singers of an idle day." Although he himself would be the first to disown any direct intention to point a moral or preach a sermon, the most casual reader can hardly fail to realize that his entire work is simply the expression, under however varied phrasing, of an intense belief in the beauty and value of idealism—the golden vein running through the world's dross and which alone can make the joy and the inspiration of living. Again and again he bids us realize that

> Above a roof,
> A chimney-pot,
> And over you and me,
> Above the humblest working day—

there is always

> A sky as pure, a sky as wide
> As ever sky of Sicily;

                                        [Les musardises]

and that the one irremediable tragedy is to keep our eyes so persistently on the street that we lose sight of the blue. We are so chary of letting ourselves go, the most of us, so fearful of what our feet may stumble over if we keep our heads too high, so desirous not to be caught straying from the solid foundations of the matter-of-fact into the foolishness of romance. We are afraid of the fate predicted by Maître Erasme for Frère Trophime—afraid we shall be excommunicated by a commonsense world that has no desire to pass beyond the limits of what it can see and touch, what its reason can account for and catalogue. It is Rostand's passionately held be-

lief, and the burden of his message to our age, that this laziness of the soul should at all costs be shaken off, and that we should, each one of us, make of his life a voyage towards a "Princesse Lointaine." The gravest reproach he brings against modern life, is the atrophy of the power of enthusiasm under the tyranny of intellectual fashion and the dictates of "good form." When Chantecler pleads in favor of the Blackbird—

> Come now, admit he is intelligent,

Patou answers:

> Ye-es—and yet not so very, for his eye
> Is never dazzled. Before every flower—
> Of whose supporting stalk he's too aware—
> He has a look that holds delight in check,
> A word that somehow makes all beauty less.

It is the regenerative and spiritually quickening power of idealism which is made the keynote of **La princesse lointaine,** and is voiced by Frère Trophime—the wise and tender monk who is the idealist in religion as Rudel is the idealist in love and Bertrand in chivalry—in his answer to the reproaches of Maître Erasme, the Prince's physician. Bitterly resentful at being stirred from a pleasant chimney-corner by the call of something so vague and glamorous, Erasme is descanting on the folly of the undertaking and ends by taking Frère Trophime to task for sanctioning with his presence an expedition which, alone in that age, was making for the East with no purpose of rescuing the Holy Sepulchre from the infidels. To which the monk replies:

> It is not this release which is God's will.
> Believe that had he cared to chase away
> The horde of infidels from round the Tomb,
> A single angel could have done it with
> Only a stirring of his mighty wings.
> But no, what God willed was to quicken those
> Living in torpor, sloth, and arrogance;
> To take them out from their dull selfishness,
> The drab indifference that kills the soul,
> And thrust them, singing, proud, among the spears,
> Drunk with devotion, eager to die afar,
> In that entire forgetfulness of self
> Of which they all had need.

And so this love of Rudel's—this love which is a dream of something unknown, pure and fair, and which has had power to waken his soul, to take him out from the little, fossilizing influences of his little court and send him to meet the larger experiences of life, hardships, danger, and even death—is working as truly for God's ends as any crusade of them all.

> Ah! inertia is the one vice, Maître Erasme,
> And the one virtue—

ERASME. Is—?

FRERE TROPHIME. Enthusiasm!

Even the rude mariners whom Rudel has hired to carry him to Tripoli—scum of the ports, pirates and cut-throats—have felt the influence that emanates from every noble and generous conception. Through storms and battles, in the midst of hunger and thirst, their courage has been sustained by the thought of this wonderful fairy-story in which they feel themselves to be taking part. There is a whole volume of suggestion in the cries with which they greet Bertrand at a moment when hope seems nearly gone.

Sir Bertrand, I am hungry—tell me more
About the gold of the Princess's hair!—
And I, Sir Bertrand, I am thirsty—tell
Me once again the deep blue of her eyes!

In his Discourse before the Academy, Rostand, defending the poetic drama, said:

> The true wit is that which lends wings to enthusiasm. . . . And this is why we need a drama through which, exalting lyrically, moralizing with beauty, consoling with grace, the poets shall be able, without doing it on purpose, to give lessons in soul. This is why we need a drama that shall be poetic and even heroic. . . . The personages of the drama are . . . intrusted with the duty of taking us out on a holiday from this eternal college which is life—taking us out in order to give us courage to go back again!

There could be no better summary than this of the nature of the place which Rostand fills. In the stress he lays upon spiritual values, in the virile force and energy of his idealism, in the transforming touch of romance he lays upon life, he is giving a lesson sorely needed—he is taking us out from the ruts of the daily routine into the holiday joys and rich possibilities that lie in fishing for the moon. (pp. 592-604)

> *Mary Arms Edmonds, "A Fisher of the Moon: An Appreciation of Edmond Rostand," in* Forum, *Vol. LI, April, 1914, pp. 592-604.*

A. G. H. SPIERS (essay date 1918)

[*In the following excerpt, Spiers discusses the triumph of idealism despite obstacles as the principal theme in Rostand's works.*]

Elected to the French Academy at the remarkably early age of thirty-five, Chevalier of the Legion of Honor, author whose works have been translated into every living language worthy of the name, deriving his art from the precepts of no particular school, yet writing the most famous play of the last eighty years, original yet commonplace, innovator and reactionary in one, Edmond Rostand is a dramatist compelling the attention of all who pretend to an interest in the history or practise of letters. And not the least curious thing about him is that, though he is now forty-nine years old, he died at the age of forty-two. Like Kipling, he is a ghost in the flesh; in the words used by Macaulay of a very different person, he has survived his own wake and overhears the verdict of posterity sitting in judgment on his life's work.

Such an author naturally suggests many subjects of study. I have chosen for discussion here merely one great characteristic which, in my opinion, has contributed not a little to his popularity. On the Place de la Concorde in Paris there is a ring of statues, each representing a different city of France. One of these is that of Strasbourg, lost to the Germans in 1870; and on this statue, draped in mourning until the opening of the present war, are engraved the following words:

> Qui vive? la France quand même!

> [Who goes there? France in spite of it all!]

Now Rostand is the poet of *quand même* ["in spite of it all"].

It takes but a superficial glance to note this fact. With the exception of the one-act play *Les deux pierrots* (1888) and *La*

Samaritaine, an "évangile en trois actes," written especially for Holy Week (1896), all his works contain this *quand même*. In *Les musardises* (1887-1893), his first volume of verse, the word itself occurs in a characteristic passage:

> Ce qu'il faut pouvoir, ce qu'il faut savoir,
> C'est garder son rêve.

> [That which it is necessary to be able to do, that which it
>   is necessary to know how to do,
> Is to preserve your dream.]

> • • • • •

> C'est avoir des yeux qui, voyant le laid,
> Voient le beau quand même;
> C'est savoir rester, parmi ce qu'on hait,
> Avec ce qu'on aime.

> [It is to have eyes which, seeing the ugliness,
> Sees the beautiful all the same;
> It is to know to stay, amongst that which you hate,
> With that which you love.]

These lines find a dramatic echo in Rostand's first play to be produced on a public stage. *Les romanesques* (1894) is the story of two romantic young people. In love with love, as well as with one another, Percinet and Sylvette undergo a series of adventures that are thoroughly to their taste. They feel that they are Romeo and Juliet all over again. As the play progresses, however, disillusionment awaits them. The obstacles they have so valiantly overcome, the wall built between their gardens, the anger of their families, yes, even the attack made upon Percinet by cruel bandits, all prove to be but a ruse invented by their experienced fathers in the hope of fostering their love. This is a cruel shock. Nevertheless, though disconcerted for a time, they suffer no permanent revulsion of feeling. They insist on marrying *quand même,* and *quand même* they will continue to cherish one another with all the sweet romance of their adventurous courtship.

And this *quand même* that appears in the first volume of verse, as it appears in the first real play, may be traced throughout Rostand's subsequent production. We find it in the next play, *La princesse lointaine* (1895), and again, although somewhat obscured, in *L'aiglon* (1900). But nowhere does it stand out more prominently than in the greatest of the plays, *Cyrano de Bergerac* (1897), and in the greatest of the poems, *Chantecler* (1910). Cyrano is a man who has made a great resolve. He will be admirable in all things; he will live up to his highest ideals as a lover, as a soldier and as a playwright. According to worldly standards, this resolve leads him to ruin. At the end of the play, his works have been plagiarized but not produced; the woman he loves has married another; and this proud swordsman who wished for death on a field of glory has been foully assassinated by those whom his independence has offended. And yet this defeat is in reality a victory. As he says himself, he has clung to his principles; he has lived without compromise; he has fought the good fight against falsehood, sham and all that diminishes the soul; and there is one thing which, unsullied, he will carry with him across the threshold of Paradise, and that is the very symbol of all for which he has contended, his plume. He has triumphed *quand même.*

Chantecler, a most beautiful poem though a bad play, is likewise imbued with the same indomitable spirit. Here it glorifies the humdrum round of daily work. Of what importance are the petty demonstrations and the limited outlook of the world? What does it matter that the world should prove our occupations useless in the scheme of the universe? There is a greater and more potent truth than that of the reason or the senses. It is just possible that on a certain morning the sun should rise uncalled by the crowing of the cock. But in the name of the greater truth, Chantecler ignores this possibility; and for the sake of his own happiness and industry, as for the sake of the happiness and industry of those about him, he insists on believing *quand même* that life's greatest blessing, the light, would vanish if he ceased to crow.

As may be seen from this superficial review, Rostand, differing from many contemporary dramatists, centers the interest of his plays not so much in the development of his plots as in the feelings of his characters. These characters are real heroes, and it is they who utter the characteristic cry of *quand même*. If, then, we wish to understand the spirit of Rostand's work, we must examine the traits with which he endows his men and women.

There enters into their moral make-up one element which is heroic, an element which recalls Corneille, whom, consciously or unconsciously, Rostand has taken as a model on more than one occasion. This is the stoic doctrine: Put your contentment in yourself and in that which depends solely on yourself. Cyrano, though done to death, is no more overcome by his enemies, he is no more crushed, than is Corneille's *Horace,* and he is only a little less happy than the same author's *Polyeucte.* Similarly, in **Les romanesques** as in **La princesse lointaine,** in **L'aiglon** as in **Chantecler,** Percinet, Mélissinde, the Duke of Reichstadt, and the cock have found within their own souls a satisfaction beyond the power of the world to take away.

It is possible, however, to be satisfied with one's life, even in adversity, for many different reasons. And there are at least two great classes into which these reasons may be divided. This satisfaction may come from within, or it may come from without. On the one hand, it may be due to a certain stolidity, a certain proud inertia of the moral fiber, which makes us indifferent to our material welfare as to the opinion of our fellows. On the other hand, it may be due to cordial or emotional suggestion, to an excitement of the heart or of the sensibilities. The characters of Corneille's plays are influenced by reasons of the first class; but those of Rostand derive their satisfaction from those of the second. If they are content with their lot, if by an attitude of mind they turn defeat into victory, it is not because they are complacent, because they have an appreciation of their own worth, but because they have acquired, as a possession no more to be wrested from them, an ideal of which they feel a spiritual need. L'Aiglon himself, the weakest of Rostand's characters, is content to die in the hands of his enemies, far from France where he had hoped to rule, because he has at least found a noble interpretation of his misery. Standing on the battle-field of Wagram, he comes to understand, as he had not understood before, the price of his father's, of Napoleon's glory. He hears the death rattle of the dying, the lament of the wounded, and the cries of the thirsty and the hungry. Then the revelation comes to him: his life is an expiatory offering. Napoleon's greatness was bought with the suffering of others; and now he, Napoleon's son, must suffer in his turn, in order that there may remain no stain upon his father's glory:

> . . . j'ai compris. Je suis expiatoire.
> Tout n'était pas payé. Je complète le prix.
> Oui, je devais venir dans ce champ. J'ai compris.

[I understand. I am an expiation.
Everything was not paid. I complete the price.
Yes, I must arise in the field. I understand.]

• • • • •

> Et je sens qu'il est juste et providentiel
> Que le champ de bataille ainsi me tende au ciel,
> Et m'offre, pour pouvoir, après cet offertoire
> Porter plus purement son titre de victoire!

[And I feel that it is just and providential
That the field of battle thus holds me out to the sky,
And offers me, in order to be able, after this offering
To carry more purely its title of victory!]

The ideals from which Rostand's characters draw their satisfaction are always immaterial and spiritual. They appeal to the heart, the imagination, and the soul. Percinet is in love with romance; Mélissinde yearns for mystic comfort and the communion of soul with soul; Cyrano seeks to satisfy to the utmost the most exacting demands of his chivalric and independent conscience; and Chantecler is the champion of work sustained by beauty and light. But Rostand is no idle dreamer; he does not forget the world. Though he has much in common with the Romantic poets of England, he is no "beautiful and ineffectual angel beating in the void his luminous wings in vain." He may live in the clouds, but he has the courage to accept the challenge of the earth; and, what is more, he purposely brings his airy forces down to meet its attack.

Critics have found one fault with Rostand which incidentally bears witness to the truth of what I have just said. They have complained of an unevenness of tone in certain plays: they would like, for instance, to separate from the rest the first act of **Les romanesques** so that it might be given alone. They object to the introduction in subsequent scenes, of a realistic, every-day element such as the unedifying quarrel between the fathers of the young people, which seems out of harmony with the purely poetic atmosphere of what procedes. But, however unfortunate this unevenness of tone may be in itself, it is due to an idea which, from the philosophic point of view, has its merits. With a characteristically French love of what Nisard calls "unevérité d'application," Rostand believes that ideals worthy of the name should stand the contact of life, and the effect of this belief is to make his characters deeper and more human.

How this contact with life is made, a beautiful line from **La princesse lointaine** will show. "On finit," says one of the characters,

> On finit par aimer tout ce vers quoi l'on rame

[One finishes by loving all that towards which one strives];

and the same thought is reaffirmed in **Chantecler** by the expression:

> L'effort, qui rend sacré l'être le plus infime.

[Effort, which makes the tiniest being sacred.]

These lines contain a profound psychological truth; to strive is to love the object of our striving, and by virtue of the effort we make we may fortify and shape for service a lofty inspiration. And it is through the operation of this truth that the ideals of Rostand's heroes are made livable.

The physical arrangement of the plays confirms this statement. It will be noticed that the big works, with the possible exception of *L'aiglon,* all affect a peculiar form of plot. In part, in general outline, they are merely tests of character. They consist of three parts. In the first part the hero takes a stand, and in the third or last, he holds very much the same position as before. In the meanwhile, however, he has been subjected to a salutary struggle. It is in the second or middle part that Rostand takes cognizance of the earth. Here he exposes his characters to an onslaught by material forces that tend to break down their lofty inspiration. He compels them to work and to suffer in defense of their ideals, and when at last they have made them secure, these ideals are stronger, nobler than before, confirmed and sanctified by the invigoration of effort and the beauty of sacrifice.

Let us take some examples. In *La princesse lointaine,* for instance, the main characters are filled with a mystic love. Joffroy Rudel and Bertran are enamored of the far-away princess whom they have never seen. Mélissinde, for her part, is given over to dreams of Rudel who sings of her in distant France, and she yearns "to reach beyond the vastness of the sea a sympathetic soul." Will this mystic love, this compound of imagination and aspiration, continue in the presence of reality? That is the question.

After an arduous journey made possible only by the enthusiastic devotion of the travellers, Bertran, leaving the sick Rudel on the galley, goes to fetch Mélissinde. He tells his errand and she understands it. But now, when body meets body and flesh meets flesh, they are both assailed by an earthly passion born of beauty of person and the luxury of an Eastern court. They are even reduced to tricking themselves. Suddenly a black sail is hoisted in the harbor. They think Rudel dead, that Rudel who has been confidently waiting for them with a look of ecstasy. Brought to their senses, they realize now how faithless they have been, not only to Rudel, but also—and especially—to their own souls. "Laissez-moi," says Mélissinde:

> . . . Laissez-moi! quels sentiments infimes!
> Voilà pourquoi, la chose horrible, nous la fîmes!—
> Mais puis-je t'accabler, malheureux, quand sur moi
> Je suis déçue hélas, encore plus que sur toi!
>
> [. . . Leave me! What low sentiments!
> That is why we did that horrible thing!—
> But can I crush you, wretched creature, when about myself
> I am deceived still more than about you!]

· · · · ·

> Hélas! grande inquiète, ô mon âme, où, comment
> Connaîtras-tu jamais l'entier rassasiement?
> Eternelle assoiffée, affamée immortelle,
> Le pain, où donc est-il? La source, où donc est-elle?
>
> [Alas! you are much uneasy, oh my soul, where, how
> Will you never know satiety?
> Eternally thirsty one, immortally famished one,
> Bread, where is it then? The spring, where is it then?]

The spell of earth is broken by this realization of its insufficiency. And when she learns that they were mistaken, that Rudel is still alive, Mélissinde, true once more to her supreme ideal, leaves her castle to go and console the poet's dying moments:

> Je viens vers toi! Je viens vers toi, Joffroy Rudel!
> Oui, je viens! Et tu m'es à cette heure dernière
> Plus cher de tout le mal que j'ai failli te faire!

> [I am coming to you! I am coming to you, Joffroy Rudel!
> Yes, I am coming! And you are to me at this last hour
> More dear on account of all the wrong that I was on the point of doing to you.]

La princesse lointaine is symbolic; *Cyrano de Bergerac* is real. In the first act Le Bret asks his friend:

> Mais où te menera la façon dont tu vis?
> Quel système est le tien?
>
> [But where will the way you live lead you?
> Which system is yours?]

To which Cyrano replies:

> J'errais dans un méandre;
> J'avais trop de partis, trop compliqués, à prendre;
> J'ai pris . . .
> LE BRET. Lequel?
> CYRANO. Mais le plus simple, de beaucoup.
> J'ai décidé d'être admirable, en tout, pour tout!
>
> [I was roving in a meander;
> I had too many courses, too complicated to take;
> I took . . .
> LE BRET. Which?
> CYRANO. But the most simple, by far.
> I decided to be admirable, on the whole, for all!]

Not five minutes later, the trials begin which will put this resolve to the test. Cyrano is tempted to sacrifice his friend Christian in order to possess Roxane, to alter his plays for the sake of having them produced, and to barter his conscience generally for material comfort and physical safety. I have already shown his attitude in the presence of these temptations and explained the triumphant cry of *quand même* with which the play ends. Cyrano himself recognizes his victory and dies content; and what is almost as important is the fact that this victory receives a beautiful confirmation from the lips of the Duke de Guiche, the great lord who has followed an opposite course, who has lived in a way to obtain what the world calls success, but who has not achieved satisfaction of the soul:

> Ne le plaignez pas trop: il a vécu sans pactes,
> Libre dans sa pensée autant que dans ses actes.
>
> [Do not be too sorry for him: he lived without contracts,
> Free in his thought as much as in his actions.]

"Oui," he continues, speaking to Roxane, who sees him to the door:

> . . . Oui, parfois je l'envie.
> —Voyez-vous, lorsqu'on a trop réussi sa vie,
> On sent—n'ayant rien fait, mon Dieu, de vraiment mal!—
> Mille petits dégoûts de soi, dont le total
> Ne fait pas un remords, mais une gêne obscure;
> Et les manteaux de duc traînent dans leur fourrure,
> Pendant que des grandeurs on monte les degrés,
> Un bruit d'illusions sèches et de regrets,
> Comme, quand vous montez lentement vers ces portes
> Votre robe de deuil traîne des feuilles mortes.
>
> [. . . Yes, occasionally I envy him.
> —You see, when one makes too much a success of one's life,
> One feels—having done nothing, my God, very wrong!—
> A thousand small disgusts about oneself, of which the total
> Does not form one remorse, but an obscure uneasiness;
> And the Duke's mantles drag along in their fur,
> While on account of greatness, one ascends the steps

A noise of barren illusions and of regrets,
As, when you slowly climb towards these doors
Your dress of mourning drags dead leaves.]

Generally speaking, there is something restrained, something quiet and internal in the pursuit of moral satisfaction, especially when it involves sacrifice. But Rostand's characters are not restrained: they are most often exuberant and noisy. Brilliant and showy, they are prompt of tongue, nimble of wit, and explosive of temperament. Though they possess the qualities of altruism, unselfishness and a steadfast devotion to immaterial ideals, theirs is no reticent or self-nourishing virtue. They feel the need of heroism, but of such a heroism as draws its strength, its protection, and its comfort from the éclat of dazzling expression and the glamor of excess. (pp. 155-62)

"Faire du luxe," that untranslatable phrase, expresses exactly the besetting sin of [Flambeau in *L'aiglon,* that] devoted, enthusiastic, and mad-headed old soldier; and it explains also that passion which, assuming different tones, animates Cyrano—Cyrano the admirer of Don Quixote, Cyrano who, for the mere beauty of the gesture, throws his full purse to the players, and Cyrano the ferocious duellist, who addresses a collective challenge to the audience of the theater. Flambeau, Cyrano, Chantecler, yes, even the weakling l'Aiglon, all "font du luxe." They all possess that exteriority, that love of effect, which the French designate by the word *panache.*

Rostand's own explanation of *panache,* though he restricts its meaning somewhat, does not conceal this love of effect:

> le panache n'est pas la grandeur, mais quelque chose qui . . . bouge au-dessus d'elle . . . c'est l'esprit de la bravoure . . . c'est comme un sourire par lequel on s'excuse d'être sublime . . . c'est souvent dans un sacrifice qu'on fait une consolation d'attitude qu'on se donne. Un peu frivole peutêtre, un peu théâtrale sans doute, le panache n'est qu'une grâce . . . mais . . . c'est une grâce que je nous souhaite.
>
> [*panache* is not greatness, but something which . . . stirs above it . . . it is the spirit of gallantry . . . it is like a smile by which one excuses oneself for being sublime . . . it is often in a sacrifice that one forms a consolation of attitude that one gives oneself. A little frivolous perhaps, a little theatrical without a doubt, *panache* is nothing but an indulgence . . . but . . . it's an indulgence that I wish for us.]

According to Rostand's own explanation, then, *panache* is unsubstantial. Therefore, we are, perhaps, surprised to see the author recommend so vigorously that which, by his own admission, is somewhat frivolous, somewhat theatrical. And especially does this *panache* seem out of keeping with the severe grandeur of the other elements with which it is associated in the character of his heroes. And yet, if we feel surprised, it is because we do not yet understand Rostand.

Philosophically considered, Rostand shows but little variety. He is not, like the writers of the seventeenth century, inspired by a spirit of observation to note objectively now this, now that, characteristic of man. He is not like Racine, he is not like Molière, he is not even in reality, very much like Corneille. Neither does Rostand resemble the writers of the present day, such as Hervieu, Curel, Donnay and the rest, who pick out now this, now that, belief or situation of the modern world to show by the logic of their plots its possibilities of sorrow or joy. Rostand draws characters, like the first; and, like

the second, he uses, to a certain extent, his plots to help bring out his meaning. But in both his character-drawing and his use of plot, he shows uniformity rather than diversity. His characters have a very marked family resemblance, and his plots all tend towards the same conclusion. Groping his way in his earlier works, then gradually becoming more and more sure of his direction in those that follow, he has moved towards a definite goal. He has but one single inspiration and his production shows it.

To begin with, Rostand was, no doubt, impelled to write by no more than a merely personal feeling. This Southerner with a dash of Spanish blood in his veins (his grandmother came from Cadiz), felt the need of expansion, of spiritual freedom, unfettered by the repression of material realities and the disheartening mockery of disillusion. In his *Musardises* (1887-1893) he evinces impatience with the cut-and-dried standards set up by unyielding doctrine or worldly success. . . . And some of the best poems are devoted to an underling of the teaching staff in his old school, a wretched, penniless drunkard whom the boys called *Pif-Luisant,* "shiny-nose." Rostand loved this man, not only for his sensitive appreciation of beauty and imagination, but also for his disdain of the rules of Boileau. The picturesque and familiar affection our poet bore him is well expressed in the lines with which he closes the first of the poems:

> Et si la mort t'a pris, ce qui vaut mieux peutêtre,
> Car tu ne souffres plus ni faim, ni froid cuisant,
> Dors tranquille, mon vieux, repose-toi, pauvre être,
> Toi que j'ai tant aimé . . . doux pochard . . . Pif-Luisant.
>
> [And if death took you, that would perhaps be better,
> Because you would no longer suffer hunger, nor sharp cold,
> Sleep tranquilly, old friend, rest yourself, poor being,
> You whom I loved so much . . . gentle drunkard . . . Pif-Luisant.]

In this same first volume of poems Rostand reveals a passion for color, for light and for the open air, and he pities the flowers grown in a city green-house:

> . . . les petites fleurs nostalgiques
> D'air pur, de lumière et de ciel.
>
> [. . . the little nostalgic flowers
> of pure air, light and sky.]

He shows further an extraordinary appreciation of contour and line, describing with remarkable distinctness, for instance, the cone of light shed by his study lamp. But he delights still more in reverie and in those delicate and fugitive sights that are the food of the spirit. . . . (pp. 163-65)

Even twenty years later, Rostand has not lost that vision in which the eye and the spirit collaborate; for it is he who speaks through Chantecler. Listen to the cock's description of things in the farmyard:

> See, the red of this geranium is never twice the same; and that wooden comb, the rake, where linger still a few hairs of the grass, how fair it is! And oh! how fair the pitchfork sleeping where it stands and dreaming of the summer hay! . . . To me an idle rake, a flower in its vase can give an ecstasy too deep for cure; and to the splendor of a morning-glory's bell I owe the rounded wonder of my eyes.

This impatience with the fetters of worldly standards, and this delight in freedom of the spirit soon took the shape of a resolve and a purpose. In the same *Musardises,* Rostand confesses to a

> . . . besoin moral
> De sentir un fond d'héroisme
> Au tableau le plus pastoral.

> [. . . moral need
> To feel a foundation of heroism
> in the most pastoral scene.]

And the application of this heroism is foreshadowed in the last poem of the collection, at least as it is now published. Meeting in his imagination Cervantes' old hero, Don Quixote, Rostand enters into conversation with him. He listens to the old Knight complaining of the modern world, a world given over to the reign of Sancho Panza and suspicious of "heroismes superflus", for, says Don Quixote:

> . . . la brise m'apporte
> Je ne sais quelle odeur de conscience morte
> Que n'aimerait pas Amadis.
> Moi qui ne vieillis pas, je sens vieillir l'Europe.

> [. . . the breeze brings me
> I don't know what odor of dead conscience
> That would not love Amadis.
> I, who does not age, I feel the aging of Europe.]

The poet is so moved by these words that he promises this "colporteur d'ideal" to help him cross the Pyrenees. He promises even more. Don Quixote has been driven out of Europe by ridicule, by laughter and by the smile that kills all generous enthusiasm. Rostand will take it upon himself to rehabilitate Don Quixote and to carry himself into France that which has been the greatest butt of ridicule, *viz.,* Don Quixote's helmet.

As early as 1893, then, before he had brought out any of the works for which he is now famous, Rostand seems to be conscious of a sociological purpose. He appears to feel that he will one day serve mankind, that he will battle against the forces of ridicule for the right to express generous impulses, and to express them with enthusiasm, yes, even with ostentation. Two years later appeared *La princesse lointaine,* and two years after that *Cyrano de Bergerac.* In both, the same idea prevails. *La princesse lointaine* contains the significant line:

> La seule vertu c'est l'enthousiasme

> [The only virtue is enthusiasm]

and Cyrano de Bergerac is the apotheosis of *panache* in the service of a lofty ideal. By 1903 all doubt has become impossible, for at this date Rostand gives us a formal statement of his views. What was at first merely a personal need he has by this time magnified to make of it a need of society as a whole. In his Discours upon being inducted into the French Academy, the same Discours in which appears the praise of *panache* already quoted, he speaks as follows:

> Le poison d'aujourd'hui . . . c'est l'essence délicieuse qui endort la conviction et tue l'énergie . . .

> [Today's poison . . . is the delicious essence which puts conviction to sleep and kills energy . . .]

It is "l'égoïsme narquois, la veulerie brillante" ["the cunning egoism, the glittering slackness"], and the enervating "silence du sourire" ["silence of the smile"].

It is just possible that Rostand had held this conviction from the outset, but had lacked either the technic or the opportunity to express it so directly. It is also possible, however—and more likely—that his reception into the Academy, or even the preparation of this Discours, led him to a more definite consciousness of his own ideas. However this may be, the fact remains that in his next work, *Chantecler,* he has brought out these ideas with a precision and clarity not to be found in any earlier play. *Chantecler* may almost be defined as a dramatization of the Discours. For the first time, the scene is laid in our own day; the animals are admittedly used to represent men and women; and we find in the play even that element of personal history which I have sought to trace, since Rostand himself has said:

> Mon coq n'est pas, à proprement parler, un héros de comédie. C'est le personnage dont je me suis servi pour exprimer mes propres rêves et faire vivre devant mes yeux un peu de moi-même.

> [My cock is not, properly speaking, a comic hero. It is the character which I used to express my own dreams and make live in my eyes a little of myself.]

In this play, enervating ridicule or *blague* (the Blackbird), malevolent flattery (the Toads), selfish indulgence (the Pheasant), all the forces that destroy the instinct and the expression of idealism, lay waste the powers of Chantecler. No more surprised by joy, bereft of the courage to proclaim the glory of his song, the cock is on the point of losing faith in his mission. Happily, the song of the nightingale wakes him from his torpor. Once more, he feels with Shelley, that call "to sympathy with hopes and fears" he heeded not. He is himself again, and when the pheasant shows him that day has risen uncalled by his crowing, he will not accept this isolated, accidental demonstration. His is the greater, the ideal world:

> Mon destin est plus sûr que le jour que je vois.

> [My destiny is more sure than the day that I see.]

If the dawn has come, it is because there still hung in the heavens some of his song of yesterday. "I am," he says, "the cock of a more distant sun. My crowing tears in the night those wounds of light that men call stars. I myself shall not see the splendor of an everlasting day. But if I sing full-throated and true, and if after me for many years each farm has a cock to crow within its yard, I believe there will be no more night."

Thus Chantecler emerges from his experience stronger, more convinced than ever. What was at first instinctive is now conscious. He has not only recovered his exuberant idealism, he has, in addition, acquired the determination to cling to it, to revel in it, as the one great principle of life, for

> . . . celui qui voit son rêve mort
> Doit mourir tout de suite ou se redresser plus fort.

> [. . . he who sees his dream die
> Must die at once or rise to greater strengths.]

The will to enthusiastic idealism, undeterred by ridicule or by material opposition, such, then, is Rostand's message. It is true that, judged by certain standards, his plays have their faults. Rostand is too Southern, too brilliant, too sensitive, perhaps, to neglect the methods, nay, even the tricks, discovered by technicians of the stage. He moves his audiences primarily, not by an appeal to the mind, but through their senses and their emotions. Perhaps even, as some affirm, he is incapable of deep psychological analysis. And for these faults he has been severely criticized. It is possible, however, that, all things considered, his plays are not only the most beautiful, but also the most beneficial product of contemporary drama. He advances no arguments and, except in the most general way, he attacks no specific problem. But he does something greater. Holding thousands of spectators spellbound in the contemplation of artistic beauty and awakening in them a potent sympathy for that which is exuberantly, frankly unselfish and high-minded, he creates a state of feeling that is more powerful than argument and may deal generously, nobly with every problem. (pp. 165-68)

A. G. H. Spiers, "Rostand as Idealist," in Columbia University Quarterly, *Vol. XX, No. 2, April, 1918, pp. 155-69.*

WILLIAM LYON PHELPS (essay date 1920)

[*An American critic and educator, Phelps was for over forty years a lecturer on English literature at Yale. His early study* The Beginnings of the English Romantic Movement *(1893) is still considered an important work and his* Essays on Russian Novelists *(1911) was one of the first influential studies in English of the Russian realists. From 1922 until his death in 1943 Phelps wrote a regular column for* Scribner's Magazine *and a nationally syndicated newspaper column. During this period, his criticism became less scholarly and more journalistic, and is notable for its generally enthusiastic tone. In the following excerpt, Phelps evaluates Rostand's achievement as a dramatist and the reasons for the depreciation of his works by French critics.*]

[One man of genius] is better than many manikins; and modern France has contributed to the literature of the world the greatest play since the days of Shakespeare, and the greatest drama since Goethe's *Faust.* From any and every point of view, Edmond Rostand is a giant. He is great in so many different ways—great as poet, dramatist, playwright, wit, humorist, romantic idealist, satirist; and as a language-virtuoso he is equally supreme. His dramatic works consist of six plays—three minor, three major; they are a permanent addition to literature; they contain characters that will last as long as the best of Victor Hugo and the best of old Alexandre Dumas, which means they will last as long as good books are read.

It is astonishing how much one man can give to his country; it is true that three plays by Rostand are not only worth all the plays written by other Frenchmen during the last thirty years, but that they represent a creative splendour in the theatre that has not been witnessed since Shakespeare. The first night of *Cyrano* was the greatest first night on any stage within the memory of living man; the first night of *Chantecler* was the prime news of the world.

Just as Normandy produced those bitter realists, Flaubert and Guy de Maupassant, whose novels and tales so perfectly illustrate the heart-killing climate of their native land, so our glorious romantic poet came from the South, and the sunshine that flooded his childhood glows on every page of his dramas. It is strange that his works should be so inspiring, for his heroes are always beaten, his best plays are all tragedies; yet, as one critic said, "Death in Rostand is more cheerful than Life in Maeterlinck." (pp. 247-49)

In the "Vorspiel auf dem Theater" to *Faust,* Goethe, in language that is as applicable in 1920 as it was when written, allows three persons to present their views. The eternal divergence of the three, and the necessity of some combination of all, have been presented with such profound wisdom and understanding of both the theatre and human nature, that no one has added anything valuable to it for a hundred years. The three debaters are the Manager, the Poet, and the Clown. The Manager insists on a play of action, that will really interest all the varieties of men and women that make up the audience; the Poet insists on Idealism, Romance, and Beauty, for the people must not only be uplifted, they must be transported; the Clown wants to make them laugh, even if it ruins the piece. The plays of Shakespeare—that is, the best of them—supremely illustrate the triple combination. They are full of poetry and beauty, alive with humour, and swift in action. The audience is amused, is excited, and is inspired.

No modern dramatist has reached this Shakespearean level except Rostand. He is equally great as poet, as humorist, as practical playwright. No man of our time has been such a creative force in literature, and possessed such a knowledge of the requirements of the stage. It is inspiring to read his dramas, as many millions of readers know; but it is even more inspiring to see his plays performed, for they were all written for the stage. The sheer dexterity of the first act of *Cyrano,* the way the throngs of people are brought in and brought off the stage, the way the general confused excitement rises to one tremendous climax, would be a model for playwrights, even if the piece were not literature. As every one knows, Cyrano fights a duel while composing a ballade, exhibiting equal skill with his hand and with his mind. It is symbolical of the author; in the very whirlwind of action, he gives us exquisite poetry.

There was a foretaste of this power in *Les romanesques,* which is a little masterpiece, and which, despite its eclipse by the later works, continues to hold the French stage, and perhaps will never become obsolete. It is beautiful, it is charming, it is humorous, but above all it is interesting. Most pieces submitted to managers are either specimens of good literary composition with no action, or else melodramas or farces of no literary value. In writing *Les romanesques,* Rostand wisely forsook subjects of temporary interest in sociology or politics, and based his work on the fundamental and therefore permanent things in human nature. In the poem "Transcendentalism," Browning compares the writer of a treatise on plants with the magician who fills a room with roses. He leaves us in no doubt as to which of these methods should characterise the poet. Many authors of modern analytical plays are like students of botany; Rostand creates flowers. He is a poet and a playwright; but above all he is a magician.

It is true that in *La princesse lointaine* and in *La Samaritaine* the poet transcends the playwright; but one of these was an experiment in tragedy, and the other a contribution to religious thought. They both helped him to write *Cyrano de Bergerac.*

In the year 1842, Browning published a lyric called "Rudel to the Lady of Tripoli." The fact that Rostand chose the same subject for *La princesse lointaine* is not important; but it is important to observe, how, not only in this play, but in *Cyrano* and in *Chantecler,* Browning's philosophy of "Success through Failure" is illustrated. The English poet and the French dramatist have much in common; they were preoccupied with love, real love; they believed that the highest success comes only through failure; they represented their teachings of optimism mainly through Tragedy. Browning might have written English words corresponding to the dying speech of Joffroy:

Ah! je m'en vais,—n'ayant à souhaiter plus rien!
Merci, Seigneur! Merci, Mélissinde!—Combien,
Moins heureux, épuisés d'une poursuite vaine
Meurent sans avoir vu leur Princesse lointaine!

[Ah! I am dying,—having nothing more to desire!
Thank you, Lord! Thank you, Mélissinde!—How many,
Less happy, exhausted from a vain pursuit
Die without having seen their Faraway Princess!]

During the last decade of the nineteenth century, plays founded on the Bible became increasingly frequent. Oscar Wilde's *Salomé* (1893), Rostand's **La Samaritaine** (1897), Sudermann's *Johannes* (1898), Stephen Phillips's *Herod* (1900) are typical illustrations of a growing fashion. The most poetic and the most reverent is certainly **La Samaritaine,** though it lacks the dramatic intensity of Wilde's short piece. The only reason why it disappoints is because no one has ever yet been able to retell a Bible story and improve it. The simplicity of the Bible narratives cannot be matched. For Rostand's verse, in all its glory, is not arrayed like one of these.

Yet **La Samaritaine** is a tenderly beautiful tribute paid by a man of genius; and I shall always regret that I never heard the melodious poetry spoken by the voice of gold.

Rostand himself was more than satisfied by the success of the play. In the printed version, he has the following foreword: "I thank Madame Sarah Bernhardt, who was a Flame and a Prayer . . . the Parisian public, whose earnestness, emotion, and intelligent excitement in responding to my most subtle meanings, have once more reassured the Poets; the Critics, who gave me noble support."

Have once more reassured the poets—it is as a rule only the minor and the unsuccessful poets who complain of the public attitude toward their work. The public is disposed to greet with enthusiasm poems of genius—nearly all great poets are properly "placed" by the public during their lifetime. The tiny poets who attack the public for not praising and appreciating their efforts would have no complaint to make if they could write better.

It is a curious thing, in the present high tide of the drama, and remembering that the glory of English literature is its poetry, that we have no great modern English dramas in verse. It is all the more remarkable because the foremost modern French dramatist and the foremost modern German dramatist wrote their masterpieces in verse form—*Cyrano de Bergerac* by Rostand and *Die versunkene Glocke,* by Hauptmann. John Masefield, when he writes plays, writes them in prose, with only slight exceptions. And so, for the most part have Synge, Yeats, Lord Dunsany and others. George Meredith might have written poetic dramas in the Elizabethan manner. Thomas Hardy's *Dynasts* is an intellectual, rather than a poetic masterpiece—it has nothing of the sublime, emotional, thrilling, transporting power of Rostand. We admire the author's mind more than the work.

Rostand was not an unconscious or an accidental Romantic. He had his own programme, and his six plays represent it. He lifted the French drama and the French spirit out of the Slough of Despond, and led them, like Greatheart, toward the Celestial City. He was disgusted with the cynicism, the sensuality, the mockery that many had come to believe were the true representation of modern French literature. In the

year 1912, I read an article by a French critic who said that nowadays the only possible intelligent attitude toward the so-called "great problems" of life was a smile. In the same year I read a good-tempered criticism of a new play in Paris, where the critic said with a yawn, "After all, Flesh is the Queen of Paris. And if there were any God, he would certainly treat our Paris as he treated Sodom and Gomorrah."

The prevailing tone of *blague* ["humbug"] was insupportable to Rostand. He knew that France needed an awakening. His plays, poems, and addresses were one protest against Mockery—when he was received into the French Academy on 4 June 1903, his speech was a call to arms, "The poison of today, with which we have no longer the right to drug the people, is that delicious essence that stupefies conviction and slays energy. We must restore passion. Yes, and emotion, too, which really is not absurd. We must remind these timid Frenchmen, who are always afraid of not being sufficiently ironical, that there can be plenty of modern wit in a resolute eye."

Little did he know how soon the spirit that he incarnated in himself, and in his poetry would be needed to save his country from slavery. Apart from the literary elevation of his dramas, *Cyrano de Bergerac* during the years of horror was worth to France a dozen generals and a million men. All the world wondered at the spirit of desperate valour and astounding tenacity exhibited by "decadent" France. But she had been regenerated by the spirit of her great poet, and the opportunity revealed the truth.

In spite of, and partly because of, his popularity, many French critics have refused him a place in the front rank. The very spirit that he fought was bound to sneer at him, knowing that the two could not live together. But that is not the chief reason for so much French depreciation. It is because, he, like Victor Hugo, fought not merely against the schoolmen, but against the national literary instinct. Many Frenchmen have never admitted the greatness of Victor Hugo, though he is one of the idols of the world; they still believe that his work is fustian. I remember in 1903 a French literary man telling me in all seriousness that Victor Hugo was mere sound and fury, signifying nothing; nor did he refer to *Ruy Blas* and *Hernani:* he said, "Fifty years hence every line of Victor Hugo will be forgotten, while Flaubert will be greater than ever." For my part, I cannot see why Frenchmen should not be proud of both; why should admiration for one lessen the other's glory? But your true Frenchman loves the lapidary style; and for this reason, many French critics cannot see Rostand, while others perhaps are afraid to surrender. I am going to quote a letter that I received from a distinguished French novelist and essayist, who is just now known all over the world. I had sent him a criticism of the theatres of Paris I wrote in 1912, which I had written after seeing five or six typical triangle plays, followed by a performance of *L'aiglon.*

21 April 1912.

I thank you for the article which you were kind enough to send me. I read it with great interest and I sympathise with your point of view. I believe your strictures are both fair and sound. But the only author whom you praise—Rostand—is one of those whom I most strongly condemn. If it is true (and I firmly believe it to be) that the theatre ought to be the mirror of its time, I cannot reproach the Parisian theatres of the boulevards for representing the brutal lack of morality characteristic of the society there represented. And from this point of view, I regard a Bataille as the most significant of the Parisian playwrights; for the best represents the moral anarchy and the extreme refinement of intelligence, where we now find the élite (a worldly élite) of an old people, very artistic, very human and very corrupt. I can consider him (and I do consider him) as an enemy; I hope for the destruction of the society that he represents: but I recognise his art and his sincerity: he does his duty like an artist: he is true to life. The Rostand of *L'aiglon* and of *La princesse lointaine* is not. The soul of his dramas consists of fanfaronnade, declamation, false heroism, false love, every sentiment false. He is a brilliant virtuoso. His work, often defective, has always éclat; but he is at his best only with the fantasies of a pianist: whenever he wants to give a fine phrase of Beethoven, a simple and profound sentiment, his inadequacy and his superficiality appear. Nor am I less severe toward the interpreter of *L'aiglon,* this Sarah Bernhardt, for I regard her as an evil influence on the French poetic drama. The radiance of her fame throws an illusion over her lack of naturalness, her faulty diction, her foreign accent, her real coldness, and her monotonous, hammered-out art. I am willing to believe that her defects are exaggerated by age; but it is precisely her defects that people admire and imitate. She has done a great deal of harm, and she makes matters worse by her deplorable taste in preferring false, offensive poetry. The hero of my novel and his author will never forgive her.

Although I have read many adverse French criticisms of Rostand, I think this letter is not only the ablest, but that the opposition to his work,—generally felt among French critics— is here expressed in an extraordinarily concise way. Although I totally disagree, it is perfectly clear why the writer of it, and so many of his fellow-countrymen, take that position. Rostand offends against their classic theories of art, their love of the sober and the self-restrained, their decided preference of irony over enthusiasm—sure mark of sophistication; they like smiles, but they hate laughter. It is for the same reason that Mr. Santayana, wholly Latin in blood and ideals, cannot endure the poetry of Browning. His poems "not only portray passion, which is interesting, but they betray it, which is odious."

But there is a great, outstanding fact to be accounted for—the conquest of the world by *Cyrano de Bergerac.* To realise now the unparalleled enthusiasm of the first night, I refer readers to Catulle Mendès; that grown-up gamin of the Boulevards, who could give any man in the world lessons in blague, skepticism, indecency and insolence, was swept into the seventh heaven of rapture—he preserved not only his own impressions in print, but collected others. The delight of the audience was so uncontrolled that the play could hardly get on— the nearest approach to it in America is the behaviour of the spectators when a touchdown is made in a football game. The applause in the theatre on that memorable night was heard next day in the remotest parts of the earth. The play appeared on every foreign stage—over half a million copies of the French text have been sold, and it has been translated into all languages. While I am writing these words, converts are being made in many countries. For the book goes everywhere.

Rostand, taking an almost forgotten historical figure, (I remember in my youth reading Henry Morley's edition of *Gul-* *liver's Travels,* with its interesting appendix on *Cyrano de Bergerac*), created a new, imperishable character in drama and in literature. Critics may sneer at Rostand's art, they may attempt to "account" for him in every way but the one true way, but they can no more drive Cyrano off the earth than they can get rid of d'Artagnan, Jean Valjean, or Falstaff. He has come to stay.

Even those who attack Rostand are puzzled by the variety and multiplicity of his accomplishments; he has all the grandeur and impromptu power of Victor Hugo, but then he abounds in what Hugo had not a trace of—humour. He has grace, dexterity, flexibility, word-magic; he uses the rigid form of the Alexandrine and makes it supple; he reaches the vertiginous heights of sublimity, heroism, self-sacrifice, and adds to the Genius of Romance the Genius of Humour. All kinds of humour—for he can defeat his rivals and leave them the choice of weapons.

It is amusing to see the critics trying to explain this. M. Blum, a French dramatic critic, says that Rostand is not a man of genius, but an extraordinary collection of diverse talents, seldom united in one person.

M. Adolphe Brisson once made a pilgrimage to Cambo, to see if he could find out from the author the reason for Cyrano's world conquest. On his way he meditated as follows, as he reports in the last chapter of *Le théâtre et les mœurs:*

> That we loved, applauded, acclaimed *Cyrano,* nothing is easier to understand; the beauties of the work justify all that. But that from day to day it spread immediately all over the world, that it was translated into all languages, played not only in large cities, but in the smallest towns and in America, and that everywhere it excited the same enthusiasm; that three hundred thousand copies of the book (1906), something unprecedented, should have been sold all over the earth, that the name of the author traversed the globe with the rapidity of a flash of lightning—all this is unique and calls for an explanation. For, after all, we have other masterpieces as brilliant, as clever as *Cyrano.* Why have they not had the same good fortune? Fame is an honest fellow, who usually walks with slow steps, and ordinarily does not place a crown except on brows mature, with whitening hair. Why, when *Cyrano* appeared, did Fame suddenly grow dizzy?

Then, being shown in the presence of M. et Mme. Rostand, he plumped the question direct, "What is there in *Cyrano* to account for its sudden universal conquest? What is it exactly that foreigners find in it?" Rostand himself had no explanation to offer; he could not explain, said M. Brisson, why it was that his piece produced exactly the same effect on people quite different, the English, the Danish, the Slavs, the Turks, the Heidelberg philosopher, and the pork-packer from Cincinnati.

> Was it the classic simplicity of the intrigue, the mingling of wit and courage, what we call *le panache,* the generosity of the hero, the contrast between his physical ugliness and his moral nobility, this antithesis which pleases men because they think that they all have something of it themselves? But these features exist in other works: Triboulet came before Cyrano, and in the plays of de Musset, there is not less feeling, French sprightliness, fantasy—*Alors. . . .*
> Mme. Edmond Rostand, who listened to my disser-

tation with a little, half-mocking smile: "There are people who exhale all around them sympathy, simply because they have charm. Don't you think it may be the same with things of the mind?" *Parbleu,* that is the best explanation, the true one! It explains nothing and it is the best one. For I believe that a work of art has a soul belonging to it, which attracts or repels, and arouses passionate feeling. One may surrender, be vanquished by a painting, a statue, a poem. Between fifteen and twenty years of age I was hopelessly in love with the Mona Lisa.

Richard Mansfield gave an admirable and highly intelligent performance of *Cyrano de Bergerac* in America; M. Le Bargy reached unexpected heights; no one will perhaps ever reach the perfection attained by Coquelin, who was a great artist, ideally fitted to the part, and who had the advantage of long and intimate discussions with the author; but the piece will never be lost to the stage, and will always awaken enthusiasm. (pp. 255-71)

No man has a soul so dead that it cannot be stirred by *Cyrano.* Its combination of lyrical beauty, passion, wit, sentiment, humour, enthusiasm, tragic force, pathos, united in one divine transport of moral beauty—the Soul! Even under those ribs of death, the boards of the French stage, Rostand awakened a soul. And in the autumnal garden, amid the falling leaves, and the chill of death, we hear the voice of that which alone is as sublime as the stars,—the human spirit.

For in all three plays we have Triumphant Failure.

Professor Nitze quotes a poem written by Rostand which was published only a few hours after his death, and harmonises with the spirit in all his work.

A scene from L'aiglon *presented at the Paris Opéra.*

Qu'un peuple d'hier
Meure pour demain,
C'est à rendre fier
Tout le genre humain!

I know I ought not to translate this, but I cannot help trying.

That yesterday's Race
Should die for to-morrow—
That gives a proud face
To all human sorrow!

Rostand did not select the figure of L'aiglon for any political or historical reason, but as an emblem of the frustration of humanity.

Grand Dieu! ce n'est pas une cause
Que j'attaque ou que je defend . . .
Et ceci n'est pas autre chose
Que l'histoire d'un pauvre enfant.

[Good God! it is not a cause
That I attack or that I defend . . .
And this is not anything
But the story of a poor child.]

The enormous difficulties of presenting *Chantecler* will probably militate against its life on the stage; but in many ways, both from the literary and spiritual point of view, it is Rostand's greatest work. We see as we saw in Wagner's *Meistersinger,* the undying hatred of every heaven-born genius for Pedantry and Affectation. Let the second-rate artists stick to the rules—they need them. Let the second-rate critics measure genius with the rules, they have no other standard. But the man of original creative power is always greater than the rules; as in the moral world, Love is greater than Law.

In the play *Chantecler,* the Peacock is like Beckmesser; the scene infallibly reminds one of the part played by the picayune pedant in the music-drama. In that famous afternoon tea—the greatest "party" ever known in literature, Victor Hugo might have poured out his scorn on the pedants and the prudes and the parlour poets; he might too have thought of the sublime scene where the Cock protects the venomous cowards from the hawk; but he could not even have imagined the marvellous humour that follows the terrific fight, like sunshine after storm. The guests are all going; Chantecler, with a fine *mot,* departs with the hen pheasant; the Guinea-hen hostess, just as the curtain is about to fall, says, "This is the most successful fête ever known!" Then, amid the *brouhaha* of leave-taking, the solemn Magpie-Usher announces an arrival:

The Tortoise!

and the curtain falls.

As every one knows, Rostand conceived the idea of this drama merely by gazing, in the course of a country walk, at a barn-yard. These humble creatures displayed human nature to the imaginative eyes of the poet.

In 1901, while taking a walk in the outskirts of Cambo, I was passing a humble farm when I suddenly stopped before the barnyard. It was just an ordinary barnyard, containing the usual pigeon loft, wire nettings, manure pile, and within, the animals, hens, ducks, guinea-fowl, geese, turkeys, a cat asleep, a dog wandering about; in brief, a common spectacle. I watched with interest, when suddenly in stalked the cock. He entered proudly, boldly, like a ruler, with disdain in his eye, and a certain rhythmic movement of the head which produced the irresistible impression of a hero. He advanced like a buccaneer, like a man in quest of adventure, a king among his subjects. In a flash I saw in this spectacle a play. I returned to the barnyard many times, and rapidly the framework of the play was constructed in my mind.

That afternoon walk was a great day in the history of literature.

We must go back to La Fontaine for anything approaching this human manipulation of the animal kingdom; and Rostand rises higher than either La Fontaine or Rudyard Kipling. For the old fabulist indicated our undeniable likeness to the instinctive selfishness of the beasts; Kipling drew his usual lesson of industry and practical wisdom; Rostand gave us a spiritual interpretation of life.

Chantecler is man doing his work in the world, doing it anyhow, doing it for the sake of the work finally, rather than for the reward; doing it first conceitedly, then despairingly, finally triumphantly. For work is more necessary to the worker than to any possible recipient of its product. The Hen-Pheasant is jealous of his absorption in his career, she wants him to put love-o' women first, but in the end she is glad to die for him. The dog is a philosopher, and a good fellow. The guinea-hen is a stupid social climber, cursed with affectations. The nightbirds prefer darkness to light, because their works are evil. The blackbird is the Parisian mocker—he may be either critic or dramatist.

The oftener one reads the three masterpieces of Rostand, the greater they seem. And curiously enough, although they abound in individual and scattered jewels of wit, wisdom and poetry, the whole is greater than the parts. In considering this unique personality, many are amazed and many doubt. But the optimism of the man should find a vibrating response in the mind of the reader. It is beyond all expression fortunate that such genius should have been given to the world, that France should have had the honour of producing a writer worthy to rank with the giant Elizabethans in England; but it is still more fortunate that, despite the nibbling tooth of criticism, the whole world should have given him homage. For he spoke directly to the conscience, the spirit, the religious life of man; the universal acclaim that greeted his voice, is proof that under all the materialism and selfishness and vulgarity and baseness of the human race there is a Soul. (pp. 273-78)

> *William Lyon Phelps, "Edmond Rostand," in his* Essays on Modern Dramatists, *The Macmillan Company, 1921, pp. 229-78.*

ELEANOR W. THOMAS (essay date 1921)

[*In the following excerpt, Thomas examines the nature of Rostand's romanticism.*]

Very early M. Rostand wrote an **"Essai sur le roman sentimental et le roman naturalist,"** and when only eighteen composed **Les romanesques,** a happy, easy little farce, which viewed seriously is an examination of the nature of the romantic. The stage direction reads: "The scene is where you will, provided the costumes are pretty." Here, at once, we meet something very unlike the minutely described and strongly localized scenes of the naturalist, his kleinmalerei. Yet the two acts which follow seem to be a burlesque of ro-

mantic comedy: the two young lovers thinking to emulate Romeo and Juliet, find themselves but the marionettes worked by too cruel and too clever fathers, and disillusioned they agree "Our poor poesy was mockery. In bursting thus before our wondering eyes, fair iridescent bubble, you are no more than a little soapsuds spattering on one's nose." Percinet's gallant rescue of Sylvette from the abducting brigand was but a mock rescue from the hired Straforel. Percinet then runs away in search of real adventure and receives many actual buffets, encounters actual dangers, and returns in rags to save Sylvette from a seemingly determined lover, the disguised Straforel. On the realization that this second rescue of a fair lady by her daring lover was but another hoax planned to gain for Straforel his delayed pay, the lovers wake up to what constitutes real romance: "Poetry, you see, is in the hearts of lovers; it comes not solely from adventures. We were fools to seek it elsewhere when it was within us." Here, then, Rostand is leaving burlesque and indicating something of the real nature of the romantic: it is subjective—"When the soul loves, she can embroider true flowers on a false woof." In the end, however, Sylvette craves indulgence for the piece, in a rondel, making fun of the conventional elements of the libretto:

> Old wall, lovers, scented thymes,
> Costumes light and easy rhymes,
> A swordsman dight in a gay mantello.

In this first play of Rostand's appears one trait of his romanticism: its literary flavor. He never hesitates to call to his assistance the suggestions of romantic art known by all; here it is *Romeo and Juliet,* but Juliet's abduction arranged as in a Watteau picture, for the romantic past suggested is not of the sixteenth, but of the eighteenth century, when men fondly imagined themselves fine figures in velvet and lace observing the rules of the game in a garden planned by LeNotre. Frolicking as the play is, it yet reveals characteristics of the author's romanticism which his greater works develop.

On April 5, 1895, at the Theatre de la Renaissance, Sarah Bernhardt and Jean Coquelin presented **La princesse lointaine,** the first work of Rostand's to prove his genius and to place him among leading romanticists. The source of the story is the twelfth century history of Joffroy Rudel, the troubadour of Provence, whose great love for the unseen and far away Mélissinde, the Lady of Tripoli, inspires his friend, the knight Bertrand, and a company of pirates, to sail with him to the East that he might catch one sight of his Lady before death closed his eyes forever. Arrived at Tripoli, Bertrand goes ashore to beseech the Lady to visit his dying friend. There he is mistaken by Mélissinde for the poet, rumors of whose love have come to her, is loved by her, and though bound straitly by his loyalty to Rudel, he loves in return. A black sail seen through the window leads them to think the poet dead, but when they find the ominous sail to be on another ship, remorse seizes them for unfaithfulness, and they reach Rudel in time for him to lift Mélissinde into the unreal world of the verge extreme of love where he dwells, so that upon his death, in an ecstacy of devotion, she and Bertrand renounce each other.

The story and its treatment reveals many elements of romanticism. It is in medieval romance that we find again and again the motive—an idealizing love for a princess never to be won—and it is medieval romance, too, which lends such incidents as Mélissinde's giving of her sleeve to Bertrand, and his killing of the goblin knight, dight so richly in green armor.

The mariners reach a land with golden beach and silver fringe of waves, whence comes the sweet fragrance of myrtles. Here later nineteenth century romanticism is responsible for the character of the details. It is a red city which lies beneath a glowing sky; Mélissinde with her lilies and bandeau of pearls suggests Rossetti, while her long hair falling in its golden wealth over the dying poet brings to mind Maeterlinck's Melisande, though the black sail conjures up the dying Tristan and the splendid approach of the Princess in her barge reminds us of that black browed beauty of Egypt floating down the Cydnus not to comfort a poet but to conquer a warrior. The closing of the window through which happiness sees duty is the sort of detail the Symbolist loves. Romantic allusion abounds, and the story embodies the theme chiefly loved by romance: that of the undaunted pursuit of an ideal, of a passion fully lived up to after the manner of passions in the world of romance. Rudel sings:

> O Love supreme that burns
> Hopeless of Love's returns;
> Tireless by night it yearns,
> And day!
> With such vain dreams that are
> Loftier than life can mar
> I love the Princess far Away.

Only romance recognizes such self devotion as that of the troubadour and such exaggerated faithfulness as leads to the final renunciation of Bertrand and Mélissinde. Yet in the midst of the exaggeration, how much of the truth of romance does Rostand give us: the influence of the ideal, of the worship of the something afar. To the scepticism of the spirit of negation, the physician Erasmus, who, however, looks less wise without cap and gown, Father Trophime affirms that "Humble folk admire what is great, and feel, untaught, the poesy of things," and to the materialist's question, What's the use of romance? gives answer:

> Every ray from the ideal sent
> Into the soul destroys an evil there.
> All noble aims bring forth a nobler aim;
> No dream suggests a dream of lower flight;

· · · · ·

> Yes, I approve adventures aiming high,
> There's but a single vice: inertia!
> And but one virtue . . .
>   That?
>   Enthusiasm!

These last words strike a note of Rostand's romanticism sounded more loudly later in his masterpiece. Rudel dies and Bertrand and Mélissinde are to give up joy, but "it is something to have wept, to have done, to have watched, seen, smelt the mystic rose, something to be wiser than the world, to be sure of a desire."

La Samaritaine, written by Rostand to be performed in Passion Week in Paris in 1897, is interesting from the point of view of romance as harking back to such religious love poetry as the mystic, erotic love poems to the Virgin of the twelfth century, to the spirit of the troubadour Court of love, and to medieval mysticism in the Francis of Assisi teaching of human love as but a stepping stone to divine love. Here again is seen Rostand's tendency to employ the methods of an earlier literature to aid him in removing us from the world of the commonplace, of disillusion, into a region of faith where ideals are believed in as working principles.

Exquisite as was *La princesse lointaine,* it was the heroic comedy of 1897, *Cyrano de Bergerac,* which entitled Rostand to rank among the first French dramatists and among the great romancers. His choice of subject was most fortunate, for the life of Savinien Cyrano de Bergerac (1619-1655) abounded in the changes, the contrasts, and the interesting events which make romance and drama. Poet, satirist, philosopher, duellist, soldier, and lover, in the Paris of the great Cardinal Richelieu, the Paris made familiar to us by Dumas as throbbing with mystery and adventure, Cyrano had a career determined by a great passion and checkered through his own sensitive and uncompromising disposition. It was a theme fit for the poetic power and dramatic instinct of Rostand.

The very name of the play is one of those that sound sweet upon the tongue, while the drama to which it gives title has connection not with the romanticist school of the end of the nineteenth century but with an older school of high romance. Though closely related to seventeenth century French fiction, it strikes the vein of old French and Spanish literature, and draws us not into a Maeterlinckian world of lonely towers by iridescent pools where there are strange movings in the wind and whisperings of coming evil from hidden vaults beneath disease stricken castles, nor into a decadent world where love is an obsession, the sole motive and end of life, but into the chivalrous world of Cervantes, the Gascon life of adventure of Dumas, the Paris of cape and sword where the poet finds not only amourous wooing but also valorous fighting, where the hero does not ignore "la douceur feminine" ["feminine sweetness"] but fails not "à sonner les verités des éperons" ["to ring the truths of the spurs"]. Rostand is careful to pay tribute to his great masters: Cyrano takes off his hat to Don Quixote and suggests that battles with wind mill sails may land one in the mud—but perhaps project one to the stars, and it is D'Artagnan who makes his bow to Cyrano on his first appearance and then leaves to him the stage.

The stage, then, is one of colorful action where men forget their heaviness and take delight in a personage larger than human, strutting it may be with a swashing and a martial outside through most varied scenes. Walter Besant joins with others in exalting cheerfulness as the necessary mood of true romance; Stevenson insists on high spirit, action, as making the romantic, and Brunetiére writes of the probable appearance of a vortex of actions, a concourse of people. These traits we find in *Cyrano:* here is exuberance of life, enthusiasm, élan, experiencing of life and pronouncing it good. The Gascon cadets are introduced by Cyrano as lying and fighting without dismay, spouting of heraldry and arms, with veins a-brimming with blood so blue—historical characters renowned for wit, courage and love of women. And the flower of them is Cyrano, the dominant personage of romance, who sweeps all forward with the rush of his spirit, a great romantic character, with exaggerated motives and powers, yet real to us as one of the most lovable male characters of fiction. Amazingly versatile, he at one moment attracts us by his wit or by his fearless bravery, and the next receives our admiration for his tenderness, his concealment of deep wounds to his spirit by jests that sleep in knavish ears. He is the lineal descendant of the great heroes of romance above all as being—it has been well said elsewhere.—

Of them who in their lips love's standards wear.

These men who do deeds play their parts in great scenes; the bustling concourse of society gathered at the Hotel de Bourgogne; the picturesque rotisserie filled with idlers coming and going; the battle field of Arras—yet is it a battle field? for here we are present at a scene out of medieval romance with seventeenth century additions; and lastly, the quiet old convent garden amid falling leaves of autumn with nuns passing and re-passing and distant sounds of the organ. How at variance is this drama of stirring life with the doctrine of Hauptmann, who predicts that action upon the stage is to give way to analysis of character and exhaustive consideration of motives which prompt men to act, or with the plays of the Symbolists "where life reveals itself in static moments and is ever menaced by the unknown."

The art of the romancer is at one with that of the realist in the accuracy of the milieu of the comedy, for Rostand in *Cyrano* rivals Thackeray in *Henry Esmond* in a faithful reproduction of the scenes, the speech, the customs, and the ideals of the century he is reviving.

Medieval motives prominent in *Cyrano* are the love of woman already spoken of and the union of grotesque and sublime. It is only at death that the sense of humor of the man with the ludicrous nose allows him to tell the woman he has worshiped:

> Grace a vous une robe a passé dans ma vie.
> Toute ma vie est là.

The play again celebrates the worthiness of battle for the unattainable:

> Mais on ne se bat pas l'espoir du succési
> Non! non c'est bien plus beau lorsque c'est inutile.
>
> [But one doesn't fight in hope of success
> No! No it is much more beautiful when it is useless.]

Mr. Charles Renault thinks of Cyrano's *panache* as symbolic of a dash that scorns to gain, of a belief in grasping after the too remote:

> O'er truth and daring floats a plume
> That is no flaunting feather vain!
> It marks for ay the hero's doom,
> O'er truth and daring floats a plume!
> It nods o'er chisel, brush, and loom,
> And consecrates the poet's strain.

In *L'aiglon,* Rostand is attracted by the modern problem of the influence of heredity, and shows the son of Napoleon as weakened at crises in his career by recognition of his Austrian inheritance, and therefore failing to carry out high purposes. This naturalist's idea, though, is clothed in romantic garb. Characters and incidents are idealized, for men and women are capable here of extreme love and devotion and the scenes and events belong to the remote world of court intrigue and military plot. Most impressive of all is the early morning scene at Wagram where the Duke hears voices of the dead, then turns to bow to his fate as symbolized by the Austrian troop. In spite of indecision, the Duke is made in part of heroic material, while Flambeau, the Grenadier, has stepped out of old romance.

Chantecler which after being long heralded, was acted in 1910, is a play *sui generis,* and yet again, even though he is writing social satire, it is Rostand the romanticist whom we must study. Though the ideas and interests of the play are those of the present day literary and social world, Rostand gives to this world the charm of remoteness by placing it in a barnyard and a forest, where humanly loyal and humanly envious birds and beasts live comedy and tragedy. With few exceptions, the symbolism of the piece is obvious. The fops, the pedants, the cynics combine against the idealists Chantecler and his friend, Patou the dog, but our sympathies are enlisted on the side of the idealists. Patou growls against the satirist whose eye never brightens with wonder and admiration, and who would kill among us love by persiflage; or against the esthete who has not "the courage of colors on his wing." The blackbird, the witty critic, seems to him but a beastly little undertaker who, after burying Faith, hops with relief and glee. As for him, he desires escape—"the fresh illusion of lapping up the stars." Chantecler finds all the world interesting and sings in praise of the transforming power of the Sun:

> Artists who making splendid the great things
> Forgets not to make exquisite the small.
> O Sun, without whose golden magic, things
> Would be no more than what they are.

As in *La princesse lointaine,* the spirit of negation is reproved and Faith and Enthusiasm triumph, for even when Chantecler finds that it is not his voice which has brought forth the sun, he is happy in the belief that he will rouse sleepers to a new day, for always must there be "in the soul a faith so faithful that it comes back even after it has been slain."

The distinguishing note of the great romantic revival is thought by leading French critics to be individualism, the ego against society, the lyrical cry; Mr. Theodore Watts thinks it to be a "renascence of wonder". *Chantecler* is remarkable as combining both these notes with a tone not usually belonging to romanticism: a tone resulting from keeness of wit, cleverness of repartee, delicious satire, a satire at times hardly escaping mockery. And yet how close akin to the great nature odes of the romantic renascence of the early 1800's are Chantecler's magnificent hymns to the Sun and the wonderfully beautiful antiphonal of the birds in the serene silence and coolness of the forest at night when they chant their gratitude to the God of Little Birds and to His Gentle Saint, the good Saint Francis, the "tender dreamer of a generous dream."

From this examination of the plays of M. Rostand, we may arrive at certain general conclusions regarding the composition of his romanticism. In the first place, eclecticism is prominent. Though steering clear of goblins and fairies and weird and mystic and gloomy effects, Rostand shows the influence of most of the other phases of the romanticism of the past hundred years. Then, secondly, there appear in his dramas traits strange to romance differentiating his romanticism from that of others. M. Rostand therefore defies classification with any one school: too much of a romancer of the healthy adventure-loving type to be one of the Neo-romanticists, he is too literary, too exquisite, a little too much of the *fin de siècle* to be altogether of the old school.

Let us review some of the outstanding features of these two traits of his work as romanticist.

Very striking is his use of satire, the play of his humor, a certain lightness of touch. Though too full of zest for life ever to be bitter, it is as if M. Rostand said: "Come, let us not take our romance too seriously. After all there is a matter of fact view of all things, and do not be mistaken about me; I see the earthly connections of these things, but I choose to believe that it is wiser and better and truer to look upward to the stars. Nevertheless, the idealist has his laughable side. My young lovers, dreaming day dreams, are hoaxed; my poet needs a wise priest as apologist; it is Cyrano's wit and virility that must save him from sentimentalism; L'Aiglon is keen enough to jest, bitterly it may be, at his helplessness—though we do not wholly acknowledge that helplessness, and Chantecler has to rise above the fear of making a fool of himself in order to do his bit in the world." The virtue of this corrective use of humor appears with great appropriateness in the death scene of *Cyrano.* The hero feels the absurdity of a man with a ridiculous nose being the central figure of a beautifully arranged death, and his jests time and again save the situation from inferior sentiment until he dies smiling that he has kept to the end his brilliancy of wit, his gaiety of soul. Here are no fine large words about untarnished honor and eternal love.

In this attitude to romance, M. Rostand is at one with the Shakespeare of *Midsummer Night's Dream,* who revels in burlesquing his own art, yet teaches "the best in this kind are but shadows and the worst no worse if imagination but mend them."

A second trait of M. Rostand's work which distinguishes him from the Neo-romanticists and Symbolists of the later nineteenth century is the joyousness, the delight in activity, which springs naturally from the sanity of a wholesome mind and which vitalizes his best creations. Gossiping on romance, Stevenson praises its presentation of men who found "everything good which accompanied their stay on earth." Though he feels sadness, Cyrano is one of these and reminds us of Dumas' Fouquet: "l'homme de bruit, l'homme de plaisir, l'homme qui n'est que parsque les autres sont" ["the man of renown, the man of pleasure, the man who is only because the others are"]. Chantecler, the indomitable, sounds the clarion call to work and even the wraiths of the soldiers of Napoleon, still stirred by devotion to an idea, cry out of their old agony: "Vive l'Empereur" ["Long live the emperor"]. The enthusiasm of the poet vents itself in a lavish expenditure of himself which has struck critics not wholly friendly to him: Mr. Norman Hapgood wrote of *Cyrano* as "a brilliant exhibition of all that M. Rostand had on hand", and Mr. Henry James, realist of realists, was pleased by the happy ease of the author of *Les romanesques* and the succeeding more serious plays. In his youthful enjoyment of life, Rostand, though less robust, is a romantic in the excellent company of Scott and Dumas, and one hardly thinks that in the next world they will ever turn upon the creator of Cyrano with his own query: "Mais que diable allait-il faire en cette galère?" ["But what the devil was he doing there?"]

It is, too, this happy exuberance which causes Mr. Chesterton to comment on the excellence of *Cyrano* as "heroic comedy" [see excerpt dated 1903], for here there is not the spiritual breakdown of tragedy but a story with death as outcome made into comedy through the strength of man's spirit. The dramatist shares with us his belief that "merriment is one of the world's natural flowers, and not one of its exotics," and yet gives us "outbursts of a human sympathy and bravado as old and as solid as the stars." The critic well remarks that death is more joyful in Rostand than life is in Maeterlinck.

This genre, heroic comedy, links Rostand with the 1830's and Alfred de Musset and Victor Hugo rather than with later romanticists, just as his use of satire and artificial verse forms suggest Banville, and his combination of romance and satire, his power of fantastic embroidery in style, Pierre de Marivaut, the opponent of Voltaire.

M. Brunetière lists as a mark of French romanticism virtuosity, the gift enabling one to appropriate the inventions or the ideas of his contemporaries with a view to transforming them and giving them definite expression. To the virtuosity of M. Rostand attention has often been called. The theme of *L'aiglon* is the contemporary problem of heredity, but M. Rostand treats it in romance. So one motive of *Chantecler* is that beloved by our quarter-century, the relative parts in life of man and woman. Ascribing to the poet lack of originality, one critic of *Cyrano* goes so far as to say that the Gascon cadets rise from the dregs of Dumas's musketeers, and another speaks of Rostand's work as Hugo brought up to date. Dear as one may hold D'Artagnan and the Three Musketeers, Cyrano is surely of a finer brand, and Hugo's romantic dramas use medieval motives, or those of the eighteenth century school of Terror far more largely than Rostand's—remote spots, secret hiding places, the hero with sin scathed brow, courting violent death for the sake of love. In this respect of indebtedness to his predecessors, Rostand's work offers comparison with the Celtic revival of romance in drama for the Celtic plays of the past two decades are racy of the soil and seek to resurrent such simplicity as was the aim of our early nineteenth century romanticist. The writings of M. Rostand, however, are redeemed from smell of the lamp by their freshness of spirit and beauty of form and poetry. He is at one with other romanticists of recent years in perfection of form. Though in *Chantecler* a squib is shot at theories of art and the pedants are rendered most ridiculous, the author himself is, when at his best, complete master of stage craft and always great poet. Only in *L'aiglon* does he fall into the error to which romanticists are prone and present situations too highly ingenious and use symbols childishly apparent.

We have already noted the slight extent to which M. Rostand bases romantic appeal on the machinery of medievalism, differing in this from his great contemporaries, Maeterlinck and Stephen Phillips, and we found in his work the individualism and the idealism, the mood of aspiration, of the romantic. The last assumes varied phases, apparent as it is in *La princesse lointaine, Cyrano, L'aiglon* and *Chantecler.* One byproduct is the attitude to death so often found in old romance. A German student of the plays comments on how the three heroes all prefer "in das geheime Haus des Todes zu stürmen, ehe der Tod sich zu ihm wagt" ["to storm into the secret house of death, before death ventures forth to him"].

Coleridge laid down as principle of successful romance that it must produce a willing suspension of disbelief and so give illusion of reality. Does Rostand give such illusion? The answer must be in the negative, and yet we must grant that he hardly attempted such accomplishment. Rather with his own Manager of *Chantecler,* he requests those who sit before what he intends that they recognize as a curtain to allow him to raise it to show them the intersting things that are immediately behind it and perhaps to suggest to them the wonders of the blue distance beyond. After all, is it not an unanswered question, this of how to present the probable so that it seem not improbable, the impossible so that it seem possible? Sir Henry Irving reprimanded a stage hand for a poor imitation of thunder, and received the defense: "Please, sir, that wasn't me that made the noise. It's the real storm outdoors; it's ragin' so and I couldn't, hear you tell me when to begin."

We were told twenty years ago that *Cyrano de Bergerac* gave no true judgment of life. Are we as sure now that Rostand's idealism is not realism? At that time the Decadents of the fin de siècle were declaring the citizens of France inapt in public and private affairs, inefficient reproducers of future generations, incapable of the devotion of deep set faith. Since then have come the days, the months, the years of 1914-1917 and the world wide admiration for a France organized once more for victory, of a France blotting out Germanized thought and making clear to us as never before the meaning of the French *élan* [spirit], the French *ame* [soul], the French love for *la gloire* [glory], the French enthusiasm for the idea, an idea to be realized in a world made safe for Democracy largely through French self-devotion. Rostand, the romanticist, the idealist, the believer in a remoter Sun, has expressed for us something of the spirit of the men who worked the miracle of the Marne and who stood firm at Verdun, letting not the enemy pass. We have heeded his appeal: "Let us call again to the somber shore the wave singing of the Ideal." (pp. 65-75)

> Eleanor W. Thomas, "The Romanticism of Rostand," in Poet Lore, *Vol. XXXII, Spring, 1921, pp. 64-75.*

EDMUND GOSSE (essay date 1923)

[*Gosse's importance as a critic is due primarily to his introduction of Henrik Ibsen's "new drama" to English audiences. He was among the chief English translators and critics of Scandinavian literature, and among his other works are studies of John Donne, Thomas Gray, and Sir Thomas Browne, and important early articles on French authors of the late nineteenth century. In the following excerpt, Gosse focuses on the contrast between Rostand's popular success during his lifetime and his uncertain reputation among critics of modern French drama.*]

The "case" of Edmond Rostand is one of the most curious in literary history. To this day his exact position has never been defined, and criticism has been shy of attempting to place him among the writers of his time. His career was brief and splendid; he flared like a comet across the sky in a blaze which lasted practically for ten years, and no more. At a moment when French poetry had become extremely subtle he astonished the world with his prodigal simplicity. While the Symbolists were occupied in describing, in veiled and difficult language, their most secret sufferings, their *minces tristesses,* Rostand shouted, like the morning star, of the joy of life in numbers intelligible to every one. He had lived by the side of Mallarmé and Verlaine without, apparently, becoming aware of their existence; he went back to an entirely different generation, to Victor Hugo, to Banville, to the early pure Romantics. He was welcomed with enthusiasm; he was played all over the world; his success seemed boundless; he was elected to the French Academy at an earlier age than any other modern candidate.

But there was a speck in the fruit and a Mordecai at the gate. While all the audiences of two hemispheres were applauding him, the inner circle of his contemporaries excluded him altogether. He has no place in the *Masques* of Rémy de Gourmont; he is not so much as mentioned in that important repertory, *Poètes d'aujourd'hui* of Van Bever and Léautaud, which includes fifty-three French and Belgian writers. The group of the *Mercure de France,* so powerful in opinion at the opening of this century, would have none of Rostand. At the moment of the triumph of *Cyrano de Bergerac,* the *Mercure* pontifically stated that M. Edmond Rostand excelled in one art, and one art only—that of writing bad French.

The "case" of Stephen Phillips is the only one which can be compared with that of Rostand, and the parallel is very imperfect. The English dramatic poet enjoyed considerable success, both with playgoers and readers, but *Paolo and Francesca* was a mild affair by the side of *Cyrano.* Phillips was the object of scornful attack, but the critics never disdained him with half the asperity which was poured out upon Rostand in the cafés of the Boulevard St. Michel. The supporters of each playwright, but particularly those of Rostand, declared that the censure was pure prejudice, and did not scruple to attribute it to envy. No one can doubt that in the case of the author of *L'aiglon* jealousy had something to do with it. A society which takes literature, and particularly poetical literature, very seriously, could not fail to contain persons who, finding their own ingenious works neglected, and those of a poet whose method was in direct opposition to all that they were admiring and teaching, lifted to the skies—it could not but be that some persons in such a society, being human and so frail, should persuade themselves that this terrible rival was an impostor and a traitor to the art.

There was an element of envy in the designation; and yet it was not altogether an unrighteous judgment which denied to Rostand the highest honours of poetical creation. It is very difficult indeed to say what it is that leaves upon the unbiassed memory a tinge of disappointment, a slightly bad taste, when we think of the six flamboyant dramas. There comes back to us the old tale of the lunatic, who said that the feasts in the asylum were magnificent and delicious, worthy of Belshazzar, but that, he could not tell why, all the dishes had a damnable smack of water-gruel.

Edmond Rostand, after one or two negligible efforts, took the stage with *Les romanesques* in 1894. This was a comedy founded on the manner of Shakespeare as seen through the gay little rhymed pieces of Banville. The plot was a sort of intentional burlesque of *Romeo and Juliet,* with touches of *A Midsummer Night's Dream.* The play sparkled with gaiety and absurdity; the comic element was carefully sustained on a high literary level, with allusions to moonlight among the honeysuckle-bowers of Stratford-on-Avon. The action was rather childish, but very merry and sentimental, and the couplets were rhymed with astonishing richness. (The richness of Rostand's rhyme was his strength and his bane from first to last.)

There followed next, in 1895, **Princess Faraway,** a coloured pageant of chivalry in the fourteenth century, contrived to display in its apogee the romantic side of Madame Sarah Bernhardt's genius. This was the old story of Rudel and the Lady of Tripoli. Here were shallops and silken sails, amorous crimson roses, a knight in emerald mail, songs—rather long songs—warbled by troubadours kneeling on one knee. It was all delicious, but too sweet; and the comic vigour of **Les romanesques** seemed to have retreated a little.

Rostand withdrew for two years, and then returned to the stage with **The Woman of Samaria.** This also was carried by the magic of Madame Bernhardt to a splendour of success, but when we read it in cold blood after a quarter of a century, something seems to have passed out of it. **The Woman of Samaria** is a mystery play, in which the solemn scenes of the Gospel are enacted against a sky which is "gold and pink." It is all very picturesque and lively, the sentiment is tender and evangelical; the poet essays no audacities, but keeps to the tradition in the story and the dogma. It is a little too brightly coloured, a little too like that variegated dainty, a Neapolitan ice—the story of Jesus as told by a troubadour, who is very skillful and charming and melodious, but essentially not spiritually minded. And then, immediately on the heels of *The Woman of Samaria,* came the prodigy of prodigies, *Cyrano de Bergerac.*

The quarter of a century which has slipped by since *Cyrano de Bergerac* took, not the town only, but the world, by storm, has tarnished a little the splendour of its triumph, but I do not think that time will ever entirely destroy its charm. Rostand has been blamed for falsifying the history and character of the actual Cyrano, who was a romantic Gascon of the seventeenth century, had a very large and disfiguring nose, and wrote plays which were good enough for Molière to steal from. All this does not seem to me to matter in the least; the famous nose by any other name would be as glowing a carbuncle, the swords and the verses would flash about with no less spirit and audacity. The modern poet had a perfect right to take as much as he wished to take, and no more, from a figure which ought to be highly gratified at being so unexpectedly lifted out of comparative oblivion.

The real point about Rostand's play is that it is an accomplished poem, and yet sustained throughout by the utmost radiance of high spirits. It is a masterpiece of heroic buffoonery, adorned and supported by the art of a masterly metrical artificer. In the earlier dramas there had been an excess of prettiness, an absence of the solid basis of feeling. In *Cyrano,* fantastic as it is, the pathos of the hero's isolation, of the contrast between his generous soul and his disfigured body, has an element of genuine tragedy, while his unselfish loyalty to the stupid Christian is a motive of novel beauty, exhibited in a manner extremely attractive. I need not dwell on this, because few modern dramas are so widely familiar, and every one who has seen or read the play will recollect the culminating scene in which Roxane hangs in agony over the corpse of Christian, kissing what she takes to be his latest letter although it was really Cyrano who had written it. This is an example of much that none but a dramatic poet of a high order could have conceived. The worst that can be said of this melodious tragedy of a clown is that the author's facetious agility is out of keeping with passion. But *Cyrano de Bergerac* is a masterpiece.

The twentieth century opened with a yet greater success. In March 1900 appeared *The Eaglet,* a long tragedy occupied with the character and the fate of the unfortunate son of Napoleon and Marie Louise, the ill-starred Duke of Reichstadt. (pp. 116-20)

As a poem *L'aiglon* is worthy of close attention. Rostand had begun with the study of Shakespeare in *Romeo and Juliet;* he comes back to it here in *Hamlet* and in *Julius Cæsar.* He is no less rich in his rhymes and agile in his versification than he was before, but he owes little now to mere ornament, and he has ceased to place his confidence in the glitter and reverberation of tirades. In *The Eaglet* love has no place, and there is little variety of intrigue; all depends on the exposition of character in rapid, appropriate, and brilliant conversation. The figures of Napoleon II., of the Empress Marie Louise, of Metternich, of Flambeau, pass before us in swift alternation, and we hurry to the inevitable tragic dénouement. The famous scene with Metternich at the mirror, which closes the third act, is melodramatic, perhaps, but of the very essence of genuine dramatic poetry.

The career of Rostand, since it was to be so brief, should have ended here. *Chanticler,* diabolically clever as it is, adds in the long run nothing to his glory. It was an attempt at the impos-

sible, this brilliant tragi-comedy in which, after the manner of La Fontaine, all the characters are birds and beasts. The famous scene in the second act, where Chanticleer explains to the adoring Pheasant that it is he who, by his clarion call, summons the sunrise every morning, is superb. . . . Yet even here—? Truly, as I permitted myself to say in the beginning of this little inadequate essay, no "case" in literary history is more curious than that of Rostand. Dowered to excess with almost every gift, was not something essential lacking to him? What was it? May it not have been the humility of a contrite spirit in the face of Nature? (p. 121)

Edmund Gosse, "Rostand's Plays," in his More Books on the Table, *William Heinemann Ltd., 1923, pp. 113-22.*

BRIAN HOOKER (essay date 1935)

[In the following excerpt, Hooker explains the requirements for a great play and how Cyrano de Bergerac *fulfills them.]*

[To] explain *Cyrano de Bergerac* is simply to explain the Theatre. It is not only a great play; it is typically and peculiarly a great play; not only literary and dramatic, but triumphantly stagy and theatrical. Its artistry makes no concealment of art; it swaggers and parades the means and methods, the powers and limitations and devices of the Theatre, as its Gascon hero flaunts his own personality: with equal frankness and with equal charm. So it is more than any other I know a play for playwrights and playgoers and all whose enjoyment increases by understanding what they enjoy. Surely no sheer theatrics ever made a play so great; nor was ever a great play so obviously of the Theatre.

This was accomplished by a meeting of minds perhaps worth mentioning; for it may not be generally known. When Rostand had written already a few plays, all cleverly beautiful but of no outstanding success, Coquelin said to him: "I am a comedian, but I am a romantic actor first: I can read poetry, I can make love and fight and die. Make me a play of all these things." So the play was made, in how mutual and intimate collaboration the work itself is evidence. I do not know how much they met nor who suggested this or that. But Coquelin was no poet outside of his own art, and Rostand wrote other plays as well but never planned one so successfully. Here were an exquisite and facile poet, and a veteran actor saturated with stagecraft; both lovers and masters of the flamboyant style and the *beau geste.* And the result was *Cyrano.*

Now a play is simply a story told in the Theatre: in action therefore and by actors then and there present to the audience: Not any story therefore; not *Paradise Lost,* nor "Anthony Adverse," nor "The Little Mermaid"; but a story such as may be seen and heard, and of that story only such parts as being seen and heard imply the rest. The actors must act, the audience enjoy and understand; and the two hours' traffic of the stage must keep in line and keep on moving.

These are restrictions; and it is interesting to note how any art does its best work and gives its greatest pleasure by taking advantage of its restrictions and turning them to its peculiar use. Of course, all arts do something of this sort; that is what art is for. Of the three narrative arts, fiction shows life as consequence; the screen as continuity; the stage as crisis. Because we must play our story complete in a series of scenes, we select the high spots, the turning points; contrasts, comparisons, ironies: in a word, all that we vaguely and naturally call

Dramatic. Whatever happens, we must hear and see; and because we so seem to hear and see the whole story actually happening (as in real life we never do), we realize life in the Theatre with a vividness and intensity beyond life itself. It is like looking through a lens: we see less; but we see it magnified.

So much for laying down the law; and now to follow out its application. We return to Rostand—and to Coquelin.

The story first; the story of a comic figure with romantic, even heroic possibilities; for he must speak poetry, and make love, and fight, and die. None better than Cyrano de Bergerac, a swaggering Gascon with literary leanings who lived in the picturesque period of Mazarin. We do not know too much about his life, and that is well; we are the freer to imagine. He wrote *A Journey to the Moon,* and was notable for his enormous nose. Theatre at once. Look how the whole gorgeous character hangs on that feature like an orient pearl. A figure visually absurd making his virtue of absurdity, conscious and eloquent of both; one who may flaunt to admiration every adornment of his soul, and we shall love him because the humor of it will save the sentimental. What a part to play!

Well, such a fellow falls in love. What would the lady do? Love him—if he were only beautiful. Dramatize that: another character, Christian, the beautiful but dumb young rival. Good, the triangle. What happens—do they fight? No, better friends; surefire—the noble old self-sacrifice; and not too trite; for Cyrano only sacrifices himself because he must. She could not love him unless he were invisible. Theatre again! The old balcony scene, with a new twist. She can see Christian and hear Cyrano. We can get away with that—with the lights. Now how to hold that situation. Why, Christian goes to war before the bridal night. Suspense, yes. Audiences like virginity. More suspense—Christian understands and is jealous. Before Roxane is told that Christian's love was Cyrano's love-making, Christian dies; and Cyrano will not take advantage. The point of honor; a weak point, but sympathetic and in character. We can make them believe that. Then for an end Roxane finds out that her love was for the soul of Cyrano. How to play that? He reads the love-letters in the dark, knowing them by heart because he wrote them. Since he has to die, he dies delirious, fighting phantoms, gloriously absurd, a new death-scene, the keynote. We have it; that will make a play: Comedie héroïque, en cinq actes, en vers! ["Heroic comedy, in five acts, in verse!"]

I wish I could go on throughout the play, examining in detail how things are done; but that would expand this introduction into a book on playmaking. The most I can do is to show you what to look for, and by illustration where to look.

The persons first; and these not as "characters" but as active parts; such parts as actors love because audiences enjoy. Action means here not merely doing something, but doing something to the audience. It may be action merely to speak: "How can you read now? It is dark." It may be action to say and do noticeably nothing, as Christian is acting when he is brought in dead. For these are actions that a man might play. What the actor does not like is being unobserved or having that within which passeth show. He wants to make a show of himself, and quite right, too; that is why he is there; and so far as his assumed character gives him that, he cares not whether it be good or evil, pleasant or unpleasant, false to life or true. Nor do we. Look then, what Rostand does for his

company. Cyrano is a great part, of course; but see how great. It is not only his range and contrast and versatility of behavior, like a dance under a spectrum of spotlights. It is that his very nature is theatrical; to wave emotion like a banner and thrust himself forward like a sword; yet with a grace and humour that takes off the curse. His own laugh follows the cheer and the tear so surely that we laugh with him and accept all three. In such a part the worst of actors must do something and the best find all that he can do. As for the others, look how the least of them affords that something to do which actor and audience agree to enjoy. The nun in the last act has her chance to be as charming as Roxane. The Duenna is as definite as Ragueneau, and for her moment as amusing. The cadet who is no more than introduced rejoices in the name of Baron Hillot de Blagnac-Saléchan de Castel-Crabioules. The Cardinal, who never speaks, dominates the whole scene upon his entrance. The page whose part is one meow gets the great star to stop and bark at him. See also how carefully those parts which play opposite are pointed up by contrast: Christian and de Guiche with Cyrano; Ragueneau and Le Bret with him and with each other; Roxane with all.

The structure now of acts and scenes; chiefly scenes, for the act is optional, a matter of convenience and convention giving sense of form. We divide our play into acts; we build it up of scenes; and the scenes do the work and tell the story. Moreover, the limits and location of an act depend upon the essential scenes therein. So our last three acts are set already: the Balcony and the Camp, of course; and for the last, the Convent will be appropriate. The Second might be set in any place where the people might meet as requisite. But its mood of course is comedy; and its main point, the compact between Christian and Cyrano, approaches fantasy. So the fantastic setting in Ragueneau's poetical pastry shop makes mere romance comparatively credible. As for the first act, its business is the character of Cyrano: we must see that before we can go on; for seeing is believing. Plausible people like Christian and Roxane and de Guiche may develop throughout the story. But upon this fellow's extraordinary behavior, the whole story turns. So we display him in a public place doing preposterous things which presently appear coherent, and so credible. Then the story begins: "Porter, the doors!"

We shall see all this better by examining single scenes; for a play is organized of scenes as the organization of ships embodies the fleet. What makes a good scene? First and last, it moves: it finds the action here and leaves it there: something has happened. There are fine scenes in fiction like that New England byway of which one said: "It don't start nowheres, nor it don't arrive to nowheres else." But such scenes are always bad Theatre. Our audience wants action; wants it so much as to be credulous of anything they understand; especially at the beginning, for the sake of the action they impatiently expect. Never argue with an audience. Never explain. All they want is to be shown; show them.

Now turn to a famous scene: the duel in Rhyme. Of course it could not happen—but who cares? It does happen; and see how much happens. Action, of course; but more than that: action which points the moral and adorns the tale. The Gascon has made good. A moment ago, he was no more than showing off; now he is a hero, and they on the stage and we in the house are all rooting for him as though he were Dizzy Dean. Something has happened to the audience. And more than that: even while we enjoy the exciting business and the showy acting, it strikes ringing the very keynote of Cyrano and of the play: Quelle sottise—mais quelle geste! ["What folly—but what heroic achievement!"]

And still more: beside its quality of action, the scene has pace and form; the pace of the fight and the form of the Ballade. Pace in a play does not mean merely speed, any more than it does in racing; but speed varied and contrasted, speed to some purpose, speed intelligent. Mere hurry does not give the effect of pace, nor mere bustle about the stage the sense of action; these are cheap substitutes which easily become boring. But see how fast the scene of Cyrano and the Busybody is played; faster than any one person could read the lines. See how the sudden pause, "And why not, if you please?" makes the part following seem faster still, although the actual lines are read more slowly; because we feel where it is going. See how the slow scene of Cyrano and Le Bret contrasts with what precedes and follows. Look how the last act never drags, because its slow movement is appropriate, and the suspense holds. That is what pace means. And by form I mean that sense of pattern in a scene evident to the audience; sometimes quite obvious as in the scene where Cyrano's "Yes, Roxane," repeats like a refrain; and the scene in the second act for the same people; and again in Cyrano's narrative which Christian interrupts with allusions to his nose; more subtly in the scenes preceding and following this last, where the rhythm of speech and action make the scene play as an orchestra plays a piece of music. A good scene is like a play in miniature, with a shape and color and climax of its own.

There is another bit of stagecraft here worth noticing for its kindness to the actor whereby his pleasure subtly becomes our own. In the scene of the noses, Cyrano is of course feeding Christian; in the scene over Christian's body, Roxane is feeding Cyrano. Generally, no actor likes to feed another; especially when he himself is playing an important part. Now in these scenes the feeder is given all the fat lines, the vivid action, while the response rings changes upon one refrain. So they are both happy and so are we. It is not that one actor must give milk from which another skims the cream; rather, the one paints a whole gorgeous sunset opposite which the other stars himself. And as actors help one another to their best effects, so the one scene, however brilliant by itself, stands higher by the support of other scenes than it could stand alone. The scene of the roses depends entirely upon the preceding scene of Christian with the Cadets and upon Cyrano's promise to Roxane. Christian is warned and dared; Cyrano has promised to be his friend; and so the scene. Without these it is nothing.

This brings us to the matter of the Plant: so named in theatrical language, and well named; for the Plant blossoms and bears fruit in the Theatre as it does nowhere else. We "plant" in the mind of our audience this or that point of plot, situation, character, what you will; later we repeat or refer to the planted idea; and by some curious crowd-psychology the audience remembers and rejoices in the sheer connection of the known and the new. I suppose the way of it is this: we tell our story on the stage in sections, in a series of high spots; whereby our audience, habituated to follow us by leaping mentally from crag to crag, does so rejoicing in its strength, discovering delightfully its own cleverness. The instinct for this is so strong that oftentimes mere repetition makes for comedy. The question whether anybody wants to buy a duck is for once no more than mildly amusing; but let the comedian repeat that innocent inquiry a few times and the crowd be-

gins to rock and roar. And even you and I among that crowd are as susceptible as the rest.

And the spell holds alike from the low comic to the highest Tragedy. Think of great tragic lines, how they are nothing in themselves but terrible in their retrospection.—"Pray you, undo this button."—"I did not know the dead could have such hair."—"Mother, give me the sun."—"The rest is silence." So in *Cyrano,* and so most obviously and often. The Balcony Scene taken alone is merely poetry. But look at what precedes. First the nose carefully made absurd, pathetic, fearfully unmentionable. Whereupon Christian mentions it. Then the pact and the love-letters. Now we actually show Christian attempting to make love for himself; so that we like him and laugh at him and begin to believe in Roxane's longing for amorous eloquence. And then and not till then the scene: its wild improbability made credible, its comedy touched with tears, and its poetry made palatable to common sense by what has gone before. So the Moon scene would be entirely boring, but that we know Christian and Roxane are being married meanwhile. So with Roxane in the fourth act, raving to Christian of the love-letters—because we know that Christian knows that Cyrano wrote them. So in this play almost everywhere.

Consider especially the planting for Cyrano's entrance in the last act. Once a week he comes most carefully upon his hour to amuse and merely to amuse Roxane. He is poor and hungry. His nose looks like old ivory. He has one coat left—his old one. He has dangerous enemies; an accident may happen to him. It has happened. He lies abed, his skull broken. The doctor who attended him for charity says that if he tries to raise his head he may die. So on the last stroke of the hour, he walks in. "After fourteen years—late for the first time." The plant here is so patent in its mechanism, so frankly trite in its material of pathos and suspense, as to lie well within the realm of Hokum; a region where playwrights and audiences rush in with mutual pleasure, where critics if not angels fear to tread. Hokum we may define as any trite and true device to arouse emotion which still affects us as intended, though we remember it a thousand times; and I will here make bold to defend it and to boast that you and I enjoy it still, despite the dear silver which shines in its hair—and now and then because of that. For after all, the trick could never have become trite if it had not been true. The grass is green and the sky blue, in the maugre of the teeth of modernists; and love is only an old scene with a new twist, and death, as Queen Gertrude originally observes, is common. And if anyone feels that I blaspheme the holiness of Art or tarnish the gold upon the gingerbread by displaying thus the manner of its making, I can assure her upon some experience of artists that they generally keep their souls to themselves and work as workmen. Art is like that because life is like that; and there is no more incongruity between its sacred ends and its necessary means than between Motherhood and diapers.

Finally as to the dialogue. In the period of the "well-made" problem play, it used to be said that plays were made, not written: that, given the precise action of the scene, the so-called "substance" of the speech, mere writing did not matter. Certainly nothing could be more absurd; for to say a thing otherwise is simply to say another thing; and because speech is action in the Theatre, there cannot be except in critical abstraction any divorce between the two. For practical proof, one need no more than glance at Shakespeare—who wrote supremely, but outside of mere narrative contrast and continuity quite seldom troubled to construct at all. Of course the truth is that sheer dialogue is as important as all the rest of stagecraft put together, since it implies and puts together all the rest. Compare play and pantomime, the silent with the speaking picture; or see a play you do not know in a language you do not understand.

And here also I can no more than illustrate. Look at the opening lines: how instantly the story moves, how many things are told in how few words. Run on through a few scenes, and see, by the continual pressure put upon you to visualize as you read, how speech is also action. Trace this quality through the turning points, the climaxes, the conclusions, of those scenes which we have already analyzed. Notice the longer speeches, the *tirades;* how each does more than give the actor a bravura passage because it is more than merely talking. The nose speech in Act I makes the scene by very exuberance of iteration. The "No Thank You" speech in Act II rolls up character and situation like a growing snowball. The contrasted styles of Cyrano and Christian are of the very essence of the play. The sheer poetry of the Balcony scene dramatizes its emotion.

Of course in all this literary phase we are seeing darkly through the glass of a translation. And to admit that is not modesty but merely truism. I know how steadily I concentrated upon theatric value; trying to follow Rostand's action scene by scene and line by line, sacrificing to that all else— and how much else! Like Ragueneau, I love a friendly audience, and am as pleased when they enjoy my cooking. But my failures are a wide open secret among all of us who care for the original. The closing lines, for instance, I fumbled abominably for want of a connotative equivalent for *panache.* The Triolets I did not really translate at all. There is a bark and growl, a sense of drums and tramplings in the very sound and rhythm of the French which I could no more achieve in English than I could make onion do for garlic:

> Oeil d'aigle, jambe de cigogne,
> Moustache de chat, dents de loups,
> Fendant la canaille qui grogne—
> Oeil d'aigle, jambe de cigogne—
> Ils vont—coiffés d'un vieux vigogne
> Dont la plume cache les trous! . .
> Oeil d'aigle, jambe de cigogne,
> Moustache de chat, dents de loups.

I gave it up. I sat me down and wrote a good colorless resonant piece of declamation to serve the purpose of the scene and let it go at that. Not Rostand; not Coquelin; but I know it! (pp. ix-xix)

> Brian Hooker, in an introduction to Cyrano de Bergerac *by Edmond Rostand, translated by Brian Hooker, The Limited Editions Club, 1936, pp. ix-xix.*

MARTIN LAMM   (essay date 1953)

[*In the following excerpt, Lamm surveys Rostand's plays, reassessing what he considers Rostand's overrated merits as a dramatist and poet.*]

Before Rostand achieved [his] tremendous success [with *Cyrano de Bergerac*] he had spent his apprentice years in the Symbolist school as a writer of lyric poetry, and later of plays which did not meet with much appreciation and did not deserve to do so.

Rostand's first play, *Les romanesques* (*The Romancers,*

1894), was an attempt to dramatize the world of Watteau. There was in his nature an element of affectation, and it was precisely in periods characterized by affectation that he found his themes, the period of the troubadour for *La princesse lointaine* (*The Faraway Princess*), the period of supreme affectation in which Cyrano is set, and the age of Rococo for *The Romancers.*

The plot of this play, in which two fathers pretend to be enemies in order to tempt their children to fall in love with each other, has also been used in a comedy by Otto Ludwig. It is not certain whether Rostand knew this work, but there is a similar situation in Musset's "A quoi rêvent les jeunes filles" ("What do young girls dream of ?").

It is of Musset and Marivaux that the play reminds us, though it lacks their psychological subtlety. The meaning is not that the young people will be cured of their romantic fancies when they have discovered how they have been puppets in their fathers' hands. The epilogue explains that they have only been deceived about the outer and unimportant appearance of things; in their hearts they have known the truth.

In his next play, *The Faraway Princess,* Rostand throws himself headlong into the most ethereal of romances. The real hero of the play, who does not appear very often on the stage, is the troubadour, Rudel. In character and style he is the perfect expression of the courtly, platonic affections of the Middle Ages. He is a character who has been treated by all the world's romantic writers, Heine, Browning, Swinburne and Carducci.

Like *Pelléas and Mélisande* the story is a variation on the Tristan theme. Rudel is at death's door, but before he dies he wishes to see Princess Mélissinde, for whom he has conceived a lofty passion through the songs of wandering minstrels. When at last he reaches Tripolis he is too weak to go ashore, and sends his friend Bertrand in his place. When the Princess catches sight of Bertrand she takes him for Rudel, and when he reads out the love poem that Rudel composed for the distant Princess she falls in love with him.

Meanwhile Rudel is still alive, though his last hour is near. During his final struggle with death the Princess and Bertrand come aboard, but the chaplain forbids Bertrand to cloud his friend's last hours by telling him of his intended deception. In a scene that is reminiscent of the end of *Hernani,* Rudel dies with his lips pressed against those of the Princess.

The plot anticipates that of *Cyrano.* Roxane is in love with the handsome face of Christian, but at the same time, and without realizing it, she loves the noble soul of Cyrano, for it was he who under the cloak of darkness made a declaration of love in Christian's name and wrote his letters for him.

Rostand's idealism is not profound, but it is genuine. The superficiality of his characterization is plainly apparent here, as well as his liking for startling stage effects. The plot is unnecessarily complicated, and the dialogue tediously wordy.

None of Rostand's early plays was particularly successful, least of all *La Samaritaine* (*The Woman of Samaria*), with its New Testament subject and the figure of Christ as an actor in the play.

Cyrano de Bergerac made him world-famous at once, and the morning after the première on 28th December, 1897, the French critics were prophesying that this date would mark a new epoch in drama as clearly as *Le Cid* and *Hernani* had done. This exaggeration was disproved by events. *Cyrano* did not turn out to be the beginning of a revolution, not even in France. The play is a vigorous and faithful revival of the great heroic drama of the French classical and romantic periods; it is in no sense a new creation.

Subject to these reservations, however, it cannot be denied that *Cyrano* exercised an influence on modern drama. Its remarkable success was convincing proof that the day of historical drama was not yet past, as critics tended to assert. The increase in the popularity of historical plays in all countries around the turn of the century is not unrelated to *Cyrano de Bergerac,* and it was never really dropped from the repertory lists of French theatres. Even in Sweden it is constantly revived, and always with success. It is unjust, too, to complain of the public's bad taste. The play is remarkable neither for its merits nor its faults. It has no unusual artistic merit, nor does it make greater concessions to the public's liking for stage effects than plays usually do.

Cyrano's struggle against a cruel fate, his ability to stand fast by his ideals in the face of opposition and defeat, his determination to put a brave face on humiliation and poverty, and finally, when all else fails, to go down with a brave gesture— all this is not something particularly French or 18th century; it is universal in its appeal. This play resembles too painstaking a copy of an old master, a typical, average piece of Dutch painting, with a few bold strokes of the brush added by Franz Hals.

Cyrano de Bergerac was a lucky shot. Rostand had found a period which perfectly matched his temperament. The early 17th century was an age of affectation, of idealism and sensibility, of gallant and elaborately turned phrases. When Rostand endowed Cyrano with his own exalted passions and his too brilliant vocabulary he gave the play its natural period flavour.

The beginning of the 17th century was also an age of military bravado, of the *Fronde* and *The Three Musketeers.* When Rostand makes D'Artagnan wish Cyrano luck and shake his hand, he clearly indicates that we are in a period where no act is too heroic to be believed. Cyrano is allowed to vanquish a hundred men and to tell the tale with his characteristic gallows humour. His long nose prevents his being taken really seriously by the audience, even when he is carrying out deeds of incredible heroism or showing a superhuman capacity for selfless resignation and exalted idealism. He has a half-mocking, half-tragic way of looking at himself, but Rostand does not allow us to witness any real soul-searching in him, and he does not even give us the impression that such a thing has ever happened.

Cyrano quickly selects the attitude which he feels honour compels him to adopt, and then abides by it stubbornly to the end. He is perfectly aware that such quixotic behaviour will not earn him esteem, but he is incapable of acting otherwise. The moral rectitude of the hero, which has been emphasized by modern dramatists from Schiller to Ibsen, practically reached its climax with Cyrano, the poet and long-nosed braggart. The effect was smaller and less convincing in him than in many of his predecessors, because he is so completely lacking in any sense of doubt. Cyrano belonged to an age when men acted more from impulse than reflection. He was created by an author who was in complete sympathy with him. This is why Rostand was able to work on audiences to

whom the heroes of Kleist, Hebbel and Ibsen, with all their introspection, will always remain incomprehensible.

Nearest to Cyrano probably come Victor Hugo's heroes, for they are based on a similar antithesis. Just as Hernani and Ruy Blas bear noble souls under their robber cloaks or servants' uniforms, so Cyrano's sensitive and poetic soul contrasts with his robust exterior and his extravagant boastfulness. The two sides of his character drive him from one deed to another, each more heroic, more wildly idealistic than the last. He resembles Hugo's heroes in their unceasing desire to excel themselves. The knowledge that Roxane loves the stupid Christian causes him to do something more positive than merely to renounce his claims nobly; he wants Roxane to have Christian and to owe her happiness to him. To do this he determines that Roxane must not realize the extent of Christian's stupidity, so he composes letters for Christian, and takes his place in the dark to make that grand avowal of love which she has demanded. These tactics make it even more certain that he will lose Roxane, but they also give him the bitter-sweet satisfaction of knowing that it is really his soul, as expressed in letters and declarations of passion, that Roxane loves. Cyrano abides by his intention even when, sorely wounded, he visits Roxane in the final act. When he reads Christian's last letter, which he himself has written, his voice betrays his feelings. But when Roxane asks him if he loved her he steadfastly denies it, whispering at the end, "No, no, my love, I did not love you." Two lives have been destroyed for a dream; in the hour of Cyrano's death they both realize this. But Cyrano also knows that this struggle for a dream has been worth while just because it was a struggle, just because more than any other struggle it has demanded courage and sacrifice. In Rudel's song in *The Faraway Princess* Rostand praised that same love, noble because of its hopelessness, "plus noble d'être vaine" ["more noble for being in vain"].

Apart from Cyrano the characters in the play are insignificant. Fair without and hollow within, Christian is the antithesis of Cyrano, in the Victor Hugo style. Roxane says in the final act of the play that she has only loved one person but has lost him twice, a thought which Hugo might have expressed in the same way. Rostand and he both revel in grand period pictures which still retain a festive quality.

Our own generation does not, however, find the play as poetic as did the audiences which filled the Théâtre Porte Saint Martin for six hundred performances, or the reading public which bought more than a million copies. What remains most firmly in the memory is probably the final act, with its autumn mood of falling leaves; the sonorous Gascon song is an imitation of a poem which was wrongly ascribed to the real Cyrano.

The play is like a rich brocade which on close examination is found to contain crudities of colour and gems which are not real, but this is less disturbing because it contains an undertone of burlesque. Less easy to forgive are the hackneyed situations of the Scribe type which occasionally occur in it.

In *L'aiglon (The Eaglet)*, which Rostand wrote three years later, we get an impression of the actor anxious to gain the applause of his audience. Here we have a loud-voiced patriotism, sentimental and full of speeches but lacking the ability to laugh at oneself that is to be found in Cyrano.

The play was written for Sarah Bernhardt, then no longer young, and was one of the attractions of the Paris Exhibition of 1900. To read it now is like being confronted in some out-of-the-way place by a vast and pretentious exhibition building, hastily constructed of shoddy material. It may be splendidly painted and equipped to please the eye during the short summer months, but seems frighteningly empty and dismal if put to longer use.

Why Rostand really failed was because he selected a profoundly tragic subject. Napoleon's unfortunate son, Frans of Reichstadt, assumed a burden that was too heavy for him when he tried to win again for France the glory that had been Napoleon's. Rostand did the same when he chose a theme that was too great for his poetic talent. One might almost believe that he realized this better than his critics when one reads his last play, *Chantecler,* where he writes with charming irony of the henhouse and its chief singer, the cock, who believes that his throat can rival that of the nightingale.

The Emperor's son, obsessed by Napoleon's dream, but lacking the power to realize it—this was the essence of the plot, but Rostand could not bring it out without resorting to theatrical devices.

Napoleon himself could not be brought on to the stage, so instead Rostand, in an unlucky moment, introduced a veteran of the Old Guard whose name was Flambeau, and who was a sort of travelling museum of Napoleon's relics. From various corners and pockets of his clothes he produces a snuff-box, a pipe and a glass, all bearing Napoleon's picture or his monogram. The tragic death of the Duke on the stage is also embellished with Napoleonic souvenirs. The cradle which the City of Paris presented at his birth is carried in, and the Grand Cross of the Legion of Honour is hung over his night-shirt. There is a statue of Napoleon in the room, and he hums the tunes of his father's day while he is receiving the sacrament.

The Eaglet is set in Scribe's period; a performance of a Scribe play is announced at a fancy-dress ball at Schönbrunn. This may explain the deliberate Scribe touches in the play, the manoeuvres and counter-manoeuvres and the endless disguises. Flambeau says somewhere that he is never satisfied simply with providing the basic needs, but has a crazy passion to 'faire du luxe.' It is this southern French characteristic which has got the better of Rostand in *The Eaglet.*

Although the faint protests against *The Eaglet* were drowned in shouts of approval, Rostand seems to have realized the validity of the criticisms. He wanted to be a poet, not just a stage technician. After *The Eaglet,* to the surprise of the public and the critics, he retired to the country, taking his family with him, and settled for ten years in a quiet corner of the Pyrenees. Rumours were rife about the great stories that he was going to dramatize, such as Faust and Don Quixote, and there was much disappointment when it was learned that he was actually writing a play about hens in a farmyard, with a cock as the hero. The idea came quite soon after *The Eaglet,* but Rostand had trouble in expressing it. In any case, he was ill at the time and was not confident about his subject. The play was not completed until 1909.

A work which had met so many obstacles and taken so long to write was awaited by public and critics alike with understandable suspicion, and the première did not dispel all doubts. Maeterlinck and his *The Blue Bird* were to triumph three years later, and *Chantecler* did not meet with the recognition it merited. In it Rostand took his revenge for *The Eaglet.* He spent ten years of his life on a play which he must

have known the ordinary public would never approve, for *Chantecler* is more of a literary drama and actually a more original piece of work than *Cyrano.*

In most European countries there is a legend to the effect that a cock believes that he causes the sun to rise because he predicts it with his crowing. This notion is elaborated by Rostand in the style of a fable. Chantecler, the name of the cock in *Roman du Renard,* is convinced that without him all would be darkness and nature sunk in eternal sleep. The jeers of envious rivals cannot shake his faith. A golden hen pheasant lures him into the forest away from all his hens, but she cannot accomplish alone her wish to make him forget his mission. She therefore summons to her aid the songster of the night, the nightingale, and at his first note Chantecler feels himself finally defeated. It is the same for him as for all who hear the song of the nightingale; they believe that they are only listening for a minute, but when the singing is ended they find they have been listening all night. The sun has risen, but Chantecler has not summoned it with his crowing. Chantecler suddenly sees that he has lost his throne. When the dog from the farmyard comes to greet him and tell him that everyone wants him back to bring up the sun, he answers in a moment of gloom, "Now they have the faith which I have lost." But his depression only lasts a moment and then he lets fly a full-throated crow. When the pheasant asks in surprise why he has done this he replies that it is his calling. The sun may have risen without his help, but it remains for him to awaken all to life, to open all eyes. "Who sees that his dream has died must die at once, or else rise up in greater strength."

This simple story has sometimes been taken to be an allegory on the fate of mankind, or in praise of the value of daily toil, or as an exhortation to all men to do their duty without too great illusions about its importance. This is a fairly widely held point of view, but we grasp the purport of the play better if we consider what the poet's function is. He cannot give life to nature, but he can open men's eyes to it, and he is most faithful to his calling when he regards himself as a worker among fellow workers. "If I sing clearly and truthfully, and if every farm has a cock who sings in his place, then there will be no more night," says Chantecler.

Rostand explained that the cock expressed his own dreams, and indeed embodied something of himself. During this ten-year period while he was working on the play he had come to realize that his merits were overrated both by himself and by others. Both in the troubadour of Rudel and in Cyrano he had shown something of himself. Cyrano's self-sacrificing idealism becomes little less than a desperate gamble, a desire to make all the noblest and most extravagant gestures himself. Chantecler is less brilliant and more natural. He is the hero of domestic virtues, the citizen and father of the family, the faithful guardian. But as with all his fellow countrymen, there is a touch of romance in his blood, and he believes that really he is something quite different. Rostand has brought out the sunny and frankly naive qualities of this Tartarin of a cock in a very human way. He is 'un brave meridional' like Tartarin, who finds it hard to see reality except through the veil of romance. Daudet blames this trait of the southern French on the burning sunshine which seems to shroud everything in a haze. So it is with Chantecler. His imagination is always a stage ahead of reality, and his sensitive soul is often wounded.

In his posthumous play, *La dernière nuit de Don Juan (Don Juan's Last Night),* Rostand writes a sequel to the Don Juan legend which leaves that most famous of all heroes morally naked. The play was not published until 1921, and it consists of a prologue and two acts which were already complete when the first world war broke out. The best scene is the one where Don Juan, released from hell, is confronted by shades of the thousand and three women whom he has seduced. He has to remember their names, but is always guessing wrong, and the shades mock him as they turn away. Finally they say that he has never known them, never possessed them—it is they who have possessed him, just to pass the time away. Romeo and Tristan are the two real lovers who have left behind something of themselves in those they loved. Don Juan is a mere intruder who has struck down those who are already wounded. He appears to have possessed all women, but in fact has possessed none. There is one single shade whom he has occasionally met but who is not on this list of conquests, the white one, the Ideal. At last the unhappy Don Juan begins to long for hell, but the cruel Devil tells him that a hell of a special sort is reserved for him. He is not destined for eternal fire but eternal theatre; he is to be one of the puppets in the Devil's collection. The play is slightly influenced by the Button-moulder episode in *Peer Gynt,* but the thought is typical of Rostand, namely that only love that is unselfish and idealistic is real. (pp. 170-78)

Martin Lamm, "The First Symbolists," in his Modern Drama, *translated by Karin Elliott, Philosophical Library, 1953, pp. 152-78.*

ANTHONY BURGESS (essay date 1970)

[*Considered one of the most prolific and versatile English novelists of his generation, Burgess has written such widely divergent works as* Tremor of Intent (1966), *an eschatological espionage story;* Nothing Like the Sun (1964), *a fictional rendering of William Shakespeare's life; and* A Clockwork Orange (1962), *an account of a futuristic dystopia narrated by a violent teenage criminal. In addition, Burgess is recognized for his vast knowledge of music and linguistics and, in particular, for his erudite criticism of James Joyce's works. In the following excerpt from his preface to his translation of* Cyrano de Bergerac, *Burgess assesses the success of Brian Hooker's translation and defends his own version.*]

The [Brian] Hooker translation [of ***Cyrano de Bergerac***] is the standard version used in America, and it was the basis of the script for the film of ***Cyrano*** in which José Ferrer starred. It has achieved a kind of literary sanctity as the Random House Modern Library of the World's Best Books definitive and undislodgeable Everybody's Cyrano, and this status is not undeserved. Hooker was a respectable minor poet and, like many minor poets, very skillful with traditional verse forms such as the ballade and the triolet—both represented in ***Cyrano***—as well as possessing a knack with blank verse. Moreover, he was humble enough to stick very close to Rostand, and he does not cut one line: his translation can very nearly be used as a key to the original. But he was not so slavish as not to recognize that certain literary references in Rostand would not easily be caught by non-French audiences. Thus, in Cyrano's long speech about his nose, he substitutes "Was this the nose that launched a thousand ships?" for the original

Enfin, parodiant Pyrame en un sanglot:
"Le voilà donc ce nez qui des traits de son maître
A détruit l'harmonie! Il en rougit, le traître!"

Here Rostand is referring to a tragedy known to a Paris audi-

ence but not to any likely to fill a theater in London, New York, or Minneapolis. Encouraged by Hooker's ingenuity, but unhappy about his failure to render the denunciatory tone of the original, I tried the following equivalent for the Pyrame parody:

And finally, with tragic cries and sighs,
The language finely wrought and deeply felt:
"Oh, that this too too solid nose would melt."

But if I had not read Hooker, I might have translated Rostand's lines more or less literally, thus losing a climax and a comic-heroic effect.

Hooker's translation, then, is both faithful and bold, but it never works on the stage, or on the late-late television screen, with the zing and bite or—since we have to use the word sooner or later when discussing ***Cyrano***—panache we have a right to expect. Hooker has produced a play in *cinq actes* ["five acts"] and in *vers* ["verse"], but he has not produced a *comédie héroïque* ["heroic comedy"]. Rostand is funny, as well as moving and pathetic, but Hooker rarely raises a laugh. For that matter, his pathos gets too close to sentimentality to be comfortable, and when we are moved it is very frequently in spite of the words. The trouble lies, I think, in Hooker's decision to use blank verse, a medium that ceased to be dramatically viable about 1630. Overwhelmingly rich in Shakespeare, solid, chunky, sometimes magnificent in Ben Jonson, packed and astringent in Massinger, blank verse became, in the nineteenth-century revivalist tradition that Hooker followed, an over-limpid or limping medium full of self-conscious Shakespearean echoes and somewhat remote—which the blank verse of the Elizabethans was not—from the rhythms of ordinary speech. Hooker makes Cyrano sound like a man speaking blank verse:

What would you have me do?
Seek for the patronage of some great man,
And like a creeping vine on a tall tree
Crawl upward, where I cannot stand alone?
No thank you! Dedicate, as others do,
Poems to pawnbrokers? Be a buffoon
In the vile hope of teasing out a smile
On some cold face?

Elizabethan characters, on the other hand, sound like men imposing their own idiolects on a fundamental beat of iambic pentameters that is, so to speak, the unconscious and disregarded pulse of the play.

Rostand, of course, wrote in rhymed Alexandrines, like the great classical French dramatists, tragic and comic alike, and this metric ought strictly to be rendered into English heroic couplets:

What would you have me do?
Seek out a powerful protector, pursue
A potent patron? Cling like a leeching vine
To a tree? *Crawl* my way up? Fawn, whine
For all that sticky candy called success?
No, thank you. Be a sycophant and dress
In sickly rhymes a prayer to a moneylender?
Play the buffoon, desperate to engender
A smirk on a refrigerated jowl?

Not, perhaps, the very regular couplets of Pope, which no living writer can easily imitate, but five-beat lines with a varying number of syllables and a regular couplet rhyming scheme. I read and saw performed Richard Wilbur's admirable translation of Molière's *Tartuffe,* in which he clings relentlessly and brilliantly to rhymed decasyllabic couplets, and, in the first draft of my version of **Cyrano,** I tried to follow his example. But for various reasons it failed to work. French Alexandrines can be used in many ways, and the classical comic way, which is Molière's, is conventional, unpoetic, arhetorical: the metric seems to symbolize the social order, it is not available for the special expressive purposes of any individual character. Rostand is romantic, and his Alexandrine, though sometimes merely traditional and conventional (the tuning-up violins in the first scene have to accommodate their *la* to it), becomes very often a highly poetic medium as well as a clever instrument of stichomythia. The English heroic couplet, with its mostly intellectual associations, cannot do as much. So I have used a variety of verse styles and even occasional passages of prose, seeing in **Cyrano** something of the quality of an opera, with set pieces like arias that require the prosy dryness of recitative before and behind them. There are in my version sprung-rhythmed heroic couplets, rhymed and unrhymed Alexandrines, blank verse breaking into occasional rhyme, verse with a free rhyming pattern (which really means lack of pattern), and—mainly in the last scene—something that can be called *vers libre* ["free verse"]. The *cinq actes* have become three (Rostand's third is my second), but *vers* remains and, it is hoped, some of the spirit of the *comédie héroïque.*

Rhyme can be a witty thing in itself, and it can bring out wit where our prose-attuned ears may fail to catch it in the ordinary realistic run of dialogue. In Hooker's version, when Ragueneau the pastrycook and his wife Lise are quarreling because he loves poets and she doesn't and she has torn up volumes of verse to make paper bags for cakes, the lines go like this:

> RAGUENEAU. Ant! Would you blame the locust for his song?
> LISE. I blame the locust for his appetite!
> There used to be a time—before you had
> Your hungry friends—you never called me Ants—
> No, nor Bacchantes!
> RAGUENEAU.   What a way to use
> Poetry!
> LISE.   Well, what is the use of it?
> RAGUENEAU. But, my dear girl, what would you do with prose?

This, being mildly scatological, ought to get a laugh, but a laugh will come only with rhyme:

> RAGUENEAU. Ant—how dare you insult these divine grasshoppers.
> LISE. Locusts, you mean, a rotten plague of locusts.
> Before you got in thick with these poet-paupers
> You never called me rotten things like ants
> And Bacchants.
> RAGUENEAU.   But—to do *that,* with *those!*
> LISE. It's all it's fit for, rotten hocus-pocus.
> RAGUENEAU. It makes me wonder what you'd do with prose.

Later in the same scene, de Guiche tells Cyrano that, Quixote-like, he is fighting windmills and that it may happen that

> —Un moulinet de leurs grand bras chargés de toiles
> Vous lance dans la boue! . . .

To which Cyrano replies: "Ou bien dans les étoiles!" Hooker has:

> DE GUICHE. Windmills, remember, if you fight with them—
> CYRANO. My enemies change, then, with every wind?
> DE GUICHE. —May swing round their huge arms and cast you down
> Into the mire.
> CYRANO.   Or up—among the stars!

This is romantic enough, the tone of a diluted Mercutio, but Cyrano is being neat as well as bold. My version goes as follows:

> DE GUICHE. If you fight with windmills—
> CYRANO.   I see what you mean:
> My enemies are the men who change with the wind.
> DE GUICHE. If you fight with windmills, they'll swing their heavy spars
> And you'll spin down to the mud.
> CYRANO.   Or up to the stars.

The other ways in which this version differs from Hooker's and, indeed, what other translations I have read, are so radical as to require some words of defense. For, directed by the director of the production, whose best defense is his aesthetic success, I have dared to make some structural alterations in the play as Rostand wrote it. Of all the characters, the least satisfactory to a modern audience is Roxane (whose name I have degallicized to Roxana). She loves Christian, and yet she rebuffs him because he cannot woo her in witty and poetic language. This must seem very improbable in an age that finds a virtue in sincere inarticulacy, and I have had to find an excuse for this near-pathological dismissal of a good wordless soldier whose beauty, on her own admission, fills Roxana's heart with ravishment. I have inserted a little speech which I hope will ring plausibly, to the effect that inarticulate brutish wooing is a mark of the aristocracy that regards a middle-class bookish pretty girl like Roxana as fair game, and that to her the advent of true love must reveal itself in divine eloquence. This perhaps adds a human substratum to Roxana's preciosity, and it seems to work dramatically.

But, adding to her lines in Act II, I have had to subtract her entire physical presence from Act III, Scene i. Her sudden appearance outside the walls of besieged Arras, with gifts of wine, cold chicken, and sausage for the starving Gascony Cadets, relieves the tension of the scene when it should remain taut to the very end, and it relieves it in an unworthy manner—through farce and the atmosphere of a fairy tale. Apart from the difficulty of staging (and it is this scene more than anything which puts good amateur companies off attempting the play), everything that is good in this phase of the action goes bad as soon as she comes on in her coach and Paris perfume. The hungry Cadets cease to be heroic and become merely foppish. They are nearly dying of starvation, and yet they have to go through the motions of taking an elegant little dinner, complete with cutlery and napery. They become mean; they make sure that de Guiche, their detested colonel, who is as ill from hunger as they are, gets nothing of their feast. We may be persuaded, with difficulty, that they now feel fine, but there is a nasty taste in our own mouths. Then comes Roxana's avowal to Christian: it is his soul she loves, not his physical beauty, and she has braved the battlefield to tell him this (the Spanish enemy has been charming and said "Pass, *señorita*"). The whole thing becomes absurd, farcical, unacceptable in terms of even the most far-fetched dramatic convention. Michael Langham [first director of Burgess's version], who had already produced **Cyrano** with this scene in it, said that it had to go, and I think he was right.

I have substituted for Roxana's personal appearance the arrival of a letter from her, which Christian can read aloud to Cyrano, or Roxana—distant and disembodied—can breathe into a microphone while the lights dim and perfume is sprayed through the auditorium. Whichever of these two ways is chosen, Cyrano has his one opportunity, while onstage, merely to listen instead of talking all the time. Having decided on the letter device, I was amused to find my judgment confirmed by a Mr. Magoo cartoon film, in which Mr. Magoo, playing Cyrano, returns amid shells and snipers from mailing the daily letter to Roxana with a letter from the beloved herself in his hand. Roxana's Platonic rhetoric comes off well enough when we can take it as epistolary literature, but—apart from all the other objections—it sounds unreal on her speaking lips.

I have made, on my own initiative, a less fundamental change in Act II. Roxana and Christian are being hurriedly married by a Capuchin duped into performing the act, and Cyrano has to prevent de Guiche—who wants Roxana as a mistress and has, through his uncle Cardinal Richelieu, power over the entire order of Capuchins—from discovering that the ceremony is taking place and stopping it. In the original, Cyrano pretends to have fallen from outer space and he insists on telling de Guiche—who does not see the nose and thinks he has been accosted by a madman—the various possible ways of getting to the moon. Since we now know how to get to the moon, there is a danger that the audience may feel very superior to Cyrano (who, incidentally, as a historical personage wrote the world's first science fiction) and ignore his ingenuity while wanting to put him right on rocketry. So I have written a couple of speeches in the satirical vein of the historical Cyrano, which may be taken as prefiguring the polemic indiscretion that (in the play, fifteen years later) is the cause of his assassination. It does not greatly matter what Cyrano does to prevent de Guiche's discovery of the clandestine marriage, since it is merely a question of filling in time entertainingly. Imaginative directors might even consider making Cyrano show his versatility by performing a mad ballet sequence. He has, after all, a couple of musicians ready at hand to accompany him.

Michael Langham suggested merging the characters of Le Bret and Carbon de Castel-Jaloux to make one meaty personage instead of two thin ones. I have done this. I also, at his behest, have the poet Lignière recite some lines from the libelous poem that is the cause of Cyrano's fight with a hundred armed ruffians. It was my own idea to make Cyrano improvise a kind of acrostic on his own name in Act I, Scene ii. For the rest, this version is close enough to the play as Rostand wrote it, except for one or two lops of Occam's razor.

The very last word spoken by Cyrano before he dies is, in the original, *panache.* This quality, he says, is the one thing that death and judgment cannot take away from him. We use the word in English, since there is no native synonym for it, but we cannot always be sure that we are using it in a Rostandian sense. Rostand was good enough to attempt a definition for the French Academy in 1901:

> Le panache n'est pas la grandeur, mais quelque chose qui s'ajoute à la grandeur, et qui bouge audessus d'elle. C'est quelque chose de voltigeant, d'excessif, et d'un peu frisé. . . . Certes, les héros sans panache sont plus désintéressés que les autres, car le panache, c'est souvent, dans un sacrifice qu'on fait, une consolation d'attitude qu'on se

donne. Un peu frivole peut-être, un peu théâtral sans doute, le panache n'est qu'une grâce; mais cette grâce . . . suppose tant de force (l'esprit qui voltige n'est-il pas la plus belle victoire sur la carcasse qui tremble?) que, tout de même, c'est une grâce que je nous souhaite.

[*Panache* is not greatness, but something which is added to greatness and which stirs above it. It is something fluttering, excessive, and a little frizzled. . . . Certainly, the heroes without *panache* are more disinterested than the others, because *panache* is often, in a sacrifice that one makes, a consolation of attitude that one gives oneself. A little frivolous perhaps, a little theatrical no doubt, *panache* is nothing but a favor; but this favor . . . grants so much strength (isn't the spirit that flies the most beautiful victory over the body that trembles?) that, all the same, it is a favor that I wish for us.]

So subtle a concept cannot easily be conveyed by any English word, except perhaps by something as symbolic as *plume,* or *white plume,* which is what Cyrano wears on his hat and is, of course, his literal *panache.* After much deliberation, I have allowed Cyrano to make his last English word the same as his last French one, but I have tried to prepare the audience for its totality of meaning by using it in various contexts throughout the play.

Cyrano de Bergerac may not be the best play ever written, and this translation certainly is highly supersessible, but Cyrano himself is surely one of the great characters of all drama, and he has qualities which ought to commend him to an age that appreciates the making of a style out of despair. It is my hope that this new version may encourage new productions, not only in Minneapolis, and that amateur companies may at last consider coming to an author they may have had cause—through no fault of their own—to neglect. On both sides of the footlights, ***Cyrano*** can be a very rewarding dramatic experience. (pp. v-xiv)

Anthony Burgess, in a preface to Cyrano de Bergerac *by Edmond Rostand, translated by Anthony Burgess, Alfred A. Knopf, 1971, pp. v-xiv.*

FURTHER READING

Besser, Gretchen R. Review of *Cyrano de Bergerac,* by Edmond Rostand. *Modern Language Journal* 61, No. 12 (January-February 1977): 78.
    Praises Christopher Fry's English version of the drama as "a marvel, a soul-satisfying translation."

Brooks, Cleanth, and Heilman, Robert B. "*Cyrano de Bergerac,* by Edmond Rostand." In their *Understanding Drama: Twelve Plays,* pp. 20-1. New York: Holt, Rinehart and Winston, 1945.
    List of questions about the themes, style, and tone of *Cyrano de Bergerac,* designed to generate discussion among students.

Brown, Calvin S. "The Deaths of Doctor Pascal and Cyrano de Bergerac." *Symposium* VII, No. 2 (November 1953): 372-74.
    Suggests that Rostand adapted the death scene from Emile Zola's novel *Doctor Pascal* for his *Cyrano de Bergerac,* based on

the similarity between Pascal's and Cyrano's announcements of their own deaths.

Burgess, Anthony. "A Mingled Chime." *Times Literary Supplement* (16 January 1976): 50.
  Criticizes both the Brian Hooker and Christopher Fry translations of *Cyrano de Bergerac,* although allowing that the Fry version has had "reported success . . . in the theatre."

Butler, Mildred Allen. "The Historical Cyrano de Bergerac as a Basis for Rostand's Play." *Educational Theatre Journal* VI, No. 3 (October 1954): 231-40.
  Compares the historical Cyrano to the character created by Rostand and outlines probable reasons for Rostand's deviations from historical fact.

———. "Sources of Plot Ideas in *Cyrano de Bergerac.*" *Western Speech* XIX, No. 2 (March 1955): 87-93.
  Evaluates a charge of plagiarism against Rostand made by Samuel Gross, concluding that while Rostand may have read Gross's drama *The Merchant Prince of Cornville,* the similarities between the two plays consist only of familiar and unoriginal metaphors and plot ideas.

Chesterton, G. K. "The Romance of Rostand." In his *The Uses of Diversity: A Book of Essays,* pp. 71-4. London: Methuen and Co., 1920.
  Defends Rostand against accusations of shallowness by illustrating the thought required to be witty and clear, and by asserting the fallacy of thinking "a thing creative because it is chaotic, and vast because it is vague."

Duclaux, Mary. "Edmond Rostand." In her *Twentieth-Century French Writers,* pp. 51-67. London: W. Collins Sons and Co., 1919.
  Praises Rostand's poetry, suggesting that future critics may look upon him as another Shakespeare.

Hamilton, Clayton. "Edmond Rostand." In his *Conversations on Contemporary Drama,* pp. 20-41. New York: Macmillan Co., 1924.
  Surveys Rostand's works and claims that Rostand is the best of the minor poets in western literature.

———. Preface to *Cyrano de Bergerac,* by Edmond Rostand, pp. ix-xvii. New York: Henry Holt and Co., 1925.
  Reminiscences about the first production of Brian Hooker's translation of *Cyrano de Bergerac,* which starred Walter Hampton.

Jung, C. G. "The Miller Fantasies: Anamnesis." In his *Symbols of Transformation: An Analysis of the Prelude to a Case of Schizophrenia,* translated by R. F. C. Hull, pp. 34-8. 1951. Reprint. London: Routledge and Kegan Paul, 1981.
  Analyzes a patient's account of attending a performance of *Cyrano de Bergerac,* in which she "identifies herself to such a degree with the wounded Christian . . . that she feels a piercing pain in her own breast, the very place where the hero receives his death wound."

Kuhns, Oscar. Introduction to *Cyrano de Bergerac,* by Edmond Rostand, pp. iii-xi. New York: Henry Holt and Co., 1899.
  General discussion of *Cyrano de Bergerac* which includes an account by the French actor Constant-Benoît Coquelin of the drama's opening night, background on the historical Cyrano, and an explanation for the play's popularity.

MacKaye, Percy. "There Is No Such Nose as That Nose." *The Literary Digest International Book Review* 11, No. 2 (January 1924): 107-08.
  Praises Brian Hooker's English translation of *Cyrano de Bergerac* for its "subtle, poetic transmutations of the French."

Miller, Nellie Burget. "Modern French Drama." In her *The Living Drama: Historical Development and Modern Movements Visualized,* pp. 225-52. New York: Century Co., 1924.
  Includes a survey of Rostand's works.

Nicoll, Allardyce. "Neo-Romanticism in the Theatre." In his *World Drama: From Æschylus to Anouilh,* pp. 611-28. New York: Harcourt, Brace and Co., 1964.
  Offers a brief discussion of Rostand's career, asserting that he created the perfect vehicle for his ideas in *Cyrano de Bergerac.*

Simon, John. "*Cyrano de Bergerac.*" In his *Singularities: Essays on the Theater, 1964-1973,* pp. 17-19. New York: Random House, 1975.
  Praises the technical merits of *Cyrano de Bergerac,* concluding that it "is not a great play, merely a perfect one."

Spiers, A. G. H. Introduction to *Cyrano de Bergerac,* by Edmond Rostand, pp. vii-xxvi. New York: Oxford University Press, 1938.
  Discusses Rostand's philosophy and theatrical techniques, asserting that he unified his plays through emotions rather than plot or character development.

Untermeyer, Louis. Foreword to *Cyrano de Bergerac,* by Edmond Rostand, pp. ix-xvii. New York: Heritage Press, 1954.
  Compares the historical Cyrano and his friends to Rostand's characters, chronicles the success of the drama, and defines the play's comedy as ironic and heroic rather than humorous.

Florencio Sánchez

1875-1910

Uruguayan dramatist.

Sánchez is considered the first major dramatist in Spanish-American literature. He is best known for plays in which he addressed social issues of the River Plate region, which lies on either side of an estuary separating Uruguay and Argentina. In these works, Sánchez produced vivid depictions of everyday life, thereby helping to introduce realism into Spanish-American drama.

Sánchez was born in Montevideo, the capital of Uruguay. Soon after his birth, Sánchez's family moved to the village of Minas, where he attended school and later worked as a reporter for the local newspaper. Returning to Montevideo, Sánchez worked as a journalist and became affiliated with the International Center of Social Studies, where he attended lectures, readings, and political discussions sponsored by an anarchist group. He later moved to Buenos Aires, Argentina, where he acted in minor theatrical productions and became increasingly interested in play writing. Sánchez's first drama, scheduled to be performed in the Argentine city of Rosario in 1902, was banned because in it he caricatured several of the city's well-known citizens. Later that year, however, his play *Canillita* was produced, and the 1903 performance of *M'hijo el dotor* in Buenos Aires represented his first major success. In that work, Sánchez portrayed the struggle between a father whose traditional mores conflict with those of his son, who has received a modern education. During the next several years, Sánchez wrote prolifically, often focusing his plays on everyday situations and on the social relations between the natives of rural Spanish America—variously called gauchos, creoles, and criollos—and gringos, immigrants to Spanish America who are usually Italian in Sánchez's dramas. Although most of his plays of this period were produced, Sánchez was unable to achieve financial security. His straitened circumstances were compounded by health problems, including tuberculosis. In 1909, Sánchez received a government grant to travel to Europe, and he died in Italy in 1910.

Sánchez's plays are considered important and innovative for their treatment of contemporary social issues, particularly the relations between gaucho and gringo. In *La gringa,* his most critically acclaimed work, Sánchez tells the story of Don Cantalicio, a gaucho who loses his land to Don Nicola, an industrious Italian immigrant. Prospero, Cantalicio's son, then works for Nicola but is fired because of his attentions to Nicola's daughter Victoria. After Cantalicio is injured and cared for by Victoria, a reconciliation is effected, and Prospero and Victoria marry. Critics maintain that the conclusion reflects Sánchez's belief that intermarriage will dissolve the hostility between the two groups. The play has also been studied for its symbolism, particularly Sánchez's use of the *ombú,* a tree representing the romantic spirit of the gaucho that is immediately cut down by Don Nicola when he gains control of the land. Ruth Richardson comments, "*La gringa* is the symbolic drama of the Argentine conscience, the epic of the invasion by the foreigner of the land of the *gaucho.*"

Critics have also applauded Sánchez for introducing realism into the theater of the River Plate region. In *La tigra,* for example, in which a mother resorts to prostitution to support her children, the family's difficulties are presented without sentimentality. Sánchez has also been commended for his insightful and convincing characterizations, especially in such family dramas as *Los derechos de la salud,* in which a dying woman sees her sister gradually assuming her own roles as mother and wife, and *Barranca abajo,* in which a gaucho loses his home and family and ultimately commits suicide. In addition, critics have praised Sánchez's naturalistic dialogue, his skill at developing character and plot with apparently insignificant details, and his ability to advance the action of a play without the use of speech, as in *Barranca abajo,* wherein the sight of an empty bed airing outside tells the audience that a character has died.

Sánchez's significance as a dramatist rests on both thematic and technical aspects of his works. Critics have praised his portrayal of the gaucho-gringo conflict as an insightful examination of an issue that has universal significance. As a result of his realistic depiction of social problems of the River Plate region, he is regarded as the progenitor of modern Spanish-American drama.

PRINCIPAL WORKS

Canillita (drama) 1902
    [*The Newspaper Boy,* 1961]
M'hijo el dotor (drama) 1903
    [*My Son the Doctor,* 1961]
Cédulas de San Juan (drama) 1904
    [published as *Midsummer Day Parents* in *Plays of the Southern Americas,* 1942]
La gringa (drama) 1904
    [published as *The Foreign Girl* in *Plays of the Southern Americas,* 1942; also published as *The Immigrant Girl,* 1961]
La pobre gente (drama) 1904
Barranca abajo (drama) 1905
    [*Down the Gully,* 1961]
En familia (drama) 1905
    [*The Family Circle,* 1961]
Mano santa (drama) 1905
    [*The Healing Hand,* 1961]
Los muertos (drama) 1905
    [published as *Los muertos* in *Yale Review,* 1928]
El desalojo (drama) 1906
    [*Evicted,* 1961]
El pasado de una vida (drama) 1906
Los derechos de la salud (drama) 1907
Moneda falsa (drama) 1907
    [*Phony Money,* 1961]
Nuestros hijos (drama) 1907
    [*Our Children,* 1961]
La tigra (drama) 1907
    [*The Tigress,* 1961]
Marta gruni (drama) 1908
Un bien negocio (drama) 1909
Teatro completo de Florencio Sánchez (dramas) 1941
Representative Plays of Florencio Sánchez (dramas) 1961

ISAAC GOLDBERG (essay date 1922)

[In the following excerpt, Goldberg surveys Sánchez's major works.]

Those of Sánchez' critics who declaim against the unliterary character of his plays are partly right. Sánchez was no closet spirit; he wrote, moreover, in haste, almost improvising. His early poverty had forced him to steal even the paper upon which he composed his pieces: he would go to the telegraph offices, pretend absorption in the writing of a telegram, and manage to make off with a block of sheets. So accustomed did he become to writing plays upon the back of these telegraph blanks that in later life, when comparative affluence was his, he would purchase blocks of them at the office, as he found it impossible to compose upon the expensive paper presented to him by admirers.

And to most of his plays there is a certain stenographic rapidity of progress that actually suggests the concise phraseology of telegraphic despatches. Even the longest of them are short, always containing a first act notable for the swiftness of the exposition. He dashed the plays off at fairly lightning speed, rarely revised or even re-read his work, did not always even spell correctly, paid little attention (as might be supposed) to the niceties of composition, and was a failure when he attempted stylistic flights. Into some of his best plays creeps an occasional speech that smacks of Echegarayan rhetoric whose death decree was signed by the "generation of 1898" across the ocean. But in recompense for these defects his dramas present us life in action; if he did not create character, he was a natural master in the depiction of types and the presentation of backgrounds.

His plays have been generally grouped as (1) portraying life in the country, (2) life in the city, especially among the lower middle class, and (3) presenting problems. He is a realist first of all, and draws chiefly upon persons and scenes that he knows intimately. Always he is preoccupied with problems that life has suggested. Now (*My Son the Doctor*) it is the conflict between new ideals and old; now (*La gringa*) the conflict between the native who must yield up his holdings to the more industrious business-like foreigner; again, as in **Barranca abajo,** or **En familia,** the portrayal of a family falling away to moral ruin because of the reverses that overtake them. Himself a sick man, he has the courage to write a harsh play like **The Rights of Health,** in which the thesis is a Nietzschean disregard of the weak.

Much of this was the application of foreign suggestion to the native drama, but such a statement should not be interpreted as implying anything like direct imitation. Sánchez had lived and seen too much to need such aid. On the other hand, intensely fond of the stage, he could not help being influenced by the 1904 season in Buenos Aires of the Italian actor, Ermete Zacconi, and the plays thus revealed. There are external resemblances in some of his plays to those of Bracco, but in theme only. Of course the critics had to talk of Ibsen, as if Ibsen were not part of the prevailing atmosphere. At this time, it will be recalled, Gorki had been brought forward by the Russian revolution of 1905.

That there is a Grand Guignol element in Sánchez is shown by Antoine's comment after witnessing a performance of **M'hijo el dotor**: "It's a piece that seems to have been written for my theatre, with an admirable sincerity of intention and simplicity of means. I almost feel like giving it in a translation at Paris."

Yet, even allowing for these varied influences, Sánchez is Sánchez. His own life had brought him face to face with the drink evil that he studies in **Los muertos**; his own experience with and against the police had brought him into contact with the low types he portrays so well in pieces like **Moneda falsa**; his personal health could have suggested the entire pessimistic facture of his plays, though it has been noted that whenever he looks toward the coming day he is optimistic. Such, for example, is the end of **La gringa,** where the son of a foreigner marries the daughter of the conquered native and prepares to build the new civilization of the future. This is the optimism of the lyrical anarchist at battle with the present; it is the optimism of a consumptive Sánchez, too—a "spes pthisica"—finding vent in his work. It is the optimism of the man who, facing a lonely death in Italy, could speak of his future labors with the accents of youthful hope.

Sánchez, in brief, was in a good sense of the term a man of the theatre. Faults his plays reveal a-plenty: in **My Son the Doctor,** for example, the son, who supposedly incarnates the new ideas, is far below the father who exemplifies the old, and the woman in the case is an impossible creature. The play, because of its historical importance, has been much overpraised by Spanish-American critics as a work of art.

It has been estimated that the actual time consumed in the writing of the author's entire output was thirty-five to forty days. Sánchez died at the beginning of his career. His plays, though they are not "literature," read well, even compellingly. Time, said the admirable Brazilian critic, Verissimo, does not respect works in which it has not been made a collaborator. Yet it might be answered, on the other hand, that the life put into a work lives in it. And though Sánchez did not make Time a collaborator, he had a faithful ally in Life. His plays mirror a certain progress not only in the Argentine drama, but in life itself in the neighboring nations. Belonging thus to history and to national development, they may safely hope to find a permanent place in the history of literature. (pp. 225-29)

Because of the importance of [*My Son the Doctor*], let us pause for a moment upon it, as upon a few of its fellows. Sánchez' dramatic personality will be the clearer for it.

My Son the Doctor, as we have seen, is representative of the eternal struggle between the old and the new; it furnishes the turning point of the Argentine theatre even as Hasenclever's *Der Sohn,* with its similar ideology, provides a rallying-point for the young German Expressionists. Julio is here the rebellious youth; Mariquita his fond, forgiving mother; Olegario, the stern, tyrannical father. Jesusa, loved by Eloy, upon whom Julio has drawn a forged check covered by Olegario, is attracted to Julio and loves him, when she discovers his attentions to Sarah. The situation is all the harder since, as might be expected, she is on the way to motherhood with Julio's child beneath her heart. The youthful doctor tries to justify his position with a somewhat preachy speech on his doctrine of moral non-responsibility. Olegario threatens to kill his son if he does not marry the seduced woman. Julio is even induced, by his mother, to wed the girl, and begins to behold in her a nobility not before apparent; Jesusa, however, fears that he will go back to Sarah after all. The end is somewhat indecisive, though Julio and Jesusa lead Olegario to believe that they will marry.

There can be no doubting the notable purpose of the drama; but the ideas suffer through insufficient and not wholly convincing characterization. Just as the old ideas are more firmly established than the new, so here the older personages seem more real than the young, erratic doctor. Julio himself does not show a real understanding of the free notions he professes. At best he is a transitory figure who has glimpsed a new truth, but has sullied it with mistaking freedom for irresponsibility. This, however, may be just what the author desired to impress. The first act has been called one of the great moments of Argentine drama; the other two, however, are far inferior. The play as a whole is important rather historically than as an example of successful artistic creation. It has been elevated to the position of a dramaturgic idol; Spanish-American critics will, as a group, recede from this untenable position to something more closely approximating an æsthetic view.

La gringa, of the following year (1904) is a mirror of the transition from indigenous to cosmopolitan outlook. Its action is characteristically swift—dramaturgic stenography, in fact—and up to the very close presents a fine theme, well-handled. The most convincing character is the old Cantalicio, as if in Sánchez there were a secret sympathy with, and a better un-

derstanding of, the older régime, just as, despite his Nietzschean *Los derechos de la salud,* he was himself a sick man and kind to the weak and oppressed. In *La gringa* no sides are taken; the foreign "intruder" and the native are seen, eventually, to merge quite as naturally as the past with the present. A similar sense of situation, a similar human insight and pathos inform *Barranca abajo* (1905), in which the hardness of character in Zoilo and his rebellious daughter and his sister, mirrors the rigidity of the theme, which recalls Giacosa's *Come le foglie.* What this play does for family degeneration in the country, *En familia* (1905) does for a like disintegration in the city. Again we have father versus son, with the son at the same time winner (morally) and loser. As usual, Sánchez is more concerned with dramatic situation than with psychology, yet he can make skillful use of situation to throw light upon character. He studies not so much the ruin of a family as the results of that ruin; not the process but the consequences.

Los muertos (1905), Sánchez' fourth play for that year, is more than simply another picture of a family's dissolution through the father's vice of drink. Here is a milieu where man's beastliness is enthroned by the tenets of social law and religious custom. The background against which Lisandro stumbles on his way to ruin is drawn with the effective, broad strokes that we come to expect of Sánchez. But what seems to have escaped his critics is that in Amelia we have one of the rare women rebels in Spanish-American drama. True, when she exchanges Lisandro for Julian, she but exchanges masters, but the quest for happiness, so long thwarted in her, at least finds vent in one mad dash for such freedom as she comprehends. She has a worthy, if more understanding, companion in the play *Liberta,* by the Cuban dramatist José Antonio Ramos.

Nuestros hijos (1908) is important for its plainly autobiographical content; it is yet another of the plays in which youth and age wage their unending battle. As so often with Sánchez, and most other playwrights engaged upon problems, the ideas are more important than the personages supposed to represent them, though here the motivation is conscientious, even if but sketchy. The economy of words is telegraphic. In contrast to *M'hijo el dotor,* here it is age and experience which see farther and more resolutely than youth and its facile conventions. The author achieves his satire of the shallow, charitable soul at the cost of exaggeration, yet a hot sincerity born of the writer's actual experience manages to fuse these touches of Ibsen, Bracco, Giacosa, and lesser social dramatists into something like a personal entity. In general outlook the piece companions Benavente's *Los Malhechores del Bien,* while in the figure of Mecha it presents another of the rare rebellious women.

Mecha, seduced and deserted by Enrique, scorns him, though she would marry him to save her family anguish. Her father is a queer, liberal-social spirit, seemingly daft upon the subject of illegitimate children. Her mother and sisters "do charity" with the automatism of most superficial dabblers engaged in that work. On the very day inaugurating the campaign in behalf of abandoned children she reveals her condition to her father. Alfredo, her brother, fights a duel with Enrique, but neither is hurt. Mecha, now the target of her aunt's moral arrows, is almost convinced to go to a convent. Her father, however, stiffens her fibre. She no longer loves Enrique, and when his mother comes with his offer to marry her after all, her father refuses in her name, afterward receiving her approbation. Mecha has now her brother's insistence to conquer, and this she does, refusing of her own free will to wed Enrique. The son threatens to have the marriage consummated by force and (as the father has foreseen) to have their obdurate parent shut up as insane. At the height of the argument the father lets slip a word about his wife's infidelity; he has letters as proof. Alfredo is too overwhelmed to reconstruct his life, but father, daughter, and unborn child go forward to a new day, a new life built upon their own truths.

It is the last of Sánchez' important plays, *Los derechos de la salud (The Rights of Health)*, 1908, that has long been the topic of excited comment. . . . *Los derechos de la salud* is a compelling, cruel play in which the hardness of the thesis appears in a certain hardness of the characters who exemplify it. It contains more than a touch of melodrama and more than one artificial situation. Nor is it so convincing as some of the other dramas in which Sánchez treats of principles and problems. But its cruelty is part of the inherent cruelty of nature, and, as in so much of what Sánchez has written, there is a singular appeal born of passionate intensity that vivifies the crudeness. (pp. 230-35)

The play itself is characteristically brief: some less than sixty pages of ordinary print. Luisa is a consumptive, the wife of Roberto; he is slowly falling in love with his sister-in-law, Renata. Luisa, with the perspicaciousness of illness, suspects her sister; Renata, learning of this, decides to leave the home—in which she serves as Roberto's amanuensis,—but Roberto is beside himself at the news. The wife, piqued at this practical demonstration of affection for the woman who loved him before she herself did, tries to reach a revolver locked in Roberto's drawer. Her death, in any event inevitable, is hastened by the domestic imbroglio. Roberto, who is a writer, and who pities his wife deeply, defends the right of health to the happiness that illness cannot provide for it. The end is foreseen; Luisa will die; Renata and Roberto will marry.

There is something in Sánchez that, to an American of the North, suggests a fleeting comparison with Eugene O'Neill. Like Sánchez, O'Neill has brought to a stage infested with unrealities a breath of the everlasting that informs all reality. To speak in text-book terminology, part of O'Neill's work represents, upon our stage, the belated arrival of European realism. But Sánchez stopped writing four years before the war began; O'Neill began writing in the year of the war and lived through those horrible years. He has learned, and quickly, what Sánchez would have learned with equal rapidity: that narrow realism is not enough. Wherefore he abandons his early melodrama for a more plastic medium, thus bridging, within the space of a few years, several distinct epochs in the evolution of dramatic form. In O'Neill, as in Sánchez, there is a certain stenographic quality born of a multifarious, restless life; in the North American, as in the American of the South, there is the same succinctness, the same sketchy psychology, the same raciness of dialogue and nearness to the soil, the same lack of "literary" graces—as if "literature" and "style," rather than extraneous ingredients that may be mixed into a work, were not organic components of the creative entity! In each, action is more important than lengthy speech; O'Neill, the equal of Sánchez in reproduction of ambient, is his superior in dramatic projection of character. Our own writer is one of the hopes of the native drama; Sánchez is, thus far, the chief dramatic glory of his continent. That glory, as we have seen, rests upon his personality, his importance to his epoch, as much as upon the plays produced

by this errant, human, striving child of the early twentieth century. Yet one would gladly surrender many a work by such "famous" playwrights as Bernstein, the later Brieux, the later Echegaray, and a number of the European mediocrities, for the crude life that pulses in the dramatic output of Florencio Sánchez. Passionate sincerity is not enough to create a work of art; it is always to be preferred, however, to that passionless excellence of the artificer who has nothing to give because he garnered nothing. Others to come will go farther than Sánchez, but they will be the stronger for his having labored. (pp. 235-37)

Isaac Goldberg, "Florencio Sánchez," in his The Drama of Transition: Native and Exotic Playcraft, *Stewart Kidd Company, 1922, pp. 218-37.*

RUTH RICHARDSON   (essay date 1933)

[*In the following excerpt, Richardson discusses various aspects of Sánchez's plays, including characterization, dramatic techniques, and themes, and assesses his contribution to Spanish-American drama.*]

Any discussion of the characters in the plays of Sánchez involves a division into two types, local and universal. The local types form, by far, the more interesting group. These characters are *gringos* and *criollos*. Don Nicola [in *La gringa*] is the outstanding *gringo* or Italian portrait. He is a pushing, successful land owner, farmer, and rancher. He keeps abreast of the times, realizes his own superiority in his work, is not deliberately cruel to his family or employees, but is thoughtless. In general, he creates a favorable impression in the reader. He is kind to those in trouble, but never sentimental; and in business he knows what belongs to him and insists upon it. He dispenses with everything that does not add to his income or to his physical comfort, hence he is the essence of efficiency. His wife, María, offers a contrast to him. She has her husband's defects but apparently none of his virtues. Mainly she lacks a sensitiveness which he has at heart, but keeps generally below the surface. Italians in other plays of Sánchez's do not vary much from the pattern used for Don Nicola and María.

Sánchez's *criollos*, too, have certain characteristics in common, but they show much individual variation, to cite a few—Don Olegario and Julio in *Nuestros hijos,* Cantalicio in *La gringa,* Don Zoilo in *Barranca abajo,* Jorge of *En familia,* and the numerous lesser figures of the *sainetes* like *Cédulas de San Juan.* The four old *criollos* offer interesting comparisons. Don Zoilo is the most tragic of them all, revealing the elements of the protagonist of old Greek tragedy. We are not led to assume that his afflictions are a direct result of mismanagement or of excesses. Rather he is a *criollo* who becomes impoverished through the changing civilization to which he cannot adapt himself. He has the sterling qualities of the type, honesty, loyalty in friendship, and a deep sense of personal honor and of family honor. In fact, when the family honor is tarnished he feels that he has nothing to live for, and he commits suicide. His sincerity of character and sense of thwarted ideals make of him the most tragic of Sánchez's characters.

Next in dignity is Don Olegario of *M'hijo el dotor.* We have in Don Olegario the simple hearted father who can look at questions from one side alone, that of honesty and personal obligation. We have an upright, straightforward individual as sure of the right course as Calderón's famous Pedro Crespo,

Alcalde de Zalamea. The latter's problem, however, was simple in comparison with Olegario's. Pedro Crespo had to take a simple fearless stand for right against a guilty man. Don Olegario, living in the late nineteenth or early twentieth century, has to combat a spurious philosophy, imperfectly understood by his son Julio. Hard as he strives to convert a recalcitrant son he makes no progress. We do not feel that he achieves a moral victory even though what he works for does finally come about. The ending is not inevitable. It probably would not have come out so in life. Perhaps Sánchez felt that that the essential aims of the *criollos* would succeed anyhow if they were willing to overlook the means and be satisfied with the end no matter how achieved. But Don Olegario is thwarted, as is every pure *criollo* of the Sánchez theatre. The *criollo* can not quicken his rate of speed for work or thought, and cannot adapt his methods or his primitive ideas of finance to the demands of the present heightened civilization. What is more tragic still is that his ideals are too high and impractical to combat the materialistic, destructive determinism of the age.

Cantalicio is a *criollo* of the same generation as Don Olegario and Zoilo; but he is not so essentially tragic. In the contact with civilization he has to sacrifice material things and traditions to which sentimental value is attached; but he does not have the bitter struggle experienced by Olegario in having to see his ethical ideals thwarted, simply because he never possessed such a high conception of duty, honor, and fundamental honesty. Cantalicion has his tragic moments, many of them, but essentially his personality is not such as to induce respect.

Don Jorge of **En familia** is the least attractive of the old *criollo* ilk. He represents the ultimate stage of the *criollo* when the contact with urban civilization has done its worst for him. He has lost every vestige of the innate nobility of his forbears. He is absolutely lacking in the sense of personal honor or of family honor, honesty, loyalty to friends or to family. He sinks so low that he prefers accepting charity to working and he fails in a matter of the highest trust. He is without a single attractive or poetic quality.

The present generation, the young *criollo* is represented by the decadent Julio of **M'hijo el dotor.** He is worse than Jorge, who is perhaps a mere sensualist. Julio goes farther. He does what he pleases regardless of its social implications, but he goes a step beyond and rationalizes, attempting to defend his despicable acts. The negative of this type is found in Eduardo of **En familia.** He lacks the *voluntad* to do anything but becomes revolting only when he tries to justify his utter worthlessness.

Of the minor local characters we have a considerable variety, the *peons* of **La gringa** who are a mixture of laziness and sentiment, the basket maker of **Marta Gruni** with his poetic philosophy of life, the opinionated old soldier of **El desalojo,** the seamstresses in **La pobre gente.**

In addition to these local types of the Rio de la Plata region, Sánchez has his universal types. Lisandro of **Los muertos** at once comes to one's mind. Drink has been a curse of all civilizations and has made wrecks of good husbands and fathers, professional men, artists, and musicians. Lisandro reacts as they all do and always have. Sánchez, however, makes him realize his moral and spiritual bankruptcy as he puts into Lisandro's mouth the dictum *"Hombre sin caracter es muerto que camina."*

Los derechos de la salud has as its principals three fairly normal individuals who in Europe or North America would probably react in the same way, given the same circumstances. The invalid wife sees her duties and her rights and then her husband's love slipping away from her to her sister. Her reactions, jealousy and the sense of being deeply wronged, would be paralleled in any part of the world. Roberto is just any normal man who lets instinct dominate his life, because it is easier and pleasanter to let instinct have play than to control it. He, like Julio of **M'hijo el dotor,** becomes *antipático* when he rationalizes.

Señora Díaz and her friends in **Nuestros hijos** are perfectly understandable types all over the world. They represent the cold, conventional women of the higher social strata who do everything to keep up appearances. Their charities, their ethics, all must be decided by "What will people say?"

Don Rogelio of **Un buen negocio** is another of these well recognized types. He is not so very common; but every community has at least one man of the sort—suave, clever, scheming. He has, through shrewd business dealings, accumulated more than his proper share of the world's goods. People know that he is dishonest, but cannot legally catch him in direct violation of the law. When he has ample money to live on comfortably for the rest of his life he determines to add a wife as evidence of his prosperity or perhaps to give the odor of respectability to his existence. He does not choose a woman of his age and with a past but instead an innocent and indigent daughter of good family who is to exchange her purity and ingenuousness for his wealth.

There are, also, several minor characters that have universal traits, but it is unnecessary to discuss them in detail. Suffice it to say that it is only in the later plays that Sánchez creates universal types. Gradually he was emerging from the rôle of observer to that of philosopher; becoming less the photographer and more the creator of character.

Any discussion of the characters in the plays of Sánchez must of necessity be limited to the masculine *dramatis personae* and to the problems which concern them. It is emphatically a man's theatre. The women . . . are not important in themselves. On finishing the reading of a Sánchez play one has no idea as to whether they are ugly or beautiful in appearance, whether they have culture, or mentality, or any inner life. They are needed to work out the plot or the thesis or to shed some light on the protagonist of the play, just as a minimum of stage furniture is required, but they are never developed and never more than abstract conceptions. Even in **Los derechos de la salud** in the triangle our interest centers in Roberto. In **Marta Gruni** we have a woman of passionate feelings who will do all for love, but even she does not reason. Since **Los derechos de la salud** came late in the production of our author and in it he attempts the study of women, we may assume that, had he lived and seen more of the European theatre, he would little by little have focussed attention on women until he made them more than figure heads.

The women in these plays with the exception of María, Martiniana, and Luísa are not real people. Reality of characterization is found only among the men. In the lesser plays— **Cédulas de San Juan, Marta Gruni, Los curdas,** as well as in **La gringa**—we find photographic characters. We feel sure that Sánchez merely uses fictitious names for persons whom he has met or known. In his other pieces there is more evidence of creative than of photographic reality. It is easier to mention the two notable characters quite lacking in reality than to list the numerous creations true to life. These two are Díaz of *Nuestros hijos,* merely the instrument of the thesis, and a contradiction of what he himself preaches—unless he is supposed to typify inconsistency—and Don Rogelio who at first is real enough, but suddenly becomes a saint. To list those characters who have so much vitality that they will always form a part of the Argentine Theatre is to include names already cited frequently. In my opinion, they are Damián, the hopelessly idealistic reformer of *En familia,* Lisandro, the drunkard of *Los muertos,* Don Zoilo of *Barranca abajo,* and Don Olegario of *M'hijo el dotor*—the last two chosen because, for all time, they record the transition stage of the *gaucho-criollo,* the fusing of old and new, and the surrender of tradition to a changing civilization and a changing morality. (pp. 183-90)

Generally speaking, we are safe in saying that Sánchez was not a stylist interested in polishing his sentences and carefully choosing his words. This is evident from the fact that he so rarely revised a manuscript. His interest lay in plot, in characterization, on occasion in thesis, and language was merely his tool. The language flows, and we never are conscious of it except in certain passages where a strictly local dialect is used. His dialogues are so free from planning and from the slightest affectation that almost no literary allusions are discoverable. Rare too, is reference to any popular Argentinian literature or folk-lore—indication again of the effortlessness of the dialogue. Sánchez, having acted in amateur theatricals from his youth, knew dramatic technique and realized how often words may retard action in a play. (pp. 192-93)

Another phase of Sánchez's style or temperament as a dramatist is that tardily he delighted in carving out the protagonists, to cite but three, Don Zoilo, Lisandro, and Luisa, for whom he converted the subordinate characters into friendly or hostile satellites. Such singularity makes them stand out in relief or silhouette against the total scenic background of the Uruguayan writer, who, by instinct a *costumbrista* and a composer of *sainetes,* natively preferred orchestral uniformity to a single soul. Sánchez in a sort of artistic tenderness loved equally all the puppets of his stage pictures.

But whence comes the vigor of a theatre like this which is not enriched by extraordinary psychic figures nor by greater novelty in the simple problems which it confronts? It springs from its intrinsic truth and scenic power. If sometimes the dramatist made mistakes, he never bored one. Good proof of the simplicity of his technique is the fact that the ends of his acts always secure applause. (pp. 195-96)

From drawing particular types Sánchez soon turned to the general, to the portrayal of racial characteristics. In choosing one of Uruguay's vital issues he departs from the specific and plants in *La gringa,* the eternal problem of all nations, that of the eventual domination of the decadent native landholder by the invading foreigner, with intermarriage as the accepted solution of racial antipathies. It is a world problem as old as the human race and one that will always be alive in some sector of our universe. Hence, the problem of *La gringa* will still be as fresh centuries ahead as it is in contemporary Uruguay, or as vital as a Shakespearian drama. Both the Elizabethan and the Uruguayan with the instinct of genius chose themes universal and permanent.

Inextricably bound up with his choice of theme is the matter of a dramatist's doctrinal tendency, which may lead to em-

phasis of thesis at the expense of a faithful portrayal of life. In the case of Sánchez we have a division of critical opinion. In fact, criticisms and discussions of the author may be divided into two general groups, those made after a single reading of the dramatist, and those based on more extensive study of the plays. It seems especially true of Sánchez that a second reading of individual plays or of the total output frequently changes one's first impression radically. (pp. 197-98)

The more penetrating critics realize that only in *Nuestros hijos* is there a play built specifically on thesis. *Los muertos* might be so considered, but although it has a definite, tangible keynote it is not mainly doctrinal.

In all his previous productions, including his best works, there is no thesis properly speaking; and it cannot be said that there is, since the author does not propose either to demonstrate or defend any idea, as he appears to have wished to do in *Nuestros hijos.* What his works give evidence of is only a manner of seeing or of facing the facts from a sociological point of view, but without departing from objective veracity. The characters are as they are in daily observable reality, and everything occurs as it occurs in reality. There are not in his works, what is inherent in the theatre of thesis, characters who preach the ideas of the author, substituting what is for what ought to be.

The protagonist of *M'hijo el dotor* could be interpreted as a type who speaks and works according to the conceptions of the author, and for that reason the play would be, definitely, a work of thesis. Carefully considered, however, it is not. This drama merely, in the background, stages the conflict of two environments and of two manifestations of conscience the father, old patriarchal *gaucho* of traditional type, and the son educated intellectually in the city, and imbued with the new ideology. . . . But, all final possibility of thesis is annulled, since the ideological person, finally resolves the moral conflict, working not according to the individualistic theories which formerly he sustained, but according to his intimate natural sentiments of piety and justice. The altruism of piety finally triumphs over the egoism of the conception, and moral duty over individual rights. The triumph of human truth over purely rationalistic theorizing, is what gives his true feeling to the work. Faithful to life, rather than to ideas, Sánchez made the character sustain his ideas; but on resolving the dramatic knot he recognized the supreme rights of life. For Sánchez the supreme truth was always in sentiment.

Since Sánchez portrays life as he sees it, without thesis, we need to remember that life for him seemed tragic. This explains his preponderance of tragedy. His characters once started are borne along by the tragic circumstances with rarely any *deus ex machina* in the form of unexpected incident or interference on the part of the author. Only once do we feel that the dramatist did not let tragedy take its course, and that is in *Un buen negocio.* [In his *Proceso Intelectual del Uruguay*] Zum Felde discusses this tragic element in Sánchez as follows:

> Throughout, the work of Sánchez is moved by the tragic fatality of the characters and the circumstances; it is a theatre of action rather than of ideas. *Barranca abajo, En familia, Los muertos*—which may be considered his masterpieces—and to those may be added *Los derechos de la salud*—are all internally moved by fatality. The protagonists seem to be impelled by psychological factors or social elements—passions, vices, misfortunes—stronger

than their wills or reason . . . Certainly this fatality is not for him, an exponent of materialism, that metaphysical, mysterious, and sacred fatality, which it was for the ancients. He tries to analyze it, to explain it, to reduce it to natural and understandable terms; his fatality is determinism.

(pp. 199-201)

In the final analysis of Sánchez, the man and the dramatist, it is impossible to separate the three factors which are integral parts of his work, actuating it in intimate unity. Joined to the truthful painter of types and regions, is ever the revolutionary sociologist who gives his interpretation of the facts; and blended with them is the poet whose emotion lives intimately in his characters. The key to his work is found in the subjective and extremely personal quality of his sentiments combined with his anarchistic ideology, and literary realism, fusing them and vivifying them, animating them with a warm human breath. His realistic method and his revolutionary thinking of themselves would have produced merely a cold cerebral product, studies of a scientific objectivity. But what humanizes, kindles, and inspires the drama of Sánchez is the deep wellspring of love for his neighbor, by virtue of which he feels and makes felt, by sharing them, the sorrow and illusion of souls.

This fundamental conception of the dramatist helps to explain his originality. As an innovator, however, he had a more definite contribution to make to the Argentine stage—realism. Up to his epoch the Rioplatense theatre had been purely romantic. Even with *gaucho* characters and South American setting the method was still that of the romantic school. It was a theatre that was false or at least unreal in that it bore no relation to the life, thought, and problems of the twentieth century in America. In fact there were two distinct dramas, the transplanted European or cultural theatre, and the popular, indigenous or *gaucho genre*. Sánchez harmonized these two elements into a truly national theatre. (pp. 206-07)

The original material of the creations of the Uruguayan writer must be sought in his rustic theatre which is the outcome of the spontaneous reaction of his creative sympathy to absolutely virgin artistic matter. Sánchez did not find models in the European rural drama, nor in the bucolic romanticism of *Martín Coronado.* His rustic dramas excepting the solitary philosophy of *M'hijo el dotor,* represent the realization of a scenic type, which is maintained even in the works specifically urban, as for example, in *Los muertos.*

In the Argentine theatre just emerging at the turn of the century, Sánchez's three works, *Barranca abajo, Los muertos,* and *Los derechos de la salud* stand out as peaks of achievement. They display three stages in the evolution of an artistic mind. And it is the first of the three works which contains the greatest essence of Americanism. *Barranca abajo* represents a new note in the universal symphony of dramatic creation. The European who experiences recognition on reading most of Sánchez's work will be distinctly surprised on meeting Don Zoilo, the tortured protagonist of *Barranca abajo*; for this figure evokes no antecedents and suggests no comparisons.

In spite of his harsh realism, Sánchez is an artist, somewhat given to repetition, and a trifle monotonous, if we recall the innumerable seduced women in his theatre and the three old men of his rustic trilogy: Olegario, Cantalicio, and Zoilo; but he was puissant and powerful, and possessed of an intuitive

scenic vision. His productions, more valuable for their intrinsic dramatic value than for their clear or meticulous construction, reveal a powerful talent with marked tendencies which on being directed to the rustic drama effected the most original innovation of the Uruguayan theatre. The sum total of his effort, because of his unvarying mental attitude, does not constitute a varicolored ensemble of *sainetes,* dramas, and comedies, but a progressive work about a nucleus whose substance evolves from the pessimism of the writer. The slight subjective glimmer scarcely caught in the marked objectivity of his art, is not the mournful note of the inconsolable romanticist, but the impassive note of the defeated stoic for whom life was a misfortune. (pp. 208-10)

> Ruth Richardson, in her Florencio Sánchez and the Argentine Theatre, *Instituto de las Españas, 1933, 243 p.*

ARTURO TORRES-RÍOSECO   (essay date 1942)

[*Torres-Ríoseco was a Chilean-born American scholar of Spanish-American literature. In the following excerpt, he discusses Sánchez's relationship to both European and Spanish-American drama.*]

Sánchez' plays are characterized by great dramatic intensity and completely real characters, and by his poetic feeling for the land of the gauchos, which is on the verge of being destroyed by 'progress.' Thus in *My Kid, the Doctor,* he dramatizes the conflict between a gaucho father and his city-educated son—the battle between the old days and the new. Indeed the spirit of the pampas pervades all his works, whether they deal with rural themes or with urban ones, as in *Dead Men.* A careful examination of all his plays brings one to the conclusion that such stories, such characters, such conflicts, could never take place in conventionally organized countries, but only in untrammelled, primitive, even barbaric ones. His themes are never those of a 'soft' decadent society, but always a product of primitive passions, of fatalistic attitudes, of basic struggles. Naturally, dramas of this sort are directed against many types of modern life: oppressors, parasites, knaves, hypocrites; while Sánchez' heroes, just as naturally, are reformers, moralists, and particularly the victims of social institutions. And all this flagellating realism is turned upon national subject matter, finding its surest theme in the basic problem of the individualist *versus* convention, the rude gaucho *versus* the city—the very clash that Sarmiento described as the struggle between civilization and barbarism.

Yet for all the gauchesque and native elements of his theatre, Sánchez' work is closely related to that of European authors. This is perhaps the essential trait of his plays, that they represent the focusing of a skilled Old World technique upon the American scene. For instance, it is possible to trace the strong influence exerted by Ibsen on Sánchez. There are numerous points of similarity in their plays. Sánchez, like Ibsen, applied his best gifts to the *drame à thèse*: heredity, the rights of woman, social problems, and even madness are themes common to both authors; like the Norwegian, Sánchez is a penetrating interpreter of modern psychology, though his tragedies are perhaps more direct and brutal than those of Ibsen. Another comparison suggests itself between the work of Sánchez and that of the great Spanish novelist Galdós. There is a great parallelism between the two, particularly in their manner of developing the struggle between good and evil, in all its gradations and all its terrible crudeness. One can even point out individual compositions, like Sánchez' *Family Life,* and Galdós' *Glory* which bear striking resemblances: In both appears the character of a strong man, who tries to guide his family on the straight path; routine and social conventions strive to destroy the original man; and parasitic relatives play an important part in both works. Similarly, one can find much in common in the writings of Sánchez and the Spanish playwright Echegaray; perhaps the influence of Ibsen is responsible for similar tendencies in the two authors.

Of course, it is not for his Ibsen-inspired stagecraft that Sánchez is most noted, but for his application of this technique to American themes. His plays mark, indeed, the fusion of indigenous subject matter with European literary methods; they exhibit a certain amount of refinement even in the most brutal tragedies. As such, Sánchez' work underlines an important phase in the development of the gauchesque genre. Previously, the man of the pampas, basically a primitive character, had been treated in equally primitive literary forms. But now the gaucho, his life, and feelings were no longer subject matter for verses improvised to the beat of a guitar, or popular epics sold in the *pulpería,* or harrowing thrillers printed in daily newspaper installments. The *gaucho,* the orphan of the plains, had become a theme worthy of accomplished writers—a subject that was to find its highest expression in the advanced technique of the modern novel. (pp. 155-56)

Arturo Torres-Ríoseco, "Gaucho Literature," in his *The Epic of Latin American Literature, Oxford University Press, 1942, pp. 133-67.*

ENRIQUE ANDERSON-IMBERT (essay date 1969)

[*Anderson-Imbert is an Argentine-born literary historian, critic, novelist, and short story writer. He has published more than twenty books of essays and criticism, including his major work* Historia de la literatura hispanoamericana *(Spanish-American Literature: A History). In the following excerpt from that work, he discusses characteristic features of Sánchez's major plays.*]

[Sánchez's] first play, *My Son the Doctor* (*M'hijo el dotor,* 1903), was an unripened fruit, but it came from a vigorous tree. It dealt with a rural reality like that of so many of the theatrical pieces of the day, except that it was more colorful, fresh and lively, with a living character—the old Creole Don Olegario—and that it had a serious purpose: to present to us in intense dialogs a conflict of souls, a set of values, a concept of life, of generations, of city and rural customs, all of which end in a crisis when Julio, the "doctor" son, seduces Jesusa and must answer for his action to Don Olegario. His next rural work, which was more ambitious and more successful, was *The Immigrant's Daughter* (*La gringa,* 1904). A dialog of great realist strength evokes the Creole ranch, the general store, the immigrant's farm, the customs of the pampa; but this dialog is at the service of an allegory: the Italian immigrants invading the land of the gaucho and the birth of a promising Italo-Creole race. The gaucho Cantalicio and son Próspero on one side, the Italian Nicola and his daughter Victoria, on the other. But the children, Próspero and Victoria, resolve the conflict with love and with the mingling of their blood in a new racial offspring. In this abstract scheme there are minor symbols, the *ombú* tree, for example, representing the strength of the pure Creole. Situations already dealt with in the theater of the day are repeated: the national-

istic resentment of the Creoles against the *gringos* or European immigrants. But the whole drama is directed toward the exaltation of the new Argentinian race.

Florencio Sánchez has respected the Creole and *gringo* points of view as equally legitimate. Cantalicio—gambler, loafer, drunkard, cantankerous, carefree, unreliable—and Nicola—stingy, distrustful—are saved through the son that Próspero has had with Victoria. Just as Próspero and Victoria unite the Creole and *gringo* worlds through instinct, Horacio unites them intellectually, through his university culture. Horacio is the progressivist, the exemplary man, understanding, good, superior and dramatically empty, as were all "reasoners" of the nineteenth-century drama. Perhaps his mockery of Victoria's romanticism and his view of the Creole as ugly are the most personal aspects of his character. The construction of *The Immigrant's Daughter* is loose. The drama takes place before our eyes: the spectator sees how Próspero's and Victoria's love begins and how Cantalicio's difficulties develop; but the presentation does not stir the spectator because the scheme is as foreseeable as a geometric theorem.

Florencio Sánchez closed his rural trilogy with *Down Hill* (*Barranca abajo,* 1905), the most somber tragedy of our theater. It does not offer a thesis: at most, it offers a problem, that of the divestiture of the lands of the old Creoles by an oligarchy armed with all the technicalities of the law and police authority. But here, Sánchez has wanted to dramatize not a social theme but the failure of an individual man. The family of Don Zoilo collapses beneath the blows of ill fortune, sickness, sordidness, the deceit of the petty lawyers, and the decadence of base passions. It is a masterpiece that gains validity on stage because it is theater and not literature. Although realist in its dialog, truthful in its rural images and in its details of customs, it is artistically composed, in a crescendo of three acts beginning and ending with deliberate effect. Here, as never before, Sánchez was in command of his scenic art. In the first scene are the four women: the wife, the sister, and Don Zoilo's two daughters. The dialog is interrupted by the apparition of Don Zoilo, who crosses the stage in silence like a phantom, and then, after Robustiana, the good daughter, has left the stage, the three women who will precipitate his downfall speak. Suddenly, Martiniana, a literary descendant of the *Celestina,* another of the Fates, adds her voice to the chorus. Like a tragic chorus, the initial conversation of the women explains the past tragedy (Ibsen's retrospective method) and the crisis which, ominously, we are going to witness. The symbols are well chosen: when Zoilo is about to hang himself, the noose becomes entwined in the nest of an *hornero* bird. He struggles in vain to loosen it and exclaims: "God's doings . . . A man's nest is more easily torn apart than a bird's nest!"

The intense pauses in the dialog are more deeply piercing than the words themselves. This dramatist who had listened to the speech of the humble people so much and so well knew the value of silence. With admirable verbal economy he contrasts the animal desire of the landowner Juan Luis for Prudencia ("Come! Woman.") with the charitableness of Aniceto who proposes marriage to the tubercular Robustiana. Occasionally a few simple words release emotions, as when Don Zoilo, in scene 5 of Act III, says to Aniceto: "Did the cross stand up all right?"—the only allusion to the death of his daughter who has just been buried. The daughter's death is announced with equally simple scenic detail: as the curtain rises in the third act, next to the door of the hut, the iron bedstead in which the tubercular has died is seen. They have taken it outdoors so that it might be cleansed by the sun. The prelude to Don Zoilo's suicide has a quiet and unequivocal effectiveness from the moment the curtain is raised on that act. Against a background of misery, in front of the dead girl's bed, Don Zoilo is waxing the rope and whistling slowly. He is whistling the melody of death: he will whistle till the final moment. Don Zoilo is a complete character, with something of old King Lear about him. A breath of solemn and universal poetry envelops **Down Hill.** The theme of the fall of the house of Zoilo is extended from the country to the city in two of Sánchez' best dramas: *The Family* (*En familia*) and *The Dead* (*Los muertos*), both of 1905. In the score of theatrical pieces he produced there are also farces, plays of suburban environment, and thesis plays *The Rights of the Healthy* (*Los derechos de la salud,* 1907), *Our Children* (*Nuestros hijos,* 1907). Realism triumphed with Sánchez; and he tasted triumph after triumph, which did not save him from the depths of poverty but gave him the intoxication of literary glory. (pp. 417-20)

> *Enrique Anderson-Imbert, "1895-1910: Florencio Sánchez," in his* Spanish American Literature: A History, Vol. 1, *edited by Elaine Malley, translated by John Falconieri and Elaine Malley, revised edition, Wayne State University Press, 1969, pp. 417-20.*

RENÉ DE COSTA (essay date 1974)

[*In the following excerpt, de Costa studies the structure of* Barranca abajo *in order to illuminate the meaning of the play. Translations in brackets are by Willis Knapp Jones.*]

Florencio Sánchez is generally considered to be the first dramatist of major importance to emerge in Spanish America since Independence. **Barranca abajo,** his best known tragedy, is unquestionably an extraordinary work. Don Zoilo, the protagonist of this modern classic, is one of the first New World dramatic personages with the stature of a complex major character. The play, first performed in Buenos Aires in 1905, and revived with almost perennial regularity, has proven itself to be an extremely successful piece of theater. Indeed, its steady passage over the years from a quaint drama of the River Plate region to a place of permanence in the theatrical repertories of the Hispanic world suggests the presence of universal dramatic qualities.

Although the continued theatrical success of the work has generated numerous reviews, the literary composition has been studied only in a most cursory fashion. To be sure, there are many informative books and articles on the life of the author and the theater of his time, yet there is a surprising dearth of serious critical attention regarding the dramaturgy of Sánchez' master works, particularly **Barranca abajo.** This phenomenon is curious, since the play at its premiere prompted a basic question regarding its structure: Was the suicide of the protagonist in the final scene a satisfactory solution to the dramatic conflict? At the time, critical concern was such that the ending was actually modified for the second performance. In the words of the play's original director, José J. Podestá:

> **Barranca abajo** fue su primer gran éxito en mi compañía; cuando me la leyó le observé que no era posible que el público aceptara lo que él sustentaba en el final: "Esa es mi idea," me contestó, "mi tesis."

> "Con ella quiero probar que cuando un hombre ya no tiene nada que hacer en esta vida, puede un amigo, un pariente, no oponerse a la voluntad de suicidarse."

[**Barranca abajo** was his first great success in my company: when he read it to me I observed that it was not possible that the public would accept what he maintained in the end: "That is my idea," he told me, "my thesis." "With it I want to prove that when a man has nothing to do in this life, a friend, a relative, cannot oppose the willingness to commit suicide."]

. . . . .

Convencido Sánchez de que su tesis no podía prosperar, aceptó la enmienda que yo le hice y que es la misma con que se representa desde la segunda función. . . . Al día siguiente del estreno de **Barranca abajo,** lo tomé en un momento de íntima satisfacción y aprobó la reforma que hice a su tesis antihumana, que concordaba con la opinión de la crítica.

[Sánchez was convinced [by me] that his thesis could not work; he accepted the emendation I made to it and that is the same with what has been presented since the second performance. . . . On the day after the premiere of **Barranca abajo,** I had a moment of private satisfaction and he approved of the revision made to his anti-human thesis, which conformed with the opinion of the critics.]

In spite of Podestá's emendation, the question of suicide has remained to haunt the critics of Argentina and Uruguay, who, unknowingly, resuscitate an antiquated notion of verisimilitude in their oft-repeated allegation that it is somehow inappropriate for an authentic *criollo* to take his own life. River Plate chauvinism continues to thwart dramatic criticism, and as a consequence, a serious literary question remains unanswered today: Do the various lines of dramatic action in **Barranca abajo** converge in such a way as to make the resolution in suicide inevitable?

In 1959, Luis Ordaz prepared an edition of the play based on manuscripts containing the original version and Podestá's revision. Since an authentic text is now available, it should be possible to reexamine Sánchez' most significant work in order to attain a deeper understanding of his dramatic art. How does **Barranca abajo** function as dramatic literature? What specific system of actions governs the character of Don Zoilo? Answers to these questions are long overdue.

The plot, organized in three acts, is essentially expository. Don Zoilo, an aging rural patriarch, through the machinations of city lawyers loses his estate. Gradually, the love and respect of his sister, wife, and one of his daughters wanes; and they prepare to abandon him. Finally, his youngest daughter dies, and in desperation and solitude he seeks an end to his own life. The principal action concerns the protagonist's repeated assertion of self in his various efforts to retain his patriarchal position. Paralleling the decline in Don Zoilo's personal fortunes vis-à-vis the new social order is another plot line: the disintegration of the family. Estrangement and suicide result. The play's organization however, does not chronicle the process of the protagonist's fall, as does *King Lear* (a work which **Barranca abajo** resembles in more than a superficial way, as will be discussed later). Rather, the action is segmented, almost episodically, into discrete dramatic units.

The familiar three-act pattern is therefore not causal, but expository; the effect is documentary.

Nevertheless, a certain sequential parallelism of action does reinforce each unit with the import of what has already occurred. Consequently, in Act I, Zoilo, unable to retain his estate, attempts to salvage his authority; he drives out his enemies and makes the decision to take his family away to a new homestead in the interior. In Act II the enemy is within; the commissioner and his cohort have already established a liaison with the younger women of the family. Zoilo is powerless to prevent his civil arrest. By Act III, the old *criollo's* position has so eroded that he can only acquiesce when his family actually does abandon him. A proud patriarch without a patriarchy, Zoilo prepares for his final attempt at self-assertion: suicide. The representation of the three acts lacks the pattern of traditional dramaturgy (exposition, complication, and denouement). Instead Sánchez depended on the device of recycling the principal action to highlight the major theme, the assertion of self, and thus gave his work a unique coherence.

In each act Zoilo chooses to leave rather than suffer a humiliating defeat. Thus, he leaves his estate, the homestead, and finally the world while the women of the family make an essentially parallel series of decisions to abandon him. Structured around the idea of separation, the play uses the divisions of the three-act form in a particularly effective way. Within each act there is an absolute continuity of time whereas between the acts time is discontinuous. As a result the actions transcend the chain of causality which usually defines the progression of realist drama. Sánchez, by limiting his dramatization to three distinct, but not unrelated moments of crisis, managed to present a most effective case-study of an individual's anguish in its full psychic potential. Perhaps it is for this reason that *Barranca abajo* has ultimately become the vehicle for Don Zoilo, certainly the most complete character ever to emerge on a Spanish American stage prior to the César Rubio of Usigli's *El Gesticulador.*

Events which are not pertinent to the principal action of self-assertion are made to occur between the acts. For example, the first act ends with Zoilo's altruistic decision to begin anew in the interior. In the second act the family is already installed in the humble homestead of Zoilo's *ahijado* Aniceto. In this way, the dramatist avoids presenting an onstage quarrel between the enraged protagonist and the women over what they surely would have considered to be a less than satisfactory solution to the family's plight. The second act concludes in a similarly hermetic fashion with the betrothal of the tubercular Robusta and Aniceto. The final act then begins with Robusta's bed on stage, "asoleándose," in mute testimony to her death between the acts. Here the dramatist has studiously avoided a scene of grief. At this point it should be noted that although Florencio Sánchez worked out of the realistic tradition of the late nineteenth century stage, he nonetheless managed to prune his work of the nonessential detail and the melodramatic circumstance so highly esteemed by his contemporaries. In so doing, he pioneered the lean plot line of the contemporary theater in South America. The scenic arrangement of *Barranca abajo* reveals not only his mastery of the techniques of the modern stage but also the highly structured nature of his original approach to dramatic art.

Like the death of Cordelia in *King Lear,* the death of Robusta is the final blow for Don Zoilo. Whereas the conventions of Shakespeare's time permitted the protagonist to come on stage carrying the body of his dead daughter, Sánchez avoids the melodramatic corpse. Instead, absorbing perhaps from the naturalists a certain studied attention to detail, he realized the dramatic potential of sublimating a stage prop into a dynamic figure. At the opening of the third act the scene is quite tersely delineated: "La misma decoración. Muestras de abandono. Contra la pared del rancho una cama desarmada asoleándose." The bed, stripped bare and left to sanitize in the sun, imposes itself as an object with an expressive function. It immediately tells the audience of Robusta's death and is a constant reminder of Zoilo's loss. Other props in the play have a similarly active role because of the forceful way in which they generate an expectation for certain kinds of action. Although occasionally the object is used in the expected fashion, following realistic convention, as when Zoilo threatens the women with his whip (I, x), at other times a seemingly decorative object advances and creates the potential for action. One might think of the play's opening: a domestic tableau in which all the women in Zoilo's family appear in the patio. Robusta is applying a plaster to her ailing mother Misia Dolores; her sister Prudencia and her aunt Rudelinda are both ironing. Through the accomplished use of a simple prop, in this case a candle, the dramatist quickly establishes the atmosphere of tension and discord which reigns in the house of Zoilo:

> MISIA DOLORES. Poneme pronto, m'hija, esos parches.
> ROBUSTA. Peresé. En el aire no puedo hacerlo. (*Se acerca a la mesa, coloca los parches de papel sobre ella y les pone sebo de la vela.*) ¡Aquí, verás!
> RUDELINDA. ¡Eso es! ¡Llename ahora la mesa de sebo, si te parece! ¿No ves? Ya gotiaste encima el paño.
> ROBUSTA. ¡Jesús! ¡Por una manchita!
> PRUDENCIA. Una manchita que después, con la plancha caliente, ensucia toda la ropa . . . Ladiá esa vela. . . .
> ROBUSTA. ¡Viva, pues, la patrona!
> PRUDENCIA. ¡Sacá esa porquería de ahí! (*Da un manotón a la vela, que va a caer sobre la enagua que plancha Rudelinda.*)
> RUDELINDA. ¡Ay! ¡Bruta! ¡Cómo me has puesto la nagua!
> PRUDENCIA. (*Displicente*) ¡Oh! ¡Fue sin querer!
> ROBUSTA. ¡Jua, jua, jua! (*Recoge la vela y trata de reanudar su tarea.*)
>
>   (I, i)

> [DOLORES. Hurry, daughter, and put those plasters on my head!
> ROBUSTIANA. Stand up. I can't do it down there. (*She goes to the table, lays out the paper plasters on it and spreads candle grease on them.*) There! Now you'll see!
> RUDECINDA. That's it! Get grease all over the table, if you feel like it! Can't you look? You dripped some on the cloth.
> ROBUSTIANA. Goodness! All that fuss over a little spot!
> PRUDENCIA. A little spot that will get all over the cloth when the iron is hot. Put that candle away!
> ROBUSTIANA. Look who's getting bossy!
> PRUDENCIA. Get that mess out of here! (*She shoves the candle, which falls on the skirt that Rudecinda is ironing.*)
> RUDECINDA. Look what you've done to my skirt, stupid!
> PRUDENCIA. (*Crossly*) I didn't mean to!
> ROBUSTIANA. Bah! (*She picks up her candle and goes back to her work.*)]

319

The ensuing argument builds in intensity. The scene functions principally to create an atmosphere rather than to convey information. Thus, when Don Zoilo enters at the peak of the argument, the mood suddenly shifts, for the women feign harmony and begin to chatter about the weather. Now, although the protagonist says absolutely nothing, his peculiar deportment and the evident effect it has on the women communicate an ominous tension in which the dialogue tells nothing but indicates all:

> *Don Zoilo aparece por la puerta del foro. Se levanta de la siesta. Avanza lentamente y se sienta en un banquito. Pasado un momento, saca el cuchillo de la cintura y se pone a dibujar marcas en el suelo.*
>
> MISIA DOLORES. (*Suspirando*). ¡Ay, Jesús, María y José!
> RUDELINDA. Mala cara trae el tiempo. Parece que viene tormenta del lao de la sierra.
> PRUDENCIA. Che, Rudelinda, ¿se hizo la luna ya?
> RUDELINDA. El almanaque la anuncia pa hoy. Tal vez se haga con agua.
> PRUDENCIA. Con tal de que no llueva mucho.
> MISIA DOLORES. ¡Robusta! ¡Robusta! ¡Ay, Dios! Traeme de una vez ese matecito. (*Zoilo se levanta y va a sentarse a otro banquito.*)
> RUDELINDA (*Ahuecando la voz*) ¡Güenas tardes! . . . dijo el muchacho cuando vino. . . .
> PRUDENCIA. ¡Y lo pior jué que nadie le respondió! ¡Linda cosa!
> RUDELINDA. Che, Zoilo, ¿me encargaste el generito pal viso de mi vestido? (*Zoilo no responde.*) ¡Zoilo! . . . ¡Eh! . . . ¡Zoilo! . . . ¿Tas sordo? Decí . . . ¿Encargaste el generito rosa? (*Zoilo se aleja y hace mutis lentamente por la derecha.*)

(I, ii)

[(*Zoilo appears through the rear door. He has just got up from his siesta. He comes forward slowly and sits on a small stool. A moment later he draws his knife from his belt and starts drawing lines on the ground.*)
DOLORES. (*Sighing*) Ah, Jesus, Mary, and Joseph!
RUDECINDA. The weather doesn't look too good. Looks like a storm is coming from the mountain.
PRUDENCIA. Hey, Rudecinda, is there a new moon yet?
RUDECINDA. The almanac announces it for tonight. Perhaps it'll bring rain.
PRUDENCIA. Just so it doesn't rain too much.
DOLORES. Robusta! Robusta! My head! (*Zoilo gets up, goes to another stool and sits there.*)
RUDECINDA. (*Lowering her voice.*) "Good afternoon!"—as the boy said when he came.
PRUDENCIA. And the worst part was, nobody answered him. Fine thing!
RUDECINDA. Say, Zoilo, did you order material for my underskirt? (*Zoilo does not reply.*) Zoilo, are you deaf? Did you order my rose material? (*Zoilo moves away, and exits slowly, right.*)]

Everything serves to draw attention to Zoilo. Not only does his unexpected silence alter the course of stage events, even his limited physical movements are used as attention-focusing devices. Furthermore, and perhaps most significantly, he uses a menacing prop in an odd way. The silent Zoilo takes out his knife and proceeds to scratch the ground with it. The mere physical presence of man and object serves a semiological function more potent and direct than any verbal

sign. Zoilo has yet to say anything. Nevertheless, from the vantage point of the stage participants as well as that of the theater public, he is the absolute center of attention.

The modern drama championed by the Podestá family in the River Plate region signaled a break with the rhetorical style of dramatic declaration employed in Spain and fostered in Spanish America by the touring companies from the peninsula. The innovation did not consist of a mere change in diction, as the colloquial flavor of the dialogue would seem to imply, but rather comprised a totally new concept of dramatic action. After Podestá's success with the mime-drama (*Juan Moreira*), it was readily apparent to all concerned that a dramatization was something more than a set of dialogues which could be acted out. Drama, not just verbal, was physical impersonation as well. A representation of an action therefore, to be truly effective, must be the result of a significant fusion of word and deed. In this new scheme of things the characters' movements and the use of stage objects passed from the domain of the acting company to that of the author. The creative possibilities of dramatic literature were thus increased immeasurably.

Florencio Sánchez was in the forefront of the innovative New World dramatists who were abandoning the hollow forms of the past in order to experiment with new and more effective means of dramatic expression. In the final act of **Barranca abajo,** when Don Zoilo is crazed with anguish over the loss of his favorite daughter and his failure to salvage the family's honor, neither a revealing soliloquy nor an intimate colloquy could adequately convey the excruciating distress of the old *criollo*. Here, the dramatist eschews such rhetorical devices in order to show the mood of impending disaster. With stage objects, physical action, and a minimum of dialogue he represents the psychic torment of the protagonist. Paralleling the pattern of the opening act and echoing its significance, the closing act begins with the women involved in discussion, while Don Zoilo is again a mute and menacing presence:

> *La misma decoración. Muestras de abandono. Contra la pared del rancho una cama desarmada asoleándose.*
>
> ### ESCENA
>
> *Al levantarse el telón, Zoilo debe estar concluyendo de ensebar un lazo; cuando termina lo enrolla y lo cuelga en el alero. Luego bebe de un jarro de agua y se aleja lentamente, silbando bajo un motivo cualquiera; monótono motivo que silba durante todo el acto.*
>
> RUDELINDA. ¡Ahí se va solo! Andá a hablarle. Le decís las cosas claramente y con firmeza. Verás cómo dice que sí; está muy quebrao ya . . . Peor sería que nos fuésemos, dejándolo solo en el estao en que se halla.
> MISIA DOLORES. Es que . . . no me animo; me da no sé qué . . . ¿Por qué no le hablás vos?
> RUDELINDA. Bien sabés que conmigo, ni palabra.
> MISIA DOLORES. ¿Y Prudencia?
> RUDELINDA. ¡Peor todavía! . . .

(III, i)

[*Same setting as Act Two, with an iron bed under the eaves near the door. It is daytime. When the curtain rises, don Zoilo is seen waxing a lasso and whistling lazily. When he finishes, he hangs the rope from the eaves. Then he goes out rear as Rudecinda and Dolores come out of the ranch house.*

RUDECINDA.   There he is, alone. Go talk to him. Explain things to him clear and firm. He'll agree, you'll see. He's all broken up now. It would be worse if we went off, leaving him in the condition he's in.
DOLORES.   I don't have the nerve. I feel queer about it. Why don't you talk to him?
RUDECINDA.   No, you know he wouldn't listen to a word from me.
DOLORES.   What about Prudencia?
RUDECINDA.   Worse yet. . . .]

The stage objects (Robusta's bed and Zoilo's noose) speak with silent eloquence, while the women's periphrastic indecision and the old gaucho's feignedly calm whistling are diverse signs whose common function is to direct attention to the protagonist and highlight his disturbed state. In the process, the words of the dialogue have been so thoroughly denuded of significance that they are scarcely needed, save to suggest the women's nervousness. The simultaneous, although uncommunicative, onstage presence of both the women and Don Zoilo brings plot lines closer to convergence. They are readying themselves to abandon Zoilo, and he is preparing to hang himself; all are making the last arrangements to carry out a decision to leave, to break the final bond, and in so doing to escape from the tragic grasp of their oppressive relationship. Desertion and suicide thus converge to complete the metaphor of the family's fall.

From one point of view, the play can be seen as a paradigm of modular structure. Like a set of Chinese boxes, each act repeats the same basic design, but on a different scale. Beginning always with a discussion among the women trailed by the disruptive presence of Don Zoilo, each dramatic unit deepens our understanding of the tense interpersonal relationships and documents the gravity of the protagonist's psychological disturbance. We have already observed certain parallels in acts I and III; the second act contains the variant which establishes the significance of the pattern: Zoilo's return to a normal state. At the opening of the second act, the family has recently arrived in the rural backlands, and in the new homestead, the aging *criollo* seems rejuvenated, a restored image of his patriarchal self. The curtain goes up on yet another family quarrel. Robusta, Cinderella-like, is grinding corn while the other women pretty themselves for a secret rendezvous:

ESCENA PRIMERA
(Robusta y Prudencia.)

ROBUSTA.   ¡Che, Prudencia! ¿Querés seguir pisando esta mazamorra? Me canso mucho. Yo haría otra cosa cualquiera.
PRUDENCIA.   Pisala vos con toda tu alma. Tengo que acabar esta pollera.
ROBUSTA.   ¡Que sos mala! Llamala a mama, entonces, o a Rudelinda.
PRUDENCIA (*Volviéndose, a voces*)   ¡Mama! . . . ¡Rudelinda! Vengan a servir a la señorita de la casa y tráiganle un trono para que esté a gusto.

ESCENA II
(Los mismos, Misia Dolores y Rudelinda)

MISIA DOLORES.   ¿Qué hay?
PRUDENCIA.   Que la princesa de Chimango no puede pisar maiz.

MISIA DOLORES.   ¿Y qué podés hacer entonces? Bien sabés que no hemos venido acá pa estarnos de brazos cruzados.
ROBUSTA.   Sí, señora, lo sé muy bien; pero tampoco viá permitir que me tengan de piona.
RUDELINDA (*Asomándose a una ventana*)   ¿Ya está la marquesa buscando cuestiones? ¡Cuándo no! . . .
ROBUSTA.   Callate vos, comadreja.
RUDELINDA.   Andá, correveidile; buscá camorra no más pa después dirle a contar a tu tata que te estamos martirizando.

(II, i-ii)

[ROBUSTIANA.   Hey, Prudencia, won't you grind this stuff for awhile? I'm awfully tired. I'd rather do anything else.
PRUDENCIA.   Do it yourself! I have to finish this sewing.
ROBUSTIANA.   How hateful you are! Call mama, then, or Rudecinda.
PRUDENCIA.   Mama! Rudecinda! Come here and wait on the young lady of the house, and bring a throne along so she can be comfortable.

(Enter Dolores and Rudecinda.)

DOLORES.   What's the trouble?
PRUDENCIA.   Oh, the Princess of Chimanga can't grind corn.
DOLORES.   Well, what can you do, then? You know very well we didn't come here to sit and fold our hands.
ROBUSTIANA.   Yes, Mother, I know that perfectly well, but I'm not going to let people make a day laborer of me, either.
RUDECINDA.   (*Looking out the window*) Her Ladyship is trying to start a quarrel. Otherwise . . .
ROBUSTIANA.   Shut up, weasel!
RUDECINDA.   Go on, tattletale. Stir up a fuss just so you can run and tell Daddy that we're tormenting you.]

This banter continues for a moment while Robusta labors, Rudelinda combs her hair, Prudencia arranges a petticoat, and Misia Dolores works on a tartan. With the approach of Zoilo all seek refuge except Robusta. Sánchez again uses a prop with telling effectiveness, not simply in the interest of a scenic naturalism but more importantly to create a nonverbal sign which has the power of communicating directly to the audience the normalization of the protagonist. Don Zoila, in complete mastery of the new situation, makes a most commanding entrance—on horseback:

ESCENA III
(Robusta y Don Zoilo.)

ROBUSTA (*angustiada*).   ¡No quieren a nadie! ¡Pobre tatita! (*Apoyada en el mortero llora un instante. Óyense rumores de la izquierda. Robusta alza la cabeza, se enjuga rápidamente las lágrimas y continúa la tarea, canturreando un aire alegre. Zoilo avanza por la izquierda a caballo, con un balde en la mano, arrastrando un barril de agua. Desmonta, desata el caballo y lo lleva fuera; al volver, acomoda la rastra.*)
DON ZOILO.   Buen día, m'hija.
ROBUSTA.   Día . . . ¡Bendición, tatita!
DON ZOILO.   ¡Dios la haga una santa! Pasó mala noche, ¿eh? ¿Por qué se ha levantao hoy?
ROBUSTA.   No; dormí bien.
DON ZOILO.   Te sentí toser toda la noche.
ROBUSTA.   Dormida, sería.

DON ZOILO. Traiga, yo acabo.
ROBUSTA. ¡No, deje! ¡Si me gusta!
DON ZOILO. Pero le hace mal. Salga.
ROBUSTA. Bueno. Entonces yo voy a ordeñar, ¿eh?
DON ZOILO. ¿Cómo? ¿No han sacao la leche entuavía?
ROBUSTA. No, señor, porque . . .
DON ZOILO. ¿Y qué hacen esas? ¿A qué hora se levantaron?

(II, iii)

[ROBUSTIANA. (*Distressed*). They don't care about anybody! Poor Daddy! (*Weeps, leaning on the stone mortar. Hearing a noise at the left, Robustiana raises her head, wipes the tears away, and continues grinding, humming a song. Zoilo rides on stage from the left with a bucket in his hand and dragging a barrel of water. He dismounts, unharnesses the horse and drives it off, then returns and straightens up the sled.*)
ZOILO. Hello, daughter!
ROBUSTIANA. Give me your blessing, Daddy.
ZOILO. God bless you, my darling! You had a bad night, didn't you? Why did you get up today?
ROBUSTIANA. No, Daddy. I slept well.
ZOILO. I heard you coughing all night long.
ROBUSTIANA. It must have been in my sleep, then.
ZOILO. Give me that. I'll finish it.
ROBUSTIANA. No, let it alone. I like to do it.
ZOILO. But it's not good for you. Off with you!
ROBUSTIANA. All right. Then I'll go and milk, eh?
ZOILO. What? Haven't they done that milking yet?
ROBUSTIANA. No, because—
ZOILO. What in the world do those women do? What time did they get up?]

The live prop serves effectively as a symbol of Zoilo's renewal. Yet, the conflict remains. Don Zoilo's family refuses to mend its ways. The patriarch again asserts himself only to fail once more to set his house in order.

The parallelism of scene and action in *Barranca abajo* would probably appear monotonous were it not for the harmony of the total structure. The dramatist has evidently planned the scenario with a view to its overall esthetic effect. Repeated patterns of action have the power to cause an observer (reader, public, characters) to take special notice of whatever differs from the norm. Hence the significance of the pattern and its deviations. In the first act Zoilo's peculiar behavior was noted not only by his family (and, one assumes, by the audience), but also by an outside observer. When Ña Martiniana—a kind of rural Celestina created by Sánchez and used as a *raisonneuse*—comes to the estate, she finds him "medio maniático" (I, iv, 38). Significantly, in the third act, after the death of Robusta, she observes that Zoilo's state has worsened: "ha quedado maniático con el golpe" (III, iv, 79). Representation and dialogue are complimentary signs. Evidently, the parallelism of the observations and their graded quality are designed to direct attention toward the psychic evolution of the protagonist.

The drama takes place on both the external, physically real plane of naturalist theater and the internal, mentally dynamic plane of psychological drama. Sánchez, in 1905, and somewhat before the advent of psychodrama, successfully represented various stages of the defeated hero's mental strain. His

protagonist does not suddenly decide to kill himself; he resolutely searches for a final solution. In this context, it is necessary to point out that the critics, so disturbed by the sociological implications of the tragic ending of *Barranca abajo,* have not only failed to assess the obvious significance of the play's title, but have also, and more seriously, tended to ignore the internal evidence of the text itself. The play is structured so as to represent the repeated failures at self-assertion. The protagonist is literally beaten down.

I realize, of course, that gauchophiles will find it even more difficult to accept the notion of a mentally exhausted Don Zoilo than the possibility of a suicidal *criollo*. Yet, the evidence is clear if the finale is analyzed in terms of the structural unity of the work and not viewed separately, as is usually the case. In fact, Zoilo's haughty self-esteem is already evident in the first act when he first learns of his family's deceit, and he resolutely drives the enemies from his house. In the second act, his setbacks are such that he begins to surrender to the cruelties of an indifferent world. And, in the final act, aware of his folly, he decides to end his meaningless life.

At this point it is well to ask if it is more than just a coincidence that this is also the familiar pattern of Shakespeare's *King Lear*. I think not, since there is sufficient external evidence to argue for an intentional allusion. The Elizabethan tragedy was on tour in South America in 1904 (only a year before *Barranca abajo* was staged), and the principal rôle was played by the great Italian Shakespearean actor Ermete Zacconi, Sánchez' constant companion in Montevideo. That the Uruguayan created in Don Zoilo a *criollo* version of the Lear legend is quite possible; that the dramatist saw in the voluntary death of the king a theatrical antecedent for the patriarch's suicide seems most probable. In the works of both Shakespeare and Sánchez, the father is disheartened as he realizes the disparate attitudes of his daughters with regard to his ruined state. Zoilo's Robusta, like Lear's Cordelia, demonstrates her filial love while the other women in the family become more distant. The series of misfortunes afflicting both fathers leads ultimately to their insanity and death, and the untimely demise of the faithful daughter is the final blow for both defeated men. Shakespeare presented the course of Lear's fall to madness; Sánchez, a case study of the stages in the psychic degradation of Zoilo.

Over the centuries though, the problem facing both authors has remained essentially unchanged: how best to represent a mental event through words and physical action? Lear's madness was shown in the conventional manner of Shakespeare's time: rashly foolish and muttering, the king comes onstage dressed absurdly in wild flowers (IV, vi). Sánchez, of course, has Zoilo do equally inappropriate things, but according to somewhat different conventions. Fundamental to an appreciation of modern dramaturgy, particularly that of the early twentieth century, is an understanding of the playwrights' renewed and even studied concern with mimesis. In the realist scheme of dramatic action, the spectators in the theater were not simply expected to empathize with the characters, but, as a consequence, to experience the same sentiments as the stage public. Thus, when the women on stage show fear of Don Zoilo silently poking at the ground with his knife (I, ii), it is presumed that the public in the theater will also feel a certain apprehension. For Shakespeare, the signs of madness were folly and the unconventional; for Sánchez, the irrational and the unexpected. Perhaps for this reason, the clues to Zoilo's strange behavior are presented with such an accumulative force at the beginning. The representation of the action permits the audience to witness the same disorienting phenomena as the stage characters, and even to wonder with Rudelinda: "Decime, Zoilo, ¿te has enloquecido endeveras?" (I, xiv). Not until the end of the first act does Zoilo finally confront his antagonists, the *arrivistes* Juan Luis and Butiérrez, who arrive uninvited at the house under the guise of a courtesy call. In fact, they are attempting to seduce Rudelinda and Prudencia. Discoursing in a calm and rational manner the master of the house begins to recall to his visitors the history of his litigation with them. However, the more he speaks, the more angry he becomes, until finally, beside himself, he throws them out, cursing them as "herejes" and "salteadores." The stage directions are most revealing. Juan Luis and Butiérrez, "confusos," are to leave slowly while Zoilo "los sigue un momento con la vista balbuceando frases incomprensibles" (I, xxi), the epitome of anger.

The psychological drama takes place in the mind of Zoilo. In the tensely emotive scene which concludes Act I all the witnesses to the action, by their confused reactions, show that they suspect him to be unbalanced. In the second act he is represented as a man enraged. Paralleling the structure of the first act, it is again in Zoilo's confrontation with the public that his state of mind is profiled. Towards the end of the second act, a representative of the law arrives to take him to town for questioning. The irrational outburst is not unexpected:

> SARGENTO.   Es que vengo en comisión [. . .] con orden de llevarlo.
> DON ZOILO.   ¿A mí? ¿A mí?
> SARGENTO.   Eso es.
> DON ZOILO.   ¿Pero han oido Vdes.?
> SARGENTO (*Paternal*)   No ha de ser por nada. Cuestión de un rato. Venga no más. Si se resiste, va a ser pior.
> ÑA MARTINIANA.   Claro que sí. Bé de ir no más a las güenas. ¿Qué saca con resistir a la autoridad?
> DON ZOILO.   ¡Callá esa lengua vos! Vamos a ver un poco; ¿no estás equivocao? ¿Vos sabés quién soy yo? ¡Don Zoilo Carabajal, el vecino don Zoilo Carabajal!
> SARGENTO.   Sí, señor. Pero eso era antes, y perdone. Aura es el viejo Zoilo, como dicen todos.
> DON ZOILO.   ¡El viejo Zoilo!
> SARGENTO.   Sí, amigo; cuando uno se güelve pobre, hasta el apelativo le borran.
> DON ZOILO.   ¡El viejo Zoilo! Con razón ese mulita de Butiérrez se permite nada menos que mandarme a buscar preso. En cambio, él tiene aura hasta apellido . . . Cuando yo le conocí no era más que Anastasio, el hijo de la parda Benita. ¡Trompetas! (*A voces.*) ¡Trompetas! ¡Trompetas, canejo!
> ANICETO.   No se altere, padrino. A cada chancho le llega su turno.
> DON ZOILO.   ¡No me'de alterar, hijo! Tiene razón el sargento. El viejo Zoilo y gracias. ¡Pa todo el mundo! Y los mejores a gatas si me tienen lástima. ¡Trompetas! Y si yo tuviese la culpa, menos mal. Si hubiese derrochao, si hubiese jugao, si hubiera sido un mal hombre en la vida, si le hubiese hecho daño a algún cristiano, paso; lo tendría merecido. Pero juí bueno y servicial; nunca cometí una mala acción, nunca . . . ¡canejo!, y aura, porque me veo en la mala, la gente me agarra pal manoseo, como si el respeto fuese cosa de poca o mucha plata.
> SARGENTO.   Eso es. Eso es.

> RUDELINDA.   ¡Ave María! ¡No exagerés!
> DON ZOILO.   ¡Que no exagere! ¡Si al menos Vdes. me respetarán! Pero ¡ni eso, canejo! Ni los míos me guardan consideración. Soy más viejo Zoilo pa Vdes., que pal más ingrato de los ajenos . . . ¡Vida miserable! Y yo tengo la culpa. ¡Yo! . . . ¡Yo! . . . Por ser demasiao pacífico. Por no haber dejao un tendal de bellacos. ¡Yo . . . tuve la culpa! (*Despues de una pausa.*) ¡Y dicen que hay Dios! . . . (*Pausa prolongada; las mujeres, silenciosas, vanse por foro. Don Zoilo se pasea.*)

(II, xvi)

> [SERGEANT.   I'm sent here as his deputy. . . . With orders to bring you in.
> ZOILO.   Me? Me?
> SERGEANT.   That's right.
> ZOILO.   Did you ever hear of such a thing?
> SERGEANT.   (*Paternally*) It won't amount to anything. It'll be a matter of a short time, I'm sure. Come along peaceably. If you resist, it'll just make things worse.
> MARTINIANA.   That's right. It's better to go willingly. What'll you get by resisting the authorities?
> ZOILO.   Shut up, you! Are you sure there isn't some mistake? You know who I am, don't you? Don Zoilo Carbajal, the citizen Don Zoilo Carbajal.
> SERGEANT.   Yes, sir, beggin' your pardon, sir, but that's what you used to be. Now you're just "Old man Zoilo." That's what they all call you.
> ZOILO.   "Old man Zoilo"?
> SERGEANT.   Yes, my friend. When a man goes broke, folks don't bother with surnames.
> ZOILO.   "Old man Zoilo." No wonder that imitation soldier Gutierrez had the nerve to send to arrest me. He has a surname of his own, now. When I first knew him, he was only Anastasio, son of the mulatta Benita! Damn it. To Hell with him!
> ANICETO.   Don't get excited, godfather.
> ZOILO.   How can I help getting excited, boy? The sergeant's right. I'm just Old man Zoilo to everybody. And everybody feels sorry for me. And it wouldn't be so bad if it had been my fault, if I'd spent my money or gambled, if I'd been a bad man or had ever harmed anybody on earth. I'd have deserved it, then. But I've never committed a crime in my life. And now because I'm down on my luck, people push me around as if being respected was simply a case of how much or how little money you have.
> SERGEANT.   That's it. That's it.
> RUDECINDA.   Come, father, don't exaggerate.
> ZOILO.   So I'm not to exaggerate? If at least you folks felt some respect for me! But Hell, no! Not even my own family has any consideration for me. I'm "Old man Zoilo" to you just like to the most ungrateful strangers. What a life! And it's my own fault. Mine! Mine for being too easy. For not having laid out cold a bunch of rascals. It's all my fault. (*After a pause*) And they say there's a God. (*Long pause. The women go silently up stage. Zoilo walks back and forth.*)]

At the point the protagonist himself clearly realizes the psycho-social significance of his change in fortune. He is no longer Don Zoilo, simply "el viejo Zoilo," Lear without his crown. The witnesses to this scene are able to realize that the greatness of the old patriarch was not in the material dimension but in the psychic realm. The cue is evidently received, for the women withdraw, as if in embarrassment, before this most intimate revelation. As a consequence, the other public, the audience, might similarly be prompted to pity.

Old Zoilo—enraged over his own impotence midway through the play—reacts at the end to the death of Robusta much like Lear to that of his daughter. In desperation, he seeks an end to his torment. Lear, in the flamboyant style of the Elizabethan stage, suddenly faints dead away; Zoilo, in the mime tradition of Podestá, elaborately prepares his noose. The melodramatic convention of suicide *circa* 1905 though would doubtless have been satisfied with a sudden offstage pistol shot as the final curtain falls. Yet Sánchez devotes an entire act to the preparation for the hanging. The structure of the play tells us why. The final deed must be understood as the only voluntary solution remaining to the hero who has repeatedly failed. In fact, as though to stress the thesis, even his finale in the amended version is a near failure:

> (*Zoilo . . . va en dirección al alero y toma el lazo que había colgado y lo estira; prueba si está bien flexible y lo arma, silbando siempre el aire indicado. Colocándose, después, debajo del palo del mojinete, trata de asegurar el lazo, per al arrojarlo se le enreda en el nido de hornero. Forcejea un momento con fastidio por voltear el nido.*) ¡Las cosas de Dios! . . . ¡Se deshace más fácilmente el nido de un hombre que el nido de un pájaro! (*Reanuda su tarea de amarrar el lazo hasta que consigue su propósito. Se dispone a ahorcarse. Cuando está seguro de la resistencia de la soga, se vuelve al centro de la escena, bebe más agua, toma un banco y va a colocarlo debajo de la horca.*)

TELÓN   (III, xix)

> [(*Zoilo goes to the eaves and takes down the lasso which he hung there. He unhooks it. He tries it to test its flexibility, then he adjusts it around his neck. All the time he is whistling tunelessly. Placing himself under the ridgepole, he throws the rope over it, getting it tangled in the ovenbird's nest. In trying to work it past, he overturns the nest.*) That's the way God does things. The nest of a man is more easily upset than a bird's nest. (*He goes back to the task of fastening the rope securely. When he is sure it is firm, he returns to the center of the stage and drinks more water. Then he starts to put a bench under the gallows.*)

CURTAIN]

Obviously, the public should not be shocked at his suicide, since it has been sympathetically conditioned to its inevitability. Robusta's bed and Zoilo's lasso, like the monotonous whistling throughout the act, are all omnipresent non-verbal signs skillfully used to prepare the audience, to elicit a certain pity for the tragic end of the desperate old man who was once the proud *criollo* Don Zoilo Carabajal.

With regard to the criticism of the suicide however, there remains a final nagging problem which is common to both the original text and to the Sánchez-Podestá revision. Many critics—undoubtedly confusing dramatic action with a preceptive notion of real life—are still concerned over the fact that Aniceto, Zoilo's faithful *ahijado,* in neither version succeeds in preventing the old man from hanging himself. We already know through Podestá that Sánchez felt such a resolution to be fundamental to his thesis ("que cuando un hombre ya no tiene nada que hacer en esta vida, puede un amigo, un pariente, no oponerse a la voluntad de suicidarse"). A literary parallel in *King Lear* may help to clarify the lingering prob-

lem of the socially-oriented critics. It is in the final scene of the Shakespearean tragedy that Lear, with the dead Cordelia in his arms, goes into a death swoon. When Edgar and others rush to help him the king's faithful servant Kent holds them all at a distance—so that Lear may die:

> LEAR.   Why should a dog, a horse, a rat, have life,
>   And thou no breath at all? Thou'lt come no more.
> Never, never, never, never, never!
> Pray you, undo this button. Thank you, sir.
> (Do you see this? Look on her! look! her lips!
> Look there, look there!) "O, O, O, O." (*He dies.*)
> EDGAR.   He faints!—My lord, my lord!
> KENT.   Break, heart. I prithee, break.
> EDGAR.   Look up, my lord.
> KENT.   Vex not his ghost. O let him pass! He hates him
> That would upon the rack of this tough world
> Stretch him out longer.

(V, iii)

The resigned attitude of Kent anticipates that of Aniceto, who also, by his inaction, sympathetically aids the death of his *padrino.* The fact that Zacconi's interpretation of this stirring scene would be immediately familiar to the 1905 audience of **Barranca abajo** is but one more example of what was probably an intentional allusion to *King Lear.*

In the final analysis though, we must not lose sight of the fact that we are dealing with a play, with the representation of an action; the dramatist is the designer of a plan to be interpreted on the stage. Sánchez' meticulous attention to the intricacies of theatrical technique and the subtleties of literary allusion goes far beyond the realist urge to imitate life, or even the naturalist attempt to study it. Acquainted with the masterworks of the modern stage, and influenced by the esthetic concerns of Hispanic modernism, he was uniquely able to communicate a dramatic sensation of reality. It is undoubtedly for this reason that the structured text of **Barranca abajo** reveals the kind of cohesion and wholeness found only in the greatest works of dramatic literature. Not only is the dialogue colloquially accurate, the stage directions carefully planned, and the settings pictorially defined, but—most significantly—the pattern of action is masterfully designed so as to raise the plight of an ordinary *criollo* to the noble dimension of tragedy. The fall of Don Zoilo Carabajal thus marks the rise of modern dramaturgy in the New World. (pp. 25-36)

René de Costa, "The Dramaturgy of Florencio Sánchez: An Analysis of 'Barranca Abajo'," in Latin American Theatre Review, *Vol. 7, No. 2, Spring, 1974, pp. 25-37.*

FURTHER READING

House, Roy Temple. "Florencio Sánchez: A Great Uruguayan Dramatist." *Poet Lore* XXXIV (Summer 1923): 279-82.
   Brief biographical and critical sketch in which House especially praises *La gringa* for its positive message.

Jones, Willis Knapp. "*La Gringa* Theme in River Plate Drama." *Hispania* 25, No. 3 (October 1942): 326-32.

Discusses the appearance and prevalence of the "gringo," or immigrant, in the drama of the River Plate region.

Schwartz, Kessel. "*La Gringa* and *The Cherry Orchard.*" *Hispania* 41, No. 1 (March 1958): 51-55.
    Compares symbolism, plot, and theme of the dramas by Sánchez and Anton Chekhov, noting that "both very clearly portray the symbolic struggle between progress and tradition, between the materialistic and what one might term the poetic or idealistic."

Shedd, Carl Eastman. "Florencio Sánchez's Debt to Eugène Brieux." *Studies in Philology* 33, No. 3 (July 1936): 417-26.
    Asserts that Brieux was the most significant European influence on Sánchez and describes similarities in theme, plot, and characterization in works by the two playwrights.

———. "Thirty Years of Criticism of the Works of Florencio Sánchez." *Kentucky Foreign Language Quarterly* 3, No. 1 (1956): 29-39.
    Bibliographic essay that addresses various issues in the criticism of Sánchez, including his place in modern drama and the extent to which he was influenced by European playwrights.

Sisto, David T. "The Gaucho-Criollo Honor Code in the Theater of Florencio Sánchez." *Hispania* 38, No. 4 (December 1955): 451-55.
    Suggests that the age of Sánchez's characters determines the ways in which they defend their honor.

Arthur Stringer

1874-1950

Canadian poet, novelist, short story writer, screenwriter, dramatist, critic, and biographer.

Stringer was one of the most popular and prolific Canadian writers of the early twentieth century. While he was best known during his lifetime for his novels of adventure, romance, and mystery, he is better remembered for his contribution to Canadian poetry. His earlier poetry addresses classical subjects in conventional poetic forms, and his later poems about Canadian life employ the techniques of free verse and dialect.

Stringer was born in Chatham, Ontario. When he was ten years old, he and his family moved to London, a larger city in the same province. An eager and industrious student in high school, where he established and edited a magazine, Stringer began to publish poems and essays in Canadian periodicals while a student at the University of Toronto. During this time, he wrote primarily poetry and published his first collection, *Watchers of Twilight, and Other Poems.* Leaving Canada in 1894, Stringer studied for a year at Oxford University and traveled extensively in Europe. He then returned to Canada, working as a journalist in Montreal and later in New York. In 1899, Stringer began earning his living as a freelance fiction writer in New York. There he met and exchanged ideas with other Canadian literary figures then living in the United States, including Bliss Carman and Charles G. D. Roberts. During this period, Stringer had several short stories and sketches accepted for magazine publication and published his first novel, *The Silver Poppy,* in 1903. Over the next two decades Stringer continued to write while pursuing various other interests: he operated a farm on the northern shores of Lake Erie, raised wheat and tobacco on a ranch in Alberta, and worked as a screenwriter in Hollywood. In 1921, he retired to a manor-house in Mountain Lakes, New Jersey, where he continued to write numerous novels and poetry collections, as well as plays, criticism, and biography. He died in 1950.

Stringer's fiction consists for the most part of romance, adventure, and detective stories. These works typically feature ordinary characters who by chance become involved in extraordinary circumstances, with ominous notes, mistaken identities, and kidnappings often responsible for the action. While Stringer's readers enjoyed his fast-paced, suspenseful novels and short stories, critics have considered his characters tenuous and plots implausible. A trilogy of novels which Stringer began writing in 1915 represents a departure from his customary genre. *The Prairie Wife, The Prairie Mother,* and *The Prairie Child* chronicle the struggles of a pioneer family in the Canadian Northwest. Although melodramatic by today's standards, these novels were praised by reviewers for their realism and insightful characterizations of women.

Stringer's poetry is considered of greater interest and merit than his fiction. His early poems, written in blank verse, were largely influenced by the works of John Keats. Though imitative in nature, these poems have been praised as fine examples

of the Romantic tradition as it endured into the twentieth century. *The Woman in the Rain, and Other Poems,* a product of this stage in Stringer's career, is considered one of his best collections. Stringer later abandoned conventional poetic meter, employing free verse in *Open Water.* Prefaced by an essay in which Stringer extolled the liberating qualities of free verse, this volume, while not considered innovative for its time, demonstrates Stringer's facility with poetic rhythms and his sentimental portrayal of life in the Canadian countryside. Stringer also wrote a well-received series of ballads which reflect the local color and folklore of Ireland. *The Old Woman Remembers, and Other Irish Poems* has been especially praised for its authentic dialect and humor. Because of its accessibility of both form and subject matter, Stringer's poetry has appealed to a wide audience. As his biographer, Victor Lauriston, noted: "He is a Canadian poet sounding to the world a note of universal humanity."

PRINCIPAL WORKS

Watchers of Twilight, and Other Poems (poetry) 1894
Pauline, and Other Poems (poetry) 1895
Epigrams (poetry) 1896
A Study in King Lear (criticism) 1897

The Loom of Destiny (short stories) 1899
Hephaestus, and Other Poems (poetry) 1903
The Silver Poppy (novel) 1903
Lonely O'Malley (novel) 1905
The Wire Tappers (novel) 1906
Phantom Wires (novel) 1907
Sappho in Leucadia (verse drama) 1907
The Woman in the Rain, and Other Poems (poetry) 1907
The Under Groove (novel) 1908; also published as *Night Hawk,* 1923
The Gun Runner (novel) 1909
Irish Poems (poetry) 1911; also published as *Out of Erin,* 1930
The Shadow (novel) 1913; also published as *Never Fail Blake,* 1924
Open Water (poetry) 1914
The Hand of Peril (novel) 1915
The Prairie Wife (novel) 1915
The Door of Dread (novel) 1916
The Man Who Couldn't Sleep (short stories) 1919
The Prairie Mother (novel) 1920
The Wine of Life (novel) 1921
The Prairie Child (novel) 1922
The City of Peril (novel) 1923
Empty Hands (novel) 1924
Manhandled [with Russell Holman] (screenplay) 1924
The Story Without a Name [with Russell Holman] (screenplay) 1924
Power (novel) 1925
In Bad with Sinbad (novel) 1926
The Wolf Woman (novel) 1928
A Woman at Dusk, and Other Poems (poetry) 1928
A Lady Quite Lost (novel) 1931
Dark Soil (poetry) 1933
Marriage by Capture (novel) 1933
Heather of the High Hand (novel) 1937
The Old Woman Remembers, and Other Irish Poems (poetry) 1938
The Dark Wing (novel) 1939
The Prettiest Woman in the World, and Other One-Act Plays (dramas) 1939
The King Who Loved Old Clothes, and Other Irish Poems (poetry) 1941
Shadowed Victory (poetry) 1943
The Devastator (novel) 1944
Red Wine of Youth: A Life of Rupert Brooke (biography) 1948

HARRY W. BROWN (essay date 1895)

[*In the following excerpt, Brown praises* Watchers of Twilight, and Other Poems *and* Pauline, and Other Poems.]

"Indian Summer"

The soft maid Summer, with her languid loins re-girt,
From earth, her love of old, withdraws her clinging arms,
Yet lingering looks again, and olden days revert
Her thoughts, and all the dread that love alone alarms
Can scarce subdue the wanton wildness of her heart.
She stays, and turns upon her ancient love her face;
Then soft her yielding arms steal round him ere they part,
And all grows dim in dreaminess of one embrace.

He who is fortunate enough to let his first glance fall upon this new and bold conception of Indian Summer will not only feel impelled to turn to other pages, but will also instinctively feel that he has found something belonging peculiarly to our own lake region with its maples and dreamy, hazy days of autumn. And when he turns over to other pages, similar striking and novel ways of offering us old familiar truths and facts in new lights and fresh colors fulfill his expectation. Our attention once drawn is held, and as our mind reverts to the author we rejoice to find a new builder working at the foundations of our national literature.

The two volumes under consideration are: *Watchers of Twilight; and Other Poems,* and *Pauline; and Other Poems,* the former published in 1894, the latter in 1895. . . . (p. 88)

The poems under consideration are not local themes of narrow bounds, but are either classical with world-wide interest or purely Canadian with national and patriotic surroundings.

In the latter class we find references to such home ideas as our Indian Summers, or the peculiar glories in our wild flowers and woods, in the goldenrod,

the queenless crown
That passing summer left behind.

the month of April,

Thou girl of many a golden tress,
Pale April, with the troubled eyes,

. . . . .

. . . in thine eyes of troubled grey
The light was soft with tears unshed,
And life was sweet some unknown way.

or as May, in her passing,

Went down among the flowers and passed away.
And left the old melodious vales forlorn,
When skies were blue and birds sang all the day.
And dew clung sweet around her feet at morn.
And falling blossoms showered her farewell ways,
While from old earth the vernal tremor went.

Who has not seen Lake Ontario in midwinter as he here depicts it?

Along the lonely shore stray snowflakes fall,
The waves crash on the shattered ice, and crush
The surging floes against a long wide wall,
Tinged gold and saffron with the sunset's flush.

Or on Lake St. Clair, we have seen how

The twilight gathers on the grey lake's breast,
And silence deepens on the reed-grown plains;
While far across the waves, from out the west,
Fly slowly in two solitary cranes.

And softly through the reeds the nightwind strays,
Half faint with odors of the marsh land's musk;
And somewhere deep within the inland haze,
A whip-poor-will cries loud across the dusk.

But all through his poems Mr. Stringer reveals to us that he has had classic thoughts and models before his eyes. He has been a close student of Keats, Shelley, Browning, and Tennyson, and although by no means imitating these poets, he has been led to look at classic subjects from a similar point of view. This perhaps may be accounted for in his coming directly from a long course of critical study of their modes of thought and means of expression. It is to his credit that he has not become an imitator; he has gone deeper in attempting to discover the source of their power, and has been successful in so far as could be expected without long years of patient toil. In the following short poem, on the old subject, **"Pygmalion and Galatea,"** we feel the same love of beauty and art, and the same passion revealed by Keats in his "Ode on a Grecian Urn":

I.

Enthralled within the sculptured stone, she sleeps;
But one long kiss the unknown barrier breaks,
And through the marble bosom warms and creeps
The blood that tingles, till the woman wakes.

II.

And looking in your eyes of summer blue,
No miracle the ancient story seems;
For was I not once waken-d thus by you
When one kiss broke through life's old clouded dreams?

III.

Though we to-day smile at the legend old,
And care not whether dream or truth the tale,
We two well know, when life or love grows cold,
That old-time Greek's one touch that cannot fail.

As if confiding to us that these were his favorite authors, he has given us a poem written on the fly-leaf of his Shelley, in which the latter appears to him as the first robin, the harbinger who assures us that the spring and summer cannot fail us; and to the questioner examining his "dog-eared volume" of Keats, he compares the poet to "a deep red, over-ripe wild strawberry," which pressed against our lips in all its color, taste and scent, will make us murmur:

"This,
The very heart of summer that I crush,"—
So poignant, through its lusciousness, it seems!

Even in his purely Canadian songs he uses classic ideals and departs from the more realistic or romantic treatment of the themes and scenes around us. The months, the seasons, the flowers, the lakes are all living souls, half hero, half god, to him. We feel they would be companions to the nymphs and gods and goddesses who dwelt about the early Grecian dales and hills.

This personification of his nature-subjects gives him an opportunity of avoiding mere photography of scenes and places, a fault so common among our Canadian poets. And when we find these familiar subjects endowed with a new life, our interest and pleasure are increased. He sees in nature what Wordsworth saw—that from her humblest flower we can draw lessons of pleasure and profit, of beauty and contentment, of patience and duty; so that we, though overcome by struggles against the unsympathizing world, can turn to her and draw first, peace of mind, then inspiration, and finally, increased activity.

But perhaps Browning is revealed more in these poems than either Keats or Wordsworth. Evidently gifted with strong artistic tastes in his yearnings both for music, whether vocal or instrumental, and for art, as revealed in his many references to these subjects, Mr. Stringer would naturally find Browning's themes congenial. The titles of some of his poems—though not the subject matter in all cases—recall the greater

writer to us at once: **"The Queen and the Slave"; "In the Art Gallery"; "A June Song"; "The Rose and the Rock"; "A Man and a Woman."** In addition to his themes, we find results of a study of Browning both in the manner in which an external object will appeal to him and in his language in its strong, forceful, and rugged expression. In reading him we are reminded of wandering among the rough Rockies, coming unexpectedly on an immense boulder, or finding suddenly a sheer descent or impassable wall confronting us, or perhaps a long, smooth, glacier surface, where the path may be easy though our surroundings are striking. In **"The Reproach of the Goddess,"** he tells us,

'Tis more the fight.
Than all the idle guerdons to be won;
It is the worship though thy gods be mute;
Turn thou thy shadowed face toward the sun,
For Art is not the goal, but the pursuit.

Just as Browning so often tells us, idleness is hateful. Better a struggle even though towards evil, than a weak vacillating fear of carrying out the promptings of our heart. In his epigrams, more than elsewhere, we feel his bold, vigorous use of words and startling ideas. Here is one, **"The Sick Man"**:

He drew too near the brink and peered below;
And mirrored in that face of pain and fear,
We saw gaunt horrors and abysmal woe,
Ere he could shrink back from the grim gulf's leer.

Even more forcible is that on **"The Anarchist"**:

From out her golden palace, Fortune thrust
A maddened dog, whose mouth foamed white with hate;
And loud he howled, and gnawed the court yard dust,
And ground his teeth upon the iron gate.

But little has been said, hitherto, of his purely lyrical poetry. Both volumes abound in short songs, of an air totally different from the poems just considered; for they lose their ruggedness and take on the simpler, though none the less poetic, language so much used by Wordsworth and Tennyson. He has attained a happy manner of carrying the reader rapidly along by various artificial devices, as in **"The Old Garden"**:

Song and golden summer dwelled,
Once within this garden old;
And a strain of music swelled,
From the casements tinged with gold,

Where a lady used to sing,
In the old forgotten Junes;
When the bird songs ceased to ring
Through the sleeping afternoons.

And the roses climbed and bloomed,
Wild, around her window-beams;
Till her chamber was perfumed
With the breathings of their dreams.

· · · · ·

And the children sometimes creep
Through the broken, crumbling wall,
Where the shadows seem to sleep,
And the bird throats seldom call;

Lingering in that lonely place,
Weaving strange and olden dreams;
But a sweet and tender face
Never from the casement gleams.

The human interest suggested in these extracts is much more

strongly emphasized in the body of the poem which is too long for insertion here.

Throughout all his lyrics there is an inspiring stimulation towards higher things, a yearning for all that is beautiful, especially for that beauty with living, even though peaceful, action. Yet the author never gives way to passion; his ideal is within reasonable attainment, and we find he prefers the dreamy, half-forgetful wanderings through the vales of life to the hardening, wearisome toilings up the endless steep slopes of Longfellow's "Excelsior." Many of his poems remind us of a lazy summer afternoon spent at the edge of a murmuring stream, with the wind softly rustling the leaves of the woods behind us, and all about us bright color, whether in the sky, the woods, the grass, or the pebbles under the water.

Perhaps the most promising and characteristic poem in these two volumes is the one which gives the title to the earlier book, **Watchers of Twilight.** It breathes forth the philosophy of hopefulness, of great confidence in the future. In the opening he takes us back to the mythological period of the world's history, "when sea and air and earth were filled with many voices of the gods . . . in the dreaming childhood of the world." But these things have passed away, and now we look back with regret "on those twilight illusions old," and "feel the sorrow of a vanished dream;" all our prophets (our poets) turn to the dead past like sad mothers

> seeing not the tristful child
> Who weeps with many a want beside her knee,
> In clasping to her breast her infant dead.

Those sacred old lands are now a waste; they never were a heaven, and were made so only in our imaginings, which had better be employed in making our own world a heaven. Since those olden days the earth has raised many altars, made many gods, but all "have grown antique along with Jove," and the earth is again in the throes of despair, and "grey-eyed sorrow walks to-day with men," but "on her footsteps goes one with dawn-light gleaming on her brow," smiling and hopeful, called by some Science, by others Philosophy, who bids Sorrow lament no more, for when the gods were on the earth they turned away their ears from men, and their voices were heard only in the wind or stream. Sorrow to-day is the companion of men, because they wander from the straight paths, and erring feet become bruised and bring suffering and death. Men are learning this, and gradually coming to turn their eyes ahead and aloft, and to toil straight onwards up the slope, bending all their energies towards the grand harvest, disdaining the petty things along the road. Thus Science comforts Sorrow, half revealing to her "how man in time shall conquer earth and sea," and "know his own strange soul, and hold at last all yet unfathomed powers." Then peace will enter man's heart, and he will be filled with ambition, and though the road is long his feet will not falter, and he will pass on to the accomplishment of things far greater than those ascribed to the gods. (pp. 88-91)

> Harry W. Brown, "Arthur J. Stringer's Poems," in The Canadian Magazine, *Vol. VI, No. 1, November, 1895, pp. 88-91.*

HARRIET MONROE (essay date 1915)

[*As the founder and editor of* Poetry, *Monroe was a key figure in the American "poetry renaissance" that took place in the early twentieth century.* Poetry *was the first periodical devoted*

primarily to the works of new poets and to poetry criticism, and from 1912 until her death, Monroe maintained an editorial policy of printing "the best English verse which is being written today, regardless of where, by whom, or under what theory of art it is written." In the following review, Monroe comments on the absence of conventional rhyme and meter in the poems collected in Open Water, *comparing them unfavorably with Stringer's earlier poetry.*]

Mr. Stringer has the over-heated enthusiasm of the convert. Having used rhyme and the usual metrical conventions since the days of **The Woman in the Rain,** he now, in an eloquent foreword to his latest book, discards them as "mediaeval apparel." The poet, he says, "must still don mail to face Mausers, and wear chain-armor against machine guns." "Rhyme has been imposed upon him," it is one of the "immuring traditions with which time and the prosodian have surrounded him." "Rhyme and meter have compelled him to sacrifice content for form, have left him incapable of what may be called abandonment."

This has a familiar ring. Milton himself was hardly more emphatic when he denounced rhyme as "the invention of a barbarous age, to set off wretched matter and lame metre." To him in the seventeenth century, as to Mr. Stringer and others today, it was "a troublesome and modern bondage," of "no true musical delight," imposed on the art by mediaeval jinglers against the authority of the "learned ancients."

As *Poetry* has been a voice crying in the wilderness for freedom from trammels and conventions, urging the public to give rein to the poet's individuality, and accord him his own gait, whether it be rhyme or *vers libre,* it would be unbecoming to complain of the presence of this Saul among the prophets. But one may reasonably note that he does not wear the prophet's robes as though to the manner born. Mr. Stringer is not yet at home with free verse, which has its own boundaries and austerities. Poetry is no easier to achieve without rhyme and iambs than with them.

Many of these new poems seem too easily written. In none of them does one find such rhythmic beauty as Mr. Stringer attained in the blank verse of **"The Woman at Dusk,"** or such adroit and accomplished art as he revealed in that poignant narrative in quatrains, **"The Girl Who Went to Ailey."** It may be that he will evolve a style in the new medium, but he does not yet convince us even by such resolute heroics as these:

> God knows that I've tinkled and jingled and strummed,
> That I've piped it and jigged it until I'm fair sick of the
>   game
> But now I want to slough off the bitterness born of it all,
> I want to throw off the shackles and chains of time . . .
> Yea, I will arise and go forth, I have said,
> To the uplands of truth, to be free as the wind,
> Rough and unruly and open and turbulent-throated!
> Yea, I will go forth and fling from my soul
> The shackles and chains of song!

Alas, one can't fling them away, those shackles. The finest poems in this new book are those in which Mr. Stringer has clung closest to the old measures. **"Sappho's Tomb"** has a delicate trochaic movement which seems to follow the light steps of the searchers. **"At Charing Cross"** is persistently iambic in its solemn march. And the beautiful wistful **"Protestations"** is as regular in form and movement as if it rhymed. Its closing lines perhaps outrank anything else in the book:

Yet the end of all is written,
And nothing, O rose-leaf woman,
You ever may dream or do
Henceforth can bring me anguish
Or crown my days with joy!
Three tears, O stately woman,
You said could float your soul,
So little a thing it seemed.
Yet all that's left of life
I'd give to know your love,
I'd give to show my love,
And feel your kiss again!

Even this, however, is not so memorable as certain earlier poems by Mr. Stringer. Thus it is with some doubt that one wishes him a *bon voyage* on his new road. May he find masterpieces along the way! (pp. 243-45)

Harriet Monroe, in a review of "Open Water," in
Poetry, *Vol. V, No. V, February, 1915, pp. 243-45.*

MARGERY MANSFIELD (essay date 1929)

[*In the following review, Mansfield discusses* A Woman at Dusk, and Other Poems *as an inferior collection of poems whose flaws are possibly related to the period in which they were written.*]

Our faults, someone said, are those of humanity, but our virtues are all our own. When the formative years of a poet's life have been spent in a community which has little literary tradition, when much of his work has been done, apparently, in places where he would have scant companionship in the art, it is perhaps pardonable and kind to let these facts account for many short-comings. It is just to point out what excellences are present, as a possible indication of better work which might have been done under different conditions.

I cannot see, however, that Arthur Stringer should be hailed as "the Keats of the Dominion." He has, to be sure, a preoccupation with the Greek myths, and with ideal beauty. He strives toward classicism, but he has not quite the right temperament for this. His Helen-and-Menelaus story—where they fish the drowned Cupid out of the pool—is almost funny. In an effort to be strong he is apt to be ludicrous. He is sometimes banal, and in his more ambitious poems always too lengthy. The title poem, in blank verse, is perhaps the best achieved as a whole—it catches a mood, paints a picture, and indicates some of the mystery of woman and of twilight. But it is a bit tedious. [*A Woman at Dusk, and Other Poems*], I might as well say frankly, is not good reading, though perhaps it would compare favorably with most of the verse written in the United States during the fallow period between 1900 and 1910. This suggests that the poet's talent is struggling through a similar fallow period in Canadian literature.

For talent I think he has, though I am almost afraid to cite evidence for fear the lines will be disappointing when not read beside verses less competent.

High Troy becomes a path for Helen's feet,
And Egypt for a kiss is thrown away.

Beauty is not immortal; in a day
Blossom and June and rapture pass away.

And at the bud of our too golden life
Eats this small canker of mortality.

Some hand unknown to us

Shook one white petal from the perfect flower,
And all the world grew old.

Yet I shall know her as she was of old,
Fashioned of moonlight and Aegean foam.

There are many more, though not so quotable. Such as they are, they constitute his claim as a poet, for the ability to write a good line is the one thing that cannot be taught. A poet can be taught not to use stilted inversions, he can be taught to shorten his work, he can be taught restraint; taste can be to some extent communicated, thought stimulated, "bunk" exposed, banalities taught self-consciousness. This can be achieved by contact with living poets and a living art. But the exalted line, the poetic image, the perfect phrase! These are the despair of teachers, and the gauge of classical talent. (pp. 108-10)

Margery Mansfield, "A Canadian Poet," in Poetry,
Vol. XXXIV, No. II, May, 1929, pp. 108-10.

VICTOR LAURISTON (essay date 1941)

[*In the following excerpt, Lauriston surveys Stringer's poetry and fiction.*]

Before the age of twenty [Stringer] had accumulated sufficient verse for his first volume, **Watchers of Twilight,** published in 1894. If there was vigor in this and the two small volumes which followed in the two ensuing years, it must be acknowledged that it, in common with all youthful poetry, was still experimental and largely derivative. We can trace the influences of Wordsworth and Browning, of William Watson and Francis Thompson. But most of all one detects the colouring of Keats.

So apparent is this Keats influence that Stringer's lines to his English master in **Pauline, and Other Poems** are little surprising. In a magazine study ten years later, Florence Henderson characterized Stringer as "The Keats of Canada." The phrase is not inappropriate. For Stringer swiftly developed a melodiousness of line, a sensuous yet objective phrasing, a warmth and richness of feeling made vocal in carefully meditated lingual cadences, and a love for classical themes made human by the exploitation of their humanity, essentially characteristic of the author of "Endymion."

With a poet so individual as Stringer, the Keats influence, obviously, could not be an enduring one. In his **Open Water** (1914) we find him abjuring rhyme and swinging over to the ranks of the *vers librists*. And he was scholar enough to articulate his reasons for his new faith.

All art has its ancestry. While it is the duty of poetry both to remember and to honour its inherited grandeurs, the fact remains that even this most convention-ridden medium of expression is a sort of warfare between the embattled soul of the artist and the immuring traditions with which Time and the prosodians have surrounded him. . . . Poetry alone during the last century seems to have remained stable. This has resulted in a technical dexterity which often enough resembles the strained postures of acrobatism and in the constantly reiterated complaint as to the aloofness of modern poetry.

Then he continues with a plea for what he calls "symphonic phrasing":

Even the effect toward emancipation is not without its value. It may serve to impress on certain minds the fact that poetry is capable of exhausting one particular form of expression, of incorporating and consuming one particular embodiment of perishable matter, and passing on to new fields. Being a living organism, it uses up what lies before it, and to find new vigor must forever feed on new forms.

It was a valorous-sounding plea for freedom. But Stringer eventually discovered that he was wrong. For in an Afterword to **Dark Soil** (1933) we find him writing:

> Two decades ago we proudly spoke of it as "Free Verse." But Time brings its changes, ending even the poet's dolorously enduring struggle between formal obligation and freedom. The Futurists are not yet in complete control of the future. And fewer lances are now broken in the cause of the Imagists. And many experimenters who may have regarded themselves as the pioneers in a new form can now be looked upon as the veterans of a war so remote we find it hard to recall either the occasion or the original cause of the conflict. . . . For, like alcohol, the foreordained outline and the expectation fulfillment of formalized verse, dangerous as it may be as an intoxicant, is not entirely valueless as a stimulant. So when I venture to quote from my earlier Foreword I must be forgiven for doing so with something not unlike the grim-eyed tolerance of a battered old General taking the salute from a march-past of his youngest and rawest militia. For Art, after all, is long. And Time teaches us that this shifted fetter known as Freedom is not always the final solution of the artist's problem.

It seems to have taken the individualistic Stringer many years to learn that rigidity of form, architectural outline, end-rhyme and material exactions were not always the obstacles he claimed them to be between feeling and expression. His free verse was not a failure. But it taught him, I think, that the twentieth century poet can no more walk alone than can the twentieth century scientist. The accretions of the past constitute a part of his heritage. He depends on the triumphs and technical accomplishments of his forebears. Those "inherited grandeurs" may not come down through the blood, but most surely they flow on through the descendants of the spirit. There is no backward path. There is no returning, as Stringer once contended, to the rudimentary chant of our campfire ancestors. The singing sons of the Psalmist may remain on earth, but they carry with them all the experiences and the adventures in artistry of all the generations of all the children of David. Stringer himself seems seeking to express this in **"A Woman Sang"**:

> Still deep entombed in her is all the Past,
> And groping from her heart to greet the day
> Are strange persistent ghosts, and from her eyes
> Peer pitiful and unperceivéd eyes.
> For once, in fires of anguish now unknown
> Was smelted this sweet silver of delight;
> In earth's deep furnace of the dead was fused
> The gold of all this careless-noted song . . .
> And women that you know not of, through you
> As through a pipe, forever cry and plead;
> Across the muffled strings of being stray
> Their ghostly hands, with all their ghostly chords . . .
> We dwell upon the Dead, and day by day
> We die a little that the world may live.
> Thought-free we can no longer fare; we are
> A haunted folk; our stillest eve is thronged

> With spectral voices; our most quiet dawn
> Is stirred with whispers from the tombéd past.

Worth quoting, these lines, not merely because they show the shifting art-tenets of the poet, but also because they reveal him in that more philosophic mood which gives depth and substance to his later verse.

No Stringer poem sounds that deeper note more triumphantly than does his **"Hephæstus,"** whose stately blank verse tells how Zeus, the father of life, gave Aphrodite to his crippled son, the god of fire and the useful arts, and how Hephæstus, finding that his wife loved and was loved by his own brother Ares, the god of war, voluntarily surrendered her to that younger and more favoured brother.

All this about gods and goddesses may sound remote; yet in it we find the far-off brought close and mythology made human. For the dramatic conflict it pictures is as modern as this morning's newspaper; conflict of personalities, of passions, of perceptions; of the material with the spiritual; of the temporal with that which passes not away: conflict of the soul with that unknown something we loosely call Fate; and conflict of the poet himself instrumenting the tumult of everyday speech into measured and memorable lines that sometimes have the sonorous organ-roll of Milton and sometimes the soft lucidity of Shelley.

> This is the woman that the dreaming hours
> Of all the world delivered unto you.
> This is the woman—look! These are the eyes
> That made the moonlight lean upon the sea
> And filled the earth with pulsing loveliness
> And turned the quiet winds of night to wine.
> These are the lips that paved the world with pain
> And threw a mist about you as you turned
> Reluctant-eyed away. This is the breast
> That made the light across the laurelled hills
> Come oversoon.

Seldom has the rapture born of man's love of woman been more majestically affirmed. The setting may be that of countless centuries ago, but both the note and the theorem are of today. They are as modern as Jesus of Nazareth, with whom the idea of renunciation is beatitude; as modern as Amiel, with whom the idea of personal sacrifice is personal dignity. Hephæstus bids Ares take this woman he can no longer hold. There will be the pang of parting, but . . .

> As Demeter mourned
> Through many-fountained Enna, I may grieve
> A time forlorn, and fare alone, and learn
> Some still autumnal twilight by the sea
> Pale gold with sunlight, to remember not.
> For as the pine foregoes the pilgrim thrush,
> I, sad of heart, yet unimpassioned, yield
> To you this surging bosom soft with dreams,
> This body fashioned of Ægean foam
> And langorous moonlight. Yet I give you not
> The eluding soul that in her broods and sleeps
> And ne'er was mine of old, nor can be yours.
> It was not born of sea and moon with her,
> And though it nests within her, no weak hand
> Of hers shall cage it as it comes and goes,
> Sorrows and wakens, sleeps and sings again.

For the loser in this duel of love, of course, is giving what can never be taken. He gives "the marble of her body touched with fire," the empty body around which mortal passion must always beat and ebb. But beyond that he cannot go. For "there is a citadel surrenders not," just as there are intimacies that can be perilous.

> And so I give you but the hollow lute,
> The lute alone, and not the voices low
> That sang of old to some forgotten touch;
> The dust I give you, the handful of blown dust
> That many a tear shall water e'er it blooms;
> The lamp I give, but not the glimmering flame
> Some fragile hand withholds, some mystic dusk
> Enisles and yet relumes beyond the last
> Receding loneliness of wave-worn eyes;
> The shell I give, O Ares, not the song
> Of murmuring winds and waves once haunting it;
> The cage, but not the wings that come and go.

Here, as elsewhere, Stringer betrays an almost Hebraic fondness for parallel clauses, a musician's passion for simultaneous vibrations. And here may be noted, not only the fluidity of the measured line, but the reiterant clause that strengthens a former clause by saying the same thing in different words, until the sense of the whole is held in suspension, a poise of thought that can wheel and hover and yet wing home to its final climax.

"Hephæstus" stands proof of Stringer's right to the purple. It has been called the best blank verse ever written by a Canadian pen. (pp. 108-15)

Stringer's *Sappho in Leucadia* is a four-act drama in blank verse. It tells a story, and is not without structure as drama. It has situation and action; it advances to a tragic climax not unsuited to theatrical uses. But, to my way of thinking, it remains a poem, a complicated and turbulent poem of passion, better suited to the study than the stage. Like *Romeo and Juliet,* it deals with the tragedy of star-crossed lovers. But it does more than this. It also exploits the timeless contest between the realistic and the rhapsodic type of mind as exemplified in the calm and calculating Pittacus and the lyric-souled singer of Lesbos.

The legends clustering about that singer of Lesbos are both numerous and contradictory. It is scarcely necessary to say that Stringer chooses the higher rather than the lower road, avoiding all direct allusion to the sexual perversion which clouds the name of this first of the Lesbians. But erotic passion he does not avoid. The drama, in fact, concerns the love of Sappho for Phaon, swart seafarer of Mytilene, across whose oar Aphrodite herself once leaned to school him in the ways of winning a wayward heart. As Sappho says of him:

> The bloom of youth was on your sunburnt cheek,
> The stream of life sang through your violet veins,
> The midnight velvet of your tangled hair
> Lured like a cooling rill my passionate hands.
> The muscles ran and rippled on your back
> Like wind on evening waters, and your arm
> Seemed one to cherish, or as sweetly crush.
> The odor of your body, sinuous
> And saturate with sun and sea-air, was
> As Lesbian wine to me.

This is all physical enough, yet the theme of *Sappho In Leucadia* reaches up into the spiritual. For that theme is treated with a delicacy of feeling that lifts it above the sordid. It becomes elemental. The artist nature in Stringer has fathomed the artist nature in Sappho. The psychology of the passion of the poetess, the "dark Sappho" of tradition, is unerringly portrayed. Even Phaon is made human and understandable. Omaphale is a definitely created character. Phocus, the

drunken and garrulous poet of Samnos, leavens the flow of sweetness with a Falstaffian strain of humour, just as the iron-souled Pittacus brings a sterner fibre to the fabric that might seem too silky in its Yeats-like mystic dreaminess and its almost over-abundant felicities of phrase. But it is Sappho who dominates this drama that loses itself in poetry, not the Sappho of Licentious fame, but the Sappho of the "Fragments" and of the Sapphic verse for which she was once crowned the Tenth Muse; not the Sappho of countless legendary amours, but the tragic and warmhearted woman whose immortal verse could not save her from the pangs of Love's immortal fires. Stringer has not white-washed her, he has reinstated her.

He has touched her with nobility. For in this Sappho, as in very few other women of distinction, the poem of nature and the poem of art seem to know a single setting. Sappho walked in beauty and at the same time remained art-conscious and articulate, holding her audience through loveliness linked with language. And, just as only loveliness of language could reincarnate her, so only a supremely lyric soul could understand and interpret a life once consecrated to lyrical expression. Within three pages of the opening act we find Sappho crying:

> I have known love, but never love like this.
> I have loved oft and lightly so at last
> I might love you. These other men were not
> A god to me; they were the trodden path
> But not the temple; they were but the key
> And not the chamber; they were but the oil
> And not the guarded lamp, the shallow tarn
> And not the mystic and impassioned sea . . .
> Look, Phaon, in my eyes and say once more
> You will not change, that you will never change!

Here again we see the same familiar amplitude of metaphor beloved of the Psalmists, the Stringer device of piling up figure on figure until the result becomes more than two-dimensional. Here, too, we see that mingled love-hunger and love-weariness, that craving for something permanent amid our mortal impermanences, to which Stringer gave such wistful expression in *A Woman at Dusk.* (pp. 116-19)

It has been claimed that the essence of poetry is emotion remembered in tranquillity, that its beauty lies in the expectation of the unexpected, "the surprise of unsurprise." But beauty it must have, the beauty of near-by things made glamorous or the beauty of old familiar things refamiliarized in fresher colours. For, in its absolute, poetry is the final perfection of painting with words. And Stringer's *Sappho in Leucadia* is filled with this sort of graphic, yet intangible, loveliness. There is scarcely a line in it that does not lure one farther. There is scarcely a passing thought that is not garmented in dreamy beauty. It must be accepted as one of the noble poetic achievements of our century.

That Arthur Stringer, himself half Celt, should be known best by his Irish poems is understandable. It is also, I think, regrettable. I say this because it is in his poems of classical allusion, his **"Hephæstus"** and **"Sappho"** and **"Helen, After Ilium"** and **"The Daughter of Demeter"** that he both shows himself the greater prosodian and achieves his greater philosophic depth. But these poems, for all the warming humanity that runs through them, are not for the man in the street. From them the scholarly mind will derive its scholarly rewards. In them the lover of poetry will discover majesty of thought wedded to the sweep of emotion. And through them the discerning reader will learn how our poet's slowly-accruing mastery of blank verse, the unrhymed iambic pentameter which Milton and Shakespeare once made the noblest utterance of our language, can still achieve an imponderable magic all its own. But these poems will and must remain caviar to the general.

It must not be assumed from this that the Irish poems are less worthy of attention. But they are more earthly and every-day, and not of the mountain tops. Their appeal is more universal. For, as Louis Blake Duff has asserted, "No one is writing Irish verse more authentic in note than Arthur Stringer's. His has the genuine taste and smell, the tears and laughter, the indefinable spirit, that mark the soul of Irish poetry."

Stringer knows Ireland and loves the Irish. He has idled about the glens and whins and chimney-corners of old Erin and has caught the colour, the wistfulness, the swift change of mood that is all Celtic. Indeed, he has caught more than this. For along with the mordant humour, the tears tangled with laughter, the small portraits so deftly executed, we get subtler and sterner connotations, a motley parade of the essential characteristics of a complex and lovable people, a revelation of the gaiety and inner grace of the Irish, and repeated evidence of that enduring compassion for the human race which we encounter in artists like Hardy and Housman.

I cannot escape the impression that in these poems Stringer stumbled into a new freedom. He locked the door on mere lyricism and through dialect escaped to what Browning first called the dramatic monologue. To him, in fact, dialect proved, what costume is to the actor, an escape from himself, a short-cut to objective ends. (pp. 123-25)

Stringer has avoided the near-brogue of the vaudeville boards and the joke-monger's column. With the passage of time, in fact, his Irish verse has approximated more and more to pure English. But through the written word he has succeeded in indicating those intonations and quirks of phrase which are as elusive as quicksilver even while they are as penetrating as turf-smoke. Taking the middle course, he has made his Irish for the eye as well as for the ear. Studying those accents, he has striven to be true to them. For, as he says:

> I love to listen to Irish voices,
> To the lilt and flow of the words,
> Consoling and quick and tumbling,
> Like the evening pother of birds.
> I love to hear my people conversing,
> Like the waters under a mill,
> Faith, never stopping to reason,
> And never entirely still.

It is there, all through the poems, deep affection united with deep understanding, a full consciousness of the contradictions, the inconsequentialities, the incongruous changes of mood, consciousness of the squalor and dissoluteness and garrulity, mingled with its salvaging humour and that inborn streak of poetry and love of beauty which has contributed to the survival of the gloomily happy sons of Erin. " 'Tis the Irish can sing through it all!"

It is in the dramatic lyric of Ireland's ancient kings, the title poem, of *The Old Woman Remembers* (1938), that Stringer best pictures this mixture of squalor and grandeur, of sordid poverty and shining poetry, characteristic of the Old Sod. For when the talk goes round to kings the old crone, huddled beside the peat fire, abruptly comes to life.

"Kings, is it, now?"
> She muttered, in a voice that'd make the croak
> Of ravens sound like music. "Kings, is it?"
> She challenged as her shrunken breast grew big.
> "Sure, we had kings a-plenty in the ould days,
> Up-standing, big-boned men with beards of red,
> And jewelled swords, faith, longer than my leg,
> Kings who'd go riding high across the hills
> With a light about their shoulders and a blade
> The sun flashed on."

But these kings, according to the old woman of the glens, were not like the kings of our degenerate days—for by candle-time they'd come:

> And ask off-hand for a spill of rushes laid
> Beside the hearth to sleep on, and a jug
> O' skim-milk and a bannock of barley-meal,
> Easing their wearied bodies of clinking mail
> And leather plates the dogs kept sniffing at
> While the childer hid away like frightened hares
> And peat was piled on the fire.

In those seven lines the poet paints a picture both graphic and unforgettable. And all through the dark and faded tapestry of this poem the Stringer flashes of poetry break and shine like sunlight through huddled clouds. These kings might sit on a three-legged stool rubbing their saddle-galls, but when they came to that cottage they were:

> Blown in like a leaf on nights of windy rain.

And these same kings who were glad enough to dry their breeks and snore beside the hob while a quick-made loaf was browning, still had their touch of grandeur

> Riding out of the mist and into the mist again
> With a cloud of gold about them.

And grandeur, too, is in their departure as the old woman depicts it, grandeur and glamour that become brighter against this background of the lowly, expressed in lowly words that break into rhapsody:

> 'Tis many a king has slept under this thatch
> With a full belly and his feet on the hearth,
> His clean sword close to his ribs, the raft of them
> With unmouthed troubles to think of, being kings;
> For at break of day they'd be blowing on the ash
> And buckling up the leather that smelt of sweat
> Over the otter skin. And off they'd be
> With a spear-shaft in their boot, bound God knows where,
> Riding out of a cloud and into a cloud again,
> 'Til the horn of hammered silver under their arm
> No longer caught the sun.

And their names came back to the old woman through the mists of time:

> Like the sound of harp strings heard on a lonely hill.

For this old woman, like Ireland herself, lived in her memories. In destitution, she found glory in dreams. The misery of today was forgotten in the splendour of times long past. It was many a moon, she laments, since the horse of a king ate meal and the chickens pecked at his dung in the courtyard. But

>   . . . Grand kings they were

> With mats of hair on their chests and thick-thewed arms,
> And a throubled world to ride for the glory of God.
> For kings, those days, were kings, and fights were fights

To face in a kingly way. And the call of a horn,
Grieving of wrong beyond some wine-dark hill,
Meant more than broken faith and a bed of silk,
And a slather of scars on a shield still held to the wind
Shone brighter than big stones set in a band of gold.

(pp. 127-30)

It is the courage to face these darker issues of life, while too many of our lyric poets remain content to sniff the clover-blossoms, that marks Stringer as of the larger mould. In **"A Rhymer's Epilogue,"** when asked if he as a singer "bared his heart for men to see," our author retorted that such a question stood a joke betwixt God and him.

> For I ten hundred hearts can claim;
> Made blends of Rogue, Ascetic, Saint,
> While virtue crowning like a flame
> Black gulfs unproved, I dare not paint?
> Villon today, tomorrow Paul,
> The wolf confounded with the lamb:
> Indeed, Dear Friend, I showed not all,
> Who know not yet the thing I am!

That the Villon strain is there was revealed long before Stringer studied the old women of Dublin. For he, like Villon, leaned over one of the blacker gulfs when he so sedulously studied that decrepit daughter of joy known as **"The Woman in the Rain."** This has been called "The Man With the Hoe in Petticoats." For, doing what Rodin did with the chisel, Stringer has not only painted the picture of the aged courtesan, but has proclaimed her an emblem of earthly woe and a symbol of our corrupted civilization. (pp. 132-33)

But Stringer, it must be remembered, has his lighter side. This is especially evident in the Irish poems, with their Celtic touch of whimsicality and their laugh that comes after a tear. Thus we have O'Hara the Bird Man, who is to be hanged for a Fenian or two he happened to kill in a bit of a fight. The friend of the murderer can lament, *more Hibernico,* the passing of so gentle a spirit:

> There's sorra hope left if they're stringin' up lads
> Wid a sowl like O'Hara's, that's sayin' the least—
> Och, what a mistake to be hangin' a man
> So fond av each little wee birdie and beast!

Then there's Terence O'Rourke, poacher and rogue and thief, his mottled career made happier by the loyalty of his old beagle, Tim, who loved that good-for-nothing as only a dog or a woman could.

> So I'm thinkin', mayhap, there's a trace av good
> Conc'aled in Terence, or no dog could
> Be wastin' his time on a murderin' lad
> From his brogans up to his midriff bad.
> But I'll take me oath if there's good in the lout
> 'Tis only a hound could be nosin' it out!

And who more adeptly than Stringer could invert a love story and depict with quieter humour the toll which time can take of even a great passion? The aged suitor in **"I Met Me Ould Love"** wanders into the cottage of his sweetheart of long ago and stares at his old storeen who had once been as slender as a fawn. She has, apparently, survived the disaster of separation. For the old boy relates:

> I marked her pewter all a-row,
> Her steamin' kettle, and her delf,
> Her fowls that did be talkin' so,
> Her clickin' needles, and Herself.

> She viewed me wid a throubled frown
> And asked me what the name might be;
> Then neatly put her knittin' down
> And "Worra, where's me specks?" sez she.

> She blinked about the clean-swept floor,
> And sat, a time, with wrinkled brow;
> Then, takin' up her wool wanst more,
> "In faith," she sez, "I mind you now!"

I cannot close this study of a poet whose life has been so eager and industrious without citing his tribute to labour, a tribute which perhaps holds the key to the mystery of his amazing accomplishment. Like Browning's "Last Duchess" he has loved whate'er he looked on, and his looks went everywhere. The blare and tumult of Broadway on New Year's Eve prompt him to exclaim:

> Austere in daily action we have stood;
> In toil, behold, we beautiful have seemed;
> But that our labour be not wholly vain
> And all the struggle empty, teach us, God,
> O teach us at the end of toil to know
> The sanctity of Laughter and the joy
> That ever walks with Beauty!

Even more eloquent of Stringer's belief in the final sanctity of labour is the proclamation of his middle-aged Pittacus who has no time for song:

> . . . I had my work,
> My work that led me on by paths austere
> And walked beside me with its patient eyes
> And seemed forever mirthless. Yet when life
> Grew wise and hard and empty, and the friends
> Of youth all fell away, 'twas in this friend,
> 'Twas in this comrade with the quiet eyes
> And solemn brow, I found my final peace.

(pp. 134-36)

• • • • •

Two marked characteristics dominate all [Stringer's] fiction—word artistry and authenticity. The artistry was partly inborn, partly acquired through an eager nature's subconscious absorption of the best his predecessors had to offer. The authenticity, the fidelity to factual circumstance, was, however, a quality neither needful nor usual in the 'nineties of the last century when he produced his first book of prose. Many popular novelists of that era enjoyed a license not permitted in a later day: the deer of imagination was too often allowed to leap the fence of fact. Hand in hand with the invention of action that had no basis in character or circumstance went the invention of backgrounds that had no basis in geography. In dialogue, a craving for high-sounding words, surviving from the sentimental romances of the 'sixties, usually submerged the slowly dawning suspicion that fiction folk might be more convincing if they talked like everyday people.

Stringer could not escape entirely these influences, though from the first his Scottish conscience and his inborn faculty of observation battled against them.

One factor in shaping his earlier prose work in book-form cannot be disregarded. Antedating even *The Loom of Destiny* and running concurrently with the long series of volumes which followed that first modest effort was a vast amount of prose writing for magazines. This helped develop in his books a compact artistry impossible had he written merely for book publication. The poetry to which he eagerly returned at every opportunity also aided the artist to survive and even to dominate the thriller epoch of his early novels.

Before this epoch, though, an experimental period produced three prose volumes meriting study: wherein the skirts of imitation still clung to the emerging figure of individuality. *The Loom of Destiny* (1899) dates from Stringer's American Press Association days, when, in odd moments snatched from diligent desk-work, he keenly observed the child life of this strange teeming city, and transmuted his observations into brief sketches of juvenile New York.

Noteworthy in this volume, a characteristic destined to emerge years later in his strikingly different novels of the prairie and the North, is Stringer's effective use of ironic contrast: as where, in **"An Essay in Equality,"** Whitney Algernon Holland in his velvet suit, surfeited in luxury and guarded by his starchy English nurse, hungers for a leveling process that will permit him to sink his bare toes in the ooze and share the mud-puddle privileges enjoyed exclusively by the ragged urchin of the slums.

A touch of Kipling reveals itself in this flashing glimpse of the forlorn little Teddie in **"Heart's Desire"**:

> His loneliness, however, did not weigh heavily upon him. He held animated discourse with bits of broken flower pots and fell into the habit of telling wonderful stories to the third step on the landing which had a crack in it, and therefore always listened best.

But the quality enabling Stringer to achieve success in the most difficult of literary tasks, child portrayal, and its most difficult phase, portrayal of the slum child, was essentially Stringer's own.

A product of his free-lancing days in the Fifth Avenue attic was Stringer's first novel, *The Silver Poppy* (1903). The artist in Stringer already disdained the sugary "happy ending" convention, and thereby gained for this novel the power which comes from a sense of inevitability. Yet his chapter openings echo the then current fiction vogue; and his dialogue, though lit with epigrammatic flashes that give promise for the future, is marked at times by a straining for melodramatic effect reminiscent of the past.

The Silver Poppy was set against the New York artistic and literary backgrounds with which Stringer—reincarnated in John Hartley, a young poet recently arrived from Oxford—had gradually familiarized himself. Current newspaper gossip mistakenly identified his Cordelia Vaugh, the lovely Kentucky novelist whose growing fame fed on the literary life blood of other writers, with a popular novelist of the day. Whatever its flaws, *The Silver Poppy* marches with a grim inevitability to its tragically ironic climax of the repentant Cordelia vainly abasing herself outside Hartley's closed door.

Stringer's third prose volume took him back to his native Ontario, to the town of Chatham, where he had played as a boy. Among all his works, *Lonely O'Malley* (1905) stands out as the most Canadian and the most definitely autobiographical. A casual reference implies a dating subsequent to the then-recent Klondike gold rush, but the story's manifest background and timing are Chatham and the Canadian Thames of the early 'eighties. With all this it has an enduring timelessness, the timelessness of recurring boyhood, which has kept and must keep it alive. (pp. 137-41)

In the year of *Lonely O'Malley* the ordeal of an hour in a New York dentist's chair diverted Stringer to a fiction field he was to cultivate for more than a decade. To the rasping obbligato of the drill, this dentist confided how a gang of wire tappers had mulcted him of half a year's earnings. Stringer, ever alert for fiction material, investigated: the outcome being *The Wire Tappers* (1906) the first of a series of crime-adventure novels having for background the picturesque but sordid New York underworld.

In the ensuing decade, Stringer's book-length fiction was limited to this narrow field. One cannot but regret that in these early years he thus restricted himself. Yet there was gain, though hardly the gain there might have been in wider fields: gain, at least, in story-telling power. Written largely for serialization, these crime stories put a premium on vigorous action with the result that Stringer's later novels in more appealing fields show a robustness not apparent in his almost contemplative earlier fiction. The contemplative detachment is not lost, but henceforth Stringer enters more fully into his tale and sits less upon the sidelines, with a resultant gain in narrative effectiveness.

Of these stories, *The Wire Tappers* is the first and in many respects the best. It possesses a subjectivity, an effective characterization and a sound motivation less evident in some of the later tales. Here, too, we catch a note that recurs again and again in Stringer's fiction, however far removed its scene from the native Ontario to which his heart still clung. Jim Durkin has been "despatcher and station agent, and ticket seller and snow shoveler, and lamp cleaner and everything else, for the Grand Trunk at Komoka, where the Tunnel trains cut off from the main line west for Chicago." Throughout his stories, glancing references such as this to Canadian scenes, the use of Canadian names, reveal that Canada is by no means forgotten.

Durkin and Frances Candler, enmeshed by the gang engaged in tapping the million wires of the great city, are human, more essentially human and more soundly motivated than Stringer's John Hartley and Cordelia Vaughan. His McNutt, his lesser crooks, his dicks and flatfeet, are real. Already he had laid a ground work in years of observation. (pp. 142-44)

Stringer's earlier observations of New York life were supplemented by specialized studies of the backgrounds with which his fiction dealt. Assiduously, Stringer gathered underworld data. To the average police officer, whatever his function, the crime story is a sorry travesty and the fiction detective a pathetic jest. It was not for nothing, therefore, that Arthur Wood, for years New York Police Commissioner, ordered his rookies and officers-in-training to read Stringer's underworld books for their authentic portrayal of criminals and criminal life. William A. Pinkerton, head of the famous detective agency, "Camera-Eye" Sheridan, and Commissioner Wood himself—and, undoubtedly, many an unsuspecting subordinate—had contributed to the fund of information which enabled Stringer to depict the New York underworld with an accuracy never before achieved.

With this fidelity to detail, Stringer combined the artistry that marked all his work. If he was faithful to his backgrounds, so, too, was he faithful to the limitations of his characters. This note of the authentic, this consciousness that the happiest ending must be merely provisional, rings in the concluding passage of *The Wire Tappers* where Durkin and Frances leave New York behind them, the man confident that their criminal past is dead:

> "Good-bye," said the woman. But it was not a challenge. It was a prayer.

And *Phantom Wires,* the sequel, sounded the same realistic note.

The period was one when the *Saturday Evening Post,* pacesetter for the magazines, eagerly featured series of complete short stories involving the same central characters. Out of such a series *The Under Groove* (1909) was loosely cobbled into a novel. Here Stringer reveals a new lightness yet sureness of touch not evident in the earlier wire-tapper stories. He has come into his full powers at a time when story telling is still glamourous, in these linked first-person tales by an old offender of his thief-catch-thief experiences. An unrivalled study of criminal psychology, *The Under Groove* leaves a sob—not of tragedy—in the reader's throat.

Similarly *The Man Who Couldn't Sleep* ties together eleven "insomniac" stories. *The Gun Runner* depicts a wireless operator playing a part in a Latin-American revolution. Current news interests are linked with later tales. *The Door of Dread* hinges on German spy activities in the United States. *The Hand of Peril* unfolds a deep-laid plot to undermine the stability of the government by a flood of counterfeit currency. *The City of Peril* deals with Bolshevik intrigue. While *In Bad With Sinbad,* last of these action stories, crowds into "one Arabian night" in Manhattan sufficient tense action to fill a book.

The Shadow (1913) later republished as *Never-Fail Blake,* falls within a different category. Technically a detective story, it is actually a Conrad-like study of character. Blake, the human blood-hound, obsessed with the insistent urge to "get his man," trails the criminal, Binhart, around the world only to discover that officialdom has double-crossed him and the case is closed. Yet the blood-hound instinct in him refuses to die. The closing scene where, on a crowded New York street corner, "Batty" Blake, the old glue-seller, at last pounces on his quarry with the chokingly triumphant cry, "I've got Binhart!" is one of the great climaxes of fiction.

Through an unsuccessful experiment in Alberta wheatgrowing, Stringer's salvaging instinct won rescue from the tightening bonds of crime fiction. True, his action stories continued even after *The Prairie Wife* (1915), but the emergence of Chaddie McKail spelled an emancipation that must have been as welcome for him as for his readers.

Chaddie McKail, the trans-Atlantic globe-trotter who becomes a prairie wife and mother, is undoubtedly the most popular of all Stringer's fiction heroines. The title, "heroine," so often misapplied, undoubtedly fits Chaddie, though in being heroic she does not cease to be human.

Critics have continuously commented on Stringer's understanding of women, his ability to see life through their eyes and define their feelings and reactions. His own disarming protest, "The man who thinks he understands women is ripe for the slaughter," finds its answer in the fact that not merely in *The Prairie Wife,* but through the two succeeding volumes of the trilogy, everything is seen and expressed through the eyes of Chaddie, the prairie wife and mother. (pp. 145-48)

The Prairie Wife stands not merely a landmark in Stringer's career, but a landmark in Canadian literature. From it dates the gradual displacement of the romantic prairie novel with its "bad men" and red-coated mounties by the novel of the West as it is. With the possible exception of Robert Stead, Stringer was almost the first fiction writer to portray a West that, with these traditional accessories relegated to their proper place and proportions, found an even greater charm for the reader in the human appeal of its characters and the actualness of its backgrounds.

The tragedy Stringer pictures in the prairie trilogy might happen, and does happen, to people of like temperaments everywhere; but in no country save Canada could it involve this particular set of dramatic personae, or emerge so naturally from such a background. (p. 149)

If Stringer occasionally, as in *The City of Peril* and *In Bad With Sinbad* went back to crime adventure, he continued steadily to work toward greater things. *The Prairie Wife* had given him a welcome opportunity to depict a new aspect of his native country to an audience far larger than Canada could offer. In *Empty Hands* (1924) he essayed yet another Canadian field he was to make peculiarly his own, the far north, in a variant of the Crusoe theme, so universal in its appeal, so alluring in its possibilities.

Claire Endicott, the self-willed product of a sophisticated civilization, and Shomer Grimshaw, the taciturn, woman-hating woodsman, are swept by the rapids of Malign Canyon into a previously untraversed wilderness. There, shut off by an insurmountable barrier from the world they have known, stark naked, empty-handed, they are compelled from Adam-and-Eve beginnings to work out their salvation or perish.

An ordinary story-teller might have been content, with an unknown country for background, to take those liberties which the utterly unknown affords the imaginative writer. For if a land has never before been visited, who has the right to challenge the story-teller's details?

Not so Stringer. If his terrain beyond the Barrier had never been visited, yet logically it must partake of the characteristics of the known North in the same latitude. Stringer was not the writer to disregard this salient fact. A vast amount of reading, and, better still, of first-hand research must have gone into the production of *Empty Hands.*

Indeed, this very fidelity to detail somewhat mars the story. There are times when you cannot see the forest of human emotion for the trees of factual exactness. One carries away the sense of a story-teller fettered by his conscious effort for fidelity in minor detail. *Empty Hands* is a big story: yet it lacks the freedom achieved in later tales of the north, such as *Marriage by Capture* (1933), and especially in *A Lady Quite Lost* (1931) probably Stringer's finest effort in this field.

In none of these stories does Stringer essay so far a leap into the romantic. *Empty Hands,* in fact, is handicapped by its very theme. Except in the opening and concluding chapters, Stringer's human characters are necessarily restricted to his two protagonists: and the third character, hostile Nature, can never take the place of those subsidiary figures, typical of the North, who add so much to his later stories in this field. (pp. 152-54)

Much of the effectiveness of these northern novels derives from their contrast, their challenge. The sophisticated man or woman is brought face to face with the challenge of the wilderness. In one novel—one of the most effective and appealing—this process is reversed, *The Wolf Woman* (1928) bringing the defiant Aurora Mary from the North to confront the social exactions and the skyscrapers of New York. (p. 154)

In any long career of fiction writing there inevitably comes some one story which, however even their artistic quality, overshadows its fellows as the mountain peak looms above even the loftiest foothills. In Stringer's fiction, this outstanding novel is *The Wine of Life* (1921). Into it enters an element not merely of sympathy and understanding, but of feeling and emotion quite unmatched in his earlier or subsequent works.

By many readers and some critics, *The Wine of Life* has been carelessly termed autobiographical, a fictionizing of Stringer's own first marriage and subsequent disillusionment. Admittedly—as is inevitable with any author—Stringer here draws much of his material from familiar Manhattan and Ontario backgrounds and characters. Admittedly, too, in this novel there is much more of genuine feeling than in any other.

Yet the similarities between Owen Storrow's career and experiences and the author's are far less marked than the divergencies. These divergencies begin by presenting Storrow as a sculptor fresh from gathering first-hand impressions in the North Woods and Torrie Throssel sitting, drying her hair, on the fire-escape of a third-rate Tenderloin hotel. And the story in its development, though replete with the elements of disillusion and heartbreak, continues to diverge widely from Stringer's own actual experience.

If Storrow's Pine Brae farm on Lake Erie is reminiscent of Stringer's Shadow Lawn, if the glimpses of the Erie shore are readily recognizable, if the Death's Curve from which the reckless Donnie Eastman plunges to destruction is the replica of a Dead Man's Curve once conspicuous on the Talbot Road, nevertheless the Owen Storrow who despite his valiant struggle to keep his light alive gradually disintegrates after Torrie leaves him, has little in common with the Arthur Stringer who, on a foundation of disillusion, built a new and greater career.

The Wine of Life, when it was published, was regarded by many critics—especially in Canada—as bold even to rashness in its handling of sex. In this respect Canadian critical standards were still somewhat mid-Victorian. Where the English novel was still recently evasive, the Continental novel has always been joyously frank. To lay down a law in such matters, to say "thus far and no farther" in an era when so many traditional barriers have crumbled, is futile. Compared with later fiction, *The Wine of Life* is conspicuous for a fine restraint, a typical Canadian reticence, a steadfast refusal to exploit sex merely for its own sake. It is honest because the story demands honesty; it is restrained because restraint represents the truer artistry.

This restraint does not apply to the treatment of sex alone. It is characteristic of the telling. With every opportunity to let go emotionally, Stringer's native artistic sense holds. His presentation and motivation of Owen, of Torrie, of the numerous secondary characters, has the utter dispassionateness of genuine literary artistry.

It is characteristic of Stringer's prose that effective quotation is difficult. No passage or chapter detached achieves the same effect as when read with its full context. For this full effect the careful preparation of the entire story is needed. A climax

such as the final chapter of *The Shadow* derives much of its power from what has gone before. So, too, the parting of Owen and Torrie, or Owen's return to the New York studio with all its nostalgia for those lost dreams and emotions in which life once had its home, derive much of their power from the entire tale of young dreams, aspirations, efforts and gradual disillusionment. Yet, even taken apart from their context, these two supreme passages can never lose all their magic.

Four years after *The Wine of Life* appeared a novel which many critics still regard as Stringer's greatest. This novel, *Power* in my opinion ranks next to *The Wine of Life.* It is essentially a man's book, yet, paradoxically, some of its keenest admirers are women. Into this personal narrative of John Rusk, the iron-souled railroad magnate who sacrifices everything for success only to discover that nothing fails like succeeding, entered much of the information garnered by Stringer as a youthful Pere Marquette car-tracer at Saginaw, nearly thirty years before. Among his novels, *Power* stands by itself. A greater achievement in its particular field than *The Wire Tappers, Empty Hands* or even *The Prairie Wife* in theirs, it still stands alone in that field. (pp. 155-59)

Individual, too, is *The Dark Wing* (1939) Stringer's sympathetic and understanding novel of a young Irish poet and the reactions he awakens in the breasts of a love-hungry mother of thirty-seven and her modernistic and frank-spoken daughter. Though plot and theme are wholly different, there is in *The Dark Wing* a note reminiscent of *The Silver Poppy.* It is interesting to set these two novels, so widely separated in time, side by side, to read them together, to study the author's progression from promising beginnings to ultimate artistic achievement, the gain in the understanding of human nature and especially of woman nature, in restraint and in the command of the colourful word and the effective phrase, that comes of more than forty years of conscious and conscientious striving. (pp. 161-62)

In any summation of Stringer's contribution to literature one returns inevitably to those two features colouring all his work, word artistry and fidelity to the actual. In all this vast volume of writing—apart from the needful vernacular dialogue—is hardly a phrase even the most captious critic could question. In so wide a variety of backgrounds, involving far-reaching research, one stands amazed at the negligible proportion of error.

We are impressed, too, with the wide scope of his writing. Yet that versatility is in itself a handicap to any accurate estimate of his literary performance. His poetic achievement, in itself a full career, is only a part, though an important and impressive part, of his activity. (p. 164)

> *Victor Lauriston, in his* Arthur Stringer: Son of the North, *The Ryerson Press, 1941, 178 p.*

EDWARD McCOURT   (essay date 1970)

[*McCourt is a Canadian novelist and critic. He describes his literary interests as focusing on "the influence of environment on character, and the translation of life into literature. I have dealt almost exclusively with the environment with which I am most familiar—that of the Canadian prairies—and have consistently attempted to illustrate the impact of that environment on both natives and aliens." In the following excerpt from his critical study* The Canadian West in Fiction, *McCourt finds that Stringer's characterization of Canadian pioneers in his Prairie trilogy is unconvincing and that the narratives are unrelated to the Canadian setting.*]

"You can't bring up a family on iambic pentameter," Stringer, a possibly frustrated poet, is reported to have said. Certainly he never shared the romantic notion that the artist should be ready to live in a garret if need be for the sake of his art. Stringer always wrote for public approval, and the measure of his success was such as to make him one of our best popular professional writers. He published over forty novels, a dozen volumes of poetry, innumerable short stories and articles, besides writing several movie scenarios. His largest audience has been in the United States, where he made his home for many years. But he was born and brought up in Canada; his themes have been prevailingly Canadian; and our claim upon him as a Canadian writer cannot be seriously questioned.

Stringer is a competent popular writer who usually writes about sophisticated people placed in unusual and difficult circumstances. When, inspired by some rather haphazard ranching experiences, he wrote a trilogy of Western novels, *The Prairie Wife*; *The Prairie Mother*; *The Prairie Child*; which won for him the largest audience he has ever enjoyed, it was not surprising that his main characters were not native Westerners but sophisticates transplanted from a society which Stringer knew well and understood. The plot of the trilogy has to do with the struggles of Chaddie and Duncan Argyll McKail to establish a home on the prairies, rear a family and win for themselves happiness and security. Their failure to do so is not Chaddie's fault. She works hard, with unfaltering good humour and courage, does more than her share of hard work at Casa Grande—as the farm is grandiloquently called—falls in love with another man but buries her secret in her heart, and, until Duncan's behaviour transgresses the utmost limits of decency, is in all things a true and loyal wife.

But Chaddie's husband, Duncan Argyll McKail, is a humourless individual with a dull, bourgeois soul. His god is Mammon; and when his grandiose schemes go awry he sulks like a small boy. Moreover, he has a wandering eye. He is handsome, susceptible to flattery. But honest Chaddie does not flatter. Neither does she share his material ambitions. So it is that the marriage at last goes on the rocks. Chaddie's love for her husband, deep and genuine though it is, dies at last of sheer starvation; and the reader leaves Duncan in the cheerless grandeur of his city mansion and returns with Chaddie to the farm on the prairies and to the other man whose wife she will be as soon as the decree becomes absolute.

That Stringer's trilogy does not rise above the level of an ephemeral popular success is not in any way due to the author's lack of technical skill. Chaddie's story is told in the first person, through the medium of letters and diary; and it is told well. Indeed, Stringer's almost urbane competence in the mechanics of story-telling is in marked contrast to the rather clumsy technique which mars the work of so many of our novelists. But the story, even though told with the utmost skill and zest, fails to convince. The characters are all either exotics or caricatures. Not one is in harmony with his environment. The heroine Chaddie is a cultured New England society girl whose wit is reminiscent of a gay nineties salon. Her knowledge of painting, music, literature and human nature—and it is much to Stringer's credit that he makes this knowledge genuinely a part of her—is encyclopaedic. "Gershom's

still in the era where he demands a story in the picture and could approach Monet and Degas only by way of Messonier and Bourgerau" is the kind of sentence that trips casually off Chaddie's tongue. After an evening of back-breaking toil, when the three children are tucked into their cots, she refreshes herself at the piano with a little Debussy, a little Chopin, and a great deal of Beethoven. And Duncan Argyll McKail, dull dour soul though he is, is quite at home in this kind of milieu. In his verbal exchanges with Chaddie—and they are numerous and prolonged—he is able to parry and riposte with a dexterity which leaves the reader painfully aware of his own conversational inadequacies. "I'm sorry you see only my bad side," says Chaddie. "But it's kindness that seems to bring out everything that is best out of us women. We're terribly like sliced pineapple in that respect: give us just a sprinkling of sugar, and out come all the juices." And Duncan replies quick as a wink: "That's a Chaddie McKail argument. And a Chaddie McKail argument impresses me as suspiciously like Swiss cheese; it doesn't seem genuine unless you find plenty of holes in it."

The Other Man, Peter Ketley, is also quite at home in the midst of this sort of thing. He carries a well-thumbed copy of *Marius the Epicurean* in his overalls pocket; and the subtlest allusion to a Henry James character does not escape him. Even the first of the Other Women, Lady Alicia Newland, although devoted chiefly to the active traditional pursuits of her class—huntin', fishin', shootin'—is familiar with Theocritus and Marcus Aurelius. And she no doubt missed the Henry James allusion only because Chaddie discreetly lowered her voice in making it.

What it all amounts to is this; that the major characters of the trilogy—particularly Chaddie—have just a little of the charm and wit of Oscar Wilde's bright young men and women. And they are even less real.

Because the protagonists are basically unreal, it is not easy to feel the tragedy of Chaddie's broken marriage. In the first two volumes of the Trilogy, *The Prairie Wife* and *The Prairie Mother,* the gradual disintegration of the marriage relationship is traced with genuine psychological insight. The difficulties and disappointments of the early years help to create tensions not easily resolved; quarrels become more and more frequent and severe; and the stubborn streak in both is broadened and deepened rather than diminished as the years go by. Duncan's jealousy of his own children, who he thinks have won Chaddie away from him and so deprived him of a companion and mistress, is realistically suggested. But we are not prepared for Duncan's complete moral collapse, for his transformation from a rather stupid but essentially good-intentioned and slightly bewildered husband into a sadistic tyrant. Nor can the transformation be wholly justified on the grounds that Duncan's appearance in his unmotivated role provides what is perhaps the most dramatic scene in the entire trilogy. Duncan, bent on horse-whipping his little son for some trivial offence, finds his way barred by an outraged Chaddie, ancient Colt revolver in hand. When he refuses to heed her command to stop she pulls the trigger. The revolver is empty; but the effect on both Chaddie and Duncan of the appalling realization that she stood ready in her moment of madness to kill the man whom she had married is described with fine dramatic skill.

The final picture of a grossly fat Duncan McKail smoking an expensive cigar and swilling alcohol before going down to the office where his paramour is waiting for him, leaving Chaddie to return by herself to the farm—where Peter is waiting for *her*—is so crudely melodramatic as to outrage the sensibilities of all but the most insensitive reader. But the picture is not without an element of poetic justice. After all, what end could be more appropriate for a tousel-headed six-footer who permits his wife to call him Dinky-Dunk?

What holds us to the trilogy—and assuredly none of its parts is ever dull—are the fine individual scenes—the prairie fire, the search for a small boy who is lost, the capture of a murderer—and the shrewd if occasionally superficial observations which Stringer makes, through Chaddie, on Western life and manners.

But in spite of occasional moments of perceptivity Stringer does not convey any strong impression of a peculiar regional atmosphere. The prairie is a convenient back-drop for the action of his stories but not an essential complement: the plot of the trilogy is one which could have been developed almost without modification in any setting the author had chosen to create. Of the profound influence of environment on human behaviour, an influence which to anyone thoroughly familiar with the Western scene is unmistakable and all-pervading, there is little evidence in Stringer's work. Perhaps this is the reason why the trilogy fails at the point which is the justification of the novel's existence. It does not communicate the sense of life. (pp. 90-4)

> *Edward McCourt, "Some Others," in his* The Canadian West in Fiction, *revised edition, The Ryerson Press, 1970, pp. 85-118.*

DON PRECOSKY (essay date 1979)

[In the following excerpt, Precosky comments on Stringer's use of free verse in Open Water.*]*

Arthur John Arbuthnott Stringer (1874-1950) is remembered, if at all, as a writer of pot-boiler novels and Hollywood screenplays. But he was also a dedicated poet and, in the Canadian context, a pioneer. His **Open Water** was the first booklength attempt at free verse by a Canadian and the foreword to it is the first statement of modernist principles by a Canadian poet. (p. 13)

In the foreword to **Open Water** poetry is compared unfavourably to the other arts. In "painting and in music, as in sculpture and the drama", Stringer says, there have been movements toward "formal emancipation" but poetry has been lagging behind. It is being held back by old forms "and with one or two rare exceptions success has been achieved through ingeniously elaborating on an already established formula and through meticulously re-echoing what has already been said."

In this same foreword Stringer offers his solution to the problem. Rhyme, he claims, was not present in ancient poetry and did not enter into English verse until after the Norman Conquest. "The one-time primitive directness of English," he laments, "was overrun by such forms as the ballade, the chant royal, the rondel, the kyriells, the rondeau, and the rondeau redouble, the virelai, and the pantoum, the sestina, the villanelle, and last, yet by no means least, the sonnet." He goes on to add that rhyme restrains the poet too much and makes him overly conscious of technique. The poet becomes unnaturally timid and will only travel the well-worn paths of a familiar rhyme scheme while forgetting that "poetry represents the

extreme vanguard of consciousness both adventuring and pioneering along the path of future progress." Henceforth rhyme must be eschewed.

Stringer next discusses rhythm. He begins by ceding that it is impossible to eliminate it from poetry but adds that the poet ought to change his approach by breaking with the rigidity of conventional metre. "Rhythmically the modern versifier has been a Cubist without quite comprehending it. He has been crowding his soul into a geometrically designed mould." The poet must abandon strictly regular rhythms as he abandons artificial rhyme schemes and "return to the more open movement of the chant, which is man's natural and rudimentary form of song."

The foreword ends with a call for the rebirth of poetry. Set rhyme schemes and metrical patterns lie in the dead past and "if men worship beauty only as he had known it in the past, man must be satisfied with worshipping that which has lived and now is dead." The clear implication is that **Open Water** offers a new birth.

The question of how Stringer was influenced by the British and American moderns is a difficult one. There are no obvious echoes of any of the great innovators in his work. The foreword is not a derivative document. Although the poems are in free verse they are not imagist nor is Stringer's foreword an imagist manifesto. His ideas appear to come more from his historical knowledge than from his reading of contemporary critics. Stringer may have heard about current experiments in poetry but he does not betray much knowledge or understanding of them in his foreword. The chief sources for his free verse are not Eliot nor the imagists but Whitman and, to a lesser extent, the Bible.

Stringer's foreword undoubtedly expresses an admirable and sincere wish, but good intentions do not always produce good poetry. So it is with much of **Open Water.** Too often the poems consist merely of dull prose chopped up into line lengths. Or they are little more than a series of clauses joined by "and". Seldom does he attain the chant-like quality endorsed in the foreword.

It is important to note that the foreword emphasizes changes in form and rhythm but makes no mention of new themes or subjects. He is often caught between the demands of his new form and the kinds of subjects he deals with in his earlier verse. A topic which lends itself to a lengthy blank verse closet drama or a highly formalized sonnet may not be so easily fitted into a basically imagist style. More than once Stringer fails to treat the thing in itself and tacks on a moral observation. **"Life"** is an example of this problem. The first two verses are stark and dramatic:

> A rind of light hangs low
> On the rim of the world;
> A sound of feet disturbs
> The quiet of the cell
> Where a rope and a beam looms high
> At the end of the yard.
>
> But in the dusk
> Of that Walled yard waits a woman
> And as the thing from its cell,
> Still guarded and chained and bound,
> Crosses that little space,
> Silent, for ten brief steps,
> A woman hangs on his neck.

Thus far it is a tense poem which appears to be rising to a climax. Unfortunately Stringer violates the poem by reducing the situation to an allegory:

> And that walk from a cell to a sleep
> Is known as Life,
> And those ten dark steps
> Of tangled rapture and tears
> Men still call Love.
>
> (pp. 15-17)

The best poetry in **Open Water** comes in pieces like **"The Last of Summer"** where Stringer combines the Canadian landscape tradition and his own good eye for nature with his new ideas about rhythm and rhyme:

> The opal afternoon
> Is cool, and very still.
> A wash of tawny air,
> Sea-green that melts to gold,
> Bathes all the skyline, hill by hill.
> Out of the black-topped pinelands
> A black crow calls,
> And the year seems old!
> A woman from a doorway sings,
> And from the valley-slope a sheep-dog barks,
> And through the umber woods the echo falls
> And faint and far the birds fly south,
> And behind the dark pines drops the sun,
> And a small wind wakes and sighs,
> And Summer, see, is done!

By appealing to the senses of sight, hearing, and touch he creates a realistic scene and captures the mood of the changing of one season into the next. (p. 18)

Stringer wrote seven more books of verse before his death. Three of them are collections of Irish verse akin to **Irish Poems. A Woman at Dusk** is his first serious collection after **Open Water.** In it he returns to regular rhyme and rhythm with no sign of the free verse he had so confidently proclaimed fourteen years earlier. (p. 19)

It is difficult to know just why his faith in free verse was so shaken. The chances are that in **Open Water** he over-stated his case and the extent of his commitment simply because he was consciously doing something rebellious and consequently felt obliged to sound a strident note. It is also probable that in the struggle between old and new attitudes which is so evident in some of the **Open Water** poems the old won out. The failure of **Open Water** to become a popular success, whereas his Irish poems were, may also have hastened his disillusionment with free verse.

Stringer's failure can be attributed to many causes. Part of the answer can be inferred from the fact that he was born in 1874. Stringer was more than a decade older than the major modernists. He was, in fact, born in the same year as G. K. Chesterton. Chronologically, he was more of an Edwardian than a modern. When Stringer brought out **Open Water** he was not a neophyte breaking into the scene with a new style and outlook but rather an oft-published veteran of forty. He was too well-trained in the old ways to take on the new: he was no Yeats. Stringer was influenced by Whitman, Carman, Service, the Victorians and Pre-Raphaelites, the nineteenth-century Canadian nature poets, and the King James version of the Bible. He does not directly reflect the influence of any of the important moderns. Stringer's Whitmanesque style may have some affinities with twentieth-century free verse, but the poets who influenced his thought were in no way

modern, and as a result his pseudo-modernist poems show a sensibility divided between old and new attitudes.

Another reason for Stringer's failure is his often sloppy handling of images. To the imagists the presentation of the concrete thing was all important. But Stringer consistently subordinates imagery to thought. He can often present us with an image which is illustrative of some important idea in a poem, but when that image is scrutinized in the mind's eye it is found to be ugly or absurd or incompletely presented. The "ample and opulent bosom" of mother earth and the speakers's heart which like the night "creeps over the hill", are but two examples. Stringer does not have this problem when he restricts himself to pure description but when he tries to inject a "deeper" meaning he usually falls down.

It may seem illogical to cite an omission as a positive achievement but one of Stringer's chief contributions to the beginnings of modernism in Canadian poetry was his refusal to be a strict follower of anyone else's doctrines. His foreward to **Open Water** is consistent with the imagist penchant for manifestoes and grand pronouncements, but in his ideas he is not a hidebound follower of any school. This independence is especially important when we consider his choice of subject matter. One of the chief features of early modernist poetry is that it is mainly set in an urban environment. This is in large part a reflection of the poets' realization that in England and The United States people were leaving the land for the cities. In Canada the process of urbanization was much less rapid. Stringer himself preferred country life. **New York Nocturnes,** his last book, is a sad one which depicts him as an exile. It is not surprising, then, that nature rather than city life provided the subject for his most successful poems. In his choice of subject matter Stringer linked the Canadian landscape tradition with twentieth-century free verse. Such a union had the potential for renewing the tradition. Aside from D. C. Scott he was the first Canadian poet to attempt such a union. Pratt, Smith, and P. R. Scott, though they are much better poets, owe a debt to this pioneer. (pp. 19-20)

> Don Precosky, "Two Early Modernists," in Journal of Canadian Poetry: The Poetry Review Vol. 2, Autumn, 1979, pp. 13-27.

A. R. KIZUK   (essay date 1986)

[*A Canadian critic and educator, Kizuk has published prolifically on Canadian literature. In the following excerpt, he discusses Stringer's contribution to the emergence of vernacular language in Canadian poetry.*]

Long before Charles Olson and the Black Mountain poets penetrated Canadian poetics through the *Tish* poets of Vancouver, Canadian poets were deeply concerned with the living, propulsive breath-measure of the speaking voice as an underlying principle of poetic organization. Tom MacInnes and Wilson MacDonald, like Pound, had made their poetic pacts with Whitman in the first decades of the century. In 1927 and 1930, Ryerson published a sort of Torontonian "Maximus Poem," Nathaniel Benson's *Twenty and After* and its sequel *The Wanderer.* Despite the work of Layton, Dudek and Souster at mid-century, the struggle to bring a recognizable speaking voice to Canadian poetry waned in the 1960s, when the myth-formalism of Reaney and Hine and the oracular or quasi-sibylline tones of Cohen and Atwood were strong. Today, poetry in Canada sports a plenitude of uniquely personal voices—what Dennis Lee has recently called the vernacular, "a sturdy, flexible tone, which draws on the resources of daily speech in Canadian English." This contemporary situation, which must be considered a net gain, has not been attained, however, without decades of struggle, the beginnings of which are . . . [discernable in the work of a minor poet] of the '20s, Arthur Stringer. . . . (p. 483)

Olson's "Projective Verse" is an appropriate place to begin because of the essay's metaphysics of place. Dating the "revolution of the ear" in 1910, Olson argues that the "place where breath comes from" is a moment of contact between man and nature in which man "achieves an humilitas sufficient to make him of use." What makes Canadian vernacular verse of use to the locality from which it springs is the promise that it will reveal secrets that have gone unheard or that have not been heard often enough in our literature. In his CBC radio-talks on "The First Person in Literature," Louis Dudek explained that since Whitman such secret knowledge has taken the form of a "tense moment of expectation" in which the " 'I' and the universal Cosmos may meet and fuse as One." This tension reifies the presupposition that knowledge will be invalid lest spoken, so that the natural universe may be said to "speak" though a fusion of self and place. For Dudek, however, this metaphysics of place had become unstuck in such a way that Canadian poets in 1966 were writing either as wielders of mythical patterns or as narcissistic anarchists. This led to a poetry without voice, a dissolution of the contract between literature and audience. Both James Reaney and the *Tish* poets had become "cut off from all public and common ground," Dudek thought, unable "to face alone the great issue of existence" and be of use: "working always for this time and this place, this self, to find the hidden meaning of all things."

Dudek fails to see that the *Tish* poets' concentration on language was their way of avoiding the solipsism that can overwhelm a poet's desire to forge an identity of self and place on the anvil of the voice. He is less than fair also to suggest that it was with the appearance of Raymond Souster, Irving Layton, Miriam Waddington, and himself that poetry in Canada first became capable of "convincing personal declaration." True, a secret-saying, truth-telling voice in poetry would be alien to the autonomous narcissism and verbal icons of either an 'anarchic' or a 'closed' verse. But 'voiced' poetry does not admit easily of the sort of periodization that Dudek implies, for this sort of voice in poetry belongs to an immemorial "world of sound." This is what Walter J. Ong calls "the I-thou world where, through the mysterious interior resonance which sound best of all provides, persons commune with persons, reaching one another's interiors in a way in which one can never reach the interior of an 'object'." In voiced poetry, words are not reduced to the status of objects; they are utterances, basic elements of what Ong calls "the cry." This cry exists in the contemporary Canadian poetry that Lee calls vernacular, it existed in the work that came out of Dudek's milieu, and it existed in Stringer's vernacular poetry of the '20s. (pp. 483-84)

Stringer is remembered for his 1914 volume, **Open Water,** which Munro Beattie described in the *Literary History of Canada* as "almost wholly unmarred by 'poetic diction,'" displaying economy and directness, and wider in scope "than other Canadian books of the period" [see Further Reading]. Beattie acknowledged the attempt in this book to emulate the verse beginning to appear in Harriet Monroe's *Poetry* in the '20s, but he felt the poems lacked the "unity that good free

verse can attain to," being "mostly gatherings of prose sentences arbitrarily divided into lines." The unity that Beattie misses here is the formal quality that does not permit what Cleanth Brooks called "The Heresy of Paraphrase," an inseparable unity of form and content in which the poet intuits whatever statement the work may make through its formal structure. This question of unity is irrelevant in discussing vernacular verse.

Stringer's poetic *oeuvre* includes legendary verse-plays and sentimental 'Irish poems' aimed at the popular market, the "un-Canadian" free verse of **Open Water,** and much voiced poetry. The work may be said to be characterized by an uneasy, often self-defeating disequilibrium between what he thought his readers' expectations were and a strong desire to rise above that sort of conditioning. This tension is mediated, moreover, by a third factor, his sensitivity to language as sensuous speech.

The Woman in the Rain (1907) contains several poems organized around a relationship between self and speech. **"The Modern Speaks,"** for example, declares that death cannot destroy self though it takes everything else,

> When I, who have joyed in my work,
> Who have loved, have taken my fling,
> Have hungered, forgotten, been glad,
> Have hated the hand that would shirk
> The honey of life for the sting,
> Have housed with the good and the bad.

These aspirated rhythms communicate the speaker's determination to have all life has to offer and face its loss in death armed with speech, the "might of a man" and a "strength that is mine as yet,"

> In the core of me, conquering still,
> This man's good might shall remain,
> And none of me, *me* shall you break.

The optimism projected here does not rely on some variety of muscular Christianity or a version of the Romantic *vates,* but rather his sense of himself and his voice as a fit measure of poetic value. In poems such as **"Non Omnis Moriar,"** **"The Wanderers,"** **"The Man Who Killed,"** and others in **The Woman in the Rain,** Stringer's emphatic ego sounds a personal note wholly characteristic of his time and his place. **"Morning in the North-West"** is another example:

> What care I here for all Earth's creeds outworn,
> The dreams outlived, the hopes to ashes turned,
> In that old East so dark with rain and doubt?
> Here life swings glad and free and rude, and I
> Shall drink it to the full, and go content.

In **"Gifts"** and **"Northern Pines,"** he pays homage to his friend and fellow expatriate Bliss Carman. Stringer admired the openness to life that he saw in Carman's verse.

Stringer's preference for *parole* as opposed to *langue,* prose sentences chopped into lines as opposed to "poetic diction" in Beattie's sense, is clear throughout **The Woman in the Rain.** A number of epigrams (often difficult to fault for their wit or execution) and longer non-mythological blank verse poems reflect a desire to reconcile trust in speech to the strictures of prosody. The epigram **"Philosophies"** records his disdain for writing that is intellectually speechless, not infused by living breath:

> We know not what doth lie beyond the Door,

But in captivity behold us grown
Enamored of our cell, in scrolling o'er
With signs and legends strange each mural stone!

Poems like **"A Woman Sang," "The Final Lesson," "Keats,"** and **"When Closing Swinburne"** deal explicitly with Stringer's ultimately confused ideas of what poetic beauty should be. The title poem, however, turns from this preoccupation to a curious and troubling analysis of the predicament of modern urban life.

In **"The Woman in the Rain,"** a bag-lady epitomizes a lost continuity between past and present. A huddled heap of rags, a "timeless thing of mumbling unconcern" with burned-out eyes, breasts fallen in, she is a woman-city who contains the embittered lives and ghostly loves of contemporary society "coffined in its agued bones." She whines and wheezes before the young, the gay, and the rich lamenting how beautiful she once was, how wild she used to be. Stringer changes tack vigorously and often in the poem, alternating between a *carpe diem* format, in which the bag-lady is a "she," and a more philosophical vein in which the woman in her decrepitude is referred to as "it." More importantly, however, she is a sphinx-like embodiment of speech. Beauty speaks and will always speak "through many-teared / Dark cities tongued with records like to her!" Her "mumbling unconcern" (the phrase is repeated in the close) symbolizes a modern loss of graceful speech. The poem's energetic voice, as opposed to prosody or thematic patterning, embodies a desire to retrieve the "breathing music of lost Nineveh" in which "through her velvet veins once musically / The mad life sang."

The bag-lady is the antithesis of the machismo self-image in **"The Modern Speaks,"** that is, the optimism, enthusiasm, and sensuality of Stringer's particular species of *brio*. Her whimpering, in which the high world of poetic beauty ends, will never swell into a resonance capable of reaching the interiors of the young and the rich to whom she speaks unheard. Under the "April thrill / imperative" of a spring rain, she is "desolately sterile." As Stringer suggests in **"The Wordless Touch,"** true communication between the inner lives of men and women requires more than language alone. It needs the body, and as speech is language in the body, the voice penetrates to a place "beyond the bourne of words."

Stringer was cosmopolitan enough to be aware of the situation of poetry abroad, yet he resisted the changes in attitude that in the '30s would make ironic and closed forms so important to Canadian poets like Leo Kennedy or A. J. M. Smith. He never let go, entirely, of the decadent concept of beauty loosely assembled in the eighteen-nineties by the initiates of Mallarmé's Tuesdays. In this "gospel of 'correspondences,' the importance of music, the use of free verse, a constant concern with technical detail, philosophical idealism, a predilection for the world of dream and legends," an idea of transcendence in which artifice reveals nature's inherent rationality, and various forms of occultism all played a part [Jean Pierrot, *The Decadent Imagination*]. Hence it is not surprising that he would try his hand at free verse and write the manifesto in **Open Water** for which he is chiefly remembered today.

On the basis that man habitually worships "beauty only as he has known it in the past," Stringer's "Forward" to **Open Water** passionately defends the vernacular in poetry as opposed to outmoded prosodic conventions. In order to revive a poetry of emotional expression, intimate moods, and subjective experiences that are "characteristically modern," poetry must shake off the immuring traditions of rhyme and metre. Intellectual timidity by which poets view the world "mathematically" imprisons poetry in a "geometrically designed mould" that leads to "an instinctive abhorrence for anything beyond the control of what he calls common sense." Stringer insists that the poet must return to the "more open movement of the chant, which is man's most natural and rudimentary form of song." The biography suggests, moreover, that his conception of the chant-line was helped along by a need to vent violent emotions surrounding the failure of his first marriage. As such, a crisis in which Stringer strove to make the private self public in his poetry bonded to his transitional modernism, and resulted in a "first step towards freedom" for open or vernacular verse in early twentieth-century Canada.

This first step, however, is a stumbling one. Stringer's desire to use his sense of voice as a principle for poetic organization is thwarted in **Open Water** by another desire to make his verse as widely read as his prose. **"The Revolt"** begins with the strong, chant-like rhythm characteristic of his verse in general. Yet the poem, by falling into two parts, one self-assertive and the other self-deprecating, expresses his ambivalence toward poetic self-discovery and literary popularity. He says that he has tinkled and jangled and piped, and is now "sick of the game." The words "I want" are repeated in a catalogue of desires that concludes,

> I want to sit down with my soul and talk straight out,
> I want to make peace with myself,
> And say what I have to say,
> While there is still time!

Stringer wants to be free from the "chains of song," "Rough and unruly and open and turbulent-throated!" He has been too long in the dungeons of Mallarméan song. Yet, "after my moment of light," he admits, he will choose "to go back to the Dark, / Since the Open still makes me afraid."

This strategy of derring-do followed by an admission of one's limitations is the same sort of thing a politician does when he attempts to win over an audience by holding forth on the issues while at the same time admitting that he is 'only human.' Audiences know what political promises really are and vote for the man behind them anyway, because of the unstated contract binding audiences to rhetorical promises of significant truths. Under the conditions of such contracts, once an audience begins to feel that the speaker 'is one of us,' they are hooked. Thus, in terms of rhetorical strategy, **"The Revolt"** is a convincing personal declaration, yet as a cry that communicates secrets objects share, the poem would seem not to have probed the issue of the self deeply enough.

In **"Sappho's Tomb,"** an aesthete study in concupiscence employing a classical décor and decadent cosmetics, the vernacular is overwhelmed by the stereotypes of artifice, that is, legendary motif-patterning, images of women's cosmetics, precious stones and metals, moonlight and water and the plant-life of dreams. (The poem is actually a choral epilogue to what he himself regarded as his *magnum opus,* the verse-play **Sappho in Leucadia,** published in 1903 and extensively rewritten for the 1949 edition.) In this sort of thing, Stringer fails to assimilate a basic presupposition of modern free verse, that underlying acceptance of the "whatness" of things, the red wheelbarrows and cool plums of everyday existence. When poems in **Open Water** manage to communicate an openness, however, the aesthete conventions are rendered in an entirely personal way. **"Autumn," "Faces," "There Is Strength in the Soil,"** and to a lesser extent the poems **"The Life on the Table"** and **"At Charing Cross,"** demonstrate how much clearer and stronger the breath-line can be when the back door of his poetic, so to speak, is open to place instead of the literary context he believed his audience demanded.

Other poems in **Open Water** are sentimental longings for home or expressions of love, loss and regret in which the verve of Stringer's breath-line degenerates in nursery-rhyme rhythms. **"Milkweed"** is an exception. Here the voice is strongly personal, infusing a lyrical and imagistic chant on homesickness among the foothills of Alberta with a real sense of a person communing with persons. The same is true of **"Chains"** and **"The Steel Worker,"** which identify industrial technology as a corrosive evil in modern life. The chant-line seems strongest in two substantial poems cathartic of violent emotion, the passionate, visceral **"Ultimata"** and **"Atavism,"** as well as a number of shorter poems exploring the relationship between love and hate.

Stringer's poetic is well represented in **Open Water.** Its cardinal points are aesthete beauty, the effects of a self-conscious desire to be popular, the consequent importance of personality, and the conception of a modern poetic language as sensuous-speech. This is an unstable combination, and in **"The Echo"** he declares that poetry is an eternal failure, "a note in the chorus . . . a wave on the deep." Everything a poet struggles to utter has been uttered before, he says, failing to realize that his sensitivity to voice in poetry would be of use in moving poetry beyond the limitations of words. In **"The Surrender"** he turns away from self and reality, having convinced himself that true poetry will be known only once "the soul falls broken" and drowns in the flood of time and death. The book closes with a series of poems on dreams in which he insists that he loves the soul and that God is with him even though he seeks the soul through flesh. In the "Afterword" to **Dark Soil,** twenty years later, Stringer recanted his challenge to convention, saying that "Time teaches us that this shifted fetter known as Freedom is not always the final solution of the artist's problem." (pp. 485-90)

Stringer's . . . verse is 'open' in the sense that inherited meter and stanza disintegrate before the verse of an everyday manner of speech. . . . [His] contribution to the genre of voiced verse derives from patterns of sound and rhythm rarely found in Canadian books in their time. . . . [His] meaning is not the product of an intellectual and prosodic encapsulation, but rather a quality of response built up in readers' aesthetic perceptions of a voice public and rhetorical as a politician's speech. Audiences will assemble an image of the personality behind the voice represented by such verse, and their response depends contractually on how interesting, serious, competent, personable and trustworthy that personality seems to be. . . . Stringer's poetry aspires to evoke an individuality of mind and heart, a high-energy construct and discharge of logopoeia through the breath, in Olson's terms, which promises two things. The first is that the poet will share with his audience "secrets objects share." The second is that the poet has learned this truth by listening "down through the workings of his own throat to that place where breath comes from." (p. 495)

A. R. Kizuk, "The Vernacular in Early Twentieth-Century Canadian Poetry: Arthur Stringer and A.

M. Stephen," in The Dalhousie Review, *Vol. 66, No. 4, Winter, 1986-87, pp. 483-96.*

FURTHER READING

Beattie, Munro. "Poetry (1920-35)." In *Literary History of Canada,* vol. II, edited by Carl F. Klinck, pp. 234-53. Toronto: University of Toronto Press, 1976.
Evaluates *Open Water* as experimental verse.

Bruce, H. A. "Canadian Celebrities." *The Canadian Magazine* XV, No. 2 (June 1900): 143-45.
Surveys Stringer's early career and favorably reviews *The Loom of Destiny.*

Cordell, Richard A. Review of *The Dark Wing,* by Arthur Stringer. *The Saturday Review of Literature* XX, No. 7 (10 June 1939): 19-20.
Summarizes *The Dark Wing* as "two-dimensional" and "incredible."

"Mr. Stringer's Arraignment of the 'Canada Fakers'." *Current Literature* XLV, No. 6 (December 1908): 642-44.
Outlines Stringer's charges against internationally famous authors who misrepresent Canada's scenery and wildlife in their writings.

Davies-Woodrow, Constance. "Who's Who in Canadian Literature: Arthur Stringer." *The Canadian Bookman* X, No. 9 (September 1928): 259-61.
Interview in which Stringer recalls his childhood.

Deacon, William Arthur. "What a Canadian Has Done for Canada." In *Our Sense of Identity: A Book of Canadian Essays,* edited by Malcolm Ross, pp. 209-16. Toronto: Ryerson Press, 1954.
Points out the many and often humorous errors Stringer commits concerning survival in the Canadian Northwest in his novel *Empty Hands.*

Lauriston, Victor. "Arthur Stringer." In *Leading Canadian Poets,* edited by W. P. Percival, pp. 255-64. Toronto: Ryerson Press, 1948.
Overview of Stringer's poetry.

Pomeroy, Elsie. "The Poetry of Arthur Stringer." In *Canadian Poetry Magazine* 14, No. 3 (Spring 1951): 22-3.
Concise survey of Stringer's poetry. Pomeroy states that, "apart from his Irish verse, Arthur Stringer's poetry remains largely unknown, although it undoubtedly constitutes a worthy and enduring contribution to our literature."

Rhodenizer, V. B. "Other Novelists, Historical and Regional." In his *A Handbook of Canadian Literature,* pp. 95-102. Ottawa: Graphic Publishers, 1930.
Biographical sketch and commentary on Stringer's trilogy *The Prairie Wife, The Prairie Mother,* and *The Prairie Child.*

Stringer, Arthur. "Letter to the Editor: A Discrepancy in Dates." *The Saturday Review of Literature* XX, No. 15 (5 August 1939): 9.
Corrects errors of fact in the review of *The Dark Wing* published in *The Saturday Review of Literature* (see Richard A. Cordell entry above). Stringer also claims that his characterization of the husband of the novel's main character was misrepresented by the reviewer. Stringer's reply is followed by a rejoinder in which the reviewer defends his appraisal of Stringer's fiction.

John Millington Synge

1871-1909

(Full name Edmund John Millington Synge) Irish dramatist, essayist, poet, and translator.

The following entry presents criticism of Synge's drama *The Playboy of the Western World,* which was first performed and published in 1907. For discussion of Synge's complete career, see *TCLC,* Volume 6.

Synge is considered the foremost dramatist of the Irish Literary Renaissance, and *The Playboy of the Western World* is regarded as his most compelling and fully developed work. Focusing on the fugitive peasant Christy Mahon, the play portrays his rise in popularity with a group of villagers in western Ireland as he recounts an act of patricide he claims to have committed. During the first production of *Playboy* at Dublin's Abbey Theatre, public and critical outrage was directed against the play's coarse language and unflattering portrayal of the Irish peasantry. Eventually surmounting these criticisms, *Playboy* is lauded for its poetic manipulation of Anglo-Irish vernacular, its ironic humor, and its inventive treatment of Christian and mythological archetypes.

Born to a middle-class Protestant family, Synge broke from his strict religious upbringing at a young age. He traveled and studied extensively in Germany, France, and Italy, intent on a career in music. After judging himself unfit for that profession, he moved to Paris and devoted himself to the study of French literature. A chance encounter with poet William Butler Yeats, a leader of the Irish Literary Renaissance, changed Synge's life. Yeats urged him to return to Ireland and to write about the peasants of the Aran Islands—advice which immediately appealed to Synge. Thereafter, he spent many summers among the peasants of western Ireland observing their customs and dialect. During one of his visits to the West, Synge learned the story of James Lynchehaun, an escaped murderer who had been harbored by peasants in the district of Connemara. The Lynchehaun case, along with an earlier account he had heard of a patricidal fugitive hidden on the Aran Islands, inspired the basic plot of *Playboy.*

Set in rural County Mayo, *The Playboy of the Western World* opens in a country shebeen, an unlicensed drinking establishment, run by Michael James Flaherty and his daughter, Pegeen Mike. Shawn Keogh, Pegeen's timid suitor, and several local peasants are gathered in the pub when newcomer Christy Mahon arrives, in flight from the civil authorities of County Kerry. Christy tells the group how he recently killed his father, and then progressively embellishes the account while the villagers respond to him as a hero and poet. A rivalry consequently develops among the local women, most notably Pegeen and Widow Quin, for Christy's attentions, and Pegeen pledges her love to the fugitive. When his father appears, injured but alive, the villagers, including Pegeen, turn against Christy because he no longer represents the romantic hero they had envisioned him to be; when he makes another attempt on his father's life, the group prepares to lynch him. Christy and his father are reconciled when Old Mahon saves his son from the lynching mob, and they leave the village to-

gether. The drama ends with Pegeen mourning the loss of Christy, "the only playboy of the western world."

In 1905 Synge joined the board of directors of the Irish National Theatre Society, which had been founded by Yeats and dramatist Lady Gregory in coalition with actors Frank and William Fay. Through the generosity of an English patron, the group had acquired Dublin's Abbey Theatre in late 1904, becoming the major force in modern Irish drama and offering Synge a ready outlet for his dramatic works. He submitted the first two acts of *Playboy* to Yeats and Lady Gregory in late 1906. Because both directors voiced reservations about instances of crude or violent language in the drama, Synge worked until the first day of rehearsal making further deletions and rewriting the third act, which ultimately underwent at least eleven revisions. Nevertheless, during the drama's first performance at the Abbey Theatre in January 1907, the utterance in the third act of the word "shift," denoting a woman's chemise, caused an uproar from members of the audience who considered it indecent to refer to a woman's undergarment on stage. A public controversy quickly arose over *Playboy* for its perceived improprieties, and at the drama's second performance, organized demonstrations developed to the extent that the police were called in to protect the players and ensure the drama's performance. Numerous hostile articles followed in the Irish press, criticizing Synge for further-ing the derogatory theatrical stereotype that typically pre-sented Irish characters as drunk, clownish, and uneducated. Irish nationalists particularly objected to the play, viewing a less than ideal depiction of Ireland as injurious to the Irish image abroad and to the goal of achieving political indepen-dence from Great Britain. Synge's ironic use of religious terms and the violent, unconventional ending of the drama additionally exacerbated public hostility. Yeats, however, stressed the play's artistic merits and insisted that it remain in performance for the scheduled week's duration.

Criticism on *The Playboy of the Western World* typically stresses the thematic opposition between reality and imagina-tion in the drama, tracing Christy's development toward self-realization as an individual and as a poetic persona. The play's portrayal of his transformation is praised for suggest-ing a variety of mythological and biblical archetypes that pro-vide models for the drama. For example, *Playboy* is often dis-cussed in terms of the central themes and plot structures of the legends surrounding the hero Cuchulain from Irish my-thology, and the drama's treatment of patricide is compared to that in Sophocles's tragedy *Oedipus Rex*. Some commenta-tors, emphasizing the rejection of Christy by his former ad-mirers in the play's third act, have argued that Synge presents him as a Christ figure. However, comic and ironic elements in *Playboy* have caused critics to debate the degree of parody involved in Synge's approach to such prototypes. Christy, for example, is also considered a mock or secularized Christ in light of the drama's pagan themes and ironic use of religious allusions and expressions.

Synge's re-creation of the speech of the Mayo peasantry is ac-claimed for revitalizing and giving dramatic validity to collo-quial Anglo-Irish language. While critics praise Synge for blending vernacular speech with rich imagery and the rhythms of formal poetry in a manner reminiscent of the Eliz-abethan dramatists, some commentators have suggested that he occasionally strained the drama's realistic aspect to create his rhythmic and symbolic effects. *Playboy* has also garnered much critical attention for eluding traditional classifications of comedy and tragedy, and is cited as an early example of the modern tragicomedy. The play's combination of natural-ism and fantasy has led critics to view the work as an illustra-tion of Synge's aesthetic tenets, which propose a synthesis of these two approaches in modern theater.

Through continued popular production, *Playboy* has gradu-ally acquired an international reputation as both a major modern drama and an essential work of the Irish Literary Re-naissance, and critics note the play's influence in the works of such Irish-born dramatists as Sean O'Casey, Samuel Beck-ett, and Brendan Behan. Of *Playboy*, Yeats concluded, "It is the strangest, the most beautiful expression in drama of that Irish fantasy which overflowing through all Irish literature that has come out of Ireland itself . . . is the unbroken char-acter of Irish genius."

(See also *Contemporary Authors*, Vol. 104, and *Dictionary of Literary Biography*, Vols. 10 and 19.)

J. M. SYNGE (essay date 1907)

[*The following is Synge's preface to the first publication of* The Playboy of the Western World.]

In writing **The Playboy of the Western World,** as in my other plays, I have used one or two words only that I have not heard among the country people of Ireland, or spoken in my own nursery before I could read the newspapers. A certain number of the phrases I employ I have heard also from herds and fishermen along the coast from Kerry to Mayo or from beggar-women and ballad-singers nearer Dublin; and I am glad to acknowledge how much I owe to the folk-imagination of these fine people. Any one who has lived in real intimacy with the Irish peasantry will know that the wildest sayings and ideas in this play are tame indeed, compared with the fancies one may hear in any little hillside cabin in Geesala, or Carraroe, or Dingle Bay. All art is a collaboration; and there is little doubt that in the happy ages of literature, strik-ing and beautiful phrases were as ready to the story-teller's or the playwright's hand, as the rich cloaks and dresses of his time. It is probable that when the Elizabethan dramatist took his ink-horn and sat down to his work he used many phrases that he had just heard, as he sat at dinner, from his mother or his children. In Ireland, those of us who know the people have the same privilege. When I was writing **The Shadow of the Glen,** some years ago, I got more aid than any learning could have given me from a chink in the floor of the old Wick-low house where I was staying, that let me hear what was being said by the servant girls in the kitchen. This matter, I think, is of importance, for in countries where the imagina-tion of the people, and the language they use, is rich and liv-ing, it is possible for a writer to be rich and copious in his words, and at the same time to give the reality, which is the root of all poetry, in a comprehensive and natural form. In the modern literature of towns, however, richness is found only in sonnets, or prose poems, or in one or two elaborate books that are far away from the profound and common in-terests of life. One has, on one side, Mallarmé and Huysmans producing this literature; and on the other, Ibsen and Zola dealing with the reality of life in joyless and pallid words. On the stage one must have reality, and one must have joy; and that is why the intellectual modern drama has failed, and peo-ple have grown sick of the false joy of the musical comedy, that has been given them in place of the rich joy found only in what is superb and wild in reality. In a good play every speech should be as fully flavoured as a nut or apple, and such speeches cannot be written by any one who works among people who have shut their lips on poetry. In Ireland, for a few years more, we have a popular imagination that is fiery, and magnificent, and tender; so that those of us who wish to write start with a chance that is not given to writers in places where the springtime of the local life has been forgotten, and the harvest is a memory only, and the straw has been turned into bricks. (pp. 174-75)

> *J. M. Synge, in a preface to his* The Complete Plays, *edited by T. R. Henn, Methuen, 1981, pp. 174-75.*

THE FREEMAN'S JOURNAL (essay date 1907)

[*The following review, which originally appeared in* The Free-man's Journal *after the first performance of* Playboy, *criticizes the drama for slander against Ireland and obscene language.*]

The Abbey Theatre is now seriously and widely recognised as a home of drama. The culture and thoughtfulness of its large and growing clientele would alone give importance to doings upon its boards. It is, therefore, necessary to take notice of things which, if done elsewhere, might possibly be dismissed on the principle that least said is soonest mended. Even in this case, one is tempted to be curt regarding the performance of Saturday night last, for it is very difficult to write with patience of J. M. Synge's piece, *The Playboy of the Western World.* A strong protest must, however, be entered against this unmitigated, protracted libel upon Irish peasant men and, worse still, upon Irish peasant girlhood. The blood boils with indignation as one recalls the incidents, expressions, ideas of this squalid, offensive production, incongruously styled a comedy in three acts. Lest these censures might appear unfair and uncalled for, a brief indication must be given of what it is all about. The action takes place in a public-house, on a wild part of the coast of Mayo. The publican, with some companions, is bound for a wake. His young unmarried daughter is to be left alone all night. A footsore, travel-stained fellow is discovered lurking near the house. One Shawn Keogh is making sheep's eyes at Margaret, the publican's daughter. He, however, is but a whining, cowardly lout. The tramp enters and reveals that he is apprehensive of the police. He believes he has murdered his father in a distant county, and has been evading pursuit. He tells how they had quarrelled when digging potatoes, and how he struck him on the head with a weapon and killed him. Instantly Christy Mahon, that is his name, becomes a hero not only with the men, but with the girl Margaret. He must be a brave, daring, splendid fellow to have done such a terrific deed. On the spot he is engaged as pot-boy, and is left to keep Margaret company in the publichouse while the others set off for their midnight spree. Margaret's shocking unnatural love for the supposed murderer develops. The repulsive theme is made the basis of what the author esteems his comedy. Mahon's fame soon spreads. The Widow Quin is smitten. She tries to snatch the treasure from Margaret. A gruesome rivalry is set up for the assassin. Other peasant girls also come to admire and make much of him. He himself fixes on Margaret. He is too comfortable in the publichouse to fall into the widow's wiles. Margaret sternly resents any others' attempts on the affections of her strong fearless young man. Her fearful love is based on a brutish admiration of his lethal prowess. She would not be afraid to go with such one poaching salmon by night in the country streams. Mahon's popularity is so great that the peasants must have him in their sports, which take place on the shore the day following his arrival. Meanwhile his father turns up. His head is bandaged. He is swearing vengeance on his son. The Widow Quin tries to get him off the scene. The sports take place. Mahon conquers all before him. The people, male and female, are delighted. Margaret's passion is at the full. Old Mahon again appears, confronts all and denounces Christy. Margaret's idol is shattered. He is not a murderer after all. His bragging was but a lie. The people round upon him. Margaret's resentment is furious. She assails him with fiendish vehemence. He pursues his father, apparently again beats him, and is followed by the peasants, who proceed to tie him with a rope. The audience had stood this revolting story thus far. Now angry groans, growls, hisses, and noise broke out while the pinioning of Mahon went on. It was not possible—thank goodness—to follow the dialogue for a time. Mahon springs forward and bites the leg of one of his captors—his rival Shawn. The girls and others rush in with the father, now in his shirt sleeves and brandishing a weapon. A brutal riotous scene takes place. The groans, hisses, and counter cheers of the audience drowned the

words, but as well as could be gathered Christy decides to depart quietly with his father, and let Mayo resume its normal state of sickening demoralisation. The mere idea can be given of the barbarous jargon, the elaborate and incessant cursings of these repulsive creatures. Everything is a b———y this or a———y that, and into this picturesque dialogue names that should only be used with respect and reverence are frequently introduced. Enough! the hideous caricature would be slanderous of a Kaffir kraal. The piece is announced to run for a week; it is to be hoped it will be instantly withdrawn. If a company of English artists attempted such an outrage the public indignation would be rightly bitter. Indeed no denunciation could be sufficiently strong. The whole affair is absolutely incomprehensible however it is examined. That such a piece should have been conceived and written is strange enough; that it could be accepted, rehearsed, and enacted at a house supposed to be dedicated to high dramatic art and truth would be past all belief but that it has actually been done. The worst specimen of stage Irishman of the past is a refined, acceptable fellow compared with that imagined by Mr. Synge, and as for his women, it is not possible, even if it were desirable, to class them. Redeeming features may be found in the dregs of humanity. Mr. Synge's dramatis personae stand apart in complete and forbidding isolation. It is not necessary to inquire whether, even if such things were true, they should be brought upon the stage. It is quite plain that there is need for a censor at the Abbey Theatre. (pp. 7-9)

A review of "The Playboy of the Western World," in The "Playboy" Riots *by James Kilroy, The Dolmen Press, 1971, pp. 7-9.*

PATRICK KENNY (essay date 1907)

[*In the following essay, a review that appeared in the* Irish Times *during the first week of the production of* Playboy *at the Abbey Theatre, Kenny praises the drama's social and psychological insights.*]

Dublin audiences are said to be very critical, and those at the Abbey Theatre are said to be the most critical of them, but they have not yet permitted themselves to see *The Playboy of the Western World,* and I hope the plucky players will play on until there is a chance to understand, when the screaming has exhausted itself. The screamers do not know what they are missing.

In a way there are two plays, one within another, and unless the inner one is seen, I am not surprised at the screaming about the outer one, which in itself is repellent, and must so remain until seen in the light of the conception out of which it arises, as when we welcome a profane quotation in a sermon, recognising a higher purpose that it is employed to emphasise. *The Playboy of the Western World* is a highly moral play, deriving its motive from sources as pure and as lofty as the externals of its setting are necessarily wild and vulgar; and I cannot but admire the moral courage of the man who has shot his dreadful searchlight into our cherished accumulation of social skeletons. He has led our vision through the Abbey street stage into the heart of Connaught, and revealed to us there truly terrible truths, of our own making, which we dare not face for the present. The merciless accuracy of his revelation is more than we can bear. Our eyes tremble at it. The words chosen are, like the things they express, direct and dreadful, by themselves intolerable to conventional taste, yet full of vital beauty in their truth to the conditions of life, to the character they depict, and to the sympathies they suggest. It is as if we looked in a mirror for the first time, and found ourselves hideous. We fear to face the thing. We shrink at the word for it. We scream.

True, a play ought to explain itself; but then, the audience has not yet permitted it to explain itself. Perhaps the externals are unworkably true to the inherent facts of life behind them; but that is a superficial matter, and though it is hard for an artist to select language less strong than the truth impelling him, I think a working modification may be arrived at without sacrificing anything essential. Mr. Synge must remember that the shock was sincere.

'Pegeen' is a lively peasant girl in her father's publichouse on the wild wayside by the Western sea, and it is arranged for her to marry 'Shaneen Keogh,' the half idiot, who has a farm, but not enough intelligence to cut his yellow hair. There is no love. Who could think of loving 'Shaneen'? Love could not occur to her through him. He has not enough intelligence to love. He has not enough character to have a single vice in him, and his only apparent virtue is a trembling terror of 'Father Reilly'. Yet there is nothing unusual in the marriage of such a girl to such a person, and it does not occur to her that love ought to have anything to do with the matter.

Why is 'Pegeen' prepared to marry him? 'God made him; therefore, let him pass for a man', and in all his unfitness, he is the fittest available! Why? Because the fit ones have fled. He remains because of his cowardice and his idiocy in a region where fear is the first of the virtues, and where the survival of the unfittest is the established law of life. Had he been capable, he would have fled. His lack of character enables him to accept the conditions of his existence, where more character could but make him less acceptable, and therefore, less happy. Character wants freedom, and so escapes, but the 'Shaneens' remain to reproduce themselves in the social scheme. We see in him how the Irish race die out in Ireland, filling the lunatic asylums more full from a declining population, and selecting for continuance in the future the human specimens most calculated to bring the race lower and lower. 'Shaneen' shows us why Ireland dies while the races around us prosper faster and faster. A woman is interested in the nearest thing to a man that she can find within her reach, and that is why 'Pegeen' is prepared to marry her half idiot with the yellow hair. 'Shaneen' accepts terror as the regular condition of his existence, and so there is no need for him to emigrate with the strong and clever ones who insist on freedom for their lives.

Such is the situation into which the 'Playboy' drifts, confessing in callous calmness that he has killed his father, and claiming sanctuary as pot boy in the publichouse—not, by the way, a convincing position in which to disguise a murderer. Women do not choose murderers for their husbands, but the 'Playboy' is a real, live man, and the only other choice is the trembling idiot, who would be incapable even to kill his father. Instinctively and immediately, 'Pegeen' prefers the murderer. Besides, there is the story of why he 'stretched his father with the loy'. The father had wanted to force him into a marriage with a woman he hated. The son had protested. The father had raised the scythe, but the son's blow with the spade had fallen first. Murder is not pleasant, but what of the other crime—that of a father forcing his son to marry a woman he hated? Were it not for this crime, the other could not have followed. A real, live man was new and fascinating to 'Pegeen', even a parricide, and the man who had killed his father, rather than marry a woman he hated, might at least be capable of loving sincerely. Then, he was a man who had achieved something, if only murder, and he had achieved the murder obviously because his better character had not been permitted to govern him. When trembling idiocy tends to be the standard of life, intelligence and courage can easily become critical, and women do not like trembling men. In their hearts, they prefer murderers. What is a woman to do in conditions of existence that leave her a choice only between the cowardly fool and the courageous criminal?

The choice itself is full of drama, the more tragic because it is the lot of a community. The woman's only alternatives are to be derilect or to be degraded; poor 'Pegeen' personifies a nation in which the 'Shaneens' prevail, and in which strong, healthy men can stay only to be at war with their surroundings. It is the revolt of Human Nature against the terrors ever inflicted on it in Connacht, and in some subtle way of his own the dramatist has succeeded in realising the distinction; so that even when the guilt is confessed, we cannot accept 'The Playboy' quite as a murderer, and we are driven back to the influences of his environment, for the origin of his responsibility, feeling that if we do not permit men to grow morally, we are ourselves to blame for the acts by which they shock us. Such are Synge's insights into life and character in Connacht. Can the Western peasantry have a truer friend than the one who exhibits to criticism and to condemnation the forces afflicting their lives?

The peasant women of Connacht are no more partial to murderers than other women in other countries, but we must take the conduct of women anywhere in the light of their environment, and we must take the conduct of men in the same way. The difference between a hero and a murderer is sometimes, in the comparative numbers they have killed, morally in favour of the murderer; and we all know how the 'pale young curate' loses his drawingroom popularity when the unmarried subaltern returns from his professional blood-spilling. It is not that women love murder; it is that they hate cowardice, and in 'Pegeen's' world it is hard for a man to be much better than a coward. Hence the half-idiot with the yellow hair, who, controlling his share of the nation's land, can inflict his kind on the community generation after generation.

The fierce truth and intensity of the dramatist's insight make strength of expression inevitable, but, confining myself strictly to the artistic interest, I feel that the language is overdone, and that the realism is overdone. They irritate, and, worse still, they are piled up to such excess in the subsidiaries of expression as to make us lose sight in some measure of the dramatic essentials. As to the discussions on feminine underclothing, I have often heard discussions more familiar among the peasantry themselves, without the remotest suggestion of immorality, and if Dublin is shocked in this connection, it is because its mind is less clean than that of the Connacht peasant women.

It itself, the plot is singularly undramatic by construction, suggesting drama rather than exploiting 'cheap' effect. We have to think down along the shafts of light into Connacht in order to realise the picture at the end of the vista, but when we see it we find it inevitable and fascinating. The play is more a psychological revelation than a dramatic process, but it is both.

I have not said much to suggest 'comedy', which is the official adjective for this play. I have tried to bring out the unseen interests that await criticism and appreciation while the Abbey street audiences scream. It is a play on which many articles could be written.

There was a large audience last night, mainly there to 'boo', but they must pay to come in, so that the management stands to make money, and to be heard in the end. (pp. 37-40)

> *Patrick Kenny, in a review of "The Playboy of the Western World," in* The "Playboy" Riots *by James Kilroy, The Dolmen Press, 1971, pp. 37-40.*

W. B. YEATS (essay date 1910)

[*The leading figure of the Irish Literary Renaissance and a major poet in twentieth-century literature, Yeats was also an active critic of his contemporaries' works. As a critic he judged the writings of others according to his own poetic values of sincerity, passion, and vital imagination. Yeats was one of the founders of the Irish National Theatre Society at the Abbey Theatre and advised Synge on the revision, rehearsal, and production of* Playboy. *In the following excerpt, Yeats recalls the controversy surrounding* Playboy *and defends the play's artistic merits.*]

On Saturday, January 26, 1907, I was lecturing in Aberdeen, and when my lecture was over I was given a telegram which said, 'Play great success.' It had been sent from Dublin after the second act of *The Playboy of the Western World,* then being performed for the first time. After one in the morning, my host brought to my bedroom this second telegram, 'Audience broke up in disorder at the word shift.' I knew no more until I got the Dublin papers on my way from Belfast to Dublin on Tuesday morning. On the Monday night no word of the play had been heard. About forty young men had sat in the front seats of the pit, and stamped and shouted and blown trumpets from the rise to the fall of the curtain. On the Tuesday night also the forty young men were there. They wished to silence what they considered a slander upon Ireland's womanhood. Irish women would never sleep under the same roof with a young man without a chaperon, nor admire a murderer, nor use a word like 'shift'; nor could any one recognise the country men and women of Davis and Kickham in these poetical, violent, grotesque persons, who used the name of God so freely, and spoke of all things that hit their fancy.

A patriotic journalism which had seen in Synge's capricious imagination the enemy of all it would have young men believe, had for years prepared for this hour, by that which is at once the greatest and most ignoble power of journalism, the art of repeating a name again and again with some ridiculous or evil association. The preparation had begun after the first performance of *The Shadow of the Glen,* Synge's first play, with an assertion made in ignorance, but repeated in dishonesty, that he had taken his fable and his characters, not from his own mind nor that profound knowledge of cot and curragh he was admitted to possess, but 'from a writer of the Roman decadence.' Some spontaneous dislike had been but natural, for genius like his can but slowly, amid what it has of harsh and strange, set forth the nobility of its beauty, and the depth of its compassion; but the frenzy that would have silenced his master-work was, like most violent things, artificial, that defence of virtue by those who have but little, which is the pomp and gallantry of journalism and its right to govern the world.

As I stood there watching, knowing well that I saw the disso-

lution of a school of patriotism that held sway over my youth, Synge came and stood beside me, and said, 'A young doctor has just told me that he can hardly keep himself from jumping on to a seat, and pointing out in that howling mob those whom he is treating for venereal disease.' (pp. 311-12)

There are artists like Byron, like Goethe, like Shelley, who have impressive personalities, active wills and all their faculties at the service of the will; but [Synge] belonged to those who, like Wordsworth, like Coleridge, like Goldsmith, like Keats, have little personality, so far as the casual eye can see, little personal will, but fiery and brooding imagination. I cannot imagine him anxious to impress or convince in any company, or saying more than was sufficient to keep the talk circling. Such men have the advantage that all they write is a part of knowledge, but they are powerless before events and have often but one visible strength, the strength to reject from life and thought all that would mar their work, or deafen them in the doing of it; and only this so long as it is a passive act. If Synge had married young or taken some profession, I doubt if he would have written books or been greatly interested in a movement like ours; but he refused various opportunities of making money in what must have been an almost unconscious preparation. He had no life outside his imagination, little interest in anything that was not its chosen subject. He hardly seemed aware of the existence of other writers. I never knew if he cared for work of mine, and do not remember that I had from him even a conventional compliment, and yet he had the most perfect modesty and simplicity in daily intercourse, self-assertion was impossible to him. On the other hand, he was useless amidst sudden events. He was much shaken by the *Playboy* riot; on the first night confused and excited, knowing not what to do, and ill before many days, but it made no difference in his work. He neither exaggerated out of defiance nor softened out of timidity. He wrote on as if nothing had happened, altering *The Tinker's Wedding* to a more unpopular form, but writing a beautiful serene *Deirdre,* with, for the first time since his *Riders to the Sea,* no touch of sarcasm or defiance. Misfortune shook his physical nature while it left his intellect and his moral nature untroubled. The external self, the mask, the *persona,* was a shadow; character was all. (pp. 328-30)

I remember saying once to Synge that though it seemed to me that a conventional descriptive passage encumbered the action at the moment of crisis, I liked *The Shadow of the Glen* better than *Riders to the Sea,* that seemed for all the nobility of its end, its mood of Greek tragedy, too passive in suffering, and had quoted from Matthew Arnold's introduction to *Empedocles on Etna* to prove my point. Synge answered: 'It is a curious thing that *Riders to the Sea* succeeds with an English but not with an Irish audience, and *The Shadow of the Glen,* which is not liked by an English audience, is always liked in Ireland, though it is disliked there in theory.' Since then *Riders to the Sea* has grown into great popularity in Dublin, partly because, with the tactical instinct of an Irish mob, the demonstrators against *The Playboy* both in the Press and in the theatre, where it began the evening, selected it for applause. It is now what Shelley's "Cloud" was for many years, a comfort to those who do not like to deny altogether the genius they cannot understand. Yet I am certain that, in the long run, his grotesque plays with their lyric beauty, their violent laughter, *The Playboy of the Western World* most of all, will be loved for holding so much of the mind of Ireland. Synge has written of *The Playboy* [see essay dated 1907]: 'Any one who has lived in real intimacy with the Irish peasantry will know that the wildest sayings in this play are tame indeed compared with the fancies one may hear at any little hillside cottage of Geesala, or Carraroe, or Dingle Bay.' It is the strangest, the most beautiful expression in drama of that Irish fantasy which overflowing through all Irish literature that has come out of Ireland itself (compare the fantastic Irish account of the Battle of Clontarf with the sober Norse account) is the unbroken character of Irish genius. In modern days this genius has delighted in mischievous extravagance, like that of the Gaelic poet's curse upon his children: 'There are three things that I hate: the Devil that is waiting for my soul; the worms that are waiting for my body; my children, who are waiting for my wealth and care neither for my body nor my soul: O, Christ, hang all in the same noose!' I think those words were spoken with a delight in their vehemence that took out of anger half the bitterness with all the gloom. An old man on the Aran Islands told me the very tale on which *The Playboy* is founded, beginning with the words: 'If any gentleman has done a crime we'll hide him. There was a gentleman that killed his father, and I had him in my own house six months till he got away to America.' Despite the solemnity of his slow speech his eyes shone as the eyes must have shone in that Trinity College branch of the Gaelic League which began every meeting with prayers for the death of an old Fellow of College who disliked their movement, or as they certainly do when patriots are telling how short a time the prayers took to the killing of him. I have seen a crowd, when certain Dublin papers had wrought themselves into an imaginary loyalty, so possessed by what seemed the very genius of satiric fantasy that one all but looked to find some feathered heel among the cobble-stones. Part of the delight of crowd or individual is always that somebody will be angry, somebody take the sport for gloomy earnest. We are mocking at his solemnity, let us therefore so hide our malice that he may be more solemn still, and the laugh run higher yet. Why should we speak his language and so wake him from a dream of all those emotions which men feel because they should, and not because they must? Our minds, being sufficient to themselves, do not wish for victory but are content to elaborate our extravagance, if fortune aid, into wit or lyric beauty, and as for the rest, 'There are nights when a king like Conchobar would spit upon his arm-ring and queens will stick out their tongues at the rising moon.' This habit of the mind has made Oscar Wilde and Mr. Bernard Shaw the most celebrated makers of comedy to our time, and if it has sounded plainer still in the conversation of the one, and in some few speeches of the other, that is but because they have not been able to turn out of their plays an alien trick of zeal picked up in struggling youth. Yet, in Synge's plays also, fantasy gives the form and not the thought, for the core is always, as in all great art, an overpowering vision of certain virtues, and our capacity for sharing in that vision is the measure of our delight. Great art chills us at first by its coldness or its strangeness, by what seems capricious, and yet it is from these qualities it has authority, as though it had fed on locusts and wild honey. The imaginative writer shows us the world as a painter does his picture, reversed in a looking-glass, that we may see it, not as it seems to eyes habit has made dull, but as we were Adam and this the first morning; and when the new image becomes as little strange as the old we shall stay with him, because he has, besides the strangeness, not strange to him, that made us share his vision, sincerity that makes us share his feeling. (pp. 336-39)

W. B. Yeats, "J. M. Synge and the Ireland of His Time," in his Essays and Introductions, *The Macmillan Company, 1961, pp. 311-42.*

MAURICE BOURGEOIS   (essay date 1913)

[*The following excerpt is from Bourgeois's* John Millington Synge and the Irish Theatre, *one of the earliest comprehensive studies of Synge's life and writings. Here, Bourgeois discusses Synge's presentation of the Irish national character in* Playboy.]

The objections against [*The Playboy of the Western World*] at large are made on religious, moral and patriotic grounds. The play, it is urged, is a specimen of blasphemous neo-Paganism in view of the continual use of expressions referring to God and the Church, and of the profane travesty on the sacrament of marriage. It must certainly be owned that in the *Playboy* even more than in *The Tinker's Wedding,* Synge, unlike Shawn Keogh, has not been afraid of Father Reilly. The justice of alleging the piece to be immoral—due to the fact that it seems to hold up patricide to admiration—may be questioned. Synge represents an admired murderer, yet in so doing he does not necessarily condone murder. But here we encounter the patriotic objection, which has been raised either by perfectly sincere Nationalists or by political coteries. The exact question is: Would real Irish peasants admire Christy Mahon?

The Irishness of the piece has been doubted. Mr. O'Donoghue is of opinion that the *Playboy* is but a dramatization of the well-known freak of Baudelaire opening a conversation in a Paris restaurant with the words, "After having assassinated my poor father," to the bewilderment of those present. The supposition is ingenious, but it seems to overlook the anecdote recorded by Synge himself, and the observations he made concerning the Aran Islanders' attitude towards criminals. The Irish peasant's instinct to shield the law-breaker against the English police (the "peelers")—a phenomenon which has its origin in the ancient Gaelic clan-spirit and in centuries of misery and oppression—is an undeniable fact. The well-known case of Lynchehaun in Achill need hardly be recalled. When Mr. Yeats first went to Aran, the people were surprised to find that he was only a peaceful tourist, not a murderer seeking sanctuary; and an Irish R.M. told the present writer the story of a man who had been hidden and protected by the very relatives of the person he had killed! Even the Irish-born policemen sometimes side with the offender—witness Lady Gregory's *Rising of the Moon.* Yet what makes the situation in the *Playboy* wholly unlikely is that we have to deal not with "a common, week-day kind of murderer," but with a man who has killed his father. Patricide is a crime abhorred in all countries; and if it is quite certain that Irish peasants would not inform against Christy, they would not for all that admire him. Above all, they would not admire the Playboy *before* he has developed his supposed deed into a "gallous tale," as is the case in the comedy.

We are thus led to assume that the play, while in a way "realistic" and sociologically accurate, contains a strong element of humorous or satirical symbolism and allegory. The Playboy might well have killed both parents instead of his father only (whom he has not even killed): it would not greatly matter. The play as a whole is Irish in view of its being an extremely searching study of the Celtic temperament, with its ever-possible imaginative perversion of ethical ideals. One cannot say that it is pro-Irish; nor that it is deliberately, intentionally anti-Irish, though we think it very unlikely that the production of the *Playboy* in various cities of England by the Abbey Theatre Company during their annual *tournée* on this side of St. George's Channel should influence English public opinion in favour of Irish Home Rule. The Irish nation as portrayed by Synge in the *Playboy*—which we positively refuse to regard as his masterpiece, in spite of the generally-received judgment and of the somewhat uncritical and conventional eulogies bestowed on the play whenever revived—are anything but fit for self-government. Synge's "comedy," when viewed in this light, certainly constitutes the most tragic exposure of his fellow-countrymen's besottedness. Is it not even rumoured in certain quarters that the management of the Abbey Theatre, which is, as we have seen, largely supported by Unionist finance, is paid to retain the *Playboy* in its repertory, and produce it in England as frequently as possible, so as to indispose against Home Rule the English public mind—which, a priori, we may suspect of anything but sympathy towards the idea of Irish autonomy—and thus prevent at any price the passing of the Government of Ireland Bill?

But to return. Synge, sitting in the auditorium of the Abbey Theatre while the row was raging and people shook their fists at him, was overheard to say, "We shall have to establish a Society for the Preservation of Irish Humour;" and also, "I don't care a rap. It's an extravaganza;" and then he relapsed into silence. Any reader of his preface to *The Tinker's Wedding* will recollect how he complains that some Irish towns are fast losing their humour, a fact which, he maintains, will bring about "morbidity of mind, as Baudelaire's mind was morbid." His intention in the *Playboy* seems therefore to have been to write a kind of humorous burlesque which, like all burlesques, is based on a thorough knowledge of unburlesqued reality—to depict poetically and allegorically, by dint of "exaltation," which in his view was the product of genuine humour, the imaginative, emotional, and sexual self-discovery of a poet's soul, burgeoning at first amidst uncongenial surroundings, and finally expanding into perfect flower of expression in the warm sunshine of public praise. Like all great poets, Christy Mahon is a liar of genius or, at the very least, an embroiderer, in the true lineal descent of Corneille's Dorante, Daudet's Tartarin, Ibsen's Peer Gynt, and Rostand's Cyrano. "It is humbugging us he is." Like all these masters, Synge personifies in his hero the romance inherent in sheer mendacity. Like all his predecessors in European drama, Christy Mahon at first believes in his own lie, and, "in the end of all," falls victim to it. The admirable gradation in his story proves him to be a true-born poet. At the beginning he "just riz the loy and let fall the edge of it on the ridge of his [Old Mahon's] skull"; finally, after a series of careful and subtle transitions which one might follow throughout the play, he transmogrifies himself into "a gallant orphan cleft his father with one blow to the breeches belt." At last the sheer intoxication of lying and of acting his lie causes him (like Henri in Arthur Schnitzler's *The Green Cockatoo*) to do in actuality what he has been doing so far only in fancy—namely, to kill his father, or at least attempt to murder him. However, at all times, Christy's character remains highly fantastic; in a way, he turns out to be almost as "stagey" and unreal a type as the stage Irishman of old—the "gossoon" and the "broth of a bhoy"—while Pegeen, who very soon becomes his equal, if not indeed his superior, in the game of imaginative lovemaking, distinctly reminds us of certain characteristic features of the Boucicaultian colleen or "slip of a girl."

Might not one go further still, and maintain that the *Playboy* is meant by Synge not only as a humorous and allegorical impersonation of poetic, creative souls in general, but also as an ironical vision of the dramatist's own personal attitude throughout his "comedy"? Is not the Playboy the playwright himself, to wit, J. M. Synge, who, like so many Irish humorists—Oscar Wilde and Mr. George Bernard Shaw in particular—chooses as his subject the crudest possible paradox, wherewith he, by a sort of perpetual *double entendre,* authorizes contradictory interpretations of his play and, as Christy did the Mayo countryfolk, constantly and consistently mystifies his public, who apparently have not yet been able to decide whether his "comedy" is a work of serious portraiture or of fanciful tomfoolery?

The play, as one must own, and as that consummate Irish humorist, Mr. "George A. Birmingham," has justly pointed out [in "The Literary Movement in Ireland," *Fortnightly Review,* 1907], is exceedingly difficult to understand—is, in fact, quite as puzzling as a play by Ibsen was at first to an average English audience. The very length of our commentary is the best proof of this necessity to explain its obscure meaning. That our double-sided construction of the play is the correct one is, we are bold enough to think, conclusively demonstrated by the very definite statement made by Synge himself, in the following unreprinted letter which he sent to a Dublin newspaper during the historic week:

> *The Playboy of the Western World* is not a play with a 'purpose' in the modern sense of the word, but, although parts of it are or are meant to be extravagant comedy, still a great deal that is in it and a great deal more that is behind it is perfectly serious when looked at in a certain light. This is often the case, I think, with comedy, and no one is quite sure to-day whether Shylock or Alceste should be played seriously or not. There are, it may be hinted, several sides to the *Playboy.*

This letter shews, among other things, that it would be a total mistake to understand the *Playboy* as a perfectly serious piece, as it is a total mistake to act it as a rollicking farce, in the fashion adopted of late years by the Abbey Theatre Company. The latter misconception would be the graver one, for Synge attached greater importance to the serious aspect of the *Playboy* than to its imaginative and poetical side. In a private letter to a friend, which is printed here for the first time, Synge emphasizes and even, we think, humorously exaggerates the serious element in his play. (We wish we were at liberty to reproduce the eloquent swearwords in the letter, but really they are not publishable. A good many of Synge's letters are in this strain—earnestness of thought mocking itself in grotesque virulence of form.)

Wednesday morning [no other date].

Dear * * *,—I can't let * * * *'s . . . rot fester in your mind. Of course *Playboy* is serious. Extravaganza theory is partly my fault: an interviewer . . . ran up and down stairs after me for two hours on the Monday night when there was the first *riot* [underlined], and I was in charge as Yeats was away. He, the interviewer, got in my way— . . . —and said, "Do you really think, Mr. Synge, that if a man did this in Mayo, girls would bring him a poulet?" The next time it was, "Do you think, Mr. Synge, they'd bring him eggs?" I lost my poor temper (. . .), and I said, "Oh well, if you like its improbable, its extravagant, its extravzance (how's it spelt?) . . . . " He hashed up what I said in a great deal worse than I expected, but I wrote next day *politely* backing out of all that was in the interview. That is the whole myth. It isn't quite accurate to say, I think, that the thing is a generalization from a single case. *If* [underlined] the idea had occurred to me I could and would just as readily have written the thing, as it stands, without the Lynchehaun case or the Aran case. My story—*in its essence* ["essence" underlined four times] is probable given the psychic state of the locality, I used the cases afterwards to controvert critics who said it was *impossible.* Amen. Go brat [for "brath," in Gaelic characters].

Yours, J. M. Synge.

That Synge does exaggerate his meaning in this curious letter, and that the **Playboy** is not so "serious" as he would have us believe, is clearly shewn by the fact that he confesses having written the comedy as a study in temperament or as an artistic reconstruction of the *possible* psychology of the people, irrespective of the actual cases by which the play happened to be borne out once written. The truth, as we have seen, is infinitely more subtle and complex, and must not be unduly simplified. On the one hand, the **Playboy** has a serious or objective side which makes it a pessimistic—some call it cynical—representation of Irish character; but this gloomy "reality" is relieved by an element of purely subjective "joy," a gift of humour and a beauty of language which make the play true not so much to Irish nature as to Synge himself, in the person of the Playboy.

Apart from this vitally personal element, one may, sociologically, regard the so-called "blackening" or "vilification" of Ireland by Synge in the **Playboy** as the direct outcome of the self-critical spirit engendered by the national revival. Leaving aside Synge's own view of life at large, which made him at times so strangely unsympathetic to Irish life in particular, it is natural enough that a literary renascence should bring about, not a complacent admiration of the national qualities, but a searching analysis of the national defects. This applies to the "pessimism" of the new Irish school of drama; indeed, it is especially true of the literatures of Celtic and Latin countries, which have a curious tendency to mirror the worse, not the better, aspect of national existence. Like the Catoblepas, the self-devouring monster in the Apocalypse, the Gaelic and Latin peoples are peculiarly self-disparaging, suicidal, self-destructive; they turn out literary works which may lead the foreign student who takes them as social documents to the gross misconception that the national life which they represent is "morbid." The French naval officer in *Fanny's First Play* makes a speech in which he "cracks up the English and runs down the French"; and we have it on the authority of Mr. Shaw that M. Raymond Lauzerte, the French actor who played the part, said that he believed every word of it.

Whatever may be thought, said, and written for and against Synge's world-famous comedy, no one will seriously contest its high intrinsic literary merits. Mr. George Moore has acclaimed it as "the most significant play of the last two hundred years," and his judgment, dithyrambic though it be, finds ever-increasing adhesion. The **Playboy** is, if not Synge's best play, at least his most important and representative contribution to the modern stage, and will long remain, for reasons literary and otherwise, the Abbey Theatre Company's centrepiece. One may say in conclusion that it is Ireland to the core in about the same degree as *Don Quixote* is Spain to

the core; while, viewed from an autobiographical standpoint, its explosive success only testifies to the overpowering gusto and vehemence of the man who wrote it. (pp. 201-12)

> *Maurice Bourgeois, in his* John Millington Synge and the Irish Theatre, *1913. Reprint by Benjamin Blom, 1965, 338 p.*

ERNEST BOYD   (essay date 1922)

[*An Irish-American writer and translator, Boyd was a prominent literary critic known for his erudite, honest, and often satirical critiques. His important survey,* Ireland's Literary Renaissance, *examines the work of Synge in relation to the Irish National Theatre. In the following excerpt from that work, Boyd evaluates the literary significance of* The Playboy of the Western World.]

The great "event" in the history of the Irish Theatre has been the discovery and universal recognition of the genius of J. M. Synge, whose brief activity of six years (from 1903 to 1909) had a decisive influence upon contemporary drama in Ireland. There can be little doubt that the peasant play, now characteristic of the National Theatre, owes its success to this writer who at the outset revealed its dramatic and poetic possibilities. In a series of masterpieces Synge established his command of this form, whether adapted to tragedy or comedy, and proved his title to rank with the great dramatists of European literature. The circumstances of his *début* all combined to strengthen the prestige which he was to lend to the folk-drama. It has already been observed that the histrionic talent of the brothers Fay, and the tradition they imparted to their group of players, were peculiarly adapted to the development of the peasant play. Add to this the fact that Synge's very first piece, **In the Shadow of the Glen,** provoked that ignorant hostility which followed his later work with increased venom, and whose manifestation could not but awaken a sense of resistance. The natural determination of intelligent minds, in the face of unreasoning prejudice, is to persevere, in obedience to the faith that is engendered by the opposition of inferiors. The stand made by W. B. Yeats for artistic freedom, when he championed Synge against mob-rule in literature, was as greatly to his credit as was his discernment in previously sensing that latent genius whose expression he had subsequently to defend so generously. Obviously such a struggle as was waged on behalf of its greatest exponent served only to enhance the claims of the folk-drama. The innumerable detractors of Synge contributed largely towards confirming his own reputation, as well as consolidating the hold of the peasant play upon a movement already predisposed in its favour. (pp. 316-17)

Until 1907 J. M. Synge was known, only to a limited public, as the author of three plays [**In the Shadow of the Glen, Riders to the Sea,** and **The Well of the Saints**], two of which had procured him a reserve of enmity, whose fullest manifestation coincided with the extension of his fame to the English-speaking world of letters in that year. The incredible history of **The Playboy of the Western World** has been exhausted by numerous commentators, and may now be left for the notes of some future compiler of "Curiosities of Literature." The peculiarly hypercritical, over-strung nature of the criticism which followed Synge from the beginning has already been alluded to. It takes on the aspect of an uninterrupted pursuit of dubious literary ancestors, for the sole purpose of bringing some discredit upon the author, on moral, religious or political grounds. Most of these researches, though ostensibly directed towards estimating Synge's literary indebtedness, were undertaken with obvious intent to create prejudice, by associating the dramatist with names not honoured in Early Victorian circles. Where the appeal is not merely to preconceived moral verdicts, there is usually some suggestion of plagiarism. On the appearance of *The Playboy* all the antagonisms were aroused to a pitch of unusual violence, a veritable cult of hostility arose, and the anti-Synge campaign was launched. The noisy proceedings of Synge's opponents secured for the play a wide hearing, which might otherwise have been deferred. The obscure dramatist found himself famous in 1907, four years after the first public production of his work—such was the recognition he obtained when thrust, by unfriendly hands, upon the attention of competent critics.

The charm of *The Playboy* lies uniquely in its verbal and imaginative qualities. To enquire what are its moral intentions, to proclaim it libellous, to discuss its basis in reality, is to confess a complete understanding of the spirit in which such masterpieces are conceived. The fable of Christy Mahon's hour of triumph, when the belief that he has killed his father makes him at last conscious of his own identity, by reaction to the effect of his exploit upon the hearers of his narrative,—this is clearly no treatise on morals, to be refuted by reference to the well-known purity of Irish life. Were all the evidence absent, which proves the Irish peasantry's very natural weakness for the fugitive from justice, the value of Synge's conception would be undiminished. If Pegeen Mike were a grotesque exaggeration, instead of a wonderfully human personality, her admiration for the alleged parricide would still be one of those profound intuitions of which genius alone is capable. The play is a pure creation of the imagination, and its language responds to the intensity of the emotion in which it was conceived. The singular beauty of the love-scenes between Christy and Pegeen Mike, the two characters in whom the exaltation of the dramatist's mood is most heightened, is the beauty of poetry in its essence. It is poetry untrammelled by the mechanism of verse, as befits the natural simplicity of the speaker. The rhythm and accent are there, coloured and emphasised by the Gaelic-English idiom, which has now become for the author a perfect instrument of poetic speech. His knowledge of Gaelic, his work of selection on the Aran Islands, and the suggestions gleaned from Hyde's *Love Songs of Connacht,* have all formed in Synge's mind a well of literary strength, from which he derives the most diversely magnificent effects. The amorous raptures of Christy, the angry interchanges of the women, the discourses of the publican—to every breath of passion there is a corresponding heightening of the key in which the language is pitched. It is evident that Anglo-Irish is to Synge a medium in which he has obtained absolute freedom, he uses it with the same effect as the Elizabethans used English. The savour and freshness of a language that is still unexploited, the wealth of imagery and the verbal magnificence of the Elizabethan tongue are felt and heard again in *The Playboy of the Western World.*

Nothing is more pathetic than to read Synge's attempted justification of this play in response to the demand for a statement of his purpose. His prefaces, and the testimony of his friends and biographers, show how averse he was to straining his art into the expression of "ideas," as the post-Shavian theory of drama demands. The stress of the riotous moment in which *The Playboy* appeared found the author unprepared. Critics and interviewers profited by his distress to drag from him some explanation of his play. He was first stampeded into

describing it as an "extravaganza," then we find him writing to say that he was mistaken, and soon the point becomes obscured by his desire to produce evidence as to the probability or possibility of the incidents denounced in his play. The effect has been to confound this evidence, which replied only to specific accusations, with a general plea on behalf of the play itself. The controversies are dead, but there still remains the doubt they have sown as to the significance of *The Playboy.* The subject has been discussed in a manner which suggests nothing less absurd than an argument to determine whether Cervantes exaggerated, when describing the adventures of Don Quixote, or whether Tartarin de Tarascon was created by Daudet to illustrate the evils of mendacity. It is, of course, easier to recognise the creations of Daudet and Cervantes as belonging to pure fantasy; they are remote from us materially, but both writers gave offence to their immediate audiences.

We have seen in *The Well of the Saints* an example of Synge's realistic treatment of a theme usually approached from the opposite direction. *The Playboy,* it may be said, is a further instance of the same kind. The scene of the play, the characterisation of the peasant types and the exteriorisation of the drama seem to indicate realism. Consequently, with the protests of the moralists and politicians in our ears, and the propagandist associations of dramatic realism to mislead us, we have attributed to Synge intentions which were never his, and to whose expression he vainly tried, at first, to adapt himself. Neither in *The Playboy* nor elsewhere did Synge attempt to contribute to the so-called theatre of ideas: "The drama," he says, "like the symphony, does not teach or prove anything." It is made serious "by the degree in which it gives the nourishment, not very easy to define, on which our imaginations live." This sentence defines exactly the serious purport of *The Playboy,* which is to nourish the imagination. The realism of the play is no more nor less than the realism of the language in which it is written. Both are the synthetic re-creation of very real elements in our life. Synge boasted that there was not a phrase of his dramatic speech but had its counterpart in the stories and conversations he heard in Gaelic Ireland, yet nobody pretends that Christy Mahon's talk is a literal transcription from life. The same is true of the play as a whole. It is a work of imaginative reconstruction, in which the moral and psychological elements are transfigured until they take on a universal significance. *The Playboy* stands in the same relation to the world of the Celtic imagination as Don Quixote did to the Spain of his day. In both cases the central figures have an existence which is at once personal, national and human. (pp. 325-29)

Ernest Boyd, "The Dramatic Movement: Second Phase," in his Ireland's Literary Renaissance, *revised edition, Alfred A. Knopf, 1922, pp. 309-43.*

DANIEL CORKERY (essay date 1931)

[In the following excerpt, Corkery examines the effect of Synge's Anglo-Irish background on his presentation of the life and language of rural Catholics.]

[The Playboy of the Western World] is Synge's most famous piece of work, so famous indeed that one can hardly deal with it without becoming entangled in legend. To grow is of the nature of legend. "There were riots in Dublin when this play was first produced," and the foreigner, not knowing these for words out of a legend, sees, in his mind's eye, a tumult-ridden

city, with chargings and counter-chargings in its streets and squares. Both inside and outside the Abbey Theatre during the first few performances of the play there certainly were squabbles and protestings, but to speak of them as riots is to use the very accents of the Playboy himself. Mr. Padraic Colum writes of the first performance [see Further Reading]:

> I remember well how the play nearly got past the dubiousness of that first-night audience. The third act was near its close when the line that drew the first hiss was spoken,—"A drift of the finest women in the County Mayo standing in their shifts around me." That hiss was a signal for a riot in the theatre. They had been disconcerted and impatient before this, but the audience, I think, would not have made any interruption if this line had not been spoken. Still, they had been growing hostile to the play from the point where Christy's father enters. That scene was too representational. There stood a man with horribly-bloodied bandage upon his head, making a figure that took the whole thing out of the atmosphere of high comedy.
>
> (p. 179)

The protest made with such heat was two-fold. It was religious. It was nationalistic. And only such outsiders as have lived in countries where an alien Ascendancy, for two centuries or more, have been casting ridicule on everything native, can really understand it. Do not psychologists tell us that if an occurrence, which causes us mental pain, is repeated, every repetition brings not only its own particular amount of pain but brings, as well, recollection of our former sufferings from the same cause, that is, brings more than the amount of pain intrinsic in the event. The *Playboy* incident, then, was not unrelated: it awakened within the national consciousness ancestral disturbances. The new protest was portion of the old. Wherever there is an alien Ascendancy there is such an attendant protest, perennial, and on occasions quickening into noise and violence. (p. 180)

The protest attending on an alien Ascendancy's callous caperings is, of course, always most active in a period of national revival. In 1907, when *The Playboy* was first produced, the Irish revival was rapidly gathering momentum—we who were then fairly young murmur when we recall the period, 'Bliss was it in that dawn to be alive,'—and therefore Ireland's young men were become, perhaps, oversensitive where the representation of the native Ireland was concerned. Religion and nationality are not separable in Ireland. If in any piece of work there occur not only incidents which reflect, or seem to reflect, on the native Ireland, but also words and phrases which hurt the religious consciousness of that Ireland, then the offence of that piece of work is reckoned, in such periods, doubly gross, and not deserving of any fine consideration or afterthought. So was it with *The Playboy*. (p. 181)

In [the drama] Synge probably did give way to a desire to shock his audience; yet of this one cannot be quite certain. It may be that he expected a Dublin audience to look at the spectacle of the play as a purely folk audience in the West, self-contained and not conscious that their neighbour in the next seat in the theatre was English-eyed, might conceivably have done, for Synge was simple about many things, and was amorous of the honest insensibility of the folk consciousness. For that sensitiveness, that touchiness, if one likes, our history has induced in us, he had but little feeling: the "harrow of sorrow" is a common phrase in Irish poetry, and a harrow

reduces to fineness. As for our religious consciousness, he was not quite unaware of it, it is true; was sometimes even touched by it—if also, at other times, estranged—but certainly he never became initiate of it. Knowing of this dullness of his to what is ever almost too alert, too quick, in our people's consciousness, we are able to conceive that he could honestly think the audience would enjoy the play even as he himself would enjoy it if another pen had written it. And his bearing in the theatre during the first performance falls in with this view of him. He is said to have remarked that it would be necessary to establish a society for the preservation of Irish humour. For humour he had an Anglo-Irish stomach, which, remembering Swift, and Lever, and Lover, and Maginn, and Prout, and George Birmingham, and Sean O'Casey, and Somerville and Ross, and St. John Ervine, and Dr. Gogarty, one thinks must be as strong, if not as naïve, as the folk stomach in all lands. On that night some of the pressmen questioned him on the play, and he answered them that certain incidents in it were improbable, that the whole thing was extravaganza. This admission his admirers at the time regarded as calamitous; and Synge himself in a short and very curious letter to the Press immediately withdrew it:

> *The Playboy of the Western World* is not a play with a 'purpose' in the modern sense of the word, but, although parts of it are, or are meant to be, extravagant comedy, still a great deal that is in it and a great deal more that is behind it is perfectly serious when looked at in a certain light. This is often the case, I think, with comedy, and no one is quite sure to-day whether Shylock or Alceste should be played seriously or not. There are, it may be hinted, several sides to *The Playboy*.

This is an honest letter. An artist makes a play and afterwards analyses his own impulses in doing so; when Synge wrote this letter he was only beginning the analysing process. Far more illuminating, however, is this passage in a personal letter of his to a friend, written about the same time:

> It isn't quite accurate to say, I think, that the thing is a generalization from a single case. If the idea had occurred to me I could and would just as readily have written the thing, as it stands, without the Lynchehaun case or the Aran case. My story—*in its essence* ["essence" underlined four times] is probable given the psychic state of the locality. I used the cases afterwards to controvert critics who said it was *impossible*.

Extravaganza, of course, was not the right word. Dionysiac would have served him better, meaning by that word the serving of the irresponsible spirit of the natural man. Between extravaganzaic and Dionysiac there is a difference, but not a world of difference: if one adds sufficient champagne, so fizzing up the mixture, one thinks the Dionysiac becomes straightway extravaganza; and *The Playboy* is drenched in poteen, which is, of course, the champagne of the Western World. We therefore cannot hold that his admission that the play was extravaganza makes any great difference. His view not only of art, but of life, was naturalistic; he had no subtler philosophy; the daemon within us must be served, as even Martin Doul and Mary Doul, illiterates though they are, come to understand through the very teaching of life itself [in *The Well of the Saints*]. What have we in *The Playboy?* Christy Mahon haphazardly becoming conscious that by serving the daemon within him he has become 'master of all fights from now.' Except his *Riders to the Sea,* Synge's entire work is an apology for the daemonic in life. Not for a moment do we think he intended *The Playboy* as a satire on the people of the West. Rather is it his tribute to them, his thank offering that, among them, the daemonic had liberty to strike out, to caper on the sands, to tumble about, even outrageously. This was for him the real spirit of the place, its psychic state. But one had to search it out. "Yet it is only in the intonation of a few sentences or some old fragment of melody that I catch the real spirit of the island, for in general the men sit together and talk with endless iteration of the tides and fish, and of the price of kelp in Connemara." Those who rail against *The Playboy* take it as Synge's picture of life in the West, a satirical picture. Prosaic themselves they want the *endless iteration,* whereas what Synge offers them is really the flash in the eyes of a young fisherman singing a passionate Irish love-song in the Irish manner, which is to say, with an intense concentration on the matter sung and no thought at all of the vulgar exploitation either of his own voice or his own personality. Were Synge to deal with any other *stratum* of life, the life of his own Anglo-Irish circle for instance, or the life of Paris or London, he would equally have sought out the daemonic urge in the heart of it. He would have given us his dramatization of the psychic state of that place, as he had read it; than which no man can do more, we, of course, understanding that no two readings of a psyche can ever be the same. In England he could take no interest, holding that life had been too whitened there to be of use to the dramatist. We may imagine he would not have found himself fully contented with any family or tribe or city or nation in the world unless that community, few or many, had, without any qualification, created the daemon within them sole arbiter of their destinies. He went sorrowing through life because no such community was to be found. He thought the lack of sophistication among the people of the West, their open-air adventurous life, their instruction at the mouth of the winds, at the strong hands of the ocean, at the eyes of the stars, their living close to the earth—that all these circumstances had fattened in their midst the roots of the golden bough of life, and kept it evergreen and flourishing. In such places life was really lived, was natural. In cities and towns it was put upon by laws and regulations as well as a multiplicity of institutions: it was strangled by them, so de-energised as to be incapable of blossoming. His choice of Mayo was therefore so much flattery of Mayo: had it contained a whole population of Playboys he would have hailed it as a bit of heaven itself! His early detractors did not understand this. His wild phrases were held up to obloquy, as if he had intended them for considered pronouncements! In reality they were his equivalent for the flashing eyes of Connacht. Synge would distil the poetry of the place into something rich and rare; his detractors, however, looked for glossy photographs of the people with their Sunday clothes upon their backs.

Remembering that the Dionysiac is the spirited and not the spiritual, it is patent that he whose quest it is will come roughly up against the people's religious susceptibilities, for their religious susceptibilities are the very flower of their labouring to keep the daemonic in check. The quester would have them be what they have always been trying not to be. In his headlong pursuit, Synge became altogether irresponsible; the cheapest thing, the most regrettable thing in *The Playboy* is the quite unnecessary flinging about of holy names and religious allusions. We are not forgetting that the religious consciousness in the Irish people overflows into curious channels; that it is to be met with in the most unexpected associations; yet Synge not only overdoes his painting of this abun-

dance, but overdoes it clumsily and without either cause or effect. One regrets he did not himself take the advice old Mahon gave his son, the Playboy: 'Leave troubling the Almighty God.' Of this perhaps somewhat slapdash abundance in the people's religious consciousness he probably became aware when reading their Irish poetry, but in the poetry the challenging phrases usually seem nothing less than forced from the singers. And naturally we come on them in the serious rather than in the humorous lyrics. They have always a striking effect, which is exactly what they have not when Synge makes use of them.

It must be allowed that every artist is partial towards the daemonic. It is the principle that opposes the mechanical, the theoretic; it is the Greek mistrust of professionalism; it is in everyman the root of honest laughter; it is in everyman the mirror of nature, answering its moods; it is the fount of heroism, it is the very colour of life itself—as ineffable as is the spirit of music; wherefore, of course, artists as such, who never will rank themselves on the side of the cut and dried, are taken by it. Yet for all that, the greater artists have never shown anything but the deepest reverence for what Goethe used to call the earnest conduct of life, which, at its best when the daemon suffuses it with warmth, becomes mere chaos when the daemon overlords it with no regard to any of the other powers within us. By so much do the greater poets differ somehow from the little terrible fry of the Bohemian *cénacles,* fanatics for theories, whether they know it or not. Synge obviously fell short of the great artist. Occasionally in his essays we find honest testimony from him to the necessity for this earnest conduct of life, and Mr. Yeats tells us he insisted that an artist, as well as anybody else, should provide for his family. Apart, however, from *Riders to the Sea,* all his art is so much laudation of one especial attribute of life, the spirited, rather than of the totality of life itself, multiple spirit as it is. Obviously, for all that, it would be quite unjust to rank him with those of the artistic *cénacles*: he didn't like them;

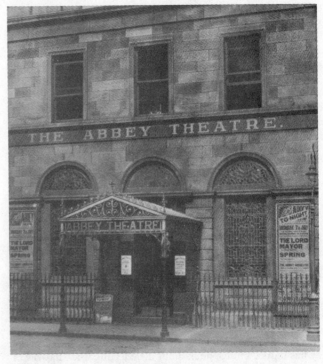

The old Abbey Theatre in Dublin.

he would have given a score of them for an Aran fisherman or a Wicklow tramp. His mind was more many-sided, therefore, than his art; he had not learnt how to master and shape forth all that he had received into it from life. But he was always ripening, which, of course, does not mean that each successive play was better than the last. Quite honestly, he expresses in *The Playboy* his idea of Connacht; yet one could show from his own essays that he knew and deeply felt other forces and other currents in the consciousness of the people. If he wrote *The Playboy,* he also wrote *Riders to the Sea*; and Shaw's flippant description of him as the Playboy himself is about as wrong as it could be. He was never a Playboy, not even while Christy Mahon was tumultuous in his brain. Molière was known as the Contemplative; and the name does not misfit John Synge by much.

Is there any reason, then, why we should take sides as between Synge and his scandalized audience? Both were honest, both consistent. If, playing the small boy, Synge did in places throw out a phrase to make them jump in their seats, they, probably knowingly and unjustly, decided to hiss at everything in the play since they had begun the rumpus at all. The critics who in cold blood, and with forensic attitudinizing, took sides seem to us to be far more erring than either Synge or his protesting audience. (pp. 183-89)

The Playboy is too fantastic, comes not easily enough within our common experience of life, to form part of the tradition of great comedy. Admitting that spirit is an unaccountable thing, miracle-working, that it dazzles with swift wings, drugs with unwonted perfumes, yet the falling of a whole countryside at the feet of a self-declared parricide simply on account of his gamey heart and his fine bit of talk, is an assumption to which we cannot give more than grudging acceptance. The readiness with which the people in the play swallow down what we cannot look at, antagonises us; and this antagonism is kept alive by constant reference to the supposed crime. From our difficulty in accepting the scheme of *The Playboy,* we may learn that the scarcely possible is not half so comfortable a basis for comedy as the almost probable; and the whole *Playboy* scheme is hardly even scarcely possible. We are all the time engaged in coercing our minds not to engage in argument against the proposition before us. Skipping this weakness we find much brain-work in the play. The point of it is the continuous upgrowth of Christy Mahon's character from nothingness to full manhood. And this 'upliftment' is due almost entirely to his meeting with Pegeen; she, however, we are to remember, is, like the others in the shebeen, drawn to him by the glamour that the great adventure of killing his father has thrown around him. Later on of course we learn from her own lips that it is not the deed itself that wins either her, or the others, it is Christy's telling of the tale, the fine bit of talk. As on a chart we can follow the Playboy's upgrowth. He was a quiet poor fellow with no man giving him heed, he tells us; only the dumb beasts in the fields were his friends (John Synge is remembering his own boyhood). To Pegeen he is only a soft lad; she treats him to bread and milk! To Widow Quin he appears as one fitter to be saying his catechism than slaying his da. To his father he was only a dirty stuttering lout, one who spent his days fooling over little birds he had, finches and felts; one who'd be off to hide in the sticks if he saw a red petticoat come swinging over the hill. In one place the Playboy remembers his own past, and Pegeen comforts him:

"What call have you to be that lonesome when

there's poor girls walking Mayo in their thousands now." "It's well you know," Christy answers grimly, "what call I have. It's well you know it's a lonesome thing to be passing small towns with the lights shining sideways when the night is down, or going in strange places with a dog noising before you and a dog noising behind, or drawn to the cities where you'd hear a voice kissing and talking deep love in every shadow of the ditch, and you passing on with an empty, hungry stomach failing from your heart."

Next to this passage, one of the most pleasing in the play, let us place his words when he knows he has won Pegeen's love:

Let you wait, to hear me talking, till we're astray in Erris, when Good Friday's by, drinking a sup from a well, and making mighty kisses with our wetted mouths, or gaming in a gap of sunshine, with yourself stretched back unto your necklace, in the flowers of the earth.

PEGEEN. (*in a low voice, moved by his tone*) I'd be nice so, is it?

CHRISTY. (*with rapture*) If the mitred bishops seen you that time they'd be the like of the holy prophets, I'm thinking, do be straining the bars of Paradise to lay eyes on the Lady Helen of Troy, and she abroad, pacing back and forward, with a nosegay in her golden shawl.

Always then we are looking at the Playboy striding forward, until, at the close, when his father would assert his authority over him, crying out: "Come on now." Christy answers:

Go with you, is it? I will then like a gallant captain with his heathen slave. Go on now and I'll see you from this day stewing my oatmeal and washing my spuds, for I'm master of all fights from now.

His astonished father can but gape, exclaiming: "Glory be to God!" Christy's upgrowth is the strong spine of meaning in the play, if we may use Mr. Galsworthy's phrase. In it, therefore, we have one more working out of the old theme that Dante knew of, that Goethe declared openly:

The indescribable, here it is done,
The woman soul leadeth us upwards and on.

—only, of course, the plane of the spiritual, in which the great ones were at home, has been exchanged for that of the spirited. Writing a comedy, as Synge was, some such difference was to be looked for, because comedy is, as Aristotle pointed out so long ago, the imitation of ignoble actions, an opinion that might be dwelt upon by those who write of *The Playboy* as if it should pass the same tests as a treatise on morals.

Christy Mahon himself is the only character that changes and grows; once it is seen for what it is, the graph of his progress is so direct as not to be interesting. Synge's sense of the psyche of place was always more subtle than his sense of the psyche of any man or woman, and of his men and women Christy Mahon is one of the simplest. One easily exhausts him. It is only when he triumphs, when he drives his stormy parent like a heathen slave before him, that he becomes fit material for great drama. For Christy Mahon lacks an abundant background within himself. He is poverty-stricken where Martin Doul is opulent. And Pegeen Mike, the only other character in the play who has a leading part, is, in background, even still more poverty-stricken. Indeed her background is to be found in theatre-land rather than in the Western World. She is the commonest thing in Synge, pert, bright-eyed, quick-witted, efficient in love-making as in bar-tending. She is the stock figure in amateur play-writing; and amateur actors revel in her type, because they know what to do with any such. Widow Quin is a thinner Mary Doul, she is a Mary Doul who speaks for effect. This feeling is all over *The Playboy.* From the Playboy himself downwards, every person is speaking for effect, an unwonted fault with Synge. Even Michael James does it, although his speech where he gives his blessing to the young pair who, one at either side, support him while he makes it, is indeed as rich as it has a right to be. So, too, one relishes old Mahon, with his pride in the atrociousness of the wound his son inflicted on him. His 'Glory be to God!' at the end of all is one of the best things in the play, far truer than Christy's carefully modulated cadences.

The two of these, old Mahon and Michael James, live, each of them, openly and unashamedly the life of the natural man. They care for nobody. They drink their fill and speak their fill, while the spirit we behold assuming sway over Christy makes of him 'a likely gaffer'—'master of all fights from now.' In the book *Wicklow and West Kerry,* Synge describes the simple people from beyond Dingle as revelling in the gaudiness of a traveling circus: a wet night did not prevent them from measuring out long miles of rough mountainy roadway to witness it. The bedizenment of the *Playboy,* the scorn of half-tones, the splashes of crude reds and yellows and apple greens, the efflorescences, the flaunting of such daemon as is either callously heroic or outrageously comic—it recalls somehow the travelling circus, posters and all. Poetry, Synge held, must become brutal again to find a way out. So too, he believed, must comedy.

It is the florid diction of the play that infects our mind somewhat as might the high colours of the circus-poster. Perhaps only those not gone far in the twenties take that diction to be quite successful. Except for the great difference in their characteristic themes, the associations that cling about them, Francis Thompson would perhaps strike us similarly; he, as well as Synge, depended on not so much the 'little more' as 'the wasteful and ridiculous excess' to lift us beyond the prosaic. Mr. T. S. Eliot quite correctly points out that "Elizabethanism was a verbal even more than an emotional debauch"; and Synge in *The Playboy* outdoes the Elizabethans. Those selfsame Elizabethans seem to have gradually replaced Racine, and indeed French drama in general, in his affections. His rhythms in *The Playboy* are more obtrusive, more rotund than in the earlier plays, as the incidents are more bustling—the whole aim is at excitement, tension, surprise. The excess of colour in his work we owe to his affection for the Elizabethans as we owe the daring, as also the homeliness, of his imagery to the Gaelic songs of Connacht, many of them truly folk songs. But both Elizabethans and Gaels had an instinct that told them that neither rapture nor intensity nor ecstasy ran to headlong verbalism. They knew when to rein in. They felt, and more especially the Gaelic poets felt, that the measure of intensity produced is in inverse ratio to the volume of the verbiage employed. In so far as you trick out your sentences with geegaw adjectives you diminish the effect the sentences produce: it is as if you were to wrap your hammer head about with webbing; let the webbing be as variegated as it may, the heart is taken out of the blow struck. Gaelic equivalents are to be found for many of Synge's most characteristic phrases, more especially for such of them as refer to religion, but the Irish phrases are always far swifter in their effect, far

more effective: the hammer head is bared, and strikes home hard and true.

> Mallacht Dé do'n té sin
> A bhain diom mo ghrádh.
>
> The curse of God on him
> Who snatched my love from me.

says the Gael, striking the nail on the head. Synge would have decorated both the curse and the beloved one, muffling the blow. There is in *The Playboy* a straining after terrible things, with not much more than a mush of colour and sweet sound resulting—a curious failure for one who would have the timber rather than the flower of poetry in his work. Adjectives, he should have known, always beat about the bush and give us time to set up defences. The Irish poets on the other hand show us no quarter, for it is not words that come hurtling against us, but the things for which the words stand—that is how it feels. With Synge, although taught of them, it is always words, words, words; and sometimes very feeble words. We do not recollect any Gaelic original for: "Aid me for to win her, and I'll be asking God to stretch a hand to you in the hour of death, and lead you short cuts through the Meadows of Ease, and up the floor of Heaven to the Footstool of the Virgin's Son." Yet, if original there be, one may be quite certain it produces an altogether different effect. Instead of the overwhelming intensity aimed at, the passage quoted has the whine of the beggar in it, whose aim it is not to make an end. One feels the tension of the mind slackening as the words flow on and on. It is like something one would find in Sean O'Casey at his worst, or is it his best? And there is hardly a page in *The Playboy* that is not stuffed with such long-winded figures, some of them, it is true, exhibiting the excess of his strength; most of them, however, exhibiting nothing more than a disturbing mannerism. Now, mannerisms, as soon as we know them for such, have an uncanny power of instantly chilling the mind; and all Synge's own interest in his puppets, his liking for them, his own innate warmth of feeling, is scarcely powerful enough to sweep us alive through those ever recurring tricks of phrase and cadence. Even while reading these word-spinnings, one suspects their efficacy as an element of dramatic technique; in the theatre itself one cannot help wondering at their ineptitude. They become thus a double distraction. Whetting our appetites, they aim at the ultimate, and achieve nothing more than the moderate, losing half their breath in calling attention to themselves.

This desire of his to go 'beyond the beyonds' accounts for his frequent introduction of phrases with religious allusions in them: if we are to challenge anyone let us challenge God himself! Still less does this obvious phrase-making of his achieve when he draws upon the religious consciousness of the people. That consciousness was, as we have before explained, terra incognita to him: he knew it only dimly, could realize it only superficially. And if we would finally satisfy ourselves as to the truth that intensity in literature is to be achieved only by getting rid of the sense of language, getting back to the thing itself, we have only to compare his refashioning of some Irish phrase or sentence with the original. Thus Synge has: "When you'll feel my two hands stretched around you, and I squeezing kisses on your puckered lips, till I'd feel a kind of pity for the Lord God is all ages sitting lonesome in His golden chair." The original we find in the lines of the well-known *Una Bhán:*

B'fhearr liomsa bheith ar leabaidh lei 'ga sior-phógadh
'Na 'mo shuidhe i bhflaitheas i g-cathaoir na Trinóide.

I'd rather be ever kissing her on a couch
Than to be sitting in heaven in the Chair of the Trinity.

This is not a good example to illustrate the difference between love poems in Irish and Synge's idea of them; nobody would think of quoting the lines to illustrate any trait in these songs; what strikes us about them in general is that whenever the nameless singers go beyond the beyonds they find themselves truly driven to it: their songs seem to have been no more made for a public than Beethoven's last quartets. Synge's phrases are literary; from that feeling we cannot escape; but how far from that feeling we are when we find 'Uch, Mac Muire na nGrás dom shaoradh' ('O, may the Son of Mary of the Graces save me!') in the well-known *Snowy-breasted Pearl* or when we come, in Liam Dall Ó h-Ifearnáin's perfect lyric: *Pé i nEirinn í* on

Cé sheolfadh Aon Mhac Dé im' líon
Ach stór mo chléibh?

Whom did the Only Son of God direct into my net
But my heart's treasure?

Synge's phrases, then, seem not alone watery to us who know the originals, but very often strike us as being also absurd. Every Catholic knows that no Connacht peasant, drunk or sober or utterly lost in ecstasy, could have used them, no more than drunk or sober or gone in our five wits, we could find ourselves asserting that two and two made five. Knowledge imbibed at our mother's knees is not to be put away from us so easily; yet to utter themselves as Synge's peasants sometimes do, such knowledge they must have forgotten; as we ourselves must forget it, if we would accept such a phrase as:—"Oh, St. Joseph and St. Patrick and St. Brigid and St. James have mercy on me now!" Such passages remind us that Synge's idea of the religious consciousness of the people was that of the outsider; for in that consciousness there is a vast chasm between the attributes of the Almighty and those of the saints. (pp. 192-99)

The Playboy of the Western World is a gaudy reckless spectacle; yet it was no small magic that raised it from the rather drab and meagre scheme of life of one of our poorest seaboards. In hidden places, and with the most crazy gear, the peasants there distil that potent spirit poteen which, Synge tells us, sends a shock of joy to the blood. No more, no less than that, did he ever wish this handful of living people to do for us. (p. 204)

> *Daniel Corkery, in his* Synge and Anglo-Irish Literature: A Study, *Cork University Press, 1931, 247 p.*

FRANK O'CONNOR (essay date 1939)

[*O'Connor was an Irish short-story writer and man of letters. His fiction is known for its realistic portrayal of small-town and city life in Ireland and its detached yet sympathetic humor regarding the human condition. Of his talents as a short-story writer William Butler Yeats once remarked, "O'Connor is doing for Ireland what Chekhov did for Russia." His critical commentary is distinguished by his insightful probing into the connections between society and individual talent as well as his attempt to analyze the creative process of the writer he is examining. In the following excerpt, O'Connor opposes Daniel Corkery's interpretation of* Playboy *(excerpted above), and praises the mythic quality of the play.*]

Since the plays of John Synge were first produced in our Theatre we have seen a revolution. In those days Synge was the wicked man, the foreigner, the atheist, the traducer of the Irish people. Now, thanks to the work of Professor Corkery, *Synge and Anglo-Irish Literature,* he has been accepted as almost an Irish writer. If he did traduce the Irish people it was unconsciously. As a Protestant, he couldn't know better! (p. 31)

Corkery dislikes ***The Playboy of the Western World*** and goes to great pains to explain and justify the riots it caused. Again it is Synge's inability to understand the deepest spiritual emotions of the Irish countryman. Shauneen Keogh's cry, "O St. Joseph and St. Patrick and St. Brigid and St. James, have mercy on me now!" shows, he tells us, that Synge's idea of the religious consciousness of the people was that of an outsider; "for in that consciousness there is a vast chasm between the attributes of the Almighty and those of the saints". From which one gathers that the author of the great lament for Patrick Sarsfield was a Protestant, since he distinctly says, "*Mo ghuidhe-se fein is guidhe Mic Mhuire leat!*—My own prayer too and the prayer of Mary's son."

But Professor Corkery seems to have come skew-ways at ***The Playboy,*** for doesn't he assume that the theme is that of Beatrice and Dante:

> The indescribable, here it is done,
> The ever-womanly leads us on,

as he quotes from *Faust?* As there seems to be some doubt about the matter, it is as well to point out that the theme of ***The Playboy*** is—as we would expect—far simpler. It is almost mythological; we develop, Synge says, in imaginations of ourselves; "Praise youth and it will prosper", the Irish proverb puts it; and so he shows us Christy Mahon, a half-idiot kept down by a tyrannical father, and who, as even half-idiots will, strikes out one day, and then flies in horror, under the impression that he is a parricide. He flies to a primitive community in the west, where outlaws are still admired, as they are in every primitive community. At the first touch of their respect Christy begins to respond; we see him becoming first loquacious, then a little vainglorious at the monstrousness of his own deed; yet not so much but that a knock at the door will send him scurrying for protection. We see that, after all, the "dirty stuttering lout" needs only a little affection and praise to turn into a likely lad. When Pegeen and the widow dispute for his affections he grows by leaps and bounds, and the curtain falls on the first act while he is murmuring, "Wasn't I a foolish fellow not to kill my father in the years gone by?"

Conscious roguery, says Professor Corkery, who seems to go wrong whenever he mentions ***The Playboy.*** An actor who spoke the curtain line with anything but earnestness and simplicity wouldn't know his job. At any rate, Professor Corkery denounces the whole thing. The theme, he says, is "hardly even possible . . . the falling of a whole countryside at the feet of a self-declared parricide . . . is an assumption to which we cannot give more than grudging acceptance". Not perhaps unless we have a deep sense of folk-life and approach it without that middle-class censoriousness which Synge abominated. Imagine trying to sing "Jesse James" with "the word 'conscience', the question of right and wrong, looming up before one's mind".

> Jesse James was a lad that killed many a man,
> He robbed the Danville train,

But a dirty little coward shot Mr. Howard
And laid Jesse James in his grave.

"The impulse to protect the criminal", Synge says in *The Aran Islands,* "is universal in the west. It seems partly due to the association between justice and the hated English jurisdiction, but more directly to the primitive feeling of these people, who are never criminals yet always capable of crime, that a man will not do wrong unless he is under the influence of a passion which is as irresponsible as a storm of the sea. If a man has killed his father and is already sick and broken with remorse, they can see no reason why he should be dragged away and killed by the law."

Professor Corkery is right when he says the second act is weak. It is, shockingly weak, but not for the reason he suggests. The fact is that when Corkery criticises the handling of Pegeen he is following Synge up the blind alley of the play. Pegeen is not a major character at all; she has not been acted upon by the dramatic machinery, and when she usurps the principal scenes in rivalry with the Widow Quin, she introduces an atmosphere of French farce which is always in conflict with folklore. Because the two characters essential to the myth are of course Christy and his father, and from the moment we become aware of the myth we know that inevitably old Mahon is still alive and are impatient for the necessary scene when the two characters who have been directly acted on by the dramatic machinery will resume their tussle on the new terms. There lies the real weakness of the second act. Nothing in it prepares us for the entrance of old Mahon, and the scenes with the young girls, with Pegeen, with Shauneen Keogh and the Widow Quin, which show us what Corkery calls "the ascending graph" of Christy's development, are perilously close to being quite irrelevant. How different to the first act, where at every instant we are made aware of old Mahon, his family, and his home! "And before I'd pass the dunghill, I'd hear himself snoring out—a loud lonesome snore he'd be making all times the while he was sleeping, and he a man would be raging all times the while he was waking, like a gaudy officer you'd hear cursing, and damning and swearing oaths." "Providence and mercy spare us all!" sighs Pegeen ecstatically, as well she might, and Christy continues, "It's that you'd say surely if you seen him, and he after drinking for weeks, rising up in the red dawn or before it maybe, and going out into the yard as naked as an ash tree in the moon of May, and shying clods against the visage of the stars till he'd put the fear of death into the banbhs and the screeching sows."

It is old Mahon's spiritual presence which keeps the whole first act so taut, and from the rise of the curtain on the second, we should be made ready for his entrance, should see that bandaged, raging man crawling up through Ireland, drawing ever nearer—perhaps it is he, surely it is; here he comes. It is the same prentice hand which, as in *The Well of the Saints,* invokes drastic dramatic machinery and then fails to exploit it.

And yet in spite of its faults, *The Playboy* is a play to which one gives one's heart. It is spontaneous, brilliant, full of joy; the myth when it transcends the clumsy intrigue has the power which only myths have of moving us profoundly. (pp. 44-9)

> Frank O'Connor, "Synge," in The Irish Theatre, edited by Lennox Robinson, Macmillan & Co. Ltd, 1939, pp. 29-52.

PATRICIA MEYER SPACKS (essay date 1961)

[*An American essayist, biographer, and educator, Spacks has written extensively on eighteenth-century poetry. In the following essay, she explores the significance of folklore and myth in* Playboy.]

Yeats said of *The Playboy of the Western World* that the inability of the original audiences to understand it represented the only serious failure of the Abbey Theatre movement [see Further Reading]. The most recent significant appearance of *The Playboy* took place off-Broadway in 1958, and its reviewers, though generally kind, revealed, like those of the past, some confusion as to the essential import of the play. Indeed, *The Playboy* seems a work destined to be forever misinterpreted. At the start of its career in 1907 it caused riots because of its alleged immorality; since then it has produced mainly perplexity. Seeing a realistic production of *The Playboy,* one is made acutely conscious of the problem which Synge himself raised during the first tumultuous week of the original Dublin performance, when he insisted he'd written "an extravaganza"—only to add later that the source of the play lay in his understanding of Irish psyche and Irish speech as they actually existed, thus claiming for the work an ultimate realism.

The dilemma of whether *The Playboy* is essentially realistic or fantastic is the one on which producers and critics have foundered ever since. Viewed as realistic drama, the play immediately begins to seem implausible. That a man should become to strangers a hero by virtue of a tale of patricide, and become in the end genuinely masterful for no readily apparent reason—the psychology of the real world is little help in interpreting these events. On the other hand, if one considers the play as fantasy, it begins to seem strangely random and undeniably hampered by its realistic elements. *The Playboy* has usually been admired for its quaintness, its poetry, or its comic force, and, though a popular anthology piece and reasonably often revived, has been universally underrated as a coherent work of art. I do not plan a full reading of it here, but wish to trace a source of the play's power which has never been insisted upon by critics or producers.

One aspect of *The Playboy* that seems disturbing is the curious tone with which it treats the theme of patricide. To be sure, the second time Christy strikes his father the spectators on stage feel that he should be hanged for his deed. But they are in no way horrified by it: they believe Christy to be potentially dangerous to them and they fear legal involvement in his crime; self-preservation motivates them. Nor, for that matter, does the revived father appear to think that there is anything extraordinary about a son who has twice tried to kill him. He resents the attempts in a personal way—as well he might—but he does not find them unnatural. The emotional weight of *The Playboy of the Western World* is on patricide as a noble deed, not as an abhorrent one.

Oedipus kills his father, and the crime brings a plague on his city. Orestes kills his mother and is pursued by furies. Patricide and matricide were for sophisticated Greeks the most dreadful of sins; Freud has brought modern readers to consciousness of the roots of the horror which the Greeks felt, and which twentieth-century audiences of Greek tragedy continue to feel. Yet Synge somehow manages to treat so dreadful a theme with apparent lightness. For parallels to this sort of treatment, one must go to the folk tale. The pages of Grimm are full of violence: giants who eat their victims, blood and bones; enchanters who turn the unwary to stone;

kings who demand the impossible and cut off the heads of those who fail to achieve it. Irish folk tales, of course, deal with the same sort of material; their heroes wade through blood to prove themselves. To be sure, this violence has a somewhat factitious quality: one is always aware that those who are turned to stone will become flesh and blood again at the end; that the frog, once its head is cut off, will turn into a prince; that however many anonymous warriors are slaughtered along the way, the true hero will accomplish the impossible and not be slaughtered himself.

In *The Playboy,* too, extreme violence is in a sense unreal. Both "murders" take place off stage. Moreover, neither of them really takes place at all: twice the father, in effect, rises from the dead, as people rise from the dead in fairy tales. Yet the symbolic violence, as in a fairy tale, shapes and defines the story: without his attempts to murder his father, one cannot imagine Christy becoming a man. One finds the same sort of pattern in many folk tales. In "The Battle of the Birds," an Irish fairy tale for which parallels exist "throughout the Indo-European world," the king's son has to undergo a series of tests before he can win Auburn Mary as a bride. Last of all, he must obtain five eggs from the top of a 500-foot tree. To get the eggs, Mary tells him, he must kill her, strip the flesh from her bones, take the bones apart, and use them as steps for climbing the tree. The prince is reluctant, but the girl insists; after the task is completed, she is rejuvenated from scattered bones and becomes his wife. The murder of the girl, then, is totally unreal, yet it is absolutely essential for the hero's winning of her.

The necessity for violence in the process of testing and maturing is, of course, frequently emphasized in folk tales: it is for precisely this reason that some modern censors have doubted the suitability of such tales for children's reading. The hero must cut off, on three successive days, the three heads of the "Laidly Beast"; or he must fight first a giant with one head, then a giant with two heads, then a giant with three heads. We feel that such obstacles are important mainly as tests, hindrances of increasing complexity and difficulty which must be overcome on the road to maturity. Ritual bloodshed is both necessary and significant: blood must be shed before the child becomes a man, before the non-entity becomes a hero. And the strange attitude toward father-murder in *The Playboy* is explainable in exactly the same way. The frivolity with which the first murder is treated is justifiable on the ground that it never in actuality takes place: it is more obviously unreal than a fantasy of murdered giants. But more importantly, the attitude of the playwright toward the murder is justifiable because the murder itself is justifiable—and more than justifiable: even necessary. It is a ritual murder, a step in the process toward maturity.

Certainly there is no question that Christy grows before our very eyes in *The Playboy.* The frightened boy who comes on stage in the first act, looking nervously about him, asking if the police are likely to come, miserably gnawing a turnip before the fire, is quite different from the Christy who departs in the last act. He leaves the stage with these words: "Ten thousand blessings upon all that's here, for you've turned me a likely gaffer in the end of all, the way I'll go romancing through a romping lifetime from this hour to the dawning of the judgment day." He recognizes the change in himself, and blesses the tavern company for having brought it about. But the responsibility is his, not theirs, and the transformation

has been accomplished through the successive murders of his father.

Characteristically in the folk tale, actions, tests, come in groups of three. The prince in "The Battle of the Birds" undergoes three tests; Conn-Eda, whose story is retold by Yeats, has to procure three magic objects; the young gardener in "The Greek Princess and the Young Gardener" has to obtain not only the golden bird he first set out for, but also the King of Morocco's bay filly and the daughter of the King of Greece. In this play, too, there are three tests, three ritual murders, not merely two, and the development of Christy's character takes place through them. The Christy with whom the play begins is described by his father, in the boy's absence, as "a dirty, stuttering lout." Christy is, old Mahon continues, "a liar on walls, a talker of folly, a man you'd see stretched the half of the day in the brown ferns with his belly to the sun." He is lazy, frightened of girls, "a poor fellow would get drunk on the smell of a pint," with a "queer rotten stomach." He is the laughingstock of all women; the girls stop their weeding when he comes down the road and call him "the looney of Mahon's."

There is something familiar about this characterization: we have here the foolish son of so many fairy tales, the male equivalent of Cinderella. Sons, in folk tales, also usually appear in threes. Two of them are reputed to be clever and brave, but they fail when they undertake the crucial quest. The youngest son is scorned by all, thought unworthy even to attempt the quest, considered foolish and stupid and cowardly, the one least likely to succeed. "A poor woman had three sons. The eldest and second eldest were cunning clever fellows, but they called the youngest Jack the Fool, because they thought he was no better than a simpleton." Given a fairy story that starts this way, one can easily predict its ending: Jack the Fool will ultimately triumph, achieving what his elders have been unable to accomplish. And the same prediction can be made about Christy.

We are told that he has brothers and sisters, and that they have not been able to free themselves from their father, even after escaping from home and leaving Christy alone with old Mahon. "He'd sons and daughters walking all great states and territories of the world," Christy says, "and not a one of them, to this day, but would say their seven curses on him, and they rousing up to let a cough or sneeze, maybe, in the deadness of the night." They are not truly free, not free as Christy in the end is free: in the nights they wake to curse their father. It remains for Christy, the foolish son, to subdue the father once and for all.

The first "murder" is nearly an accident, and its maturing effects are stumbled upon by accident. Christy strikes his father almost in self-defense, after an argument over whether he is to marry the rich old widow his father wants for him. He tells his story in the tavern largely because his pride is touched by the suggestion that he is wanted by the police for commonplace reasons. His true realization of what the murder means grows only gradually, fostered by the reactions of those to whom he tells his story. Soon, as a result of it, he comes to think of himself as, in effect, a poet: the equation between poetry and violence remains constant throughout the play. "I've heard all times it's the poets are your like," Pegeen says, "fine fiery fellows with great rages when their temper's roused." The image appeals to Christy, and becomes his picture of himself. To himself, to the rest of the world, he had hitherto seemed, in his own words, "a quiet, simple poor fellow with no man giving me heed." But now, to himself and to the rest of the world, he is a "fine fiery fellow"—a poet and a hero. Christy has apparently achieved freedom and power with the greatest ease: he remarks to himself that he was a fool not to have killed his father long before. His new assurance carries him to triumph in the games even though his father has actually appeared before then: he relies on the Widow Quin to protect him, and assumes that people's belief in him as a father-murderer is as good as the reality.

But when Christy and his father are brought into conjunction, in the third act, it becomes immediately clear that manhood is not so easily won. The old man starts beating his son, and the passive Christy is reviled and ridiculed by all. His grandiose self-image is destroyed: he defends himself finally not on the basis of his achievement, but because he has never hurt anyone, except for his single blow. But the man of no violence, as Christy is soon brought to see, is no poet and no hero; he is the eternal victim, the scapegoat. Understanding for the first time what failure means, he can no longer accept it willingly. His rejection by the company makes Christy see that his earlier success has been an illusion, based, as he says, on "the power of a lie," and that he has substituted for loneliness the company of fools. Yet the effects of the first "murder" make the second one possible: Christy bolsters himself with the memory of his physical and rhetorical triumphs and, so strengthened, dashes out to kill his father again.

W. H. Auden [in "The Wish Game," *The New Yorker,* March 16, 1957] has suggested that one of the distinguishing characteristics of the fairy tale is its stress on the power of the wish: the wish is the main cause of fairy tale events. "The cause of all wishes is the same," he writes—"that which is should not be. . . . When a scolded child says to a parent, 'I wish you were dead,' he does not mean what he actually says; he only means 'I wish I were not what I am, a child being scolded by you.' " Christy's attempts to murder his father are fairy-tale-like enactments of such a wish: not so much that the old man should be dead as that he, Christy, should no longer be in a position to be humiliated by his father—and, by extension, humiliated by the rest of the world. But the second "murder" is different from the first. The first is a spontaneous reaction to humiliation; the second is a calculated and aware reaction. The wish has turned to will: Christy has perceived—or thinks he has perceived—that actual violence is necessary for social acceptance. And violence, after all, is still a simple matter. He has but to strike his father once again, and the impossible will be accomplished: Pegeen will be properly won, and Christy will be at last truly free.

The blow is struck, and Christy expects his reward, as the fairy tale hero after each trial is likely to think that trial the last. The Widow Quin warns him that he will be hanged, but he indignantly rejects the suggestion. "I'm thinking," he says, "from this out, Pegeen'll be giving me praises the same as in the hours gone by." And, a bit later: "I'm thinking of my luck to-day, for she will wed me surely, and I a proven hero in the end of all." But it is Pegeen herself who drops the rope over his head, Pegeen who calls his act "a dirty deed," Pegeen who burns his leg as he lies bound on the floor. For Pegeen and the others this "killing" has none of the symbolic richness of the "gallous story" Christy told of his first murder, the story which seemed to identify him as a man of great stature and great passions. The storyteller as hero is another familiar figure in Irish folk lore. In "Conal Yellowclaw," the hero wins freedom for his three doomed sons by telling three stories;

"The Story-Teller at Fault" constructs an elaborate fiction around the dilemma of a storyteller with no tale to tell. And Christy as man in action seems less heroic than Christy as storyteller. The second attack on his father has been too transparently motivated by the desire for approval; it is in no way heroic. Christy's mistake, however, is rectified as a result of the attack on him it causes. The first "murder" made the second one possible, in typical fairy tale fashion, and so does the second bring about the third. For as a result of being totally rejected by those who have previously praised him, Christy discovers for the first time that he doesn't *need* these fools.

The third "murder" takes place before our eyes, and is entirely verbal and symbolic in its enactment: Christy discovers he can give his father orders, shove him out the door, tell him that their relation now is to be that of "a gallant captain with his heathen slave." Having achieved, as a result of experience, genuine self-confidence, he can manage a real triumph, without violence, and one not based on a lie or motivated by desire for approval. Christy has yearned to escape the domination of his father and others; he fulfills his wish at last in appropriate terms, freeing himself not by physical murder, but by asserting his own power to dominate. The stupid son has become a hero, has inherited the kingdom and claimed his rights as ruler. If, contrary to the convention of the fairy tale, he does not win the princess, it is only because she is not worthy of him: he could have her now that he scorns her. It is Pegeen, indeed, who underscores his triumph, breaking into lamentations for her loss of one who, she realizes at last, is after all "the only Playboy of the Western World."

The word "playboy" is defined, in effect, by the action of the drama; it comes finally to mean the hero in the sense of a man who can "play" successfully with language, triumph in the "play" of athletic contests, excel in the "play" of flirtation and courtship. As he leaves the stage for the last time, Christy has become a playboy indeed, the man and the pose finally identical. And here the word "playboy" is used of him for the first time without ironic overtones. It has previously been employed to stress the disparity between Christy's pose and the actuality. The word is first spoken by Widow Quin, laughing at Christy, who has been huddled in terror behind the door while she talks with his father. She observes, "Well, you're the walking Playboy of the Western World, and that's the poor man you had divided to his breeches belt." The Widow Quin uses the word a second time in the context of Christy's victory in the games, still with the irony of her superior awareness. She tells old Mahon that the people are cheering "the champion Playboy of the Western World," and the old man is thereby led to think that this could not possibly be his worthless son. The fact that Christy's father is still alive is revealed to the crowd, and they jeer at the lad by calling out, "There's the playboy!" And when, in the curtain speech, Pegeen wails, "Oh my grief, I've lost him surely. I've lost the only Playboy of the Western World," the import of the phrase depends upon our knowledge of its previous ironic uses. Now at last it is spoken without irony, and now at last it *can* be applied without irony: Christy has won the right to the title.

Pegeen's final lamentations are preceded by her final rejection—with a box on the ear—of Shawn, her official suitor. Shawn, the true fool of the play, points up by contrast all the way through not only the superior richness of Christy's character, but the importance to that character of the father-murders. Father-destruction is, after all, an archetypal theme, and the primitive *necessity* of father-murder is stressed in *The Playboy* by the character of Shawn, who is totally unable to free himself from authority. He pleads for himself, in the second act, that he doesn't *have* a father to kill. But Shawn is clearly—and ridiculously—dominated by a father-figure, the priest, Father Reilly. When other characters in the play refer to Shawn, it is almost always in conjunction with Father Reilly; the lad is notoriously under the thumb of the priest, whose authority he is always citing, and of whom he is admittedly afraid. The priest is his excuse for lack of courage and imagination, for unwillingness to do the unexpected. None of his neighbors respect him; his subjection is too complete. Pegeen's father admits that he'd rather have Christy's children for grandsons than Shawn's, who would be only "puny weeds." The man who is dominated is a weakling; he must assert his individuality—must metaphorically kill his father—before he is to be respected. Both positively and negatively, then, the point is stressed. The idea of father-murder is the thematic center of the play, a center with precisely the sort of mythic overtones that are so often found in folk tales.

The ritual power of the "murders" in the play is reinforced by the ritual power of the language. Susanne Langer has suggested the essential similarity between the symbolism of metaphor and the symbolism of ritual; a sense of this intimate relation between language and ritual dominates *The Playboy of the Western World.* If it can be said that Christy is created as a man by his successive "murders" of his father, it can be said with equal truth that he is created by the force of language. The murder of his father represents, from the beginning, a sort of metaphor of achievement; Christy's verbal metaphors also define a pattern of achievement. Symbols are brought to life in this play in a rather special way. It has been commonplace, at least since Freud, that for primitive people the relation between word and thing is close, that the magic of spells depends upon the notion of this close tie. In *The Playboy* language seems to have power in the real world, as spells have power—as language in the folk tale has power. As Christy develops self-command, he develops also command of language; his increasingly poetic speech reflects his increasingly imaginative perception, and with the final subduing of his father comes a final control of language. Yet in another sense it might be said not that Christy comes to control language, but that language comes to control him.

The idea of himself as a poet, suggested by Pegeen, comes to have great importance for Christy; it is for him and the others inextricably connected with the idea of the hero. When the young man makes his first appearance, his speech has the strong folk rhythm of all the characters and some flashes of imagination, but he is essentially prosaic. Deciding to stay, he says, "It's a nice room, and if it's not humbugging me you are, I'm thinking that I'll surely stay." His reaction, in short, is that of the practical man—or the man trying to be practical. Left alone with Pegeen, after the suggestion that he is a poet has been made, he describes his father "going out into the yard as naked as an ash tree in the moon of May, and shying clods against the visage of the stars till he'd put the fear of death into the banbhs and the screeching sows." The father flings clods at the stars and gets a response from pigs; the disproportion between stimulus and response suggested marks the situation of Christy himself, a dreamer by inclination whose life has hitherto been bounded by the most mundane details. Stars and moon are the typical material of his expanding metaphors. Pegeen, annoyed with him, seems to drive him away; as he goes to the door, he describes himself

as "lonesome, I'm thinking, as the moon of dawn," and Pegeen is won to call him back. His metaphors grow more extravagant as his confidence develops. He speaks of Pegeen as having "the star of knowledge shining from her brow," and connects her repeatedly, in his references to her, with "the heavens above." In the wooing scene, he appeals to her with elaborate images of love-making beneath the moon and stars, and insists on the superiority of Pegeen to anything offered by the Christian heaven: he talks of "squeezing kisses on your puckered lips, till I'd feel a kind of pity for the Lord God in all ages sitting lonesome in his golden chair." Finally, at the height of Christy's first illusory triumph, Pegeen's father reports Father Reilly as saying that the dispensation has come in the nick of time, so he'll wed Pegeen and Shawn in a hurry, "dreading that young gaffer who'd capsize the stars." There has been no evidence that Father Reilly is an imaginative man; indeed, he seems to stand for all that is opposed to imagination. When he makes this comment about Christy, we feel as though the youth's most extreme metaphors have become fact, have formed the facts: as though it were indeed conceivable that Christy should overturn the stars, unlike his father, whose attempts at the stars only arouse the farm animals. Similarly, in a slightly earlier scene, old Mahon, not recognizing his son, comments, "Look at the mule he has, kicking the stars." Christy has somehow been created a true giant—and created partly by the power of his metaphors.

The same pattern of development from prose to extravagant poetry is repeated in miniature in the brief scene between Christy's humiliation by his father and his second murder attempt. It is repeated again, with a difference, between the second "murder" and the third. Once more, Christy's language develops in power as the lad develops in self-realization, but this time the self-realization is successful, and the language has an entirely new quality. No longer dependent on the opinion of others, Christy gains a new freedom; his speech, too, gains new freedom, a quality of pure joy different from anything it has had before. He talks of hell now as he had talked of heaven, but without the sense of unreality that clings to his earlier metaphors. The fusion of joy and reality that Synge spoke of as one of his goals in the play is complete at the very end. Christy leaves us with his vision of "a romping lifetime," couched in romping language.

So *The Playboy of the Western World* presents essentially the vision of a man constructing himself before our eyes. Not only does Christy construct himself: he creates his princess. Pegeen is, after all, a matter-of-fact girl with a hot temper. But she is not that sort of girl after a conversation with Christy. As Christy's images grow more and more compelling, Pegeen becomes more and more gentle and eloquent herself. She, too, seems to be changing before our eyes. Finally she comments on the phenomenon: "And to think it's me is talking sweetly, Christy Mahon, and I the fright of seven townlands for my biting tongue. Well, the heart's a wonder." But it seems to be the sheer power of language that has won Pegeen, and she apparently recognizes the fact herself when she says she'd not wed Shawn, "and he a middling kind of a scarecrow, with no savagery or fine words at all."

The importance of the idea of Christy as a constructed man is stressed by the fact that it is the main source of the play's humor as well as of its serious import. The comedy of *The Playboy* depends heavily on the ironic conjunctions between the felt ritual importance of the Playboy's role and the evidence of his incompetence or pettiness in the real world. The girls come to do him homage, bearing gifts, deducing from his boots that he is one who has traveled the world; they find him indulging in petty vanity with the looking glass. Christy describes himself as "a gallant orphan cleft his father with one blow to the breeches belt"; immediately afterwards he staggers back in terror at the sight of his living father. The young man is enjoying his triumph; his father comes in and starts beating him. Over and over the device is employed, to insist on Christy's efforts to make appearance and reality coincide, the name of hero correspond to the actuality. And as the central action of the ritual "murders" is reflected by the patterns of Christy's language, so the ironic conjunctions of the action are symbolized by such verbal patterns as the one we have noted around the word "playboy."

The sense of the fairy tale which one is likely to get from **The Playboy** does after all, then, provide clues for a reading of the play which solves the problem of the relation between realism and fantasy in it, and also suggests the sources of its strange power. The themes, the language, the import of the play resemble those of folk tale and myth; its "serious" aspects and its comic ones alike, it seems, may be largely accounted for by this relation. (pp. 314-23)

> Patricia Meyer Spacks, "The Making of 'The Playboy'," in Modern Drama, *Vol. 4, No. 3, December, 1961, pp. 314-23.*

T. R. HENN (essay date 1963)

[*Henn was an Irish-born English educator and critic who wrote numerous studies of Anglo-Irish literature and edited* The Plays and Poems of J. M. Synge. *In the following excerpt from his introduction to* Playboy, *Henn examines irony and ambivalence in the drama.*]

The Playboy does not lend itself readily to classification; as we revolve it in our hands many facets take light and fire. In one mood we may suggest that it is sheer extravagant comedy, with elements of strong farce in the "resurrection" of Christy Mahon's father, and in the deflation of the boastful man, the revelation of a massive and mock-heroic lie. As such, it embodies the classic elements of reversal and recognition. Yet it is comedy that might have ended (for we are prepared from the first for a possible wedding) with Pegeen winning her Playboy and Old Mahon marrying the Widow Quin; comedy which at the end is edged, skilfully and unexpectedly, into a semi-tragedy. From another point of view we may call it "free" comedy, in which moral issues are reversed, transcended or ignored in the desire for "energy", though this view will be only part of the truth. It is helpful to quote Yeats:

> In a country like Ireland, where personifications have taken the place of life, men have more hate than love, for the unhuman is nearly the same as the inhuman, but literature, which is a part of that charity that is the forgiveness of sins, will make us understand men however little they conform to our expectations. We will be more interested in heroic men than in heroic actions, and will have a little distrust for everything that can be called good or bad in itself with a very confident heart. [*Explorations, 1962*]

Again we may see **The Playboy** (carrying Yeats' thought a stage further) as a Dionysiac comedy, in which the instincts are, within Synge's conventions, given uninhibited play; this in keeping with his demand for what is "superb and wild in reality". So the Playboy himself becomes a country Don Juan, rejoicing in his new-found power to excite the admiration of women, and the very growth of the language, "richly flavoured as a nut or an apple", reflects his desire for "an imagination that is fiery and magnificent and tender".

We turn the play on its axis, and satire seems to predominate. It is a satire (but with more than a hint of approval) on the proverbial willingness of the West to give shelter to the malefactor and murderer, which goes back to the Elizabethan wars of conquest, the shipwrecked sailors of the Armada, and beyond. Then the Playboy may become a comic Oedipus, "the man who killed his da"; the mutual descriptions of each other by father and son give some point to the classic situation. There is satire in the pursuit of man by woman, the comic reversal of the conventional view; we may remember how Shakespeare and Shaw turned that theme to account, and the additional flavour lent to it by the romantically fostered idea of modest Irish womanhood. Indeed, we may carry the idea of the mock-heroic still further, and see in Christy Mahon an Odysseus, the wanderer cast up and seeking refuge; his triumph in the sports on the sea-shore a parody of the Greek games. We might then have a tragi-comic piece with the Widow Quin as Nausicaa, a chorus of girls, the village pub for a palace. But again we may see it, if we will, as tragedy. The Playboy finds his soul through a lie, the "gallous story" of his parricide. Under the stimulus of heady admiration from men and women he grows in stature and in poetry. Detail is elaborated, the fatal blow struck by the potato-spade (we may note the irony) becomes more final, more heroic. He is indeed of the company of poets, "fine fiery fellows with great rages when their temper's roused". Under the shock of his father's reappearance (and the old man's account of his son's character has prepared the audience for this) he staggers, weakens and is finally reconciled; though with a new certainty of himself. He is "master of all fights from now". His father accepts the situation: "Glory be to God!" (*with a broad smile*) "I am crazy again." The final "turn" reminds us of the end of [**The Shadow of the Glen**]: "By the will of God, we'll have peace now for our drinks." But it is Pegeen who is the heroine-victim. She has found her man, made him, won him in the teeth of opposition from her own sex. The marriage has been approved, in a superb drunken half-parody of the traditional blessing, by her father. From that marriage would come, because of Christy's heroic and virile virtues which have grown, mushroom-like, out of the tale of parricide, a band of "little gallant swearers by the name of God". At the end Pegeen's loss is absolute, beyond comfort, for she has lost her illusion of greatness in her man, and his body too; the complacent Shawn has seen the obstacle to his marriage removed.

> Oh my grief, I've lost him surely. I've lost the only Playboy of the Western World.

Synge intended that the play should run its course between antinomies. It is, for all its apparent simplicity of plot, a delicately balanced system of ironies, ambivalences, both of words and situation. We may quote his letter to the press after the storm of abuse which its production aroused:

> **The Playboy** is not a play with a "purpose" in the modern sense of the word,

(he is thinking perhaps of Shaw, Brieux, and the then current misrepresentations of Ibsen as a didactic dramatist)

> —but, although parts of it are or are meant to be

extravagant comedy, still a great deal that is in it and a great deal more that is behind it is perfectly serious when looked at in a certain light. This is often the case, I think, with comedy, and no one is quite sure today whether Shylock or Alceste should be played seriously or not. There are, it may be hinted, several sides to *The Playboy.*

We may examine first the direct consequences of these "several sides" of the play. Synge's conflict with outraged Irish morality had begun as early as 1903, when the portrait of Nora in *The Shadow* was felt to be a slur on Irish womanhood. But the week that followed the first production of *The Playboy* on 26 January 1907 was a continuous riot, with a hysteria that recalls the first production of Victor Hugo's *Hernani* (with its violation of the formal Alexandrine) or the reception of Ibsen's *Ghosts* in London. We may quote from Lady Gregory:

> There was a battle of a week. Every night protestors with their trumpets came and raised a din. Every night the police carried some of them off to the police courts. Every afternoon the paper gave reports of the trial before a magistrate who had not heard or read the play and who insisted on being given details of its incidents by the accused and by the police . . . There was a very large audience on the first night . . . Synge was there, but Mr Yeats was giving a lecture in Scotland. The first act got its applause, and the second, though one felt that the audience were a little puzzled, a little shocked at the wild language. Near the end of the third act there was some hissing. We had sent a telegram to Mr Yeats after the end of the first act "Play great success"; but at the end we sent another—"Audience broke up in disorder at the word shift". [*Our Irish Theatre;* see Further Reading]

We may attempt first to set out the main causes of offence, however innocent they may appear to a modern audience. As a background it is well to remember the image of Romantic Ireland, sedulously fostered in the 90's: the Land of Saints, the country whose Literary Renaissance would save European culture, Ireland was the home of the most ancient Christian tradition; her women were models of chastity and purity. Against this are to be set the "heroic" aspects of homicide, countless jests on the subject during the agrarian troubles, the Phoenix Park murders, the raw material of the play itself:

> An old man on the Aran Islands told me the very tale on which *The Playboy* is founded, beginning with the words: "If any gentleman has done a crime we'll hide him. There was a gentleman that killed his father, and I had him in my own house six months till he got away to America." [William Butler Yeats; see excerpt dated 1910]

As for the "wild language", Lady Gregory and the actors had indeed protested against its coarseness before the play was produced. But it was, at least overtly, an indelicacy rather than a blasphemy that triggered off the riot:

> . . . a drift of chosen females, standing in their shifts itself, maybe, from this place to the eastern world.

The rancour of the mob centres on the fatal *shift;* in an access of outraged modesty, Victorian in character, but connected somehow with the idea that the very word was insulting to the womanhood of Ireland, whose chastity and purity had become a national myth, even as the saintliness of the island as

a whole. It is probable that the audience, in their bewilderment at the more subtle ironies of the play, missed the full point of the phrase. The picture of Mayo maidens perceived in terms of a slave market, or a throng of Eastern houris, is made yet more fantastic in that the term *drift* is applied to a drove of heifers; and it is possible that they took the point of the *eastern* world (Leinster or Dublin) as opposed to the Western of Connemara or Mayo. (pp. 56-61)

It seems to me likely that the offensive word was no more than a catalyst for the general but indeterminate unease caused by a number of other factors in the play; and these factors in this are themselves complicated by Synge's technique of producing, deliberately, an ebb and flow in the audience's response to character and situation. The perception of ironies and ambivalences will, of course, vary with the type of audience, its age and its environment. It is worth noting, for example, that *The Playboy* was more popular in England, *The Shadow* in Ireland; and the Dublin audiences in 1907 might well have been particularly sensitive to anything provided by the "Anglo-Irish Ascendancy" group of writers. The more subtle, dispassionate and balanced the irony the less likely it is that the general pattern will be perceived, and the more probable that overt points of conventional distaste will be selected for attack. In *The Tinker's Wedding* Synge pleaded, unavailingly, for the recognition of a humour without malice. That of *The Playboy,* fantastic as it may be, was probably too close to observation to be taken lightly.

Synge's attitude to Ireland and to the Irish peasantry was highly ambivalent: insight combined with toleration, love without passion. We may think of broadly similar positions taken up by Swift, Shaw, Yeats. Love and understanding are not inseparable from a detached mockery. But the union of these may be so subtle, so fluctuating and yet so integral to the whole system of values in the play, that we may examine briefly some of the instances.

His irony is founded most often on incongruity, the perception of polar opposites; and within the broad rhythm of the play's construction, the manipulation of character so that it rises and falls, retreats and advances in the sympathy of the audience, to form its characteristic patterns. The irony may go unperceived, or be furiously rejected, when one of the poles from which the current passes is felt by the audience to be unacceptable; whether as involving religion, womanhood, King Lear's "nature", drunkenness, or aesthetic delicacy. (Curiously enough, the morbid, particularly of the churchyard, seems to go unchallenged; the accessories or instruments of death have a perennial attraction for a peasantry.)

It was a lady novelist of the early nineteenth century who noted the proclivity of the Irish for swearing, and on those somewhat tenuous grounds asserted the Grecian origin of the Milesians. "It is certain that the habit of confirming every assertion with an oath is as prevalent among the Irish as it was among the ancient, and is among the modern Greeks" [Sydney Owenson, *The Wild Irish Girl*]. In the Notes to these plays I have drawn attention to some instances of a pleasant and at best devotional practice in this respect. But rapid and violent verbal conjunction may give quite another aspect. Consider, for instance:

> . . . or Marcus Quin, God rest him, got six months for maiming ewes—

Maire O'Neill (Molly Allgood) as Pegeen Mike in the 1907 production of The Playboy of the Western World.

("God rest him" is the normal pious expletive concerning the dead, but here a little incongruous with his crime)

> —and he a great warrant to tell stories of holy Ireland . . .

—where the second clause links "holy Ireland" with "God rest him", and both combine ironically with the "six months for maiming ewes". But set against this triangle there are two background references: to the Moonlighters and the agrarian troubles with their horrible practice of maiming cattle, horses, sheep by hamstringing or cutting off their tails. The second is to the juxtaposition of "holy Ireland", the kind of reference embodied in Yeats' poem whose title is the first three words:

> Beautiful lofty things: O'Leary's noble head;
> My father upon the Abbey stage, before him a raging crowd:
> "This Land of Saints," and then as the applause died out,
> "Of plaster Saints;" his beautiful mischievous head thrown back.

Something of the same metaphysical conjunction (which emerges only when distanced) is in Shawn's agonized cry "Oh, Father Reilly and the saints of God, where will I hide myself today?" Sometimes we have a double counterpointing, when the romantic, the religious and the realistic meet in a vortex characteristic of Synge's technique:

> Amn't I after seeing the love-light of the star of knowledge shining from her brow, and hearing words would put you thinking on the holy Brigid speaking to the infant saints, and now she'll be turning again, and speaking hard words to me, like

an old woman with a spavindy ass she'd have, urging on a hill.

or,

> There's poetry talk for a girl you'd see itching and scratching, and she with a stale stink of poteen on her from selling in the shop.

More subtle and less definable is Sara's speech as she tries on the boots:

> There's a pair do fit me well, and I'll be keeping them for walking to the priest, when you'd be ashamed this place, going up winter and summer with nothing worth while to confess at all.

—when the ideas of confession and barefoot penance have a kind of subtle and uneasy association. It is the same with the convolutions of the plot. *The Playboy*'s epic blow grows steadily in narration; but it is counterpointed and parodied by Pegeen's account of how the Widow Quin killed *her* man:

> She hit himself with a worn pick, and the rusted poison did corrode his blood the way he never overed it, and died after. That was a sneaky kind of murder did win small glory with the boys itself.

and yet again Pegeen's

> And to think of the coaxing glory we had given him, and he after doing nothing but hitting a soft blow and chasing northward in a sweat of fear.

There are the overt attacks on custom; the terrifying description of Kate Cassidy's wake is balanced against Michael's drunken blasphemy:

> . . . aren't you a louty schemer to go burying your poor father unbeknownst when you'd a right to throw him on the crupper of a Kerry mule and drive him westwards, *like holy Joseph in the days gone by,* the way we would have given him a decent burial, and not have him rotting beyond, *and not a Christian drinking a smart drop to the glory of his soul?*

Now the uneasiness set up in an audience is caused, not by the extravagance of these syntactical conjunctions, but because each one of them is, *in itself,* perfectly natural and in common use, and is therefore elusive. It is Synge's art, which has something in common with Pope's, of suggesting value or its depreciation in this manner. Much the same is true of the plot, with its fantastical propositions. Does murder become heroic just because the blow is a good one, or because it and its context are narrated poetically? Granted that the police, together with the "khaki cut-throats", are natural enemies of the community, embodying "the treachery of the law", is it a moral act to shelter wrong-doers? Is a murderer likely to be a proper protector for Pegeen while the others are out? Is his reported valour a sufficient counterweight to the impropriety of his being left alone with her? If women are so easily won by poetical speech combined with inferred virility, what is the position of the conventional timid man as represented by Shawn Keogh?

Old Mahon boasting of his drink and lechery, his treatment in hospital, is in some sense a counterpart to the boasting of his son. They go off together, united in an utter reversal of this relationship.

Go with you, is it? I will then, like a gallant captain
with his heathen slave.

and old Mahon's comment, that oblique and perhaps profound comment on metaphysics:

Glory be to God! I am crazy again.

So Synge's art makes the characters and the themes advance
and retreat from the audience. Outrageous statements become logical, and the language of hyperbole makes them still
more credible, in relation to the reality which is being questioned.

It is being questioned, of course, in the very title. A geographer could fix the scene of *The Playboy* with some accuracy.
It is obviously in north-west Mayo, within sight of the sea-
shore, and of the dominant mountain Nephin. It is not far
from Belmullet and Castlebar. The Western World is the land
lying westward of the Shannon; proverbial for its 'wildness'
and poverty; isolated from the civilized East and South, and
the dour virtues of the 'black North'. Perhaps there are connotations of the Holy Islands, the Country of the Sunset, St
Brandon. Yet it is a *world,* fantastic, romantic, brutal and
sentimental, all at once. In the play Synge's own ambivalent
attitude is fully apparent:

I once said to John Synge, "Do you write out of
love or hate for Ireland?" and he replied, "I have
often asked myself that question . . ." [William
Butler Yeats, *Letters*]

Let us be frank about it. Synge's satiric view is constantly focused, with more or less directness, towards certain aspects
of the peculiar blend of paganism and Roman Catholicism
that he saw in the West. The pious ejaculations can, by juxtaposition and contrast, become loaded with ironies that demand both distance and an Anglo-Irish viewpoint to imagine
their full implications. The unseen Father Reilly hovers in the
background of *The Playboy* as the guardian of peasant morality, the supporter of the cowardly and feeble Shawn; whose
comments on each situation are yet those of the ordinary
moral man. Against settled and dull convention and a religion which can be made to appear superficial there are set
Synge's tinkers, tramps, fishermen, publicans, in their actual
or potential vitality. Yeats recognized the potential conflicts
in a letter to Ricketts:

I notice that when anybody here writes a play it always works out, whatever the ideas of the writer,
into a cry for a more abundant and intense life.
Synge and "AE" the poet are staying here, and
though they have come to their task from the opposite sides of the heavens they are both stirring the
same pot—something of a witches' cauldron, I
think.

The Playboy exists as a work of art, and in a sense all comments on it are futile or irrelevant. The complexity that gives
it life must be apprehended with all our senses. Its verbal har-
monies and disharmonies are integral with its verbal rhythms
and idiom, its characters with the waves and currents of the
plot. We stand back from it, and we may remember Shaw [in
his *The Matter with Ireland*]:

. . . the admirable comedies of Synge, who, having
escaped from Ireland to France, drew mankind in
the manner of Molière, and discreetly assured the
public that this was merely the human nature of the
Blasket Islands, and that, of course, civilized people

never admired boastful criminals nor esteemed
them according to the atrocities they pretended to
commit. The Playboy's real name was Synge; and
the famous libel on Ireland (and who is Ireland that
she should not be libelled as other countries are by
their great comedians?) was the truth about the
world.

(pp. 61-67)

*T. R. Henn, in an introduction to "The Playboy of
the Western World," in* The Plays and Poems of
J. M. Synge, *edited by T. R. Henn, Methuen & Co
Ltd., 1963, pp. 22-78.*

HOWARD D. PEARCE (essay date 1965)

[*In the following essay, Pearce discusses Christy Mahon as a
mock Christ figure.*]

Even though critics frequently grant *Riders to the Sea* or
Deirdre of the Sorrows to be the "greatest" of Synge's plays,
Playboy of the Western World has for many the most hearty
appeal of all. One may wonder, though, at reasons for such
popularity in view of the profound gulf that separates the two
most commonly held interpretations of the Playboy himself:
on the one hand he is thought to become a hero in the final
act, and on the other a mock-hero. I find little attempt among
the critics to justify one view or the other, on the contrary the
fundamental understanding of his character usually colors or
generates a concept of the play. Alan Price, in the most thorough and recent study of Synge [see Further Reading], thinks
of Christy as a hero, seeing in this play, in contrast to *The
Well of the Saints,* Synge's fusion of the "dream" and the
"actuality," watching Christy develop through the action
"from weakling to hero." [In *The Irish Dramatic Movement,*
1939] Una Ellis-Fermor likewise sees him developing, "not
merely into 'a likely man,' but into a poet-hero, 'the only
playboy of the western world.' " H. N. MacLean devotes an
article [excerpted in *TCLC,* Vol. 6, pp. 437-38] to exploring
Christy's Christ archetype, which makes of Christy a myth-
generated hero. I have severe doubts about rigorously applying archetypal patterns to the play, but it might be interesting
to look at the Christ parallel again to see if Synge has not used
the myth to ironic purposes not entirely consistent with
MacLean's reading.

Even though it seems a minority voice, there certainly exists
an ironic interpretation of Christy. Krause sees the "mock-
heroic treatment of Christy" as deriving from the Ossian prototype [see Further Reading]. He in addition finds in Synge
a "counterpoint of idealism and irony," where "lyric and satiric modes are played against each other." [Ronald Peacock
in his *Poet in the Theatre,* 1946] in the same way proposes a
far more subtle comprehension of Synge's vision in the play
than that which makes Christy simply a hero:

The basis of the comic here is a delicate and capricious mockery at the very idea of fine language,
closely related as it is to fine ideas. Synge plays in
this comedy with his own discovery. Through his
mock-hero Christy Mahon he allows his instrument to elaborate its most splendid ornaments.

Here, then, is an evasive hero whose similarities to Christ
should perhaps be seen in the same light.

Christy Proteus-like shifts before our eyes, before his associates' eyes, and before his own. He has always tried to see

himself, has not simply begun doing so when we catch him with the mirror at the beginning of Act II. Mahon deprecates his eternal romancing, including "making mugs at his own self in the bit of glass we had hung on the wall." Where he has been seen a hero in general by the Mayo people, Mahon makes him a frightened rabbit, a "looney," which we of course suspected from our first glimpse. There is in the final action the obviously diametrical movement of Christy upward in the eyes of the audience and downward in the eyes of the Mayo people. Yet it is not an unqualified movement. The truth lies not in one pair of eyes, but in the reality of the contradictions that result from the shifting perspective. Surely the antithetical views achieved by Christy himself and Pegeen should leave the spectator a range in which to see the irony of Christy's self-glorification and Pegeen's disillusion.

One of the most fundamental ironies in the play rises from the apotheosis of an ostensible murderer. Christy's coming strikes fear into the hearts of the folk in the shebeen, especially Shawn, who has heard (or felt) him "groaning wicked like a maddening dog" in the ditch above. Yet when they have learned that he is a murderer, Pegeen is ready to take him as her defender for the night, and Philly and Jimmy reinforce her argument. They create of him a champion of discord and conflict. Killing his father is admired as an act of courage qualifying him as defender *against* the law and champion of gaming competition. When the Widow Quin first proposes him for the sports, Sara says, "I'll bet my dowry that he'll lick the world"—not that he will save it, but lick it. The Widow later applies to him the epithet "champion of the world." Mahon, of course, seeing him from a different angle considers him an anti-Christ. He asks, " . . . and isn't it by the like of you the sins of the whole world are committed?" Christy declares himself delighted with and devoted to his own evil at last, again a kind of anti-Christ. In the fracas of Act III, when Shawn thinks he will die from being bitten by Christy, Christy answers with delight, "You will then, the way you can shake out hell's flags of welcome for my coming in two weeks or three, for I'm thinking Satan hasn't many have killed their da in Kerry, and in Mayo too." The full force of the irony strikes in Michael's eloquent concession to Pegeen's avowed marriage to Christy instead of to Shawn. He joins their hands, pronouncing his blessing: "A daring fellow is the jewel of the world, and a man did split his father's middle with a single clout, should have the bravery of ten, so may God and Mary and St. Patrick bless you, and increase you from this mortal day." That baroque Christ-epithet "jewel of the world" is coupled with the grotesquely visualized "split his father's middle with a single clout," achieving the mockery of lyricism observed by Peacock.

A more comprehensive irony may be seen in that generally speaking Christy does offer a kind of salvation to his devotees. His power of romancing seems so much more finely tuned than theirs that he comes to embody the illusion which they try to turn to practicality. The Widow Quin's schemes show the severity and immediacy of her need for him as he is. When he romanticizes Pegeen, the Widow Quin says, "There's poetry talk for a girl you'd see itching and scratching, and she with a stale stink of poteen on her from selling in the shop." And though Pegeen can follow him in romantic flights, her hold on the illusion is so weak, so tentative, that it takes only one assertion by old Mahon to prove to her that Christy is a liar and "nothing at all."

We can see in terms of this dream Christy bears to them that

in fact there is a ground for dramatic irony in his paralleling Christ. Where He was adored in His Epiphany, His people turned on Him at last and destroyed Him. For Christy, a lusty sex idol, the adoration of the Magi becomes the adoration of the local girls. Christy thinks they trekked four miles to see him, until Pegeen informs him that they came no distance at all "over the river lepping the stones." The gifts they bear—"a brace of duck's eggs," "a pat of butter," "a little cut of cake," and "a little laying pullet"—effectively parody the gifts of the Magi. Sara even teases Christy about his divinity, asking, when he will not use his right hand to touch the gifts, "Is your right hand too sacred for to use at all?" The betrayal comes, of course, when the people lose their illusion and become again fearful of the law.

Certainly, as MacLean argues, this betrayal turns Christy into a mythic scapegoat figure. He comes to them as sufferer, Pegeen as king, "Aren't you destroyed walking with your feet in bleeding blisters, and your whole skin needing washing like a Wicklow sheep." But after his moment of glory with them they reject him when Mahon turns up alive and threatening vengeance on Christy—first Pegeen, then all. He turns at last to the Widow Quin, who declares that her "share is done," then to the others, and Sara mocks him with advice to turn to Pegeen again. After he has again "killed" his father, they do not merely reject, but set about destroying him to protect themselves. Michael says, "If we took pity on you, the Lord God would, maybe, bring us ruin from the law today," and Pegeen echoes him with "take him on from this, or the lot of us will be likely put on trial for his deed today."

Around this scapegoat idea plays the theme of mock-sacrifice which illuminates a serious depth in the play. A good bit of "saving" goes on in the play, but far earlier and more frequently not "saving" but bribery. Both of these grow from the essential selfishness of human nature seen in the various reasons for accepting Christy in the first place: Pegeen likes and wants him, Michael wants to get out of the house, Philly thinks he will keep the peelers away. Christy reveals his father's secret motive in trying to marry him to the Widow Casey, " . . . letting on I was wanting a protector from the harshness of the world, and he without a thought the whole while but how he'd have her hut to live in and her gold to drink." Further, much of the plot turns upon bribery. Mahon will tell Philly and Jimmy of his "murder" if they will give him a supeen. Shawn tries to bribe Christy to go away, and when that fails tries to bribe the Widow Quin, who skillfully turns the affair into, not bribery, but sacrifice. He asks what she will do if he promises her a ewe, she answering, "A ewe's a small thing, but what would you give me if I did wed him and did save you so?" The Widow Quin offers the same kinds of bribes to lure Christy away from Pegeen—not wealth but leisure, since Christy is such a lazy fellow—but when he in turn asks the Widow to help him win Pegeen, to "aid and save [him] for the love of Christ," she again agrees for the payment of "a right of way . . . , a mountainy ram . . . , and a load of dung at Michaelmas."

Yet the Widow Quin's mock-sacrifice takes a strange turn in the final action. The Widow seems all along one who has been almost entirely free of illusions about Christy. She admires him less for the lie than for the reality—he is a handsome lad. Thus it is not surprising that when the illusion dies she does not betray him. (Admittedly, Sara leagues with the Widow, but her admiration for Christy seems, like the Widow's, less dependent on his story than on his face.) Of course it is Christy's father who finally "saves" him from the avengers—the so-called "savior" is at last saved. But the Widow, aided by Sara, tries to save him as well. Seemingly her motives are still practical and selfish, but on the other hand she appears poignantly aware of that Syngean vision of the mutability of youth and beauty, trying to save him not merely for herself, but because it would be a shame for him to die. She offers him finer sweethearts than Pegeen, again bribing him away, then, when he refuses to give up the illusion and takes a stool to them all, she goes out saying to Sara, "It's in the mad-house they should put him, not in jail, at all. We'll go by the back-door, to call the doctor, and we'll save him so." If Widow Quin lacks the sparkle and romance of Christy, nevertheless her actions, grounded in actuality, in such sharp contrast to Christy's, which are irremediably floating in the dream vision, point up Synge's ironic detachment. His impetus arises not merely from love or hate, resulting in neither simply romance nor bitter satire, but some complex interrelationship of the two.

This view of Synge is necessary in order to avoid oversimplifying his characters and as a result the entire play. In suggesting that those parallels with the Christ myth illuminate the play, my purpose is to show Christy as a mock-Christ, a mock-hero. We see facets in this way which cannot be seen from one perspective. If we take his recognition in the last scene as a simple thing, then we are led to oversimplify Synge's vision. Certainly he admired the rambunctious self-assurance and glamor Christy has put on in espousing the dream. But I think that, especially through such elements as the implicit grace of Widow Quin's final action, it is obvious that Synge saw Christy's affirmation as no absolute answer to the conflict. Price seems to come dangerously near such an oversimplification in his assertion of the paradox that the dream becomes the actuality. The matter is not simply Pegeen's inability to grasp the dream. The sad truth is that the dream and the actuality remain as disparate here as in *Deirdre of the Sorrows.*

Christy comes into this Western World an innocent and a romancer, and he goes out of it the same, influenced by that world primarily to self-confident braggadocio. It may be that he loses innocence, but even here the conversion seems only partial. He shows a naiveté early in the play which makes him kin to such other characters as the Tramp in *In the Shadow of the Glen.* Christy is, of course, like the Tramp in that they share the romantic vision and are wanderers and free men, but they are further alike in having a kind of innocence that leaves them astounded by and vulnerable to the shocks they receive from other men. The Tramp is unbelieving when Dan would put Nora out of the house: "It's a hard thing you're saying for an old man, master of the house, and what would the like of her do if you put her out on the roads?" When Dan shows himself adamant, the Tramp suggests that Michael Dara might then take her, an idea absurd to all the realists, for she now has no dowry to offer Michael. Christy, too, only with difficulty understands the viciousness of mankind. In Act II, when Pegeen has tormented him with the story of the hanging (which is her way of repaying him for accepting naively and promiscuously the attentions of other females), he complains, "What joy would they have to bring hanging to the likes of me?" He is no more knowledgeable about man's laws than about those "queer joys" which make men torment others. In recounting his past adventures in poaching, he says, "I was a devil to poach, God forgive me, (*very naively*) and I near got six months for going with a dung fork and stab-

bing a fish." His innocence of females is the source of much humor in the play, of course, Mahon revealing his being the butt of jokes and having the title "the looney of Mahon's." And he does not give up this innocence easily. Even after Pegeen's complete rejection of him, he still expects her to relent, accepting the truth only after she says that she will burn him.

Corollary to this innocence is his utter romanticism. Mahon declares him "a liar on walls, a talker of folly, a man you'd see stretched the half of the day in the brown ferns with his belly to the sun." He romanticizes Pegeen and himself, even innocently supposes that he has found a pastoral idyll among the good people of Mayo. The romancing, of course, grows beyond proportion, until he imagines in the last scene his own hanging: ". . . the day I'm stretched upon the rope with ladies in their silks and satins snivelling in their lacy kerchiefs, and they rhyming songs and ballads on the terror of my fate." This declaration far better shows the ridiculous lining of his romanticism than does the frequently quoted line about "romancing through a romping lifetime."

I asserted above that Christy only partially loses his innocence and naiveté. This can be seen in the quality of his "tragic recognition." Far from arriving at some deeper truth, he gains a superficial self-assurance without the more profound understanding which would accompany a tragic hero's "reversal." His final affirmation is on a grand scale, but it remains grand comedy, a mockery of Maurya's acceptance, Deirdre's heroic passion, and Nora's pathetic realization of the imperfection in the Tramp's promise of life. What Christy specifically learns is that Mayo is not the fulfillment of his dream. He came thinking the promise of peace which Pegeen offered him was attainable, thinking that "You're decent people . . . and yourself a kindly woman." He thought he had found perfection on earth, " . . . a clean bed and soft with it, and it's great luck and company I've won me in the end of time," " . . . a fine place to be my whole life talking out with swearing Christians . . . , smoking my pipe and drinking my fill, and never a day's work." Nature is idyllic still in the duet of love he and Pegeen sing in Act III.

But he had known all along the imperfection of the people of Clare: "Oh, they're bloody liars in the naked parish where I grew a man," as he had known of the bleakness of nature, the "cold, sloping, stony, divil's patch of a field" where he killed his "da." Thus what he learns when Pegeen deserts him and the crowd cheers Mahon against him is that people are fools, an opinion echoed by Mahon as they go off together: " . . . my son and myself will be going our own way, and we'll have great times from this out telling stories of the villainy of Mayo, and the fools is here." Christy has realized merely that the people of Mayo are no better than those of Clare, that he has not found the dream. But he goes on naively seeking the dream, with no sounder justification for the search nor any improved chance of finding it. His new daring holds little promise of changing the world or the people in it.

Yet there is joy in his affirmation. We applaud his act of domination, perhaps for the comic justice in it, the underdog's winning the day, perhaps for the gusto itself. It is ironic that our sympathy has grown for Christy not because of his pride, domination, and rejection of the world, but for the opposite: his pathetic need to find a place in it. Christy before his triumph often seems to come close to the perception of Nora, who in accepting the Tramp's offer recognizes the stark reality of her action: "I'm thinking it's myself will be wheezing that time with lying down under the Heavens when the night is cold; but you've a fine bit of talk, stranger, and it's with youself I'll go." Christy's speech, ". . . it's a lonesome thing to be passing small towns with the lights shining sideways when the night is down . . . " is now famous. The sadness which is part of the wanderer's lot is not unknown to him—all the more ironic his exuberant blindness in the end, thinking that lot is nothing but joy. Before the reversal, the lonesomeness of the Widow Quin causes him to see, "You're like me, so." Then as he faces his rebelling devotees, he bares the horns of the dilemma of human existence with the pathetic realization that " . . . you're setting me now to think if it's a poor thing to be lonesome, it's worse maybe to go mixing with the fools of the earth." (His is essentially the plight of Huck Finn, who comes up with a similar, and no better, solution to this conflict.) One may have love, escaping loneliness, or one may have freedom, escaping the evils bred in man, but he may not have both. He may flee, and thus dominate, or succumb, but not both. Christy has here stated the dilemma but has remained blind, or perhaps grown even blinder, to the loss involved in making a choice, a loss which Synge shows a full awareness of in his other plays.

Thus even though Christy is made into a deity, the apotheosis contains ironies. Since he comes as a Christ-destroyer, rather than saving he in fact in actuality destroys, overpowers, "licks" his people (with words, at least, though obviously he is instrumental in Pegeen's destruction) instead of sacrificially succumbing to their destroying him. As he grows to a heroic affirmation, there remains mockery implicit in the disparity between the grandeur of it and the degree of ignorance that engenders it. The danger is that the spectator may be taken in by the apotheosis as the good people of Mayo were by the Epiphany. To avoid becoming subject to the simple assertion of this hero, one must maintain a finely tuned ear for the lyric and the mockery of it, the heroic and the mock-heroic, and the discrepancy between the actuality and the dream. (pp. 303-10)

> Howard D. Pearce, "Synge's Playboy as Mock-Christ," in Modern Drama, Vol. VIII, No. 3, December, 1965, pp. 303-10.

DIANE E. BESSAI (essay date 1968)

[*In the following essay, Bessai examines* Playboy *in the context of Irish mythology and the comic tradition in Irish Literature.*]

[In M. J. Sidnell's "Synge's Playboy and the Champion of Ulster"; see Further Reading] it has been suggested that the central action of *The Playboy of the Western World,* the blow on the head, can be read as a modern version of the beheading game as it appears in "The Championship of Ulster". The comparison is an apt one: indeed, in discussing the links between the saga material of ancient Ireland and Synge's play, Professor Sidnell does not go far enough. In using this motif for his drama, the playwright himself is taking a role very much like that of the inaugurator of the beheading action, the traditional poet figure, Bricrui. As Bricrui manipulates the men of Ulster at his famous feast, sometimes with comically malicious intent, so does Synge, I would suggest, manipulate his Irish peasant characters in a sustained mock-heroic vein; at the same time, he provides one character who, like Cuchulain, nicely survives and even transcends the machinations. In both cases the rest of the characters are in various ways made to look ridiculous.

When Shaw once wrote that "The Playboy's real name was Synge", another way of saying that the playwright himself was the real hoaxer and mischief-maker, he pointed the way to clarification of Synge's specific ironic dimension in the play. On the other hand, Frank O'Connor, in his posthumous study of Irish literature, *The Backward Look* [see Further Reading], insists on what he calls Synge's great structural mistake in the play when he does not reveal at the very first that Old Mahon is alive. He argues that the audience should grasp the irony of Christy's tale-spinning as soon as possible. Surely, however, there is a strong indication in Synge of what Yeats describes generally as an Irish habit of mind with its "mischievous extravagance", a hidden malice which delights when someone is willing to "take the sport for gloomy earnest". Thus at the very beginning *The Playboy* audience is deliberately placed into something of the same absurd position as the villagers in the comedy.

To be swept along by the glories of romance rather than by the plain fare of reality is a universal human tendency, but it is one that Synge saw as particularly and richly Irish. Synge's game is to show up audience and characters alike by letting both get involved in what is essentially a mock-heroic situation. Christy is lauded for killing his father, though—unlike the events in "The Championship of Ulster"—no one literally loses his head. No one in *The Playboy* among either audience or characters—not even Christy himself—knows that no murder has been committed. The other characters are of course directly, if unwittingly, involved in creating the fable, but the audience with its lack of essential knowledge is caught up as well.

The first audiences took Synge's sport for gloomy earnest because they resented having to tolerate an immoral situation which they believed to be a falsification of Irish peasant life. They were perhaps too much concerned with the superficialities of the national image, no doubt preferring the nobilities of *Kathleen ni Houlihan* or the nostalgia of *The Land of Heart's Desire*. What they failed to perceive was that the Irish peasant was not in himself the object of attack, nor indeed [as A. E. Malone declared in his *Irish Drama*] did Synge heap scorn on the head of his hero, Christy Mahon. On the contrary, to Synge the vigour of the Irish tradition was in the keeping of the highly imaginative peasant with whom he so frequently associated. But at the same time in this particular play he seems to have used his peasant material for a further purpose than in his previous work. On one level at least, he created an effective comment on what he seems to have considered the unrealistic preoccupation of the Celtic renaissance.

Several years earlier he had written, in reply to the Celtic point of view expressed by his friend Stephen MacKenna, that "no drama can grow out of anything other than the fundamental realities of life which are never fantastic, are neither modern nor unmodern and, as I see them, rarely 'springday-ish, or breezy or Cuchulainoid'." And, he went on to affirm, "Ireland will gain if Irish writers deal manfully, directly and decently with the entire reality of life." One might go as far as to suggest that paradoxically Synge chose to point this out by indirection in *The Playboy.* Perhaps because he was aware of the absurdities in a nationalist movement that saw in Cuchulain the spirit of a new as well as the old Ireland, he gave his Irish audience a mock-heroic version of the Red Branch buried in the framework of a peasant comedy. In so doing he demonstrated in the final triumph of Christy Mahon that self-knowledge and self-realization were necessary to achieve a national as well as a personal destiny. This is the "reality" of *The Playboy of the Western World,* or perhaps one of the "several sides" to it hinted at by Synge himself in his letter to *The Irish Times* shortly after the play's riotous première.

The evidence for such a reading becomes apparent with an examination of elements of the Ulster hero story other than those that are dealt with by Professor Sidnell. Nevertheless, his citing of the beheading game, when Cuchulain becomes the Champion of Ulster, as the parallel for the central action for which Christy is named Champion Playboy of the Western World, is the significant starting point for further argument. Throughout the play, Synge maintains the mock-heroic tone in two ways: the comic analogies to the Cuchulain lore, sustained by the continuing humour of the modern-peasant/ancient-nobleman inversion, and sometimes by the direct ironic reversal of mythical incident and personality.

It is illuminating, first of all, to examine the father-son relationship in terms of the Ulster material. While, in keeping with the beheading motif, Old Mahon is a Curoi figure, Curoi is not described in the Ulster cycle as Cuchulain's parent. There are several conflicting accounts in the birthtale of Cuchulain as to the identity of his father. Lady Gregory follows the oldest tradition, which as much as says that he is the god Lug of the Long Hand. Dechtire, sister of King Conchubar, is always the mother, but in one version Conchubar himself is the father; in another it is Sualtim, Dechtire's husband. In any case there are a number of heroic father and authority figures in Cuchulain's life—those mentioned above, other guardians and tutors, as well as those with whom he comes into direct conflict, such as Forgall, father of Emer, Curoi Mac Daire, and Culain the Smith. Lug of the Long Hand is largely unknown to his earthly son, but on one memorable occasion when Cuchulain has been for weeks holding off the armies of Maeve of Connaught single-handed, Lug makes a miraculous appearance to give the severely pressed hero a rest from his trials.

Christy knows only too well who his father is, having been plagued and bullied by him all his young life; yet Christy is the kind of son who has grown up never really knowing his parent in an intimate way. Therefore [Herbert in his *Irish Writers, 1880-1940;* see Further Reading] Howarth, sees Christy's unconscious view of Old Mahon as of a "god and object of worship". Certainly in the first telling of his tale of parricide, Christy exposes his mixed feelings of fear, awe, and reluctant pride towards the old man. The more we see and hear of Old Mahon, the more we realize that while Pegeen is busy creating a man out of Christy and he in turn is trying to match her image of himself, the old father is everything that Christy is not. While it may seem extreme to call him a god, Old Mahon is unquestionably heroic in dimension. Although to us he is comically heroic, a loud-mouthed, grasping, greedy, drunken old brawler, he is one who might have been more socially acceptable in the spacious days of the Red Branch. In him we see Synge's version of "romantic Ireland", neither "dead and gone", nor imprisoned between the covers of a translation. And it is significant to the Cuchulain parallel that the reprehensible old father makes his most dramatic entrance in the play just at the point when Christy is hard pressed by the ire of a whole community.

The motivating action of *The Playboy* is Christy's blow on his father's head. The myth of Christy's heroics arises out of

his belief that he has actually killed Mahon, but the comic irony of the play reaches its climax when the old man appears before the Widow Quin, battered but very much alive. This leads to the Widow's sarcastic remark "Well, you're the walking Playboy of the Western World". Christy's real triumph occurs at the end, when he accepts the return challenge that Old Mahon thrusts at him, in the presence of all Christy's former admirers, and batters him a second time. This is the act which to his father demonstrates Christy's real worth as "Playboy of the Western World". It therefore takes the time between these two events for Christy to re-establish himself, not as the hoaxer the Widow Quin implied him to be, nor even, as he later becomes, a "champion of the world" at sports. Ultimately he has to become "the likely gaffer" who has the dare-devil power to defy all the fools who have suddenly renounced the hero they themselves helped to create. Mock-heroics have been transformed into reality when Christy can handle himself and all comers. Moreover, father and son have been reunited with a mythically appropriate reversal of their positions.

Another strand of the Ulster hero story to be found in the play is the reference to the naming of the hero. Cuchulain first comes to public attention when he is only a little fellow aged seven. His given name is Setanta. He insinuates himself into Conchubar's Boy Troop by virtue of his superior skill at games, particularly hurling. The first major event in his life occurs when he acquires the name by which he is to be known to fame: the killing of the fierce hound of Culain the Smith. When Culain is angered by his loss, the boy volunteers to serve the smith as protector of his goods until he can seek and train a new dog. Thus he becomes known as Hound of Culain, often shortened affectionately to Little Hound. He is a popular figure at Emain Macha, and although excessively proper as a child, he is much loved and admired by the women of Ulster for his beauty of face, sweetness of speech, and athletic prowess. So much so, that he is hardly out of adolescence when the men of Ulster decide they must protect themselves by finding him a wife.

In direct mock-heroic contrast, Christy Mahon is a timid little peasant weakling, physically "a small low fellow," a lazy worker and a dreamer; he is afraid of girls and when it comes to athletic prowess is "the fool of men." His father tells that he is therefore universally known to the district as "the looney of Mahon's." Also he has so little appeal to the opposite sex that he is "the laughing joke of every female woman where four Baronies meet".

Cuchulain's taking of arms occurs when he is still a child. He chooses an auspicious day, one for which it is prophesied that he who takes arms will die young, and live on in immortal fame. Only King Conchubar's weapons satisfy the boy, and he goes off to prove his worth against three fierce sons of Nechtan. He defeats the first with his iron hurling ball, the second with his sword, and the third with his spear, employing in each case the athletic prowess for which he has already become well known. He returns home with the three heads for trophies, as well as two stags that he chased on foot and a flock of white swans that he captured alive. Since his battle-anger is still upon him as he approaches Emin Macha, steps have to be taken to subdue his wildness before it is safe to welcome him.

The comparable event in Christy's career occurs at a later time in his life, but then Synge in any case crowds Christy's heroic activity into a period of about ten days. Christy's unexpected success at the local athletic competition represents his triumphant initiation into combat. His borrowed arms are the borrowed clothes of Shawn Keough and his trophies the bagpipes, fiddle, and blackthorn which he wins for jumping, leaping, and racing. Here he has really earned the Widow's now unironic compliment when she calls him "the Champion Playboy of the Western World" in the sense of being successful at sports. He is still a hoaxer in his parricidal claims, but he has acquired the courage and bravado to keep up the front. He has yet to win his true championship, the one that is comparable, in comic terms, to Cuchulain's triumph of courage in the beheading game.

Another important event in the life of Cuchulain is "The Wooing of Emer," a tale which in Lady Gregory follows the taking of arms. Since the men of Ulster have been unsuccessful in finding him a wife to his liking, the youth seeks out the distinguished maiden Emer, daughter of Forgall Manach the Wily, feeling that she alone is worthy of his birth, education, and reputation for strength and skill in combat. Emer has the "six gifts" of beauty, voice, sweet speech, skill at needlework, wisdom, and chastity.

Part of Cuchulain's wooing is couched in traditional mythological metaphor, ostensibly devised for the occasion to prevent Emer's maidens from understanding his intent and reporting to Forgall, who is against him. Emer herself, however, is interested in the hero's suit, but warns him that he will have to accomplish several difficult feats in order to overcome her reluctant father. When the wily parent discovers Cuchulain's intent, he tricks Conchubar into sending the young aspirant to the woman-warrior Scathach on the pretext of further training in combat, but actually he hopes that Cuchulain will perish on the journey. While Cuchulain is away, Forgall finds another suitor for Emer—Lugaid, a king of Munster. When Emer explains that she loves Cuchulain, Lugaid is reluctant to take her, for he is afraid of Cuchulain's reputation for strength. Emer's recalcitrant father continues to resist at the expense of his life when Cuchulain returns to win his bride.

Christy is attracted to Pegeen early in their acquaintance, but it is his success at sports that gives him the courage to seek her hand in earnest. She herself has prepared the way by turning him into a hero almost the moment she hears what he did to his father. In comic contrast to Emer, who is surrounded by the warrior world, she is starved for exciting action and therefore has to make her own. She starts with the traditional idea of associating hero with poet, displaying the equally traditional awe and admiration for such a figure: "and I've heard all times it's the poets are your like—fine fiery fellows with great rages when their temper's roused." She has already noted Christy's supposedly aristocratic "small feet" and "quality name, the like of what you'd find in the great powers and potentates of France and Spain". Here one recalls not only the noble lineage of Cuchulain but also that his childhood tutor was Amergin, "fighter and poet", who taught him—as he tells Emer—courage to stand up to any man and poetic skill in making "praises for the doings of a king". Christy's first telling of his own "doings" is timid and reluctant, but encouraged by the admiration of Pegeen, his description of the "battle rage" which was supposed to have led to his father's death becomes increasingly imaginative. This warrior too has the voice of the poet.

Christy finds in Pegeen the several gifts which Cuchulain admires in Emer. We find that the shebeen-keeper's daughter

has her own peasant version of the "six gifts". To the Playboy she is "a lovely handsome woman"; he admires the "sweetness" of her voice and speech. She is even skilled at needlework: the cover that she puts over Christy on the night of his stay "I'm after quilting a while since with my own two hands." But in some way these and the other "gifts" also operate in comic reversal: the Widow Quin sees her as undistinguished in physical charm, "itching and scratching, and she with the stale stink of poteen"; of her sweet speech, Pegeen herself admits she can be "the fright of seven townlands for my biting tongue"; there are a number of examples of her less than lovely voice, as for example when she berates Christy for his response to the other girls, or when she discovers the lie of her lover's reputation. Although Pegeen's chastity is never in doubt, she is, in the view of Shawn, immodest in her determination to house Christy overnight unchaperoned. Wisdom she later acquires, but too late, when she realizes "I've lost the only Playboy of the Western World".

Christy's words of wooing to Pegeen are universally celebrated for the richness of their poetry. They are more overt in their implications and intentions than Cuchulain's elaborate metaphor and poetic formality, but there is a kind of measured ceremony in the lovers' dialogue, which, as Alan Price has noticed [in his *Synge and Anglo-Irish Drama;* see Further Reading], gives "the impression of ritual". More specifically, Christy also uses the lore of belief and tradition in his speech, though his metaphors are of course relevant to his own time. An example is his extravagant avowal: "If the mitred bishops seen you that time, they'd be the like of the holy prophets, I'm thinking, do be straining the bars of Paradise to lay eyes on the Lady Helen of Troy—and she abroad, pacing back and forward, with a nosegay in her golden shawl."

Pegeen, like Emer, has another suitor who is approved by her father. However, in contrast to Forgall, Michael James does give at least temporary consent. He is suddenly impressed by Christy's spirit, which leads him to dream of "a score of grandsons growing up little gallant swearers". Again in contrast to Forgall, who dies resisting Cuchulain as a son-in-law, Michael James claims that if necessary he will happily risk an untimely grave in order to make Christy a part of his family. Needless to say he changes his mind and is the first at hand with a rope to apprehend the denigrated hero.

Cuchulain's visit to Scathach is a prelude to the trials of strength which win him Emer for his bride. Scathach is a renowned woman warrior who also has the druid power of prophecy. Her "sunny house" is on an island "in the east of Alban" where she lives in the company of beautiful maidens. One of these is her daughter Uactach who falls in love with the Ulster hero at first sight. She sends him to her mother whom Cuchulain immediately seizes and holds at swordpoint until Scathach agrees to teach him her great skill at arms. In return Scathach has good service from Cuchulain during his stay: he becomes Uacthach's temporary husband, and in defeating the fierce woman warrior Aoife, saves Scathach's two sons from the enemy. In some ways, then, Scathach is the wise old woman in Cuchulain's life: she tutors him and trains him, tries to protect him from harm during his stay, and receives assistance from him in return. As he leaves for Ulster she uses her druid power, making a forecast of the dangers of his career, his victories, fame, and how "he would die in his full strength". On his return home, Cuchulain kills the required number of opponents in his determination to fulfil his word to Emer and for this is given "the headship of the young men of Ulster".

Christy's counsellor and aid to his success is the Widow Quin. She is the one who signs him up for the sports in which he triumphs and is the first to pronounce him "Playboy of the Western World". When she discovers that his story of parricide is an error, she does everything in her power, in return for the promise of certain favours, to deceive both the villagers and Old Mahon. Thus she functions as a kind of parody of the wise old-woman figure with her greater knowledge of the situation and her shrewd sense of how to handle it for her own ultimate benefit.

In keeping with the idea of comic contrast, she starts out by wanting the Playboy for herself rather than for any of the young girls in whose company she is frequently found. She offers the young man the comforts of her version of the "sunny house", the "houseen" described in scathing terms by Pegeen as a decrepit dwelling, where "leaky thatch is growing more pasture for her buck goat than her square of fields". The most significant feature to be found in the Widow Quin, in comic parallel to Scathach, is that as Scathach and Cuchulain have a common bond as warriors of repute, so, in Synge's terms, do the Widow and Christy. Years ago she "destroyed" her man who died of blood poisoning after she had hit him "with a worn pick". Again in scathing terms, Pegeen comments that it was "a sneaky kind of murder did win small glory with the boys itself ". But Christy does not wish to cement their bond, and when the Widow sees that her case is hopeless, she strikes the bargain to help him win Pegeen; and when Christy loses his bride in the end, it is through no lack of effort on her part.

The final scuffle, which in *The Playboy* is comparable in its sequence of events to Cuchulain's slaughter of the protectors of Emer for which Scathach helped him prepare begins inauspiciously. Mahon makes his third appearance, as if from the dead, and begins beating his son with a stick. When he can no longer deny that this is his "murdered" father, Christy runs to the Widow for protection. But she can do nothing, and so, faced with the loss of his new reputation and lady love, Christy confronts his tormentors. Out of the undignified turmoil which follows, Christy really does acquire by mock-heroic means a modern form of heroic stature; it is achieved at the expense of a bride but at the gain of wisdom and self-knowledge. His title is secure.

It has been suggested here that Synge has, in a comic-satiric way, made a special use of the revival of ancient lore current in the contemporary literary movement. Yet Vivian Mercier's recent study [*The Irish Comic Tradition,* 1962] would place Synge "almost entirely outside the Gaelic literary tradition", the author of a new "genre" in Irish literature: "Unlike the class-conscious Gaelic poets and satirists, Synge sympathizes with the underdog and the outcast, be he tramp or tinker, parricide or blind beggar." That such an association does not necessarily rule out the traditional connection for *The Playboy* is most modestly argued by Professor Sidnell, according to whom "*The Playboy* may be seen as the story of the Championship of Ulster after it had passed through the literary guts of an Irish Tramp". This is certainly a way to see interest in the contemporary peasant and the heroic tradition as not being mutually exclusive, though it does not particularly illuminate the question of Synge's relationship to the Irish comic tradition.

Use may now be made of Mercier's rather cogent general insights into the comic tradition of Irish literature to show that Synge, specifically in *The Playboy,* did in fact belong to that tradition, and on Mercier's terms. Mercier writes that "the most striking, single fact about Irish literature in either Gaelic or English is the high proportion of satire which it contains." He goes on to refer to the probable magical origins of satire, pointing to evidence that in Old Irish the general word for the genre must have originally meant "spell" or "enchantment". Fear of a power which must have been inherited from the Druids enhanced the prestige of the poet-satirist, his "spell-derived" abuse having the power of curse. This can be substantiated from the record in the *Mythological Cycle* of the first satire composed in Ireland, down to Douglas Hyde's Gaelic play *The Twisting of the Rope*. The potency of the poet-satirist should already be evident in Synge himself in his role described above as analogous to that of Bricrui, Ulster satirist and trouble-maker; and perhaps the awe with which Pegeen beholds her poet-hero can also be traced to this tradition.

Among major elements in Irish comic and satiric writing, both past and modern, Mercier lists the fantastic, the macabre, and the grotesque. The comic use of fantasy is related to magical events such as shape-changing, transformation, and miracle. The stories of "Manannan at Play" recorded in Lady Gregory's *Gods and Fighting Men* are good examples of fantastic humour. Certainly the transformations of Cuchulain to and from his battle rages were not intended to be humorous, but Synge could be said to draw on this tradition in a comic way, with the magic of Christy's lightning-quick changes from snivelling coward to man of violence. Even the comic hints of the traditional beheading-game motif suggest the humorous handling of the marvellous. Fantasy can also be a pretext for sexual ribaldry, says Mercier, although "purely erotic writing does not come naturally to the modern Irish". The closest example of this in *The Playboy* lies in the possible titillation of Christy's once controversial speech: "It's Pegeen I'm seeking only, and what'd I care if you brought me a drift of females, standing in their shifts itself, maybe, from this place to the eastern world?"

Concerning the macabre and the grotesque, Mercier describes the effect of one as a defence mechanism against the idea of death, the other as a means of belittling the awe inspired by life. With regard to the macabre elements in *The Playboy,* he briefly mentions that Synge has developed "the comic possibilities of parricide with a thoroughness unparalled elsewhere in literature", rightly seeing the father-son conflict as macabre in a universal rather than a specifically Irish sense. But it should be added that Synge, as a deliberate technique, backs away from the macabre when he makes his peasants so horrified at the spectacle of Christy's second murder attempt, and that he does this to make his comic-satiric point about the contemporary Irishman who balks when faced with actions comparable in violence to the old heroic tales; that, while the peasant loves to hear and repeat macabre stories, "there's a great gap between a gallous story and a dirty deed." Thus, of a piece with the psychological climate which makes a sensation of the hearsay murder of Mahon we have Philly's account of his boyhood Sunday game of playing with the skeleton of a man "who had thighs as long as your arms", and Jimmy Farrell's "skulls they have in the city of Dublin, ranged out like jugs in a cabin of Connaught". It is all mere matter for goose-bumps; and in no way matched by a capacity to stomach real bloodshed and corpses. In this way, Synge comments ironically within the framework of his play on one aspect of the Irish literary movement, in whose enthusiasts a story like that of Cuchulain playing hurley with the head of the dead half-man might invoke equally delicious thrills.

But the most conspicuous traditional comic characteristic reinforcing the central action of the parricide in *The Playboy* is Synge's handling of the grotesque. The grossness of some of Old Mahon's self-confessed indulgences may have more than a faint ring of the character and behaviour of the Dagda, ancient father god of the Tuatha de Danaan, whose crude exploits have a strongly comic note even in their earliest forms. He is quick in temper, fierce in battle, gross in appearance, lusty in behaviour, and later in his career he is duped out of his dwelling by his son Angus Og.

Less is known and recorded of the Dagda's female counterpart, the Sheela-na-gig, goddess of creation and destruction, usually considered a primitive prototype of the Great Queen and war goddess, the Morrigu. In surviving statuary the Sheela-na-gig is a grotesque combination of skeleton ribs, enlarged sex organ, and a big scowling or sometimes laughing mouth. There is some debate over the size or even presence of bosom on the typical Sheela-na-gig, although one interpretation of her name is "Sheila of the Breasts." There is evidence that the name was used in modern times in an area of Cork to mean "hag", and of course, the hag-figure plays a predominant role in Irish hero lore. The most conspicuous hag figure who also has Sheela-na-gig aspects in *The Playboy* is one who never makes an appearance on stage, but is described thus: "A walking terror from beyond the hills, and she two score and five years, and two hundred weights and five pounds in the weighing scales, with a limping leg on her and a blinded eye, and she a woman of noted misbehaviour with the old and young." This is the widow Casey whom Christy's father wants him to marry for his own mercenary reasons. But the young man is horrified; not only is she "a hag this day with a tongue on her has the crows and seabirds scattered, the way they wouldn't cast a shadow on her garden with the dread of her curse," but even worse "when all know she did suckle me for six weeks when I came into the world."

In the Ulster Cycle, Cuchulain has various adventures with vicious one-eyed hags. During his stay with Scathach, he meets Ess Enchenn, "blind of the left eye", who is anxious to kill him in revenge for the death of her three sons. After the battles of the Cattle Raid of Cooley, the three one-eyed daughters of Calatin pursue him to his near peril. Towards the end of his career, three hags, also blind in the left eye, force him to break his taboo and eat roasted hound, with fatal consequences. The Morrigu herself becomes his sworn enemy during the Cooley conflict when, in the guise of a red woman, she offers herself to him and is rejected. When he answers her threats with his sword, the woman disappears "and all he saw was a black crow, and it sitting on a branch, and by that he knew it was the Morrigu had been talking with him."

The Widow Quin has some resemblance to both the hag and Morrigu figures. She has a reputation for grotesque female behaviour, such as the suckling of a ewe which recalls Sheila of the Breasts. She has a warlike fierceness which led to the death of her man, and she is anxious to wed the young Christy. She also has a crafty quality, but this is of no personal avail; circumstances and the hero's preferences defeat her. She even fails in her unhaglike attempt to save him from his inevitable fate, in contrast to the three hags who drive Cuchulain to his doom. But Christy's fortune is happier than

that of his ancient counterpart. Cuchulain's price of fame is his young life, while Christy, whose heroic days are also over, will nevertheless live on to enjoy his own 'immortality'. The price is the loss of his beautiful romance with the lovely Pegeen. But while she is left to lament her folly, "the likely gaffer" she has helped to self-fulfilment will "go romancing through a romping lifetime from this hour to the dawning of the judgement day."

Thus, Synge may be said to have written *The Playboy* out of materials in which the ancient Irish tradition and contemporary country lore manage to coincide. But the one is a remote shadow of the other; and it is in the psychological disparity between them that the play finds its ironic centre. (pp. 372-83)

> Diane E. Bessai, "Little Hound in Mayo: Synge's *Playboy* and the Comic Tradition in Irish Literature," in The Dalhousie Review, *Vol. 48, No. 3, Autumn, 1968, pp. 372-83.*

MARY ROSE SULLIVAN   (essay date 1969)

[*In the following essay, Sullivan focuses on Synge's treatment in* Playboy *of the demythologizing process central to* Oedipus Rex.]

Of all the twentieth-century dramas attempting to re-work classical myth, John Millington Synge's *The Playboy of the Western World* seems to have the most tenuous connection with its original. The boisterous Irish comedy of bungled attempts at father-killing is so far removed in tone and spirit from the austerely beautiful *Oedipus Rex* that one is tempted to assume it is a parody, in which the hyperactive Celtic peasant imagination transforms the Theban king's awful crime into an act of derring-do—except that a reading of it as parody does not stand up, either. With no attempt to imitate Sophocles' style, and with a plot and characterization remarkable for their vigor and freshness, the comic effect is clearly independent of any familiarity with the original. And even a casual reader is caught by the sense that, beneath the humor, Synge is in some way engaged with a significant and sobering truth about the human situation.

What, then, is the relationship between the two plays? For Synge clearly wants us to recall Sophocles' play as we read *The Playboy of the Western World.* How else explain his persistent emphasis on his protagonist as parricide: the phrase, or variation of it, "the man who killed his father," is used to describe Christy Mahon more than a dozen times in the course of the play, until it assumes the quality of a Greek-like epithet; details of description link the two killings (Christy's accounts of the attack with a blunt instrument—"I hit a blow on the ridge of his skull, laid him stretched out"—echo Oedipus' version: "By one swift blow from the staff in his hand he was rolled right out of the carriage, on his back"). Synge even seems to be giving a passing nod to the second aspect of Oedipus' crime, marriage to his mother, when he has Christy protest in horror his father's plans to marry him to the Widow Casey, since "all know," he claims, "she did suckle me for six weeks when I came into the world."

What Synge is doing in sounding these distant but insistent echoes of Sophocles' play is, it seems to me, drawing our attention to a profounder thematic similarity, which might otherwise go unrecognized, in his comedy and *Oedipus Rex.* Both plays deal with a man who enters a society as a stranger to everyone—even to himself—to be hailed as a savior by that society because of some distant epic deed that has renewed the barren land; however, in the course of attempting to learn the facts about his own identity and the mysterious deed, the hero uncovers a truth which proves too harsh for the society to accept—with the result that he is forced to leave it as he came, a stranger and alone. Looked at thus, Synge's comedy can be read as a deliberate re-working, despite its vastly different tone, of Sophocles' tragedy in its exploration of the role of myth in human affairs. He is showing the continuing truth of how myth, as a "constructive lie," operates to allow the man with heroic potential to perform a redemptive social role and in the process find his own identity. But he is also showing that, after the myth has done its creative work, the heroic potential is fully realized only when a man is capable of taking the next step, penetrating it and piercing to the truth, however unpalatable, at its core. As it is in this demythologizing that Oedipus' greatness lies, in his insistence on finding and accepting, despite its terrible cost, the truth about who he really is, so, I believe, is Synge pointing out that his protagonist's heroic stature depends finally on his ability to do what the ordinary man cannot do—unmake the myth and accept the truth it had hidden.

Necessarily, in making a comedy rather than a tragedy, Synge works toward the same goal as Sophocles by an entirely different method, inverting the basic situation, and demonstrating not just the destruction of the myth but the process of its creation as well. Christy Mahon is the very antithesis of the Aristotelian tragic hero—"a small, low fellow," the laughing-stock of the village, "a dirty, stuttering lout"—and much of the play's humor springs from the unexpected endorsement given his crime by the villagers. In contrast to talk in *Oedipus* of "the accursed defiler of this land," Christy's deed wins almost universal acclaim ("Well, you're a marvel! Oh, God bless you! You're the lad surely!"). Oedipus in his shame fears for his children's ruined marriage hopes ("who shall be the man, my daughters, that will hazard taking unto himself such reproaches . . . ?"); Christy is promised Pegeen Mike's hand and gets the lavish blessings of her father as well ("a man did split his father's middle with a single clout, should have the bravery of ten, so may God and Mary and St. Patrick bless you, and increase you from this mortal day.") This comic inversion, and the fact that Synge's writing for an audience less attuned to the mythic function than his predecessor's means he has to telescope into the play's action both the making and the unmaking of the myth, account for what appears to be a greater emphasis on the gain than on the cost to the hero in seeking the truth. But if Sophocles could depend on his audience's knowledge of the beneficent aspects of the Oedipus myth—his solving the riddle and saving the land from the monster—and was thus free to concentrate all his tragic power on showing the dissolution of the myth, Synge is, within his comic perspective, just as uncompromisingly insistent on the need for demythologizing, and on the heavy price it exacts from the hero. His Christy Mahon is, on his own more modestly-dimensioned terms, engaged in as inexorable a pursuit of the painful truth about himself as the great king of Thebes. But while critics have come to such a reading of *Oedipus* (that the question of whether the hero is victim of fate or flaw is less relevant than the recognition that his victory lies in the relentless pursuit of truth for its own sake), they have been led, by traditional assumptions about Synge's play as a satire on Irish romanticizing, to overlook what he sought to make clear by linking

his play with *Oedipus Rex,* that his hero's victory is of the same kind, if not degree, as that of Sophocles' hero.

Not only the theme, but even the action of his play bears out such a conclusion. In both plays, the hero's quest for self-identity consists of a series of encounters with other persons; in each case, exposure to an alien viewpoint forces the hero to re-adjust his own image of himself to conform to some unexpected revelation, until he arrives at what is virtually a new identity. With Oedipus, each successive encounter—with Teiresias, the Messenger, the Herdsman—loosens further the scales from his eyes until he finds himself face to face with the shattering knowledge that he is indeed the cursed killer. For Christy, the admitted "father-killer," the process works in an opposite direction, as in his successive encounters with others—the tavern men, Pegeen, Widow Quin, the village girls—he adopts their different view of himself only temporarily, almost like a near-sighted man trying on various spectacles until he finds a pair that provides a satisfactory view. Once the "creative lie" has done its work, however, and Christy has found in it release for his latent powers as poet and "playboy," he too must endure the dissolution of the myth, putting aside the borrowed viewpoints and facing unflinchingly the stark truth about himself.

The brilliance of Sophocles' plot for showing the revelatory process at work has long been recognized; how Synge goes about his similar task is well worth examining too, in some detail. To begin with, he sees the making of myth as a social act comprising two distinct elements: first, the potential hero's need for an image of greatness to conform to, an image he can only derive from the accepted values of the community in which he finds himself; and second, the need of that same community for a man capable of embodying its preconceived image of greatness, who can then liberate it from a sense of limitation by performing high exploits with such ceremonial or ritualistic style that they take on a semi-religious or transcendent dimension. To demonstrate the first part of this proposition, that the potential hero is entirely dependent on society to provide him with the standards of heroic behavior, that he can in fact work out his own identity only by conforming to the prevailing communal values, Synge introduces his protagonist Christy Mahon as a young man suffering from such a poorly defined sense of self that he is extraordinarily susceptible to any outside view of himself. On first arriving at the Mayo tavern as a frightened fugitive from justice, he bitterly admits his confused state to Pegeen—"It's little enough I'm understanding myself"—after a lifetime of being ignored or scorned. "Up to the day I killed my father, there wasn't a person in Ireland knew the kind I was, and I there drinking, waking, eating, sleeping, a quiet, simple poor fellow with no man giving me heed," he tells her. "There wasn't anyone heeding me in that place saving only the dumb beasts of the field." If the villagers noticed him at all, it was to roar at him and call him "the looney of Mahon's." Desperate to reject their assessment of him—"Oh, they're bloody liars in the parish where I grew a man"—he has nothing to replace it with, until the unexpected response of the tavern crowd to his confession of father-killing presents an intriguing new possibility. His initial disbelief at the favorable impression he is making as a murderer ("Is it me?" he exclaims delightedly at Pegeen's praise of his "noble brow") gives way almost immediately to the welcome conviction that he is indeed of the stuff of heroes: "and I a seemly fellow with great strength in me and bravery. . . . "

To reinforce this point, that the incipient hero needs an out-side view of himself to actualize his heroism, Synge makes use of various stage devices, such as properties, costumes, and the grouping or linking of characters, as a means of measuring Christy's advance toward genuine self-knowledge. Sophocles had done the same thing with his hero by using image patterns of sight and sightlessness to foreshadow Oedipus' literal blindness when he finally sees the truth; in keeping, however, with his protagonist's still rudimentary level of understanding, Synge relies on the simple, concrete, and mundane object, to show how important external appearance is to Christy's structuring of a self-image. The looking-glass, for instance, which figures prominently in the second act, when the village girls come to admire "the man who killed his father," is a means by which he can literally see himself from outside. As he habitually resorted to it at home—one of his father's complaints is that he wasted so much time "making mugs at his own self in the bit of a glass we had hung on the wall"—he now, in the first excitement of his transformation, instinctively moves to confirm in it his revised self-estimate; interestingly enough, he attributes the change to the new mirror and not to himself, feeling that it merely reflects more accurately what he always suspected to be true: "Didn't I know rightly I was handsome, though it was the divil's own mirror we had beyond, would twist a squint across an angel's brow. . . ." Caught in the act by the visiting girls, he tries to hide the mirror behind his back but, once discovered, he brings it out and unselfconsciously uses it as a tray on which they pile the gifts of eggs, cake, and chicken they have brought; the gesture seems to indicate that, for him, the very substantial evidence of others' admiration serves to validate and complete the partially-objective image of the mirror. Pegeen's anger, when she notices the misplaced glass, suggests that even she, much as she wants Christy a hero, recognizes that his continuing efforts to objectify his self-image will eventually destroy his dependence on her approval.

In a somewhat similar manner, the clothes he wears serve as a means by which Christy can learn more about how he appears to other people and therefore how he should appear to himself. (In fact, wearing apparel plays a significant part in establishing status and determining behavior for everyone in the play: in the opening lines Pegeen orders her trousseau for her marriage to Shawn Keogh and then sees the move as a sign that she should marry Christy instead, "with my gowns bought ready, the way that I can wed you, and not wait at all"; Shawn's loss is foreshadowed when, fleeing the tavern in terror of temptation, he leaves his coat behind and Pegeen has to recover in chagrin "her property"; in still another instance of the symbolic value attached to clothing, Sara surreptitiously tries on Christy's boots to see if she can by contact develop a touch of the murderer's daring.) On Shawn's offering his new rival his best hat, breeches, and coat as a bribe to give up Pegeen, the transformation in Christy's personality is instantaneous: he shows a "new arrogance" speaks "almost pugnaciously," even before he gets so much as the hat on his head and, once attired in the natty outfit, he "swaggers" and preens himself "as proud as a peacock," until the Widow Quin says, "If you seen yourself now, I'm thinking you'd be too proud to speak to us at all. . . ." In fact, Christy *is* "seeing himself" now, the clothes providing him with another clue as to what is expected of him. He is like an actor for whom the costume defines the role; next, he dons a new "jockey's suit" to enter the races and, looking like a champion, he proceeds to behave like one, winning every contest in sight. Only in the last scene do we see him able to distinguish

between the apparel and his inner self; as the crowd turns on him threateningly, he rejects the Widow Quin's efforts to help him escape by disguising him in shawl and petticoat, because to accept the ignominious costume would be to deny his new stature: "And I a proven hero in the end of all." Besides indicating that he is no longer solely dependent on external appearance to define his role, however, the rejection shows that he is, even at this stage, still associating appearance with behavior; he will be truly self-actualized only at that point when he can see himself a hero while the jeering crowd binds him and drags him off to be hanged.

Having thus established that the first element in the myth-making is present, the hero's need for an image to conform to, Synge makes the second ingredient, the community's need for a hero, quite as patent. Like the plague-ridden Thebans who hailed Oedipus as savior, the Mayo peasants are ready to accept with open arms anyone who can brighten their bleak lives. "The broken harvest and ended wars" have made a meanness and deformity seem a general affliction in "this place where you'll meet none but Red Linahan, has a squint in his eye, and Patcheen is lame in his heel, or the mad Mulrannies were driven from California and they lost in their wits." The great men of yesterday are all gone; as Pegeen asks, "Where now will you meet the likes of Daneen Sullivan knocked the eye from a peeler, or Marcus Quin, God rest him, got six months for maiming ewes, and he a great warrant to tell stories of holy Ireland till he'd have the old women shedding down tears about their feet. Where will you find the like of them, I'm saying?"

Into this situation comes Christy as, not just a killer, but the killer of his own father. In making him an acknowledged parricide, Synge artfully exploits all the psychological implications of the father-figure as a symbol of repression, the obstacle to an individual's achieving full human potential, and he emphasizes the people's sense of oppression by having Christy's crime an object of general envy as well as approbation. Everybody wishes he had the courage to do the same. Pegeen admits, somewhat ruefully, "I never killed my father. I'd be afeard to do that. . . ." The Widow Quin tries to claim a kinship with Christy on the strength of having, even indirectly, "destroyed her man." And even the convention-bound Shawn Keogh confesses to a jealousy of Christy for having had such an opportunity: "Oh, it's a hard case to be an orphan and not to have your father that you're used to, and you'd easy kill and make yourself a hero in the sight of all." All agree that the father-killing establishes Christy as one worthy to be entrusted with great responsibility. "Bravery's a treasure in a lonesome place," observes Jimmy Farrell, "and a lad would kill his father, I'm thinking, would face a foxy divil with a pitchpike on the flags of hell." Surely, he concludes, on Pegeen's behalf, "herself will be safe this night, with a man killed his father holding danger from the door. . . ."

The only disapproval comes from Father Reilly. This authoritarian figure, who never appears in person but is constantly invoked (no less than six times in the first scene alone by the fear-ridden Shawn) on all ethical and religious questions, represents an extension of the repressive father-symbol beyond the family into the larger sphere of the community. "I'm afeard of Father Reilly," is Shawn's constant refrain, until Pegeen has to order him to "Stop tormenting me with Father Reilly"; but for all his fear Shawn rightly sees the clerical authority as his staunchest ally against the danger posed by

An Abbey Theatre production of The Playboy.

the feeling prevails that his act acquires a transcendent and universal meaning not just despite, but in some sense because of, its outraging of all the established moral and social conventions.

This surrounding of the extraordinary moral act with religious significance, an indispensable element in the myth-making process, must be accompanied with a sense of ritualization and prescribed form, Christy further discovers, if it is to produce the full-blown hero who, "mounted on the springtide of the stars of luck," will become the playboy of the western world. The act of raw violence by itself is not enough to make the heroic deed; it needs to be informed by an aesthetically satisfying pattern of such epic proportions as to inspire mystery and awe. The Widow Quin, after all, had killed her husband, but she is outside the pale nevertheless because the doing of it displayed no imaginative style; as Pegeen describes it scornfully, "She hit himself with a worn pick, and the rusted poison did corrode his blood the way he never overed it, and died after." Christy's initial description of his deed is equally crude—"I just riz the loy and let fall the edge of it on the ridge of his skull, and he went down at my feet like an empty sack, and never let a grunt or groan from him at all"—but, driven by his dangerous position to be wary, he takes refuge in vagueness—"Oh, a distant place," he describes the spot, "a windy corner of high, distant hills"—and immediately discovers how the mystery lends enchantment to the tale. By the second narration, he knows how to give his audience exactly what it wants: "With that the sun came out between the cloud and the hill, and it shining green in my face. 'God have mercy on your soul,' says he, lifting a scythe; 'or on your own,' says I, raising the loy. . . . He gave a drive with the scythe, and I gave a lep to the east. Then I turned around with my back to the north, and I hit a blow on the ridge of his skull, laid him stretched out, and he split to the knob of his gullet." His poet's instinct released by the fascinated response of his listeners ("That's a grand story"; "He tells it lovely"), he expands on the natural setting, builds suspense with epic speeches and dramatic gestures, increases tension and suggestiveness by the rhythmic parallels ("says he," "says I"), the touch of the preternatural (the sun "shining green"), and ritualistic movement (the turns to the east and north, the exchange of prayers).

Once given this aesthetic form, all the narration needs to firmly establish its mythical dimensions is repetition. Pegeen can complain that he has told her "that story six times since the dawn of day," but Christy can no more stop repeating it, once he has discovered its almost incantatory power, than he can reject the new image of himself that it implies. The villagers note that even in the midst of his concrete triumph in the races, he is "not able to say ten words without making a brag of the way he killed his father, and the great blow he hit with the loy." The fact that he sees so clearly how important mystery and ritual are to preserving the myth—a few half-hearted and quite futile attempts to frighten people with the loy confirm his guess that it is not repetition of the *act* that is needed, but repetition of the *tale*—proves that when Christy finally attempts to repeat the original deed, he is really aware that the second killing will not satisfy Pegeen and the villagers who will find it only a "dirty deed": his doing it anyway indicates that he has reached the stage of self-knowledge where he can begin to transcend the need for others' approval and face their ultimate rejection.

Christy's non-conformity. To Pegeen's lament that the great men are all gone, he replies emphatically that "Father Reilly has small conceit to have that kind walking around talking to the girls"—a sign that he recognizes the antipathy natural between the guardians of the established order and the new hero. His view is borne out by the report that the priest rushed the dispensation to marry Shawn and Pegeen: he would "wed them in a hurry, dreading that young gaffer who'd capsize the stars." The threat Christy offers to the existing system is in fact no small part of his appeal to the villagers. In his defiance of convention, he begins to take on the look of a man set to slay the dragon that has been holding them in thrall. No matter that his father-killing and his wooing of Pegeen are less acts of social benefit than of personal aggrandizement; everybody feels that in some way they redound to the general welfare, that the common man shares in the good flowing from any individual act of genuine heroism. This feeling, that in injecting a note of excitement into their drab lives, Christy is at the same time liberating them from stifling cultural sanctions, accounts for the way they tend to attach a kind of religious value to his violent act. From the exclamations of "Glory be to God!" or "God bless you!" which invariably greet his re-telling of the killing, to Christy's own pious summary of how he managed to do away with his father—"With the help of God I did surely, and that the Holy Immaculate Mother may intercede for his soul"—

At this point, Synge is ready to show the process of demythologizing at work. Unlike the making of the myth, it is not a cooperative effort of hero and community: the common man resists the effort required to penetrate the myth and fears the result. Jocasta's anguished cry to Oedipus "Mayst thou never come to know who thou art!"—represents the ordinary human tendency to turn away from harsh truth into illusion or evasion; the crowd which turns on Christy so quickly in anger and frustration is revealing the same reaction. By showing their protagonists capable of rising above this human need for a softening of reality, both Sophocles and Synge are calling attention to the ineluctable loneliness of heroic stature. Just as they served notice, through their respective use of sight imagery and the devices of the looking-glass and the clothing, that man needs the support of society's values to learn his potential, so also they are now reminding us, by their separation of the hero from the supporting community, that the true hero merely "borrows" the viewpoint of others until he is strong enough to survive without dependence on any values outside himself. The final test of heroism is thus the ability to bear the burden of truth in lonely exile. This is, of course, recognizably the archetypal pattern of all mythical heroes: the savior is betrayed or abandoned by the society he redeemed and the grandeur in his lonely end is recognized by society only in retrospect. Oedipus' greatest trial—more than loss of wife, sight, kingdom—is *exile,* and his most heroic act the pronouncing of sentence on himself: "Cast me out of this land with all speed, to a place where no mortal shall be found to greet me more." And, in fact, it is Christy's victory, too, that he can finally choose to leave the place where he found himself and, as he says, "go back into my torment" of a solitary existence.

Although the enormity of Oedipus' fate makes it hard to see Christy's as comparable, Synge presents convincing evidence of the torment of solitude for his protagonist. He shows him from the first eloquently lamenting his state: "I was lonesome all times, and born lonesome, I'm thinking, as the moon of dawn"; trying to explain his difference from other people: "What would any be but odd men and they living lonesome in the world?"; rejoicing to discover he is at last accepted: "And I not lonesome from this mortal day," and even, in the excitement of that discovery, able to pity "the Lord God in all ages sitting lonesome in his golden chair." To dramatize the extent of Christy's need for acceptance into the community, he shows his repeated anxious efforts to link himself with other persons through some shared experience or attitude. He wants to find a likeness in himself to the sturdy, sharp-tongued Pegeen, but she will have none of it. "I never cursed my father the like of that," she tells him, not without envy, "though I'm twenty and more years of age." When he tries to explain his oddity, she responds, "I'm not odd, and I'm my whole life with my father only." And when he notes a similarity in their attitudes toward marriage, her not entirely irrelevant answer is, "I never killed my father. I'd be afeard to do that, except I was the like of yourself . . . ," voicing the common man's need to have the hero set apart from mundane reality. The Widow Quin, on the other hand, is only too happy to link Christy with herself: "It's of the like of you and me you'd hear the penny poets singing in an August Fair," she tells him, in allusion to her "destroying her man." She complacently agrees with the village girls who pair them off— "You're heroes surely, and let you drink a supeen with your arms linked like the outlandish lovers in the sailor's song"— making Christy drink with arms entwined in hers. Significantly, however, she admits that their likeness rests less in their daring than in their loneliness; "You'll be doing like my-

self, I'm thinking," she tells him, "when I did destroy my man," brooding on the past and doomed to "long years living alone." To his interested reply, "You're like me, so," her agreement is prompt: "I am your like, and it's for that I'm taking a fancy to you. . . ." But this kind of sharing Christy rejects, since it is based on their common status as outcasts from that larger community he still needs.

What the Widow Quin recognizes is that she and Christy are both essentially realists who understand the nature of myth and its limitations: having discovered the falsehood of his father-killing story as soon as he did, she is no more surprised by his subsequent racing victories than he is. Both understood that they must keep the secret of Old Mahon's reappearance from Pegeen and the other villagers who need the myth and who will turn on Christy as soon as it appears in jeopardy. But the Widow is no hero nevertheless; just as her "destroying her man" was not the sort of thing penny poets would sing of in an August Fair, she has no tongue to make it into a "gallous story." Awed by Christy's rhetoric ("There's poetry talk"; "There's praying"), she is still quite content to let others dream of finding "a Jew-man, with ten kegs of gold" while herself settling for a thatched hut, a mountainy ram, and a load of dung. The lack of imagination is no disadvantage when it comes to driving a shrewd bargain, but it costs her the loss of Christy as surely as Pegeen's romanticism does. The last we see of her, having misunderstood the nature of Christy's metamorphosis and mistaking his new confidence for madness, she is vainly trying to rescue him from the crowd's anger; in contrast, Pegeen recognizes clearly, although too late, that Christy has gone far beyond the need for their protection or assistance.

The sign that the change has taken place is Christy's acknowledgment to the sullen crowd that although the myth has regenerated him, he is ready now to let it die and accept the lonely truth. "For if you're after making a mighty man of me this day by the power of a lie," he tells them, "you're setting me now to think if it's a poor thing to be lonesome, it's worse maybe to go mixing with the fools of earth." Their calling him "idiot" cannot obscure the knowledge that he won the races and heard his voice "this day saying words would raise the topknot on a poet in a merchant's town." As the myth disintegrates, the villagers move to disassociate themselves from the consequences of his deed, as before they had sought to share in its glory; Pegeen speaks for the disillusioned community when she orders Christy expelled from their midst: "Take him on from this, or the lot of us will be likely put on trial for his deed today." But by now, Christy is not only able to accept his difference from others, he sees it in truth as a proof of superiority and he revels in it, frightening the crowd with great full-mouthed curses in which he promises to have "a gay march down" to the gallows, taking some of them along for a "gallous jaunt" through Limbo with his father's ghost; boasting of the depth of his outlawry: "for I'm thinking Satan hasn't many have killed their da in Kerry, and in Mayo too." Unshaken by still another reappearance of his resilient father, he is secure enough in his new status as hero to let the old man free him from his prisoner's bonds and then tell him that he will return home with him only as a "gallant captain with his heathen slave." That his father accepts the reversal of situations with delighted surprise (his "Is it me?" echoes Christy's first apprehension of a new identity) shows that the wheel has come full circle and Christy's sense of his own identity is now strong enough that he can impose it on others. His last statement sums up all that he has learned about himself and about the need for making and unmaking myth—"Ten thousand blessings upon all that's here, for you've turned me a likely gaffer in the end of all, the way I'll go romancing through a romping lifetime from this hour to the dawning of the judgment day"—and Pegeen's wild lamentation, after he has gone, acknowledges society's belated recognition of all that it has lost in clinging to the myth and evading the truth.

What one is left with as a result of reading Synge's play in the light of Sophocles' is the conviction that Synge was indeed concerned to show his kinship with the great classic dramatist in their belief that although man needs myth to discover his heroic potential, it is only in unmaking the myth that he can realize that potential. When one considers that, beyond the disillusioned view of reality such a belief entails, it must have brought the dramatist face to face with the largest and most profound questions about his own role as artist—that is, as constructor of the "creative lie"—with all its implications for the artistic creation as a means to some greater truth, it is not difficult to attribute the seriousness underlying the surface gaiety of *The Playboy of the Western World* to Synge's realization that even in comedy he was moving to the very borderline of tragedy. (pp. 242-53)

> *Mary Rose Sullivan, "Synge, Sophocles, and the Un-Making of Myth," in* Modern Drama, *Vol. 12, No. 3, December, 1969, pp. 242-53.*

ROBIN SKELTON (essay date 1972)

[*Skelton is an English-born Canadian poet, essayist, and editor, whose poetry reflects the duality of his geographic background and his wide-ranging interests in art and music. A renowned scholar of the Irish Literary Renaissance, Skelton has edited volumes of Synge's dramas and poetry, and has written extensive studies on Synge's life and works. In the following excerpt, he discusses the stylistic devices of* Playboy *and elaborates on the drama's central themes and characters.*]

As with *In the Shadow of the Glen, The Tinker's Wedding,* and *The Well of the Saints,* Synge chose for *The Playboy of the Western World* a story that at first blush seems proper only for treatment as farce. The story of the young man who is welcomed as a hero by the Mayo peasants because he is believed to have killed his father with the blow of a spade, and, on the reappearance of the dead man, ridiculed as an imposter, is similar to many folk tales of many lands. Synge chose to complicate it somewhat by making two women rivals for his playboy's affections, and by arranging for the father to be again "killed" in the sight of the peasants, who are then outraged by the reality that they had previously admired in their imaginations. He also chose to imitate the stories he had heard in Aran by filling his play with echoes of other stories. He himself, in commenting on the play in a letter, referred to *Don Quixote* as being similarly extravagant, and, in a note to the press, to *The Merchant of Venice* and *Alceste* as being similarly poised between comedy and seriousness. It is easy to see that Christy Mahon is similar to Don Quixote in transforming commonplace actuality by means of his imagination, and in involving others in his poetic version of the world. In *The Merchant of Venice* the bargain of the pound of flesh is accepted largely as a joke until it becomes actuality, just as Christy Mahon's act of murder is regarded as heroic until it is repeated in full view of the peasants. Alceste, who, when her husband was about to die, offered her life for his, and was eventually brought back from Hades by Hercules, is a less obvious parallel, though Pegeen Mike in hiding Christy from the police and in wishing to devote her life to him does perform a slightly similar role. Synge was not, however, concerned to echo these earlier stories directly: he was interested in reflecting them in a slightly distorted manner, and, in his comments, suggesting to those that had the intelligence to take the hint that the play develops thematic richness from the use of allusion and parody. It is notable, however, that while hinting at this general characteristic of the play, he did not think it wise to refer to the most powerful allusions of all, those to the life of Jesus Christ.

The play forces us to admit the presence of these allusions by its continual use of religious epithets and phrases. These are used with rich incongruity and inappropriateness by all the characters but the Widow Quinn. The first hint that this is intended to do more than indicate the confusion of religion with superstition in the mind of the Mayo peasant comes when Shawn Keogh reports to Pegeen Mike that he has heard a fellow "above in the furzy ditch . . . groaning out and breaking his heart" but was afraid to go and see what ailed him. Shawn being excessively god-fearing and blatantly pious, this must remind us of the parable of the Good Samaritan, especially as shortly after this disclosure is made and Pegeen promises to tell no one of Shawn's encounter, the men enter the public house saying "God Bless you. The blessing of God on this place." When Christy Mahon does arrive and tells his story the village girls bring him gifts, thus parodying the Epiphany, and tell him "Well you're a marvel! Oh, God bless you! You're the lad surely!" When Christy rides to triumph in the sports and then comes back into the inn his glory is short-lived, for Old Mahon turns up and identifies himself. The dialogue that follows has strong biblical echoes, with its reference to the "sins of the whole world" and to "Almighty God"; and Pegeen herself echoes Pontius Pilate when she tells Old Mahon,

> Take him on from this, for I think bad the world should see me raging for a Munster liar and the fool of men.
>
> MAHON. Rise up now to retribution, and come on with me.
>
> CROWD. (*Jeeringly*) There's the playboy! There's the lad thought he'd rule the roost in Mayo. Slate him now, Mister.
>
> CHRISTY. (*Getting up in shy terror*) What is it drives you to torment me here, when I'd ask the thunders of the might of God to blast me if I ever did hurt to any saving only that one single blow.
>
> MAHON. (*Loudly*) If you didn't, you're a poor good-for-nothing, and isn't it by the like of you the sins of the whole world are committed?
>
> CHRISTY. (*Raising his hands*) in the name of the Almighty God. . . .

The binding and wounding of Christy after he has "killed" his father a second time echoes the binding and wounding of Christ, and Christy's last speech, in its assertion of his immortality and the good his "crucifixion" has done, is also a near-parody of Christ's claims after his resurrection:

> Ten thousand blessings upon all that's here, for you've turned me a likely gaffer in the end of all,

the way I'll go romancing through a romping lifetime from this hour to the dawning of the judgement day.

If this parallelism is accepted, it must be realized that the
drama has political as well as moral overtones of considerable
seriousness. Christy's killing of his father must be seen in the
context of Shawn Keogh's constant awed references to Authority in the form of Father Reilly and the Holy Father in
Rome. Christy has rebelled against Authority, and as long as
the rebellion is purely verbal, a "gallous story," it arouses the
appreciation of the Irish: when, however, it becomes an actual rebellion, support for it falls away. It is the story of many
Irish rebellions, including that of 1916 which Synge did not
live long enough to see. It is the story of Parnell who remained the "Chief" as long as he did not too obviously offend against puritanical morality; when he was accused of
adultery he was abandoned and Ireland's greatest hope of
freedom was destroyed. Words are, to Synge's Irishmen,
more important than facts: it is the fine poetic speech of
Christy that makes him a hero, and not the actuality upon
which the poetry is based. Here, as in Synge's earlier comedies, the central figure is the vehicle of a poetic vision that
transfigures the commonplace and makes the mundane narrowness of country life bearable. Whereas in *In the Shadow
of the Glen, The Tinker's Wedding,* and *The Well of the
Saints,* this poetic vision is regarded as being a sign of spiritual health, in *The Playboy of the Western World* we are shown
that poetic sensibility and moral integrity need not necessarily go together.

The Playboy of the Western World differs from the earlier
plays in other respects also. In those earlier plays, even including *Riders to the Sea,* the central figure is not aware of
his or her heroic stature. The pathos of the Douls is intensified by their laying claim to lesser dignities than they in fact
possess by being so committed to the life of the inward vision
and so resolutely opposed to the big world of materialism.
Sarah Casey does not understand the nature of the battle she
herself wages. Norah Burke is unaware that her rebellion
raises a standard of general importance, and Maurya does not
see herself as representative of all bereaved motherhood.
Christy Mahon, however, at first deluded into believing himself a hero, becomes a hero because he is given the opportunity to play the role, and, after his downfall, understands not
only his own personal strength, but also its symbolic importance, as Pegeen Mike herself recognizes it when she cries out
in desperation,

Oh my grief, I've lost him surely. I've lost the only
playboy of the western world.

Christy is a hero to Mayo, however, not simply because of his
poetry, but because he symbolizes in his murderous act the
peasant's attitude towards moral and political authority.
When he first hints of his crime, Jimmy thinks he may be in
trouble for having followed "a young woman on a lonesome
night," and Philly suggests that "maybe the land was grabbed
from him and he did what any decent man would do," or perhaps that he was on the run because he had fought against
the English in the Boer War and was now liable to be "judged
to be hanged, quartered and drawn." All are sure that the police would be afraid to arrest him. The girls also show the
Mayo approach to legality when they tell Christy and the
Widow Quin (who is popularly supposed to have murdered
her husband):

You're heroes surely, and let you drink a supeen

with your arms linked like the outlandish lovers in
the sailor's song. There now. Drink a health to the
wonders of the western world, the pirates, preachers, poteen-makers, with the jobbing jockies, parch-
ing peelers, and the juries fill their stomachs selling
judgements of the English law.

This speech reveals the Mayomen's love of roguery and their
cynical unbelief in the lawmakers and processes of law. Michael, in spite of Shawn Keogh's wealth, prefers Christy as
a husband for his daughter, for he thinks it better to breed
"little gallant swearers" than "puny weeds."

Shawn Keogh serves to show the materialism and greed of
the peasants by attempting to bribe the Widow Quin to marry
Christy, and he also indicates his own cowardice and treachery by admitting:

I'd inform again him, but he'd burst from Kilmain-
ham and he'd be sure and certain to destroy me. If
I wasn't so Godfearing, I'd near have courage to
come behind him and run a pike into his side.

The portrait of the Mayo peasants that Synge presents is, one
may surely now admit, quite as savage as his earliest critics
felt. Though he enjoys the vigor of their speech, their wildness, their simplicity, he exposes their moral weakness, their
hypocrisy, and their greed also. He does however in Pegeen
Mike create yet another heroine animated by a passionate desire to escape from the constrictions of her way of life, and
fully committed to her vision. She fights wholeheartedly for
her man, accepting him totally, and when she discovers the
truth she attacks him with equal wholeheartedness, leading
in the binding of him, and herself burning him with the fire.
She is herself heroic in the extremity of her feelings, and in
the savagery of her pride. Desperation stirs in her: she is
forced by emotional necessity to grab every chance of escape
from the world of Mayo. Intemperate in speech, vital in action, she is capable of that kind of violence to which Christy
lays claim, and so she recognizes something of herself in him,
and when forced by pride to reject him, she realizes that she
has thrown away part of herself.

The Widow Quin, on the other hand, is almost exactly an opposite to Pegeen. A spectator of the action, she is delighted
to connive at Christy's deceit and send Old Mahon on a fool's
errand. Blandly amoral, she is the wise and cynical woman
of the play, reminding one of Mary Byrne in her understanding of the ways of the human heart. Oddly enough, she is the
only character who does not take the name of God in vain
at every available opportunity: she finds this pseudo-religious
verbiage amusing. When Christy appeals to her to help him
win Pegeen her retort is coolly mocking.

CHRISTY.   . . . Aid me for to win her, and
                I'll be asking God to stretch a
                hand to you in the hour of death,
                and lead you short cuts through
                the Meadows of Ease, and up the
                floor of Heaven to the Footstool of
                the Virgin's Son.
WIDOW QUIN.   There's praying!

The Widow Quin, however, is unlike Mary Byrne in that her
vision of the world, because cynical, fails to appreciate the
real importance of all the high-sounding words. She does not
understand that the man accepted as hero becomes hero; she
does not appreciate that the religious imprecations and the
glorification of violence both arise from a desperate need to

give life significance and dignity; she cannot share in either the pathos or the glory, and is unable to see why Christy is in love with Pegeen Mike for, she tells him, "Come I'll find you finer sweethearts at each waning moon," and thinks him fit for the madhouse rather than the gaol when he insists that he must marry Pegeen.

It was the stark harshness of Pegeen Mike at the close of the play which disturbed George Moore and other critics, and yet it is completely in character and, of course, essential to the theme of rejection which Synge was again concerned to present.

The theme of rejection in *The Playboy of the Western World* is handled more comprehensively than elsewhere in his work. The second killing of Old Mahon is especially significant, for it is this actual attack against authority which causes him to be rejected by those very people who have, it seems, a profound need themselves to reject the authorities set over them, and who talk continually of the heroic rebels amongst them. In this Christy himself parallels Synge's own rebellions and betrayals: *In the Shadow of the Glen* was condemned by those very people who were most concerned to bring Ireland freedom, dignity, and a proper understanding of her predicament; *The Well of the Saints* was condemned by critics who were themselves busy raising a standard of revolt against the authority of the establishment. The harshness of Synge's play is, possibly, to some extent due to his own sense that he himself, as a man whose every work was written at least partly in a desire to assist the regeneration of his country, had been condemned by those very people who shared his patriotism and should logically have applauded his endeavors.

In commenting upon Synge's drama in his essay, "J. M. Synge and the Ireland of his Time," W. B. Yeats told how he explained to Synge that he preferred *The Shadow of the Glen* to *Riders to the Sea,* because the latter was "too passive in suffering" [see excerpt dated 1910]. He wrote:

> Synge answered: "It is a curious thing that *Riders to the Sea* succeeds with an English but not with an Irish audience, and *The Shadow of the Glen,* which is not liked by an English audience, is always liked in Ireland, though it is disliked there in theory." Since then *Riders to the Sea* has grown into great popularity in Dublin, partly because with the tactical instinct of an Irish mob, the demonstrators against *The Playboy* both in the Press and in the theatre, where it began the evening, selected it for applause. It is now what Shelley's "Cloud" was for many years, a comfort to those who do not like to deny altogether the genius they cannot understand. Yet I am certain that, in the long run, his grotesque plays with their lyric beauty, their violent laughter, *The Playboy of the Western World* most of all, will be loved for holding so much of the mind of Ireland. . . . It is the strangest, the most beautiful expression in drama of that Irish fantasy which overflowing through all Irish literature that has come out of Ireland itself (compare the fantastic Irish account of the Battle of Clontarf with the sober Norse account) is the unbroken character of Irish genius.

Whether or not one accepts Yeats's view of the nature of "Irish genius," this prophesy of 1910 as regards the coming popularity of *The Playboy* has been amply fulfilled. Yeats's comments, however, also suggest in what way *The Playboy* differs from the earlier works. It contains more of "the mind

of Ireland." Whereas, in the short plays Synge had only space to imply the complexity of his characters and suggest the most basic of their emotional problems, in *The Playboy of the Western World* he was able to make the gradual uncovering of the paradoxes and confusions of his main characters an integral part of the movement of the play. Instead of repeating key images, he elaborated and developed them. Thus, the hypocrisy of Shaun Keogh is not so static a component of the play as is the simple sincerity of the Saint in *Well of the Saints,* or the timorous cupidity of the young man in *The Shadow of the Glen;* it develops and intensifies until it achieves the outrageous grotesquerie of the last act. Similarly, the conflicts of interests in the earlier drama are easily identifiable: desire opposes desire in straightforward confrontation. In *The Playboy of the Western World,* however, the motives of the Widow Quin, of Pegeen Mike, and of Christy Mahon himself are less simple to define. The Widow Quin, in particular, appears to be moved as much by her relish for the farcical and ironic as by her sexual greed, and there is an element of Narcissism in both Pegeen Mike and Christy Mahon which qualifies and to some extent vitiates the urgency of their more outward-looking desires.

The Playboy of the Western World is not merely more complex in characterization than the earlier drama; it is organized dramatically in terms of the changing nature of personal beliefs, desires, and commitments in a situation calculated to provoke such change. It is the last of a series of plays each of which concerned itself more with the uncovering of dramatic conflicts within the individual characters than did its predecessor. Thus the "lyric beauty" and "violent laughter" of which Yeats speaks are products not of different kinds of events but of the presence in each individual of elements of glory and absurdity which the events uncover. This distinction is most obvious when we see how Christy Mahon can wax lyrical over matters we ourselves might think trivial or even gross, and how the intensity of his feelings betrays him into absurdity on occasions which are not in themselves absurd. It was Synge's realization that the wellspring of his drama was to be found more in character than in event that enabled him to make of an anecdote scarcely more substantial than those he had used for *Riders to the Sea* and *In the Shadow of the Glen,* a full-length drama which remains one of the greatest comedies of the world. He did it by seeking, Yeats wrote, "not through the eyes or in history, or even in the future, but . . . in the depths of the mind." (pp. 59-70)

Robin Skelton, in his J. M. Synge, *Bucknell University Press, 1972, 89 p.*

BRUCE M. BIGLEY (essay date 1977)

[*In the following essay, Bigley interprets* Playboy *as a drama that opposes the conventions of both comedy and tragedy.*]

Let me begin with a few observations on John Millington Synge's *The Playboy of the Western World* and its critical acceptance. It seems safe to assert that *The Playboy* is Synge's best play; although some prefer *Riders to the Sea,* they will agree that *The Playboy* is more characteristic and that it is the best full-length play. *The Playboy* is also one of the classics of modern British theater, probably the most anthologized modern full-length play written in English. More arguably, it is the finest play written in English in a couple of centuries. Hence we may say that it is highly regarded, it has worn well, it is worth study and rereading, and it has as unanimous a critical acclaim as one is likely to find in a twentieth-century author.

Yet there is little agreement on how to read the play or react to its title character. Is he a hero, a buffoon, a fraud, a Christ figure, a mock Christ, a Promethean figure, a demonic figure, an Oedipal figure, the last hero of the decadent West? Is he even the protagonist? And how are we to react to the peculiar ethics of the play: is parricide so good a thing as it seems to be? There is as little agreement critically about the genre of the play. Is it comedy, as Synge subtitles it; an extravaganza, as he called it in an unguarded moment; a comedy with an anticlimactic ending; tragicomedy; a comedy with a tragic ending (comitragedy?)? Northrop Frye avoids classifying it in the [*Anatomy of Criticism*], although he does remark elsewhere that Christy is a mutation of the *miles gloriosus* ["Boastful soldier"]; but his disciples Foulke and Smith in *The Anatomy of Literature* touch all of Frye's mythoi by describing it in the following manner: "a romantic hero has been built out of a tragic idea and immersed in a society that turns out to be ironic, yet this complex vision of human motives still ends in an exuberant celebration of the possibilities of life—elsewhere."

So on the level of character, of ethics, of genre, the play refuses to fit our categories; it constantly breaks down the barriers we have erected and then believed real. Probably for this reason our initial reaction to the play is, more often than delight, a puzzlement, if not anger. The play was disliked not only by the Irish nationalists who led the riots at its première, but also by such sympathetic viewers as George Moore and Lady Gregory [see Further Reading]. Moore objected to the ending as uncomic, although he later grew to see that it was right; and Lady Gregory became one of the play's champions on the first American tour. She could write in 1913 on *The Playboy*'s reception in America, "But works of imagination such as those of Synge could not be suppressed even if burned in the market place." Both recognized that the play would not fit into the comic scheme it invites us to impose, and eventually both seemed to understand that this quality is not a flaw, but the genius of the play. *The Playboy of the Western World* is actually less a mixture of comic and tragic elements than a denial of either convention, a kind of anticomedy and an anti-tragedy, indeed a kind of antidrama. The tonal shift toward the serious and brutal after the reentrance of Old Mahon in Act Three is only the final wrench to a play that keeps us uncomfortable from beginning to end. It is not a play written in ignorance of generic or ethical conventions. It depends for its effect on its rejection of convention. It is thus related to the tradition of theatricalist drama, to *The Rehearsal, The Green Cockatoo, Six Characters in Search of an Author,* and *Marat/Sade.* But it does not, like these plays, violate the illusion of the stage, although it does lead us to deny the naturalistic premise that we are determined by our environment, our stage setting. More importantly it violates the generic conventions, the expectations it fosters in the audience, just as *Troilus and Cressida* repeatedly builds up and denies heroic expectations, or as *Bonnie and Clyde* encourages us to see crime as a joy ride and then shocks us with the inevitable blood [see Gerstenberger in Further Reading]. Synge carefully and skillfully manipulates our response to the material of the play in at least two ways: through our responses to generic convention he forces us into uncomfortable moral positions; and through our conventional moral responses he keeps us from settling into comfortable aesthetic attitudes.

For an example let us look at Christy's first entrance. Christy Mahon enters into this village which is imaginatively starved by harsh, uncompromising poverty. The village is represented so far by Pegeen Mike, longing after Daneen Sullivan and Marcus Quin, two violent storytellers; by Shawn Keogh, with his borrowed vision of a theocracy in which the meek like himself will inherit their promised due; and by Michael James and his companions, who seek solace in drink. When Christy, his feelings hurt by Pegeen's accusation of innocence, and threatened by a beating, announces his crime—parricide—Pegeen Mike leads the others in offering admiration and awe. He becomes for each of them, except for Shawn, of course, the answer to a wish. Michael James and his companions see in him the solution to the immediate problem, finding a protector for Pegeen Mike for the night. Beyond this immediate goal he would provide the shebeen with protection from the peelers, since (according to their logic) the police are afraid of Christy. For Pegeen herself, he seems the embodiment of the rebel and the poet: he has struck his blow against authority, and he demonstrates, once drawn out, a way with language that will come to surpass them all. He is eligible to boot.

It is only Shawn who has his doubts about Christy, doubts that audiences and critics have shared since the appearance of the play. While Pegeen and the others feel awe, we feel with Shawn a certain horror for Christy's crime. But we are loath to associate our position with that of the village coward. The credibility of the villagers' acceptance of parricide as an admirable act, an acceptance we are forced uneasily to entertain, has been the main critical crux of the play. Synge recorded in *The Aran Islands* a similar instance, but the islanders only harbored a fugitive parricide rather than lionizing him. We naturally feel uneasy about the wholehearted acceptance of parricide as hero that the play seems to ask of us. With this uneasiness begins a carefully controlled counterpoint between the reactions of the villagers, Christy's audience on the stage, and the response of an audience in the theater. The audience on the stage reverse their earlier glorification when the act of parricide is re-performed in their presence; and they thereby lose their right to possess the Playboy of the Western World. The audience in the theater are spared the sight of an actual enactment of parricide, successful or not, and we can thus count ourselves on the winning side of Christy rather than on the losing side of Pegeen Mike. But we recognize quite surely at the end of the play that we probably belong with the lamenting Pegeen if not with the blind Shawn Keogh. So the dilemma of the audience in the first act persists throughout, although we are allowed some respite in the second act when we learn of the failure of the parricide. Our sympathies are in conflict and our reactions are ambivalent.

Christy's transformation and transcendence of the limits of reality in the Western World are based on his acceptance as actual of what the others were willing to accept as tall tale: an act in the imagination, if real, then distanced by time and space, without actual involvement for them, a gallous tale. When the act is re-performed in their presence, when they are called upon to reaffirm their complicity in a deed become real (apparently), they flee back to the world of the shebeen, bow to the authority of the English law and rejoin Shawn's patriarchal society. The audience in the theater, since their sympathies have been separated from the beginning from Christy's audience on the stage, are left with the implicit responsibility to choose between Christy Mahon (and the uncomfortable implications of that choice, which range from parricide in Act I to a rejection of "reality" in Act III) and Shawn Keogh (and the stifling implications of that choice, which always means bondage to "reality" or naturalism). The act of the imagination which frees Christy from the tyranny of the actual is revolutionary; and although the political currents in this play are less clearly relevant to the Irish Question than some have assumed, this revolution has social and political as well as psychological and epistemological implications.

"There's a great gap between a gallous story and a dirty deed," Pegeen Mike declares in one of the pivotal scenes of the last act, and most critics have seized upon this speech as somehow crystallizing the theme of Synge's problem play. Yet if we stop to measure it against the resolution of the plot, we must conclude, at the least, that for a character such as Christy Mahon has become by the end of the play, it is the story that determines reality: both the reality of character and the dominion of character over phenomenal reality. He learns, just as Synge's favorite poet learns in the course of *The Prelude,* "to what point, and how, / The mind is lord and master—outward sense / The obedient servant of her will." Just as the "spots of time" teach and continually remind Wordsworth that the imagination rightfully has dominion over phenomenal nature, so in another way Christy is taught to bridge the gap between the gallous story he tells and his own reality. But for Christy the experience means he must leave the social milieu which failed to learn this lesson even as it taught him. That a gallous story, a mere fiction, might be more important than what we so often think of as reality, the world of legal and economic obligations, is as disturbing a notion for us as it is for the inhabitants of the Western World in the play, and I would suggest that it is this element that is responsible for the peculiar reactions the play often elicits, not only the famous riots attending its première at the Abbey Theatre in 1907 and its first American tour in 1911, but also the discomfort we still feel today. Audiences are uncomfortable with the ambivalence of **The Playboy,** and they have too often preferred to reject the play rather than to consider the questions it raises. It is surely relevant that the riots on the première night occurred not in Act II at the first appearance of the offending word *shifts,* but directly after the second parricide, when the implication of the audience in the dilemma the play presents is most complex.

It is, of course, no accident that the deed that frees Christy from his dependence and allows him to grow into independent maturity is parricide. Whether we read Freud or Frazier or Blake, the resonance of that act is clear. But whatever we think of the symbolic nature of the act, what is important in the play is that it is a real act to Christy insofar as he twice strikes the blow and is prepared, the second time, and if need be a third time, to accept the consequences, both positive and negative. It is not, I think, the theme of parricide that disturbs us, but rather that the play teaches us that the reality we live in is not necessarily so well-founded as we believed. By accepting the implications of his dirty deed—even after he knows the deed itself to be false—Christy frees himself from what we usually call reality, a subjection to parental domination and its extensions in Church, state and society. That domination of a materialistic vision forces Pegeen into a marriage with Shawn, even though he is a nonentity, because of his comparative wealth. This dependence on the materialistic has brutalized the imaginations of these villagers until, in reaction, their denied craving for something other leads them to drink, to slavish religiosity, or to the fascination with vio-

lence that imbues all their anecdotes to make a hero of a Marcus Quin, who maims ewes, not to mention Christy, the parricide. For the inhabitants of the Western World it is a confusion between the reality and the fiction that makes them goad Christy into the second murder and then assert the great gap between the story and the deed. For them the story of the murder was a tale separated from them by time, distance and a narrator. The difference between Christy the epic hero and his creator, Christy the epic bard, is not understood, since for them whatever occurs outside the narrow world represented on the stage by the shebeen is unreal.

This distinction between Christy as hero and Christy as narrator is clear if we compare an early scenario with the play as it developed. Draft "E" of Act I ends after Christy leaves in disgrace with his father in the following dialogue:

> BALLAD MAN. (*Singing as he comes in*)
> Young Christopher the daddy man
> came walking from Tralee
> And his father's bloody ghost the
> while did keep him company. . . .
> SHAWN. (*Jostling him*) Hold your jaw there
> his father's not murdered at all.
> BALLAD MAN. Oh, God help me and I after spending the half of me day making of his deed.
> SHAWN. He's not murdered I'm saying and we want none of your lies.
> BALLAD MAN. But it's a lovely song. . . .
> PEGEEN. What do we want with lies.
> BALLAD MAN. Well I'll sing it other roads where he's not known at all.
> It's a lovely song surely.
> SHAWN. Come on now to the green. (*Pipes are heard behind*). There's the piper and we'll have great dancing till the fall of night.

Here the narrator-ballad singer transforms the deeds of Christy into a poem which has a raison d'être apart from its truth. He is only a step from the narrators of epic theater, the Stage Manager of *Our Town,* the narrator in *The Caucasian Chalk Circle,* or Tom in *The Glass Menagerie.* And he is closely related to the rumor mongers in Lady Gregory's *Hyacinth Halvey* and *Spreading the News.* But Synge goes on to identify Christy the protagonist with the narrator so that Christy the protagonist becomes an invention of Christy the narrator. The real action of the play is narration; and Christy learns that the craft of narration is independent of category truth. To be sure he needs the encouragement of an audience. And his audience on the stage are made up of inveterate storytellers, so in Act I they give Christy object lessons about the transformation of a dirty deed into a gallous story. But they never learn the relationship between truth and fiction.

Christy is able to learn because for him the first murder was real, until his father appears: the story has always had a basis in fact, even though it becomes more heroic with each retelling. He is ethically implicated, and he is willing to accept not only the reward, but the punishment. The shifting responses of the villagers to his story allow him to learn that the gap between a dirty deed and a gallous story is not so wide as to be unbridged. He proceeds to make a gallous story out of his hanging rather than collapse into a whimpering mass resigned to his fate (his reaction to Act II to a lesser threat and now Shawn's reaction to Christy's bite):

> CHRISTY. If I can wring a neck among you, I'll

have a royal judgment looking on the
trembling jury in the courts of law. And
won't there be crying out in Mayo the
day I'm stretched upon the rope with ladies in their silks and satins snivelling in
their lacy kerchiefs, and they rhyming
songs and ballads on the terror of my
fate? (*He squirms round on the floor and
bites* SHAWN's *leg.*)

SHAWN. (*Shrieking*) My leg's bit on me! He's the
like of a mad dog, I'm thinking, the way
that I will surely die.

CHRISTY. (*Delighted with himself*) You will then,
the way you can shake out hell's flags of
welcome for my coming in two weeks or
three, for I'm thinking Satan hasn't
many have killed their da in Kerry, and
in Mayo too.

It is crucial that this affirmation occurs before Old Mahon re-
enters; Christy's growth is complete before we know that Old
Mahon survives and therefore in no way dependent on Old
Mahon's second survival, although presumably his own survival is, as is the ambivalent tonality of the play. Without
Mahon's survival, the play would veer off into ironic tragedy,
like *Bonnie and Clyde.*

In other words, Christy has learned that what we usually regard as literal reality is in fact unliteral, unliterary, or the raw
material of an imaginative reshaping of it into a fiction. He
teaches us to believe our ears, not our eyes, since our eyes tell
us that Christy and the set remain the same through three
acts, while our ears tell us that Christy has grown up and that
the set changes for him as his vision of himself and reality expands. In Act I the shebeen is a refuge from the police, but
also a piece of real estate distinctly less desirable than his father's Kerry farm. In Act II, as he counts the wealth represented by jugs and glasses, it has become a place of comfort,
potentially a dowry to be acquired. But by the love duet of
Act III, it has become too confining a locale for Christy, so
he offers Pegeen a "poacher's kind of love" in a natural setting. By his final exit he has learned that neither the shebeen
nor Pegeen is worth having.

Significantly in the starkly naturalistic setting, the shebeen,
almost nothing happens except narration, as if the poverty we
see oppresses all other action. All the "real" events take place
outside, in an unconfined setting, both of the murders and the
games. Moreover the reference of the speeches, except for
Christy's inventory in Act II, is always beyond the shebeen.
Only the final skirmish takes place within the set, and it is at
this point, when the action moves inside, that the reality becomes too much for the villagers and sometimes for the audience in the theater. Hence they respond in the brutally defensive way of Michael James: "It is the will of God that all
should guard their little cabins from the treachery of law and
what would my daughter be doing if I was ruined or was
hanged itself?" True reality in this play exists only beyond
the back wall of the stage, and we can perceive it only indirectly, through the storytellers, the fabulists, mainly Christy,
but also the others. In the race scene we perceive it in a sort
of instant replay as told by Old Mahon, Widow Quin, Jimmy
and Philly. The villagers' imaginations are constantly expanding beyond the back wall to the bishops and the courts
of Rome, to the polygamist Luthers of the preaching north,
to the man who bit the yellow lady's nostril on the northern
shore, to the parricide in Kerry. When that reality loses its
comfortable distance and invades the shebeen, they retreat to

the protection of Father Reilly, the English Courts, and the
bottle. The audience in the theater, on the other hand, do not,
because they have been not only educated along with Christy
in the poetic process, but also spared an immediate vision of
the reality out there. But Christy has been out there—
although he does not realize it until he stumbles into the shebeen and learns with the help of these naturalistic victims
that he need not simply react to reality, that he can shape it
to suit his desires. He can shape an otherwise dirty deed into
a gallous story.

Christy's ability to transform reality through the story, this
apparent lack of connection with the facts, may incline us to
dismiss the play and Synge as escapist. But we must recognize
a theme which weighs against this dismissal. Christy's reality
beyond the stage wall, like Deirdre's in Synge's last play
[**Deirdre of the Sorrows**], is not totally arbitrary like the reality of Algernon in *The Importance of Being Earnest.* It is a natural order. One can grasp this point by comparing Christy to
Hjalmar Ekdal in Ibsen's *Wild Duck,* a character who also
uses words to reduce an unhappy "reality" to a kind of story
with himself as hero (although Hjalmar's preferred genre is
melodrama, not epic). But Hjalmar's imaginative world, his
green world as it were, centers in a garret filled with some old
Christmas trees, chickens, rabbits, and a wild duck quickly
becoming domestic. Christy's green world is nature and the
inspiration of his language is natural. It is a world which includes, besides the natural pleasures, winter and hunger and
cold and aging and death. Most of all it includes loneliness.
These aspects are implicit in the **Playboy,** especially in Christy's natural imagery, but they are explicit in **Deirdre of the
Sorrows.** In the latter, Deirdre voluntarily ends a "playgirl"
existence and seeks certain death; she chooses to avoid the
waning of love and beauty which is inescapable, though the
inhabitants of Emain Macha try to deny that natural process.
The theme is also clear in Synge's first play, **In the Shadow
of the Glen,** where the tramp invites Nora to leave her dull,
jealous husband to join him in a vagrant existence that includes both pleasures and pains:

> We'll be going now, I'm telling you, and the time
> you'll be feeling the cold and the frost, and the great
> rain, and the sun again, and the south wind blowing
> in the glens, you'll not be sitting . . . in this place,
> making yourself old with looking on each day and
> it passing you by. You'll be saying one time, 'It's
> a grand evening by the grace of God,' and another
> time. 'It's a wild night, God help us, but it'll pass
> surely.'

On the other hand it is the world we usually call realistic, represented by Byrne's cottage, Emain Macha, and O'Flaherty's
shebeen, that tries to deny the reality of time and death and
pain. A whole series of characters in Synge from Dan Byrne
in **The Shadow** through Widow Casey in the **Playboy** and
Conchubar in **Deirdre** try to purchase the youth they have
wasted in "realistic" matters through grotesquely younger
spouses: Nora, Christy, and Deirdre. Material wealth in
Synge is always used as an attempt to buy time, and Christy
is most disappointing at the beginning of Act II, where he
seems to believe the shebeen with its "power of glasses" is
enough to make him happy. Parricide, real or symbolic, becomes necessary when an older generation tries through
power or wealth to deny time by subjugating the younger
generation whose time has come. It is the villagers in the
Western World, materially so poor, who are afraid to accept
the reality of time and the passing of power from one genera-

tion to the next. Old Mahon accepts with a broad smile and a "Glory be to God!"

Many of the difficulties the play presents can be resolved by seeing it, not as a comedy, which we are invited to do, but as a *Bildungsdrama* in which Christy grows from a timid lad, dominated by his father, something like Shawn Keogh, to a confident, self-reliant artist, like his father, master of his circumstances, chiefly through his mastery of language. He flees his home to wander in the world and finds the needed impetus for his growth in the admiration of the villagers and of Pegeen Mike for him and for his "gallous story." But by the last scene he has liberated himself from dependence on them just as surely as he had from dependence on the truth of his story and earlier from dependence on his father. He will "go romancing through a romping lifetime from this hour to the dawning of the judgement day"; or, to qualify his hyperbole, until he becomes subject to the natural limitations of aging, just as his father has become subject to one of those hazards, a son who asserts his independence. This limited qualification of Christy's assertion is implicit in his language, because he rejects allegiance never to the natural reality of time and mutability, but only to the social realities of the world as represented by the shebeen and its grudging submission to Father Reilly and the English law.

This pattern is one we are used to in fiction, especially in the tradition of the *Bildungsroman,* in which typically a hero moves from a position of social and familial conformity to the freedom of a conscious independence from that conformity. One might mention the roughly contemporaneous Stephen Daedalus or Hans Castorp. But this pattern of plot is much less common in drama, where there is a stronger pressure toward social conformity which is inherent in the very mode of theater and the mechanics of its performance. Christy changes more radically than almost any character in drama—the only similar transformation I can think of is Sigismund in Hofmannsthal's *Der Turm,* although Wagner's Siegfried and Giraudoux's Electre also grow to maturity before our eyes. The problem of making Christy's rapid transformation believable explains some of the measures Synge had to take, most significantly Christy's passivity as protagonist.

Our most traditional dramatic patterns also turn on the conflict of an individual with society, but society usually triumphs. Even where there is a conflict between two individuals, it is the individual most attuned to social values who triumphs. If this characterization of drama is fair, then clearly the *Playboy* is unusual as traditional drama. It would more clearly fit the pattern if the society of the village and Pegeen had been able to forgive Christy his unwitting lie after either of Old Mahon's resurrections, so that Christy's extravagances might have been integrated into the society as comic tall tales; or alternatively, if Christy had left as either a fugitive, a prisoner of the police, or just an exile, but without our approval and Pegeen's lament. But it is clear from Synge's revisions that he consistently moves away from the traditional comic situation toward more and more ambiguous patterns. The play seems to fit into the very typical ironic comic pattern of *Tartuffe* or *Volpone,* in which the imposter is finally unmasked and rejected as society closes its ranks, but for the fact that *The Playboy of the Western World* leaves the audience, like Pegeen, feeling trapped in the ranks of a restrictive society and longing for the freedom of the imposter. The implications of this "comedy" are antisocial, hence uncomic

and undramatic in a fundamental way. If we consider that the only action central to the play is narration and that the community created by the play is a community only in its sharing of an aesthetic response to Christy's story, not in any sharing of an interpretation of the facts, the ethics, or even the genre of the play, we can conclude that *The Playboy of the Western World* is truly antidrama, a form which undercuts its own conventions and refuses to resolve the problems it raises. (pp. 157-66)

    Bruce M. Bigley, " 'The Playboy of the Western World' as Antidrama," in Modern Drama, *Vol. 20, No. 2, June, 1977, pp. 157-67.*

JAMES C. PIERCE   (essay date 1981)

[In the following essay, Pierce focuses on the character of Widow Quin and her significance in the drama.]

After seventy years of critical attention, there still exists fundamental disagreement over interpretation of Synge's most famous play, *The Playboy of the Western World.* The debate, of course, focuses on Christy Mahon, the playboy. Most critics have seen Christy in purely comic terms as either the bona fide hero of a comic romance, or as the mock hero of a romantic farce. A brave few, however, have argued that Christy is an anti-hero, and *The Playboy* a tragicomedy. Indeed, it is difficult to view the play in purely comic terms. What seems to develop along the traditional lines of comedy concludes in a manner quite the opposite of comedy: rather than the expected marriage of comic hero and heroine and the unification of society, there is estrangment, and, although youth does triumph over age, the effect of this triumph is hardly comic unity.

A partial solution to the problem is to accept Synge as the modernist that he most emphatically is. Synge's plays cannot be expected to accommodate simple generic classification because Synge's vision is not simply comic or tragic; it is tragicomic, ironic. Misinterpretation of or refusal even to consider Synge's ironic sensibility has been the source of much confusion about all Synge's plays, especially *The Playboy.* An even greater problem lies in discovering a consistent sense to Synge's irony, and a consistent point-of-view in *The Playboy.* The potential for conflicting ironic interpretation appears at every turn: what Synge treats with warmth at one point he treats with cold derision at another; and what before was viewed negatively is suddenly presented in positive terms. Ultimately, the play appears at one moment to embrace a form of romantic idealism, but at another moment takes on tones of naturalistic cynicism.

The Playboy requires a touchstone to the ironic vision and tragicomic structure of the play—a consistent interpreter of this playboy and this western world. And there is good reason to expect one, for Synge provides such a touchstone in his other plays: Maurya, in *Riders to the Sea;* Nora, in *The Shadow of the Glen;* Mary Byrne in *The Tinker's Wedding;* Mary Doul in *The Well of the Saints;* and Deirdre in *Deirdre of the Sorrows* each act in this capacity; each provides a consistent, *all*-encompassing point-of-view that unifies, if not resolves, the play's contradictory, otherwise ambiguous perspectives. A touchstone for *The Playboy* does exist in the character of the Widow Quin. In fact, the Widow may be seen, *should* be seen, as a kind of ironic "backdrop" to the play against which all other of the play's points-of-view are shown to be incomplete—and without which the play would remain a hopelessly ambiguous puzzle. Through the Widow we may penetrate the apparent contradictions of *The Playboy* in order to discover that contradiction itself is thematically central to the play.

Surprisingly little attention has been paid to the characterization of the Widow Quin and her significance to *The Playboy of the Western World*. The Widow is usually passed off as a delightfully comic old schemer, a kind of "parody of the wise old woman figure with her greater knowledge of the situation and her shrewd sense of how to handle it for her own ultimate benefit" [see the excerpt by Diane Bessai dated 1968]. Critics see her as a comic foil, otherwise useful for establishing and furthering plot, but serving only minor thematic function.

Three reasons encourage such consistently oversimplified interpretation. First, critics tend to accept Pegeen's condemnation of the Widow as a woman who committed "a sneaky kind of murder did win small glory with the boys itself "; as a woman who lives in "leaky thatch is growing more pasture for her buck goat than her square of fields"; as a woman who the world knows "reared a black ram at . . . her breast, so that the Lord Bishop of Connaught felt the elements of a Christian and he eating it after in a kidney stew." Second, critics naturally tend to associate the Widow Quin with the Widow Casey, the woman Christy says his father would have forced him to marry had it not been for Christy's "fatal" blow, and whom Christy describes as:

> A walking terror from beyond the hills, and she two score and five years, and two hundredweights and five pounds in the weighing scales, with a limping leg on her, and a blinded eye, and she a woman of noted misbehavior with the old and young . . . [who] did suckle me for six weeks when I came into the world, and she a hag this day with a tongue on her has the crows and sea birds scattered the way they wouldn't cast a shadow on her garden with the dread of her curse.

And, third, there is the simple and undeniable fact that the Widow Quin *is* a shrewd woman who, above all, has concern for her own well-being. It is no wonder that the Widow so often seems a selfish, lecherous, vulgar, ugly old hag whose proposal to Christy we must certainly find disgusting.

The actual characterization of the Widow Quin, however, gives us quite a different picture. In the first place, she is neither old nor ugly. The play's cast of characters describes her as "a woman of about thirty." According to Christy's self-satisfied appraisal of his situation at the end of the first act—"it's great luck and company I've won me in the end of time . . . [with] two fine women [Pegeen and the Widow] fighting for the likes of me"—she is still an attractive woman, quite comparable to Pegeen. The Widow is, in fact, Pegeen's only real rival for Christy, and we must therefore view anything Pegeen says about her with great suspicion. We are left, then, with only the fact of the Widow Quin's shrewdness and her concern for her own well-being. In *The Playboy*'s world, this constitutes no criticism at all, for all of the play's characters seek, in one way or another, to protect *their* own well-being. The Widow Quin, simply, is more aware than anyone else of just what her well-being consists of, and more willing to pursue it directly and consciously.

The Widow Quin, the only realist in this Mayo community, serves as the touchstone of the play, the only reliable com-

mentator on *The Playboy* world. Synge indicates her importance by presenting her as the last major character, except Old Mahon, to enter the stage. So, her cynically comic observations serve as a kind of undercutting final commentary to the characterizations and situation introduced in the first act. The Widow Quin appears on the stage only a few minutes in the first act, but in that short time she firmly establishes the ironic course and tone of the play.

We are, of course, most interested in the effect the Widow has on Christy, for we should by this time be thoroughly confused about Christy's heroic, pathetic character. And, if we have been led to think that Christy's true nature is that of a hero, that he has just now entered an environment that offers him the inspiration he needs to mature heroically, we must now have second thoughts. Christy has just finished retelling his story, which takes on more heroic embellishments with each recounting, and has just proclaimed himself "a seemingly fellow with great strength in me and bravery of . . . " when he hears a knocking at the door. Immediately thrown into a state of terror, he clings to Pegeen for protection crying, "Oh, glory! it's late for knocking, and this last while I'm in the terror of the peelers and the walking dead. . . . " The Widow Quin has only knocked at the door, but already she has revealed to us Christy's more likely character. More to the point, however, is the Widow's unromanticized first assessment of Christy. The Widow has not heard Christy's story firsthand, but she has heard it from Shawn Keogh, and we may surmise that Shawn's version has made Christy out to be an even more terrible character than Christy makes himself out to be. But the Widow displays only warmly humorous curiosity, a trait which immediately separates her from the other, more easily impressed citizens of Mayo. Synge indicates that she sizes Christy up immediately for what he is: "*Looking at him with half-amused curiosity,*" the Widow says,

> Well, aren't you a little smiling fellow? It should have been great and bitter torments did rouse your spirits to a deed of blood . . . it'd soften my heart to see you sitting so simple with your cup and cake, and you fitter to be saying your catechism than slaying your da.

The Widow's first estimation of Christy is based solely upon intuition, but from what we have seen of Christy so far, and what we shall see in the second act, her intuitions are well founded.

The consistent "rightness" of the Widow Quin cannot be denied. In this short scene she not only sizes up Christy just by looking at him, but she also warns, in terms that the audience must surely recognize as likely, that Pegeen, with her bad temper and her sharp tongue, will "be rating at your own self when a week is by? . . . [And] let you be wary, there's right torment will wait you here if you go romancing with her like. . . . " In fact, the Widow proves to be right about everything and everyone in Mayo. She knows the immature, flighty, headstrong kind of girl Pegeen is. She immediately recognizes the not particularly heroic, but quite human qualities of Christy. And, though she never complains of it, she seems quite aware of the potential cruelty of the Mayo people.

Perhaps the best explanation for the dependable accuracy of the Widow Quin's perspective is that she is a woman of experience. As she herself explains, she is "a woman has buried her children and destroyed her man." That is terrible knowl-

" PLAYBOY "

**Last Night's Scenes
in New York**

**HISSING DROWNED BY
APPLAUSE**

Roosevelt Present

UNDER POLICE PROTECTION

In New York as in Dublin

Synge's Malodorous "Playboy"

THE RIOT IN THE THEATRE

The "Man that Killed his Da"

OFFENSIVE INCIDENTS CAUSE UPROAR

Headlines on The Playboy's *production in New York in November 1911.*

edge to carry of the world, for she has come to know violence not simply as a romanticized fantasy, as her Mayo neighbors do, but as a cruel reality. Another part of the Widow's experience, one not so obvious but of equal significance, is that she knows loneliness. A woman of only about thirty, not so old that she no longer has hope or need of romantic fulfillment, of intimate personal communion, she is old enough, especially in peasant Ireland, that her hopes of romantic communion are dwindling, even while her conscious need grows stronger. The Widow knows the cruelty of the world and she knows her prospects in that world, but her experience and her knowledge have not made her bitter. Rather, they have made her the most compassionate, the most sympathetically human of all the people of this western world.

The most effective indication of both the sympathetic qualities and the realistic perspective of the Widow Quin may be the almost soothing tone with which Synge surrounds her characterization. Never found to be vindictive or even angry, the Widow often has reason to be, especially considering Pegeen's abuse of her. The personification of sympathetic good humor, often a tease but never cruelly so, the Widow is, in fact, the only one among the villagers who is not fascinated by the cruelty of others. This aspect of the Widow's character—this sort of objective understanding of and slightly distanced participation in a society that she knows better than anyone else—makes the Widow Quin the touchstone for Synge's satiric but not unsympathetic assessment of Mayo society—and perhaps all of society.

The Widow Quin's vastly more experienced view extends the boundaries of reality beyond the shallow vision, the romantic fantasies, of the rest of Mayo—the community that, without the Widow, would be our only measure of Christy's growth.

The "vision" of Mayo, when placed alongside that of the Widow Quin, proves extremely suspect; therefore, Christy's romantic stature, his heroic image, diminishes considerably. The most concrete example of this effect is the scene of the Widow's proposal to Christy, which may be argued as the high point of **The Playboy** in terms of thematic development, though not in terms of plot development.

As the scene opens, Old Mahon has just gone off, tricked by the Widow into thinking that Christy has already passed through; and Christy, *"nearly speechless with rage,"* curses his father for not having died as he was supposed to:

> To be letting on he was dead, and coming back to his life, and following me like an old weasel tracing a rat, and coming in here laying desolation between my own self and the fine women of Ireland, and he a kind of carcass that you'd fling upon the sea. . . . May I meet him with one tooth and it aching, and one eye to be seeing seven and seventy divils in the twists of the road, and one old timber leg on him to limp into the scalding grave.

Both scandalized and greatly moved by Christy's apparently sincere hatred, the Widow asks "What ails you?" And Christy replies:

> Amn't I after seeing the love-light of the star of knowledge shining from her [Pegeen's] brow, and hearing words would put you thinking on the Holy Brigid speaking to the infant saints, and now she'll be turning again, and speaking hard words to me, like an old woman with a spavindy ass she'd have, urging on a hill.

Christy is conscious of the fact that, without his one violent deed, he will be looked upon just as he was before. He also seems to have accepted his new romantic image as his real self; only the failure of the act itself separates him from the romantic existence broadly represented by "the fine women of Ireland" and, specifically, by Pegeen. It is equally significant that he compares himself, without society's praise, to a "rat" and an "ass"; and, again, that he compares Pegeen, without the reason to praise him, with an "old woman" driving him with "hard words." Christy has recognized some of the parts to an absurd world, but he has not put them together so that he can recognize the absurdity itself. He has seen that heroic praise depends not upon virtue but upon imagined virtue; however, he refuses to recognize the shallowness of such romantic illusions or the blindness of people who pursue them.

The Widow Quin suffers from no such blindness. She knows the real world from the fantasy world and points out to Christy just how unsuited his romantic vision of Pegeen is to the real Pegeen. "There's poetry talk," she says, "for a girl you'd see itching and scratching, and she with a stale stink of poteen on her from selling in the shop." A harsh view, and one undoubtedly influenced by the rivalry of the two women, it is much closer to the truth, however, than Christy's view. And, as we discover from the Widow's response to Christy's distress over what he would do if he loses Pegeen, such a view comes from a woman who understands much better than Christy the pathetic implications of his potential loss, no matter how unromantic the actual substance of that loss:

> You'll be doing like myself, I'm thinking, when I destroy my man, for I'm above many's the day, odd times in great spirits, abroad in the sunshine, darning a stocking or stitching a shift, and odd times again looking out on the schooners, hookers, travelers, is sailing the sea, and I thinking on the gallant hairy fellows are drifting beyond, and myself long years living alone.

The Widow knows the unromantic substance of the real world, but she knows also the reality of man's romantic longings and the desperate emptiness of a life without the comforts of imaginative companionship. Her talk fascinates Christy, for he cannot fail to recognize the loneliness that his threatened return to preheroic existence represents. The Widow has struck a sympathetic chord and having, if but for a moment, gained Christy's interest, she proposes:

> I am your like, and it's for that I'm taking a fancy to you, and I with my little houseen above where there'd be myself to tend you, and none to ask were you a murderer or what at all. . . . I've nice jobs you could be doing, gathering shells to make a whitewash for our hut within, building up a little goose house, or stretching a new skin on an old curragh I have, and if my hut is far from all sides, it's there you'll meet the wisest old men, I tell you, at the corner of my wheel, and it's there yourself and me will have great times whispering and hugging. . . .

If there has been any doubt before the Widow Quin is attracted to Christy, in spite of seeing through his heroic facade, there can be none now. She has seen Old Mahon, heard from him the pathetic truth of Christy's past, and has seen Christy cower in his presence. But, far from being disappointed, as Pegeen will be when she learns the truth, the Widow appears even more attracted, for she has seen too much of the world and knows too well the unheroic nature of violence to pursue a romantic fantasy. She is attracted to Christy simply because

he is a man—not less because he is an unheroic man, but more because he is a sensitive man. And she has offered to him a real life based, not on romantic idolatry, but on human affection. She has offered Christy everything that he himself has professed to value—a secure life, good company, and womanly affection—everything, that is, except the fantasy of being a romantic hero idolized by a romantic heroine. For that romantic fantasy, however, Christy rejects the Widow's offer.

Christy's rejection of the Widow's proposal closes what we may logically expect to be her last opportunity to obtain the sympathetic companionship that she alone seems to recognize as mankind's one comfort against the destructive forces of the natural world, against time. There can be no doubt that the Widow understands this, just as she understands the lonely and empty life that lies ahead of her. This is most certainly a kind of tragic recognition. But, supportable as this aspect of the Widow's character is, Synge only indirectly focuses upon it in the play. We are likely to ignore her more tragic side, preferring the comically material side of the Widow's character. Still, the invitation to "project" tragedy out of what on the surface appears merely comic remains, and this sense of potential tragedy forms what is probably Synge's most illusive structural irony.

Such projected potential is not new to Synge's drama. T. R. Henn found similar implications in *The Shadow of the Glen,* noting that the play is neither comedy nor tragedy but a combination of the "elements of comedy which are not fully exploited in the present [and the] elements of tragedy which are, perhaps, projected into the future after the curtain has fallen." Such ambiguous combinations also exist in *The Tinker's Wedding* and *The Well of the Saints.* However, in all three of these earlier plays, Synge makes the tragic potential fairly obvious: it is almost impossible not to recognize the tragic fate that awaits Nora Burke or Mary Byrne or Mary Doul, for we are specifically told of their probable fates. But, in *The Playboy of the Western World,* except for the personal tragedy of the Widow Quin, such potential never becomes so obvious. Its presence is asserted not so much by declarative language as by anxiety created out of the contradiction between what we are told will happen and what seems likely to happen, as by the uneasy feeling that things have not really worked out so well as they seem to have; as by the feeling that, no matter how comically things have thus far come to pass, there must sometime in the future be a tragic confrontation with what has so far only been dimly understood.

This more subtle form of irony affects our interpretation of *The Playboy* most obviously, perhaps, to the extent that it alters our assessment of Christy. This reassessment comes directly out of the Widow's personal tragedy. The Widow has offered Christy a real life, based upon honest affection, imaginative communion, and acceptance of his real, unromanticized self. In this sense, the Widow represents acceptance of the real or unromanticized world and self, and Christy's rejection of the Widow must be seen as a rejection of reality in favor of his illusory vision of heroism. On its most obvious level, the tragic, and satiric, consequences of his rejection are first made evident of all by Christy's failure to win Pegeen, the romantic object of his heroic fantasies, because he has not really committed the murder that made him a hero in the first place; and, then, after he has killed his father a second time and made himself "a proven hero in the end of time," by Pegeen's inability to live up to the ideal of heroine that is the necessary price of Christy's romantic quest; and, finally, after he has witnessed society's and Pegeen's confrontation with the deed that they heartily approved of so long as it remained only an "ideal," revealed by Christy's inability to reject an ideal that has proven itself false.

We may sense tragic potential in Pegeen also, especially in view of her anguished words at the end of the play; but, unless we are willing to accept as real Christy's heroism, we are probably at a loss to explain Pegeen as a tragic heroine. A major reason for this is that we are likely to pass over the possibility of any sympathetic relationship between Pegeen and the Widow and see them simply as comic adversaries. In reality, they have much more in common than not; and, just as with Christy, our assessment of Pegeen depends primarily upon our understanding of the Widow. The greatest difference between them, perhaps the only difference of real significance, is age—Pegeen is twenty and the Widow is about thirty. This single difference, and the difference in experience and awareness that it implies, forms the basis of their personality differences—mainly that Pegeen is youthfully and sometimes cruelly impetuous, whereas the Widow is patiently and sympathetically mature. But the same difference also allows us to see Pegeen as a younger version of the Widow.

What the Widow Quin and Pegeen Mike most obviously have in common is that they are the liveliest and most personally demanding women in the village. They demand more of life than any man in Mayo can provide. Moreover, both have demonstrated their determination not to bow to the oppressively mundane existence of Mayo life. Pegeen is still too young to understand fully her own needs; and her needs are only immaturely expressed by her craving for a more exciting life and by her constant threats of violence against anyone who appears an obstruction to her. The Widow's calmer disposition, and her concern about Christy's welfare as the villagers threaten to hang him, do not lead us to think of her in terms of violent potential; but she did kill her husband, though accidentally, and the calm disposition that she now displays is best explained as the result of having experienced the consequences of the ultimate violent act—the lonely remorse of having destroyed a companion. This, too, may be seen as a reflection of the projected experience of Pegeen. For Pegeen's declaration, after having witnessed what appears to be an actual murder, that "there's a great gap between a gallous story and a dirty deed," reveals a partial recognition of the unromantic reality of violence. However, since she follows her new awareness with a violent deed of her own, her "recognition" can hardly be considered complete.

Perhaps the strongest evidence for the likeness of Pegeen Mike and the Widow Quin is their common basis of attraction to Christy Mahon. Of course, all the village girls are attracted to Christy, but their reasons seem purely superficial: they see him only as a violent, vainglorious, heroic romancer, and they never look beyond this illusory image. But, as noted before, the Widow Quin, though interested in him at first simply because he is a "curiosity man," finally proposes to him when she discovers the lonely desperation and, perhaps, the potential poet that lies beneath his fantasies of romantic heroism. Pegeen Mike is at first attracted to Christy for the same reasons as the rest of Mayo—because Christy represents a curious break from the dull monotony of Mayo life. But, like the Widow Quin's, Pegeen's curiosity transforms into romantic longing when she discovers, during her private conversation with Christy in the first act, that he has not been the gal-

lant romancer that she and the others of Mayo have thought. Pegeen is at first disappointed when Christy tells her that "Up to the day I killed my father, there wasn't a person in Ireland knew the kind I was." But, when he tells her of the terrible existence he suffered under his father's rule, of the lonely and "bitter life he led me till I did up a Tuesday and halve his skull," Pegeen seems more drawn to him than ever. "*Putting her hand on his shoulder*," she tells him, "Well, you'll have peace in this place, Christy Mahon, and none to trouble you, and it's near time a fine lad the like of you should have your share of the earth."

Though she barely realizes it herself, Pegeen has discovered in Christy the same depth of feeling that the Widow Quin later discovers—the warmth and sensitivity that are the essentials of a truly romantic companion. But Pegeen does not understand, as the Widow does, the significance of her discovery. Her recognition of Christy's truly romantic worth—and therein her own truly romantic needs—is only momentary. And her rejection of Christy—first because he has not and then because he has killed his father—foretells a life as tragically lonely and insecure as the Widow Quin's. In the end, only Shawn Keogh is left her, and she truly has lost "the only playboy of the western world."

The tragedy implicit in the characterization of Pegeen Mike remains only a "projected" tragedy because Pegeen has not yet fully realized what she has lost; she does not yet understand that Christy's real value was human, and not heroic. Pegeen's tragic flaw—a very naturalistic sort of tragic flaw—is that, when she most needed the mature understanding necessary to make a mature judgment, she was too young and too inexperienced to fully understand or to satisfactorily judge. She has, like Christy, achieved some awareness of herself and her world, but her awareness remains as incomplete as Christy's. Both have achieved a greater understanding than most of the Mayo villagers, but neither has achieved the "complete" awareness of the Widow Quin.

This is Synge at his ironic best: in ***The Playboy of the Western World*** we not only can but *must* accept the existence of seemingly contradictory interpretations. Christy has lived up to the romantic ideals of the western world—and he is therefore a hero. Yet, in terms of the play's broader perspective, the ideals of the western world are empty fantasies, not worth living up to—and he is therefore not a hero. Christy and Pegeen have come to a new understanding of themselves and their society which does make them reject as inadequate the ideals they had held in such high esteem; and they do suffer at the loss of those ideals—therefore, they may be seen as tragic hero and heroine. Yet, in terms of the broader implications of the play, in comparison to the Widow Quin, their new understanding is incomplete. They have not fully recognized the shallowness of the heroic ideal itself—and they are therefore not tragic hero and heroine. Only the Widow Quin seems fully aware, and her tragic "moment" has already passed, since she has rejected the shallow fantasies of this falsely romantic world even before the start of the play. Moreover, the overriding tone of the Widow Quin's presentation is not tragic but satirically comic, just as the overriding structure of the play is not that of tragedy but of ironic romance. Only implied in this play, tragedy is projected only as a probable outcome to any realistic extension of the play beyond its own loosely comic, but ultimately ironic boundaries. (pp. 122-33)

James C. Pierce, "Synge's Widow Quin: Touchstone

to the Playboy's *Irony,"* in *Eire-Ireland, Vol. XVI, No. 2, 1981, pp. 122-33.*

HUGH KENNER (essay date 1983)

[*A Canadian-born American critic, Kenner is the foremost chronicler and commentator on literary Modernism. He is best known for* The Pound Era (*1971*), *a massive study of the Modernist movement, and for his influential works on Samuel Beckett, T. S. Eliot, James Joyce, and Wyndham Lewis. In addition to his reputation as an important scholar, Kenner is also noted for his often eccentric judgments and a critical style that relies on surprising juxtapositions and wit. In the following excerpt from his study* A Colder Eye: The Modern Irish Writers, *he elaborates on the development of* Playboy *through successive draft versions and discusses Synge's use of folk rhythm in representing the speech of western Ireland.*]

The plays [Synge] started writing in 1902 came from stories he had been told. He set them in places he had visited and made up the dialogue, laborious sentence by sentence, out of phrases he had heard. It was the way James Joyce worked too, though not Yeats, and it was a check against vagueness. Though a time would come when Yeats's verse could describe a piece of lapis lazuli with museum-catalogue accuracy, on the whole his aversion to particularity, save for sudden effect, seemed constitutional. "I have read in some old book," he would intone, or "A friend of my father's used to say . . ." When he and Lady Gregory received Synge's *Aran Islands* typescript, a lively prose account of four visits, it was Yeats's immediate counsel that details should be blurred, even the names of the islands omitted, in the service of "a curious dreaminess" Synge had no interest whatever in attaining: Synge who held the setting of *In the Shadow of the Glen* so clearly in mind his biographers have had no trouble identifying Nora Burke's actual cottage, inhabited when Synge was up there in 1897 by two brothers and their sister, name of Harney. When Willie Fay would ask during rehearsal, "Was Dan standing where he is on the right, behind the table, when he said those lines?" Synge would say, "No, he was on the right-hand side of the table with his hand on it." Not for him the indifference that could let whole orderings of the visible vanish on the instant at whim, or envisage the setting and groupings of [Yeats's drama] *The Land of Heart's Desire* in two quite different ways and vacillate between them from reprinting to reprinting.

Not for him either the rapid poet's pen to catch fleeting thoughts for reworking. Taking a play through a dozen drafts or more, he composed with much premeditation on the queer little typewriter with twenty-seven keys and shifts for FIG and CAP. He bought it in 1899 for his Aran Islands book, and because each keystroke had first to rotate the printwheel and then slam it forward it was not a machine on which you could get up speed: transcribing thirteen hundred words was a day's work. We must assume that he welcomed its slow staccato, its stubborn interposition between brain and paper, forcing deliberate attention to every preposition, every mark of punctuation. "Good evening kindly, stranger" differs substantially from "Good evening, kindly stranger," which was how a London printer in 1905 commenced Nora's first speech in *Shadow.* Though other printers have followed him, the first version is what Synge typed at least twice.

Unlike most of the Abbey playwrights, he was a writer at heart, not a talker; the commonest perception of Synge in company was that he hardly ever spoke. The speech in his plays is as synthetic as Shakespeare's, something Thomas MacDonagh was wincing at when he found it "too full of rich phrases." You might say the same of any speech of Falstaff's, if what you expected was to hear the way English knights talk. In a time with poetic conventions so introspective they were all but useless on stage, and a prose of no more interest than a polished plate-glass pane, Synge had glimpsed a way to stylize words for speaking aloud, and it got mistaken for malicious misreporting.

When John Quinn, in New York, thought of buying the *Playboy* manuscript Synge described what it was like.

> I work always with a typewriter—typing myself—so I suppose it has no value? I make a rough draft first and then work over it with a pen until it is nearly unreadable; then I make a clean draft again, adding whatever seems wanting, and so on. My final drafts—I letter them as I go along—were "G" for the first act, "I" for the second, and "K" for the third! I really wrote parts of the last act more than eleven times, as I often took out individual scenes and worked at them separately. The MS., as it now stands, is a good deal written over, and some of it is in slips or strips only, cut from the earlier versions—so I do not know whether it has any interest for the collector.

It had; and the typescript Quinn bought is now at Indiana University. Later Synge made two more drafts of Act II, so the Indiana copy is "K."

The plays gained density slowly. A notebook draft of what was still called *The Fool of Farnham* has the pubkeeper's daughter writing out an order: "Three barrels of porter with the best compliments of the season." (Synge disliked using any but authentic phrases, and "wishing you the best compliments of the season" was a flourish from a letter a girl on Aran wrote him.) By typescript "D" this had become "Two dozens of Powers Whiskey. Three barrels of porter. And soda as before." In the margin of draft "E" (23 May 1905) he prompted himself: "Open out? Try making her order her trousseau?" and flipping the page he jotted a trousseau: "Six yards of yellow silk ribbon, a pair of long boots, bright hat suited for a young woman on her wedding day, a fine tooth comb to be sent. . . . " His pen hovered over this. "Long boots" became "pair of shoes with English heels"; then "English" became "big," "big" became "long," "long" became "lengthy," and in the printed text that copies typescript "G" *The Playboy of the Western World* begins:

> PEGEEN. (*Slowly, as she writes*): Six yards of stuff for to make a yellow gown. A pair of lace boots with lengthy heels on them and brassy eyes. A hat is suited for a wedding day. A fine tooth comb. To be sent with two barrels of porter in Jimmy Farrell's creel cart on the evening of the coming fair to Mister Michael James Flaherty. With the best compliments of this season: Margaret Flaherty.

Sharp eyes will notice that "the season" became "this season," exactly the wording of the letter of the girl from Aran. No detail was too minute for pondering. As late as the final typescript of Act III the "drift of chosen females" was standing "stripped itself," and when Synge at the last minute draped them in the notorious shifts he thought he had adjusted an outrageousness. His model was the thirty virgins arrayed in the old story, to quench Cuchulain's bloody rage with the sight of their stark nakedness: the hero paid them nearly Victorian courtesy.

Some elements were never changed at all. One of the things he knew from the first about his playboy hero was that his name was Christy: a mock-Christ who puts an end to crucifixion by killing the Father. Brought up in a Scriptural family which had even preceded him to the Aran Islands in the person of a reverend uncle with a mission to reform papists' ways ("I have succeeded in putting a stop to the ball match that used to go on here every Sunday"—1851), the sardonic John Millington Synge made free in his plays with Scriptural motifs. *The Well of the Saints* is about a canonical miracle, blindness cured, which proves unwanted ("It's a power of dirty days, and dark mornings, and shabby-looking fellows we do have to be looking on when we have our sight"). *In the Shadow of the Glen* turns on a resurrection, also unwanted; when the "dead" husband leaps from his bed no one present, including his wife, is anything but chagrined. And *The Playboy* has a resurrection too, for good measure a pair of them, the slain and risen figure both times not the son but the father, whom Synge after several deleted tries surnamed Mahon, pronounced Ma'on, approximately Man: not a "meaning," no, an agnostic author at play.

In this topsy-turvy gospel Christy the Son of Mahon was as abstemious as you'd want ("poor fellow would get drunk on the smell of a pint") and so chaste he ran from the sight of a distant girl (when "you'd see him shooting out his sheep's eyes between the little twigs and the leaves") and indeed had every virtue you can list save being any use; and when his old rascal of a father instructed him that his next move in life, after these potatoes were dug, should be to wed the Widow Casey, Christy would have none of that idea at all. For the Widow Casey was "a walking terror from beyond the hills, and she two score and five years, and two hundred weights on her, and a blinded eye, and she a woman of noted misbehaviour with the old and young." In all but not being skinny she was the Sheela-na-gig, the old Irish effort at a fertility goddess, a skeleton with huge pudenda, grinning like death [Vivian Mercier, *The Irish Comic Tradition*].

So Christy banged his father with the spade, saying later he'd split his skull to the knob of his gullet and still later that he'd split him to the breeches belt; but in fact by the word of the resurrected father, "Weren't you off racing the hills before I got my breath with the start I had seeing you turn on me at all?"

That was in Kerry, where the Kerrymen come from about whom the Irish tell their Polish jokes; the way the Kerryman broke his leg was he fell out of the tree raking leaves, so you know murder is a thing he'd botch. Christy next ran and walked for eleven days all the way north to the mean bleak country toward Belmullet in County Mayo. (Did it amuse Synge, as it would have amused James Joyce, that to get there he must have trudged past Lady Gregory's Coole?)

Northwest Mayo was as sinister overpopulated wilderness, bogs, stones and hovels, the heart of the Congested Districts that stretched down the Atlantic Coast from Donegal to Dingle and were the special concern of a Board charged with bureaucratic countermeasures to starvation. This blind corner of Ireland stunned even the optimistic AE. It was from Belmullet itself AE had written to Synge in 1897 how he was disheartened out of words. There was nothing to write about save the distress and that was "a disgrace to humanity" and "not cheerful subject matter for a letter."

Synge was first in Belmullet in September 1904, and made

there the first sketches for all three acts of *The Murderer (A Farce)*, four titles later *The Playboy of the Western World*. The people thereabouts, his journal recalls, were "debased and nearly demoralized by bad housing and lodging and the endless misery and rain." Any girl's usual costume was "a short red petticoat over bare feet and legs, a faded uncertain bodice and a white or blue rag swathing the head," and the town was "squalid and noisy, lonely and crowded at the same time and without any appeal to the imagination." It was in a like place he heard an old boatman's lament: "I don't know what way I'm going to go on living in this place that the Lord created last, I'm thinking, in the end of time; and it's often when I sit down and look around on it I do begin cursing and damning, and asking myself how poor people can go on executing their religion at all." That was the Western World, so called to contrast it with the Dublin or eastern side of the island, and Christy Mahon fetches up there. Nowhere was it less likely that the pure and exalted peasantry of Nationalist myth might be found, chaste in action, chaste in speech, united in simple love of Ireland and Holy Church and Father Reilly.

That was true even if Synge had been content to depict them naturalistically. The region had a long history of strife. It was there in 1880 that Captain Boycott got boycotted, and that was a mild dealing. Reprisals were normally brutal. Twenty-nine Mayo men, by a story Synge heard there and made a ballad of, once decided it was high time to deal with a hell-raiser named Danny,'d capsize the stars:

> But we'll come round him in the night
> A mile beyond the Mullet;
> Ten will quench his bloody eyes,
> And ten will choke his gullet.

W. B. Yeats's sister Lollie declined to set this in type. Synge's ballad particularized what damage Danny did the lads who ambushed him, but it was dozens to one, and

> . . . seven tripped him up behind
> And seven kicked before,
> And seven squeezed around his throat
> Till Danny kicked no more.
>
> Then some destroyed him with their heels,
> Some tramped him in the mud,
> Some stole his purse and timber-pipe,
> And some washed off his blood.
>
> • • • • •
>
> And when you're walking out the way
> From Bangor to Belmullet,
> You'll see a flat cross on a stone
> Where men choked Danny's gullet.

The pious X-marks-the-spot is a fine touch. And between Belmullet and Bangor, that would not be far off from where we might look for the shebeen (low pub) Christy Mahon, reputed murderer, stumbles into after getting his wind in a ditch.

Synge's first thought had been to dramatize a story he was told on Aran, about how folk in a remote place will shelter a fugitive. When W. B. Yeats himself first visited Aran in 1896 there were islanders who thought from his oblique eye he was a killer in need of refuge instead of a tourist with a skew cornea. "If any gentleman has done a crime we'll hide him," Yeats was told meaningfully. And an old man, the oldest on Inishmaan, more than once told Synge a story out of living memory "about a Connaught man who killed his father with the blow of a spade when he was in a passion, and then fled to this island and threw himself on the mercy of some of the natives. . . . They hid him in a hole—which the old man has shown me—and kept him safe for a week, though the police came and searched for him, and he could hear their boots grinding on the stones over his head." Then they got him off to America. Synge reflected:

> This impulse to protect the criminal is universal in the west. . . . Such a man, they say, will be quiet all the rest of his life, and if you suggest that punishment is needed as an example, they ask, "Would any one kill his father if he was able to help it?"

But the first sketches he set down in Belmullet in late 1904 already eschew this sententious note. He had commenced to amuse himself with the notion of a folk who might not simply shield a murderer but glorify him. For whom did Irishmen glorify? Looking round at their current heroes he saw Fenians, the Phoenix Park murderers—thugs, dynamiters, knifers; also the literary cult of Cuchulain the skull-basher.

So in Act I we should see the bang on the head itself, out in that Kerry potato-field. Then in Act II—this was pivotal— the murderer would be a feisty talker; himself it was would dictate the terms of glory. He would tell of the deed at every provocation, and his eloquence would boss the show. They would elect him county councillor! (When Synge was feeling sardonic his thoughts turned ritually to politicians, though never did any of these windbags survive into a finished play.) In Act III the father—not dead after all—would turn up to spoil the victory speech by calling his son a liar. "Son attacks father and is handcuffed. . . . " This was *The Murderer* (*A Farce*), and whether Synge judged it more farcical to disgrace this politician or reinstate him we cannot know, since the next leaf is torn from the notebook.

It is trivial, but so are all Synge's projects in the notebook stage beyond which most of them were never carried. His way, in four of the six plays he finished—the exceptions are *Deirdre* and *Riders to the Sea*—was to start from something like a sophomore's joke and endow it slowly with human range and weight: blind folk who treasure their blindness, dead men who will not stay dead, tinkers who crave the blessing of the parish priest and end up tying him in a sack. It was while *The Playboy* was still a jeu d'esprit that he let a simple point of stagecraft impose a crucial decision. The opening scene, the killing in the potato-field, was deleted. For to keep an audience from seeing the blank side walls of the Abbey's box a set-dresser would have to arrange canvas frames, called wings, on which he would have painted—what but trees? So, as Yeats explained to an audience at Harvard, "Synge gave up the intention of showing upon the stage a fight between 'The Playboy' and his father, because he would not have six large trees, three on each side, growing in the middle of a ploughed field." That was impeccable Irish logic.

Consequently *The Playboy* has but the one set, the shebeen Pegeen helps her father run, and now Synge was able to get interested in an idea he might otherwise have dropped, since we in the audience no longer know what happened in the field as we listen to Christy, so his eloquence can work on us the way it does on the men and girls of Mayo. This greatly alters the effect envisaged in *The Murderer*, where we'd have seen a braggart inflaming silly folk we were free to feel superior to. Now Christy's talk can create an heroic world.

CHRISTY. (*Impressively*) With that the sun came

out between the cloud and the hill, and it shining green in my face. "God have mercy on your soul," says he, lifting a scythe. "Or on your own," says I, raising the loy.
SUSAN. That's a grand story.
HONOR. He tells it lovely.
CHRISTY. (*Flattered and confident, waving bone*) He gave a drive with the scythe, and I gave a lep to the east. Then I turned around with my back to the north, and I hit a blow on the ridge of his skull, laid him stretched out, and he split to the knob of his gullet. (*He raises the chicken bone to his Adam's apple.*)
GIRLS. (*Together*) Well, you're a marvel! Oh, God bless you! You're the lad surely!

Indeed it's a grand story and he tells it lovely, guided by a playwright who knew with what ceremonies of formal speech and specificity of clinical detail *The Iliad* tells such things, or how Ulysses, famous for his lies, entranced the Phaiacians over drinks with wondrous tales. The equipoise between language and heroics in Homer would eventually occupy Joyce, and Synge had no doubt that eloquence the like of Nora Burke's tramp's could limn for the deprived some land of heart's desire. *The Playboy,* one of the first self-cancelling plays, is a great iridescent bubble we watch blown, and admire till the moment it bursts, and regret after. It is we, and not only Pegeen in that forlorn last speech, who have lost the only Playboy of the Western World. We shall have him back as surely as the curtain can be persuaded to rise on another performance.

But tucks will appear in a fabric however well woven. If on the opening night the wrongness that offended the patriots was not wrong with the play but with their ideology, still there was something else wrong, to be sensed as dogs sense ozone far from thunder, and that was a subtle wrongness with Synge's whole sense of even the most brutalized Catholic peasantry. Though he used, he said, barely a word that he hadn't heard, still it was by him the words were arranged, and the oaths and invocations seem not so much overnumerous as disconcertingly placed. They bubble at the crests of good-humored vigor; and a cheerful vigor in that continuum of poverty is the daydream of a scion of Bible-readers who trusts that elsewhere, despite all, there exist people the rhythm of whose "Providence and Mercy, spare us all!" bespeaks chthonic energies.

Among such people there will be poltroons of course, afeard of Father Reilly and fussing about a dispensation to marry; that was a way to characterize Shawn Keogh, and it did not trouble Synge that there was no intelligible reason why a dispensation should be needed. Prof. Henn thinks it is necessary because Pegeen and Shawn are being married in Lent, but Lent is in March and Synge's note beneath the list of characters states plainly that the play is set in the autumn. No, "dispensation" for Synge is a piece of Papist rigmarole Father Reilly can worry Shawn Keogh with: a trivial detail but indicative of a surface beneath which his knowledge of Kerry and Mayo did not penetrate.

Or cast a cold eye on the speech with which Pegeen's father greets Christy in Act III:

> The blessing of God and the holy angels on your head, young fellow. I hear tell you're after winning all in the sports below; and wasn't it a shame I didn't bear you along with me to Kate Cassidy's wake, a fine stout lad, the like of you, for you'd

never see the match of it for flows of drink, the way when we sunk her bones at noonday in her narrow grave, there were five men, aye, and six men, strained out retching speechless on the holy stones.

That is not the talk of the Congested Districts but of a fantasy land as like Mayo as Shakespeare's bear-plagued seacoast of Bohemia is like the Adriatic strand. Shakespeare had the advantage over Synge, that no one from Bohemia was likely to be at the Globe.

The speech assembles much verifiable detail: that spirits flow at a wake, that one measure of a spirituous deluge is the body-count of the prostrate, that these if conscious will retch, that a grave is narrow, that God and the holy angels may get ceremonially invoked. Yet as the utterance of a Mayo pubkeeper it is implausible, and Synge though he defended his local accuracies ("one or two words only that I have not heard") never claimed a play made of such speeches was plausible. "An extravaganza," he said, and we'd best believe him, noting how like are its mechanics to those of well-made French farce, abundant in contrivances to hustle someone—in France the deceived husband, here the aggrieved father—back and forth through doors so he'll not meet someone else.

Synge's extravagances are propelled by his love of dizzying contrasts:

> MAHON. . . . . (*With hesitation*) What's that? they're raising him up. They're coming this way. (*With a roar of rage and astonishment*) It's Christy, by the stars of God! I'd know his way of spitting and he astride the moon.

This has literary analogues more cogent than the dubious folk ones Synge half-claimed. The stars of God, spitting, the moon: heterogeneous ideas yoked by violence together: a taste for such effects was coalescing, and we may reflect that the play was finished only six years before Grierson's edition of Donne inaugurated the new century's resurrection of that yeasty poet. "Metaphysical" qualities have since been noted in the way Jimmy Farrell tells how madness is a fright:

> It's a fright, surely. I knew a party was kicked in the head by a red mare, and he went killing horses a great while, till he eat the insides of a clock and died after.

Horses, an indigestible clock: if we think of lovers and a pair of "stiff twin compasses" we spot something astir in the sensibility of that decade, that would soon welcome "A Valediction, Forbidding Mourning," despised nearly two hundred years. Or "The Relique":

> When my grave is broke up again
> Some second guest to entertain
> —For graves have learned that woman-head
> To be to more than one a bed—
> And he that digs it, spies
> A bracelet of bright hair about the bone. . . .

Soon T. S. Eliot would marvel at the "telescoping of images," "the sudden contrast of associations of 'bright hair' and of 'bone,' " and in a similar connection would adduce "that surprise which has been one of the most important means of poetic effect since Homer," poetic effect having been delivered from Tennyson. Yeats concurred. "Donne could be as metaphysical as he pleased . . . because he could be as physical as he pleased." And Synge:

> —Did you ever hear tell of the skulls they have in

the city of Dublin, ranged out like blue jars in a cabin of Connaught?
> —And you believe that?
> —Didn't a lad see them, and he after coming from harvesting in the Liverpool boat? "They have them there," says he, "making a show of the great people there was one time walking the world. White skulls and black skulls and yellow skulls, and some with full teeth, and some haven't only but one."
> —It's no lie, maybe, for when I was a young lad there was a graveyard beyond the house with the remnants of a man who had thighs as long as your arm. He was a horrid man, I'm telling you, and there was many a fine Sunday I'd put him together for fun, and he with shiny bones, you wouldn't meet the like of these days in the cities of the world.

He labored through many drafts of a poem for his fiancée Molly Allgood that evokes near a churchyard full of whitening bones a sexual resurrection of the body. In verse, though, he was too near the Victorians to attempt direct speech save at the bony lines. In one draft we find,

> . . . With what new gold you'd gilded all the moon
> With what rare anthem raised the river's tune
> Where bees fetch honey for their swarming cribs
> And we're two skulls and backs and forty ribs. . . .

Meter, until the skulls and ribs poke through, confines him in Georgian diction; he was right to give up his early fumblings toward verse drama. It was out of rhythms the pentameter does not permit that his idiosyncratic effects arose.

Yet a governing rhythm, which entails a convention for speaking, was one ground of Elizabethan stage success, and Synge's high ambitions left him soon uncontented with anything less than a modern equivalent. Yeats noted as early as *The Well of the Saints* that "all his people would change their life if the rhythm changed," and *The Playboy,* so often rewritten in quest of a form for its verbal designs, offers one audacious experiment, the presence from the opening words to the closing of a persistent recurrent tune, an Irish tune with remote Gaelic credentials, marked by a rhythmic figure that troubles actors because its jaunty beat can be neither obeyed nor suppressed. When Yeats wrote that Synge "made word and phrase dance to a very strange rhythm," difficult for players "till his plays have created their own tradition," *The Playboy* was still in the making, and no actor had yet confronted the challenge of delivering Christy Mahon's exit-speech, that summation of a romping future with his da:

> CHRISTY. Ten thousand blessings upon all that's here, for you've turned me a likely gaffer in the end of all, the way I'll go romancing through a romping lifetime from this hour to the dawning of the Judgement Day.

Something wants to force the last clauses into a quatrain:

> The way I'll go romancing
> through a romping lifetime
> from this hour to the dawning
> of the *Judge ment Day.*

Nor is that unique; more are easily collected.

> I did not then.
> Oh, they're bloody liars
> in the naked parish
> where I grew a man.

Each of the following is within a page of the next:

> It should have been great
> and bitter torment
> did rouse your spirits
> to a *deed of blood.*

· · · · ·

> That was a sneaky
> kind of murder
> did win small glory
> with the *boys it self.*

· · · · ·

> And that there isn't
> my match in Mayo
> for thatching, or mowing,
> or shearing a sheep.

· · · · ·

> Till I'm thinking this night
> wasn't I a foolish fellow
> not to kill my father
> in the *years gone by.*

These are all from Act I, and once we have picked up the pattern—three syncopated measures, then a thudding three-stress termination—we may come to think it omnipresent. We may even find its elements, with free interpolation dividing them, in Pegeen's opening words:

> Six yards of stuff
> for to make a yellow gown
> A pair of lace boots with lengthy
> heels on them and brassy eyes.
> A hat is suited
> for a *wed ding day.*

"For a *wed / ding / day*"; "in the *years / gone / by*"; "of the *Judge / ment / Day*"; that triple terminal beat: where can we have heard it before? It is possible we are remembering its debasement in the anthology piece about the bells of Shandon on the *ri / ver / Lee.*

> On this I ponder
> Where'er I wander
> And thus grow fonder,
> Sweet Cork, of thee:
> With thy bells of Shandon
> That sound so grand on
> The pleasant waters
> Of the river Lee.

Those over-familiar lines of Francis Mahony (1804-1866) dance to a persistent tune indeed: they echo "The Groves of Blarney" by Richard Milliken (1767-1815), who was parodying something anonymous called "Castlehyde," which went to Irish music that once had Gaelic words, now lost. Synge was a fiddler. Did he somewhere pick up the old tune? Was it merely "The Bells of Shandon" that rang in his head?

Surely not. Fiddle-music or no, he could have found Irish assonantal stanzas like the one that degenerated into "Shandon" exhibited in Douglas Hyde's *Songs Ascribed to Raftery* (1903), with deft English imitations, as for instance:

> There's a lovely posy lives by the roadway
> Deirdre was nowhere beside my joy,
> Nor Helen who boasted of conquests Trojan,
> For whom was roasted the town of Troy.

Try that again: "The *town / of / Troy*": "for a *wed / ding / day*": yes, it's close. A folk rhythm, then, known to Sassenachs in its "Bells of Shandon" debasement.

That he built this rhythm (and others) into speech after speech of *The Playboy* is indisputable. How he judged it we cannot know. Like much other Irish, it had been rendered banal already by English parody. A banality, then, to establish Christy's banality? A lilt, to endear? More likely, a token of how Christy and his da and Pegeen and the rest are bound into one community of lilting rogues.

Had he lived we'd know more of the drama he intuited: prose knitted by cross-rhythms insistent as any verse. He wrote but six plays, and in a brief time, 1902-1909, the last months of which were also taken up with dying. William Shakespeare's sixth play (of thirty-odd) was merely *Titus Andronicus.* (pp. 127-39)

> Hugh Kenner, "The Living World for Text," in his *A Colder Eye: The Modern Irish Writers,* Alfred A. Knopf, 1983, pp. 113-43.

FURTHER READING

Akin, Warren, IV. " 'I Just Riz the Loy': The Oedipal Dimension of *The Playboy of the Western World.*" *SAB (South Atlantic Bulletin)* XLV, No. 4 (November 1980): 55-65.
  Discusses Christy Mahon's maturation in terms of the Oedipal complex of Freudian psychology.

Benson, Eugene. *"The Playboy of the Western World."* In his *J. M. Synge,* pp. 112-36. New York: Grove Press, 1983.
  Examines major themes and dramatic techniques in *Playboy.*

Bowen, Zack R. "Synge: *The Playboy of the Western World.*" In *A J. M. Synge Literary Companion,* edited by Edward A. Kopper, Jr., pp. 69-86. New York: Greenwood Press, 1988.
  Addresses themes, images, and language presented in the play, summarizing the interpretations of prominent critics. The essay also outlines the hostile public reception of the drama during its debut production at the Abbey Theatre.

Bushrui, S. B., ed. *A Centenary Tribute to John Millington Synge, 1871-1909: Sunshine and the Moon's Delight.* New York: Barnes & Noble, 1972, 356 p.
  Contains two essays on *Playboy:* "*The Playboy of the Western World:* Christy Mahon and the Apotheosis of Loneliness" by Augustine Martin, which addresses the conflict faced by Christy between loneliness and domination by society, and "The *Playboy* Riots" by Richard M. Kain, which examines political and aesthetic views involved in the controversy surrounding the production of the play at the Abbey Theatre.

Chaudhuri, Una. "The Dramaturgy of the Other: Diegetic Patterns in Synge's *The Playboy of the Western World.*" *Modern Drama* XXXII, No. 3 (September 1989): 374-86.
  Concludes that the diegetic mode of dramatic signification—the mode of absence and otherness—is given precedence in *Playboy.*

Colum, Padraic. "Leinster." In his *The Road Round Ireland.* pp. 339-415. New York: Macmillan Co., 1926.
  Includes personal remiscences of Synge and the production of *Playboy.*

Cusack, Cyril. "A Player's Reflections on *Playboy*." *Modern Drama* 4, No. 3 (December 1961): 300-05.
Personal notes on performing the role of Christy Mahon with the Abbey Theatre from 1932 to 1945.

Ditsky, John. "Synge's Savage Sermon: *The Playboy of the Western World*." In his *The Onstage Christ: Studies in the Persistence of a Theme*. pp. 46-58. Totowa, N. J. : Barnes & Noble, 1980.
Asserts that Synge's treatment of religious allusion is parodic and interprets Christy Mahon as a secularized Christ who serves to critique Irish social and sexual mores of the era.

Estill, Adelaide Duncan. "*The Playboy of the Western World*." In her *The Sources of Synge*, pp. 29-33. Folcroft, Pa.: Folcroft Press, 1939.
Provides summarizing commentary and notes the drama's sources in Synge's travel essays of western Ireland.

Fay, William G. "*The Playboy of the Western World*." In *J. M. Synge: Interviews and Recollections*, edited by E. H. Mikhail, pp. 48-54. New York: Barnes & Noble, 1977.
Personal recollections of events surrounding the drama's 1907 debut by a cofounder of the Abbey Theatre who played the role of Christy Mahon in the original production.

Foster, Leslie D. "Heroic Strivings in *The Playboy of the Western World*." *Éire-Ireland* VIII, No. I (Spring 1973): 85-94.
Examines heroic elements in *Playboy* that suggest an Irish national epic.

Gerstenberger, Donna. "A Hard Birth." In her *John Millington Synge*. pp. 75-93. New York: Twayne Publishers, 1964.
Examines the early critical and public reception of *Playboy* and focuses on Synge's presentation of Christy's self-realization.

———. "Bonnie and Clyde and Christy Mahon: Playboys All." *Modern Drama* 14, No. 2 (September 1971): 227-31.
Compares *Playboy* with Arthur Penn's film *Bonnie and Clyde*, exploring parallel subject matter and audience response.

Gorki, Maxim. "Observations on the Theatre." *The English Review* XXXVIII (March 1924): 494-98.
Praises Synge's portrayal of the hero in *Playboy* and relates the play to modern drama.

Greene, David H., and Stephens, Edward M. "*The Playboy* Riots." In their *J. M. Synge, 1871-1909*, pp. 234-71. New York: Macmillan Co., 1959.
Details the controversy over *Playboy* during its original performances in Ireland and abroad in a major biographical study of Synge coauthored by Synge's nephew and friend, Edward M. Stephens (1888-1955).

Gregory, Lady. *Our Irish Theatre: A Chapter of Autobiography*. Rev. ed. New York: Oxford University Press, 1972, 279 p.
Chronicle of the Irish Literary Theatre and the Irish National Theatre Society at the Abbey Theatre by one of its cofounders, offering personal accounts of Synge during the writing of *Playboy* and of the drama's controversial debut in Ireland in 1907 and production in the United States from 1911 to 1912. The work also contains appendixes excerpting American reviews of *Playboy* and interviews with Gregory.

Grene, Nicholas. "Approaches to *The Playboy*." In his *Synge: A Critical Study of the Plays*. pp. 132-45. Totowa, N. J. : Rowman and Littlefield, 1975.
Outlines critical approaches to the drama and examines its structure.

Grubgeld, Elizabeth. "Verbal Geographies: Synge's *Playboy of the Western World*." *The University of Mississippi Studies in English* 6 (1988): 194-205.
Argues that the drama explores the potentiality of words and "reveals their power to restructure the landscape."

Gutierrez, Donald. "Coming of Age in Mayo: Synge's *The Playboy of the Western World* as a Rite of Passage." *Hartford Studies in Literature* VI, No. 2 (1974): 159-66.
Describes Christy's growth from boyhood to manhood as an archetypal "puberty rite of passage."

Harmon, Maurice, ed. *J. M. Synge Centenary Papers. 1971*. Dublin: Dolmen Press, 1972, 202 p.
Contains two essays focusing primarily on *Playboy*: "Synge's Poetic Use of Language" by Seamus Deane, which explores Synge's devices of composition and how they function as linguistic structures, and "Synge and Modernism" by Thomas Kilroy, which relates Synge's dramatic art to the Irish Dramatic Movement and European dramatic modernism.

Hart, William E. Introduction to *The Playboy of the Western World* in *"The Playboy of the Western World" and "Riders to the Sea"*, by John Millington Synge, edited by William E. Hart, pp. ix-xxvi. New York: Meredith, 1966.
Offers introductory overview of the sources, language, and humor of the drama and describes opposing reactions to the play's production at the Abbey Theatre in the Irish press.

———. "Synge's Ideas on Life and Art: Design and Theory in *The Playboy of the Western World*." *Yeats Studies*, No. 2 (1972): 35-51.
Argues that "Synge's ideas on life and art generated a theory of poetry and drama which determined the formal design of his play."

Hirsch, Edward. "The Gallous Story and the Dirty Deed: The Two *Playboys*." *Modern Drama* XXVI, No. 1 (March 1983): 85-102.
Elaborates on the critical debate over the degree of naturalism in *Playboy*.

Hogan, Robert, and Kilroy, James. "1907." In their *The Modern Irish Drama: A Documentary History—Vol. III. The Abbey Theatre: The Years of Synge, 1905-1909*. pp. 123-91. Dublin: Dolmen Press, 1978.
Provides an in-depth account of the public and critical controversy over the production of *Playboy* at the Abbey Theatre, quoting extensively from Irish periodicals of the era and allowing "the story to be told, as much as possible, by the players and playwrights and playgoers themselves."

Holder, Heidi J. "Between Fiction and Reality: Synge's *Playboy* and Its Audience." *Journal of Modern Literature* 14, No. 4 (Spring 1988): 527-42.
Asserts that Synge's presentation of the conflict between reality and fantasy in the drama affected the hostile audience response to the Abbey Theatre debut of *Playboy* and that Synge's emphasis on the conflict shaped the play's themes and characters during revision.

Howarth, Herbert. "Edmund John Millington Synge, 1871-1909." In his *The Irish Writers, 1880-1940: Literature under Parnell's Star*, pp. 212-44. London: Rockliff, 1958.
Discusses *Playboy* in the context of Synge's literary career and suggests the influence of his works on the fiction of James Joyce.

Howe, P. P. "The Plays, II" and "Men and Women." In his *J. M. Synge: A Critical Study*. pp. 61-99, 158-98. London: Martin Secker, 1912.
Focuses on Synge's characterization techniques in *Playboy* and provides character analyses.

Johnson, Toni O'Brien. "*The Playboy of the Western World*: Medieval Analogues." In her *Synge: The Medieval and the Grotesque*, pp. 54-69. Totowa, N. J. : Barnes & Noble, 1982.
Posits that the drama shares motifs with the Irish folktale "Bricriu's Feast" and with *Sir Gawain and the Green Knight*.

Kelsall, Malcolm. "The *Playboy* before the Riots." *Theatre Research International* I, No. 1 (October 1975): 29-37.
Suggests that the realistic approach of the Abbey Theatre company's original production of the drama influenced the subse-

quent riots by exacerbating "possibilities of brutality latent in the text."

Kiberd, Declan. "Synge and Irish Literature—Saga, Myth and Romance" and "Synge, the Gaelic League and the Irish Revival." In his *Synge and the Irish Language,* pp. 95-121, 216-60. Totowa, N. J. : Rowman and Littlefield, 1979.
    Includes two chapters addressing *Playboy*: the first discussing Synge's treatment of the Irish myth of Cuchulain in *Playboy,* the second examining the extent of the Gaelic League's involvement in the Abbey Theatre demonstrations against the drama.

Kilroy, James F. "The Playboy as Poet." *PMLA* 83, No. 2 (May 1968): 439-42.
    Interprets Christy Mahon as representing "the gradual development of the poet's craft."

King, Mary C. "Metadrama in *The Playboy of the Western World.*" In her *The Drama of J. M. Synge.* pp. 133-59. London: Fourth Estate, 1985.
    Expounds on the theme of language in *Playboy* and addresses metadramatic elements in the drama.

Krause, David. " 'The Rageous Ossean': Patron-Hero of Synge and O'Casey." *Modern Drama* 4, No. 3 (December 1961): 268-91.
    Asserts that Celtic warrior-bard Oisin, in his dialogue with St. Patrick in Irish mythology, shaped the conflict between pagan and Christian values in *Playboy,* and that Synge and Irish dramatist Sean O'Casey (1880-1964) "shared the pagan temperament and values of Oisin."

Lucas, F. L. "John Millington Synge: *The Playboy of the Western World.*" In his *The Drama of Chekhov, Synge, Yeats, and Pirandello.* pp. 201-24. London: Cassell, 1963.
    Outlines the public reception of the play during its early productions in Ireland and abroad, provides summarizing commentary on the drama, and praises it as "a miraculous example of the power of style."

Mikhail, E. H. "Two Aspects of Synge's *Playboy.*" *Colby Library Quarterly* IX, No. 6 (June 1971): 322-30.
    Argues that the drama was the product of extensive rewriting by Synge and asserts thematic correspondences between *Playboy* and Henrik Ibsen's drama *Peer Gynt.*

Nethercot, Arthur H. "The *Playboy* of the *Western World.*" *Éire-Ireland* XIII, No. 2 (1978): 114-20.
    Studies the implications of the specific terms "playboy" and "western world" as they are developed in the drama.

O'Casey, Sean. "Song of a Shift." In his *Drums under the Windows,* pp. 168-90. New York: Macmillan Co., 1946.
    Humorous narrative recounting the public uproar over the production of *Playboy* at the Abbey Theatre in 1907.

O'Connor, Frank. *The Backward Look: A Survey of Irish Literature,* pp. 170 ff. London: Macmillan, 1967.
    Discusses *Playboy* within the context of Synge's literary career. For a more extensive evaluation of the drama by O'Connor, see excerpt dated 1939.

Parker, Randolph. "Gaming in the Gap: Language and Liminality in *Playboy of the Western World.*" *Theatre Journal* 37, No. 1 (March 1985): 65-85.
    Applies the anthropological concept of liminality to the drama and expounds on the play's ambiguous relation to traditional dramatic expectations of theme, character, setting, and comedy.

Price, Alan. "Longer Plays: *The Playboy of the Western World.*" In his *Synge and Anglo-Irish Drama.* 161-80. London: Methuen & Co., 1961.
    Charts the development of Christy's imagination as it transforms dream into actuality and analyzes Synge's use of language and irony in the drama.

Rollins, Ronald G. "O'Casey and Synge: The Irish Hero as Playboy and Gunman." *The Arizona Quarterly* 22, No. 3 (Autumn 1966): 217-22.
    Parallels *Playboy* with Sean O'Casey's drama *The Shadow of a Gunman* as they address "the Irishman's extreme fondness for heroes and heroic speech and action."

Saddlemyer, Ann. Introduction to *J. M. Synge and Modern Comedy.* pp. 5-31. Dublin: Dolmen Press, 1968.
    Treats the thematic opposition between imagination and reality in *Playboy* and observes elements of European comedy in Synge's dramas.

———. Introduction to *J. M. Synge: Collected Works, Vol. IV—Plays,* by John Millington Synge, edited by Ann Saddlemyer, pp. xi-xxxiii. London: Oxford University Press, 1968.
    Offers a detailed discussion of the writing process of *Playboy* and gives an account of the riots at the Abbey Theatre. Early drafts and revisions of the drama are included in an appendix.

Salmon, Eric. "J. M. Synge's *Playboy:* A Necessary Reassessment." *Modern Drama* 13, No. 2 (September 1970): 111-28.
    Elaborates on central themes of the drama "from the point of view of the play as a piece of theater-in-performance."

Setterquist, Jan. "*The Playboy of the Western World: Peer Gynt—The Wild Duck—The Master Builder.*" In his *Ibsen and the Beginnings of Anglo-Irish Drama, Vol. I: John Millington Synge,* pp. 52-70. Cambridge, Mass.: Harvard University Press, 1951.
    Parallels Synge's play with Henrik Ibsen's dramas *Peer Gynt, The Wild Duck,* and *The Master Builder* in a study that suggests Ibsenian models for each of Synge's dramatic works.

Sidnell, M. J. "Synge's Playboy and the Champion of Ulster." *The Dalhousie Review* 45, No. 1 (Spring 1965): 51-9.
    Asserts similar motifs in *Playboy* and the story of "The Championship of Ulster" from Irish mythology and argues that Synge "managed to express, through his organic metaphor, the tension existing between past and present." For related criticism on this topic, see the essay by Diane E. Bessai dated 1968.

Skelton, Robin. *J. M. Synge and His World.* New York: Viking Press, 1971, 144 p.
    Biographical study offering relevent background to *Playboy,* including Synge's relationship with Abbey Theatre actress Molly Allgood during the writing of the drama and the public reception of the play's production in Ireland and England.

———. "*The Playboy of the Western World.*" In his *The Writings of J. M. Synge,* pp. 114-31. Indianapolis: Bobbs-Merrill Co., 1971.
    Describes the writing process of the drama, discusses major critical interpretations, and examines its central parallels in Christianity and mythology.

Styan, J. L. "Making Meanings in the Theatre: *The Playboy of the Western World.*" In his *The Elements of Drama,* pp. 48-63. Cambridge: Cambridge University Press, 1960.
    Discusses Synge's use of irony in *Playboy* as it affects audience response, focusing on the first act.

Sultan, Stanley. "A Joycean Look at *The Playboy of the Western World.*" In *The Celtic Master: Contributions to the First James Joyce Symposium Held in Dublin, 1967,* edited by Maurice Harmon, pp. 45-55. Dublin: Dolmen Press, 1969.
    Describes the drama's presentation of the motif of the betrayed messiah, maintaining that Christy Mahon represents "one example of many in an Anglo-Irish tradition of rejected and betrayed would-be deliverers from political or even spiritual oppression."

Waters, Maureen. "The Comic Hero." In her *The Comic Irishman,* pp. 58-81. Albany: State University of New York Press, 1984.
    Discusses major themes of *Playboy* as they illustrate the development of the comic hero in Anglo-Irish literature.

Yeats, William Butler. "The Irish Dramatic Movement: On Taking *The Playboy* to London." In his *Plays and Controversies,* rev. ed., pp. 197-98. New York: Macmillan Co., 1924.

Essay from 1907 discussing the drama's controversial reception in Ireland and defending the proposed production of the play in London. For a more extensive defense of the work, see the excerpt by Yeats dated 1910.

Benedict Wallet Vilakazi

1906-1947

(Full name Benedict Wallet Bambatha Vilakazi) South African (Zulu) poet, novelist, critic, linguist, and essayist.

Vilakazi is a pioneering figure in the creation of Zulu literature. In his poetry, he combined elements of the tribal oral tradition with European poetic techniques. While he also described the Zulus' way of life in his fiction and promoted their literature in his essays, his poems are considered his most eloquent and effective expression of black African concerns.

Vilakazi was born at the Groutville Mission Station near Stranger, Natal, to parents who were Zulu tribe members and devout Christians. He attended the mission school until he was about ten years old and then began classes at St. Francis College, Mariannhill, a Roman Catholic monastery outside Durban. After obtaining his teaching certificate in 1923, he instructed classes at Mariannhill College and later at the Catholic seminary in Ixopo. During this period, Vilakazi wrote his first novel and first volume of poetry, both of which received immediate critical acclaim. He continued his studies and earned a B.A. from the University of South Africa in 1934. Because the University of Witwatersrand was the only institution to provide advanced courses in Zulu language and literature, Vilakazi's chosen field, he postponed further study until 1936 when he was given a language assistantship in their Bantu Studies Department, becoming the first black South African to teach white South African students at the university level. Along with his growing fame as a poet and novelist, Vilakazi was developing a reputation as a linguistics scholar, publishing respected essays on Zulu language and literature. With the head of the department, C. M. Doke, Vilakazi wrote a Zulu-English dictionary and in 1946 became the first black South African to earn a Ph.D. He died a year later of meningitis.

Vilakazi's novels are most often praised for their accurate depiction of Zulu life. *Noma nini,* one of the first works of fiction written in Zulu to treat modern subject matter, tells the story of a young Zulu couple who decide to marry, but are forced to separate when the man moves to the city to earn "bride money." After several years of waiting, the woman accepts another suitor only to have her original fiancé return just before her marriage. All ends happily when she finds another bride for her second suitor and she marries the first. Although the novel has been criticized for its simplistic plot and themes, its fusion of the European ideal of romantic loyalty with Zulu pragmatism is unique in Zulu literature. Vilakazi extended his representation of Zulu life in *Nje nempela,* which has been praised for its depiction of traditional life in a polygamous household.

As a poet, Vilakazi was strongly influenced by the European Romantics, whose sense of alienation and belief in individual freedom and the perfectibility of humanity matched Vilakazi's feelings about the subjugation of black South Africans and his optimism about change. The influence is most evident in such early poems as "Inqomfi" ("The Lark") and "We moya" ("Hail, Wind"), which are patterned after Percy Bysshe Shelley's "To a Skylark" and "Ode to the West

Wind," respectively. *Inkondlo kaZulu* (*Zulu Songs*), his first collection of poetry, combines rhyme and stanza forms, unknown in traditional Zulu verse, with elements of the oral praise poem, the *izibongo,* including praise of ancestors and tribal leaders, allegory, and dramatic tone. Traditional components played a larger role in Vilakazi's second volume of poetry, *Amal'eZulu* (*Zulu Horizons*), in which he rejected his experiments with rhyme and followed more closely the form of the *izibongo.* His themes increasingly reflected the concerns not only of modern Zulus, but of black South Africans regardless of tribal affiliation. Vilakazi protested the exploitation of blacks in such poems as "Ezinkomponi" ("In the Gold Mines"). Considered one of his best poems, "In the Gold Mines" expresses the frustration, humiliation, and powerlessness of those compelled to work in the mines.

Vilakazi's essays and scholarly studies of Bantu language and literature command great respect. These works include analyses of the Bantu languages Zulu and Xhosa, literary critiques of the oral traditions and newly developing written literatures in these languages, and explanations of Vilakazi's own poetic innovations in Zulu. While his scholarly achievements advanced the study and respectability of South African tribal literature, Vilakazi's poetry remains his most important legacy, eloquently expressing modern Zulu hopes and concerns in works that preserve the spirit of the Zulu oral tradition.

PRINCIPAL WORKS

Inkondlo kaZulu   (poetry)   1935
   [*Zulu Songs* published in *Zulu Horizons,* 1962]
Noma nini   (novel)   1935
UDingiswayo kaJobe   (novel)   1939
Nje nempela   (novel)   1944
Amal'eZulu   (poetry)   1945
   [*Zulu Horizons* published in *Zulu Horizons,* 1962]
Zulu-English Dictionary   [with Clement Martyn Doke]
   (dictionary)   1948
Zulu Horizons   (poetry)   1962

J. DEXTER TAYLOR   (essay date 1935)

[*In the following excerpt, Taylor praises* Inkondlo kaZulu.]

By the publication of ***Inkondlo kaZulu,*** a little book of Zulu poems by Mr. B. Wallet Vilakazi, B.A., the Bantu Studies Department of the Witwatersrand University has once more done great service to the cause of Bantu progress. Mr. Vilakazi has, for a number of years, been publishing in the Native newspapers the product of his meditations and imagination and these bits and others are here gathered into a worthy little book. The University deserves hearty commendation for making possible this first venture of a South African Native in the field of poetry. The title-page bears the title "The Bantu Treasury," and gives promise of a series to be, in which the best literary work of Bantu writers in their own languages shall be made available for their natural audience, and so shall become a stimulus to intellectual and spiritual growth. There is a steadily increasing group of young Africans who are possessed of literary talent and are working hard to perfect themselves in various media of expression. The invitation that the title-page of this first volume of a projected series holds forth will be to them an open door of opportunity. Lacking a large reading constituency and lacking facilities for publication, the only recourse of the ambitious Bantu writer has been the newspaper. This series should draw the best African effort in poetry, fiction, essay and drama and should be of immense encouragement to the race. The success of the series will depend in large measure upon the support given it by African readers. African authors of ability will not appear and grow to a significant stature except they have an eager public to read what they write.

The title of Mr. Vilakazi's little book ***Inkondlo,*** is the name of a certain Zulu dance. Its significance lies in the fact that the emotions of a people who lack means of literary expression find outlet in the dance. Mr. Vilakazi, the first of his race, seeks to make Zulu experience dance to the music of his words. And yet not the first. It has often been said that the only literature the Bantu people possess is the *Izibongo*. These are flattering descriptions of chiefs and their exploits, composed for declamation accompanied with action, on state occasions. They have a certain rhythm, are couched in imaginative language and are essentially poetry. Mr. Vilakazi in the richness of his Zulu vocabulary, in the truly African flavour of his imagery and in the exuberant extravagance of some of his descriptions is a true descendant of the *imbongi*. But the background of his thought is not that of the *imbongi*. He is not much concerned with warlike prowess. Aggrey is a greater hero to him than Shaka. The clay pot family heirloom, the song of the lark, the train that dashes by in the night, leaving him vainly waiting—all the little incidents of daily life serve as starting points for the flow of his verse. He is the human poet rather than the Zulu poet also in the attention he pays to his own emotions and those he observes in others. It is the *imbongi* come to consciousness of the abstract and of the inner self, through contact with the work of other poets and through the unconscious influence of education and European culture.

His technique also is not that of the pagan *imbongi*. He attempts rhyme, but with limited success, as Zulu syllables, invariably, ending in vowels, do not present the variety of sound and tone that makes successful rhyming possible. Even the forms of English rhythm that he uses do not supply a perfect medium, for Zulu accents and stresses refuse to be bent into conformity with the beat of the music. But Mr. Vilakazi is an experimenter in a new field and is to be congratulated on the large measure of his success, rather than criticized for small failures. He will perhaps, as he grows surer in his art, develop a technique more indigenous and more pliable to the Zulu words. The Zulu in which the poems are written will be the delight of the linguist and the despair of the tyro. His sensitiveness to words is remarkable and he has gathered a vocabulary which must enrich the Zulu speech.

But it is when one turns to the emotional content of the poems that the real talent of the author is revealed and a new respect must be felt for the capacity of the Zulu mind and heart. (pp. 163-64)

A fine appreciation of spiritual values appears in the first poem ***Umkhuleko wesiphoxo* ("The Fool's Prayer").** It is the story of a "simple" made to pray for the amusement of a thoughtless crowd. The prayer so reveals the pathos of the misused soul that the fool becomes the wise man and the wise men fools. (p. 164)

[Mr. Vilakazi's] appreciation for sound and its values comes out clearly in his poem to the Lark **"Ingomi"** which is reminiscent here and there of Shelley, in its ideas not in its music. The quaint comparison, in one of its stanzas, of the lark with certain Zulu musicians is a pretty tribute to his fellows. The underlying sense of frustration in the African mind combined with the consciousness of a soul above the birds and beasts appear in [this poem]. . . .

A word must be said about the outward appearance of the book. The dignity of its simple blue cloth binding, with the seal of the University on the cover, the clear print and perfect proof-reading are not only a credit to the Editors and to the Lovedale Press, but they are a quiet testimony to the recognition given to these poems as real literature, worthy of preservation and of presentation to their readers in a form of beauty. (p. 165)

J. Dexter Taylor, "Inkondlo kaZulu," in Bantu Studies, *Vol. IX, No. 2, 1935, pp. 163-65.*

B. W. VILAKAZI   (essay date 1938)

[*In the following excerpt, Vilakazi explains his reasons and methods for adapting the rhyme schemes and poetic forms of European poetry to poetry written in the Zulu language.*]

Steere, in his preface to *Swahili Tales,* criticises [rhyming in Swahili poetry] on the ground that "the rhyme is to the eye more than to the ear, as all the final syllables being unaccented, the prominent sounds often destroy the feeling of rhyme." I am inclined to agree with Steere in such criticism when I look at Zulu, because in rhyming the Bantu syllables one has to take into account the penultimate syllable which not only has prominence to the ear because the succeeding final syllable is generally (in Zulu) devocalised, but also attracts the eye in that the poet will run his rhyming through two syllables: the penultimate and the final.

I tried to use such a rhyme system when I wrote some of my poems in ***Inkondlo kaZulu.*** I shall illustrate here what I mean by such rhyme.

Sengiyokholwa ukuthi sewafa	a
Um' ukukhala kwezinyoni zaphezulu	b
Nobusuku obuqhakaz' izinkanyezi zezulu	b
Um' inkwezane yokusa nezinkanyezi	c
Ezikhanyis' umnyama njengonyezi	c
Sezanyamalal' ungunaphakade.	d

Such a system of rhyming I am trying to develop for Zulu. At the beginning I found it to be rude and forcible; but since that I have composed very smoothly with it, once I have begun my poem and made up my mind in a certain way. By trying to adopt this rhyming I have found that there is a feeling among European critics that Zulu can achieve only a limited success with rhyming, since most of the words in Zulu end in vowels, and thus do not permit variety of sound that makes successful rhyming possible.

This system does not take only the vowel of the penultimate into account but combines such a vowel with its governing consonant, e.g. *"Zulu"* cannot rhyme with *"mulu"* for fricative alveolars have no ear-relation or even phonetic relation with nasal bilabials. . . . Here then, the question, what consonants have to rhyme, is to be answered.

Before this question is answered, I must first prove the necessity and desirability of rhyme in Zulu. Poetry is art, and the end of art is to create or reveal beauty. Art must have form which is the beauty of the poem; that beauty must give aesthetic pleasure to both the writer and the reader. I do not believe in form; I rely more on the spirit of poetry. Form tends to reduce everything to mechanical standards and mathematical formulae. But we have to use some form to embody or clothe the beautiful spirit of our poetry. We have no definite form so far, and our starting point will be at the standards given us by the Western education we have imbibed at college. We are beginning the work which may be given perfect form in generations to come. After all, our language is old and is fast accumulating new words and concepts. I believe therefore it is absolutely necessary that, in composing some poems, we ought to rhyme and decorate our poetic images with definite stanza forms.

My rhyme system is this: The rhyme begins with the penultimate syllable.

    (a)   *Bi-labial Consonants : ph, p; b, b;* all are perfect rhymes, e.g.

i*ph*aba	i*mb*obo	i*mp*uphu
u*b*aba	u*p*opo	i*mb*ubu
uku*b*aba		

I rhyme all these consonants in simple or combined forms except where phonetic changes due to palatalisation have taken place. *M* seems to stand alone, because of nasalisation, whereas other bilabials have implosion and explosion. But when *m* is combined with the other bilabials the rhyming is smooth.

    (b)   *Denti-labial Consonants:* Here we have two, the unvoiced *f* and the voiced *v* and these rhyme well, e.g.

*v*ela	*f*ula	wathi *fof*o, etc.
*f*ela	*v*ula	ama*vov*o

    (c)   *Alveolars : t, th* and *d* run together, while *s* and *z* agree, and *l* and *r* rhyme. *R* is creeping into the language, and provision for it has to be made.

    Examples :

(i)	ama*t*ata	in*t*andi	i*tw*etwe
	ama*th*atha	aku*nt*anti	isi*dw*edwe
	ama*d*ada		
(ii)	um*s*izi	uku*s*usa	
	um*z*isi	uku*z*uza	
(iii)	ukwe*l*ula	uku*l*ola	
	uku*r*ula	uku*r*ola	

The nasal alveolar *n* stands by itself.

    (d)   *Prepalatals: Sh* and *tsh* present some difficulty. Fricative *sh* rhymes well with the alveolar *s* whereas the affricate *tsh,* because of its ejective pronunciation, differs a lot from *s.* It suggests rather the ejected *t.* In this case I not only rhyme *sh* with *tsh,* but also rhyme *sh* with *s* and *tsh* with *t.* In combination with *n* I would rhyme *ntsh* with *nt* because they are both ejective. *Nt* goes further because it rhymes also with *nd.*

    Examples :

ika*tsh*ana	ika*tsh*ana	isikha*sh*ana
isikha*sh*ana	ukukwene*t*ana	ubi*s*ana

Again the voiced prepalatal *j* raises difficulty. Being a voiced affricate it does not agree with any other unvoiced affricates and, because of its voiced quality, I would either rhyme it with the voiced alveolar *d* which itself, under rules of palatalisation in forming diminutives, changes into *j.* The voiced prepalatal suggests rhyming with the voiced velar *g* in which case I would not hesitate to rhyme the two.

    Examples :

    (i)   *j* with *d*

ama*J*uda	uku*b*eja
uku*d*uda	uku*b*eda

    (ii)   *j* with *g.*

ama*J*uda	ama*j*ele	uku*g*eza
uku*g*uda	izi*g*ele	uku*j*eza

    (e)   *Velar Consonants : K', k, kh,* and *g* rhyme very smoothly. The velar semi-vowel *w* stands alone, and I would not suggest rhyming it even when used with vowels. Its suggestiveness of bilabial quality takes it away from the unvoiced glottal fricative *h* with which rhyming would be possible.

    Examples of Velars :

amaga*g*asi	ukugu*g*uza
amakhosi*k*azi	ukukhu*kh*usa
ama*kh*asi	ukusu*k*uza

(f) *Glottals:* There are only two; the fricative unvoiced *h* and the voiced *h*.

Now there remain the click consonants. The basic physiological mechanism of the Zulu click, is in general one. According
to Professor C. M. Doke, the Zulu clicks are "produced by
the formation of a partial vacuum between the tip and the
back of the tongue, so that when the tip or the side (as is the
case with the lateral clicks) of the tongue is released from
contact with the palate etc., air rushes momentarily into the
rarefaction, and causes the smacking sound." In pronouncing
a click there is a forward and a back release. Because of this
scientific discovery I do not propose to separate the clicks but
to treat them as related.

(i)   The radical and the aspirated forms of the den-
tal, palatoalveolar and lateral clicks could rhyme
without differentiation. E.g.

Radical	*Aspirated*
I*cala*	uku*chuma*
uku*qala*	uku*qhuma*
uku*xhala*	uku*xhuma*

(ii) The voiced click consonants in all combinations would have to rhyme. E.g.

Uku*gxuma*
Uku*gquma*.

The reason for my advocacy of rhyme is that in Zulu there
are fewer primitive words than derivatives. The derivative
formatives are mostly dissyllabic, and some of them rhyme
splendidly. The diminutive formative of nouns and the reciprocal formative of verbs rhyme well; the perfective of some
verbs in *ela* rhymes with the verbal applied formatives; the
augmentative is the same as the feminine formative *kazi*. The
language is elastic and because of this quality, I would not
give in to those who advance that rhyme is foreign to Zulu.
It seems to me there is a feeling for rhyme among the Zulus,
when one studies their music in its ending verses, for there
will always be recurrence of certain sounds for the sake of
rousing emotion.

There is a long poem in my book where this rhyme system
has been tried—but without much success—because I disregarded the penultimate consonant in preference to its vowel,
and therefore produced the rhyming of final syllables and the
vowels preceding such syllables. But this was a mistake which
served to confirm my view of rhyme having its beginning in
the whole of the penultimate syllable, as in the stanza quoted
above. The following from the same publication will illustrate
my meaning of a mistaken Zulu rhyme:

*Wen' obange namahl*athi
*Abecash' iziny*athi
*Wandundulel' amal*iba

*Wawamba wawagq*iba
*Ngob' ugqilaz' amath*ongo
*Ezizwana zakoMhl*ongo
*Ezathi zala nam*anzi

*Zanganqob' umhlab' ob*anzi
*Zithi ngek' ube nenk*athi

*Yokuziginga njengenhlw*athi.

(You, who rivalled forests
Which hid buffaloes

You, who piled graves upon one another
Digging and covering them
You enslave ancestral spirits
Of the tribes of the Mhlongo people
Who having refused to give you water,
Failed to conquer a wide world,
Thinking that you would have no chance
To swallow them like a python.)

The future poetry of the Zulus must reflect two things:—

(i) The indomitable Zulu spirit, which was described by Dr. Charles S. Wesley, professor of history in Howard University, U.S.A., most adequately, in 1931, in an article in *Southern Workman*. He
wrote: "A people with a warlike background as this
cannot do otherwise than express their emotion in
song. The note of defiance is frequent in their singing. There is the warrior pose and the thrust of the
spear, the shout of battle and the song of victory.
There seem to be few sorrow songs in the music of
the Zulus. There are funeral songs, but even in
these, there are the majestic strains without the
plaintive minor so well known in our American
music." What Professor Wesley wrote about music
after hearing Mr. R. T. Caluza's Zulu Double
Quartett perform in England in 1930, applies
equally to Zulu poetry. Professor Wesley mentioned in the same article that "Rhythm and melody go together, and song and dance as well seem to
be in union. . . . . The physical movements cannot
be recorded and reproduced with music for truly
they are parts of the singing."

(ii) The power of a Black man's mind and heart to
rise above all circumstances imposed on him by
conquest and subjugation to Western conditions.
The Black man has a test to pass to prove his ability
for what Emerson calls "the ability of man to stand
alone." By this I do not indicate the isolation of the
Black man, but that the Black man, who is introduced into Western social and political systems,
may keep unscarred his personal independence and
integrity. The Black man has something to contribute to the world's literature, for he has yet to interpret his conception of the end of human existence
and the meaning of life. He has yet to consider the
impact of the whole disordered world and tell us
how he will resist the temptation to discourage-
ment, and even to despair, when he looks upon the
behaviour of contemporary civilisation and Western culture. Educated poets have yet to produce
more famous lines than the one found in the primitive song, composed in 1906 after Bambatha's Rebellion:—

Mlungu, kawunoni
Ngezingane zawobaba!

(White man, thou dost not grow fat
Because of our fathers' children!)

The breakdown of the family system and the lamentation of
the married women in deserted kraals, whence husbands
have gone to Johannesburg not to return, is found in a new
type of Zulu music, which is sold broadcast in Johannesburg
music saloons. The feature of the songs is that they are composed to a verse, e.g.

Wo Sebenz' ubuye!

(Please work and return home!)

We expect our poets to tell us the truth—the greatest achievement of any poet—for if we are to believe and teach other races of humanity to believe our tale, the poets must be truthful. Just as face answers to face, so does the heart of man to man. In the Black man's failures and his successes, in his littleness and his bigness, the poet must be clear, simple, passionate, and glitter with a lustre of his own. (pp. 127-33)

Every great literature of the nations has contributed to the universal meaning of life. This is found in its poetry, and here again I feel the heavy burden laid on our poets by the impact of Western conditions. In Negro literature where the Black man has sung of human ingratitude, atrocious servitude and crude brute power, the whole thing has been summed up in two lines, in the most triumphant manner and power. The lines are sublime in simplicity and in depth of universal meaning:

> Nobody knows the trouble I see—
> Glory, hallelujah!

(p. 133)

> B. W. Vilakazi, "The Conception and Development of Poetry in Zulu," in Bantu Studies, Vol. XII, 1938, pp. 105-34.

D. McK. MALCOLM (essay date 1962)

[In the following excerpt, Malcolm discusses the evolution of Vilakazi's poetic aims and techniques.]

There are quite a number of Zulu poets, the works of some of whom have been published but the best of them all is undoubtedly Dr B. W. Vilakazi. (p. xiii)

It was when Vilakazi was studying for his B.A. degree that he became aware of the English poets of the Romantic period and was fired with the ambition of doing for Zulu literature what they had done for English. His early works show their influence upon him. Such pieces as **"Ukhamba luka Sonkomose"** ("Sonkomose's Bowl"), **"Inqomfi"** ("The Lark"), and **"We moya!"** ("Hail Wind!")** belong to this category.

At first he strove to model his poetry on the English style but found that rhyme did not suit the Zulu language, and after some experimental pieces he decided that he would base his style on the traditional blank verse of the Zulu praise poems (*Izibongo*). The first edition of his national songs contained four pieces which were omitted when the second edition was published. They were of an experimental nature and were replaced by other poems. It is the second edition that is being used for this translation.

The first volume of his poems is therefore of unequal quality. Those in which he used the traditional Zulu mode are most successful. **"Inkelekele yakivaXhoza"** ("The Xhosa Calamity—1856"), **"UShaka KaSenzangakhona"** ("Shaka, Son of Senzangakhona")** and **"Phezu kwethuna likaShaka"** ("The Grave of Shaka")** are examples. **"UNokufa"** ("Death")** is one of the best of Vilakazi's earlier works but it suffers from a lack of logical arrangement and rather meanders. He is preoccupied with the subject of death and writes several elegies, in which some of his most poignant lines occur.

The most beautiful of his poems in this first volume is the one describing the Victoria Falls. Vilakazi felt that one of his missions in life was to teach the Zulu people an appreciation of the beauties of nature. It is something which receives scant attention under tribal conditions and whenever he can appro-

priately do so, he draws the Zulu's attention to it. It is another result of his study of the Romantic period in English verse.

When we turn to the second volume we find a more mature and confident poet. From the first piece we get the cue to Vilakazi's source of inspiration. In a vision he imagines himself waiting outside the palisades of Dukuza, the large grass palace built by Shaka on the present site of the town of Stanger. It is customary for Zulu royalty to keep visitors waiting for long periods outside, but his singing of the praises of the Zulu kings eventually brings Mnkabayi, Shaka's aunt, to the gates to admit him and she lays upon him the task of singing the sagas of the victorious battles in Zulu history.

From that time on he regarded himself as the poet appointed by the ancestral spirits to speak for his nation. We find further reference to the same idea in that short poem entitled **"Tell Me!"** in which he expresses his sense of being lost when he finds himself in the great city of Johannesburg and, bewildered as a Zulu bride in the strange home of her husband, he hears the Zulus saying: "Be our voice!"

There are two poems in this volume that stand out: **"Mamina"** and **"Ezinkomponi"** ("The Gold Mines")**. In the first, Vilakazi seeks to capture Mamina "The Spirit of Poetry". Long and earnestly he pursues her. Often he communes with her. But always she eludes him. One gets the impression, as one reads this poem, of being a listener to a telephone conversation. Only by implication does the poet let us hear what she is saying to him and this adds to the intrigue with which we follow the continually changing situations.

In the second poem we have a stark picture of what life in the compound of a gold mine means to an African labourer. From the comparative peace and dignity of his life in his rural homeland he comes to the roar and machine-like routine of manual labour. No green of the rolling hills to rest the eyes upon, only the whirling dust of the mine dumps. No matter how hygienically fed and housed he may be he feels that he has left his manhood behind him and he has become a 'boy' to his master. Inevitably he thinks of the glorious past of the Zulu nation and compares it with its present poverty and depression.

To sum up: Vilakazi stands supreme amongst Zulu poets. His lofty idealism, his loyalty to the traditions of his forefathers, his anxiety to find the most appropriate form of expression, his appreciation of the beauties of nature, his flights of fancy even into the outer space of the Milky Way, the brilliant manner in which he represents Zulu thought and culture, and his sensitive sharing in the present growing pains of his nation, all combine to make the study of his poetry a matter of the deepest interest. (pp. xiv-xv)

> D. Mck. Malcolm, in an introduction to Zulu Horizons by Benedict Wallet Vilakazi, translated by Florence Louie Friedman, Witwatersrand University Press, 1973, pp. xiii-xv.

ALBERT S. GERARD (essay date 1971)

[Gérard is a Belgian essayist and scholar who has contributed to surveys of African literature and to literary journals in the Congo and South Africa. In the following excerpt, he examines the form and themes of Vilakazi's works.]

[The] best Zulu writer so far is Benedict Wallet Vilakazi, who was born on 6 January 1906. . . . (p. 240)

In 1932, he had submitted a novel entitled *Noma nini (For Ever)* for the third competition of the International African Institute; this was awarded a prize in 1933. The book was printed in Mariannhill in 1935. The story takes place in the late nineteenth century during the reign of Mpande, when the first missionaries reached Groutville. It deals with a girl whose lover goes to work in Durban for bride money; she promises to wait for him as long as will be necessary. But during his absence, which lasts several years, the missionaries settle in Groutville, the girl becomes a Christian, and she works at the mission station, where a nice young man falls in love with her. She rejects him at first, but as the years pass and she has no news of her fiancé, she comes to think that the latter has forgotten her, and she agrees to marry her new suitor. But just as the marriage is about to take place, the young man returns from Durban after all sorts of misadventures and delays. He has never stopped thinking about the girl, and he is fortunately in time to marry her. The bride manages to find another suitable girl to bring solace to her second lover. This sentimental and rather pointless story is a good example of acculturation literature, where the Western concept of romantic love and the Christian ideal of premarital constancy are oddly fused with the much more matter-of-fact African view of marriage. Further, as one recent Zulu critic says, "characterization is not convincing," and the narrative "is overburdened with unrelated and irrelevant details of historical accounts." Nevertheless, *Noma nini* had the merit of being the first piece of imaginative fiction to handle modern subject matter in Zulu.

More important is Vilakazi's first collection of poetry, *Inkondlo kaZulu (Zulu Songs)* which was printed in 1935 by the University of the Witwatersrand Press as number 1 in their Bantu Treasury series. The first volume of poetry to appear in Zulu, it contains poems that had been published in native newspapers over a number of years. Some research should be done to establish their chronology, as many of them apparently reflect phases in the poet's evolution. The title, J. Dexter Taylor explained in a long review article [see excerpt dated 1935] "is the name of a certain Zulu dance. Its significance lies in the fact that the emotions of a people who lack means of literary expression find outlet in the dance." Actually, even in their illiterate days, the Bantu did not lack means of literary expression, but the words, the music, and the dance were not kept apart. The title, therefore, means that Vilakazi envisioned himself as a poet in the tradition of the tribal bard, the imbongi, but with an important difference that Taylor pointed out when he said that "Vilakazi in the richness of his Zulu vocabulary, in the truly African flavour of his imagery and in the exuberant extravagance of some of his descriptions is a true descendant of the *imbongi*. But the background of his thought is not that of the *imbongi*."

To begin with, as [C.L.S.] Nyembezi observed [in *A Review of Zulu Literature*], "unlike the traditional poet who recited the praise of chiefs and heroes, Vilakazi wrote on a variety of subjects." This widening of the scope of vernacular poetry was a common feature throughout Africa. It does not mean that traditional topics were abandoned; there are several poems about Chaka in the volume. It means that praise poetry was used for illustrious people other than tribal chiefs and heroes, even though Taylor may have been somewhat rash in asserting that "Aggrey is a greater hero to [Vilakazi] than Shaka." It also means that apart from praise poetry, the modern Bantu author deals with other subjects as well: "the clay pot family heirloom," says Taylor, "the song of the lark, the train that dashes by in the night, leaving him vainly waiting—all the little incidents of daily life serve as starting points for the flow of his verse." One of the best-known poems in the collection is a descriptive piece about the Victoria Falls, which, it is reported, Vilakazi never saw; it was translated by Taylor as an appendix to his review of the book.

A third difference lies in the emotional tenor of the poetry. Traditional poetry was fairly impersonal; because of the limitations in subject-matter, the only emotions it was called upon to convey and stimulate were admiration and wonder. But Vilakazi introduces the lyrical modes he had found in English poetry. In the words of Miss Beuchat [in *Do the Bantu Have a Literature?*], he "has been able to convey his feelings of frustration, of longing for the past, his aspirations and deceptions, in a style of his own, which is not that of the traditional poems, and not that found in any European either." Because of this unique African flavor, Taylor considers Vilakazi as "the *imbongi* come to consciousness of the abstract and of the inner self, through contact with the work of other poets and through the unconscious influence of education and of European culture."

As to form, Nyembezi has noted [in *A Review of Zulu Literature*] that Vilakazi "was mainly responsible for developing poetry whose form departed radically from the traditional Izibongo (or praise). Instead of adopting the style and pattern of the Izibongo, he experimented with European forms. He divided his poems into regular stanzas. He also experimented with rhyme." For this, as we know, he was to be severely rebuked by Herbert I. E. Dhlomo. But already in his review article of 1935, Taylor offered a balanced appraisal of Vilakazi's endeavors in prosody: "He attempts rhyme, but with limited success, as Zulu syllables, invariably, ending in vowels, do not present the variety of sound and tone that makes successful rhyming possible. Even the forms of English rhythm that he uses do not supply a perfect medium, for Zulu accents and stresses refuse to be bent into conformity with the beat of the music. But Mr. Vilakazi is an experimenter in a new field and is to be congratulated on the large measure of his success, rather than criticized for small failures."

The section entitled "Future of Zulu Poetry," in Vilakazi's article of 1938 in *Bantu Studies* [see excerpt above], was presumably written as a rejoinder to Taylor's mild strictures. The poet noted that "there is a feeling among European critics that Zulu can achieve only a limited success with rhyming, since most of the words in Zulu end in vowels, and thus do not permit variety of sound that makes successful rhyming possible." Indeed, Vilakazi stressed his agreement with Steere's remark, in his Preface to *Swahili Tales,* that in Bantu languages "the rhyme is to the eye more than to the ear, as all the final syllables being unaccented, the prominent sounds often destroy the feeling of rhyme." To obviate these difficulties, Vilakazi explained that he had evolved his own system, based on the notion that "in rhyming the Bantu syllables one has to take into account the penultimate syllable," so that "the poet will run his rhyming through two syllables: the penultimate and the final," thus achieving both the desired eye and sound effects. Vilakazi's poetic credo at that early stage in his evolution was defined as follows:

> Form tends to reduce everything to mechanical standards and mathematical formulae. But we have to use some form to embody or clothe the beautiful spirit of our poetry. We have no definite form so far, and our starting point will be at the standards

given by the Western education we have imbibed at college. We are beginning the work which may be given perfect form in generations to come. After all, our language is old and is fast accumulating new words and concepts. I believe therefore it is absolutely necessary that, in composing some poems, we ought to rhyme and decorate our poetic images with definite stanza forms.

It is worthy of note, however, that already in 1938, Vilakazi was aware that better education and the influence of Stuart's Zulu books were combining to turn would-be Zulu poets back to the virtues of the traditional izibongo.

Vilakazi's experiments with rhyme and stanza form should not be viewed as ritualistic imitations of English prosody, but as a brave attempt to enrich Zulu poetic technique and to make Zulu poetry intelligible and acceptable by Western standards. Obviously, **"Inqomfi" ("The Lark")** was inspired by Shelley's "To a Skylark" and **"We moya" ("Hail, Wind")** by the "Ode to the West Wind," and echoes from "Mont Blanc" can easily be detected in **"Impophoma yeVictoria" ("The Victoria Falls")**. Romantic influence on Vilakazi—and later on Herbert Dhlomo—should not be solely accounted for by the prominence of romantic poetry in the school curriculum. The sensitive African suffers under a sense of alienation and nourishes a yearning for a better world, which make him share in the fundamental *Weltschmerz* and *Sehnsucht* of Western romanticism. Just as Western romantics— from Walter Scott to James Fenimore Cooper and Victor Hugo, and from James Macpherson to the Grimm brothers—turned to folklore and to history for images of happiness and grandeur, so the Zulu poet, for all his innovations, remained profoundly faithful to the inspiration of the tribal imbongi. The best pieces in *Inkondlo kaZulu* are genuine praise poems, as allusive as, but less elliptic than the traditional izibongo. Indeed, if we compare the Chaka image in several of those poems with the portrait offered by Dube in *Insila kaTshaka*, it is clear that the younger writer, far from attempting any balanced moral valuation, reverts to the unreservedly encomiastic attitude of the old bards. He likens Chaka to Caesar and Charlemagne as the great conqueror, the military and administrative genius, the welder of many nations into one mighty empire. He strangely revels even in the sufferings inflicted by Chaka on the conquered tribes:

> Let us tell how peoples reeled
> And died, their blood congealed with terror.

For him, Chaka is an outsize figure, whose stature makes moral judgment irrelevant:

> How unpredictable were you!
> You whose ambition slaughtered infants,
> Babies born and unborn babies.

The reason for this unexpected leniency in a poet so imbued with the Christian religion is that Chaka is presented as the instrument and the embodiment of past Zulu unity and greatness, and a source of everlasting inspiration:

> Still today we speak of you
> And swear by you with utmost faith;
> And all the problems of the Council,
> Discussed by those whom you inspired—
> Those you bequeathed to Zululand—
> We who are not deaf, hear clearly.

Indeed, in **"Khalani maZulu" ("Weep, You Zulu")**, a dirge written on the death of King Solomon in 1933, the decline

and enslavement of the Zulu nation are ascribed to the divisiveness and internecine strife in the post-Chaka era, as symbolized in the battle of Ndondakusuka in 1856:

> Have you forgotten what happened:
> The slaughter of one by another,
> The ruin at Ndondakuzuka?
> You died and the future was barren.
> Now see all the young ones
> Of Whites who despoiled us
> Suckled by cows almost famished,
> Those that were meant for the children—
> The offspring of Senzangakhona
> Who sired the breed of Cetshwayo?
>
> Do you forget then
> Our share of the penance
> Is this: to remember and ever
> Be haunted by Ndondakusuka?

The poem celebrates Chief Solomon's tireless efforts to restore the "Inkatha," the secret tribal emblem of Zulu solidarity, which now takes the shape of a fund constituted by the various Zulu chieftains in order to carry out such national projects as the building of a school for the education of chiefs' sons:

> For years counting thirty and seven,
> Did Solomon scheme,
> And plans for uniting the nation
> He formed, and he showed it the ways
> Of peace, and in place of the spears,
> The use of the armour of knowledge.
> He planned and constructed a school
> Where those highly born should become
> The pillars of African progress.

This leads us to the second main theme of *Inkondlo kaZulu.* For the world has changed, and if the Zulu are to restore anything like their former glory, it cannot be through warlike deeds, but through learning:

> How does it serve to brood upon the past
> As though this period of enlightenment
> Offers no more than darkness and confusion?

This was the lesson taught by Dr. Aggrey, whose lectures in 1921, as a member of the Phelps-Stokes Commission sent out from the United States to survey the problems and prospects of African education, had made a deep impression on Bantu audiences, even though he had been received with contempt by the Afrikaner section of the population:

> And from the Rand, Paul Kruger's people
> Derided and belittled you,
> Seeing, they thought, a little jackal,
> No different from the other jackals,
> Black, white-toothed, this country's own!

In this praise poem addressed to Aggrey, Vilakazi recalls how

> I turned from you because I feared you,
> Dreaded to have my ignorance revealed,
> My nakedness displayed,
> When I had thought that I was learned.

But, he adds,

> When you had gone away, I stayed,
> Saw, with new eyes, my native land,
> How men stood firmly on their feet
> And packed their bags and went to learn.

And he proudly records the educational achievements of his

people throughout southern Africa, at Lovedale and at Morija, at Amanzimtoti and Ohlange. Characteristically, the last poem in the volume is a long ode in celebration of the fiftieth anniversary of the monastery founded by Catholic missionaries from Germany and Austria. In traditional Zulu phrasing, Vilakazi sings of those white educators as

> the sons
> Who left their homes
> To wander far and wide;
> Knotted their bundles and escaped,
> Never to return again.
> The dwellings of their ancestors,
> The kinsmen tied to them by blood,
> The soil that nourishes the fruit,
> The noon-day heat of summer days,
> The moonlight's glow on winter nights—
> All this they left behind them.
> They crossed the waters of the sea,
> They reached the place of assegais

to help the Zulu gratify

> . . . the longing
> Of their souls,
> The longing for the flaming torch
> Already lighted in the South [i.e. among the Xhosa]
> And carried high by Grout
> And Lindley too and Adams.

These were the American missionaries who had come from the United States in 1840. The Reverend A. Grout had founded the Groutville mission, where Vilakazi was born; the Reverend Lindley had founded the Inanda mission, home of John Dube; and Dr. Newton Adams had established the college at Amanzimtoti. Vilakazi's gratitude for devoted service to the Zulu people extends to Protestants and Catholics alike.

The years immediately preceding World War II were filled with feverish activity for Vilakazi, who had become by now the first Zulu man of letters with a full university education. His work on the Zulu language for a B.A. had earned him a bursary from the University of South Africa and he started working for an M.A. degree in African Studies. The only place that offered senior courses in African Studies was the University of the Witwatersrand, which, at the time, was in need of an African language assistant for the Department of Bantu Studies. Vilakazi was appointed to this post in 1936, thus becoming the first African to teach at university level outside Fort Hare. Because of his literary activities, he was invited to attend the first two African Authors' Conferences of 15 October 1936 and 30 September 1937, where he, together with Herbert Dhlomo, represented emergent Zulu writing. In 1938 he was awarded an M.A. degree with a study on **"The Conception and Development of Poetry in Zulu,"** the substance of which was printed in *Bantu Studies*. Simultaneously, he wrote a biographical novel about Shaka's protector, *UDingiswayo kaJobe* (*Dingiswayo, Son of Jobe*), and carried on a controversy with Dhlomo about the nature of traditional izibongo, the significance of Zulu drama, and the future of Zulu prosody. But, as Nyembezi recalls:

> Vilakazi's appointment to the University of the Witwatersrand aroused opposition among a section of the Africans in the Transvaal. Its effect was to make him recoil into his shell so that he appeared to shun the company of Africans of his class. He became a controversial figure among the African people. The educated Africans respected him for his academic achievements and for his contribution to

Zulu literature. But they regarded him as cold, aloof, haughty—a man who was not easily approachable. They found him abrupt in his manner and sometimes deliberately rude. The illiterate Africans on the other hand, found him a pleasant character and easily approachable. . . . Yet . . . there were those who accused him of being insufficiently conscious of their sufferings and disabilities. He did not take an active part in politics. It was his firm belief that he could not serve two masters and that he could not participate in politics and still perform his academic work satisfactorily.

We have seen Vilakazi's somewhat abrupt, haughty manner during his controversy with Dhlomo. His sense of isolation found utterance in the poetry of those years, which he collected in 1945 under the title *Amal'EZulu* (*Zulu Horizons*). A poem like **"Imfundo ephakeme"** (**"Higher Education"**) traces his evolution from his youthful hopes of smooth synthesis between tradition and novelty to the more mature awareness of inherent conflict, which grew in him as a result of his experience of life in Johannesburg:

> When my thinking was but folly,
> Then I dreamed of satisfaction
> If I read my books and studied,
>
> Pondered learning, mused on wisdom,
> Striving for some understanding:
> Now, to-day, my mind is weary.
>
> I have spent so many years
> Turning over leaves of books
> Whose authors' skins were white;
> And every night I sat alone
> Until the new day's sun arose:
> But now, to-day, my eyes are throbbing.
>
> And poets who were black I called on,
> Those who sang of kings' ambitions,
> Those who praised our brimming bowls,
> And their wisdom too, I thought on,
> Mixing it with white men's teachings:
> Now my mind's a battle-field.

This intellectual confusion leads him to doubt the value of learning:

> He who does not know these things,
> And sleeps untroubled through the night,
> Never reading till the dawn,
> Not knowing Cicero or Caesar,
> Shaka, Ngqika or Moshoeshoe:
> He, to-day, is light of heart.

A further source of despondency is his estrangement from other Africans, the prosperous bourgeois class, who have fully embraced the white man's creed of material success:

> Those I grew with, those unlettered,
> When they meet me, they despise me,
> Seeing me walk on naked feet
> While they travel in their cars,
> Leaving me to breathe their dust:
> These to-day are chiefs and masters.

This tragic inner conflict finds resolution in acceptance of both the costs and the rewards that go with the author's dedication to learning and poetry:

> So I absorb and add and store
> Wisdom for the Zulus' children.
> The day may come to have discussions

And learn from all my nightly writings,
Never written from ambition:
For you, ancestral spirits, urged me,
Inspiring me through hours of darkness!

But then I shall be here no longer.

The main direction in Vilakazi's development, therefore, lay in ever deeper reverence for the Zulu tradition. Many of the poems in this second volume deal once more with the great events and figures of the past, the beauty of the Natal landscape, the cult of the ancestors, African respect for the wisdom of old age, or the mission of the poet in Zulu society. The writer's technique also demonstrates that he was not happy with his experiments in the earlier collection. He now discards rhyme almost completely, thus rallying to the views expressed by Taylor and Dhlomo.

But a new orientation also emerges as Vilakazi shows himself more subtly aware of the complex pathos in the modern African's situation. He describes the bewilderment of the tribesman who is compelled to leave his kraal and come to the white man's city of brick and concrete:

Tell, O tell me, white-man's son,
The reason you have brought me here!
I come, but O my knees are heavy
And, as I think, my head is swimming;
Darkness descends for me at noon
And each day's sun becomes a moon.

In **"Ukuhlwa" ("Nightfall")**, he evokes the filth and insecurity of the native locations:

Now, as the streets are lit,
I fear the lurking thieves
Who seek their prey like hunters.

Here, there is no grass,
But dust from off the mine-dumps
Like smoke is drifting skyward.

In **"Imifula yomhlaba" ("The Rivers of the World")**, he relives in a dream the occupation of African land by the white invaders:

And then I saw Retief and all his men
Scurrying, hurrying through the land,
To scatter generations
Of the nations of the white man.
They wash in waters of the Orange,
They cleanse themselves of filth;
And we, the peoples who are black,
Accepted that calamity,
That evil weight that bowed our heads.

In **"Izinsimbi zesonto" ("Church Bells")**, he underscores the irony of Christianity, which first seemed to threaten with extinction the African's cherished beliefs and values:

I heard the bells, the white man's bells!
At first I heard them sullenly,
Heard them toll with rising anger,
Rage consumed me—then it left me.

but which has now become—unheeded by the white man, hypocritical, materialistic, and blind—the instrument of a new African awakening:

Ring out, O bells, O white man's bells!
John Dube and his friends have risen
And brought to life the black men's minds.
Your call does not awaken them—

Those looking on, the while they rang you!
They waken us, yes us in darkness,
Hidden in the white man's shadow.
Ring out! the charge is yours, O bells!

And in **"Ngoba . . . sewuthi" ("Because . . . You Say")**, he denounces—in terms which are reminiscent of Dhlomo's article, if only because they are a commonplace of African experience and thinking—the comfortable blindness of the white man, who chooses to remain unaware of the black man's sufferings and revolt:

Because I smile continually,
Because I even seem content
And sing with all my voice
Although you trust me underground
Beneath the wealth so fabulous
Of earth stained blue with diamonds—
You say that I am like a post,
A thing that feels no pain?
. . . .
Because I am, in truth, a dupe
Who suffers through my ignorance,
Not understanding all these laws,
Though knowing I am used and plundered,
And though the hut in which I live
I've built beneath the mountain crags—
My own true home is made of grass
My own true garment is a sack:
Because of this, you think me lifeless,
Having not a tear to shed
That issues from a living heart
To fall within the spotless hands
Of spirits holy and all-seeing.

Although Vilakazi did not engage actively in politics, it is clear that his experience of township life in Johannesburg, because of the contrast it offered with the sheltered seclusion of Natal mission schools and with the comparative humaneness of life in Durban, prompted him toward more explicit protest through his chosen medium. This second orientation reached its climax in what is commonly considered his best poem, **"Ezinkomponi" ("In the Gold Mines")**, which deals with the black laborer's life on the Rand. Vilakazi's mood and attitude are very close to those of Dhlomo in *The Valley of a Thousand Hills*. The main difference is that Dhlomo, writing in Durban, found his symbols of oppression in the "commercial dells" of the modern mercenary city, whereas Vilakazi, writing in Johannesburg, found apt emblems of man's inhumanity to man in the industrial society and in the roaring machines that remain deaf

To black men groaning as they labour—
Tortured by their aching muscles,
Gasping in the foetid air,
Reeking from the dirt and sweat—
Shaking themselves without effect.

Yet, the poet feels pity for the machines, that were brought from their faraway native land:

You had no choice, you had to come;
And now roar, revolve and toil,
Till, thrown away, worn out, you rot
On some neglected rubbish-plot.

But the miner's fate is even worse:

We too, grow old and rusty in the mines;
Our strength soon goes, our lungs soon rot,
We cough, we cannot rest—We die!
But you are spared that coughing—why?

Although Vilakazi's description of the cruel injustice of South African society is heartfelt and eloquent, it does not lead him to rebellion, but merely to what Mphahlele has aptly recognized as "romantic escapism." The poet can only dream ineffectually of "that far day" when

> we, at last, will cry: "Machines!
> You are ours, the black men's, now!
> • • • • •
> "Dream that this land—my father's land—
> Shall be my fathers' sons' again."

For the present, his feeling is one of frustration and helplessness:

> But now I have no place to rest
> Though wealth is everywhere around me;
> Land that my fathers owned is bare
> And spreads untilled before my eyes;
> And even if I had some wealth,
> This land my fathers' fathers owned
> I may not purchase or possess.
> • • • • •
> Every day this land of yours [i.e. the ancestral spirits']
> Is seized and spoiled by those who rob us:
> These foreign breeds enrich themselves,
> But all my people and myself
> Are black, and, being black, have nothing.
> • • • • •
> Our hands are aching, always aching,
> Our swollen feet are aching too;
> I have no ointment that might heal them—
> White men's medicines cost much money.
> • • • • •
> Well have I served the rich white masters,
> But oh, my soul is heavy in me!

The mood, however, remains elegiac, impervious to the revolutionary potentialities of the situation, and the only hope that the black miner entertains, as he once more addresses the machines at the end of the poem, is forgetfulness on earth and a better life hereafter:

> Roar less loudly, let me slumber,
> Close my eyes and sleep and sleep
> And stop all thinking of tomorrow.
> Let me sleep and wake afar,
> At peace where all my forebears are
> And where, no more, is earthly waking!
> Let me sleep in arms long vanished,
> Safe beneath the world's green pastures.

It is noteworthy that the word "Zulu" does not occur in this poem. Vilakazi's move to Johannesburg had confronted him with greater misery, exploitation, and oppression than he could have witnessed in Natal. As the mining labor force on the Rand was multitribal, his turning to the social theme also meant a reorientation from Zulu particularism toward a new sense of all-African solidarity. It is true that he remained faithful to his Zulu inspiration in his third and last novel, *Nje nempela* (*Truly, Indeed*). The book has been described as "one of the finest expositions of the Bhambatha Rebellion of 1906," and has also been singled out by Zulu anthropologist Absalom Vilakazi as an outstanding depiction of traditional life in a polygamous household, with the rivalries between co-wives, the suspicion, the everpresent quarrels, and the tense relations marked by spiteful speeches and public reprimands. But while writing this novel, Vilakazi was also working on a doctoral dissertation about **"The Oral and Written Literature of the Nguni,"** which made him the first African to obtain a Ph.D. degree of the University of the Witwatersrand

on 16 March 1946. The Nguni are the branch of the Southern Bantu which includes both the Zulu and the Xhosa; the two peoples speak kindred languages, and unsuccessful efforts had been made in the previous two decades to bolster African unity by fusing Zulu and Xhosa into one single language. This was also the purpose of Vilakazi, who studied the traditional and the modern literatures of both groups as if they were one nation. Although the dissertation has never been published, it is the most important single source of historical information for modern Xhosa and Zulu literature. (pp. 241-56)

> Albert S. Gérard, "Zulu Literature," in his Four African Literatures: Xhosa, Sotho, Zulu, Amharic, *University of California Press, 1971, pp. 181-270.*

MARIA K. MOOTRY (essay date 1973)

[*In the following excerpt, Mootry demonstrates how Vilakazi combined elements from the European Romantic tradition and the Zulu oral tradition in order to write poetry of "protest and resistance."*]

What is the role of an intellectual whose people are an oppressed group struggling for new or renewed nationhood? How can he, from a position inherently disengaged and analytical, involve himself immediately and vitally in that struggle? This question Frantz Fanon answers in his handbook for black revolution, *The Wretched of the Earth*. Recognizing the spiritual, cultural, and psychological, ravages of the colonizer on the colonized, Fanon places the onus of recovery on the intellectual. To legitimize the people's past; to restore the people's image; to reflect the people's evolution to national consciousness—these are the intellectual's tasks. But, in Fanon's view, he must first undergo a process of evolution himself. This evolution consists of three stages. In the first, the intellectual assimilates the colonizer's culture; in the second, he rejects this culture violently, often embracing negative stereotypes of his people in his effort to rebel; in the last, he frees himself from mere reaction to create a national literature or art based on the dynamic fight for freedom. Within this framework the concept of negritude or 'black is beautiful' becomes an anathema, as much as poetry in imitation of Shakespeare or art after Renoir. The mythologization of the people, based on the oppressor's exaggerations, simply expresses a new form of degradation.

As with all formulae, when applied to actual literary achievements Fanon's categories are inelastic. His assumption is that an intellectual's thought and its expression could not reflect two or three stages of evolution at once. . . . [My purpose is to demonstrate how the Zulu poet Benedict Wallet Vilakazi] fused the elements of the European Romantic tradition with . . . [his] oral legacy to create poetry of protest and resistance. (p. 112)

All critics of Vilakazi . . . [stress his] artistic debt to the English Romantic poets—a debt expressed in form and sentiment. D. Mck. Malcolm, in the introduction to *Zulu Horizons,* [see excerpt dated 1962], explains that in studying for his undergraduate degree, Vilakazi 'became aware of the English poets of the Romantic period and was fired with the ambition of doing for Zulu literature what they had done for English'. When the characteristics of the Romantic writers are listed it is clear that their style and thought, in some areas, was peculiarly appropriate for a Zulu poet in the first half of the twentieth century. On an ideological level, the Romantic tradition was characterized by a faith in the imagination and in intuition which was most frequently expressed in the tendency to read meanings into landscapes. Along with this went a strong sense of man's oneness with nature. The poet was regarded as a kind of high-priest. In his uncompromising individualism, he denounced industrial development, all forms of institutions, and all sources of human oppression. He was preoccupied with revolution, often taking a leftist political stance and believing in man's perfectibility; but at the same time he was prone to a powerful sense of disillusionment which reflected his perfectionist standards.

On a formal level, the poet presented himself with a direct appeal to his reader rather than through ironic detachment, often using a dramatic tone. He used images full of nuance and suggestion. In line with his iconoclastic stance, he mixed his styles at will, including the elegiac, the lyrical and the meditative.

The Romantic tradition, then, contained escapist as well as involved proclivities. The clouded view of nature as sympathetic to man and as an automatic source of inspiration and well-being denies the necessary social condition of man. Persistent sombre notes of despair, melancholy, confusion, and unrest, are often signs of a failure to deal with reality. The emphasis on individualism and anti-institutionalism, in one sense, is an escape from the acknowledgment of communal origin and destiny. On the other hand, the aura of revolution emanating from the Romantic tradition was entirely relevant to the needs of the Zulu peoples; seemingly everywhere the downtrodden revolted, championed by the English poet: Greek against Turk, Italian against Austrian, Black against White (San Domingo); and Frenchman against Frenchman. The emphasis was on activism:

> Wordsworth interested himself in the abolition of the slave trade, Coleridge once dreamed of founding a utopian community in the New World, Blake saw existing European churches and governments as the engines of Satan, Shelley and Byron envisioned a new Hellas rising out of the ashes of the Old Greece, and Byron himself, after aiding for some time the Italian underground, died in Greece trying to bring the new Hellas about.

The poets' anti-industrialism paralleled protest against the economic exploitation of black Africans by Englishmen and Afrikaners. And, finally, the view of the poet as 'unacknowledged legislator of the world', is analogous to Fanon's demand that the artist/intellectual assume the role of leader and legitimizer.

The question then arises of the matter of selection and emphasis. Vilakazi explored the Romantic tradition intensely, with positive and negative results. Weighted by Romantic escapist sensibility, sometimes his poetry loses its originality and power altogether. At other times, even though he uses rhyme and addresses a lark or an urn, Vilakazi introduces images and ideas from his Zulu heritage, creating a syncretic work which derives potency from its unique expression. (pp. 113-14)

[Three poems by Vilakazi] are often pointed out as directly influenced by Keats and Shelley. **'Ukhamba luka Sonkomose'** ('Sonkomose's Bowl'), **'Inqomfi'** ('The Lark') and **'We moya!'** (**Hail Wind!'**) are presumably modelled on Keats's 'Ode to a Grecian Urn', and Shelley's 'To a Skylark' and 'Ode to the West Wind', respectively.

The inspiration of **'Sonkomose's Bowl'** was an old family pot from which the poet's grandfather had drunk. As the poet gazes at the bowl, memories of the past burst upon his consciousness, creating a sense of communion with his grandfather. This interaction with the object immediately establishes a relationship very different from that of Keats with his urn. The main thrust of Keats's poem is on the artistic distance of the urn. It is a 'cold pastoral' which preaches an abstract truth. Vilakazi's initial apostrophe establishes an atmosphere of warmth and immediacy; a very *human* encounter. In a dramatic tone, he speaks to his ancestor:

> Grandsire, although I did not know you,
> Yet I can commune with you
> And even though I cannot see you,
> This I see: the bending backs
> Of those who say you are their sire,
> And they have given me this insight.

The bowl, no simple *objet d'art,* has been used by the grandfather:

> Here, before me, is a bowl,
> And, from this vessel, once you drank,
> You, son of the Mzwangedwa tribe,
> You who went your ways alone
> And did not ever think to own
> That in its depths were precious secrets.

The poem also incorporates two formal characteristics from the *izibongo,* i.e. the naming of the person addressed or use of epithet ('son of the Mzwangedwa tribe') and the use of repetition plus extension of statement through a consecutive tense:

> You, son of the Mzwangedwa tribe,
> You who went your ways alone
> And did not ever think to own, etc.

The third stanza expresses the happy sense of communion of past, present, and future. In the fourth stanza the use of names derives from the oral tradition in much of Africa. Professor Klaus Wachsmann, in his lectures, has commented on the special emotional potency of names in oral recitations. Vilakazi himself wrote of names that 'stab us like spears: each one is magic'. Thus, the three names in the stanza function in a way unknown to the European written tradition:

> Vessel, in you I see the hills
> Whose name is yours, O Sonkomose,
> Inherited by your son, Mkhwethu,
> Scattered with many herds of cattle,
> Which, by Nkombose my father's daughter,
> Proclaim you 'Encircler of the Hills.'

The fifth stanza includes a direct quotation from a praise epithet:

> I fear not even seers and sages
> Whose lips have touched this bowl,
> Can praise the Mkhwethus in these words:
> 'The ravenous beast whose growl was heard
> That time it stirred and fed at Bulawayo
> Where gorgeous crimson grasses grow.'

Here, interestingly, the poet defies his customs by praising his family on his mother's side (the Mkhwethu) who turned grass crimson with blood as great warriors and founded the Matabele nation in Southern Rhodesia.

The sixth and final stanza reiterates the poet's concept of the bowl and its goblet as retainers of his Zulu heritage. The amber liquid of the goblet reminds him of yet another ancestral figure whom he names, Qwabe, brother of Zulu, founder of the Zulu tribe. The closing lines, addressed to the goblet, beautifully complete the personal veneration of the poet for the bowl and what it symbolizes:

> You are wedded to this vessel
> And everything this vessel holds.

'Inqomfi' ('The Lark'), written in two parts at different times, is a less successful poem. Since the first six stanzas were composed as a unit and can be considered a complete poem, only these will be discussed. The remaining stanzas are rather superfluous, adding little to either the thought or form. In comparing this poem with Shelley's, a case similar to the above analysis could be made. But here it is less the verbal form that varies than the imagery, detail and sensibility. Shelley's bird is pure spirit ('Bird thou never wert') and as such knows only pure joy. Shelley's theme is his plea that the bird teach him the secret of its music so that the world would be compelled to listen to him. Vilakazi's lark, though it represents spirit, is deliberately linked to the African soil. It leads no idyllic existence, but suffers from the menace of the iguana and the deadly mamba snake, hawks, and poisoned Bushman arrows. It eats tasty locusts, which for Shelley's lark is inconceivable. In the end the bird symbolizes less a remote disembodied spirit than an oracle, a tool of the supernatural forces which govern the destinies of men. The following stanzas are illustrative:

> Oh, you who lay those eggs of dappled colours,
> Hiding them well within the grassy tufts
> Where neither iguana comes nor mamba glides,
> Sing clear above them songs inspiring courage
> And drive away the hawks that would consume them
> During your flights in search of tasty locusts.
>
> What meaning has that rich and fadeless colour,
> That splash of glowing crimson on your throat;
> Who pierced you with those sharp and fatal arrows,
> Known to Bushmen in their rocky caves?
> Your symbol this, a flag of flame
> To scorch the deaf who spurn your counselling!
>
> If you should fly before a traveller,
> The elders say that his affairs will prosper;
> But woe to him when you behind
> Shall soar across his path, and, like the buzzard,
> Sing when the clouds conceal the sun. Ill omen!
> You are an oracle, bird, you prophesy!

Of the three poems, **'We moya!' ('Hail Wind!')** is closest to the European tradition. In it Vilakazi shows the same concept of nature as Shelley in his 'Ode to the West Wind'. To Shelley, the rough wind is a destroyer and preserver, to which he prays for artistic rebirth:

> Scatter, as from an unextinguish'd hearth
> Ashes and sparks, my words among mankind!
> Be through my lips to unawaken'd earth
>
> The trumpet of a prophecy!

Like Shelley, Vilakazi apostrophizes the wind, ending with a plea for a union with it that will revive the poet. Returning to Fanon's categories, this poem falls easily into assimilationist literature or what Jahnheinz Jahn termed 'apprentice literature'. Its pervasive melancholy is trite; its imitative language lacks the strength of original imagery. Only two stanzas attain any power of expression, and these contain details derived from the poet's background. By way of illustration, the two stanzas labelled *a* and *b* can be compared with those that follow:

> (a) Come soon, the sun has risen
> And pleasant is the hill
> Where you in strength can rival
> The houses of the Ngangas.
>
> Come let us both be merry
> And feel that strong desire
> That's born of restlessness
> Whose enemy is sloth.

> (b) And you foretell the rain,
> (Wafting the scent of melons
> That ripen with the pumpkins)
> For mealie plants and berries,
>
> Come, wind! O come and lighten
> My heart that feels so heavy
> And let me die when you die.

Elements from the *izibongo* found in Vilakazi's first volume and used even more extensively in the second are: the use of names and praise-names; the use of metaphors, similes and imagery from Zulu plant and animal life; the use of a dramatic tone; the use of a confident epic tone; the use of parallel structures; and the use of repetition. In the interest of time and space, four poems from **Inkondlo kaZulu** (the first volume in **Zulu Horizons**) will be used to illustrate the prevalence of these techniques. They are (*a*) **'Inkelekele yakwa Xhoza' ('The Xhosa Calamity')**; (*b*) **'Khalam maZulu' ('Weep, You Zulus')**; (*c*) **'UShaka kaSenzangakhona' ('Shaka, Son of Senzangakhona')** and (*d*) **'Phezu kwethuna lika Shaka' ('Over the Grave of Shaka')**. Here are the examples.

A. Use of names:

> (a) Ah! speak and tell me, where are *Tshiwo*
> And other chiefs, men like *Hanahana*
> *Xiniha, Menziwa,* and *Hahabe,*
> *Manxa, Nukwa* and *Nqabisile?*
> Where do they sleep, the maids of *Xhosa,*
> *Sutho, Joli, Nomalizo?*
> Speak and tell me, where are *Hintsa,*
> The *Xhosa* chiefs, the *Xhosa* women—
> Adorned with feathers, vulture, ostrich—
> Who danced at *Qonce* and at *Monti?*

(Note the cumulative effect of a catalogue of names.)

> (b) The great bird has died, and there rotted
> The bones of the children of *Qwabe.*
> And then came a man, *Dinuzulu,*
> Who lived at the place, *Sikhwebezi,*
> The home of the leading *uSuthu;*
> A new one at *emaHhashini*
> He built on a hill near *Nongoma.*

(Note powerful effect of having names at end of each line.)

> (c) You, *Shaka,* were the very image
> Of sages whom we know today,
> Fighting all the would-be traitors.
> Many opposed you, all were hurled
> Upon the assegais and clubs.
> *Zwide* fell; he fell because
> He sought to elevate himself
> Above you. Broken and crushed he fell
> And all his followers disputed:
> They, like *Matiwane* quarrelled.

(Note the structuring function of the names.)

(*d*) Come to your children again, O *Zulu!*
Greatest of all the *uSuthu* Chiefs,
So that the world may see once more,
O fearless son of *Menzi,*
The power of your famous forbears,
The fame the *Qulusis* still retain.

(Again, note the structuring function of the names.)

B. Use of Praise-names:

(*a*) The great bird has died . . .

To the mountain that shelters the Lion
From the fear of the thundering heavens.

And some saw Monase
Who gazed at Mahhashini
And wept like the abaQulusi. . . .

(Note extension through a grammatical unit dependent
upon the statement and through a consecutive tense.)

(*b*) . . . . the mighty Cub
Of Phunga and of Xaba who was borne
Upon the shoulders of the sun,
Cared for and nurtured by the moon,
For he was destined to discover trails
Of Zulus bound for Pondoland.

(Note statement, extension, development, and conclusion.)

(*c*) Your tombstone has displaced them, Shaka,
Mountain whose spirit is a lion
Sheltering from the storms of heaven!
You who drank from clear deep pools,
As though a honeysucker, also
Drank from shallow muddy water
That soils the tufted bending head
And stains the tips of trailing wings.

(Note lyricism and imagery of harmless, delicate, animal,
which is also characteristic of pre-Shakan praise-poem.)

C. Metaphors, similes and imagery from Zulu plant and animal life:

(See above examples which contain references to
bird, hill, mountain, lion, cub, sun, moon, pool, and
honeysucker.)

D. Use of dramatic address:

(*a*) Battalions of Zulus, awaken!
Gather your weapons and listen!
Awaken, uSuthu detachments!
And yours Mandlakazi, awake!
What manner of sleep has benumbed you?
Can you not hear that the Zulus
Are seething as though they were maggots?

(*b*) Listen to me, you simpletons,
You who hear me speak
Until I waste to thinness of a rake . . .

Listen to me, you useless men!

You, Shaka, were the very image
Of sages whom we know today . . .

(Shaka is addressed throughout.)

(*c*) Come to your children again, O Zulu!
Greatest of all the uSuthu chiefs . . .

Ring out the bells,

You Zulu chiefs . . .

Rise from beneath that tomb, O Shaka

E. Use of a Confident Epic-like tone:

(See examples of direct address.)

The confident tone derives primarily from contemplation
of past; examples are numerous but this stanza offers a
typical rendering:

(*d*) And one who fled was grey-haired Nxaba;
He scaled the great uBombo mountains.
But in the land of the Basutos
Mshweshe was a scourge: he plundered!
He lured them into uBusiko,

Establishing new rules and customs
For the baKgatla and the Pedi,
Giving no ground and spreading Northward.
Time passed and all the nations feared him;
Great were his gains and he a marvel.

(This is the intellectual exalting and legitimizing his past;
his attitude might be contrasted to Mofolo's moralizing
against Shaka in his historical novel, *Chaka*. Jahn rightfully called this type of poetry 'indirect protest.')

F. Use of parallel structures and repetition:

(*a*) Oh you who would hinder the Zulus,
Oh you who would conquer their kingdom,
All, all will be slaughtered and perish.

(*b*) Later inherited by Shaka:
He who devoured the rich and poor,
He who destroyed the forests, herds and rushes.

He dwelt among the Portuguese
Where still his people could survive,
Free from the terrors of the night,
Free from the marching of the troops,
Free from the clashing of the shields.

(*c*) Those stones at Nkandla cover him,
Him, not helped across the river,
Him his people doomed through envy,
Him they branded as a tyrant.

Interestingly, while Zulu critics such as D. D. T. Jabavu and
C. L. S. Nyembezi admit that Vilakazi made some use of the
oral tradition, especially in his second volume of poetry, they
emphasize the European influence on the poet. It is partially
in reaction to their assessment that the above analysis has attempted to show that, even where Vilakazi used European
rhyme and stanza form, i.e. in his first volume of poetry, elements from the *izibongo* were a substantial part of the verse.
Jabavu describes this volume as an example of 'English influence *in excelsis*'; this he attributed to 'its outright imitation
of English modes (metres long, short, and common; all varieties of stanzas, elegiacs, sonnets, rhymes and even the heroic
couplet reminiscent of Pope and Dryden) all punctiliously
observed'. Nyembezi emphasized Vilakazi's 'Europeanness'
when he observed,

And yet among the Zulus Vilakazi is remembered
more as a poet than as a prose-writer; he was mainly responsible for developing poetry whose form departed radically from the traditional *izibongo* (or
praises). He experimented with European forms.
He divided his poems into regular stanzas. He also
experimented with rhyme.

Unfortunately, Vilakazi's poetic theory probably contributed to his critics' judgements. In **'The Conception and Development of Poetry in Zulu'**, [see excerpt dated 1938], he called for faithful imitation of the colonizer's form. 'Educated poets,' he felt, had to study the standards of Classical or European poetry; these standards would help to arouse 'finer and deeper feelings' because of the impact of the 'outer world' on their sensitive souls. He added emphatically:

> I do not believe in form; I rely more on the spirit of poetry. Form tends to reduce everything to mechanical standards and mathematical formulae. But we have to use some form to embody or clothe the beautiful spirit of our poetry. We have no definite form so far, and our starting point will be at the standards given us by the Western education we have imbibed at college. We are beginning the work which may be given perfect form in generations to come. I believe, therefore, it is absolutely necessary that, in composing some poems, we ought to rhyme and decorate our poetic images with definite stanza forms.

What conclusions can be drawn from Vilakazi's use of historical themes and techniques from the oral tradition relative to the question of political consciousness? One thing is clear. The use of historical themes or praise-poem structure does not automatically indicate escapism, nor does it automatically create protest or a militant stance. In other words, varied uses can be made of an oral tradition. Looking into the past can create a sense of regret and immobility, as when Vilakazi addressed Shaka in disillusionment, crying 'Would that our times were yours, O Shaka!' The structure of the praise-poem can be used to flatter the colonizer (almost all missionaries and other whites have had praise-poems made for them), or to deride him (the oft-quoted mock-praise by Mqhayi is a famous example). In the latter case, the form achieves a level of satirical protest, or better yet, protest-through-satire. One fascinating example of this use of the praise-poem appeared in the Xhosa journal, *Isigidimi* (1871). It was written by UHadi Waseluhlangeni ('The Harp of the Nation'), whom A. C. Jordan described as a writer of great intellectual integrity, widely read by literate Black South Africans. 'Hadi' protested against the journal's support of whites and bias against its own people and suggested that this poem be a model for other poets:

> Arise, ye sons of the Mountain-at-Night!
> The hyena howls, the white hyena,
> All ravenous for the bones of Moshoeshoe,
> Of Moshoeshoe who sleeps high up on the mountain.
>
> Its belly hangs heavy and drags on the ground,
> All gorged with the bones of warrior-kings;
> Its mouth is red with the blood of Sandile.
>
> Awake, rock-rabbits of the Mountain-at-Night!
> She darts out her tongue to the very skies,
> That rabbit-snake with female breasts
> Who suckled and fostered the trusting Fingos,
> Thereafter to eat them alive.

Except that Sandile is a Xhosa chief and the rabbit-snake represents Queen Victoria, not much commentary is needed here.

But to return to Vilakazi: it seems that he used his Zulu heritage largely on an artistic basis and with the purpose of recapturing the past. As indicated earlier, this might have been due to his temperament, which seems to have been melancholy

and resigned. His most famous and overt protest poem, **'In the Gold Mines'**, significantly is neither in the Romantic nor the praise-poem tradition, but in simple dramatic stanzas. Equally significant, however, is the poet's use of the allegorical mode characteristic of his oral tradition. As in UHadi's poem quoted above, black men are represented as rock-rabbits, but these rock-rabbits have been turned into moles who burrow deep into the earth. The machines are brothers of the black men but they are luckier: they face no prospect of lung disease. Even here Vilakazi's overall tone is plaintive; he feels confused, dispirited. Once this plaintive note rises to defiance, when the poet is bolstered by thoughts of his past:

> Take care! Though now our arms are weak,
> Once their power made dark the skies,
> And earth was torn and nations reeled,
> The Great White Queen lost many sons,
> Paul Kruger's children too we slaughtered.
> Then we, the conquerors, were defeated.
> And now I dream, Oh thing of Iron!
> Dream that this land—my fathers' land—
> Shall be my fathers' sons' again.

But then Vilakazi slips back into his plaintive mode, calling on his fathers to end his wretchedness. After receiving no answer, he concludes his poem with a startling, chilling, plea for withdrawal into death. (pp. 114-23)

> *Maria K. Mootry, "Literature and Resistance in South Africa: Two Zulu Poets," in* African Literature Today: A Review, Poetry in Africa, *edited by Eldred Durosimi Jones, Heinemann, 1973, pp. 112-29.*

ABSOLOM L. VILAKAZI (essay date 1975)

[*Vilakazi is a Zulu anthropologist. In the following excerpt, he investigates the social and historical impetus for Vilakazi's poetry.*]

Friedman's translation of Vilakazi's Zulu poems [*Zulu Horizons*] is not only an artistic achievement, it is clearly an inspired work as well. In Daniel McK. Malcolm's apt phrase Friedman's "wizardry with the English language" has captured the native poetry of Vilakazi's words—so much so that, reading the translations without the benefit of the Zulu version to refer to, this reviewer could still recall the magic of the Zulu words as, in stanza one of **"The Valley of a Thousand Hills,"** he could respond to the translation by breaking out in ecstatic Zulu: "Sizigqume ngomoya omanzi wasolwandle" (lines 3, 4 and 5); or, on reading **"Mamina"** he could join Vilakazi's invitation to the maid, to steal out of the house in the fashion of a lovesick Zulu girl as if to draw water, to go downstream where she would find me:

> Phansi kwazihlahla zomdoni
> Zithelile zithe yeyeye
> Zijuz'umpe (stanza two, lines 4, 5, 6)

In assessing Vilakazi's poetry, it is perhaps to miss the point entirely to dwell on the details of style, meter and rhyme. These are important as techniques which merely "gild the lily."

We share completely Lucien Goldmann's view, (as elaborated by Scott Sanders in *Telos*, No. 18, pp. 116-17) that the significance of a literary work does not reside in the details of style or character but in the mental structures which bind it together; for it is these mental structures, these habits of thought and feeling which have been elaborated by the human group in the course of shared experiences, which give us its real meaning and significance. The task of the critic, therefore, becomes one of isolating the significant categories of thought which "shape both the consciousness of a group and the imagery universe created by the writer." This, then, is our approach to an evaluation of Vilakazi's poetry. We seek to discover the essential meaning of the poetry, and whether it reveals the mental categories which give it structure. The intent of such analysis is to "uncover historical rather than purely literary, and social rather than individual" phenomena in his work. While Vilakazi did not elaborate a social theory of literature, he would have agreed with the proposition that the poet springs from the bosom of his social group and therefore reflects the historical social experiences of that group. That this was indeed his perception of a poet as "the voice of his people" is shown by the fact that he sought inspiration from "waiting outside the palisades of Dukuza." It was from here that he heard his people saying: "Be our voice."

The African elites (and there were many) who thought that Vilakazi was not involved in the people's struggle, never really understood him; nor did they read his poetry—understandably because the intellectual elites of his time disdained vernacular literature (and the disdain lingers on in South Africa, particularly in the cities where literature is only that which is written in a European language).

Any reading of Vilakazi's poetry shows, as Professor Nyembezi points out, that he had an intense identification with "the struggles, fears, aspirations, sacrifices and the unconquerable spirit of his people" [see Further Reading].

His poem **"Ezinkomponi" ("The Gold Mines")** is a searing criticism of the dehumanizing and socially destructive process of industrialization as represented by the system of migrant labor which supports the mining industry. And on the subject of the destruction of African families as a result of this system, he has this peasant but poignant characterization of the situation:

> Where I come from, far away,
> The lands are free of towering buildings
> Whose tops I stretch my head to see;
> But when I return there, clutching my bundle,
> All I can find are shrivelled stalks
> And empty huts: I scratch my head and ask about my family
> They answer: "Ask your white employer."
> I close my mouth in weary silence.

One notes, in Vilakazi's poetry, a very strong commitment to Christianity and the use of Christian symbols. He came from a generation of proud mission-station Africans who held steadfastly to what they perceived to be superior values and to visions of progress inculcated by missionaries. A post-World War II and post-African independence generation, which thinks it discovered African nationalism, may sneer and snivel at his **"Easter," "The Historic Home of Grout"** or **"The Bells of the Church."** But it is well to remember that he was writing as an African in a South Africa of baffling contradictions which have been graphically portrayed by the Xhosa poet Mqhayi. . . . Mqhayi complained of Great Britain:

> You sent us the preacher, you sent us the bottle
> You sent us the Bible and barrels of Brandy!
> Ah, roaring Britain, which must we embrace?
> You sent us the truth, you denied us the truth

> You sent us life, you deprived us of life;
> You sent us light, we sit in the dark
> Shivering benighted in the bright noonday sun!

This reviewer welcomes Friedman's translations which make Vilakazi's poetry available to the international scholarly community. . . . (pp. 134-36)

> *Absolom L. Vilakazi, in a review of "Zulu Horizons," in* Research in African Literatures, *Vol. 6, No. I, Spring, 1975, pp. 134-36.*

CHERIE MACLEAN   (essay date 1986)

[*In the following excerpt, Maclean analyzes the themes and imagery in Vilakazi's poems "Sengiyokholwa-ke" ("Now I Will Only Believe") and "Sengiyakholwa" ("Now I Do Believe").*]

'Sengiyokholwa-ke' and **'Sengiyakholwa'** are sad, sincere, and beautiful [poems]. The poet loves his father so much that it takes him ten years (the interval between the writing of the two poems) after the old man's death to believe that he has gone forever.

The title of the first poem, **'Sengiyokholwa-ke'**, containing the remote future infix '-yo-' and the enclitic '-ke-', meaning 'then', sets the tone of the poet's disbelief that his father is dead and the conditions he lays down for the remote possibility of his believing it in the future. The title of the second poem, **'Sengiyakholwa'**, containing the auxiliary infix '-ya-', which indicates the final or long form of the present tense, positive, tells us that at last the poet believes his father is dead.

Grief is the overriding theme in both poems but there is a difference in tone. In **'Sengiyokholwa-ke'** the tone is angry. The poet throws down a challenge—the sun and moon must die, must be annihilated, before he will believe his father is dead. It is an unreasonable defiance, especially since his father died in his very hands. But clearly, the only way he can live with his tremendous grief is to reject the belief that the tragedy ever occurred.

In **'Sengiyakholwa'** the tone is calmer. Further experiences of death of people very close to him—Mandlakayise, his elder brother, and Nomasomi, his sister, to name but two—gradually have brought him to the realization of the finality of death. Signs of his own aging, such as greying hair, remind him that this happened to his father, too. He actually watched his father slowly fading away from then on. These are things he forgot in the anguish he felt immediately after his father's death, but now that he has accepted the inevitability of death, he has become aware of the guiding presence of his father in his dreams, which is a consolation to him.

The term of address in **'Sengiyokholwa-ke'** could be direct (*to* his father) or indirect (*about* his father) since the 'wa' grammatical morpheme relating to the remote past tense can refer to the second person singular (you) as well as to the third person singular (he/she/it). Either way, directly or indirectly, the term of address does not alter much the sense of the poem.

In **'Sengiyakholwa'**, though, there are parts of the poem in which the poet is clearly addressing his father (or someone else?) directly, as well as other parts, again in the remote past tense, in which it is not clear to this reader whether the address is direct or indirect. For instance, in stanza four:

2nd or 3rd person:	Ngingekholwa kanjan' se*wafa*
definitely 2nd:	Um' umgwaqo wakh*o u*vulekile,
then 2nd or 3rd:	Ngibon' iminyaka yonk' *ub*hudulekile
definitely 2nd:	*W*ena kungathi *wa*hamba umnyang' uvuliwe
then 2nd or 3rd:	Khon' abanye beyophuma sengathi badiniwe
definitely 2nd:	Kanti sebelandela *wena* bangabuyi.

This whole stanza could be addressed to Vilakazi's father, indeed, the whole poem. I would like to suggest, however, that the recurrent phrase 'sewafa' means '*he* is now dead' rather than '*you* are now dead' and that the term of address changes from indirect (he) to direct (you) in stanzas four and eight in this poem. I suggest further that in this sense the 'you' refers not to Vilakazi's father but to Jesus. I have three reasons for this.

Firstly, we know that Vilakazi taught at the Mariannhill Roman Catholic Mission and so religious belief surrounding the parting words of Jesus . . . 'I go to prepare a place for you . . .' may have influenced the poet's phrasing in the fourth stanza and therefore his address in the second person singular:

Ngingekholwe kanjan' ukuthi sewafa
Um' umgwaqo wakho uvulekile,
Ngibon' iminyaka yonk' ubhudulekile
Wena kungathi wahamba umnyang' uvuliwe
Khon' abanye beyophuma sengathi badiniwe
Kanti sebelandela *wena* bangabuyi.

(How can I not believe that he is dead
When *your* road is open in front of me?
I see all the years you have worn away
It seems as if your own going opened the door
For others to go out when they were tired,
Indeed they are following you and not returning.)

Secondly, in the eighth and last stanza the words:

Ungiweza ngamasango namazibuko
Obuhlakani nezindlela zenkalipho;
Nodondolo lwakho ngiluzwa lugqula
Phambi kwamehl' ami ngingakuboni.

(You make me to cross over through gateways and fords
Of wisdom and awareness;
I can hear your guiding staff tapping
In front of me although I cannot see you.)

are reminiscent of the 23rd Psalm from the Old Testament of the Bible:

. . . He leadeth me in the paths of righteousness
for his name's sake. Yea, though I walk through the
valley of the shadow of death, I will fear no evil: for
thou art with me; thy rod and thy staff they comfort
me . . . (with 'He' and 'thy' referring to 'The
Lord').

Thirdly, the locativization and capitalization of sleep ('kwaButhongo') earlier on in this last stanza give sleep such significance that we might associate the condition with Death—since the poem is about death—and, again, with the 23rd Psalm quoted above:

Yea, though I walk through the valley of *the shad-*

ow of death . . . thy rod and thy staff they comfort me . . .

Sustaining my suggestion of a religious reference in **'Sengiyakholwa'**, I note another possible one in the last stanza of **'Sengiyokholwa-ke'**:

Uma ilanga nenyanga sekwafe,
Kwawel' enhlabathini yamagade,
Kwashabalala ungunaphakade.

(If the sun and moon die,
Fall down to the very earth of sods,
Annihilated for ever and ever.)

'Falling down to the very earth of sods' is reminiscent of the burial service from the Book of Common Prayer or any Christian burial service:

We therefore commit his body to the ground; earth
to earth, ashes to ashes, dust to dust; in sure and
certain hope of the Resurrection to eternal life.

In a sense, the last stanza of **'Sengiyokholwa-ke'** is linked to the last stanza of **'Sengiyakholwa'**: in order that a soul be resurrected, the body must first die. By the end of the first poem Vilakazi has not yet accepted the fact that his father will not return to him in his bodily form. By the end of the second poem, however, his awareness of his father (Father?) in his sleep can be seen as his father's 'resurrection' to eternal life, following the necessary acceptance by his son that he has in fact died.

The refrain 'ungunaphakade' (for ever and ever) at the end of the first, second, and last stanzas of **'Sengiyokholwa-ke'**, as well as at the end of the last stanza of **'Sengiyakholwa'**, is suggestive of the traditional conclusion to Christian prayer: 'For ever and ever, Amen'. The refrain is a link between the two poems, as is the recurrent beginning to several of the stanzas in each: 'Sengiyokholwa ukuthi sewafa' in the first poem, and 'Sengiyakholwa ukuthi sewafa' in the second.

An interesting changeover in contrast between distance and immediacy occurs within and between the poems. In the first, the effect on the poet of his father's recent death is immediate and close: his father died in his very hands. Yet the cosmic imagery incorporated in the surviving son's challenge creates a sense of vast distance in time and space:

'Sengiyokholwa ukuthi sewafa . . .' (I will only believe that he is dead) if the crying of the birds above,
the night, the stars, the mountains and flowing rivers, the winds, the seasons, and the sun and the
moon disappear for ever and ever.

Death has been very close at hand in the first poem and, by contrast, the imagery is distant. In the later poem, though, ten years have passed since the poet's father's death so the death itself is distant in time. Correspondingly, the landscapes are close, tangible for the most part. For instance, the red soils, the big fig tree, Frans's grave, the bell above the cemetery, and the grey hairs on his head.

Another contrast is in the solitariness of the poet relative to the rest of the world. In the first poem the impression we get is that after his father's death there is no one but him in the world of natural phenomena. In the second poem he says:

Wena kungathi wahamba umnyang' uvuliwe
Khon' abanye beyophuma sengathi badiniwe
Kanti sebelandela wena bangabuyi.

Ababuyi wena weqhawe lase Mzwangedwa.
Bavalelisa ngime bangishiye ngedwa.

(It seems as if your own going opened the door
For others to go out when they were tired,
Indeed they are following you and not returning.

They don't return or you, hero of umZwangedwa.
They bade farewell and left me standing here alone.)

'Ilanga nenyanga' (the sun and the moon) are powerful in contrast to the lamenter's powerlessness; *they* are able to turn the blackness of night into light while 'Konke ukubona kwami kulize leze'—all of his vision is now a nothing of nothing. That is, he is unable to brighten the darkness of his despair because his father's light—the light of his own life—has been extinguished in death. In the third stanza of **'Sengi-yokholwa-ke'** the imagery of the infinite height of the sky ('phezulu kude'—far and wide), the width of the coast, and the vast quantity of grains implicit in "izihlabathi zolwandle" (the sands of the sea), again, contrast vividly with the relative height, width, and singularity of the dying man.

The climax in imagery appears in stanza three of **'Sengi-yokholwa-ke'** with the falling of his father's body likened to the falling of the wild banana trees which surround the coast. These trees grow closely together in their natural habitat so when one of them falls it does not do so in a direct way, but slowly, because the trunk's progress is checked and supported by the trunks of the other trees in the direction of its fall. Vilakazi's father died in his arms so, too, the body like the tree fell slowly and irregularly, supported in its progress by the son. The bereaved's shock at this event is described as 'Ngawubona kuhle kwephupho' (I saw it as if in a dream); it does not seem real; he cannot believe it. Similarly, in 'Sengiyakholwa' he has the same reaction to the deaths of his brother and sister. In stanza two:

Ngambon' elele bengakamembesi.
Ngalibon' iphupho liz' emini.

(I saw him lying down not yet covered up.
I saw a dream coming in the middle of the day.)

And in stanza three:

Nango Nomasomi kwabanjalo.

(And so it was also with Nomasomi.)

Vilakazi's father's place of burial is not mentioned in the first poem but in **'Sengiyakholwa'** the poet spends some time in describing the places where his other relatives have been buried in the meantime. Indeed, the only touch of humour in the two poems appears in stanza five of the latter one, in 'the graveyard scene'. Vilakazi calls the nuns of Mariannhill 'hens' and this does conjure up in the imagination a rather sweet picture of motherly creatures looking after others who cannot fend for themselves:

Abanye ngibatshala eMhlatuzane,
Lapho befukanyelw' izikhukuzana . . .

(Others I have planted at Mariannhill,
There they are sheltered by the hens . . .)

'Sengiyakholwa' is a longer poem than **'Sengiyokholwa-ke'**, having eight stanzas to the latter's five. It begins slowly with the poet observing animals grazing in the early part of the day, and moves on slowly through his memories of his other relatives' deaths. The imagery of the graves at Mariannhill

being sheltered by hens begins to speed up the movement of the poem. The imagery of the soils competing for redness in the sunset leads us on to the climax of movement in this poem, which is the remembered words of grandfather Frans:

Shayan' ingelosi
Ebusika nasehlobo ikhal' ingalingozi!

(Let us ring the angelus
Winter and summer it rings without grief!)

This heightened movement correlates with the poet's own progress on the path to self-recovery; he realizes that the bell above the burial ground rings only to waken the nuns to pray, not to wail in grief for the dead. It seems he is able to distance himself somewhat from his grief now. (Ten years earlier he would have believed the bells rang only for the dead.) After this, the movement of the poem slows down again, as indicated by Vilakazi's vision of his father coming towards him with a 'cool' heart, 'tapping' his guiding staff in front of Vilakazi, who is 'like a blind person . . . '.

Although the longer poem moves more slowly than the shorter one, there is much more movement in its actual happenings—of dawn, animals grazing, sorrowing relatives, burying of the dead, the bell ringing, sunset, and the poet lying down on the ground next to Frans's grave—than in the actual happenings in **'Sengiyokholwa-ke'**. In the latter poem, the only actual happening is that of the gradual fall of the old man as he died, and the gradual cooling of his body. As mentioned earlier, this is also the climax of the poem.

However, in the imagery employed in the first poem, the movement is spectacular! For instance, in the first stanza one of the conditions laid down by the poet for his belief that his father is dead is the disappearance for ever and ever of the night which *bursts* into stars above:

Nobusuku *obuqhakaz'* izinkanyezi zezulu . . .

Movement in the second stanza, as felt in the flowing rivers and blowing winds, is slower and more controlled. In stanza three occurs the climax of the imagery:

Njengenkanyez' edilika phezulu kude,
Nomzimba wawa . . .

(Just like a star which falls from high and far,
So did his body fall . . .)

This is an ultimate contrast in movement within the poem because, as we know, a falling star is a magnificent sight which lasts for only a few seconds, and the falling of a dying man's body—slowly and heavily—is a tragic sight. The poet might even have been thinking of the symbolic gradual fall of man from 'the state of grace' in his graphic description of the death itself. Stanza four moves very slowly, in the final stages of the old man's death; the son feels the life fading out of his father's body and his being coming to an end. He waits with the corpse as it gradually cools.

The poem ends in a climax of figurative illustration with the very strong demand that the sun and moon fall out of the sky—down to the very sods of the earth—and be annihilated for ever and ever. Can there be any more energetic a movement than that? Indeed, Vilakazi has succeeded in creating in this poem an overwhelming sense of grief, a great deal of movement, vast space, and eternity in time, all within a tight structure of only five stanzas, which is to my mind a mark of his genius as a poet.

Secondary to the theme of grief is the 'blindness' associated with that grief. As mentioned before, because his father was the light of his life, his father's death was an extinction of that light. Afterwards, Vilakazi could see nothing ('Konke uku-bona kwami kulize leze'). Ten years later, he is still terribly sad but at least he has regained his sight, figuratively speaking, because now, when the sun lights up the earth in the morning, he can see animals grazing, whisking their tails—which are white, just like those of the cows at home. Still, however, it is sometimes dusk for him at midday—giving the impression of grief clouding his vision; he cannot 'see' for grief. Death itself and blindness are synonymous in his description of Nomasomi's death:

> Izinkanyezi zamehlo zacimeza
> Wabanda wehlulw' ukuzifudumeza . . .
> Ngilunguz' ubuso bakhe buhwelela,
> Nobuhle bengaba banqifiphalela.

> (The stars of her eyes were closed,
> She became cold and failed to warm up again . . .
> I took a quick look, her face became dusk,
> And her astonishing beauty became obscured for me.)

Again, in the last stanza of **'Sengiyakholwa'** he says to the guide he becomes aware of in his sleep:

> . . . ngingakuboni.
> Nginjengempumputhe ngamehl' omzimba.

> (. . . I cannot see you.
> I am like a blind person with my bodily eyes.)

I would like now to mention the form of the two poems. **'Sengiyokholwa-ke'** contains six lines in each of the first two stanzas; the third stanza has five lines, and the fourth and fifth stanzas have four lines each. In **'Sengiyakholwa'** the first, second, third, fourth and sixth stanzas have six lines each; the fifth and eighth stanzas have ten lines each, and the seventh has seven. We can see from this structure that neither of the two poems has a regular pattern.

There is a rhyme stress in both the penultimate and ultimate syllables of the last word of most lines but, because of the varying number of lines in the stanzas, the pattern is slightly irregular overall although it is the same in stanzas composed of the same number of lines. Using the traditional structure of poetry in English literature as the basis of his own Zulu poetry, Vilakazi has a problem in rhyming the last words of lines because, Zulu word stress falling on the penultimate syllable, he has to rhyme the final *two* syllables instead of only the ultimate one, as in English. He has employed other poetic devices to make his poetry flow. For instance, as previously mentioned, the title of each poem is repeated at the beginning of each of several stanzas within the poem. The use of the refrain 'for ever and ever' at the end of some lines has also been noted, indicating continuity in the poet's imagination both in actual time and in the structure of the poems. Another instance of this continuity is to be found in the use of the word 'emini' (at midday) at the end of two consecutive stanzas in **'Sengiyakholwa'**. A variation on this use is that the last word of its fourth stanza, 'bangabuyi' (they are not returning), is

used again in a slightly different construction at the beginning of the next stanza: 'Ababuyi' . . . ' (They don't return . . .). One can read the heaving sobs implicit in the words . . .

But it is in the actual reading out loud of Vilakazi's poetry that his skill in phrasing can best be appreciated. This is readily understandable when one recalls that it is only very recently—in the last fifty years—that Zulu literature has found a written expression. Until now it has had only an oral tradition, and even today, far more stories are still told at the hearth than are ever read by the Zulu people. So it is only in the *saying* (from **'Sengiyokholwa-ke'**) of:

> Phezu kwalokho angiyukolwa neze,
> Konke ukubona kwami kulize leze.

> (On top of this I cannot believe *anything*,
> All of my vision is now a *nothing* of nothing.)

that one can feel the yearning inherent in . . . 'kulize leze' and hear the richness in the words' rise and fall. Indeed, the spoken words of these two poems of Vilakazi must surely be even more heartbreaking than those which are read; but either way they are, for me, unforgettable. (pp. 70-9)

Cherie Maclean, "Laments for His Father: Zulu Poems of B. W. Vilakazi," in Theoria, *Pietermaritzburg, Vol. LXVI, May, 1986, pp. 66-79.*

FURTHER READING

Mphahlele, Ezekiel. "Black on Black." In his *The African Image,* pp. 194-289. New York: Praeger Publishers, 1974.

> Includes a discussion of Vilakazi's poem "In the Gold Mines," identifying it as a protest against the economic exploitation of black Africans.

Nyembezi, C. L. S. In his Biographical Note to *Zulu Horizons,* by Benedict Wallet Vilakazi, pp. xvii-xx. Johannesburg: Witwatersrand University Press, 1973.

> Biographical sketch which includes a discussion of Vilakazi's contribution to Zulu literature and his image as a spokesperson for black South Africans.

Pieterse, Cosmo. "Conflict in the Germ: William Plomer and Benedict Vilakazi." In *Protest And Conflict in African Literature,* edited by Cosmo Pieterse and Donald Munro, pp. 1-25. New York: Africana Publishing Corporation, 1969.

> Compares the themes of Vilakazi's poetry to those in William Plomer's South African novel *Turbott Wolfe.*

Vilakazi, B. W. "Some Aspects of Zulu Literature." *African Studies* 1, No. 4 (December 1942): 270-74.

> Surveys Zulu literature.

Yevgeny Zamyatin

1884-1937

(Full name Yevgeny Ivanovich Zamyatin; also transliterated as Zamiatin and Zamjatin) Russian novelist, short story writer, dramatist, essayist, and critic.

For further discussion of Zamyatin's career, see *TCLC,* Volume 8.

One of the most influential Russian writers in the decade following the Russian Revolution, Zamyatin is best remembered for his anti-utopian novel *My (We).* While his early writings satirize the philistinism of provincial life, his works written after the Revolution criticize obedience to dogmatic authority. Throughout his career Zamyatin experimented with form and language, renouncing the straightforward representation of life advocated by the nineteenth-century Russian realists, and his work is praised for its arresting language, grotesque imagery, and ironic viewpoint.

The son of an orthodox priest, Zamyatin was born in the central Russian town of Lebedyan. As a child, he had few friends and occupied himself reading the works of such classic Russian authors as Fyodor Dostoevsky, Ivan Turgenev, and Nikolai Gogol. Zamyatin entered the Polytechnical Institute of St. Petersburg (now Leningrad) in 1902 to study naval engineering. His studies were interrupted when he was arrested and temporarily exiled for revolutionary activities in 1905, a sentence that was reenacted in 1911. Zamyatin graduated in 1908, remaining with the institute as a lecturer in the Department of Naval Architecture. During this time, he began writing short fiction, and a few of his efforts were published in local journals. With the publication in 1913 of *Uezdnoe (A Provincial Tale),* a satire on Russian provincial life, Zamyatin was acknowledged as an important literary figure in his country. His satiric portrayal of military life *Na kulichkakh (At the World's End)* appeared in the following year, offending czarist authorities who accused him of anti-militarism and subversion, charges which were eventually dropped.

Zamyatin worked in England during World War I, designing and supervising the construction of Russian ships. His contact with British society is reflected in his two satires of the English bourgeoisie, *Ostrovityane (Islanders)* and "Lovets chelovekov" ("The Fisher of Men"). Zamyatin returned to Russia just before the October Revolution of 1917, which he supported, although he later became disenchanted with the Soviet government's insistence on artistic conformity to standards of realism and political didacticism. In 1920 he wrote what many consider his most important work, the novel *We.* Though it is not documented that *We* was a reaction specifically against Soviet communism, Zamyatin's attack on the communists' vision of a collectivist civilization is hardly concealed, and *We* was banned from publication in the U.S.S.R. He continued to write and lecture on literary subjects during the 1920s, having a particular influence on the Serapion Brothers, a group of young Russian writers that included formalist critic Viktor Shklovsky and short story writer Mikhail Zoshchenko. Although diverse in their aesthetic tenets, the Serapions shared an emphasis on the autonomy of art from political commitment and on experimentation with literary

technique. In 1929 the Soviet government forbade publication of Zamyatin's works after an unauthorized portion of *We* appeared in the Soviet Union through a Russian émigré journal based in Prague. He subsequently wrote to Soviet leader Joseph Stalin asserting his independence as a writer and requesting emigration. Through the appeals of socialist-realist author Maxim Gorky, Zamyatin was permitted to leave the country in 1931 and lived in Paris until his death in 1937.

Commentators generally divide Zamyatin's literary career into four periods. The first, which includes such works as *A Provincial Tale* and *At the World's End,* is characterized by stories and novellas with provincial settings and themes. In these works Zamyatin satirized the philistinism of rural society by focusing on characters whose coarse, prosaic lives are devoid of any cultural or moral qualities. Employing the *skaz* manner of narration, which incorporates local dialects and colloquialisms, these works feature grotesque images and metonymies, often attributed to the influence of Nikolai Gogol. The second period of Zamyatin's career begins with the publication of the novella *Islanders* in 1917 and ends with the completion of *We.* The works of this phase are characterized by urban settings and depart from the *skaz* form of narration. Zamyatin's fiction of this period is noted for stylistic and formal innovations, including the use of a central, integrating metaphor. As illustrated by *We,* Zamyatin shifted his concerns from provincial backwardness to the automatization of human life and the alienation of humanity from nature. Marked by an elliptical narrative and a rich network of imagery, the novel is esteemed for further developing the style and themes of utopian works by H. G. Wells and for illustrating the critique of utopian ideals in the fiction of Dostoevsky. *We* is also recognized as a significant precursor of such dystopian works as George Orwell's *1984* and Aldous Huxley's *Brave New World.*

The transitional third stage of Zamyatin's literary career, from 1922 to 1927, reflects his search for new literary forms. "Rasskaz o samom glavnom" ("A Story about the Most Important Thing") presents actions on multiple planes of existence and is often interpreted as stressing the relative nature of all systems of meaning. The story is considered characteristic of Zamyatin's efforts to base a literary structure on the aesthetic theories presented in his essays, which emphasize continual revolution and dialectical conflict, rather than an adherence to any ultimate ideology. He also wrote several dramatic works during this time, most notably *Ogni svyatogo Dominika (The Fires of Saint Dominic).* Set in Spain during the Inquisition, the drama elaborates his concept of the heretic. According to Zamyatin, a heretic is one who, though persecuted for his views, upholds energy and truth against all forms of entropy, represented by religious, political, and artistic dogmas. In the final phase of his literary career, which spans from 1928 until his death, Zamyatin returned to fiction based on stylistic simplicity, objective narration, and surprise endings. Critics regard works of this period as powerful expressions of the author's tragic conception of life.

For the most part Zamyatin's essays advocate rebellion against all forms of tradition and authority and have contributed to his status as an uncompromising artist. Despite his relative obscurity in the Soviet Union after his death, he is recognized as a major influence on Russian writers who have appeared since the 1920s. Although commentators criticize Zamyatin's fiction for excessive verbal effects and for focusing on central metaphors at the expense of character development, his writing is esteemed for its powerful imagery and satire. *We* remains prominent as a quintessential anti-utopian novel, and Zamyatin's work as a whole is viewed as central to the transitional period that established modernism in Russian literature.

(See also *Contemporary Authors,* Vol. 105.)

PRINCIPAL WORKS

Uezdnoe   (novella)   1916
   [*A Provincial Tale* published in *The Dragon,* 1966]
Bolshim detyam skazki   (fables)   1922
Ogni svyatogo Dominika   [first publication]   (drama)   1922
   [*The Fires of Saint Dominic* published in *Five Plays by Yevgeny Zamyatin,* 1971]
Ostrovityane   (novellas and short stories)   1922
   [*Islanders* (partial translation) published in journal *Russian Literature Triquarterly,* 1972]
Na kulichkakh   (novellas and short stories)   1923
   [*At the World's End* (partial translation) published in *The Dragon,* 1966; also published as *A Godforsaken Hole* (partial translation) 1988]

Blokha   (drama)   1925
   [*The Flea* published in *Five Plays by Yevgeny Zamyatin,* 1971]
Obshchestvo pochetnykh zvonarey   (drama)   1926
   [*The Society of Honorary Bell-Ringers* published in *Five Plays by Yevgeny Zamyatin,* 1971]
*My   (novel)   [partial publication] 1927; published in journal *Volya Russy*
   [*We,* 1924]
Nechestivye rasskazy   (short stories)   1927
Sobranie sochineny. 4 vols.   (autobiography, drama, fables, novellas, and short stories)   1929
Navodnenie   (novella)   1930
   [*The Flood* published in *The Dragon,* 1966]
Bich Bozhy   (unfinished novel and short stories)   1939
†Atilla [first publication]   (drama)   1950; published in journal *Novy zhurnal*
Litsa   (essays)   1955
Povesti i rasskazy   (autobiography, novellas, and short stories)   1963
The Dragon   (letters, novellas, and short stories)   1966
Yevgeny Zamyatin: A Soviet Heretic   (autobiography, essays, and letters)   1970
Five Plays by Yevgeny Zamyatin   (dramas)   1971

*This work was written in 1920 and not published in its entirety until 1952.

†This work was written from 1925 to 1927.

YEVGENY ZAMYATIN   (essay date 1924)

[*What follows is Zamyatin's essay "On Literature, Revolution, and Entropy."*]

Ask the question point-blank: what is revolution? You get a variety of replies. Some people will answer in the style of Louis XIV: *la révolution, c'est nous* ["the revolution, it is we"]. Others turn to the calendar, giving you the day and the month. Still others spell it out letter by letter. But if we go one stage beyond the alphabet and articulate our answer, this is what we get:

Two dead, dark stars collide with a deafening but unheard crash and spark into life a new star: that's revolution. A molecule breaks loose from its orbit, invades a neighboring atomic universe and gives birth to a new chemical element: that's revolution. With one book Lobachevsky cleaves the centuries-old walls of the Euclidean world and opens the way to the infinities of non-Euclidean space: that's revolution.

Revolution is everywhere and in all things; it is infinite, there is no final revolution, no end to the sequence of integers. Social revolution is only one in the infinite sequence of integers. The law of revolution is not a social law, it is immeasurably greater, it is a cosmic, universal law—such as the law of the conservation of energy and the law of the loss of energy (entropy). Some day an exact formula will be established for the law of revolution. And in this formula nations, classes, stars—and books will be expressed as numerical values.

Red, fiery, death-dealing is the law of revolution; but that death is the birth of a new life, of a new star. And cold, blue as ice, as the icy interplanetary infinities, is the law of entropy. The flame turns from fiery red to an even, warm pink, no longer death-dealing but comfort-producing; the sun ages and becomes a planet suitable for highways, shops, beds, prostitutes, prisons: that is a law. And in order to make the planet young again, we must set it afire, we must thrust it off the smooth highway of evolution: that is a law.

The flame, true enough, will grow cold tomorrow or the day after tomorrow (in the Book of Genesis days are years and even aeons). But already today there should be somebody who can foresee that; there should be somebody today to speak heretically of tomorrow. Heretics are the only (bitter-tasting) remedy for the entropy of human thought.

When (in science, religion, social life, art) a flaming, seething sphere grows cold, the fiery molten rock becomes covered with dogma—with a hard, ossified, immovable crust. In science, religion, social life and art, dogmatization is the entropy of thought; what has been dogmatized no longer inflames, it is merely warm—and soon it is to be cool. The Sermon on the Mount, delivered beneath the scorching sun to upstretched arms and rending sobs, gives way to slumberous prayer in some well appointed abbey. Galileo's tragic *"E pur si muove"* gives way to calm calculations in some well-heated office in an observatory. On the Galileos the epigones build—slowly, coral upon coral, forming a reef: this is the path of evolution. Till one day a new heresy explodes and blows up the dogma's crust, together with all the ever so stable, rock-like structures that had been erected on it.

Explosions are not comfortable things. That is why the exploders, the heretics are quite rightly annihilated by fire, by axes and by words. Heretics are harmful to everybody today, to every evolution, to the difficult, slow, useful, so very useful, constructive, process of coral reef-building; imprudently and foolishly they leap into today from tomorrow. They are romantics. It was right and proper that in 1797 [French agitator François-Noël] Babeuf had his head cut off: he had leaped into 1797, skipping one hundred and fifty years. It is equally right and proper that heretical literature, literature that is damaging to dogma, should also have its head cut off: such literature is harmful.

But harmful literature is more useful than useful literature: because it is anti-entropic, it militates against calcification, sclerosis, encrustedness, moss, peace. It is Utopian and ridiculous. Like Babeuf in 1797 it is right one hundred and fifty years later.

We know Darwin, we know that after Darwin came mutations, Weismannism, neo-Lamarckism. But these are only penthouses and balconies while Darwin is the building itself. And the building contains not only tadpoles and toadstools, it also contains man. Fangs grow sharp only if there is someone to gnaw on; the domestic hen's wings serve only to flap with. Ideas and hens obey the same law: ideas which feed on minced meat lose their teeth just as civilized men do. Heretics are necessary to health. If there are no heretics, they have to be invented.

Live literature does not set its watch by yesterday's time, nor by today's, but by tomorrow's. Live literature is like a sailor who is sent aloft; from the masthead he can descry sinking vessels, icebergs and maelstroms which are not yet visible from the deck. You can drag him down from the mast and put him to work in the boiler-room or on the capstan, but that won't change a thing: the mast is still there and from the

masthead another sailor will be able to see what the first sailor has seen.

In stormy weather you need a man aloft. And right now the weather is stormy. SOS signals are coming in from all directions. Only yesterday the writer was able to stroll calmly on deck, taking snapshots of "real life"; but who wants to look at pictures of landscapes and scenes from daily life when the world has taken on a forty-five degree list, when the green waves are threatening to swallow us and the ship is breaking up? Right now we can look and think only as men do in the face of death: we shall die—and what then? How have we lived? If we are to live all over again in some new way, then by what shall we live, and for what? Right now we need in literature the vast philosophical horizon, the vast sweep from the masthead, from the sky above, we need the most ultimate, the most fearsome, the most fearless "Whys?" and "What nexts?"

Those are the questions that children ask. But children are after all the boldest of philosophers; they come into life naked, not covered by one single small leaf of dogma or creed. That is why their questions are always so ridiculously naive and so frighteningly complicated. The new people, who are right now coming into life, are naked and fearless as children, and they too, like children, like Schopenhauer, Dostoevsky, Nietzsche, are asking their "whys" and "what nexts." Philosophers of genius, children and ordinary people are equally wise—because they ask equally stupid questions. Stupid for civilized man who possesses a well-furnished apartment, with a magnificent bathroom, and a well-furnished dogma.

Organic chemistry has blurred the dividing-line between living and dead matter. It is a mistake to divide people into the living and the dead: there are live-dead people and live-live people. The live-dead people also write, walk, talk, act. But they do not make mistakes; only machines produce without mistakes, but they produce only dead things. The live-live people are all mistakes, searchings, questions, torments.

So too what we write also walks and talks, but it can be live-dead or live-live. The genuinely live, stopping at nothing, brooking no obstacle or hindrance, searches for the answers to foolish, "childish" questions. The answers may be wrong, the philosophy erroneous—but errors are of greater value than truths: truth is machine-like, error is alive, truth reassures, error unsettles. And even if the answers are quite impossible, so much the better: to ask answered questions is the privilege of minds constructed on the same principle as the cow's stomach which is ideally suited, as well we know, to chewing the cud.

If there were in nature something fixed, if there were truths, all this would, of course, be wrong. But happily all truths are erroneous. This is precisely the significance of the dialectic process: today's truths become tomorrow's errors; there is no final integer.

This (one and only) truth is only for the strong: weak-nerved minds unfailingly require a finite universe, a final integer, they require, as Nietzsche said, "the crutches of assurance." The weak-nerved do not have the strength to include themselves in the dialectic syllogism. True, this is difficult. But it is the very thing that Einstein did succeed in doing: he managed to remember that he, Einstein, with watch in hand observing motion, was also moving; he succeeded in looking at the earth's movements *from outside.*

That is precisely how great literature—literature that knows no final integer—looks at the earth's movements.

The formal characteristic of live literature is the same as its inner characteristic: the negation of truth, that is, the negation of what everyone knows and what I knew up to this moment. Live literature leaves the canonical rails, leaves the broad highway.

The broad highway of Russian literature, worn shiny by the giant wheels of Tolstoy, Gorky, Chekhov, is realism, real life: consequently we must turn away from real life. The rails, sanctified and canonized by Blok, Sologub, Bely, are the rails of symbolism—symbolism which turned away from real life: consequently we must turn towards real life.

Absurd, isn't it? The intersection of parallel lines is also absurd. But it's absurd only in the canonical, plane geometry of Euclid; in non-Euclidian geometry it's an axiom. The one essential is to cease to be flat, to rise above the plane. Today's literature has the same relation to the plane surface of real life as an aircraft has to the earth: it is nothing more than a runway from which to take off and soar aloft from real life to reality, to philosophy, to the realm of the fantastic. Leave the carts of yesterday to creak along the great highways. The living have strength enough to cut off their yesterdays.

We can put a police officer or a commissar in the cart, but the cart will still remain a cart. And literature will still remain the literature of yesterday, if we drive real life—even "revolutionary real life"—along the well-traveled highway—even if we drive it in a fast troika with bells. What we need today are automobiles, airplanes, winged flight, seconds, dotted lines.

The old, slow, soporific descriptions are no more. The order of the days is laconicism—but every word must be supercharged, high-voltage. Into one second must be compressed what formerly went into a sixty-second minute. Syntax becomes elliptical, volatile; complicated pyramids of periods are dismantled and broken down into the single stones of independent clauses. In swift movement the canonical, the habitual eludes the eye: hence the unusual, often strange symbolism and choice of words. The image is sharp, synthetic, it contains only the one basic trait which one has time to seize upon from a moving automobile. The lexicon hallowed by custom has been invaded by dialect, neologisms, science, mathematics, technology.

There is a rule, if you can call it a rule, that the writer's talent consists in making the rule the exception; but there are far more writers who turn the exception into the rule.

The business of science and art alike is the projection of the world onto coordinates. Differences in form are due to differences in the coordinates. All realist forms involve projection onto the fixed, plane coordinates of the Euclidian world. These coordinates have no existence in nature. This finite, fixed world does not exist; it is a convention, an abstraction, an unreality. And therefore realism—be it "socialist" or "bourgeois"—is unreal: immeasurably closer to reality is projection onto fast-moving, curved surfaces—as in the new mathematics and the new art. Realism which is not primitive, not *realia* but *realiora*, consists in displacement, distortion, curvature, non-objectivity. The lens of the camera is objective.

A new form is not intelligible to all, for many it is difficult. Maybe. The habitual, the banal is, of course, simpler, plea-santer, more comfortable. Euclid's world is very simple and Einstein's world is very difficult; nevertheless it is now impossible to return to Euclid's. No revolution, no heresy is comfortable and easy. Because it is a leap, it is a rupture of the smooth evolutionary curve, and a rupture is a wound, a pain. But it is a necessary wound: most people suffer from hereditary sleeping sickness, and those who are sick with this ailment (entropy) must not be allowed to sleep, or they will go to their last sleep, the sleep of death.

This same sickness is common to artists and writers: they go contentedly to sleep in their favorite artistic form which they have devised, then twice revised. They do not have the strength to wound themselves, to cease to love what has become dear to them. They do not have the strength to come out from their lived-in, laurel-scented rooms, to come out into the open air and start anew.

To wound oneself, it is true, is difficult, even dangerous. But to live today as yesterday and yesterday as today is even more difficult for the living. (pp. 372-78)

Evgeny Zamyatin, "On Literature, Revolution and Entropy," translated by Walter N. Vickery, in Partisan Review, *Vol. XXVIII, Nos. 3 & 4, May-June, 1961, pp. 372-78.*

VIKTOR SHKLOVSKY (essay date 1924)

[*A Russian critic and novelist, Shklovsky was a member of the Serapion Brothers, a group influenced by Zamyatin's literary theories. In his criticism, which has been characterized as brilliant and aggressive, if sometimes paradoxical, Shklovsky is concerned with the form and structure of a literary work and not with its content. The following essay was written after Joseph Stalin granted political amnesty to Shklovsky, a situation that may have altered his favorable opinion of Zamyatin, who was out of favor with Soviet leaders. Here, he discusses* We *and* Islanders.]

Every airplane has its ceiling, the height above which it cannot rise, spread out like an invisible horizontal surface. The one-sided ability of Zamyatin most likely creates this ceiling for him.

The usual tragedy of a writer is the question of his method.

Zamyatin has a novel, *We,* which probably will appear soon in an English translation.

Since this novel is still not published in Russian, due to accidental circumstances, I will not analyze it in detail.

The novel represents a social utopia. Strange as it seems, this utopia recalls a certain parody of utopia by Jerome Jerome. This applies even in minor correspondences, for example, the clothes of the future people, both with Zamyatin and Jerome Jerome, is a grey tunic. The names of the people are replaced by numbers: even for men, odd for women, etc.

In its basic intent and construction, the thing is most closely connected with *The Islanders (Ostrovitiane).*

The whole setting represents a development of the word "integration."

The country's social system is a realization of "Vicar Dooley's Testament of Compulsory Salvation."

One of the heroines, U, plays approximately the same role in the thing as Mrs. Dooley, etc.

The heroes are not only square, but they think, in the main, about the equality of their angles.

All the heroes have their themes which, so to say, constrain them: one, for example, is "scissors," and he doesn't talk, he "snips."

In my opinion, the world into which Zamyatin's heroes have fallen is not so much similar to a world of failed socialism, as a world constructed by the Zamyatin method.

That is, in general, we are examining not the universe, but its instruments.

This world (per Zamyatin), no matter what it may be, is a bad and boring world.

It seems to me, all the same, that this is the Zamyatinian ceiling. The author is helpless when he breaks out of it.

In *We* there is a remarkable heroine, her brows cross in such a way as to form an X, she thus signifies in this equalized world—X.

Of course, her brows are mentioned every time she appears.

Sometimes the heroine leaves the equalized world, goes into the old world, the "Old House." In this Old House she puts on a silk dress, silk stockings. A statue of Buddha stands in the corner.

I fear that "Apollon" will be lying on the desk, or maybe "Stolitsa i Usad'ba." [In a footnote, the editor notes that "the first was the most luxurious pre-revolutionary cultural journal (St. Petersburg, 1909-17), the second devoted to "the capital and the manor."]

Probably this happens because Zamyatin is unable to construct a world outside of his categories.

The people who oppose the equalization call themselves "Mephi," an abbreviation of Mephistopheles, because Mephistopheles signifies inequality.

They bow down to this Mephistopheles. And also to a statue of [nineteenth-century sculptor Mark Matveevich] Antokolsky.

In vain.

There is nothing worse in the world than Antokolsky. Despite a number of successful details in *We,* the whole thing is a failure and a clear indication that Zamyatin, within his old manner, has reached his ceiling. (pp. 49-50)

> *Viktor Shklovsky, "Evgeny Zamyatin's Ceiling,"*
> *translated by Gary Kern, in* Zamyatin's "We": A
> Collection of Critical Essays, *edited by Gary Kern,*
> *Ardis, 1988, pp. 49-50.*

GEORGE ORWELL   (essay date 1946)

[*An English novelist and essayist, Orwell is renowned for his unwavering commitment, both as a man and an artist, to personal freedom and social justice. His unpretentious self-examination and his ability to perceive the social effects of political theories inspired Irving Howe to call him "the greatest moral force in English letters during the last several decades." Foremost among Orwell's works is his dystopian novel* Nineteen Eighty-Four *(1949), one of the most influential books of the century. An attack on totalitarianism, it warns that absolute power in the hands of any government can deprive a people of all basic freedoms. In the following excerpt, Orwell favorably reviews* We *and praises the novel's political insight.*]

Several years after hearing of its existence, I have at last got my hands on a copy of Zamyatin's *We,* which is one of the literary curiosities of this book-burning age. Looking it up in Gleb Struve's *Twenty-Five Years of Soviet Russian Literature,* I find its history to have been this:

Zamyatin, who died in Paris in 1937, was a Russian novelist and critic who published a number of books both before and after the Revolution. *We* was written about 1923, and though it is not about Russia and has no direct connection with contemporary politics—it is a fantasy dealing with the twenty-sixth century AD—it was refused publication on the ground that it was ideologically undesirable. A copy of the manuscript found its way out of the country, and the book has appeared in English, French and Czech translations, but never in Russian. The English translation was published in the United States, and I have never been able to procure a copy: but copies of the French translation (the title is *Nous autres*) do exist, and I have at last succeeded in borrowing one. So far as I can judge it is not a book of the first order, but it is certainly an unusual one, and it is astonishing that no English publisher has been enterprising enough to reissue it.

The first thing anyone would notice about *We* is the fact—never pointed out, I believe—that Aldous Huxley's *Brave New World* must be partly derived from it. Both books deal with the rebellion of the primitive human spirit against a rationalised, mechanised, painless world, and both stories are supposed to take place about six hundred years hence. The atmosphere of the two books is similar, and it is roughly speaking the same kind of society that is being described, though Huxley's book shows less political awareness and is more influenced by recent biological and psychological theories.

In the twenty-sixth century, in Zamyatin's vision of it, the inhabitants of Utopia have so completely lost their individuality as to be known only by numbers. They live in glass houses (this was written before television was invented), which enables the political police, known as the "Guardians", to supervise them more easily. They all wear identical uniforms, and a human being is commonly referred to either as "a number" or "a unif" (uniform). They live on synthetic food, and their usual recreation is to march in fours while the anthem of the Single State is played through loudspeakers. At stated intervals they are allowed for one hour (known as "the sex hour") to lower the curtains round their glass apartments. There is, of course, no marriage, though sex life does not appear to be completely promiscuous. For purposes of love-making everyone has a sort of ration book of pink tickets, and the partner with whom he spends one of his allotted sex hours signs the counterfoil. The Single State is ruled over by a personage known as The Benefactor, who is annually re-elected by the entire population, the vote being always unanimous. The guiding principle of the State is that happiness and freedom are incompatible. In the Garden of Eden man was happy, but in his folly he demanded freedom and was driven out into the wilderness. Now the Single State has restored his happiness by removing his freedom.

So far the resemblance with *Brave New World* is striking. But though Zamyatin's book is less well put together—it has a rather weak and episodic plot which is too complex to summarise—it has a political point which the other lacks. In

Huxley's book the problem of "human nature" is in a sense solved, because it assumes that by pre-natal treatment, drugs and hypnotic suggestion the human organism can be specialised in any way that is desired. . . . The aim is not economic exploitation, but the desire to bully and dominate does not seem to be a motive either. There is no power hunger, no sadism, no hardness of any kind. Those at the top have no strong motive for staying at the top, and though everyone is happy in a vacuous way, life has become so pointless that it is difficult to believe that such a society could endure.

Zamyatin's book is on the whole more relevant to our own situation. In spite of education and the vigilance of the Guardians, many of the ancient human instincts are still there. The teller of the story, D-503, who, though a gifted engineer, is a poor conventional creature, a sort of Utopian Billy Brown of London Town, is constantly horrified by the atavistic impulses which seize upon him. He falls in love (this is a crime, of course) with a certain I-330 who is a member of an underground resistance movement and succeeds for a while in leading him into rebellion. When the rebellion breaks out it appears that the enemies of The Benefactor are in fact fairly numerous, and these people, apart from plotting the overthrow of the State, even indulge, at the moment when their curtains are down, in such vices as smoking cigarettes and drinking alcohol. D-503 is ultimately saved from the consequences of his own folly. The authorities announce that they have discovered the cause of the recent disorders: it is that some human beings suffer from a disease called imagination. The nerve-centre responsible for imagination has now been located, and the disease can be cured by X-ray treatment. D-503 undergoes the operation, after which it is easy for him to do what he has known all along that he ought to do—that is, betray his confederates to the police. With complete equanimity he watches I-330 tortured by means of compressed air under a glass bell:

> She looked at me, her hands clasping the arms of the chair, until her eyes were completely shut. They took her out, brought her to herself by means of an electric shock, and put her under the bell again. This operation was repeated three times, and not a word issued from her lips.
>
> The others who had been brought along with her showed themselves more honest. Many of them confessed after one application. Tomorrow they will all be sent to the Machine of The Benefactor.

The Machine of The Benefactor is the guillotine. There are many executions in Zamyatin's Utopia. They take place publicly, in the presence of The Benefactor, and are accompanied by triumphal odes recited by the official poets. The guillotine, of course, is not the old crude instrument but a much improved model which literally liquidates its victim, reducing him in an instant to a puff of smoke and a pool of clear water. The execution is, in fact, a human sacrifice, and the scene describing it is given deliberately the colour of the sinister slave civilisations of the ancient world. It is this intuitive grasp of the irrational side of totalitarianism—human sacrifice, cruelty as an end in itself, the worship of a Leader who is credited with divine attributes—that makes Zamyatin's book superior to Huxley's.

It is easy to see why the book was refused publication. The following conversation (I abridge it slightly) between D-503 and I-330 would have been quite enough to set the blue pencils working:

"Do you realise that what you are suggesting is revolution?"

"Of course, it's revolution. Why not?"

"Because there can't *be* a revolution. *Our* revolution was the last and there can never be another. Everybody knows that."

"My dear, you're a mathematician: tell me, which is the last number?"

"What do you mean, the last number?"

"Well, then, the biggest number!"

"But that's absurd. Numbers are infinite. There can't be a last one."

"Then why do you talk about the last revolution?"

There are other similar passages. It may well be, however, that Zamyatin did not intend the Soviet régime to be the special target of his satire. Writing at about the time of Lenin's death, he cannot have had the Stalin dictatorship in mind, and conditions in Russia in 1923 were not such that anyone would revolt against them on the ground that life was becoming too safe and comfortable. What Zamyatin seems to be aiming at is not any particular country but the implied aims of industrial civilisation. I have not read any of his other books, but I learn from Gleb Struve that he had spent several years in England and had written some blistering satires on English life. It is evident from *We* that he had a strong leaning towards primitivism. Imprisoned by the Czarist Government in 1906, and then imprisoned by the Bolsheviks in 1922 in the same corridor of the same prison, he had cause to dislike the political régimes he had lived under, but his book is not simply the expression of a grievance. It is in effect a study of the Machine, the genie that man has thoughtlessly let out of its bottle and cannot put back again. This is a book to look out for when an English version appears. (pp. 72-5)

George Orwell, "Review of 'We'," in The Collected Essays, Journalism and Letters of George Orwell: In Front of Your Nose, 1945-1950, Vol. IV, *edited by Sonia Orwell and Ian Angus, Harcourt Brace Jovanovich, 1968, pp. 72-5.*

CHRISTOPHER COLLINS   (essay date 1967)

[*In the following essay, Collins discusses* Islanders *and its protrayal of alienation in modern society.*]

The years 1916 and 1917 found Zamyatin living abroad for the first time. He had been sent to England to supervise the construction of Russian icebreakers. His stay there resulted in three works set in England, *Islanders (Ostrovityane)*, **"Fisher of Men" ("Lovets chelovekov")**, and (a play based on *Islanders*), *The Society of Honorary Bell Ringers (Obshchestvo pochetnykh zvonarey)*. England must not be regarded as the target of these works so much as the artistically appropriate setting for the phenomena being satirized.

Islanders will be read here as a study of alienation in modern society. The term has been used by so many modern critics, philosophers, and writers in such a variety of contexts that a working definition must be made before proceeding. One view expressed in Western letters today is that the modern writer must be alienated if he is to be a good writer. Alienation in this context means alienation from the society surrounding the writer, disagreement with the values and standards accepted by society at large. A writer in complete agreement with his society, with commonly held standards and values would have very little to say, and very little impetus to say it. This concept of the writer as heretic is not new and was heartily affirmed by Zamyatin in his critical essays.

It is, of course, psychically unhealthy to be alienated from society at large, and we should partially sympathize with pleas for recognition of the modern writer's martyrdom in the name of art and truth; but there are other, more destructive forms of alienation which only the heretic may escape. If adherence to the values of modern bourgeois society leads to alienation from Self, nature, or God, then the individual, the writer-heretic, or the writer's protagonist-heretic may find a more meaningful, unalienated life in rejecting society. He necessarily suffers some alienation from society as a result, but he avoids alienation in more important respects and benefits from his healthy relationship and integration with the other elements of his existence.

In *Islanders* traditional British reserve, conformity, and propriety are seen joined with the modern industrial age to alienate the protagonist, Campbell, and most of his fellow citizens, from Self and from nature.

One might suppose that a work set in twentieth-century urban England and dealing with alienation might include comments (or diatribes) found so frequently in other contemporary literary or philosophical works on the city—the anonymity, the loneliness, the slums, the garish advertising, the atmosphere of the fast buck, the all-pervasive noise and filth, the violence, the absence of wildlife, trees, and grass. Such is not the case here. Zamyatin's fictional English city is an exciting place to live in for people like the Irish lawyer and Don Juan, O'Kelly, and for the striptease dancer, Didi. Away from the city they would certainly sink into the provincial muck of Zamyatin's early stories. The city does not alienate them from Self or from nature. Far from discouraging their free sexual expression, the city, in its anonymity, gives them privacy. Nor, as will be seen below, does the city stop them from responding to nature.

The three most important forces in the story—traditional propriety, modern industrialism, and freedom and integration with Self and nature—are represented in three key images that appear throughout the narrative. These images are, respectively, the portrait of Campbell's late father, Sir Harold Campbell, the electric iron (which Campbell must purchase before he can consider marriage or sexual relations with Didi), and Didi's porcelain pug, Johnny. Each of these objects occupies an honored position on the mantel above the fireplace in the apartments of their respective owners. (Fire is Zamyatin's usual image for Energy and passion, and as such, is nearly holy. There is always a fire in the fireplace in Didi's apartment, but there are no fires in Campbell's or in Lady Campbell's apartments.)

In position and importance these objects can be considered as holy images, a kind of icon. Lady Campbell, Campbell, and Didi each have their revered icons. Campbell's rejection of Didi's icon and the placing of his icon on the mantel next to it is symbolically an indication of the attempted replacement of one religion by another in the life of Didi.

When Lady Campbell's apartment is first described, the portrait on the mantel of her late husband, Sir Harold, is one of the few objects mentioned. Her first words in the story are:

"My late husband, Sir Harold, always used to speak out against. . . . " Aside from appeals to the authority of her late husband, she has very little else to say. When others discuss her son's "disgraceful" participation in a boxing match and the resulting injuries, her only comment is: "All I can think is: what would my late husband, Sir Harold, say. . . ." When the Vicar Dewley and his flock, the Society of Honorary Bell Ringers, discuss Campbell's plans to marry a striptease dancer having an affair with another man, Lady Campbell again is capable only of: "My God, what would your deceased father, Sir Harold, say. . . . " Her last words in the story, like most of her other words, include a reference to her late husband as an absolute moral authority. The icon of Sir Harold is the holy image of British propriety. The deadness of the saint in the icon is emphasized in many ways. The portrait is of a person physically dead, belonging to a dead past. His title and the fact that he is dead are emphasized in each of Lady Campbell's utterances. The absence of the slightest conjugal or filial affection for the departed husband and father is an indication of the deadness of even his actual life with them in the past. Although dead, he exercises great power over Lady Campbell, as indicated by her reverent invocations, and by her head being frequently jerked back, as if by unseen reins. Lady Campbell is a death figure herself, with her "mummy" shoulders and décolleté, her gray dress, gray hair, and especially her lips "wriggling like worms."

The resemblance between Campbell and his late father is mentioned several times; each has the same square, solid chin. Campbell has a high opinion of his mother and does not wish to offend her. In response to an "indecent" question by Didi he echoes his mother's allegiance to the dead authority of propriety: "What if my mother could. . . . "

Sir Harold, the law, and propriety are related to each other and with death. When Campbell is commanded by his mother to sit down and listen to the instructions of the Corporation of Honorary Bell Ringers—a sort of kangaroo court sitting in moral judgment—the portrait of the late Sir Harold is invoked first. Only at this point is it noted that the portrait shows Sir Harold in his wig and robe, the first reference to his profession. He was literally a judge, and he is here metaphorically a judge presiding over the trial of his own son in this moral court, and the judgment leads to the eventual execution of his son as prescribed by an actual court. In *Islanders* the law does not exist to protect man from criminals, big business, or big government, or even to serve as the arm of the powerful and the privileged. The law as shown here is concerned solely with propriety. The references to points of law in the work are: the insistence that, as a matter of form, Didi's ex-husband ought to pay her alimony, even though she was unfaithful to him; O'Kelly's remark that he had invented a portable, inflatable suitcase to circumvent the law requiring a couple registering in a hotel to possess at least one suitcase; and the execution of Campbell, considered by the "decent" people more a matter of propriety than one of moral or social justice. O'Kelly sums it up: "In the final analysis, the role of the law is nothing more than the role of your dresses, ladies?" That is, the purpose of each is to restrain the natural, cover it up, and impose a mask of propriety on it. That O'Kelly is a lawyer does not indicate that he has any interest in joining the late jurist Sir Harold in the support of the rule of law, but rather his wish and talent for circumventing the law in his own interests and in the interests of his clients.

The second icon is the electric iron Campbell purchases as the first important step in setting up a household for himself and his future bride, Didi. There are to be no sexual relations and no wedding until he has enough money to rent a house and furnish it properly.

The chapter dealing with the arrival of spring, with flowers and trees in bloom, is entitled "The Electric Iron." For Campbell, the iron is far more important than the stirring of external nature, or the stirring of Didi's sexual desire. Didi complains of the heat, unbuttons her blouse, and puts Campbell's hand on her breast. He is tempted, but "Campbell, thank God, grips the steering wheel again and steers steadily toward the little house with the electric iron. Campbell withdrew his hand." Campbell's first sentence to Didi when she visits him after secretly spending the night with O'Kelly is "Iron." They then go shopping. Campbell has been full of doubts inspired by the anonymous letter he received, but he is completely reassured by the shopping trip; this is what a happy marriage is to be about. The iron is bought first, then other things, including night clothes for Didi. "With each purchased thing Didi became more and more his wife." By mocking contrast, Didi had already become (sexually) the wife of O'Kelly the night before, without benefit of clothes or electric iron. In fact, the same King Street which provides Campbell the electric iron also provides O'Kelly flowers to grace the room where he makes love to Didi.

Campbell and Didi return from shopping to Didi's apartment. When O'Kelly arrives he finds the iron on the mantel next to Didi's icon, the porcelain pug. " 'Next to Johnny?' he looked reproachfully at Didi." Didi is now quite unhappy. The iron has been purchased and placed on a level with her icon, her beloved porcelain pug. Campbell's open dislike for the pug bodes ill for the future.

Didi then spends the afternoon aimlessly tearing up lined paper. O'Kelly explains that these lines are considered of the utmost importance in the city of Jesmond, that they are the rails along which the proper life ought to move. As a symbol, the electric iron is related to, and perhaps sums up, the metaphors of the rails used here and frequently by the Vicar Dewley, as well as the entire concept of enforced, mathematically, mechanically perfect happiness preached by the Vicar. Whereas the portrait of Sir Harold represents the dead hand of tradition, the iron represents what Edward J. Brown calls [in "Zamjatin and English Literature," 1963; see Further Reading] "a symbol of conventional propriety, as well as of a life neatly pressed and patterned." It also refers to the dehumanization of man in the age of the assembly line and the age of mass consumption, for, like the ubiquitous, nameless Sunday Gentlemen, with their equally nameless and indistinguishable wives, children, and houses, and like "buttons, Fords, and *The Times.*" the iron is produced by the thousands. Industry depends not only on mathematics and mechanics, and on the interchangeable parts of the assembly line, but on reliability, efficiency, and strict scheduling. Industry depends on, and therefore encourages, a consumer goods mentality in the society as a whole. As contemporary writers and philosophers argue frequently, what is good for industry and trade may not necessarily be good for people, since people tend to become dehumanized and alienated when they function as cogs in a great economic machine. The Vicar's concept of enforced mathematical happiness and strict adherence to schedule owes something both to the Grand Inquisitor and to the efficiency expert of the twentieth century.

Another obvious metaphor relating to the iron, and to the age of the machine and mechanical happiness, is that of Campbell as a truck. Campbell's initial appearance is as a truck. He proceeds slowly, deliberately, "like a heavily loaded truck. . . . " Early references to him include: " . . . the truck traveled only on pavement"; " . . . you could hear how the heavy truck puffs, unable to move from the spot"; "Paper—that's something defined. The fog in Campbell's head cleared. The truck pulled its cargo swiftly and surely along the well-traveled highway"; and " . . . now the truck will start moving. . . . " When Campbell departs the world of propriety and mechanical happiness, as he does briefly in the boxing match, in his partly suppressed desire for Didi, and in his flight from discovering Didi in bed with his rival, his thoughts and emotions are described in terms of a car or truck plunging ahead without steering.

Didi's icon is her porcelain pug Johnny. Unlike the other icons, Johnny makes no demands, he just smiles incessantly at Didi and her love life, just as the moon smiles on lovers in the park: "The bushes were intensively alive all night, they stirred, whispered, and all night the moon walked about over the park with a monocle in his eye and looked down with the beneficent irony of the porcelain pug." The pug is further identified with the moon, when "the moon plunged into the light batiste clouds," while Johnny plunges into the white batiste and rosy waves of Didi's breasts. Johnny is more physically alive than the other icons. He comes down from the mantel frequently, to be caressed and talked to by Didi. He is wet by her tears and kisses and warmed by her touch. In his smile, friendliness, and ugliness, he is said to bear a remarkable resemblance to the human being O'Kelly—"two drops of water." Not only more alive than the other icons, he is more alive than Campbell. After Campbell evades sexual relations with Didi, she presses Johnny to her breast and he kisses her. . . . As the icon of the all-wise, all-understanding, all-loving life, Johnny is even able (although reluctantly) to kiss the Vicar Dewley.

It is Johnny to whom Didi turns shortly after her divorce from her first husband to beg him not to be angry if again she gets "a little bit" (*nemnozhko*) married. Johnny, never one to make a moral judgment, does not object. The same Johnny seems to approve when, in the following chapter, Didi asks him if she may go to O'Kelly.

Campbell instantly senses Johnny's values and the threat to his world of propriety and electric irons: " . . . there were immediately established, without any visible reason, poor relations between Campbell and Johnny." As Campbell lies in Didi's bed (alone) recovering from the boxing match, "the whole night the porcelain pug guarded Campbell with a grin and disturbed his thinking." Didi's sexual desire and the identical smiles of Johnny on the mantel and the monocled moon in the window annoy Campbell to the point where he leaps up angrily and turns Johnny's face to the wall. Didi will not permit her icon to be so treated and puts it to her breast. Campbell then sullenly juts out his square chin at the moon.

Thus, the portrait of the deceased Sir Harold is an image of dead propriety, and the equally lifeless electric iron is a symbol of the age of the machine; and both are symbols of the pursuit of status and serve for their owners and worshipers as images, models, and moral authorities for alienation from the spontaneous, the natural, the free, especially free sexual expression, and, in short, from the Self. But Johnny the porcelain pug comes down from the mantel, and even though it is an inanimate object, it enters into a complex web of relationships and identities with nature, animals, and people. For Didi and for O'Kelly the porcelain pug serves as a symbol of, and a moral authority for, their spontaneous, natural, free life, in which propriety and social or economic status are not factors, a life in which the Self is neither crushed nor covered over.

A symbolism of clothes is also of importance as regards alienation. First, clothes cover the natural body. Bourgeois society regards the natural, naked body as indecent. Campbell won't remove his jacket for the doctor in the presence of a lady, even though he is seriously, or even, for all he knows, mortally injured as the result of an accident. And he never removes his square shoes. To do so would be to expose his bare feet. (The foot is often considered in dream or myth a phallic symbol. For a discussion of the preference Englishmen in the story *Islanders* have for waterproof shoes, see below.) Didi, the incarnation of the natural life, is appropriately a striptease dancer by profession. The bare body, the natural, is capable of exerting a powerful influence on even those as well-clothed and well-indoctrinated as Campbell. It is the sight of her body on stage that leads to his otherwise unthinkable infatuation and his appearance in a boxing match. The second and last sight he has of her body, in bed with his rival, leads to murder and to Campbell's consequent execution. Related is the obvious symbolism of Mrs. Dewley's pince-nez—with it on she is cool and reserved. When it is off or lost, as it is when Campbell becomes a patient in her home, and when he is executed, Mrs. Dewley becomes human, emotional, and loving.

Second, the wearing of conservative, neat clothes, properly selected for the social occasion, displays one's respect for tradition and one's conformity in taste and morals with one's fellow citizens. The Sunday Gentlemen all wear identical suits and top hats. Their wives are all dressed in pink and blue. By contrast O'Kelly's jacket is a mess, and often unbuttoned. On the occasion of Lady Campbell's dinner party, O'Kelly "spoils" everything by appearing in a morning coat instead of the proper attire. And in his enthusiastic, spontaneous gesturing and talking he grossly spills sauce on his clothes.

Lastly, one notes the white flannel nightcap of the Vicar and his fellow citizens, an image of comfortable complacency, apathy, and isolation. The nightcap certainly discourages marital sexual relations. It is pulled over the ears to keep out the birds' singing. And the night before Campbell's execution, when human beings ought to be taking action, or, at the least, unable to sleep because of human concern, the Vicar, in flannel nightcap, "with arms folded on his chest, as prescribed in 'The Doctrine,' snored peacefully . . . the whole world slept peacefully, snoring, in its flannel nightcap. . . ."

As in the case of Turgenev's *Fathers and Sons* the degree of alienation from Self is partly demonstrated by the relation with external nature. Zamyatin's story, unlike most of Turgenev's works, is set in the city, and hence the possibilities for relationship with external nature would appear to be limited. There are no gardens, no fields, no forests, not even grass underfoot. One might expect all the characters, whether alienated from Self or not, to suffer from the artificial environment of the city, and seek to escape it. But through the extensive use of a symbolism involving sun, weather, and water, Zamyatin is able to indicate the characters' alienation from, or relatedness to, nature, and therefore to imply the degree of alienation from Self.

When outdoors, the Vicar Dewley frowns from "the too bright sun, and the impermissible racket of the sparrows." Indoors, he is much happier with sunlight diffused and softened by window panes. Lady Campbell objects to bright sun and pulls down her blinds so that the sunlight becomes "more moderate and decent." Her son, reflecting the self-alienation of his mother and of bourgeois society at large, also objects to bright sun. In his apartment he pulls down the blinds to shut out the sun. Up to this point the lustful Didi has managed to remain faithful to her fiancé, Campbell, despite his repeated refusal to have sexual relations with her and despite his steady talk of buying furniture and the iron. But the closing of the blinds to shut out the sun is the crucial action that leads immediately to Didi's resolution to offer herself to O'Kelly:

> "But I want sun," Didi jumped up.
>
> "But dear, you know very well I'm working so that we can begin buying the furniture as soon as possible, and after that. . . ."
>
> Didi suddenly broke out laughing, did not hear the rest, and went to her own room. She put the pug on the mantel, looked into his charmingly ugly mug.
>
> "What do you think, Johnny?"
>
> Johnny obviously thought the same thing. Didi began to pin on her hat in a hurry. . . .

Didi then goes with O'Kelly to the beach at *Sun*day-By, where the sun "made the blood boil." She soon agrees to spend the night with him.

References to the weather, the clouds, rain, the seasons of the year occur frequently. The Vicar includes "the taking of fresh air" in his weekly schedule. (We can well suppose he would enthusiastically endorse H. G. Wells's hopes, satirized in *My,* for weather control.) But for the most part the Vicar and his fellow Jesmondians simply prefer to isolate themselves from the weather and from the seasons: "At night came a flood of bird-singing, not taking any account of the fact that at 10 o'clock decent people went to bed. Decent people angrily slammed their windows shut and thrust themselves into their white nightcaps." A similar isolation from the rain and from the night air is one of the key symptoms of alienation of the protagonist in Ivan Bunin's "Gentleman from San Francisco."

The Sunday Gentlemen's standard greeting to each other is "Fine weather, isn't it?" They go home and discuss the weather and little else with their families. The weather remains only a subject of polite conversation with them; they are never involved with it. They do not sweat or shiver from temperature extremes, and the weather and the seasons do not have the slightest effect on their work, leisure, or emotions. The Vicar Dewley's great social presence of mind is indicated by the remark that even while dozing he is always prepared to open his eyes and say "Fine weather, isn't it?"

In her longing for Campbell, Mrs. Dewley comes to a partial realization of her alienation: "Mrs. Dewley went somewhere, with the pink and blue ladies, spoke of the weather, and meanwhile the clouds kept rushing along and swelling." Before Campbell's arrival, she is bored by the Vicar's puerile enthusiasm for efficiency and schedules and sits glumly by the window watching the "swift, swelling clouds." After Campbell is injured in an accident, brought to her house, and nursed back to health, she becomes human and longs for him. Now she sits at the breakfast table, looks past the Vicar "perhaps at the clouds" and smiles. Campbell is never able or willing to perceive her love, and his recovery results in his leaving the house. She feels she should act, but is unable to act: ". . . she looked out the window, the swift, swelling clouds rushed on, and one ought to run after them, one ought to do just that. . . ." The implications of the cloud images will be discussed at greater length below in the discussion of water symbolism.

While the Sunday Gentlemen in top hats remain unaffected by the heat, and Campbell flushes only from embarrassing social situations, O'Kelly is the only one present who pants and sweats freely from the heat at Lady Campbell's dinner party. While "decent" people slam their windows on the spring, others spend the night in the park, and keep the bushes alive; Didi commits adultery in her first marriage, she confesses, simply because the weather was nice; and the June weather is directly related to Didi's increasing lust. She complains of the heat and unbuttons her blouse in Campbell's presence. The heat of the sun mentioned above is involved in her increasing sexual desire for O'Kelly at the beach.

The bourgeoisie are very much antiwater. It is noted at almost every one of her appearances that Lady Campbell's ribs stick out like a broken umbrella. Mr. MacIntosh, as his name suggests, is interested in keeping out the water. (In the play adaptation of *Islanders* he is a raincoat dealer.) O'Kelly notes that Englishmen are fond of waterproof shoes. A connection between the passion for waterproof shoes, Campbell's refusal to remove his shoes when injured, and the ultimate meaning of the desire for isolation from water is suggested in Mr. MacIntosh's enthusiastic proposal (approved by the Honorary Bell Ringers) that the church journal increase its advertising revenue by accepting advertisements for rubber prophylactics—whose purpose, of course, is to isolate and render ineffective the life-giving moisture.

Didi and O'Kelly do not isolate themselves from the water. After they have sunned themselves well at the beach, they plunge eagerly into the surf. Leaping into the water is the necessary action when overheated by the sun. Buffeted by waves, and by her desire, Didi is unable to resist and agrees to sleep with O'Kelly.

The association of water and sexual expression is made more explicit in other images. Didi's breasts are termed "white and pink waves." and the breasts-clouds parallel was noted above. Didi's short, wet, curly hair is mentioned twice with strong sexual associations. Full of unsated desire, Didi smells sweet and pungent, like the *levkoy* flower "dry from lack of rain." There is no direct description of Didi and O'Kelly's lovemaking, but the night they spend together is described metaphorically: "Heat slept. There stood a milky, wet fog."

In conclusion, the unhappy protagonist, Campbell, the Vicar and Mrs. Dewley, Lady Campbell, and other Honorary Bell Ringers are thoroughly alienated from Self and from the natural world. Their alienation is seen in their everyday life and is symbolically emphasized in their choice of holy images, their clothes, their rejection of nature, and particularly their isolation from water.

Like D-503 in *My,* Campbell makes an unsuccessful attempt to break out of his prison. He enters a boxing match, becomes infatuated with a striptease dancer, but is unable to escape the alienation-imposing values of his bourgeois society, loses his fiancé, murders his rival, and is executed.

The other Honorary Bell Ringers do not even attempt to escape their prison. They avoid the boredom of alienation by becoming spectators. Just as they were spectators of the weather and seasons rather than participating in them, they are spectators of life. The mob of spectators, metaphorically an enormous serpent, appears both at the boxing match to witness real human conflict and to yell for blood, and at the prison gate to be present at real human death and to yell for an execution. (They are the *Honorary* Bell Ringers—the real bell ringer tolls the bell as the signal for the hangman to spring the trapdoor and hang Campbell.)

The Honorary Bell Ringers, and especially MacIntosh, the specialist in moral problems, are always ready to forego their sterile talk of the weather and to smack their disapproving lips over the scandal of the boxing match and over Didi's affair, and even to intervene enthusiastically in such a way that murder is not a totally unexpected result. The murder and the execution are further grist for the spectators' mill.

Didi and O'Kelly, although they may be somewhat socially alienated in being more or less ostracized by the "decent" people, do not suffer the slightest loneliness thereby, and, more important, are not alienated in the slightest from Self or nature. They never talk about weather or the private lives of others; they are too busy leading their own spontaneous, free, private lives. But modern bourgeois society, argues Zamyatin, finds such lack of alienation from Self and nature both an intolerable insult and rich fare for gossip. Ostracism and meddling are the natural consequences and, in this case, lead inevitably to the unhappy end of Campbell and O'Kelly. (pp. 209-20)

Christopher Collins, "Islanders," in Major Soviet Writers: Essays in Criticism, *edited by Edward J. Brown, Oxford University Press, Inc., 1973, pp. 209-20.*

STANLEY EDGAR HYMAN   (essay date 1968)

[*As a longtime literary critic for the* New Yorker, *Hyman achieved a prominent position in American letters during the middle decades of the twentieth century. He is noted for his multidisciplinary approach to modern literary criticism, and many of his best reviews and essays rely on his application of theories gleaned from such disciplines as cultural anthropology, psychology, and comparative religion. In the following excerpt, he evaluates* We *and favorably reviews Zamyatin's short stories in* The Dragon.]

There appears to be a growing interest in the work of Evgeny Zamyatin. Eight translations of his only novel, *We,* have appeared over the past decade. A selection of Zamyatin's stories recently appeared in a translation by Mirra Ginsburg as *The Dragon.* A monograph on Zamyatin by D. J. Richards was published in England in 1962, [See *TCLC,* Vol. 8, pp. 546-49], and now the first American monograph, *The Life and Works of Evgenij Zamjatin,* by Alex M. Shane, has appeared [See *TCLC,* Vol. 8, pp. 551-54]. This growth of interest may be attributed largely to the mushrooming field of Russian studies, but some part of it is the recognition that the Soviet 1920s—with Babel, Olesha, Pilnyak, Mandelstam, and others—were a literary renaissance, and some part of it is due to the peculiar attractiveness of Zamyatin as writer and man. (p. 248)

We, written in 1920 and never published in the Soviet Union (a recent Russian critic acknowledged it as "a malicious pamphlet on the Soviet government") makes curious reading today. It is a story of the breakdown of the utopian state after a thousand years, when the flowers of freedom, "that bloom only once a thousand years" (all my quotations are from the Gregory Zilboorg authorized 1924 English translation that was the book's first publication) burst into blossom. The book's protagonist and narrator, D-503, the sober designer of the state's first spaceship, under the influence of such archaic symptoms as love, jealousy, and dreams, cooperates with the underground conspiracy and goes so far as to proclaim "We must become insane as soon as possible!" He is saved by a kind of lobotomy, to become the conspiracy's happy betrayer. *We*'s innumerable progeny, prominent among them Huxley's *Brave New World* (Huxley always denied any indebtedness, but in a series of inconsistent statements that invite disbelief) and Orwell's *1984,* have made all this material overfamiliar, and the novel now seems terribly dated.

The principal weaknesses of *We* are that the wonderful heroine, I-330, has no personality but is simply a mouthpiece for Zamyatin ("There is no last revolution, their number is infinite"), that too little is clearly stated and too much implied in unfinished sentences (always a weakness of the author's), and that the book's contrast to the regimented life in the United State is pure pastoral romance: a naked people, their bodies "silky-golden and diffusing an odor of different herbs," eating ripe fruit and drinking sparkling wine out of wooden cups. The strengths of *We* are its subversive sensuality (all art derives from sex, Zamyatin wrote to a friend) and the author's craft. The eroticism of I-330 undressing, for example, is so charged that it is clearly revolutionary. Zamyatin's craft is best shown in wild, almost surrealist, tropes and in fierce parodies of Soviet rhetoric (a paean to the New Poets, whose "lyre is the morning rubbing-sound of the electric tooth-brushes"; the state paper's argument that counting dissenting votes would be like taking coughing in a concert hall to be part of the symphony).

In 1920, *We* was prophetic, visionary. While Stalin was still an insignificant figure, Zamyatin saw a future world "like steel—a sun of steel, trees of steel, men of steel." D-503, before he falls into sin, represents the New Man (and not only the Soviet New Man) as the death of the imagination: He sees clouds as so much steam, defines inspiration as "an extinct form of epilepsy," is horrified by irrational numbers and blots, finds nothing beautiful in flowers, and enjoys the reassuring feeling of an eye watching over his shoulder. How the book would have delighted Marx, an earlier Scythian humanist.

The 15 stories and tales in *The Dragon* show a considerable range. The first of them, *A Provincial Tale,* written in 1912, is a museum of the horrors of provincial life: ignorance, grossness, boredom, cruelty, superstition, servility, chicanery. Its protagonist, Anfim Baryba, rises to the exalted rank of police sergeant by the betrayal of every friend and benefactor, the nasty hero of this nasty sty. Other stories are tragic, such as **"The North,"** where the idyllic joy, "the intolerable happiness," of the giant Marey with the Lapp girl Pelka is slowly undermined by her death-wish until she leaves them disarmed before an infuriated bear, which kills them both. Other stories are mainly ironic, such as **"A Story about the Most Important Thing"** ("the most important thing" is pro-

gressively understood as "to crush the others," to survive, "to bloom," and, finally, to love sacrificially). Some stories neatly blend tragedy and irony, such as *The Flood,* where the murderer Sofya gives birth, "running over with juices"; confesses her murder, running over with words; then sleeps, "breathing evenly, quietly, blissfully, her lips parted wide." Other short pieces are grotesques, such as **"The Dragon,"** a portrait of a 1918 Soviet soldier as "a dragon with a gun" (by 1923, in **"The Most Important Thing,"** the same image has become "an ant with a rifle").

Zamyatin's style in the stories is equally varied. In *A Provincial Tale* it is portentous: A lamp dies "in long, slow anguish"; Baryba is seen at the end as "an idol from an ancient burial mound." The style of **"X"** is effervescent comedy: A deacon repents of religion in order to replace his wife with the round-heeled Martha, revealing that he is a convert not to Marxism but to Marthism (this enables the author to lecture us on Martha's generous bosom as Marxist superstructure; elsewhere Marx is confused with the planet Mars and the god Mars). At times **"X"** is a marvel of what Kenneth Burke calls "perspective by incongruity": We see militiamen in a ballet class; a doctor's tombstone lists his visiting hours.

The current Soviet writer most visibly influenced by Zamyatin is Andrei Sinyavsky, who has published abroad as "Abram Tertz." The works of "Tertz" are Zamyatin's monument, but far more so was Sinyavsky's fearless eloquence at his trial. Evgeny Zamyatin, who believed in new life out of death, lives on in the Soviet Union, and his long-quiescent flowers of freedom may yet blossom everywhere. (pp. 250-52)

Stanley Edgar Hyman, "A Scythian Humanist," in his The Critic's Credentials: Essays & Reviews, *edited by Phoebe Pettingell, Atheneum, 1978, pp. 248-52.*

SUSAN LAYTON   (essay date 1976)

[In the following essay, Layton offers a close examination of "The Cave."]

Evgenij Zamjatin is best known for the fantastical, antiutopian novel *We,* which was a forerunner of *Brave New World* and *1984.* Of equal interest, however, are short stories such as **"The Cave," "Mamaj"** and **"The Dragon"** in which he dealt with the Bolshevik revolution in a nonrealistic manner. As does *We,* the stories oppose the optimism of the Marxist view of man and doctrine of historical progress, and they helped to establish Zamjatin's reputation in the Soviet Union as an anti-Bolshevik writer. However, it is inadequate to describe them narrowly as political works written in opposition to communism. Zamjatin had a revolutionary fervor which had led to a brief involvement with the impulse for radical political and social change in Russia. While he was a student in the early 1900's he joined the Bolshevik Party; arrested for his revolutionary activities, he was imprisoned for several months in 1905-1906, but by 1908 he had left the Party. As an artist Zamjatin continued to uphold an anarchistic, bohemian concept of revolution, and he opposed the encroachment upon freedom of expression in the Soviet Union as one of the signs of a dogmatization of Bolshevism. In several essays and articles in the 1920's he protested against demands that the artist serve the state and provide a chronicle of the progressive development of socialism in the U.S.S.R. Attacking journalistic writing that followed the current Party line, he stated that genuine literature must have a symbolic dimension; it must be "artistically realized philosophy." Repeatedly Zamjatin defended this notion that the artist must rise above the chaotic day-by-day progression of events and deal with the realities of being. Comparing the function of genuine art to a sailor on the watchtower of a ship [see essay dated 1924], he wrote that

> In stormy weather you need a man aloft. And right now the weather is stormy. S.O.S. signals are coming in from all directions. . . . Right now we can look and think only as men do in the face of death: we shall die—and what then? How have we lived? If we are to live all over again in some new way, then by what shall we live and for what? Right now we need in literature the vast philosophical horizon, the vast sweep from the masthead, from the sky above; we need the most ultimate, the most fearsome "Whys?" and "What nexts?"

"The Cave" is one of the most richly symbolic works in which Zamjatin placed the contemporary within a framework of universal experience. Concerned with the difficulty of maintaining traditional values and civilized behavior under harsh conditions in Russia after the revolution, **"The Cave"** depicts a grim regression of life. Focusing upon Martin Martinych and his wife Masha, the story covers approximately twenty-four hours during the winter of 1919-1920. Martin Martinych is desperate to get some firewood—especially because his wife, who is ill and weak, hopes to burn the stove throughout her nameday. When his request to borrow some logs from a neighbor is denied, Martin Martinych steals the wood; and his suffering over the meaning of that act is the essential material of **"The Cave."** Certainly there are realistic details in the story that point to the new political system. In the years of War Communism, supplies of food and fuel were minimal, and people literally lived in the dark much of the time because the government had to regulate strictly the use of electricity. Most directly to the point, the central occurrence of the story was drawn from Zamjatin's own experience in Soviet Petersburg. In the essay **"Behind the Scenes"** he relates:

> One winter night in 1919 I was on watch duty in our yard. My partner—a frozen, half-starved professor—complained about the lack of firewood: "Sometimes I am even tempted to steal some wood! But the trouble is that I cannot do it. I'd rather die than steal." On the following day I sat down to write **"The Cave."**

While Zamjatin clearly was dealing with the material of experience in contemporary society in this story, as in *We* and other works of this period of his career in **"The Cave"** he has transformed the particulars of life in Soviet Russia in order to make current history speak of the human condition.

The title, **"The Cave,"** poses the central metaphor which extends throughout the story—and transforms contemporary Petersburg into a nightmarish world of fear and suspicion: life in a cave is a framing device that refers to natural history and renders the society of 1919 as alien and distant. With no direct reference to a city or to men, the first lines describe a snow-swept wasteland with a starkness that is heightened by the compressed, often elliptical sentences:

> Glaciers, mammoths, wastes. Black nocturnal cliffs, somehow resembling houses; in the cliffs, caves. And no one knows who trumpets at night on the stony path between the cliffs, who blows up white snow-dust, sniffing out the path. Perhaps it

is a gray-trunked mammoth, perhaps the wind. Or is the wind itself the icy roar of the king of mammoths?

This god-forsaken wasteland in which winter seems eternal is preeminently a realm of necessity:

> And you must clench your teeth as tightly as possible to keep them from chattering; and you must split wood with a stone axe; and you must carry your fire every night from cave to cave, deeper and deeper; and you must wrap yourself into shaggy animal hides, more and more of them.

As for their prehistoric ancestors, for the people inhabiting the fearfully transformed Petersburg, existence is essentially a struggle to survive.

Zamjatin presents Martin Martinych and Masha as the inhabitants of one of the caves. Unable to keep their entire apartment heated, they have retreated to the bedroom and light a fire in the stove for a few hours each day. In this situation the hero emerges as a life-like individual whose behavior has a complex psychological and philosophical basis—even though Zamjatin does not analyze his motivations. However, in exploring the predicament of that freezing professor whom he had encountered, Zamjatin represents Martin Martinych in a symbolic manner. There is no complete physical description of Martin Martinych, and he is not identified by full name or profession. Appearing as a figure of everyman, he undergoes a struggle which is referred back beyond the trials of the contemporary social upheaval. Existing now as cave men means being devoted to a fight for the material necessities; but in opposition to this terrifying realm, the story evokes another mode of being and suggests that the soul is the universally distinctive feature of humanity. Standing in **"The Cave"** as a remembered ideal, this world of spirit is summoned by references to love, art and Christian legend.

The hero in **"The Cave"** is a man who attributes primary value to the spiritual dimension of existence. Considered within this broad tendency, his name suggests an association with Henride St. Martin, the man whose books exerted a major influence in the mid-eighteenth century upon the first Russian Masons. Zamjatin's hero can be regarded as a son of these original "Martinists"—the name which Catherine the Great applied to Novikov and his followers, only in the most general sense, of course. Martin Martinych professes no specific doctrines, but he, like the Masons, believes that authentic reality is the world of the spirit. As the only reference in the story to his physical appearance emphasizes, he is acutely aware that the soul is being lost in the realm of the cave: "his face is crumpled, claylike: many people had clay faces now—back to Adam." Compounding the image of the cave man, this biblical reference suggests that man attains fully human being only when animated by a divine inner spirit.

The cave of this person who has spiritual longings is a chaotic world that contains all manner of things and centers around a deity invented by man:

> In the Petersburg bedroom-cave things were much as they had been in Noah's ark not long ago: a confusion of beasts, clean and unclean, thrown together by the flood. A mahogany desk; books; stone-age pancakes that seemed to have been made of potter's clay; Scriabin, Opus 74; a flat-iron; five potatoes, scrubbed lovingly to gleaming whiteness; nickel

bedsteads; an axe; a chiffonier; firewood. And in the center of this universe—its god, the shortlegged, rusty-red, squat, greedy cave god: the cast-iron stove.

The jumbled, disordered quality of Martin Martinych's existence is not described essentially in terms of social upheaval—but is conveyed through the allusion to immemorial chaos—the Flood. The fact that the hero has retained a place in his life for things which are not necessary for physical survival underlines that he, like Noah, is notable as a man with a soul. Zamjatin juxtaposes the objects which belong to the realm of the cast-iron god with products of civilization, indicating a discrepancy between Martin Martinych's spiritual aspirations and the possibilities of realizing them in his present existence.

The participation of Martin Martinych and Masha in the world of the soul is conveyed mainly through their personal recollections of the past. In opposition to the wintry realm of necessity, the world in which the spirit can thrive is summoned in the hero's thoughts by symbolic reference to the other seasons of the year. In the bedroom-cave the fire as a source of warmth is associated with spring, as the glow of the flames seems to regenerate Martin Martinych: "For a single hour it was spring in the cave; for one hour the animal hides, claws, fangs were discarded, and green shoots—thoughts—struggled up through the ice-crusted cortex of the brain." References to autumn and summer elaborate upon this allusion to a specifically human world of mind, emphasizing not the intellectual but the spiritual, irrational faculty. Masha breaks into her husband's contemplation, accusing him of forgetting that tomorrow is her saint's day. Not answering immediately, he continues to dream, now recalling summer as a lost ideal and autumn as the falling away:

> In October, when the leaves have yellowed, withered, drooped, there are sometimes blue-eyed days; you throw back your head on such a day, so as not to see the earth, and you almost believe that joy, that summer are still here. And so with Masha now: if you close your eyes and only listen to her voice, you can still believe she is the same, the old Masha.

As evoked further in Masha's recollections on her nameday, the ideal world of spring and summer is a creation of love. Speaking in her "voice of old," she recalls a distant evening when their warm, beautiful "universe had been created":

> Do you remember, Mart: my blue room, and the piano with the covered top, and the little wooden horse, the ashtray, on the piano? I played, and you came up to me from behind. . . .
>
> Do you remember, Mart—the open window, the green sky and below, out of another world, the hurdy-gurdy man? . . .
>
> And on the quay—remember? The branches still bare, the rosy water and a last ice floe, like a coffin floating by. And the coffin only made us laugh, for we would never die. Remember?

In contrast to the grim world that is ruled by cold and hunger, this recollected universe stands in **"The Cave"** as an eternal ideal; experiencing love, Zamjatin's characters express a sense of immortality.

In contrast to Martin Martinych and Masha, other creatures are at home in the kingdom of the cast-iron god. Obertyshev

is the cave man most in harmony with the environment in which only the fittest survive. When Martin Martinych goes to him to beg for firewood, Obertyshev opens the door—his face appearing as a "wasteland overgrown with rusty, dusty weeds." For Obertyshev to smile is like the scurrying of a lizard: "Through a tangle of weeds—yellow, stony teeth, and between the stones, a flick of a lizard's tail." Recurrently, the prominence of his teeth is noted, and this motif stresses his kinship with the mammoths of the frozen wasteland that is summoned in the opening paragraphs. As this episode procedes, the underlying metaphor of Obertyshev as a subhuman, animal-like person is "realized" so that he appears essentially as a monster trying to impersonate a man. As Martin Martinych anticipates his refusal to give him any firewood, "all of Obertyshev was sprouting teeth, and they grew longer and longer"; later, after he has stolen some wood, the hero imagines the fury of Obertyshev, "all of him overgrown with teeth." Appearing increasingly grotesque, Obertyshev presents the most horrible aspect in **"The Cave"** of a man who is not human. Similarly, while the house chairman Selikhov does display some sympathy for Martin Martinych, Zamjatin also characterizes him by motifs of dehumanization that connect him with the mammoths and with the cast-iron stove and shows his ready adaptation to the laws of the harsh realm of Soviet cave men.

Unlike Obertyshev and Selikhov, Martin Martinych and his wife are conscious of their reduction in the realm of the cave. Throughout the story Masha appears "flat, cut-out of paper" and is never fully described. The suggestion that she is less than a vital, three-dimensional person is realized in her own words. At the end of **"The Cave"** she begs her husband to give her the single dose of poison that he has, as though to commit suicide would be to acknowledge her virtual death: " 'There is nothing left of me anyway. This is no longer I. . . .' " Reduced to a helpless, irritable creature, Masha is now unrecognizable as the fully human woman who is preserved in memory. During the critical twenty-four hour period that is portrayed in **"The Cave,"** the old Martin Martinych also ceases to exist. As conveyed by motifs that externalize his mental state, he is falling to pieces and eventually seems annihilated spiritually. Unknown to Masha on the eve of her saint's day, their wood supply has been totally exhausted. Martin Martinych's anxiety about this is shattering: he hears the sound of Obertyshev's chopping logs and the "stone axe was splitting Martin Martinych into pieces." One part of him smiles at his wife while "another piece—like a bird that has flown into a room out of the open—dashed itself blindly, stupidly against the ceiling, the windows, the walls: 'Where can I get some wood—some wood—some wood?' " Flying to pieces, Martin Martinych desperately asks Obertyshev for some logs: "The strayed bird could be heard fluttering up, rustling, darting left, right—and suddenly, desperately, it dashed its breast against the wall." The metaphor of a shattered personality is realized when the hero stands alone before the big wood pile after Obertyshev has refused to give him any logs: ". . . two Martin Martinychs locked in mortal combat: the old one, who had loved Scriabin and who knew he must not, and the new one, the cave dweller, who knew—he must." The cave man throttles the old self, and Martin Martinych with the logs "bounded upstairs with great, animal leaps." By stealing, he believes that he has destroyed his former self and degenerated into a subhuman creature.

Virtually annihilated as a man from his own point of view, Martin Martinych appears increasingly like a clay figure.

Even before the theft, the motif of the clay figure suggests not a human who still can respond to the external world but inanimate material that can be molded. When he first enters Obertyshev's apartment, the "clay Martin Martinych painfully struck his side against the wood—a deep dent formed in the clay." After the theft of the logs, the image of the clay figure is central in conveying what it means for the hero to have lost his soul. "Cold, blind, made of clay, Martin Martinych stumbled against the things piled in confusion, out of the flood." Similarly, he is described as "mechanical, far-away," but "still going through some motions." Lost in despair Martin Martinych is transformed finally into an android figure.

Throughout the story Masha appears oblivious to her husband's suffering, and her anger at him brings the blackest moment for him. Stumbling about numbly, Martin Martinych knocks the tea kettle and pan from the stove, arousing his wife's irritation: " 'Get out! Get out at once. I don't need anybody, I don't need anything—I want nothing, nothing!' " As if the cry "nothing, nothing" overwhelms him, he now takes the vial of poison from the desk. At first he intends to drink it himself, but his wife catches sight of the vial. When she then asks for the poison, Martin Martinych hesitates in his own misery but does give it to her—perhaps thinking that to abandon Masha would be more dishonorable than the theft of firewood. For the pitiful Masha death is associated with a journey away from the wintry realm to a land of the sun. Almost joyfully she prepares to drink and appears "rosy, immortal—like the river at sunset long ago." In the name of the woman and of the entire joyful existence which are etched in memory, Martin Martinych allows his wife to escape from the cave. His own anguish is unrelieved, however. At his wife's request he goes outside, leaving her to die. The icy wasteland described in the opening paragraph of **"The Cave"** is represented once again, and the hero is left alone in a hostile universe of blizzards, ice and monster mammoths.

While surely the most sombre of any of Zamjatin's works, **"The Cave"** nevertheless does attest to the greatness of the human soul. Precisely because of his despair about falling from the ideal of the truly human, Martin Martinych transcends the realm of the cave men. Unlike Obertyshev and Selikhov, who exist as animals, experiencing no spiritual torment, he has lived with a sense of good and evil. By reducing him to the state in which his best choice is to mercifully kill his wife, Zamjatin very starkly underlines his hero's struggle to retain a residual humanity. As do many of Zamjatin's works, this story also represents passionate love as a peak of human experience.

When **"The Cave"** first appeared in the Soviet Union in 1920, Marxists interpreted it strictly in ideological terms; and, since Zamjatin did not celebrate the Bolshevik revolution, he was berated. He was attacked for compassionately depicting those "disappearing people who are unfit for life." Zamjatin was well aware that works such as **"The Cave"** would provide grounds for this kind of charge from Communists. But instead of avoiding forbidden themes, he insisted that literature must arouse readers by exploring fundamental questions about life. Believing that the artist must consider all aspects of the revolution, he did draw upon the reality of contemporary Russia to depict the tragedy of an individual overwhelmed by history. Writing the story of a man who steals firewood in October 1919 in Petersburg, Zamjatin subsumed the realistic elements in philosophical speculation about what it means to be human. (pp. 455-61)

Susan Layton, "The Symbolic Dimension of 'The Cave' by Zamjatin," in Studies in Short Fiction, *Vol. XIII, No. 4, Fall, 1976, pp. 455-61.*

EDWARD J. BROWN   (essay date 1976)

[*Brown is an American critic who has written extensively on postrevolutionary Soviet literature. Notable among his studies are* Russian Literature since the Revolution *(1963), which some critics consider the standard work on the period, and* "Brave New World," "1984," *and* "We": An Essay On Anti-Utopia. *In the following excerpt from the latter work, Brown expounds on the thematic concerns, philosophical thought, and aesthetic tenets presented in Zamyatin's essays and major works.*]

While Zamyatin's range of thematic interest seems at first sight very wide, reaching from a military outpost in the Far East to a study of social organization in a state of the distant future, a closer inspection reveals his organic attachment to one particular theme. Zamyatin might be characterized as a writer who persistently negates "the city" and who finds his own most congenial matter for esthetic formulation among the precivilized and the primitive. Not only does he describe people like Baryba in **Provincials,** who has hardly a trace of civilized moral sense, who steals from his benefactors and bears false witness against his friends, or a Potifona in **"Ala-tyr,"** or Captain Arancheev in **In the Backwoods,** that fantasy of lust and gluttony; but he takes literary interest also in naive and charming primitives, the fisherman Fedor Volkov in **"Afrika"** where "Elephants? But why not: you just sit on him and he takes you wherever you want to go. He'll be running along, then he plays on a silver trumpet and the way he plays you just can't hear enough of it, and he carries you off to undiscovered lands," and of course the wonderfully appealing Marei in **"The North"** with his animal-like mate Pelka. In the story **"Rus'"** the characters and scenes upon which Zamyatin's imagination lingers are "No prospects measured off by Peter's ruler—no: that's Petersburg, 'Rossiia.' Here you have the real Russia (*Rus'*), narrow little streets that go up and down so the noisy kids will have a place to slide in winter—alleys, streets that lead nowhere, gardens, and fences, lots of fences." And Zamyatin's enthusiastic appreciation of Jack London, published as a preface to the *Universal Literature* (*Vsemirnaia literatura*) edition of London's works, reveals the characteristic preoccupation of Zamyatin himself:

> Our city life is already obsolete. Cities, like old men, bundle up against the bad weather in asphalt and iron. Cities, like old men, fear excessive movement and substitute machines and push-buttons for all healthful muscular work . . . But if a man still has his young blood burning in him and if the hard iron power of his muscles is looking for a way out, for struggle, then that man runs away from the decrepit cities . . . runs wherever his eyes lead him, anywhere: to the field, or the forest or the sea, to the north or the south.

It should surprise no one that those lines came from the pen of the man who wrote **Islanders** and **We.** The "city" when it does occur in Zamyatin's writings is a monster of mechanical efficiency, London in **Islanders** or the "city-state" in **We,** or else it is the fog-bound snow-covered haunt of mammoths, dragons, and cave-dwellers. The possibility of a normal "realistic" city is never admitted in the art of Zamyatin. And always, in those impossible, dream-like cities, there are characters who rebel against them and try to find their way to the free air "outside the wall." There is in his work a long series of escapes or attempted escapes from one level of organized life to a lower, less organized and supposedly more free level. This notion of escape is a constantly recurring theme and is deeply characteristic. O'Kelley and Didi, the bohemian individualists in *Islanders,* resist the pressures of the bourgeois world and remain outside its pale of respectability in a kind of half-world of their own. In *We,* I-330 and her lover D-503 similarly attempt to escape the conventions of their time by finding their way outside the glass wall to the hairy creatures who still live among the "debris" of nature. On a much lower level the primitive fisherman Marei attempts an escape with his mate from the world of the merchant Kortoma, who, in burlesque form, embodies "Piter" and rational organization: "Kortoma's accounts are in strict order—not just any old way, but by a system of triple bookkeeping. 'It's time we lived in accordance with the West European nations,' such was Kortoma's favorite saying." Similar to these escapes is that of Fedor Volkov, for whom "Afrika" is Canaan and Goshen. Dashutka's letter home describing the cultural wonders of city life is full of simple yearning for the country: "How I would like to go out now barefoot into the garden, and have the dusty ground under my feet." These words might have served as a motto for the revolutionaries in *We.*

Though Zamyatin described himself as a "neo-realist" it will be obvious that his characteristic thematic interest might rather be labelled "romantic."

• • • • •

Zamyatin's work before the revolution offers no evidence of a consistent philosophical position, other than a vaguely Rousseauistic urge toward the unspoiled primitive. And Zamyatin's Rousseauism is much more esthetic than it is philosophical. He is drawn to the primitive and the prerational because the life he finds—or, better, imagines—outside the "wall" offers both piquancy of dialect and novelty of character. In Zamyatin's subjective apprehension, with which he completely infects the reader, Marei and Pelka are more interesting than Kortoma, O'Kelley and the music-hall girl Didi than Vicar Dooley; and D-503's atavistic hair lends to him a possibility of irrational adventure that should not exist for the good citizen of a well-ordered state.

The manner in which Zamyatin utilized fugitive subjective impressions of reality in creating both character and situation he revealed himself in the essay **"Backstage" ("Zakulisy")**:

> I woke up at some little station near Moscow and raised the shade. Right in front of my window, just as though in a frame, the physiognomy of the station policeman floated past me: a low overhanging forehead, little bear-like eyes, jawbones frightfully square. I managed to read the name of the station: Barybino. Right there the novella *Provincials* and its hero Anfim Baryba took form.

In view of this frank statement it is unsound to assume that Baryba in Zamyatin's story has anything in common with that actual police official whom the author chanced to glimpse, or even that his story tells us anything useful about provincial police officials as a class, and it is risky to interpret the work of such a writer in tendentious or topical terms. And when Mr. Richards in his excellent book on Zamyatin [*Zamyatin: A Soviet Heretic,* 1962] offers the opinion that "the final picture of the drunken Baryba, rejected by the father and

mocked by the onlookers as he blunders along, heavy, grunting, and helpless, symbolizes the state, not only of provincial life but of old Russia itself," one should, it would seem, view such an interesting idea with great reserve.

As a leading member of the Serapion Brothers in the early twenties Zamyatin insisted that literature be free of social or political tendency, and while it has been suggested that this apolitical position was a mask for political hostility, it seems not unlikely that Zamyatin, in spite of his early membership in the Russian Social Democratic Workers Party, was genuinely indifferent to actual political events and the philosophies that motivated them. He wrote two stories dealing with the events of 1905, but one could not assume from a mere reading of the stories that the author of them was involved in politics. He wrote two novellas, the setting of which was England during the First World War, but there is no allusion whatever to the war in *Islanders,* and the Zeppelin raid in **"Fisher of Men"** is a noisy and colorful interlude in the story whose function in the plot is to break down Mrs. Lory's cool reserve and make her accessible to her lover. The First World War as an event of some historical importance was simply not part of Zamyatin's artistic consciousness at the time he wrote those stories. And in the stories he wrote about Petrograd at the time of the revolution and the civil war his attention is directed to the poignant but petty tragedies of individual human beings rather than to the tremendous historical event, whether viewed as triumph or as tragedy. Contemporary history provided him with material for artistic treatment, but as an honest artist he refrains from direct political or philosophical commentary.

Yet Zamyatin's work of the twenties has given rise to the idea

Drawing of Zamyatin in 1921 by Yuriy Annenkov.

that he is an important philosophical writer. The literary works that contain his thought are *We* (1920), *The Fires of St. Dominic* (1922), "A Story about the Most Important Thing" (1924), *Attila* (1928), and the posthumously published unfinished novel *The Scourge of God* (1939). Let us consider them briefly as philosophical statements. *We,* as we have seen, is closely related to *Islanders,* and its basic theme is rebellion against a rigid and universally enforced code of correct behavior. In both novels this rebellion is given philosophic motivation as an effort to free human emotions from their confinement in a rigidly rational social structure. The London Vicar Dooley's plan for "universal salvation" is mathematically perfect, involving the rational organization of every human activity. The electric iron which the character Campbell would buy Didi for their establishment is a symbol of conventional propriety, as well as of a life neatly pressed and patterned. The Sunday gentlemen strolling properly in a proper British uniformity are an early sketch for the citizens of *We* marching in ranks on their daily walk. The intellectual preoccupations of Zamyatin are essentially the same in *Islanders* as in *We,* where one of the gods of rationalism is the American industrial efficiency expert F. H. Taylor.

But there is an important difference between *Islanders* and *We.* For the latter work Zamyatin, perhaps influenced by the polemical ambience of the period, has devised an explicit philosophical statement, which is expressed in the impassioned speeches of the revolutionary young woman I-330. Statements very much like hers appear in the article "Tomorrow" ("Zavtra"), written at approximately the same time, and in the article entitled "On Literature, Revolution and Entropy" ("O literature, revoliutsii, i entropii") [see essay dated 1924], published in 1924 as part of the collection *Writers about Literature and about Themselves* (*Pisateli o literature i o sebe*). To summarize in a rational system the points made in that essay would do violence to the spirit of the work. It is a series of subjective apercus, each one a fragment of thought, the whole bound together by a central subjective intuition expressed in the terminology of the science ("*nova,*" entropy, relativity) and the philosophy (Hegelian dialectics) contemporary to Zamyatin. It is highly personal and poetic—is, as a matter of fact, a literary production, and is directed in the main against the dogmatic rationalism which Zamyatin felt was developing in the Russia of his day. Against the ruthlessly mechanical rationalism of the dogmatists Zamyatin urges the view, neither original nor unfamiliar, that the life process proceeds by way of dialectical movement, that all "established" values are relative, and that in human societies heretics are the necessary agents of change.

> Fiery, crimson, and deathdealing is the law of revolution; but the death it brings is the embryo of new life, of a new star. Cold and blue as ice, blue as the icy interplanetary infinities is the law of entropy. The flame that was crimson becomes pink and warm—no longer death-dealing but comfortable; the sun ages into a planet suitable for roads, stores, beds, prostitutes and jails: such is the law . . .

> Let the flame grow cold tomorrow or the day after tomorrow (in the Book of Genesis days equal years, centuries). But someone should see today what's about to happen tomorrow, and speak heretically even today about tomorrow. Heretics are the only medicine (a bitter one) against the entropy of human thought . . .

> All truths are mistaken; the dialectical process

means precisely that today's truths are tomorrow's errors; there is no final number.

The play *The Fires of St. Dominic,* like the essays mentioned and the two novels, provides a telling commentary on dogmatic authority and in the person of the Spanish Inquisitor shows the extent to which such authority corrupts human beings. Brilliantly and courageously Zamyatin dissects the motivations and the mode of operation of a police power responsible only to itself. As we have already seen, the story "A Story about the Main Thing" presents in symbolic form a statement about the relativity of all values.

In the play *Attila* and in the novel *The Scourge of God* Zamyatin has transferred to an actual historical setting his single, idiosyncratic literary theme, and given it a philosophic motivation. Attila and his Huns, a new and fresh force from the outer limits of the civilized world, are contrasted with the effete and enervated Romans of the "City," whose minds and bodies have grown soft with decay. As in the novel *We,* Zamyatin has here contrived a situation in which vital and primitive beings violently disturb the entropic calm of the arch-City itself.

To summarize, Zamyatin's philosophy, a mixture of his basic romanticism with modern scientific vocabulary and Hegelian dialectics, does not appear in his work until the twenties. The earliest attempt to formulate that philosophy is the novel *We,* and perhaps its clearest literary formulation is the novel *The Scourge of God.* That philosophy seems to the present writer to have been an artificial intellectual superstructure developed in answer to the insistent demand upon writers—even by the most liberal of critics—that they take a definite ideological position. It is not a connected or coherent system but a series of brilliant poetic insights. Stated in the simplest terms, it was a philosophy designed to uphold the independence and integrity of the artist by insisting on his right to be a heretic.

• • • • •

Zamyatin on at least two occasions attempted to analyze and explain his own creative processes. The lectures he delivered in the *House of Arts* in 1920, two of which have been published ["Contemporary Russian Prose" ("Sovremennaia russkaia proza") and "The Psychology of Creativity" ("Psikhologiia tvorchestva") in *Grani,* 1956] and an article appearing in the collection *How We Write* (*Kak my pishem*) reveal with unusual clarity and originality not only his own approach to the craft of writing, but the philosophical assumptions and esthetic theories of the group with whom he identified himself: the "neorealists." Students of Soviet literature have pointed out that Zamyatin's lectures in Petrograd on the art of writing were an important seminal event in the history of Soviet prose of the twenties. It should be emphasized that the "craft" he taught was not that of the realistic writers nor of the symbolists or futurists, but almost exclusively of the "neorealists." The examples of literary language and device which he uses come from a rather narrow range of Russian authors, and the names which occur most frequently are those of Bely, Remizov, and Zamyatin himself. Zamyatin uses their works as textbooks of modern literary form, just as he would have taught modern physics from the works of Einstein.

In the lecture entitled "Contemporary Russian Literature" ("Sovremennaia russkaia literatura") Zamyatin traces a dialectical development from the realists, whose attention was focused on men as particular earth-bound facts, through the symbolists, who saw "man in general" as part of some higher reality, and at last to the "neorealists," who represent a kind of unity of opposites in that they attempt generalization while still dealing with concrete human reality (*byt*). The scheme he sets up is both interesting and suggestive and is characteristic of the Hegelian forms in which his mind operated. Those he lists as neorealists in some, at least, of their work are—in addition to Bely and Remizov—Sologub, Sergeev-Tsensky, Prishvin, Aleksei Tolstoi, and Zamyatin himself.

He observes that the attraction to provincial life and language, his own principal theme, is characteristic to some extent of all the neorealists and Zamyatin explains this interest of theirs in terms which apply equally to himself:

> Life in big cities is like that in factories: it de-individualizes, makes people somehow all the same, machine-like. And so it happened that many of the neo-realists, in their urge to create the most striking images, turned their faces away from the great city and looked to the provinces and backways.

Other characteristics of the neorealists are their search for a more "real" reality through fantasy and distortion, their tendency to an impressionistic style, and their use of popular dialect material. And in their technique there is a kind of cooperative effort on the part of writer and reader, the former furnishing fragmented thoughts and impressions which the latter actively "creates."

Zamyatin's remarks on the psychology of creativity reveal his conviction that the rational part of man plays only a secondary role in artistic creation, which, he maintains, takes place in the sphere of the subconscious. In his essay **"Backstage"** Zamyatin compares the condition of a mind disposed to creative activity with a railway sleeping-compartment lighted only by the blue night lamp, when objects are visible but not in their normal daylight shapes and colors. In such a state the "fantasy" creates dreamlike images that have at the same time a quality of vividness denied to objects seen in rational daylight.

In the materials that we have Zamyatin did not attempt a detailed analysis of the psychological factors operating in literary creation, but from the examples he gives of his own experience the literary images he characteristically created were the result, not of any conscious cerebral purpose, but of a complex interaction of memory and association with passing impression and subjective feeling. A conscious philosophic and perhaps polemic purpose entered, as we have seen, into the creation of certain important works of the twenties, and the psychological factors at work in them might be the subject of analysis.

Zamyatin's stylized language is his own most original esthetic resource. His stories of the provinces probably do not provide an accurate account of provincial speech, and on his own admission he knew nothing of the actual locale and personnel portrayed in the story **In the Backwoods.** But in their selection of occasional local words (or even words not necessarily native to the locality but strange to the literary ear), by the generous employment of forms, diminutives for instance, which are felt as non-literary, and by simplicity and colloquial casualness of syntax, those stories do artfully contrive to produce in the sophisticated reader an illusion of immediate contact with the deeply primitive. Similarly, the stories **"The Sign"** and **"The Monk Erasmus"** suggest the language of

church chronicles, the former in an extremely primitive form. The stories **"Afrika"** and **"Ela"** contrive an impression of the dialect spoken in the fishing villages of the far north; and in the story *Islanders,* as Zamyatin has said, the language is deliberately stylized so as to suggest a translation from English. And in the novel *We* with its clipped telegraphic manner and swift ellipses he attempts to suggest the rationalized thought and simplified language of the twenty-ninth century, disturbed, it's true, by constant interference. The delight experienced by readers of Zamyatin is to a large extent bound up with the consciousness he conveys of linguistic vigor, variety, and possibility. The style he cultivated is, of course, *skaz,* and his closest contemporary Russian relatives were Remizov and Bely.

We have seen the attraction of Zamyatin to the primitive and prerational in the matter of his stories; it is now clear that a similar preoccupation governed his manner. He avoids in them the organized method of rational statement in favor of impression, suggestion, and image, conveyed in a language as free as possible of syntactic complexity. (pp. 20-37)

> *Edward J. Brown, in* "Brave New World," "1984," *and* "We": An Essay on Anti-Utopia (Zamyatin *and English Literature*), Ardis, *1976, 61 p.*

MARC SLONIM   (essay date 1977)

[*Slonim was a Russian-born American critic who wrote extensively on Russian literature, including his study* Soviet Russian Literature: Writers and Problems, 1917-1977. *In the following excerpt from that work, he outlines Zamyatin's literary career and discusses his influence on postrevolutionary Russian literature.*]

Two writers exerted a strong influence on post-revolutionary literature between 1918 and 1925. One was Andrey Bely, the symbolist, whose imprint was so obvious in Pilnyak; and the other was Evgeny Zamyatin who spread Remizov's neorealism and his own brand of expressionism among the younger generation. At the beginning of the Soviet regime Zamyatin occupied a unique position: in his early thirties, he could not be identified with the "fathers" who had been swept away or had emigrated, and at the same time he was above the "children" who looked up to him because of his artistic maturity, brilliant craftsmanship, critical integrity, and independence of judgment. He naturally acted as a master, and a combination of personal and literary qualities made him one of the most original figures of the civil war and NEP era.

Zamyatin was born in 1884 in Lebedyan, a seventeenth-century town of Central Russia. "Lebedyan," he says in his autobiographical sketch, "was famous for its card sharpers, gypsy horse-market fairs, and most forceful Russian language, and Tolstoy and Turgenev wrote about it." The thoroughly national environment of Lebedyan gave Zamyatin an intimate knowledge of provincial Russia. In 1902 he entered the Polytechnic in St. Petersburg, traveled as a student across the country and in the Near East, became involved in politics, joined the Bolshevik faction of the Social Democratic Party, was arrested and sentenced to exile, but succeeded in graduating as a naval engineer in 1908. By this time the designs of a torpedo boat and mathematical charts were mixed on his desk with the sheets of his poems and stories. In 1911 Zamyatin's **Tale of a District,** a description of life in a Northern province, written in a new sharp manner, suddenly stirred readers and critics; in two months it was being discussed in some three hundred reviews. Three years later his *At the World's End,* a short novel, also attracted general attention. It dealt with the weird happenings in a military garrison located in a god-forsaken town in Eastern Siberia, and its details were so realistic that nobody believed Zamyatin had never been in the army. The Tsarist authorities sued the author for anti-militarism and subversion.

The two novels, as well as the short stories that followed, were distinctly satirical and attacked the coarseness and brutishness of the lower and middle classes. But their originality lay in the union of a colorful style, ironic observation, and a particular system of images. In each work Zamyatin emphasized a key image, or a "Mother metaphor" (Mirsky), which is used as a visual leitmotif. In the tale **"North,"** Kortoma, a fat, ignorant merchant drinks innumerable tumblers of tea at his samovar—and the curved sides of the copper utensil reflect his face, a distorted ludicrous image; in Kortoma's mind the world is like his own face as mirrored in the samovar: distorted and ugly, and this simile reappears throughout the story. The way Zamyatin treated images corresponded to his carefully planned composition. In his autobiography he mentions his literary beginnings: "In Nikolayev I constructed several bulldozers and a few short stories." A builder of icebreakers and a professor of ship construction, Zamyatin went about his writing with the spirit of a skilled professional: just as he could not permit any miscalculations in his naval blueprints, he could not overlook any flaws in the composition of his novels, tales, and plays. Whatever he wrote was well-planned, well-proportioned, and smoothly finished. He believed that aesthetic forms were subject to laws—not unlike the laws of physics and hydraulics—and so he demanded thorough organization of material, full control of devices, and a "purposeful selection of words."

Some critics believe that this method imparted a certain detachment and a chilly brilliance to his writings. This could have been true with another writer, but Zamyatin, despite all his external dryness and tongue-in-cheek humor, was a warm and sensitive person. During World War I he had gone to Great Britain on a mission to build ice-breakers for Russia, and afterwards friends teased him, contending that English composure was now added to his innate self-control. Alexander Blok called him with friendly mockery "the Englishman from Moscow." Lean, clean-shaven, with reddish hair parted on the side, always wearing tweeds and with an "unextinguishable" pipe in his wide generous mouth, he indeed resembled an Englishman. He spoke in an even voice, hardly changing his inflections when throwing out a sarcastic hint or an ironic allusion; his manners were reserved, and to those who knew him but little he seemed all "buttoned up," a man who kept an "unmelting icicle" inside—some hard core of perfect self-mastery, strong will, and keen intelligence. But this gentleman was an independent artist and a fearless thinker. He combined logic and imagination, precision and fantasy. The technician who preached "functional expressionism" and taught young men how to write a compact, economical prose, was a man of strong passions. Under his balanced exterior were national traits of intensity and deep inner life. Like many people with a scientific background, he loved dreams and irrational flights, and glorified man's desire to overcome all limitations. An enemy of conventional rules and dogmatic structures he had a romantic devotion to freedom and individualism and exposed whatever endangered them. These qualities were expressed with particular vigor in his *The Islanders* (1917) and **"The Fisher of Men."** The first gave an

image of provincial British people who are afraid of Mrs. Grundy and want to exclude "surprising or unexpected emotions" from a well-patterned routine of respectability. The vicar Dewly, author of "Precepts of Compulsory Salvation," demands that everybody live according to a fixed schedule, which would indicate days of prayer and repentance, and the precise times for meals or copulation, for charity or the "intake of fresh air." Lady Kemble finds the sun "shockingly impudent"; she is moreover indignant when the faces and habits of the people she meets are too uncommon. Her son, however, abandons the straight road, falls in love with a show girl, Didi, and kills the gay unconventional Irishman O'Kelly when it turns out that he is Didi's lover. The young man is hanged in the courtyard of the local prison, and everything returns to calm and tradition in the little town. In **"The Fisher of Men,"** Craggs, who speaks of his gains on the stock exchange, actually makes money blackmailing couples who make love in the parks of London. In both tales hypocrisy and mechanical rules are opposed by genuine impulses—open and therefore fatal in young Kemble, hidden and repressed in Lory, Craggs's wife. What made *The Islanders* (as well as other tales written in the 1917-22 period) a model of new literary technique, was not only its compactness and perfect composition, but also the device of significant details and symbolic central images. Young Kemble is like a tractor, he is square, he moves and thinks in straight lines; sudden passion ruins this simple machine. His mother has thin lips, like worms, and the repetition of this comparison serves to delineate her portrait. This stylization gave the works of Zamyatin a structural unity; there was something angular, almost cubistic, in their outlines, and the use of movie-like flashes, of grotesque and ironical dialogue enhanced their theatrical expressionism. In a way Zamyatin's devices were similar to those of modern painting: not only did he render the psychological through the visual, but he also utilized surrealist multiplane composition and symbolic representation of unconscious drives. In his *Flood* (1926), a short novel about a woman suddenly overcome by passion, the emotional awakening is made analogous to the Neva river inundating the banks and islands of Leningrad. The short story **"Mamai"** (1920) starts with the sentence: "In the evening and at night there are no more houses left in Petersburg: only six-storeyed stone ships." This image is then expanded: "The ships, solitary six-storeyed worlds, scud along the stone waves in the midst of other solitary, six-storeyed worlds; the ships gleam with the lights of numberless cabins into the agitated ocean of streets."

The Islanders was published in 1918, while other tales by Zamyatin, including **"North," "The Fisher of Men," "Mamai,"** and **"The Cave,"** appeared in 1922. In the two latter (as well as in his sketches **"The Dragon,"** 1918, **"The Eyes,"** 1918, and in **"The Tale of the Most Essential,"** 1928), Zamyatin described the initial stage of the Communist regime. He portrayed intellectuals being caught up unaware by the revolutionary hurricane and perishing in the frozen cities like the passengers of a ship sinking at sea (the simile of **"Mamai"**). For Martin Martynovich, the hero of **"The Cave,"** revolution meant a step backward into pre-history. He subsists in a cavernous icy cold room and sheds all his moral standards in the struggle for existence. He steals wood for his god—an ugly potbellied stove—but cannot endure his degradation, and prefers death to yielding and becoming a barbarian. Soviet critics attacked Zamyatin for concentrating only on the negative sides of contemporary actuality, but the rift between Zamyatin and the rulers of the day was much more profound.

The censors were annoyed with every work published by the ironic writer. His *Impious Tales* (collected in a book form in 1927) or *Tales for Adult Children* were filled with malicious hints, as were his other stories which seemed to adhere to Anatole France's slogan: "Teach men to laugh at the stupid and the vicious, less we fall prey to the weakness of hating them." Zamyatin presented Soviet bureaucrats as narrow-minded replicas or Tsarist officials; they try to solve all problems, including disasters and epidemics, by posting decrees and regulations ("Famine is strictly forbidden," "Cholera is hereby officially proscribed"). One of Zamyatin's stories dealt with the adventures of a deacon who joined the Bolsheviks and wanted to study Marx, but since at the same time he was in love with a pretty girl called Martha, he was torn between Marthism and Marxism.

Communist critics found most irritating the fact that along with his satirical sketches Zamyatin wrote serious articles claiming that his verbal and compositional experiments were closer to the spirit of the Revolution than the naturalistic snapshots of proletarian writers. His concept of the Revolution [see essay dated 1924] did not coincide with current formulas.

> When two extinguished stars collide with a deafening crash we do not hear and ignite a new star—that is revolution. When Lobachevsky [the Russian mathematical genius] crumbles with his book the walls of the millennial Euclidean world and opens a path into numberless non-Euclidean space, that is revolution. Revolution is everywhere, in everything; it is infinite; the last revolution, the last number does not exist. Social revolution is just one of innumerable numbers: its law is not a social law but an immeasurably greater one—universal, cosmic, similar to that of entropy, of the conservation and disintegration of energy.

What he saw around him stirred him to indignation: he could not call revolution the regimentation and cruelty of a government that was becoming more and more abusive. "Dogma," said Zamyatin, "is the hard crust which imprisons the fiery magma, that molten material from which the hard rock is formed." A former Socialist, he saw Communists becoming dogmatic authoritarians who ruled by oppression and executions and as replacing Tsarist autocracy with Marxist ideocracy. Zamyatin could not accept despotism and pretense, and with all the idealism of a humanitarian intellectual and the devastating irony of a temperamental artist, he fought for the rights of freedom and reason. In his *Fires of St. Dominic* (1922), a historical drama probably inspired by Dostoevsky's "Legend of the Grand Inquisitor," he portrayed the Spanish Inquisition, and under this thin disguise, attacked the Communist terror and the "righteous puritans of the Revolution" who were killing men in order to save mankind.

Zamyatin's articles exposed what he called false art dominated by frisky, sly individuals who knew when to sing hymns to the Tsar and when to the hammer and sickle. "True literature," proclaimed Zamyatin, "can be created only by madmen, hermits, heretics, dreamers, rebels, sceptics, and not by efficient and loyal functionaries . . . I am afraid we won't have true literature unless we are cured of some kind of new catholicism which gets frightened by any heretical word. And if this illness is incurable, I am afraid Russian literature will have but one future: its past." He laughed at the attempts of proletarian writers to bring about a "new literature" which

he dubbed as a "retreat to the 'sixties of the last century." When the extremists demanded "party art" and threatened the non-conformists with repressive measures, Zamyatin defined *October,* the monthly which made the most vicious attacks against "bourgeois writers," as "a periodical which has to do only with one of all the arts: with the military art; its writing is simply a new weapon, in addition to well known mines and gas bombs." Obviously, such "repartees" created what Zamyatin called "negative popularity": he was singled out by the Party press as a dangerous subversive. His dissonant voice, however, was heard far and wide. Zamyatin became a leading figure in Petrograd (and later Leningrad) literary circles; he founded various, and usually short-lived, periodicals, he gave courses and conferences, and he taught techniques of fiction in the "House of Art" to the group of Serapion Brethren. Among those who felt strongly his influence and were to a certain extent his disciples were Vsevolod Ivanov, Konstantin Fedin, Nikolay Nikitin, Mikhail Zoshchenko, Venyamin Kaverin, Yefim Zozulya, Mikhail Slonimsky, Yuri Olesha, and many others. Later Zamyatin said with his usual grin: "I taught them how to write with ninety proof ink." There was a moment when it looked as if Zamyatin would become the head of a whole literary school. He contended that literature was also subject to the laws of dialectics and that from the opposition of naturalism (thesis) and symbolism (antithesis) a new trend had been born, the synthesis of the first two. This neo-realism, or expressionism, he wrote, was legal heir of the past. But Zamyatin's own literary activity was soon curtailed. Branded as an enemy of the regime, Zamyatin endured arrest, persecution, and vituperation, particularly toward the end of the 'twenties. The Communist press offensive against him reached its peak in 1929 because of the publication abroad of his novel *We.*

In 1920 Zamyatin had felt that Communist society might degenerate into an ant heap, into a new, planned, and inescapable state slavery; in this mood he wrote *We,* a satirical picture of a collectivistic utopian city from which individuality and freedom are excluded. The city is roofed over with glass to avoid the intemperate freaks of weather and the insubordination of the climate; the inhabitants are designated by numerals and letters (vowels for females and consonants for males); they wear gray-blue uniforms; their work, thought, and leisure are regulated by the "wise authorities" headed by the Well-Doer or Benefactor; and they can make love only on days and at hours strictly prescribed and designated on special pink tickets issued by government agencies. The houses are of glass and therefore transparent, so the police can see what is going on in each dwelling; microphones pick up conversations; mechanical "eyes" and "ears" are erected in the streets, and the behavior and utterances of all citizens are watched and recorded from the cradle to the grave; electrocution takes care of the few rebels. One of these, D-503, a mathematician and builder of the Integral, a cosmic ship, dares to challenge the Bureau of Guardians and its Day of Unanimity: he commits the crimes of free thought and true love, at one point taking his mistress beyond the Green Wall that separates the city from unadulterated nature, from uncontrolled plants, animals, and menlike beings. But his attempt at revolt is duly liquidated: D-503 undergoes the Great Operation which makes him betray all other Enemies of Happiness and deliver his beloved to the Executors. Reason wins out, and the numbers are isolated from the world of chaos and improvisation by a new high-voltage fence. In *We* Zamyatin again emphasizes the opposition of mechanical rationalism and natural instincts of being. This is one of his main themes: the natural man, with all the variety of his emotions and capacities, with all his glow of imagination and thirst for infinity, is bound to clash with dogmatics, builders of robots and prisons, and with artifical regulations and limitations. Parenthetically, it may be mentioned that *We* was published in English in 1924, thus preceding a score of amazingly similar works by Aldous Huxley, George Orwell, and other social satirists.

Publication of *We* in the Soviet Union was, of course, impossible, but Zamyatin read it at one of the meetings of the Writers' Union in 1924. It went around in manuscript copies, and several Soviet authors referred to it as "one of the most earnest and jocular works Zamyatin ever wrote." In 1927 *We* was about to be translated into Czech, this writer who at that time was the literary editor of *Volia Rossii,* an *émigré* monthly in Prague, got hold of the Russian manuscript of the novel and printed it in his monthly. The introductory note preceding the text stated that this was a re-translation into Russian from the Czech, and to give weight to this assertion the editor had to change or distort Zamyatin's beautiful prose. The subterfuge, however, did not work. The Communist press, which had not paid much attention five years before to the appearance of *We* in English, this time accused its author of impudently challenging the authorities. Dubbed a counter-revolutionary, Zamyatin was compelled to resign from professional organizations and was completely ostracized. Soviet periodicals refused to print one line of the great criminal, the publication of his collected works in several volumes was suspended, and *The Fly,* a comedy Zamyatin adapted from a tale by Leskov, was banned from the theaters despite its huge success with hundreds of performances. As he said later, he became "the Devil of Soviet literature, and since to spit on the Devil is considered a good deed, all the critics did nothing but spit on me as viciously as they could." This sentence was part of a letter Zamyatin addressed to Stalin in 1931 asking for permission to go abroad and "to rest awhile from baiting and persecution." This message to the General Secretary of the Party (never divulged in the Soviet Union) reflected its author's rectitude, courage, and dignity. "I know," Zamyatin wrote, "that I have a very uncomfortable habit of saying not what seems most advantageous at this particular moment or that, but whatever I believe is the truth. Among other things I have never concealed what I think about literary servility, obsequiousness, and turning one's coat. I have always thought, and I continue to think, that such things are as humiliating to the writers as they are to the Revolution . . . I have been sentenced without trial to what amounts, for a writer, to capital punishment—silence . . . I beg that I be allowed to go abroad for a time—so that I may come home as soon as it is possible in our literature to express devotion to great ideas without crawling before small men, and as soon as our attitude toward the artist of the word changes." Thanks to Gorky's intervention, the authorization to leave Russia, was, to the general surprise, granted to Zamyatin and his wife five months later. In 1932 they settled in Paris. He wrote a few stories and scenarios, made a successful film with Jean Renoir of Gorky's *The Lower Depth,* and finished the first part of *Attila,* a historical novel in which the fall of the Roman Empire was described with many concealed references to the current European scene. His health, however, undermined by privations and by the nervous tension under which he lived for years, declined rapidly, and he died of a heart ailment in March 1937. No obituaries in the Soviet press marked his passing; his former friends and disciples were afraid to send their condolences to his widow. The official silence which isolated Zamyatin from Russian readers

during his lifetime continued after his death. It lasted twenty-five years—and while it is being broken now in some critical circles, the works of this brilliant writer are still banned in his native land, and no surveys of Soviet literature dare to give a fair appraisal of the role he played in contemporary Russian prose.

The main impact of Zamyatin in the 'twenties was that of a master who had trained a new generation in craftsmanship. He also was a satirist and the head of that brand of neo-realism closest to European expressionism. His enemies called him a formalist: he actually was a literary professional who loved to experiment in words and plots but put above everything "a well-made story." The reason he provoked such deep antagonism in the Soviet press was due, probably, to the fact that he jeered and laughed when writers were required to sing "hosannah." Moreover, he was a liberal and a socialist, who maintained the best traditions of the Russian intelligentsia, and could not accept a new regime divorced from individual freedom. To a great extent Zamyatin and his friends carried on the ideology of the Russian non-Communist left, and this was why they were so badly treated. Communist dogmatics knew that monarchists and reactionaries represented a lost cause and that the real threat to the dictatorship could come only from traditional Russian socialism, which expressed the dreams of the masses. It was this potential danger that determined the intransigent attitude toward, and the ostracism of, Zamyatin. But the day is not far off, when, regardless of political struggle, new Russian readers will value Zamyatin as an excellent and truly independent writer. (pp. 82-91)

Marc Slonim, "Evgeny Zamyatin: The Ironic Dissident," in his Soviet Russian Literature: Writers and Problems 1917-1977, *second revised edition, Oxford University Press, 1977, pp. 82-91.*

EDWARD W. R. PITCHER (essay date 1981)

[*In the following excerpt, Pitcher analyzes symbolism in* We *and examines its thematic significance.*]

To complement the several general commentaries on the quality and kind of novel which Yevgeny Zamyatin's *We* has been declared to be, I will analyze closely the novel's symbols in this essay and argue for the importance of paying close attention to the text before arriving at judgments of Zamyatin's intent or accomplishments. (p. 252)

[*We*] explores the interplay between the individual and the state as utopian and dystopian fiction inevitably must. The central protagonist is D-503, numbers having replaced names in the closed society conceived by Zamyatin, and the reader follows his progress from unquestioning citizen of the One State to unwilling violator of its laws (seduced to disobedience by I-330, the Mata Hari of the novel and member of the subversive group Mephi), from uncomfortable participant to questioning, passion-inspired collaborator in acts of rebellion (including the conspiracy to seize control of the state's ultimate instrument for domination, an airship called the *Integral*), until finally D-503, fearful of capture, death, and loss of sanity, betrays those who have recruited him, is brainwashed into a new and absolute conformity, and dispassionately witnesses the failure of the Mephi rebellion. However, Zamyatin is as much concerned with the psychological as with the social or political implications of D-503's rebellion, and the symbolism more than the plot directs us to this complex level of the novel's meaningfulness.

Admittedly, one approaches any explication of symbolism with caution when treating a translation of the novel; one cannot assume that even a translator as experienced and careful as Mirra Ginsburg has wholly captured the denotations and connotations, or the metaphoric and symbolic nuances in the original. Nonetheless, where there is a repetitive and emphatic use of specific images and words, we may be justified in undertaking a closer investigation into their function. A casual reader of *We* would surely take some note of its highly "literary" style and the frequent uses of colors, wind and storm, glass and mirrors, fires, electricity, fogs, clouds, waves, eyes, lips, abstract shapes, geometric and algebraic symbols, numerals and letters. The problem for the critic is to discover the key to this profusion of images and symbols, and to judge the appropriateness and effectiveness of the manner of writing to the themes, ideas or dramatized impressions of the novel.

Following one circle of Zamyatin's web of symbols, we find that sky-cloud images reflect the changes in the character and life of D-503. As he moves from complacent acceptance of the One State, through stages of passionate interest in I-330, to conscious individualism precipitated by sexual jealousy and possessiveness, to subversive action, doubt and hesitation, and then back to conformity and un-imagination, we find an analogous movement from calm, blue skies, to lightly clouded skies, to iron-grey clouds, to ever increasing wind and storm, then subsiding of storm and restoration of calm (order) following personal defeat. One finds no difficulty constructing Fretag's pyramid of rising and falling action to represent the stages in this novelesque tragedy.

Similarly, Zamyatin has encircled the "meaning" of the novel by a series of images that can be related to the seasonal shifts from spring to autumn, and therefore to fertility and fruition. Early in the novel (Second Entry), the air is filled with spring pollen that films the lips, leaving a sweet taste. The mouth and lips become a symbol of the female sexual orifice, and by extension the face is an index to sexual passion in D-503's impressionistic descriptions. In the First Entry he feels his "cheeks burning" with the desire "to unbend the wild, primitive curve": "This must be similar to what a woman feels when she first senses within herself the pulse of a new, still tiny, still blind little human being. It is I, and at the same time, not I." The dawning of passion in him, the compulsive attraction to the "sweet" lips of I-330, to consummation of desire, leads to an apparent birth of self, of soul, an "I" beneath the "We." It is a birth reflected both in the rebellion against the state and in the psychological torment within D-503. And like any birth, there is pain and the fear of pain, symbolized by D-503's focus on the teeth behind I-330's inviting lips, the fire within the depth of her eyes, and the fascinating *X* of her features (an impressionistic intersecting of lines in her face).

The sexual imagery penetrates, radially, to the center of the novel. The fertile vegetative world behind the Green Wall is reached by entering an Ancient House with its dark-red walls, past the old woman with the "ingrown" mouth and wrinkled lips from which all the lines of her face radiate outward in a "beaming" smile, inward to a chaos of objects and colors, a huge fireplace and large mahogany bed, and a "closet" that leads secretly downward and up to the other side of the wall. In the Seventeenth Entry, D-503 seeks I-330 at the Ancient House, kisses the "ingrown, soft, mossy mouth" of the old woman who tells him I-330 is there, runs "directly to the bedroom," enters, seeing "the wide bed—smooth, untouched," finds the key in the keyhole of the closet, hears only "drops falling hurriedly into the washstand from the faucet," thinks himself pursued by S (the *betrayer within* the One State), enters the closet and falls: "Slowly, softly, I floated down somewhere, my eyes turned dark, I died."

Of course, "it was a state of temporary death, familiar to the ancients" (orgasm), and he revives, noting "blood on [his] finger" and his "broken, quivering breath." He has arrived on the inside, in tunnels where lights "tremble" as he also soundlessly trembles, and he finds I-330: "Her eyes opened to me—all the way; I entered." She laughed and "sprayed [D-503] with laughter, and the delirium was over, and drops of laughter rang, sparkled all around and everything, everything was beautiful." They return with I-330 "pressed . . . all of her" against D-503, silently, blindly: "she walked just as I did, with closed eyes, blind, her head thrown back, her teeth biting her lips. . . ." He "comes to" as from a dream, returning from a symbolic journey of sexual adventure, having discovered, he believes, the kinship between passion and "soul."

The centrality of his discovery is asserted in a passage that associates the Ancient House with the face of the old woman and with both I-330 and sexual passion: "The starting point of all the coordinates in this entire story is, of course, the Ancient House. It is the centre of all the axial lines of all the X's, Y's and Z's on which my whole world has been built of late." However, Zamyatin clearly intimates that D-503 is experiencing the wild fervor, the fire, of spring passion without regard to true fruitfulness and growth. It is 0-90 who becomes pregnant with real life, not I-330. Her teeth, the presence of the "blade-sharp" doctor who "speaks with scissors," and the threat felt by D-503 sensing I-330's fiery nature, are qualifications and contradictions for one seeking to make too much of the "soul" that D-503 is said to have discovered.

The water dropping in the washstand slips wastefully into the drains. The old woman at the Ancient House is infertile and withered as surely as I-330 is promiscuous and a Mata Hari seductress. I-330, like U (who is also infertile), would use D-503 like a child or dupe, because "love must be ruthless" and revolution must be bloody. The wind of change brings sweet honey pollen to the lips but also dries the mouth; it brings innocent white clouds and "cast-iron slabs," the promise of life-giving rain, and destruction, storm, and sterility. In this world, D-503 is buffetted and drowned and burnt—a pawn and victim of a Nature turned against him, a Nature where $L = f(d)$ and Nature demands "dissolution" of self in the universe as much as Reason demanded a dissolution of self in the One State.

Looking outward from the center of the web, the labyrinth, D-503 confronts the unknown and the irrational. For dramatic reasons, Zamyatin focuses mystery in I-330 (the X dissects her face), and she is the vehicle of the unknown "truths" that are progressively disclosed to D-503—"truths" of passion, jealousy, possessiveness, irrationality, and individuality. The X of I-330 is supplanted, however, by another web centered in the Ancient House, seen as a symbol of the historical past, of paganism and passion, false gods and beliefs, and a life in tune with Nature. It is not the Nature of Thompson or Wordsworth or Goethe, but the Nature of Melville, Hardy and Lawrence—it is the wild energy of the treacherous ocean, the untamed garden, the passion of instinct and desire. It is lawless, permissive, aggressive, and irresistible.

The city-state within the glass wall is shut off from this Nature, but it functions within individuals, suppressed, caged, like the energy latent in a body of water. In the One State, the "energy residing in the waves" has been turned from beast to "domestic animal." Indeed this is exactly what happens to the numbers (citizens), each of whom represents "one of the innumerable waves in this mighty stream." The "blue waves of unifs" in the auditoriums and during the exercise marches are imaged time and again as Zamyatin establishes not only the "quality" of life in the One State, but also focuses upon the dominant symbol of the novel. As we shall see, D-503 conceived of himself fundamentally as at one with the state, as a single wave in the sea, and as this sense of identity is challenged by the discovery of passion, the result is figured forth as an explosive intermixing of fire and water.

Zamyatin emphasizes moments when D-503 feels himself behaving in a manner contrary to state ethics by introducing water symbolism. In the auditorium lecture of the Forth Entry, the anecdote of the Savage and the barometer clearly links "rain" ("algebraic rain") with order and mathematics; D-503 is distracted and shuts out "the vitalizing stream that flowed from the loud-speakers" until "sobered" as the person next to him emits "a tiny bubble of saliva" that "burst" on his lips. Being a drop of water in the sea of numbers, D-503 is unconsciously responsive ("sobered") to the symbolic destruction of that drop of saliva. Liquidation (literally being turned to water) is always a threat for those who stray from state regulation.

When he follows I-330 to the Ancient House (Sixth Entry), he is introduced to the fire burning within her. When she suggests that they fraudulently solicit a sickness excuse slip, D-503 feels obliged by state law to report her, but he is reluctant to destroy the budding relationship. Consequently, his dream at the outset of the Seventh Entry of "sap" flowing over the objects of the Ancient House, leaves him with "some strange, sweet, mortal terror." In the Seventh Entry he is resigned to his "treachery" and I-330 has established a hold over him that becomes a death-grip in later chapters.

In the Eighth Entry, D-503 explains his abhorrence for the irrational through recollections of early mathematical training and his introduction to the square root of minus one. What often is wholly overlooked, however, is that this early period in his mental training was also a period when he developed a subliminal association between water and rational order. The teaching machine was nicknamed Plapa because when "he" was plugged in "the loudspeakers would always start with 'Pla-pla-pla-tsh-sh-sh' and only then go on to the day's lesson." This watery "plash" of sound might easily be passed over were not the passage immediately followed by D-503's conversation with R-13, the poet, whose "rush of words . . . spurt out in a torrent and spray comes flying from his thick lips. Every 'p' is a fountain; 'poets'—a fountain." We are advised, moreover, that D-503 had been instructed in law by a man whose voice came through the loudspeaker like "blasts of violent wind." R-13 had failed in mathematics and subverted the law program by stuffing his speaker with spitballs, but D-503 stored his lessons in mathematical orderliness (water) and state law (wind) in the deeper recesses of his mind.

In the Ninth Entry we are given D-503's account of an execu-

tion in the Cube Plaza. An atomizing ray reduces a "number" to a small puddle of "chemically pure water" and the Benefactor is "wet with spray" from the liquidated "enemy." D-503 accepts the stern order of the state, impressionistically seeing the Benefactor as a man with huge hands that move in "cast-iron" gestures, but the associations between water and death reinforce his earlier learning. The following day he feels "freshly distilled" (an echo of the "chemically pure water" remaining after the purge of the "superfluous" number). He meets with I-330 and is seduced into drinking prohibited alcohol, feeling as a result as one poised over "a seething, scarlet sea of flame" that is also deep "within" himself.

At night his "bed rose and sank and rose again under me, floating along a sinusoid." He fears that he will perish; the sea has turned to flame, "liqueur" is found to be "fiery poison"; fire and water intermingle, struggle to dominate each other, and begin the slow process of self-dissolution as vapors (mist, fog, cloud) inevitably result. The exercise of the Cube Plaza is repeated hereafter on the psychological level and with painful slowness.

From the Eleventh Entry to the Thirteenth Entry, we are moved from "a light mist" to a pervading "fog." The fog seems (to D-503) to dissolve the "glass walls" and even the "gray unifs." It is an acidic fog, sprung from the fire/water elemental confusion in D-503, a fog like "swirling smoke, as in a silent, raging fire." He at once hates and loves it, according to I-330, because it permits him to dissolve (be free of state law). He drank the fire of I-330's lips, "poured" himself into her and "drank her in" in return, and felt "full . . . to the very brim!" In such moments, there is "no State" in his conscious thoughts, but there is always the emblem of the State, the mist and fog, that the fiery sun cannot wholly evaporate. On the day O-90 visits (Fourteenth Entry), the orderliness of State life is resumed, but mist outside implies his thoughts are elsewhere, and he knows that "by nightfall the fog would probably be dense again."

Returning to work on the *Integral,* D-503 rediscovers the secure comfort of collective work, like floating "on the mirror-like untroubled sea," but when questioned about his previous absence and illness he feels that he is "drowning" or "doomed to burn forever." The sea becomes deadly, fiery, vengeful. In the newly discovered world of passion and betrayal of the One State, D-503 finds himself without "rudder" or "controls," directionless, but sure to crash into the ground "or up—into the sun, into the flames." He is alienated, "cast out by a storm upon a desert island," and he senses, unconsciously, that his identity is being eroded away as if by "drops falling slowing from the washstand faucet" or an "impermeable substance softened by some fire"—images repeated in the Seventeenth Entry when he discovers the tunnels below the Ancient House.

The water symbolism flowing from the reflecting and subconscious mind of D-503 becomes increasingly threatening and desperate as his anxiety is heightened. In the Eighteenth Entry, he dreams "like an overturned, overloaded ship. A heavy, dense mass of swaying green water." He dreams of I-330 undressing behind the closet door and himself making love to her. In that moment he sees (in the dream) "a sharp ray of sunlight breaking like a flash of lightning on the floor . . . and now the cruel, gleaming blade fell on the bare outstretched neck of I-330." The crisis has come. D-503 has imaged the destruction (appropriately by fire) of I-330; his subconscious mind seeks its own survival, its liberation from the fear of death by water (the One State), or madness induced by the irrational.

In the following entries, D-503 makes deliberate but ill-sustained efforts to return to normality, but even O-90 subverts his intention as she begs him, with words flowing "like a stream over the dam," to give her a child. After obliging her, he cannot resist following I-330's invitation to the Ancient House (Twenty-first Entry), although he rationalizes his reasons for going. He goes "against a strong wind" (recall the law instructor's windy voice), in a state of suspension and frozen will, and as he approaches the Ancient House, the city is seen initially as "blue blocks of ice," then under the shadow of a cloud, as ice heaving, breaking up to "burst, spill over, whirl, and rush downstream." He fails to find I-330 but views the house "as through water, at the bottom of a deep lake," and searches until "sharp, salty drops of sweat crept down my forehead into my eyes." Then, behind him, he hears the "splashing steps" of S, and feels threatened, alien, under the eyes of this Guardian of the One State. S "plashed away" but leaves a warning that heightens D-503's anxiety and dread. D-503 returns to his rooms and listens "constantly to the wind as it flapped its dark wings against the window."

Despite D-503's subsequent, impassioned encounters with I-330 and his recurrent feeling of dissolving in her like a crystal in water (forgetting all threats from the State), we are repeatedly reminded by Zamyatin's symbols that there is still "the wind flapping huge wings" and always, increasingly, cloudiness, storm, imminent disaster. D-503's "true" self is restored, from time to time, as he cools his passions; "Quick—cold water, logic. I pour it by the pailful, but logic hisses on the red-hot bearings and dissipates into the air in whiffs of white elusive steam."

When the state is openly threatened (as in the "election" of the twenty-fifth entry), he anticipates instantaneous recriminations because his guilt makes him feel complicity in any "crime." The very air appears to him as "transparent cast iron"—an association with the benefactor, lawmaker and executioner. Later D-503 remarks that where "mephi" had been put on the wall people shied away "as if a pipe had burst there and cold water were gushing out . . . and I was also showered with cold water, shaken, thrown off the sidewalk." From his guilt-ridden perspective, the "water" of the state threatens him most, hits him directly. Most significantly, he is not heated by the "fever" of revolution; like the *Integral* he can be fired up, but he carries a ballast of water.

The abortive attempt to take over the *Integral,* and the effort of the State to put down revolution through the Great Operation, leave D-503 with a compulsive desire to be finally cured. Initially he wants to kill U, the informer, but he realizes (through her misinterpretation of his intentions) that the urge to kill is linked to the sexual passions that have been part of his "sickness." He pursues her with "dry" mouth, down "stairs disgustingly slippery, liquid," while the wind howls outside, but he realizes the absurdity of U's sexual submission to him, knows he has been "locked within the same circle" (symbolized by the glass steel hoop of a bandage about his head), and finally is purged of passion.

He goes to the Benefactor (Thirty-sixth Entry) and learns that perhaps I-330 had merely used him. He struggles not to accept this hint of ultimate betrayal, but the wedge is in and the "edges of the crack spread wider." In the moment of his struggle, the Mephi break down the Glass Wall and open rebellion in the State provides an analogy for the psychological turmoil in D-503. In one last meeting with I-330, he tremblingly pours a glass of water, tremblingly resists her, tries to drink the water and is nauseated, but manages to break the hold she has over him (her lips now are cold). The next day, his reconstruction is complete, and he is able to seize and gulp "greedily" the glass of water left from the previous day. He goes to the Guardians to betray I-330 and cleanse his conscience, but in a final twist, Zamyatin has him interviewed by S, and D-503 realizes that S is an agent of the Mephi—that treachery is housed in the very heart of the One State, that the corruption is *within*. The only means of rooting it out is to submit to the surgical solution provided by the Great Operation.

Throughout the course of his narration, D-503 has repeatedly represented his struggle and the struggle between the Mephi and the One State as an opposition between contradictory, wholly incompatible philosophies and perspectives on life. The opposition between the rational and irrational, between mathematical orderliness in the harmoniously functioning collective and passion-based individualism in the anarchic world of "Nature" is symbolized as an opposition between water and fire, between the present and past, stability and flux. In the words of I-330, the opposition is between energy and entropy: the party of "energy" is dedicated to the maintenance of dissimilar forces or the collision of like forces "to get fire, explosion"; the party of "entropy" is dedicated to the dissipation of energy by the orderly spreading of uniformity, sameness. The one sacrifices ease and contentment for struggle and ecstasy; the other sacrifices struggle and ecstasy for ease and contentment. The polarized viewpoints are, in Zamyatin's representation of them, mirror images of each other, or even constituent parts of the same reflecting mirror.

In a pluralistic world, opposites truly exist; they are realities to contend with. In Zamyatin's *We,* D-503 thought he underwent a personal experience of those opposites colliding, internally and externally in self and state. It is an experience figured forth as a perilous, exciting intermixing of fire and water, individualism versus collectivism, passion versus reason, the "natural" versus the artificial, fertility versus infertility. For D-503 it is also an experience that necessitates a choice between order and disorder, between a sureness of identity and a confusion and madness. He is psychologically incapable of conceiving of identity based upon an embracing or straddling of the opposites within himself or within the State. The "wall" is utterly essential and "white cannot at the same time be black." For D-503 it is a sickness of "soul" or excess of treacherous "imagination" that allows one to conceive of the universe as inherently uncontainable, undefinable, infinite and ineffable. For citizens of the One State, such thinking constitutes a form of psychological suicide.

D-503 did indeed have the necessary "sickness of soul," but it was more than he could withstand. When he is fired by passion, he *walls* out thought of the One State (water) from his consciousness. The exercise is futile, of course, as the unconscious mind spills over with images of threatening water, sap, fog, wind. He struggles to balance and synthesize the warring elements, seeing "a sea of flame" or "molten drops" of self, but he cannot achieve a new monism, a "single firewater," and opts for the surgical removal of imagination in order to rediscover the old monism. He could not play the double role of I-330 or S-4711, and he could not resist contemplating the other side of each "wall"—that which lies beyond the fixed and finite.

In *We,* the choice is not between the Natural World and the One State, the Garden and the City, because D-503 is not free to choose, and representatives of both worlds are shown to be vicious, ruthless, and self-seeking pseudophilosophers. D-503's dilemma is the human dilemma; we cannot opt for one or other side of the polarized positions in the novel. We cannot wall in an idea and think that truth has been circumscribed; we cannot conceive of a finite universe without immediately asking what lies beyond the area circumscribed by logic or mathematical calculation. However, we must retain the wisdom and the psychological capacity to live with the ineffable, the irresolvable, the ambiguous and the irrational. We must forego the belief in utopia (Eden or the New Jerusalem) without relinquishing the dream. (pp. 252-60)

> *Edward W. R. Pitcher, "That Web of Symbols in Zamyatin's 'We',"* in Extrapolation, *Vol. 22, No. 3, Fall, 1981, pp. 252-61.*

GORMAN BEAUCHAMP (essay date 1983)

[*Beauchamp is an American critic who has written numerous studies of fantasy, science fiction, and utopian fiction. In the following excerpt, he focuses on the intellectual precedents of* We *and examines its mythic structure.*]

The dystopian novel, in formulating its warning about the future, fuses two modern fears: the fear of utopia and the fear of technology. If, as Zamiatin's fellow émigré Nicholas Berdyaev claims, in that passage made famous as epigraph to *Brave New World,* twentieth-century society is moving toward utopia, then it is doing so through the agency of modern technology. The utopian ideations of the past, that once seemed impossible of historical actualization, appear in our century not only possible, but perhaps inevitable, given the increasing array of techniques for social control made available by our science. As these venerable idola—Plato's *Republic,* say, or Tommaso Campanella's *City of the Sun* or Etienne Cabet's *Voyage to Icaria*—threatened, in modernized form, to replace the societies they had criticized, the image of utopia loomed more ominous, its darker implications for human freedom and initiative more apparent. What could be entertained on paper with detachment proved more disturbing when projected or practiced on flesh-and-blood subjects. Having himself lived through, and supported, a revolution of utopian aspirations, Zamiatin early on perceived its pernicious consequences—a decade before the rise of Stalin—and portrayed them with prophetic insight: so prophetic, indeed, that the Soviet regime has never allowed his novel to be published in Russia. But the satire in *We* is inclusive of much more than a specific regime or a particular revolution: it comprehends modes of thought, millennial expectations, chiliastic dogma, a mechanistic Weltanschauung that have come increasingly to characterize Western culture and of which Soviet Marxism is only one manifestation, albeit an important and portentous one. (pp. 56-7)

Over the United State depicted in *We,* a glass-enclosed city separating its strictly regimented inhabitants from the natural world, hovers the oppressive spirit of the Grand Inquisitor, Feodor Dostoevsky's crypto-political spokesman for utopian authoritarianism. His heretical betrayal of Christianity, ironically presented in the parable of Ivan in *The Brothers Karamazov,* has become the inflexible orthodoxy of the United State; and he is reincarnated in Zamiatin's figure of the Well-Doer, the godlike ruler who takes all freedom into his own hands and offers a mindless contentment in its place. From the Grand Inquisitor, through the Well-Doer, stems that line of spokesmen for dystopia that runs from Mustapha Mond in Aldous Huxley's *Brave New World* and O'Brien in George Orwell's *1984* to the Darling Dictator of L. P. Hartley's *Facial Justice,* Captain Beatty of Ray Bradbury's *Fahrenheit 451* and Wei of Ira Levin's *This Perfect Day.* In his rejection of the benevolent tyranny of the Grand Inquisitor, Zamiatin must be counted among Dostoevsky's most ardent followers. But if the Grand Inquisitor (cum the Well-Doer) is the perverted god of Zamiatin's negative utopia, Frederick Winslow Taylor is his prophet. Taylor, the father of scientific management, plays a role in *We* analogous to that of Henry Ford in *Brave New World:* the exponent of a philosophy of industrial efficiency that reduces man to an appendage of his machines. In *We* Zamiatin meshes utopian social theory with the principles of scientific management, the Grand Inquisitor with Frederick Taylor, as the ideological antagonists of his satire.

The apologia of the Grand Inquisitor embodies arguments, ironically but not inaccurately, for a paternalistic *Führerprinzip* ["leader principle"] that both sums up and anticipates a pervasive impulse of the utopian imagination. From Plato's philospher-kings, Campanella's Hoh, and Francis Bacon's Fathers of the House of Solomon to the scientific elites of H. C. de Saint-Simon and Auguste Comte, the Samurai of H. G. Wells, Lenin's Central Party, and B. F. Skinner's behavioral engineers, the benevolent dictator who will control men's destinies for them has been a hallmark of authoritarian utopias. The rationale for the utopian abrogation of individual freedom, for the imposition of a ruling elite on the weak and muddled mass of mankind nowhere receives starker articulation than in the words of the Grand Inquisitor; but brutal as his diagnosis of the human condition is, it only makes overt the assumptions that lurk, draped by benevolence, in the subtext of utopia.

Chief of these assumptions holds that man cannot cope with freedom: "Nothing has ever been more insupportable for a man and a human society," the Grand Inquisitor declares, "than freedom." He will willingly relinquish it for security, for contentment, for bread. "No science will give them bread so long as they remain free. In the end they will lay their freedom at our feet, and say to us, 'Make us your slaves, but feed us.' " (pp. 57-8)

In the Grand Inquisitor's philosophy are to be found the informing principles of Zamiatin's United State. Its citizens rejoice in their non-freedom, in their childlike yielding to omnipotent authority. "Why is the dance beautiful?" muses the novel's narrator. "Answer: because it is *unfree* movement. Because the deep meaning of the dance is contained in its absolute, ecstatic submission, in the ideal of nonfreedom." Or again: "It is pleasant to feel that somebody's penetrating eye is watching you from behind your shoulder, lovingly guarding you from making the most minute mistake, from the most minute incorrect step." The eye over the shoulder belongs to the Bureau of Guardians, the Well-Doer's secret police who monitor and correct any deviation from the state's norms. So deeply has D-503—the narrator—internalized these norms that the rumor that some of his fellow citizens seek "liberation from the beneficial yoke of the State" horrifies him:

> Liberation! It is remarkable how persistent human

criminal instincts are! I use deliberately the word "criminal," for freedom and crime are as closely related as—well, as the movement of an aero and its speed: if the speed of an aero equals zero, the aero is motionless; if human liberty is equal to zero, man does not commit any crime. That is clear. The way to rid man of criminality is to rid him of freedom.

These passages illustrate Zamiatin's filiation with Dostoevsky in the articulation of a proto-totalitarian social theory that permeates his dystopia: the Grand Inquisitor, then, is one antagonist. But the language of the narrator suggests the second antagonist, an ultratechnocratic rationalism for which Frederick Taylor stands as Zamiatin's synecdoche.

Early in the novel, D-503 describes the daily regimen of the Numbers, as the citizens of the United State are designated:

> Every morning, with six-wheeled precision, at the same hour, at the same minute, we wake up, millions of us at once. At the very same hour, millions like one, we begin our work, and millions like one, we finish it. United into a single body with a million hands, at the very same second, designated by the Tables, we carry the spoons to our mouths; at the same second we all go out to walk, go to the auditorium, to the halls for Taylor exercises, and then to bed.

This passage provides not only the novel's first reference to Taylor but an encapsulation of the effect of Taylorism extended throughout an entire society. From the publication of his *Principles of Scientific Management* in 1911, Taylor's system for the structuring of industrial operations enjoyed a considerable vogue in both the United States and Europe, particularly in the years immediately after World War I. In his first months in power Lenin strongly endorsed Taylorism as the best means of enhancing Soviet economic power. "The Soviet Republic must at all costs adopt all that is valuable in the achievements of science and technology in this field," he wrote. "We must organize in Russia the study of teaching of the Taylor system and systematically try it out and adapt it to our purposes." Himself a naval engineer and faculty member of the Saint Petersburg Polytechnic Institute, Zamiatin clearly recognized the appeal that Taylorism made to the emerging technocratic elite of the Soviet Union, eager to consolidate its political revolution with an industrial one.

Beyond its promise of increased industrial capacity, however, Zamiatin saw that Taylorism embodied basic utopian ideals, only expressed in new terminology; indeed, were Plato or Cabet or Edward Bellamy—or the Grand Inquisitor—transported to the twentieth century, he would have found a kindred spirit in Frederick Taylor. For Taylor had adapted to the factory the model of the organic, conflict-free society—hierarchically structured, with strict division of labor and the reduction of individuals to cogs in a rationally regulated machine—that marked utopias in the Platonic tradition. Zamiatin, in turn, reconverts the factory model into a social one, drawing out the dystopian implications of commitment to a purely rational efficiency. (pp. 59-60)

In the sociomachia of his dystopia, then, Zamiatin establishes as his coantagonists utopian social theory, as redacted by the Grand Inquisitor, and the scientific management of Frederick Taylor, which symbolizes the reductio ad absurdum of the technological world-view. The techniques of the latter made the reification of the former appear only too possible to Zamiatin, who at a propitious moment in history fused these elements into a fictive projection of a nightmare future when man had been transformed into a machine, an efficient, obedient, mindlessly content robot incapable of freedom. Or almost incapable: for a band of rebels makes one last stand against the utopian technique of the United State. In them are embodied the protagonistic values of Zamiatin's novel—freedom, spontaneity, fancy, the individual's own foolish will.

Just as Dostoevsky provided, in the figure of the Grand Inquisitor, one antagonistic force for *We,* so in *Notes from Underground* he provides a figure whose arguments against utopian authoritarianism and technocratic mechanization are echoed distinctly by the rebels against the United State—I-330, R-13, even D-503 in his awakened or "sick" state: indeed, if the Well-Doer is a reincarnation of the Grand Inquisitor, D-503 is clearly an avatar of the Underground Man. In addition, just as Zamiatin fuses arguments from a literary source with those from a sociohistorical source—the Grand Inquisitor with Taylorism—in establishing the thesis in his dialectic, so in establishing its antithesis he unites the literary anarchism of the Underground Man with the theories of the historical Anarchists that Russia so plentifully bequeathed to a reluctant Europe throughout the latter part of the nineteenth century. Michael Bakunin is the representative figure here, symbolic, like Taylor, of a world-view contesting for dominance in the modern age; as such, his anti-statist, anti-authoritarian, anti-technocratic stance dominates Zamiatin's dystopia. *We* is, in its ideological stance, clearly anarchistic.

Notes from Underground launches a polemic against the technocratic utopianism of the mid-nineteenth-century *raznochintzi* or so-called Nihilists, whose ideas were disseminated most widely in the soddenly didactic novel of N. G. Chernyshevsky, *What Is To Be Done?* Chernyshevsky argues for a theory of "rational egotism," a belief that people invariably act from selfish motives, but that, once they are enlightened by science, the selfish and the rational will become identical: to know the good will be to do the good. Creating a "rational" environment thus becomes the first priority of the *raznochintzi,* for once society is scientifically structured, man could not act unreasonably if he wanted to, since to do so would violate his basic (selfish) nature. The result will be utopia—a utopia, as presented in the famous Fourth Dream of Vera Pavlovna, like the Crystal Palace of 1851: "Glass and steel, steel and glass." In this Crystal Palace everyone is happy, rational, moral; machines do all the work: the millennium has arrived on the wings of scientific determinism and the hedonic calculus.

The notion that man will inevitably act according to rationally calculated advantage strikes Dostoevsky's Underground Man as both absurd and pernicious. Nothing in human history, he protests, supports the claim that man will ever learn to live by reason alone, or even wants to: instead, he seeks to follow his "own foolish will!" (pp. 62-3)

For the Underground Man the Crystal Palace signifies not the true culmination of man's desires, but a prison that encloses him in its rigid system of reason: utopia raises a wall, and the Underground Man rejects all walls. Zamiatin, who sets his nightmare dystopia in the glass-walled Crystal Palace of Chernyshevsky's fantasy, echoes this rejection. The Green Wall that separates the United State from the natural world is one of Zamiatin's central symbols throughout the novel, palpable evidence of utopia's denial of freedom; thus it becomes the target of the rebels who conspire to destroy the Green Wall "and all other walls, so that the green wind may blow over all the earth, from end to end." In this creative/destructive act, as in all their anti-utopian program, Zamiatin's protagonistic rebels appear clearly as the ideological descendants of Dostoevsky's Underground Man.

Thus when D-503 awakens from his utopian torpor to discover the Underground dimension of his own personality, this "sickness" conveys the novel's positive values. These are the values of the heretic, of the nay-sayer to all orthodoxies, of Zamiatin himself. Repeatedly in his essays, Zamiatin affirms that "the world is kept alive by heretics," that "heretics are the only (bitter) remedy against the entropy of human thought." If, in his praise of the heretic as the exemplar of anarchic freedom and creative energy in a world of stultifying systems, Zamiatin shows himself the spiritual heir of the Underground Man, he also demonstrates his filiation with the political Anarchists, particularly with Bakunin, who, like Zamiatin, resolutely rejected the imposition of all orthodoxy, all system on life. (p. 64)

In particular, he shares with Bakunin two motifs that figure centrally in *We:* a dread of technocratic tyranny and a celebration of Satanic rebellion against the enforced perfection of paradise. In the century when science was assuming the status of a new religion and scientists enjoyed unrivaled prestige, Bakunin's was one of the few voices raised against the potential for tyranny that science and scientists posed; he foresaw and decried the rise of technocracy. Suppose, he suggests in *God and the State,* in a scenario of social Taylorism with Baconian overtones,

> a learned academy, composed of the most illustrious scientists, were charged with the lawful organization of society, and that, inspired by the purest love for truth, it framed only laws in absolute harmony with the latest discoveries of science. Such legislation, I say, and such organization would be a monstrosity. . . . [A] society which obeyed legislation emanating from a scientific academy, not because it understood its rational character but because this legislation was imposed by the academy in the name of science which the people venerated without comprehending it, would be a society not of men but of brutes.

Such a state as Bakunin hypothesizes here describes precisely the United State in *We* where the rule of scientific rationalism results not in autonomous individuals capable of thinking for themselves, but in the sheeplike Numbers, parroting slogans of reason and science that they do not understand. It is the old paradox of Plato's *Republic* in which the great majority of men must rest content with *eikasia* ["image"], while the handful of philosophic rulers alone achieve *noesis* ["intelligence"]. Under such an authoritarian system as science would impose, Bakunin contends, "the State becomes the patrimony of the bureaucratic class and then falls—or, if you will, rises—to the position of a machine." This perception of the state as a bureaucratic machine is graphically realized in Zamiatin's dystopia.

Throughout much of the nineteenth century the mythic figure that embodied revolutionary aspirations was Prometheus, the rebellious fire-bringer: Marx himself employed the mythic Titan for this symbolic purpose. But for others—Pierre Joseph Proudhon, for example—Satan proved the truer archetype for the individual in rebellion against tyrannical authority. Bakunin was of Satan's party: he believed that the instinct to revolt—lèse majesté—made up one of the basic

Drawing of Zamyatin in 1927.

"moments" in the development of humanity, and thus he pays homage to Satan as the original rebel, enemy of the God-State, true friend of human freedom. His version of the Fall of Man is a *felix culpa* with a distinctly unorthodox twist: "To entice man to eat of the forbidden fruit of the tree of knowledge, God had but to command him: 'Thou Shalt Not!' This immoderation, this disobedience, this rebellion of the human spirit against all imposed limits, be it in the name of science, be it in the name of God, constitutes his glory, the source of his power and of his liberty." This ironic inversion of the Myth of the Fall, with all its value signs reversed, provides the central structural metaphor of *We.* In his own ironic redaction of Genesis, Zamiatin pits the antagonistic forces sketched above—the utopian political theory of the Grand Inquisitor and the mechanistic social order of Taylor, meshed in the image of the United State as neo-Eden with the Well-Doer as the new Jehovah—against the protagonistic forces represented by the Underground Man and Bakunin: anarchism, heresy, the "sinful" quest for freedom and knowledge. Significantly, the rebellious Numbers of *We* are called the *Mephi,* followers of Mephistopheles. In dystopia, where the state claims the omniscience and omnipotence of God, the Party of Satan becomes the only hope of those who resist becoming robots.

In its narrative structure, *We* is a log or series of Records of D-503, begun as a testimonial to the perfect order of the United State. As the designer of the spaceship *Integral,* whose mission "is to subjugate to the grateful yoke of reason the unknown beings who live on other planets, and who are still perhaps in the primitive state of freedom," he intends his log to convey to them what "we" think: "*We,* therefore, shall be the title of my records." When the reader first encounters him, D-503 is seemingly a well-adjusted Number, worshipful of the Well-Doer, content in his glass cubicle under the watchful eyes of the Bureau of Guardians, moving effortlessly in the clockwork rhythm of the regimen set by the Tables of Hours. For the few Private Hours in the week, he has an assigned sex partner, O-90; but the Private Hours represent the one remaining defect in the design of the state, due for elimination in the final "celebration of *all* over *one,* the *sum* over the *individual.*" Otherwise, the Well-Doer's in his heaven and all's right with the United State: no change in the social order is conceivable, the petrifaction of paradise reigns. "The ideal (it's clear) is to be found where nothing *happens,*" writes D-503, but then "something *happened* to me." What *happens* to him is I-330.

In the dystopian novel there must be, as Irving Howe notes [in his *Decline of the New,* 1970], a flaw in the perfection of the perfect. I-330, a strangely enigmatic Number, who appears to D-503 "like an irrational component of an equation that you cannot eliminate." represents the flaw in the United State's perfection. She seduces D-503, literally and figuratively, away from his loyalty to the Well-Doer by awakening in him the sense of his instinctual, animal self—a sexual self-awareness that, Zamiatin implies, is the strongest source of man's individualism. Whether or not Zamiatin had read Freud, he invests the conflict in *We* with a decidedly Freudian substructure: that is, he motivates D-503's revolt against the rationalism of utopia by positing in his protagonist a subconscious, irrational-erotic drive that surfaces to consciousness through the sexual temptations of I-330. The eternal seductress beneath the drab Unif, I-330 has charms that prove stronger than the state's mathematical formulae. She tempts D-503 to sexual disobedience, and he falls: "Suddenly her arms were around my neck . . . her lips grew into mine, even somewhere much deeper, much more terrible."

The experience proves shattering:

> I became glass-like and saw within myself. There were two selves in me. One, the former D-503, Number D-503; and the other. . . . Before, that other used to show his hairy paws from time to time, but now that whole other self left his shell. The shell was breaking.

The other (unconscious) self emerging from the shell that civilization had constructed around it now begins to dream, a phenomenon symptomatic among the Numbers of mental disorder. And, indeed, by the utopian standard of the United State, D-503 has become "sick."

> I *felt* myself. To feel one's self, to be conscious of one's personality, is the lot of an eye inflamed by a cinder, or an infected finger, or a bad tooth. A healthy eye, or finger, or tooth is not felt; it is non-existent, as it were. Is it not clear, then, that consciousness of oneself is sickness?

The question is, of course, ironic, since D-503's "sickness," like that of the Underground Man, constitutes for Zamiatin the human essence, that which separates man from the robot. And sexuality he presents as the force that liberates consciousness, frees man from the utopian state's repression of his instincts, and gives rise to his individualism, his imagination. "I know that I have imagination," the post-lapsarian D-503 realizes, "that is what my illness consists of. And more than that: I know that it is a wonderful illness—one does not want to be cured, simply does not want to!"

What I have described so far of the mythos or plot of the novel will have suggested the myth that underlies it: Zamiatin is ironically rehearsing the Myth of the Fall. His dramatis personae are the cast of Genesis, with their value signs reversed: D-503 is Adam, I-330 is Eve, and the Well-Doer Jehovah—an identification made explicit in the description of his appearance on the Day of Unanimity: "This was always the most magnificent moment of our celebration: all would remain sitting motionless, joyfully bowing our heads under the salutary yoke of that Number of Numbers" as "He descend[ed] to us from the sky, He—the new Jehovah—in an aero, He, as wise and lovingly cruel as the Jehovah of the ancients." Indeed, Zamiatin has the poet R-13 (secretly a Mephi) spell out, with conscious irony, the parallel between Eden and the United State.

> That legend referred to us of today, did it not. Yes. Only think of it for a moment. There were two in paradise and the choice was offered to them: happiness without freedom or freedom without happiness. No other choice. . . . They, fools that they were, chose freedom. Naturally, for centuries afterward they longed for fetters, for the fetters of yore. . . . For centuries! And only we found the way to regain happiness. . . . The ancient god and we, side by side at the same table! We helped god to defeat the devil definitely and finally. It was he, the devil, who led people to transgression, to taste pernicious freedom—he, the cunning serpent. And we came along, planted a boot on his head, and . . . squash! Down with him! Paradise again! We returned to the simple-mindedness of Adam and Eve.

But this Adam and Eve, true to prototype, reject the security of paradise for the dangerous knowledge of good and evil. The rest of *We* is the tale of their rebellion.

I-330's motive for rebellion is overtly political: a leader of the Mephi, she is dedicated to the overthrow of the Well-Doer, to the collapse of the United State, to the destruction of the Green Wall. Through her, Zamiatin voices his own anti-utopian, anti-rationalistic, anti-mechanistic attitudes. She combines a faith in cultural primitivism with a Bakuninesque attachment to apocalyptic anarchy, that creative desire to destroy the mechanical order of utopia in the hope of freeing the Numbers for a fuller, more natural existence. Beyond the Wall lives a race of "savages," the antithesis of the denatured Numbers within it; they represent, I-330 tells her lover, " 'the half we have lost,' " the instinctual half without which the purely intellectual man is incomplete: " 'these two halves must be reunited'." The reintegration of the Numbers with nature constitutes the Mephi's program.

Under the sexual spell of I-330, D-503 becomes a rebel for reasons of passion rather than of politics; his treason is that of a man blindly following his heart. "I want to be with I-330. I want her every minute, every second, to be with me, with no one else. All that I wrote about Unanimity is of no value. . . . For I know (be it sacrilege, yet it is the truth) that a Glorious Day is possible only with her and only when we are side by side." She has, in fact, robbed him of his reason; after spending an ecstatic night with I-330, he struggles to rationalize his confused sensations: "Of course it is clear that in order to establish the true meaning of a function one must establish its limit. It is also clear that yesterday's 'dissolution in the universe' taken to its limit is death. For death is exactly the most complete dissolution of self in the universe. Hence: $L = f(d)$, love is the function of death." Such a "reasonable" conclusion would leave a healthy Number no alternative but to reject the fatal allure of love—as D-503 tries spasmodically to do, for he is a reluctant rebel. But, "the horror of it is that even now, when I have integrated the logical function, when it becomes evident that the function contains death hidden within it, still I long for it with my lips, my arms, my heart, with every millimeter." Eros aroused in him, D-503 is no longer a healthy Number; he will sacrifice everything, Adam-like, for his obdurate Eve.

He agrees to turn over to the Mephi the *Integral,* to be used to destroy the Wall and topple the Well-Doer. But their plans for the spacecraft fail, thwarted by the Gestapo-like Bureau of Guardians, and even though they manage to breach the Wall and foment an uprising, it too appears doomed to failure at the novel's end. D-503 is captured by the Guardians and forced to undergo the Great Operation, a kind of lobotomy by X-ray, that leaves the Numbers "perfect . . . mechanized." His "fancy" thus removed, D-503 reverts to perfect Numberhood: docile, content, unable to feel love for any but the Well-Doer, again a smoothly functioning cog in the machine state. Sitting beside the Well-Doer, he watches blankly as I-330 is tortured to death: "When they began pumping the air from under the Bell she threw her head back and half-closed her eyes; her lips were pressed together. This reminds me of something. She looked at me, holding the arms of the chair firmly. She continued to look until her eyes closed." He cannot remember who she is, but is convinced that her death is right, "for reason must prevail." The Great Operation, the United State's "final solution," has rendered further rebellion impossible in this glass and steel new Eden; D-503's has been man's last disobedience.

The single grace note in the novel's pessimistic conclusion comes, faintly, from O-90, who, in violation of the state's "maternal norms," has conceived a child by D-503 and fled beyond the Wall to give it birth. Her natural primitivism—centered in the womb, in the nurturing instinct of a mother—thus manages a modest victory over utopia, which from Plato on has shown a marked hostility toward mothers. As with the "proles" in *1984,* whatever hope the novel holds lies with the primitives, with the savages beyond the Wall who have escaped the yoke of Reason. (pp. 65-70)

> *Gorman Beauchamp, "Zamiatin's 'We',"* in No Place Else: Explorations in Utopian and Dystopian Fiction, *Eric S. Rabkin, Martin H. Greenberg, Joseph D. Olander, eds., Southern Illinois University Press, 1983, pp. 56-77.*

PATRICK A. McCARTHY (essay date 1984)

[*McCarthy is an American critic specializing in modern English and Irish literature. In the following essay, he addresses Zamyatin's presentation of technology and the Romantic imagination in* We.]

In a 1918 essay entitled **"Scythians?"** Yevgeny Zamyatin set forth his belief that the reach of the true revolutionary should exceed his grasp. The question mark in his title signifies that Zamyatin doubted that the ideologue Ivanov-Razumnik and other "Scythians" (*Skify*) were upholding the romantic ideals of the nomadic tribe from which this association of writers and intellectuals took its name. Reasserting the belief in perpetual revolution that the Scythians embraced before the Bolshevik Revolution of October 1917, Zamyatin defined the Scythian as "an eternal nomad" whose being revolts against the constraints of civilized existence. Thus, for Zamyatin, the Scythian is "the spiritual revolutionary, the romantic"; like the crucified Christ, he is the emblem of freedom. His enemy or antitype, however, is the oppressive, institutionalized Christ, "the grand inquisitor" whose mission is to stamp out freedom wherever it arises. Challenging the judgment of Ivanov-Razumnik, Zamyatin cites the writer Alexey Remizov as an example of a Scythian; as the grand inquisitor, we have N. V. Krylenko, a public prosecutor and a type of the people who, Zamyatin says, "have covered Russia with a pile of carcasses, who are dreaming of socialist-Napoleonic wars in Europe—throughout the world, throughout the universe!" For Zamyatin, the true writer must be a Scythian, that is, a heretic and revolutionary constantly in revolt against the Krylenkos of the world. Inevitably, as Alex Shane observes [in his *Life and Works of Evgenij Zamjatin,* 1968], Zamyatin regarded the fate of the writer-prophet as "a Faust's eternal dissatisfaction with the present and the attainable."

Similar ideas appear in a 1923 essay entitled **"On Literature, Revolution, Entropy, and Other Matters"** [see essay dated 1924], where the Krylenko types are recognizable in what Zamyatin there calls the "dead-alive" people, those who are like machines in that they "make no mistakes" and "produce only dead things." The heretics, on the other hand, are like the Scythians: they are "alive-alive" people, "constantly in error, in search, in questions, in torment." Errors, Zamyatin asserts, "are more valuable than truths: truth is of the machine, error is alive." Truth, however, can never really be fixed and mechanical, for "today's truths become errors of tomorrow; there is no final number."

Between these two essays, Zamyatin wrote, but was denied permission to publish, his anti-utopian novel *We,* which made its first appearance, in English translation, in 1924. Several ideas in these essays figure prominently in *We:* the reference to people who dream of socialist wars "throughout the universe" foreshadows the building of the spaceship *Integral,* whose mission is to help spread the gospel of Reason to other planets in order to release their inhabitants from the primitive state of freedom; the dichotomy of energy and entropy, introduced in the later essay, had already been developed as an important theme in *We;* and the declaration that "there is no final number" is logically derived from the conversation of I-330 and D-503 in chapter 30 of the novel.

Such connections are obvious; less obvious, I believe, are the ways in which the essays might help us to reconcile the political and technological levels of meaning in Zamyatin's futuristic nightmare fantasy, a novel that Zamyatin described as "a warning against the twofold danger which threatens humanity: the hypertrophic power of the machines and the hypertrophic power of the State." The logic behind that dual warning seems to be implied by the machine imagery used throughout *We,* and by the Promethean sequence in the novel that apparently developed out of Zamyatin's involvement with the Scythian writers during the early years of the Soviet state.

1. Criticism of *We* has tended to focus on one side of Zamyatin's warning or on the other. George Orwell, for example [see excerpt dated 1946], called the novel "in effect a study of the Machine, the genie that man has thoughtlessly let out

of its bottle and cannot put back again." Some other critics, emphasizing the political satire in the book, have regarded it as essentially an anti-Bolshevik tract, a protest against the growing totalitarianism of Soviet Russia. In retrospect, however, it is possible to see that the focus on technological politics—or on the political implications of technology—is evident from the first page of *We,* where the narrator, D-503, opens the first page of his diary by copying, "word for word," the State newspaper's announcement of the purpose of the *Integral* and the need for Numbers (citizens) to compose essays, poems, or other writings "on the greatness and beauty of the United State"; these compositions, in turn, will be the *Integral's* first cargo, a barrage of propaganda aimed at those unfortunate free beings who may live on other planets. Reduced at the beginning of his diary to the most mechanical of literary activities—copying an official announcement—D-503 soon declares his intent to record what *he* sees and thinks, and to offer the result as "a derivative of our life, of our mathematical, perfect life in the United State." Mechanical copying has given way to the expression of personal feelings; yet in keeping with his political conditioning D-503 is unable to admit that he really enjoys the freedom of expression that a diary record will allow him: the diary, he insists, will record not just what *he* sees and thinks but, "to be more exact, the things *we* think." To reassure himself of the orthodox nature of his undertaking, he entitles the record *We.*

Throughout the book, D-503 is almost always conscious of a desire to support the heavily regimented or mechanical structure of life in the United State, on the grounds that the life developed there is most consistent with reason and economy. The movement of the lathes and other machines used in building the *Integral,* for example, seems to him beautiful "because it is an *unfree* movement. Because the deep meaning of the dance [of the machines] is contained in its absolute, ecstatic submission, in the ideal *non-freedom.*" The mechanical ideal of non-freedom extends to all of society; and although some people have been known to revert to the primitive values of freedom and individualism, this "is only a case of small parts breaking; these may easily be repaired without stopping the eternal great march of the whole machine." Later he notes with displeasure that "some Number has impeded the smooth running of the great State machine." Throughout the book, the people of the State seem to be machines or parts of machines, a role that is suggested by the petroleum food they eat. Nor does D-503 initially see this situation as undesirable: on the contrary, having awakened from a dream, he is horrified that his brain, which he had thought mechanically perfect—"this precise, clean, glittering mechanism, like a chronometer without a speck of dust on it"—could be subject to the irrational influence of the imagination.

The model for the orderly scheduling of life in the United State is the Tables, which in turn are comparable to "that greatest of all monuments of ancient literature, the Official Railroad Guide." Like the railroads of Zamyatin's day, the Numbers of the United State run on schedule:

> The Tables transformed each one of us, actually, into a six-wheeled steel hero of a great poem. Every morning, with six-wheeled precision, at the same hour, at the same minute, we wake up, millions of us at once. At the very same hour, millions like one, we begin our work, and millions like one, we finish it. United into a single body with a million hands, at the very same second, designated by the Tables, we carry the spoons to our mouths; and at the same

> second we all go out to walk, go to the auditorium, to the halls for the Taylor exercises, and then to bed.

In short, the people are like automatons. Much of the conditioning needed to turn people into machines has been accomplished through the implementation of measures derived in large part from Frederick Winslow Taylor's *Principles of Scientific Management* (1911) and other writings. Not only are there several specific references to Taylor, but Taylor's priorities of efficiency and standardization, his desire to bring the principles of shop management to bear upon the home, and his interest in "a control so extensive and intensive as to provide for the maintenance of all standards" are all reflected in Zamyatin's United State. That the references to Taylorism have a general political significance is obvious enough; but they are also specifically directed against Lenin, who, in three essays published in April and May, 1918, praised the Taylor system and argued for its immediate introduction into the Soviet economy.

Lenin's admiration for the Taylor system's combination of "the refined brutality of bourgeois exploitation" and "scientific advancements" might surface in *We* in another context. Several times D-503 compares some aspect of life in the United State with something from "ancient times"; and, like the comparison of the Tables to the Official Railroad Guide, the point always is that life is being perfected under the United State. Thus, he rejects the charge that the Operation Department—a sophisticated torture chamber—is akin to the Inquisition; to say this, he contends, "is as absurd as to compare a surgeon performing a tracheotomy with a highway cutthroat" simply because the scalpel is a kind of knife. In one sense, of course, the argument is altogether false: the surgeon's purpose in cutting the patient's throat has nothing in common with the highwayman's intentions, but the Operation Department and the Inquisition, as different as they may be in technological sophistication, are essentially alike in their purpose. In another sense, however, D-503 is basically right to argue that one should judge a technology primarily by the ends for which it exists. What he fails to recognize is that the machines, and the rigid mentality that they serve and perpetuate, have become the masters of humanity. Ironically, the technological situation here bears little resemblance to the ideal of Leninist thought; instead, it is more like the decadent capitalist state that Marx protested against, in which "machines, invented to help man, have ended by becoming the symbols of his servitude."

2. The dual vision of the machine as man's potential liberator and his actual master helps to explain the strange account of the Prometheus myth given in *We.* As the rebellious demigod who was punished for stealing fire from the gods and giving it to man, Prometheus has always been an ambiguous figure in Western literature, for his act may be regarded as Satanically defiant and subversive or as Christ-like in its self-sacrifice. For the Romantics, however, the myth typically assumed two related forms, both positive:

> The re-creation of the mythic culture-hero followed two main lines. One was the conception of Prometheus as the archetype of the free creative artist, the original genius, the half-divine "maker" . . . The other conception, more familiar and more enduring, was that of the heroic, isolated rebel against repressive authority, divine and human. These interpretations, which could readily merge together, symbolized and strengthened the Romantic exalt-

ing of self-expression over neoclassical restraints, and, later and more largely, the revolutionary struggle against political, social, and religious oppression and reaction. [Douglas Bush, *Pagan Myth and Christian Tradition in English Poetry,* 1968]

In various ways, such writers as Blake, Byron, Goethe, and (above all) Shelley found the plight of Prometheus to be an appropriate symbol of the artist's desire to express himself proudly and freely, and of the battle between imaginative energy and the rational or institutional restraints upon the imagination; typically, too, the Romantics associated sexual desire with the Promethean fires of the imagination. Given what Shane calls Zamyatin's "essentially romanticist philosophy," it is unsurprising that D-503 exhibits several Promethean characteristics. Yet he is generally a timid rebel, a Prometheus *malgré lui,* his desire to express his feelings and ideas in his journal is subverted by his conditioned aversion to personal and idiosyncratic elements; his sexual experience with I-330 develops erratically, and he is led by her into adventures whose consequences he fears; and in the end, he accepts the hard rock of Reason, undergoing a lobotomy on his imagination rather than struggling against his fate in true Promethean fashion. To read events as D-503 reads them is therefore to accept the limitations of his essentially orthodox viewpoint, so that in the brief episode where the Prometheus myth is explicitly described we need to regard the incident from a somewhat different angle.

Significantly, the Promethean theme surfaces during a public event at the Plaza of the Cube, where people feel somewhat like "the ancients . . . during their 'church services' "; D-503 adds, however, that while the ancients "served their nonsensical, unknown god," the people of the United State serve a "rational god" who "gives us absolute truth." Again the narrator has made a distinction between his era and ours, but has only succeeded in reinforcing the parallel between blind submission to orthodox Christianity and blind subservience to the United State. More importantly, however, the emphasis on their service to a god, even a rational one, puts the audience at the opposite end of the spectrum from the rebellious Prometheus, and makes it impossible for the Numbers assembled at the Cube to interpret the following events in their true light.

The occasion is the execution of a criminal, apparently someone who has dared to assert his individuality against the will of the State. The execution is carried out by the Well-Doer, or head of government; his instrument is the Machine, a device that dissolves the human body into its constituent elements through a "dissociation of matter." Before the actual execution, however, a state poet reads some "iambic brass verses" which D-503 cannot well remember, although he is convinced that "one could not choose more instructive or more beautiful parables." What he does remember is the following:

> [The verses] dealt with the man who, his reason lost and lips like glass, stood on the steps and waited for the logical consequences of his own insane deeds. . . . A blaze. . . . Buildings were swaying in those iambic lines, and sprinkling upward their liquefied golden substance, they broke and fell. The green trees were scorched, their sap slowly ran out and they remained standing like black crosses, like skeletons. Then appeared Prometheus (that meant *us*):

> " . . . he harnessed fire
> With machines and steel
> And fettered chaos with Law . . . "

> The world was renovated; it became like steel—a sun of steel, trees of steel, men of steel. Suddenly an insane man "unchained the fire and set it free," and again the world had perished. . . .

Superficially, the passage might appear to depend on a simple reversal—the reference to Prometheus as the law-giver and protector of the status quo rather than as the revolutionary figure or liberator who is here regarded as an "insane man." The reference to the "black crosses," however, calls to mind the interpretation of Prometheus as a type of Christ and suggests that Zamyatin's essay on the Scythians, with its distinction between the crucified Christ and the institutionalized Christ, might provide us with a gloss on this passage. The "insane man" who liberates the fire is the Prometheus who resembles the crucified Christ: like the true Scythian, he is an emblem of freedom, and therefore an object of fear to those who cannot face the insecurity and responsibility of human liberty. As in the Romantic conception of Prometheus, he is a Christ-like figure whom the political establishment will regard, mistakenly, as Satanic. Yet the other figure, who creates a technology and builds a civilization upon it, is also Prometheus: originally a figure of energy and of the imagination, he evolves naturally into a rigid systematizer, much as Blake's Orc (Prometheus) first revolts against, and then becomes, Urizen (Jupiter). The political-technological connection is especially apparent in this poem, whose two figures parallel those on the stage: in his revolt against the rigidity of the State, the condemned man attempts, like the "insane man" of the poem, to set free the fire of the human imagination, while the Well-Doer, who is in charge both of the literal machine (the instrument of execution) and the machine of the State government, resembles the "Prometheus" of the poem in his attempt to restrain the imaginative energies.

3. That every revolution is capable of degenerating into a narrowly conformist and doctrinaire state is one implication of the Promethean sequence in *We.* As a corollary to this observation, we might add that the machinery we create—and this applies to the machinery of government as well as to technological marvels like the *Integral*—is in its inception the product of the open and lively imagination, but its end may be to thwart the kind of inquiring mentality that gave it birth. Translated into the political arena, the requirements of the machine shop—dependability, standardization, simple efficiency—become mediocrity, conformism, and the loss of aesthetic awareness. Raised in this environment, D-503 cannot "see anything beautiful in flowers," since he believes that "Only rational and useful things are beautiful." This prejudice against natural beauty is a symptom of the sterile thought fostered by a machine-like state.

Most of the events I have described so far occur rather early in *We,* before D-503 begins his love affair with I-330 and ventures outside the Green Wall that surrounds the United State. Throughout the remainder of the novel, D-503 is torn between his instinctive desire for freedom and individual love, and his conditioned dependence upon the State. He never becomes a true rebel, unlike Winston Smith in Orwell's *1984;* and his confusion and ambivalence are resolved only when he is forced to submit to the operation that removes his imagination and makes him, at the end of the novel, little more than a robot. Ironically, in this final state D-503 never could design anything so brilliant as the *Integral*, a triumph not only of technology but of the imagination. Earlier, when a doctor said that D-503 should have the operation to remove his fancy, another doctor observed that he might need it to build the *Integral*. Again, the point is that technology is a product of the imagination, even through it may have the effect of impairing imagination in others.

Meanwhile, without the operation D-503 has failed to be what he believes he should be: a perfectly rational, and therefore mechanical, being. He entitles his record *We,* intending, like the Proletarian writers of Zamyatin's day, to glorify "the collective and the machine," but instead emphasizes the individual and the human; inside this Proletarian writer is a Scythian trying to avoid suffocation. The struggle of the imagination to free itself is dramatized most obviously in D-503's two trips beyond the Green Wall: first a trip underground, during which D-503 seems for the first time to come alive; then the flight of the *Integral,* in which he and the revolutionary forces, the Mephi, fail in their attempt to seize control of the spaceship. The two episodes are related, for in the first scene, a visionary or dreamlike sequence in which D-503 first encounters the Mephi, he is really confronting forms of his own unfettered imagination, while in the second episode, the recapture of the *Integral* by forces of the United State signals the failure of the imagination to free itself and to gain control over the technology it has created. The same idea is played out in different form when a dream about his lover, I-330, changes to nightmare: a ray of sunshine falling on her neck becomes a "cruel ray blade" that seems about to behead her as he awakens. The lesson that D-503 draws from this nightmarish sequence is that he is unfortunately subject to irrational influences; we might more accurately see that the sunlight's transformation into a cruel blade is typical of the way the political and technological products of the imagination may become horrors.

From Zamyatin's fundamentally Romantic point of view, the entire society of the United State, with its carefully regulated activity, its abolition of privacy, its repression of all opposition, and especially its resistance to all change, is the true nightmare. Early in the novel, D-503 records his orthodox opinion that "the history of mankind . . . is a history of the transition from nomadic forms to more sedentary forms." The "sedentary forms" are apparent throughout the novel; the "nomadic forms," however, exist only beyond the Green Wall, among the Mephi, who are clearly Zamyatin's fictional version of the Scythian writers, Promethean figures whose imagination roves continually. The polar opposition of nomadic and sedentary forms is expressed elsewhere as the dichotomy of energy and entropy; here, as in his essay **"On Literature, Revolution, Entropy, and Other Matters,"** Zamyatin demonstrates his opposition to the entropic state of perfect equilibrium, which in political terms means quietude and a collectivist mentality. Similar to Dostoevsky's *Notes from Underground* in its rejection of a perfectly rational society modeled upon the Crystal Palace and the ant heap (which in *We* become the *Integral* and "all the cells of the gigantic hive", Zamyatin's novel is at heart a protest against the sterile and rigid concept of a final revolution, or a static society—against a world, that is, ruled by a mechanism rather than by the human spirit. It is against this idea that man should emulate the machine—not against the machines themselves, but against the ascendancy of technology over the imagination that created it—that Zamyatin very effectively directs his satire. (pp. 122-27)

Patrick A. McCarthy, "Zamyatin and the Nightmare of Technology," in Science-Fiction Studies, *Vol. 11, No. 33, July, 1984, pp. 122-29.*

ANDREW BARRATT (essay date 1984)

[*In the following excerpt, Barratt discusses the narrative technique of* We *and what it reveals about the relationship between the central characters of the novel.*]

My is a novel in which two of the most important trends in early Soviet fiction are combined. In the first place, it is one of many works to display the influence of popular adventure writing. Zamyatin was, in fact, one of the first Soviet writers to extol the virtues of so-called 'low' fiction, and *My* is the work which most clearly meets the demand for interesting story-telling which he voiced in many of his critical articles. Following in the footsteps of H. G. Wells, who was in this respect one of his most revered writers, Zamyatin relied heavily in *My* on the devices of popular fiction to supply the excitement and tension that he felt to be so conspicuously absent from the works of many of his contemporaries.

At the same time, *My* also belongs to the large group of ironic first-person *skaz* narratives which flourished so vigorously in the early 1920s. Although stylistically quite different from the type of *skaz* favoured by such writers as Zoshchenko and Babel' (and by the younger Zamyatin himself, for that matter), *My* nevertheless displays exactly the kind of 'double meaning' that Viktor Shklovsky has identified as the hallmark of *skaz* technique: '*Skaz* complicates the literary work. Two levels result: I) what the person narrates; 2) what emerges seemingly by chance from his narrative.' Zamyatin makes this tension between ostensible purpose and unwitting achievement quite explicit on a number of occasions in *My,* the most striking of which is to be found in Entry 18, where D-503 notes: 'I see with regret that instead of a harmonious and strict mathematical poem in honour of the One State, my work has turned out to be some sort of fantastic adventure novel.'

D-503's rueful comment serves not only to identify the two strands in the narrative—the propaganda message on behalf of the One State, and the 'fantastic' story of his relationship with I-330—it also indicates the most fundamental irony of the novel, namely, that the propagandist purpose is totally undermined by the presence of this 'extraneous' material. It should also be noted that, whilst the role of propagandist is one that D— takes on willingly, the task of writing an 'adventure novel' is forced upon him by circumstance. Nevertheless, once he becomes involved in the chain of mysteries which accompany his liaison with I—, he is quite prepared to accept that he has a new and more irksome 'authorial duty', which is to discover and explain to his unknown readers precisely what is going on. But this is a role to which he proves totally unsuited. From the very outset, he displays obvious deficiencies of understanding. When, for example, he finds himself in Auditorium 112, exactly as predicted by I-330, his only thought is that the mathematical odds against this happening are 3:20,000. Later, when he mentions the newspaper reports of growing political opposition within the One State, he fails even to speculate that this might somehow be connected with his recent strange experiences.

To begin with, D-503's inadequacies would appear to be the mark of nothing more serious than an absence of imagination, a natural enough consequence of living in the inhibiting intellectual environment of the One State. But, in the light of his subsequent behaviour, this initial opinion stands in need of radical revision. The turning point comes in Entry 10. By this time it is quite obvious that I-330 is a member of the opposition movement, a Mata Hari figure, who has been using her sexual attractiveness as a means of luring D-503 away from his allegiance to the One State. (As a prominent engineer, and one engaged on the prestigious *Integral* project to boot, D— is, of course, a natural 'target' for her attentions.) I—'s tactics will be instantly recognizable to any aficionado of spy stories. First, she inveigles the unsuspecting D— into committing an act of disobedience. Then she is in the position to blackmail him into aiding her cause. Once her objective is achieved, she tells D— quite openly: 'Now you are in my hands'. Nothing could be more plain, and D— accompanies his account of this crucial scene with a comment that leaves no doubt that he has understood perfectly what has occurred: 'Like a small boy, foolishly, like a small boy, I had fallen for it. . . . '

No sooner does D— acknowledge the truth, however, than he blocks it from his consciousness. From this point onwards, he behaves as if I— had never explained herself to him at all and their relationship involved no ulterior motive on her part. Rather than swallow the bitter pill, he retreats into the comforting illusion that I-330 is interested in him only as a sexual partner.

In committing so blatant an act of self-deception, D-503 vitiates his professed pursuit of understanding, driving a wedge between himself and his readers. The narrative which follows is peppered with instances of the most astonishing incomprehension, which are explicable solely in terms of his self-imposed blindness. He refuses to take the obvious hints that he is far from being the only object of I—'s affections; he continues to believe that S-4711 is a loyal Guardian, even though the latter's behaviour is clearly inconsistent with the proper exercise of his duties; and he fails to draw the logical conclusion when he encounters I— and the other Mephi conspirators in the subterranean chamber, even half-convincing himself afterwards that the entire episode may have been a figment of his imagination.

That D-503's journal is above all a monument to the folly of its author there can be no doubt, yet the engineer is not quite the naive 'sixteen-year-old' the Benefactor takes him for. This will become clear if we examine more closely the role of I-330. Despite what the Benefactor says about her, there is more to I— than mere cynical Machiavellianism. Let us repeat: she *does* use her female wiles to ensnare D—; this is an important part of the Mephi plot to take over the *Integral*. There is even a suggestion that she derives a degree of malicious pleasure from the spectacle of D—'s subjugation. It is certainly difficult, for example, to imagine her words 'You know perfectly well that you will do what I tell you' being spoken with anything other than cruel satisfaction. But, for all that, I— is not content simply to blackmail D— into participating in the Mephi cause. Once she has him in her power, she sets out to convert him intellectually as well. This second task is a matter not of coercion, but of *education*.

The most obvious sign of I-330's educative purpose is the famous scene in which she expounds to D— the theory of Energy and Entropy as an illustration of her belief in permanent revolution. But the same urge to instruct is also present, although in a more insidious form, in the ambiguous remarks with which she taunts the literal-minded engineer from their very first meeting. Both techniques are designed to serve the same end, which is to ensure that D— will transfer his intellectual allegiance from the One State to the Mephi. An active rebel is of far more use to the cause than an unwilling accessory.

On the face of it, I—'s efforts are amply rewarded. Not only does D— eventually express a desire to know something about the Mephi, he also shows signs of a growing rebelliousness. He intercedes physically when he sees a group of Mephi prisoners being led away to custody by the Guardians. He helps I-330 to escape after the protest action at the Day of Unanimity. He makes a bold, revolutionary speech when I— takes him to the other side of the Green Wall. And when, in a crucial scene, his two 'teachers', I— and Yu— (the latter actually is a teacher by occupation) come into open conflict, it is I— who emerges the victor in the battle for the engineer's soul.

The external marks of D-503's transformation from loyal subject of the One State into Mephi revolutionary are impressive, yet they remain, in the final reckoning, external marks only. But this is something that I-330 is unable to see. Due, no doubt, to an excess of educative zeal, she seriously misinterprets D—'s behaviour and becomes—no less than D— himself—a victim of delusion. Once again, the narrative perspective is the source of irony, only this time it is at the expense of I-330. As readers of D-503's journal, we are privy to information which casts an entirely different light upon his behaviour and provides a powerful corrective to I—'s illusions about him.

Let us take the first example of D—'s new-found 'rebelliousness'—his attempt to intercede for the Mephi prisoners. The account of the affair contained in the diary makes it clear that D—'s sole motive in undertaking this bold act was *to rescue I-330,* whom he had wrongly identified as the woman protester. I-, of course, has no way of knowing this, a circumstance which lends an ironic piquancy to her subsequent praise of D-'s action: 'For that one folly of yours—for what you did yesterday during the promenade—I love you even more, even more'. More important even than I-330's display of ignorance is the fact that, quite unconsciously, she has responded here in terms which are bound to *reinforce D-503's delusive view of her.* In her own mistaken belief that D— has become a rebel, she supplies him with the very reward he most desires: the 'fearless hero' receives a protestation of 'love' from the 'grateful heroine'. Without realizing it, therefore, D— and I— have become engaged in what the psychologists call *collusion,* a 'game of mutual self-deception', as R. D. Laing has defined it, in which I-'s false impression of D— as a revolutionary causes her to bolster his own false image of her as his romantic partner. Once the 'game' has begun, it speeds under its own momentum to an inevitably tragic conclusion. (pp. 347-49)

Collusion of the kind in which D— and I— indulge is a risky enterprise, as the participants in the 'game' constantly run the risk of having their delusions uncovered. . . . [However], both of Zamyatin's characters prove to be adept 'players', who deftly sidestep the dangers as they present themselves. But collusion can withstand only so much pressure from reality, and the turning point comes, inevitably, with the flight of the *Integral.* D— has now been fully apprised of the Mephi plot and his allegiances are subjected to the ultimate test. His behaviour throughout the test flight is, however, suspiciously ambiguous. He plays no active part in the attempt to highjack the rocket and, when the conspiracy is easily foiled by the waiting Guardians, I— draws what seems to her the only logical conclusion—that D— must have acted as an informer.

The collusion between D— and I— breaks down, then, because the abortive coup brings their delusions into a conflict so fundamental that they can no longer be accommodated within the framework of the 'game'. By charging D— with treachery, I— signals her unwillingness to continue as a 'player'. But, although she has withdrawn from this particular 'game', this does not mean that she is no longer prone to misapprehension. It is, in fact, quite obvious that she has *failed* to discern the truth about D-'s part in recent events. Her assumption that he has played the Judas, although understandable, is quite mistaken. What she has done, therefore, is to replace one delusion with another. She has 'changed the rules', as it were, thereby substituting a new 'game' in place of the old one. In this new 'game' D— is no longer the hero, the 'revolutionary convert'; he is the villain, the 'traitor to the cause'.

It must again be emphasized that I-330's false impression of the engineer, like her original delusion, is the product of circumstances rather than deliberate evasion on her part. Yet this second delusion, once established in her mind, proves equally resistant to the promptings of contrary evidence. As it turns out, the second delusion—although painful—is nevertheless a brilliant invention, because it protects I— from experiencing the greater pain that would have resulted from perceiving the truth. By choosing to believe that D-503 has deliberately betrayed her, she absolves herself of the need to question her own behaviour in attempting to recruit the engineer to the Mephi movement in the first place. By believing herself to be the victim of deception, she can conveniently ignore the evidence of her own self-deception. This way she can at least die a martyr to the cause. She does not have to acknowledge that her entire endeavour has been a tragic error. This would explain why she displays such unwillingness to understand D— when he endeavours to inform her of the truth during their last meeting.

I—'s rapid switch of the ground rules naturally has a profound effect on D-503, her partner in collusion. Once he has recovered from his initial shock and despair, he directs all his energies towards restoring the status quo, so that the original 'game' may be resumed. To do this, he has to convince I-330, first, that her charge of treachery is groundless, and, second, that he really *is* a revolutionary, despite all that has happened. This is the logic that inspires his grotesque scheme to murder Yu—, by which means he hopes to resolve both issues at a single stroke: he will expose the real informer (Yu— had, of course, passed on the information she had gleaned from D—'s journal), and act as the avenging arm of the Mephi at the same time. The plan misfires, however, due to Yu—'s failure to conform to the role that D— had invented for her. At the crucial moment, she mistakes D—'s murderous intent for a sexual advance, and the insane project declines into farce.

D-'s subsequent visit to I—'s apartment building is equally unsatisfactory; the engineer arrives there only to find that she is not at home. But a chance event provides him with an alternative solution to his dilemma. As he wanders aimlessly about the room, he discovers a batch of the pink coupons which entitle the citizens of the One State to exercise their sexual rights. Most importantly, they indicate that, unbeknown to him, she has been conducting an 'affair' with a certain F—. The engineer's reaction is as extreme as it is unex-

pected. Where previously he had chosen to ignore I—'s 'infidelities', he now behaves like the traditional deceived lover, stamping his foot on the fateful coupons in a typical—and inadvertently comic—melodramatic gesture. D—'s new vision of I— the 'unfaithful lover' is, of course, just as false as her image of him as 'traitor to the cause'. Furthermore, the secondary delusion performs exactly the same psychological function for both characters. If he accepts the idea that he has been betrayed by I—, D— too is spared the necessity of facing up to a reality even more unpalatable, which, in his case, is that I— never actually loved him at all.

The final scene in this tragic psycho-sexual drama occupies Entry 38. Here I-330 displays a grim determination not to be moved from her secondary delusion; no matter what D— might say, he will remain the traitor in her eyes. The engineer himself seems unconsciously aware of this, and he is left with no alternative but to fall back on his own secondary delusion. The sign that he has done so is the physical punishment he inflicts upon I— for her 'infidelity':

> And suddenly . . . Sometimes it happens that you're completely immersed in sweet, warm sleep, when suddenly you're pricked by something, you shudder and your eyes are wide open again . . . So it was now: on the floor of her room are the trampled coupons, and on them the letter F— and some numbers . . . They knotted together to form a bundle within me, even now I am unable to say what sort of feeling it was, but I squeezed her so hard that she cried out in pain.

The simile is totally inappropriate: D— has not 'opened his eyes' at all, he has merely sunk into a different sort of delusive sleep. As for I—, once she has been punished by D—, she is quite happy to return the compliment. After she has 'extracted' the information she requires from the 'traitor' (the very readiness with which D— supplies this information gives the lie to I—'s opinion of him), she offers him her cold lips in a final gesture of vengeance, to remind him of the 'passion' they will no longer share.

In short, the relationship between D-503 and I-330 is inauthentic from beginning to end. D—'s initial act of self-deception leads directly to a sustained piece of collusion, which gives way in turn to an equally delusive severance. Such is the tragic story which forms the core of *My*. It now remains to explore some of the implications of these findings for the broader issues raised in the novel.

The most important consequence of the foregoing discussion is that it suggests the need for a fundamental reappraisal of I-330. Oddly enough, her role in the novel has not attracted much in the way of critical comment. By and large, the literature on *My* has been characterized by the (usually unspoken) assumption that I— is a positive character, if not the 'heroine' of the piece. It is not difficult to see why this should have been so. Many of the views expressed by I— in the novel bear an unquestionable resemblance to opinions set forth elsewhere by Zamyatin himself. Most significant in this respect is her argument about Energy and Entropy, which virtually repeats the opening sections of the author's most famous article, **'O literature, revolyutsii i entropii'** [see essay dated 1924]. It is essential, however, to distinguish between what I-330 says and what she does, for her defence of heresy does not entirely correspond with the part she plays in *My*.

This point will become clearer if we review briefly what Zamyatin has to say about the heretic in '**O revolyutsii** . . .'. The heretic, in this description, is the archetypal outsider, a person whose thoughts or creations are so innovative as to represent a radical challenge to the status quo. Such individuals are encountered only very rarely; Zamyatin's list includes Galileo, Darwin, Babeuf, Schopenhauer, Dostoyevsky, Einstein, and Nietzsche. The mention of Nietzsche in this context is most revealing, for Zamyatin—in true Neitzschean fashion—quite consciously divides humanity into two unequal groups: heretics, who constitute a tiny élite of 'supermen'; and the vast mass of mankind (the 'market-place rabble' as they are termed in *Also sprach Zarathustra*), which is typified by a slavish acceptance of received values. (pp. 350-53)

Like a true heretic, I-330 is quite prepared both for martyrdom, and for the fact that her heresy may be the fount of tomorrow's conservatism. Yet, for all that, her own story illustrates a tragedy quite different from that adumbrated in her (and, of course, Zamyatin's) theory. Her main activity in the novel has no counterpart in the account of heresy contained in '**O revolyutsii** . . .'. In fact, her revolutionary endeavour runs counter to the very 'law' of human existence expounded there. She preaches heresy, we should remember, with a view to destroying the innate slavishness of those, like D-503, whose acquiescence in the face of tyranny is the cause of their own enslavement. In the terms of the article, she is striving to achieve the impossible. For what is she attempting, if it is not to wean a man of 'weak-nerved brains' away from his reliance on the 'crutches of certainty'?

I—'s relationship with D— demonstrates the operation of that cruel law, defined in '**O revolyutsii** . . .', which insists that such reforms cannot be realized. The tragic outcome of their liaison is, therefore, quite inevitable. It must be stressed, however, that this tragedy is not only the product of D—'s inability to rise to the challenge offered by I— (although this is commonly held to be so); it is also—and perhaps even in greater measure—the result of I—'s own failure to understand that her efforts to emancipate the slave disregard a principle of human nature as immutable as the laws of physics. As we have seen, she goes to her death with this misapprehension intact. In her own eyes, she dies a martyr; in the eyes of the reader, she dies the victim of a delusive faith in the revolutionary ideal.

It has been suggested to me that the inclusion of the Energy-Entropy argument is a fundamental weakness of *My.* Certainly, Zamyatin does leave himself open to the charge of having borrowed inappropriately from his article. However, this is a point for others to decide. What I would suggest, however, is that the inclusion of those passages where I-330 speaks in the language of '**O revolyutsii** . . .' has been the source of major critical misunderstanding of her role. We have here a striking example of the dangers involved in relying too heavily upon external evidence to support textual interpretation. The story of D-503 and I-330 may be most readily understood, then, as a reverse metaphor of that romantic conception of revolution which deals in the inspiring image of the revolutionary hero or heroine leading the enslaved masses to freedom. In Russian literature this revolutionary romanticism had already found expression, most notably in the legend of Danko, the second of the two stories told in Gor'ky's famous tale, 'Starukha Izergil'. Danko is the youth with the blazing heart, which he tears from his breast in order to light the path so that others may find their way out of the

dark forest. Although he dies at journey's end, he does so in the knowledge that those he has saved will now be able to begin a new life. Zamyatin almost certainly alludes to Gor'ky's legend when he describes the emblem of the Mephi as a crudely drawn depiction of a winged youth with a 'dazzling, crimson, smouldering ember' in place of his heart. It might be added that D-503's 'revolutionary' speech, with its eulogy of 'madness', recalls another of Gor'ky's works, 'Pesnya o Sokole', which has the repeated refrain: 'To the madness of the brave we sing our song'.

In *My* Zamyatin challenges this romantic conception of revolution by striking at its weakest link. In effect, he is asking: how is the freedom-loving revolutionary actually to bring about a qualitative change in the nature of those lesser mortals who make up the bulk of mankind? The romantic would reply that the answer lies in education and the example of others. Once again, it was Gor'ky who gave this idea literary form, both in his short fable 'Tovarishch!', and—more notoriously and at greater length—in the novel *Mat'*. Zamyatin offers an alternative perspective which is considerably less alluring, especially as it is rendered with far greater psychological conviction. Such changes, he tells us in *My,* cannot come about because revolutionaries and slaves are incapable of making common cause together.

The most disturbing aspect of the tragic misalliance between Zamyatin's hero and heroine, however, is that I-330's attempt to convert D-503 is founded on a paradox. Her ultimate aim, as we saw above, is to arouse in the engineer a love of freedom and an independence of spirit. Yet her initial act—absolutely necessary, of course, if she is to bring D— within the Mephi sphere of influence—was to *enslave* him by luring him against his will into compromising his allegiance to the One State. The thrust of Zamyatin's critique is more pragmatic than ethical. This is not an argument against the principle that the ends justify the means. Zamyatin's paradox suggests something altogether different: that the means employed ensure that the end *cannot* be achieved. (pp. 354-56)

This conflict is a logical consequence of the inauthentic relationship between D-503 and I-330. Having adopted the role of compliant slave, D—'s instinct is to avoid the responsibilities that I— thrusts upon him in her delusive belief that he has become a rebel. He is, however, aware of the need to resolve the issue of his divided allegiances, but, rather than confront the dilemma head on, as I— wishes him to do, he is more readily attracted to solutions which will allow him to slip between its horns. One such solution has already been encountered in a different context—his hopeless dream of running away with I-330 to live beyond the Green Wall. The advantage of this plan is that it would absolve him of the need to revolt actively against the One State and, at the same time, remove I— to an environment where she might be just a sexual partner, which is all he desires of her. The newspaper announcement of the Great Operation, which he greets with hyperbolic enthusiasm ('Saved'), seems to offer a similar prospect of wish fulfilment. Submission to the Operation (in his naivety he imagines that I— will obey the One State's command as willingly as he) will have two positive benefits: no longer a criminal liable to punishment, he will be merely a sick man who has been 'cured', and who is now able to continue as I—'s lover *within* the protective framework of the One State.

That these two solutions imply political stances which are diametrically opposed does not concern him; indeed, it does not even occur to him. Inside the One State or beyond the Green Wall, it is all the same to him, so long as he can have I— as his lover without having to accept the responsibility of being a rebel. But I— is not to be shaken from her commitment to the revolutionary cause and she finally succeeds—with tragic consequences for them both—in forcing D— into a position of responsibility from which he cannot escape.

Discussion of D-503's divided personality would be incomplete without at least brief reference to what many commentators have seen as its most striking surface manifestation—the language of the novel. That D—'s journal is characterized by a disjunction between two radically different types of discourse, the one distinguished by logical thought patterns and strictly referential language, the other elliptical and rich in imagery—has been established by many critics. And this stylistic disharmony has commonly been viewed in terms of a conflict within D— between his 'old' and 'new' self, between the scientist and the artist. The present discussion inclines towards a different conclusion—that the growth of D—'s artistic spirit, no less than the growth of the spirit of rebellion (to which it is often supposed to be related), is more apparent than real. The stylistic opposition can, in fact, be quite adequately explained as a product of D-503's initial act of self-deception. As we saw above, D—'s journal is self-defeating: its surface form—the quest for understanding—is undermined by the engineer's deeper psychological need to preserve his illusions at all costs. The language of logic is the one he uses to conduct this delusive search for knowledge. The elliptical style, on the other hand, attests to the constant pressure of the censored material upon his consciousness. The leaps of lateral association, the interconnecting systems of imagery and mythic references, the startling reversals of meaning all combine not only to remind D— where the truth really lies, but also to perform a *predictive* function, pointing clearly to the inevitable end that awaits him and his erstwhile mistress. (pp. 357-58)

> *Andrew Barratt, "Revolution as Collusion: The Heretic and the Slave in Zamyatin's 'My'," in* The Slavonic and East European Review, *Vol. 62, No. 3, July, 1984, pp. 344-61.*

FURTHER READING

Aldridge, Alexandra. "Myths of Origin and Destiny in Utopian Literature: Zamiatin's *We.*" *Extrapolation* 19, No. 1 (December 1977): 68-75.
  Discusses *We* as it reflects the biblical myths of the Garden of Eden and the New Jerusalem, arguing that the novel thus presents a prototype for subsequent anti-utopian works.

Alexandrova, Vera. "Yevgeny Zamyatin (1884-1937)." In her *A History of Soviet Literature,* translated by Mirra Ginsburg, pp. 84-96. Garden City, N.Y.: Doubleday & Co., 1963.
  Charts Zamyatin's literary career, maintaining that he was "not only one of the pioneers of the Soviet period of Russian literature, but one of the most interesting and original Russian writers of the twentieth century."

Angeloff, Alexander. "The Relationship of Literary Means and Alienation in Zamiatin's *We.*" *Russian Language Journal* XXIII, No. 85 (June 1969): 3-9.
  Describes the literary techniques with which Zamyatin presents alienation in *We.*

Barker, Murl G. "Onomastics and Zamiatin's *We.*" *Canadian-American Slavic Studies* 11, No. 4 (Winter 1977): 551-60.
  Discusses the significance of the alphanumeric character names in *We.*

Barratt, Andrew. "The X-Factor in Zamyatin's *We.*" *The Modern Language Review* 80, Part 3 (July 1985): 659-72.
  Examines the function of X-imagery in *We.*

Bayley, John. "Them and Us." *The New York Review of Books* XIX, No. 6 (19 October 1972): 18-21.
  Review of *We* and *A Soviet Heretic* emphasizing Zamyatin's theories on revolution.

Beauchamp, Gorman. "Of Man's Last Disobedience: Zamiatin's *We* and Orwell's *1984.*" *Comparative Literature Studies* X, No. 4 (December 1973): 285-301.
  Discusses *We* and George Orwell's *Nineteen Eighty-Four* as they reflect the biblical myth of the Fall and Sigmund Freud's theories on civilization and instinctual repression.

———. "Future Words: Language and the Dystopian Novel." *Style* 8, No. 3 (Fall 1974): 462-76.
  Addresses the function of language in dystopian novels, arguing that both *We* and *Nineteen Eighty-Four,* "provide a convincing illusion of linguistic change that reflects the political/technological realities of their nightmare futures."

Beaujour, Elizabeth Klosty. "Zamiatin's *We* and Modernist Architecture." *The Russian Review* 47 (January 1988): 49-60.
  Explores Zamyatin's views on modernist architecture as reflected in his essays and *We.*

Beehler, Michael. "Yevgeny Zamyatin: The Essential, the Superfluous, and Textual Noise." *Substance* XV, No. 2 (1986): 48-60.
  Focuses on Zamyatin's aesthetic ideals and treatment of the irrational in his essays and *We,* arguing that his writing maintains an ambiguous relationship to his concepts of revolution and heresy.

Billington, James H. "The Uncertain Colossus: Crescendo—Apocalypticism." In his *The Icon and the Axe: An Interpretive History of Russian Culture,* pp. 504-18. New York: Alfred A. Knopf, 1966.
  Asserts that *We* is "a culmination of the essentially anti-Christian preoccupation with Prometheanism and sensualism in the late imperial period" of Russian history.

Blake, Patricia. "Literature as a Lash." *The New York Times Book Review* (26 February 1967): 1; 32-34.
  Offers an overview of Zamyatin's literary career and its significance in a favorable review of *The Dragon.*

Borman, Gilbert. "A New Look at Eugene Zamyatin's *We.*" *Extrapolation* 24, No. 1 (Spring 1983): 57-65.
  Interprets the alphanumeric character names in *We* as coded references to biblical verses and suggests the relevance of the allusions.

Brown, Edward J. "Zamjatin and English Literature." In *American Contributions to the Fifth International Congress of Slavists: Vol. II, Literary Contributions,* pp. 21-39. The Hague: Mouton & Co., 1963.
  Examines Zamyatin's creative process and literary production, themes and philosophy, and affinity with such English writers as H. G. Wells, Aldous Huxley, and George Orwell.

———. "Eugene Zamjatin as Critic." In *To Honor Roman Jakobson: Essays on the Occasion of His Seventieth Birthday,* Vol. I, pp. 402-11. The Hague: Mouton & Co., 1967.
  Survey of Zamyatin's criticism asserting that his importance as a critic lies in his search for new literary forms and in his defense "of the *modern* accent in literary art."

Carden, Patricia. "Utopia and Anti-Utopia: Aleksei Gastev and Evgeny Zamyatin." *The Russian Review* 46, No. 1 (January 1987): 1-18.
Discusses *We* as a satire on the favorable presentation of technology and labor in the essays and works of Soviet poet Aleksei Gastev.

Collins, Christopher. "Zamyatin, Wells, and the Utopian Literary Tradition." *The Slavonic and East European Review* 44, No. 103 (July 1966): 351-60.
Compares *We* to utopian works by H. G. Wells, finding that "where Wells combined the social satire of Swift, the Utopianism of Plato, the science fantasy of Verne, and the English travel-adventure of Defoe, Zamyatin took Wells' entire amalgam and stirred in the psychology and existential revolt of Dostoyevsky, as well as his own brand of 20th-century expressionistic style."

Connolly, Julian W. "A Modernist's Palette: Color in the Fiction of Evgenij Zamjatin." *Russian Language Journal* XXXIII, No. 115 (Spring 1979): 82-98.
Studies the development of color imagery in *Uezdnoe*, "Sever," and *Navodnenie*.

Connors, James. "Zamyatin's *We* and the Genesis of *1984*." *Modern Fiction Studies* 21, No. 1 (Spring 1975): 107-24.
Argues that the major thematic and political concerns of *Nineteen Eighty-Four* differed from those in *We* and were present in Orwell's thought before he was exposed to Zamyatin's work.

Deutscher, Isaac. "*1984*—The Mysticism of Cruelty." In his *Russia in Transition, and Other Essays*, pp. 230-45. New York: Coward-McCann, 1957.
Discusses similarities in the themes and plots of *We* and George Orwell's *Nineteen Eighty-Four*.

Doyle, Peter. "Zamyatin's Philosophy, Humanism, and *We*: A Critical Appraisal." *Renaissance and Modern Studies* XXVIII (1984): 1-17.
Examines Zamyatin's essays and *We*, suggesting that his philosophical ideas are "derivative, negative, and at variance with his humanistic statements."

Ehre, Milton. "A Free Imagination." *The New Leader* L, No. 6 (13 March 1967): 22-3.
Favorable review of Zamyatin's short stories in *The Dragon*.

Elliott, Robert C. "The Fear of Utopia." In his *The Shape of Utopia: Studies in a Literary Genre*, pp. 84-101. Chicago: University of Chicago Press, 1970.
Broad overview of the central themes of *We* in an essay charting the development of anti-utopian fiction.

Garson, Judith M. "The Idea of Freedom in the Work of Yevgeni Zamyatin." In *Columbia Essays in International Affairs: Vol. IV— The Dean's Papers, 1968*, edited by Andrew W. Cordier, pp. 1-24. New York: Columbia University Press, 1969.
Outlines Zamyatin's theories on revolution and freedom as presented in his major works.

Ginsburg, Mirra. Introduction to *The Dragon: Fifteen Stories*, by Yevgeny Zamyatin, edited and translated by Mirra Ginsburg, pp. v-xi. Chicago: University of Chicago Press, 1976.
Discusses Zamyatin's literary career and aesthetic tenets.

Hayward, Max. "Pilnyak and Zamyatin: Two Tragedies of the Twenties." *Survey*, No. 36 (April-June 1961): 85-91.
Describes the suppression of works by Zamyatin and novelist Boris Pilnyak (1894-1937?) in the Soviet Union.

Howe, Irving. "The Fiction of Anti-Utopia," *The New Republic* 146, No. 17 (23 April 1962): 13-16.
Compares *We*, George Orwell's *Nineteen Eighty-Four*, and Aldous Huxley's *Brave New World*, outlining the general themes and structures of the anti-utopian novel.

Hutchings, William. "Structure and Design in a Soviet Dystopia: H. G. Wells, Constructivism, and Yevgeny Zamyatin's *We*." *Journal of Modern Literature* 9, No. 1 (1981-1982): 81-102.
Examines the narrative structure and technique in *We*, contrasting the novel's form and content with those of works by H. G. Wells, and extrapolates Zamyatin's views on Russian futurist poetry and the Constructivist movement in Soviet architecture.

Jackson, Robert Louis. "E. Zamyatin's *We*." In his *Dostoevsky's Underground Man in Russian Literature*, pp. 150-57. The Hague: Mouton & Co., 1958.
Views the Single State in *We* as "a realization of the utopia outlined by the Underground Man" in Fyodor Dostoevsky's *Notes from the Underground*.

Kern, Gary, ed. *Zamyatin's "We": A Collection of Critical Essays*. Ann Arbor, Mich.: Ardis Publishers, 1988, 306 p.
Includes essays by Richard A. Gregg and Alexander Voronsky (see *TCLC*, Vol. 8, excerpts dated 1965 and 1922), Edward J. Brown, Christopher Collins, M. M. Kuznetsov, and Susan Layton. The collection also contains an editor's introduction discussing the literary components of *We*, and offers previously unavailable essays and letters by Zamyatin.

La Bossière, Camille R. "Zamiatin's *We*: A Caricature of Utopian Symmetry." *Riverside Quarterly* 6, No. 1 (August 1973): 40-3.
Interprets *We* as a satire on the regularity and order of Enlightenment thought and nineteenth-century utopian fiction.

Leatherbarrow, W. J. "Einstein and the Art of Yevgeny Zamyatin." *The Modern Language Review* 82, Part 1 (January 1987): 142-51.
Observes the influence of Albert Einstein's theory of relativity on Zamyatin's thought and, consequently, on the composition of *We*.

"A New Soviet Novelist." *The Living Age* 343, No. 4,393 (October 1932): 160-63.
Unsigned interview in which Zamyatin comments on life and literature in postrevolutionary Russia.

McClintock, James I. "United State revisited: Pynchon and Zamiatin." *Contemporary Literature* 18, No. 4 (Autumn 1977): 475-90.
Compares *We* and Thomas Pynchon's *Gravity's Rainbow* (1973), asserting that "in reaction against the scientized State characterized by unholy alliances between science, technology, bureaucracy, and despotism, Zamiatin and Pynchon use similar concepts, myths, symbols, and structural devices."

Mapplebeck, John. "Russian Llareggub." *The Listener* 112, No. 2,888 (13 December 1984): 27-8.
Review of "*Islanders*" and "*The Fisher of Men*," noting a "distinct Celtic edge to Zamyatin's imagination" as expressed in these works.

Mihailovich, Vasa D. "Critics on Evgeny Zamyatin." *Papers on Language and Literature* 10, No. 3 (Summer 1974): 317-34.
Summarizes significant critical studies and essays, both from the Soviet Union and abroad, on Zamyatin's major works. The essay also provides an extensive bibliographic footnote.

Mihajlov, Mihajlo. "Evgeny Zamyatin: The Chagall of Russian Literature." In his *Russian Themes*, translated by Marija Mihajlov, pp. 288-97. New York: Farrar, Straus and Giroux, 1968.
Praises Zamyatin's literary career, paralleling his work with that of contemporary Soviet writers and with the paintings of Marc Chagall.

Oulanoff, Hongor. *The Serapion Brothers: Theory and Practice*. The Hague: Mouton & Co., 1966, 186 p.
Surveys the principal aesthetic tenets and literary styles of the Serapion Brothers discussing Zamyatin's metonymic representation of characters in *Ostrovityane* and "The Dragon."

Parrinder, Patrick. "Imagining the Future: Wells and Zamyatin."

In *H. G. Wells and Modern Science Fiction*, edited by Darko Suvin, pp. 126-43. Lewisburg, Pa.: Bucknell University Press, 1977.

Compares the depiction of future societies in *We* and works by H. G. Wells, examining their narrative technique and use of language, and evaluating them as models of science fiction.

Pekar, Harvey. "The Captain's Wife." *Book World* (*Washington Post*) XVIII, No. 32 (17 August 1988): 8.

Favorable review of *A Godforsaken Hole*.

Richards, D. "Four Utopias." *The Slavonic and East European Review* 40 (December 1961-June 1962): 220-28.

Compares the philosophical, psychological, and political ideas presented in *We,* Fyodor Dostoevsky's "The Legend of the Grand Inquisitor," Aldous Huxley's *Brave New World,* and George Orwell's *Nineteen Eighty-Four.*

Rooney, Victoria. "Nietzschean Elements in Zamyatin's Ideology: A Study of His Essays." *The Modern Language Review* 81, Part 3 (July 1986): 675-86.

Asserts thematic parallels in Zamyatin's essays and the philosophy of Friedrich Nietzsche, stressing Nietzsche's impact on Zamyatin's theory of the Heretic and concept of the irrational.

Rosenshield, Gary. "The Imagination and the 'I' in Zamjatin's *We*." *The Slavic and East European Journal* 23, No. 1 (Spring 1979): 51-62.

Outlines "the theme of the imagination as manifested in the narrative structure" of *We.*

Russell, Robert. "Literature and Revolution in Zamyatin's *My*." *The Slavonic and East European Review* LI, No. 122 (January 1973): 36-46.

Explores "the link between Zamyatin's idea of eternal revolution and his view of the rôle of literature" in *We* as represented by R-13, D-503, and the revolution of the Mephis.

Sheldon, Richard R. "Sklovskij, Gor'kij, and the Serapion Brothers." *The Slavic and East European Journal* XII, No. 1 (Spring 1968): 1-13.

Notes Zamyatin's role within the Russian literary group the Serapion Brothers, focusing on the literary influence of Maxim Gorky and Viktor Shklovsky on the circle.

Thomson, Boris. *The Premature Revolution: Russian Literature and Society, 1917-1946,* pp. 16ff. London: Weidenfeld and Nicolson, 1972.

Discusses Zamyatin and *We* in the context of postrevolutionary Russia.

Walsh, Chad. *From Utopia to Nightmare.* New York: Harper & Row, 1962, 191 p.

Provides summarizing commentary on *We* in a survey of major dystopian works of the nineteenth and twentieth centuries.

Warrick, Patricia. "The Sources of Zamyatin's *We* in Dostoevsky's *Notes From Underground*." *Extrapolation* 17, No. 1 (December 1975): 63-77.

Contends that major images and themes of Fyodor Dostoevsky's *Notes from the Underground* influenced those in *We,* and that Dostoevsky's protagonist, "by a process of ironic inversion, serves in great detail as a model for D-503" in *We.*

Watt, Alan. "George Orwell and Yevgeny Zamyatin." *Quadrant* XXVIII, Nos. 7-8 (July-August 1984): 110-11.

Maintains that *We* influenced George Orwell's *Nineteen Eighty-Four* and claims that "Zamyatin's book is essential reading for anyone interested in Orwell's themes."

Weber, Harry. "A Note on Zamjatin's 'The Dragon'." *The Slavic and East European Journal* 21, No. 4 (Winter 1977): 564-65.

Argues that allusions to the Book of Revelations in "The Dragon" indicate Zamyatin's views on Russia's October Revolution during its first year.

Woodcock, George. "Utopias in Negative." *The Sewanee Review* LXIV, No. 1 (January-March 1956): 81-97.

Discussion of *We* as the first significant anti-utopian novel and predecessor of Aldous Huxley's *Brave New World* and George Orwell's *Nineteen Eighty-Four.*

Yarwood, Edmund. "A Comparison of Selected Symbols in 'Notes from the Underground' and *We*." *Proceedings: Pacific Northwest Conference on Foreign Languages* XXI (3-4 April 1970): 144-49.

Observes the similarity of symbols used to portray irrationality in *We* and Fyodor Dostoevsky's *Notes from the Underground.*

Zamiatin, Eugene. *We.* Translated by Gregory Zilboorg. New York: E. P. Dutton & Co., 1959, 218 p.

Includes the original 1924 foreword by Zilboorg discussing Zamyatin's life and the presentation of the individual and society in *We* (see *TCLC*, Vol. 8, excerpt dated 1924); a preface by Marc Slonim offering personal reminiscences of Zamyatin's literary career and personality; and an introduction by Peter Rudy examining Zamyatin's life and the thematic concerns of *We.*

Zavalishin, Vyacheslav. "Stylists and Stylizers: Zamyatin, Shklovski, Babel', Pil'nyak." In his *Early Soviet Writers,* pp. 179-201. New York: Frederick A. Praeger, 1958.

Discusses Zamyatin's literary career in the context of postrevolutionary Russia.

Twentieth-Century Literary Criticism

Cumulative Indexes
Volumes 1-37

This Index Includes References
to Entries in These Gale Series

Contemporary Literary Criticism

Presents excerpts of criticism on the works of novelists, poets, dramatists, short story writers, scriptwriters, and other creative writers who are now living or who have died since 1960. Cumulative indexes to authors and nationalities are included, as well as an index to titles discussed in the individual volume.

Twentieth-Century Literary Criticism

Contains critical excerpts by the most significant commentators on poets, novelists, short story writers, dramatists, and philosophers who died between 1900 and 1960. Cumulative indexes to authors, nationalities, and titles discussed are included in each new volume.

Nineteenth-Century Literature Criticism

Offers significant passages from criticism on authors who died between 1800 and 1899. Cumulative indexes to authors, nationalities, and titles discussed are included in each new volume.

Literature Criticism from 1400 to 1800

Compiles significant passages from the most noteworthy criticism on authors of the fifteenth through eighteenth centuries. Cumulative indexes to authors, nationalities, and titles discussed are included in each new volume.

Classical and Medieval Literature Criticism

Offers excerpts of criticism on the works of world authors from classical antiquity through the fourteenth century. Cumulative indexes to authors, titles, and critics are included in each volume.

Short Story Criticism

Compiles excerpts of criticism on short fiction by writers of all eras and nationalities. Cumulative indexes to authors, nationalities, and titles discussed are included in each new volume.

Children's Literature Review

Includes excerpts from reviews, criticism, and commentary on works of authors and illustrators who create books for children. Cumulative indexes to authors, nationalities, and titles discussed are included in each new volume.

Contemporary Authors Series

Encompasses five related series. *Contemporary Authors* provides biographical and bibliographical information on more than 92,000 writers of fiction, nonfiction, poetry, journalism, drama, motion pictures, and other fields. Each new volume contains sketches on authors not previously covered in the series. *Contemporary Authors New Revision Series* provides completely updated information on active authors covered in previously published volumes of *CA*. Only entries requiring significant change are revised for *CA New Revision Series*. *Contemporary Authors Permanent Series* consists of updated listings for deceased and inactive authors removed from the original volumes 9-36 when these volumes were revised. *Contemporary Authors Autobiography Series* presents specially commissioned autobiographies by leading contemporary writers. *Contemporary Authors Bibliographical Series* contains primary and secondary bibliographies as well as analytical bibliographical essays by authorities on major modern authors.

Dictionary of Literary Biography

Encompasses three related series. *Dictionary of Literary Biography* furnishes illustrated overviews of authors' lives and works and places them in the larger perspective of literary history. *Dictionary of Literary Biography Documentary Series* illuminates the careers of major figures through a selection of literary documents, including letters, notebook and diary entries, interviews, book reviews, and photographs. *Dictionary of Literary Biography Yearbook* summarizes the past year's literary activity with articles on genres, major prizes, conferences, and other timely subjects and includes updated and new entries on individual authors. A cumulative index to authors and articles is included in each new volume.

Concise Dictionary of American Literary Biography

A six-volume series that collects revised and updated sketches on major American authors that were originally presented in *Dictionary of Literary Biography*.

Something about the Author Series

Encompasses three related series. *Something about the Author* contains heavily illustrated biographical sketches on juvenile and young adult authors and illustrators from all eras. *Something about the Author Autobiography Series* presents specially commissioned autobiographies by prominent authors and illustrators of books for children and young adults.

Yesterday's Authors of Books for Children

Contains heavily illustrated entries on children's writers who died before 1961. Complete in two volumes.

Literary Criticism Series
Cumulative Author Index

This index lists all author entries in the Gale Literary Criticism Series and includes cross-references to other Gale sources. References in the index are identified as follows:

AAYA: *Authors & Artists for Young Adults,* Volumes 1-3
CAAS: *Contemporary Authors Autobiography Series,* Volumes 1-11
CA: *Contemporary Authors* (original series), Volumes 1-130
CABS: *Contemporary Authors Bibliographical Series,* Volumes 1-3
CANR: *Contemporary Authors New Revision Series,* Volumes 1-29
CAP: *Contemporary Authors Permanent Series,* Volumes 1-2
CA-R: *Contemporary Authors* (revised editions), Volumes 1-44
CDALB: *Concise Dictionary of American Literary Biography,* Volumes 1-6
CLC: *Contemporary Literary Criticism,* Volumes 1-58
CLR: *Children's Literature Review,* Volumes 1-21
CMLC: *Classical and Medieval Literature Criticism,* Volumes 1-4
DLB: *Dictionary of Literary Biography,* Volumes 1-92
DLB-DS: *Dictionary of Literary Biography Documentary Series,* Volumes 1-7
DLB-Y: *Dictionary of Literary Biography Yearbook,* Volumes 1980-1988
LC: *Literature Criticism from 1400 to 1800,* Volumes 1-13
NCLC: *Nineteenth-Century Literature Criticism,* Volumes 1-27
SAAS: *Something about the Author Autobiography Series,* Volumes 1-9
SATA: *Something about the Author,* Volumes 1-59
SSC: *Short Story Criticism,* Volumes 1-5
TCLC: *Twentieth-Century Literary Criticism,* Volumes 1-37
YABC: *Yesterday's Authors of Books for Children,* Volumes 1-2

A. E. 1867-1935 . . . . TCLC 3, 10
See also Russell, George William
See also DLB 19

Abbey, Edward 1927-1989 . . . . . . CLC 36, 59
See also CANR 2; CA 45-48;
obituary CA 128

Abbott, Lee K., Jr. 19??- . . . . CLC 48

Abe, Kobo 1924- . . . . CLC 8, 22, 53
See also CANR 24; CA 65-68

Abell, Kjeld 1901-1961 . . . . CLC 15
See also obituary CA 111

Abish, Walter 1931- . . . . CLC 22
See also CA 101

Abrahams, Peter (Henry) 1919- . . . . . CLC 4
See also CA 57-60

Abrams, M(eyer) H(oward) 1912-... CLC 24
See also CANR 13; CA 57-60; DLB 67

Abse, Dannie 1923- . . . . CLC 7, 29
See also CAAS 1; CANR 4; CA 53-56;
DLB 27

Achebe, (Albert) Chinua(lumogu)
1930- . . . . CLC 1, 3, 5, 7, 11, 26, 51
See also CLR 20; CANR 6, 26; CA 1-4R;
SATA 38, 40

Acker, Kathy 1948- . . . . CLC 45
See also CA 117, 122

Ackroyd, Peter 1949- . . . . CLC 34, 52
See also CA 123, 127

Acorn, Milton 1923- . . . . CLC 15
See also CA 103; DLB 53

Adamov, Arthur 1908-1970 . . . . . . CLC 4, 25
See also CAP 2; CA 17-18;
obituary CA 25-28R

Adams, Alice (Boyd) 1926- . . . CLC 6, 13, 46
See also CANR 26; CA 81-84; DLB-Y 86

Adams, Douglas (Noel) 1952- . . . . . . CLC 27
See also CA 106; DLB-Y 83

Adams, Henry (Brooks)
1838-1918 . . . . TCLC 4
See also CA 104; DLB 12, 47

Adams, Richard (George)
1920- . . . . CLC 4, 5, 18
See also CLR 20; CANR 3; CA 49-52;
SATA 7

Adamson, Joy(-Friederike Victoria)
1910-1980 . . . . CLC 17
See also CANR 22; CA 69-72;
obituary CA 93-96; SATA 11;
obituary SATA 22

Adcock, (Kareen) Fleur 1934- . . . . . . CLC 41
See also CANR 11; CA 25-28R; DLB 40

Addams, Charles (Samuel)
1912-1988 . . . . CLC 30
See also CANR 12; CA 61-64;
obituary CA 126

Adler, C(arole) S(chwerdtfeger)
1932- . . . . CLC 35
See also CANR 19; CA 89-92; SATA 26

Adler, Renata 1938- . . . . CLC 8, 31
See also CANR 5, 22; CA 49-52

Ady, Endre 1877-1919 . . . . TCLC 11
See also CA 107

Agee, James 1909-1955 . . . . TCLC 1, 19
See also CA 108; DLB 2, 26;
CDALB 1941-1968

Agnon, S(hmuel) Y(osef Halevi)
1888-1970 . . . . CLC 4, 8, 14
See also CAP 2; CA 17-18;
obituary CA 25-28R

Ai 1947- . . . . CLC 4, 14
See also CA 85-88

Aickman, Robert (Fordyce)
1914-1981 . . . . CLC 57
See also CANR 3; CA 7-8R

Aiken, Conrad (Potter)
1889-1973 . . . . CLC 1, 3, 5, 10, 52
See also CANR 4; CA 5-8R;
obituary CA 45-48; SATA 3, 30; DLB 9,
45

Aiken, Joan (Delano) 1924- . . . . CLC 35
See also CLR 1; CANR 4; CA 9-12R;
SAAS 1; SATA 2, 30

Ainsworth, William Harrison
1805-1882 . . . . NCLC 13
See also SATA 24; DLB 21

Ajar, Emile 1914-1980
See Gary, Romain

Akhmadulina, Bella (Akhatovna)
1937- . . . . CLC 53
See also CA 65-68

Akhmatova, Anna 1888-1966. . . . CLC 11, 25
See also CAP 1; CA 19-20;
obituary CA 25-28R

Aksakov, Sergei Timofeyvich
1791-1859 . . . . NCLC 2

Aksenov, Vassily (Pavlovich) 1932-
See Aksyonov, Vasily (Pavlovich)

Aksyonov, Vasily (Pavlovich)
1932- . . . . CLC 22, 37
See also CANR 12; CA 53-56

Akutagawa Ryunosuke
1892-1927 . . . . TCLC 16
See also CA 117

Alain-Fournier 1886-1914 . . . . TCLC 6
See also Fournier, Henri Alban
See also DLB 65

Alarcon, Pedro Antonio de
1833-1891 . . . . NCLC 1

Alas (y Urena), Leopoldo (Enrique Garcia)
1852-1901 . . . . TCLC 29
See also CA 113

Albee, Edward (Franklin III)
1928- . . . CLC 1, 2, 3, 5, 9, 11, 13, 25, 53
See also CANR 8; CA 5-8R; DLB 7;
CDALB 1941-1968

Alberti, Rafael 1902- . . . . CLC 7
See also CA 85-88

Alcott, Amos Bronson 1799-1888 . . NCLC 1
See also DLB 1

Alcott, Louisa May 1832-1888 . . . . NCLC 6
See also CLR 1; YABC 1; DLB 1, 42;
CDALB 1865-1917

Aldanov, Mark 1887-1957 . . . . TCLC 23
See also CA 118

Aldington, Richard 1892-1962 . . . . . . CLC 49
See also CA 85-88; DLB 20, 36

Aldiss, Brian W(ilson)
1925- . . . . CLC 5, 14, 40
See also CAAS 2; CANR 5; CA 5-8R;
SATA 34; DLB 14

Alegria, Fernando 1918- . . . . CLC 57
See also CANR 5; CA 11-12R

Aleixandre, Vicente 1898-1984 . . . CLC 9, 36
See also CANR 26; CA 85-88;
obituary CA 114

Alepoudelis, Odysseus 1911-
See Elytis, Odysseus

Aleshkovsky, Yuz 1929- . . . . CLC 44
See also CA 121

Alexander, Lloyd (Chudley) 1924- . . CLC 35
See also CLR 1, 5; CANR 1; CA 1-4R;
SATA 3, 49; DLB 52

Alger, Horatio, Jr. 1832-1899 . . . . . NCLC 8
See also SATA 16; DLB 42

Algren, Nelson 1909-1981 . . . . CLC 4, 10, 33
See also CANR 20; CA 13-16R;
obituary CA 103; DLB 9; DLB-Y 81, 82;
CDALB 1941-1968

Alighieri, Dante 1265-1321 . . . . CMLC 3

Allen, Edward 1948- . . . . CLC 59

Allen, Roland 1939-
See Ayckbourn, Alan

Allen, Woody 1935- . . . . CLC 16, 52
See also CANR 27; CA 33-36R; DLB 44

Allende, Isabel 1942- . . . . CLC 39, 57
See also CA 125

Allingham, Margery (Louise)
1904-1966 . . . . CLC 19
See also CANR 4; CA 5-8R;
obituary CA 25-28R

Allingham, William 1824-1889 . . . NCLC 25
See also DLB 35

Allston, Washington 1779-1843 . . . . NCLC 2
See also DLB 1

Almedingen, E. M. 1898-1971 . . . . . . CLC 12
See also Almedingen, Martha Edith von
See also SATA 3

Almedingen, Martha Edith von 1898-1971
See Almedingen, E. M.
See also CANR 1; CA 1-4R

Alonso, Damaso 1898- . . . . CLC 14
See also CA 110

Alta 1942- . . . . CLC 19
See also CA 57-60

Alter, Robert B(ernard) 1935- . . . . . . CLC 34
See also CANR 1; CA 49-52

Alther, Lisa 1944- . . . . CLC 7, 41
See also CANR 12; CA 65-68

Altman, Robert 1925- . . . . CLC 16
See also CA 73-76

Alvarez, A(lfred) 1929- . . . . CLC 5, 13
See also CANR 3; CA 1-4R; DLB 14, 40

Alvarez, Alejandro Rodriguez 1903-1965
See Casona, Alejandro
See also obituary CA 93-96

Amado, Jorge 1912- . . . . CLC 13, 40
See also CA 77-80

Ambler, Eric 1909- . . . . CLC 4, 6, 9
See also CANR 7; CA 9-12R

Amichai, Yehuda 1924- . . . . . . CLC 9, 22, 57
See also CA 85-88

Amiel, Henri Frederic 1821-1881 . . NCLC 4

Amis, Kingsley (William)
1922- . . . . . . CLC 1, 2, 3, 5, 8, 13, 40, 44
See also CANR 8; CA 9-12R; DLB 15, 27

Amis, Martin 1949- . . . . CLC 4, 9, 38
See also CANR 8; CA 65-68; DLB 14

Ammons, A(rchie) R(andolph)
1926- . . . . . CLC 2, 3, 5, 8, 9, 25, 57
See also CANR 6; CA 9-12R; DLB 5

Anand, Mulk Raj 1905- . . . . CLC 23
See also CA 65-68

Anaya, Rudolfo A(lfonso) 1937- . . . . CLC 23
See also CAAS 4; CANR 1; CA 45-48

Andersen, Hans Christian
1805-1875 . . . . NCLC 7
See also CLR 6; YABC 1

Anderson, Jessica (Margaret Queale)
19??- . . . . CLC 37
See also CANR 4; CA 9-12R

Anderson, Jon (Victor) 1940- . . . . . . CLC 9
See also CANR 20; CA 25-28R

Anderson, Lindsay 1923- . . . . CLC 20

Anderson, Maxwell 1888-1959 . . . . . TCLC 2
See also CA 105; DLB 7

Anderson, Poul (William) 1926- . . . CLC 15
See also CAAS 2; CANR 2, 15; CA 1-4R;
SATA 39; DLB 8

Anderson, Robert (Woodruff)
1917- . . . . CLC 23
See also CA 21-24R; DLB 7

Anderson, Roberta Joan 1943-
See Mitchell, Joni

Anderson, Sherwood
1876-1941 . . . . . . TCLC 1, 10, 24; SSC 1
See also CAAS 3; CA 104, 121; DLB 4, 9;
DLB-DS 1

Andrade, Carlos Drummond de
1902-1987 . . . . CLC 18
See also CA 123

Andrewes, Lancelot 1555-1626 . . . . . . LC 5

Andrews, Cicily Fairfield 1892-1983
See West, Rebecca

Andreyev, Leonid (Nikolaevich)
1871-1919 . . . . TCLC 3
See also CA 104

Andrezel, Pierre 1885-1962
See Dinesen, Isak; Blixen, Karen
(Christentze Dinesen)

Andric, Ivo 1892-1975 . . . . CLC 8
See also CA 81-84; obituary CA 57-60

Angelique, Pierre 1897-1962
See Bataille, Georges

Angell, Roger 1920- . . . . CLC 26
See also CANR 13; CA 57-60

Angelou, Maya 1928- . . . . CLC 12, 35
See also CANR 19; CA 65-68; SATA 49;
DLB 38

Annensky, Innokenty 1856-1909 . . . TCLC 14
See also CA 110

Anouilh, Jean (Marie Lucien Pierre)
1910-1987 . . . . . . CLC 1, 3, 8, 13, 40, 50
See also CA 17-20R; obituary CA 123

Anthony, Florence 1947-
See Ai

Anthony (Jacob), Piers 1934- . . . . . . CLC 35
See also Jacob, Piers A(nthony)
D(illingham)
See also DLB 8

Antoninus, Brother 1912-
See Everson, William (Oliver)

Antonioni, Michelangelo 1912- . . . . CLC 20
See also CA 73-76

Antschel, Paul 1920-1970
See Celan, Paul
See also CA 85-88

Anwar, Chairil 1922-1949 . . . . TCLC 22
See also CA 121

Author Index

Author Index

Author Index

Dexter, Pete 1943- . . . . **CLC 34, 55**
See also CA 127

Diamond, Neil (Leslie) 1941- . . . . **CLC 30**
See also CA 108

Dick, Philip K(indred)
1928-1982 . . . . **CLC 10, 30**
See also CANR 2, 16; CA 49-52;
obituary CA 106; DLB 8

Dickens, Charles
1812-1870 . . . . **NCLC 3, 8, 18, 26**
See also SATA 15; DLB 21, 55, 70

Dickey, James (Lafayette)
1923- . . . . **CLC 1, 2, 4, 7, 10, 15, 47**
See also CANR 10; CA 9-12R; CABS 2;
DLB 5; DLB-Y 82

Dickey, William 1928- . . . . **CLC 3, 28**
See also CANR 24; CA 9-12R; DLB 5

Dickinson, Charles 1952- . . . . **CLC 49**

Dickinson, Emily (Elizabeth)
1830-1886 . . . . **NCLC 21**
See also SATA 29; DLB 1;
CDALB 1865-1917

Dickinson, Peter (Malcolm de Brissac)
1927- . . . . **CLC 12, 35**
See also CA 41-44R; SATA 5

Didion, Joan 1934- . . . . . **CLC 1, 3, 8, 14, 32**
See also CANR 14; CA 5-8R; DLB 2;
DLB-Y 81, 86

Dillard, Annie 1945- . . . . **CLC 9**
See also CANR 3; CA 49-52; SATA 10;
DLB-Y 80

Dillard, R(ichard) H(enry) W(ilde)
1937- . . . . **CLC 5**
See also CAAS 7; CANR 10; CA 21-24R;
DLB 5

Dillon, Eilis 1920- . . . . **CLC 17**
See also CAAS 3; CANR 4; CA 9-12R;
SATA 2

Dinesen, Isak 1885-1962 . . . . **CLC 10, 29**
See also Blixen, Karen (Christentze
Dinesen)
See also CANR 22

Disch, Thomas M(ichael) 1940- . . . **CLC 7, 36**
See also CAAS 4; CANR 17; CA 21-24R;
DLB 8

Disraeli, Benjamin 1804-1881 . . . . . **NCLC 2**
See also DLB 21, 55

Dixon, Paige 1911-
See Corcoran, Barbara

Dixon, Stephen 1936- . . . . **CLC 52**
See also CANR 17; CA 89-92

Doblin, Alfred 1878-1957 . . . . **TCLC 13**
See also Doeblin, Alfred

Dobrolyubov, Nikolai Alexandrovich
1836-1861 . . . . **NCLC 5**

Dobyns, Stephen 1941- . . . . **CLC 37**
See also CANR 2, 18; CA 45-48

Doctorow, E(dgar) L(aurence)
1931- . . . . **CLC 6, 11, 15, 18, 37, 44**
See also CANR 2; CA 45-48; DLB 2, 28;
DLB-Y 80

Dodgson, Charles Lutwidge 1832-1898
See Carroll, Lewis
See also YABC 2

Doeblin, Alfred 1878-1957 . . . . **TCLC 13**
See also CA 110; DLB 66

Doerr, Harriet 1910- . . . . **CLC 34**
See also CA 117, 122

Donaldson, Stephen R. 1947- . . . . . . **CLC 46**
See also CANR 13; CA 89-92

Donleavy, J(ames) P(atrick)
1926- . . . . **CLC 1, 4, 6, 10, 45**
See also CANR 24; CA 9-12R; DLB 6

Donnadieu, Marguerite 1914-
See Duras, Marguerite

Donne, John 1572?-1631 . . . . **LC 10**

Donnell, David 1939?- . . . . **CLC 34**

Donoso, Jose 1924- . . . . **CLC 4, 8, 11, 32**
See also CA 81-84

Donovan, John 1928- . . . . **CLC 35**
See also CLR 3; CA 97-100; SATA 29

Doolittle, Hilda 1886-1961
See H(ilda) D(oolittle)
See also CA 97-100; DLB 4, 45

Dorfman, Ariel 1942- . . . . **CLC 48**
See also CA 124

Dorn, Ed(ward Merton) 1929- . . . **CLC 10, 18**
See also CA 93-96; DLB 5

Dos Passos, John (Roderigo)
1896-1970 . . . **CLC 1, 4, 8, 11, 15, 25, 34**
See also CANR 3; CA 1-4R;
obituary CA 29-32R; DLB 4, 9;
DLB-DS 1

Dostoevski, Fedor Mikhailovich
1821-1881 . . . . **NCLC 2, 7, 21; SSC 2**

Doughty, Charles (Montagu)
1843-1926 . . . . **TCLC 27**
See also CA 115; DLB 19, 57

Douglas, George 1869-1902 . . . . **TCLC 28**

Douglass, Frederick 1817-1895 . . . . **NCLC 7**
See also SATA 29; DLB 1, 43, 50;
CDALB 1640-1865

Dourado, (Waldomiro Freitas) Autran
1926- . . . . **CLC 23**
See also CA 25-28R

Dove, Rita 1952- . . . . **CLC 50**
See also CA 109

Dowson, Ernest (Christopher)
1867-1900 . . . . **TCLC 4**
See also CA 105; DLB 19

Doyle, (Sir) Arthur Conan
1859-1930 . . . . **TCLC 7, 26**
See also CA 104, 122; SATA 24; DLB 18,
70

Dr. A 1933-
See Silverstein, Alvin and Virginia B(arbara
Opshelor) Silverstein

Drabble, Margaret
1939- . . . . **CLC 2, 3, 5, 8, 10, 22, 53**
See also CANR 18; CA 13-16R; SATA 48;
DLB 14

Drayton, Michael 1563-1631 . . . . **LC 8**

Dreiser, Theodore (Herman Albert)
1871-1945 . . . . **TCLC 10, 18, 35**
See also CA 106; SATA 48; DLB 9, 12;
DLB-DS 1; CDALB 1865-1917

Drexler, Rosalyn 1926- . . . . **CLC 2, 6**
See also CA 81-84

Dreyer, Carl Theodor 1889-1968 . . . . **CLC 16**
See also obituary CA 116

Drieu La Rochelle, Pierre
1893-1945 . . . . **TCLC 21**
See also CA 117; DLB 72

Droste-Hulshoff, Annette Freiin von
1797-1848 . . . . **NCLC 3**

Drummond, William Henry
1854-1907 . . . . **TCLC 25**

Drummond de Andrade, Carlos 1902-1987
See Andrade, Carlos Drummond de

Drury, Allen (Stuart) 1918- . . . . **CLC 37**
See also CANR 18; CA 57-60

Dryden, John 1631-1700 . . . . **LC 3**

Duberman, Martin 1930- . . . . **CLC 8**
See also CANR 2; CA 1-4R

Dubie, Norman (Evans, Jr.) 1945- . . **CLC 36**
See also CANR 12; CA 69-72

Du Bois, W(illiam) E(dward) B(urghardt)
1868-1963 . . . . **CLC 1, 2, 13**
See also CA 85-88; SATA 42; DLB 47, 50;
CDALB 1865-1917

Dubus, Andre 1936- . . . . **CLC 13, 36**
See also CANR 17; CA 21-24R

Ducasse, Isidore Lucien 1846-1870
See Lautreamont, Comte de

Duclos, Charles Pinot 1704-1772 . . . . . **LC 1**

Dudek, Louis 1918- . . . . **CLC 11, 19**
See also CANR 1; CA 45-48

Dudevant, Amandine Aurore Lucile Dupin
1804-1876
See Sand, George

Duerrenmatt, Friedrich
1921- . . . . **CLC 1, 4, 8, 11, 15, 43**
See also CA 17-20R; DLB 69

Duffy, Bruce 19??- . . . . **CLC 50**

Duffy, Maureen 1933- . . . . **CLC 37**
See also CA 25-28R; DLB 14

Dugan, Alan 1923- . . . . **CLC 2, 6**
See also CA 81-84; DLB 5

Duhamel, Georges 1884-1966 . . . . **CLC 8**
See also CA 81-84; obituary CA 25-28R

Dujardin, Edouard (Emile Louis)
1861-1949 . . . . **TCLC 13**
See also CA 109

Duke, Raoul 1939-
See Thompson, Hunter S(tockton)

Dumas, Alexandre (Davy de la Pailleterie)
(pere) 1802-1870 . . . . **NCLC 11**
See also SATA 18

Dumas, Alexandre (fils)
1824-1895 . . . . **NCLC 9**

Dumas, Henry (L.) 1934-1968 . . . . **CLC 6**
See also CA 85-88; DLB 41

Du Maurier, Daphne 1907- . . . **CLC 6, 11, 59**
See also CANR 6; CA 5-8R;
obituary CA 128; SATA 27

Dunbar, Paul Laurence
1872-1906 . . . . **TCLC 2, 12**
See also CA 104, 124; SATA 34; DLB 50,
54; CDALB 1865-1917

Engel, Marian 1933-1985......... **CLC 36**
See also CANR 12; CA 25-28R; DLB 53

Engelhardt, Frederick 1911-1986
See Hubbard, L(afayette) Ron(ald)

Enright, D(ennis) J(oseph)
1920-.................. **CLC 4, 8, 31**
See also CANR 1; CA 1-4R; SATA 25;
DLB 27

Enzensberger, Hans Magnus
1929-...................... **CLC 43**
See also CA 116, 119

Ephron, Nora 1941-...... **CLC 17, 31**
See also CANR 12; CA 65-68

Epstein, Daniel Mark 1948-........ **CLC 7**
See also CANR 2; CA 49-52

Epstein, Jacob 1956-............ **CLC 19**
See also CA 114

Epstein, Joseph 1937-............ **CLC 39**
See also CA 112, 119

Epstein, Leslie 1938-............ **CLC 27**
See also CANR 23; CA 73-76

Erdman, Paul E(mil) 1932-....... **CLC 25**
See also CANR 13; CA 61-64

Erdrich, Louise 1954-......... **CLC 39, 54**
See also CA 114

Erenburg, Ilya (Grigoryevich) 1891-1967
See Ehrenburg, Ilya (Grigoryevich)

Eseki, Bruno 1919-
See Mphahlele, Ezekiel

Esenin, Sergei (Aleksandrovich)
1895-1925 .... **TCLC 4**
See also CA 104

Eshleman, Clayton 1935-.......... **CLC 7**
See also CAAS 6; CA 33-36R; DLB 5

Espriu, Salvador 1913-1985........ **CLC 9**
See also obituary CA 115

Estleman, Loren D. 1952-........ **CLC 48**
See also CA 85-88

Evans, Marian 1819-1880
See Eliot, George

Evans, Mary Ann 1819-1880
See Eliot, George

Evarts, Esther 1900-1972
See Benson, Sally

Everett, Percival L. 1957?-........ **CLC 57**
See also CA 129

Everson, Ronald G(ilmour) 1903-... **CLC 27**
See also CA 17-20R

Everson, William (Oliver)
1912-.................... **CLC 1, 5, 14**
See also CANR 20; CA 9-12R; DLB 5, 16

Evtushenko, Evgenii (Aleksandrovich) 1933-
See Yevtushenko, Yevgeny

Ewart, Gavin (Buchanan)
1916-.................... **CLC 13, 46**
See also CANR 17; CA 89-92; DLB 40

Ewers, Hanns Heinz 1871-1943 ... **TCLC 12**
See also CA 109

Ewing, Frederick R. 1918-
See Sturgeon, Theodore (Hamilton)

Exley, Frederick (Earl) 1929-.... **CLC 6, 11**
See also CA 81-84; DLB-Y 81

Ezekiel, Tish O'Dowd 1943-....... **CLC 34**

Fagen, Donald 1948-.............. **CLC 26**

Fair, Ronald L. 1932-............ **CLC 18**
See also CANR 25; CA 69-72; DLB 33

Fairbairns, Zoe (Ann) 1948-....... **CLC 32**
See also CANR 21; CA 103

Fairfield, Cicily Isabel 1892-1983
See West, Rebecca

Fallaci, Oriana 1930-............ **CLC 11**
See also CANR 15; CA 77-80

Faludy, George 1913-............ **CLC 42**
See also CA 21-24R

Farah, Nuruddin 1945-............ **CLC 53**
See also CA 106

Fargue, Leon-Paul 1876-1947 ..... **TCLC 11**
See also CA 109

Farigoule, Louis 1885-1972
See Romains, Jules

Farina, Richard 1937?-1966........ **CLC 9**
See also CA 81-84; obituary CA 25-28R

Farley, Walter 1920-............ **CLC 17**
See also CANR 8; CA 17-20R; SATA 2, 43;
DLB 22

Farmer, Philip Jose 1918-....... **CLC 1, 19**
See also CANR 4; CA 1-4R; DLB 8

Farrell, J(ames) G(ordon)
1935-1979 .... **CLC 6**
See also CA 73-76; obituary CA 89-92;
DLB 14

Farrell, James T(homas)
1904-1979 .... **CLC 1, 4, 8, 11**
See also CANR 9; CA 5-8R;
obituary CA 89-92; DLB 4, 9; DLB-DS 2

Farrell, M. J. 1904-
See Keane, Molly

Fassbinder, Rainer Werner
1946-1982 .... **CLC 20**
See also CA 93-96; obituary CA 106

Fast, Howard (Melvin) 1914- ...... **CLC 23**
See also CANR 1; CA 1-4R; SATA 7;
DLB 9

Faulkner, William (Cuthbert)
1897-1962 .... **CLC 1, 3, 6, 8, 9, 11, 14,
18, 28, 52; SSC 1**
See also CA 81-84; DLB 9, 11, 44;
DLB-Y 86; DLB-DS 2

Fauset, Jessie Redmon
1884?-1961............... **CLC 19, 54**
See also CA 109; DLB 51

Faust, Irvin 1924-................. **CLC 8**
See also CA 33-36R; DLB 2, 28; DLB-Y 80

Fearing, Kenneth (Flexner)
1902-1961 .... **CLC 51**
See also CA 93-96; DLB 9

Federman, Raymond 1928- ...... **CLC 6, 47**
See also CANR 10; CA 17-20R; DLB-Y 80

Federspiel, J(urg) F. 1931-........ **CLC 42**

Feiffer, Jules 1929-............ **CLC 2, 8**
See also CA 17-20R; SATA 8; DLB 7, 44

Feinberg, David B. 1956-........ **CLC 59**

Feinstein, Elaine 1930-............ **CLC 36**
See also CAAS 1; CA 69-72; DLB 14, 40

Feldman, Irving (Mordecai) 1928-.... **CLC 7**
See also CANR 1; CA 1-4R

Fellini, Federico 1920-............ **CLC 16**
See also CA 65-68

Felsen, Gregor 1916-
See Felsen, Henry Gregor

Felsen, Henry Gregor 1916-....... **CLC 17**
See also CANR 1; CA 1-4R; SAAS 2;
SATA 1

Fenton, James (Martin) 1949-...... **CLC 32**
See also CA 102; DLB 40

Ferber, Edna 1887-1968.......... **CLC 18**
See also CA 5-8R; obituary CA 25-28R;
SATA 7; DLB 9, 28

Ferlinghetti, Lawrence (Monsanto)
1919?-........... **CLC 2, 6, 10, 27**
See also CANR 3; CA 5-8R; DLB 5, 16;
CDALB 1941-1968

Ferrier, Susan (Edmonstone)
1782-1854 .... **NCLC 8**

Feuchtwanger, Lion 1884-1958 ..... **TCLC 3**
See also CA 104; DLB 66

Feydeau, Georges 1862-1921...... **TCLC 22**
See also CA 113

Ficino, Marsilio 1433-1499 .... **LC 12**

Fiedler, Leslie A(aron)
1917-............ **CLC 4, 13, 24**
See also CANR 7; CA 9-12R; DLB 28, 67

Field, Andrew 1938-............ **CLC 44**
See also CANR 25; CA 97-100

Field, Eugene 1850-1895 .... **NCLC 3**
See also SATA 16; DLB 21, 23, 42

Fielding, Henry 1707-1754 .... **LC 1**
See also DLB 39

Fielding, Sarah 1710-1768 .... **LC 1**
See also DLB 39

Fierstein, Harvey 1954-........ **CLC 33**
See also CA 123

Figes, Eva 1932-................. **CLC 31**
See also CANR 4; CA 53-56; DLB 14

Finch, Robert (Duer Claydon)
1900-.................... **CLC 18**
See also CANR 9, 24; CA 57-60

Findley, Timothy 1930-........... **CLC 27**
See also CANR 12; CA 25-28R; DLB 53

Fink, Janis 1951-
See Ian, Janis

Firbank, Louis 1944-
See Reed, Lou
See also CA 117

Firbank, (Arthur Annesley) Ronald
1886-1926 .... **TCLC 1**
See also CA 104; DLB 36

Fisher, Roy 1930-................. **CLC 25**
See also CANR 16; CA 81-84; DLB 40

Fisher, Rudolph 1897-1934 .... **TCLC 11**
See also CA 107; DLB 51

Fisher, Vardis (Alvero) 1895-1968.... **CLC 7**
See also CA 5-8R; obituary CA 25-28R;
DLB 9

FitzGerald, Edward 1809-1883 .... **NCLC 9**
See also DLB 32

Fitzgerald, F(rancis) Scott (Key)
1896-1940 .... **TCLC 1, 6, 14, 28**
See also CA 110, 123; DLB 4, 9; DLB-Y 81;
DLB-DS 1

Fuller, Roy (Broadbent) 1912-.... **CLC 4, 28**
See also CA 5-8R; DLB 15, 20

Fulton, Alice 1952-.............. **CLC 52**
See also CA 116

Furphy, Joseph 1843-1912........ **TCLC 25**

Futrelle, Jacques 1875-1912 ...... **TCLC 19**
See also CA 113

Gaboriau, Emile 1835-1873 ...... **NCLC 14**

Gadda, Carlo Emilio 1893-1973 .... **CLC 11**
See also CA 89-92

Gaddis, William
1922- ...... **CLC 1, 3, 6, 8, 10, 19, 43**
See also CAAS 4; CANR 21; CA 17-20R;
DLB 2

Gaines, Ernest J. 1933-...... **CLC 3, 11, 18**
See also CANR 6, 24; CA 9-12R; DLB 2,
33; DLB-Y 80

Gale, Zona 1874-1938 .... **TCLC 7**
See also CA 105; DLB 9

Gallagher, Tess 1943-............. **CLC 18**
See also CA 106

Gallant, Mavis
1922- .... **CLC 7, 18, 38; SSC 5**
See also CA 69-72; DLB 53

Gallant, Roy A(rthur) 1924- .... **CLC 17**
See also CANR 4; CA 5-8R; SATA 4

Gallico, Paul (William) 1897-1976 ... **CLC 2**
See also CA 5-8R; obituary CA 69-72;
SATA 13; DLB 9

Galsworthy, John 1867-1933....... **TCLC 1**
See also CA 104; DLB 10, 34

Galt, John 1779-1839............. **NCLC 1**

Galvin, James 1951-.............. **CLC 38**
See also CANR 26; CA 108

Gamboa, Frederico 1864-1939..... **TCLC 36**

Gann, Ernest K(ellogg) 1910- ...... **CLC 23**
See also CANR 1; CA 1-4R

Garcia Lorca, Federico
1899-1936 .... **TCLC 1, 7**
See also CA 104

Garcia Marquez, Gabriel (Jose)
1928- .... **CLC 2, 3, 8, 10, 15, 27, 47, 55**
See also CANR 10; CA 33-36R

Gardam, Jane 1928-.............. **CLC 43**
See also CLR 12; CANR 2, 18; CA 49-52;
SATA 28, 39; DLB 14

Gardner, Herb 1934- .... **CLC 44**

Gardner, John (Champlin, Jr.)
1933-1982 .... **CLC 2, 3, 5, 7, 8, 10, 18,
28, 34**
See also CA 65-68; obituary CA 107;
obituary SATA 31, 40; DLB 2; DLB-Y 82

Gardner, John (Edmund) 1926-..... **CLC 30**
See also CANR 15; CA 103

Garfield, Leon 1921-.............. **CLC 12**
See also CA 17-20R; SATA 1, 32

Garland, (Hannibal) Hamlin
1860-1940 .... **TCLC 3**
See also CA 104; DLB 12, 71

Garneau, Hector (de) Saint Denys
1912-1943 .... **TCLC 13**
See also CA 111

Garner, Alan 1935-.............. **CLC 17**
See also CLR 20; CANR 15; CA 73-76;
SATA 18

Garner, Hugh 1913-1979......... **CLC 13**
See also CA 69-72; DLB 68

Garnett, David 1892-1981 .... **CLC 3**
See also CANR 17; CA 5-8R;
obituary CA 103; DLB 34

Garrett, George (Palmer, Jr.)
1929- .... **CLC 3, 11, 51**
See also CAAS 5; CANR 1; CA 1-4R;
DLB 2, 5; DLB-Y 83

Garrigue, Jean 1914-1972 .... **CLC 2, 8**
See also CANR 20; CA 5-8R;
obituary CA 37-40R

Gary, Romain 1914-1980 .... **CLC 25**
See also Kacew, Romain

Gascar, Pierre 1916-............. **CLC 11**
See also Fournier, Pierre

Gascoyne, David (Emery) 1916- ... **CLC 45**
See also CANR 10; CA 65-68; DLB 20

Gaskell, Elizabeth Cleghorn
1810-1865 .... **NCLC 5**
See also DLB 21

Gass, William H(oward)
1924- ...... **CLC 1, 2, 8, 11, 15, 39**
See also CA 17-20R; DLB 2

Gautier, Theophile 1811-1872 ..... **NCLC 1**

Gaye, Marvin (Pentz) 1939-1984 ... **CLC 26**
See also obituary CA 112

Gebler, Carlo (Ernest) 1954-....... **CLC 39**
See also CA 119

Gee, Maggie 19??- .... **CLC 57**

Gee, Maurice (Gough) 1931-...... **CLC 29**
See also CA 97-100; SATA 46

Gelbart, Larry (Simon) 1923- ...... **CLC 21**
See also CA 73-76

Gelber, Jack 1932-........... **CLC 1, 6, 14**
See also CANR 2; CA 1-4R; DLB 7

Gellhorn, Martha (Ellis) 1908- ..... **CLC 14**
See also CA 77-80; DLB-Y 82

Genet, Jean
1910-1986 ... **CLC 1, 2, 5, 10, 14, 44, 46**
See also CANR 18; CA 13-16R; DLB 72;
DLB-Y 86

Gent, Peter 1942-................ **CLC 29**
See also CA 89-92; DLB 72; DLB-Y 82

George, Jean Craighead 1919-...... **CLC 35**
See also CLR 1; CA 5-8R; SATA 2;
DLB 52

George, Stefan (Anton)
1868-1933 .... **TCLC 2, 14**
See also CA 104

Gerhardi, William (Alexander) 1895-1977
See Gerhardie, William (Alexander)

Gerhardie, William (Alexander)
1895-1977 .... **CLC 5**
See also CANR 18; CA 25-28R;
obituary CA 73-76; DLB 36

Gertler, T(rudy) 1946?- .... **CLC 34**
See also CA 116

Gessner, Friedrike Victoria 1910-1980
See Adamson, Joy(-Friederike Victoria)

Ghelderode, Michel de
1898-1962 .... **CLC 6, 11**
See also CA 85-88

Ghiselin, Brewster 1903-......... **CLC 23**
See also CANR 13; CA 13-16R

Ghose, Zulfikar 1935-............. **CLC 42**
See also CA 65-68

Ghosh, Amitav 1943- .... **CLC 44**

Giacosa, Giuseppe 1847-1906 ...... **TCLC 7**
See also CA 104

Gibbon, Lewis Grassic 1901-1935... **TCLC 4**
See also Mitchell, James Leslie

Gibbons, Kaye 1960- .... **CLC 50**

Gibran, (Gibran) Kahlil
1883-1931 .... **TCLC 1, 9**
See also CA 104

Gibson, William 1914-........... **CLC 23**
See also CANR 9; CA 9-12R; DLB 7

Gibson, William 1948-........... **CLC 39**
See also CA 126

Gide, Andre (Paul Guillaume)
1869-1951 .... **TCLC 5, 12, 36**
See also CA 104, 124; DLB 65

Gifford, Barry (Colby) 1946-....... **CLC 34**
See also CANR 9; CA 65-68

Gilbert, (Sir) W(illiam) S(chwenck)
1836-1911 .... **TCLC 3**
See also CA 104; SATA 36

Gilbreth, Ernestine 1908-
See Carey, Ernestine Gilbreth

Gilbreth, Frank B(unker), Jr.
1911- .... **CLC 17**
See also CA 9-12R; SATA 2

Gilchrist, Ellen 1935-......... **CLC 34, 48**
See also CA 113, 116

Giles, Molly 1942-............... **CLC 39**
See also CA 126

Gilliam, Terry (Vance) 1940-
See Monty Python
See also CA 108, 113

Gilliatt, Penelope (Ann Douglass)
1932-............... **CLC 2, 10, 13, 53**
See also CA 13-16R; DLB 14

Gilman, Charlotte (Anna) Perkins (Stetson)
1860-1935 .... **TCLC 9, 37**
See also CA 106

Gilmour, David 1944-
See Pink Floyd

Gilroy, Frank D(aniel) 1925-........ **CLC 2**
See also CA 81-84; DLB 7

Ginsberg, Allen
1926- .... **CLC 1, 2, 3, 4, 6, 13, 36**
See also CANR 2; CA 1-4R; DLB 5, 16;
CDALB 1941-1968

Ginzburg, Natalia 1916-...... **CLC 5, 11, 54**
See also CA 85-88

Giono, Jean 1895-1970......... **CLC 4, 11**
See also CANR 2; CA 45-48;
obituary CA 29-32R; DLB 72

Giovanni, Nikki 1943- .... **CLC 2, 4, 19**
See also CLR 6; CAAS 6; CANR 18;
CA 29-32R; SATA 24; DLB 5, 41

Giovene, Andrea 1904-............. **CLC 7**
See also CA 85-88

Green, Henry 1905-1974 .... **CLC 2, 13**
See also Yorke, Henry Vincent
See also DLB 15

Green, Julien (Hartridge) 1900- .. **CLC 3, 11**
See also CA 21-24R; DLB 4, 72

Green, Paul (Eliot) 1894-1981...... **CLC 25**
See also CANR 3; CA 5-8R;
obituary CA 103; DLB 7, 9; DLB-Y 81

Greenberg, Ivan 1908-1973
See Rahv, Philip
See also CA 85-88

Greenberg, Joanne (Goldenberg)
1932- .... **CLC 3, 7, 30**
See also Green, Hannah
See also CANR 14; CA 5-8R; SATA 25

Greenberg, Richard 1959?- .... **CLC 57**

Greene, Bette 1934- .... **CLC 30**
See also CLR 2; CANR 4; CA 53-56;
SATA 8

Greene, Gael 19??- .... **CLC 8**
See also CANR 10; CA 13-16R

Greene, Graham (Henry)
1904- ..... **CLC 1, 3, 6, 9, 14, 18, 27, 37**
See also CA 13-16R; SATA 20; DLB 13, 15;
DLB-Y 85

Gregor, Arthur 1923- .... **CLC 9**
See also CANR 11; CA 25-28R; SATA 36

Gregory, Lady (Isabella Augusta Persse)
1852-1932 .... **TCLC 1**
See also CA 104; DLB 10

Grendon, Stephen 1909-1971
See Derleth, August (William)

Greve, Felix Paul Berthold Friedrich
1879-1948
See Grove, Frederick Philip
See also CA 104

Grey, (Pearl) Zane 1872?-1939 ..... **TCLC 6**
See also CA 104; DLB 9

Grieg, (Johan) Nordahl (Brun)
1902-1943 .... **TCLC 10**
See also CA 107

Grieve, C(hristopher) M(urray) 1892-1978
See MacDiarmid, Hugh
See also CA 5-8R; obituary CA 85-88

Griffin, Gerald 1803-1840 .... **NCLC 7**

Griffin, Peter 1942- .... **CLC 39**

Griffiths, Trevor 1935-......... **CLC 13, 52**
See also CA 97-100; DLB 13

Grigson, Geoffrey (Edward Harvey)
1905-1985 .... **CLC 7, 39**
See also CANR 20; CA 25-28R;
obituary CA 118; DLB 27

Grillparzer, Franz 1791-1872...... **NCLC 1**

Grimke, Charlotte L(ottie) Forten 1837-1914
See Forten (Grimke), Charlotte L(ottie)
See also CA 117, 124

Grimm, Jakob (Ludwig) Karl
1785-1863 .... **NCLC 3**
See also SATA 22

Grimm, Wilhelm Karl 1786-1859 .. **NCLC 3**
See also SATA 22

**Grimmelshausen, Johann Jakob Christoffel
von** 1621-1676 .... **LC 6**

Grindel, Eugene 1895-1952
See also CA 104

Grossman, Vasily (Semenovich)
1905-1964 .... **CLC 41**
See also CA 124

Grove, Frederick Philip
1879-1948 .... **TCLC 4**
See also Greve, Felix Paul Berthold
Friedrich

Grumbach, Doris (Isaac)
1918- .... **CLC 13, 22**
See also CAAS 2; CANR 9; CA 5-8R

Grundtvig, Nicolai Frederik Severin
1783-1872 .... **NCLC 1**

Grunwald, Lisa 1959-............. **CLC 44**
See also CA 120

Guare, John 1938- .... **CLC 8, 14, 29**
See also CANR 21; CA 73-76; DLB 7

Gudjonsson, Halldor Kiljan 1902-
See Laxness, Halldor (Kiljan)
See also CA 103

Guest, Barbara 1920-............. **CLC 34**
See also CANR 11; CA 25-28R; DLB 5

Guest, Judith (Ann) 1936-....... **CLC 8, 30**
See also CANR 15; CA 77-80

Guild, Nicholas M. 1944-......... **CLC 33**
See also CA 93-96

Guillen, Jorge 1893-1984........... **CLC 11**
See also CA 89-92; obituary CA 112

Guillen, Nicolas 1902-1989 .... **CLC 48**
See also CA 116, 125

Guillevic, (Eugene) 1907-.......... **CLC 33**
See also CA 93-96

Gunn, Bill 1934-1989 .... **CLC 5**
See also Gunn, William Harrison
See also DLB 38

Gunn, Thom(son William)
1929- .... **CLC 3, 6, 18, 32**
See also CANR 9; CA 17-20R; DLB 27

Gunn, William Harrison 1934-1989
See Gunn, Bill
See also CANR 12, 25; CA 13-16R

Gurney, A(lbert) R(amsdell), Jr.
1930- .... **CLC 32, 50, 54**
See also CA 77-80

Gurney, Ivor (Bertie) 1890-1937... **TCLC 33**

Gustafson, Ralph (Barker) 1909-.... **CLC 36**
See also CANR 8; CA 21-24R

Guthrie, A(lfred) B(ertram), Jr.
1901- .... **CLC 23**
See also CA 57-60; DLB 6

Guthrie, Woodrow Wilson 1912-1967
See Guthrie, Woody
See also CA 113; obituary CA 93-96

Guthrie, Woody 1912-1967 .... **CLC 35**
See also Guthrie, Woodrow Wilson

Guy, Rosa (Cuthbert) 1928-..... **CLC 26 13**
See also CANR 14; CA 17-20R; SATA 14;
DLB 33

Haavikko, Paavo (Juhani)
1931- .... **CLC 18, 34**
See also CA 106

Hacker, Marilyn 1942- .... **CLC 5, 9, 23**
See also CA 77-80

Haggard, (Sir) H(enry) Rider
1856-1925 .... **TCLC 11**
See also CA 108; SATA 16; DLB 70

Haig-Brown, Roderick L(angmere)
1908-1976 .... **CLC 21**
See also CANR 4; CA 5-8R;
obituary CA 69-72; SATA 12

Hailey, Arthur 1920- .... **CLC 5**
See also CANR 2; CA 1-4R; DLB-Y 82

Hailey, Elizabeth Forsythe 1938-... **CLC 40**
See also CAAS 1; CANR 15; CA 93-96

Haines, John 1924-................. **CLC 58**
See also CANR 13; CA 19-20R; DLB 5

Haley, Alex (Palmer) 1921-...... **CLC 8, 12**
See also CA 77-80; DLB 38

Haliburton, Thomas Chandler
1796-1865 .... **NCLC 15**
See also DLB 11

Hall, Donald (Andrew, Jr.)
1928- .... **CLC 1, 13, 37, 59**
See also CAAS 7; CANR 2; CA 5-8R;
SATA 23; DLB 5

Hall, James Norman 1887-1951 ... **TCLC 23**
See also CA 123; SATA 21

Hall, (Marguerite) Radclyffe
1886-1943 .... **TCLC 12**
See also CA 110

Hall, Rodney 1935- .... **CLC 51**
See also CA 109

Halpern, Daniel 1945-............. **CLC 14**
See also CA 33-36R

Hamburger, Michael (Peter Leopold)
1924-..................... **CLC 5, 14**
See also CAAS 4; CANR 2; CA 5-8R;
DLB 27

Hamill, Pete 1935-............... **CLC 10**
See also CANR 18; CA 25-28R

Hamilton, Edmond 1904-1977....... **CLC 1**
See also CANR 3; CA 1-4R; DLB 8

Hamilton, Gail 1911-
See Corcoran, Barbara

Hamilton, Ian 1938-............. **CLC 55**
See also CA 106; DLB 40

Hamilton, Mollie 1909?-
See Kaye, M(ary) M(argaret)

Hamilton, (Anthony Walter) Patrick
1904-1962 .... **CLC 51**
See also obituary CA 113; DLB 10

Hamilton, Virginia (Esther) 1936-... **CLC 26**
See also CLR 1, 11; CANR 20; CA 25-28R;
SATA 4; DLB 33, 52

Hammett, (Samuel) Dashiell
1894-1961 .... **CLC 3, 5, 10, 19, 47**
See also CA 81-84

Hammon, Jupiter 1711?-1800? .... **NCLC 5**
See also DLB 31, 50

Hamner, Earl (Henry), Jr. 1923- ... **CLC 12**
See also CA 73-76; DLB 6

Hampton, Christopher (James)
1946-..................... **CLC 4**
See also CA 25-28R; DLB 13

Hamsun, Knut 1859-1952....... **TCLC 2, 14**
See also Pedersen, Knut

Author Index

Holt, Victoria 1906-
  See Hibbert, Eleanor (Burford)

Holub, Miroslav 1923-............ **CLC 4**
  See also CANR 10; CA 21-24R

Homer c. 8th century B.C.-....... **CMLC 1**

Honig, Edwin 1919-.............. **CLC 33**
  See also CANR 4; CA 5-8R; DLB 5

Hood, Hugh (John Blagdon)
  1928-.................... **CLC 15, 28**
  See also CANR 1; CA 49-52; DLB 53

Hood, Thomas 1799-1845........ **NCLC 16**

Hooker, (Peter) Jeremy 1941-...... **CLC 43**
  See also CANR 22; CA 77-80; DLB 40

Hope, A(lec) D(erwent) 1907- .... **CLC 3, 51**
  See also CA 21-24R

Hope, Christopher (David Tully)
  1944-....................... **CLC 52**
  See also CA 106

Hopkins, Gerard Manley
  1844-1889 .... **NCLC 17**
  See also DLB 35, 57

Hopkins, John (Richard) 1931-...... **CLC 4**
  See also CA 85-88

Hopkins, Pauline Elizabeth
  1859-1930 .... **TCLC 28**
  See also DLB 50

Horgan, Paul 1903- .... **CLC 9, 53**
  See also CANR 9; CA 13-16R; SATA 13;
  DLB-Y 85

Horovitz, Israel 1939- .... **CLC 56**
  See also CA 33-36R; DLB 7

Horwitz, Julius 1920-1986........ **CLC 14**
  See also CANR 12; CA 9-12R;
  obituary CA 119

Hospital, Janette Turner 1942-..... **CLC 42**
  See also CA 108

Hostos (y Bonilla), Eugenio Maria de
  1893-1903 .... **TCLC 24**
  See also CA 123

Hougan, Carolyn 19??-........... **CLC 34**

Household, Geoffrey (Edward West)
  1900-1988 .... **CLC 11**
  See also CA 77-80; obituary CA 126;
  SATA 14

Housman, A(lfred) E(dward)
  1859-1936 .... **TCLC 1, 10**
  See also CA 104, 125; DLB 19

Housman, Laurence 1865-1959..... **TCLC 7**
  See also CA 106; SATA 25; DLB 10

Howard, Elizabeth Jane 1923- ... **CLC 7, 29**
  See also CANR 8; CA 5-8R

Howard, Maureen 1930- ..... **CLC 5, 14, 46**
  See also CA 53-56; DLB-Y 83

Howard, Richard 1929- ...... **CLC 7, 10, 47**
  See also CANR 25; CA 85-88; DLB 5

Howard, Robert E(rvin)
  1906-1936 .... **TCLC 8**
  See also CA 105

Howe, Fanny 1940- .... **CLC 47**
  See also CA 117; SATA 52

Howe, Julia Ward 1819-1910 ..... **TCLC 21**
  See also CA 117; DLB 1

Howe, Tina 1937-................ **CLC 48**
  See also CA 109

Howell, James 1594?-1666......... **LC 13**

Howells, William Dean
  1837-1920 .... **TCLC 7, 17**
  See also CA 104; DLB 12, 64, 74;
  CDALB 1865-1917

Howes, Barbara 1914-............ **CLC 15**
  See also CAAS 3; CA 9-12R; SATA 5

Hrabal, Bohumil 1914-............ **CLC 13**
  See also CA 106

Hubbard, L(afayette) Ron(ald)
  1911-1986 .... **CLC 43**
  See also CANR 22; CA 77-80;
  obituary CA 118

Huch, Ricarda (Octavia)
  1864-1947 .... **TCLC 13**
  See also CA 111; DLB 66

Huddle, David 1942- .... **CLC 49**
  See also CA 57-60

Hudson, W(illiam) H(enry)
  1841-1922 .... **TCLC 29**
  See also CA 115; SATA 35

Hueffer, Ford Madox 1873-1939
  See Ford, Ford Madox

Hughart, Barry 1934-............. **CLC 39**

Hughes, David (John) 1930- .... **CLC 48**
  See also CA 116; DLB 14

Hughes, Edward James 1930-
  See Hughes, Ted

Hughes, (James) Langston
  1902-1967 ..... **CLC 1, 5, 10, 15, 35, 44**
  See also CANR 1; CA 1-4R;
  obituary CA 25-28R; SATA 4, 33;
  DLB 4, 7, 48, 51

Hughes, Richard (Arthur Warren)
  1900-1976 .... **CLC 1, 11**
  See also CANR 4; CA 5-8R;
  obituary CA 65-68; SATA 8;
  obituary SATA 25; DLB 15

Hughes, Ted 1930- ..... **CLC 2, 4, 9, 14, 37**
  See also CLR 3; CANR 1; CA 1-4R;
  SATA 27, 49; DLB 40

Hugo, Richard F(ranklin)
  1923-1982 .... **CLC 6, 18, 32**
  See also CANR 3; CA 49-52;
  obituary CA 108; DLB 5

Hugo, Victor Marie
  1802-1885 .... **NCLC 3, 10, 21**
  See also SATA 47

Huidobro, Vicente 1893-1948 ..... **TCLC 31**

Hulme, Keri 1947- .... **CLC 39**
  See also CA 123

Hulme, T(homas) E(rnest)
  1883-1917 .... **TCLC 21**
  See also CA 117; DLB 19

Hume, David 1711-1776............. **LC 7**

Humphrey, William 1924-......... **CLC 45**
  See also CA 77-80; DLB 6

Humphreys, Emyr (Owen) 1919-.... **CLC 47**
  See also CANR 3, 24; CA 5-8R; DLB 15

Humphreys, Josephine 1945-.... **CLC 34, 57**
  See also CA 121, 127

Hunt, E(verette) Howard (Jr.)
  1918-..................... **CLC 3**
  See also CANR 2; CA 45-48

Hunt, (James Henry) Leigh
  1784-1859 .... **NCLC 1**

Hunter, Evan 1926- .... **CLC 11, 31**
  See also CANR 5; CA 5-8R; SATA 25;
  DLB-Y 82

Hunter, Kristin (Eggleston) 1931-... **CLC 35**
  See also CLR 3; CANR 13; CA 13-16R;
  SATA 12; DLB 33

Hunter, Mollie (Maureen McIlwraith)
  1922-..................... **CLC 21**
  See also McIlwraith, Maureen Mollie
  Hunter

Hunter, Robert ?-1734............. **LC 7**

Hurston, Zora Neale
  1891-1960 .... **CLC 7, 30; SSC 4**
  See also CA 85-88; DLB 51

Huston, John (Marcellus)
  1906-1987 .... **CLC 20**
  See also CA 73-76; obituary CA 123;
  DLB 26

Huxley, Aldous (Leonard)
  1894-1963 .. **CLC 1, 3, 4, 5, 8, 11, 18, 35**
  See also CA 85-88; DLB 36

Huysmans, Charles Marie Georges
  1848-1907
  See Huysmans, Joris-Karl
  See also CA 104

Huysmans, Joris-Karl 1848-1907 .. **NCLC 7**
  See also Huysmans, Charles Marie Georges

Hwang, David Henry 1957-........ **CLC 55**
  See also CA 127

Hyde, Anthony 1946?-............ **CLC 42**

Hyde, Margaret O(ldroyd) 1917- ... **CLC 21**
  See also CANR 1; CA 1-4R; SATA 1, 42

Ian, Janis 1951- .... **CLC 21**
  See also CA 105

Ibarguengoitia, Jorge 1928-1983.... **CLC 37**
  See also obituary CA 113, 124

Ibsen, Henrik (Johan)
  1828-1906 .... **TCLC 2, 8, 16, 37**
  See also CA 104

Ibuse, Masuji 1898-.............. **CLC 22**

Ichikawa, Kon 1915-............. **CLC 20**
  See also CA 121

Idle, Eric 1943-
  See Monty Python
  See also CA 116

Ignatow, David 1914-...... **CLC 4, 7, 14, 40**
  See also CAAS 3; CA 9-12R; DLB 5

Ihimaera, Witi (Tame) 1944-....... **CLC 46**
  See also CA 77-80

Ilf, Ilya 1897-1937 .... **TCLC 21**

Immermann, Karl (Lebrecht)
  1796-1840 .... **NCLC 4**

Ingalls, Rachel 19??-............. **CLC 42**
  See also CA 123

Ingamells, Rex 1913-1955 .... **TCLC 35**

Inge, William (Motter)
  1913-1973 .... **CLC 1, 8, 19**
  See also CA 9-12R; DLB 7;
  CDALB 1941-1968

Innaurato, Albert 1948-........... **CLC 21**
See also CA 115, 122

Innes, Michael 1906-
See Stewart, J(ohn) I(nnes) M(ackintosh)

Ionesco, Eugene
1912-........ **CLC 1, 4, 6, 9, 11, 15, 41**
See also CA 9-12R; SATA 7

Iqbal, Muhammad 1877-1938 ..... **TCLC 28**

Irving, John (Winslow)
1942-................. **CLC 13, 23, 38**
See also CA 25-28R; DLB 6; DLB-Y 82

Irving, Washington
1783-1859 .... **NCLC 2, 19; SSC 2**
See also YABC 2; DLB 3, 11, 30, 59, 73,
74; CDALB 1640-1865

Isaacs, Susan 1943- .... **CLC 32**
See also CANR 20; CA 89-92

Isherwood, Christopher (William Bradshaw)
1904-1986 .... **CLC 1, 9, 11, 14, 44**
See also CA 13-16R; obituary CA 117;
DLB 15; DLB-Y 86

Ishiguro, Kazuo 1954- ...... **CLC 27, 56, 59**
See also CA 120

Ishikawa Takuboku 1885-1912 .... **TCLC 15**
See also CA 113

Iskander, Fazil (Abdulovich)
1929-...................... **CLC 47**
See also CA 102

Ivanov, Vyacheslav (Ivanovich)
1866-1949 .... **TCLC 33**
See also CA 122

Ivask, Ivar (Vidrik) 1927- .... **CLC 14**
See also CANR 24; CA 37-40R

Jackson, Jesse 1908-1983 .... **CLC 12**
See also CA 25-28R; obituary CA 109;
SATA 2, 29, 48

Jackson, Laura (Riding) 1901-
See Riding, Laura
See also CA 65-68; DLB 48

Jackson, Shirley 1919-1965........ **CLC 11**
See also CANR 4; CA 1-4R;
obituary CA 25-28R; SATA 2; DLB 6;
CDALB 1941-1968

Jacob, (Cyprien) Max 1876-1944 ... **TCLC 6**
See also CA 104

Jacob, Piers A(nthony) D(illingham) 1934-
See Anthony (Jacob), Piers
See also CA 21-24R

Jacobs, Jim 1942- and **Casey, Warren**
1942-...................... **CLC 12**

Jacobs, Jim 1942-
See Jacobs, Jim and Casey, Warren
See also CA 97-100

Jacobs, W(illiam) W(ymark)
1863-1943 .... **TCLC 22**
See also CA 121

Jacobsen, Josephine 1908-......... **CLC 48**
See also CANR 23; CA 33-36R

Jacobson, Dan 1929- .... **CLC 4, 14**
See also CANR 2, 25; CA 1-4R; DLB 14

Jagger, Mick 1944-............... **CLC 17**

Jakes, John (William) 1932-....... **CLC 29**
See also CANR 10; CA 57-60; DLB-Y 83

James, C(yril) L(ionel) R(obert)
1901-1989 .... **CLC 33**
See also CA 117, 125

James, Daniel 1911-1988
See Santiago, Danny
See also obituary CA 125

James, Henry (Jr.)
1843-1916 .... **TCLC 2, 11, 24**
See also CA 104; DLB 12, 71, 74;
CDALB 1865-1917

James, M(ontague) R(hodes)
1862-1936 .... **TCLC 6**
See also CA 104

James, P(hyllis) D(orothy)
1920-.................... **CLC 18, 46**
See also CANR 17; CA 21-24R

James, William 1842-1910..... **TCLC 15, 32**
See also CA 109

Jami, Nur al-Din 'Abd al-Rahman
1414-1492 .... **LC 9**

Jandl, Ernst 1925- .... **CLC 34**

Janowitz, Tama 1957- .... **CLC 43**
See also CA 106

Jarrell, Randall
1914-1965 .... **CLC 1, 2, 6, 9, 13, 49**
See also CLR 6; CANR 6; CA 5-8R;
obituary CA 25-28R; CABS 2; SATA 7;
DLB 48, 52; CDALB 1941-1968

Jarry, Alfred 1873-1907....... **TCLC 2, 14**
See also CA 104

Jeake, Samuel, Jr. 1889-1973
See Aiken, Conrad

Jean Paul 1763-1825 .... **NCLC 7**

Jeffers, (John) Robinson
1887-1962 .... **CLC 2, 3, 11, 15, 54**
See also CA 85-88; DLB 45

Jefferson, Thomas 1743-1826 .... **NCLC 11**
See also DLB 31; CDALB 1640-1865

Jellicoe, (Patricia) Ann 1927-...... **CLC 27**
See also CA 85-88; DLB 13

Jenkins, (John) Robin 1912-....... **CLC 52**
See also CANR 1; CA 4Rk; DLB 14

Jennings, Elizabeth (Joan)
1926-.................... **CLC 5, 14**
See also CAAS 5; CANR 8; CA 61-64;
DLB 27

Jennings, Waylon 1937-.......... **CLC 21**

Jensen, Laura (Linnea) 1948- ...... **CLC 37**
See also CA 103

Jerome, Jerome K. 1859-1927..... **TCLC 23**
See also CA 119; DLB 10, 34

Jerrold, Douglas William
1803-1857 .... **NCLC 2**

Jewett, (Theodora) Sarah Orne
1849-1909 .... **TCLC 1, 22**
See also CA 108; SATA 15; DLB 12, 74

Jewsbury, Geraldine (Endsor)
1812-1880 .... **NCLC 22**
See also DLB 21

Jhabvala, Ruth Prawer
1927-................... **CLC 4, 8, 29**
See also CANR 2; CA 1-4R

Jiles, Paulette 1943-........... **CLC 13, 58**
See also CA 101

Jimenez (Mantecon), Juan Ramon
1881-1958 .... **TCLC 4**
See also CA 104

Joel, Billy 1949-................. **CLC 26**
See also Joel, William Martin

Joel, William Martin 1949-
See Joel, Billy
See also CA 108

Johnson, B(ryan) S(tanley William)
1933-1973 .... **CLC 6, 9**
See also CANR 9; CA 9-12R;
obituary CA 53-56; DLB 14, 40

Johnson, Charles (Richard)
1948-.................... **CLC 7, 51**
See also CA 116; DLB 33

Johnson, Denis 1949-............. **CLC 52**
See also CA 117, 121

Johnson, Diane 1934-........ **CLC 5, 13, 48**
See also CANR 17; CA 41-44R; DLB-Y 80

Johnson, Eyvind (Olof Verner)
1900-1976 .... **CLC 14**
See also CA 73-76; obituary CA 69-72

Johnson, James Weldon
1871-1938 .... **TCLC 3, 19**
See also Johnson, James William
See also CA 104, 125; DLB 51

Johnson, James William 1871-1938
See Johnson, James Weldon
See also SATA 31

Johnson, Joyce 1935-............ **CLC 58**
See also CA 125

Johnson, Lionel (Pigot)
1867-1902 .... **TCLC 19**
See also CA 117; DLB 19

Johnson, Marguerita 1928-
See Angelou, Maya

Johnson, Pamela Hansford
1912-1981 .... **CLC 1, 7, 27**
See also CANR 2; CA 1-4R;
obituary CA 104; DLB 15

Johnson, Uwe
1934-1984 .... **CLC 5, 10, 15, 40**
See also CANR 1; CA 1-4R;
obituary CA 112; DLB 75

Johnston, George (Benson) 1913- ... **CLC 51**
See also CANR 5, 20; CA 1-4R

Johnston, Jennifer 1930-.......... **CLC 7**
See also CA 85-88; DLB 14

Jolley, Elizabeth 1923-............ **CLC 46**

Jones, D(ouglas) G(ordon) 1929-.... **CLC 10**
See also CANR 13; CA 113; DLB 53

Jones, David
1895-1974 .... **CLC 2, 4, 7, 13, 42**
See also CA 9-12R; obituary CA 53-56;
DLB 20

Jones, David Robert 1947-
See Bowie, David
See also CA 103

Jones, Diana Wynne 1934- .... **CLC 26**
See also CANR 4; CA 49-52; SATA 9

Jones, Gayl 1949-.............. **CLC 6, 9**
See also CA 77-80; DLB 33

Jones, James 1921-1977.... **CLC 1, 3, 10, 39**
See also CANR 6; CA 1-4R;
obituary CA 69-72; DLB 2

Jones, (Everett) LeRoi
    1934- . . . . CLC 1, 2, 3, 5, 10, 14, 33
    See also Baraka, Amiri; Baraka, Imamu
    Amiri
    See also CA 21-24R

Jones, Madison (Percy, Jr.) 1925- . . . CLC 4
    See also CANR 7; CA 13-16R

Jones, Mervyn 1922- . . . . CLC 10, 52
    See also CAAS 5; CANR 1; CA 45-48

Jones, Mick 1956?-
    See The Clash

Jones, Nettie 19??- . . . . CLC 34

Jones, Preston 1936-1979 . . . . CLC 10
    See also CA 73-76; obituary CA 89-92;
    DLB 7

Jones, Robert F(rancis) 1934- . . . . . . CLC 7
    See also CANR 2; CA 49-52

Jones, Rod 1953- . . . . CLC 50

Jones, Terry 1942?-
    See Monty Python
    See also CA 112, 116; SATA 51

Jong, Erica 1942- . . . . CLC 4, 6, 8, 18
    See also CANR 26; CA 73-76; DLB 2, 5, 28

Jonson, Ben(jamin) 1572-1637 . . . . . . LC 6
    See also DLB 62

Jordan, June 1936- . . . . CLC 5, 11, 23
    See also CLR 10; CANR 25; CA 33-36R;
    SATA 4; DLB 38

Jordan, Pat(rick M.) 1941- . . . . CLC 37
    See also CANR 25; CA 33-36R

Josipovici, Gabriel (David)
    1940- . . . . CLC 6, 43
    See also CA 37-40R; DLB 14

Joubert, Joseph 1754-1824 . . . . NCLC 9

Jouve, Pierre Jean 1887-1976 . . . . . CLC 47
    See also obituary CA 65-68

Joyce, James (Augustine Aloysius)
    1882-1941 . . . . . . TCLC 3, 8, 16, 26, 35;
                                                    SSC 3
    See also CA 104, 126; DLB 10, 19, 36

Jozsef, Attila 1905-1937 . . . . TCLC 22
    See also CA 116

Juana Ines de la Cruz 1651?-1695 . . . . LC 5

Julian of Norwich 1342?-1416? . . . . . . LC 6

Just, Ward S(wift) 1935- . . . . CLC 4, 27
    See also CA 25-28R

Justice, Donald (Rodney) 1925- . . CLC 6, 19
    See also CANR 26; CA 5-8R; DLB-Y 83

Kacew, Romain 1914-1980
    See Gary, Romain
    See also CA 108; obituary CA 102

Kacewgary, Romain 1914-1980
    See Gary, Romain

Kadare, Ismail 1936- . . . . CLC 52

Kadohata, Cynthia 19??- . . . . CLC 59

Kafka, Franz
    1883-1924 . . . . TCLC 2, 6, 13, 29; SSC 5
    See also CA 105, 126; DLB 81

Kahn, Roger 1927- . . . . CLC 30
    See also CA 25-28R; SATA 37

Kaiser, (Friedrich Karl) Georg
    1878-1945 . . . . TCLC 9
    See also CA 106

Kaletski, Alexander 1946- . . . . CLC 39
    See also CA 118

Kallman, Chester (Simon)
    1921-1975 . . . . CLC 2
    See also CANR 3; CA 45-48;
    obituary CA 53-56

Kaminsky, Melvin 1926-
    See Brooks, Mel
    See also CANR 16; CA 65-68

Kaminsky, Stuart 1934- . . . . CLC 59
    See also CA 73-76

Kane, Paul 1941-
    See Simon, Paul

Kanin, Garson 1912- . . . . CLC 22
    See also CANR 7; CA 5-8R; DLB 7

Kaniuk, Yoram 1930- . . . . CLC 19

Kant, Immanuel 1724-1804 . . . . . . NCLC 27

Kantor, MacKinlay 1904-1977 . . . . . . CLC 7
    See also CA 61-64; obituary CA 73-76;
    DLB 9

Kaplan, David Michael 1946- . . . . . . CLC 50

Kaplan, James 19??- . . . . CLC 59

Karamzin, Nikolai Mikhailovich
    1766-1826 . . . . NCLC 3

Karapanou, Margarita 1946- . . . . . . CLC 13
    See also CA 101

Karl, Frederick R(obert) 1927- . . . . . CLC 34
    See also CANR 3; CA 5-8R

Kassef, Romain 1914-1980
    See Gary, Romain

Katz, Steve 1935- . . . . CLC 47
    See also CANR 12; CA 25-28R; DLB-Y 83

Kauffman, Janet 1945- . . . . CLC 42
    See also CA 117; DLB-Y 86

Kaufman, Bob (Garnell)
    1925-1986 . . . . CLC 49
    See also CANR 22; CA 41-44R;
    obituary CA 118; DLB 16, 41

Kaufman, George S(imon)
    1889-1961 . . . . CLC 38
    See also CA 108; obituary CA 93-96; DLB 7

Kaufman, Sue 1926-1977 . . . . CLC 3, 8
    See also Barondess, Sue K(aufman)

Kavan, Anna 1904-1968 . . . . CLC 5, 13
    See also Edmonds, Helen (Woods)
    See also CANR 6; CA 5-8R

Kavanagh, Patrick (Joseph Gregory)
    1905-1967 . . . . CLC 22
    See also CA 123; obituary CA 25-28R;
    DLB 15, 20

Kawabata, Yasunari
    1899-1972 . . . . CLC 2, 5, 9, 18
    See also CA 93-96; obituary CA 33-36R

Kaye, M(ary) M(argaret) 1909?- . . . . CLC 28
    See also CANR 24; CA 89-92

Kaye, Mollie 1909?-
    See Kaye, M(ary) M(argaret)

Kaye-Smith, Sheila 1887-1956 . . . . . TCLC 20
    See also CA 118; DLB 36

Kazan, Elia 1909- . . . . CLC 6, 16
    See also CA 21-24R

Kazantzakis, Nikos
    1885?-1957 . . . . TCLC 2, 5, 33
    See also CA 105

Kazin, Alfred 1915- . . . . CLC 34, 38
    See also CAAS 7; CANR 1; CA 1-4R

Keane, Mary Nesta (Skrine) 1904-
    See Keane, Molly
    See also CA 108, 114

Keane, Molly 1904- . . . . CLC 31
    See also Keane, Mary Nesta (Skrine)

Keates, Jonathan 19??- . . . . CLC 34

Keaton, Buster 1895-1966 . . . . CLC 20

Keaton, Joseph Francis 1895-1966
    See Keaton, Buster

Keats, John 1795-1821 . . . . NCLC 8

Keene, Donald 1922- . . . . CLC 34
    See also CANR 5; CA 1-4R

Keillor, Garrison 1942- . . . . CLC 40
    See also Keillor, Gary (Edward)
    See also CA 111; DLB 87

Keillor, Gary (Edward)
    See Keillor, Garrison
    See also CA 111, 117

Kell, Joseph 1917-
    See Burgess (Wilson, John) Anthony

Keller, Gottfried 1819-1890 . . . . . . NCLC 2

Kellerman, Jonathan (S.) 1949- . . . . . CLC 44
    See also CA 106

Kelley, William Melvin 1937- . . . . . . CLC 22
    See also CA 77-80; DLB 33

Kellogg, Marjorie 1922- . . . . CLC 2
    See also CA 81-84

Kelly, M. T. 1947- . . . . CLC 55
    See also CANR 19; CA 97-100

Kelman, James 1946- . . . . CLC 58

Kemal, Yashar 1922- . . . . CLC 14, 29
    See also CA 89-92

Kemble, Fanny 1809-1893 . . . . NCLC 18
    See also DLB 32

Kemelman, Harry 1908- . . . . CLC 2
    See also CANR 6; CA 9-12R; DLB 28

Kempe, Margery 1373?-1440? . . . . LC 6

Kempis, Thomas á 1380-1471 . . . . . . LC 11

Kendall, Henry 1839-1882 . . . . NCLC 12

Keneally, Thomas (Michael)
    1935- . . . . . . CLC 5, 8, 10, 14, 19, 27, 43
    See also CANR 10; CA 85-88

Kennedy, John Pendleton
    1795-1870 . . . . NCLC 2
    See also DLB 3

Kennedy, Joseph Charles 1929- . . . . . CLC 8
    See also Kennedy, X. J.
    See also CANR 4; CA 1-4R; SATA 14

Kennedy, William (Joseph)
    1928- . . . . CLC 6, 28, 34, 53
    See also CANR 14; CA 85-88; DLB-Y 85;
    AAYA 1

Kennedy, X. J. 1929- . . . . CLC 8, 42
    See also Kennedy, Joseph Charles
    See also DLB 5

Krumgold, Joseph (Quincy)
1908-1980 .... CLC 12
See also CANR 7; CA 9-12R;
obituary CA 101; SATA 48;
obituary SATA 23

Krutch, Joseph Wood 1893-1970 .... CLC 24
See also CANR 4; CA 1-4R;
obituary CA 25-28R; DLB 63

Krylov, Ivan Andreevich
1768?-1844 .... NCLC 1

Kubin, Alfred 1877-1959 .... TCLC 23
See also CA 112

Kubrick, Stanley 1928- .... CLC 16
See also CA 81-84; DLB 26

Kumin, Maxine (Winokur)
1925- .... CLC 5, 13, 28
See also CANR 1, 21; CA 1-4R; SATA 12;
DLB 5

Kundera, Milan 1929- ..... CLC 4, 9, 19, 32
See also CANR 19; CA 85-88

Kunitz, Stanley J(asspon)
1905- .... CLC 6, 11, 14
See also CA 41-44R; DLB 48

Kunze, Reiner 1933- .... CLC 10
See also CA 93-96; DLB 75

Kuprin, Aleksandr (Ivanovich)
1870-1938 .... TCLC 5
See also CA 104

Kurosawa, Akira 1910- .... CLC 16
See also CA 101

Kuttner, Henry 1915-1958 .... TCLC 10
See also CA 107; DLB 8

Kuzma, Greg 1944- .... CLC 7
See also CA 33-36R

Labrunie, Gerard 1808-1855
See Nerval, Gerard de

Laclos, Pierre Ambroise Francois Choderlos
de 1741-1803 .... NCLC 4

La Fayette, Marie (Madelaine Pioche de la
Vergne, Comtesse) de
1634-1693 .... LC 2

Lafayette, Rene
See Hubbard, L(afayette) Ron(ald)

Laforgue, Jules 1860-1887 .... NCLC 5

Lagerkvist, Par (Fabian)
1891-1974 .... CLC 7, 10, 13, 54
See also CA 85-88; obituary CA 49-52

Lagerlof, Selma (Ottiliana Lovisa)
1858-1940 .... TCLC 4, 36
See also CLR 7; CA 108; SATA 15

La Guma, (Justin) Alex(ander)
1925-1985 .... CLC 19
See also CA 49-52; obituary CA 118

Lamartine, Alphonse (Marie Louis Prat) de
1790-1869 .... NCLC 11

Lamb, Charles 1775-1834 .... NCLC 10
See also SATA 17

Lamming, George (William)
1927- .... CLC 2, 4
See also CANR 26; CA 85-88

LaMoore, Louis Dearborn 1908?-
See L'Amour, Louis (Dearborn)

L'Amour, Louis (Dearborn)
1908-1988 .... CLC 25, 55
See also CANR 3; CA 1-4R;
obituary CA 125; DLB-Y 80

Lampedusa, (Prince) Giuseppe (Maria
Fabrizio) Tomasi di
1896-1957 .... TCLC 13
See also CA 111

Lampman, Archibald 1861-1899 .. NCLC 25

Lancaster, Bruce 1896-1963 .... CLC 36
See also CAP 1; CA 9-12; SATA 9

Landis, John (David) 1950- .... CLC 26
See also CA 112

Landolfi, Tommaso 1908-1979 ... CLC 11, 49
See also obituary CA 117

Landon, Letitia Elizabeth
1802-1838 .... NCLC 15

Landor, Walter Savage
1775-1864 .... NCLC 14

Landwirth, Heinz 1927-
See Lind, Jakov
See also CANR 7; CA 11-12R

Lane, Patrick 1939- .... CLC 25
See also CA 97-100; DLB 53

Lang, Andrew 1844-1912 .... TCLC 16
See also CA 114; SATA 16

Lang, Fritz 1890-1976 .... CLC 20
See also CA 77-80; obituary CA 69-72

Langer, Elinor 1939- .... CLC 34
See also CA 121

Lanier, Sidney 1842-1881 .... NCLC 6
See also SATA 18; DLB 64

Lanyer, Aemilia 1569-1645 .... LC 10

Lapine, James 1949- .... CLC 39

Larbaud, Valery 1881-1957 .... TCLC 9
See also CA 106

Lardner, Ring(gold Wilmer)
1885-1933 .... TCLC 2, 14
See also CA 104; DLB 11, 25

Larkin, Philip (Arthur)
1922-1985 ... CLC 3, 5, 8, 9, 13, 18, 33,
39
See also CA 5-8R; obituary CA 117;
DLB 27

Larra (y Sanchez de Castro), Mariano Jose de
1809-1837 .... NCLC 17

Larsen, Eric 1941- .... CLC 55

Larsen, Nella 1891-1964 .... CLC 37
See also CA 125; DLB 51

Larson, Charles R(aymond) 1938- ... CLC 31
See also CANR 4; CA 53-56

Latham, Jean Lee 1902- .... CLC 12
See also CANR 7; CA 5-8R; SATA 2

Lathen, Emma .... CLC 2
See also Hennissart, Martha; Latsis, Mary
J(ane)

Latsis, Mary J(ane)
See Lathen, Emma
See also CA 85-88

Lattimore, Richmond (Alexander)
1906-1984 .... CLC 3
See also CANR 1; CA 1-4R;
obituary CA 112

Laughlin, James 1914- .... CLC 49
See also CANR 9; CA 21-24R; DLB 48

Laurence, (Jean) Margaret (Wemyss)
1926-1987 .... CLC 3, 6, 13, 50
See also CA 5-8R; obituary CA 121;
SATA 50; DLB 53

Laurent, Antoine 1952- .... CLC 50

Lautreamont, Comte de
1846-1870 .... NCLC 12

Lavin, Mary 1912- ...... CLC 4, 18; SSC 4
See also CA 9-12R; DLB 15

Lawler, Raymond (Evenor) 1922- ... CLC 58
See also CA 103

Lawrence, D(avid) H(erbert)
1885-1930 .... TCLC 2, 9, 16, 33; SSC 4
See also CA 104, 121; DLB 10, 19, 36

Lawrence, T(homas) E(dward)
1888-1935 .... TCLC 18
See also CA 115

Lawson, Henry (Archibald Hertzberg)
1867-1922 .... TCLC 27
See also CA 120

Laxness, Halldor (Kiljan) 1902- .... CLC 25
See also Gudjonsson, Halldor Kiljan

Laye, Camara 1928-1980 .... CLC 4, 38
See also CA 85-88; obituary CA 97-100

Layton, Irving (Peter) 1912- ..... CLC 2, 15
See also CANR 2; CA 1-4R

Lazarus, Emma 1849-1887 .... NCLC 8

Leacock, Stephen (Butler)
1869-1944 .... TCLC 2
See also CA 104

Lear, Edward 1812-1888 .... NCLC 3
See also CLR 1; SATA 18; DLB 32

Lear, Norman (Milton) 1922- ..... CLC 12
See also CA 73-76

Leavis, F(rank) R(aymond)
1895-1978 .... CLC 24
See also CA 21-24R; obituary CA 77-80

Leavitt, David 1961?- .... CLC 34
See also CA 116, 122

Lebowitz, Fran(ces Ann)
1951?- .... CLC 11, 36
See also CANR 14; CA 81-84

Le Carre, John 1931- ... CLC 3, 5, 9, 15, 28
See also Cornwell, David (John Moore)

Le Clezio, J(ean) M(arie) G(ustave)
1940- .... CLC 31
See also CA 116

Leduc, Violette 1907-1972 .... CLC 22
See also CAP 1; CA 13-14;
obituary CA 33-36R

Ledwidge, Francis 1887-1917 ..... TCLC 23
See also CA 123; DLB 20

Lee, Andrea 1953- .... CLC 36
See also CA 125

Lee, Andrew 1917-
See Auchincloss, Louis (Stanton)

Lee, Don L. 1942- .... CLC 2
See also Madhubuti, Haki R.
See also CA 73-76

Lee, George Washington
1894-1976 .... CLC 52
See also CA 125; DLB 51

Megged, Aharon 1920-............ **CLC 9**
See also CANR 1; CA 49-52

Mehta, Ved (Parkash) 1934-....... **CLC 37**
See also CANR 2, 23; CA 1-4R

Mellor, John 1953?-
See The Clash

Meltzer, Milton 1915-......... **CLC 26 13**
See also CA 13-16R; SAAS 1; SATA 1, 50;
DLB 61

Melville, Herman
1819-1891 .... **NCLC 3, 12; SSC 1**
See also DLB 3; CDALB 1640-1865

Mencken, H(enry) L(ouis)
1880-1956 .... **TCLC 13**
See also CA 105; DLB 11, 29, 63

Mercer, David 1928-1980.......... **CLC 5**
See also CA 9-12R; obituary CA 102;
DLB 13

Meredith, George 1828-1909...... **TCLC 17**
See also CA 117; DLB 18, 35, 57

Meredith, William (Morris)
1919-.............. **CLC 4, 13, 22, 55**
See also CANR 6; CA 9-12R; DLB 5

Merezhkovsky, Dmitri
1865-1941 .... **TCLC 29**

Merimee, Prosper 1803-1870...... **NCLC 6**

Merkin, Daphne 1954-............ **CLC 44**
See also CANR 123

Merrill, James (Ingram)
1926-........ **CLC 2, 3, 6, 8, 13, 18, 34**
See also CANR 10; CA 13-16R; DLB 5;
DLB-Y 85

Merton, Thomas (James)
1915-1968 .... **CLC 1, 3, 11, 34**
See also CANR 22; CA 5-8R;
obituary CA 25-28R; DLB 48; DLB-Y 81

Merwin, W(illiam) S(tanley)
1927-...... **CLC 1, 2, 3, 5, 8, 13, 18, 45**
See also CANR 15; CA 13-16R; DLB 5

Metcalf, John 1938-............. **CLC 37**
See also CA 113; DLB 60

Mew, Charlotte (Mary)
1870-1928 .... **TCLC 8**
See also CA 105; DLB 19

Mewshaw, Michael 1943-.......... **CLC 9**
See also CANR 7; CA 53-56; DLB-Y 80

Meyer-Meyrink, Gustav 1868-1932
See Meyrink, Gustav
See also CA 117

Meyers, Jeffrey 1939-............ **CLC 39**
See also CA 73-76

Meynell, Alice (Christiana Gertrude
Thompson) 1847-1922 .... **TCLC 6**
See also CA 104; DLB 19

Meyrink, Gustav 1868-1932....... **TCLC 21**
See also Meyer-Meyrink, Gustav

Michaels, Leonard 1933-........ **CLC 6, 25**
See also CANR 21; CA 61-64

Michaux, Henri 1899-1984 ...... **CLC 8, 19**
See also CA 85-88; obituary CA 114

Michelangelo 1475-1564.......... **LC 12**

Michener, James A(lbert)
1907-...............**CLC 1, 5, 11, 29**
See also CANR 21; CA 5-8R; DLB 6

Mickiewicz, Adam 1798-1855..... **NCLC 3**

Middleton, Christopher 1926-...... **CLC 13**
See also CA 13-16R; DLB 40

Middleton, Stanley 1919-........ **CLC 7, 38**
See also CANR 21; CA 25-28R; DLB 14

Migueis, Jose Rodrigues 1901-..... **CLC 10**

Mikszath, Kalman 1847-1910 ..... **TCLC 31**

Miles, Josephine (Louise)
1911-1985 .... **CLC 1, 2, 14, 34, 39**
See also CANR 2; CA 1-4R;
obituary CA 116; DLB 48

Mill, John Stuart 1806-1873..... **NCLC 11**

Millar, Kenneth 1915-1983 .... **CLC 14**
See also Macdonald, Ross
See also CANR 16; CA 9-12R;
obituary CA 110; DLB 2; DLB-Y 83

Millay, Edna St. Vincent
1892-1950 .... **TCLC 4**
See also CA 104; DLB 45

Miller, Arthur
1915-....... **CLC 1, 2, 6, 10, 15, 26, 47**
See also CANR 2; CA 1-4R; DLB 7;
CDALB 1941-1968

Miller, Henry (Valentine)
1891-1980 .... **CLC 1, 2, 4, 9, 14, 43**
See also CA 9-12R; obituary CA 97-100;
DLB 4, 9; DLB-Y 80

Miller, Jason 1939?-................ **CLC 2**
See also CA 73-76; DLB 7

Miller, Sue 19??-................ **CLC 44**

Miller, Walter M(ichael), Jr.
1923-................... **CLC 4, 30**
See also CA 85-88; DLB 8

Millhauser, Steven 1943-....... **CLC 21, 54**
See also CA 108, 110, 111; DLB 2

Millin, Sarah Gertrude 1889-1968 .. **CLC 49**
See also CA 102; obituary CA 93-96

Milne, A(lan) A(lexander)
1882-1956 .... **TCLC 6**
See also CLR 1; YABC 1; CA 104; DLB 10

Milner, Ron(ald) 1938-............ **CLC 56**
See also CANR 24; CA 73-76; DLB 38

Milosz Czeslaw
1911-........... **CLC 5, 11, 22, 31, 56**
See also CANR 23; CA 81-84

Milton, John 1608-1674............ **LC 9**

Miner, Valerie (Jane) 1947-........ **CLC 40**
See also CA 97-100

Minot, Susan 1956-.............. **CLC 44**

Minus, Ed 1938-................ **CLC 39**

Miro (Ferrer), Gabriel (Francisco Victor)
1879-1930 .... **TCLC 5**
See also CA 104

Mishima, Yukio
1925-1970 .... **CLC 2, 4, 6, 9, 27; SSC 4**
See also Hiraoka, Kimitake

Mistral, Gabriela 1889-1957 .... **TCLC 2**
See also CA 104

Mitchell, James Leslie 1901-1935
See Gibbon, Lewis Grassic
See also CA 104; DLB 15

Mitchell, Joni 1943-.............. **CLC 12**
See also CA 112

Mitchell (Marsh), Margaret (Munnerlyn)
1900-1949 .... **TCLC 11**
See also CA 109; DLB 9

Mitchell, S. Weir 1829-1914...... **TCLC 36**

Mitchell, W(illiam) O(rmond)
1914-...................... **CLC 25**
See also CANR 15; CA 77-80

Mitford, Mary Russell 1787-1855.. **NCLC 4**

Mitford, Nancy 1904-1973 .... **CLC 44**
See also CA 9-12R

Miyamoto Yuriko 1899-1951...... **TCLC 37**

Mo, Timothy 1950-............. **CLC 46**
See also CA 117

Modarressi, Taghi 1931- .... **CLC 44**
See also CA 121

Modiano, Patrick (Jean) 1945-..... **CLC 18**
See also CANR 17; CA 85-88

Mofolo, Thomas (Mokopu)
1876-1948 .... **TCLC 22**
See also CA 121

Mohr, Nicholasa 1935-............ **CLC 12**
See also CANR 1; CA 49-52; SATA 8

Mojtabai, A(nn) G(race)
1938-............**CLC 5, 9, 15, 29**
See also CA 85-88

Moliere 1622-1673 .... **LC 10**

Molnar, Ferenc 1878-1952........ **TCLC 20**
See also CA 109

Momaday, N(avarre) Scott
1934-................... **CLC 2, 19**
See also CANR 14; CA 25-28R; SATA 30,
48

Monroe, Harriet 1860-1936...... **TCLC 12**
See also CA 109; DLB 54

Montagu, Elizabeth 1720-1800 .... **NCLC 7**

Montagu, Lady Mary (Pierrepont) Wortley
1689-1762 .... **LC 9**

Montague, John (Patrick)
1929-................... **CLC 13, 46**
See also CANR 9; CA 9-12R; DLB 40

Montaigne, Michel (Eyquem) de
1533-1592 .... **LC 8**

Montale, Eugenio 1896-1981... **CLC 7, 9, 18**
See also CA 17-20R; obituary CA 104

Montgomery, Marion (H., Jr.)
1925-...................... **CLC 7**
See also CANR 3; CA 1-4R; DLB 6

Montgomery, Robert Bruce 1921-1978
See Crispin, Edmund
See also CA 104

Montherlant, Henri (Milon) de
1896-1972 .... **CLC 8, 19**
See also CA 85-88; obituary CA 37-40R;
DLB 72

Montisquieu, Charles-Louis de Secondat
1689-1755 .... **LC 7**

Monty Python................... **CLC 21**

Moodie, Susanna (Strickland)
1803-1885 .... **NCLC 14**

Mooney, Ted 1951-.............. **CLC 25**

O'Flaherty, Liam 1896-1984 ..... **CLC 5, 34**
See also CA 101; obituary CA 113; DLB 36;
DLB-Y 84

O'Grady, Standish (James)
1846-1928 .... **TCLC 5**
See also CA 104

O'Grady, Timothy 1951- .... **CLC 59**

O'Hara, Frank 1926-1966 ..... **CLC 2, 5, 13**
See also CA 9-12R; obituary CA 25-28R;
DLB 5, 16

O'Hara, John (Henry)
1905-1970 .... **CLC 1, 2, 3, 6, 11, 42**
See also CA 5-8R; obituary CA 25-28R;
DLB 9; DLB-DS 2

O'Hara Family
See Banim, John and Banim, Michael

O'Hehir, Diana 1922- .... **CLC 41**
See also CA 93-96

Okigbo, Christopher (Ifenayichukwu)
1932-1967 .... **CLC 25**
See also CA 77-80

Olds, Sharon 1942- .... **CLC 32, 39**
See also CANR 18; CA 101

Olesha, Yuri (Karlovich)
1899-1960 .... **CLC 8**
See also CA 85-88

Oliphant, Margaret (Oliphant Wilson)
1828-1897 .... **NCLC 11**
See also DLB 18

Oliver, Mary 1935- .... **CLC 19, 34**
See also CANR 9; CA 21-24R; DLB 5

Olivier, (Baron) Laurence (Kerr)
1907- .... **CLC 20**
See also CA 111

Olsen, Tillie 1913- .... **CLC 4, 13**
See also CANR 1; CA 1-4R; DLB 28;
DLB-Y 80

Olson, Charles (John)
1910-1970 ..... **CLC 1, 2, 5, 6, 9, 11, 29**
See also CAP 1; CA 15-16;
obituary CA 25-28R; CABS 2; DLB 5, 16

Olson, Theodore 1937-
See Olson, Toby

Olson, Toby 1937- .... **CLC 28**
See also CANR 9; CA 65-68

Ondaatje, (Philip) Michael
1943- .... **CLC 14, 29, 51**
See also CA 77-80; DLB 60

Oneal, Elizabeth 1934-
See Oneal, Zibby
See also CA 106; SATA 30

Oneal, Zibby 1934- .... **CLC 30**
See also Oneal, Elizabeth

O'Neill, Eugene (Gladstone)
1888-1953 .... **TCLC 1, 6, 27**
See also CA 110; DLB 7

Onetti, Juan Carlos 1909- .... **CLC 7, 10**
See also CA 85-88

O'Nolan, Brian 1911-1966
See O'Brien, Flann

O Nuallain, Brian 1911-1966
See O'Brien, Flann
See also CAP 2; CA 21-22;
obituary CA 25-28R

Oppen, George 1908-1984 .... **CLC 7, 13, 34**
See also CANR 8; CA 13-16R;
obituary CA 113; DLB 5

Orlovitz, Gil 1918-1973 .... **CLC 22**
See also CA 77-80; obituary CA 45-48;
DLB 2, 5

Ortega y Gasset, Jose 1883-1955 ... **TCLC 9**
See also CA 106

Ortiz, Simon J. 1941- .... **CLC 45**

Orton, Joe 1933?-1967 .... **CLC 4, 13, 43**
See also Orton, John Kingsley
See also DLB 13

Orton, John Kingsley 1933?-1967
See Orton, Joe
See also CA 85-88

Orwell, George
1903-1950 .... **TCLC 2, 6, 15, 31**
See also Blair, Eric Arthur
See also DLB 15

Osborne, John (James)
1929- .... **CLC 1, 2, 5, 11, 45**
See also CANR 21; CA 13-16R; DLB 13

Osborne, Lawrence 1958- .... **CLC 50**

Osceola 1885-1962
See Dinesen, Isak; Blixen, Karen
(Christentze Dinesen)

Oshima, Nagisa 1932- .... **CLC 20**
See also CA 116

Oskison, John M. 1874-1947 ...... **TCLC 35**

Ossoli, Sarah Margaret (Fuller marchesa d')
1810-1850
See Fuller, (Sarah) Margaret
See also SATA 25

Otero, Blas de 1916- .... **CLC 11**
See also CA 89-92

Owen, Wilfred (Edward Salter)
1893-1918 .... **TCLC 5, 27**
See also CA 104; DLB 20

Owens, Rochelle 1936- .... **CLC 8**
See also CAAS 2; CA 17-20R

Owl, Sebastian 1939-
See Thompson, Hunter S(tockton)

Oz, Amos 1939- ... **CLC 5, 8, 11, 27, 33, 54**
See also CA 53-56

Ozick, Cynthia 1928- .... **CLC 3, 7, 28**
See also CANR 23; CA 17-20R; DLB 28;
DLB-Y 82

Ozu, Yasujiro 1903-1963 .... **CLC 16**
See also CA 112

Pa Chin 1904- .... **CLC 18**
See also Li Fei-kan

Pack, Robert 1929- .... **CLC 13**
See also CANR 3; CA 1-4R; DLB 5

Padgett, Lewis 1915-1958
See Kuttner, Henry

Padilla, Heberto 1932- .... **CLC 38**
See also CA 123

Page, Jimmy 1944- .... **CLC 12**

Page, Louise 1955- .... **CLC 40**

Page, P(atricia) K(athleen)
1916- .... **CLC 7, 18**
See also CANR 4, 22; CA 53-56; DLB 68

Paget, Violet 1856-1935
See Lee, Vernon
See also CA 104

Palamas, Kostes 1859-1943 .... **TCLC 5**
See also CA 105

Palazzeschi, Aldo 1885-1974 .... **CLC 11**
See also CA 89-92; obituary CA 53-56

Paley, Grace 1922- .... **CLC 4, 6, 37**
See also CANR 13; CA 25-28R; DLB 28

Palin, Michael 1943- .... **CLC 21**
See also Monty Python
See also CA 107

Palma, Ricardo 1833-1919 .... **TCLC 29**
See also CANR 123

Pancake, Breece Dexter 1952-1979
See Pancake, Breece D'J

Pancake, Breece D'J 1952-1979 .... **CLC 29**
See also obituary CA 109

Papadiamantis, Alexandros
1851-1911 .... **TCLC 29**

Papini, Giovanni 1881-1956 ...... **TCLC 22**
See also CA 121

Parini, Jay (Lee) 1948- .... **CLC 54**
See also CA 97-100

Parker, Dorothy (Rothschild)
1893-1967 .... **CLC 15; SSC 2**
See also CAP 2; CA 19-20;
obituary CA 25-28R; DLB 11, 45

Parker, Robert B(rown) 1932- ...... **CLC 27**
See also CANR 1, 26; CA 49-52

Parkin, Frank 1940- .... **CLC 43**

Parkman, Francis 1823-1893 ..... **NCLC 12**
See also DLB 1, 30

Parks, Gordon (Alexander Buchanan)
1912- .... **CLC 1, 16**
See also CANR 26; CA 41-44R; SATA 8;
DLB 33

Parnell, Thomas 1679-1718 .... **LC 3**

Parra, Nicanor 1914- .... **CLC 2**
See also CA 85-88

Pasolini, Pier Paolo
1922-1975 .... **CLC 20, 37**
See also CA 93-96; obituary CA 61-64

Pastan, Linda (Olenik) 1932- ...... **CLC 27**
See also CANR 18; CA 61-64; DLB 5

Pasternak, Boris 1890-1960 ... **CLC 7, 10, 18**
See also obituary CA 116

Patchen, Kenneth 1911-1972 ... **CLC 1, 2, 18**
See also CANR 3; CA 1-4R;
obituary CA 33-36R; DLB 16, 48

Pater, Walter (Horatio)
1839-1894 .... **NCLC 7**
See also DLB 57

Paterson, Andrew Barton
1864-1941 .... **TCLC 32**

Paterson, Katherine (Womeldorf)
1932- .... **CLC 12, 30**
See also CLR 7; CA 21-24R; SATA 13, 53;
DLB 52

Patmore, Coventry Kersey Dighton
1823-1896 .... **NCLC 9**
See also DLB 35

Ransom, John Crowe
1888-1974 .... **CLC 2, 4, 5, 11, 24**
See also CANR 6; CA 5-8R;
obituary CA 49-52; DLB 45, 63

Rao, Raja 1909- .... **CLC 25, 56**
See also CA 73-76

Raphael, Frederic (Michael)
1931- .... **CLC 2, 14**
See also CANR 1; CA 1-4R; DLB 14

Rathbone, Julian 1935- .... **CLC 41**
See also CA 101

Rattigan, Terence (Mervyn)
1911-1977 .... **CLC 7**
See also CA 85-88; obituary CA 73-76;
DLB 13

Ratushinskaya, Irina 1954- .... **CLC 54**

Raven, Simon (Arthur Noel)
1927- .... **CLC 14**
See also CA 81-84

Rawley, Callman 1903-
See Rakosi, Carl
See also CANR 12; CA 21-24R

Rawlings, Marjorie Kinnan
1896-1953 .... **TCLC 4**
See also YABC 1; CA 104; DLB 9, 22

Ray, Satyajit 1921-............... **CLC 16**
See also CA 114

Read, Herbert (Edward) 1893-1968 .. **CLC 4**
See also CA 85-88; obituary CA 25-28R;
DLB 20

Read, Piers Paul 1941- ...... **CLC 4, 10, 25**
See also CA 21-24R; SATA 21; DLB 14

Reade, Charles 1814-1884 .... **NCLC 2**
See also DLB 21

Reade, Hamish 1936-
See Gray, Simon (James Holliday)

Reading, Peter 1946- .... **CLC 47**
See also CA 103; DLB 40

Reaney, James 1926- .... **CLC 13**
See also CA 41-44R; SATA 43; DLB 68

Rebreanu, Liviu 1885-1944 .... **TCLC 28**

Rechy, John (Francisco)
1934- .... **CLC 1, 7, 14, 18**
See also CAAS 4; CANR 6; CA 5-8R;
DLB-Y 82

Redcam, Tom 1870-1933 .... **TCLC 25**

Redgrove, Peter (William)
1932- .... **CLC 6, 41**
See also CANR 3; CA 1-4R; DLB 40

Redmon (Nightingale), Anne
1943- .... **CLC 22**
See also Nightingale, Anne Redmon
See also DLB-Y 86

Reed, Ishmael 1938-.. **CLC 2, 3, 5, 6, 13, 32**
See also CA 21-24R; DLB 2, 5, 33

Reed, John (Silas) 1887-1920 ...... **TCLC 9**
See also CA 106

Reed, Lou 1944-.................. **CLC 21**

Reeve, Clara 1729-1807 .... **NCLC 19**
See also DLB 39

Reid, Christopher 1949-........... **CLC 33**
See also DLB 40

Reid Banks, Lynne 1929-
See Banks, Lynne Reid
See also CANR 6, 22; CA 1-4R; SATA 22

Reiner, Max 1900-
See Caldwell, (Janet Miriam) Taylor
(Holland)

Reizenstein, Elmer Leopold 1892-1967
See Rice, Elmer

Remark, Erich Paul 1898-1970
See Remarque, Erich Maria

Remarque, Erich Maria
1898-1970 .... **CLC 21**
See also CA 77-80; obituary CA 29-32R;
DLB 56

Remizov, Alexey (Mikhailovich)
1877-1957 .... **TCLC 27**
See also CA 125

Renan, Joseph Ernest
1823-1892 .... **NCLC 26**

Renard, Jules 1864-1910 .... **TCLC 17**
See also CA 117

Renault, Mary 1905-1983 .... **CLC 3, 11, 17**
See also Challans, Mary
See also DLB-Y 83

Rendell, Ruth 1930-.......... **CLC 28, 48**
See also Vine, Barbara
See also CA 109

Renoir, Jean 1894-1979 .... **CLC 20**
See also obituary CA 85-88

Resnais, Alain 1922-............. **CLC 16**

Reverdy, Pierre 1899-1960 .... **CLC 53**
See also CA 97-100; obituary CA 89-92

Rexroth, Kenneth
1905-1982 ...... **CLC 1, 2, 6, 11, 22, 49**
See also CANR 14; CA 5-8R;
obituary CA 107; DLB 16, 48; DLB-Y 82;
CDALB 1941-1968

Reyes, Alfonso 1889-1959 .... **TCLC 33**

Reyes y Basoalto, Ricardo Eliecer Neftali
1904-1973
See Neruda, Pablo

Reymont, Wladyslaw Stanislaw
1867-1925 .... **TCLC 5**
See also CA 104

Reynolds, Jonathan 1942?- ...... **CLC 6, 38**
See also CA 65-68

Reynolds, Michael (Shane) 1937- ... **CLC 44**
See also CANR 9; CA 65-68

Reznikoff, Charles 1894-1976 .... **CLC 9**
See also CAP 2; CA 33-36;
obituary CA 61-64; DLB 28, 45

Rezzori, Gregor von 1914-........ **CLC 25**
See also CA 122

Rhys, Jean
1890-1979 ...... **CLC 2, 4, 6, 14, 19, 51**
See also CA 25-28R; obituary CA 85-88;
DLB 36

Ribeiro, Darcy 1922-............. **CLC 34**
See also CA 33-36R

Ribeiro, Joao Ubaldo (Osorio Pimentel)
1941- .... **CLC 10**
See also CA 81-84

Ribman, Ronald (Burt) 1932- .... **CLC 7**
See also CA 21-24R

Rice, Anne 1941- .... **CLC 41**
See also CANR 12; CA 65-68

Rice, Elmer 1892-1967......... **CLC 7, 49**
See also CAP 2; CA 21-22;
obituary CA 25-28R; DLB 4, 7

Rice, Tim 1944- .... **CLC 21**
See also CA 103

Rich, Adrienne (Cecile)
1929- .... **CLC 3, 6, 7, 11, 18, 36**
See also CANR 20; CA 9-12R; DLB 5, 67

Richard, Keith 1943- .... **CLC 17**
See also CA 107

Richards, David Adam 1950-....... **CLC 59**
See also CA 93-96; DLB 53

Richards, I(vor) A(rmstrong)
1893-1979 .... **CLC 14, 24**
See also CA 41-44R; obituary CA 89-92;
DLB 27

Richards, Keith 1943-
See Richard, Keith
See also CA 107

Richardson, Dorothy (Miller)
1873-1957 .... **TCLC 3**
See also CA 104; DLB 36

Richardson, Ethel 1870-1946
See Richardson, Henry Handel
See also CA 105

Richardson, Henry Handel
1870-1946 .... **TCLC 4**
See also Richardson, Ethel

Richardson, Samuel 1689-1761 .... **LC 1**
See also DLB 39

Richler, Mordecai
1931- .... **CLC 3, 5, 9, 13, 18, 46**
See also CA 65-68; SATA 27, 44; DLB 53

Richter, Conrad (Michael)
1890-1968 .... **CLC 30**
See also CA 5-8R; obituary CA 25-28R;
SATA 3; DLB 9

Richter, Johann Paul Friedrich 1763-1825
See Jean Paul

Riding, Laura 1901-............. **CLC 3, 7**
See also Jackson, Laura (Riding)

Riefenstahl, Berta Helene Amalia
1902- .... **CLC 16**
See also Riefenstahl, Leni
See also CA 108

Riefenstahl, Leni 1902- .... **CLC 16**
See also Riefenstahl, Berta Helene Amalia
See also CA 108

Rilke, Rainer Maria
1875-1926 .... **TCLC 1, 6, 19**
See also CA 104

Rimbaud, (Jean Nicolas) Arthur
1854-1891 .... **NCLC 4**

Ringwood, Gwen(dolyn Margaret) Pharis
1910-1984 .... **CLC 48**
See also obituary CA 112

Rio, Michel 19??-................. **CLC 43**

Ritsos, Yannis 1909-........ **CLC 6, 13, 31**
See also CA 77-80

Ritter, Erika 1948?-............. **CLC 52**

Rivera, Jose Eustasio 1889-1928... **TCLC 35**

Rivers, Conrad Kent   1933-1968 . . . . . . **CLC 1**
   See also CA 85-88; DLB 41

Rizal, Jose   1861-1896 . . . . **NCLC 27**

Roa Bastos, Augusto   1917- . . . . **CLC 45**

Robbe-Grillet, Alain
   1922- . . . . . . **CLC 1, 2, 4, 6, 8, 10, 14, 43**
   See also CA 9-12R

Robbins, Harold   1916- . . . . **CLC 5**
   See also CANR 26; CA 73-76

Robbins, Thomas Eugene   1936-
   See Robbins, Tom
   See also CA 81-84

Robbins, Tom   1936- . . . . **CLC 9, 32**
   See also Robbins, Thomas Eugene
   See also DLB-Y 80

Robbins, Trina   1938- . . . . **CLC 21**

Roberts, (Sir) Charles G(eorge) D(ouglas)
   1860-1943 . . . . **TCLC 8**
   See also CA 105; SATA 29

Roberts, Kate   1891-1985 . . . . **CLC 15**
   See also CA 107; obituary CA 116

Roberts, Keith (John Kingston)
   1935- . . . . **CLC 14**
   See also CA 25-28R

Roberts, Kenneth   1885-1957 . . . . . . **TCLC 23**
   See also CA 109; DLB 9

Roberts, Michele (B.)   1949- . . . . **CLC 48**
   See also CA 115

Robinson, Edwin Arlington
   1869-1935 . . . . **TCLC 5**
   See also CA 104; DLB 54;
   CDALB 1865-1917

Robinson, Henry Crabb
   1775-1867 . . . . **NCLC 15**

Robinson, Jill   1936- . . . . **CLC 10**
   See also CA 102

Robinson, Kim Stanley   19??- . . . . **CLC 34**
   See also CA 126

Robinson, Marilynne   1944- . . . . **CLC 25**
   See also CA 116

Robinson, Smokey   1940- . . . . **CLC 21**

Robinson, William   1940-
   See Robinson, Smokey
   See also CA 116

Robison, Mary   1949- . . . . **CLC 42**
   See also CA 113, 116

Roddenberry, Gene   1921- . . . . **CLC 17**
   See also CANR 110

Rodgers, Mary   1931- . . . . **CLC 12**
   See also CLR 20; CANR 8; CA 49-52;
   SATA 8

Rodgers, W(illiam) R(obert)
   1909-1969 . . . . **CLC 7**
   See also CA 85-88; DLB 20

Rodriguez, Claudio   1934- . . . . **CLC 10**

Roethke, Theodore (Huebner)
   1908-1963 . . . . . . **CLC 1, 3, 8, 11, 19, 46**
   See also CA 81-84; CABS 2; SAAS 1;
   DLB 5; CDALB 1941-1968

Rogers, Sam   1943-
   See Shepard, Sam

Rogers, Thomas (Hunton)   1931- . . . . **CLC 57**
   See also CA 89-92

Rogers, Will(iam Penn Adair)
   1879-1935 . . . . **TCLC 8**
   See also CA 105; DLB 11

Rogin, Gilbert   1929- . . . . **CLC 18**
   See also CANR 15; CA 65-68

Rohan, Koda   1867-1947 . . . . **TCLC 22**
   See also CA 121

Rohmer, Eric   1920- . . . . **CLC 16**
   See also Scherer, Jean-Marie Maurice

Rohmer, Sax   1883-1959 . . . . **TCLC 28**
   See also Ward, Arthur Henry Sarsfield
   See also CA 108; DLB 70

Roiphe, Anne (Richardson)
   1935- . . . . **CLC 3, 9**
   See also CA 89-92; DLB-Y 80

Rolfe, Frederick (William Serafino Austin
   Lewis Mary)   1860-1913 . . . . . . **TCLC 12**
   See also CA 107; DLB 34

Rolland, Romain   1866-1944 . . . . **TCLC 23**
   See also CA 118

Rolvaag, O(le) E(dvart)
   1876-1931 . . . . **TCLC 17**
   See also CA 117; DLB 9

Romains, Jules   1885-1972 . . . . **CLC 7**
   See also CA 85-88

Romero, Jose Ruben   1890-1952 . . . **TCLC 14**
   See also CA 114

Ronsard, Pierre de   1524-1585 . . . . **LC 6**

Rooke, Leon   1934- . . . . **CLC 25, 34**
   See also CANR 23; CA 25-28R

Roper, William   1498-1578 . . . . **LC 10**

Rosa, Joao Guimaraes   1908-1967 . . . **CLC 23**
   See also obituary CA 89-92

Rosen, Richard (Dean)   1949- . . . . . . **CLC 39**
   See also CA 77-80

Rosenberg, Isaac   1890-1918 . . . . **TCLC 12**
   See also CA 107; DLB 20

Rosenblatt, Joe   1933- . . . . **CLC 15**
   See also Rosenblatt, Joseph

Rosenblatt, Joseph   1933-
   See Rosenblatt, Joe
   See also CA 89-92

Rosenfeld, Samuel   1896-1963
   See Tzara, Tristan
   See also obituary CA 89-92

Rosenthal, M(acha) L(ouis)   1917- . . . **CLC 28**
   See also CAAS 6; CANR 4; CA 1-4R;
   DLB 5

Ross, (James) Sinclair   1908- . . . . **CLC 13**
   See also CA 73-76

Rossetti, Christina Georgina
   1830-1894 . . . . **NCLC 2**
   See also SATA 20; DLB 35

Rossetti, Dante Gabriel
   1828-1882 . . . . **NCLC 4**
   See also DLB 35

Rossetti, Gabriel Charles Dante   1828-1882
   See Rossetti, Dante Gabriel

Rossner, Judith (Perelman)
   1935- . . . . **CLC 6, 9, 29**
   See also CANR 18; CA 17-20R; DLB 6

Rostand, Edmond (Eugene Alexis)
   1868-1918 . . . . **TCLC 6, 37**
   See also CA 104, 126

Roth, Henry   1906- . . . . **CLC 2, 6, 11**
   See also CAP 1; CA 11-12; DLB 28

Roth, Joseph   1894-1939 . . . . **TCLC 33**

Roth, Philip (Milton)
   1933- . . . . . . **CLC 1, 2, 3, 4, 6, 9, 15, 22,**
                         31, 47
   See also CANR 1, 22; CA 1-4R; DLB 2, 28;
   DLB-Y 82

Rothenberg, James   1931- . . . . **CLC 57**

Rothenberg, Jerome   1931- . . . . **CLC 6**
   See also CANR 1; CA 45-48; DLB 5

Roumain, Jacques   1907-1944 . . . . . **TCLC 19**
   See also CA 117

Rourke, Constance (Mayfield)
   1885-1941 . . . . **TCLC 12**
   See also YABC 1; CA 107

Rousseau, Jean-Baptiste   1671-1741 . . . **LC 9**

Roussel, Raymond   1877-1933 . . . . . **TCLC 20**
   See also CA 117

Rovit, Earl (Herbert)   1927- . . . . **CLC 7**
   See also CANR 12; CA 5-8R

Rowe, Nicholas   1674-1718 . . . . **LC 8**

Rowson, Susanna Haswell
   1762-1824 . . . . **NCLC 5**
   See also DLB 37

Roy, Gabrielle   1909-1983 . . . . . . **CLC 10, 14**
   See also CANR 5; CA 53-56;
   obituary CA 110; DLB 68

Rozewicz, Tadeusz   1921- . . . . **CLC 9, 23**
   See also CA 108

Ruark, Gibbons   1941- . . . . **CLC 3**
   See also CANR 14; CA 33-36R

Rubens, Bernice   192?- . . . . **CLC 19, 31**
   See also CA 25-28R; DLB 14

Rudkin, (James) David   1936- . . . . . . **CLC 14**
   See also CA 89-92; DLB 13

Rudnik, Raphael   1933- . . . . **CLC 7**
   See also CA 29-32R

Ruiz, Jose Martinez   1874-1967
   See Azorin

Rukeyser, Muriel
   1913-1980 . . . . **CLC 6, 10, 15, 27**
   See also CANR 26; CA 5-8R;
   obituary CA 93-96; obituary SATA 22;
   DLB 48

Rule, Jane (Vance)   1931- . . . . **CLC 27**
   See also CANR 12; CA 25-28R; DLB 60

Rulfo, Juan   1918-1986 . . . . **CLC 8**
   See also CANR 26; CA 85-88;
   obituary CA 118

Runyon, (Alfred) Damon
   1880-1946 . . . . **TCLC 10**
   See also CA 107; DLB 11

Rush, Norman   1933- . . . . **CLC 44**
   See also CA 121, 126

Rushdie, (Ahmed) Salman
   1947- . . . . **CLC 23, 31, 55**
   See also CA 108, 111

Rushforth, Peter (Scott)   1945- . . . . . **CLC 19**
   See also CA 101

Ruskin, John   1819-1900 . . . . **TCLC 20**
   See also CA 114; SATA 24; DLB 55

Schmitz, Ettore 1861-1928
See Svevo, Italo
See also CA 104, 122

Schnackenberg, Gjertrud 1953-..... **CLC 40**
See also CA 116

Schneider, Leonard Alfred 1925-1966
See Bruce, Lenny
See also CA 89-92

Schnitzler, Arthur 1862-1931 ..... **TCLC 4**
See also CA 104

Schorer, Mark 1908-1977 .... **CLC 9**
See also CANR 7; CA 5-8R;
obituary CA 73-76

Schrader, Paul (Joseph) 1946-..... **CLC 26**
See also CA 37-40R; DLB 44

Schreiner (Cronwright), Olive (Emilie
Albertina) 1855-1920........ **TCLC 9**
See also CA 105; DLB 18

Schulberg, Budd (Wilson)
1914-..................... **CLC 7, 48**
See also CANR 19; CA 25-28R; DLB 6, 26,
28; DLB-Y 81

Schulz, Bruno 1892-1942......... **TCLC 5**
See also CA 115, 123

Schulz, Charles M(onroe) 1922-.... **CLC 12**
See also CANR 6; CA 9-12R; SATA 10

Schuyler, James (Marcus)
1923-..................... **CLC 5, 23**
See also CA 101; DLB 5

Schwartz, Delmore
1913-1966 .... **CLC 2, 4, 10, 45**
See also CAP 2; CA 17-18;
obituary CA 25-28R; DLB 28, 48

Schwartz, John Burnham 1925- .... **CLC 59**

Schwartz, Lynne Sharon 1939-..... **CLC 31**
See also CA 103

Schwarz-Bart, Andre 1928-....... **CLC 2, 4**
See also CA 89-92

Schwarz-Bart, Simone 1938-........ **CLC 7**
See also CA 97-100

Schwob, (Mayer Andre) Marcel
1867-1905 .... **TCLC 20**
See also CA 117

Sciascia, Leonardo
1921-1989 .... **CLC 8, 9, 41**
See also CA 85-88

Scoppettone, Sandra 1936-........ **CLC 26**
See also CA 5-8R; SATA 9

Scorsese, Martin 1942- .... **CLC 20**
See also CA 110, 114

Scotland, Jay 1932-
See Jakes, John (William)

Scott, Duncan Campbell
1862-1947 .... **TCLC 6**
See also CA 104

Scott, Evelyn 1893-1963........... **CLC 43**
See also CA 104; obituary CA 112; DLB 9,
48

Scott, F(rancis) R(eginald)
1899-1985 .... **CLC 22**
See also CA 101; obituary CA 114

Scott, Joanna 19??-.............. **CLC 50**
See also CA 126

Scott, Paul (Mark) 1920-1978....... **CLC 9**
See also CA 81-84; obituary CA 77-80;
DLB 14

Scott, Sir Walter 1771-1832 ..... **NCLC 15**
See also YABC 2

Scribe, (Augustin) Eugene
1791-1861 .... **NCLC 16**

Scudery, Madeleine de 1607-1701..... **LC 2**

Sealy, I. Allan 1951- .... **CLC 55**

Seare, Nicholas 1925-
See Trevanian; Whitaker, Rodney

Sebestyen, Igen 1924-
See Sebestyen, Ouida

Sebestyen, Ouida 1924-........... **CLC 30**
See also CA 107; SATA 39

Sedgwick, Catharine Maria
1789-1867 .... **NCLC 19**
See also DLB 1

Seelye, John 1931-............... **CLC 7**
See also CA 97-100

Seferiades, Giorgos Stylianou 1900-1971
See Seferis, George
See also CANR 5; CA 5-8R;
obituary CA 33-36R

Seferis, George 1900-1971....... **CLC 5, 11**
See also Seferiades, Giorgos Stylianou

Segal, Erich (Wolf) 1937- .... **CLC 3, 10**
See also CANR 20; CA 25-28R; DLB-Y 86

Seger, Bob 1945-................. **CLC 35**

Seger, Robert Clark 1945-
See Seger, Bob

Seghers, Anna 1900-1983....... **CLC 7, 110**
See also Radvanyi, Netty Reiling
See also DLB 69

Seidel, Frederick (Lewis) 1936-..... **CLC 18**
See also CANR 8; CA 13-16R; DLB-Y 84

Seifert, Jaroslav 1901-1986..... **CLC 34, 44**

Selby, Hubert, Jr. 1928- ..... **CLC 1, 2, 4, 8**
See also CA 13-16R; DLB 2

Senacour, Etienne Pivert de
1770-1846 .... **NCLC 16**

Sender, Ramon (Jose) 1902-1982 .... **CLC 8**
See also CANR 8; CA 5-8R;
obituary CA 105

Senghor, Léopold Sédar 1906-...... **CLC 54**
See also CA 116

Serling, (Edward) Rod(man)
1924-1975 .... **CLC 30**
See also CA 65-68; obituary CA 57-60;
DLB 26

Serpieres 1907-
See Guillevic, (Eugene)

Service, Robert W(illiam)
1874-1958 .... **TCLC 15**
See also CA 115; SATA 20

Seth, Vikram 1952-.............. **CLC 43**
See also CA 121

Seton, Cynthia Propper
1926-1982 .... **CLC 27**
See also CANR 7; CA 5-8R;
obituary CA 108

Seton, Ernest (Evan) Thompson
1860-1946 .... **TCLC 31**
See also CA 109; SATA 18

Settle, Mary Lee 1918- .... **CLC 19**
See also CAAS 1; CA 89-92; DLB 6

Sevigne, Marquise de Marie de
Rabutin-Chantal 1626-1696..... **LC 11**

Sexton, Anne (Harvey)
1928-1974 ..... **CLC 2, 4, 6, 8, 10, 15, 53**
See also CANR 3; CA 1-4R;
obituary CA 53-56; CABS 2; SATA 10;
DLB 5; CDALB 1941-1968

Shaara, Michael (Joseph) 1929- .... **CLC 15**
See also CA 102; obituary CA 125;
DLB-Y 83

Shackleton, C. C. 1925-
See Aldiss, Brian W(ilson)

Shacochis, Bob 1951-............. **CLC 39**
See also CA 119, 124

Shaffer, Anthony 1926- .... **CLC 19**
See also CA 110, 116; DLB 13

Shaffer, Peter (Levin)
1926-................. **CLC 5, 14, 18, 37**
See also CANR 25; CA 25-28R; DLB 13

Shalamov, Varlam (Tikhonovich)
1907?-1982.................. **CLC 18**
See also obituary CA 105

Shamlu, Ahmad 1925- .... **CLC 10**

Shammas, Anton 1951-........... **CLC 55**

Shange, Ntozake 1948-....... **CLC 8, 25, 38**
See also CA 85-88; DLB 38

Shapcott, Thomas W(illiam) 1935- .. **CLC 38**
See also CA 69-72

Shapiro, Karl (Jay) 1913- ..**CLC 4, 8, 15, 53**
See also CAAS 6; CANR 1; CA 1-4R;
DLB 48

Sharpe, Tom 1928-............... **CLC 36**
See also CA 114; DLB 14

Shaw, (George) Bernard
1856-1950 .... **TCLC 3, 9, 21**
See also CA 104, 109, 119; DLB 10, 57

Shaw, Henry Wheeler
1818-1885 .... **NCLC 15**
See also DLB 11

Shaw, Irwin 1913-1984....... **CLC 7, 23, 34**
See also CANR 21; CA 13-16R;
obituary CA 112; DLB 6; DLB-Y 84;
CDALB 1941-1968

Shaw, Robert 1927-1978 .... **CLC 5**
See also CANR 4; CA 1-4R;
obituary CA 81-84; DLB 13, 14

Shawn, Wallace 1943- .... **CLC 41**
See also CA 112

Sheed, Wilfrid (John Joseph)
1930-................. **CLC 2, 4, 10, 53**
See also CA 65-68; DLB 6

Sheffey, Asa 1913-1980
See Hayden, Robert (Earl)

Sheldon, Alice (Hastings) B(radley)
1915-1987
See Tiptree, James, Jr.
See also CA 108; obituary CA 122

Starbuck, George (Edwin) 1931-.... **CLC 53**
See also CANR 23; CA 21-22R

Stark, Richard 1933-
See Westlake, Donald E(dwin)

Stead, Christina (Ellen)
1902-1983 .... **CLC 2, 5, 8, 32**
See also CA 13-16R; obituary CA 109

Steele, Timothy (Reid) 1948-....... **CLC 45**
See also CANR 16; CA 93-96

Steffens, (Joseph) Lincoln
1866-1936 .... **TCLC 20**
See also CA 117; SAAS 1

Stegner, Wallace (Earle) 1909-... **CLC 9, 49**
See also CANR 1, 21; CA 1-4R; DLB 9

Stein, Gertrude 1874-1946... **TCLC 1, 6, 28**
See also CA 104; DLB 4, 54

Steinbeck, John (Ernst)
1902-1968 ... **CLC 1, 5, 9, 13, 21, 34, 45**
See also CANR 1; CA 1-4R;
obituary CA 25-28R; SATA 9; DLB 7, 9;
DLB-DS 2

Steiner, George 1929-............. **CLC 24**
See also CA 73-76

Steiner, Rudolf(us Josephus Laurentius)
1861-1925 .... **TCLC 13**
See also CA 107

Stendhal 1783-1842............. **NCLC 23**

Stephen, Leslie 1832-1904 .... **TCLC 23**
See also CANR 9; CA 21-24R, 123;
DLB 57

Stephens, James 1882?-1950 .... **TCLC 4**
See also CA 104; DLB 19

Stephens, Reed
See Donaldson, Stephen R.

Steptoe, Lydia 1892-1982
See Barnes, Djuna

Sterling, George 1869-1926 .... **TCLC 20**
See also CA 117; DLB 54

Stern, Gerald 1925- .... **CLC 40**
See also CA 81-84

Stern, Richard G(ustave) 1928-... **CLC 4, 39**
See also CANR 1, 25; CA 1-4R

Sternberg, Jonas 1894-1969
See Sternberg, Josef von

Sternberg, Josef von 1894-1969..... **CLC 20**
See also CA 81-84

Sterne, Laurence 1713-1768......... **LC 2**
See also DLB 39

Sternheim, (William Adolf) Carl
1878-1942 .... **TCLC 8**
See also CA 105

Stevens, Mark 19??-............. **CLC 34**

Stevens, Wallace 1879-1955..... **TCLC 3, 12**
See also CA 104, 124; DLB 54

Stevenson, Anne (Katharine)
1933- .... **CLC 7, 33**
See also Elvin, Anne Katharine Stevenson
See also CANR 9; CA 17-18R; DLB 40

Stevenson, Robert Louis
1850-1894 .... **NCLC 5, 14**
See also CLR 10, 11; YABC 2; DLB 18, 57

Stewart, J(ohn) I(nnes) M(ackintosh)
1906- .... **CLC 7, 14, 32**
See also CAAS 3; CA 85-88

Stewart, Mary (Florence Elinor)
1916- .... **CLC 7, 35**
See also CANR 1; CA 1-4R; SATA 12

Stewart, Will 1908-
See Williamson, Jack
See also CANR 23; CA 17-18R

Still, James 1906-................. **CLC 49**
See also CANR 10; CA 65-68; SATA 29;
DLB 9

Sting 1951-
See The Police

Stitt, Milan 1941-............. **CLC 29**
See also CA 69-72

Stoker, Abraham
See Stoker, Bram
See also CA 105

Stoker, Bram 1847-1912 .... **TCLC 8**
See also Stoker, Abraham
See also SATA 29; DLB 36, 70

Stolz, Mary (Slattery) 1920-....... **CLC 12**
See also CANR 13; CA 5-8R; SAAS 3;
SATA 10

Stone, Irving 1903-1989........... **CLC 7**
See also CAAS 3; CANR 1; CA 1-4R;
SATA 3

Stone, Robert (Anthony)
1937?- .... **CLC 5, 23, 42**
See also CANR 23; CA 85-88

Stoppard, Tom
1937- ...... **CLC 1, 3, 4, 5, 8, 15, 29, 34**
See also CA 81-84; DLB 13; DLB-Y 85

Storey, David (Malcolm)
1933- .... **CLC 2, 4, 5, 8**
See also CA 81-84; DLB 13, 14

Storm, Hyemeyohsts 1935- .... **CLC 3**
See also CA 81-84

Storm, (Hans) Theodor (Woldsen)
1817-1888 .... **NCLC 1**

Storni, Alfonsina 1892-1938 .... **TCLC 5**
See also CA 104

Stout, Rex (Todhunter) 1886-1975 ... **CLC 3**
See also CA 61-64

Stow, (Julian) Randolph 1935- .. **CLC 23, 48**
See also CA 13-16R

Stowe, Harriet (Elizabeth) Beecher
1811-1896 .... **NCLC 3**
See also YABC 1; DLB 1, 12, 42;
CDALB 1865-1917

Strachey, (Giles) Lytton
1880-1932 .... **TCLC 12**
See also CA 110

Strand, Mark 1934- .... **CLC 6, 18, 41**
See also CA 21-24R; SATA 41; DLB 5

Straub, Peter (Francis) 1943- ..... **CLC 28**
See also CA 85-88; DLB-Y 84

Strauss, Botho 1944- .... **CLC 22**

Straussler, Tomas 1937-
See Stoppard, Tom

Streatfeild, (Mary) Noel 1897- ..... **CLC 21**
See also CA 81-84; obituary CA 120;
SATA 20, 48

Stribling, T(homas) S(igismund)
1881-1965 .... **CLC 23**
See also obituary CA 107; DLB 9

Strindberg, (Johan) August
1849-1912 .... **TCLC 1, 8, 21**
See also CA 104

Stringer, Arthur 1874-1950 ...... **TCLC 37**
See also DLB 92

Strugatskii, Arkadii (Natanovich)
1925- .... **CLC 27**
See also CA 106

Strugatskii, Boris (Natanovich)
1933- .... **CLC 27**
See also CA 106

Strummer, Joe 1953?-
See The Clash

Stuart, (Hilton) Jesse
1906-1984 .... **CLC 1, 8, 11, 14, 34**
See also CA 5-8R; obituary CA 112;
SATA 2; obituary SATA 36; DLB 9, 48;
DLB-Y 84

Sturgeon, Theodore (Hamilton)
1918-1985 .... **CLC 22, 39**
See also CA 81-84; obituary CA 116;
DLB 8; DLB-Y 85

Styron, William 1925- .. **CLC 1, 3, 5, 11, 15**
See also CANR 6; CA 5-8R; DLB 2;
DLB-Y 80

Sudermann, Hermann 1857-1928 .. **TCLC 15**
See also CA 107

Sue, Eugene 1804-1857 .... **NCLC 1**

Sukenick, Ronald 1932-..... **CLC 3, 4, 6, 48**
See also CA 25-28R; DLB-Y 81

Suknaski, Andrew 1942- .... **CLC 19**
See also CA 101; DLB 53

Sully-Prudhomme, Rene
1839-1907 .... **TCLC 31**

Su Man-shu 1884-1918........... **TCLC 24**
See also CA 123

Summers, Andrew James 1942-
See The Police

Summers, Andy 1942-
See The Police

Summers, Hollis (Spurgeon, Jr.)
1916- .... **CLC 10**
See also CANR 3; CA 5-8R; DLB 6

Summers, (Alphonsus Joseph-Mary Augustus)
Montague 1880-1948 .... **TCLC 16**
See also CA 118

Sumner, Gordon Matthew 1951-
See The Police

Surtees, Robert Smith
1805-1864 .... **NCLC 14**
See also DLB 21

Susann, Jacqueline 1921-1974....... **CLC 3**
See also CA 65-68; obituary CA 53-56

Suskind, Patrick 1949-........... **CLC 44**

Sutcliff, Rosemary 1920- .... **CLC 26**
See also CLR 1; CA 5-8R; SATA 6, 44

Sutro, Alfred 1863-1933.......... **TCLC 6**
See also CA 105; DLB 10

Sutton, Henry 1935-
See Slavitt, David (R.)

Svevo, Italo 1861-1928........ **TCLC 2, 35**
See also Schmitz, Ettore

Swados, Elizabeth 1951- .... **CLC 12**
See also CA 97-100

Timrod, Henry   1828-1867 . . . .   NCLC 25

Tindall, Gillian   1938- . . . .   CLC 7
See also CANR 11; CA 21-24R

Tiptree, James, Jr.   1915-1987 . . .   CLC 48, 50
See also Sheldon, Alice (Hastings) B(radley)
See also DLB 8

Tocqueville, Alexis (Charles Henri Maurice
Clerel, Comte) de   1805-1859 . .   NCLC 7

Tolkien, J(ohn) R(onald) R(euel)
1892-1973 . . . .   CLC 1, 2, 3, 8, 12, 38
See also CAP 2; CA 17-18;
obituary CA 45-48; SATA 2, 32;
obituary SATA 24; DLB 15

Toller, Ernst   1893-1939 . . . .   TCLC 10
See also CA 107

Tolson, Melvin B(eaunorus)
1900?-1966 . . . .   CLC 36
See also CA 124; obituary CA 89-92;
DLB 48, 124

Tolstoy, (Count) Alexey Nikolayevich
1883-1945 . . . .   TCLC 18
See also CA 107

Tolstoy, (Count) Leo (Lev Nikolaevich)
1828-1910 . . . .   TCLC 4, 11, 17, 28
See also CA 104, 123; SATA 26

Tomlin, Lily   1939- . . . .   CLC 17

Tomlin, Mary Jean   1939-
See Tomlin, Lily
See also CA 117

Tomlinson, (Alfred) Charles
1927- . . . .   CLC 2, 4, 6, 13, 45
See also CA 5-8R; DLB 40

Toole, John Kennedy   1937-1969 . . . .   CLC 19
See also CA 104; DLB-Y 81

Toomer, Jean
1894-1967 . . . . .   CLC 1, 4, 13, 22; SSC 1
See also CA 85-88; DLB 45, 51

Torrey, E. Fuller   19??- . . . .   CLC 34
See also CA 119

Tournier, Michel   1924- . . . . . .   CLC 6, 23, 36
See also CANR 3; CA 49-52; SATA 23

Townshend, Peter (Dennis Blandford)
1945- . . . .   CLC 17, 42
See also CA 107

Tozzi, Federigo   1883-1920 . . . .   TCLC 31

Trakl, Georg   1887-1914 . . . .   TCLC 5
See also CA 104

Transtromer, Tomas (Gosta)
1931- . . . .   CLC 52
See also CA 117

Traven, B.   1890-1969 . . . .   CLC 8, 11
See also CAP 2; CA 19-20;
obituary CA 25-28R; DLB 9, 56

Tremain, Rose   1943- . . . .   CLC 42
See also CA 97-100; DLB 14

Tremblay, Michel   1942- . . . .   CLC 29
See also CA 116; DLB 60

Trevanian   1925- . . . .   CLC 29
See also CA 108

Trevor, William   1928- . . . . .   CLC 7, 9, 14, 25
See also Cox, William Trevor
See also DLB 14

Trifonov, Yuri (Valentinovich)
1925-1981 . . . .   CLC 45
See also obituary CA 103, 126

Trilling, Lionel   1905-1975 . . . .   CLC 9, 11, 24
See also CANR 10; CA 9-12R;
obituary CA 61-64; DLB 28, 63

Trogdon, William   1939-
See Heat Moon, William Least
See also CA 115, 119

Trollope, Anthony   1815-1882 . . . . .   NCLC 6
See also SATA 22; DLB 21, 57

Trotsky, Leon (Davidovich)
1879-1940 . . . .   TCLC 22
See also CA 118

Trotter (Cockburn), Catharine
1679-1749 . . . .   LC 8

Trow, George W. S.   1943- . . . .   CLC 52
See also CA 126

Troyat, Henri   1911- . . . .   CLC 23
See also CANR 2; CA 45-48

Trudeau, G(arretson) B(eekman)   1948-
See Trudeau, Garry
See also CA 81-84; SATA 35

Trudeau, Garry   1948- . . . .   CLC 12
See also Trudeau, G(arretson) B(eekman)

Truffaut, Francois   1932-1984 . . . .   CLC 20
See also CA 81-84; obituary CA 113

Trumbo, Dalton   1905-1976 . . . .   CLC 19
See also CANR 10; CA 21-24R;
obituary CA 69-72; DLB 26

Tryon, Thomas   1926- . . . .   CLC 3, 11
See also CA 29-32R

Ts'ao Hsueh-ch'in   1715?-1763 . . . .   LC 1

Tsushima Shuji   1909-1948
See Dazai Osamu
See also CA 107

Tsvetaeva (Efron), Marina (Ivanovna)
1892-1941 . . . .   TCLC 7, 35
See also CA 104, 128

Tunis, John R(oberts)   1889-1975 . . .   CLC 12
See also CA 61-64; SATA 30, 37; DLB 22

Tuohy, Frank   1925- . . . .   CLC 37
See also DLB 14

Tuohy, John Francis   1925-
See Tuohy, Frank
See also CANR 3; CA 5-8R

Turco, Lewis (Putnam)   1934- . . . . . .   CLC 11
See also CANR 24; CA 13-16R; DLB-Y 84

Turgenev, Ivan   1818-1883 . . . .   NCLC 21

Turner, Frederick   1943- . . . .   CLC 48
See also CANR 12; CA 73-76; DLB 40

Tutuola, Amos   1920- . . . .   CLC 5, 14, 29
See also CA 9-12R

Twain, Mark
1835-1910 . . . .   TCLC 6, 12, 19, 36
See also Clemens, Samuel Langhorne
See also DLB 11, 12, 23, 64, 74

Tyler, Anne
1941- . . . .   CLC 7, 11, 18, 28, 44, 59
See also CANR 11; CA 9-12R; SATA 7;
DLB 6; DLB-Y 82

Tyler, Royall   1757-1826 . . . .   NCLC 3
See also DLB 37

Tynan (Hinkson), Katharine
1861-1931 . . . .   TCLC 3
See also CA 104

Tytell, John   1939- . . . .   CLC 50
See also CA 29-32R

Tzara, Tristan   1896-1963 . . . .   CLC 47
See also Rosenfeld, Samuel

Uhry, Alfred   1947?- . . . .   CLC 55
See also CA 127

Unamuno (y Jugo), Miguel de
1864-1936 . . . .   TCLC 2, 9
See also CA 104

Underwood, Miles   1909-1981
See Glassco, John

Undset, Sigrid   1882-1949 . . . .   TCLC 3
See also CA 104

Ungaretti, Giuseppe
1888-1970 . . . .   CLC 7, 11, 15
See also CAP 2; CA 19-20;
obituary CA 25-28R

Unger, Douglas   1952- . . . .   CLC 34

Unger, Eva   1932-
See Figes, Eva

Updike, John (Hoyer)
1932- . . . . . .   CLC 1, 2, 3, 5, 7, 9, 13, 15,
23, 34, 43
See also CANR 4; CA 1-4R; CABS 2;
DLB 2, 5; DLB-Y 80, 82; DLB-DS 3

Urdang, Constance (Henriette)
1922- . . . .   CLC 47
See also CANR 9, 24; CA 21-24R

Uris, Leon (Marcus)   1924- . . . .   CLC 7, 32
See also CANR 1; CA 1-4R; SATA 49

Ustinov, Peter (Alexander)   1921- . . . .   CLC 1
See also CANR 25; CA 13-16R; DLB 13

Vaculik, Ludvik   1926- . . . .   CLC 7
See also CA 53-56

Valenzuela, Luisa   1938- . . . .   CLC 31
See also CA 101

Valera (y Acala-Galiano), Juan
1824-1905 . . . .   TCLC 10
See also CA 106

Valery, Paul (Ambroise Toussaint Jules)
1871-1945 . . . .   TCLC 4, 15
See also CA 104, 122

Valle-Inclan (y Montenegro), Ramon (Maria)
del   1866-1936 . . . .   TCLC 5
See also CA 106

Vallejo, Cesar (Abraham)
1892-1938 . . . .   TCLC 3
See also CA 105

Van Ash, Cay   1918- . . . .   CLC 34

Vance, Jack   1916?- . . . .   CLC 35
See also DLB 8

Vance, John Holbrook   1916?-
See Vance, Jack
See also CANR 17; CA 29-32R

Van Den Bogarde, Derek (Jules Gaspard
Ulric) Niven   1921-
See Bogarde, Dirk
See also CA 77-80

Vandenburgh, Jane   19??- . . . .   CLC 59

Vanderhaeghe, Guy   1951- . . . .   CLC 41
See also CA 113

Ward, Arthur Henry Sarsfield 1883-1959
  See Rohmer, Sax
  See also CA 108

Ward, Douglas Turner 1930-........ CLC 19
  See also CA 81-84; DLB 7, 38

Warhol, Andy 1928-1987.......... CLC 20
  See also CA 89-92; obituary CA 121

Warner, Francis (Robert le Plastrier)
  1937-......................... CLC 14
  See also CANR 11; CA 53-56

Warner, Marina 1946-
  See also CANR 21; CA 65-68

Warner, Rex (Ernest) 1905-1986.... CLC 45
  See also CA 89-92; obituary CA 119;
  DLB 15

Warner, Sylvia Townsend
  1893-1978 .... CLC 7, 19
  See also CANR 16; CA 61-64;
  obituary CA 77-80; DLB 34

Warren, Mercy Otis 1728-1814... NCLC 13
  See also DLB 31

Warren, Robert Penn
  1905-1989 ... CLC 1, 4, 6, 8, 10, 13, 18,
                  39, 53, 59; SSC 4
  See also CANR 10; CA 13-16R. 129. 130;
  SATA 46; DLB 2, 48; DLB-Y 80;
  CDALB 1968-1987

Washington, Booker T(aliaferro)
  1856-1915 .... TCLC 10
  See also CA 114, 125; SATA 28

Wassermann, Jakob 1873-1934..... TCLC 6
  See also CA 104; DLB 66

Wasserstein, Wendy 1950-...... CLC 32, 59
  See also CA 121; CABS 3

Waterhouse, Keith (Spencer)
  1929-......................... CLC 47
  See also CA 5-8R; DLB 13, 15

Waters, Roger 1944-
  See Pink Floyd

Wa Thiong'o, Ngugi
  1938-................ CLC 3, 7, 13, 36
  See also Ngugi, James (Thiong'o); Ngugi wa
  Thiong'o

Watkins, Paul 1964-............. CLC 55

Watkins, Vernon (Phillips)
  1906-1967 .... CLC 43
  See also CAP 1; CA 9-10;
  obituary CA 25-28R; DLB 20

Waugh, Auberon (Alexander) 1939-.. CLC 7
  See also CANR 6, 22; CA 45-48; DLB 14

Waugh, Evelyn (Arthur St. John)
  1903-1966 ... CLC 1, 3, 8, 13, 19, 27, 44
  See also CANR 22; CA 85-88;
  obituary CA 25-28R; DLB 15

Waugh, Harriet 1944-............. CLC 6
  See also CANR 22; CA 85-88

Webb, Beatrice (Potter)
  1858-1943 .... TCLC 22
  See also CA 117

Webb, Charles (Richard) 1939-..... CLC 7
  See also CA 25-28R

Webb, James H(enry), Jr. 1946-.... CLC 22
  See also CA 81-84

Webb, Mary (Gladys Meredith)
  1881-1927 .... TCLC 24
  See also CA 123; DLB 34

Webb, Phyllis 1927-............. CLC 18
  See also CANR 23; CA 104; DLB 53

Webb, Sidney (James)
  1859-1947 .... TCLC 22
  See also CA 117

Webber, Andrew Lloyd 1948-...... CLC 21

Weber, Lenora Mattingly
  1895-1971 .... CLC 12
  See also CAP 1; CA 19-20;
  obituary CA 29-32R; SATA 2;
  obituary SATA 26

Wedekind, (Benjamin) Frank(lin)
  1864-1918 .... TCLC 7
  See also CA 104

Weidman, Jerome 1913-........... CLC 7
  See also CANR 1; CA 1-4R; DLB 28

Weil, Simone 1909-1943.......... TCLC 23
  See also CA 117

Weinstein, Nathan Wallenstein 1903?-1940
  See West, Nathanael
  See also CA 104

Weir, Peter 1944-................ CLC 20
  See also CA 113, 123

Weiss, Peter (Ulrich)
  1916-1982 .... CLC 3, 15, 51
  See also CANR 3; CA 45-48;
  obituary CA 106; DLB 69

Weiss, Theodore (Russell)
  1916-.................. CLC 3, 8, 14
  See also CAAS 2; CA 9-12R; DLB 5

Welch, (Maurice) Denton
  1915-1948 .... TCLC 22
  See also CA 121

Welch, James 1940-........ CLC 6, 14, 52
  See also CA 85-88

Weldon, Fay
  1933-........ CLC 6, 9, 11, 19, 36, 59
  See also CANR 16; CA 21-24R; DLB 14

Wellek, Rene 1903-............. CLC 28
  See also CAAS 7; CANR 8; CA 5-8R;
  DLB 63

Weller, Michael 1942-........ CLC 10, 53
  See also CA 85-88

Weller, Paul 1958-.............. CLC 26

Wellershoff, Dieter 1925-......... CLC 46
  See also CANR 16; CA 89-92

Welles, (George) Orson
  1915-1985 .... CLC 20
  See also CA 93-96; obituary CA 117

Wellman, Manly Wade 1903-1986 .. CLC 49
  See also CANR 6, 16; CA 1-4R;
  obituary CA 118; SATA 6, 47

Wells, Carolyn 1862-1942 .... TCLC 35
  See also CA 113; DLB 11

Wells, H(erbert) G(eorge)
  1866-1946 .... TCLC 6, 12, 19
  See also CA 110, 121; SATA 20; DLB 34,
  70

Wells, Rosemary 1943-........... CLC 12
  See also CLR 16; CA 85-88; SAAS 1;
  SATA 18

Welty, Eudora (Alice)
  1909- .... CLC 1, 2, 5, 14, 22, 33; SSC 1
  See also CA 9-12R; CABS 1; DLB 2;
  DLB-Y 87; CDALB 1941-1968

Wen I-to 1899-1946 .... TCLC 28

Werfel, Franz (V.) 1890-1945 ...... TCLC 8
  See also CA 104

Wergeland, Henrik Arnold
  1808-1845 .... NCLC 5

Wersba, Barbara 1932-........... CLC 30
  See also CLR 3; CANR 16; CA 29-32R;
  SAAS 2; SATA 1; DLB 52

Wertmuller, Lina 1928- .... CLC 16
  See also CA 97-100

Wescott, Glenway 1901-1987....... CLC 13
  See also CANR 23; CA 13-16R;
  obituary CA 121; DLB 4, 9

Wesker, Arnold 1932- .... CLC 3, 5, 42
  See also CAAS 7; CANR 1; CA 1-4R;
  DLB 13

Wesley, Richard (Errol) 1945-...... CLC 7
  See also CA 57-60; DLB 38

Wessel, Johan Herman 1742-1785 .... LC 7

West, Anthony (Panther)
  1914-1987 .... CLC 50
  See also CANR 3, 19; CA 45-48; DLB 15

West, Jessamyn 1907-1984 ...... CLC 7, 17
  See also CA 9-12R; obituary CA 112;
  obituary SATA 37; DLB 6; DLB-Y 84

West, Morris L(anglo) 1916-.... CLC 6, 33
  See also CA 5-8R; obituary CA 124

West, Nathanael 1903?-1940 .... TCLC 1, 14
  See also Weinstein, Nathan Wallenstein
  See also CA 125; DLB 4, 9, 28

West, Paul 1930- .... CLC 7, 14
  See also CAAS 7; CANR 22; CA 13-16R;
  DLB 14

West, Rebecca 1892-1983 .. CLC 7, 9, 31, 50
  See also CANR 19; CA 5-8R;
  obituary CA 109; DLB 36; DLB-Y 83

Westall, Robert (Atkinson) 1929-... CLC 17
  See also CLR 13; CANR 18; CA 69-72;
  SAAS 2; SATA 23

Westlake, Donald E(dwin)
  1933-.................... CLC 7, 33
  See also CANR 16; CA 17-20R

Westmacott, Mary 1890-1976
  See Christie, (Dame) Agatha (Mary
  Clarissa)

Whalen, Philip 1923-........... CLC 6, 29
  See also CANR 5; CA 9-12R; DLB 16

Wharton, Edith (Newbold Jones)
  1862-1937 .... TCLC 3, 9, 27
  See also CA 104; DLB 4, 9, 12;
  CDALB 1865-1917

Wharton, William 1925-........ CLC 18, 37
  See also CA 93-96; DLB-Y 80

Wheatley (Peters), Phillis
  1753?-1784............... LC 3
  See also DLB 31, 50; CDALB 1640-1865

Wheelock, John Hall 1886-1978 .... CLC 14
  See also CANR 14; CA 13-16R;
  obituary CA 77-80; DLB 45

Whelan, John 1900-
See O'Faolain, Sean

Whitaker, Rodney 1925-
See Trevanian

White, E(lwyn) B(rooks)
1899-1985 .... **CLC 10, 34, 39**
See also CLR 1; CANR 16; CA 13-16R;
obituary CA 116; SATA 2, 29;
obituary SATA 44; DLB 11, 22

White, Edmund III 1940- .... **CLC 27**
See also CANR 3, 19; CA 45-48

White, Patrick (Victor Martindale)
1912- .... **CLC 3, 4, 5, 7, 9, 18**
See also CA 81-84

White, T(erence) H(anbury)
1906-1964 .... **CLC 30**
See also CA 73-76; SATA 12

White, Terence de Vere 1912- ...... **CLC 49**
See also CANR 3; CA 49-52

White, Walter (Francis)
1893-1955 .... **TCLC 15**
See also CA 115, 124; DLB 51

White, William Hale 1831-1913
See Rutherford, Mark
See also CA 121

Whitehead, E(dward) A(nthony)
1933- .... **CLC 5**
See also CA 65-68

Whitemore, Hugh 1936- .... **CLC 37**

Whitman, Sarah Helen
1803-1878 .... **NCLC 19**
See also DLB 1

Whitman, Walt 1819-1892 .... **NCLC 4**
See also SATA 20; DLB 3, 64;
CDALB 1640-1865

Whitney, Phyllis A(yame) 1903- .... **CLC 42**
See also CANR 3, 25; CA 1-4R; SATA 1,
30

Whittemore, (Edward) Reed (Jr.)
1919- .... **CLC 4**
See also CANR 4; CA 9-12R; DLB 5

Whittier, John Greenleaf
1807-1892 .... **NCLC 8**
See also DLB 1; CDALB 1640-1865

Wicker, Thomas Grey 1926-
See Wicker, Tom
See also CANR 21; CA 65-68

Wicker, Tom 1926- .... **CLC 7**
See also Wicker, Thomas Grey

Wideman, John Edgar
1941- .... **CLC 5, 34, 36**
See also CANR 14; CA 85-88; DLB 33

Wiebe, Rudy (H.) 1934- ...... **CLC 6, 11, 14**
See also CA 37-40R; DLB 60

Wieland, Christoph Martin
1733-1813 .... **NCLC 17**

Wieners, John 1934- .... **CLC 7**
See also CA 13-16R; DLB 16

Wiesel, Elie(zer) 1928- ..... **CLC 3, 5, 11, 37**
See also CAAS 4; CANR 8; CA 5-8R;
DLB-Y 87

Wiggins, Marianne 1948- .... **CLC 57**

Wight, James Alfred 1916-
See Herriot, James
See also CA 77-80; SATA 44

Wilbur, Richard (Purdy)
1921- .... **CLC 3, 6, 9, 14, 53**
See also CANR 2; CA 1-4R; CABS 2;
SATA 9; DLB 5

Wild, Peter 1940- .... **CLC 14**
See also CA 37-40R; DLB 5

Wilde, Oscar (Fingal O'Flahertie Wills)
1854-1900 .... **TCLC 1, 8, 23**
See also CA 104; SATA 24; DLB 10, 19,
34, 57

Wilder, Billy 1906- .... **CLC 20**
See also Wilder, Samuel
See also DLB 26

Wilder, Samuel 1906-
See Wilder, Billy
See also CA 89-92

Wilder, Thornton (Niven)
1897-1975 ...... **CLC 1, 5, 6, 10, 15, 35**
See also CA 13-16R; obituary CA 61-64;
DLB 4, 7, 9

Wiley, Richard 1944- .... **CLC 44**
See also CA 121

Wilhelm, Kate 1928- .... **CLC 7**
See also CAAS 5; CANR 17; CA 37-40R;
DLB 8

Willard, Nancy 1936- .... **CLC 7, 37**
See also CLR 5; CANR 10; CA 89-92;
SATA 30, 37; DLB 5, 52

Williams, C(harles) K(enneth)
1936- .... **CLC 33, 56**
See also CA 37-40R; DLB 5

Williams, Charles (Walter Stansby)
1886-1945 .... **TCLC 1, 11**
See also CA 104

Williams, Ella Gwendolen Rees 1890-1979
See Rhys, Jean

Williams, (George) Emlyn
1905-1987 .... **CLC 15**
See also CA 104, 123; DLB 10

Williams, Hugo 1942- .... **CLC 42**
See also CA 17-20R; DLB 40

Williams, John A(lfred) 1925- .... **CLC 5, 13**
See also CAAS 3; CANR 6, 26; CA 53-56;
DLB 2, 33

Williams, Jonathan (Chamberlain)
1929- .... **CLC 13**
See also CANR 8; CA 9-12R; DLB 5

Williams, Joy 1944- .... **CLC 31**
See also CANR 22; CA 41-44R

Williams, Norman 1952- .... **CLC 39**
See also CA 118

Williams, Paulette 1948-
See Shange, Ntozake

Williams, Tennessee
1911-1983 .... **CLC 1, 2, 5, 7, 8, 11, 15,
19, 30, 39, 45**
See also CA 5-8R; obituary CA 108; DLB 7;
DLB-Y 83; DLB-DS 4;
CDALB 1941-1968

Williams, Thomas (Alonzo) 1926- ... **CLC 14**
See also CANR 2; CA 1-4R

Williams, Thomas Lanier 1911-1983
See Williams, Tennessee

Williams, William Carlos
1883-1963 .... **CLC 1, 2, 5, 9, 13, 22, 42**
See also CA 89-92; DLB 4, 16, 54

Williamson, David 1932- .... **CLC 56**

Williamson, Jack 1908- .... **CLC 29**
See also Williamson, John Stewart
See also DLB 8

Williamson, John Stewart 1908-
See Williamson, Jack
See also CANR 123; CA 17-20R

Willingham, Calder (Baynard, Jr.)
1922- .... **CLC 5, 51**
See also CANR 3; CA 5-8R; DLB 2, 44

Wilson, A(ndrew) N(orman) 1950- ... **CLC 33**
See also CA 112; DLB 14

Wilson, Andrew 1948-
See Wilson, Snoo

Wilson, Angus (Frank Johnstone)
1913- .... **CLC 2, 3, 5, 25, 34**
See also CANR 21; CA 5-8R; DLB 15

Wilson, August 1945- .... **CLC 39, 50**
See also CA 115, 122

Wilson, Brian 1942- .... **CLC 12**

Wilson, Colin 1931- .... **CLC 3, 14**
See also CAAS 5; CANR 1, 122; CA 1-4R;
DLB 14

Wilson, Edmund
1895-1972 .... **CLC 1, 2, 3, 8, 24**
See also CANR 1; CA 1-4R;
obituary CA 37-40R; DLB 63

Wilson, Ethel Davis (Bryant)
1888-1980 .... **CLC 13**
See also CA 102; DLB 68

Wilson, John 1785-1854 .... **NCLC 5**

Wilson, John (Anthony) Burgess 1917-
See Burgess, Anthony
See also CANR 2; CA 1-4R

Wilson, Lanford 1937- .... **CLC 7, 14, 36**
See also CA 17-20R; DLB 7

Wilson, Robert (M.) 1944- .... **CLC 7, 9**
See also CANR 2; CA 49-52

Wilson, Sloan 1920- .... **CLC 32**
See also CANR 1; CA 1-4R

Wilson, Snoo 1948- .... **CLC 33**
See also CA 69-72

Wilson, William S(mith) 1932- ..... **CLC 49**
See also CA 81-84

Winchilsea, Anne (Kingsmill) Finch, Countess
of 1661-1720................. **LC 3**

Winters, Janet Lewis 1899-
See Lewis (Winters), Janet
See also CAP 1; CA 9-10

Winters, (Arthur) Yvor
1900-1968 .... **CLC 4, 8, 32**
See also CAP 1; CA 11-12;
obituary CA 25-28R; DLB 48

Wiseman, Frederick 1930- .... **CLC 20**

Wister, Owen 1860-1938 .... **TCLC 21**
See also CA 108; DLB 9

Witkiewicz, Stanislaw Ignacy
1885-1939 .... **TCLC 8**
See also CA 105

Literary Criticism Series
Cumulative Topic Index

This index lists all topic entries in the Gale Literary Criticism Series *Contemporary Literary Criticism,* *Literature Criticism from 1400 to 1800, Nineteenth-Century Literature Criticism,* and *Twentieth-Century Literary Criticism.*

TCLC Cumulative Nationality Index

AMERICAN

Adams, Henry **4**
Agee, James **1, 19**
Anderson, Maxwell **2**
Anderson, Sherwood **1, 10, 24**
Atherton, Gertrude **2**
Austin, Mary **25**
Barry, Philip **11**
Baum, L. Frank **7**
Beard, Charles A. **15**
Belasco, David **3**
Benchley, Robert **1**
Benét, Stephen Vincent **7**
Benét, William Rose **28**
Bierce, Ambrose **1, 7**
Black Elk **33**
Bourne, Randolph S. **16**
Bradford, Gamaliel **36**
Bromfield, Louis **11**
Burroughs, Edgar Rice **2, 32**
Cabell, James Branch **6**
Cable, George Washington **4**
Cather, Willa **1, 11, 31**
Chandler, Raymond **1, 7**
Chapman, John Jay **7**
Chesnutt, Charles Waddell **5**
Chopin, Kate **5, 14**
Comstock, Anthony **13**
Cotter, Joseph Seamon, Sr. **28**
Crane, Hart **2, 5**
Crane, Stephen **11, 17, 32**
Crawford, F. Marion **10**
Crothers, Rachel **19**
Cullen, Countee **4, 37**
Davis, Rebecca Harding **6**
Davis, Richard Harding **24**
Day, Clarence **25**
DeVoto, Bernard **29**
Dreiser, Theodore **10, 18, 35**

Dunbar, Paul Laurence **2, 12**
Dunne, Finley Peter **28**
Fisher, Rudolph **11**
Fitzgerald, F. Scott **1, 6, 14, 28**
Fletcher, John Gould **35**
Forten, Charlotte L. **16**
Freeman, Douglas Southall **11**
Freeman, Mary Wilkins **9**
Futrelle, Jacques **19**
Gale, Zona **7**
Garland, Hamlin **3**
Gilman, Charlotte Perkins **9, 37**
Glasgow, Ellen **2, 7**
Goldman, Emma **13**
Grey, Zane **6**
Hall, James Norman **23**
Harper, Frances Ellen Watkins **14**
Harris, Joel Chandler **2**
Harte, Bret **1, 25**
Hawthorne, Julian **25**
Hearn, Lafcadio **9**
Henry, O. **1, 19**
Hergesheimer, Joseph **11**
Higginson, Thomas Wentworth **36**
Hopkins, Pauline Elizabeth **28**
Howard, Robert E. **8**
Howe, Julia Ward **21**
Howells, William Dean **7, 17**
James, Henry **2, 11, 24**
James, William **15, 32**
Jewett, Sarah Orne **1, 22**
Johnson, James Weldon **3, 19**
Kornbluth, C. M. **8**
Kuttner, Henry **10**
Lardner, Ring **2, 14**
Lewis, Sinclair **4, 13, 23**
Lewisohn, Ludwig **19**
Lindsay, Vachel **17**
London, Jack **9, 15**

Lovecraft, H. P. **4, 22**
Lowell, Amy **1, 8**
Marquis, Don **7**
Masters, Edgar Lee **2, 25**
McCoy, Horace **28**
McKay, Claude **7**
Mencken, H. L. **13**
Millay, Edna St. Vincent **4**
Mitchell, Margaret **11**
Mitchell, S. Weir **36**
Monroe, Harriet **12**
Muir, John **28**
Nathan, George Jean **18**
Nordhoff, Charles **23**
Norris, Frank **24**
O'Neill, Eugene **1, 6, 27**
Oskison, John M. **35**
Porter, Gene Stratton **21**
Rawlings, Marjorie Kinnan **4**
Reed, John **9**
Roberts, Kenneth **23**
Robinson, Edwin Arlington **5**
Rogers, Will **8**
Rölvaag, O. E. **17**
Rourke, Constance **12**
Runyon, Damon **10**
Saltus, Edgar **8**
Sherwood, Robert E. **3**
Slesinger, Tess **10**
Steffens, Lincoln **20**
Stein, Gertrude **1, 6, 28**
Sterling, George **20**
Stevens, Wallace **3, 12**
Tarkington, Booth **9**
Teasdale, Sara **4**
Thurman, Wallace **6**
Twain, Mark **6, 12, 19, 36**
Van Dine, S. S. **23**
Van Doren, Carl **18**

Title Index to Volume 37